OTES

HIS is a

er, Jame

w of Pa

"Professo
can philos
observer
as Willia
Bergson,
The sec
sponden
Woodrow W
appreciated."

50 pages,

ps, 2 vo

DICTIONARY

OF

PHILOSOPHY AND PSYCHOLOGY

THE MACMILLAN COMPANY
NEW YORK · BOSTON · CHICAGO
ATLANTA · SAN FRANCISCO

MACMILLAN & CO., Limited
LONDON · BOMBAY · CALCUTTA
MELBOURNE

THE MACMILLAN CO. OF CANADA, Ltd.
TORONTO

DICTIONARY

OF

PHILOSOPHY AND PSYCHOLOGY

INCLUDING

MANY OF THE PRINCIPAL CONCEPTIONS OF ETHICS, LOGIC, AESTHETICS,
PHILOSOPHY OF RELIGION, MENTAL PATHOLOGY, ANTHROPOLOGY,
BIOLOGY, NEUROLOGY, PHYSIOLOGY, ECONOMICS, POLITICAL
AND SOCIAL PHILOSOPHY, PHILOLOGY, PHYSICAL
SCIENCE, AND EDUCATION

AND GIVING

A TERMINOLOGY IN ENGLISH, FRENCH, GERMAN, AND ITALIAN

WRITTEN BY MANY HANDS

AND EDITED BY

JAMES MARK BALDWIN

PH.D. (PRINCETON), HON. D.SC. (OXON.), HON. LL.D. (GLASGOW)
STUART PROFESSOR IN PRINCETON UNIVERSITY

*WITH THE CO-OPERATION AND ASSISTANCE OF AN INTERNATIONAL
BOARD OF CONSULTING EDITORS*

IN THREE VOLUMES

WITH ILLUSTRATIONS AND EXTENSIVE BIBLIOGRAPHIES

VOL. I

NEW EDITION, WITH CORRECTIONS

New York
THE MACMILLAN COMPANY
1911

Norwood Press :

Berwick & Smith Co., Norwood, Mass., U.S.A.

COLLABORATORS

Ethics.

(J. S.)   Professor JAMES SETH, Edinburgh University.
(W. R. S.)   Professor W. R. SORLEY, Cambridge University.

Psychology.

(J. McK. C.)   Professor J. McK. CATTELL, Columbia University.
(E. C. S.)   President E. C. SANFORD, Clark University.
(E. M. S.)   Mrs. H. SIDGWICK, Principal, Newnham College, Cambridge.
(G. F. S.)   Dr. G. F. STOUT, University Reader, Oxford.
(E. B. T.)   Professor E. B. TITCHENER, Cornell University.
(H. C. W.)   Professor H. C. WARREN, Princeton University.
(J. M. B.)   The Editor.

Philology.

(B. I. W.)   President B. I. WHEELER, University of California.

Physical Science and Mathematics.

(J. S. A.)   Professor J. S. AMES, Johns Hopkins University.
(E. W. D.)   Professor ELLERY W. DAVIS, University of Nebraska.
(H. B. F.)   Professor H. B. FINE, Princeton University.
(S. N.)   Professor SIMON NEWCOMB, Washington.

Mental Pathology and Anthropology.

(J. J.)   Professor J. JASTROW, Wisconsin University.
(A. M.)   Dr. ADOLF MEYER, Worcester, Mass., Insane Asylum.

Biology.

(C. B. D.)   Professor C. B. DAVENPORT, Carnegie Institution of Washington.
(E. S. G.)   E. S. GOODRICH, Lecturer, Oxford University.
(C. S. M.)   Professor C. S. MINOT, Harvard University.
(C. Ll. M.)   Principal C. LLOYD MORGAN, University College, Bristol.
(E. B. P.)   Professor E. B. POULTON, Oxford University.
(W. F. R. W.)   Professor W. F. R. WELDON, Oxford University.

Economics.

(A. T. H.)   President A. T. HADLEY, Yale University.

Political and Social Philosophy.

(J. B.)   Dr. JAMES BONAR, Civil Service Commission, London.
(F. H. G.)   Professor F. H. GIDDINGS, Columbia University.
(F. C. M.)   F. C. MONTAGUE, Oriel College, Oxford.
(W. D. M.)   Dr. W. D. MORRISON, London.

Law.

(S. E. B.)   Judge S. E. BALDWIN, Governor of Connecticut; Professor, Yale University.

Philosophy of Religion.

(E. G. B.)   E. G. BROWNE, Lecturer, Cambridge University.
(J. E. C.)   Rev. J. ESTLIN CARPENTER, Manchester College, Oxford.
(A. T. O.)   Professor A. T. ORMOND, Princeton University.
(R. M. W.)   Professor R. M. WENLEY, Michigan University.

Education.

(C. DE G.)   Professor C. DE GARMO, Cornell University.

Aesthetics.

(J. R. A.)   Professor JAMES R. ANGELL, Chicago University.
(J. H. T.)   Professor J. H. TUFTS, Chicago University.

Neurology and Physiology.

(H. H.) [1]   { President C. L. HERRICK, University of New Mexico.
          { Professor C. J. HERRICK, Denison University.
(C. F. H.)   Professor C. F. HODGE, Clark University.

Bibliography.

(B. R.)   Dr. BENJ. RAND, Harvard University.

[1] Joint authorship.

EDITOR'S PREFACE

I.

IT may be well, before proceeding to define the scope and present some of the features of this work, to indicate the objects which were entertained in preparing it. It may be said, in general, that two purposes are combined in it, which may be distinguished without attempting to decide which was more important in the execution: first, that of doing something for the thinking of the time in the way of definition, statement, and terminology; and second, that of serving the cause of education in the subjects treated.

As to the former of these intentions, the details of the contents of the work, as described below in this introduction, may give some preliminary light; especially in the way of securing judgment from the reader on what is attempted rather than on what is not. In all attempts to improve terminology or to settle the meanings of terms, one finds oneself in the presence of such manifold pitfalls, that the assumption of failure is commonly made from the start. And this assumption is just, when made with reference to attempts of certain types. If one aims at securing the adoption of new meanings or of new terms, one is in most cases doomed to failure. If one presumes to settle arbitrarily the relative claims of conflicting usages, one's failure is wellnigh as sure. If one attempts to reach a consensus of authoritative opinions, that does not succeed, for the minority may after all be those who establish the future course. So evident is all this that it requires some hardihood to set out on such an undertaking at all; and the chance of coming off with reasonable success seems to be in proportion to the unimportance of what is attempted.

We have, therefore, essayed none of these things. Our task has not been to originate terms or to make meanings; not to enlarge our vocabulary or to suppress synonyms. We are, on the contrary, undertaking a more moderate and, withal, a more reasonable task,—a task which, as regards the use of terms, is twofold: to understand the meanings which our terms have, and to render them by clear definitions,—this on the one hand; and to interpret the movements of thought through which the meanings thus determined have arisen, with a view to discovering what is really vital in the development of thought and term in one,— this on the other hand. So much may be said without presenting a dissertation on the philosophy of language, or suggesting the outline of a would-be science of Semantics. In most cases, the success of this attempt depends upon the state of discussion of the subject-matter, here or there. Often we have found, for instance, that there were real distinctions, which closer definition availed to disclose, justifying both of two usages, or making it plain that one of them rested on a misapprehension. Again, it often happens that an older term has been wrested from its place by a mistaken assertion of novelty by a writer uninformed, or by its undiscriminating use with a meaning slightly at variance with the earlier. These instances may be taken as typical of the sorts of ambiguity and irrelevancy which the student of this subject is constantly meeting, and which may often be cleared away by concise and authoritative definitions.

Authoritative, it should be said: for despite the fact that authority may not keep usage true, nevertheless it is often authority which makes usage false; and it is the part of authority, once definitions and discriminations are reached, to establish and maintain them. Hence, in this work, authority is invoked; not merely the use of authority as representing the highest ability in the matters taken up, but also bare authority as a force,—what would be called by Professor Durkheim the social force of 'constraint.' This has been argued recently by Professor Tönnies, in his discussions of the theory of terminology and its reform, and acted upon by Lady Welby in her efforts to convene conferences of eminent men. Indeed, the idea of the former writer, to the effect that an International Academy for Scientific Terminology might have an important function, is in so far quite correct. We, in this work, are not an Academy, of course, but we are an international committee. Not to dwell upon the excellent work of individuals in the several departments, we may recall the fact that the American Psychological Association has a newly appointed committee on terminology; and that the neurologists have been aiming to do something, both in Germany and in the United States, by similar committees. Despite the independence of single writers—often of the highest position—who will not conform to what committees do, this would seem to be a way of making progress, however slowly, at any rate so far as it succeeds, by sharply defining the alternatives of usage and, in so far, making ambiguity less likely. We do not expect that our recommendations will have more success than may be realized through such general processes and social influences; and that some of our preferences will turn out unwise is not only likely, but quite certain.

As to the other purpose spoken of above—the pedagogical—that is more properly the object of a dictionary than of any other work not a textbook, because it aims to state formulated and well-defined results rather than to present discussions. The fulfilment of this function has given form and set limits which might not, from other points of view, have seemed altogether most desirable. We may mention in this connection especially the shorter bibliographies appended to most of the articles. These are planned to furnish to the student, who is not yet the practised man of research, leaders and first guides to the literary sources. Such a person would be lost in the maze of titles given in the bibliographical volume (iii), as in a general index he always is. Furthermore, the criticism of the scope of the work should have before it the knowledge of this pedagogical purpose; for the introduction to a large subject—philosophy, indeed, is the largest subject—must needs include various details of knowledge of other branches of science and information, and of methods, preliminary to its proper task. It is for this pedagogical reason that a glossary of the nervous system furthers the treatment of psychology for the beginner, that definitions of physical terms aid the student of the moral sciences, and that accounts of the latest biological discoveries serve the worker in social philosophy. And this quite apart from the legitimate question of the scope of philosophy itself: indeed, the consciousness of the necessity of meeting the pedagogical demand has relieved the Editor of undue anxiety as to this last-suggested matter. For he has been able to say: 'This or that might possibly be excluded, if we held to a strict understanding that only the materials of these and those problems were to be included; but it cannot be omitted from a work which aims to fit the student to approach the problems, as well as to explain to him the possible solutions of them.'

II.

The subject-matter of the Dictionary is Philosophy and Psychology. These disciplines are what we set out to treat. By philosophy is understood the attempt to reach statements, in whatever form, about mind and nature, about the universe of things, most widely conceived, which serve to supplement and unify the results of science and criticism. It is necessary to say criticism, as well as science, because all the thought which defines, estimates, devises methods, and sets categories for science,—which, to use a comprehensive term, 'justifies' knowledge and life,—together with all the ways of coming into relation to things other than by knowledge,—all this is involved with the matter of science. If there is a dispute about the function of philosophy, it arises, we take it, through two main ways of regarding the problem of philosophy: of which the one makes philosophy a rethinking and deeper formulating of the results safely come to by science; and of which the other makes philosophy the criticism—in Herbart's phrase, the 'rectification'—of the conceptions upon which science proceeds, and upon which, with all its values and interests, rests life no less than knowledge. The one assumes knowledge, and aims to systematize it; the other criticizes knowledge, and aims to idealize it. The one begins with facts, with things as they are, and aims to understand them so thoroughly that one insight will cover them all; the other lays claim to the insight, the ideal, the universal, and says: 'Whatever things may *seem* to be for science and for experience, *this* is what, for good and all, they really *are* and *mean.*'

However inadequate this distinction may be to reflect the ways of approaching the world in the name of philosophy, it may illustrate our undertaking. We are treating both of the philosophy that is science, and of the philosophy that criticizes and transforms science with a view to the demands of life. In either case, however, the data of science, broadly conceived, are there with their claim. It is one of the safest sayings of philosophy, at the close of the outgoing century, that whatever we may become to end with, we must be naturalists to begin with,—men furnished with the breastplate of natural knowledge. We must know the methods as well as the results of science; we must know the limitations of experiment, the theory of probability, the scientific modes of weighing evidence and treating cases. Lack of these things is the weakness of many a contemporary writer on philosophy. Such a one criticizes a science which he does not understand, and fails to see the significance of the inroads science is making into the territory which has so long seemed to be exempt. Note the application of biological principles, in however modified form, to psychological facts; the treatment of moral phenomena by statistical methods; and the gradual retreat of the notion of purpose before the naturalist, with the revised conception of teleology which this makes necessary. And these things are but examples.

We have aimed, therefore, to present science—physical, natural, moral—with a fullness and authority not before undertaken in a work of this character. In the selection of the topics, in the form and length of treatment, in the bibliographical lists, this emphasis will be found throughout. Furthermore, the newer advances in scientific method have been made the subject of longer articles, as a reference to the topic Variation—where the statistical treatment of biological phenomena is explained—or to the topic Probability, will show. Both these topics are becoming of especial importance to the psychologist, the moralist, and the student of life.

An additional and more positive reason for the wide inclusion of science is to be found in the present state of psychological studies, of which more is said below. As to philosophy proper—the discipline which calls itself by that name—certain of our aims should be clearly defined, especially on the side of their limitations. In the first place, this work is not, and does not include, a history of philosophy. The writers, one and all, approach their topics from a historical point of view; this is one of the distinguishing features of the work. They trace historical movements when this is necessary for the exposition or justification of the definitions made or the usages recommended; and the history of thought is comprehensively illustrated through the selection of topics over the whole vocabulary of philosophy. Yet no one of these things has been made an end in itself; rather have we aimed at truth to history, and fair appreciation of the spirit of historical research. More particularly, also, is it the history of conceptions rather than that of terms that has concerned us. Lexicographical and linguistic determinations are largely foreign to our task. Meanings, with their historical development, together with the terms which have expressed them and their variations,—these are the essentials of our quest.

And secondly, we have subjected ourselves to another very definite and evident limitation on the side of exclusion. It would be useless to attempt in any compass, short of an independent work as large as this, to make a Dictionary of Greek and Scholastic Philosophy. It should be done ; it is much needed : but we have not attempted it. We include special articles on Greek and Latin Terminology, with select glossaries of representative terms ; and it will be found that many of the finer distinctions of scholastic as well as of ancient thought are brought out in connection with the terms which in our modern vocabulary express or represent them. Yet when all is said, the student of scholastic thought, as of Greek thought, will find so many gaps that it is only just to our limited purpose to warn him of them in advance. It is a change which has come into the subject,—this facing of philosophy towards science and modern life, instead of towards logic and ancient life,—and in consciously accepting the change we accept as well the inevitable criticism it will bring upon us.

As to the prominent place given to psychology, no further justification of it is required than the statement that this is what we set out to do,—to prepare a work devoted to philosophy and psychology. The association of these two subjects is traditional and, as to their contents, essential. Psychology is the half-way house between biology with the whole range of the objective sciences, on the one hand, and the moral sciences with philosophy, on the other hand. The claim to this place laid by psychology to-day is no more plain than is the proof of it which the results in this department of research make good. The rise of experimental and physiological psychology has caused the science to bulk large towards the empirical disciplines, as it always has towards the speculative ; and the inroads made by psychological analysis and investigation into the domains where the speculative methods of inquiry, spoken of above, were once exclusively in vogue, render permanent and definite the relation on that side as well. In biology, in sociology, in anthropology, in ethics, in economics, in law, even in physics, the demand is for sound psychology ; and the criticism that is making itself felt is psychological criticism. How could it be otherwise when once it is recognized that science is the work of mind, and that the explaining principles by which any science advances beyond the mere cataloguing of facts are abstract conceptions made by processes of thought ?

It will be found, therefore, that it is upon the psychology of this work that most of its lines converge ; and it is in its psychology that many of the hopes of its producers centre. That the psychology be found less adequate than it might be,—that is only to be expected ; that it be found less adequate than it should be,—that is the judgment we wish most of all to escape.

III.

Coming now to more particular features of the work, we may make certain explanations. The Editor has had responsible charge and, in the negative sense of control, nothing in these volumes is outside of his responsibility. He has used this responsibility freely. He has assigned and reassigned articles, supplemented articles, rewritten articles, rejected articles. But it has been his universal rule— departed from only in cases of trivialities or of cosmic obstacles like those of time and space—to exercise these prerogatives under the checks and controls supplied by the board of consulting editors. This board has been an indispensable part of the Dictionary organization. Certain of the members have read the articles of one another and of the other writers, either in manuscript or in proof; they have passed and repassed suggestions, criticisms, and emendations; they have laboured on definitions, equivalents, literature, with a patience and self-denial which leads one to accept Aristotle's high estimate of philosophers. Accordingly there is hardly anything in the work which has not the support of a group of men of the highest authority. This should be remembered by the single writer or student who finds this or that point unsatisfactory. He is one; we are many. And this, the co-operative feature, has been a leading—if not the leading—methodical feature of the work from its first inception.

It has been the especial function of the consulting board to supply the recommendations as to foreign equivalents for all the terms defined in the work. This undertaking, while extremely difficult, has been on the whole gratifyingly successful. Of course, the developing state of philosophical terminology makes conventions ineffective, notably as between different languages,—to say nothing of the artificial character of convention as such in matters linguistic; but it is our hope and belief that in this feature, thanks to the enormous pains and toil devoted to it by our consulting editors and contributors, we are making a measure of gain for international science and philosophy. The thanks of all readers of the book are due in the fullest measure—not at all to underthank any of the others—to Professor Morselli and Professor Flournoy, members respectively of the Italian and French committees.

As to the preparation of the articles, more specifically, the plan has been as follows. Two authorities determined upon the terms in a given department in the first instance, and divided the topics between them. As their work advanced, they exchanged their manuscripts for suggestion and consultation. After this, the important articles were submitted to other authorities also especially versed in these topics. Passing then through the hands of the editor, the copy went, in those cases in which matters of detail remained still unsettled, to one or other of the consulting editors for his opinion and counsel, and to the foreign boards for their revision, and especially for the consideration of the foreign equivalents and the supplementing of the select literature lists. Further than this, the proofs have gone both to the authors—in most cases of joint authorship to all of the authors—and to the foreign editors. Of course, after all this, much has remained for the Editor to decide, notably in the matter of collation and selection; and he has been obliged to use his best judgment. Wherever he has been mistaken, it has been not because the view adopted was not well supported, but because there were alternatives, both or all of which had good support. And he wishes to say to the collaborators, one and all, that wherein their contributions are not just what they might desire, this is not by reason of arbitrary rulings of the Editor, but by reason of general adjustments, in which each authority is recognized in his own sphere—the Editor no more than others—and so far as possible consulted. This is the more to be said, seeing that it has not been possible in each case to state the alternatives in the text, or to indicate the authorities pro and con by name. Yet in cases of important emendation second proofs were sent to the writers. So far, however, as actual authorship goes, the writers' names are in all cases appended. The distribution of responsibility in cases of joint signature conforms to the rules which follow.

When an article is signed by one set of initials only (A.B.C.), the author is responsible for the whole article, except the recommendations as to foreign equivalents; these, though possibly the same as those originally suggested by the writer of the article, are nevertheless inserted as recommendations of the board of consulting editors. In cases in which a recommendation of a distinctly original or novel usage is due to any one of the staff, or is taken from a printed authority, the source, whether personal or public, is indicated, in connection with the term recommended, in the form: Evocation (P.J.).   When lacking this indication, a topic-term is itself due to the writer who signs the article, e. g. Autotelic, signed (J.M.B.).

In cases of actual joint authorship of an article or part of an article, two cases will be found: either—and where possible—each contributor's initials are added to his section of the article, or the two sets of initials, joined by a hyphen, are set at the end, thus: (A.B.C.-X.Y.Z.).   In most cases this form of signature indicates that the article was originally written by A.B.C. (the signature standing first), but has undergone more or less important modification to meet the criticisms or suggestions of X.Y.Z.   In many cases the contribution of X.Y.Z. is decidedly less than that of A.B.C.; but in all cases it was judged sufficient to justify the citing of the article as the product of the two writers together.   The articles by President and Professor Herrick are all of joint authorship, and are signed (H.H.).

Another case is the signature by two persons with a comma—not a hyphen—between them: (A.B.C., X.Y.Z.)   This indicates that the article was written by A.B.C. and accepted without alteration by X.Y.Z., who thus adds the weight of his authority to it.   This feature has not in general been deemed explicitly necessary, but is limited to cases of positive teaching on disputed points or of topics about which combined authority is considered, for any other reason, of great importance.   A case in point is the article on Heredity, in which positive views are expressed over and above the scientific definition.   Throughout the range of topics in general psychology many such double signatures will be found.   In this latter subject, a detailed and prolonged series of conferences has led to the formulation of a series of definitions and expositions to which two of the writers at work have found it possible to add their joint signatures in one or other of the two forms here explained.   And the experimental psychology has been treated with equal care.

The treatment is primarily, as has been said, that of a dictionary; not that of an encyclopedia.   The articles are of three sorts: first, concise definitions; second, such definitions with the addition of certain historical and expository matter, running to several hundred words;   third, articles called 'special,' on topics which seemed, in view of either of the general purposes set forth above, to call for extended treatment.   These last are of encyclopedic character, varying in length from 1,000 to 5,000 words.   Important movements in the history of philosophy, the general divisions of the topic Philosophy itself, and select subjects in all of the general departments of science, have this special treatment.   In most cases these select articles have the further justification that they are written with a view to gathering into a general presentation and _résumé_ many of the subordinate topics treated in a more detached way in their respective places.   The article Vision may be cited in illustration both of the nature and we trust also of the utility of this feature.

A closer examination of the relative importance given to each of the departments represented—whether calculated from the average length of the articles or from the entire space devoted to the subject—will show that there is a more or less logical and intentional adjustment about the central subjects Philosophy and Psychology.   The figure given below presents in a rough way an idea of this adjustment.   The vertical ordinates 1, 2, 3, &c., vary in length from the centre outwards in both directions.   It will be seen that Mental Pathology and Anthropology, for example, have generous treatment; this for the practical reason —apart from other justification—that the topics have not been well written up for the student of philosophy and psychology, and that the sources are scattered and relatively unavailable.   In these and other subjects the intention has been to emphasize what the student of philosophy ought to know, rather than what he does know.   On both sides the curve sinks rapidly, and terminates with departments in which relatively few terms are treated, and these in the briefest form. Of course, the actual relations of the several departments are but roughly indicated in this curve.

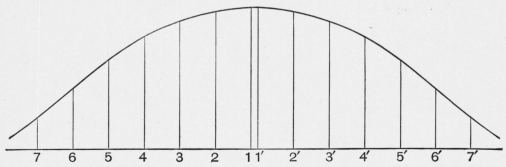

1, 1'. Philosophy and Psychology.
2, 2'. { Ethics and Anthropology.
{ Mental Pathology and Neurology.
3, 3'. Aesthetics and Logic.
4, 4'. Philosophy of Religion and Biology.
5, 5'. { Sociology and Political Philosophy.
{ Economics and Physiology.
6, 6'. Philology and Law.
7, 7'. Education and Physics (Mathematics).

Biography is not made a prominent feature—quite the reverse. Only the outstanding biographical facts are recorded, which any reader of philosophy should know, or know where to find, if he is to be educated. Seeing that the volume of bibliographies is arranged by authors' names, the titles of their works are not given in the biographies; and seeing that in the articles on the important movements of thought the names of prominent thinkers are given, separate accounts of authors' views are not generally attempted. There has resulted, therefore, simply by reason of this incidental division of the material commonly put under the biographical heading, a certain meagre look to the biographies, which is sure to strike the reader.

The bibliographical feature, on the contrary, has been given excessive pains and care. The plan is to include the best references—both magazine articles and select books—under the topic in each case, even though in many instances this repeats the entries of book titles made in the volume (iii) of general bibliographies. Yet the fact that the titles of all such independent publications are given in full, and with date of publication, in the separate volume devoted to it, makes it unnecessary that the same details should be given in the select lists. Thus some inconsistency in the details of citation (as of dates), and some lack of uniformity in the references to editions, will be found in the select lists. They have been printed very largely as originally sent in by the writers, except that abbreviations have been reduced to the form given in the lists tabulated at the beginning of this volume (i). When the writers include dates of publication, these are allowed to stand, although they are also given in Vol. iii; for whatever saves the reader time and trouble is, in so far, good, and consistency should not be made a fetich. The place of publication, however, has not been given in the select lists except in departments, notably Neurology, which are not represented in the general bibliographies. The writers' direct responsibility for these select lists is, however, not the same as for the articles; for the Editor and his associates have taken a free hand in supplementing and completing them. The references in the volumes (i and ii) of text, made in the form 'see BIBLIOG. A, I, c,' are to the general bibliographies of Vol. iii.

As to the general bibliographies, an editorial word may well be added; to the effect that the Editor's responsibility for these is not the same as for the matter in the other volumes. It was not a part of the original plan to compile such extensive bibliographies; and it was only by the good fortune that Dr. Rand had them already largely prepared that we were able to secure them. This fact made it impossible for the editorial management to bring them entirely within the scheme of execution of the whole. So far as possible, they have been made an intrinsic part of the work, and in their terminology and general character they maintain its form consistently. But the actual results, as respects relative fullness, the division of topics, the form of citation, &c., were determined independently in the first instance, and to change them in a material way would have been to make the lists over. They are, therefore, in a sense supplementary to the Dictionary. The same sort of statement may be made also regarding their quality; they have not been through the same forms of criticism, and are, therefore, more largely the independent work of one man.

In regard to future bibliographies, we may say that it is intended to continue the issue of the *Psychological Index* in its present form both as a part of the *Psychological Review* and as a supplement to this Dictionary. The issues beginning with that of April, 1901 (No. 7), incorporate certain changes in classification made by arrangement with the foreign journals *Zeitschrift für Psychologie* and *Année Psychologique*, which publish the same lists,—changes which make the *Index*, as respects both terminology and divisions, identical with the scheme printed in this work under the topic Psychology. This scheme of classification, resulting as it has from the long experience of professional workers, and gradually improved by international co-operation, is recommended to librarians and bibliographers generally. Other bibliographical annuals are the excellent lists printed by the *Archiv für systematische Philosophie* and the *Revue Néo-Scolastique*.

IV.

In matters of lexicography, use has been made, by permission, of both the *Century* and the *Standard* Dictionaries; in the derivations the *Century* has generally been followed. The rules of composition and orthography of the Clarendon Press, for which Dr. Murray, editor of the *New English Dictionary*, is largely responsible, have been adopted, except in certain specific matters, and the results are thus in general accord with the recommendations of this last-named work. Indebtedness should also be acknowledged to Eisler's *Wörterbuch der philosophischen Begriffe*, which by reason of its plan of giving large numbers of quotations (though mainly from German authors), and its comprehensive scope and recent appearance, has been more available than any other Dictionary of Philosophy proper. Other indications are made by the individual writers themselves of the sources found by them respectively to be most available; and very frequent reference will be found to the good but unfortunately fragmentary *Geschichte der philosophischen Terminologie* of Professor Eucken. Useful earlier books which, in this feature or that, cover our territory, and on which we have drawn, are Noack's *Philosophie-geschichtliches Lexikon* (1879), used especially for biographical material; Krug's *Encyklopädisch-philosophisches Lexikon* (2nd ed., 1833); Franck's *Dictionnaire des Sciences philosophiques* (1844), which contains, in the preface, a historical note on earlier attempts at Dictionaries of Philosophy; and the *Vocabularies* devoted to particular authors, certain of which are named in the articles on the terminology of the great philosophers (Kant's, Hegel's, Greek Terminology, and Latin and Scholastic Terminology). Additional references to the sources of Scholastic usage are to be found in the article on Patristic Philosophy and in that on St. Thomas.

As in the case of most works of this kind, it has been found impossible to keep all the threads equally taut as the manufacture has proceeded; and certain evidences of this will be open to the eye of the careful observer. In particular, it has been found advisable to keep the 'polls open' as long as possible in the matter of recommendations as to equivalents, &c.; and in order to do this, the term Terminology has itself been made a topic in its alphabetical place. Under various sections of that article—'German,' 'French,' &c.—discussions are to be found of certain terms which present difficulty. The recommendations therein made will not be found—unless there be especial declaration to that effect—to contradict those given respectively under the main English topics. They serve the rather to supplement them, and to settle points left indefinite or undecided in the earlier pages. Indeed, the resource which this procedure makes available is openly resorted to in many instances. Further, the development in the plan of the Dictionary made incidental changes necessary in one or two departments—e. g. the expansion of certain subjects after articles upon them had already been written. The Editor recognizes particularly the goodness of Principal Lloyd Morgan and Professor Titchener for permitting this in connection with certain of their topics.

After these explanations, no doubt some one will say that this is not a Dictionary of Philosophy; and if it would help matters to call it rather a 'dictionary for philosophers,' to that there would be no objection. What we care to make plain is that we do not wish to be considered as having prepared a work in support of any academic view of philosophy, but rather as having wished to present materials and definitions which workers in philosophy and science generally might find useful and reliable.

V.

Obligations of so extensive and manifold a character, extending over seven years, have been contracted by the Editor and his associates, that only a general declaration of habitual and generous gratitude can reach all to whom it is due. In particular, speaking for themselves, the contributors desire to thank each of those who have given advice to them or made suggestions. The department of anthropology extends more specific thanks to Professor F. Boas, of Columbia University. The Editor finds himself, apart from his great obligation to the consulting editors, grateful to those contributors of special articles who have generously given their work without financial compensation. Some of the longest and most important articles in the work have thus been given without recompense. To Professor Warren he owes thanks for unreckoned and unstinted aid in many matters; and to Mrs. Baldwin, who collated the corrected proofs and gave much general assistance.

During the progress of our work we have lost the presence and active aid of Professor Henry Sidgwick, from whose active co-operation we gained much, and to whose counsel we had learned to look. He gave his time ungrudgingly to the criticism and revision of the articles in ethics, at the same time requesting that what he did should be counted as editorial, and so should not be set off with his name. The writers in ethics, as well as the Editor, who sought his advice in many matters besides, feel in an especial way the loss of his masterly thought, and miss his genial and kindly personality. He illustrated at its fullest the spirit of judicial inquiry and fair criticism which the rest of us have aimed to make the ideal of our work; and his going is a loss not only to us, but to the whole philosophical world.

The Editor finds it a peculiarly pleasant task to acknowledge the many personal, no less than professional, courtesies extended to him during his year of residence at Oxford for the printing of the Dictionary at the Clarendon Press. Of the personal, it is not here the place to speak; but for the very unusual arrangements to meet his needs and to facilitate his work made by the Librarian, the late Sir Henry Acland, and the other authorities of the Radcliffe Library,—extending to the liberal purchase of books which he required,—and by the Controller of the Press in the many ways in which the resources of such a great institution may be made more available,—for these things he is sincerely grateful. It may be taken to show, perhaps (not in any way to intimate that this sort of thing is unusual in Oxford and in England, or on this side of the water in the case of men from the other side), that the idea of international co-operation which the Dictionary embodies extends not alone to the tasks in hand, but finds confirmation in a large spirit of recognition and encouragement. The Cambridge people, with the lamented Henry Sidgwick and with James Ward at their head, responded in the same spirit; and it may not be judged a violation of the proprieties of a preface to suggest to any literary Christian who is bearing a pack—say an editorial pack, which is the heaviest of all—that if he go to Oxford or Cambridge he will find his 'yoke made easy and his burden light' in a very material way. While being so personal, the Editor may also be allowed to extend the reference to his own University, and to thank President Patton and the Board of Trustees for the leave of absence for a year, granted expressly for the prosecution of this work.

Finally, the Editor must express verbally his apologies for the evident short-comings of the book. No one man, of course, could compass the field mapped out for the Dictionary; the present Editor least of all. He has been the mouth-piece of his collaborators in their respective specialties, and the work is as much theirs as his. His opinion has counted only as one among many; it has been sacrificed oftener probably than that of any one else; and it has changed time and again, as the consultations have advanced. May the future Dictionary of Philosophy profit somewhat by our labours, and if it profit also by our mistakes, that will be no less a point of justification for our endeavour.

It is intended to issue the remainder of the text—completing the alphabetical treatment of topics—together with full indices of Greek, Latin, German, French, and Italian terms, in Vol. ii, and to devote Vol. iii exclusively to the general bibliographies. Short prefatory notes are to be found at the beginnings of Vol. ii and Vol. iii.

Readers are requested to send to the Editor, at Princeton, New Jersey, U.S.A., corrections or suggestions of alterations of any sort, with a view to the possible issue of another edition, if the sale of the work should justify it. And to those who adopt the recommendations of the text it may not be too much to suggest that a note be printed in their publications saying that they follow in whole or part the scheme of terminology recommended in the Dictionary. Editors of journals often find uniformity of usage desirable on the part of their con-tributors; and in case the Dictionary system prove an advance in the matter, it would seem but fair recognition of the work and encouragement to the publishers, who have generously taken upon themselves the cost of publication and the payment of the contributors, to request their writers to conform, so far as may be possible, to the usages here suggested. The recommendations of foreign equivalents have been made in part to meet the urgent needs of translators—a need which the most competent are the first to feel—and in cases in which the renderings here given are followed, it may not be improper to ask that a note be printed to that effect. The same suggestion in kind may be made also concerning the lists of Abbreviations immediately following the Table of Contents; they have been prepared on the basis of earlier schemes, and in a conservative spirit.

THE EDITOR.

PRINCETON UNIVERSITY,
June, 1901.

CONTENTS

(See the detailed Table of Contents in Volume III.)

ABBREVIATIONS

I. ABBREVIATIONS OF TERMS OCCURRING IN TITLES OF JOURNALS AND OTHER PUBLICATIONS

a.	= aus, an.	Cent.	= Century.
Abhandl.	= Abhandlung.	Centralbl.	= Centralblatt.
Abstr.	= Abstract.	Chir., Cirug.	= Chirurgical, &c.
Abth.	= Abtheilung.	Chrét., Christ.	= Chrétienne, Christian, &c.
Acad., Accad., Akad.	= Academy, &c.	Cien.	= Ciencia.
Addr.	= Addresses.	Circ.	= Circulars.
Adv.	= Advancement.	Cirug.	= Cirugía.
Aesth.	= Aesthetic, &c.	Clin.	= Clinical, &c.
Ak.	= Akustik.	Co., Comp.	= Company.
Alien.	= Alienist.	Comm.	= Commission.
allg.	= allgemein.	Comm'r, Comm'rs.	= Commissioner, &c.
Amer.	= American.	Commun.	= Communication, &c.
Anat.	= Anatomy, Anatomical, &c.	Compar.	= Comparative.
angew.	= angewandt.	Cong.	= Congress.
Ann.	= Annals, &c.	Contemp.	= Contemporary.
Anthropol.	= Anthropological, Anthropology, &c.	Contrib.	= Contributions.
		Corresp.	= Correspondenz.
Anthropom.	= Anthropometry.	Crim.	= Criminal, &c.
Antiq.	= Antiquities.	Criminol.	= Criminology.
Antol.	= Antologia.	Crit.	= Critical.
Anz.	= Anzeiger.	Cyc.	= Cyclopedia.
Aphor.	= Aphorismen.		
Arb.	= Arbeiten.	d.	= de, der, &c.
Arch., Ark.	= Archives, &c.	Descrip.	= Descriptive.
Archaeol.	= Archaeological, &c.	deutsch.	= deutscher, &c.
art.	= article.	Devel.	= Development(al).
Assoc.	= Association.	Dict.	= Dictionary, &c.
Aufl.	= Auflage.	Dis.	= Disease.
Augenh.	= Augenheilkunde.	Diss.	= Dissertation.
Ausg.	= Ausgabe.		
		Eccles.	= Ecclesiastical.
Beitr.	= Beiträge.	Econ.	= Economics, Economy, &c.
Belg.	= Belgique, &c.	ed.	= edited, edition.
Ber.	= Bericht.	Educ.	= Education, &c.
Berl.	= Berliner.	Electr.	= Electric, &c.
Bib.	= Biblical.	Electro-biol.	= Electro-biology, &c.
Bibliog.	= Bibliography, Bibliographical, &c.	Encyc. Brit.	= Encyclopaedia Britannica.
		Eng. trans.	= English translation.
Biblioth.	= Bibliothèque.	Enseignem.	= Enseignement.
Biog.	= Biography, &c.	Entomol.	= Entomology, &c.
Biol.	= Biological, &c.	Entwickelungsmech.	= Entwickelungsmechanik.
Bk.	= Book.	Ét.	= Étude.
Bl.	= Blatt.	Eth.	= Ethical, Ethics.
Bost.	= Boston.	Ethnol.	= Ethnology.
Brit.	= British, Britannica.	Exam.	= Examination.
Brux.	= Bruxelles.	Exper.	= Experimental, &c.
Bull., Boll.	= Bulletin, &c.	Explan.	= Explanatory.
C. R.	= Comptes Rendus.	f.	= für.
Cal.	= California.	Fasc.	= Fascicule.
Canad.	= Canadian.	Filos., Filoz.	= Filosofia, &c.
Cathol.	= Catholic, &c.	Fortn.	= Fortnightly.

Fortsch.	= Fortschritt.		Mém.	= Mémoires.
Fr.	= French.		Mens.	= Mensuel, -elle.
Franç.	= Français.		Ment.	= Mental, &c.
Freniat.	= Freniatria.		Met., Mét.	= Metaphysics, &c.
			Meth.	= Method.
Gaz., Gac.	= Gazette, &c.		Microg.	= Micrographic. &c.
Geb.	= Gebiet.		Microsc., mikr.	= Microscopy, Microscopical,
Gen.	= General.			mikroskopisch, &c.
Geneesk.	= Geneeskunde.		Mitth., Mitt.	= Mittheilungen.
Geol.	= Geology, &c.		Mo.	= Monthly.
Ger.	= German.		Mod.	= Modern, &c.
gerichtl.	= gerichtlich.		Monatsbl.	= Monatsblatt.
ges.	= gesammt.		Monatsh.	= Monatsheft.
Gesch.	= Geschichte.		Monatssch.	= Monatsschrift.
Gesell.	= Gesellschaft.		Monog.	= Monograph.
Gior.	= Giornale.		Mor.	= Morals, Moral.
			Morphol.	= Morphology, &c.
H.	= Heft.		Münch.	= Münchener.
Habil.	= Habilitationsschrift.		Mus.	= Museum.
Handb.	= Handbook, Handbuch.			
Handwörterb.	= Handwörterbuch.		N. S.	= New Series.
Heilk., -hk.	= Heilkunde.		N. Y.	= New York.
Hist.	= History, &c.		Nat.	= Natural.
Hôp.	= Hôpital.		Natnl.	= National.
Hosp.	= Hospital.		Natural.	= Naturalist, &c.
Hypnot.	= Hypnotism, &c.		Naturf.	= Naturforscher.
			Naturw.	= Naturwissenschaft.
I, Ist.	= Istituto.		nederl.	= nederlandsch.
Icon.	= Iconoclast, Iconography,		Néo-Scol.	= Néo-Scolastique.
	&c.		Nerv.	= Nervous, &c.
imman.	= immanent, &c.		Nervenh.	= Nervenheilkunde.
Inaug.	= Inaugural.		Neurasth.	= Neurasthenia, &c.
Inebr.	= Inebriates, Inebriety.		Neurol., Névrol.	= Neurology, &c.
Inq.	= Inquiry.		Neurot.	= Neurotomy, &c.
Insan.	= Insanity.		Nic.	= Nicomachaean.
Inst.	= Institute, Institution, &c.		No.	= Number.
Int.	= International.		Norm.	= Normal.
Interméd.	= Intermédiaire.		Nouv.	= Nouveau, &c.
Intermed.	= Intermediate.		Nov.	= Novum.
Interpret.	= Interpretation.			
Introd.	= Introduction.		Ocul.	= Oculiste, &c.
Ital.	= Italian.		Offenb.	= Offenbarung.
			Ohrenh.	= Ohrenheilkunde.
J.	= Journal.		Ophthal., Ottal.	= Ophthalmology, Ophthal-
Jahrb.	= Jahrbuch.			mic, &c.
Jahresber.	= Jahresbericht.		Org.	= Organum.
Jahrg.	= Jahrgang.		Orific.	= Orifical.
Just.	= Justinian.		Osp.	= Ospedale.
			Osteol.	= Osteology, &c.
k., kgl.	= königlich.		Otol.	= Otology, &c.
Kantstud.	= Kantstudien.			
klin.	= klinisch.		Päd.	= Pädagogik, &c.
krim.	= kriminal.		Pathol., Patol.	= Pathology, &c.
Kriminol.	= Kriminologie.		Pedag.	= Pedagogy, &c.
krit., Krit.	= kritisch, Kritik, &c.		Perc.	= Perception.
			Phar.	= Pharyngologie.
Lab.	= Laboratory.		Philol.	= Philology, &c.
Lanc.	= Lancisiana.		Philos.	= Philosophy, &c.
Laryng.	= Laryngoscope, Laryngo-		Phys.	= Physical.
	tomy, &c.		Physiol.	= Physiology, &c.
Laryngol.	= Laryngology, -ist, &c.		Pogg.	= Poggendorff.
Lects.	= Lectures.		Policl.	= Policlinic, &c.
Legisl.	= Legislation.		Polit.	= Political.
Lehrb.	= Lehrbuch.		Pop.	= Popular.
Lfg.	= Lieferung.		Pract.	= Practical.
Linn.	= Linnaean.		prakt.	= praktisch.
Lit.	= Literary, Literature.		Pref.	= Preface.
			Pres.	= Presidential.
Mag.	= Magazine.		Presb.	= Presbyterian.
Med., Méd.	= Medicine, Medical, &c.		Princ.	= Principles.
Med.-Chir.	= Medico-Chirurgical, &c.		Proc.	= Proceedings.
Med.-Psychol., &c.	= Medico-Psychological, &c.			

Prog.	= Program, Programmab- handlung.	Suppl.	= Supplement, &c.
		Surg.	= Surgery, Surgical.
Psych.	= Psychic, Psychical.	Syst.	= System.
Psychiat.	= Psychiatry, &c.	System.	= Systematic, systematisch,
Psychol., Psicol., &c.	= Psychology, &c.		&c.
Pt.	= Part.		
Publ., publ.	= Publications, published by.	Theol.	= Theology, &c.
		Therap.	= Therapeutic, &c.
Quart.	= Quarterly.	Thom.	= Thomiste.
Quest.	= Questionnaire, Questions.	Tijd.	= Tijdskrift.
Quind.	= Quindicinale.	trad.	= traduit.
		Trans.	= Transactions.
R.	= Reale (Ital.).	trans. (Eng. &c.)	= translation (English, &c.).
Rdschau.	= Rundschau.	Trav.	= Travaux.
Rec.	= Record, Recueil.	Treat.	= Treatise.
Ref.	= Reference, Reformed.	Trib.	= Tribune.
Rendic.	= Rendiconti.	Trimest.	= Trimestriel.
Rep.	= Report.		
Rep'r.	= Reporter.	ü.	= über.
Res.	= Research.	u.	= und.
Rev.	= Review, &c.	Uebers.	= Uebersetzt.
rev.	= revised.	Univ.	= University.
Rhinol.	= Rhinology.	Univl.	= Universal.
Riv.	= Rivista.	Untersuch.	= Untersuchungen.
Roy.	= Royal.		
		v.	= von.
S.	= Series.	Ver.	= Verein.
Samml.	= Sammlung.	verb.	= verbesserter.
Schol.	= Scholastic.	Verh.	= Verhandlung.
Sci.	= Science.	verm.	= vermehrte.
Scient.	= Scientific.	Vocab.	= Vocabulary.
Sciol.	= Sciolism, Sciolistic.	vol.	= volume.
Sem.	= Seminary, Seminar.	Vortr.	= Vorträge.
Semej.	= Semejotica.	Vorw.	= Vorwort.
Sent.	= Sentiments.	Vtljsch.	= Vierteljahrsschrift.
Sitzber.	= Sitzungsbericht.		
Skand.	= Skandinavian.	Wien.	= Wiener.
Smithson.	= Smithsonian.	Wisc.	= Wisconsin.
Soc.	= Society, Social.	Wiss., wiss.	= Wissenschaft, wissen- schaftlich.
Sociol.	= Sociology.		
Span.	= Spanish.	Wochensch.	= Wochenschrift.
Specul.	= Speculative.	Wörterb.	= Wörterbuch.
spek.	= spekulativ.		
Sperim.	= Sperimentale (Italian).	z.	= zur, zum.
Staatswiss.	= Staatswissenschaft.	Zool.	= Zoology, &c.
Stat.	= Station.	Zeit.	= Zeitung.
Statist.	= Statistics, &c.	Zeitsch.	= Zeitschrift.
Stud.	= Studies, Studien.		

II. ABBREVIATIONS OF TITLES OF JOURNALS AND OTHER PUBLICATIONS

Abhandl. d. k. sächs. Gesell. d. Wiss.
Abhandl. d. physiol. Gesell. zu Berlin
Abhandl. z. Philos.
Acad. R. Méd.-Chir. d. France
Addr. and Proc. Natnl. Educ. Assoc.
Alien. and Neurol.
Allg. Päd.
Allg. Wien. med. Zeit.
Allg. Zeitsch. f. Psychiat.
Amer. Anthropol.
Amer. J. Med. Sci.
Amer. J. of Insan.
Amer. J. of Ophthal.
Amer. J. of Physiol.
Amer. J. of Psychol.
Amer. J. of Sci.
Amer. J. of Sociol.
Amer. Med.-Surg. Bull.
Amer. Natural.
Amer. Phys. Educ. Rev.
Amer. Presb. Rev.
Anat. Anz.
Anat. Hefte
Ann. Amer. Acad. Polit. and Soc. Sci.
Ann. Clin. de Bordeaux
Ann. d. Mal. de l'Oreille
Ann. d'Ocul.
Ann. d. Physik u. Chemie (or Wiedemann's Ann.)
Ann. d. Sci. Nat.
Ann. d. Sci. Psych.
Ann. de Microg.
Ann. de Philos. Chrét.
Ann. de Psychiat.
Ann. di Freniat.
Ann. di Neurol.
Ann. di Otol.
Ann. di Ottal.
Ann. of Otol., Rhinol., and Laryngol.
Ann. Méd.-Psychol.
Ann. Soc. Roy. d. Sci. Méd. et Nat. de Brux.
Année Biol.
Année Philos.
Année Psychol.
Année Sociol.
Annual Encyc.
Anomalo
Anthropol.
Antiq. Rom. Syntagma
Arch. Clin. de Bordeaux
Arch. d'Anat. Microsc.
Arch. d'Anthropol. Crim.
Arch. de Neurol.
Arch. d'Ophthal.

Arch. de Physiol.
Arch. di Psichiat.
Arch. f. Anat. u. Entwickelungsgesch.
Arch. f. Anat. u. Physiol.—Physiol. Abth.
Arch. f. Anat. u. Physiol.—Anat. Abth.
Arch. f. Augenh.
Arch. f. d. ges. Physiol. (or Pflüger's Arch.)
Arch. f. Entwickelungsmech.
Arch. f. exper. Pathol.
Arch. f. Gesch. d. Philos.
Arch. f. krim. Anthropol.
Arch. f. Laryngol. u. Rhinol.
Arch. f. mikr. Anat.
Arch. f. Ohrenh.
Arch. f. Ophthal. (or v. Graefe's Arch.)
Arch. f. pathol. Anat. (or Virchow's Arch.)
Arch. f. Psychiat.
Arch. f. Religionswiss.
Arch. f. syst. Philos.
Arch. Int. de Laryngol. et d'Otol.
Arch. Ital. d. Biol.
Arch. Ital. di Laringol.
Arch. of Neurol. and Psychopathol.
Arch. of Ophthal.
Arch. of Otol.
Arena
Atlantic Mo.
Atti R. Accad. d. Lincei
Atti Soc. Rom. di Antropol.

Beitr. z. Ak. u. Musikwiss.
Beitr. z. Augenh. (Deutschmann's)
Beitr. z. exper. Psychol.
Beitr. z. pathol. Anat.
Beitr. z. Psychol. u. Philos.
Ber. d. k. sächs. Gesell. d. Wiss.
Ber. d. Senckenberg. Naturf.-Gesell.
Berl. klin. Wochensch.
Bern. Stud. z. Philos.
Bibliog. Anat.
Biol. Centralbl.
Biol. Lectures
Biol. Untersuch. (Retzius's)
Blackwood's Mag.
Boll. d. Soc. di Natural. in Napoli
Boll. d. Policlin. Gen. di Torino
Boll. d. Soc. Lanc. d. Osp. di Roma
Boll. d. Soc. Med.-Chir. di Pavia
Boston Med. and Surg. J.
Brain
Brit. Med. J.
Brit. Quart. Rev.
Bull. Acad. de Méd.

Bull. Amer. Acad. Med.
Bull. Johns Hopkins Hosp.
Bull. Méd.
Bull. Mus. Compar. Zool. Harvard Coll.
Bull. Soc. d'Anthropol. d. Paris
Bull. Soc. d. Méd. Ment. d. Belg.
Bull. Soc. Franco-Belg.
Bull. Soc. Roy. d. Sci. Méd. et Nat. d. Brux.
Bull. Soc. Zool. d. France
Bull. Univ. of Wisc.

Cathol. Univ. Bull.
Cellule
Centralbl. f. allg. Pathol. u. pathol. Anat.
Centralbl. f. Anthropol.
Centralbl. f. med. Wiss.
Centralbl. f. Nervenh. u. Psychiat.
Centralbl. f. Physiol.
Centralbl. f. prakt. Augenh.
Century Mag.
Child-Study Mo.
Cleveland Med. Gaz.
Columbia Univ. Bull.
Columbia Univ. Contrib. to Philos.
Commun. all' Accad. Med.-Chir. di Napoli
Compar. Embryol.
Contemp. Rev.
Corresp.-Bl. d. deutsch. anthropol. Gesell.
Course in Exper. Psychol.
C. R. Acad. d. Sci.
C. R. Acad. d. Sci. Mor. et Pol.
C. R. Soc. de Biol.

Deutsch. Arch. f. klin. Med.
Deutsch. med. Wochensch.
Deutsch. med. Zeit.
Deutsch. Rdschau.
Deutsch. Rev.
Deutsch. Zeitsch. f. Nervenh.
Dict. de Physiol.

Edinburgh Med. J.
Education
Educ. Rev.
Encyc. Brit.
Ét. publ. p. Pères Comp. d. Jésus
Eth. Nic.
Eth. of Nat.

Field Columbian Museum—Anthropol. Ser.
Folk-Lore
Fortn. Rev.
Fortsch. d. Med.
Forum
Friedreich's Bl. f. gerichtl. Med.

Gac. Méd.
Gen. Corresp.
Gen. Meth.
Gen. Morphol.
Gesch. d. Aesthetik
Gesch. d. christl. Eth.
Gesch. d. Philos.
Gior. di Patol. Nerv. e Ment.
Glasgow Med. J.

Handb. d. Physiol.
Handb. of Mor. Philos.
Handwörterb. d. Staatswiss.
Hist. of Eth.
Hygeia

Inaug. Diss.
Inland Educ.
Int. J. of Ethics
Int. Med. Mag.
Int. Monatssch. f. Anat. u. Physiol.
Int. Sci. Ser.
Interméd. d. Biol. et d. Méd.
Interméd. d. Neurol. et d. Alién.
Iowa Med. J.

J. Amer. Folklore
J. Amer. Med. Assoc.
J. Anthropol. Inst.
J. Asiatic Soc.
J. Boston Soc. Med. Sci.
J. de l'Anat. et de la Physiol.
J. de Neurol. (et d'Hypnol.)
J. de Physiol. et Pathol. Gén.
J. de Physique
J. Int. d'Anat. et de Physiol.
J. Linn. Soc.
J. N. Y. Entomol. Soc.
J. N. Y. Microsc. Soc.
J. of Anat. and Physiol.
J. of Compar. Neurol.
J. of Educ.
J. of Exper. Med.
J. of Laryngol., Rhinol., and Otol.
J. of Ment. Sci.
J. of Morphol.
J. of Nerv. and Ment. Dis.
J. of Ophthal., Otol., and Laryngol.
J. of Orific. Surg.
J. of Pedag.
J. of Physiol.
J. of Polit. Econ.
J. of Specul. Philos.
Jahrb. f. Philos. u. spek. Theol.
Jahrb. f. Psychiat. u. Neurol.
Jena. Zeitsch. f. Naturwiss.
Johns Hopkins Hosp. Rep.
Johns Hopkins Univ. Circ.
J. Roy. Statist. Soc.

Kansas Univ. Quart.
Kantstud.
Klin. Monatsbl. f. Augenh.
Klin. Vortr. a. d. Geb. d. Otol. u. Phar.-Rhinol.
Krit. d. prakt. Vernunft
Krit. d. reinen Vernunft

La Nature
La Parole
Lancet
Laryngol.
Lects. on Met.
Lehrb. d. Psychol.
Linn. Soc. J. Zool.
Linn. Soc. Trans.
Lyon Méd.

Mag. Nat. Hist.
Manicomio Mod.
Manual of Psychol.
Med. Jahrb., Wien
Med.-Leg. J.
Med. Mag.
Méd. Mod.
Med. Record
Med. Times
Mem. Amer. Acad. Arts and Sci.

Mem. Amer. Mus. of Nat. Hist., N. Y.
Mem. Bost. Soc. Nat. Hist.
Mém. Soc. d'Anthropol. Paris
Mém. Soc. Zool. d. France
Ment. Devel. in the Child and the Race
Ment. Dis.
Meth. of Eth.
Mind
Mitteil. d. zool. Stat. zu Neapel
Monatssch. f. Ohrenh.
Monatssch. f. Psychiat. u. Neurol.
Monist
Mor. and Legisl.
Mor. Sent.
Morphol. Arb. (Schwalbe)
Morphol. Jahrb.
Münch. med. Wochensch.

Nat. Sci.
Nature
Natur u. Offenb.
Naturw. Wochensch.
Neurol. Centralbl.
New World
Nineteenth Cent.
Nordiskt Med. Arkiv.
Norsk Mag. f. Laegevid.
North Amer. Rev.
Northwest. Lancet
Nouv. Icon. de la Salpêtrière
Nov. Org.
Nuova Antol.
N. Y. Med. J.
N. Y. State Hosp. Bull.

Open Court
Ophthal. Rec.
Ophthal. Rev.

Päd. Monatsh.
Pedag. Sem.
Pediatrics
Philos. Aphor.
Philos. d. Griechen
Philos. Jahrb.
Philos. Mag.
Philos. of Educ.
Philos. Rev.
Philos. Stud.
Philos. Trans. Roy. Soc.
Philos. Zool.
Physical Rev.
Physiol. d. Geruchs
Physiol. Optik
Physiol. Psychol.
Polit. Sci. Quart.
Pop. Sci. Mo.
Pract. Eth.
Presb. and Ref. Rev.
Presse Méd.
Presse Méd. Belg.
Princeton Contrib. to Philos.
Princeton Contrib. to Psychol.
Princ. of Econ.
Princ. of Eth.
Princ. of Psychol.
Princ. of Sci.
Princ. of Sociol.
Proc. Acad. Nat. Sci.
Proc. Amer. Acad. Arts and Sci.
Proc. Amer. Assoc. Adv. Sci.

Proc. Amer. Med.-Psychol. Assoc.
Proc. Amer. Philos. Soc.
Proc. Amer. Psychol. Assoc.
Proc. Cambridge Philos. Soc.
Proc. Entomol. Soc.
Proc. Manchester Lit. and Philos. Soc.
Proc. Roy. Soc.
Proc. Soc. Psych. Res.
Proc. Zool. Soc.
Progrès Méd.
Przeglad Filoz.
Przeglad Lekarski
Psicol. Contemp.
Psychiater
Psychische Stud.
Psychol. als Wiss.
Psychol. Arb.
Psychol. Exper.
Psychol. Rev.
Publ. Amer. Acad. Polit. and Soc. Sci.

Quart. Med. J.
Quart. J. Microsc. Sci.
Quart. J. of Inebr.

Real-Encyc.
Rec. d'Ophthal.
Rendic. R. I. Lombard.
Rep. Brit. Assoc. Adv. Sci.
Rep. Bureau Ethnol.
Rep. Comm'r Educ.
Rep. Smithson. Inst.
Rev. Bleue
Rev. d. Deux Mondes
Rev. d. Quest. Hist.
Rev. d. Quest. Scient.
Rev. d. Rev.
Rev. de l'Enseignem.
Rev. de l'Hypnot.
Rev. de l'Univ. de Brux.
Rev. de Méd.
Rev. de Med. y Cirug. Pract.
Rev. de Mét. et de Mor.
Rev. de Mor. Sociale
Rev. de Paris
Rev. de Psychiat., de Neurol. et de Psychol. Expér.
Rev. de Psychol. Clin. et Thérap.
Rev. Encyc.
Rev. Gén. des Sci.
Rev. Gén. d'Ophthal.
Rev. Int. de l'Enseignem.
Rev. Int. de Sociol.
Rev. Méd. de la Suisse Romande
Rev. (Mens.) de l'École d'Anthropol.
Rev. Néo-Scol.
Rev. Neurol.
Rev. Pédag.
Rev. Philos.
Rev. Scient.
Rev. Thom.
Rev. Trimest. Microg.
Riv. di Filos. Scient.
Riv. di Patol. Nerv. e Ment.
Riv. di Sci. Biol.
Riv. Filos.
Riv. Icon. Policl. Gen. di Torino
Riv. Ital. di Filos.
Riv. Ital. di Sociol.
Riv. Mens. di Psich. Forens., Antropol. Crim., ecc.

Riv. Quind. di Psicol.
Riv. Sperim. di Freniat.

Science
Sci. of Educ.
Sci. Progress
Scient. Amer. Suppl.
Semaine Méd.
Semej. malat. ment.
Sitzber. Akad. Wiss. Berlin
Sitzber. Akad. Wiss. München
Sitzber. Akad. Wiss. Wien
Skand. Arch. f. Physiol.
Social and Eth. Interpret.
Sperimentale
Stud. in Educ.
Stud. Yale Psychol. Lab.
Syst. Dis. Eye
Syst. d. Philos.
System. Theol.

Texas Acad. of Sci.
Toledo Med. and Surg. Rep'r.
Trans. Amer. Microsc. Soc.
Trans. Amer. Philos. Soc.
Trans. Canad. Inst.
Trans. Illinois Soc. Child-Study
Trans. Roy. Soc. Canada
Trans. Roy. Soc. Edinburgh
Trib. Méd.
Tuke's Dict. of Psychol. Med.
Twentieth Cent. Pract of Med.

Univl. Cyc.
Univ. Med. Mag.
Univ. of Cal. Stud.
Univ. of Chicago Contrib. to Philos.
Univ. of Iowa Stud. in Psychol.

Univ. of Toronto Stud.—Psychol. Ser.

Verh. d. Berl. Gesell. f. Anthropol.
Vocab. of Philos.
Voprosi Philos.
Vrach
Vtljsch. f. gerichtl. Med.
Vtljsch. f. Musikwiss.
Vtljsch. f. wiss. Philos.

Weekbl. v. h. nederl. Tijd. Geneesk.
West London Med. J.
West. Reserve Univ. Bull.
Westminster Rev.
Wien. klin. Rdschau.
Wien. klin. Wochensch.
Wien. med. Presse
Wien. med. Wochensch.
Wisc. Geol. and Nat. Hist. Survey Bull.
Wörterb. d. philos. Begriffe
Wörterb. d. philos. Grundbegriffe

Zeitsch. f. angew. Mikr.
Zeitsch. f. Augenh.
Zeitsch. f. Biol.
Zeitsch. f. Ethnol.
Zeitsch. f. Hypnot.
Zeitsch. f. imman. Philos.
Zeitsch. f. kathol. Theol.
Zeitsch. f. klin. Med.
Zeitsch. f. Krim.-Anthropol.
Zeitsch. f. Ohrenh.
Zeitsch. f. päd. Psychol.
Zeitsch. f. Philos. u. Päd.
Zeitsch. f. Philos. u. philos. Krit.
Zeitsch. f. physiol. Chemie
Zeitsch. f. Psychol.
Zeitsch. f. wiss. Zool.
Zool. Anz.
Zool. Jahrb.

A

A (in logic). Symbol for the universal affirmative judgment—All men are mortal.

Literature : notes on the origin of this and the other symbols of formal logic are to be found (sub verbis) in EISLER, Wörterb. d. philos. Begriffe. See also PRANTL, Gesch. d. Logik. (J.M.B.)

A = A. The logical formula for IDENTITY (q.v.). (J.M.B.)

A, Ab, or **Abs; A** or **An.** The former (*A, Ab,* or *Abs*), a prefix of Latin origin, denotes separation, deviation, or departure from, as in *amentia*, a departure from normal mental endowment ; *abnormal*, deviating from what is typical or normal : the latter (*a* or *an*), a prefix of Greek origin (known as à privative), denotes absence or lack of, and is equivalent to the English *un* or *less*, as in *amnesia*, loss or lack of memory ; *anaesthesia*, loss or lack of sensation. (J.J.)

Abacus (logical) [from the letters A, B, C] : Ger. *Rechentisch* ; Fr. *abaque* ; Ital. *abbaco*. Mechanical arrangement, resembling the arithmetical abacus, by which may be exhibited (1) the total combinations of a number of simple logical terms with their several negatives, (2) the effect produced on such combinations by subjecting the terms involved to any restrictions or defined relations.

Term and thing are used by Jevons. See his *Pure Logic and other Minor Works* (1890), 80, 113 ff., 117 ff., 151. Called also LOGICAL MACHINE (q.v.). (R.A.)

Abano, Pietro d' (Petrus de Apono, or — Aponne, or — de Padua). (1246–1315 or 1316.) Studied at Constantinople, Padua, and Paris : settled at Padua, where he practised astrology and alchemy, after methods of Averroës, and medicine, after methods of the Arabs. Denounced as a sorcerer, possessor of the philosopher's stone, &c., by the clergy, he received a death sentence from the Inquisition, but died a natural death at Padua.

Abbadie, Jacques. (1657–1727.) Scholar and divine. Received degree of D.D. at the age of seventeen. Pastor of the French church at Berlin : accompanied Marshal Schomberg to England in 1688 : minister of the French church in the Savoy, London : having received episcopal ordination, he was made dean of Killaloe, Ireland, by King William. Best known for his religious treatises.

Abdalatif, or **Abd-el-Latif,** or **Abd-ul-Lateef.** (1162–1231.) An Arabian historian and physician. He wrote on Egypt.

Abélard, or **Abailard, Pierre.** (1079–1142.) French philosopher and dialectician. Studied dialectics under the Nominalist Roscellinus and under the Realist William of Champeaux, theology under Anselm of Laon. Taught in Paris chiefly. He varied little from NOMINALISM (q.v.), being one of the founders of SCHOLASTICISM (q.v.).

Abercrombie, John. (1780–1844.) Practised medicine in Edinburgh. Writer on moral and intellectual philosophy.

Abercromby, David. (Latter half of 17th century.) Scottish metaphysician, who wrote on the practice of medicine, on the pulse, on theological and philosophical themes, &c.

Aberration (chromatic) [Lat. *aberrare*, to wander, to deviate] : Ger. *chromatische Aberration* ; Fr. *aberration chromatique* ; Ital. *aberrazione cromatica*. A result of the different degrees of refraction which lights of different wave-lengths experience in traversing a lens. It is possibly of psychological importance, as influencing the perception of distance. See VISION, and SPACE (perception of).

Literature: HELMHOLTZ, Physiol. Optik (2nd ed.), 156; SANFORD, Course in Exper. Psychol., expt. 109. (E.B.T.)

Aberration (mental): Ger. *Geistesstörung, Irrsinn*; Fr. *aberration mentale, aliénation*; Ital. *aberrazione mentale*. A term of somewhat indefinite scope denoting a more or less serious departure from normal soundness of mind; also used to indicate any form of mental disorder or insanity. (J.J.)

Ability and **Inability** (in theology) [Lat. *a + habilis*, expert]: Ger. *Fähigkeit, Unfähigkeit*; Fr. *capacité, incapacité*; Ital. *abilità, inabilità*. These terms designate the sinner's power, or want of it, to do what is good in the sight of God. ' Man by his fall into a state of sin hath wholly lost all ability of will to any spiritual good accompanying salvation; so, as a natural man, being altogether adverse to that of good, he is not able by his own strength to convert himself, or to prepare himself thereunto ' (*Westminster Confession*). The problem has close connection with the dogma of original sin.

The Pelagians hold the view of ' plenary ability '; the Arminians, that of ' gracious ability '; and the school of Edwards, that of ' natural ability.'

Literature: HAGENBACH, Hist. of Doctrine, ii. 214 f.; A. H. STRONG, System. Theol., 342 f. (R.M.W.)

Abiogenesis: see BIOGENESIS.

Ablaut [Ger. *ab*, off, denoting substitution, + *laut*, a sound]. A German term in general scientific use to denote those variations of vowel in Indo-European roots, suffixes, and endings, which are solely dependent upon phonetic conditions in the mother-speech. Its best English equivalent is ' vowel-gradation.'

The phenomena of ablaut first noted and classified in connection with the historical study of Teutonic grammar, e.g. *sing, sang, sung*, were in the early days of linguistic science conceived of as developed to serve the purpose of the differentiated meanings; but the later perception that they are simple inheritances from the mother-speech disconnected from any phonetic conditions active or discernible in the separate languages, and further, that the same variations appear in suffixes and endings as in roots; that, e. g. *precor* : *procus* in Lat. is the same thing as λέγω : λόγος in Greek, and *singen* : *gesang* in Ger., and that φέρομεν : φέρετε is the same thing as ἵππος : ἵππε, and as λέλοιπα : λείπω,

determined the present view that ablaut is a purely phonetic phenomenon, and that its variations have been merely *utilized* by language; as notably, owing to decay of endings, in the Teutonic languages, for the distinguishing of meanings. See UMLAUT. (B.I.W.)

Abnormal [Lat. *ab + norma*, rule]: Ger. *abnorm, unregelmässig*; Fr. *anormal*; Ital. *anormale*. Distinctly deviating from a more or less precisely determined norm, standard, or type. (J.J.)

Abnormal Psychology: Ger. *pathologische Psychologie, Psychologie der Geistesstörungen*; Fr. *psychologie des anormaux, psychologie pathologique*; Ital. *psicologia morbosa (or patologica)*. That division of psychology which treats of such mental processes and manifestations as deviate in various ways and to a more or less serious extent from what is regarded as normal or usual. It is desirable to give to this term a wide significance, making it one of the large divisions of PSYCHOLOGY (q.v.), including the study of all that is irregular or unusual in mental phenomena. It would thus embrace the study of the various forms of illusions and hallucinations; of the phenomena of trance, hypnotism, automatism, and allied states; of the psychic effects of drugs or intoxicants and of diseased bodily conditions; of the impairment of the faculties in old age; of the unusual mental manifestations of individuals or classes under the dominance of special or extreme emotions (fright, panic, psychic epidemics); of real or alleged manifestations purporting to transcend the ordinary laws and limitations of human intelligence (possession, telepathic phenomena), as well as of the more specific types of lack of development, irregular development, or loss or impairment of faculty, constituting the various forms of mental disorder or insanity. This last division is commonly known as MENTAL PATHOLOGY (q. v.) or Psychopathology. See also PSYCHIATRY.

Literature: see the several topics referred to, and BIBLIOG. G, 1, *g*. (J.J.)

Aborigines [Lat. *ab + origo*, origin]: Ger. *Urbewohner*; Fr. *aborigènes*; Ital. *aborigeni*. Primitive inhabitants of the earliest known period. (J.J.)

Aboulia [Gr. ἀ + βουλή, will]: Ger. *Abulie, Willenlosigkeit* (-*schwäche*); Fr. *aboulie*; Ital. *abulia*. Loss or lack of the power to exercise will. The defect appears in a variety of forms, which are discussed in the article WILL (defects of). (J.J.)

Abscissa: see CURVE.

2

Absent-mindedness: Ger. *Zerstreutheit*; Fr. *distraction, absence*; Ital. *distrazione*. (1) A condition of inattention to certain parts of the conscious field resulting from positive attention to other parts.   (J.M.B.–G.F.S.)

This is a popular term applicable to states of mental preoccupation of all sorts, whether from DISTRACTION (q.v.) or from absorption in or concentration upon a train of thought. The popular emphasis is placed on the incongruities of action, speech, &c., which result in the view of the onlooker. See ATTENTION.   (J.M.B.)

(2) *Abnormal.* A more habitual condition of abstraction or preoccupation. It is characterized by inattention to one's surroundings and a forgetfulness of or failure to realize what would ordinarily easily and naturally enter the field of consciousness. If we regard as the normal attitude of the attention one in which a limited group of perceptions occupies the focus of consciousness while at the same time a wide penumbra of outlying perceptions is less definitely present, and in which the transition is easy from one focal group to another, then we may describe the condition of absent-mindedness as characterized by a very sharp concentration of the attention upon a narrow area, the penumbra of perceptions fading away, and the transition from one to another of the several components of the stream of consciousness becoming difficult and uncertain. This deviation from the normal distribution of the attention is familiar as a transitory experience; but in some individuals, or again as a mark of senescence, becomes more or less habitual and characteristic. It is then more or less abnormal. The condition is probably allied to such states as DISTRACTION (q.v.) and ECSTASY (q.v.), as well as to states of vagueness of consciousness, such as reverie, 'brown-study,' and the like. See ATTENTION (defects of).   (J.J.)

Absolute and **The Absolute** [Lat. *ab* + *solvere*, to loose]: Ger. *absolut, das Absolute*; Fr. (*l'*)*absolu*; Ital. (*l'*) *assoluto*. That which is not relative is Absolute; and the ultimate principle of explanation of the universe is The Absolute.

This meaning is the common element in the various uses of Absolute as an adjective, covering the narrower connotations of 'not dependent,' 'unconditioned,' 'necessary'; e.g. absolute (perfect, immediate) knowledge or truth; absolute (independent) existence; absolute (undetermined) freedom; absolute (not relative) validity; absolute (ultimate) categories; absolute (inherent) necessity; absolute position (the positing of what is not relative); absolute spirit (see MIND, in philosophy); absolute (noumenal) space, time, ego (see KANTIAN TERMINOLOGY); absolute (inherent, unconditional) value.

The Absolute, as a substantive, has three great connotations in the philosophical systems; it is an ultimate principle (1) as all-comprehensive, i.e. including all possible distinctions, the universal; and (2) as immediate, i.e. escaping all possible definition or distinction; for this necessarily implies negation. This latter connotation covers the absolute as noumenal (or unknowable to those who consider knowledge a relation in which the object, as constituted, is *ipso facto* phenomenal). (3) As world-ground: first cause, *primum movens, natura naturans*, i.e. relatively absolute. In modern philosophy NEO-HEGELIANISM or absolute IDEALISM and PANTHEISM represent (1); KANTIANISM and AGNOSTICISM represent (2); epistemological REALISM, MATERIALISM, SPIRITUALISM, and THEISM represent (3).

Besides the principal discussions under RELATIVE AND ABSOLUTE, INFINITE, and PHENOMENON, see the other topics printed in large type above.   (J.M.B., G.F.S.)

The Absolute in sense (1) is independently real; having a reality not imparted or otherwise conditioned by other reality. It is accordingly that which is entirely of itself, and as such (in the view of the metaphysical monists who chiefly use the term) it must comprise all reality; for if there were any reality external to it, the two would stand in mutual relations conditioning both. It follows that there is only one thing in the world, all apparently distinct things being parts or aspects without an independent reality. Thus the Absolute is simply the universe, with the added connotation that its principle of being is necessarily but one.

The Absolute has figured both in idealistic and in realistic systems. In the former it is necessarily psychic in nature; in some of them it is conceived as a cosmic consciousness in which human and brute, and whatever other consciousness may exist, are embraced as parts. Personality is sometimes asserted of it, sometimes expressly denied. This 'Absolute Spirit' is conceived as transcending time, that is (according to one conception), as including within itself all the streams of temporal experience in the myriad minds of the world, not in one moment (for the serial procession of moments is present as such), but in unity of consciousness, in a single experience. The idealistic Absolute plays its most notable rôle in the theories of Fichte, Schelling, and Hegel, and attains with the last named its greatest elaboration. Still the sum of things, its connotation is gradually enriched by the process of logical or 'dialectical' development based on Hegel's conception of the concrete and organic character of universals. The Absolute in this process takes to itself predicate after predicate until it appears as embodying the perfect harmony of the objective world with reason and of reason with itself.

In the British realistic speculation of Hamilton and Herbert Spencer the term has been used in other senses. It has sometimes been taken as implying freedom from all relation — sense (2) above — even the internal relation of the parts to the whole, or to each other; and sometimes in its proper sense as implying only freedom from external and necessary relation, i. e. independence. Hamilton, in defining the Absolute (*Discussions*, 14), dismisses one sense of the word and gives a second, as follows: '*Absolutum* means *finished*, *perfected*, *completed*; in which sense the Absolute will be what is out of relation, &c., as finished, perfect, complete, total, and thus corresponds to τὸ ὅλον and τὸ τέλειον of Aristotle. In this acceptation – and it is that which for myself I exclusively use — the Absolute is diametrically opposed to, is contradictory of, the Infinite.' With Hamilton's follower, Mansel (*Limits of Religious Thought*), we find: 'By the Absolute is meant that which exists in and by itself, having no necessary relation to any other being.' A definition compatible, as Mansel intends, with infinity in the thing defined, and consistent with the meaning (3) given above. Herbert Spencer writes (*First Principles*, 38): 'Thus the First Cause must be in every sense perfect, complete, total: including within itself all power, and transcending all law. Or, to use the established word, it must be absolute.' Among recent thinkers in which various mediating positions are combined with these great tendencies respectively may be mentioned in chronological order Lotze (3), Bradley (2), and Royce (1). See BIBLIOG. B, 2, *a*. (R.H.S.—J.M.B.)

Absolute Ethics: see RELATIVE AND ABSOLUTE ETHICS.

Absolution [Lat. *absolutio*, from *absolvere*, to loose from]: Ger. *Absolution* or *Lossprechung*; Fr. *absolution*; Ital. *assoluzione*. The name commonly given to the phrase, 'I absolve thee from thy sins,' pronounced by a priest upon a penitent who has confessed. It is regarded as a judicial act. The Roman Catholic sacrament of Penance requires the payment of a debt of temporal punishment for sin. This takes the form of pious works, and used to be discharged partly by public penances. The essential points to be noted are that a priest alone can give absolution, and that he is able to do so only after confession.

Literature: S. J. HUNTER, Outlines of Dogmatic Theol., iii. 297 f.; JEROME, Op., xi. 499; BASIL, Op., ii. 492; BINTERIM, Denkwürdigkeiten, i. 1, 3; KLEE, Die Beichte; SIEMERS, Die Sacrament Beichte. (R.M.W.)

Absolutism (aesthetic): Ger. *aesthetischer Absolutismus*; Fr. *absolutisme esthétique*; Ital. *assolutismo estetico*. The doctrine that beauty is something objective and absolute, i.e. not relative to the observer, and hence that there is a fixed absolute standard of criticism.

The theory appears first as a part of Plato's system of idealism (see PLATONISM), in which it is held that any aesthetic criticism or comparison of individual beautiful things presupposes some standard of absolute beauty. It has in general been maintained by intuitionists in philosophy, and attacked by those who consider beauty merely a kind of pleasure, and hence dependent on the individual's organization. The absolutist would explain differences in individual judgment, by the fact that individuals may differ in their capacity to discover and appreciate. An intermediate position is that of Kant, that beauty is subjective, but that the judgment 'this is beautiful' is always made *as if* an objective standard existed. See BEAUTY. Begg, *The Development of Taste* (1887), and Marshall, *Pain, Pleasure, and Aesthetics* (1894), represent the two opposed standpoints. (J.H.T.)

Absolutism (political): Ger. *Absolutismus*; Fr. *absolutisme*; Ital. *assolutismo*. The absolute or unlimited rule, usually of one man; virtually equivalent to DESPOTISM (q.v.). (F.C.M.)

Absorption (in education) [Lat. *ab* + *sorbere*, to suck in]: Ger. *Vertiefung*; Fr. *absorption*; Ital. *assorbimento*. The complete occupation of the attention with an object of knowledge.

According to Herbart, the twofold process of culture is that of mental absorption and its removal through reflection. He calls absorption and reflection the inspiration and expiration of the soul. In the former the mind loses itself momentarily in the contem-

4

plation of new experiences; it forgets its normal order of thought through its absorption in what is novel, strange, or wonderful. Absorption is followed by reflection, which is a conscious process of APPERCEPTION (q.v.): the new experience takes its place henceforth as a mental possession. The comprehension of these two processes is of the utmost importance to the art of instruction. The Hegelian equivalent of absorption is SELF-ESTRANGEMENT (q.v.).

Literature: HERBART, Sci. of Educ. (trans. by Filkin), 123; DE GARMO, Essentials of Method, 40–42, and Herbart and the Herbartians; ROSENKRANZ, Philos. of Educ., 27. (C.DE G.)

Abstract (term, &c.): Ger. *abstrakt, abgezogen*; Fr. *abstrait*; Ital. *astratto*. Abstract is a relative designation, probably implying throughout its various uses, (*a*) the isolation of an aspect, quality, or relation from the whole in which it is directly apprehended, and (*b*) the employment of the isolated factor as the subject of an assertion, and therefore the assignment to it of a certain measure of independent, substantive existence. The second feature is prominent in the grammatical distinction of abstract from concrete terms.

The treatment of abstract terms begins with Aristotle, who contrasts the processes ἀφαίρεσις and πρόσθεσις, and takes his examples mainly from the contrast between mathematics and physics. In Aristotle, also, appears the general mark of abstraction, as departure from the immediate data of sense. Modern formal logic has tended to view the function of abstracting as a subordinate though necessary part of the process of GENERALIZATION (q.v.). The sounder view, psychologically, which rejects the distinction of kind between sense-apprehension and thought, cannot admit that there is only one group of notions or terms, entitled to claim for itself the designation abstract.

Literature: works on logic; MEINONG, Hume-Studien (1877–8); MEINONG-HÖFLER, Logik, 21 ff.; HUSSERL, in Philos. Monatshefte, xxx. 159 ff. (R.A.)

Abstract Idea: Ger. *abstrakte Vorstellung*; Fr. *idée abstraite*; Ital. *idea astratta*. When that view of an object which is gained by way of ABSTRACTION (q.v.) is regarded as a permanent possession of the mind, it is called an abstract idea. (G.F.S.–J.M.B.)

In a GENERAL IDEA (q.v.), like characters are apprehended as repeated, or capable of repetition, in a plurality of distinct instances. But the like nature thus repeated has

itself an internal constitution, which may be considered without reference to its particularization in a plurality of special cases. So considered, it forms an abstract universal, and the mode of thought by which it is apprehended is called an abstract idea or abstract conception. See CONCEPTION.

Man is a general concept or idea; humanity is an abstract concept or idea. Humanity consists in a group of characters found in each and every man. When we consider this group of characters *per se*, without reference to its repetition in a plurality of particular cases, we obtain the abstract idea of humanity. The general idea of course involves abstraction, inasmuch as the general nature is distinguished from its particular embodiments; but the abstract idea depends on a further abstraction performed upon the general idea. In this further abstraction the fact of generality is disregarded, and only the group of characters which possesses the generality is attended to. The object of an abstract concept is a universal, and a universal belonging to a general concept. But the universal is not the unity of particular instances or examples: it is rather the unity of the characters or attributes belonging to each instance or example.

In the language of logic the abstract concept is the connotation of a general term considered apart from its denotation. Mill defines an abstract name as a 'name which stands for an attribute of a thing.' Thus 'white is a name of a thing, or rather of things; whiteness is the name of a quality or attribute of those things. Man is a name of many things; humanity is a name of an attribute of those things.' He protests against the practice of 'applying the expression abstract name to all names which are the results of abstraction or generalization, and consequently to all general names, instead of confining it to the names of attributes.' (G.F.S., J.M.B.)

Literature: BERKELEY, Princ. of Human Knowledge, Introd., §§ 6–25, 97–100; HUME, Treatise on Human Nature, § 7; RIBOT, L'évolution des idées générales; VON KRIES, Ueber die Nature gewisser mit den psychischen Vorgängen verknüpfter Gehirnzustände, Zeitsch. f. Psychol. u. Physiol. d. Sinnesorgane, viii. S. 1; and Zur Psychologie des Urteils, Vtljsch. f. wiss. Philos., xxiii. Heft 1, S. 7; JAMES, Princ. of Psychol., i. 468, 508, ii. 48; WARD, art. Psychology, in Encyc. Brit., xx. 75–6; STOUT, Analytic Psychol., i. 78–91; BALDWIN, Ment. Devel. in the Child and the Race, chap. xi, with quotation from Royce, 330. See Bibliog. C, 2, *a*, and systematic works on psychology. (G.F.S.)

Abstraction [Lat. *ab + trahere*, to draw]: Ger. *Abstraktion*; Fr. *abstraction*; Ital. *astrazione*. Concentration of attention on those parts or characters of an object which are treated as relevant to the special interest of the moment, and its consequent withdrawal from those which are irrelevant.

Sometimes those characters which are specially attended to are said to be abstracted, viz. separated from the whole to which they belong. But so far as this language is accurate at all it applies to all selective interests. It is essential to abstraction to be prepared to recognize and disregard the irrelevant, and what is recognized as irrelevant is *ipso facto* abstracted from.

The interest on which abstraction depends must be of a certain kind. Something being initially presented as part of a given context, abstraction occurs only when the interest of thought lies in following out its relations, not within, but outside this context. To this end its relations within the given context must be as far as possible ignored; and when they obtrude themselves, they must be recognized as irrelevant, and for that reason disregarded. Such a process may demand more or less strenuous effort or 'resistant concentration' (Sully). A child may attend predominantly to the 'lustre of sunlit water' simply because it is the most impressive item within the context of its sense experience at the moment. In this case there is no process of abstraction. But abstraction is present in a well-marked form when a psychologist attends to the lustre of the water, because he is interested in analysing the perception of lustre in general, whatever may be the particular circumstances of its occurrence.

Abstraction is to be distinguished from analysis. The governing interest in analysis lies in discerning partial constituents within a given complex. The governing interest in abstraction lies in relating the partial constituents of a complex to partial constituents of other complexes. (G.F.S., J.M.B.)

Genetically, abstraction seems to be an adaptive function. The vague 'general' with which the child may be thought to start out in his treatment of an object is found to lead him into difficulties—notably in cases in which he adopts a word from his social fellows and applies it too widely, by the broad inclusion of similars. He is forced to adapt himself to differences, and this is genetically, no doubt, the beginning of abstraction. So in the case given above, when the child finds that the lustre of the water disappears so soon as he changes his position, the process of abstracting lustre has begun. He does not intentionally seek for a given quality in similar objects; that would require the abstract idea beforehand ready-made. On the contrary, he acts upon his concrete perception or image, and finds differences compelling him to drop out inconsistent details, which then become in so far irrelevant to his future use of the idea. This growth in intention at the expense of extension gradually results in the relative isolation of this or that mark or quality, according to the exigencies of this or that interest from moment to moment. It has been called a sort of 'erosion' or wearing down. When the mental habit of comparison and logical analysis has been acquired, this process is less important, giving way to deliberate exclusion and inclusion of marks. (J.M.B., G.F.S.)

Literature: A. Meinong, Vtljsch. f. wiss. Philos. (1888), 329 ff.; general works on psychology. (G.F.S.–J.M.B.)

Absurd (in logic): Ger. *sinnlos*; Fr. *absurde*; Ital. *assurdo*. See Fallacy, and Reductio ad absurdum.

Academy and **New Academy** [Gr. Ἀκαδέμος, proper name]: Ger. *Akademie*; Fr. *académie*; Ital. *accademia*. See Schools of Greece, and Renaissance.

Acatalepsy [Gr. ἀκαταληψία]. Unknowableness; a term used by the Greek Sceptics. See Unknowable, and Scepticism. (J.M.B.)

Acatamathesia (or **Akat-**) [Gr. *a + κατά + μαθεῖν*, to learn]: Ger. *Akatamathesie*; Fr. *aprosexie* (inability to attend); Ital. *acatamatesi*. Inability to comprehend ordinary conversation, accompanied by a blunting of the perceptions. It appears as a degenerative symptom in various forms of chronic Insanity (q.v.). (J.J.)

Acataphasia (or **Akat-**) [Gr. *ἀ + κατά + φάναι*, to speak]: Ger. *Akataphasie*; Fr. *paraphasie* (see Aphrasia — P.J.); Ital. *acatafasia*. A disorder of speech appearing as an inability to connect words properly in sentences; a disorder of the syntactical arrangement of words. It is thus an aphasic defect which involves the most complicated components of spoken language. The coarse outlines of speech—words and their meanings—are understood and spoken, but their finer relations in the sentence are confused. The term was suggested by Steinthal and adopted by Kussmaul, *Störungen der Sprache*, chap. xxx. See SPEECH AND ITS DEFECTS. (J.J.)

Acceleration (law of): Ger. *Heterochronie* (Haeckel); Fr. *loi d'accélération de développement, tachygénèse*; Ital. *legge di acceleramento ontogenetico*. 'All modifications and variations in progressive series tend to appear first in the adolescent or adult stages of growth, and then to be inherited in successive descendants at earlier and earlier stages according to the law of acceleration, until they either become embryonic, or are crowded out of the organization, and replaced in the development by characteristics of later origin' (Alphaeus Hyatt).

This 'law' was put forth independently by A. Hyatt and E. D. Cope, who lay much stress on its importance. Meynert regards acceleration in the embryological development of an organ as definitely correlated with the biological importance of that organ. (C.LL.M.)

Darwin called this principle that of 'earlier inheritance.' A very similar principle of ontogenetic acceleration has also been made use of by Haeckel ('heterochrony') and by Lankester ('precocious segregation') to explain the early appearance of certain characters in embryos. (E.S.G.)

Literature: A. HYATT, Mem. Bost. Soc. Nat. Hist. (1866), 193; E. D. COPE, Trans. Amer. Philos. Soc. (1866), 398; The Origin of the Fittest (1887); The Primary Factors of Organic Evolution (1896); ERNST MEYNERT, Biomechanik erschlossen aus dem Princip der Organogenese (1898). (C.LL.M.)

Also E. HAECKEL, Anthropogenie, 3. Aufl. (1877); E. R. LANKESTER, Notes on Embryology and Classification, Quart. J. Microsc. Sci., N. S., xvii. (1877). (E.S.G.)

Accent [Fr. *accent*, from Lat. *accentus*, blast or tone]: Ger. *Accent*; Fr. *accent*; Ital. *accento*. A term employed in phonology, with some confusion of use, to denote the varying quality, pitch, or stress of vowel-sounds. It may also be applied to the conventional marks for denoting the same; as in French or Greek.

The Greek προσῳδία (πρός, in addition, + ῷδή, song), of which the Lat. *accentus* (*ad* + *cano*, sing) is a mere translation, was used by the Greek grammarians to include all the written signs, the marks of quantity, the breathings, the three accents proper, the hyphen, the apostrophe, &c., which were added to the letters to guide pronunciation. The Greek

word-accent was a matter of varying pitch, accompanied also undoubtedly by some distinction of stress. That which the French accents mark is only a variety of quality, and that now often only of historical value; *é* is usually close *e*, *è* open. The English word-accent is distinguished most prominently by stress, or relative force of expulsion. The term accent is also loosely used to denote a peculiar colouring of pronunciation in the dialect of an individual or a community. (B.I.W.)

Accentuation (in psychology): Ger. *Betonung*; Fr. *accentuation*; Ital. *accentuazione*. The subjective emphasis put upon certain terms of a series in consciousness, which makes the series more or less rhythmical. (J.M.B.–G.F.S.)

The German equivalent is used by Wundt (*Outlines of Psychol.*, § 11, B) in discussing auditory tone series. See RHYTHM. (J.M.B.)

Acceptance [Lat. *acceptatio*]. Recommended to replace the word recognition, sometimes used as translation of the German Anerkennen (-ung). Cf. Hegel's use of Anerkennung in his *Philos. of Mind*; and Eisler, *Wörterb. d. philos. Begriffe*, sub verbo. (J.M.B.)

Accessory: see PRINCIPAL.

Accident: see ESSENCE AND ACCIDENT, and CHANCE.

Accident (1) and **Accidental** (2) [Lat. *ad* + *cadere*, to fall]: Ger. *Accidenz* (1), *zufällig* (2); Fr. *accident*(-*el*); Ital. *accidente* (-*tale*). (1) That which is not essential or substantial. See ESSENCE, and SUBSTANCE; also the equivalent terms in the Latin and Greek glossaries under TERMINOLOGY.

(2) From this the further meaning of that which is disconnected with substance, and so uncaused and fortuitous. A 'pure accident' or the 'purely accidental' indicates that which is uncaused, and which thus illustrates chance in the old sense of the Greek τύχη. As the word chance has come to mean subject to the law of probability, and hence not fortuitous, this meaning of accident should be retained. (J.M.B.)

Accidentalism. The theory that events may occur absolutely without cause. In ethics it is INDETERMINISM (q. v., also for foreign equivalents); in metaphysics it is TYCHISM. Cf. ACCIDENT, and CHANCE. (J.M.B.)

Accidenter: see PER ACCIDENS.

Acclimatization: see ACCOMMODATION (in biology).

Accommodation (in biology): Ger. *Accomodation, Anpassung*; Fr. *accommodation, adaptation*; Ital. *adattamento*. (*a*) The process by which an organism reaches functional adaptation. (*b*) The state attained by the process (*a*). These meanings were suggested by J. Mark Baldwin (1896). Cf. *Nature*, lv. 558. (C.LL.M.)

The term applies to any acquired alteration of function resulting in better adjustment to environment; and to the functional changes which are thus effected. For special cases we have the terms Acclimatization (accommodation to new climatic conditions), Naturalization (accommodation of an organism as a whole to new bionomic conditions), and Equilibrium or Balance (a state of relatively good adjustment due to structural adaptation of the organism as a whole). On the distinction between accommodation and ADAPTATION see the latter term. See also MODIFICATION.

Literature: DE VARIGNY, art. Acclimatation in Richet's Dict. de Physiol. (with literature); CONTAULIN, Accommodation des Plantes, &c., Bull. Soc. France-Belg., xxx. 489; Les Végétaux et les Milieux cosmiques (1897); DAVENPORT, Exper. Morphol., ii ; BALDWIN, Ment. Devel. in the Child and the Race (1895). Also under MODIFICATION. (J.M.B.)

Accommodation (in psychology) [Lat. *ad + commodus*, fit]: Ger. *Accomodation* ; Fr. *accommodation* ; Ital. *accomodazione*. The determination of a function as modified by the incorporation of new elements. A single case of such incorporation is an accommodation, and the generalization that the mind's progress and growth is by such modifications is the law or principle of accommodation.

Analysis shows that the element most prominently involved is conation; and the conation involved in the function passes from an initial stage of less voluntary, or perhaps completely non-voluntary, conation up to more voluntary conation, culminating in intensely felt effort. This progressive modification of the conditions of determination through a series of stages is, when considered as characteristic of mental progress, a genetic principle the reverse of HABIT (q.v.). As habit is the principle of mental 'conservation of type,' so accommodation is the principle of modification of type. This sort of determination has been called by Stout 'relative suggestion' (*Analytic Psychol.*). He now restricts this phrase, however, to accommodations resulting in modifications in trains of thought. The process by which accommodation is secured is said to be 'adaptive.' The term adaptation, however, is ambiguous. See ADAPTATION (in biology). The process is one of attention, and has been

variously described as SELECTION (mental), SELECTIVE THINKING, &c. See those terms.

Literature: see SELECTION, and HABIT; also BIBLIOG. G, 1, *f*, and 2, *f*. (J.M.B.–G.F.S.)

Accommodation (visual) : Ger. *Accomodation* ; Fr. *accommodation* ; Ital. *accomodamento*. The adjustment of the eye to objects at different distances by alterations in the distance between the lens and the retina (Cephalopods, Fish, Amphibians, and Snakes) or in the convexity of the lens by the contraction or relaxation of the ciliary muscle (Chelonians, Crocodiles, Lizards, Birds, Mammals). (C.LL.M.–E.S.G.)

Literature: M. FOSTER, Textbook of Physiol. (5th ed.), 1151 ; LECONTE, Sight (2nd ed.); TH. BEER, Proc. Int. Physiol. Cong. (1898) ; J. of Physiol., xxiii. (1898–9) ; WERTHEIMER, art. Accommodation in Richet's Dict. de Physiol. (with bibliography); NORRIS and OLIVER'S System of Diseases of the Eye, i. 501. See Eye under VISION, and LABORATORY AND APPARATUS (phakoscope). (E.S.G.–J.M.B.)

The true theory of accommodation dates from Descartes (HELMHOLTZ, Physiol. Optik, 2nd ed., 154). See WALLER, Human Physiol., 414 ; WUNDT, Physiol. Psychol. (4th ed.), ii. 107 ; ARRER, in Philos. Stud., xiii. 116, 222 ; SANFORD, Course in Exper. Psychol., expts. 105–8. (E.B.T.)

Also M. TSCHERNING, Le mécanisme de l'accommodation, Rev. Gén. des Sci. (1894), 80 f.; Étude sur le mécanisme de l'accommodation, Arch. de Physiol. (1894), 158 f. ; Recherches sur les changements optiques de l'œil pendant l'accommodation, Arch. de Physiol. (1895), 158–69, 181–94. (L.M.)

Accommodation (principle of, in theology). A term commonly used in connection with biblical interpretation. A doctrine is set forth, not absolutely and in its full meaning and consequences, regardless of all other considerations, but in relation to the circumstances or capacities of those for whom the teaching is intended. Primarily, it may be viewed as an integral part of divine grace condescending to human frailty. Secondarily, it is often employed in relation to all kinds of instruction connected with religion. Parable, metaphor, analogy are common instances of it.

Literature: ZACHANIA, Essay upon the Condescension of God toward Man (1763). See ESOTERIC. (R.M.W.)

Accompanying Movements : for foreign equivalents see CONSENSUAL. Involuntary or indirectly stimulated movements accompanying or associated with voluntary or directly stimulated movements.

Physiologically such movements are secondary to the reactions which the stimulus normally excites, or correlated with them; such as symmetrical movements of both sides, two arms, &c., when the stimulus is applied to the apparatus of one side only. The phenomenon is held to illustrate the irradiation of nervous discharges, particularly under intense stimulation. In voluntary movements they are more marked when effort is intense.

Literature: VIERORDT, Physiol. d. Kindesalters; MÜNSTERBERG, Beitr. z. exper. Psychol., iv; BALDWIN, Ment. Devel. in the Child and the Race, chap. iv. § 1; citations under LOCALIZATION (cerebral); the textbooks of physiology. (J.M.B.)

Accountable [ME. *accompt*, from Lat. *computum*]: Ger. *verantwortlich*; Fr. *comptable, responsable*; Ital. *responsabile*. The relation of the agent to some judge in respect to his action.

The term is jural in origin; but its application is extended when transferred to ethics. The accountableness is regarded sometimes as social or legal (e.g. a man is accountable to the laws of his country), or theological (he is accountable to God—a quasi-legal conception). Sometimes a purely personal significance is given to the conception. Thus a man is said to be accountable to his own conscience, which passes judgment upon his conduct by reference to an ideal code of rules, or to an ideal self, conformity to which he acknowledges to be his duty. A late statement in terms of the ideal self is that of Baldwin (*Social and Eth. Interpret.*, chap. ix). See OBLIGATION. (W.R.S.)

Accuracy of Discrimination. See DIFFERENCE (just noticeable), and cf. WEBER'S LAW.

Achenwall, Gottfried. (1719–72.) German writer on statistics; professor of philosophy at Göttingen. He introduced the term Staatswissenschaft.

Achilles Argument: see ZENO (of Elia).

Achillini, Alessandro. (1463–1512.) Celebrated lecturer in medicine and in philosophy, chiefly in Bologna: was styled the second Aristotle. He and Mundinus were the first, after the permission given by Frederick II, to dissect dead bodies.

Achromatopsia [Gr. $\dot{a}$ + $\chi\rho\hat{\omega}\mu a$, colour, + $\check{o}\psi\iota s$, sight]: Ger. *Achromatopsie*; Fr. *achromatopsie*; Ital. *acromatopsia*. A defective perception of colour: COLOUR BLINDNESS (q.v.). See also VISION (defects of). (J.J.)

Aconative. Not involving CONATION (q.v.). Cf. ACTION, and NON-VOLUNTARY (also for foreign equivalents). (J.M.B., G.F.S.)

Acosmism [Gr. $\dot{a}$ + $\kappa\acute{o}\sigma\mu os$, world]: see PANTHEISM.

Acoumetry [Gr. $\dot{a}\kappa o\acute{u}\epsilon\iota\nu$, to hear, + $\mu\acute{e}\tau\rho o\nu$, measured]: Ger. *Akumetrie*; Fr. *acoumétrie, acumétrie*; Ital. *acumetria*. The quantitative determination of hearing capacity, e.g. of the distance at which a sound of standard loudness is heard with variations according to direction. The standard clinical instrument is Politzer's acoumeter, in which a c^2 is given by the drop of a steel point upon a steel rod. In psychological laboratories the telephone is often adapted to this purpose (Münsterberg, Cattell).

Literature: SANFORD, Course in Exper. Psychol., expt. 61. (E.B.T.–J.M.B.)

Acoumetry is also used to include the investigation of the hearing of pitch and timbre. (J.McK.C.)

Acousma [Gr. $\check{a}\kappa o\nu\sigma\mu a$, from $\dot{a}\kappa o\acute{u}\epsilon\iota\nu$, to hear]: Ger. *Akusma*; Fr. *illusion ou hallucination auditive*; Ital. *acusma*. A form of auditory hallucination. See HALLUCINATION, and ILLUSION. (J.J.)

Acoustics (psychological) [Gr. $\dot{a}\kappa o\nu\sigma\tau\iota\kappa\acute{o}s$, relating to hearing]: Ger. *Akustik*; Fr. *acoustique*; Ital. *acustica*. The science of HEARING (q.v.). (J.M.B.)

It rests upon (1) the physical doctrine of sound, and (2) the results of anatomical and physiological investigation into the structure and function of the auditory apparatus. It includes (1) the psychophysics of simple tone and noise; (2) the psychophysics and psychology of the perception of sound; and (3) the psychology of music. (E.B.T.)

Literature: HELMHOLTZ, Sensations of Tone, trans. from the 4th ed. (1877) of the German work (Tonempfindungen) by A. J. Ellis (last ed., 1895); STUMPF, Tonpsychologie, i (1883) and ii (1890), and Beitr. z. Ak. u. Musikwiss., i. ii. (1898); HENSEN in Hermann's Handb. d. Physiol., iii. 2 (1880); KÖNIG, Quelques expériences d'acoustique (1882). (E.B.T.)

Acoustics (physiological): see HEARING.

Acquired (in psychology) [Lat. *ad* + *quaerere*, seek]: Ger. *erworben*; Fr. *acquis*; Ital. *acquisito*. Added during the individual's life to the original or innate equipment of the mind; experiential.

This term had considerable currency during

the early controversy on innate ideas, in the phrases 'acquired' ideas, perceptions, notions, judgments, capacities. It was made much of by the Scottish philosophers, indicating what was not 'intuitive' (Reid, Hamilton, McCosh). It thus came to mean 'due to experience' in discussions which discriminated sharply between what was 'native' and what 'acquired.' It is analogous to the use of the same term in biology—in the phrase ACQUIRED CHARACTERS (q.v.)—as contrasted with those which are congenital. Cf. INNATE IDEAS.

Literature: HAMILTON, Metaphysics, chap. xviii; REID, Active Powers, and Essays, iii. Pt. I. chap. iii; McCosh, Cognitive Powers, chap. i. §§ 12–14. (J.M.B.)

Acquired (1) and (2) **Congenital Characters**: Ger. *erworbene und congenitale Eigenschaften*; Fr. *caractères acquis et caractères innés*; Ital. *caratteri acquisiti e caratteri congeniti*. (1) Those modifications of bodily structure or habit which are impressed on the organism in the course of individual life. (C.Ll.M.)

(2) Those characters or properties with which the organism is originally endowed. (E.S.G.)

Acquired characters are logically, but not practically, distinguishable from congenital characters. An organism being the result of the interaction between its innate or congenital qualities and its environment, every particular character is developed under the influence of certain stimuli, and so partakes of the nature both of an acquired and of a congenital character (cf. Delage, *Structure du Protoplasma*; Roux, *Kampf der Theile im Organismus*). Some go so far on the strength of this as to contend that all characters are alike 'acquired' (Ortmann, *Biol. Centralbl.*, Feb. 15, 1898). When the complex of stimuli, which constitute the normal environment, are sufficiently altered (to upset that balance established between environment and innate qualities resulting in the production of a normal individual) to produce an appreciable change, such a modification or 'difference' (Sedgwick, Pres. Addr. Brit. Assoc., *Nature*, Sept. 21, 1899) may be called an acquired character. The response to a stimulus is determined, apart from the properties of the stimulus itself, by the degree of plasticity of the organism (its responsiveness). Acquired characters may be grouped in three classes: (1) Mutilations; (2) Modifications brought about directly by the environment (the cause of evolution according to Buffon and Saint-Hilaire); (3) Modifications brought about indirectly through use and disuse, Use-Inheritance (Ball) or Kinetogenesis (the cause of evolution according to Lamarck's theory). The transmissibility of acquired characters depends in the first place on whether they persist after the cessation of the stimulus under the influence of which they arose, or whether they disappear or become obliterated by the modifications called forth by the succeeding stimulus. In the latter case there can be no question of hereditary transmission. On the other hand, if a stimulus can so affect an organism as to leave an impress, which persists, and is not obliterated by the effect of succeeding stimuli, such modification would obviously affect succeeding generations in cases of fission and budding, and possibly also in cases of sexual generation, by its supposed effect on the germ-cells (or embryo in viviparous forms). For further discussion see HEREDITY, and VARIATION.

Although Prichard, in 1826, had clearly distinguished between acquired and congenital characters, and had denied the transmissibility of the former, and Galton, in 1875, had independently come to the same conclusion, it was not till 1883 that the inheritance of modifications was seriously questioned by zoologists. (E.S.G.–J.M.B.)

Up to 1883 the inheritance of modifications played a leading part in the conception of organic evolution as presented by Lamarck and expounded by Herbert Spencer, but held a subordinate position in that formulated by Darwin.

In that year Weismann denied the possibility of hereditary transmission of such acquired characters. Weismann claims, in the first place, that there is no sufficient evidence that modifications are transmitted, and in the second place that, on the CELL-THEORY (q.v.) as now understood, the line of hereditary continuity and descent is through the germinal cells, and not through those which compose the substance of the rest of the body. It is claimed, on the other hand, by those who still adhere to the view that acquired characters are (sexually) transmitted, that, although the body-cells are not in the line of direct hereditary transmission, they may none the less in some way influence the germ-plasm so as to impress upon it the tendency to give rise to variations similar to the modifications acquired by the body-cells. Darwin's view was that they throw off gemmules which are collected in germ-cells (see PANGENESIS). W. K. Brooks remodelled the theory in 1883, but modern investigation lends little support to this view. Weismann held that the modifications of the cell-substance of the unicellular organisms were transmitted. Even this is denied by those who hold that the CHROMOSOMES (q.v.) of the nucleus are independent of the cell-substance; but in cases of fission (as said above) modifications must be carried on. (C.LL.M.)

Various names have been suggested for acquired and congenital characters; for the latter, the terms blastogenic, centrifugal, inborn, innate, and inherent character are used; for the former, the terms somatogenic and centripetal character. (E.S.G.)

Literature: J. C. PRICHARD, Researches into the Physical History of Mankind (2nd ed., 1826) (cf. E. B. POULTON, A Remarkable Anticipation of Modern Views on Evolution, Sci. Progress, 1896); A. WEISMANN, Ueber Vererbung, in Essays, i; The Germ-Plasm (1893); C. DARWIN, Animals and Plants under Domestication (1st ed., 1868); W. K. BROOKS, The Law of Heredity (1883); The Foundations of Zoology (1899); TH. EIMER, Organic Evolution, trans. by J. T. Cunningham (1890); HERBERT SPENCER, Princ. of Biol. (2nd ed., 1899), also Contemp. Rev. (Feb. and March, 1893); J. DELAGE, L'Hérédité (1895); G. J. ROMANES, Darwin and after Darwin; W. HAACKE, Gestaltung und Vererbung (1893), and Grundriss der Entwicklungsmech. (1897); O. HERTWIG, Zeitsch. u. Streitfragen d. Biol. (1894); K. GROOS, Die Spiele der Thiere (1896; Eng. trans., 1898); E. B. WILSON, The Cell (1896); E. D. COPE, The Primary Factors of Organic Evolution (1896); A. SEDGWICK, Pres. Addr. Brit. Assoc. (Section Zoology, 1899); G. WOLFF, Beitr. z. Krit. d. Darwin'schen Lehre (1898). (C.LL.M.–E.S.G.)

Acquisitiveness [Lat. *acquisitus*, from *acquirere*, to acquire]: Ger. *Habsucht* (1), *Lernfähigkeit* (2); Fr. *instinct d'appropriation* (1), *faculté d'acquisition* (2); Ital. *istinto di appropriazione* (1), *appropriatività* (2). (1) In general; the propensity to appropriate objects so as to make them part of one's personal belongings. (G.F.S.)

(2) In psychology; relative ease of acquiring or learning, considered usually as part of a person's natural endowment. (J.M.B.)

Acro- [Gr. ἀκρο-, combining form of ἄκρος, high, extreme]: Ger. (not used); *Höhenfurcht* (acrophobia); Fr. *acro-*; Ital. *acro-*. A prefix used to express an extreme form of a condition, such as *Acroaesthesia*, exaggerated sensitiveness; *Acromania*, pronounced or un-

curable insanity. It has a more literal sense in *Acrophobia*, a term used (by Verga) to indicate an extreme or morbid dread of being at a great height and a marked uneasiness when in such positions. See PHOBIA. It is further used in its original sense of high, as in *Acrocephalic*. (J.J.)

Acroamatic [Gr. ἀκρόαμα, things heard]. ESOTERIC (q.v.). Applied to the more private lectures and teachings given by Aristotle to his pupils. (J.M.B.)

Act [Lat. *actio*, a deed, an action]: Ger. *That*; Fr. *acte*; Ital. *atto*. A deed performed with some foresight and deliberation, whether carried out in muscular movement or not. See ACTION (in psychology), meaning (1). (J.M.B.–G.F.S.)

Act (in ethics). An event which is due to human ACTIVITY (q.v.) and is not merely the result of the laws of nature. It includes any volition, whether an external effect follows the 'inner act' or 'act of will,' or not.

In more popular usage the term is applied not only to changes brought about by a volition or 'act of will,' but also to those due to organic reflexes. Hence the distinction of voluntary and involuntary acts. It is commonly held that morality, as distinct from law, takes cognizance only of the former. Cf. CONDUCT.

Literature: KANT, Werke (ed. Hartenstein), vi. 125–6, and Theory of Ethics, Abbott's trans. (3rd ed.), 337–8; POLLOCK, First Book of Jurisprudence, Pt. I. chap. vi. (W.R.S.)

Act (in law): Ger. (1) *That, Handlung*; (2), (3) *Acte* (Act of the German Confederation, *Bundesacte*; Act of Accusation, *Anklageacte*); (4) *Rechtsgeschäft*; Fr. (1), (2), (3) *acte*; (2) *loi*; (4) *acte juridique*; Ital. *atto*. (1) A determination of will, producing an external effect in the world of sense. See FACT. (2) An act of legislation; a statute. *Public Acts* are statutes passed to regulate matters of general concern, and all subjects of the enacting power are bound to know them. *Private Acts* are statutes passed to regulate private interests, and the general public are not presumed to know them. (3) Rarely (except on the Continent of Europe), an act of administrative government, as a notarial protest, or an act of accusation (equivalent to indictment). (4) *Juristic Act*, an act producing an effect which was intended by the doer (Holland, *Jurisprudence*, 100; Markby, *Elements of Law*, chap. vi. § 235). *Act of God*, any event resulting from forces beyond human control, and which a man cannot be expected to foresee, or foreseeing, to prevent or oppose; *Vis maior* (Hohenmacht). Cf. a somewhat broader definition in Pollock on *Contracts*, chap. vii. 366 : 'Under the term *act of God* are comprehended all misfortunes and accidents arising from inevitable necessity, which human prudence could not foresee or prevent.' Williams *v.* Grant, 1 Conn. Law Reports, 491. 'Vis maior, quam Graeci θεοῦ βίαν, id est, vim caelestim appellant' (*Dig.* xix. 2, *Locati Conducti*, 25, § 6). It excuses a man from the performance of what would otherwise be a legal duty, unless he has bound himself by contract to the contrary. It is a legal maxim that *Actus dei nemini facit iniuriam.*

Literature: POLLOCK, First Book of Jurisprudence, chap. vi. 132 f. (1896); ZITELMANN, Irrtum und Rechtsgeschäft : eine psychologisch-juristische Untersuchung (1879). (S.E.B.)

Act of God : see ACT (in law).

Actio ad Distans : see GRAVITATION.

Action (in law): Ger. *Rechtshandel, Process, Klage* (civil action, *Civilklage*; criminal prosecution, *Kriminalklage*); Fr. *action, procès*; Ital. *azione giudiziaria*. A lawsuit; a particular right growing out of the violation of other rights, and given by law, either to put a stop to such violation, or to give redress for the injury already suffered, or both. Redress is secured sometimes through restitution, sometimes through compensation. An action *in personam* seeks to enforce a right against a person; an action *in rem*, a right to a thing against all persons whatsoever. *Chose in action*, a thing to which a person is entitled who is not in possession of it. The moving party in an action *in personam* is styled the actor, plaintiff, complainant, demandant, petitioner, orator (in equity suits), libellant (in admiralty); the party against whom he moves, the *reus*, defendant, or respondent (in equity suits).

Austin, in his *Jurisprudence* (Lectures xx, xxiv, xxv), considers the liability of a wrongdoer to an action at law as the sanction imposed by law for its transgression, and so a penalty for disobedience. Cf. Holland, *Jurisprudence*, chap. xiii. (S.E.B.)

Action (in psychology): Ger. (1) *Action, Thätigkeit* (general, contrasted with *Passion*), (2) *Thätigkeit* (e. g. *Reflexthätigkeit*); Fr. *action*; Ital. *azione*. (1) A general term for deeds or ACTS (q. v.) and the doing of them. See CONDUCT. (2) Used also in phrases for various sorts of motor processes, as (q. v.) REFLEX ACTION, VOLUNTARY ACTION. See also REACTION.

We recommend the following scheme of terms for the different sorts of action; it is carried out under the various headings: actions are (1) 'Voluntary,' (2) 'Non-voluntary,' (3) 'Involuntary.' Voluntary actions are those which (*a*) are and (*b*) may be performed by an act of will, i. e. (*a*) 'Volitional,' and (*b*) 'Unvolitional' or 'Spontaneous.' Non-voluntary are those which are performed quite in independence of the will, i. e. 'Reflex,' 'Automatic' actions. Involuntary actions are those which are opposed by the will; they occur in spite of a volition to the contrary. See VOLITION, and Veto under FIAT. In terms of conation, actions are: (1) 'Conative,' (2) 'Aconative,' (3) 'Contra-conative.'

Literature: general works on psychology and ethics. (J.M.B., G.F.S.)

Action and Reaction (law of): Ger. *Einwirkung und Gegenwirkung, Action und Reaction, Reactionsprincip*; Fr. *action et réaction*; Ital. *azione e reazione*. The law that whenever one body, *A*, exerts a mechanical force or system of forces upon another body, *B*, the latter exerts an equal force or system of forces on *A* in the same lines but in the opposite direction. For example, when the foot presses down upon the ground, the latter presses upward against the foot with equal force. First clearly stated by Newton in his *Principia*. See FORCE. (S.N.)

Action Current : see NEGATIVE VARIATION.

Active Powers : Ger. *Actionsvermögen*; Fr. *facultés actives*; Ital. *facoltà attive*. The capacities of impulse and desire which lead to or determine human action, as distinguished from the capacities of reasoning, judging, conceiving, &c. (called Intellectual or Cognitive Powers). It is no longer in use as a technical term.

The distinction is derived from Aristotle's analysis of the capacities or powers (δυνάμεις) of living beings into nutrition, appetite, perception, movement, and reason. Of these, reason is held to be peculiar to man, in whom, however, appetite (including desire, sensuous impulse, and will) partakes of reason in the sense of being able to obey it. On the distinction thus reached between the appetitive and the purely rational functions of man was founded the distinction of moral and intellectual virtues. Aristotle's fivefold distinction of powers was adopted by Aquinas, but he discussed in detail only the intellectual and appetitive powers—the latter including desire and will.

Thomas Reid gave currency to this dual division in the early philosophical literature of the 19th century, although the psychologists preceding Kant had substituted a tripartite division by the separation of feeling and activity. Thus Tetens reckons three fundamental powers of the soul: feeling, understanding, and active power. Later writers who retain a twofold division (e. g. McCosh) include feeling among the active or 'motive' powers. Cf. CLASSIFICATION (of mental functions), and CONATION. Reid distinguished will from the principles of action, and included under the latter (1) mechanical principles (instinct and habit); (2) animal principles (appetite, desire, &c.); (3) rational principles (e. g. duty, rectitude).

Literature: ARISTOTLE, De Anima, ii. 3; Eth. Nic., i. 7, 13; REID, Intellectual Powers (1785), and Active Powers (1788); TETENS, Versuche über die menschliche Natur (1777), i. 625; McCOSH, Motive Powers, and Cognitive Powers. (W.R.S.)

Activity [Lat. *activitas*]: Ger. *Thätigkeit, Activität*; Fr. *activité*; Ital. *attività*. (1) The state of any being at the time when it is changing. (2) Any operation or change itself. In the first sense one says that the object is 'in activity.' In the second sense one speaks of the 'activities' of the mind; or of bodies, as in the phrase *actio ad distans*, action over an intervening space. (3) In case of those who regard activity and real being as essentially the same thing, to be *in actu*, or sometimes to be active, has on occasion meant the same as to be real. (4) Activity, in Aristotle's list of the categories, is opposed to such categories as substance, quality, &c. It is here a name for a doing, as opposed to a being, a character, or a passive state. Physical Activity is the operation of a being in the physical world. Mental Activity is a process supposed to be directly observable, or else otherwise verifiable, in mental life—a process whereby either the 'mind' or 'Ego' acts, or else an operation occurs, for which see ACTIVITY (mental). Self-activity is variously used to mean: (1) the activity of something whose operation is solely the result or effect of its own nature; (2) the activity of a being already called, for other reasons, a Self. See SELF-ACTIVITY, and SELF.

The whole history of the term activity, and of its related terms, has been greatly influenced by an unfortunate ambiguity in Aristotle's terminology. Act, or actuality (ἐνέργεια), in Aristotle's sense, is first opposed to potential being, or to what is merely possible. Yet, as thus opposed, ἐνέργεια is not the category ποιεῖν. But since Aristotle's account of God makes him, in the terms used by the scholastics, *actus purus*, or purely actual, this expression, and its Greek originals, have suggested that to be real, and to be active, must mean precisely the same thing, and by contrast the passive has even thus been sometimes confused with the merely possible. Apart from this historical misfortune of terminology, the idea of activity goes back of course to primitive speech, and to popular interpretations of experience. Two regions of experience especially gave origin to the notion of activity, and have controlled its development. On the one hand, physical things (e. g. the sun, or fire) appeared to affect or to act upon other things in observable ways. On the other hand, the process of effort and volition, as observed within, suggested the existence and the nature of active processes in a very complex but interesting way. Primitive thought brought these two sets of facts, the outer and the inner 'active' processes, into a close relation in the animistic interpretation of nature. Thought has ever since been busy, as science and reflection have developed, (1) in trying to distinguish and to contrast the two sorts of 'active processes' which animism confused; (2) in trying in various ways once more to synthesize the two, or to reduce one of them, despite the recognized distinction, to the other as its source, basis, or explanation; or finally, (3) in trying to explain how the activities, whatever they may be as activities, are related to the other modes of reality, such as Matter, Soul, Qualities, Relations, &c. The story of these efforts would involve the greater part of the history of psychology and philosophy. See IMMANENT AND TRANSIENT, and CAUSE. (J.R.)

Literature: the general works on metaphysics. Recent: LOTZE, Metaphysics; LADD, Theory of Reality (1899), chaps. v, x; WARD, Naturalism and Agnosticism; WUNDT, Syst. d. Philos., and Logik; ORMOND, Basal Concepts in Philos.; PAULSEN, Introd. to Philos.; HODGSON, Metaphysics of Experience. (J.M.B.)

Activity (mental): Ger. *psychische Activität, Thätigkeit, Action*; Fr. *activité mentale*; Ital. *attività mentale*. If and so far as the intrinsic nature of conscious process involves tendency toward a TERMINUS (q. v.), it is active process, and is said to have activity. See END, and TENDENCY. (G.F.S.-J.M.B.)

It is a disputed point whether a distinctive

activity-experience exists other than sensations of motor strain and the like. Our definition leaves that question unanswered, and relates to activity considered as a form of process and not as a peculiar experience. The older conception of active process is well expressed by Locke (*Essay on Human Understanding*, Bk. II. chap. xxi. § 72) : ' The active power of motion is in no substance which cannot begin motion in itself, or in another substance, when at rest. So likewise in thinking, a power to receive ideas or thoughts, from the operation of any external substance, is called a power of thinking : but this is but a passive power or capacity. But to be able to bring into view ideas out of sight at one's own choice, and to compare which of them one thinks fit, this is an active power.' We have generalized this view so as to include all direction toward a terminus as well as explicit choice. Older psychologists often draw a sharp line of distinction between active processes and passive processes. Some limit activity to practical activity, and regard the cognitive side of our nature as purely passive. Reid, e. g., distinguishes between intellectual and ACTIVE POWERS (q. v.). The modern tendency is to regard the distinction as one of degree rather than of kind, the element of conation being in some measure present in both. In recent times there has been much discussion concerning the nature and even the existence of mental activity. Ward regards it as a simple and ultimate datum of consciousness. According to him it is essential to all consciousness, and no account of it can be adequate which does not emphasize the concept of efficiency. The notion of causal efficiency in general is ultimately derived from mental activity. Wundt speaks of an ' immediate feeling of activity' (*Thätigkeitsgefühl*). Bradley, on the other hand, regards the experience of activity as a comparatively late and complex product of mental development. It is difficult to say whether he regards in the same way activity itself in distinction from the experience of it. Shadworth Hodgson entirely denies validity to the conception of mental activity. Activity-experiences are, according to him, indications of the existence of an activity which is not mental, but neural. We have tried to evade these debated questions by defining activity as a certain form of process which appears certainly to exist, whatever we may think of its origin and implications. The limiting cases would seem to be (1) so-called ' anoetic' or ' passive' consciousness, in which the whole question of ' conscious process,' as

a narrower term than ' conscious experience,' would be in debate, and (2) cases of nonvoluntary process, of such an automatic or habitual kind that the concept of terminus loses its application.

Literature: JAMES, Princ. of Psychol., i. 296–305 ; WUNDT, Grundzüge der physiologischen Psychologie, Syst. d. Philos.; REHMKE, Allg. Psychol., 348–425 ; BRADLEY, Appearance and Reality (2nd ed.), 96–100 603–7 ; Mind, O.S., 43, 47 ; HÖFFDING, Wiedererkennen, Association und psychische Activität, Vtljsch. f. wiss. Philos., xiv. ; WARD, Mind, O.S.; STOUT, Analytic Psychol., i. Bk. II. chap. i ; BALDWIN, Handb. of Psychol., Senses and Intellect, 64, 69, and Psychol. Rev., i. 6.   (G.F.S.–J.M.B.)

Actuality and **Actual** [Lat. *actus*] : Ger. *Actualität, Wirklichkeit* ; Fr. *actualité* ; Ital. *attualità ed attuale*. That which is in phenomenal reality or fact is actual, and is said to have actuality. The terms are opposed to POTENTIAL, and POTENTIALITY (q.v.). See also REAL AND ACTUAL, and HEGELIAN TERMINOLOGY, VI.   (J.M.B.)

Actuality Theory. The theory that all existence is activity ; opposed to substantiality. In psychology it makes the essence of the mental life entirely activity or process. For further discussion and literature, see SUBSTANTIALITY.   (J.M.B.)

Actus (**purus,** and in other phrases) : see ACTIVITY, and LATIN AND SCHOLASTIC TERMINOLOGY (glossary).

Adam [Heb. *Ādām*, human beings (Gen. i); personal name of the first man (Gen. ii); probably connected with Assyrian *adâmu*, to build, form]. Adam occupies an important place in that section of doctrinal theology which treats of man in his actual and ideal relations to God. Here the dogmas of the Fall and of the Imputation of Adam's Guilt may be regarded as principal sources of sin. In connection with this arises the dogma of the means of deliverance from God's wrath and its penalty—of a universal condemnation to eternal perdition. This dogma constitutes the objective aspect of God's relation to man in connection with reconciliation, just as ' conversion ' constitutes the subjective.

Literature: EDWARDS, Works, ii. 303 f.; J. MÜLLER, Origin of Sin ; KAHNIS, Dogmatik, ii. 107 f. ; VAN OOSTERZEE, Christian Dogmatics, 466 f., 628 f. ; O. PFLEIDERER, Philos. of Religion, iv. 10 f.   (R.M.W.)

Adaptation [Lat. *adaptare*]: Ger. *Anpassung* ; Fr. *adaptation* ; Ital. *adattamento*. (1) A word signifying adjustment or fitness ; as of means to ends, organ to function, &c. (2) In biology, adaptation is a general term used to signify the adjustment of the organism or its organs to the environment, with especial reference to other organisms. (J.M.B.)

The doctrine of evolution has rendered the study of adaptation of scientific importance. Before that doctrine was formulated, natural adaptations formed part of the mystery of special creation, and played a great rôle in natural theology through the use of the argument from 'design in nature.' The term, as now employed, includes both that which is hereditary and that which is acquired. In view of modern biological theory and discussion, two modes of adaptation should be distinguished : (1) adaptation through variation (hereditary) ; (2) adaptation through modification (acquired). For the functional adjustment of the individual to its environment (2, above), J. Mark Baldwin has suggested the term ACCOMMODATION (q. v.), recommending that adaptation be confined to the structural adjustments which are congenital and hereditary (1, above). On this distinction adaptations are phylogenic (and blastogenic), and accommodations are ontogenic (and somatogenic). (C.LL.M.)

Before the formulation of the principle of natural selection, the existence of special adaptations so called was a great difficulty to the theory of evolution ; now cases of lack of adaptation are cited as furnishing objection to the principle of natural selection. Darwin very early considered that adaptations were the real difficulty to be met by one who would attempt to solve the problem of evolution. He expresses this in the Introduction to the *Origin of Species*, and more epigrammatically in his letter to Asa Gray (Sept. 5, 1857) : 'The facts which kept me longest scientifically orthodox are those of adaptation—the pollen-masses of asclepias—the mistletoe, with its pollen carried by insects, and seed by birds—the woodpecker, with its feet and tail, beak and tongue, to climb the tree and secure insects. To talk of climate or Lamarckian habit producing such adaptation to other organic beings is futile. This difficulty I believe I have surmounted' (*Life and Letters*, J. Linn. Soc., 1858). (E.B.P.)

Literature: H. SPENCER, Princ. of Biol. (2nd ed., 1898); CH. DARWIN, Origin of Species (1859); A. WEISMANN, Essays on Heredity (1889); J. MARK BALDWIN, Nature, lv. 588; POULTON, Charles Darwin, 42, 43, 68. See also under EVOLUTION, DESIGN, and NATURAL SELECTION. (C.LL.M.)

Adaptation (visual) : Ger. *Adaptation* ; Fr. *adaptation*; Ital. *accomodazione* (*visiva*—E.M.) Adjustment of the eye to altered objective illumination, which takes place through change in the size of the pupil and in the sensitiveness of the retina. (J.McK.C.)

(1) If the retina is exposed continuously to the same objective stimulus, sensation tends towards a medium degree of brightness, and, so far as colour is involved, towards neutrality. This is 'general adaptation' (Hering). If the edges of adjacent fields, that differ in brightness or colour tone or both, are fixated, a similar mutual compensation takes place: Hering's 'local adaptation' (Ebbinghaus, *Psychol.*, 230). This is brought under fatigue or 'partial' adaptation by many.

(2) To be distinguished from this is the adaptation to a faint illumination, which takes place in from fifteen minutes to half an hour, and which has been connected with the production of visual purple (rod-purple or rod-pigment) in the rods of the retina. Experiments on direct and indirect vision, with adaptation to light and darkness, are theoretically important, e. g. as possibly aiding us to distinguish the sense functions of rods and cones. Cf. v. Kries, in *Zeitsch. f. Psychol.*, xiii. 241, and see COLOUR-MIXTURE, VISION, and PURKINJE PHENOMENON. (E.B.T.–C.L.F.)

Literature: AUBERT, Physiol. d. Netzhaut, 25 ; Grundzüge d. Physiol. Optik (1876), 483 ; SANFORD, Course in Exper. Psychol., expt. 123 ; H. PARINAUD, La sensibilité de l'œil aux couleurs spectrales ; fonctions des éléments rétiniens et du pourpre visuel, Ann. d'Ocul. (1895), cxii. 225 f. ; Rev. Scient. (1895), iii. 4e s., 709 ff. ; iv. 134 f. (cf. J. of Ophthal., Otol., and Laryngol., 1896, viii. 15 f.) ; and (especially) La Vision (1898) ; A. CHARPENTIER, L'adaptation rétinienne et le phénomène de Purkinje, Arch. d'Ophthal., xvi. 188 ff. (E.B.T.–L.M.)

Adaptive (mental process) : Ger. *sich anpassend*; Fr. *adaptif*; Ital. *adattabile*. Mental activity is adaptive if and so far as its mode of pursuing its end is varied in accordance with varying conditions. The process of adaptation is still going on so long and so far as its modes take the form of trial and failure upon variations of content. The completed state of adaptation has been reached when no further trials are required. See ACCOMMODATION, SELECTIVE THINKING, and DETERMINATION (mental). (G.F.S.–J.M.B.)

Adaptive Characters: see CONVERGENCE.

Adelard of Bath. Lived in England in

the 12th century. Wrote *De Rerum Naturis*, and translated Euclid from Arabic into Latin.

Adendritic [Gr. *ἀ + δενδρίτης*, pertaining to a tree]: Ger. *adendrit*; Fr. *sans dendrites*; Ital. *adendritico*. Without dendrites or protoplasmic processes. Said of a nerve-cell when giving rise only to a neurite, or axis-cylinder process. Cf. NEUROCYTE. Embryonic nerve-cells are often adendritic, but it is doubtful if such a cell can function perfectly. (H.H.)

Adequate [Lat. *ad + aequus*, equal]: Ger. *adäquat*; Fr. *adéquat*; Ital. *adeguato*. (1) Used of the DEFINITION (q.v.) in which the 'generic and specific marks' are sufficiently determined.

(2) The term has also been applied by individual philosophers to knowledge, ideas, causes, to indicate sufficiency or exactness in various ways. Locke and Hume (*Treat.*, ii. § 2) discuss the adequacy of ideas to their objects. Leibnitz (*Op.*, ed. Erdmann, 29) considers knowledge adequate when 'all that is contained in the concept is unfolded.' See these and other citations in Eisler, *Wörterb. d. philos. Begriffe*, sub verbis. Spinoza uses adequate to express the 'intrinsic' characters of a true idea as opposed to the 'extrinsic' agreement of the idea and its object (*Ethics*, Pt. II, def. 4). (J.M.B.)

Adevism [Lat. *a + deus*, God] (no foreign equivalents in use). Adevism designates denial of gods, as contrasted with Atheism—denial of God. It is applied by F. Max Müller to consequences of the teaching of the Vedanta Philosophy. True science (Vidya) conquers Nescience (Avidya) with its accompaniment of Adevism.

Literature: F. MAX MÜLLER, Gifford Lectures (1892), chap. ix; The Vedanta Philos., 100 f. (R.M.W.)

Adiaphora [Gr. *ἀδιάφορα*]: see INDIFFERENCE, and STOICISM.

Adiaphoristic Controversy [Gr. *ἀδιάφορος*, indifferent]: Ger. *adiaphoristischer Streit*; Fr. *controverse adiaphoristique*; Ital. *controversia adiaforistica*. The 'Form of Concord' was the name given to the latest of the Lutheran Creeds or Confessions (1577–80). Its tenth article grew out of the Adiaphoristic controversy. Substantially it teaches that rites and ceremonies which the Scriptures do not impose or forbid are indifferent (*neutra*), although in certain circumstances they may become affairs of conscience and adhesion to principle.

After Luther's death, the 'hard' Protestants revolted from the observance of Roman Catholic rites and ceremonies required by the 'Augsburg Interim,' and especially by the 'Leipzig Interim,' which the Elector Maurice passed in 1548 with the active support of Melanchthon, whose humanistic tendencies kept him from extremes. Flacius, Amsdorf, and other zealous Lutherans could not bring themselves to view as 'indifferent' the Mass, Feasts, Images, Extreme Unction, Confirmation and Ordination by bishops, to all of which Melanchthon had temporarily assented for the sake of peace. Flacius in particular attacked Melanchthon and his associates as 'the dangerous rabble of Adiaphorists.' With the civil and religious changes effected by the Treaty of Augsburg (1555) the question ceased to be part of ecclesiastical practical politics.

Literature: GIESELER, Church Hist., iv. 193 f., 201 f., 435; Die Theol. d. Concordien-formel, iv. 1 f. (R.M.W.)

Adjective: see SUBSTANTIVE AND ADJECTIVE.

Adjective Law: Ger. *zum Rechtsverfahren gehörig* (*Rechtsverfahren*, as contrasted with *Wesen des Rechts*); Fr. *loi de procédure*; Ital. *diritto processuale* (as contrasted with *diritto positivo*). The law defining or creating the means of enforcing rights, as distinguished from the law defining or creating the rights themselves (*substantive law*); the law of procedure. (S.E.B.)

Adjudication [Lat. *adiudicatio*]: Ger. *gerichtliche Zuerkennung*; Fr. *jugement, arrêt, jurisprudence des tribunaux*; Ital. *aggiudicazione*. The sentence of a judicial tribunal—a final judgment.

In Great Britain and the United States adjudication is a recognized source of law, when it ascertains something which before was uncertain. It cannot vary or abrogate a law previously established by the legislature, but it may fix upon it a particular meaning. It may assert that to be a rule of the common or unwritten law, which was never before stated in form, but which, in the opinion of the judges, is properly deducible from other rules of that law, which are generally acknowledged as obligatory. A rule thus asserted or affirmed by courts of last resort becomes the law of the jurisdiction, and may affect past transactions as well as future ones. Such decisions are known as judicial precedents, and out of them most of the private law of England and the United States has been judicially built up. The Roman law gave them no such force.

'Non exemplis, sed legibus iudicandum.' Code VII. 45, *de Sententiis et Interlocutionibus Omnium Iudicum*, 13. (S.E.B.)

Adjustment of Observations: see OBSERVATION (experimental).

Administrative Law: Ger. *Verwaltungsrecht*; Fr. *droit administratif*; Ital. *diritto amministrativo*. That branch of public law defining or creating the way in which the active exercise of the powers of government is maintained and conducted.

Under the influence of Montesquieu's *l'Esprit des Lois*, it became a common belief of publicists and framers of Constitutions in the 18th century that the functions of government could be reduced to three divisions—executive, legislative, and judicial. Experience has taught that a considerable body of law, in all civilized communities, must exist which is not strictly referable to either of these heads. Most of it is now termed administrative. See *In re* Application of Clark, 65 Connecticut Law Reports, 38 ; Norwalk Street Railway Company's Appeal, 69 Connecticut Law Reports, 597, 606. (S.E.B.)

Admiralty Jurisdiction: Ger. *Admiralitätsgerichtbarkeit*; Fr. *la connaissance des affaires relatives à la marine, la compétence de la cour de l'amirauté*; Ital. *giurisdizione marittima*. The jurisdiction exercised by Courts of Admiralty : in England confined to dealing with acts done upon the high seas, and demands for seamen's wages or on bottomry bonds ; in the United States extending also over all navigable waters of the United States, salt or fresh, and to all contracts for maritime service, or respecting maritime transactions or casualties, wherever executed ; on the Continent of Europe, generally as wide as in the United States, or wider. See Insurance Company *v.* Dunham, 1 Wallace's United States Reports. The forms of proceeding in general are similar to those of the Civil Law. Process is issued both *in rem* and *in personam*. If admiralty jurisdiction attaches to a ship, the decree, in case of a sale, will bind the ship and all interested in her, in any country into which she may afterwards come (Woolsey's *Int. Law,* §§ 141, 143).

Modern admiralty practice rests on the foundations of the Roman law, which in turn embodied part of the maritime law of Rhodes (*Dig.* xiv. 2, *de Lege Rhodia de Iactu*). A compilation of the sea-laws of the Mediterranean (*Il Consolato del Mare*) of the 13th century has also had great authority. (S.E.B.)

Admiration [Lat. *admiratio*] : Ger. *Bewunderung*; Fr. *admiration*; Ital. *ammirazione*. (1) Feeling as going out in active approval. (2) Aesthetic feeling as so going out.

The term originally denoted primarily WONDER (q.v.) or amazement, or was used to characterize the mingled intellectual and aesthetic feeling. The feeling now denoted by the term may contain in varying degree the element of wonder, but this latter cannot be regarded as an essential constituent.

Literature : MARTINEAU, Types of Ethical Theory (2nd ed., 1886), ii. 152–60. See also under FEELING. (J.H.T.)

Adolescence (psychological) [Lat. *ad* + *olescere*, from *alere*, to nourish, grow] : Ger. *Jünglingsalter*; Fr. *adolescence* ; Ital. *adolescenza*. A period in the development of the individual introductory to the attainment of maturity. Legally, it is from 12 in girls and 14 in boys to 21 ; physiologically, to about 25 for boys and 21 for girls.

General usage makes adolescence apply to the time between beginning of puberty and maturity. Clouston would confine the term to the later part of this period, i. e. from '18 to 25' (Clouston, *Ment. Diseases*, 542). (J.J.–C.F.H.)

The term is usually, but not exclusively, confined to human developmental stages. It is customary to distinguish the periods of infancy, childhood, puberty, adolescence, the adult state, and senescence ; a distinction between the early and the later periods of adolescence seems also desirable. The more distinctive characteristics of adolescence are of a physiological nature related in great part to the unfoldment of sexual functions; but the accompanying secondary psychological tendencies are hardly less characteristic and important. The appearance of the beard, the change in voice, the assumption of the adult form, the more pronounced differentiation of sex characteristics, the final consolidation of the bones, the appearance of latent propensities, the change of features to show new characters, the prominence of hereditary influences, as well as other less objective and more subtle changes, serve to distinguish adolescence. The period appears earlier in the female than in the male, and its advent is somewhat affected by racial and social influences.

The psychological traits of adolescence are prominent, but their variability and complexity render an adequate description difficult. In thought and feeling, as well as in appearance, the boy becomes specifically masculine and the girl feminine. There is in both a fundamental change and expansion of the emotional life. The mind is filled with hopes and ideals, dreamy longings and fervid passions. Ethical, religious, and intellectual motives become more cogent; conscientiousness and seriousness inspire action. Great emotional fluctuations occur; periods of enthusiastic energy and spasmodic attempts at high achievement giving place at times to languor and depression, to doubt, dissatisfaction, and morbid rumination. It is a period of violent affections for the opposite sex, of intense friendships, of pledges and vows. It is a period when home surroundings begin to seem narrow, and the desire to wander, to do and dare, seizes the adolescent enthusiast. It is the period of adventure, of romance and poetry and artistic sensibility. In its later stages it may usher in the period of doubt and speculation, of the desire to reform existing evils, and the ambition to accomplish great things. Many deeds and movements of historical importance found their origin in the impulses and strivings of adolescents, while the description of this period in their own career or in that of others has offered an inviting field for the biographer and the novelist. The storm and stress periods of Goethe and John Stuart Mill, of Tolstoi and Marie Bashkirtseff, no less than the masterly delineations of George Eliot's Gwendolen Harleth and Maggie Tulliver, form a valuable and suggestive contribution to the psychology of adolescence. The period has been recognized by primitive peoples, and in past civilizations by special rites and cults. In its educational as well as psychological aspect the study of adolescence is of great importance; the utilization of the enthusiasms and good impulses and the avoidance of the dangers and excesses of this period form a part of the duty of the educator, the physician, and the parent, to which renewed attention is being directed.

Literature: CLOUSTON, Ment. Diseases, 542 ff., and art. Developmental Insanities, in Tuke's Dict. of Psychol. Med., i. 360–71; also, Neuroses of Devel.; BURNHAM, The Study of Adolescence, Pedag. Sem., i. 174–95; LANCASTER, The Psychology and Pedagogy of Adolescence, Pedag. Sem., v. 61–129 (with literature); A. MARRO, La pubertà studiata nell' uomo e nella donna (1898); W. WILLE, Die Psychosen des Pubertätsalters (1898); H. P. BOWDITCH, The Growth of Children, Mass. State Board of Health Rep. (Boston, 1877); LOUIS N. WILSON, Bibliog. of Child Study (1898, for numerous references). (J.J.–C.F.H.)

Adoptionism [Lat. *adoptare*, to choose, select]: Ger. *Adoptionismus*; Fr. *adoptionisme*; Ital. *adottazionismo*. The doctrine according to which Christ is viewed, in his human nature, as the Son of God by adoption only.

The union of two natures, divine and human, in the person of Christ has given rise to many difficulties, which, in turn, have occasioned numerous controversies. Of these last, 'adoptionism' is one. Similar tendencies manifested themselves early, and still continue to exist. Adoptionism proper was formulated near the close of the 8th century, vigorously opposed by Alcuin in particular, and condemned by the Council of Frankfort in 1794. It arose in Spain, where its chief exponents were Eliphantus, archbishop of Toledo, and Felix, bishop of Urgel. Their teaching substantially was that, in his divine nature, Christ is the real Son of God; in his human nature he is the Son by adoption only. This view probably recommended itself to the Spanish dignitaries, because of the emphasis it put upon the human element, and the consequent access of power with which Christian doctrine could be pressed upon a Mohammedan community. The difficulty of the non-divinity of the human nature was supposed to be lessened by the doctrine that it won God's adoption by its inherent virtue. From the standpoint of the Church, this view was heretical, because it implied a manhood separated completely from God before the right to adoption had been earned. And the Church was so far correct in this judgment; for the implied independence of the human nature involved an irreducible dualism. Several centuries earlier germs of a similar view are to be found in the teaching of Theodore, bishop of Mopsuestia (400 A.D.). With him the difficulty of the independence of the human nature is removed by the supposition that, through the indwelling of the Logos, the man Jesus became the second Adam; this indwelling (and here lies the important point) is distinctively ethical. It is obvious that, whenever ethical considerations, especially such as imply normal development, predominate, parallel problems must arise; naturally these made their influence most felt after the Reformation.

Literature: DORNER, Hist. of the Devel. of the Doctrine of the Person of Christ (Eng. trans.), Division II, i. 248 f., ii. 338 f., iii. 301 f. (R.M.W.)

Adoration [Lat. *adoratio*]: Ger. *Anbetung*; Fr. *adoration*; Ital. *adorazione*. An act of solemn worship, accompanied by suitable observances, usually paid to divine, or quasi-divine, beings, and later to gods or God

In the course of history, the Roman Catholic Church has come to differentiate adoration of God from the secondary adoration paid to the Host, the Virgin, the saints and martyrs of the Church, the crucifix. Protestant teaching regards all this, with the exception in some cases of the last, as idolatry. (R.M.W.)

Adrastus. Supposed to have lived in 1st or 2nd century A.D. A Greek commentator on Aristotle, and author of an extant work on music.

Advent [Lat. *adventus*, from *ad + venire*, to approach]: Ger. *Advent*; Fr. *avent* (in opposition to *carême*), *avènement* (in opposition to the 'second coming'); Ital. *avvento*. The time of the 'Christian Year' which immediately precedes Christmas; the period of the Nativity.

In the Roman Catholic and Anglican Churches Advent has come to be recognized as beginning on the Sunday nearest to St. Andrew's Day, November 30. This custom probably dates from so early a period as the 4th century. Two centuries later the custom of regarding Advent as the beginning of the 'Christian Year' became prevalent. In the Eastern Church Advent dates from St. Martin's Day, November 11. (R.M.W.)

Advent (the second): see MILLENNIUM.

Advocate [Lat. *advocatus*]: Ger. *Advokat*; Fr. *avocat*; Ital. *avvocato*. One who makes it his profession to conduct the trial of causes before judicial tribunals. Especially used for admiralty lawyers who conduct the trial, as distinguished from admiralty lawyers, known as proctors, who prepare the cause for trial.

Advocacy as a profession was first developed at Rome. The patrons were naturally advocates of the causes of their clients, but their position was a political one, and implied no special legal education. Servius Sulpicius, a contemporary of Cicero, was the first great pleader of causes (*orator*), who also was a learned jurisconsult (*Dig.* i. 2, *de Origine Iuris*, &c., 43). (S.E.B.)

Aedesius. A Neo-Platonist, follower of Iamblichus. Born in Cappadocia in the time of Constantine, he became the tutor of Constantine and other famous men.

Aegidius of Colonna (Aegidius-a-Columna). (Died 1316.) Native of Rome, educated for theology under Thomas Aquinas in Paris. Became tutor to the Dauphin of France, Philippe le Bel. He was very prominent as a theologian, and wrote a philosophical work called *De Regimine Principis*.

Aeneas of Gaza. A follower of Plato, who lived in the latter half of the 5th century A.D. He became a Christian, and wrote *Theophrastus*, combining Christian and Platonic ideas.

Aenesidemus. A sceptical philosopher, born at Gnossus (or Cnossus) in Crete; supposed to have lived in the 1st century of the Christian era.

Aeon [Gr. αἰών, age]. That which exists from eternity. A term of the Gnostics denoting a subordinate or dependent deity or semideity, mediating—especially in the process of creation—between the world and the supreme Deity. Cf. the literature cited under GNOSIS. (J.M.B.)

Aepinus, John. (1499–1553.) A Protestant divine, disciple of Luther, the most influential theologian in the north of Germany, and a great polemical writer.

Aesthesia [Gr. αἴσθησις, perception by the senses]: Ger. *Empfindlichkeit*; Fr. *sensibilité*; Ital. *sensibilità, estesia*. A synonym of sensibility. As ANAESTHESIA (q.v.) denotes the absence of the capacity to have sensation, so Aesthesia denotes its normal presence. (J.J.)

The term is also used to denote the general power and process of feeling, in opposition to kinesia, the power of movement. See Arndt, *Lehrb. d Psychol.*, and Morselli, *Semej. malat. ment.*, ii. (E.M.)

Aesthesiogen, Aesthesiogenic [Gr. αἴσθησις, feeling, + γενης, producing]: Ger. *aesthesiogen, gefühlserregend*; Fr. *esthésiogène, esthésiogénique*; Ital. *estesiogeno*. (1) Having the capacity to stimulate or produce sensation; analogous in its use to DYNAMOGENIC (q.v.). (2) Specifically used, in connection with experiments upon hypnotized subjects, to denote the apparent power of certain substances—for instance, a magnet—to produce by mere contact or proximity peculiar forms of sensation and nervous action, such as the transference of a cataleptic attitude from one side of the body to the other. See HYPNOTISM. (J.J.)

The term dates from the researches of Bury and his school on 'metalotherapy' and aesthesiogenic processes, and has only lately and indirectly been introduced into the study of hypnotism. (P.J.)

Literature to (2): BINET and FÉRÉ, Animal Magnetism, 125 and elsewhere; MYERS, Proc. Soc. Psych. Res. (Oct. 1886), 127, and succeeding papers; SEPPILLI and BUCCOLA, Riv. di Freniat. (1880). (J.J.)

Aesthesiometer: see LABORATORY AND APPARATUS, III, B. (c), (1), (3).

Aesthesodic [Gr. αἴσθησις, sensation, + ὁδός, road]: Ger. *reizleitend, aesthesodisch* (applied to spinal ganglia, not to cortical centres—H.M.); Fr. (not used); Ital. *estesiodico*. Receptive rather than centrifugal or initiatory.

An aesthesodic centre is one which receives stimuli from a centripetal nerve, especially a cortical centre forming the central end-organ for a sensory tract. See KINESODIC. A more inclusive term than 'sensory' in the same connections, and not implying that the stimuli necessarily participate in sensation.   (H.H.)

Aesthetic and **Aesthetics** [Gr. αἰσθητικός, from αἰσθήσεσθαι, to perceive]: Ger. *aesthetisch, Aesthetik*; Fr. *(l')esthétique, science du beau*; Ital. *estetico, l'estetica*. Relating to the beautiful in the broadest sense, i.e. as including (q.v.) the SUBLIME, COMIC, TRAGIC, PATHETIC, UGLY, &c., as in the phrases Aesthetic Feeling, Aesthetic Fancy, &c. Cf. FEELING, FANCY, EMOTION, SENTIMENT (aesthetic). The aesthetic is related to the agreeable, the useful, and the morally good, in that all are experienced as values. The qualities by which it is distinguished from these are stated variously by different authorities, but there is general agreement that the value experienced in the aesthetic field is regarded as objective (as contrasted with the agreeable), shareable, intrinsic (as contrasted with the useful), and is appreciated in a contemplative as opposed to a practical attitude of consciousness (as contrasted with the moral). Aesthetics is the science of the beautiful. See BEAUTY.

I. The term was introduced by Baumgarten (*Aesthetica*, 1750–8) to signify the science of sensuous knowledge, supplementary and parallel to logic, the science of 'clear thinking,' or of the higher faculty, the intellect. Both sciences were regarded as rather propaedeutic to philosophy than as included within it. In the current psychology of that time the characteristic quality of sensuous knowledge was held to be its 'confused' or obscure nature. It is felt or 'sensed,' rather than known. As the peculiar excellence or goal of clear thinking, with which logic is concerned, is truth, so the end or perfection of sensuous knowledge as such was held to be beauty. Beauty was declared to be the province of aesthetic. Kant, in his *Critique of Pure Reason* (1781), still used the word in the sense of a science of sensuous knowledge, but rejected the special turn given to the term by Baumgarten; because Kant then held that there could be no science of the beautiful in the strict sense. He accordingly gave to the term the new content of a science of the *a priori* principles or forms of the sensibility, viz. space and time. In the *Critique of Judgment* (1790), having, as he supposed, discovered a rational basis for the treatment of our judgments as to the beautiful, he discussed them under the title 'Critique of the Aesthetic Judgment,' to indicate that they are judgments as to feeling. Since Kant there has been general uniformity in usage.

II. *Scope and Divisions of Modern Aesthetics*. Aside from the question as to the relation of beauty to ultimate reality, which is more properly a problem of metaphysics than of aesthetics, modern aesthetics deals with two main sets of problems: *A*, those of aesthetic appreciation; *B*, those of artistic production. These of course cannot always be kept distinct. Under *A* may be considered (1) psychological and physiological problems, such as the origin and nature of aesthetic feeling, its relation to imagination and sensation, and the influence of association; the physiological basis and conditions of the aesthetic thrill, including the relation of the stimulus to the sensation, the mathematical relations of harmonious tones, the relation of aesthetic feeling to other pleasurable feeling, and to the vital processes; finally, the biological significance of aesthetic feeling in the development of the organism and of the race. (2) Problems arising from analysis of the form and content of objects judged beautiful, or of the nature of the aesthetic judgment and of the categories of beauty; such as the question as to the 'objective' character of beauty, that of valid art criticism, &c. Under *B* fall questions as to (1) the end or essential nature of art; (2) the nature of art-impulse; (3) the imagination and its relation to the execution of the idea; (4) the origin and function of the art-impulse in the development of the race; (5) the evolution of art. The two main groups of problems, *A* and *B*, are often spoken of as respectively concerning art from the 'spectator's point of view' as contrasted with art from the 'producer's point of view.'

III. *Methods*. The problems under *A* (2) are analogous to logical and ethical problems, and demand similar methods of analysis and criticism. The remaining problems are largely psychological or historical, and therefore employ the methods of those sciences. More particularly, in addition to the older method of introspection, the experimental investigation of the structure and formation of the special sense-organs and the corresponding qualities of sensation, or of the physiological basis of all pleasure and pain, and the relation of stimulus to response studied by psychophysics. The historical or genetic method is throwing much light on the origin and development of the arts; and the attempt has been made to apply this method to the origin of aesthetic pleasures, such as the delight in colour, the pleasure of the comic, &c. For specific illustrations, see under BEAUTY V, and ART IV. The historic treatment of aesthetic problems will be found chiefly under the articles ART AND ART THEORIES, BEAUTY, CLASSIFICATION (of the fine arts), COMIC, SUBLIME, TRAGIC. See álso FEELING (aesthetic), ASSOCIATION (aesthetic).

Literature: historical works are given in connection with the topics named; special monographs are also named in connection with articles on special topics. Many recent works are named in sec. V of article on BEAUTY, and sec. IV of article on ART. A selection is given here of general works, and of essays on the general subject. (1) On the general field of aesthetics: SULLY, On the Possibility of a Science of Aesthetics (essay xiii in Sensation and Intuition, 1874); and art. Aesthetics, in Encyc. Brit.; LADD, Introd. to Philos. (1890), chap. xii; VOLKELT, Die gegenwärtigen Aufgaben der Aesthetik (vi. in Aesthetische Zeitfragen, 1895); KÜLPE, Introd. to Philos. (1895, Eng. trans.), § 10; JERUSALEM, Einleitung in die Philos. (1899), V. Absch.; MARSHALL, Aesthetic Principles (1895).

(2) Systematic and other works. (*a*) Brief or popular works: SCHASLER, Aesthetik (1886); KNIGHT, Philos. of the Beautiful (1891-3); GAUCKLER, Le Beau et son Hist. (1873); VÉRON, Aesthetics (trans. by Armstrong, 1879); VAN DYKE, The Principles of Art (1887); SANTAYANA, The Sense of Beauty (1896); GROOS, Einleitung in die Aesthetik (1892). (*b*) More comprehensive works: CARRIÈRE, Die Aesthetik (3rd ed., 1885); VON HARTMANN, Aesthetik (1886-7); LAUD, Nederlandsche Aesthetika (1881); ZEISING, Aesthetische Forschungen (1855); VISCHER, Aesthetik (3 vols., 1846-57); ZIMMERMANN, Aesthetik (1858-65); KÖSTLIN, Aesthetik (1869); CHAIGNET, Les Principes de la Sci. du Beau (1860); LÉVÊQUE, La Science du Beau (2nd ed., 1872); MARSHALL, Pain, Pleasure, and Aesthetics (1894).

The first volume of KNIGHT contains a very full bibliography of important works. Cf. also GAYLEY and SCOTT, Guide to the Literature of Aesthetics (1890), and Introd. to the Meth. and Materials of Literary Criticism (1899). See BIBLIOG. D. (J.H.T.)

Aesthetic (transcendental): see KANTIAN TERMINOLOGY, cf. also the preceding topic (I).

Aesthetic Standard: Ger. *aesthetischer Massstab*; Fr. *règle esthétique autoritative*; Ital. *misura estetica*. A principle or criterion of criticism, which must be presupposed if a work of art is pronounced good or bad, or if any aesthetic object is compared with another and estimated as more or less beautiful. See CRITICISM. (J.H.T.)

Aetiology [Gr. αἰτία, cause, + λόγος, discourse]: Ger. *Aetiologie*; Fr. *étiologie*; Ital. *etiologia*. The theory of CAUSE (q.v.). (J.M.B.)

Mainly used in medicine, where it is the science that deals with the causes or origin of disease; the description of the factors which produce or predispose toward a certain disease or disorder. Compare, for example, what is said of the aetiology of insanity under INSANITY AND SANITY. (J.J.)

Affect [Lat. *ad + facere*, to do]: Ger. *Triebfeder*, or *affectiver Bewegungsreiz*; Fr. *motif affectif*, *mobile* (cf. TERMINOLOGY, French); Ital. *motivo affettivo*. A stimulus or motive to action which is AFFECTIVE (q. v.) or felt, not presented as an end.

Suggested by Baldwin (*Handb. of Psychol.*, Feeling and Will, 313, 319, 354). The same distinction is made by Mackensie (*Manual of Ethics*, 62 f.). See also Wundt, *Outlines of Psychol.*, 714 (and the German original). The two cases indicated in the definition are those respectively of non-voluntary and voluntary action; only in the latter case is the affect a MOTIVE (q. v.). Wundt uses Triebfeder for the affective element in every Motiv, the presented or intellectual element being the Beweggrund. Judd's translation of these respectively by Impelling Force and Moving Reason (see END) is clumsy. Impelling force loses the implication of feeling altogether. The earlier English ethical term Spring of Action (Martineau) is too comprehensive, and is besides complicated by being 'lower' and 'higher.' We accordingly fall back upon affect. (J.M.B., G.F.S.)

Affection (1) and **Affective** (2): Ger. (1) *elementares Gefühl*, (2) *Gefühls-* (in comp., as *Gefuhlston*); Fr. (1) *affection, sensibilité*, (2) *affectif*; Ital. (1) *sentimentalità*, (2) *affettivo*. (1) The hypothetical elementary form of feeling. (2) Belonging or pertaining to feeling of all sorts. Affection is also a popular word for LOVE (q.v.) or tender feeling, with the adjective affectionate. The adjective form (meaning given under 2) was used before the substantive, notably by the French psychologists (cf. Rabier).

See FEELING, EMOTION, and AFFECTION (in ethics and theology).

This usage seems best since there is no adjective formed from 'feeling.' The demand for the noun Affection seems to have come from those analysts who desired to avoid using the ambiguous word Feeling. The term is useful, and the same is true of CONATION (q.v.), provided one guards against the evident danger of taking them to mean real things, and of thinking that complex mental states are at all explained when stated in terms of them. Sufficient care is not always exercised in distinguishing the English affective from the German Affekt, the equivalent of emotion.

In Titchener's translation of Külpe's *Outlines of Psychol.*, § 52, there is the complication that affection is made equivalent to Gemüths-in the term Gemüthsbewegung—a direct confusion of what is affective with what is conative, seeing that the German Gemüthsbewegung includes both feelings and impulses. Judd seems to have Wundt's endorsement of the same rendering (trans. of Wundt's *Outlines of Psychol.*, 109, 187, and Glossary); but it does violence to English usage. It revives the confusion of feeling and action seen in the older terms 'Active' and 'Motive Powers': as in Judd's translation (loc. cit., 168), where Gefühlslage is rendered by the same adjective ('affective state') used for Gemüthsbewegung ('affective process') and Gemüthslage (or Gemüthszustand, 'affective state') in other passages (cf. Judd, loc. cit., Glossary). Cf. TERMINOLOGY (German).   (J.M.B.–G.F.S.)

Literature: HAMILTON, Lectures on Metaphysics; RABIER, Leçons de Psychol.; BIBLIOG. G, 2, e.

Affection (in ethics). (1) Any states of pronounced feeling. In English usage, the term applies both to the more permanent sentiments (Ger. *Gefühle*), and to passing emotional states (Ger. *Affecte*). The best writers distinguish it from passion, as having less vehemence, and as less distinctly, if at all, connected with a sensuous basis. (2) Sometimes it is restricted to feelings which have persons for their object. The first definition is, however, more in accord with psychological usage. See AFFECTION AND AFFECTIVE, AFFECT, and EMOTION.

St. Augustine, as quoted and adopted by Aquinas, says: 'Those mental states (*motus animi*) which the Greeks call πάθη, and Cicero *perturbationes*, are by some called *affectus*, or *affectiones* by others, keeping to the literal rendering of the Greek *passiones*.' This equivalence of *passio* and *affectus* is still found in Descartes. There is a wider use in Spinoza, by whom the term *affectus* is made to cover purely rational sentiments. And this wider application is characteristic of the British moralists, in whose writings the word affection is of very frequent occurrence. Shaftesbury uses it in the widest sense as above defined. But other writers draw a distinction between affection and passion: Hutcheson, on the ground that the former does not necessarily—whereas the latter does—involve uneasiness; Price, because of the distinct presence of a sensuous element in passion, which also indicates greater vehemence of active tendency; while, according to Gay, passion is the 'pleasure or pain arising from the prospect of future pleasure or pain,' and affection is 'the desire consequent thereupon.' The narrower usage (2) is sanctioned by Reid, who defines affections as the 'various principles of action in man, which have persons for their immediate object, and imply, in their very nature, our being well or ill affected to some person, or, at least, to some animated being.' This usage is followed by Sidgwick. A. F. Shand defines affections as feelings for, not in, an object; and says: 'The terms sentiment, interest, and affection do not seem to mark any important difference. We speak of the sentiment of justice, truth, and the moral sentiment generally, of the sentiment of friendship; but of affection for our friends rather than sentiment, and of interest in our health or business rather than either: the difference turning upon the different character of the object.'

Literature: AUGUSTINE, De Civ. Dei, ix. 4; AQUINAS, Summa Theol., II. i. Q. 22; DESCARTES, De Pass. Animae; SPINOZA, Ethica, iii. 58 ff.; HUTCHESON, Essay on the Passions, § 2; PRICE, Princ. Quest. and Difficulties of Morals, chap. iii; GAY, Dissertation prefixed to Law's transl. of King's Origin of Evil, § 3; HUME, Human Nature, I. i. 2; REID, Active Powers, Essay III, Part II. chaps. iii–v; SHAND, Mind, N.S., v. 214 ff.   (W.R.S.)

Affection (in theology) [Lat. *affectio*]: Ger. *Neigung*; Fr. *affection*; Ital. *affetto*. (1) The affections (plural usually) are the sentiments of personal inclination that give rise to love. (2) The motive forces in an individual that render him consistently devoted to some one aim. The subject falls within the province of Christian ethics, and, especially in the latter aspect, involves controversial questions concerning the will.

(1) The affections, especially as they produce love to God, are natural and healthy. The extreme of mysticism, which offers devotion

to the Deity as if he stood in need of it, is to be avoided. Similarly, the love which, sure of its object and satisfaction, remains thereafter quiescent, is to be condemned. The ideal lies in a *unio caritatis*, whereby the opposition between individual and universal is ended. (2) To be turned to their essential uses, the affections must be enlisted for high ends. Human action is not the result merely of affections that have always held rule, or which remain fixed; it depends upon their transformation by the Christian ideal. Man is naturally perverse and selfish, hence the need for the process of moralizing the affections or of rendering them holy; only thus can they furnish motives for correct moral action. In recent years the aspects involved in (1) have attracted greatly preponderating attention.

Literature: for (1) see the treatment of love in any systematic treatise on Christian Ethics, e. g. by DORNER; for (2), such a work as JONATHAN EDWARDS' Religious Affections. (R.M.W.)

Affective Tone or **Feeling Tone**: Ger. *Gefühlston*; Fr. *élément affectif, ton émotionnel*; Ital. *elemento affettivo, tono sentimentale*. The ingredient of feeling that attaches to a mental state of any kind. (J.M.B., G.F.S.)

The term was introduced, in its German form, by Wundt, who distinguished sensation from its affective tone, supposing that every sensation has with it a certain qualitative sense-feeling. To some (Ward) it appears to be vague organic sensation accompanying special sensation. Other writers fail to find such feeling, and consider the so-called affective tone of sensation as pleasure and pain; yet others consider all feeling a state of compounded pleasure and pain (see FEELING). To them affective tone is simply the presence of pleasure and pain. It is best, on the whole, to confine affective tone—or feeling tone—to qualitative differences of the affective order everywhere; to leave it as a further question as to whether sensations have such affective tone; and to use the phrase HEDONIC TONE (q.v.) for the pleasure-pain colouring throughout.

Literature: WUNDT, Physiol. Psychol., chap. x; Outlines of Pyschol., § 7; WARD, Encyc. Brit., art. Psychology; LADD, Psychol. Descrip. and Explan., chap. ix; Elements of Physiol. Psychol., 514 f.; BALDWIN, Handb. of Psychol., Feeling and Will, chaps. iii, iv; STOUT, Analytic Psychol., i. chap. vi. (J.M.B.–G.F.S.)

Affinity (chemical): see CHEMICAL SYNTHESIS.

Affirmation and **Affirmative**: Ger. *Be-*

hauptung; Fr. *affirmation*; Ital. *affermazione*. See JUDGMENT.

A fortiori [Lat.] (the same in the other languages). With stronger reason; hence, more conclusive, as applied to an argument. (J.M.B.)

After-image: Ger. *Nachbild*; Fr. *image consécutive*; Ital. *immagine persistente* (or *consecutiva*). (1) AFTER-SENSATION (q. v.). (2) After-sensation of sight. These may be classified as (*a*) positive and negative, according as they retain the relations of light and shade of the original stimulus or reverse them; (*b*) same-coloured, complementary, and variable, according as their colour-tone stands related to the stimulus colour; and (*c*) monocular, binocular, or transferred, according as they are set up in the stimulated eye or eyes, or in the unstimulated eye.

The negative and complementary after-image ('the' after-image of popular parlance) is explained by Fechner and Helmholtz as a phenomenon of retinal fatigue (Helmholtz, *Physiol. Optik*, 2nd ed., 534). Hering regards it as a phenomenon of ADAPTATION (q.v.), as significant of a return to equilibrium of the antagonistic visual processes (Ebbinghaus, *Psychol.*, 258). Positive and same-coloured after-images, resulting from brief and intensive stimulation, are explained as due to a continuation of excitation after removal of stimulus; but there are difficulties. Between primary sensation and this (positive and same-coloured) image is sometimes seen a positive and complementary after-image: the explanation is doubtful (Ebbinghaus, loc. cit., 244). See AFTER-SENSATION. The variable after-image shows the 'flight of colours' (e. g. solar after-image), which must be indicative of highly complicated excitatory processes. The transferred after-image depends apparently on the existence of a sensory reflex arc in the binocular visual apparatus (Titchener, *Philos. Stud.*, viii. 231). Altogether, the after-image chapter is one of the least satisfactory in current visual theory. Cf. VISION; also LABORATORY AND APPARATUS (optical). (E.B.T.)

Both the 'explanations' (Helmholtz' and Hering's) are merely restatements of what a complementary or an antagonistic colour is, in the given theory—i. e. a residuum, when one colour is removed from white, or a 'reversed' colour-process.

It has sometimes been supposed that after-images are due to processes of fatigue or of restitution in the visual centres of the brain, higher or lower—not in the retina. This view is based upon the fact that an after-image due to stimulation of one eye may, under proper conditions, sometimes seem to be seen with the other. Experiments show, however, that in such cases the after-image is really seen with the eye first stimulated; other considerations, together with Exner's experiments on retinal and optic nerve stimulation, support the retinal location (Sanford, *Course in Exper. Psychol.*, expt. 27). (C.L.F.)

Literature: works cited above. Also VON KRIES, Zeitsch. f. Psychol., xii. 81; HERING, Pflüger's Arch., xlii. 488, xliii. 264, 329; Arch. f. Ophthal., xxxvii. 3, 1; xxxviii. 2, 252; HESS, Arch. f. Ophthal., xxxvi. i. 1; Pflüger's Arch., xlix. 190; FICK and GÜRBER, Arch. f. Ophthal., xxxvi. 2, 245, xxxviii. 1, 118; S. BIDWELL, Proc. Roy. Soc., lvi, No. 337, 132; FRANZ, Mon. Supp. to Psychol. Rev., No. XII; and general references under VISION.

After-sensation: Ger. *Nachempfindung*; Fr. *sensation consécutive*; Ital. *persistenza della sensazione*. In various senses, brief stimulation of the peripheral organ results in (1) a primary sensation, (2) a short blank interval after the stimulus ceases, and (3) a secondary sensation, called after-sensation.

Literature: KÜLPE, Outlines of Psychol., § 9. Pressure: GOLDSCHEIDER, Abhandl. d. physiol. Gesell. zu Berlin (Oct. 31, 1890). Temperature: DESSOIR, Du Bois-Reymond's Arch. (1892). Tone: URBANTSCHITSCH, Pflüger's Arch., xxv. (1881). Sight: see AFTER-IMAGE. Touch: SPINDLER, Psychol. Rev., iv. 632 f.

(2) The name is also given to the continuance of sensation without pause after removal of stimulus.

Literature: Temperature: GOLDSCHEIDER, Du Bois-Reymond's Arch. (1885), Suppl.-Bd. Tone: STUMPF, Tonpsychologie, i. 213 (not admitted). Sight: 'fall' of sensation (cf. Ebbinghaus, Psychol., 241); SANFORD, Course in Exper. Psychol., expts. 11, 13, 19, 64, 124–8. (E.B.T.)

Agamogenesis [Gr. ἀ + γάμος, marriage, and γένεσις, birth]: Ger. *ungeschlechtliche Fortpflanzung*; Fr. *agamogenèse, génération asexuée*; Ital. *agamogenesi, riproduzione agamica*. The process of asexual multiplication (or Monogony) in animals and plants. Compare GAMOGENESIS (or Amphigony).

Four modes of agamogenesis have been distinguished: (1) Where the organism divides into two more or less similar organisms by binary FISSION (q.v.), as in the amoeba and other unicellular organisms [and occasionally in higher forms (Schizogamy of Annelids). (2) Where the organism divides into a num-ber of minute bodies or spores, each of which can develop into the adult form (sporulation), as in plants and unicellular animals. (E.S.G.)]

(3) Where buds are produced by GEMMATION (q.v.), as in many plants, and among the Coelenterata and many other, especially sessile and colonial, animals. (4) By the development of unfertilized ova (see PARTHENOGENESIS). In many animals and plants reproduction by both processes, gamogenetic and agamogenetic, prevails. Thus hydra, when the conditions are favourable, reproduces by gemmation; but under the indirect influence of cold or from insufficient nutrition, it gives rise to ova or spermatozoa. See PROTOZOA, ALTERNATION OF GENERATIONS, and PARTHENOGENESIS. (C.LL.M.)

Whether organisms can continue for an indefinite number of generations reproducing asexually, is a question which has a very important bearing on the subject of the origin and significance of sex, senility, and death. Maupas found that in the case of the Infusoria (unicellular animals) an occasional return to AMPHIMIXIS (q.v.) is necessary to prevent degeneration and eventual death. Nevertheless, there are groups of lowly organized animals and plants amongst which agamogenetic reproduction only is known to occur. See DEATH.

Literature: E. MAUPAS, Recherches expérimentales sur la multiplication des infusoires ciliés, Arch. Zool. Exp. et Gén. (1888). (E.S.G.)

Agency (in law) [Med. Lat. *agentia*]: Ger. *Agentschaft, Agentur, Stellvertretung*; Fr. *procuration, agence*; Ital. *procura*. A contractual relation, whereby one person is authorized to act for another in such a manner as to confer upon the latter new rights or impose upon him new obligations. The wife's authority to act for her husband so far as to bind him for the purchase of necessaries for her support was originally an incident of her legal relation to him, but is now treated as proceeding from his implied consent. The absence of authority may be supplied by a subsequent ratification. By some jurists agency is considered to involve a delegation of power to exercise some discretion in determining the manner of action, so that the juristic act, which is the result of the agency, is performed by the agent: in this view a mere messenger is not a true agent, for in his case the juristic act is concluded by the principal, and there is no real representation as to the latter (Sohm's *Institutes of Roman Law*, § 32). He for whom another is an agent is termed the *principal*.

Agency is a development of the law of the family, where all act in subjection to its head, and on his account. Its basis has gradually changed from that of *status* to that of contract. It played but a small part in Roman law, so far as it depended on contractual relations (Sohm's *Institutes of Roman Law*, § 32 ; Phillimore's *Principles and Maxims of Jurisprudence*, xx). The Roman *mandatarius* bound himself personally as to the third party with whom he might deal for his principal, the *mandator*.

Literature : MOREY, Outlines of Roman Law, 370 ; CUF, Institutions Juridiques des Romains (1891), 649. A scholarly discussion of the history of agency in English law, by Chief Justice Holmes, of Massachusetts, will be found in the Harvard Law Review, iv. 345, v. 1. (S.E.B.)

Agent [Lat. *agens*, acting] : Ger. *wirkendes Wesen, Agent* ; Fr. *agent* ; Ital. *agente*. That which manifests ACTIVITY (q.v.) in any of the senses given under that term. The more special meanings immediately follow. (J.M.B.)

Agent (free). One who exercises FREEDOM (q.v.). The agent is said, in general, to be free when the act is not performed under external constraint, or by mere physiological reflex. The degree to which threat of pain or deception or ignorance interferes with free agency is a disputed question (cf. Aristotle, *Eth. Nic.*, iii. 1). (W.R.S.—J.M.B.)

Agent (in law) [Lat. *agens*] : Ger. *Agent, Geschäftsführer* ; Fr. *mandataire, gérant* ; Ital. *agente*. One authorized to act for another (who is termed his principal) in such a manner as to give the latter new rights or impose upon him new obligations.

See AGENCY. An agent is juristically identified with his principal. *Qui facit per alium facit per se.* (S.E.B.)

Agglutination (linguistic) [Lat. *ad*, to, + *glutinare*, to paste] : Ger. *Agglutination* ; Fr. *agglutination* ; Ital. *agglutinazione*. A method of formation in language, whereby a modification of meaning or of relation is given to a word through a significant element or elements attached to it or contained in it.

The method is widely applied in language, and is abundantly illustrated in English (e. g. in *circlet, leaflet, ringlet*, the element *-let* is distinctly and separately significant), and can be applied in the formation of new words, as *priestlet* ; so *-ess* in *goddess, baroness, authoress* ; so *-ed* in *sounded, hated, 'suicided'* ; or *ex-* in *ex-president, ex-convict*. This, which is in English and generally in inflectional languages one of various devices used for modifying the meaning of words or fitting them to their function in the sentence, appears in a large number of languages, known as the agglutinative, and of which the Turkish, the Japanese, and the Bantu languages are typical examples, as the dominant principle of structure. Like elements are with a high degree of consistency used for like modifications, and hence the structure is in general simple and regular, making the minimum of demand upon the memory. Such languages appear to have been originally developed in adjustment to the needs of scattered populations within which intercourse was maintained at low tension. Psychologically they represent a grammatical consciousness awake to the necessity of indicating simply and unmistakably every turn of thought, and are so distinguished from inflectional languages, but most widely and radically from the monosyllabic or isolating languages like the Chinese. (B.I.W.)

Agglutination (in psychology). A term used by the early associationists for cases of close or 'adhesive' association of ideas. Also by Wundt for the simplest form of apperceptive combination (*Verbindung*). Its use is not recommended. (J.M.B., G.F.S.)

Aggregate [Lat. *ad* + *grex*, flock] : Ger. *Aggregat, Zusammen* (for Herbart's use, see COMPLEX) ; Fr. *agrégat* ; Ital. *aggregato*. (1) A collection of individuals considered as aggregated or loosely gathered together (see AGGREGATION). (2) In psychology, an Aggregate Idea or Concept is a general idea of a class or group taken collectively rather than abstractly. In the aggregate or collective idea the multiplicity of separate units is held before the mind. Cf. GENERAL AND ABSTRACT IDEA, and NOTION.

Judd (trans. of Wundt's *Outlines of Psychol.*, Glossary and 260), following Titchener (ibid. 260 note), uses Aggregate Idea to render Wundt's Gesammtvorstellung, an alternative expression being Idea of Imagination, an apperceptive compound which is distinguished from Fusion and Association by being voluntary and selective. The English word Concept would seem to render this meaning sufficiently well, provided we do not follow Wundt (loc. cit.) in using its equivalent (Begriff) for a special case of Gesammtvorstellung. The aggregate idea is a GENERAL (see that term for the foreign equivalents) that is the idea of an aggregate, not an idea that is itself 'aggregated or complex.' For this latter we have the terms Composite and Complex, which may be used (cf. Titchener's recommen-

25

dation, *Amer. J. of Psychol.*, vii. 82) for the intellectual framework of the Concept as covered by Gesammtvorstellung. (J.M.B., G.F.S.)

Aggregation (in sociology) : Ger. *Aggregat* (1), *Haufen* (2) ; Fr. *agrégat, agrégation* ; Ital. *aggregazione.* (1) A collection of beings taken together, considered as a unit or as made up of units. See UNIT (social).

It is a general term for the different cases often designated by the term ASSOCIATION (social) (q.v.). It is recommended that aggregation and (social) GROUP (q.v.) take the place of ' social association,' for reasons given under Association (social), in sociology (the point of view of the onlooker) ; and that CO-OPERATION (q.v.) be used in the same general way for all sorts of Aggregation and of Groups when looked at from the point of view of the actor in the group. We should then have Aggregation (general) determined in different Groups (special), as Family, Church, Commercial, &c., in sociology, and Co-operation determined as Instinctive, Spontaneous, Intelligent, &c., in social psychology.

Literature : see SOCIOLOGY, and SOCIAL PSYCHOLOGY. (J.M.B., G.F.S.)

(2) A term of demography or of statistics of population, meaning a grouping of individuals in one place or territory.

Hobbes (*De Corpore Politico*, Pt. II. chap. ii. § 1) uses the phrase ' a multitude considered as an aggregate.' Genetic and congregate aggregation are terms introduced by Giddings (*Princ. of Sociol.*, 1896), with the following meanings : genetic aggregation = a grouping of kindred by common descent ; congregate aggregation = a grouping by immigration of either unrelated or related individuals. (F.H.G.)

Agnoiology [Gr. ἄγνοια, ignorance, + λόγος, discourse]. The theory of human ignorance, its extent, limits, and conditions ; a term used by Ferrier (*Instit. of Met.*, 48) to indicate a discipline between epistemology and ontology. (R.H.S.)

Agnosticism [Lat. *a + gnoscere*, to know] : Ger. *Agnosticismus, Agnosie* ; Fr. *agnosticisme* ; Ital. *agnosticismo.* The class of philosophical or scientific theories which recognize an intrinsically UNKNOWABLE (q.v.).

The term is due to Huxley, with whom, and many other scientific men (cf. Du Bois-Reymond, *Ueber d. Grenzen d. Naturerkenntniss*), it means rather a habit of mind which considers metaphysics futile. In philosophy it has been applied especially to Spencer and the Positivists (see POSITIVISM), to Kant (see KANTIANISM), and to those (e.g. Hamilton, Brad-

ley) who draw agnostic conclusions from the doctrine of the RELATIVITY OF KNOWLEDGE (q.v.).

Literature : see UNKNOWABLE, POSITIVISM, EPISTEMOLOGY ; especially KANT, ' Transcendental Dialectic,' in Critique of Pure Reason ; HUXLEY, Collected Essays, i, and ' Hume' ; SPENCER, First Principles ; STERLING, Textbook to Kant ; WARD, Naturalism and Agnosticism ; BIBLIOG. E, 2, *a*. (J.M.B., G.F.S.)

Agnosticism (in theology). A word primarily descriptive of any theory which denies that it is possible for man to acquire knowledge about God.

While theologians almost unanimously unite in opposing agnosticism, they have not been unaffected by cognate tendencies. The problem, ' How far can a finite being know the absolute Being?' invariably raises difficulties that often lead to conclusions of a partially agnostic character. These difficulties are inseparable from the manner in which theology states the problem. (1) As against the doctrine of ' traditionalism,' which holds that man needs the aid of a supernatural revelation to arrive at a knowledge of the being of God, the Roman Catholic Church authoritatively teaches that ' by the natural light of human reason' the fact of God's existence can certainly be ascertained. But, on the other hand, as against the theory of ' ontologism'—that man is able of himself to know God directly, and that all knowledge is nothing more than a mode of this knowledge of deity—it upholds a modified agnosticism. In condemning the tendencies to pantheism, which are alleged to be traceable in such a writer as, say, Rosmini, it was necessary to declare that from nature man does not obtain any insight into the essence of God's being. The direct perception of the nature of God is reserved for the blessed in another life. Here God can be known only ' reflected in a mirror.' While, then, man can know that God is by an effort of mere reason, he cannot know what God essentially is. (2) Christian theism is also partially agnostic. It holds that man has knowledge of God, but denies that God is one with the universe. It therefore infers that the absolute Being transcends the universe, and that human knowledge of him, while always progressing, can never be complete. (3) Mansel furnishes the classical instance of agnosticism in theology. His conception is that, while man must believe in the infinity of God, he is unable to comprehend it. Faith and knowledge are thus necessarily divorced. For, as knowledge always attaches predicates in order to obtain definiteness, and as predicates limit, there cannot be any real knowledge of the infinite existence in which, nevertheless, man must believe. (4) The most recent form of agnosticism in theology is to be found in the teaching of A. Ritschl and some of his school. It reposes upon a specialized theory of knowledge, derived partly from one interpretation of Kant and partly from Lotze, according to which man knows only phenomena. As God is not a phenomenon, he is not known by man. Theology therefore deals not with the *causa efficiens*, but with the *causa finalis*. That is to say, it treats of God not as a being, but as an 'attractive ideal' which, by impressing a man subjectively with its value for him, leads him to adopt it. God is thus unknowable in himself—even in divine revelation it would seem; man is aware of him only in so far as appreciative of the value of his nature (which is love) for the purposes of moral and religious elevation. (R.M.W.)

Literature: see BIBLIOG. E, 2, *g*, *a*.

Agoraphobia [Gr. ἀγορά, market-place, + φοβία, fear]: Ger. *Platzfurcht, Platzangst*; Fr. *agoraphobie, topophobie*; Ital. *agorafobia*. A morbid uneasiness or fear in crossing open places. The term *Platzfurcht* or Agoraphobia is due to Westphal. The symptom is one of a group of excessive fears (see PHOBIA) characteristic of states of nervous debility or of persons with nervous diathesis. It is also symptomatic of mental degeneration and of neurasthenia. Open spaces, parks, squares, and the like are avoided. When it is necessary to cross them the patient follows the surrounding houses or trees or clings to a companion. There is no vertigo, but the legs feel weak, the heart palpitates; there may be coldness or numbness and profuse sweating. The patient may realize the groundlessness of the fear, but none the less feels alarm and apprehension. At times it cannot be overcome, and momentarily inhibits action (cf. ABOULIA). (J.J.)

Literature: H. SAURY, Étude clinique sur la folie héréditaire (1886); BENEDIKT, Allg. Wien. med. Zeit., xl; WESTPHAL, Arch. f. Psychiat. u. Nervenh.(1872); KAAN, Der neurasthenische Angstaffekt; Jahrb. f. Psychiat. u. Neurol., xi. 149; SUCKLING, Amer. J. Med. Sci., xcix. 476-83; LEGRAND DU SAULLE, Étude clinique sur la peur des espaces (1878); DECHAMBRE, Dict. Encyc. des Sci. Méd. (sub verbo); CORDES, Arch. f. Psychiat. u. Nervenh. (1872); DUHAUT, Considérations sur l'agoraphobie (1879); M. DE GRAIN, Délire chez les dégénérés (1886); V. MAGNAN, Leçons sur les délires (1897). (L.M.–J.M.B.)

Agraphia [Gr. ἀ+γράφειν, write]: Ger. *Agraphie*; Fr. *agraphie*; Ital. *agrafia*. The loss or impairment of the power to express oneself by written symbols. It is one of a group of the diseases of language (Aphasia) with intricate and important relations to the growth and decay of other speech functions, treated under the article SPEECH AND ITS DEFECTS (q.v., also for *Literature*). (J.J.)

Agreeableness and **Disagreeableness**: see PAIN AND PLEASURE, and PLEASANTNESS AND UNPLEASANTNESS.

Agreement [O.F. *agrement*]: Ger. (1) *Uebereinstimmung*, (2) *Gleichheit*, (3) *Uebereinstimmung, Consistenz*; Fr. (1) *convenance*, (2) *similitude*, (3) *compatibilité*; Ital. (1) *concordanza*, (2), (3) *accordo*. (1) Concord, harmony; (2) similarity, likeness, or sameness; analogy, or connectedness of meaning in case of ideas; (3) logical consistency in case of judgments.

Locke (*Essay concerning Human Understanding*, Book IV, chap. i) defines knowledge as 'the perception of the connection and agreement, or disagreement and repugnancy, of any of our ideas.' He then names four sorts of 'agreement or disagreement': (1) identity, or diversity; (2) relation; (3) coexistence; (4) real existence. The first is the particular relation between two ideas, which makes them called the same or not the same. The second refers to abstract relations which exist between ideas such as are still not identical; e.g. the relation of equality or inequality between two different quantities. The third has to do with the relation in concrete substances, between their various qualities; e.g. fusibility and yellowness coexist in gold. The fourth refers to the agreement or disagreement of any idea 'with real existence,' e. g. one may affirm God is. This view of the conception of agreement, and of its relation to judgment and to knowledge, was later much discussed.

Literature: FRASER'S edition of Locke's Essay, ii. 120 (with references). (J.R.)

Agreement (legal): see CONTRACT.

Agreement (method of): Ger. *Methode der Uebereinstimmung*; Fr. *méthode de concordance*; Ital. *metodo di concordanza*. The process of using a number of instances of constant conjunction amid differences as basis for inference to a real connection, most commonly of cause and effect. The rule defining the kind of conjunction required is expressed in Mill's enunciation thus: 'If two or more instances of the phenomenon under investigation have only one circumstance in common, the circumstance in which alone all these instances agree is the cause (or effect) of the given phenomenon.' The Method of Agreement is substantially that inculcated by F. Bacon as 'comparentia ad intellectum instantiarum quae in eadem natura conveniunt per materias licet dissimillimas' (*Nov. Org.* ii. 11). Modern logic recognizes more fully than Bacon did the characteristic imperfection of the method due to the possibility of PLURALITY OF CAUSES (q. v.), and more fully than Mill did the practical difficulties involved in application of the method to unanalysed experience. The method as a test or criterion of the sufficiency of evidence is pre-eminently but not exclusively applicable to data of observation.

Literature: BACON, Nov. Org.; J. S. MILL, Logic; VENN, Empirical Logic, chap. xvii; BRADLEY, Princ. of Logic, Bk. II. Pt. II. chap. iii; HOBHOUSE, Theory of Knowledge, Pt. II. chap. xv.　　　　　　　　(R.A.)

Agricultural Stage: Ger. *Kulturstufe der Ackerbauer*; Fr. *état agricole*; Ital. *stato agricolo*. That stage of economic development in which agriculture is of the greatest relative importance, when the pastoral or nomadic stage is over, and manufactures and commerce are still restricted.　　　　　　　　(F.C.M.)

Grosse (*Die Formen der Familie*) distinguishes a 'lower' from a 'higher' agricultural stage.　　　　　　　　(K.G.)

Agrippa, Henry Cornelius, of Nettesheim. (1486–1535.) A German physician, philosopher, and astrologer. Lectured in theology in Cologne and elsewhere, and practised medicine in France.

Ahrens, Heinrich. (1808–74.) Educated in Göttingen, he fled to Paris, and there lectured on the history of German philosophy. He was professor of philosophy in Brussels (1834), of law and political economy at Graz (1850), and of practical philosophy and political science in Leipzig (1859). Wrote on law and politics.

Ahrimân. The principle of evil in Persian philosophy. See ORIENTAL PHILOSOPHY (Persian).　　　　　　　　(J.M.B.)

d'Ailly (or **Ailli**), **Pierre.** (1350–cir. 1420.) A French churchman and reformer. Chancellor of the university of Paris after 1389; archbishop of Cambray after 1395; cardinal after 1411. He presided at the trial of John Huss before the Council of Constance. He exposed and condemned the abuses and impurities of the Church.

Aim [Lat. *aestimare*, to estimate]: Ger. *Ziel*; Fr. *fin, but*; Ital. *scopo*. A more remote or general project in voluntary action. Syno-

nymous most nearly with PURPOSE (q.v.), and having a less exact meaning than the terms END and MOTIVE (cf. those terms).　(J.M.B., G.F.S.)

Aim (in education): Ger. *Ziel*; Fr. *but*; Ital. *fine*. A stage in Herbartian METHOD (in education; q. v.); the end to be attained in a given exercise.

It is thought to conduce greatly to successful instruction if the end, or aim, towards which it moves is brought clearly to the consciousness of the pupil. That the aim may be both clear and important, Herbartian writers urge that the subject-matter of instruction should be so grouped that each subdivision may be considered a unit, or whole, for method. The aim for each unit, or method-whole, is simply the leading purpose for teaching it. Thus, in introducing a lesson upon the motions of the earth, the teacher may say: 'We have found that the earth is a great ball suspended in space; let us see whether it is at rest or in motion.' See METHOD-WHOLE.

Literature: McMURRY, The Method of the Recitation, 98–109.　　　　　　(C.DE G.)

Akinesis [Gr. ἀ + κίνησις, motion]: Ger. *Bewegungslosigkeit*; Fr. *paralysie, parésie*; Ital. *acinesi*. See PARALYSIS.

Alalia and **Dyslalia** [Gr. ἄλαλος, from ἀ + λαλεῖν, to talk]: Ger. *Alalie*; Fr. *alalie*; Ital. *alalia*. (1) Partial or complete loss of the power to articulate, or imperfect articulation, due usually to paralysis of one or other of the groups of muscles (lips, tongue, larynx) used in speaking. Similarly, dyslalia is used to refer to faulty articulation, or, which is better, complete loss of that power (Séglas, *Troubles du Langage*), which defect, when confined to a few special sounds, is termed mogilalia, and which, when the sound uttered is different from the one intended, may be termed paralalia. In these cases the defect is called peripheral, although the cause of it (paralysis) may be in the centres below the cortex. The difficulties in pronouncing *r, th, s,* &c., peculiar to individuals or races, are cases of mogilalia, and these in turn have been given special names, according to the letter involved—rhotacism, &c. These terms are used and illustrated by Kussmaul (*Störungen der Sprache*, chap. xxxv) and Morselli (*Semej. malat. ment.*, ii), but have not been generally adopted by other writers. Such normal difficulties of pronunciation are purely peritheral. (2) Loss of the elements of speech due to cerebral disease; i. e. a central defect. This is less usual and less desirable. See distinctions given under SPEECH AND ITS DEFECTS. (J.J.)

28

Alanus (or **Alan**), **Johann.** (1565–1631.) A Danish professor of philosophy, and author of philosophical works.

Albertists: followers of ALBERTUS MAGNUS (q.v.). See also THOMISTS, and PATRISTIC PHILOSOPHY.

Albertus Magnus. (1193–1280.) Sometimes called Albert von Bollstädt, 'Doctor Universalis.' One of the most learned men of the Middle Ages. He introduced the complete system of Aristotle to his age by a loose reproduction of Arabic versions and commentaries. Lectured at Cologne and in Paris, Thomas Aquinas being one of his pupils. He was a Dominican and became bishop, but found the office uncongenial and resigned.

Albo, Joseph (or **José**). (died 1428.) A Jewish scholar, disputant, and polemical writer, who continued the work of Maimonides. He considered the existence of God, the law of Moses, and the future life the fundamental dogmas of JUDAISM (q.v.).

Alcoholism [Arab. *al-koh'l*]: Ger. *Alkoholismus*; Fr. *alcoolisme*; Ital. *alcoolismo*. A morbid condition with marked physiological and psychological symptoms, brought about by excessive indulgence in alcoholic liquors.

The effects of alcohol vary considerably according to the duration, manner, and degree of imbibition, and the predisposition and general condition of the individual. The term Acute Alcoholism is reserved for a very distinctive group of symptoms which occurs at times after an excessive debauch, at times as an incident in the development of chronic alcoholism, and at times in predisposed patients as the consequence of severe mental or physical strain. This condition is also known as delirium tremens. Chronic Alcoholism is a condition resulting from the effects of the abuse of alcohol taken for a long period. Drunkenness is a transitory condition resulting from an excessive dose of alcohol; its synonyms are Inebriation or Intoxication. DIPSOMANIA (q.v.) is strictly an intermittent, irresistible craving for liquor, being a defect of inhibition similar in nature to other manias, but is often used as synonymous with drunkenness or alcoholism, as dipsomaniac is used for drunkard.

The morbid symptoms of alcoholism present a wide variation. The hereditary predisposition is a most important aetiological factor which influences as well the nature of the symptoms. Alcoholic poisoning seems to attack the region of least resistance, and, though slow and insidious in its onset, is certain to undermine the vigour of the nervous system. The nervous disorders pass, as the disease proceeds, from the periphery to the centre, appearing first as sensory and motor derangement, and later besieging the intellectual and moral faculties. The sensory troubles appear as pseudo-sensations in the extremities, itching, creeping, or pricking; at times hyperaesthesia, but more usually a progressive loss of sensibility occurs. The eyes lose their visual acuteness, and are prone to pseudo-sensations. Of the motor disorders, which likewise proceed from periphery to centre, the most salient symptom is a tremor, at first slight and occasional, then more marked and constant. Such tremors are exaggerated under nervous strain or effort, appear in the articulation, and frequently lead to more serious motor neuroses (spasms, cramps, convulsions, and paralyses). The intellectual disorders are usually described as falling into two periods, the second period exhibiting the typical picture of insanity (mania and dementia), while the first reveals the effects of a less serious but comprehensive intellectual decline. The excitability of the nervous centres leads to violent outbursts of anger, irritability, suspiciousness, or recklessness. Moral sensibilities are blunted, and the general plane of mental life gradually declines. The final stages of alcoholic dementia present complete decay of all the mental faculties, with pronounced stammering, tremor, and paralysis (see DEMENTIA).

Acute alcoholism (delirium tremens) is the sharp outbreak of a predisposed nervous system under the influence of alcoholic poisoning, and is in many cases an exacerbation of a chronic condition. The attack is generally foreshadowed in a prodromic period marked by cerebral exaltation, rapid flow of ideas, excitement, excessive sensitiveness, fear, irritability, and the like; and sensory illusions, fantastic and persistent, and regularly increasing at night, render the sleep of the sufferer a protracted nightmare of gruesome scenes and fearful catastrophes. The delirium itself is the culmination of the prodromic symptoms, the illusions passing into more constant and varied hallucinations; the patient, no longer a spectator but an actor in the fancied horrors, becomes the victim of numberless fears and torturing sensations, particularly affecting sight and touch. In drunkenness likewise there are two periods—one of excitement and the other of depression. A lively imagination, exuberance of spirits, loquacity, lack of reserve, are characteristic of the first stage, while in the ensuing stage are observed confusion of thought, difficulty in speech and in the finer motor co-ordinations, vertigo, sense-illusions. This is followed by a period of deep sleep—a recuperative period of heaviness and stupor gradually leading to the normal condition. The condition, like other forms of alcoholic poisoning, varies considerably with the individual and the nature of the dose. The study of alcoholism has an importance beyond its medical and psychological interest. It has contributed to much of the degradation of individuals and races, and the regulation of its use has been for generations one of the most important sociological problems. The tendency to this excess has passed into our heredity, and is recognized as one of the significant marks of a degenerate diathesis.

Literature: LEGRAIN, articles Alcoholism, Chronic Alcoholism, Delirium Tremens, in Tuke's Dict. of Psychol. Med.; BONHOEFFER, Der Geisteszustand des Alcoholdelirienten, Wernicke's Psychiatrie, App. 6 (1898); C. F. HODGE, Experiments on the Physiology of Alcohol, Pop. Sci. Mo. (1897), l. 594–603, 769–812. An extensive bibliography of alcoholism has been compiled by J. S. BILLINGS (1894). (J.J.)

Also V. MAGNAN, Recherches sur les Centres Nerveux, 1e série (1876), 2e série (1893); Leçons Cliniques sur les Maladies Mentales (1893); De l'Alcoolisme (1874); Des diverses formes de Délire alcoolique et de leur Traitement; DECHAMBRE, Dict. Encyc. des Sci. Méd. (sub verbo); J. DEJERINE, De l'Hérédité dans les Maladies du Système Nerveux (1886); M. LEGRAIN, Hérédité et Alcoolisme (1889). (L.M.)

Also HUSS, Alkoholismus; E. FAZIO, L'Ubriachezza (1878–92); ZERBOGLIO, Alcoolismo (1896). (E.M.)

Alcott, Amos Bronson. (1799–1888.) American transcendental philosopher; contributed to *The Dial*, and published works on a wide range of speculative and practical themes.

Alcuin (or **Alkuin**), **Flaccus Albinus Alcinus.** (cir. 735–804.) An English churchman, 'the most learned man of his age.' He became (782) member of the court of Charlemagne, with whom he sustained an intimate friendship until his death. Assisted the king in founding and maintaining schools, was head of the court school, and was made (796) abbot of St. Martins at Tours.

d'Alembert, Jean le Rond. (1717–83.) A French geometer and philosopher: educated in the Mazarin College, his favourite study being geometry. He wrote on dynamics, fluids, and a number of important literary and philosophical themes. With Diderot, he was one of the ENCYCLOPEDISTS (q.v.).

Alexander, Archibald. (1772–1851.) President of Hampden-Sidney College; pastor in the Presbyterian Church; professor in the Theological Seminary of Princeton. He was noted as a pulpit orator and as a writer on theology and the evidences of Christianity.

Alexander, James Waddell. (1804–59.) Son of Archibald Alexander, educated in Princeton College and Seminary. Pastor, editor of *The Presbyterian* (1830–3); professor of rhetoric and belles-lettres at Princeton (1833–44); pastor, New York (1844–9 and 1851–9); professor of church history and government in Princeton Theological Seminary (1849–51).

Alexander, Joseph Addison. (1809–1860.) Son of Archibald Alexander, educated at Princeton. Distinguished for oriental learning, he became professor of biblical criticism and ecclesiastical history in Princeton Theological Seminary (1833), and professor of biblical and ecclesiastical history after 1852.

Alexander of Aphrodisias. A teacher of the Peripatetic philosophy at Athens in the end of the 2nd and beginning of the 3rd centuries A.D. Wrote commentaries on the works of Aristotle, which were translated by the Arabians, and published later in the Aldine edition of Aristotle's works (1495–8) and, in part, in more recent times.

Alexander of Hales. (died 1245.) Named 'Doctor Irrefragabilis' and also 'Fons Vitae': a celebrated English theologian of the 13th century. Trained in the monastery of Hales, he relinquished an archdeaconry to study in Paris, where he received the doctor's degree and became famous as a teacher of philosophy and theology. Among his pupils was Bonaventura (but not Duns Scotus or Thomas Aquinas, as has been asserted). Entered the order of Minorite Friars. His most famous book, *Summa Theologiae*, is based on the *Sentences* of Peter Lombard.

Alexandrian School: Ger. *Alexandrinische Schule*; Fr. *école d'Alexandrie*; Ital. *scuola alessandrina*. The phrase has been used in two distinct senses—a literary and a philosophico-theological. In the former sense, with which we need not deal here, it is applied to the literary tendencies dominant during the age of the Ptolemies (322–30 B.C.) In its philosophico-theological usage it indicates that junction between Eastern and Western thought which took place at Alexandria and produced a new series of doctrines which mark an entire school. Although these tendencies may be traced as far back as 280 B.C., it is convenient to date the *floreat* of the school from 30 B.C. to 529 A.D.

East and West met and commingled at Alexandria. The operative ideas of the civilizations, cultures, and religions of Rome, Greece, Palestine, and the further East found themselves in juxtaposition. Hence arose a new problem, developed partly by occidental thought, partly by oriental aspiration. Religion and philosophy became inextricably mixed, and the resultant doctrines consequently belong to neither sphere proper, but are rather witnesses to an attempt at combining both. These efforts naturally came from two sides. On the one hand, the Jews tried to accommodate their faith to the results of Western culture, in which Greek elements predominated. On the other hand, thinkers whose main impulse came from Greek philosophy attempted to accommodate their doctrines to the distinctively religious problems which the eastern nations had brought with them. From whichever side the consequences be viewed, they are to be characterized as theosophical rather than purely philosophical, purely religious, or purely theological.

(1) The beginnings of the movement are almost entirely lost in obscurity. Some profess to find traces of it so early as the Septuagint (280 B.C.), but it is usual to date the first overt traces from Aristobulus (160 B.C.). The Jewish line culminated in Philo (fl. 40 A.D.), who accepts Greek metaphysical ideas and, by the method of allegorical interpretation, finds their justification in the Hebrew Scriptures. Philo's system falls into three main portions: (*a*) The existence and nature of God. (*b*) God's relation to the world, embodying the very important and influential doctrine of the Logos. This doctrine is Philo's most distinctive contribution to the history of thought, and is a determining element in the teaching of the school in all its branches. (*c*) Man's life in the light of his own and of God's nature. Philo's significance is to be sought rather in what he attempted than in what he accomplished, and the same may be said of the Jewish Alexandrians as a whole. These thinkers are significant phenomena, not permanent figures.

(2) In the more strictly philosophical line the doctrine of the Alexandrian school goes by the name Neo-Platonism. Here, once more, great obscurity prevails regarding the earlier history. It may be said generally that the Neo-Platonists are deflected from philosophy proper by their adoption of the contemporary religious and apocalyptic longings of mankind, and by their tacit agreement to view these theosophical movements as originating the problems which it was most essential for philosophy to solve. Consequently, their interpretation of the universe and of life is not unbiassed, but is conducted in the interest of the great question of salvation from this present evil world. Philosophically viewed, the school is eminently eclectic. Although relying upon Plato for its first principles, and especially for its dualism, it agrees with the post-Aristotelian sceptics in its contempt for knowledge; with the Stoics in its manifold tendencies towards pantheism, and in its regard for an ascetic morality; it bears traces too of the influence of Aristotle, especially in some aspects of its statement of the problem of the relation of God to the world. According to generally accepted opinion the school was founded by Ammonius Saccas (fl. 200 A.D.). His doctrines well illustrate the general scheme of its teaching. The human soul forms the central subject of investigation. Its pure origin, its falling away, and the means of its return to its first estate constitute the principal subjects discussed. The entire attitude is mystical. That is to say, the beginning lies in a transcendent sphere, and there the end is to be found also. Man must needs get beyond experience, and this by exceptional means. By cultivating freedom from the trammels of sense, a man may at length achieve a condition of ecstasy in which he will become one with God. With Plotinus Neo-Platonism attains its highest development and, very specially, its clearest and least irrational teaching. Porphyry (fl. 280 A.D.) was Plotinus' greatest pupil, and he always remained a pupil. He departed from the theoretical severity of the master and emphasized the practical element more, with a view to combating the rising power of Christianity. After him the theosophical interest predominates, as in Iamblichus, Sopater, Maximus, and many others. The members of the school became religious teachers charged with a mission on behalf of Paganism against Christianity. After the death of Julian 'the Apostate' (363 A.D.), the power of the Church gradually increased, and that of Pagan theosophy waned correspondingly. Alexandria and Rome ceased to be the head quarters, and Greek thought

found its last refuge in the old home, Athens. Plutarch (fl. 425 A.D.) and Proclus (fl. 470 A.D.) are the most distinguished representatives of this branch. Naturally, under the changed conditions, the general aspect of the school was once more altered. Its scholars tend to emphasize accurate historical knowledge of previous systems, and, on the basis of this, they try to resystematize the entire body of Greek thought, relying at the same time upon Plotinus for the general framework. With Proclus dialectic comes to occupy a prominent position again. Neo-Platonism may be said to end with Damascius, who was head of the Athenian school when it was closed, by order of Justinian, in 529 A.D. Boethius is the last eminent thinker to be affected by it.

(3) Owing to the historical circumstances in which they found themselves, rather than to the influence of Neo-Platonism as a formal system, some Christian thinkers were profoundly swayed by ideas characteristic of the Alexandrian school. Of these T. Flavius Clemens (fl. 200 A.D.) and Origen (fl. 240 A.D.) were the most distinguished. Clemens was a pupil of Pantaenus, the first great teacher of this branch—the catechetical—of the school; he was also a convert from Paganism to Christianity. His main importance in the history of thought lies in his perception of the value of philosophy to religion, which had become obscured, or even lost, during the conflict of the Church with the Gnostics. Coming so early as he did, he was unable to realize the full significance of the problems that turned upon an alliance between Christianity and Greek thought, while his lack of system gave an air of accommodating syncretism to his doctrines. He attempted to combine purity of life (as against some Gnostics) with freedom of thought (as against Church tendencies). The former takes from Christian conceptions, the latter from Greek. Origen is the great systematizer and scholar of the theological line of the school. In his combination of the Christian religion with Greek philosophy, the practical tendency of the former counteracts the mystical implications of the latter. He has his theory of the universe and his rule of life, like the Neo-Platonists, but he founds them on the Scriptures, and by his peculiar interpretations contrives to bring about harmony. Hence his theory of one teaching for the people and another for those 'who are able to bear it.' The whole truth is too high and difficult for the masses. He evinces marvellous skill in harmonizing the varied elements, so much so that, at a later time, opposing theological factions agreed in appealing to him, and with equal show of reason. The best example of this skill is to be found in his treatment of the Logos. Origen had no successor of equal intellectual rank, though Athanasius must have known something of current speculation. At the end of the 4th century the philosophical writings of Synesius of Ptolemais show how close might still be the bond between Christianity and Neo-Platonism.

The value of the work done by Clemens, and especially by Origen, is often underestimated. They saved Christianity from the extremes of fanaticism and superstition, due to early apocalyptic ideas, and strove, by inculcating the Fatherhood of God, to unify the conception of the revelation in Christ with the older notion of a revelation in nature. In this connection, the continuation of their work by Augustine deserves close attention.

The comparatively recent researches and contentions of A. Ritschl, and particularly of A. Harnack and his co-workers, have renewed interest in these problems by showing their great importance for the history of the development of dogma in the Christian Church.

Literature: (1) GFRÖRER, Philo u. d. Alex. Theosophie; DÄHNE, Darstellung d. jüd.-alex. Religionsphilos.; ZELLER, Philos. d. Griechen, iii. 2; HEINZE, D. Lehre vom Logos; DRUMMOND, Philo-Judaeus. (2) ZELLER, op. cit.; HEINZE, op. cit.; UEBERWEG, Hist. of Philos., i; VACHEROT, Hist. de l'école d'Alexandrie. (3) AUGUSTINE, Confessions, vii. 9–21; any good Church History, e.g. NEANDER, F. C. BAUR; HARNACK, Hist. of Dogma; VOGT, Neuplatonismus u. Christenthum; KEIM, Aus d. Urchristenthum; KEIM, Augustinus; REDEPENNING, Origenes; PATRICK, Apology of Origen; A. RITSCHL, Theol. u. Met.; BIGG, Christian Platonists of Alexandria; HATCH, Hibbert Lectures; the new editions of Early Christian Literature (especially Origen) by HARNACK and his associates. See PATRISTIC PHILOSOPHY, V. (R.M.W.)

Alexia [Gr. ἀ + λέγειν, to read]: Ger. *Alexie*; Fr. *alexie*; Ital. *alessia*. Loss or impairment of the power to read; i.e. to understand the meaning of the visual symbols expressed in printed or written words. It forms one of a group of the diseases of speech with intimate and important relations to other defects. See SPEECH AND ITS DEFECTS. Forms of alexia are termed word-blindness, text-blindness; and it is related to, though not synonymous with, mental or mind-blindness, called also Psychic Blindness (q. v.). (J.J.)

Alexinus of Elis. Lived in the 4th century B.C. A logician, follower of Eubulides, who attacked Aristotle and Zeno the Stoic.

Alfarabi or **Alfarabie** (Lat. **Alfarabius**). Died 950 A.D. A distinguished Arabian scholar and philosopher who lived in Damascus. He is said to have known seventy languages; and wrote treatises on the sciences and on Aristotle.

Al-Gazzali or **Al-Ghazzali.** (1058–1111.) Moslem theologian and philosopher. A prolific writer, who taught in Nishapoor and Bagdad. Lived in Syria, and travelled (or visited) in Egypt.

Algedonic Aesthetics [Gr. ἄλγος, pain, + ἡδονή, pleasure]: Ger. *algedonische Aesthetik, Gefühlsaesthetik*; Fr. *esthétique algédonique*; Ital. *estetica*. Aesthetics considered as a special branch of the science of hedonics, or, more broadly, of the science of pleasure and pain. The term was suggested by Marshall, in *Pain, Pleasure, and Aesthetics* (1894), chap. vi. (J.H.T.)

Algesia [Gr. ἀλγεῖν, to have pain]: Ger. *Schmerzempfindlichkeit*; Fr. *algésie*; Ital. *algesia*. The capacity for having pain. As Analgesia (q. v.) expresses the absence of the sense of pain, algesia expresses its normal presence; it is also used (Tuke) as a synonym of Hyperaesthesia (q.v.). See Pleasure and Pain (also for *Literature*). (J.J.)

Algometer or **Algesimeter:** see Laboratory and Apparatus, III. B, (c). (C.)

Algorism (and, erroneously, **Algorithm**). The Arabic or decimal system of numeration, and hence arithmetic; so called from the name of the Arabian writer on Algebra, whose work, in translation, introduced the decimal system into Europe early in the 9th century. Cf. Murray's *Eng. Dict.*, sub verbo. (J.M.B.)

Alienist (1), **Alienism** (2), **Alienation** (3) [Lat. *alienus*, belonging to another, estranged]: Ger. *Irrenarzt* (1), *Psychiatrie* (2), *Geistesstörung* (3); Fr. *aliéniste* (1), *psychiatrie* (2), *aliénation* (3); Ital. *alienista* (1), *psichiatria* (2), *alienazione mentale* (3). A medical specialist in the study and treatment of mental diseases. Alienism is the name for such study, while Alienation is a generic name for the various forms of insanity or mental derangement. (J.J.)

Alison, Archibald. (1757–1839.) A Scottish writer, best known for his *Essays on the Nature and Principles of Taste.*

Alkindi, Abu Yusuf (also **Alchendius**). Lived in the first half of the 10th century, and

died after 961. The most encyclopedic writer among the Arabs. He wrote on nearly every science and every branch of philosophy, and was one of the earliest translators and commentators on Aristotle. He represented the first philosophic revolt against Mohammedanism.

All [AS. *all, alle*]: Ger. *All*; Fr. *tout*; Ital. *tutto*. (1) As noun, a name for the whole universe, 'The all.' Also, in general, for the whole of anything. (2) As adjective, with distributive force, the characteristic adjective prefixed to the plural form of the subject of any universal affirmative judgment; and equivalent to 'every' followed by the singular of the same subject: e. g. 'All men are mortal.' (3) As collective adjective, the sign that a number of objects are regarded as forming a single collective individual: e. g. 'All the angles of a triangle taken together are equal to two right angles.'

The use of τὸ πᾶν as a philosophical term for the universe dates back to the Pythagoreans and Plato. See, for Plato's usage, *Timaeus*, 28c., and elsewhere. The universal judgment, with its character as the judgment which affirms the predicate of every member of the subject class, was distinguished as one of the forms of judgment by Aristotle. Modern logic and Epistemology, ever since the discussion of the categories of Allheit by Kant, have been concerned with a discussion of the grounds upon which any universal judgment could be founded; and a distinction has grown up between the adjective 'all' when used with reference to a numerable class or collection of individuals found in experience, and when used with reference to every member of an ideally defined class whose representatives may be infinitely numerous. Cf. Sigwart, *Logik*, Bk. I. § 27. See also Induction, Universal, and Judgment. (J.R.)

Allaesthesia [Gr. ἄλλος, belonging to another, elsewhere, + αἴσθησις, feeling]: Ger. *Allaesthesie*; Fr. *allesthésie*; Ital. *allestesia, eterestesia*. See Allochiria.

Allamand, Jean Nicolas Sebastian. (1713–87.) Swiss philosopher and naturalist. Professor of philosophy, and later of natural history, at Leyden.

Allegiance [L. Lat. *ligius*, duty of a tenant]: Ger. *Unterthanenpflicht, Fehdepflicht*; Fr. *allégeance*; Ital. *fedeltà, sudditanza*. The obligation due from a subject to a sovereign. Also, the sense of such obligation. Extended to denote obligation of any inferior to any superior, or the sense of it. Cf. Fealty,

I.

D

LOYALTY. It may be (1) 'natural and perpetual' as of a citizen, or (2) local and temporary as of a mere resident (Wharton, *Law Lexicon* (1892)). (J.B.)

Allochiria or **Allocheiria** [Gr. ἄλλος, elsewhere, + χείρ, hand]: Ger. *Allochirie*; Fr. *allochirie*; Ital. *allochiria*. A disorder of tactile sensibility of central origin (see Janet, *Nervoses et idées fixes*) in which a touch on one side of the body is felt and located on the opposite side. Also termed allaesthesia. (J.J.)

Alogia [Gr. ἀ + λόγος, reason]: Ger. *Alogie*; Fr. *alogie*; Ital. *alogia*. Inability to speak due to intellectual defect; i.e. a disorder in the formation of thought whereby speech is not acquired or becomes impossible. It is therefore not properly an aphasic but a mental difficulty. See SPEECH AND ITS DEFECTS. (J.J.)

Séglas, *Troubles du Langage* (1892), suggests Dyslogia. (J.M.B.)

Alphabet [Gr. ἄλφα + βῆτα, the first two letters]: Ger. *Alphabet*; Fr. *alphabet*; Ital. *alfabeto*. A set of symbols used for writing a given language by a more or less exact indication of its sounds. The term is sometimes also used loosely in application to symbols that denote things, not sounds. Thus the Chinese characters, which are partly ideographic, partly phonetic, are called the Chinese alphabet.

This term, formed from the names of the first two Greek letters, *alpha* and *beta*, after the manner of our *a, bee, cee*, originally denoted the series of letters by which the Greek language was written, and was then extended, first to the various types of the Greek alphabet in use throughout Europe, secondly to like sets of symbols of non-Greek origin. The alphabets of Eastern Europe in the domain of the Orthodox Greek Church are modifications of the Cyrillic alphabet, itself based upon the Greek writing of the 9th century A.D. Those of Western Europe, including our own, are essentially the Roman form of the Greek. The Romans received not the common Ionian form of the Greek alphabet, but the Chalcidian, in which the 3rd letter was C, not Γ, the 12th L, not Λ, the 20th P, not P, the 23rd V, not Y, and in which the 6th letter F and *koppa*, Q=Q, were in use, and X had the value *ks*, not *ch*. It gave C the value of *k*, using K but little, gave F the value of *f* instead of *w*, created G, a modification of C, in the value of *g*, and gave it the place of disused *zeta*, and finally in the Augustan age introduced the Ionian *upsilon*, Y, with value *ü*, and the *zeta*, and set them at the end of the alphabet. The letter J is a modern differentiation out of I established in usage in the 17th century A.D., and the letter W represents the attempt, in the earlier use of the Roman alphabet among Germanic peoples, to indicate the consonantal *u* (= *w*) by doubling the Roman V. Neither the number nor the order of the symbols is adjusted to phonetic considerations, but both are dependent on tradition with slight makeshift alterations. The order remains essentially that of the Phoenician alphabet, in which it was apparently originally rational, being in part at least determined by the names given the letters from their fancied resemblance to natural objects; thus, groups were formed like *aleph* (=ox), *bēth* (=house), *gimel* (=camel), *daleth* (=door), i. e. A, B, C, D; or *mēm* (=water), *nūn* (=fish), i. e. M, N; or *ayin* 'o' (=eye), *pē* (=mouth), i. e. O, P; or *kōph* (=head, rear), *rēsh* (=head, side), *shin* (=tooth), i. e. Q, R, S. Groups like B, C (*g*), D, and M, N, L, on the other hand, point towards phonetic arrangement. The Phoenician standard order was continued in the Greek and Roman alphabets, meaningless as it was for them, merely on account of the use of the letters as numeral signs. The Greek names of the letters also were meaningless echoes of their Semitic originals. The Phoenician alphabet, like the earlier Hebrew writing, had no means of indicating vowels. Its symbols were evidently developed from ideographs, and these from hieroglyphs, presumably the Egyptian. The common order of development is the soundsign from the syllable-sign, the syllable-sign from the word-sign, the word-sign from the picture of an object. The Sanskrit alphabet offers an example of a series of symbols carefully, almost scientifically adjusted to the phonetic material, and arranged in a phonetic order.

Literature: TAYLOR, The Alphabet, 2 vols. (1883, ed. 1899); BALLHORN, Alphabete der orientalischen und occidentalischen Sprachen (12th ed., 1880); LARFELD, Müller's Handbuch d. Altertumswiss. i. 494 ff.; SCHLOTTMANN, Riehm's Handwörterb., s. v. Schrift; BERGER, Hist. de l'écriture dans l'antiquité (1891). (B.I.W.)

Alphabet Method (in education). A synthetic method of teaching reading, by the construction of syllables and words from the letters of the alphabet.

This was formerly the usual method of teaching pupils to read, as it must ever remain the ultimate one. Modern teachers,

34

however, introduce the subject by presenting at first a limited number of words as wholes. These are learned as such, only afterwards to be analysed in order to arrive at the ultimate units, the letters. These are then used in the old way to build up words. See METHOD (in education). (C.DE G.)

Alter [Lat. *alter*, other]: Ger. *der Andere*; Fr. *autrui*; Ital. *l'altro*. An individual's thought of another self as such. (J.M.B.–G.F.S.)

The term is generally used as correlative with EGO (q.v.), and emphasizes the distinction, seen in the term ALTRUISM (q.v.), between 'self and other,' within the individual's consciousness. In social psychology the alter is the social other as the self at the moment apprehends him. It is accordingly a shifting content growing with the growth of the ego, whatever theory may be held as to the method of this growth. See also SELF-CONSCIOUSNESS.

Literature: see under EGO, and SELF-CONSCIOUSNESS. (J.M.B.–G.F.S.)

Alternating Insanity: Ger. *circuläres Irresein*; Fr. *folie circulaire, folie à double forme*; Ital. *pazzia circolare*. A form of insanity characterized by periods or cycles of radical emotional and intellectual variation, as the change from exaltation (mania) to depression (melancholia). See RECURRENT INSANITY.

Literature: art. Circular Insanity, in Tuke's Dict. of Psychol. Med. (J.J.)

Also V. MAGNAN, Recherches sur les centres nerveux, 2ᵉ série (1893); Leçons cliniques sur les maladies mentales (1893); KRAEPELIN, Psychiatrie. (L.M.)

Alternation of Generations [Ger. *Generationswechsel*; Fr. *alternance de générations*; Ital. *generazione alternante*. The alternation of gamogenetic and agamogenetic reproduction in the life history of certain animals and plants. See GAMOGENESIS, AGAMOGENESIS, PARTHENOGENESIS, and METAGENESIS. First discovered among animals by Chamisso in the Salpidæ and supported by Sars in Aurelia. Ably treated by Streenstrup and Leuckart.

Balfour says: 'It would perhaps be convenient to classify the cases of alternations of sexual and gemmiparous generations under the term metagenesis, and to employ the term heterogamy for the cases of alternation of sexual and parthenogenetic generations.'— Work cited below, p. 13. (C.LL.M.)

Botanists generally restrict the term to designate the regular alternation of dissimilar spore-forming and sexual generations. Amongst Protozoa are found cases of (perhaps irregular) alternation of spore-forming and sexual generations; amongst Protozoa and Annelids, alternation of generations produced sexually and by fission; amongst Coelenterates, Platyhelminths (Flat-worms and Flukes), Ascidians, &c., alternation of generations produced by budding and sexually; amongst Arthropods are found cases of heterogamy. Finally, some worms show examples of more or less regularly alternating unisexual and hermaphrodite generations; for instance, among the Ostracoda (Cypris) a varying number of parthenogenetic generations are interpolated between the sexual generations, among the Cladocera (Daphnia) parthenogenetic generations occur in spring and summer, sexual generations in the cold weather only. (E.S.G.)

Literature: for the phenomena among different groups of plants see BAYLEY BALFOUR, art. Botany, in Encyc. Brit. (9th ed.), iv. 159. For animals see HUXLEY, Invertebrated Animals, 33; CLAUS, Zoology, i. 123; and F. M. BALFOUR, Compar. Embryol., i., Introd.; ALB. DE CHAMISSO, De animalibus quibusdam, see Fac. i. De Salpa Berolini (1819); J. J. S. STREENSTRUP, Ueber den Generationswechsel, übersetzt von C. Thonenzen (1842); LEUCKART, Ueber Metamorphose, ungeschlechtliche Vermehrung, Generationswechsel (1851). For recent treatment in animals see L. C. MIALL, Address to Section D (Zoology), Brit. Assoc., Toronto meeting (1897); and in plants, D. H. SCOTT's address to Section K (Botany), Brit. Assoc., Liverpool meeting (1896); and F. O. BOWER, Address to Section K, Brit. Assoc., Bristol meeting (1898); A. WEISMANN, Germ-Plasm (1893).

Althusen, Johann (or **Althusius, Johannes**). (1556–1638.) A Dutch jurist who advocated the doctrine that supreme power is the right of the people.

Altruism (in psychology) [Lat. *alter*, other, through the Fr. *autrui*]: Ger. *Altruismus*; Fr. *altruisme*; Ital. *altruismo*. Attitudes or dispositions having as their conscious end the advantage of an ALTER (q.v.) or other self are termed altruistic, and constitute altruism.

This definition follows that of alter, and defines the term in contrast with EGOISM (q.v.). Altruism and egoism are correlative terms representing an opposition within self-consciousness, which arises only when the two sorts of attitude are submitted to some degree of reflection. It is opposed to the usage which applies either of those words (1) to spontaneous or unreflective action, which to the onlooker appears generous or selfish, but does not represent an opposition in the consciousness of the actor, and (2) to instinctive or merely biological phenomena of gregariousness and collective ill or welfare.

Literature: see the general works under ETHICS, and SOCIOLOGY; many of the text-books of psychology, and BIBLIOG. F, 2, *a*. (J.M.B.)

Altruism (in ethics). Interest in others for their own sake. More precisely, the term is used for the ethical theory according to which the moral end of conduct is the good of others, however conceived.

The tendencies to action which have the interest of others as their direct object are called 'altruistic'; and, logically, they should be called altruistic whether it is the good or the evil of others to which they tend. But in practical usage, it is only the tendencies to the good of others that are called altruistic. Altruistic are distinguished from egoistic tendencies, which have self-interest as their direct object. The use of the word is due to Comte, who maintained that 'the chief problem of our existence is to subordinate as far as possible egoism to altruism,' in accordance with his fundamental precept, *vivre pour autrui*. It was adopted by H. Spencer, who discusses the opposition between egoism and altruism. Disinterested (or benevolent) and self-regarding are the corresponding terms with older moralists.

Literature: COMTE, Système de politique positive, i. Introd., chap. iii., ii. chap. ii; SPENCER, Princ. of Eth., Part I, Data, xi–xiv; the general works under ETHICS. (W.R.S.–H.S.)

Amalric, Amauric, or **Amauri, of Bena.** Lived in the 12th and 13th centuries. A scholastic philosopher who attempted to reconcile theology with Averroës' materialistic interpretation of the metaphysics of Aristotle. He was forced to recant, but founded a pantheistic and mystical sect who rejected the Church and its sacraments.

Amaurosis [Gr. $\dot{a} + \mu a i \rho \epsilon \iota \nu$, to shine]: Ger. *Amaurose*; Fr. *amaurose*; Ital. *amaurosi*. A somewhat vague term for a form of total loss of vision, in which the eyes, when examined by the ophthalmoscope and otherwise, show no ostensible lesion or defect.

Gutta serena was an older term for this disorder. A condition of similar nature, in which the loss of vision is not total, is termed AMBLYOPIA (q.v.). In typical cases the defect is due to some abnormality of function

of the central nervous system. See VISION (defects of). (J.J.)

Ambidextrous [Lat. *ambi*, both, + *dexter*, right hand]: Ger. *Ambidextrie*; Fr. *ambidextre*; Ital. *ambidestro*. Possessing equal or nearly equal facility and skill in the use of either hand. It is differentiated from the normal superiority of the right hand (right-handedness) and the exceptional superiority of the left hand (left-handedness). It is opposed to DEXTRALITY (q.v.).

Literature: references under DEXTRALITY; also LOMBROSO, Antropologia criminale. (J.J.)

Ambiguity [Lat. *ambo* + *agere*, to act]: Ger. *Zweideutigkeit*; Fr. *ambiguïté*; Ital. *ambiguità*. A source of verbal fallacy, depending on the fact that the same word or words may have come historically to bear more than one sense, or may have a meaning that varies with the context. See FALLACY. (R.A.)

Amblyopia [Gr. $\dot{a}\mu\beta\lambda\dot{v}s$, dull, + $\ddot{\omega}\psi$, eye, sight]: Ger. *Schwachsichtigkeit, Amblyopie*; Fr. *amblyopie*; Ital. *ambliopia*. A partial enfeeblement or obscurity of vision, in which no lesion or defect of the organs of vision can be recognized by the ophthalmoscope or otherwise. It is apt to be connected with an abnormality of function of the central nervous system. See also AMAUROSIS, and VISION (defects of). (J.J.)

Ambrosius, Sanctus (or **Saint Ambrose**). (cir. 340–97.) The son of a Roman noble in Gaul, he became governor of Liguria and later archbishop of Milan. He served with 'unequalled ability, zeal, and disinterestedness' from 374 until his death. His great influence humbled King Theodosius into performing public penance.

Amelius (or **Amerius**). Lived in the last half of the 3rd century A.D. The disciple of Plotinus, he became an Eclectic. His own writings are lost.

Ametropia [Gr. $\dot{a} + \mu\epsilon\tau\rho\sigma\nu$, measure, + $\ddot{\omega}\psi$, eye]: Ger. *Ametropie, Refraktionsstörung*; Fr. *amétropie*; Ital. *ametropia*. A general term for a refractive error or abnormality in the eye; the opposite of EMMETROPIA, or normal refraction. MYOPIA, ASTIGMATISM (q.v.), &c., are special forms of Ametropia. See VISION (defects of). (J.J.)

Literature: DONDERS, Refractum, edited by Oliver (1899); NORRIS and OLIVER, Diseases of the Eye, iv. 401–81.

Amimia [Gr. $\dot{a} + \mu\dot{\iota}\mu\sigma s$, a mimic]: Ger. *Amimie*; Fr. *amimie*; Ital. *amimia*. An aphasic symptom involving the loss of the power to use gestures and other pantomimic means of expression of thought.

Certain aphasic patients, when unable to express themselves by spoken words, can still communicate to some extent by descriptive, imitative, or conventional signs and gestures; can nod the head for 'yes,' shake it for 'no'; express numbers with the fingers, and the like. Amimia involves the loss of this power.

If the gestures are inappropriately or incorrectly used there is paramimia. The defect is of cortical origin, and represents the motor aspect of the function which, when sensorily disordered, produces ASEMIA (q.v.). A defect of similar nature involving a subcortical centre presents an inability to correctly imitate or repeat gestures and the like. Such a defect may also be regarded as a form of amimia, but is not usually included in the use of the word as applied to aphasic disorders. See SPEECH AND ITS DEFECTS; also MIMETISM, and the classification given under RESEMBLANCE.

Literature: SÉGLAS, Troubles du Langage; BALDWIN, Ment. Devel. in the Child and the Race, chap. xiii. § 4; KUSSMAUL, Störungen der Sprache; MORSELLI, Semej. malat. ment., ii. Also literature cited under AGRAPHIA, and SPEECH AND ITS DEFECTS. (J.J.)

Amitosis [Gr. *ἀ* + *μίτος*]: Ger. *Amitose*; Fr. *amitose*; Ital. *amitosi*. Direct nuclear division in the cell without those complex changes known as karyokinesis or mitosis. First applied by Flemming (1882). (C.LL.M.)

The nucleus remains in the resting stage, without the formation of chromosomes, and simply divides into two similar daughter-nuclei. This process of direct nuclear division, discovered by Remak (1855), was at first considered to be the normal method of division; but it has since been found to be relatively rare, occurring chiefly in degenerate, and in very highly specialized cells, or in pathological growths. (E.S.G.)

Literature: FLEMMING, Zellsubstanz; WILSON, The Cell in Devel. and Inheritance (1896). (C.LL.M.)

Amixia [Gr. *ἀ* + *μίξις*, a mixing]; Ger. *Amixie*; Fr. *amixie*; Ital. *amissia*. A term denoting the absence of free intercrossing. Cf. PANMIXIA.

The term was proposed by Weismann (*Ueber den Einfluss der Isolirung auf die Artbildung*, 1872) for the prevention of interbreeding between groups, by geographical isolation. Delbœuf has advanced mathematical considerations to show that any such separation of groups must result in divergence of characters; and Romanes makes much use of the principle in his theory of ISOLATION (q.v.).

Literature: WEISMANN (as cited); ROMANES, Darwin and after Darwin, Pt. III (with quotation on p. 13, from DELBŒUF). (C.LL.M.–J.M.B.)

Ammonius Saccas. Died about 241 A.D. A Greek philosopher, born in Alexandria, who founded Neo-Platonism. He taught Plotinus, Origen, and Longinus. Born of Christian parents, he preferred heathenism. See ALEXANDRIAN SCHOOL.

Amnesia [Gr. *ἀ* + *μιμνήσκειν*, to remind, remember]: Ger. *Amnesie*; Fr. *amnésie*; Ital. *amnesia*. Loss or impairment of memory. See MEMORY (defects of). (J.J.)

Amoeba [Gr. *ἀμοιβή*]: Ger. *Amoebe*; Fr. *amibe*; Ital. *ameba*. A genus of unicellular organisms characterized by indefinite movements and changes of form.

Von Rosenhof described the Proteus animalcule in 1755. Ecker drew attention to the contractility involved, and compared it with that of muscle. Later observers gradually recognized in the amoeba the beginnings of all the essential physiological processes, such as contractility, irritability, assimilation, metabolism, respiration, and reproduction. The term amoeboid is applied to movements (e.g. in white blood-corpuscles) like those of the amoeba.

The common species, *Amoeba proteus*, consists of a little mass of naked semi-fluid protoplasm containing a nucleus, but with no further permanent differentiation of the cell substance. The amoeba alters its shape and moves by means of pseudopodia, processes formed by the outflowing of the protoplasm at any point, and capable of being withdrawn again into the body. Nutrition takes place by the ingestion into the substance of the amoeba of food particles, which undergo digestion within food-vacuoles. A pulsating contractile vacuole periodically becomes filled with liquid and emptied to the exterior, acting perhaps as an excretory organ. The amoeba is known to reproduce by simple binary fission of the body, with accompanying division of the nucleus. Amoebae live an active life in stagnant water. Under certain conditions they secrete a closed protective cyst. Cf. PROTOZOA, and UNICELLULAR ORGANISMS. (E.S.G.)

Literature: MARSHALL and HURST, Pract. Zool.; M. FOSTER, Textbook of Physiol., Introd.; T. J. PARKER, Elementary Biol., art. Protozoa, Encyc. Brit. (9th ed.). (C.LL.M.–E.S.G.)

Amortization [Lat. *amortisatio*]: Ger. *Amortisation*; Fr. *amortissement*; Ital. *amortizzamento*. The practice of setting aside a fixed sum out of current income for the sake of extinguishing a debt (or other form of liability) within a determinate period. The sums thus set aside, with the interest accruing upon them, constitute what is known as a sinking fund.

Amortization seems to have been first applied to the public debt of England early in the 18th century, and to have been introduced into French public finance almost immediately afterward. The amortization of industrial enterprises began with the English 'turnpike trusts'; but it has been far more extensively applied in France and Germany than in England or America. The term originally signified alienation in mortmain; but the meaning here given has gradually superseded the older one. (A.T.H.)

Ampère: see UNITS (electrical).

Amphibology or **Amphibolia** [Gr. ἀμφιβολία]: Ger. *Amphibolie*; Fr. *amphibologie*; Ital. *anfibologia*. A verbal fallacy, arising from the double interpretation of any proposition, rendered possible by some want of clearness or definiteness in the grammatical construction of the statement. See Aristotle, *Soph. Elenchi*, chap. iv. (R.A.)

Amphigony: see GAMOGENESIS.

Amphimixis: Ger. *Amphimixie*; Fr. *amphimixie*; Ital. *anfimissi*. The mingling of the substance IDIOPLASM (q.v.) from two individuals so as to effect a mingling of hereditary characteristics. See SEXUAL REPRODUCTION.

The term is due to Weismann, and includes the phenomena of conjugation and fertilization amongst unicellular and multicellular organisms. Weismann also makes amphimixis the main source of congenital VARIATIONS (q.v.).

Literature: A. WEISMANN, Essays on Heredity, ii. No. XII (1891); Germ-Plasm (1893); F. Galton, A Theory of Heredity, J. Anthropol. Instit., v. 5 (1875), and Contemp. Rev. (1875); v. BENEDEN, Recherches sur la maturation de l'œuf, Arch. de Biol., iv. (1883). (C.LL.M., E.S.G.)

Ampliative: Ger. *Erweiterungs- (urteil)*; Fr. *ampliatif*; Ital. *ampliativo*. Ampliative Judgment is one in which the predicate adds something not already contained in the notion of the subject. It is contrasted with explicative or ANALYTIC JUDGMENT (q.v.). (R.A.)

Amulet [Lat. *amuletum*]: Ger. *Amulet*; Fr. *amulette*; Ital. *amuleto*. A charm to ward off evils. Gems and other stones, pieces of metal, both usually engraved or stamped with some design; pieces of parchment bearing sacred writing like the Jewish phylacteries—all are common forms of the amulet. Although the word is first used by Pliny, there can be no doubt that the custom of wearing amulets is a very ancient one.

When spirits, heavenly bodies, and occult powers were believed to work evil upon man, these charms were used to ward off or minimize the effects. Witchcraft was a potent cause of their employment, and still is, in Africa for example. Superstition so dominates the human mind that amulets were by no means uncommon even amongst adherents of the more spiritual religions, such as Judaism and Christianity. Early Christians wore the fish-symbol; and we find Chrysostom and Augustine protesting against similar usages. While common still amongst Eastern peoples and half-civilized tribes, and even amongst the superstitiously inclined of civilized peoples, amulets were condemned by the Christian Church as early as the Council of Trullo (692 A.D.) (R.M.W.)

Amusia [Gr. ἀ + μοῦσα, a muse]: Ger. *Amusie*; Fr. *amusie*; Ital. *amusia*. The loss of the power to understand or to execute music; a defect in regard to music, analogous to aphasia in regard to speech. It presents types and varieties analogous to the types of speech disorders.

The defect may be motor, as in a loss of the power to execute music by singing or by performing upon an instrument (motor amusia); or the loss of ability to comprehend and appreciate music (sensory amusia); or there may be a perverted musical sense (paramusia). Loss of musical memories constitutes amnesic amusia.

In almost all cases, amusia involves some degree of aphasia, but cases of sensory and amnesic amusia (musical recognition) occur without aphasia. This fact, and the frequency with which the musical powers are retained in cases of aphasia, tend to establish the existence of a separate musical centre, situated usually in the left hemisphere, with close anatomical and functional connections with the centre of speech. Corresponding to word-deafness would be tone-deafness; and to word-blindness would be note-blindness. A subnormal capacity for the appreciation of music is very common in normal individuals in complete health and in the absence of any nervous defect; such persons lack 'a musical ear,' and in extreme cases approximate to a condition of amusia. (J.J.—J.M.B.)

Literature: ELDER, Aphasia, chap. x; BASTIAN, Aphasia, 289–98; BRAZIER, Rev. Philos. (Oct. 1892); WALLASCHEK, Zeitsch. f. Psychol., xii. 1; MORSELLI, Semej. malat.

ment., iv; BALDWIN, Ment. Devel. in the Child and the Race, chap. xiv. § 2 (with bibliography); EDGREN, Brit. Med. J. (1894), ii. 1441; IRELAND, J. of Ment. Sci., xl. 354. Also citations under SPEECH AND ITS DEFECTS. (J.J.)

An sich (Hegel): see HEGELIAN TERMINOLOGY, V. 6.

An und für sich [Ger.]. 'In and for itself'; first used, it is said, by Baumgarten. See the glossaries under KANTIAN TERMINOLOGY (ding an sich) and HEGEL'S TERMINOLOGY. (J.M.B.)

Anabaptists [Gr. ἀνά, again, + βαπτίζειν, to baptize]: Ger. *Anabaptisten, Wiedertäufer*; Fr. *Anabaptistes*; Ital. *Anabattisti*. The name of the most extreme sect of the Reformation period. Setting out from the rejection of the sacrament of infant baptism, on the ground that personal profession, with baptism as the seal, alone suffices to salvation, they eventually aimed at a complete overthrow of the existing social order, and the establishment of a Christian theocracy on the basis of community of goods and of absolute personal equality.

The principal names connected with the movement, which originated in Germany and had its most considerable influence there, are Thomas Münzer, Lutheran pastor of Zwickau, in Saxony (1521); Nikolaus Storch, the 'prophet' of Wittenberg; Rothmann, of Münster, in Westphalia; and, above all, 'John of Leyden' (Johann Bockhold), who ruled Münster for a year (1534–5), and, along with his followers, gave himself over to unbridled licence. He was put to death in 1536. The movement was closely connected with the 'Peasants' War' in Thuringia (1525). After the Bockhold rising had been suppressed with terrible severity, the sect disappeared; but some of its teachings were soberly continued by Menno Simmons, the founder of the sect known as Mennonites. (R.M.W.)

Anabolism [Gr. ἀναβολή, a throwing up]: Ger. *Anabolismus*; Fr. *anabolisme*; Ital. *anabolismo*. The constructive or synthetic metabolism whereby more complex chemical substances are elaborated in the cell; associated with a storage of energy, which is liberated by the opposite process of katabolic METABOLISM (q.v.).

This term, which was suggested by Michael Foster and used by Gaskell in 1886, has served to bring out clearly the distinction between the constructive and disintegrating changes which occur in the cell. Geddes and Thomson have elaborated the thesis that the ovum is predominantly anabolic, the spermatozoon katabolic, thus giving these processes a rôle in evolution; and have extended this both to the female and male organisms—the former being supposed to have a predominantly anabolic, the latter a katabolic diathesis —and to species.

Literature: W. H. GASKELL, On the Structure, Distribution, and Function of Visceral Nerves, J. of Physiol., vii. (1886), 47; M. FOSTER, art. Physiology, in Encyc. Brit. (9th ed.), xix; GEDDES and THOMSON, Evolution of Sex (1889). (C.LL.M.)

Anaemia or **Anemia** [Gr. ἀ + αἷμα, blood]: Ger. *Anämie, Blutarmuth*; Fr. *anémie*; Ital. *anemia*. Bloodlessness, deficiency of blood: acute, when due to haemorrhage; chronic, when caused by a pathological condition of the blood. See VASO-MOTOR SYSTEM.

Literature: Richet's Dict. de Physiol., art. Anémie. (C.F.H.)

Anaesthesia [Gr. ἀ + αἴσθησις, feeling]: Ger. *Unempfindlichkeit, Anästhesie*; Fr. *anesthésie*; Ital. *anestesia*. A loss or impairment of sensibility; a condition characterized by such loss.

Anaesthesia may be the result of a lesion in the nerve centres, or in the nerves supplying a given part, or of a functional interference with any portion of the mechanism for receiving sense impressions (as by the action of drugs or anaesthetics). Anaesthesia usually involves loss of tactile sensibility, of pain (analgesia), and of temperature sensations, but in exceptional cases any one of these may be lost and the others remain unimpaired. Several varieties of anaesthesia are distinguished; according to its origin, it is central or peripheral; to its extent, general or local; to its degree, complete or incomplete; it may be unilateral (hemi-anaesthesia) when due to lesion of the spinal cord on the opposite side; it may be associated with severe pain in the part affected (anaesthesia dolorosa). Muscular anaesthesia indicates a loss of the muscle sense without loss of other sensations; one form of it appears as an awkwardness in movement, and an inability to perform certain movements unless guided and controlled by the eyes (see ATAXIA). Optical, auditory, gustatory, olfactory, thermal, and tactile anaesthesia (known as anaphia or apselaphesia) are sometimes used in reference to a loss of the special sense denoted. Psychic anaesthesia is a term (used by German writers) to denote a condition of impassiveness or apathy—a dullness or lack of response to the usual motives, feelings, and impressions of life. It occurs in conditions of extreme preoccupation, ecstasy, grief, melancholia, and the like. See also ANAESTHETICS. (J.J.)

Literature: RICHET, Recherches sur la Sensibilité; JANET, Les Stigmates Mentaux des Hystériques (1893); MOEBIUS, Diagnostik d. Nervenkrankheiten, 185 ff. Also extended bibliography in Richet's Dict. de Physiol., art. Anesthésie, and references under PLEASURE AND PAIN. (J.M.B.)

Anaesthetics: Ger. *Betäubungsmittel*; Fr. *anesthésiques*; Ital. *anestetici*. Substances producing diminished sensibility in general, and especially to pain (ANALGESIA, q.v.).

Anaesthetics are administered by inhalation, injection, or local application. They differ considerably in their mode of action as well as in the accompanying physiological and psychic symptoms which they induce. Of prime importance is the distinction between general anaesthetics, which produce a general condition of insensibility with loss or profound modification of consciousness (ether, chloroform, nitrous oxide gas, &c.), and local anaesthetics, which are applied to, and affect directly, the part to be anaesthetized (ether spray, cocaine, &c.). (J.J.)

Chloroform was discovered and first used as an anaesthetic for an operation by Sir J. Simpson, in Edinburgh, 1847. Sulphuric ether was used for operation in Boston in 1846. Cf. Simpson, *J. Med. Soc.*, viii. 415, and *Works* (1871), ii. 23. The term anaesthetic was proposed by Oliver Wendell Holmes. (J.M.B.)

Literature: for the history, methods of use, and specific effects of anaesthetics, consult article by J. T. CLOVER and G. H. BAILEY, in Quain's Dict. of Med.; Nineteenth Cent. Pract. of Med. (sub verbo); BUXTON, Anaesthetics (1892); TURNBULL, The Advantages and Accidents of Artificial Anaesthesia (1890). Also citations under ANAESTHESIA, PSYCHIC EFFECT OF DRUGS, and literature there cited. (J.J.)

Anagogic Interpretation [Gr. ἀναγωγικός, mystical + Lat. *interpretatio*]: Ger. *erhebende Erklärung*; Fr. *interprétation anagogique*; Ital. *interpretazione anagogica*. One of the ways of interpreting the so-called (in mediaeval times) 'fourfold sense' of Scripture. As contrasted with allegorical interpretation, which refers to redemption as it is already known, anagogic extracts references to future revelations of things heavenly.

This factitious kind of interpretation was known so early as the beginning of the 5th century (Eucherius), and continued in use more or less till the Reformation. It is traceable probably to the fixity of dogma which left theologians little of essential interest to work upon. The following lines throw some light upon modes of approaching the Scriptures then prevalent:—

'Litera gesta docet, quid credas allegoria,
Moralis quid agas, quo tendas anagogia.'
(R.M.W.)

Analgesia or **Analgia** [Gr. ἀ + ἄλγος, pain]: Ger. *Schmerzlosigkeit, Analgie, Analgesie*; Fr. *analgésie*; Ital. *analgesia, analgia*. Impairment or loss of the sense of pain.

It may occur without involving the loss of tactile sensibility. It occurs in the torpor induced by ANAESTHETICS (q.v.), in certain forms of poisoning, in brain diseases (epilepsy, hysteria), &c., and in diseases of the spinal cord. Emminghaus uses the term Psychic Analgesia to indicate a lowered sensibility, an apathy and indifference to the opinions and feelings of others, or again, to indicate a loss of the finer moral, aesthetic, and social sensibilities. See ANAESTHESIA. (J.J.)

Literature. Physiological: Richet's Dict. de Physiol., art. Anesthésie. Psychological: see PLEASURE AND PAIN. (J.M.B.)

Analogical Characters: see CONVERGENCE.

Analogies of Experience. The *Analogien der Erfahrung* of Kant are the rules according to which 'unity of experience arises out of the multiplicity of perceptions' (*Krit. d. reinen Vernunft*). They are the *a priori* principles which constitute the persistence of substance and the relations of causality and change in the phenomenal world. Cf. KANTIAN TERMINOLOGY, 11, 19, and KANTIANISM.

Literature: citations in EISLER, Wörterb. d. philos. Begriffe; LAAS, Kant's Analogien d. Erfahrung; the textbooks to Kant by CAIRD, WATSON, STIRLING, and the histories of philosophy. (J.M.B.–K.G.)

Analogies of Sensation: see SYNAESTHESIA.

Analogon rationis. Used by Leibnitz and Wolff for what appears to be reason in the animals. See citations in Eisler, *Wörterb. d. philos. Begriffe*, sub verbo. (J.M.B.)

Analogous Organs: Ger. *analoge Organe*; Fr. *organes analogues*; Ital. *organi analoghi*. Those parts or organs of animals or plants which are similar in function though of different origin in development; or, in other words, of different phylogenetic history. See HOMOLOGOUS ORGANS. (C.LL.M.–E.S.G.)

The term in its present biological use, as contrasted with homologous, was introduced by Richard Owen (*The Archetype and Homologies of the Vertebrate Skeleton*, 1848). (C.LL.M.)

Analogy [Gr. ἀναλογία, proportion]: Ger. *Analogie*; Fr. *analogie*; Ital. *analogia*. (1) Agreement or similarity in general. (2) Proportion, i. e. agreement or equivalence between the ratios or relationships present in different cases or objects. (3) Such agreement in relationship between two objects as gives real or apparent warrant for an argument from ANALOGY, in logic (q. v.). (4) Such agreement between objects as leads to a use of analogous names, or to a naming of objects according to analogy.

'Αναλογία is used by Plato. By Aristotle the term is defined (*Eth. Nic.*, v. 3) as an equality of ratios, hence requiring for its expression four terms; only, in case of such an expression as ' *A* is to *B* as *B* is to *C*,' the terms may be only virtually four, since *B* is taken twice. But as the application to the case of distributive justice at once shows, where the equal or fair distribution of two objects to two persons is in question, Aristotle does not conceive his ratio as necessarily merely quantitative, although he uses the cases of geometrical proportion as illustrative instances. As a fact, the equality of qualitative ratios is very frequent in Aristotle's usage. So in the instance (*Metaph.* ix. 6, 7) where Aristotle speaks of actual and potential being as the ' same by analogy ' in all things, because the statue is to its material as the waking man is to the sleeper. The usage of analogy thus defined is the one that has since become universal. The scholastic use of the adjective analogous, of terms equivocal in usage and applied to objects because of some analogy between them, has an obvious basis in the Aristotelian usage.

Analogous terms or names : equivocal terms, or names of double meaning, where the doubleness is due not to chance or to arbitrary choice, but to a known connection or analogy between the objects thus homonymously named. (J.R.)

Analogy (in logic). A kind of resemblance. All derivative uses of the term bear traces of the original restriction to resemblance in relations. Generally it may be defined as resemblance in any feature that does not form part of the constitutive or defining marks whereby the classes to which the things compared are determined. Analogical reasoning is therefore always external in character, and is suggestive rather than probative. Briefly : a form of argument in which, by reason of the identity or similarity between the relationships believed or known to be present in two or more objects, we argue from characters observed or known to co-exist in one of them, to a similar co-existence, not yet observed, in the other, and so predict that this other, if corresponding to the first object in some features, will also correspond in still other features. (R.A.–J.R.)

'Αναλογία is used by Aristotle in the specific sense of identity of ratios, but its cognates were employed by him with the same general meaning which they bear among modern writers. He did not designate any special type of reasoning analogical (though syllogisms turning on relations of proportion were recognized by the commentators); what in his scheme corresponds most closely to analogical reasoning is the argument from 'example' (παράδειγμα), Aristotle, *Anal. Pr.*, ii. 4.

Kant (*Logik*, Werke III. 320, ed. R. u. S.) defines induction as inference from what is found in many particulars to the same as universally present, and analogy as inference from many points of resemblance between two things to their resemblance in some other point. Mill (*Logic*, Bk. III. chap. xx) rightly rejects the Kantian distinction as artificial, and makes the distinctive worth of analogy the absence of knowledge or of assumption that the known features of resemblance from which the argument starts are connected by any general law with the points as to which inference is made.

Literature : ARISTOTLE, KANT, MILL, as cited ; JEVONS, Princ. of Sci., chap. xxviii ; SIGWART, Logik, § 98 ; BOSANQUET, Logic, Bk. II. chap. iii ; HOPPE, Die Analogie (1873) ; W. STERN, Die Analogie im volksthümlichen Denken (1893). (R.A.)

Analogy (linguistic). Construction or adaptation of the mechanism of language in conformity with what is felt to be a predominant type of mechanism for the expression of like ideas.

The earliest grammatical system of the ancient Greeks, which was concerned preeminently with demonstrating that grammar is an art or τέχνη governed by canons (κανόνες), used the term *analogy* to express conformity to the established canons or inflectional schemes of the language ; in the rhetorical schools the *analogist* came to be what we should now call a *purist*. In distinction from the older grammar, which was descriptive grammar, because it sought to record and arrange the facts, and artistic because it sought to establish canons, the modern historical grammar seeks to understand the facts in accordance with their lines of descent and the historical causes that gave them being. It uses the term, therefore, not in reference to conformity to canons, but to those historical changes of word-form and expression which arise under the operation of certain great psychological principles. Not being concerned with the notion of correctness or incorrectness, it cannot speak of 'false' analogy. When *threble* appears in place of *treble*, under influence of *three*, it is no more 'false' than *female* in place of **femel* (Fr. *femelle*), under influence of *male*. *Chinee* in place of *Chinese* (sing.), or *shay* in place of *chaise*, is determined by the ratio *tree : trees*, or *sea : seas*, precisely as *cherry* in place of **cherris* (Fr. *cerise*), or *pea* in place of **peas* (Fr. *pois*). All association of form in language is found to rest ultimately in association of ideas. Things and their names are indissolubly connected in the folk-consciousness. The natural instinct is therefore to express the like by the like. Association of idea leads therefore directly to association of form. The assignment of the naming material to the idea material being guided by what is immediately present to consciousness, and not by a complete summary of the existing historical material, leads readily to associations which pervert historical conditions. Thus in Latin *meridialis*, 'southern,' and *septentrionalis*, 'northern,' the common vowel *i* induced a distribution which caused that *meridi-* in the one, and *septentri-* in the other, should carry the body of the meaning. Consciousness of like function in the endings then extended *-onalis* from the latter to the former with the result *meridionalis*.

Likeness of idea may be first suggested by resemblance of form, and this suggested likeness of idea then result in complete adaptation of form. Such are the common phenomena of folk-etymology : thus, *causey* (Fr. *chaussée*) suggests that *-ey* may be intended to denote the same thing as *way*, and *causeway* results; but still it is the association of idea, not that of form, which is ultimately responsible for the change. Mere resemblance of external form is never found to effect association without the intervention of ideas. The tendency of analogy is to eliminate the purposeless variety of form-material which mixture of dialect and the destructive action of phonetic laws have produced, and with which tradition offers to endow language, and to introduce unity and simplicity in place of diversity.

Literature : H. PAUL, Principien d. Sprachgesch. (3rd ed., 1898), v; STRONG-LOGEMAN-WHEELER, Introd. to the Study of the Hist. of Language (1891), v; B. I. WHEELER, Analogy and the Scope of its Application in Language (1887). (B.I.W.)

Analogy of Experience. A class-name given by Kant (*Analogie der Erfahrung*) to the three *a priori* principles of substantiality, causality, and reciprocity or interaction. Cf. KANTIAN TERMINOLOGY (Erfahrung). (J.R.)

Analogy of Faith, and **of Doctrine** (in theology) : Ger. *Analogie* (*des Glaubens*); Fr. *analogie* (*de la foi*); Ital. *analogia* (*di fede*). Phrases that sprang up in connection with the interpretation of Scripture. Analogy of doctrine is set forth by Augustine in the principle that the interpretation ought to explain the more obscure passages by reference to the 'essential contents of Christian doctrine.' When definite interpretation cannot be obtained, in spite of observance of this rule, it is to be inferred that the matter lies without the sphere of the essential doctrines of the Christian faith. Analogy of faith is regarded differently by Roman Catholics and Protestants respectively; for the latter restrict the sphere of faith to the Bible.

The Council of Trent strictly prohibited all interpretations which were not in agreement with the unanimous opinion of the Fathers. This opinion constituted a norm from which the analogy of faith set out. After the Reformation, the analogy of faith was defined as 'the fundamental articles of faith, or the principal chapters of the Christian faith, collected from the clearest testimony of the Scriptures.' In other words, interpretation ought to proceed, in doubtful cases, upon the analogy to be drawn from the consensus of Scripture in its perfectly lucid passages. These form the basis of faith. But the Reformed Church did not always hold to this attitude. It is notorious that tradition has been reinstated once more, and this in the form of creeds, of which many examples still exist. For *Literature* see EXEGESIS. (R.M.W.)

Analysis [Gr. ἀνάλυσις, from ἀνά + λύειν, to loose] : Ger. *Analyse*; Fr. *analyse*; Ital. *analisi*. The isolation of what is more elementary from what is more complex by whatever method. Cf. the following terms. (J.M.B., G.F.S.)

Analysis (in logic) : Ger. *logische Analyse*; Fr. *analyse logique*; Ital. *analisi logica*. Literally a resolution, an unloosening of that which has been combined. The kinds of analysis may therefore be analogous, but each will have its special character determined by the nature of the combination to be resolved.

Even within the sphere of logic, this difference is observable. Analysis means, in one sense, the exhibition of the logical form involved in concrete reasoning. In another sense, it is logical in kind, when the attempt is made to show the common character involved in all special cases where the procedure is of the nature of resolution of a given whole.

That Aristotle called the central portion of his logical work *Analytical Research* indicates that in his view the problem of logic was to resolve the concrete facts of reasoning and demonstration into their elements. He distinguished Prior Analytics (theory of inference) from Posterior Analytics (theory of proof). The Greek mathematicians worked out in detail the relations of the analytical to the synthetical method (cf. Pappus, *Coll. Math.*, Bk. VII), and Descartes' general description of his method (see *Port Royal Logic*, Pt. IV) is an attempt to apply the same general conceptions as the Greek mathematicians had used to the whole sphere of knowledge. Modern logic exhibits the tendency, not wholly justified, to identify analysis with induction and synthesis with deduction.

Literature: D. STEWART, Philos. of the Human Mind, Pt. II. viii; DUHAMEL, Méth. dans les Sci. de Raisonnement; G. C. ROBERTSON, Philos. Remains, 82–99; WUNDT, Logik, II. 1, i; BIBLIOG. C, 2, *l*. (R.A.)

Analysis (linguistic): see SYNTHESIS (linguistic).

Analysis (method of, in education). The separating of a whole into its component parts, in order to discover their relations; as the analysis of a sentence, or of a chemical compound.

The proper use of analysis in instruction depends upon the nature of the subject-matter and the age of the pupils. Herbartian writers often use the term in a peculiar sense, as denoting the preparation of the pupil's mind for the ready assimilation of new knowledge. The knowledge already possessed is 'analysed' in order to bring to the front the most appropriate ideas and feelings. See METHOD (in education).

Literature: REIN, Das erste Schuljahr, 40–41; HERBART, Sci. of Educ. (trans. by Filkin), 154–8. (C.DE G.)

Analysis (psychical or mental): Ger. *psychische Analyse*; Fr. *analyse mentale*; Ital. *analisi mentale*. The mental function which proceeds by the progressive discrimination of the parts or aspects of any kind of whole. (G.F.S., J.M.B.)

Wolf defines analysis as follows: 'The resolution of a notion into the notions of those things which enter into its composition' (*Psychologia*, 339). The attempt to give precision to the concept of mental analysis, however, is modern.

Literature: STUMPF, Tonpsychologie, i. 96 ff.; MEINONG, Beiträge zur Theorie der psychischen Analyse, in Zeitsch. f. Psychol., vi. 340 and 417; H. CORNELIUS, Über Verschmelzung und Analyse, in Vtljsch. f. wiss. Philos., xvi. (1892), 404 ff.; xvii. (1893), 30 ff.; JAMES, Princ. of Psychol., ii. 344. Also the text-books of psychology, in which the mental function of analysis is often treated under CONCEPTION or ABSTRACTION (q.v.). (G.F.S.—J.M.B.)

Analysis (psychological): Ger. *psychologische Analyse*; Fr. *analyse psychologique*; Ital. *analisi psicologica*. A general method of psychological study, giving what is known as analytic psychology.

Analysis or analytic procedure in psychology consists in the reduction of complex states of mind to the simpler elements or factors which compose them. This is the object of all science, psychological or other, and any method which accomplishes it is available. Inasmuch, however, as all psychological results are, in the last resort, brought to consciousness for verification, and this verification requires a more or less independent analysis by introspection, the process of using introspection for purposes of analysis has become a recognized method called analysis, or introspective analysis (and its results analytic), in distinction from description (and descriptive). As a body its results are contrasted with those of genetic and those of experimental psychology. It is important that this should be distinguished from psychical or mental analysis (see topic above)—a distinction for which terms in the four languages are recommended. It is an instance of the general distinction between the terms PSYCHICAL (or mental) AND PSYCHOLOGICAL (q.v.).

Literature: the textbooks of psychology. (J.M.B., G.F.S.)

Analytic (transcendental): see KANTIAN TERMINOLOGY.

Analytic and Synthetic Judgment: Ger. *analytisches und synthetisches Urteil*; Fr. *jugement analytique et synthétique*; Ital. *giudizio analitico e sintetico*. An analytic judgment is one in which the predicate is obtained or obtainable by analysis of the notion of the subject; a judgment therefore which on the one hand requires no appeal to a ground in experience, and on the other hand has as its sufficient test the principle of contradiction.

The name was introduced by Kant, and the distinction between analytic and synthetic judgments is fundamental in his theory of knowledge. The distinction is hardly of logical worth (cf. Sigwart, *Logik*, § 18). See KANTIAN TERMINOLOGY. (R.A.)

The synthetic judgment, on the other hand, is one of which the predicate is not obtainable by analysis of the subject, but is something added to the subject in the act of judging. The predicate is, therefore, either obtained by experience or contributed by the mind, the latter being the alternative which Kant discusses and affirms in his 'synthetic judgments *a priori.*' See KANTIAN TERMINOLOGY.

The value of the distinction would seem to depend largely upon one's view of JUDGMENT (q.v.); i.e. upon whether judgment is psychologically a function of change in mental content or one of mere recognition of such change as takes place in conception. If the latter—as in varying forms is the later and more adequate view—then the growth of conception, involving both analysis and synthesis, covers at once the two contrasted cases; and judgment in all of its forms represents analysis. The synthetic aspect of conception is simply the growth of experience itself; and the identification of, e.g., AB (the later experience) with A (the earlier), giving $A = AB$, an apparently synthetic judgment, is psychologically only the recognition by analysis of the growth of A into AB. This view, which may be called the conceptual interpretation of judgment, applies to the combination of judgments in the syllogism (cf. the writer's *Handb. of Psychol.*, i. chap. xiv). In cases of the so-called 'synthetic *a priori*,' what is 'added' is not content, but character or relation, i.e. universality, and this again is not a matter of judgment. To have a universal is not to judge the particular differently, but to think what is not particular; so judgment again here is but the recognition in analytic terms of what is thought (J.M.B.)

A distinction partially corresponding to that between analytic and synthetic judgments, but by no means coincident with it, plays a most important part in the philosophies of Locke and Hume. Hume states it as follows: 'There are seven different kinds of philosophical relations [of relations considered as objects of consciousness], viz. resemblance, identity, relations of time and place, proportion in quantity or number, degrees in any quality, contrariety, and causation. These relations may be divided into two classes: into such as depend entirely on the ideas which are compared together, and such as may be chang'd without any change in the ideas. 'Tis from the idea of a triangle that we discover the relation of equality which its three angles bear to two right ones; and this relation is invariable as long as our idea remains the same. On the contrary, the relations of contiguity and distance betwixt two objects may be changed merely by an alteration of their place, without any change in the objects themselves or in their ideas; and the place depends on a hundred different accidents that cannot be foreseen by the mind.' The first class of relations are called by Hume 'relations of ideas,' and the second class 'matters of fact.'

The Humian distinction, inherited from Locke, is not coincident with the Kantian. For instance, the proposition $2 + 2 = 4$ is not an analytic judgment in the Kantian sense; for the concept of $2 + 2$ need not include, as part of its recognized content, equality to 4. But the proposition expresses what Hume calls a relation of ideas; for it lies in the intrinsic nature of $2 + 2$ and 4 to be equal to each other. The same holds true of all mathematical identities. Similarly, Hume would rank many geometrical judgments under the same head, though there is no reason to suppose that he would have admitted them to be analytical in the Kantian sense.

It may be maintained that the Locke-Hume distinction, or a distinction framed on similar lines, is of far more vital importance to the theory of knowledge than the distinction between synthetic and analytic judgments as formulated by Leibnitz and Kant. J. Bergmann has criticized the Kantian system from this point of view, though without reference to Hume (*Gesch. d. Philos.*, 32-7). Riehl's distinction between Urtheile and begriffliche Sätze (*Vtljsch. f. wiss. Philos.*, xvi. 13 f.), and the analogous distinction of von Kries between Real - Urtheile and Beziehungs-Urtheile, are akin to that of Hume between relations of ideas and matters of fact. The antithesis between 'bare conjunction' and 'necessary connection,' which plays so large a part in the philosophy of Bradley, is framed on similar lines (see in particular 'Contradiction and the Contrary,' *Mind*, N.S., No. 20, reprinted in Appendix to *Appearance and Reality*, 2nd ed.). (G.F.S.)

Analytic Method: Ger. *analytische Methode*; Fr. *méthode analytique*; Ital. *metodo analitico*. See ANALYSIS (psychological) and METHOD.

Anamnesis [Gr. ἀνάμνησις]: see REMINISCENCE.

Anaphase [Gr. ἀνά + φάσις, appearance]; Ger. *Anaphase*; Fr. *anaphase*; Ital. *anafasi*. The later phase of mitosis, or complex nuclear-division, in which the chromosomes are drawn apart so as to divide their substance between the daughter-nuclei. See REPRODUCTION. It was first used by Strasburger in 1884.

Literature: STRASBURGER, Neue Untersuchungen über den Befruchtungsvorgang bei den Phanerogamen, als Grundlage für eine Theorie der Zeugung; E. B. WILSON, The Cell in Devel. and Inheritance (1896, with full bibliography). (C.LL.M.)

Anaphia [Gr. ἀ + ἀφή, touch]: Ger. *Anaphe*, *Anaphie*; Fr. *anaphie* (rarely used; special forms as *paresthésie, anesthésie tactile*, &c.); Ital. *anafesia*. See ANAESTHESIA. (J.J.)

Anarchism [Gr. ἀ + ἀρχή, government]: Ger. *Anarchismus*; Fr. *anarchisme*; Ital. *anarchismo*. The doctrine that every form of government is noxious, and that the individual should be absolutely free to act as he thinks proper. Godwin's *Political Justice* (1793) puts forward, first in modern times, as the ultimate goal of political progress, 'the dissolution of political government, of that brute engine, which has been the only perennial spring of the vices of mankind' (Bk. V. chap. xxiv, end). (F.C.M.–H.S.)

The growth of modern anarchism as such may be dated from the writings of Pierre Joseph Proudhon (1809-65). Proudhon is best known by his youthful essay, *Qu'est-ce que la propriété ?*—containing the famous answer: 'La propriété c'est le vol.' His principal work was *La Philosophie de la Misère*, published in 1846. Himself a labouring man, Proudhon felt deeply the wretchedness of his class, which he explained, much as socialists have done, by capitalist competition and capitalist monopoly. No satisfactory state of things was attainable, he thought, until the labourer should receive the whole produce of his labour. But he looked for the remedy in unlimited individual freedom, not in state control. The next eminent teacher of anarchism was the German schoolmaster, Caspar Schmidt (1806-56), who took the *nom de plume* of

Max Stirner, and expounded his doctrine in *The Individual and his Property*, published in the same year as *The Philosophy of Misery*. Not a man of action, but a philosopher bewildered with much thinking, Max Stirner rejected not only all existing authorities secular or ecclesiastical, but every idea, such as God or humanity, which tended to limit the absolute self-determination of the individual. 'I derive all right and justification from myself alone; for I am entitled to everything which I have power to take or to do.' But these reveries also failed to take hold on the public. For many years after 1848 anarchism appeared to be on the decline, and certainly was not a political force. The revival of anarchism, and the fullest development of whatever brutal and destructive tendencies may be implicit in it, are the work of Russian revolutionists. Of noble birth, and at first an officer in the Russian army, Michael Bakunin (1814-96), before reaching the age of thirty, had convinced himself that anarchy was the only tolerable state of man, and the destruction of all existing laws, institutions, and beliefs the most imperative, indeed the one imperative, duty. Bakunin's writings, though numerous, are fragmentary. But it is he and his school who have done most to prompt the many murders and attempts to murder characteristic of anarchism at the present day. The eminent geographer Élisée Réclus, a singularly upright and amiable man, cherishes the pleasing fancy that all men are, like himself, anxious to further the welfare of humanity. Auberon Herbert disapproves of compulsory taxation, and would trust the maintenance of the State to voluntary liberality. Even from the writings of Herbert Spencer passages might be extracted almost as startling in their restriction of the province of government. Thus anarchism, like its counterpart socialism, admits of innumerable degrees. The crimes which in recent years have marked the course of anarchism may be explained (1) by the savage fanaticism which Russian anarchists have infused into the party ; (2) by the pressure of misery in Russia, and, to a less extent, in Spain and Italy; and (3) by the spread of a moral malady, not confined to anarchists, which makes many people regard assassination as a venial method of promoting and advertising political changes. See SOCIALISM.

Literature: E. V. ZENKER, Anarchism, a Criticism and History of the Anarchist Theory (with bibliographical references); L PROAL, Political Crime; LOMBROSO and

Loschi, Le Crime Politique; Sernicoli, L'Anarchia; Garofalo, Criminologie; Tosti, in Polit. Sci. Quart., xiv. 3. (f.c.m.)

Anarthoscope: see Position and Movement (illusions of).

Anarthria [Gr. ἀ + ἄρθρον, a joint]: Ger. *Anarthrie*; Fr. *anarthrie*; Ital. *anartria*. Loss of, or extreme difficulty in, articulation, especially from difficulty in moving the tongue, owing to paralysis of the hypoglossus nerve.

It is a characteristic symptom in bulbar paralysis; is a muscular and wholly peripheral defect; and involves no cerebral or central aphasic symptoms. Of special forms of anarthric defects may be mentioned: (1) Lalling (q. v.), an indistinct utterance due to lack of precision in articulation, which would be normal in childhood, but should disappear with education (see also Alalia); (2) Stammering (q. v.), and also Stuttering (q. v.); and (3) Aphthongia, a rare disorder in which speech is impossible owing to a spasm of the hypoglossus, which sets in whenever speech is attempted. Cf. Bastian, *Aphasia* (1898), chap. iv. See Speech and its Defects (also for *Literature*). (j.j.)

Anaxagoras. (cir. 500–428 b.c.) Ionian philosopher. Spent nearly 30 years in Athens, where he enjoyed the friendship of Pericles; was finally banished on a charge of impiety. See Pre-Socratic Philosophy (Ionics).

Anaxarchus. Lived in the 4th century b.c. A Greek philosopher, born in Abdera. An intimate of Alexander the Great.

Anaxilaus. Lived during the 1st century b.c. A physician and Pythagorean philosopher, born in Larissa. His skill in natural philosophy brought upon him the charge of practising magic, for which he was banished from Rome by Augustus.

Anaximander. (cir. 610–546 b.c.) The second of the Ionian physical philosophers; a pupil and friend of Thales, the first. He is said to have invented the sundial, and to have taught the obliquity of the ecliptic, the globe-shape of both the earth and the sun, and the infinitude of worlds. See Pre-Socratic Philosophy (Ionics).

Anaximines. Lived probably about 500 b.c. An eminent Ionian physical philosopher, whose opinions are recorded by Theophrastus. See Pre-Socratic Philosophy (Ionics).

Ancestor Worship [OF. *ancestre*, from Lat. *antecessor*, one who goes before]: Ger. *Ahnencult*; Fr. *culte des ancêtres*; Ital. *culto degli antenati*. The worship of dead ancestors. (j.m.b., g.f.s.)

The whole question of ancestor worship is still in a transition stage. It is prevalent among peoples of the Indo-European, the Mongolian, and, in some degree, the Semitic stock. But the precise relation of this social and family idea to the prevalent religion, and the reasons for the growth of the custom, are as yet in dispute.

Literature: Caland, Ueber Totenverehrung bei einigen d. indog. Völker; Robertson Smith, Religion of the Semites; F. B. Jevons, Introd. to the Hist. of Religion; Maine, Early Law and Custom; H. Spencer, Sociology; F. Max Müller, Anthropol. Religion; v. Adrian, Der Höhenkultus asiatischer u. europäischer Völker; de Beaurepaire, Du culte des ancêtres chez les Romains; Boüinais and Paulus, Culte des Morts dans l'Emp. Céleste et l'Annam; E. Caird, Evolution of Religion, i. 239 f. (r.m.w.)

Ancestral Inheritance: see Gaston's Law (of ancestral inheritance).

Andronicus Rhodus (of Rhodes). He lived about 80 b.c.; collected and arranged the writings of Aristotle. See Peripatetics.

Angel, Angelology [Gr. ἄγγελος, a messenger, + λόγος, discourse]: Ger. *Engel, Angelologie*; Fr. *ange, angélologie*; Ital. *angelo, angelologia*. A messenger, i.e. one entrusted with a special mission; but, in theology, either a theophany or, more usually, a spiritual being intermediate between God and man. Angelology is a systematic discussion of the nature and office of angels.

The conception of angels may be said to have flourished in three main periods: (1) that represented by the scriptures of the Old and New Testaments; (2) the period of the Alexandrian school and of the early 'heretics'— the Gnostics and Manichaeans; (3) in the mediaeval thought of the Latin Church. Parallel beings are, of course, incident to many pre-Christian faiths.

Literature: Schultz, Bib. Theol. of the Old Testament; Weiss, Bib. Theol. of the New Testament; works on the Alexandrian School (q.v.); Matter, F. C. Baur, Lipsius, and Mansel on Gnosticism (q.v.); works of F. C. Baur, Beausobre, Trechsel, Flügel, Geyler, and Kessler on Manichaeism (q. v.); Aquinas, Summa Totius Theol., i. 44–74, 99, 105–15; S. J. Hunter, Dogmatic Theol., ii. 265 f.; P. d'Ercole, Il Teismo (1884); relative arts. in Herzog, Hastings, Cheyne (Dictionaries). (r.m.w.)

Anger [ME. *anger*]: Ger. *Zorn*; Fr. *colère*; Ital. *collera*. A painful emotion essentially characterized by the tendency to destroy or to break down opposition.　　(G.F.S.—J.M.B.)

Anger is usually considered one of the primitive emotions, closely associated with fear, and is thought to have arisen in connection with the reactions of defence which situations of fear would call out. Both psychologically and in its muscular (and other) expressions, however, it tends to supersede fear, taking on forms of positive opposition and aggression, where fear alone results in inaction or flight. The expressions of anger —apart from organic changes—involve the muscles of the eyebrows and jaws, facts which suggest the utilities of clear vision with protection of the eyes, and biting. The vasomotor changes are those of intense flushing ; rather than the reverse, as in cases of extreme fear. Cf. EMOTIONAL EXPRESSION.

Literature: BAIN, Emotions and Will, chap. ix ; DARWIN, Expression of Emotions, 240 f. ; JESSEN, Versuch ü. Psychol. ; JAMES, Princ. of Psychol., ii. 409, 460, 478 ; H. M. STANLEY, Evolutionary Psychol. of Feeling, chap. x ; STOUT, Manual of Psychol., 307 f. (J.M.B.,G.F.S.)

Angiosthenia : see ASTHENIA.

Angles of Displacement : Ger. *Erhebungswinkel und Seitenwendungswinkel (des Blickes*) ; Fr. *angle ascensionnel du regard et angle de déplacement latéral (de l'œil*) ; Ital. *angoli di spostamento visuale.* The angles of vertical and lateral displacement (see DONDERS' LAW) are used by Helmholtz to determine the direction of the line of regard. The former measures the departure of the plane of regard, upwards or downwards, from the primary position ; the latter is the angle made by the present line of regard with the median line of the plane of regard.

Literature: HELMHOLTZ, Physiol. Optik (2nd ed.), 617.　　(E.B.T.)

Anglo-Catholic (or Oxford) Movement : see TRACTARIANISM.

Anima : see TERMINOLOGY (Latin).

Anima Mundi [Lat.] : see WORLD SOUL.

Animal [Lat.] : Ger. *Thier* ; Fr. *animal* ; Ital. *animale.* There is no short and simple definition by which the animal can be so labelled as to be clearly distinguished from the plant. Perhaps the nearest approach we can make to such a concise definition is that an animal is a living organism which is unable to manufacture protoplasm from inorganic materials. Cf. LIFE, and VITAL PROPERTIES.

For a sketch of the earlier stages in the concept 'animal,' Huxley's article (see below),

'On the Border Territory between the Animal and Vegetable Kingdoms,' should be consulted. At present the higher animals are readily distinguished from the higher plants by the nature of their life-history and mode of development, by the manner of their nutrition, by the distribution of energy rendered possible by a more or less developed nervous system, and by the relative preponderance of certain qualities of the protoplasm which is common to both animals and plants. Only among some of the lower organisms do we find any difficulty. And it is now generally agreed that 'in grouping organisms as plants or as animals, we are not called upon to apply a definition, but to consider the multifarious evidences of historical evolution' (Lankester). 'The real question at issue in determining the position of any doubtful organism is not the possession of this, that, or the other character which may have been used to ticket the animal or vegetable kingdom, but whether the whole life-history of the organism indicates a nearer blood-relationship to groups of undoubted plants or undoubted animals. All simple forms should be regarded as so far common property that they should be studied equally by zoologists and botanists' (D. H. Scott).

Literature: HUXLEY, Collected Essays, viii, Essay vi ; HAECKEL, Phylogenie der Protista u. Pflanzen ; TIEGHEM, Traité de Botanique (2nd ed.) ; LANKESTER, art. Protozoa, Encyc. Brit. (9th ed.).　　(C.LL.M.)

Animal Heat : Ger. *thierische Wärme* ; Fr. *chaleur animale* ; Ital. *calore animale.* The heat of the living animal body is a continuous evolution of energy due in ultimate analysis to combustion of constituents of the tissues or food materials.

Animals were formerly divided into warmblooded (mammals and birds) and cold-blooded. A more exact designation, now generally used, classes them as : (1) homothermous (of uniform body temperature), birds and mammals, and (2) poikilothermous (of variable temperature), all other animals. Homothermous animals maintain a uniform body temperature by means of heat-regulating mechanisms which control both heat production (contraction of muscles, shivering) and heat dissipation (fluffing up of feathers or hair, perspiration), paling or blushing of the skin (see VASO-MOTOR SYSTEM). The normal temperature for man is about 37·1°C. (98·8°F.) for the armpit, 37·3°C. in the mouth, 37·6°C. in the rectum. Muscle is the great heat-producing tissue ; the large glands, notably the liver, rank next; and the brain has also been proved to be an important heat-producing organ.

Literature: A. Mosso, Die Temperature des Gehirns (Leipzig, 1894); general works given under Physiology. (C.F.H.)

Animal Magnetism: see Hypnosis.

Animal Psychology: Ger. *Thierpsychologie*; Fr. *psychologie animale*; Ital. *psicologia animale*. See Comparative Psychology, and Psychology.

Animal Worship: Ger. *Verehrung der Thiere, Thierverehrung*; Fr. *culte des animaux*; Ital. *culto degli animali*. As the name indicates, Animal Worship implies either (1) that animals are believed to possess in some crude sense deities worthy of worship; or (2) that they are associated with some sacred person, conception, or custom, and are therefore sanctified.

(1) This is the earlier phase, and is intimately connected with the psychological ideas incident to primitive Animism (q.v.). In this early stage, too, social reasons, whatever they may have been, especially in connection with Totemism (q.v.), were potent. (2) At a later stage, when Fetichism (q.v.) was fully developed, certain animals came to be regarded as incarnations of divinities or, still later, as specially sacred to some god. The ancient Egyptian religion, Brahmanism, and contemporary Hinduism are the most noted instances of this. The entire subject is still obscure.

Literature: Tylor, Primitive Culture, i. 467 f.; ii. 229 f. The view which excludes the influence of Totemism is represented by Wiedemann in Die Religion d. alten Aegypter, 94 f. See also Frazer, The Golden Bough, and many notes in his edition of Pausanias. (R.M.W.)

Animalcule [Lat. *animalculum*, little animal]: Ger. *Tierchen*; Fr. *animalcule*; Ital. *animaletto, animalculo*. (1) A vague term for a microscopic organism, now called microorganisms; generally applied to the infusoria.

Used in early times for any small animal. More speaks of flies and gnats and such-like bold animalcula; and Carlyle calls the spiders the basest of created animalcules. The use of the microscope caused a narrowing of the usage. (C.L.M.)

(2) Used by Leeuwenhoeck and his pupils (1677) for the preformed germ of man, and other animals, in the spermatozoon. See Animalculist. (E.M.)

Animalculist: Ger. *Präformist*; Fr. *spermatiste, animalculiste*; Ital. *animalculista*. One who believes that the male germinal cell or spermatozoon is or contains a miniature model of the organism into which it is to develop.

Ludwig Hamm, a pupil of Leeuwenhoeck (1677), is credited with the discovery of the spermatozoon. By many it was regarded as a parasitic animal; and Johann Müller, in 1842, regarded the question as undecided. But Spallanzani (1786) showed that the fertilizing power lay not in the fluid but in the contained spermatozoa. The animalculist believed that each spermatozoon contained in miniature the future organism which, in the early stages of its development, received nutriment from the ovum. Together with the ovists they are classed as preformationists or preformists. The development of the modern cell-theory has made the animalculist hypothesis, in anything like its original form, quite untenable. Cf. Preformation.

Literature: Y. Delage, Protoplasma . . . et l'Hérédité (1895). (C.Ll.M.)

Animism (in anthropology) [Lat. *anima*, soul]: Ger. *Animismus*; Fr. *animisme*; Ital. *animismo, dottrina animistica*. There are three more or less current uses of the term Animism in ethnology and the science of religions: (1) it signifies belief in the animation of all nature, which does not imply the existence of agents distinct from visible bodies; (2) the belief in something dwelling in bodies but distinct from them; this something, however, may still be material; (3) the belief that bodies are animated or inhabited by the ghosts of departed men. The second usage is in the main that of Tylor; the third view is developed in the Ghost-theory (q.v.) of Spencer. It is the second meaning which — especially in its higher form, and independently of the truth of the ghost-theory—illustrates the principle of Personification (q.v.). (L.M.–J.M.B.–G.F.S.)

Animism, in some of its forms, is one of the most important principles pervading the philosophy of primitive peoples, and has left its traces upon customs and habits of thought in all stages of culture down to the present. Its most specific application was to the explanation of the forces of nature. Everything not obviously to be accounted for by material causes was believed to be in some way animated. The sun and moon, the winds and rains, the harvest and dearth, good and ill fortune, sickness and death were conceived of as animate beings to be feared and appeased, to be worshipped and attended.

The theory of animism of Herbert Spencer (3) includes the belief in the existence of a human spirit apart from the body and surviving the death of the body in a life after death. This conception may have been suggested by the experiences of dreams and trance, of visions, and by the attacks of nervous disease. Around it has developed an elaborate variety of customs and beliefs affecting almost all the exigencies and fortunes of life. The worship of ancestors, the transmigration of souls, the doctrine of the life beyond the grave, the magical influencing of other persons and events by sorcery and witchcraft, the intercourse with demons and fairies, and a host of superstitious customs and rules of conduct, all find a more or less definite origin in one or another of the ramifications of this primitive conception. These two doctrines—the existence of powerful spirits or deities in nature and of individual souls as separate from and surviving the body —form the two great dogmas of developed religious animism.

A specific development of this general belief is known as FETICHISM (q.v.); in this doctrine the connection of the spirit or force with some material representative becomes of fundamental importance. The meaning of the fetich is, however, in dispute. Cf. also MAGIC, EJECTION, and INTROJECTION. (J.J.–J.M.B.)

Literature: A. RÉVILLE, Prolégomènes de l'Hist. des Religions; GOBLET D'ALVIELLA, L'idée de Dieu d'après l'Anthropol. et l'Hist.; TYLOR, Primitive Culture, chapters on Animism; also in briefer form in the art. Animism in Encyc. Brit., and in chap. xiv of Tylor's Anthropology; H. SPENCER, Princ. of Sociol.; F. B. JEVONS, An Introd. to the Hist. of Religion; GIRARD DE RIALLE, Mythol. Comparée (1878); J. G. FRAZER, The Golden Bough (1890). (L.M.–J.J.)

Animism (in philosophy). The view that the soul (anima), however conceived, is the cause or principle of life.

Applied to Aristotle's theory of the relation of soul and body, and held by the Stoics. The point of view was developed and refined by the scholastics, without, however, losing the material connotation of the term which attaches to the Greek conception. Applied also to the theory of WORLD SOUL (q.v.), and illustrated in HYLOZOISM (q.v.). It is attributed to Leibnitz (see MONADOLOGY); and finally it is used to express the form of VITALISM (q.v.), which makes life (or life and mind) the directive principle in evolution and growth. Logically considered, philosophical animism is

an early and cruder form of the monism which takes on a more refined phase in SPIRITUALISM (q.v.).

Literature: see the citations in EISLER, Wörterb. d. philos. Begriffe, sub verbo; WUNDT, Syst. d. Philos., 210; PAULSEN, Introd. to Philos. (Eng. trans.). (J.M.B.)

Anisometropia [Gr. *ὰ* + *ἴσος*, equal, + *μέτρον*, a measure, + *ὤψ*, the eye]: Ger. *Anisometropie*; Fr. *anisométrie*; Ital. *anisometropia*. An inequality in the refractive mechanism of the two eyes. See VISION (defects of). (J.J.)

Ankle Clonus: Ger. *Fussclonus*; Fr. *clonus du pied*; Ital. *clono del piede*. A tendon reflex (see REFLEX ACTION) diagnostic of lateral SCLEROSIS (q.v.), spastic PARALYSIS (q.v.), and other diseases of the spinal cord. It is produced by artificially flexing the foot at the ankle, and consists of rhythmical contractions of the muscles of the calf of the leg. (H.H.)

Anlage [Ger.]: there is no adequate French term, the best translation is *rudiment* (Y.D.); Ital. *rudimento* (E.M.). See RUDIMENT, and cf. DISPOSITION. It is contrary to the genius of the English language, and especially to scientific usage, to introduce non-classical words, such as Anlage, preserving the inflections. Its use is, therefore, not recommended. See TERMINOLOGY (German). (H.H.)

Annett or **Annet, Peter.** (died 1769.) An English deistical writer.

Annihilation [Pat. Lat. *adnihilare*, *ad* + *nihil*, to bring to nought]: Ger. *Vernichtung*; Fr. *annihilation*; Ital. *annientamento*. The doctrine which teaches complete destruction of the wicked or 'unregenerate,' as opposed to their eternal punishment in the world to come, is called Annihilationism.

This dogma has never been formally incorporated in any creed, but has been taught from time to time by various theologians, though seldom in its full force. (Cf. CONDITIONAL IMMORTALITY.) Arnobius of Sicca (cir. 310 A.D.) and Faustus Socinus are its older representatives. In modern times E. White, of Hereford, England (1846), and C. F. Hudson, of New England, have written the most important books on the subject. Richard Rothe is the most distinguished theologian who has paid attention to it. It was held by Whately and Isaac Barrow, and Locke made reference to it.

Literature: SALMOND, The Christ. Doctrine of Immortality, 594 f.; for Locke, see LORD KING, Life of Locke, ii. 139 f. (R.M.W.)

Annunciation [Lat. *annunciatio*, *ad* +

nuntiare, to announce to]: Ger. *Verkündigung*; Fr. *annonciation*; Ital. *annunziazione*. The name given to the visit of the angel Gabriel to Mary, when he announced the beginning of the Incarnation.

The origin of the Church feast-day is unknown. Documentary evidence for it exists so far back as 492 A.D. It is now observed on March 25, though December 18 and the fourth Sunday in Advent were assigned by the Council of Toledo (656) and the Milan Church respectively. The controversy on the subject raged in the Latin Church from the 12th till the 15th century, and was finally ended by Sixtus IV, in 1480, when the feast was sanctioned with a special office. It thus passed from the Eastern into the Western Church. (R.M.W.)

Anodyne [Gr. ἀ + ὀδύνη, pain]: Ger. *schmerzstillendes* (or *linderndes*) *Mittel*; Fr. *anodin*; Ital. *anodino*. A remedy which relieves pain by lowering the irritability of local nerves or of the brain; called also analgesic (T. Lauder-Brunton). (C.F.H.)

Anoia, Anoea, Anoesia [Gr. ἄνοια, want of understanding]: Ger. *Blödsinn, Anoia*; Fr. *idiotie, imbécillité*; Ital. *anoia, idiozia*. See IDIOCY. (J.J.)

Anomalous Colour-system. A suggested rendering of the German *Anomales Farbensystem*. Colour equations which hold for one individual hold also with very slight exceptions for nearly every other individual; the exceptional cases also all belong, so far as yet known, to a single type called the Anomalous System.

Such individuals are few in number; out of seventy persons examined in this respect by König and Dieterici three only had the exceptional colour-system. They were first noticed by Lord Rayleigh, later by Donders, and they have been thoroughly tested by means of spectral light equations by König and Dieterici. The abnormality exists only in red and green, and it may be described by saying that the curve for the green constituent of white light has a transitional position between the red curve and the green curve of the normal eye. To make yellow out of red and green they require only one-third as much green as do individuals with normal eyes.

Literature: HELMHOLTZ, Physiol. Optik (2nd ed.), 359; RAYLEIGH, Nature (1881); KÖNIG and DIETERICI, Zeitsch. f. Psychol. (1892). (C.L.F.)

Anomaly (mental) [Gr. ἀ + ὁμαλός, even, from ὁμός, same, common]: Ger. *geistige Abnormität*; Fr. *anomalie mentale*; Ital. *anomalia mentale*. A marked deviation from the normal or typical mental endowment or functioning; any such irregularity implying something exceptional or unusual. The term anomaly is used in reference to physical structures and functions, to mental processes and traits, as well as to general occurrences. Many of the traits and symptoms studied in abnormal psychology can be characterized as mental anomalies. (J.J.)

Anorthopia [Gr. ἀ + ὀρθός, straight, + ὤψ, eye]: Ger. *Anorthopie*; Fr. *strabisme*; Ital. *anortopia*. Obliquity of vision; squinting. See VISION (defects of). (J.J.)

Anorthoscope: see LABORATORY AND APPARATUS, III. B. (*a*), (9).

Anosmia [Gr. ἀ + ὀσμή, smell]: Ger. *Anosmie, Anosmia*; Fr. *anosmie*; Ital. *anosmia*. Lack, loss, or impairment of the sense of smell; olfactory anaesthesia. Like all defects of the special senses, it may be due to disorder of or interference with the function of any portion of the sense-mechanism from centre to periphery. Aside from local disorders and injuries to the head, it may result from tumours, or from the decline of sensibility with old age, and may be associated with other symptoms of loss of function in other parts of the cerebral mechanism.

Literature: ROSS, Dis. of the Nerv. Syst. (1881–5); ZWARDEMAKER, Physiol. d. Geruchs; ARONSOHN, Zur Physiol. d. Geruchs (1886); J. PASSY, Sur les sensations olfactives, Année Psychol., ii. 382 f. (J.J.)

Anschauung [Ger.]: see TERMINOLOGY (German).

Anselm, Saint. (1033–1109.) A pupil of Lanfranc at the abbey of Bec in Normandy, where he became a monk and succeeded Lanfranc as prior. He became abbot of Bec and archbishop of Canterbury. See ONTOLOGICAL ARGUMENT, and THEISM.

Anselmian Argument (for the existence of God): see ONTOLOGICAL ARGUMENT. From Anselm, of Canterbury.

Antagonism [Gr. ἀντί + ἀγωνίζεσθαι, to struggle against]: Ger. *Antagonismus, Antagonisten* (of muscles or nerves); Fr. *antagonisme* (*musculaire et nerveux*), *poisons antagonistes* (of drugs); Ital. *antagonismo*. Used of muscles which oppose the action of other muscles, e. g. flexors and extensors, adductors and abductors, inspiratory and expiratory, sphincters and dilators. See MUSCLE.

The word is used also to designate nerves which cause opposite effects on the same organ, as the inhibitory and accelerator nerves of the heart, the constrictor and dilator nerves of the iris and of the blood-vessels.

A third physiological use of the term relates to opposing actions of drugs, notable examples being muscarin and atropin, strychnin and atropin or chloroform.

Literature: antagonistic physiological action is fully discussed in Richet's Dict. de Physiol. See also WALLER, Human Physiol., and the general works given under PHYSIOLOGY. For antagonism of drugs see T. LAUDER-BRUNTON, Pharmacology, 495. (C.F.H.)

Antagonistic Colour: Ger. *Gegenfarbe*; Fr. *couleur antagonistique*; Ital. *colore antagonistico*. Hering's term for COMPLEMENTARY COLOUR (q. v.). Cf. VISION. (E.B.T.)

Antecedent (in logic) [Lat. *ante + cedo*]: Ger. *vorhergehend* (general), *antecedens* (in logic); Fr. *antécédent*; Ital. *antecedente*. Literally, antecedent is that which goes before, primarily in space, then in time.

In logic, the sense of precedent in time is still retained when the term appears in the treatment of inductive reasoning, otherwise the derived meaning of GROUND (q.v.) or condition is the most common. The antecedent as statement of that from which the logical CONSEQUENT (q. v.) is asserted to follow, forms one element of every hypothetical judgment. (R.A.)

Antenna [Lat. *antenna*, a sail-yard]: Ger. *Fühlhorn*; Fr. *antenne*; Ital. *antenna*. A jointed appendage of the head in some arthropods. In insects the antennae probably represent the anterior paired metameric appendages, modified for use as organs of sense. (C.Ll.M.–E.S.G.)

In the antennae of ants and bees there are, according to Lubbock, at least eight different types of sensory organs, consisting of modified hairs or sensillae (Whitman) and pits. Some are tactile, some probably auditory, others gustatory; while of others the sensory value is unknown.

Literature: LUBBOCK, The Senses of Animals (1888); E. KORSCHELT and K. HEIDER, Lehrb. d. vergl. Entwicklungsgesch. d. wirbellosen Thiere; WHITMAN, Woods Holl Biol. Lectures (1898); WHEELER, Contrib. to Insect Morphology, J. of Morphol., viii. (1893). (C.Ll.M.)

Anthropoid [Gr. ἄνθρωπος, man, + εἶδος, form]: Ger. *Menschenaffen, menschenähnliche Affen*; Fr. *anthropoïdes*; Ital. *antropoidi*. In the broader sense the sub-order of the Primates, which includes man; in the narrower sense, the family which comprises the manlike apes.

As now defined, the sub-order Anthropoidea contains five families, viz.: (5) Hominidae (man); (4) Simiidae (apes); (3) Cercopithecidae (baboons); (2) Cebidae (American monkeys); (1) Hapalidae (marmosets).

The family of the Simiidae or anthropoid apes includes the gibbons of S E. Asia, the orangs of Sumatra and Borneo, the gorillas of W. Equatorial Africa, the chimpanzees of W. and Central Equatorial Africa. Probably none of these are on the direct line of human descent. In their teeth the gibbons, in their brain-structure the orangs, in their size the gorillas, and in the sigmoid curvature of the vertebral column the chimpanzees most closely resemble man. (C.Ll.M.)

The families Cercopithecidae, Simiidae, and Hominidae form the group Catarrhini, distinguished by the possession of a narrow nasal septum, a skull with the auditory bulla not swollen and a long external auditory meatus, a dentition of 32 teeth, each side of each jaw having 2 premolars and 3 molars, and a completely opposable pollex.

In their general structure the apes (Simiidae) approach very closely to man, as in the absence of tail, the semi-erect posture (resting on finger-tips or knuckles), the vertebral column, the shape of the sternum and pelvis, the adaptation of the arm for pronation and supination, the presence of a long vermiform appendix to the short caecum of the intestine, the size of the cerebral hemispheres, and the complexity of their convolutions. Yet in certain respects, as in the proportion of the limbs, the development of the bony ridges of the skull, the adaptation of the foot as a climbing and grasping organ, the higher apes represent a line of development from which the human has diverged.

Man differs from the anthropoid apes chiefly in the reduction of the hairy covering and its special local development on the scalp and face; in the development of a large lobule to the external ear; in the fully erect attitude in walking, the flattened walking foot with a large non-opposable hallux, the straightened limb-bones, widened pelvis, and pronounced sigmoid curve of the vertebral column; in the perfected structure for the rotation of the arm and fore-arm, and the further adaptation of the hand as a delicate organ of prehension and touch; in the small size of the canine teeth, and diminution in size of the molars from before backwards; in the arrangement of the teeth in a continuous crescentic or horseshoe-shaped row without diastema; in the development of a mental prominence (chin) on the lower jaw, and the small size of the jaws relatively to the immense development of the brain-case, accompanied by the shortening of the basi-cranial axis, shifting forward of the foramen magnum, and elevating of the facial region into an almost vertical plane; in the reduction of the supraciliary ridges, and development of a projecting nose.

Most of the differences between man and the apes in the structure of the skull and shape of the head are directly related to the great increase in size of the human brain. The average cranial capacity of man is about 1500 c.c., and that of the higher apes about 490 c.c. (the maximum in the gorilla being 621 c.c.). The cranial capacity of man is therefore roughly three times that of the apes.

The relative weight of the human brain, as compared with the weight of the whole body, is very superior to that of other orders of Mammalia; but inferior to that of many of the smaller Primates. The superiority of the human brain in absolute weight is, however, very great. Whereas the average weight of the brain of the larger apes is at most 400 gr., that of man is about 1400 gr. The average human brain is, therefore, more than three times the weight of the average simian. The minimum weight of the normal human brain is rarely, if ever, less than double that of the maximum simian.

In the brain of man the hemispheres are relatively larger and more convoluted, principally in the frontal region, which appears to be more especially concerned with the exercise of the higher faculties and with speech. The anthropoid brain is generally distinguished by the presence of a conspicuous transverse groove (simian fissure) between the parietal lobes and the overlapping edge of the occipital lobe. Cf. BRAIN (comparative anatomy).

The gap between man and the ape has to a considerable extent been bridged over by the discovery of remains of fossil men, and of an extinct Primate, *Pithecanthropus*, which appears to be intermediate in structure between the two. The fragments of *Pithecanthropus erectus*, Dubois, were found by E. Dubois in Java (Pleistocene?), and consist of a femur, teeth, and the upper region of a skull (calvarium), not necessarily belonging to the same individual. The skull appears to have been low and depressed, with strong supraciliary ridges, elongated (cephalic index 70), and with an estimated capacity of 855 c.c. The corresponding brain-weight is estimated at 750 gr. The teeth are very large, and the femur quite human. *Pithecanthropus* is believed by some authors to be on the direct line of human descent.

The most important remains of fossil (Quaternary) men are the Neanderthal calvarium from near Elberfeld (Prussia), a lower jaw from La Naulette near Dinant (Belgium), fragments of crania from La Denise (France), skeletons found at Spy (Belgium) and in Kent (Galley Hill Terrace Gravels). All these remains show, so far as their condition allows, a low elongated cranium of essentially normal capacity, with large supraciliary ridges; the molars decrease not at all or very little from before backwards; and the mental prominence is rudimentary in the lower jaws of Spy, and absent in the jaw of La Naulette.   (E.S.G.)

Literature: T. H. HUXLEY, Man's Place in Nature (1863); FLOWER and LYDEKKER, Mammals Living and Extinct (1891); P. TOPINARD, L'Homme dans la Nature (1891); R. HARTMANN, Anthropoid Apes (1885); A. H. KEANE, Ethnology (1895); E. DUBOIS, Pithecanthropus erectus, eine Uebergangsform aus Java (1894); also in Proc. 4th Int. Cong. of Zool. (1899); O. C. MARSH, Amer. J. of Sci. [4] i. (1896); J. FRAIPONT and M. LOHEST, La Race Humaine de Néanderthal ou de Candstadt en Belgique, Arch. de Biol., v. 7 (1887); HAECKEL, Natürliche Schöpfungsgeschichte, and Anthropogenie; MORSELLI, Antropol. gen.: Lezioni sull' Uomo (Turin, 1888–1900).   (C.LL.M.–E.S.G.)

Anthropology [Gr. ἄνθρωπος, man, + λόγος, discourse]: Ger. *Anthropologie*; Fr. *anthropologie*; Ital. *antropologia*. The science of man, or the natural history of mankind.

The term anthropology has fluctuated in usage considerably; and even at the present day is somewhat differently conceived by different nations and authors. The term was used by Aristotle, but somewhat inexactly. In the 16th to 18th centuries it was frequently employed in a purely physical sense, as synonymous with human anatomy and physiology; and by another school of writers in a psychological and also in an ethical and religious sense. Kant, while considering in other connections the origin of races, devotes his treatise on Anthropology to a specifically psychological discussion. Although it had been, for a long period, theoretically defined as the science and natural history of mankind, it was not generally used in this sense until the beginning of the present century. There was, and still is.

a tendency amongst Germans to regard the term as synonymous with physical anthropology or SOMATOLOGY (q. v.), and amongst the French to use the expression *anthropologie générale* for the science in its broadest aspects. With many French writers anthropology is the physical description—mental also, but mainly physical— of the different races of man; the study of the manners, customs, habits, religions, &c., belongs to ethnography or ethnology. In the description here given, an attempt is made to interpret the most authoritative consensus regarding the significance of the term in current usage.

The most general, as well as the most desirable, use of the term gives it a significance broad enough to include the various lines of interest and study which contribute to a knowledge of the nature of man and the story of his development and occupation of the earth; and yet definite enough to give the study of anthropology a specific, consistent, and useful place among the sciences. It will contribute to a clearer conception of anthropology to bear in mind that a science receives its distinctive characteristics quite as much from the point of view from which it approaches its facts, and from the purposes and guiding conceptions which dominate it, as from the nature of the groups of facts which make up its material content; and likewise that one science should not be regarded as including in its own domain one or more other sciences because it utilizes or depends for certain classes of facts upon the results contributed by such sciences. Anthropology and anatomy both study minutely the physical characteristics of the human body, but the points of view, and the purposes of the two, are quite different; nor does anthropology in any legitimate sense include anatomy because its progress in certain directions depends upon the data which the latter supplies. In other directions a similar relation obtains between anthropology and geology, psychology, physiology, sociology, linguistics, history, and other departments of study. ' Anthropology should not too ambitiously strive to include within itself the sciences which provide so much of its wealth,' but ' it is the office of anthropology to collect and co-ordinate [the results concerning man furnished by other sciences], so as to elaborate as completely as may be the synopsis of man's bodily and mental nature, and the theory of his whole course of life and action from his first appearance on earth ' (Tylor).

More specifically, anthropology may be described as that department of knowledge which renders an account of man's origin and distribution over the earth, and his relation to other animals; of the various types, races, or varieties of mankind and their relations, historical, physical, and psychological, to one another; of the development of the arts and sciences, industries, and occupations of the human race; of the organization of man in society, and the complex and endlessly variable forms of custom and belief in which such organization finds expression; of man's mental nature and the various forms of thought-habits and tendencies, myths and superstitions, rites and cults, in which it is reflected; and furthermore, anthropology assumes the task of interpreting, in all these respects, the relics of man's most ancient and primitive occupation, and of collecting similar data in regard to the undeveloped peoples now extant. The historically recorded phases of these subjects must logically also be included within the realm of anthropology; but it is the peculiar function of that science to consider the prehistoric phases, utilizing as comparative aids the data of history.

In common with all the biological sciences, anthropology has shared in the renaissance which has come from the application of evolutionary and developmental conceptions to the problems of origin and growth. The discussion of man's place in nature and his derivation from less developed forms of animal life, which is sometimes known as anthropogenesis or anthropogeny, formed one of the first and most hotly contested discussions in the history of the doctrine of evolution, while no consensus has as yet been reached in regard to the derivation of his mental endowments from those of the higher animals, or the precise relation of the two to each other. The comparative method has likewise been fertile in anthropology not only in tracing kinship and migrations of races and thought-habits, in suggesting intercommunication and the order and direction of customs and beliefs, but as well in exhibiting the general similarities and specific differences of the arts and sciences, the mental and material occupations of mankind under different and independent conditions. The comparative method has also been serviceable in furnishing to anthropological studies a sense of reality by revealing numerous and salient points of similarity between the customs and beliefs suggested by the relics of primitive peoples or found current amongst savages, and those in vogue in past civilizations or surviving from these into our own times. (J.J.)

It is convenient to recognize certain main divisions of anthropology, and to recognize as well that these are frequently not sharply separated from one another, and stand in constant and intimate relations to other sciences. Amid the very great diversity in the mode of drawing these distinctions, the following stand out as the most usual and important.

On the one hand, human individual anatomy and physiology are generally excluded as belonging to the wider science of biology, in its zoological division, and, on the other hand, psychology and philology are generally given independent rank. Omitting these, the following scheme (which should be compared with that given under BIOLOGY) will suffice to indicate the subdivisions of the science.

1. *Natural History of Man*: *a*. Physical characteristics (Anthropography, ANTHROPOMETRY: sometimes called somatology); *b*. Relations to other organisms and to environment (Anthroponomics).

2. *Distribution* in space and time: Geographical and Historical Ethnography.

3. *Aetiology* and *Evolution*: The descent of man and the origin of races (ETHNOLOGY).

4. The relations of man in *Social Communities*, with psychological variations, descriptive and aetiological (SOCIOLOGY, CRIMINAL ANTHROPOLOGY, and RACE PSYCHOLOGY, by many regarded as separate branches of science).

5. His progress as represented in things and institutions (ARCHAEOLOGY, History of Culture). See the terms in heavy type; also FOLKLORE. (C.LL.M.–J.M.B.–J.J.)

Literature (general): E. B. TYLOR, Anthropology (consult selected list of books there given); also art. Anthropology, in Encyc. Brit. (9th ed.), and Researches in the Early History of Mankind; RANKE, Der Mensch; PRITCHARD, Nat. Hist. of Mankind; HUXLEY, Essays, vii; P. TOPINARD, Anthropology; BUCKLAND, Anthropol. Stud.; DE QUATREFAGES and HAMY, Crania ethnica; VERNEAU, Les races humaines; E. MORSELLI, Antropol. Gen., Turin (1888–1900); HERVÉ and HOVELACQUE, Précis d'Anthropol. (1887); KEANE, Ethnology, and Man, Past and Present (1899); RATZEL, Völkerkunde, i. (1895); ACHELIS, Moderne Völkerkunde (1896); WAITZ, Introd. to Anthropol. (Eng. trans., i. only, 1863).

For special departments of anthropology, see special terms and bibliographies given in the larger treatises, in the journals devoted to Anthropology, for a list of which, as well as for detailed references, see 'Anthropology,' &c., in Index Catalogue of the Surgeon-General's Library, i. (1880), and second series i. (1896). Recent more popular works are HADDON, The Study of Man (1897); and DENIKER, The Races of Man (1899). (J.J.)

Anthropology (in theology). The name given to that section of doctrinal or dogmatic theology which treats of man in his actual and ideal relations to God, or of man the 'subject' of the kingdom of God.

The history of the subject as a whole relates mainly to the articulation of anthropology with the other parts of the doctrinal system. Among the most noteworthy of the varying arrangements are those of Calvin, Cocceius, Schleiermacher, Hagenbach, Lipsius, and I. A. Dorner. A. Ritschl and his followers have developed a view of the subject-matter which leaves the lines customary hitherto.

Literature: VATKE, D. menschl. Freiheit; V. OOSTERZEE, Christ. Dogmatics (Eng. trans.), 355 f. (gives literature of special topics); HASTINGS, Dict. of the Bible, art. Man; E. CAIRD, Evolution of Religion, i. 21 f., 70 f., 188 f., 205 f. (R.M.W.)

Anthropometry [Gr. ἄνθρωπος, man, + μέτρον, measure]: Ger. *Anthropometrie*; Fr. *anthropométrie*; Ital. *antropometria*. The science that deals with the measurements, proportions, and physical characteristics of the human body.

The two dominant interests in anthropometrical investigations and results are the anthropological and sociological, and the developmental. The anthropologist uses anthropometric measurements to aid him in the differentiation of races and peoples and in the various problems of ethnology. This description of man as a member of a zoological species is best (although not invariably) termed Physical Anthropology or SOMATOLOGY (q. v.); also see ANTHROPOLOGY. Physical anthropology is therefore a broader term than anthropometry, including the study of man's origin and place in nature, the differentiation of races, variation of types, &c.

Anthropometry, on the other hand, includes the application of bodily measurements to individual development, to the effects of social influences, of environment, of special training and the like. The development of anthropometric research is a recent acquisition of science. Apart from the accurate description of the physical characteristics of man and their correlation with one another, anthropometry has been fostered by the study of the growth and development of the body (and its correlations with mental characteristics); by its practical applications in gymnastic and athletic training; by its connections with medical research, and the study of climatic, hereditary, and social influences. Cf. TESTS (psychophysical).

A division of anthropometry of special importance in ethnological research is CRANIOMETRY (q.v.). A further application of bodily measurement and description to the identification of criminals has recently been introduced with some success. Cf. A. Bertillon, in whose volume, *Identification anthropométrique*, new edition (1893), with atlas, a complete account of these methods is given. For a special study with a similar purpose see F. Galton, *Finger Prints, Finger-print Directories*. Cf. Criminal Anthropology under CRIMINAL.

Literature: CHARLES ROBERTS, A Manual of Anthropom. (1878), and the complete literature, largely of special studies, reprinted and enlarged from J. H. Baxter; Statistics, Med. and Anthropol., of the Provost-Marshal-General's Bureau, 2 vols. (1875). Among more recent contributions are EMIL SCHMIDT, Anthropol. Meth. (1888); MEGRET, Anthropom. Normale (1895); HRDLICKA, Anthropometry, Amer. J. of Insan. (1897), liii. 521. R. THOMA, Untersuchungen über die Grösse und das Gewicht der anatomischen Bestandtheile des menschlichen Körpers (1882), is to be recommended, and includes a bibliography. See also DORSEY in Science, N.S., vi. 110. (J.J.)

Anthropomorphism [Gr. ἄνθρωπος, man, + μορφή, form]: Ger. *Anthropomorphismus*; Fr. *anthropomorphisme*; Ital. *antropomorfismo*. The assumption of human beings that their own characteristics are present in beings or facts widely different from themselves, more particularly in gods or in the forces of nature. It is a dominant trait in certain forms of the animistic conception of nature, and is discernible in more elaborate religious and philosophical systems. (R.H.S.–J.J.)

Anthropomorphism is a narrower conception than ANIMISM (q.v.); it finds illustrations in each of the three meanings given under the latter term, since it indicates the special form of animation—often human analogy—but is not limited to the spiritual, or even to any sort of existence distinct from visible bodies. The GHOST THEORY (q.v.) applies to the quasi-spiritual form of anthropomorphism; but the ghost may, in particular cases, be a refined material shape; and the use of the dream-ghost itself rests on an earlier cruder animism. Cf. the topics EJECT and PERSONIFICATION; and see the next topic. (J.J.–J.M.B.)

Anthropomorphism (in religion). The name applied to that tendency which endows the gods, or God, with the nature of men or of man. The ancient Greek religion is usually cited as a typical instance.

The history of the subject is too intricate to be summarized briefly. But it may be said that anthropomorphism marks a stage in the history of religions superior to Fetichism, Nature Worship, and Shamanism. The extremest anthropomorphists in the history of Christianity were the Andians, who flourished in the 4th and 5th centuries. They were literalists in biblical interpretation, and held that all passages of Scripture attributing eyes, ears, and the like to God were to be taken in their strictest sense. At the present time interest in anthropomorphism centres in the consequences of the view, favoured by many philosophers, that this tendency is necessarily involved in the attribution of Personality to God. At this point the discussion touches upon the ultimate problems of pantheism and theism, with their metaphysical accompaniments of immanence and transcendence.

Literature: NÄGELSBECK, Die Homerische Theol.; CAMPBELL, Religion in Greek Lit.; TIELE, Elements of the Sci. of Religion, ii. 100–21; E. CAIRD, Evolution of Religion, i. 239 f., 367 f.; A. LANG, Myth, Ritual, and Religion (2nd ed.); L. MARILLIER, L'origine des Dieux, Rev. Philos. (1899); A. REVILLE, Prolégomènes de l'Hist. des Religions; ROMANES, Mind and Matter, and Monism; BALDWIN, Social and Eth. Interpret., chap. viii. § 5, and chap. x. § 4. (R.M.W.–L.M.)

Antichrist [Gr. ἀντί, against, + Χριστός, Christ]: Ger. *Antichrist*; Fr. *antéchrist*; Ital. *Anticristo*. The apocalyptic conception of a personal power operating specially to defeat the scheme of salvation dependent upon Christ. The subject belongs properly to the eschatological section of doctrinal theology.

The idea had its origin during the religious fermentation in the early years of the Roman Empire. From time to time theologians have identified the 'Man of Sin' with historical personages or movements. Instances of this are:—Antiochus Epiphanes in *Daniel*; Nero in *Revelation*; Mohammed with the Christians of the dark ages; the Pope with some Protestants; Napoleon III and the modern sceptical movement, especially in its 'realistic' aspects, with some dogmatists.

Literature : RENAN, L'Antéchrist ; DE LA SAUSSAYE, Studien, i. 65 f. ; Commentaries on the Apocalypse, Thessalonians, Daniel ; POURCHET, Antichrist ; REUSS, Hist. of Christ. Theol. in the Apostolic Age, i. 115, ii. 192, 448. (R.M.W.)

Anticipation [Lat. *ante*, before, + *capere*, to take] : Ger. (1) *Erwartung*, (2) *vorzeitige Reactionen, negativen Werth* (*Reaction vom*) ; Fr. (1) *anticipation*, (2) *réaction anticipée* ; Ital. (1) *anticipazione*, (2) *reazione anticipata*. (1) A state of mental readiness for a coming event, on whatever ground it may rest. (2) A voluntary reaction to a stimulus before the latter occurs. See also PROLEPSIS.

(1) 'Expectation' has been used (by the translator of Külpe's *Outlines of Psychology*) in the general sense, but that term (q. v.) has a special signification. Cf. the usage of Reid, *Inquiry*, ii. § 24. Terms which emphasize more special phases of this state of mind are expectant attention (see ATTENTION) and PRE-PERCEPTION (q. v.).

(2) The number of anticipations in experiments in the laboratory is greater in so-called 'muscular reaction.' In German (Wundt) these cases are called 'negative values.' For theories of such anticipations and methods of treating results containing them, see the references given under REACTION-TIME. (J.M.B., G.F.S.)

Anticipations of Experience. Kant's expression (Anticipationen der Wahrnehmung) denotes the principles of knowledge (Erkenntnis) by which I am able to recognize and determine *a priori* anything that is known empirically (zur empirischen Erkenntnis gehört, *Krit. d. reinen Vernunft*, 103), and especially, of these principles, the second of the 'Grundsätzen des reinen Denkens,' which reads : Every object of sensation has intensive magnitude, i.e. degree. (J.M.B.–K.G.)

Antinomianism [Gr. ἀντί, against, + νόμος, law] : Ger. *Antinomismus* ; Fr. *antinomisme* ; Ital. *antinomismo*. A forcible separation between the 'gospel' and the 'law,' or between faith and works, whereby the latter are expelled from their due place in an ethico-religious unity.

Beginning with Paul, this controversy has come down through the ages to the present time. The contest was acute among the Reformers, of whom Arnsdorf was the most extreme. At present, and from the point of view of philosophy of religion, the interest of the question centres in the tendency (probably unconscious) of some among the evangelical churches to raise subscription, or orthodoxy, above life.

Literature : DORNER, Syst. of Christ. Doctrine, iv. 24 f., 77, 233 ff. ; FRANK, Theol. d. Konkordienformel. (R.M.W.)

Antinomy : Ger. *Antinomie* ; Fr. *antinomie* ; Ital. *antinomia*. A logical contradiction between two accepted principles or between conclusions drawn rightly from premises which have equal claim to objective validity.

The term, not in common use, though it is to be found in application to cases of conflict of positive laws and in controversial theological literature, has acquired a definite place in philosophy from the employment of it by Kant, to indicate the position in which reason is placed when it endeavours, taking the cosmos as a given and determinate subject, to lay out systematically the general predicates by which it must be characterized. Cf. KANTIANISM, and KANTIAN TERMINOLOGY. (R.A.)

Antinomy (ethical). Any conflict of moral principles, each so comprehensive that no appeal to a third principle can decide between them.

The term is used by Kant with reference to a special conflict to which his ethical criticism leads. On the one hand the Summum Bonum involves a combination of happiness and virtue, and the promotion of the Summum Bonum is *a priori* a necessary object of the will and thus inseparably attached to moral law ; on the other hand, happiness and virtue are conceptions which have nothing in common and which depend on different conditions : so that their connection cannot be brought about either analytically (one involving the other) or synthetically (one being the cause of the other). The antinomy is solved by Kant by reference to the postulate of God's existence. Cf. KANTIAN TERMINOLOGY. The phrase Social Antinomy is applied to the conflict between the individual's sense of duty and the practical formulations of society. See SOCIAL ETHICS.

Literature : KANT, Krit. d. prakt. Vernunft, I. ii. 1–2 ; BALDWIN, Social and Eth. Interpret. (W.R.S.)

Antiochus of Aegae in Cilicia. A Greek sophist of about 200 A. D.

Antiochus of Ascalon. A Greek Platonist who lived in the first half of the 1st century B.C., teaching in Athens, Alexandria, and Rome. The friend and teacher of Cicero ; the pupil and later the successor of Philo as head of the New Academy. He taught philosophy in Athens and later in Alexandria.

He sought to refute the scepticism of Philo and Carneades, and to unite the principles of the New Academy with Stoicism.

Antiochus of Laodicea. A sceptic of the 1st or 2nd century; disciple of Zeuxis.

Antiochus of Saba or **Seba.** He lived in the early part of the 7th century and wrote a treatise on Christian morals.

Antipathy [Gr. ἀντί, against, + πάθος, feeling]: Ger. *Abneigung, Antipathie*; Fr. *antipathie*; Ital. *antipatia.* A deep-seated and unreasoning mental aversion. See APPE-TENCE.

Antipathy falls under the general history of IMPULSE (q.v.). It has reference to an object, generally an individual person, toward which the aversion is felt. Its unreasoning character is expressed often by the words 'unaccount-able,' 'unreasonable,' 'instinctive,' and even 'physical' (when the physical signs of aversion are marked). As contrasted with aversion, it is intensive.

It arises (1) through association of ideas (Spinoza), or (2) from inherited predisposi-tion. (J.M.B.–K.G.)

Antisthenes. Lived probably in the later part of the 5th and early part of the 4th cen-turies B.C. Founder of the Cynic school of Greek philosophers. A friend and pupil of Socrates, teacher of Diogenes, but hostile to Plato.

Antitheistic Theories. More important philosophical theories which oppose THEISM (q.v.), more particularly PANTHEISM (q.v.) and MATERIALISM (q.v.). (J.M.B.)

Antithesis [Gr. ἀντί, against, + θέσις, thesis]: Ger. *Antithese*; Fr. *antithèse*; Ital. *antitesi.* Logical or verbal opposition; also, the second of two opposed propositions, the first of which is the thesis. See THESIS, OPPOSITION, and HEGELIAN TERMINOLOGY.

Anxiety [Lat. *anxius*, anxious, from *angor*, distress]: Ger. *Angst, Beängstigung*; Fr. *an-xiété, délire anxieux, inquiétude*; Ital. *ansietà.* (1) Relatively strong apprehension or fear of the type described under HOPE AND DESPAIR (q.v.).

(2) Pathological: solicitude, mental distress or agitation; either in dread or anticipation of some sorrow or trial, or as a general appre-hensiveness of misfortune. Its specific expres-sions may be recognized in the worried aspect of the features and attitude, and in a feeling of constriction and distress in the praecordial region. It is a frequent symptom in various forms of nervous weakness and of mental disease. (J.J.)

It characterizes conditions of degeneracy, and is a symptom of Morel's 'emotional delirium' —délire émotif. (L.M.)

Literature: cf. V. MAGNAN, Recherches sur les Centres nerveux (2nd series); and Leçons cliniques sur les Maladies mentales (1893); Mosso, Fear (Eng. trans.). (L.M.)

Apagogue (in logic) [Gr. ἀπαγωγή]: see REDUCTIO AD ABSURDUM.

A parte ante and **A parte post** [Lat.]. Scholastic expressions for those aspects of the eternal life of God whereby it is thought as without limits in the past (ante) and in the future (post). Cf. ETERNITY OF GOD. (J.M.B.)

Apathy [Gr. ἀ + παθεῖν, to suffer, feel]: Ger. *Apathie*; Fr. *apathie*; Ital. *apatia.* Lack or suppression of normal emotional sensibility.

It is a frequent symptom in conditions of physical and nervous weakness as well as of mental impairment. It appears in the mental states of MELANCHOLIA (q.v.) when character-ized by stupor rather than by agitation; and in states of dementia. See Féré, *Pathol. des émotions* (1892); cf. NEURASTHENIA. (J.J.)

Apathy (in ethics). The being unmoved by any motive other than reason.

Apathy expresses the negative ideal of the wise man in the Stoic philosophy. The wise man is regarded as unmoved by the effects which external excitations produce upon the feelings. In this consists the rule or hegemony of reason in the soul. Reason (νοῦς), seeing that the violence of the πάθη is contrary to its nature, refuses to be hurried along by them. The wise man thus overcomes the impulses which external stimuli tend to originate, and prevents them from becoming his πάθη. In overcoming these impulses his personality re-mains unmoved. Pleasure or pain may arise: but, as he refuses to call pleasure good or pain evil, he remains self-sufficient.

A similar conception appears in modern writers, e. g. Spinoza; and it appears as a general characteristic of ORIENTAL PHILO-SOPHY (q.v.). But the modern use of the term apathy is rather popular than technical; although it has the same signification of emotionlessness.

Literature: ZELLER, Philos. d. Griechen, III. i. 8; and cf. STOICISM. (W.R.S.)

Apeiron [Gr. τὸ ἄπειρον]. The unlimited or indeterminate of Anaximander. See PRE-SOCRATIC PHILOSOPHY, and GREEK TERMINO-LOGY. Cf. the citations in Eisler, *Wörterb. d. philos. Begriffe*, sub verbo. (J.M.B.)

Apelt, Ernst Friedrich. (1812–59.) Professor of metaphysics at Jena; writer on induction, metaphysics, and the philosophy of religion. Studied under J. F. Fries, adopting his method.

Aphakia [Gr. ἀ + φακός, lentil, taken for lens]: Ger. *Aphakie*; Fr. *aphacie*; Ital. *afachia*. Absence of the crystalline lens in the eye; the condition may result from an operation for cataract. See VISION (defects of). (J.J.)

Aphasia [Gr. ἀ + φάναι, speak]: Ger. *Aphasie*; Fr. *aphasie*; Ital. *afasia, disfasia*. Loss or impairment of any or all of the faculties concerned in the understanding or use of spoken or written language; such loss being dependent upon injury to the nervous centres involved, and being independent of any serious mental incapacity, and of any disease or paralysis of the organs concerned in articulation.

The term is thus a most general one, and includes the various forms of speech defect—sensory and motor, complete and partial, defects in speaking and in comprehension, in reading and writing—that depend upon a lesion in any of the centres involved, a breaking down of the connection between any two of these centres or of the paths entering or leaving them; or again upon an impairment of the imitative and reflex functions of speech. The term has been used in more specialized and somewhat different senses, but the usage here given is at once the most useful and general. Dysphasia is sometimes used as synonymous with aphasia. For an account of the various forms of aphasia and all other details see SPEECH AND ITS DEFECTS. (J.J.–J.M.B.)

Aphasia (motor): Ger. *motorische Aphasie*; Fr. *aphasie motrice, aphasie de Broca, aphémie*; Ital. *afasia motrice, afasia del tipo Broca*. Loss or impairment of the power to express oneself in spoken or written language, due not to a defect in articulation or in general intelligence, but to an inability to effect the proper innervations for language or to reinstate the proper KINAESTHETIC EQUIVALENTS (q.v.) of the muscular order.

It is used in contrast with sensory aphasia, and is the form of aphasia most frequently associated with the general term. Its relations to other forms of speech defect are considered under SPEECH AND ITS DEFECTS (q.v.). (J.J.–J.M.B.)

Aphasia (sensory): Ger. *sensorische Aphasie*; Fr. *aphasie sensorielle*; Ital. *afasia sensoriale, afasia del tipo Wernicke*. Loss or impairment of the power to comprehend spoken or written language, either (1) purely

sensory, as in PSYCHIC BLINDNESS or DEAFNESS (q.v.) for words, or (2) amnesic, due to impairment or loss of verbal memories other than muscular.

Theoretically, it is independent of any defect of sensation or articulation. It is contrasted with motor aphasia, and has intimate and important relations to the other factors of language which are considered under SPEECH AND ITS DEFECTS (q.v.). (J.J.–J.M.B.)

Aphemia [Gr. ἀ + φήμη, voice]: Ger. *Aphemie*; Fr. *aphémie*; Ital. *afemia*. Loss or impairment of the power of vocal speech; practically equivalent to motor aphasia, which term has in large measure been substituted for aphemia. Aphemia is used in slightly different senses. (Cf. Trousseau, *Leç. cliniques*; Tamburini, *Disturbi del linguaggio* (1875); Bastian, *Aphasia*, 62, 180.) The term was (Broca) and is sometimes used as synonymous with aphasia in general, but this use is not desirable. For its relations to the various forms of aphasia, see SPEECH AND ITS DEFECTS. (J.J.–J.M.B.)

Aphonia or **Aphony** [Gr. ἀ + φωνή, voice]: Ger. *Stimmlosigkeit, Aphonie*; Fr. *aphonie*; Ital. *afonia*. Loss of the power of vocal utterance, due not, as in aphasia, to not knowing how to speak, nor, as in anarthria, to inability to articulate, but to the inability to produce the sound, from paralysis or imperfect approximation of the vocal cords. Whispering is usually possible.

Hysterical aphonia or mutism ('mutisme hystérique'—Janet, *Les Stigmates mentaux des Hystériques*) is a term applied to this condition when occurring as a symptom in cases of HYSTERIA (q.v.). Baldwin has suggested (*Ment. Devel. in the Child and the Race*, chap. xiv. § 1) the term Psychic Dumbness, co-ordinate with psychic blindness and deafness. Cf. MUTISM, and SPEECH AND ITS DEFECTS. (J.J.–L.M.)

Aphrasia [Gr. ἀ + φράσις, speech]: Ger. *Aphrasie*; Fr. *aphrasie*; Ital. *afrasia*. (1) A disorder of speech in which the patient can speak single words or expressions, but cannot make use of connected phrases; in this sense partially equivalent (Kussmaul) to acataphasia. In French, 'acataphasie' designates incapacity to construe phrases, in opposition to 'autonomasie,' difficulty of associating words.

(2) Most frequently used to denote speechlessness due to lack of intelligence, or the stubborn silence due to voluntary restraint or some insane motive for not speaking (aphasia

paranoica). Cf. Séglas, *Troubles du langage*; Morselli, *Semej. malat. ment.*, ii.

(3) Used by Broca as synonymous with aphasia in general (Tuke). Cf. SPEECH AND ITS DEFECTS. (J.J.–P.J.–J.M.B.)

Aphthongia [Gr. *à* + *φθόγγος*, voice, sound]: Ger. *Aphthongie*; Fr. (not used); Ital. *aftongia*. A term used by Kussmaul. See ALALIA. (E.M.)

Aplasy or **Aplasia** [Gr. *à* + *πλάσις*, formation]: Ger. *Aplasie*; Fr. (not in use); Ital. *aplasia*. Failure of an organ or tissue to develop by reason of operative interference or disease. See ATROPHY. (H.H.)

Apocalypse [Gr. *ἀπό* + *καλύπτειν*, to reveal]: Ger. *Apokalypse*; Fr. *Apocalypse*; Ital. *Apocalisse*. In the history of religion, the name given to certain Jewish and Jewish-Christian writings, extending from the 'Book of Enoch' (200 B.C.) to the 'Sibylline Oracles' (350 A.D.).

Apocalyptic literature fills the gap between the prophetic and the Christian writings. It betrays several leading characteristics. (1) Interest centres in a supramundane sphere. (2) A pessimistic view of the world prevails. (3) The future is predetermined by God, i.e. the interpretation is mechanical. (4) Authorship is pseudonymous. The literature was called forth by the difficulty of reconciling present suffering with continued confidence in the divine order of the universe.

Literature: SCHÜRER, Hist. of the Jewish People, Div. II. iii. 44 f. (Eng. trans.); THOMSON, Books that influenced our Lord; DRUMMOND, The Jewish Messiah; HILGENFELD, Die jüdische Apokalyptik. The best account of this subject is by CHARLES, art. Apocalyptic Literature, in Cheyne's Encyc. Biblica. (R.M.W.)

Apodictic (-tical) (spelt also apodeiktic) [Gr. *ἀποδεικτικός*, demonstrative]: Ger. *apodictisch*; Fr. *apodictique*; Ital. *apodittico*. Capable of clear demonstration, hence necessary, as applied to statements, truths, or judgments. Kant distinguishes judgments as problematical, assertorical, and apodictical, the last being judgments expressing necessary truth. So a syllogism in which the conclusion follows with logical certainty is apodictical.

Literature: MANSEL, Prolegom. Logica, vii. 252; CAIRD, Crit. Philos. of Kant, II. iii. 242. (J.M.B.)

Apogamy [Gr. *ἀπό* + *γάμος*, marriage]: Ger. *Apogamie*; Fr. *apogamie*; Ital. *apogamia*. For (1) the foreign equivalents are not in general use. (1) That indiscriminate mode of ISOLATION (q.v.) which gives rise to separate breeding in an isolated group of animals. Cf. HOMOGAMY. The term was suggested by Romanes (*Darwin and after Darwin*, iii., 1897). (C.LL.M.)

(2) A term also used by botanists to denote the substitution of a vegetative, asexual, mode of reproduction for the usual sexual mode. (E.S.G.)

Apokatastasis [Gr. *ἀπό* + *κατά*, down, + *ἱστάναι*, to set]: Ger. *Apokatastase*; Fr. *rétablissement universel*; Ital. *apocatastasi*. The doctrine which teaches the restitution of all sinful beings to the life of happiness with God (Acts, iii. 21).

Origen is the originator of this teaching, but he regarded it as esoteric only. Gregory of Nazianzen and other Eastern theologians also advocated it. Erigena was its first supporter in the West. He was followed by certain of the Mystics, such as the Brethren of the Free Spirit; by some of the Anabaptists; by F. C. Oetinger, the Pietist; and by Schleiermacher. Rothe and Martensen are its most formidable modern critics. It is closely connected with UNIVERSALISM (q.v.).

Literature: the article in Herzog's Real-Encyc.; HARNACK, Hist. of Dogma (Eng. trans.), ii. 275, iii. 186 f., vii. 128 f. (R.M.W.)

Apolar Cell: Ger. *apolare Zelle*; Fr. *cellule apolaire*; Ital. *cella apolare*. A cell without processes. Such are the youngest NEUROBLASTS (q.v.). Probably no functional nerve-cells are apolar. See NERVOUS SYSTEM (Histology). (H.H.)

Apollinarianism: Ger. *Apollinarismus*; Fr. *Apollinarisme*; Ital. *Apollinarismo*. The name given to one of the many attempted solutions of the difficulties incident to the union of two natures, a divine and a human, in one person—Christ. So called after its originator, Apollinarius the Younger, bishop of Laodicea (d. 390).

From being an orthodox upholder of Athanasianism, Apollinarius promulgated the heretical theory that two natures, one altogether divine and one altogether human, could not be unified in a single personality. To get over this problem, Apollinarius reduced the human element to a body and an animal (or irrational) soul, while he held that the Logos took the place of the human (or rational) soul. Hence the heretical conclusion, that Christ was no more than a man to whom God has given inspiration. The doctrine met with universal opposition and soon gave way before the NESTORIAN CONTROVERSY (q.v.).

Literature: DRÄSCHKE, Apollinarius v.

Laodicea (in Gebhardt and Harnack, Texte u. Untersuchungen); HARNACK, Hist. of Dogma (Eng. trans.), chaps. iii, iv, especially chap. iii. (R.M.W.)

Apollonius of Chalcis. A Stoic philosopher who lived in the 1st and 2nd centuries A.D. Invited to Rome because of his moral attainments to teach Marcus Aurelius, who commends his powers.

Apollonius Tyanaeus. A Neo-Pythagorean philosopher, native of Cappadocia, who lived in the time of Christ. He has been compared by enemies of Christianity to Christ, for his miracles. Probably a moral reformer in Greece and Rome. He was accorded divine honours for four centuries.

Apologetics [Gr. ἀπολογητική]: Ger. *Apologetik*; Fr. *apologétique*; Ital. *apologetica*. One of the three main divisions of systematic theology. It is used in two senses —a wider and a narrower. (1) In the wider signification it includes any consideration that may be adduced in support of the particular system for which apology is being made. (2) In the narrower and usual acceptation it includes all pleas for the divine origin and authority of Christianity.

Apologetics naturally takes a prominent position when Christianity is the object of attack. Hence the main periods of its history are :—(1) the Early Church, with Origen's *Against Celsus* as the typical work; (2) the 18th century, with the Deists and Butler as conspicuous actors; (3) the 19th century, especially since 1835—the year of Strauss's *Leben Jesu*—from which time may also be dated the scientific movement in its Positivist aspects. It should be noted that, till the time of Strauss, apologetics occupies a very small place in German religious literature.

Literature: A. B. BRUCE, Apologetics; FLINT, Sermons and Addresses, 299 f.; ORR, Christ. View of God and the World; WENLEY, Preparation for Christianity; the relative art. in Herzog's Real-Encyc., where the literature is given at length. (R.M.W.)

Apology (Christian): see APOLOGETICS.

Apoplexy [Gr. ἀπό, off, + πλήσσειν, to strike]: Ger. *Schlag, Apoplexie*; Fr. *ictus, apoplexie*; Ital. *colpo, apoplessia*. A sudden seizure, or 'stroke,' involving loss of consciousness, sensation, and the power of movement, due to the effusion of blood in the brain (cerebral haemorrhage). The term is also used to describe a similar group of symptoms due to other causes, particularly stoppage of a blood-vessel—thrombus or embolism.

During the apoplectic attack there is usually profound coma; the face is flushed, the lips livid, the head and neck in perspiration, the pulse full and slow; the muscles are relaxed, the limbs dropping when raised, as if inert. A further characteristic symptom is the conjugate deviation of the eyes with rotation of the head and neck. While the typical apoplectic attack comes without warning, other forms of it are preceded by such premonitory symptoms as headache, dizziness, numbness, twitching, &c. The seriousness of the attack depends largely upon the place and size of the lesion; and it is frequently fatal. When recovery takes place mental symptoms may ensue similar to those of senile dementia, or mental weakness not amounting in degree and kind to a condition properly termed insanity in the legal sense. Conditions of depression or excitement with delusions may supervene with progressive dementia and emotional weakness. Paralysis, particularly on one side of the body (hemiplegia), is quite constantly present, and some form of aphasic disorder is equally likely to occur. A considerable number of cases of disorders of speech (see SPEECH AND ITS DEFECTS) are those in which the aphasia was sequential to apoplexy.

Literature: ROSS, Nervous Dis.; GRASSET, Traité du système nerveux (with bibliography); ROBERTSON, art. Post-apoplectic Insanity, in Tuke's Dict. of Psychol. Med.; LEVOFF, Étude sur les troubles intellectuels liés aux lésions circonscrites du cerveau; MINGAZZINI, Riv. di Freniat. (1897). (J.J.)

A posteriori [Lat.]: see A PRIORI.

Apostolics [Gr. ἀπό, away, + στέλλειν, to send forth]: Ger. *Pastoraltheologie*; Fr. *théologie pastorale*; Ital. *teologia pastorale*. The division of Practical Theology devoted to questions concerning the propagation of religion—to missions, in short. Other names for the same subject are Halieutics and Keryktics. (R.M.W.)

Apotheosis [Gr. ἀποθεοῦν, to deify; ἀπό + θεός, god]: Ger. *Apotheose, Vergötterung*; Fr. *apothéose*; Ital. *apoteosi*. The name given to the reception of a great man, or ruler, into the Pantheon.

The most familiar case is that of Augustus Caesar. For this there were precedents in the East, in Egypt, in Greece, and even in Rome. The general sentiment is best set forth in Virgil and Horace (especially *Carm.*, iii. 5; iv. 5, 14).

Literature: FUSTEL DE COULANGES, La

Cité Antique, 21 f.; FRIEDLÄNDER, Darstellung a. d. Sittengesch. Roms, iii; HAUSRATH, Hist. of New Test. Times, and The Times of the Apostles, ii. 31 f.; BOISSIER, La Religion Romaine d'Auguste aux Antonins, i. 109 f.; BACK, De Graecorum caeremoniis in quibus deorum homines vice fungebantur; NITZSCH, De apotheosis apud Graecos vulgatae caussis dissert.; DEL MAR, The Worship of Augustus Caesar. (R.M.W.)

Apparatus (psychophysical): see LABORATORY AND APPARATUS.

Apparition [Lat. *apparere*, to appear]: Ger. *Geistererscheinung, Gespenst*; Fr. *apparition*; Ital. *apparizione*. An unusual, marvellous, or preternatural appearance or phenomenon. See HALLUCINATION, and ILLUSION. (J.J.)

Appearance: see PHENOMENON, and SEMBLANCE.

Apperception [Lat. *ad* + *percipere*, to perceive]: Ger. *Apperception*; Fr. *apperception*; Ital. *appercezione*. The process of attention in so far as it involves interaction between the presentation of the object attended to, on the one hand, and the total preceding conscious content, together with preformed mental dispositions, on the other hand. (G.F.S.—J.M.B.)

Leibnitz, who introduced the concept of apperception into philosophy, understood by it the apprehension of an object as distinguished from and related to the self. His actual meaning is practically coincident with that of attention in modern psychology.

Kant's view resembles that of Leibnitz. He distinguishes transcendental and empirical apperception. Transcendental apperception is awareness of an object as involving self-consciousness. But the self of transcendental apperception is not the concrete self as constituted by a flow of specific states and processes; it is the pure subject implied in the base possibility of an object's being presented. Empirical apperception, on the other hand, is a cognition which has for its special object the concrete self with its states and processes. Cf. KANTIAN TERMINOLOGY, and KANTIANISM.

The treatment of apperception by Herbart forms a turning-point in the history of the subject. Apperception, for him, is the process by which a mass of presentations (Apperceptions-masse) assimilates relatively new elements, the whole forming a system (Apperceptions-system). The new material assimilated may be either given in sensation, or reproduced by the internal working of the psychological mechanism; and attention, in the broad sense of noticing an object, coincides in the main, but not altogether, with the apperceptive process. Relation to the self is, on this view, involved in apperception because, according to Herbart, the self is a product constituted by the mental modifications left behind by previous experience. Wundt's theory of apperception emphasizes the formal or functional side of the attention-process and gives a definition largely in terms of conation. It seems to include both the Leibnitzian and Herbartian views. According to Pillsbury (*Amer. J. of Psychol.*, viii. No. 3), Wundt's apperception consists of four elements. '(1) Increase of clearness in the idea directly before the mind, accompanied by the immediate feeling of activity (Thätigkeitsgefühl); (2) inhibition of other ideas; (3) muscular strain sensations, with the feelings connected with them, intensifying the primary feeling of activity; (4) the reflex effect of these strain sensations, intensifying the idea apperceived.' Our definition follows Herbartian lines in giving prominent place to the 'mechanism of presentations,' i.e. the psychical interactions involved in the process of attention.

Literature: LEIBNITZ, Princ. de la Nat. (Erdmann), 4 Opp., 715a, and Monadologie, 23–30 (Erdmann, 707); KANT, Krit. d. reinen Vernunft; HERBART, Psychol. als Wiss., zweiter Theil, erster Absch., cap. 5; VOLKMANN, Lehrb. d. Psychol., ii. 175–211; STEINTHAL, Einleitung in die Psychol. u. Sprachwiss., 164–263; ERDMANN, Vtljsch. f. wiss. Philos., x. 320; WUNDT, Physiol. Psychol. (successive editions); LIPPS, Grundthatsachen des Seelenlebens, 390–410; BALDWIN, Handb. of Psychol., Senses and Intellect, 65–6, and Ment. Devel. in the Child and the Race, 308 ff.; STOUT, Analytic Psychol., ii. chap. viii; PILLSBURY, Amer. J. of Psychol., viii. 3; STAUDE, Philos. Stud., i. 149 ff.; HEINRICH, Mod. Theorien d. Aufmerksamkeit; VILLA, Psicol. Contemp. (1899); EISLER, Wörterb. d. philos. Begriffe, sub verbo (with many quotations). (G.F.S.—J.M.B.)

Apperception (in education). The interpretation of new knowledge in the light of that previously obtained: mental assimilation.

The term is largely used by educational writers to characterize the synthesis of new with old experiences. New acquisitions of knowledge become significant only to the extent of the interpreting power of our former acquisitions. This being the case, the apperceptive power of the mind is a constantly developing capacity as the child increases in years, knowledge, and mental alertness. Modern child-study emphasizes the fact that the subject-matter of instruction, together with the sequence of its topics, and the time of its presentation, should be governed by the child's power to apperceive. Furthermore, methods of teaching and of moral training should take their cue from the same changeable power. See METHOD (in education).

Literature: works in modern psychology; LANGE, Apperception; DE GARMO, Essentials of Meth., 24–44; MCMURRY, Gen. Meth., 106–21; HARRIS, Herbart and Pestalozzi compared, Educ. Rev. (May, 1893).   (C. DE G.)

Appetence [Lat. *appetentia*]: Ger. *Streben* (*nach Erlangung eines lustbetonten Zustandes*), *Begierde* (Eisler); Fr. *appétition*; Ital. *appetenza* (appetite), *desiderio* (desire). Conations which find satisfaction in some positive state or result are called appetences. An appetence may be either innate or acquired. It is contrasted with aversion, which has for its terminus the avoidance or removal of some disturbing condition. Cf. CONATION, IMPULSE, and APPETITE; also TERMINOLOGY (German).   (G.F.S.–J.M.B.)

Appetite [Lat. *ad + petere*, to seek]: Ger. *sinnliches Begehren, Verlangen*; Fr. *appétit, besoin physique*; Ital. *appetito*. (1) An organic need represented in consciousness by certain sensations described below. (2) Applied to conative tendencies of all sorts, for which the terms appetence (or appetency) and impulse are better. (3) 'Acquired appetite' is used for tendencies either physical or mental which have arisen in the individual's experience. This usage is not good; it should be limited to the physical.

Appetite is distinguished from instinct, in that it shows itself at first in connection with the life of the organism itself, and does not wait for an external stimulus, but appears and craves satisfaction. The movements, however, by which an appetite is gratified are mostly reflex and instinctive. For example, the child has the imperfect instinct of sucking to satisfy the appetite for food. Appetite is not equivalent to impulse, in that the organic process is well defined and deep-seated, and is only to a very limited degree subject to voluntary control or modification. The appetites generally recognized are those of hunger, thirst, and sex; yet the need of air, the need of exercise, and the need of sleep come under the definition.

Psychologically the progress of an appetite is about as follows : (1) A state of vague unrest involving, when extreme and when satisfaction is deferred, painful sensations of definite quality and location (largely in the organs by which the gratification is to be secured). (2) Pleasant sensations coming from the organs securing the appropriate stimulation, together with sensations from the reflex motor processes which are involved in the organic reaction. (3) Presentations or ideas of the objects or events which afford the stimulation; these modify consciousness on future occurrences of the appetite. (4) A complex state of tension of all the motor and other elements whenever the appetite is aroused either (*a*) by the direct organic condition of need, or (*b*) indirectly through the presence or memory of the object.

The gratification of an appetite is pleasurable both in immediate, more local, and generally in its remote, more systemic, effects; thus, in the case of hunger, both the taste and the general digestion effects are pleasant.

Literature: REID, Active Powers, Essay III, Pt. II. chap. i; STEWART, Active Powers, Bk. I. chap. i; BAIN, Senses and Intellect (4th ed.), 360 f.; BEAUNIS, Les Sensations Internes, chap. ii ff. (Besoins); LADD, Psychol. Descrip. and Explan., 576.   (J.M.B.–G.F.S.)

Applied Ethics: see ETHICS, and SOCIAL ETHICS.

Appreciation (and **Description**) [Lat. *ad + pretium*, price]: Ger. *Bewerthung, Würdigung*; Fr. *appréciation*; Ital. *apprezzamento*. A way of formulating the distinction between judgments involving value and those of science, which latter pertain to fact.

Terms due to Royce (*Religious Aspect of Philos.*), who brings under them the current oppositions between 'ought' and 'is,' 'practical' and 'pure' reason, ethics and science. The ethics of the matter is discussed à propos of Huxley's *Evolution and Ethics* in papers by several writers in the *International Journal of Ethics* (1895), and the psychology of it is covered, by the present writer, under the broader distinction between 'prospective' and 'retrospective' points of view (*Psychol. Rev.*, Nov. 1895). Cf. ORIGIN vs. NATURE, and see WORTH (also for *Literature*).   (J.M.B., G.F.S.)

Appreciation (economic): see DEPRECIATION.

Apprehension [Lat. *apprehensio*, from *ad + prehendere*, to seize]: Ger. *Auffassung, Apprehension* (Kant); Fr. *appréhension*; Ital. *apprendimento*. (1) The intellectual act or process by which a relatively simple object is understood, grasped, or brought before the mind. (2) A relatively simple or elementary intellectual act itself (without regard to its object), as opposed to a complex act, such as judgment, or a more finished sort of knowledge, such as comprehension. (3) An act of imagination or of presenting to knowledge the image of an object. (4) A comparatively simple belief, understanding, or opinion, especially one for which no explicit reasons are now forthcoming. If such a belief is later judged false it is called a misapprehension. The second meaning given is that to which good usage tends to confine the word, without allowing closer definition. It is thus almost synonymous, for psychology, with bare consciousness of an object. (J.M.B.–G.F.S.)

In Aristotle's theory of the types of knowledge, stress is laid upon the assertion that only judgments are properly true and false, while thought (νοῦς), on precisely its highest levels, deals with objects which it is possible either to grasp directly, or to grasp not at all, but which it is impossible any longer to grasp falsely, or to misjudge, when one knows them. This act of attaining direct acquaintance with truth Aristotle metaphorically calls θιγεῖν, a touching, or direct contact, with truth. It is equivalent to what has often been later called 'intuitive knowledge.' It is compared by Aristotle himself to seeing. (On this Aristotelian usage see Bonitz, *Commentary to Aristotle's Metaphysics, Pars Posterior*, 410, of his edition of that work. The Aristotelian passages in question are especially *De Anima*, iii. 6; *Metaph.*, ii. 10, xii. 7.) The term apprehension, in scholastic usage, is a translation of the Aristotelian θιγεῖν. But the term has been from the outset of its usage extended to apply to various sorts of direct or simple knowledge, or knowledge involving acquaintance with objects, as opposed to complex, indirect, or discursive knowledge. The Aristotelian contrast between the knowledge capable of truth or falsity and the simple knowledge or apprehension incapable of truth or falsity has indeed been frequently retained, at least by more technical usage. But apprehension, even in case of such retention, has meant very frequently not higher grades of intuition, but rather sensory knowledge, or presentation, too simple to be a matter of truth or falsity. And other usage has abandoned altogether the contrast to judgment or belief, so that an apprehension becomes merely a comparatively simple cognition (see Hamilton's note to Reid's *Inquiry*, chap. ii. sect. 3), whether involving judgment or not.

Kant, in the *Critique of Pure Reason*, defines apprehension as the synthetic act whereby the contents of a perception (Anschauung) are given their temporal and spatial form, and are prepared for the higher activity of the understanding. This act is more fully called the 'synthesis of apprehension.' (J.R.)

Apprehension (moral). The APPREHENSION (q. v.) of the moral value of action or character.

This is the most generic term in use for what is more specifically spoken of as moral sense, moral judgment, or CONSCIENCE (q. v.). The term is commonly used so as to convey, less than any other term, any theory as to the specific nature of the power by which moral value is 'apprehended.' (W.R.S.)

Apprenticeship [Lat. *apprehendere*, to learn]: Ger. *Lehrlingswesen*; Fr. *apprentissage*; Ital. *noviziato*. The learning of a trade or craft under a contract which gives the teacher the right to avail himself of the services of the pupil for a specified term—usually a rather long one.

In the middle ages the right to exercise a craft was a valuable legal franchise, and those who enjoyed that right were jealous of any addition to their numbers, which would make their monopoly of the craft less valuable. The craft gilds and other industrial corporations of the middle ages were powerful enough to secure the passage of laws relating to apprenticeship devised in the interest of their monopolies rather than of the public at large. Many of these laws survived the power which had been instrumental in their creation (cf. Adam Smith, *Wealth of Nations*, Bk. I. chap. x). The beginning of the 19th century witnessed the downfall of the obnoxious features of the system. (A.T.H.)

Approbation (moral) [Lat. *approbatio*]: Ger. *ethische Billigung*; Fr. *approbation morale*; Ital. *approvazione morale*. The recognition of conduct or character as morally good.

The term is in most frequent use with Hutcheson and succeeding British moralists, who discuss the questions whether moral approbation is innate or the result of experience of consequences, and how it is related to sensation, to reasoning, and to aesthetic appreciation. Adam Smith (*Theory of the Moral Sentiments*) discusses the social character of moral approbation. It is commonly distinguished from aesthetic appreciation by the differentia that the former does, whereas the latter does not, involve merit or demerit. See CONSCIENCE (also for *Literature*). (W.R.S.)

Appropriation [Lat. *ad + propriare*, to take to oneself]: Ger. *Zueignung*; Fr. *appropriation*; Ital. *appropriazione*. A term used technically by Protestant, especially Calvinistic, theologians with reference to the believer's relation to 'Grace' and to the 'Word of God.' The believer 'appropriates' the 'Grace of the Scriptures' by faith (West, *Shorter Catechism*, quest. 90); he 'appropriates' the 'Word of God' by reading and meditation. Biblical interpretation, conducted in consonance with principles, and applied practically in life, discovers the ground of the appropriation. Cf. FAITH, and HERMENEUTICS. (R.M.W.)

Apraxia [Gr. *à + πράσσειν*, do]: Ger. *Apraxie*; Fr. *apraxie*; Ital. *aprassia*. (1) The loss of the power to use or appreciate the nature of common objects.

It involves no sensory disorder, but a purely psychical one. As aphasia expresses incapacity to handle words correctly, so apraxia expresses a similar incapacity in regard to common objects. The apraxic patient mistakes the use of objects; e.g. he may no longer be able to recognize coins and their use, may mistake a fork for a spoon, or a brush for a cane. The condition is contrasted with ASEMIA (q.v.), in which there is a general receptive defect, and to the condition termed (mental) BLINDNESS (q.v.), the defect in apraxia being primarily motor. Cf. SPEECH AND ITS DEFECTS. (J.J.–J.M.B.)

(2) A term used by Morselli for the loss or suspension of psychomotor activity; a variety of dispraxia, or general derangement of conduct. Other pathological varieties are hyperpraxia, parapraxia, and hypopraxia. See Morselli, *Semej. malat. ment.*, ii. (1895). (E.M.)

Literature: E. CLAPARÈDE, l'erception stéréo-gnostique et stéréo-agnosie, Année Psychol., v. 65 f.; the literature of aphasia given under SPEECH AND ITS DEFECTS (q.v.). (J.J.)

A priori and **A posteriori** (in logic) [Lat.]: Ger., Fr., Ital., the same. A reasoning is *a priori* when it proceeds to the determination of a proposition from or on the ground of the notion in which the essence of a subject, its constitutive marks, is supposed to be given. It is therefore, independent of experience so far as attainment of the conclusion is concerned, being thus DEDUCTIVE (q.v.), and of experience altogether if the notion be itself held to be due to the mind itself. (R.A.)

A posteriori is contrasted with *a priori* in both these meanings. It designates reasoning, which is INDUCTIVE (q.v.), as opposed to deductive, and also applies to notions which are due to experience (i. e. making appeal to experience), rather than to the mind itself. Extended citations from literature on the contrast are to be found in Eisler, *Wörterb. d. philos. Begriffe*. (J.M.B.)

Although the definite use of the contrast *a priori* and *a posteriori* in reference to reasoning goes back only to Albert of Saxony, in the 14th century (cf. Prantl, *Gesch. d. Logik*, iv. 78), the contrast itself is as old as Aristotle. Reasoning *a priori* is that based on insight into the essence or form of the subject, an insight which might in order of time be preceded, even necessarily preceded, by the collection of particulars from sense perception, but which, once attained, constitutes the source of necessary predications respecting the subject. The Aristotelian doctrine, interpreted by such Platonizing moderns as Cudworth, who identified the essence with innate ideas (see *Eternal and Immutable Morality*, Bk. III. chap. iii. § 5), is evidently closely akin to the later Kantian view, the distinctive mark of which is its definite statement of what it is that mind contributes from itself to experience, and how the contributing is to be conceived. In Hume and Clarke may be seen the more special sense of *a priori* as that which can be evolved, without appeal to special experience, by inspection of ideas themselves. The term is used very sparingly by Hume in the *Treatise on Human Nature*, and frequently in the *Essays*. Cf. KANTIAN TERMINOLOGY. (R.A.)

Aprosexia [Gr. *à + προσέχειν*, to give heed]: Ger. *Aprosexie*; Fr. *aprosexie*; Ital. *aprosessia*. Inability to fix the attention. See ATTENTION (defects of). (J.J.)

Aptitude [Lat. *aptitudo*, from *aptus*, fit]: Ger. *Begabung, Neigung*; Fr. *aptitude*; Ital. *attitudine*. A natural or acquired capacity for a certain kind of activity.

Like the words faculty, trait, nisus, bent, the term usually indicates an endowment of nature strengthened, it may be, by training, experience, or circumstance; as an aptitude for sports, for games of skill, for music, for business affairs, &c. In connection with the problems of human faculties—their nature and distribution, the parts played by nature and nurture in our intellectual growth—the term becomes significant. (J.J.)

Aquinas, Thomas. (1227–74.) Of royal family, he became a Dominican at the age of sixteen, and was instructed by Albertus Magnus. Refused ecclesiastical preferment, and spent his life in teaching and writing. He was canonized in 1323. See ST. THOMAS (philosophy of).

Arabian Philosophy : see SCHOLASTICISM, MOHAMMEDANISM, AVERROISM, and AVICENNISM.

Arbitrage : Ger. *Arbitrage* ; Fr. *arbitrage* ; Ital. *arbitraggio.* The profit which can be realized from the difference in market price of the same article in different places at the same time ; contrasted with the *speculative* profit due to the variation in price at different times.

Before the invention of the telegraph the operations of arbitrage required great skill and involved large possible profit or loss. At present the conditions of different markets are so far known to buyers and sellers the world over that the risks and profits of arbitrage have been greatly reduced. But at the same time, the sphere of operation of arbitrage brokers has extended itself more widely than ever. (A.T.H.)

Arbitration [Lat. *arbitratio*] : Ger. *schiedsrichterliche Beurteilung und Entscheidung* ; Fr. *arbitrage* ; Ital. *arbitrato.* The determination of a matter in dispute by a third person acting by authority voluntarily conferred upon him by the agreement of the parties to the difference.

Its voluntary character distinguishes it from judicial proceedings. Statutes exist in many states by which, if the parties who agree to submit their dispute to arbitration agree further to ask the aid of the Government to enforce the award (or sentence), such aid may be given by judicial process. This is sometimes, though incorrectly, termed Compulsory Arbitration. The arbitration is not compulsory, but at the voluntary request of the parties compulsory force is given to the award.

The *actiones arbitrariae* in Roman law paved the way for modern arbitration. In those the *judex*, though appointed by the court, was called an arbiter, and could decide according to his view of justice and equity, and grant specific relief if money damages would not afford adequate redress. He was appointed on the defendant's demand (*Instit. of Just.*, iv. 6, *de Actionibus*, 31 ; Gaius, iv. § 163). (S.E.B.)

International Arbitration, or arbitration between nations, does not differ in principle from that between private individuals, except that there can be no mode of enforcing the award by law. Their agreement to a resort to arbitration (submission, *compromis*) implies, however, a mutual engagement to submit in good faith to the decision rendered, provided it be one within the jurisdiction conferred upon the arbitrators. See Title IV,

De l'arbitrage international, of the 'Décisions de la Conférence de la Paix,' held at the Hague in 1899 ; Corsi, *Arbitrato Internazionale* (Pisa, 1893) ; Darby, *Int. Tribunals* (London, Peace Society, 1899).

Arborization [Lat. *arbor*, tree] : Ger. *Endbäumchen* ; Fr. *arborisation* ; Ital. *arborisazione.* Terminal ramifications of the processes of a NEUROCYTE (q. v.) or nerve-cell. See NERVOUS SYSTEM (histology). (H.H.)

Arcana [Lat. *arcanus*, hidden] : Ger. *Arcana* ; Fr. *mystères* ; Ital. *arcani*, (*l'*) *occulto.* Applied generally to anything hidden or unknown, but usually to the esoteric. Used most frequently now by esoteric Buddhists and by theosophists.

The chief historical interest centres in the *arcana disciplina* of the early Christian Church. Converts from other systems went through a lengthened catechumenate. When they were so far instructed as to be ready for baptism, the *arcana disciplina*—consisting of the Creed and the Lord's Prayer—were made known to them. The more essential parts of the service were closed to catechumens. About the 6th century, owing to the altered circumstances of the Church, this custom seems to have lapsed. Cf. MAGIC. (R.M.W.)

Arcesilaus or **Arkesilaus.** (316–241 B.C.) A Greek sceptical philosopher; founder of the New or Middle Academy. He studied philosophy under Theophrastus and Polemon. Cf. SCHOOLS OF GREECE.

Archaeology and **Prehistoric Archaeology** [Gr. ἀρχαῖος, ancient, + λόγος, discourse, lore] : Ger. (*prähistorische*) *Archäologie* ; Fr. *archéologie* (*préhistorique*); Ital. *archeologia preistorica.* Archaeology is the science which attempts to reconstruct the history of man from the relics and records of the past.

While a generic similarity of purpose characterizes the various departments of archaeology, they differ in method and in the character of their fundamental problems according to the nature of the material relics at command. The most important distinction is that which separates prehistoric (a word due to Sir Daniel Wilson) from historic archaeology ; for in spite of the fundamental continuity between the two periods, the presence in the latter period of written records and the endless possibilities of illumination which a civilization capable of written records may reveal, and the total absence of these in the former period, result in significant differences of method, material, and problems. Prehistoric archaeology, considered as a department of ANTHROPOLOGY

(q. v.), finds its material in the relics of earth and bone, of stone and metals, of fibre or sinew, which have escaped the ravages of time, and perhaps by their geological location, or internal evidence of conjunction with animal remains and the like, suggest the period of their original construction or deposit. The two most general problems in regard to prehistoric man are the determination of the time of his first appearance, and the division of the periods that elapsed between then and his emergence into historic times. The presence of quaternary man coeval with the mammoth at the opening of the glacial epoch is quite universally admitted; while his presence in still earlier geological periods, though by no means impossible, has not as yet been satisfactorily established. The oldest age indicated by human relics is termed the Stone Age, and is subdivided into the palaeolithic or old stone age (the pleistocene period), and the neolithic or new stone age (the prehistoric period). These names are derived from the character of man's most primitive implements, the palaeolithic (usually chipped) being of a cruder type of workmanship than the neolithic (frequently polished). These, especially when found *in situ* and in connection with the relics of man himself and his monuments, mounds, graves, kitchen-middens, and the like, serve to fix a more or less definite grade of development, which, however, indefinitely shades into, and may be overlapped by, the neolithic age. Relics of palaeolithic man have been found in almost all portions of the earth where competent investigation has been carried on, and frequently in situations suggestive, if not demonstrative, of a fairly definite location in time.

Yet it should be mentioned that recent discussion has called in question the validity of the criterion between chipped and polished implements as an index of sequence in time; for there is some evidence not only that the two arts may have been carried on together, but that, with certain materials or in certain places, the rubbing may have been more primitive than the chipping. Caution demands that stone implements of a palaeolithic appearance without other corroborative evidence should not be too readily accepted as belonging to the earliest period of man's occupation.

Following the Stone Age was the age of metal, which is usually divided in Europe into the Bronze and Iron ages; the former characterizing the general period of culture concomitant with simple metallurgic processes, while the latter suggests a period of far greater advance. The former undoubtedly overlaps the neolithic period, while the age of metal naturally forms an easy transition to the culture stages of historic times. The problems here discussed as prehistoric archaeology are not infrequently considered under the heads of ETHNOLOGY or ETHNOGRAPHY (q.v.).

Literature: KEANE, Ethnology (1896), 442; SIR DANIEL WILSON, art. Archaeology, in Encyc. Brit. (9th ed., 1875); and Prehistoric Man (2 vols., 1875); LUBBOCK, Prehistoric Times (4th ed., 1878), 655; J. C. SOUTHALL, The Epoch of the Mammoth (1878), 430; W. BOYD DAWKINS, Early Man in Britain (1880), 537; N. JOLY, Man before Metals (1883), 365; DE BAYE, L'Archéol. Préhistorique; G. DE MORTILLET, Le Préhistorique (1883); MORSELLI, Antropol. gen. (1890); SOPHUS MÜLLER, Nordische Alterthumskunde (1898); NADAILLAC, L'Amér. Préhistorique (1883); RANKE, Der Mensch (2nd ed., 1896); HÖRNES, Urgesch. des Menschen (1892). For more detailed and special works see the literature under ANTHROPOLOGY.   (J.J.)

Arche [Gr. ἀρχή]. Aristotle's term for first principle or source, in the sense of formal and final CAUSE (q.v.), in his scheme of causes.   (J.M.B.)

Archelaus of Miletus. Surnamed Physicus. Lived about 450 B.C. A Greek philosopher devoted to physical science. The pupil of Anaxagoras, and probably the teacher of Socrates.

Archetype [Gr. ἀρχή, chief, + τύπος, form]: Ger. *Archetyp*, *Urbild*; Fr. *archétype*; Ital. *archetipo*. A Platonic word meaning the perfect or absolute idea (cf. PLATONISM, and IDEALISM) of each thing after its kind. See references to Plato (*Republic*, Jowett's trans., vi. 507, and ibid. v. 472, and others in Fleming-Calderwood, *Vocab. of Philos.*, sub verbo).   (J.M.B.)

Archimedes. (cir. 287-12 B.C.) The greatest geometer of antiquity. He is said to have been a pupil of Canon of Egypt, and a relative of Hiero II, king of Syracuse. He was profoundly versed in mechanics and hydrostatics.

Architectonic: see ARCHITECTURE. Applied to principles of construction and to the science of such principles in all theoretical work. By a secondary meaning it is applied to what is extremely schematic, formal, and logical. Kant's usage illustrates the first meaning, and his philosophy illustrates the second.   (J.M.B.)

Architecture [Gr. ἀρχι + τέχνη, art] : Ger. *Baukunst*; Fr. *architecture*; Ital. *architettura*. The science and art of building. See CLASSIFICATION (of the fine arts).

Archytas. Lived about 350 B.C. Greek philosopher, mathematician, and general. He belonged to the Pythagorean school; is said to have been the first to apply geometry to mechanics, and to have saved Plato from the wrath of Dionysius the tyrant.

Argument [Lat. *argumentum*]: Ger. *Argument* (*Argumentiren, Argumentation*), *Beweis*; Fr. *argument*; Ital. *argomento*. A reasoning in which the relation between grounds and conclusion is explicit.

Argumentum seems at first with Cicero to have had the more special sense of ground on which a conclusion might be based, and hence was frequently identified with the middle term in a syllogism. But the more general meaning coexisted with the other, and gradually gained wider acceptance. Argumentatio is quite a common equivalent for argumentum among the later Latin logicians. (R.A.)

For the various sorts of argument see DEDUCTION, INDUCTION, A PRIORI, A FORTIORI, CIRCULUS IN PROBANDO, REDUCTIO AD ABSURDUM, SORITES, FALLACY, and PROOF.

Argumentation : see REASONING.

Arianism : Ger. *Arianismus*; Fr. *Arianisme*; Ital. *Arianismo*. The name given to the Christological theory of Arius (fl. 318 A.D.).

The Arian doctrine must be traced to the apparently contradictory statements of the Alexandrian theologians, especially Origen, regarding the relation between the Father and the Son. The Alexandrians taught, on the one hand, the eternity of Christ; on the other, his separate 'essence,' and, by consequence, his inferiority to the Father. Arius accepted the latter alternative. This contrast was expressed by the 'full' Arians in the term *hetero-ousios*. The 'semi-Arians' used the term *homo-ousios*—admitting identity of 'essence,' but denying identity of 'substance.' Some of them, like Eunomius, employed the term *anomoios*, thus emphasizing the differences rather than the identity. The orthodox formula, associated with the Nicene Creed, is expressed in the term *homo-ousios*, and implies the coequality of Father and Son. The whole subject is intimately bound up with the difficult problems surrounding the Alexandrian theory of the LOGOS (q. v.). The classical period of the controversy is from 318–81. The discussion broke out again in England in 1720, with Samuel Clarke; and in New England, in 1747, with Jonathan Mayhew.

Literature: GIBBON, Decline and Fall of the Roman Empire, chap. xxi ; KÖLLING, Gesch. d. Ar. Häresie ; GWATKIN, Stud. of Arianism ; HARNACK, Hist. of Dogma (Eng. trans.), iii, iv; the relative article in Herzog's Real-Encyc. (with literature). For modern times, see STEPHEN, English Thought in the 18th Century; PATTISON, Tendencies of Religious Thought in England (1688–1750) ; M. STUART, Letters; NORTON, Statement of Reasons. (R.M.W.)

Aristippus. (425–cir. 366 B.C.) Greek philosopher, founder of the Cyrenaic school. A pupil of Socrates, he differed from Socrates in philosophic teachings. He passed some years at the court of Dionysius. See SCHOOLS OF GREECE (Cyrenaics).

Aristobulus. Lived in Egypt between 181 and 117 B.C.; but dates of birth and death are not certain. A Jew who tried to identify Greek philosophical conceptions with the Jewish religion. He is the first representative of Hellenic Judaism, or Jewish Alexandrianism. His reputed *Commentaries on the Writings of Moses* are quoted by the patristic Fathers.

Aristocles or Aristokles. (1) Of Messana or Messina. A Greek Peripatetic of the 2nd century A.D. Wrote on ethics. (2) Of Pergamus (cir. 100–35 A.D.). A rhetorician and Peripatetic philosopher; pupil of Herodes Atticus.

Aristocracy : Ger. *Aristocratie*; Fr. *aristocratie*; Ital. *aristocrazia*. (1) A form of government in which the sovereign power is vested in a select number of individuals. (2) Those individuals and the class to which they belong.

By derivation 'government of the best,' either singular or plural. Plato and Aristotle distinguish it from oligarchy (government of the few, in a bad sense), and it has still a better flavour. The commonest sense now is a class superior in birth and breeding to the other classes in a state, whether retaining special political privileges or not. For the difficulty of an exact definition see C. Lewis, *Polit. Terms*, x. 73.

Literature: MONTESQUIEU, Esprit des Lois, II. iii, cf. III. iii, iv; ARISTOTLE, Pol., iv. 6 ; HALLECK, Int. Law, i. chap. vi. § 1. (J.B.)

Ariston or Aristo. (1) An Athenian, son of Aristocles, and father of Plato. (2) Of Alexandria (cir. 30 B.C.). A philosopher (see

PERIPATETICS). (3) Of Ceos (cir. 230 B.C.). Succeeded Lycon as head, or scholarch, of the Peripatetic school. (4) Of Chios (cir. 275 B.C.). Surnamed the Siren for his eloquence. A Stoic, disciple of Zeno, who opened a school at Athens and lectured on ethics. He differed from Zeno. He despised logic, rejected natural philosophy, and regarded indifference to everything except virtue and vice as the highest good, and a clear, well-informed, healthy habit of mind as the only virtue.

Aristotelian Logic: see FORMAL LOGIC.

Aristotle. (384–22 B.C.) In point of intellect alone, probably the most remarkable of men. His father, Nicomachus, was a physician. Left an orphan early, he was placed under a guardian, Proxenus, who had him carefully educated. At seventeen, according to the best account, he visited Athens, and, when Plato returned from Sicily, joined the latter's school. He remained in Athens twenty years. He did not fully agree with his master in opinions. Married Pythias, the daughter (by adoption) of Hermias, prince of Atarneus in Asia Minor. Upon the assassination of the prince, he fled with his wife to Mitylene for two years. Became the tutor of King Philip's son, Alexander. Aristotle opened a school in Athens called the Lyceum. Accused of impiety he withdrew to Chalcis in Euboea, where he died. He wrote on all the sciences of his time and created new ones. The frequent mention of his name in the main articles of this or of any philosophical or scientific dictionary shows his extraordinary influence upon human thought. Cf. the topics following.

Aristotle's Dictum: Ger. *dictum de omni et nullo* (Lat. form); Fr. (Lat. form); Ital. (Lat. form). The so-called *Dictum de Omni et Nullo*, the general axiom of categorical syllogism: ' Quidquid dicitur universum de aliquo subiecto, affirmatur de quovis contento sub illo, quidquid negatur de aliquo universaliter accepto negatur de omnibus de quibus illud alterum affirmatur,' is rightly assigned to Aristotle, though his enunciation of it (1 b, 10–15; 24 b, 26–30) gives less prominence to the aspect of extension than do the ordinary scholastic formulas.

Explicit recognition of the *Dictum* as the general principle of syllogism occurs first in Boethius (see Prantl, *Gesch. d. Logik*, i. 652, 659).

Literature: On the relation of the *Dictum* to other axioms of syllogism, HAMILTON, Logic, ii. App. VI; MILL, Logic, Bk. I. chap. ii; LOTZE, Logik, § 97 f.　　　　(R.A.)

Aristotle's Experiment: Ger. *Versuch von Aristoteles*; Fr. *expérience d'Aristote*; Ital. *experimento d'Aristotile*. The second finger of either hand is crossed over the first, in such a way that its tip is brought upon the thumb-side of the latter. A marble or other round object is inserted between the crossed tips: the single marble is ' felt ' as two objects. Sometimes, if the subject is eye-minded, only one object is ' felt,' despite the fact that two sensitive surfaces are affected which, under ordinary circumstances, can be affected only by two distinct objects. The illusion is assisted by slight movement of the finger-tips.

Literature: SANFORD, Course in Exper. Psychol., expt. 3; RIVERS, Mind (1894), 583; HENRI, Raumw. d. Tastsinnes, and Année Psychol., iii. 225 f. (1898); ARISTOTLE, On Dreams (De Insomniis), chap. ii.　　(E.B.T.)

Aristotle's Terminology: see GREEK TERMINOLOGY, passim.

Aristoxenus of Tarentum. Lived about 330 B.C. A Greek philosopher, pupil of Aristotle. He wrote many works, nearly all of which are lost.

Arithmetical Mean: see MEAN.

Arithmomania [Gk. ἀριθμός, number, + μανία, madness]: Ger. *Arithmomanie*; Fr. *arithmomanie*; Ital. *aritmomania*. A marked or morbid tendency to count or keep tally, or to be anxious about and speculate in numerical relations. Cf. MANIA.　　(J.J.)

Literature: H. SAURY, Étude clinique sur la folie héréditaire (1886); V. MAGNAN, Recherches sur les centres nerveux, 2e série; and Leç. clin. sur les mal. ment. (1893); LEGRAIN, Délire chez les dégénérés (1886). (L.M.)

Arius. (cir. 250–336 A.D.) The founder of ARIANISM (q.v.). Ordained deacon by the patriarch Peter, and promoted to the highest rank among the clergy by Alexander, he was exiled to Illyricum, after the Council of Nicaea (or Nice), by Constantine. The ´sentence was revoked after two or three years, and he would have been restored to communion, after avowing his submission to the creed adopted by the Council, had he not suddenly died. Arius left several valuable theological discussions and treatises.

Arminianism: Ger. *Arminianismus*; Fr. *Arminianisme*; Ital. *Arminianismo*. The most celebrated form of the reaction against the extreme or supralapsarian interpretation of the Calvinistic dogma of predestination. So called from its originator, Jacobus ARMINIUS (q.v.) of Leyden (1560–1609).

The rigid Calvinistic dogma of predestination—taught by Th. Beza of Geneva, among others, under whom Arminius studied—inculcates that eternal life is foreordained for some, eternal damnation for others; and that these are ends which exist for the revelation of God's attributes. Against this view the Arminians drafted the *Remonstrance* (1610) to the States of Holland; hence their other name, Remonstrants. In its five articles the *Remonstrance* sets forth: (1) Election conditional upon faith; (2) the death of Christ for all; (3) the dependence of man upon grace, and his insufficiency without it; (4) the indispensableness of grace for goodness, yet its failure in some cases; (5) participation in Christ's Spirit as the means of salvation, although all may not persevere in the use of it as an instrument for the defeat of Satan. Hugo Grotius, the philosopher, was the most eminent adherent of Arminianism. The Calvinistic and Arminian theories represent respectively determinism and indeterminism of the will. The Arminian view is represented to-day by the theologians of the Wesleyan or Methodist Episcopal Church. (R.M.W.–J.M.B.)

Literature: BANGS, Life of Arminius; LIMBORCH, Theol. Christiana; G. S. FRANCKE, De Hist. Dogmatum Armin.; J. MÜLLER, Lehre v. d. Sünde, Bk. IV. chap. iii. (also Eng. trans.); DORNER, Hist. of Protestant Theol. (Eng. trans.), i. 420 f. (R.M.W.)

Arminius, Jacobus. (1560–1609.) A Dutch theologian who founded ARMINIANISM (q.v.). His Dutch name was Jacob Harmensen. Educated at Marburg, Leyden, and Geneva, he also visited Rome. He was ordained minister at Amsterdam. Doubts as to the Calvinistic doctrine of predestination led to the charge of heterodoxy. The Supreme Court of the Hague listened to a discussion between Arminius and Gomar. He left several able theological treatises.

Arnauld, Antoine. (1612–94.) Doctor of the Sorbonne, a celebrated French theologian and philosopher. He was always a determined antagonist of the Jesuits, whose enmity finally drove him into exile, where he died. He became a zealous Jansenist. He wrote many works on theology, logic (*The Port Royal Logic*), and philosophy. He produced a reform in the style of French theologians, Pascal and Bossuet following his purer taste.

Arnobius ('the elder'). Lived probably about 302 A.D. An eloquent converted apologist for Christianity. He was the teacher of Lactantius. Wrote a strong and sarcastic work against Paganism.

Arnold, Daniel Heinrich. (1706–75.) Professor of philosophy and divinity at Königsberg.

Arnold, Johann Christian. (1724–65.) Professor of philosophy, and afterwards of physics, at Erlangen.

Arnott, Neil. (1788–1874.) Scottish physician and eminent experimenter in natural philosophy. A pupil of Sir Everard Home, he practised in London; lectured and wrote on natural philosophy. Became a Fellow of the Royal Society, and in 1854 received the Rumford medal for his inventions.

Arrian. An eminent Greek historian who lived during the 2nd century A.D. The pupil and friend of Epictetus, he published the master's works. Under Hadrian he was prefect of Cappadocia, and consul under Antoninus Pius.

Art and **Art Theories** [Lat. *ars*]: Ger. *Kunst und Kunsttheorien*; Fr. (*théories de l'*) *art*; Ital. (*teorie dell'*) *arte*. (1) In the broadest sense, any activity or production involving intelligence and skill. In this sense it is opposed to 'nature' on the one hand, and to unskilful production on the other; while it is distinguished from science as doing from knowing. (2) In a narrower sense, equivalent to fine art, an activity or a product of activity, which has aesthetic value or (in the broadest sense of the term) is beautiful. (3) In a still narrower sense it is sometimes restricted to sculpture and painting, but this is liable to objection as the word is needed in the broader sense of (2).

Under this topic there is given a sketch of general theories only, except where a particular art may illustrate a general point of view. For the various classifications of the arts see CLASSIFICATION (of the fine arts); and for closely related problems see AESTHETICS, and BEAUTY.

Theories of art fall, for the most part, under three classes according as they examine (*a*) the end sought by art, as to imitate nature, to express an ideal, to give delight; or (*b*) the social or educational value of art, and its relation to morality and religion; or (*c*) the psychological impulses out of which art has sprung, as the instinct of play, of self-exhibition, of decoration, &c.

I. *Ancient Theories.* Greek theory regarded imitation as the essential nature of fine art. According to Plato, God creates an 'idea,' or a world after the pattern of 'ideas'; the artisan resembles God in that he makes real things 'in accordance with the idea,' i.e. he has to have a scientific knowledge of his products; but the artist (e.g. the painter or poet) imitates the products of others without necessarily having any scientific knowledge of the thing imitated. He is thrice removed from the truth. He has as his pattern not the eternal 'idea,' the true reality, but the thing of sense. A copy of this is inferior in value to the original. Moreover, the artist is satisfied to present an appearance: he does not necessarily penetrate to the truth. Just for this reason art is dangerous in education. Additional objections are that poets often convey faulty ethical and religious conceptions, and that imitation of undesirable states of mind through music, or of evil passions and characters in acting, must react on the person imitating, and, by sympathy, upon the spectator. Art, however charming, should not be admitted unless it can be proved to be for the good of the state. When used to adorn noble sentiments, music and all art may have the highest educational value. For art springs from certain primitive instincts, which in animals find expression in play and cries of various kinds—an overflowing of activity or surplus of energy—but which in man have the additional element of order, i.e. of rhythm and harmony, and so find expression in the choral dance and song.

Imitation is for Aristotle both a source of art, at least of poetry and painting, and the means of its enjoyment. It is natural to man to imitate and to delight in imitations. We say this is so-and-so; and this pleasure of learning is the chief element aside from that produced by the colouring or some similar cause. But although art is called imitation, and even music is styled the most imitative of the arts, the term has with Aristotle the significance, not of copying existing things or actions, but of representing more or less idealized (i.e. intensified or modified by imagination) emotions, characters, or situations. Poetry should relate not what has occurred, but what might occur, what is possible in accord with general laws. It is therefore more philosophical and more elevated than history. Tragedy seeks to represent men better than they are, comedy worse; and the same difference appears in the work of different painters.

As regards the end and the educational value of art, Aristotle makes the end of all the fine arts (as contrasted with the useful arts) to give pleasure or to serve 'diagoge'—that rational enjoyment or ideal employment of leisure which the man of culture and elevation of mind delights in. Art is thus distinguished from play or pastime, which gives merely recreation, though music may indeed serve this latter end also. Only music is treated in detail with respect to its educational value, but painting and tragedy have incidental mention. The especial educational value of music is as a means to rational enjoyment, but it has also moral power by bringing us into sympathy with states of mind like courage, gentleness, &c. It should have a threefold use: the ethical melodies for education, the lax for recreation in old age, the enthusiastic for purging the emotions. For persons specially liable to the emotions of compassion, fear, or enthusiasm, 'after listening to melodies which raise their soul to ecstasy, relapse into their normal condition.' 'They experience a purging and a pleasurable feeling of relief.' A similar catharsis of the passions is effected by tragedy. Cf. CATHARSIS, and TRAGIC.

II. *Theories in the 17th and 18th centuries.* The same general principle that art is imitation appears as the basis of early French and English theories. The formula received a different emphasis in consequence of the actual tendencies of art (genre and landscape painting), and as Imitation of Nature was given general statement by Batteaux (1746). Another formula emphasized truth as the end of art, 'Rien n'est beau que le vrai'; but 'truth,' which with Boileau (1674) had meant nearly the same as the rational 'clearness and distinctness' of Descartes, came to mean, with the growth of 'Naturalism,' a representation of the variety of nature, or of its life and fullness (Diderot, 1765).

The 'strictest imitation of nature' is also a standard with Shaftesbury (*Characteristics*, 1711), but his watchword of 'truth' is supplemented by 'unity of design,' and the painter 'knows that he is even then unnatural when he follows nature too close and strictly copies life.' In his further statement that the artist avoids what is peculiar and seeks to form his idea from many objects, we have the suggestion of the theory which holds that art is to express an ideal, and that the ideal is to be found in what is most characteristic, not of the individual, but of the species. So Reynolds (1759). Winckelmann, also, in his *History of Ancient Art* (1765), held that the Greeks aimed to express ideal beauty by making their works of art general rather than individual. Ideal beauty would be like pure water with no individual characteristics. Expression is detrimental to beauty. On the other hand, he notes, besides the 'beautiful' style (or style of grace), the 'grand' style, which is beautiful as the expression of a tranquil soul, and again says, 'Beauty without expression would be colourless, expression without beauty unpleasant.' The antithesis between (formal) beauty and expression, which has been prominent in all subsequent theory, was thus definitely stated. Lessing restricted formative art (sculpture and painting) to beauty, but admitted the representation of the ugly into poetry, as the latter art need not dwell permanently upon the painful impression. Lessing also (in his *Laocoön*, 1769) defined sharply the provinces of the arts of form, on the one hand, and of poetry on the other, by their respective media. Sculpture and painting, employing coexisting signs (shape and colour), can represent bodies, but only suggest actions ; poetry, using successive signs (tones), represents actions, but depicts bodies by suggestion only.

III. *Theories growing out of the Romantic movement.* Various tendencies, social and political as well as aesthetic, found expression in a revolt from classic forms, in a demand for freedom in art as in life, in Rousseau's enthusiasm for the natural as opposed to the conventional or artificial, and in the appreciation of Shakespeare, of Gothic architecture, and of romantic poetry. What had been called 'wild' or 'unordered' was given aesthetic value under the conception of the sublime or significant. This found theoretic expression in Goethe's essay on German architecture (1773), in which he contrasts 'beautiful' art with 'characteristic' art to the advantage of the latter.

This doctrine was carried further by Hirt (1797), and the essence of art was declared to be the characteristic. Art should aim to present what nature intended to produce in a given species, and to present this by means selected expressly for their fitness for this end. This was in turn criticized by Goethe, who asserted that the characteristic must be modified by beauty (formal) in order to be really individual (as contrasted with the generic or abstract), and to become perfect art (i. e. the beautiful conceived in a narrower sense, not including necessarily the significant).

This same general movement toward freedom and enlargement in art found more systematic expression in Kant's *Critique of Judgment*

(1790). It is the essence of art that while known to be art, and not nature, it yet must seem like nature in being free from all constraint of rules or set purpose. Beautiful art is free ; it is the production of genius, and the essence of genius is that it works not according to models imposed, but by originating products which serve as models. Genius embodies in art aesthetic ideas ; and an aesthetic idea is a creation of the imagination which, instead of being formed by rule, suggests more than can be exhausted by any definite concept. On the other hand, a 'normal idea,' formed by making a composite of various particulars, is merely correct, not beautiful. The end of all aesthetic art is to give pleasure : if in the mere sensations, it may be called pleasant or entertaining art; if in modes of cognition, beautiful art.

Schiller expressed another aspect of the art consciousness of his time in terming ancient art NAÏVE (q. v.) and modern 'sentimental.' In the former the artist *is* nature ; in the latter he *seeks* nature, is consciously apart from it, is subjective rather than objective—a thought which was further developed by Schlegel in his conception of IRONY (q. v.). Schlegel also asserted the essence of modern art to be not the beautiful, but the interesting, including the piquant, the striking, the ugly, &c. ; and again later asserted that the beauty of art lies in its significant content, and hence that its essence is the symbolic. Schiller's most important service lay in his treatment of the function of art in the education of the race (*Letters on the Aesthetic Educ. of Man*, 1793–5).

The aim of education is to bring the individual into harmony with universal law. It is just the characteristic of art and beauty that this is accomplished—that the individual becomes the ideal—not by compulsion, but in freedom. For art is play. It is an activity which is autotelic (not controlled by outside ends), and at the same time perfectly harmonious (the expression of an ordering principle). This aesthetic play is indeed not to be identified with physical play, but it may be regarded as an outgrowth, since the freedom which is its prerogative has its analogy in the surplus of energy exhibited in the play of animals. The necessity which calls this out is not external, but lies in their own fullness of life. Schopenhauer gives a similar value to art, as silencing the desires, and enabling the individual to transcend himself, to contemplate or embody the 'Ideas' which are the objectifications of Will, the ultimate reality.

Schelling and Hegel give the thought of Kant and Schiller a more metaphysical turn. Art, according to Schelling, is that complete union of subject and object which philosophy seeks; it is therefore superior to philosophy as expression of the absolute. According to Hegel, art is the revelation of truth in sensuous form, and a more adequate expression of the idea than can be made through nature. It is therefore on the same plane with religion and philosophy; but as embodying the idea in sensuous form, it is fitted to be, as it has been, the first instructress of peoples. It has embodied and shown to them the spiritual values of their lives. The various periods of symbolic, classic, and romantic art are determined by the expression found for the ideal.

IV. *Recent art theories.* Recent writers have concerned themselves largely with the psychological and anthropological origins of art, or with its social and moral functions. As regards the nature of art, theories may again be related to the actual development of art itself. This has been chiefly in music and landscape painting on the one hand, and in the novel on the other. Of these, the former tend to bring into prominence the pleasures of sensation and form, the latter the representation of a significant content. Impressionism (as a theory of the aim of art, not of the means by which this shall be secured) has its motives in the former. Pater (*Fortn. Rev.*, October, 1877, reprinted in *The Renaissance*) urges that music is the type of all art, the ideally consummate art. Taine leans, in his definition, to the emphasis of content. 'The end of a work of art is to manifest some essential or salient character. . . . It does this by employing a group of connected parts.' Ruskin emphasizes especially the value of characteristic expression, and by the insistence on sincerity and truth tends often to transform aesthetic into ethical categories. Guyau seeks to combine both sides: 'Art is expression of the highest idea in the language which thrills the senses most deeply, and thus stirs all emotions, higher and lower.' If art is defined as the embodiment of the beautiful, the same antithesis may be repeated according as the beautiful is understood to include or to exclude expression or significance. Cf. FORMALISM.

Finally, there may be noted here the application of Lange's theory (see under BEAUTY, V) to art, by which art is defined to be a capacity to give to others a pleasure free from practical interests and resting on a conscious self-illusion. This conscious illusion, 'make-believe,' or SEMBLANCE (q. v.), whether in imitation of nature or in the production of an emotional state, is the 'constant factor in art.'

As regards the moral and social relations of art, Ruskin has emphasized its earnestness as above noted, Morris (*Hopes and Fears for Art*, 1881) its dependence on social conditions. Guyau (*L'art au point de vue sociologique*, 1889) regards artistic emotion as in its nature social, and the end of art to be not only the production of agreeable sensations, but the expression of life. This last includes especially the expression of the social sentiments, sympathy, interest, pity, &c. Tolstoi would limit art to the production of simple pleasures shareable by all, or to the representation of sentiments of universal fraternity.

Another set of writers have treated especially the origin of art, and frequently in connection with this its value to the individual or the race. Spencer (*Princ. of Psychol.*, ii) adopts and develops the play and 'surplus-energy' theory of Plato and Schiller. Baldwin Brown emphasizes the festal origin of art. Marshall (*Pain, Pleasure, and Aesthetics*, 1894; *Aesthetic Princ.*, 1895) seeks its origin in impulses to attract the attention and good will of others, called by J. Mark Baldwin 'self-exhibiting impulses.' Grosse (*The Beginnings of Art*, 1897) emphasizes the close relation of primitive art to the activities of the hunter, and shows its value in the struggle for existence. He also maintains that instead of one art-impulse there are several, and as against Spencer's view of the gradual differentiation of the arts maintains that all the main arts exist in distinct though crude form among primitive peoples. Groos (*The Play of Animals*, 1898, Ger. trans. 1896) attacks the 'surplus-energy' theory, and shows that play (and hence art) is rather in the nature of a necessity than a luxury, as providing exercise of the faculties which have later their serious use. Lange (*Zeitsch. f. Psychol.*, xiv, 1897) points out the social value of art in the employment and cultivation of activities and sentiments which are useful to the society, but which do not always find a field for exhibition in earnest, e.g. the value of music or poetry in kindling patriotism. J. Mark Baldwin (*Social and Eth. Interpret.*, 1897) emphasizes the social value of imitation and self-exhibition, and Tarde (*Rev. Philos.*, xxx. 1) compares artistic enjoyment with economic consumption.

Lee and Thomson also (*Contemp. Rev.*, 1897) criticize the 'surplus-energy' theory from the experimental standpoint. For these last theories in their relation to the origin of specific arts see CLASSIFICATION (of the fine arts).

Literature: General works dealing incidentally with art theories as well as other aesthetic problems will be found under AESTHETICS, BEAUTY, and CLASSIFICATION (of the fine arts).

(1) *Historical*: BOSANQUET, Hist. of Aesthetic (1892); SCHASLER, Krit. Gesch. d. Aesthetik (1872); WALTER, Gesch. d. Aesthetik im Alterthum (1893); E. MÜLLER, Gesch. d. Theorie d. Kunst bei den Alten (1834); EGGER, Essai sur l'Hist. de la Critique chez les Grecs (3rd ed., 1887); BUTCHER, Aristotle's Theory of Poetry and Fine Art (1895); BÉNARD, L'Esthétique d'Aristote (1887); DÖRING, Die Kunstlehre des Aristoteles (1876); SVOBODA, Gesch. d. Ideale mit besonderer Berücksichtigung d. bildenden Kunst (1886); LOTZE, Gesch. d. Aesthetik in Deutschland (1868); HARTMANN, Aesthetik, Historisch-krit. Theorie (1886); BASCH, Essai critique sur l'esthétique de Kant (1896); COHEN, Kant's Begründung d. Aesthetik (1889); CAIRD, Crit. Philos. of Kant (1889); BERGER, Die Entwicklung v. Schiller's Aesthetik (1894); KEDNEY, Hegel's Aesthetics (1885); BOSANQUET, Hegel's Philos. of Fine Art (trans. of the Introd. with pref. essay, 1886); MILSAND, L'Esthétique anglaise (1864, on Ruskin); KANT, Crit. of Judgment (trans. Bernard, 1892); SCHILLER, Essays, Aesthetic and Philos. (Bohn Lib.); HEGEL, Aesthetische Werke (1833–48), x.

(2) *Systematic*: in addition to those named under IV above and under AESTHETICS, G. BALDWIN BROWN, The Fine Arts (1891); COLLINGWOOD, Philos. of Ornament (1883); KER, The Philosophy of Art, in Essays in Philos. Criticism (ed. by Seth and Haldane, 1883); FIERENS-GEVAERT, Essai sur l'Art contemporain (1897); GUYAU, Les Problèmes de l'Esthétique contemporaine (4th ed., 1897); HADDON, Evolution in Art (1895); MORRIS, The Lesser Arts, in Lectures on Art (1882); PROUDHON, Du Principe de l'Art et de sa Destination sociale (1865); SÉAILLES, Essai sur le Génie dans l'Art (2nd ed., 1897); RIEGEL, Die bildenden Künste (4th ed., 1895); VOLKELT, Aesthetische Zeitfragen (1895); WALLASCHEK, Primitive Music (1893); Aesthetik der Ton-Kunst (1886); SULLY, Sensation and Intuition (1874); GURNEY, The Power of Sound (1880), and Tertium Quid (1887); PRUDHOMME, L'expression dans les Beaux-Arts (1883); VISCHER, Krit. Gänge, esp. Heft vi (1873); CARRIERE, Die Kunst im Zusammenhange der Kulturentwickelung, u. die Ideale d. Menschheit (3rd ed., 1885); ALT, Syst. d. Künste (1888); SEMPER, Der Stil in den technischen u. techtonischen Künsten (2nd ed., 1878–9). (J.H.T.)

Art Impulse: Ger. *Kunsttrieb*; Fr. *instinct esthétique*; Ital. *istinto* (or *impulso*) *artistico*. The impulse which manifests itself in the production of works of art.

Like the play impulse, it is generally held to be free and spontaneous, and not directly determined by material needs. It is distinguished from the play impulse in that for its satisfaction it requires expression in a rational, ordered, and significant activity.

For the various theories as to the specific impulses assigned as the origin of art see ART, and CLASSIFICATION (of the fine arts).

Literature: Recent works giving especial attention to the subject are: SPENCER, Psychology, ii; BROWN, The Fine Arts (1891); GROSSE, Die Anfänge d. Kunst (1893, Eng. trans. 1897); MARSHALL, Pain, Pleasure, and Aesthetics (1894); GROOS, The Play of Animals (1898, Ger. 1896), and The Play of Man (1900, Ger. 1899); RIBOT, La Psychol. des Sentiments (1896); BALDWIN, Social and Eth. Interpret. (1897). (J.H.T.)

Artery [Gr. ἀρτηρία, the windpipe, a survival of the ancient notion that these vessels contained air]: Ger. *Arterie*, *Schlagader*; Fr. *artère*; Ital. *arteria*. A vessel which carries blood from the heart to a system of capillaries. See VASO-MOTOR SYSTEM. (C.F.H.)

Articular Sensation [Lat. *articularis*, pertaining to the joints]: Ger. *Gelenkempfindung*; Fr. *sensation articulaire*; Ital. *sensazione delle giunture*. A sensation, whose adequate stimulus is movement of the one joint-surface upon the other, or pressure and counter-pressure of the two surfaces. The sensation is of great importance, as the basis of the perceptions of movement and position of the limbs, of resistance, &c. It possesses local signature (see LOCAL SIGNS), and seems to show constancy of absolute sense discrimination.

Literature: KÜLPE, Outlines of Psychol., 140 ff., 341 ff.; SANFORD, Course in Exper. Psychol., expts. 39, 40, 43; GOLDSCHEIDER, Du Bois-Reymond's Arch. (1889), 369, 540, and Suppl.-Bd. (1889), 141; Centralbl. f. Physiol. (1887 and 1889); E. CLAPARÈDE, Du Sens musculaire (1897). (E.B.T.)

Articulation (vocal) [Lat. *articulatio*, a joining together]: Ger. *Artikulirung*; Fr.

articulation; Ital. *articolazione.* The act of co-operation among the organs of speech in larynx and mouth, whereby, through modification or check of the breath-current, distinct speech-sounds are produced.

The character of speech-sounds is determined by the noises generated as the breath-current passes the articulated organs, or by the resonance dependent on the form of the resonance cavity in mouth and nose created in the articulation, or by both. See Vietor, *Elemente d. Phonetik,* 2nd ed., §§ 1 ff. Whitney's definition (*Proc. Amer. Philol. Assoc.,* 1881, 22) is: 'Articulation is virtually syllabication—a breaking of the stream of utterance into joints, by the intervention of closer utterances or consonants between the opener utterances or vowels.' This does not represent with any exactness the present scientific use of the term, though it may be etymologically more correct. (B.I.W.)

Artificial Selection : Ger. *künstliche Auswahl* (or *Selektion*); Fr. *sélection artificielle* (or *méthodique*); Ital. *selezione artificiale* (or *metodica*). The selection by man of certain animals or plants from which to breed, with a view to securing certain chosen or desirable characters.

It is treated by Darwin under the heads (1) 'Methodical Selection': 'That which guides a man who systematically endeavours to modify a breed according to some predetermined standard.' (2) 'Unconscious Selection': 'That which follows from men naturally preserving the most valued and destroying the less valued individuals without any thought of altering the breed.' The term unconscious is somewhat unfortunate. The distinction is between selecting with conscious intention of improving or altering the breed, and selecting for various other reasons of utility, convenience, &c., with no thought of the breed. See SELECTION, where recommendations regarding various meanings of the English word selection are to be found. (C.LL.M.–J.M.B.)

Darwin's *Animals and Plants under Domestication* contains a store of facts relating to artificial selection. This process differs in its method from that of natural selection in that man selects the fittest from which to breed, the 'fit' being those individuals which already show the desired character and the process leading to the accumulation of variations along artificially chosen lines, while nature eliminates the unfit in the struggle for existence without the element of conscious choice,

which thus constitutes the great difference. The distinction as between the fit, in the one case, and the unfit in the other, is largely a matter of degree. In SOCIAL SUPPRESSION (q. v.) the unfittest, from a distinctly social point of view (e. g. criminals), are isolated or suppressed. (C.LL.M.–J.M.B.)

Literature: DARWIN (as cited); G. J. ROMANES, Darwin and after Darwin, i. (1892). See also under SELECTION.

Aryan [Sansk. *Árya,* noble]: Ger. *Arier, arisch*; Fr. *Aryen*; Ital. *Ariano.* A term used by anthropologists and historians to designate the speech-family commonly called among philologists of England, America, and France the Indo-European, and of Germany Indogermanisch.

In the stricter usage of present-day philologists the term is limited in its application to the Indo-Iranian speech-family, i. e. the family whose chief ancient representatives are the Sanskrit and Avestan (Zend). As the use of the term Indo-Iranian, however, has now practically displaced it in this value, the value given it by anthropologists may well be regarded as its standard meaning, in which sense its brevity commends it to general use. (B.I.W.)

Asceticism (in ethics and philosophy) [Gr. ἄσκησις, exercise or training]: Ger. *Asceticismus*; Fr. *ascétisme*; Ital. *ascetismo.* A system of conduct in which the realization of the moral life is attempted by means of a complete subjugation of sensuous impulse and worldly desire.

Asceticism is not so much the name of a moral theory as of a practical method of realizing morality. But it implies this element of theory, that the true good for man is something outside of and opposed to his animal nature and the ordinary interests of mundane life. The regulation of the impulses which morality requires is not possible without a subjugation of lower impulses in presence of higher needs. And the life of mere impulse (which is non-moral) has its most obvious antithesis in a complete subjugation of impulse. Hence asceticism is an early factor in the demand for a higher life. In particular it has characterized most oriental religions; and in them, abstinence from fleshly and worldly desire was commonly accompanied by various methods of actively mortifying the body. The Jewish religion is in this respect exceptional amongst oriental faiths: in it there were only slight traces of asceticism, although the Deity was frequently approached by fasting, as well as by prayer—until the rise of the sect of the Essenes, shortly before the Christian era.

The most complete system of ascetic morality is to be found in Buddhism, in which creed it is held that the struggle against impulse is continued by the individual soul in successive incarnations; and it is characteristic of this system that the victory over impulse is held to be capable of perfect attainment only in the complete submergence of the individual consciousness. In modern thought a similar view is to be found in the pessimistic morality of Schopenhauer: the self-annihilation of the will to live involves the destruction of consciousness, along with that which gives birth to consciousness. On the other hand, the Christian ascetics have mortified the flesh and the world for the sake of spiritual perfection; and their renunciation of the pleasures of this life has always been accompanied by a foretaste of the spiritual joys of a future state of existence.

Asceticism was, on the whole, hostile to the spirit of Greek ethics: but it appeared in the Pythagorean life, and in the contempt of pleasure which characterized at least the more extreme forms of Cynicism and Stoicism. Plato also, in the *Phaedo*, looked upon the bodily life as a mere clog and obstacle to the true destiny of the soul, and held that life should be a practice of death. In the *Republic*, however, he reached a broader view, and sketched the moralization of civic life: although this moralization was only brought about by a reorganization of the state, under the rule of philosophers, in which the conflict of interests arising from appropriation was to be eliminated and individual activities were to be subjected to strict regulation. In the Neo-Platonic systems the contemplative life carried with it an ascetic attitude.

Elements of asceticism were present from the beginning amongst the Christians, and the ascetic spirit manifested itself in the second century in the recommendation to CELIBACY (q.v.). The Gnostics and writers influenced by them worked out a contemplative or mystical ideal of life in which the flesh had no part but to be subdued and kept under. The ascetic tendencies of the Church were further developed in opposition to the growing corruption of society. Of this movement monasticism was the most striking result. The ascetic ideal was put forward by Rufinus, Sulpicius Severus, Cassian, and Prudentius in the 4th century, and by many later writers. The ideal included various forms of abstinence, such as celibacy, poverty, frequent fasting, and, as the distinctive mark of monasticism, solitude. Connected with it was the distinction of two modes of life — that of ordinary Christian morality, and the higher stage marked chiefly by celibacy and withdrawal from the world—a Christian form of the distinction in Greek ethics between civic and philosophic virtue.

Asceticism has found its most constant antagonist in the Hedonistic morality. Cf. HEDONISM. But the view of Bentham (*Princ. of Mor. and Legisl.*, chap. i), who contrasts his own doctrine with the ascetic, and describes the latter as taking pain instead of pleasure for its *summum bonum*, is—and was perhaps meant to be—a caricature.

Literature: LECKY, Hist. of European Mor., chap. iv; LUTHARDT, Hist. of Christ. Eth., §§ 34 ff. (W.R.S.)

Asceticism (in religion). The view which teaches that maceration of the body, extirpation of passion, and the like, are essential to salvation. It is commonly connected with an APOCALYPTIC (q.v.) conception of the world, involving a low estimate of the present life, and a belief in the essentially evil nature of matter.

Asceticism is found in association with the doctrines of Buddhism; of some forms of Hinduism; of the Jewish Essenes; of the Egyptian Therapeutae; of the Alexandrian Neo-Platonists. Through the last it came into contact with Christianity, and, favoured by certain superstitions current in the early Christian centuries, effected a permanent lodgement in the Christian system. Some writers, chiefly Roman Catholic, assign a special place to ascetic theology, which, as distinguished from dogmatic, mystic, and moral theology, offers directions for a more intimate walk with God than is necessary for all.

Literature: ZÖCKLER, Krit. Gesch. d. Askese; DORNER, Christ. Eth. (Eng. trans.), 405 f. (R.M.W.)

Aschenmayer, Adam Karl. (1768–1852.) A German mystical philosopher, born in Neuenberg, Würtemberg. He became professor of philosophy and medicine at Tübingen in 1811, and was transferred to the chair of practical philosophy in 1818. In 1836 he moved to Kirchheim, where he died. He is best known for a work on the philosophy of religion.

Aseitas [Med. Lat. *a se*, being for oneself]. A term incident to the scholastic discussions of the metaphysical essence of God. It may be translated by the words 'self-existent,' or 'uncaused.'

The metaphysical essence of anything is that which is special or peculiar to it. The Scotists maintained that infinity is the metaphysical essence of God; some of the followers of Aquinas assign this to God's complete self-knowledge; the prevalent view maintains that aseitas (or life in himself, John v. 26) is the attribute to which all others must be referred. The question has naturally entered into the quasi-metaphysical discussions concerning the relation of the Son to the Father. It dates back to Dionysius the Areopagite.

Literature: DORNER, Doctrine of the Person of Christ, I. div. i. 83, and *passim*; OOSTERZEE, Christ. Dogmatics, 256; CLARKE, Discourse concerning the Being and Attributes of God. (R.M.W.)

Asemia or **Asemasia** [Gr. ἀ + σῆμα, a sign]: Ger. *Asemie*; Fr. *asémie* (little used); Ital. *asemia* (a variety of *dissemia*). Loss of the power to form or to understand any sign or symbol, whether word or gesture or other action.

The essential nature of this defect is the same as in aphasia, but the term covers a wider field of application. The essential processes of speech are the comprehension and expression of thought by an acquired system of symbolization. Apart from the spoken or written systems (languages), gesture signs, facial and other forms of expression are employed; feeling is conveyed by music; and conventional forms of greeting and other social customs are readily interpreted. Asemia implies the loss of the power to interpret any of these systems, or indeed to interpret any group of sensations as the sign or symbol of a thought or feeling. The term Asemia is used by Steinthal, Kussmaul, and others; Hamilton proposes Asemasia; Finckelnburg, Asymbolia. The loss of any special set of symbols may be referred to by appropriate adjectives: Asemia graphica, loss of writing; Asemia mimica, loss of gesture signs; Asemia verbalis, loss of verbal symbols. If the defect extends to the mishandling and confusion of objects, it becomes APRAXIA (q. v.). The defect has also relations to BLINDNESS (mental, q. v.) and to SPEECH AND ITS DEFECTS (q. v., also for *Literature*).

Literature: SÉGLAS, Les troubles du langage; HEILBRONNER, Asymbolie (1897); MORSELLI, Semej. malat. ment., ii. (J.J.)

Asexual Reproduction (or multiplication). Reproduction without sex in animals and plants. See AGAMOGENESIS. (J.M.B.)

Asonia or **Tone-Deafness**: see HEARING (defects of).

Aspirate: see PHONETICS.

Aspiration [Lat. *ad + spirare*, to breathe upon]: Ger. *Aspiration*; Fr. *aspiration*; Ital. *aspirazione*. In the system of Christian ethics, aspiration is an integral element in the theory of the genesis of Christian character.

Faith in the Gospel possesses, as one of its most important consequences, a power of generating aspiration, i. e. either a 'longing desire' for reconciliation with Christ, or an 'overmastering determination' to lead the Christian life so far as possible.

Literature: DORNER, Christ. Eth. (Eng. trans.), 363 f. (R.M.W.)

Assent [Lat. *ad + sentire*, to feel]: Ger. *Bewilligung*; Fr. *assentiment*; Ital. *adesione*. Agreement with a judgment presented to one for acceptance. This meaning of the term replaces its use loosely for various forms of judgment, belief, affirmation. (J.M.B.–G.F.S.)

Assertion [Lat. *assertio*]: Ger. *Bejahung*; Fr. *assertion*; Ital. *asserzione*. See BELIEF, JUDGMENT, and PROPOSITION.

Assignment (in law) [Med. Lat. *assignamentum*]: Ger. *Übertragung eines Rechtes, Überweisung*; Fr. *transport, cession*; Ital. *cessione*. The transfer of a right: less often, the transfer of a thing in possession. A General assignment is a transfer of all a man's rights of property for the benefit of his creditors. An Involuntary assignment is one made by operation of law, without the owner's consent.

By the common law of England and America an assignment cannot pass a legal title to anything of which the person assigning is not at the time in possession, that is, to choses in action. An equitable title, however, might thus be gained. The Roman law was originally the same (Gaius, ii. 38). (S.E.B.)

Assimilation (in physiology) [Lat. *ad + similis*, like]: Ger. *Assimilation*; Fr. *assimilation*; Ital. *assimilazione*. The process of converting food materials into living protoplasm. See ANABOLISM, and METABOLISM. (C.F.H.)

Assimilation (in psychology). (1) The union of elements in consciousness by which certain contents (those assimilated) take the form of or contribute material to the formation of others (those which assimilate). (J.M.B.–G.F.S.)

(2) Association between like elements and compounds (Wundt).

Wundt (reference below) uses the term in the special sense (2), which is not recommended. A better usage is (1), in which it serves to indicate the content side of the Herbartian form of the notion of APPERCEPTION (q.v.).

Assimilation describes what takes place in any case of mental synthesis from the point of view of how the elements of presentation behave. It is a convenient term, since the various cases of contrast, fusion, association (of all sorts), with consciousness of identity and resemblance, recognition, &c., can be construed as involving assimilation of different modes. Cf. Ward (art. Psychology, in *Encyc. Brit.*), who speaks of 'assimilation or recognition' of an impression in the process of perception. On the nervous side it rests upon the direct coalescence of sensory processes (James) or their indirect union through the synergy (Münsterberg, Baldwin) of motor processes.

Literature: WUNDT, Philos. Stud., vii. 345 ff., and Outlines of Psychol., 228 ff.; LEWES, Problems of Life and Mind; WARD, art. Association and Assimilation, in Mind (July, 1893, and Oct., 1894); BALDWIN, Ment. Devel. in the Child and the Race, 308 ff. (J.M.B., G.F.S.)

Assimilation (linguistic). A process by which contiguous sounds in language tend to approximate or become alike. Thus *hands* becomes *handz*, the voiceless *s* assuming the voiced quality of *d*; *hemp* from O. Eng. *henep*.

The organs of speech, in passing from one mode of ARTICULATION (q.v.) to another, either carry forward somewhat of the position necessary for the former, or by anticipation draw back somewhat of the latter. (B.I.W.)

Assistance or **Concurrence**: Ger. *Concurrenz*; Fr. *concurrence*; Ital. *concorrenza*. The act of God in maintaining the relation of mind and body on the theory of PRE-ESTABLISHED HARMONY (q.v.). (J.M.B.)

Associate Points: see CONGRUENT.

Association (experiments on); for derivation and equivalents, see ASSOCIATION (of ideas). Experimental work upon association of ideas falls under the following heads:

(1) Classificatory (types of association).

Literature: WUNDT, Physiol. Psychol. (4th ed.), ii. 455; TRAUTSCHOLDT, Philos. Stud., i. 213; GALTON, Brain (1879); BOURDON, Rev. Philos., xxxv; MÜNSTERBERG, Beiträge, i. and iv. Cf. HÖFFDING, LEHMANN, and WUNDT, Philos. Stud., v, vii, viii, and Vtljsch. f. wiss. Philos., xiv; CALKINS, Psychol. Rev., Monograph Suppl., 2 (1896); ZIEHEN, Die Ideenassoziation des Kindes (Berlin, 1898); WAHLE, Vtljsch. f. wiss. Philos. (1885); RIBOT, Rev. Philos., xxxi. 35 ff.

(2) Analytic (mechanics of association).

Literature: SCRIPTURE, Philos. Stud., vii; MÜNSTERBERG, Beiträge, iv; W. G. SMITH, Z. Frage v. d. mittelbaren Assoc.,

Diss. (Leipzig, 1894); HOWE, Amer. J. of Psychol. Cf. BOURDON, Rev. Philos., xxxi; HÖFFDING, LEHMANN, WUNDT, as above; CALKINS, loc. cit.; ASCHAFFENBURG, Exper. Stud. ü. die Assoc., Psychol. Arb., i. 209 ff., ii. 1 ff.

(3) REACTION TIME (q.v., for literature).

(4) Scattered experiments only exist upon associativeness, i. e. the conditions under which ideas are liable to be associated, and upon the capacity of a given idea to arouse an associated idea.

Literature: MÜNSTERBERG, loc. cit.; PILLSBURY, BIRCH, in Amer. J. of Psychol., &c. See KÜLPE, Outlines of Psychol., §§ 27–33. (E.B.T.)

Association (in aesthetics). As an aesthetic principle, association is used to explain aesthetic value by deriving the pleasure felt in the presence of the beautiful or sublime, not directly from the form or constitution of the object as such, nor from the sensations it excites, but from the recall or revival of pleasure previously experienced in connection with the same or a related object or quality; e.g. a red cheek suggests youth and health, and is beautiful; red hands suggest disagreeable labour, and are ugly.

The principle of association has been used to explain either all or only a part of aesthetic value. Some writers have had in mind the accidental associations which individuals have formed in their particular experience; others, the universal relations of natural processes and qualities. Buffier (1724) and Reynolds (1759), in connection with the view that the beautiful in nature is a fixed form for each species toward which nature inclines—a sort of mean or average—and that the ugly is a departure therefrom, drew the conclusion that 'the effect of beauty depends on habit alone, the most customary form in each species of things being invariably the most beautiful.' We admire beauty for no other reason than that we are used to it. Alison (*Essay on the Nature and Principles of Taste*, 1790), while recognizing that association cannot account for the effect of beauty unless the associated elements have intrinsic pleasing quality, developed the working of the principle in great detail, and was followed by Jeffrey, who asserted that 'beauty is not an inherent property or quality of objects at all, but the result of the accidental relations in which they may stand to our experience of pleasures or emotions.' Any object may become beautiful in this way. Stewart

(1810), while rejecting the extreme form of the theory as held by Reynolds, agreed in the main with Alison, and made a specific application of the principle to explain how the word 'beauty,' which originally referred to objects of sight only, came to be applied 'transitively' to perceptions of other senses. Spencer (*Princ. of Psychol.*, ii) accepts the general principle 'under an expanded form,' which would include not merely our own individual associations, but those of the race, transmitted by heredity. Spencer, however, does not use this as the sole principle of explanation.

The same is true of Fechner (*Vorschule d. Aesthetik*, 1876), who has given the most extended recent discussion. He emphasizes especially the constant and universal associations found in nature—colours with grass, sky, or fire—as contrasted with accidental or individual experiences. The principle, so far as it implies a conscious recollection, was criticized by Volkelt (*Der Symbolbegriff in d. neuesten Aesthetik*, 1876), and has been reaffirmed in the sense not of conscious recollection or comparison of separate elements, but as 'the implicit relation existing between different ideas,' by Stern (*Einfühlung u. Assoc. in d. neueren Aesthetik*, 1898). See also Thomas Brown, *Philos. of the Human Mind*, 124 ff.

Literature: The work of STERN, cited above, contains a sketch of recent discussions in Germany. BEGG, The Devel. of Taste, 1887, and STEWART, Essays, in Works, ed. Hamilton, v, contain some historical material. See also GURNEY, Power of Sound, chap. vi; SANTAYANA, Sense of Beauty (1896), Pt. IV; and the authors named in the text. HARTLEY, Observations on Man (1749), and JAS. MILL, Anal. Phenom. Human Mind (1829), treat aesthetic association briefly. (J.H.T.)

Association (in education). A purposive comparison of newly presented facts with other related facts already known; a phase of inductive teaching that leads to the perception of a general truth; a stage in Herbartian method. See METHOD (in education).

Literature: MCMURRY, The Meth. of the Recitation, chap. vii. (C.DEG.)

Association (of ideas) [Lat. *ad + socius*, companion]: Ger. (*Ideen-*) *Association*; Fr. *association* (*d'idées*); Ital. *associazione*. A union more or less complete formed in and by the course of experience between the mental dispositions corresponding to two or more distinguishable contents of consciousness, and of such a nature that when one content recurs, the other content tends in some manner or degree to recur also. (G.F.S.—J.M.B.)

Aristotle, in his treatise on *Memory and Reminiscence*, recognizes the principle of association, and distinguishes association by similarity, by contrast, and by contiguity. The doctrine is further explained and illustrated by ancient commentators on Aristotle and by the Schoolmen. In the period of the Renaissance, Ludovicus Vives is distinguished by his careful treatment of this topic. It occupies a very prominent place in the psychology of Hobbes. The phrase 'association of ideas' was first introduced by Locke; but he seems to have had no insight into its general psychological importance. Berkeley was the first to extend the principle of association so as to make it cover not merely the sequence of ideas in train, but also the formation of percepts and higher states. Hartley proceeds further in the same direction, and so becomes the founder of modern ASSOCIATIONISM (q. v.).

Literature: for a compact history of the subject see CROOM ROBERTSON, Philos. Remains, 102 f.; FERRI, La Psychol. de l'Assoc., is also historical; HOBBES, Leviathan, chap. iii, and Human Nature, chap. iv; SPINOZA, Ethics, Bk. II, Prop. xviii (applied in Bk. III to theory of emotion); HARTLEY, Observations on Man, *passim*; JAMES MILL, Anal. Phenom. Human Mind; BAIN, Senses and Intellect (4th ed.), 336–40, and the exceedingly detailed and instructive exposition which follows throughout the rest of the book; SPENCER, Princ. of Psychol., chaps. vii and viii, especially § 120; SULLY, Human Mind, i. 185–205; S. HODGSON, Met. of Experience, iii. chaps. i and ii; JAMES WARD, Encyc. Brit., xx. 60; JAMES, Princ. of Psychol., i. chap. xiv; FRIES, Neue Krit., 159; VOLKMANN, Lehrb. d. Psychol., i. 73–9; LIPPS, Grundthatsachen des Seelenlebens, Pt. II, chap. vi; KARL DEFFNER, Die Aehnlichkeitsassociation, in the Zeitsch. f. Psychol., xviii. Heft 3; WUNDT, Physiol. Psychol., ii. chap. xvi; Grundriss, 265 f.; STRICKER, Stud. ü. die Assoc.; TAINE, On Intelligence, Pt. I. Bk. II. chap. ii; FOUILLÉE, La Psychol. des idées-forces, i. Bk. III. chap. ii; BRADLEY, Stud. in Logic; VILLA, Psicol. Contemp. (1899). Also the textbooks cited under PSYCHOLOGY; EISLER, Wörterb. d. philos. Begriffe (for many quotations); and BIBLIOG. G, 2, *l*. (G.F.S.)

Association (nervous). The process by

which the activities proper to several centres of the central nervous system are brought into a state of mutual influence or interdependence. The process of neural association is probably at the bottom of all mental processes more complex than the simplest sense presentation, and is accordingly much wider than the psychological term association of ideas. Cf. ASSOCIATION FIBRES. (H.H.)

Association (social): Ger. *Association* (1), *Verein, Gesellschaft* (2); Fr. *association* (1), *compagnie* (2); Ital. *associazione*. (1) The spontaneous being together of creatures, in regular ways, without regard to the mental states which actuate them; that is, without regard to the presence or absence of Co-

the science of 'the association of ideas' with sociology as the science of 'the association of individuals.' For a direct working out, however, of an analogy between the two, see Bosanquet, *Philos. Theory of the State*, chap. vii.

Literature: see the titles given under SOCIOLOGY. (J.M.B., G.F.S.)

(2) An organization to promote an object or to realize a purpose, e. g. The British Association for the Advancement of Science, The American Psychological Association. Legalized or chartered associations are called Companies.

Rousseau first clearly distinguished between association and aggregation. In his *Contrat Social*, chap. v. § 1, he says of a society held

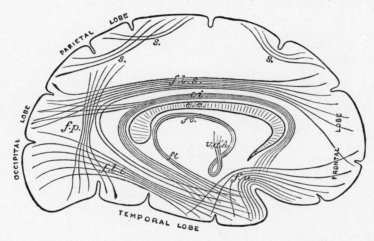

Diagram of the Association Fibres of the cerebrum. *s.*, short fibres connecting adjacent gyres; *f. l. s.*, superior longitudinal, *f. l. i.*, inferior longitudinal, *f. u.*, uncinate (to the uncinate gyre), and *f. p.*, perpendicular fasciculus; *ci.*, cingulum; *fo.*, fornix; *fi.*, fimbria; *v. d'A.*, bundle of Vicq d'Azyr. After Schäfer-Meynert, from Mill's *Nervous System and its Diseases*.

OPERATION (q. v.) on their part, or to its degree when present.

Association used in this sense is a sociological rather than a psychological term. It applies to social and gregarious life looked at by an outsider rather than as involving the recognition of it by the beings themselves. When used at all—it were better avoided altogether, unless qualified as 'social'; cf. AGGREGATION—it should be very carefully defined, seeing that one of the elements of conscious social and gregarious life is the association of ideas, a very different conception; and the confusion of the two is sometimes made. For example, Giddings (*Princ. of Sociol.*) contrasts psychology as

together by force, 'c'est, si l'on veut, une agrégation, mais non pas une association.' 'In the situation of an ignorant labourer . . . associating with no one except his wife and his children, what is there that can teach him to co-operate?' (J. S. Mill, *Diss. and Discussions*, i. 193). This usage continually recurs with reference to all possible modes of friendly and useful association in the *Nicomachean Ethics* of Aristotle. (F.H.G.)

Association Fibres. Those fibres which connect different parts of the brain. More specifically fibres (usually collaterals) which unite different areas of the same hemisphere of the cerebrum as contrasted with commissural fibres, such as connect corresponding parts of the opposite hemisphere via the callosum and precommissure. For a diagram of the latter relation see SPINAL CORD (Fig. 4). For illustration of the course of the more definite association tracts cf. the figure on p. 79.

The association fibres apparently develop late in the ontogeny, and the perfection with which the higher processes of perception, conception, judgment, &c., are performed may reasonably be supposed to be conditioned on the completeness with which the neural associations are provided for. Senile return to the simpler range of associations may result from the atrophy of the more remote connections.

Literature: MEYNERT, Neue Studien über die Associationsbündel des Hirnmantels, Sitzber. d. kais. Akad. d. Wiss. Wien, ci. (1892), 361–79; BECHTEREW, Zur Frage ü. d. äusseren Associationsfasern der Hirnrinde, Neurol. Centralbl. (1891); FLECHSIG, Zur Entwickelungsgeschichte des Associationssystems im menschlichen Gehirn, Berichte u. Verh. d. kgl. sächs. Gesell. d. Wiss. (1894); FLECHSIG, Gehirn u. Seele, Rede (2nd ed., 1896); BARKER, The Sense-areas and Association-centres in the Brain as described by Flechsig, J. of Nerv. and Ment. Dis., xxiv. 6, 326–56 (1897); SOURY, Le Syst. nerv. centr. (1900), ii. See also BRAIN, and NERVOUS SYSTEM. (H.H.)

Associationism: Ger. *Associationspsychologie*; Fr. *associationisme*; Ital. *dottrina psicologica dell' associazione*. The theory which, starting with certain simple and ultimate constituents of consciousness, makes mental development consist solely or mainly in the combination of these elements according to certain laws of ASSOCIATION (q. v.). According to this theory, rigidly carried out, all genesis of new products is due to the combination of pre-existing elements. Cf. COMPOSITION THEORY, and MIND-STUFF THEORY. (G.F.S.–J.M.B.)

We may quote from Hartley (*Observations on Man*, 1749) as at once the founder and, together with James Mill, the most typical representative of modern associationism: 'Sensations may be said to be associated together when their impressions are either made precisely at the same instant of time or in the contiguous successive instants. . . . Any sensations, *A*, *B*, *C*, &c., by being associated with one another a sufficient number of times, get such a power over the corresponding ideas *a*, *b*, *c*, &c., that any one of the sensations *A*, when impressed alone, shall be able to excite in the mind *b*, *c*, &c., the ideas of the rest'

(Pt. I, prop. 10). By frequent repetition of this reproductive process 'the simple ideas of sensation run into clusters and combinations; and each of these will at last coalesce into one complex idea, by the approach and commixture of the several compounding parts. . . . If the number of simple ideas which compose the complex one be very great, it may happen that the complex idea shall not appear to bear any relation to these its component parts. . . . The reason of this is that each single idea is overpowered by the sum of all the rest. . . .' as 'in very compound medicines the several tastes and flavours of the separate ingredients are lost and overpowered by the complex one of the whole mass. . . . One may hope, therefore, that by pursuing and perfecting the doctrine of association, we may some time or other be enabled to analyse all that vast variety of complex ideas, which pass under the name of ideas of reflection and intellectual ideas, into their simple compounding parts, i. e. into the simple ideas of sensation, of which they consist' (prop. 12). 'Admitting the powers of leaving traces and of association, compounds of mental changes will arise from simple bodily ones by means of words, symbols, and associated circumstances' (prop. 33). 'The passions must be aggregates of the ideas, or traces of the sensible pleasures or pains; which ideas make up, by their number and mutual influence upon one another, for the faintness and transitory nature of each singly taken' (prop. 89). Hume, whose *Treatise on Human Nature* was first published ten years before Hartley's *Observations*, is the first among English writers clearly to distinguish between association by contiguity and association by similarity. He adds to these causality, and considers himself to have given a complete list of the conditions of association. The chief interest of his work, however, lies in his attempt to give an explanation on the lines of associationism of the psychological origin of the categories of causality and individual identity. James Mill (1773–1836) works in an original manner on the lines of Hartley. In him associationism culminates. Its later representatives, J. S. Mill and A. Bain, are by no means pure associationists. J. S. Mill breaks away from the old tradition in his doctrine of 'mental chemistry,' and Bain does the same in a different way by laying stress on the importance of subjective selection as determining motor activity and attention. (G.F.S.)

Literature: see ASSOCIATION.

Assumption [Lat. *ad + sumere*, to take]: Ger. *Voraussetzung*; Fr. *assomption*; Ital. *assunzione*. In modern logic, an Assumption is the statement of a proposition, the truth of which is taken as granted for the purpose of the argument into which it enters. It is the more general type of which POSTULATE and HYPOTHESIS (see these terms) are the more important varieties.

Assumption among the earlier Latin logicians, from Boethius onwards, was the technical name for the minor premise. See Hamilton, *Logic*, i. 281, 284.　(R.A.)

Assumption (in theology): Ger. *Mariä Himmelfahrt*; Fr. *Assomption*; Ital. *Assunzione*. In Roman Catholic usage, particularly, Assumption means direct reception into heaven. Like freedom from original sin (though not with the same dogmatic certainty) it is viewed by the Roman Catholic Church as one of the 'privileges of the Virgin.' The feast of the name is celebrated on August 5.　(R.M.W.)

Assurance [OF. *assurance*, from Pat. Lat. *assecurare*, to secure to one]: Ger. *Zuversicht*; Fr. *assurance*; Ital. *certezza*. A term which came into general use at the time of the Reformation. In its technical sense it means personal certainty of grace or, more commonly, of salvation (cf. Rom. viii. 38; xiv. 5; Col. ii. 2; iv. 12; 2 Tim. i. 12; Heb. vi. 11; x. 22). See also INSURANCE.

Historically, three great theological groups have expressed themselves on the subject:— (1) the Reformers; (2) the Council of Trent; (3) the Wesleyans. (1) With Luther, the assurance of salvation is one distinctive feature of 'saving faith.' Knowledge of the faith brings sure and firm consolation to pious minds; the foundation is individualistic. With Calvin, the same doctrine holds true; belief in Christ's imputed righteousness implies assurance. (2) The Council of Trent, consistently with the Roman Catholic and scholastic position, allows the possibility of assurance, but treats it as a purely private affair. The Virgin and Jesus are the only subjects of a certain revelation on the matter. For, if thus favoured, the believer would be freed from obligation to the offices of the Church. (3) Wesley held a doctrine closely akin to that of the Reformers. 'Witness of the Spirit' is the source of this assurance in the evangelical churches. Cf. JUSTIFICATION.

Literature: DORNER, Hist. of Protestant Theol. (Eng. trans.), i. 227, 292; CUN-NINGHAM, The Reformers and the Reformation Theol., 124; HUNTER, Outlines of Dogmatic Theol., iii. 127.　(R.M.W.)

Assyria (religion in): see ORIENTAL PHILOSOPHY (Babylonio-Assyria).

Ast, Georg Anton Friedrich. (1778–1841.) A German philosopher and philologist.

Astasia: see ATAXIA.

Asthenia [Gr. ἀ + σθένος, strength]: Ger. *Asthenie*; Fr. *asthénie*; Ital. *astenia*. Lack or impairment of strength or vitality; general debility; also used in combination, as in neurasthenia, lack of nervous vigour. The term angiosthenia is used for lack of muscular force.　(J.J.–E.M.)

Asthenopia [Gr. ἀ + σθένος, strength, + ὤψ, eye]: Ger. *Asthenopia*; Fr. *asthénopie*; Ital. *astenopia*. A visual weakness due to the susceptibility to fatigue of the muscular mechanism concerned in the accommodation or in the general movements of the eyes. It may result from special strain or weakness in the accommodation mechanism or in the ocular muscles, or as a symptom of more general disorder. Cf. VISION (defects of). A retinal asthenopia is also spoken of. See Norris and Oliver, *Syst. Dis. Eye* (1900), iv; Clarke, *Eye Strain* (1892).　(J.J.)

Astigmatism [Gr. ἀ + στίγμα, a point]: Ger. *Astigmatismus*; Fr. *astigmatisme*; Ital. *astigmatismo*. A defect in the refractive mechanism of the eye, owing to which not all the rays of light which proceed from a single point are brought to a single point on the retina.

In regular astigmatism, one of the refracting surfaces, generally the cornea, is ellipsoidal instead of spherical; that is, it has meridians of maximum and minimum curvature at right angles to each other, though in each meridian the curvature is regular. When this is the case, the rays proceeding from a single luminous point are brought to a focus earliest when they lie in the meridian in which the surface is most convex; the pencil of rays will therefore have two linear foci at right angles to each other separated by a space in which the cone of rays is first elliptical, then circular, and then again elliptical. (An excellent binocular diagram of the course of such rays is given by Bowditch in Howell's *Amer. Textbook of Physiol.*) The defect may be detected by simple tests: if straight lines drawn in various directions through a common point cannot all be seen with equal distinctness at the same time, it is evident that the eye needs to be differently accommodated to focus rays in different meridians—i.e. it is astigmatic. The degree of astigmatism may be accurately determined by the ophthalmometer. The defect is corrected by the use of appropriate cylindrical lenses. Nearly all eyes are slightly astigmatic. Helmholtz could see sharply a vertical and a horizontal line at the same time if the former was 65 cm. and the latter 54 cm. distant; for Thomas Young (who first studied the defect) the sense of the error was reversed. The name was proposed by Whewell.

In irregular astigmatism there is a lack of homogeneousness in the refracting media (or else their curvatures in certain directions are not arcs of circles or ellipses). It is incapable of correction. It is the cause of monocular polyopia—of the several images which most people see of the horns of the crescent moon, for instance—and also of the rayed appearance of stars and of distant streetlights. See VISION (defects of).   (C.L.F.)

Literature: HELMHOLTZ, Physiol. Optik (2nd ed.), 169; RUEL, in Richet's Dict. de Physiol. i. 779; WALLER, Human Physiol., 422; BURNETT, Astigmatism (1887); DONDERS, Refraction (ed. by Oliver, 1900); LE CONTE, Sight (2nd ed.), 46.   (E.B.T.–J.J.)

Asymbolia [Gr. $\dot{a}$ + $\sigma\acute{v}\mu\beta o\lambda o\nu$, symbol]: Ger. *Asymbolie*; Fr. *asymbolie*; Ital. *asimbolia*. Loss of the power of forming or understanding signs or symbols of expression. The term is also used by Finkelnburg as a general synonym of aphasia. Cf. ASEMIA.   (J.J.–E M.)

Asymmetry [Gr. $\dot{a}$ + $\sigma\acute{v}\nu$ + $\mu\acute{\epsilon}\tau\rho o\nu$, a measure]: Ger. *Asymmetrie*; Fr. *asymétrie*; Ital. *asimmetria*. An unusual degree of unlikeness in structure or function in the two corresponding organs or halves of the body.

A large degree of symmetry is the rule in all but the lower forms of animal life, and seems to be related to the constant direction of progressive locomotion characteristic of such organisms. Yet symmetry is not complete, and the term asymmetry may be used to denote its normal lack of completeness, as well as an abnormal deviation in parts usually alike or nearly so. The nervous system and sense-organs share in this general symmetry, but more precise observation reveals slight or marked divergences. The two eyes are rarely alike in visual acuteness nor the ears in delicacy of hearing. The tendency to right-handedness is doubtless the most marked of the functional asymmetries, and is related to a greater development of the left hemisphere of the brain. Unusual asymmetries of structure or function—such as marked differences in the shape of the two sides of the head—are cited as signs of degeneration, and have been noted in the insane and criminal classes. See also DEXTRALITY and literature there cited.

Literature: HALL and HARTWELL, Bilateral Asymmetry of Function, in Mind, ix. 93, 899; VAN BIERVLIET, L'homme droit et l'homme gauche, in Rev. Philos. (1899); V. MAGNAN, Recherches sur les centres nerveux.   (J.J.–L.M.)

Lombroso (*L'Uomo delinquente*) and the Italian school of criminal anthropologists have investigated all forms of somatic and physiological asymmetry in lunatics, epileptics, and criminals. Cf. CRIMINAL.   (E.M.)

Asymmetry (in aesthetics). The absence of SYMMETRY (q.v.).

Asymmetry (in vision; of ocular movements). (1) Movements of ocular CONVERGENCE (q.v.) may be symmetrical or asymmetrical. In the former case the point fixated is in the median plane of the head; in the latter case it is outside that plane, and the lines of regard make unequal angles with that plane. Asymmetrical convergence is confined to transverse movements of the eyes; since they are in a horizontal line, asymmetry of movement upward and downward would be inconsistent with convergence, and hence it does not occur in normal eyes.

Literature: WUNDT, Physiol. Psychol. (4th ed.), ii. 165 f.

(2) Asymmetrical innervation of the muscles of an eye (e.g. paresis of the abducens) leads to wrong localization in the field of that eye. When the patient is required to turn the eye in the direction of the normal action of the paralyzed muscle there is displacement of objects in the visual field, despite the fact that the eye has not moved. The phenomena of displacement have been turned to account for theories of visual localization. Cf. LOCAL SIGN.

Literature: WUNDT, Physiol. Psychol. (4th ed.), i. 424.

(3) Normal asymmetry of muscular innervation in the vertical and horizontal directions is thought to account for certain geometrical OPTICAL ILLUSIONS (q.v.).

Literature: WUNDT, Physiol. Psychol. (4th ed.), ii. 137.   (E.B.T.)

Asynergia [Gr. $\dot{a}$ + $\sigma\acute{v}\nu$ + $\dot{\epsilon}\rho\gamma\epsilon\hat{\iota}\nu$, to work]: Ger. *Asynergie*; Fr. *asynergie*; Ital. *asinergia*.

Defective muscular co-ordination. See ATAXIA, and SYNERGY.

The term refers to the lack of central co-ordination in the innervation processes involved, as in paraphasia. (J.J.—J.M.B.)

Atavism [Lat. *atavus*, a distant ancestor]: Ger. *Atavismus*; Fr. *atavisme*; Ital. *atavismo*. Reversion to a more primitive type shown by the reappearance by hereditary transmission of ancestral characters, which normally are no longer developed. The cases of atavism may be classed in two main groups: (1) the reappearance in the progeny of a character (normal or abnormal) absent in its immediate progenitors, but present in its more remote ancestors; (2) the reappearance in a race or individual of a character originally derived by the crossing of more or less remote ancestors from another race. Atavism often accompanies intercrossing, or a pronounced change in the conditions of life. In practice, however, atavism is not always distinguishable from the recurrence of variation of like character, or from the direct effect of external influences on plastic organisms. Indeed, it is probable that the latter may act as stimulating conditions under which the atavistic characters arise. (E.S.G.—E.B.P.)

Literature: CH. DARWIN, Animals and Plants under Domestication (1888); A. WEISMANN, Germ-Plasm (1893); Y. DELAGE, L'Hérédité (1895). (C.LL.M.)

The theory of atavism has recently been applied in criminal anthropology (see CRIMINAL); a class of criminals being considered, on the ground of certain apparently atavistic physical characters, as owing their criminal propensities to reversion through heredity. See the literature given under CRIMINAL (anthropology), especially the works of the Italian school, Lombroso, Ferri, Garofalo, &c. (J.M.B.)

Ataxia [Gr. *à* + τάσσειν, to order, to arrange]: Ger. *Ataxie*; Fr. *ataxie, tabes*; Ital. *atassia*. Although the term ataxia indicates any irregularity of function, its use is practically restricted to inco-ordination of muscular action; a difficulty or inability in co-ordinating voluntary movements. Furthermore, as locomotor ataxia is the most common form of the disorder, the single term ataxia is frequently used as synonymous with that form; and again, as locomotor ataxia is the most characteristic symptom of a disease of the spinal cord known as tabes dorsalis, the term locomotor ataxia is frequently used as a synonym of the disease of which it is the prominent symptom.

This last usage, however, is certainly not desirable; and it is well, in order to differentiate the several forms of ataxia, to retain that term in its general sense. Asynergia is another term used to designate this general defect of co-ordination. Ataxia is distinguished as static, or motor; the former appearing as an irregularity in the maintenance of attitudes and positions, while the latter becomes evident in the difficulty and lack of precision of movements. As forms of static ataxia (also symptomatic of tabes) may be mentioned the excessive swaying and tottering which occurs when one is standing still with the eyes closed, the inability to balance the body on one leg, or to extend the arm steadily (also called astasia).

Motor or muscular ataxia is much more striking and varied; it much more frequently affects (and in tabes usually first affects) the legs than any other organ of movement, and is then locomotor ataxia. As examples of ataxia of the upper extremities may be mentioned the shakiness of the handwriting, difficulty in handling objects, in grasping and pointing, in playing upon an instrument, and in all actions which require skill in manipulation. The difficulty becomes greatly emphasized if any of the simpler co-ordinations is attempted with the eyes closed. A similar disorder affecting speech would be termed atactic aphasia or ataxophemia. The signs of locomotor ataxia have been carefully studied. The ataxic gait is most characteristic; walking with the eyes closed becomes impossible, and sticks or crutches are depended upon. The normal pendular swing of the leg is replaced by a jerky lifting and propulsion of the foot to be advanced, which is then frequently brought down with a thump. The body is not well balanced, and the trunk is elevated unduly in shifting the weight of the body from one leg to the other. In less pronounced cases walking is less seriously affected, but there is considerable uncertainty in starting out, or in suddenly rising from a chair and walking, in starting and stopping at command, in turning about, in going down stairs, &c. These and other tests have been used to detect the incipient stages of tabes dorsalis. Cf. TABES.

Literature: P. BLOCQ, Les troubles de la marche dans les maladies nerveuses; PICK, art. Ataxie, in Eulenberg's Real-Encyk., ii. 409; GRASSET et RANGIER, Traité pratique des maladies nerveuses (4th ed., 1894, also for bibliography). (J.J.)

Athanasian Creed: Ger. *Athanasianisches Glaubensbekenntnis*; Fr. *symbole d'Athanase*; Ital. *simbolo di Atanasio*. A pseudonymous document, chiefly remarkable as an orthodox summary of the conclusions arising from the great Christological discussions which broke out at the time of Arius, and continued till the 5th century. This creed is notorious for its damnatory clauses.

The origin of this formula is unknown; it was certainly not written by Athanasius. Internal evidence would seem to relegate it, in its present form, to a period after the 5th century. Although often so classed, it cannot any longer be regarded as an Oecumenical creed, for it is rejected by the Greek Church and the American Episcopal Church, and has been seriously questioned by the Church of England. Its main value lies in the precision with which it summarizes the decisions of Oecumenical Councils and the doctrines of AUGUSTINIANISM (q.v.) in regard to the Trinity and the Incarnation. In these matters it is more dogmatic and abstruse than the Nicene Creed, of which it may be regarded as a development.

Literature: SCHAFF, Church Hist., iii. 689, and Creeds of Christendom, i. 34; OMMANNEY, Early Hist. of the Athanasian Creed; LUMBY, Hist. of the Creeds; HARNACK, Hist. of Dogma (Eng. trans.), iv. 133 f. (R.M.W.)

Athanasius, Saint. (cir. 296–373 A.D.) A famous Greek Father, the pupil and friend of Archbishop Alexander. His zeal and eloquence against Arius made him prominent in the Council of Nice. As archbishop of Alexandria, he is said to have refused to restore Arius to communion as ordered by Constantine I. Accused of sacrilege, he was condemned and exiled without proof, restored by Constantine II, and again deposed by Constantius. The Synods of Rome and Sardica approved his cause and doctrines, and he returned to Alexandria, but was again exiled by Julian, and lastly by Valens. The last five years of his life were spent in possession of his see. He was the firm and efficient champion of the 'orthodox party' which centred in the doctrine of the Trinity. Cf. ARIUS, and ATHANASIAN CREED; and see PATRISTIC PHILOSOPHY.

Atheism (theological use of) [Gr. *à* + *θεός*, God]: Ger. *Atheismus*; Fr. *athéisme*; Ital. *ateismo*. Within recent years theologians have so far departed from their ancient usage as to concentrate discussion upon the historical question: 'Are there atheistic peoples or tribes?' Great interest, too, has recently surrounded the view of God as a subjective phenomenon, issuing from the Ritschlian school. But neither question falls within the range of theology proper; the first belongs to anthropology and the science of religions, the second to psychology and metaphysics. Although, as a rule, theologians have employed the term with reprehensible looseness, especially in controversy, it may be said that, strictly speaking, from the necessarily dualistic standpoint of theistic theology, atheism can be applied to one theory only: Pancosmism is, for orthodox theology, the sole atheism.

Literature: ROSKOFF, Religionswesen d. rohesten Naturvölker; ORR, Ritschlian Theol.; WENLEY, Contemp. Theol. and Theism; FLINT, Anti-theistic Theories; HARRIS, Philos. Basis of Theism; MAINLÄNDER, Philos. d. Erlösung; GARVIE, Ritschlian Theol.; D'ERCOLE, Teismo, i (1883). (R.M.W.)

Athenagoras. Lived in the 2nd century. A Greek philosopher converted to Christianity, who wrote *An Apology for the Christians*, together with other theological works.

Âtman [Sansk.]. The Sanskrit term for the inner principle of that conception of unity which occupies so conspicuous a place in the Rig-Veda and especially in the Brahmanas.

Four senses in which the term has been used are traceable: (1) meaning life, particularly animal life, when the word often appears in the form 'tman'; (2) meaning the life principle—much in the same sense as the Aristotelian expression, 'soul is the primary reality of organism'; (3) meaning the individual subject or ego, with an emphasis, making it comparable to the scholastic conception of 'essence'; (4) meaning the soul of the world or universe. The former two may be called poetical, the latter philosophical, usages. In later Sanskrit (3) and (4) are the common meanings. Cf. ORIENTAL PHILOSOPHY (India).

Literature: OLDENBERG, Buddha, 25; MAX MÜLLER, Ancient Sanskrit Lit., 18. (R.M.W.)

Atom and **Atomic Theory** (material): see MATTER.

Atom and **Atomism** (mental): see MIND-STUFF THEORY, and COMPOSITION THEORY.

Atom and **Atomism** (philosophical): see PRE-SOCRATIC PHILOSOPHY (Atomists), and MONADOLOGY. Cf. extensive literary citations in Eisler, *Wörterb. d. philos. Begriffe*, 'Atom' and 'Atomistik.' Cf. also MATTER. (J.M.B.)

Atomic Weight: see CHEMICAL AFFINITY.

Atonement [ME. *at-one-ment*, probably]: Ger. *Versöhnung* (Anselm), *Acceptationstheorie* (Eisler); Fr. *expiation*; Ital. *espiazione*. The term used to characterize Christ's redeeming relation to mankind. The relative terms in the Old Testament embody the idea of 'satisfaction' and 'ransom'; in the New Testament, those of 'expiation,' 'redemption by blood,' 'release' (from the law), and 'ransom.' In the field of theology discussion of the subject falls within the doctrinal division of systematic theology, and is the chief problem in the section which treats of God's relation to man under historical conditions.

On a philosophical analysis it may be said that the history of the doctrine has always depended upon (1) the dominant religious conceptions of the day, with their philosophical presuppositions and accompaniments; (2) upon the nature of the answers given to these three questions: (*a*) What is the nature of Christ? (*b*) From what does man stand in need of being saved? (e. g. from sin? from guilt? from evil?). (*c*) What is the nature of God? On this basis it may be said very generally (1) that with the Fathers (especially the Greek Fathers) a *metaphysical* conception predominated; reunion of mankind with God was the end of atonement. (2) As speculative interest waned, and social and ecclesiastical organization became more fixed, a *juridical* conception emerged (Anselm) which, nevertheless, like the former, still left the personal, or subjective, element largely out of account. The purport of Abelard's *moral influence* theory was to recognize this subjective side; but, owing to the circumstances of the time, it exercised small formative influence: on the whole, scholasticism remained steadfast to the objective juridical idea. (3) With the Reformation the subjective element, in the shape of *personal conviction of guilt*, altered the entire trend of the discussion. Extreme theories tended to be formulated, of which Kant's may be taken as a reasoned type. (4) The metaphysical tendency of the earliest theories was resuscitated at the beginning of the 19th century, mainly by Hegel and his school; union of mankind with God once more became the leading problem. Objective ideas of a more specially theological character were promulgated by Hugo Grotius, whose scheme, known as the *governmental theory*, became the official 'New England' theology; by McLeod Campbell, a mediating theory of an ethico-penal character. (5) The chief modern representative of the subjective tendency was Schleiermacher, according to whom Christ transmits to men a new spiritual life of fellowship with God through his personal power over them. This theory may be termed mystical. Other notable modern discussions are those of Dorner and Rothe, the former being conspicuous for knowledge and analytic power, the latter for spiritual insight; both attempt to combine the subjective and objective elements. Finally, Ritschl has reiterated a subjective view by teaching that men are able to judge of sin only through the impression made upon them by the life of Christ. From a purely philosophical standpoint it cannot be said that the personal subjective and metaphysical objective elements have been adequately reconciled as yet. The contact of the reforming subjectivity with the objective conclusions derived from evolution and other recent conclusions serves to make this the plainer. Many prominent theologians recognize the existence of the difficulty.

Literature: the relative article in Herzog's Real-Encyc. (with literature); DORNER, Syst. of Christ. Doctrine (Eng. trans.), Pt. II, first main division (with literature); BRUCE, Humiliation of Christ; ORR, Christ. View of God and the World. (R.M.W.)

Atrophy (-ia) [Gr. ἀτροφία, lack of nourishment]: Ger. *Atrophie*; Fr. *atrophie*; Ital. *atrofia*. Reduction in size or efficiency in an organ or mechanism of the body as a result of disuse, injury, or disease. Atrophy differs from degeneration in that the latter implies an actual destruction of the tissue. It is also distinguished from aplasy by careful writers. Cf. APLASY, and DEGENERATION. (H.H.)

In connection with the theory of evolution the term atrophy is now used for the diminution of an organ or tissue owing to its being useless (through change of habit or environment), or through its being superseded by some other organ. The inheritance of atrophy due to disuse is one of the tenets of the Lamarckian school of evolutionists.

Literature: art. Atrophy, Encyc. Brit. (9th ed.); J. DEMOOR, J. MASSART, and E. VANDERVELDE, Evolution by Atrophy (1899). (C.LL.M.)

Attention [Lat. *ad* + *tendere*, to stretch]: Ger. *Aufmerksamkeit*; Fr. *attention*; Ital. *attenzione*. The mind at work or beginning to work upon its object. Cf. Janet, ref. below. (G.F.S.—J.M.B.)

The attention is commonly described by such expressions as 'being occupied with,' 'concentrating upon,' 'absorbed in,' &c.

The two sorts of attention commonly distinguished are: 'reflex,' 'passive,' sometimes inappropriately called 'spontaneous,' on the one hand; and 'voluntary' or 'active' on the other hand—attention being reflex when drawn without the subject's foreknowledge by an unexpected stimulation, and voluntary when (1) it follows a purpose to attend, or (2) pursues an object intrinsically interesting. If we call the first of these cases 'volitional,' the latter may be named 'unvolitional' or 'spontaneous,' both being 'voluntary.' Cf. the recommendations made under ACTION. This main distinction, between reflex and voluntary attention, marks so clear a fact that it should be preserved (as against, e. g., Stumpf, *Tonpsychologie*, ii. 283).

To these may be added, though not correlative with them, Primary Attention (cf. Ladd), which indicates the supposed form of attention, or its organic analogue, in organisms so low as to be incapable of having a life of presentation. If attention be used with this meaning (cf. Ward, *Encyc. Brit.*, art. Psychology) it is better to qualify it by some such word as 'primary.'

Other distinctions are marked by the phrases: (1) Expectant Attention, or Pre-attention, with the variations Preperception (Lewes) and Ideational Preparation (Bain, *Emotions and Will*, 373; James, *Princ. of Psychol.*, i. 438; Münsterberg, *Die Willens-handlung*, 67), with (2) Diffused or Scattered Attention, characteristic of states of Indifference, lack of Interest, and Apathy, terms of degree used (in contrast with Strained, Concentrated, Effortful Attention) in reference to mental objects which are clearly taken in but quickly passed over. (3) Selective Attention, having reference to the outcome, on which see SELECTION (mental).

States of attention are also distinguished with reference to their objects as (1) Sensorial (attention to a sensation) and (2) Ideational, Ideal, or Intellectual (attention to an idea). For the one Sensorial is preferable to 'sensible,' as a translation of the German 'sinnlich,' and for the other Ideational is recommended. In regard to attention directed to the motor functions we find that it facilitates strictly voluntary functions, but interferes with and retards those which are automatic or tending to become so.

With some notable exceptions (Wolff, Kant, and James Mill) the attention was greatly neglected until more modern times, notably by the English empiricists (cf. James, *Princ.*

of Psychol., i. 402). It was considered an unanalysable attribute of the soul, and direct evidence of the independent activity of the mental principle (Hamilton, Carpenter, McCosh). With Leibnitz it was the essential mode of receiving new experiences which he termed apperception.

Recent literature, however, is full of theories of attention, which may be grouped under certain headings. There are (1) the affective theories (Horwicz, Ribot); (2) the 'psychical energy' and 'original activity' theories (Lotze, Wundt, Stumpf, Ward, Ladd, Jodl); (3) the conative and motor theories (Bain, Lange, Münsterberg, Stout, Baldwin); (4) the 'intensity' and 'reinforcement' theories (Condillac, G. E. Müller, Bradley); (5) the 'inhibition' theory (Ferrier, Obersteiner).

The differences of opinion on the question as to whether attention is a separate or independent faculty or a function of the content in mind, are now reflected in the question as to whether it be, if a function, a common and constant, or a variable and specialized function. It has recently been argued, in opposition to the 'constant function' view, that attention is a variable function: that we have not one attention, but many attentions. On this view, while there is a constant element in the different reactions of attention to different contents, there are nevertheless both 'typical' (visual, auditory, &c.) and also individual or special elements characteristic of each. The discussion of the question is facilitated by the use of symbols put in a formula:—

Att (attention) $= A + a + a$: a formula showing the mental elements which enter into an act of attention, apart from the object attended to, in which the symbols have the following significance:

$A =$ elements common to all acts of attention.

$a =$ elements special to acts of attention to different classes of objects, but common to acts of attention to all the objects of each class.

$a =$ elements special to acts of attention to each single object, but common to repeated acts of attention to the same object.

The advantage of the symbols is that they can be used in the discussion of any of the theories of attention; that is, they can be given motor, affective, or intellectual values. It does not even require the view that all the symbols have positive values; for on the theories which consider attention as a constant faculty or function, the formula reduces itself to $A = A$, the other symbols being each zero (cf. Baldwin, *Ment. Devel. in the Child and the Race*, chap. x. § 3; chap. xi. § 2; chap. xv).

Literature: CHR. WOLFF, Psychol. Empirica, § 245; JAMES MILL, Analysis of the Phenomena of the Human Mind; BAIN, Emotions and Will, 373 f.; BRADLEY, Mind, xi. 305 ff.; WARD, art. Psychology, in Encyc. Brit. (9th ed.); STUMPF, Tonpsychologie, i. 33, and ii. 208 ff.; MÜNSTERBERG, Beitr. z. exper. Psychol., i, ii, and Die Willenshandlung; G. E. MÜLLER, Zur Theorie d. sinnlichen Aufmerksamkeit; LADD, Psychol. Descrip. and Explan., chap. v; JAMES, Princ. of Psychol., ii. chaps. xi, xxvi; WUNDT, Physiol. Psychol., ii. chaps. xv, xvi; LEWES, Problems of Life and Mind, 3rd series, Prob. 2, chap. ix. 106, and chap. x. 184; RIBOT, La Psychol. de l'Attention; PIERRE JANET, art. Attention in Richet's Dict. de Physiologie, and Névroses et idées fixes, i. 69; WAITZ, Lehrb. d. Psychol., § 55; VOLKMANN, Lehrb. d. Psychol., ii. § 114; BALDWIN, Handb. of Psychol., Feeling and Will, chaps. xii, xvi, and Ment. Devel. in the Child and the Race; N. LANGE, Philos. Stud., v. 413; MARILLIER, Rev. Philos., xxvii. 566; FERRIER, Functions of the Brain, §§ 102 f.; OBERSTEINER, Brain, i. 439 ff.; HEINRICH, Die mod. physiol. Psychol. in Deutschland; STOUT, Analytic Psychol., i. 180 ff.; EISLER, Wörterb. d. philos. Begriffe (for German references). (J.M.B., G.F.S.)

Attention (defects of). Inasmuch as the normal exercise of attention, considered in both its spontaneous and volitional forms, involves the ability to concentrate the intellectual processes in a desired direction, and also a susceptibility to the influence of a large and variable number of impressions, any marked deviation from these may be regarded as defects of the attention. Abnormalities in the former direction would involve a deficiency of voluntary attention, and in the latter direction its excessive concentration, and consequently an undue limitation of its field.

Deficiency of Attention. 'As attention is the great conditioning factor in our intellectual life,' any serious impairment of intelligence will naturally bring with it a defect of the attention. This is well marked in IDIOCY (q. v.) and IMBECILITY (q. v.), as also in the waning of the mental powers in SENESCENCE (q. v.) and DEMENTIA (q. v.). In the former case, the very limited capacity, which is normal in childhood, to direct the line of intellectual

effort for any considerable period, never passes beyond the undeveloped stage; while in the latter case the normal range of attention has been established, but has again become unduly contracted. A subnormal capacity to fix the attention is also characteristic of several varieties of functional derangements of the nervous system, particularly in cases of brain exhaustion (cf. NEURASTHENIA). Sufferers from this disorder find great difficulty at certain times in concentrating their efforts in a given direction; a few minutes of reading may bring on feelings of mental confusion and distress, or there may result a 'swimming' of the page, the words floating by without conveying a meaning. Talking, or listening to conversation, may unduly strain the weakened power of the attention, and cause vague feelings of mental uneasiness or positive pains (headache, &c.). While this defect is intimately related to defects of the will (see WILL, defects of), it is well to note that many neurasthenics have appearance of energy and desire to work, but the actual effort brings on speedy exhaustion. Purely physical fatigue, or abstinence from food, defective nutrition, weakness from illness, may also produce similar symptoms of a more or less temporary character.

The cerebral intoxication induced by the action of drugs (cf. PSYCHIC EFFECTS OF DRUGS) is frequently characterized by a wandering of the attention and difficulty of concentration. This is true of the effects of large doses of alcohol, and perhaps even more of opium and its related medicaments. That such drug habits may bring with them a permanent impairment of the mental powers, in which attention is markedly affected, is sufficiently indicated by accounts of alcoholism and opium-eating (De Quincey, *Opium Eater*; cf. Carpenter, *Ment. Physiol.*). A form of attention may also appear in normal men of gifted intellectual ability and high originality, whose minds overflow with plans and projects, but for whom the effort of execution and definite concentration seems almost impossible, which is yet not a defect. It has been called 'fluid attention,' and described by Baldwin (*Story of the Mind*, chap. viii. 3) as characteristic of the 'motor type.'

No definite pathology of the attention has been made out, and may by the very nature of the case be impossible; but there is considerable evidence (from disease and injury, from artificial experiments, and from comparative development) for regarding the functions of the frontal lobes of the brain as intimately connected with the power of attention.

Literature: D. FERRIER, Functions of the Brain; and the titles given under PSYCHIC EFFECTS OF DRUGS, and under LOCALIZATION (cerebral). (L.M.)

The name aprosexia has been given by Guye (*Brit. Med. J.*, 1889, 709) to an impairment of the attention due to nasal obstruction. Most of the cases occur in boys and young men of the student class. Aprosexia is also used in a more general sense for the inability to fix the attention; when due to neurasthenia, it would be neurasthenic aprosexia; when due to nasal obstruction, nasal aprosexia.

Fixed Attention. A typical example is furnished by the insistent or FIXED IDEA (q. v.), which occupies the narrowed field of attention and prevents the access of other impressions. Such a condition is frequently characteristic of the brooding phases of grief or melancholia, and likewise of conditions of undue excitement and the delusions of monomania. States of ECSTASY (q. v.) and deep religious absorption may present longer or shorter periods of intense oblivion to outer impressions. Many writers regard the hypnotic condition as involving by suggestion a similar cramp of the attention upon the suggested action or idea, and a consequent lack of receptivity to all other impressions.

Literature: P. JANET, Névroses et idées fixes, i, ii (1898), and L'automatisme psychol. (1889); RIBOT, Psychol. of Attention (Eng. trans., 1890); Dis. of the Will (Eng. trans., 1884); CARPENTER, Ment. Physiol. (Eng. trans., 6th ed., 1891), chap. iii, &c.; MAUDSLEY, Physiol. of Mind (1878), and Body and Will (1884), chap. iii; FERRIER, Functions of the Brain; EXNER, Psychische Erscheinungen, chap. iv; SOLLIER, Psychol. de l'Idiot et de l'Imbécile (1891); L. MARILLIER, Remarques sur le mécanisme de l'attention, Rev. Philos. (1889), and Du rôle de la pathologie mentale dans les recherches psychologiques, Rev. Philos. (1893). (J.J.–L.M.)

Also PAOLO RICCARDI, L'Attenzione nella serie animale (1876); G. BUCCOLA, Leggi del tempo nei fenomeni del pensiero (Milano, 1883); DE SANCTIS, Patologia dell' Attenzione (Rome, 1896). See also ATTENTION (above and below). (E.M.)

Attention (experiments on). The experimental investigations upon attention may be grouped under the following heads:—

(1) FLUCTUATIONS of attention (see that topic).

Literature: URBANTSCHITSCH, Centralbl. f. med. Wiss. (1875); Pflüger's Arch., xxvii; N. LANGE, MARBE, PACE, ECKENER, LEHMANN, in Philos. Stud.; MÜNSTERBERG, in Beiträge, ii; WUNDT, Physiol. Psychol. (4th ed.), ii. 295 ff.; HEINRICH, Anz. d. Akad. d. Wiss. in Krakau (Nov., 1898); COOK, Amer. J. of Psychol. (1899).

(2) COMPLICATION (see that topic). Cf. Wundt, *Physiol. Psychol.* (4th ed.), ii. 389 ff.; von Tschisch, *Philos. Stud.*, ii; Pflaum, *Philos. Stud.*, xv; Pierce and Angell, Jastrow, *Amer. J. of Psychol.*, iv, v.

(3) Range of Attention (see SPAN OF CONSCIOUSNESS). Cf. Wundt, *Physiol. Psychol.* (4th ed.), 286 ff.; Cattell, Dietze, in *Philos. Stud.*; Bechterew, in *Neurol. Centralbl.* (1889).

(4) DISTRACTION of attention (see that topic).

(5) Influence of attention on the estimation of time intervals (see TIME-SENSE). Cf. Wundt, *Physiol. Psychol.* (4th ed.), 409 ff.

(6) Reaction-time experiments (see REACTION TIME).

(7) Attention and concomitant processes, physiological and psychological.

Literature: Breathing and pulse: DELABARRE, Rev. Philos., xxxiii. 639; LEHMANN, Philos. Stud., ix; MÜNSTERBERG, Beiträge; WUNDT, Physiol. Psychol. (4th ed.), ii. 297; MENTZ, Philos. Stud., xi. Muscle sensations: MÜNSTERBERG, Beiträge. Adaptation of organ (eye): HEINRICH, Zeitsch. f. Psychol., ix, xi; MAC DOUGALL, Psychol. Rev., iii. 158; ANGELL and MOORE, Psychol. Rev. (1896), iii. 245; (ear): HEINRICH, Physiol. Centralbl. (1896); Wien. med. Wochensch. (1896). Organic processes: ANGELL and THOMPSON, Psychol. Rev. (1899), vi. 32.

(8) Effects of attention.

Literature: MÜNSTERBERG, Psychol. Rev., i; LALANDE and PAULHAN, Rev. Philos., xxxv; HAMLIN, Amer. J. of Psychol., viii. Cf. JAMES, Princ. of Psychol., i. 424. (E.B.T.)

Attitude [Lat. *aptus*, fit]: Ger. *Haltung*, *Einstellung* (cf. PREDISPOSITION); Fr. *attitude*; Ital. *attitudine*. Readiness for attention, or action, of a definite sort. A mental attitude is thus a motor or attentive DISPOSITION (q. v.) which represents a definite, relatively independent, and conscious function.

Attitude is used of both mind and body. Mentally, it is a state of the attention primarily, and secondarily an expression for habitual tendencies and interests. A physical attitude is primarily a state of partial stimulation to action of a definite kind, and secondarily an expression of HABIT (q.v.).

The theoretical question concerning mental attitudes is as to their relation to the respective mental contents or objects to which they have reference. A mental attitude is always directed towards something in mind: is the attitude a function of this, or is this content brought up by the attitude? Put this way, the question presupposes, however answered, a vital connection between content of whatever kind and attitude with its resulting action.

Psychologists distinguish between voluntary and non-voluntary attitudes, and for the latter class it is held that both attitudes of the attention and those of action result from mental contents (purely physical attitudes being due to habit or to direct organic stimulation). With reference to attitudes toward action, most contemporary psychologists hold that they are revivals of earlier actions brought about by the perception or thought of the object to which they are appropriate (James, Münsterberg, Wundt lately, Baldwin). Some, however, still hold (Ladd, Ward) that the mind may take a quite original attitude, which is not a function of the content, and realize action or new thought from this attitude. With this latter position is associated the view (Wundt formerly, Ladd, Waller) that this original mental attitude has its seat in the motor centres of the brain, whose discharge in action is accompanied by 'sensations of innervation' and 'feeling of effort.' See INNERVATION (sensations of). James holds that higher intellectual and moral attitudes are original and initiative of action (*Princ. of Psychol.*, i. 453 f.), a view which is not reconciled with his other position that effort is due to kinaesthetic sensations and is ultimately attention.

The tendency to consider attitudes apart from contents was practically universal in psychology until very recently. But felt attitudes are now considered on a par with presented contents as elements of analysis, under the terms 'motor elements,' 'dispositions,' &c. Münsterberg, Fouillée, Royce, Stout, Baldwin, have worked out theories which recognize motor attitudes as links of association in mental compounds (Münsterberg), as dynamic units correlative with ideas (Fouillée), as the unifying and the general, in all the mental life, contributing the subjective phase to various psychoses, such as recognition, judgment, belief (Bain, Royce, Stout, Baldwin). Further, in genetic psychology the view has been worked out that the organizing and conserving of experience on which mental development proceeds are due to two typical attitudes, under which all those of attention and action may be subsumed, the attitudes of HABIT and ACCOMMODATION (see these terms). See also SELECTION (mental).

Literature: see the titles given under the special headings cited in this article. Also BAIN, Emotions and Will (3rd ed.), 505 ff.; JAMES, Princ. of Psychol., i. chap. xi, and ii. chap. xxvi; and The Will to Believe; MÜNSTERBERG, Beitr. z. exper. Psychol., i; FOUILLÉE, La Psychol. des Idées-Forces, and Rev. Philos., xxviii. 561 f.; LADD, Psychol. Descrip. and Explan., chaps. v and xi; STOUT, Analytic Psychol., Bk. II, chaps. i, iii, vii, viii, xi; BALDWIN, Ment. Devel. in the Child and the Race, chaps. viii, xv. (J.M.B.–G.F.S.)

Attraction and **Repulsion** [Lat. *attractio et repulsus*]: Ger. *Anziehung und Abstossung*; Fr. *attraction et répulsion*; Ital. *attrazione e ripulsione*. Attraction is a force exerted between two bodies or particles tending to bring them together or to prevent their separation.

When the two bodies in question are at an appreciable distance apart attraction always varies inversely as the square of the distance, as in the case of GRAVITATION (q.v.) and magnetic and electric attraction. When the attracting particles are in contact, the result may be *cohesive attraction*, keeping the parts of a body together; *surface tension*, a contractile force between the surface molecules of a liquid which makes a drop of liquid assume its spherical form; or *capillary attraction*, between a solid and a liquid. The laws governing the various forms of cohesive attraction are essentially different from the law of gravitation, because two particles could not cohere by virtue of an attraction which did not increase more rapidly than the inverse square of the distance.

Repulsion is the opposite or algebraic negative of attraction, and is a force tending to separate two particles or bodies. Its most familiar forms are the tendency of two like magnetic poles, or two bodies electrified by like electricities, to move away from each other. As in the case of attraction, the intensity of the force is inversely as the square of the distance between the repelling particles.

The impenetrability of matter, or the resistance which it offers to compression, is, so far as its manifestation goes, of the nature of a repulsive force, the negative of molecular or cohesive attraction. (S.N.)

Attribute [Lat. *ad + tribuere*, to assign]: Ger. (1) *Attribut*, (3) *Eigenschaft*; Fr. *attribut*; Ital. *attributo*. (1) An essential characteristic of a being. Without its attributes, the existence of a thing is unthinkable. It is opposed to QUALITY, MODE, ACCIDENT. Cf. these terms.

Used in this sense by the Scholastics as a translation of the Aristotelian συμβεβηκὸς. Usually applied by them to the essential characteristics of the Deity. The term is still in use in theology. The 17th century philosophers apply the term to substance. Extension and thinking are the two attributes which we may know. It is defined by Spinoza: 'That which the intellect perceives of substance as constituting its essence.' The precise meaning of the term in Spinoza's system is disputed. K. Fischer makes 'attribute' equivalent to a force proceeding from the substance which he conceives as a *causa efficiens*; J. Erdmann considers the 'attributes' as forms under which the limitations of the finite mind compel us to view the infinite substance (*Hist. Philos.*, iii. 72).

(2) The logical predicate is sometimes called 'an attribute' or said to be attributive.

(3) Loosely, any quality or property is called attribute; an incorrect use of the word. (R.H.S.)

Attributes (of God, doctrine of): Ger. (*die Lehre der*) *göttlichen Eigenschaften*; Fr. *attributs de Dieu*; Ital. *attributi divini*. An integral part of the division of systematic theology devoted to discussion of the nature of God. An attribute is a quality which may, or must, be joined to the conception; but junction with a conception by no means implies that it is merely subjective. Cf. ESSENCE, PROPERTY.

(1) From the Christian standpoint, other religions inevitably lead to partial or abstract views; e.g. Judaism to undue exaltation of holiness, heathenism to a merely physical conception. (2) In early Christian thought the subject was not systematically explored. Knowledge of God, and the fact of the divine unity (as against Gnostics and Manichaeans), constituted the centres of interest. (3) With the rise and spread of Christological and Trinitarian controversies, systematic treatment of the attributes became necessary; the relation of unity (of nature) to diversity (of attributes), and of unity (of substance) to diversity (of persons), now became the central problems. On them the mediaeval and scholastic theories of God converged. The tendency was to elaborate the intellectual aspects and to pass lightly over the ethical. (4) Even after the Reformation this tendency continued, thanks (*a*) to the special Christology of the Reformers and to its prominence, and (*b*) to the Deistic controversies. Similar leanings were present in the Mystics, the most marked difference being traceable to the doctrine of knowledge termed the 'beatific vision.' (5) In the 19th century the influence of the idealistic movement (Herder to Hegel) and of Schleiermacher at length brought systematic theologians face to face with the entire problem, on the ethical as well as on the intellectual side. The analyses of Philippi, Thomasius, Nitzsch, and others, more particularly Dorner, are the most adequate presentations of the subject as a whole. Much has been done, from a more specially philosophical standpoint, by I. H. Fichte and his group (including Lotze). As concerns philosophy of religion, the central problem still remains that of the reconciliation of immanence with transcendence, and at the present moment it is attracting increased attention.

Literature: DORNER, Syst. of Christ. Doctrine (Eng. trans.), i. 187, 324, 344, 453; Person of Christ (Eng. trans.), i. division i. 88; Hist. of Protestant Theol. (Eng. trans.), ii. 452; HUNTER, Outlines of Dogmatic Theol., ii. 50; S. CLARKE, Discourse concerning the Being and Attributes of God; WEBER, Vom Zorne Gottes; BRUCH, Lehre von den göttlichen Eigenschaften; HARNACK, Hist. of Dogma (Eng. trans.), iii. 244 f., v. 110 f. (R.M.W.)

Attrition [Lat. *attritus*, from *atterere*, to rub]: Ger. *Attrition*; Fr. *attrition*; Ital. *attrizione*. There are degrees of sorrow for sin—conviction of guilt, implying contrition, being the highest. Attrition is the name given to sorrow proceeding from some lower motive, e.g. fear of future consequences. (R.M.W.)

Atwater, Lyman Hotchkiss. (1813–83.) An American divine, graduate of Yale College and of the New Haven Divinity School. Held a Congregational pastorate at Fairfield, Conn., and chairs in Princeton College in turn in mental and moral philosophy, logic, and moral and political science. He was, for a time, acting president at Princeton. He published several discussions, and an elementary work on logic.

Audition and **Auditory Sensation**: see HEARING.

Audition Colorée [Fr.]: Ger. *farbiges Hören*; Fr. as in topic; Ital. *udizione colorata*. See SYNAESTHESIA. (J.J.)

Aufklärung [Ger.]: see ENLIGHTENMENT.

Augsburg Confession: Ger. *Augsburgische Konfession*; Fr. *Confession d'Augsbourg*; Ital. *Confessione di Augusta*. The Augsburg Confession is the most authoritative of the Lutheran creeds. It was prepared by Melanchthon in 1530, with the approval of Luther, and at the request of the Emperor Charles V.

Its main value to the student of history of thought lies in the admirable moderation with which it sets forth the points of agreement and difference between the Reformers and the Church. This Confession drew a ' Confutation' from Eck and other Catholic divines, which the emperor approved. Melanchthon in turn prepared a confutation of this, known as the Apology of the Augsburg Confession. This is a more valuable document for the history of thought than the Confession—of which it is the authoritative exposition. It was completed fourteen months after the Confession.

Literature: SCHAFF, Creeds of Christendom, i. 225; iii. 3. (R.M.W.)

Augustine, Saint. (353–430 A.D.) See AUGUSTINIANISM, and PATRISTIC PHILOSOPHY.

Augustinianism: Ger. *Augustinianismus*; Fr. *Augustinianisme*; Ital. *Agostinianismo*. The name given to the doctrines of Aurelius Augustinus, bishop of Hippo.

Augustine was the founder of Christian philosophy in the West, and by far the most important of patristic writers, holding a supremacy among the Latin Fathers which even Origen by no means enjoyed among the Greek.

In the course of his long career Augustine passed through several distinct stages of intellectual and spiritual experience; these have left their mark on his work everywhere. (1) After receiving a good education, he devoted himself to the principal higher study of his time, rhetoric; was aroused to the pursuit of truth by Cicero's *Hortensius*, and, to this end, studied the Scriptures in Latin translations, his knowledge of Greek being very defective. (2) Dissatisfied with the results of this inquiry, he turned to the MANICHAEANS (q. v.) for aid, and belonged to their sect for ten years (till 383). (3) Having gone to Rome, he was there appointed to a professorship of rhetoric at Milan. In his new home he listened, first

as a rhetorician and for practical purposes, to the eloquent preaching of Ambrose, but soon passed from connoisseurship of its manner to consideration of its matter. This, with special study of Paul's writings, led to his conversion in 386, and baptism in 387. (4) Passing once more to his native Africa, he lived as a recluse for several years, in marked contrast to his former laxity. In 391 he was ordained priest at Hippo, in 395 coadjutor-bishop, and six months later succeeded to the full bishopric. The rest of his career, coincident with his episcopate of 35 years, was spent in Africa, where ecclesiastico-religious conditions exerted an important influence over his thought and writings. He was prominent in three great controversies —with the MANICHAEANS (q.v.), the DONATISTS (q. v.), and the PELAGIANS (q. v.). Opposition to the teachings of the first and last was of particular importance in moulding his views, especially of God and the Trinity, and of Grace and Free Will. His ignorance of Greek left him independent of previous doctrinal controversies, while his training as a rhetorician lent peculiar force to his speech, and elegance to his writing.

Three main elements combine in the formation of his opinions : (1) The personal, consisting in vivid spiritual experiences, and in remarkable talent for self-analysis; (2) the philosophical, emanating chiefly from the pursuits and training incident to his pre-Christian period, and destined to exercise more influence in his earlier than in his later ecclesiastical life; (3) the religious, traceable partly to his early struggles, partly to his conception of the Catholic Church, and partly to the difficulties of Christian doctrine which he was compelled to face as a controversialist. This element, particularly as connected with the idea of the Church, grew in force, and finally became paramount. In his philosophy, Augustine starts from the principle of the immediate certainty of knowledge. Even doubt cannot but testify to the fact of knowledge. Thence he at once passes to show that the existence of God is necessarily involved in this first principle. With these two normative principles he has a firm basis, and finds himself able to unite the individual and the universal. Here the influence of Plato exercises marked influence, especially in the proof that all knowledge is ultimately knowledge of God. Proceeding to fill out the conception of Deity, Augustine at once shows his tendencies as a master of introspection by adopting the will as central characteristic; and in this what is commonly known as Augustinianism has its source. The world was created by God's free choice; the Timeless created the world in time, and upon God it ever depends for continued existence. Evil was not created by God, and is good only in so far as it must exist with God's permission, and because he can cause good to grow out of it. Human souls are essentially personal or individual, and come into existence along with their bodies. Memory, intellect, and will are the soul's principal faculties, and they serve to reflect the triune nature of God. This psychological theory immediately passes over into an ethical one. Individuality and will are intimately related. Hence, free will is the foundation of the possibility of morality. Free will implies freedom of choice, or, in another aspect, exemption from evil—which may be expressed also as freedom for good. In the latter sense —which predominates as concerns this life— freedom is wholly dependent upon the grace of God. Here philosophy passes over into theology. Man was free at the first, and therefore had the capacity to sin from choice. This Adam did, and, through him, all men lost freedom; it became impaired as concerned the soul's most vital interest. Man could not attain salvation because of original sin. But God in his grace had elected some to salvation; before the beginning of the world he had pre-determined the saved. But this grace can be received only through the Church. The conceptions of God, original sin, and the Church are therefore organic to each other, and serve to explain at once one another and man's worldly vocation. Freedom of the will and Predestination are the two *foci* of Augustine's theology. By means of the former, he triumphs over heretics; by means of the latter he is able to furnish a systematized Weltansicht. Christian subjectivity and Greek objectivity lie side by side. The development of Augustine's influence, especially in Aquinas and the Reformers, shows that the two sides had not been completely united.

Literature: art. in Herzog's Real-Encyc. (with literature); any history of mediaeval philosophy—STÖCKL, WINDELBAND, ERDMANN, HÖFFDING; HARNACK, Hist. of Dogma (Eng. trans.), v. (R.M.W.)

Aura [Gr. αὔρα, breeze]: Ger. *Aura*; Fr. *aura*; Ital. *aura*. (1) Any subjective sensory or motor phenomenon that ushers in a nervous seizure such as epilepsy or hysteria; (2) specifically, the subjective sensation as of a current of air rising from some part of the body to the head, which is a frequent premonition of an epileptic attack; (3) a supposed emanation or fluid assumed by believers in mesmeric or similar forces as the medium of conveyance of such forces.

The premonitory symptoms of epilepsy are frequently spoken of as the *aura epil ptica*, and of hysteria as the *aura hysterica*. The forms of aura are extremely various. They may be motor, such as local tremors, twitchings, or spasms, deviations of the eyes, contortions of the face, &c.; they may be sensory, as a general feeling of heat or cold, tingling, numbness, pain, dizziness, as well as subjective auditory and visual sensations; they may be visceral or vaso-motor sensations, blushing, choking, burning in the stomach, excessive salivation; and they may be mental, such as sudden fright or apprehensiveness. The nature and development of the aura is at times of importance in detecting the precise nature of the malady. See EPILEPSY (also for literature), and HALLUCINATION. (J.J.)

Literature: PARISH, Hallucinations and Illusions (1897); MAGNAN, Leçons clin. sur les maladies ment. (1893); MARINESCO and SENEUX, Essai sur la pathogénie et le traitement de l'épilepsie (1895); CH. FÉRÉ, Les épilepsies et les épileptiques (1896), particularly chap. vi. (L.M.–J.J.)

Austrian School (of political economy): see CONSUMPTION, and MARGINAL INCREMENT.

Authenticity [Gr. αὐτοέντης, αὐθέντης, one who does anything with his own hand; Ger. *Authenticität*, *Echtheit*; Fr. *authenticité*; Ital. *autenticità*. A main problem of 'higher,' as distinguished from 'lower' (or merely textual), criticism, involving all questions of authorship and title; of genuineness, compilation, and forgery; of tradition with respect to authorship. Possibly the most vivid practical example of the problem is to be found in Bentley's work cited below. Cf. CANON, CRITICISM, and EVIDENCE (external and internal).

Literature: BENTLEY, Diss. on the Epistles of Phalaris (Wagner's ed., 1883). (R.M.W.)

Authority (in religion) [Lat. *auctoritas*, a decree]: Ger. *Autorität*, *Zeugnis* (of writings); Fr. *autorité*; Ital. *autorità*. The term has several meanings. (1) Ecclesiastical. (*a*) The Roman Catholic view, of an infallible Church, implies that an external organization, being universal, submerges the individual, or at least sets the bounds within which conclusions reached by individuals must fall. Pushed to an extreme it falls into a one-sided legalism, and this is always its prevalent tendency.

(b) According to the Protestant view, the Church (in its creed chiefly) and the Bible are norms from which the individual sets out; but their influence, *qua* authoritative, is dependent upon his personal response and willing co-operation. This view often runs the danger of rating belief higher than life, just as the Roman Catholic rates conformity.

(2) Theological. (a) The creed of a Church, or the theory of ecclesiastical organization, and the scriptural records are the norms from which the theologian starts; they provide the implicit subject-matter, the principles of which he is to render explicit.

(b) In Speculative Theology, which approaches most closely to philosophy, the norms are the facts of God's existence, his relation to the universe, and his peculiar nature. Here the authority may lie either in a common or universal reason, held to be revealing itself in the universe, according to the liberal interpretation; or in certain dogmas—which stand in need of being systematically rationalized—according to the conservative view. In recent years, owing to the influence of philosophy, such writers as Dorner, Sterrett, the authors of *Lux Mundi*, and others, have tended to fuse these two views.

Literature: WATERSWORTH, Faith of Catholics; MARTINEAU, Seat of Authority in Religion; OETTINGER, Die Autorität; DORNER, Hist. of Christ. Doctrine (Eng. trans.), i. 79; STERRETT, Reason and Authority in Religion; GORE (editor), Lux Mundi; BALFOUR, Foundations of Belief; LEWIS, Authority in Matters of Opinion.   (R.M.W.)

Auto- (in compounds) [Gr. αὐτός, self]. A prefix denoting reference to self.

Examples (q.v.): AUTOMATIC, AUTONOMOUS, AUTOSUGGESTION.   (J.M.B.)

Autocracy [Gr. αὐτοκράτωρ]: Ger. *Selbstherrschaft*; Fr. *autocratie*; Ital. *autocrazia*. A form of government in which the sovereignty is vested in one individual absolutely.

The Greek means 'ruling by oneself'; and the adjective (αὐτοκρατής) often means 'independent.' But αὐτοκράτωρ is used of absolute rule as well as of simple independence. In post-classical times it was translated dictator, and later still imperator in the sense of emperor. The typical autocracy is Russia, and the Russian word, Императоръ, was borrowed from Byzantine Greek.   (J.B.)

Autokinesis [Gr. αὐτός, self, + κινεῖν, move]: Ger. *Autokinese*; Fr. *mouvements spontanés* or *involontaires*; Ital. *autocinesi*. Movements due to causes within the organism. See MOVEMENT.   (J.J.)

Automatic and **Automatism** [Gr. αὐτόματος, self-moving]: Ger. *automatisch, Automatismus*; Fr. *automatique, automatisme*; Ital. *automatico, automatismo*. A machine which shows complex adjustments is automatic, and its action illustrates automatism.

1. In physiology: the adjective automatic is applied, in a strict sense, to those functions of the living organism which are independent of external stimuli, finding their stimulus in the conditions of the organism itself—such processes, e. g., as the circulation of the blood, respiration, the beating of the heart.

Literature: general works on physiology; especially FOSTER, Textbook of Physiol.; WALLER, Human Physiol.; VERWORN, Gen. Physiol.   (A.S.P.P.–J.M.B.)

2. In neurology: the terms are frequently used in a wider sense, to include what are more strictly known as REFLEX (q. v.) reactions. See AUTOMATIC ACTION (in psychology). It then indicates the performance of responsive acts independently of higher cerebral control.   (C.LL.M.–J.M.B.)

Literature: LLOYD MORGAN, Compar. Psychol. (1894), Monist (1896), and Habit and Instinct (1896); HARTLEY, Essay on Man; CARPENTER, Ment. Physiol.   (C.LL.M.)

3. In philosophy: automatism characterizes the whole behaviour of a living organism, so far as that is not influenced by conative consciousness.

Many of the actions of men and other animals fall admittedly under this category, and the question has been raised whether the whole life-experience of animals may not be so explained. This theory, called Automatism or the Automaton Theory, was propounded by Descartes in regard to the lower animals, whose actions he explained throughout on purely mechanical principles, going so far, apparently, as to deny to them any consciousness accompanying the changes which transpired in their bodies. During the last half-century the attempt has been made by Huxley, D. Spalding, Shadworth Hodgson, and others to apply the same theory to man, in whose case, however, it is impossible to deny consciousness accompanying the bodily changes. The theory of conscious automatism does not seek to ignore the irreducibility of conscious facts to terms of matter and motion, but it regards consciousness as, in its own language, an EPIPHENOMENON (q. v.), an inactive accompaniment of a series of molecular changes which form in themselves a closed circle of causes or real conditions. In Huxley's words

(Essay on 'Animal Automatism,' *Collected Essays*, i. 244), 'our mental conditions are simply the symbols in consciousness of the changes which take place automatically in the organism; and, to take an extreme illustration, the feeling we call volition is not the cause of a voluntary act, but the symbol of that state of the brain which is the immediate cause of the act.' As Shadworth Hodgson insists, states of consciousness not only do not cause material movements; they are not even the causes of other conscious states. They are 'effects of the nature, sequence, and combination of the nerve states without being themselves causes either of one another or of changes in the nerve states which support them' (*Theory of Practice*, i. 336). 'The doctrine that we are essentially nervous machines, with a useless appendage of consciousness somehow added' (Sully, *The Human Mind*, ii. 368), seems to involve the contradiction of an effect which costs its cause nothing; for transformations of energy are supposed to go on entirely in the bodily sequence. The mental accompaniment is either mere surplusage or it must absorb some of the energy of the material system. The DOUBLE ASPECT THEORY (q. v.), which in some of its statements closely resembles automatism, endeavours to avoid this inconsequence by referring both series conjointly to the causation of a single substance. It is to this group that Clifford more properly belongs, though sometimes cited as an automatist. Cf. PARALLELISM, and MIND-STUFF THEORY.

4. Aristotle uses the term τὸ αὐτόματον in a special sense to designate what would now be called the contingent—events which, as he explains, are not due to the purposive power of nature, but which occur, as it were by the way, as by-products, in consequence of some action which was purposive. See also MONISM. (A.S.P.P.)

Literature: cf. MIND AND BODY. The best exposition is contained in SHADWORTH HODGSON, Met. of Experience, ii. chap. ii. § 6; see also HUXLEY, Sci. and Culture, 199 ff. The best criticism is contained in HERBERT, Mod. Realism. See also LEWES, Problems of Life and Mind, 2nd series, and The Physical Basis of Mind, 307 ff.; WARD, Naturalism and Agnosticism, Lect. 12; JAMES, Princ. of Psychol., i. chap. v. (G.F.S.)

Automatic Action (in psychology). A succession of acts in response to repeated or continuous excitation, proceeding in more or less complete independence of attention. Cf. CONSCIOUS-REFLEX. (G.F.S.)

We owe to Hartley the distinction between 'primarily' and 'secondarily' automatic actions. Under the first head he includes all congenital reflex actions; under the second head, those actions which we perform without attention because we have become used to them. The typical cases of primarily automatic actions are the rhythmical organic processes, such as breathing (Hartley, *Observations on Man*, Introd., and props. 19 and 21). We adopt Waller's distinction between the simple reflex and the automatic process. The automatic process is a serial effect of serial stimuli (cf. Waller, *Physiol.*, 293). The word automatic is also sometimes used in the sense of self-moving or spontaneous. This clashes with the commoner usage, and should be discarded, except so far as the physiological usage given under (1) above is meant, in which case, however, the reactions are due to constant stimulating conditions.

Literature: see general works on psychology and physiology. (G.F.S.—J.M.B.)

Automatic Writing: Ger. *automatisches Schreiben*; Fr. *écriture automatique*; Ital. *scrittura automatica*. The name given to a form of writing that is recorded without the complete and conscious co-operation of the individual who writes; it is an elaborate and consequently less usual form of automatic movement which seems to be associated with obscure functional disorders of the nervous system (hysteria, &c.), but also occurs in persons who are healthy and entirely normal.

While really of the same general character as the unconscious movements involved in MUSCLE-READING (q.v.), it goes beyond these in involving not merely a definite direction of movement, or number and combination of movements, as in 'table-turning' or 'table-rapping,' but also a constant and complex as well as conventional co-ordination of the movements necessary to form letters, words, and sentences. In a typical but simple case, a pencil placed in the hands of the automatist will begin to write apparently of its own accord; the automatic character of the result being indicated by the fact that the writing proceeds the more successfully the more the subject is distracted from the action (by being directed to read aloud or by being engaged in conversation), and frequently, too, by the content and character of the writing. Such an experiment is still more likely to succeed when several persons co-operate by placing their hands upon a planchette or similar instrument, for then the slightest automatic tendency of any one of the party is apt to remain unchecked by the writer, and to be taken up and encouraged by the movements of the others. In a typical hysterical case, in which, according to the testimony of the normal consciousness, a hand or other member of the body is anaesthetic, the psychical character of such anaesthesia is revealed by the record automatically produced in response to touches upon the anaesthetic member. Much more elaborate and obscure forms of automatic writing have been recorded, which it is difficult to comprehend psychologically, and in which an element of unconscious deception is not excluded. It seems proper to speak of the directing intelligence of such writing and to endeavour to determine its relation to the conscious normal intelligence. The most usual theory ascribes the automatic expressions to the agency of a subconscious personality, which has become dissociated from the main conscious stream of thought, a secondary personality split off from the main personality, and accessible only by psychological means like hypnotism, or by automatic writing which reveals as 'out of gear' the usual co-ordinating relations of the highest cerebral centres. Much study and ingenuity have been expended upon the description of the phenomena, but no very satisfactory explanation has as yet been reached.

Literature: A. BINET, Alterations of Personality; P. JANET, Automatisme Psychol. (1889), and Névroses et idées fixes; JAMES, Princ. of Psychol., chap. x; MYERS, series of articles in Proc. Soc. Psych. Res., especially May, 1885; FLOURNOY, Des Indes à la planète Mars (1900); W. R. NEWBOL, Pop. Sci. Mo., xlix. See PERSONALITY (disorders of). (J.J.)

Automatism (psychic, psychological): Ger. *psychischer Automatismus*; Fr. *automatisme psychologique*; Ital. *automatismo psicologico*. The performance of actions apparently involving some degree of psychological determination, without the consciousness of the personal subject.

This term has gained currency from the usage of P. Janet in his work *Automatisme Psychologique*, which is devoted to the study of the phenomena described more fully under PERSONALITY (disorders of) and AUTOMATIC WRITING. The aspect emphasized by the term is that of the analogy to nervous automatic movement, in which no conscious control or initiative is exercised. Here the movements, &c., though apparently involving psychological processes, are nevertheless psychically or mentally unconscious, and are variously ascribed to 'secondary,' 'split-off,' 'low,' 'unconscious' forms of mentality resident in restricted portions or areas of the nervous system. Following the usage recommended under PSYCHIC AND PSYCHOLOGICAL, psychic or mental automatism is the more exact expression. Cf. the literary references made under the terms cited. (J.M.B.)

Automatograph: see LABORATORY AND APPARATUS, III. B. (*c*), (5).

Autonomy [Gr. αὐτονομία, independence]: Ger. *Autonomie*; Fr. *autonomie*; Ital. *autonomia*. (1) Independence, self-determination, freedom from external restraint or authority.

(2) By autonomy of the will may be meant either the actual freedom of the will (i. e. its freedom from causal necessity), or its relative freedom from externally suggested or imposed motives, such as social or theological restraints. In the latter sense a believer in necessity could still speak of the relative autonomy of the will of an independently minded man.

(3) In Kantian terminology, the character belonging especially to the rational will as such, the character, namely, of being altogether its own lawgiver. The law that the will or the practical reason gives to itself is in Kant's view, namely, quite independent of experience, as well as of all ordinary forms of authority. This autonomy implies metaphysical freedom. Cf. the next topic. (J.R.)

Autonomy (ethical). The characteristic of a moral being in virtue of which he is said to be a 'law to himself'; not in the sense of following his desires, but because the law which he recognizes as morally binding upon him is the law laid down by his own moral consciousness. (W.R.S.)

In this sense the term is used by Kant, *Grundl. d. Met. d. Sitten*, ii; *Krit. d. prakt. Vernunft*, I. i. 1, §§ 7, 8. He distinguishes between the true or rational self and the natural self with its content of sense and desire. This true self, which is practical reason, is at the same time will, and determines itself by its own law, which is the moral law. In other passages, however, it should be remembered (e. g. *Krit. d. prakt. Vernunft*, 229–31, ed. Rosenkranz), empirical character is referred to the 'causality of the noumenon.' All other ethical systems, inasmuch as they rely upon a law or end outside the rational will, are classed by him as systems of Heteronomy. (W.R.S.–H.S.)

Autosuggestion: Ger. *Autosuggestion*; Fr. *autosuggestion*; Ital. *autosuggestione*. The process of bringing about in oneself hypnotic or analogous suggestive states. Cf. SUGGESTION, and HYPNOSIS.

Wundt uses the term Fremdsuggestion for the contrasted and usual process of suggestion from another person. The analogous Greek formation would be Heterosuggestion. (J.M.B.)

Autotelic (1) and (2) **Heterotelic** [Gr. αὐτός, self, and ἕτερος, other, + τέλος, end]. (1) Autotelic: having or being its own end, existing 'for its own sake,' as contrasted with (2) Heterotelic: having or serving a foreign or external end.

Autotelic is suggested as serving, in the phrases autotelic function, process, &c., the meaning indicated by the German Selbstzweck, especially in recent discussions of the aesthetic. According to certain theories, the aesthetic and play impulses are autotelic. It is analogous to autonomic (in contrast with heteronomic), but narrower in its connotation. The distinction is important also in discussions of ethics and TELEOLOGY, under which it is further illustrated. (J.M.B., G.F.S.)

Avarice [Lat. *avaritia*]: see SENTIMENT (ethical).

Avatar. In Hindu mythology, the name used to signify each of the ten incarnations of Vishnu.

Vishnu became specially prominent in later Brahmanism for his incarnations. These were not THEOPHANIES (q.v.), nor demi-gods, but men in whom the god was actually present. The doctrine is that of a theanthropos. But the rich mythology has included beasts and monstrosities among the Avatars.

Literature: BARTH, Religions of India, 170; HOPKINS, Religions of India, 468. (R.M.W.)

Avempace of Saragossa. Died 1138. One of the leaders of Arabian thought in Spain. A physician, a mathematician, a philosopher, and an astronomer. Lived also in Grenada and in Africa.

Avenarius, Richard Heinrich Ludwig. Son of Eduard Avenarius, a German publisher and bookseller in Paris, where Richard was born in 1843. The family removed to Leipzig, and soon after to Berlin. Here began his education, continued later at Leipzig, where he was especially influenced by Carl Ludwig, Drobisch, and Zarncke. He was one of the founders of the Akademisch-Philosophischer Verein of Leipzig. He became Docent at the same university in 1876, and founded the *Zeitschrift für wissenschaftliche Philosophie*. He succeeded Windelband as professor of philosophy at Zurich in 1877, where he died, August 18, 1896. His philosophical system, called Empiriocriticism, has gained considerable currency (cf. the general account, biographical and expository, by Carstanjen, in *Zeitsch. f. wiss. Philos.*, xx, 1896, 361 ff., with references to the writings of Avenarius). An extended criticism of the system is by Wundt, in *Philos. Stud.*, xiii, 1897.

Average and **Average Error:** see ERRORS OF OBSERVATION, PSYCHOPHYSICAL METHODS, and VARIATION.

Averroës, or **Averrois,** or **Averois,** or **Averoys,** or **Averrhoës.** (1126–98.) The greatest of the Arabian philosophers and physicians. The pupil of Avempace and of Avenzoar, he became cadi (judge) at Seville and Cordova, enjoying great favour at the court at Morocco. He wrote commentaries on Aristotle and numerous works on medicine, theology, law, logic, &c. See the next topic, and the remarks on Arabian philosophy under SCHOLASTICISM.

Averroism (Ibn Roschd): Ger. *Averroismus*; Fr. *Averrhoïsme*; Ital. *Averroismo*. The doctrine of Averroës, the last great thinker of the Muslim world in the West.

In Averroës' thought, as in that of other Muslim thinkers, three main elements meet. (1) The philosophy of Aristotle. (2) Neo-Platonism as deflected through eastern Muslim thought, which was indebted chiefly to the NESTORIANS (q.v.). (3) The influences incident to Islam as a religion. Averroës is thus at once a philosopher, a theologian, and a theosophist. But in him, more than in any other, the philosophic tendency predominates, thanks to his faithfulness to Aristotle. His peculiar and normative tenets are: (1) the eternity of matter and of the universe, thus eliminating creationism; (2) the unity of the intellect of the individual man with the universal spirit, involving a denial of immortality, and a doctrine of return to an 'over-soul.' This 'over-soul' (Erdgeist) is not God, but an emanation from God. Averroës was thus a speculative rationalist. As such he came into collision with Islamic orthodoxy and was rejected; for the same reasons he was attacked by Albertus Magnus and Aquinas. Through Maimonides he exerted widespread and profound influence; lived again in the teaching of the school of Padua, of which Pomponatius (1495) was the most brilliant ornament. Roger Bacon, Duns Scotus, John Baconthorpe, Walter Burley, and Michael Scott, the 'wizard of the North,' were all affected by him.

Literature: UEBERWEG, ERDMANN, STÖCKL, Histories of Philos.; AVERROËS, Philos. u. Theol. (Ger. trans. by Müller); MUNK, Mélanges de Philos. juive et arabe; RENAN, Averroës et l'Averroïsme. (R.M.W.)

Aversion [Lat. *a + vertere*, to turn]: Ger. *Aversion, Abneigung*; Fr. *aversion*; Ital. *avversione*. See APPETENCE, and ANTIPATHY. (J.M.B.)

Avesta. Avesta, Avesta-Zend, or, as it is popularly and incorrectly termed, Zend-Avesta, is the name applied to what remains of the sacred writings of Zoroastrianism. 'Avesta' probably means 'law'; 'Zend' (Zand) means 'commentary.'

What remains in the Avesta is but a fraction of a great literature, which probably perished during, or after, the destruction of the Persian power by Alexander the Great. The fragments date back possibly as far as the 6th century B.C. What then remained was gathered carefully together under the Sassanians (213 A.D.). This, with further losses incident to the Muslim conquest, was made known to the Western world by Du Person in 1771. It may be divided into six parts. (1) Yasna and Gathas—liturgy and hymns. (2) Visperad—invocations. (3) Yashts—hymns to angels and heroes. (4) Smaller texts—prayers and 'doxologies.' (5) Vendidad—the law directed specially against demons. (6) Other fragments.

Literature: Sacred Books of the East, iv, xxiii, xxxi; F. SPIEGEL, Eranische Alterthumskunde. For other literature see TRÜBNER, Amer. and Oriental Lit. Rec. (July 20, 1865); TIELE, Hist. of Ancient Religions, 160; JACKSON, Zoroaster. For a philosophical interpretation see JULIA WEDGWOOD, Moral Ideal, chap. ii. (R.M.W.)

Avicebron, Salomon Ibn Gabirol. (cir. 1020–70.) A Spanish Jew who applied Aristotelian principles to the doctrines of Moses. He was distinguished also as a religious poet.

Avicenna, Ibn Sina. (980–1037.) An Arabian physician and philosopher. See AVICENNISM.

Avicennism. The doctrine of Avicenna, the greatest thinker of the Muslim world in the East.

Avicenna's philosophy consists mainly of Aristotelianism plus Neo-Platonism; but the mystic elements drawn from the latter are affected by MAZDAISM (q. v.). He is thus interested mainly in philosophy on its religious side, and his system is a doctrine of Being, based on Aristotle. God is necessary being; space, time, and the like, which receive necessity from God, are actual being; while the objects of the physical sciences are possible being. God is thus shot through all things, and the doctrine of emanation mediates between a crude creationism and an equally crude materialism. Hence Avicenna's doctrine of an 'active' intellect, common to all men, imparted to them, and destined to return again to God. In spite of this, Avicenna holds personal immortality. His doctrines had wide influence in mediaeval thought. Those who opposed Averroës respected Avicenna, not perceiving that the later thinker only drew the logical conclusions to which the earlier unconsciously pointed. It should be noted that his influence is most marked in Dante and the Mystics.

Literature: UEBERWEG, Hist. of Philos., i. 107; Encyc. Brit., sub verbo; ERDMANN, Hist. of Philos., i. 362. It should be pointed out that existing literature is far from exhausting the subject. (R.M.W.)

Award (in law) [Old Fr. *esguart*]: Ger. *Schiedspruch, Entscheidung*; Fr. *jugement arbitral*; Ital. *arbitrio*. (1) The final sentence pronounced by an arbitrator upon the matter submitted to his determination. (2) That which is to be said or done according to this sentence. An award differs from a judgment in that upon its publication the authority by which it is pronounced terminates, and therefore does not extend to its enforcement. Cf. ARBITRATION. (S.E.B.)

Axiom [Gr. ἀξίωμα, dignity]: Ger. *Axiom, Grundsatz*; Fr. *axiome*; Ital. *assioma*. A proposition, general in import, and held as standing in no need of, or indeed as incapable of, proof. Axioms are self-evident truths.

Aristotle uses ἀξίωμα in the sense of ultimate principles, which were regarded by him as being of two kinds: common, i. e. principles ultimate as regards any kind of reasoning or knowledge, such e. g. as the law of contradiction; special, i. e. principles which unfolded the ultimate nature of some type or kind of real existence. Such ultimate nature he took to be apprehensible, even if approached through the subordinate offices of sense-perception, by the intuitive grasp of reason. The same term ἀξίωμα was afterwards used by the Stoics to denote merely a proposition, and this usage was followed by the Ramist logicians and partly by Bacon, who, however, takes *axiomata*

I.

H

more in the sense of generalized statements. With Kant, axioms are synthetical propositions only, self-evident and intuitively apprehended. In his view, therefore, axioms are possible only within the sphere of intuition, i.e. of space and time. Round such axioms, much modern discussion is concentrated. (R.A.)

In mathematics, the term is commonly restricted to the self-evident propositions on which geometry is based, and those facts of general experience which are so familiar that every one must admit them. (S.N.)

Literature: CROOM ROBERTSON, Philos. Remains, 119–134; B. ERDMANN, Die Axiome d. Geometrie; EISLER, Wörterb. d. philos. Begriffe, sub verbo. (R.A.)

Axion. The central nervous system or cerebro-spinal axis; cf. NEURAXIS. To be distinguished from Axon, used by Wilder for the longitudinal skeletal axis of the vertebrate body and by Kölliker for the NEURITE (q. v.). (H.H.)

Axis Cylinder: Ger. *Primitivband, Axen-cylinder*; Fr. *cylindre-axe*; Ital. *cilindrasse*. The central nervous axis of a nerve fibre. Cf. NERVOUS SYSTEM, NERVE. For axis-cylinder process, see NEURITE. Sometimes abbreviated to 'axis' (Howell and Huber). Opinion differs as to whether the axis cylinder consists of an outgrowth of a single cell. There is much evidence in favour of the view that the longer peripheral nerves are formed by a moniliform union of many neuroblasts or ganglioblasts. (H.H.)

Azymites (and **Prozymites**) [Gr. ἀ + ζύμη, leaven]. Azymite is one of the names which arose during the dispute between the Eastern and Western Churches. It was applied by the Greeks to the Latins, because the latter used unleavened bread in the celebration of the Eucharist. The Latins retorted upon the Greeks with the epithet Fermentarii or Prozymites (1051 A.D.).

Literature: PICKLER, Gesch. d. kirch. Trennung zwischen d. Orient u. Occident, i. 255; NEANDER, Church Hist. vi. 337. (R.M.W.)

B

Baader, Franz Xavier von. (1765–1841.) German philosopher and Roman Catholic theologian, a follower of Jacob Böhme and opponent of Hegel and Schelling. He was professor of philosophy at Munich.

Bâbüsm: see SUNNITES AND SHI'ITES.

Babylonia (religion in): see ORIENTAL PHILOSOPHY (Babylonio-Assyrian).

Bacon, Francis. (1561–1629.) Studied at Trinity College, Cambridge, and there formed a dislike for Aristotle's philosophy. Visited France to study law and was admitted to the bar in 1582; became counsel-extraordinary to the queen in 1590. Elected to Parliament in 1584, he sat in every Parliament until 1614. The Cecils procured the reversion of registrar of the Star Chamber for him; it fell to him during the reign of King James. Knighted in 1603, he became one of the counsel of King James I. Married in 1606; became solicitor-general, 1607; attorney-general and member of the privy council, 1613; keeper of the great seal, 1617; lord high chancellor of England, 1618; in this year he became Baron Verulam and took his seat in the House of Peers; Viscount St. Albans, 1620. After his sixtieth birthday, he pleaded guilty to the charge of having accepted bribes as judge, and retired on a pension of £120,000, devoting his time until death to study. His great influence was all directed toward the 'new era' of science; but his real services are variously estimated. See BACONIAN METHOD.

Bacon, Roger. (1214–cir. 1292.) An English philosopher and monk, possibly the greatest philosopher of the 13th century. Educated at Oxford and Paris, he joined the Franciscan order at the former place. In 1278 a Franciscan council condemned his writings and committed him to prison, where he remained for ten years.

Baconian Method. The method of investigating experience which proceeds from given particular facts, and applies no general conceptions that have not themselves been gained from and tested by comparison with particulars. See INDUCTION. In the more special sense it names the special form of induction advocated by Francis Bacon.

The salient features are: (*a*) the investigation begins with a collection of particular instances, and for its perfect working out requires an exhaustive collection; (*b*) from the collected instances there are excluded by comparison all elements that do not accompany the phenomenon investigated; (*c*) the result of the exclusion or elimination of the non-essential is to disclose that simpler 'form' or more general characteristic of reality of which the phenomenon investigated is a specification; (*d*) the work of exclusion is a gradual one, and explanation therefore proceeds regularly from less to more general propositions; (*e*) were the collection of instances exhaustive, the comparison and exclusion would lead in all cases to a true result. Bacon's method is defective on two sides; his conception of nature retains so much of the Aristotelian and scholastic doctrine of causes (though his 'forms' are intended to be physical and are not abstractions) that his rules for exclusion are too narrowly framed; he did not allow for the free action of thought and its necessary function in theorizing. It is to be said also that Bacon's total failure to grasp the significance of the mechanical element in natural process prejudices his view and method.

Literature: ELLIS in the Introd. to vol. i

of Ellis and Spedding's ed. of Bacon's Works; FOWLER, ed. of Bacon's Nov. Org. (1878); LIEBIG, Fr. Bacon (1863); SIGWART, in Preuss. Jahrb. (1863); HEUSSLER, Fr. Bacon u. seine geschichtl. Stellung (1889); NATGE, F. Bacon's Formenlehre (1891); LEUCKFELD, Arch. f. Gesch. d. Philos., viii. (R.A.)

Baer, Karl Ernst von. (1792–1876.) A Russian naturalist belonging to a German family. Professor in zoology at Königsberg in 1819. Became librarian of the Academy of Sciences at St. Petersburg in 1834. Cf. v. BAER'S LAW.

v. Baer's Law: Ger. *Baer'sches Gesetz*; Fr. *loi de Baer*; Ital. *legge di Baer* (*dello sviluppo*). In the development both of the organism and of its parts there is progress from the simple to the complex, and from an unspecialized to a more specialized condition. The embryo passes through a series of stages in which it resembles the embryos of lower forms.

This generalization, based upon careful observation and prolonged research, Agassiz among the anti-evolutionists and Haeckel among the evolutionists regarded as of fundamental importance in organic development. See RECAPITULATION.

Literature: v. BAER, Beobachtungen u. Reflexionen ü. die Entwickelungsgesch. d. Thiere (1829); LOUIS AGASSIZ, Zool. Gén. (1854); ERNST HAECKEL, Gen. Morphol. (1866); A. SEDGWICK, On the Law of Development, Quart. J. Microsc. Sci., xxxvi. (1894). (C.LL.M.)

Bahnsen, Junius Friedrich August. (1830–81.) A German philosopher. Educated at Kiel and at Tübingen, he became a disciple of Schopenhauer, and an ardent advocate of his doctrines.

Balance (in aesthetics) [Lat. *bi-lanx*, two scales]: Ger. *Gleichgewicht*; Fr. *équilibre*; Ital. *bilancio, equilibrio*. Equivalence of value in the respective parts of a spatial or temporal whole, when contrasted or set over against each other with alternating attention.

It is an important factor in harmony. Its aesthetic value is probably closely connected with the feelings arising from bodily equilibrium and the rhythm of respiration.

It does not, like symmetry, imply an exact correspondence of point with point, nor does it refer primarily to the relation of part to whole, but rather involves that the general impression of the one part shall be of equivalent strength to that of the other. It is applied to the divisions of a line or surface, as in architecture, to the disposition of figures in painting and sculpture, to the strength of different parts of an orchestra or chorus, and to the parts of a line, stanza, or period in verse or prose. Cf. HARMONY, PROPORTION, and SYMMETRY. (J.H.T.)

Balance of Trade: Ger. *Handelsbilanz*; Fr. *balance du commerce*; Ital. *bilancio del commercio*. The difference between the value of the merchandise exported from a given country within a specified period, and the value of the merchandise imported into the same country during the same period. When the exports exceed the imports the balance is said to be favourable; in the reverse case it is said to be unfavourable.

Most of the economists of the 17th and 18th centuries thought that the exports of a country corresponded to the sales of a merchant, and its imports to the purchases of a merchant; that the net income of the merchant or of the country was represented by the excess of sales over purchases; that if a country had such an excess, it would be prosperous, and get gold or silver from other nations; that if it had a deficiency instead of an excess, it was unprosperous, and would lose its gold and silver. These views constituted what is known as the *mercantile system*. Their fallacy was exposed by the Physiocrats, by Adam Smith, and by J. B. Say. These writers showed that many other elements besides exports and imports combined to determine the movement of the precious metals; and also that this movement was a far less important index of national prosperity than the adherents of the Mercantile System had supposed.

Literature: COSSA, Introd. to the Study of Polit. Econ. (3rd ed., trans. by Dyer), 201–10; SMITH, Wealth of Nations, Bk. IV; GOSCHEN, The Theory of the Foreign Exchanges. (A.T.H.)

Balfour, James (of Pilrig). (1705–95.) A Scottish jurist and philosophical writer. He was appointed professor of moral philosophy in Edinburgh University, 1754, and of law, 1764. He became the friend of Hume.

Balfour, Robert. (cir. 1550–cir. 1625.) A Scottish philosopher of the 17th century, who wrote commentaries on Aristotle and edited the works of Cleomedes. Professor of Greek and principal of Guienne (cir. 1586).

Bamalip: see MOOD (in logic).

Baptism [Gr. βαπτίζειν, to dip]: Ger. *Taufe*; Fr. *baptême*; Ital. *battesimo*. Baptism is one of the seven sacraments recognized by the Roman Catholic Church, and one of the two sacraments recognized by the majority of Protestants. Its detailed treatment belongs to the doctrinal department of systematic theology, and there falls in the section dealing with the functions of the Church.

From the point of view of theology, baptism is a condition of salvation. Its due treatment involves these considerations: (1) the material—water; (2) the form or formula, including the question of institution by Jesus; (3) the result—regeneration, or gift of new life; (4) the subjective condition requisite for its reception. According to the Roman Catholic doctrine, baptism gives entrance to the Church, outside of which there can be no salvation. With Protestants it is a sign, which has no effect in itself, but depends on the co-operant faith of the recipient. Cf. SACRAMENTS.

Literature: for full treatment and literature, see Herzog's Real-Encyc.; on the philosophical aspects of the matter, see MOZLEY, Review of the Baptismal Controversy. (R.M.W.)

Baptists: Ger. *Täufer, Baptisten*; Fr. *Baptistes*; Ital. *Battisti*. Those who regard baptism as the ceremony special to a public confession of belief in the central dogmas of Christianity, and make use of the custom of 'dipping' or submersion, not that of sprinkling.

From the standpoint of history of religions, the matter has interest on its mainly philological and archaeological side.

Literature: art. in Herzog's Real-Encyc.; the works of W. WALL, MOSES STUART, E. BEECHER, A. CARSON, A. CAMPBELL, T. J. CONANT, J. W. DALE, on Baptism. (R.M.W.)

Barbara: see MOOD (in logic).

Bardesanes of Edessa, or Bar-Daisan. (cir. 155–223). An orthodox Christian who enjoyed great favour at the court at Edessa. An astrologer, and strongly influenced by the Gnosticism of Valentinus. Missionary to Armenia in 217.

Bardili, Christoph Gottfried. (1761–1808.) A German philosopher, who opposed Kant and favoured a philosophy of identity. Professor of philosophy at Stuttgart, 1794.

Bargain: Ger. *handeln*; Fr. *marchander*; Ital. *patteggiare*. To offer a low price for a commodity with the contemplated possibility of paying a higher one; or conversely, to ask a high price for a commodity with the contemplated possibility of accepting a lower one. Opposed to the one-price system.

In isolated transactions bargaining is all but universal. If *A* wishes to sell a house of a peculiar character, and *B* is the only man who, for the moment, wishes to buy that kind of house, it may happen that the maximum price which *B* is willing to pay is greater than the minimum which *A* is willing to accept. In view of this possibility, *A* is reluctant to name the lowest price at which he will sell until he sees whether *B* cannot be induced to pay more, while *B* is equally reluctant to name his highest price until he sees whether *A* may be induced to sell for less. But if there are other house-owners in the same situation as *A*, or other buyers in the same situation as *B*, the matter assumes a different aspect. *A* is afraid to ask an exorbitant price for fear *B* may buy of some one else; *B* is afraid to begin with an unduly low figure for fear *A* may sell to some other buyer. Competition tends to take the place of bargaining. (A.T.H.)

Baroco (Barocco, Baroque) [a rough pearl; deriv. uncertain]: Ger. *Barok*; Fr. *baroque*; Ital. *barocco*. Odd, wilfully peculiar; more specifically in aesthetics, a species of the peculiar or abnormal, in which this effect of peculiarity seems to be intentionally or systematically sought.

The term has been applied especially to the architecture of the 17th and 18th centuries. At its best, this was characterized by grandeur, massiveness, picturesqueness of effect, and richness of detail; often, however, by exaggeration, over-luxuriance, contorted scrollwork, and generally inorganic ornamentation. Cf. Lübke, *Hist. of Art* (Eng. trans., 1877), ii. 159 ff. (J.H.T.)

Baroco (in logic): see MOOD (in logic).

Barter [O.F. *barat*]: Ger. *Naturaltausch, Naturalwirthschaft*; Fr. *troc*; Ital. *baratto*. The exchange of one commodity or group of commodities for another without the intervention of MONEY (q. v.).

The difficulties attendant upon a system of barter are so great as to make extensive trade by this method impossible. It requires 'a double coincidence of wants and possessions.' If a hat is to be bartered for a pair of shoes, there must be at once a producer of shoes who wants a hat, and a producer of hats who wants a pair of shoes. As a natural consequence, we find the invention and use of money to have been almost coincident with the development of exchange; and where money is lacking, we see a resort to some form of credit, however insecure, rather than a lapse into the régime of barter. (A.T.H.)

Barthélemy-Saint-Hilaire, J. (1805–95.) A French philosopher, statesman, and oriental scholar. He first held office under the Minister of Finance, contributing meanwhile to the *Globe* and the *Nation*. In 1838 he was elected to the chair of Greek and Roman philosophy in the Collége de France. In 1839 he became a member of the Academy of Moral and Political Science. In 1848 he entered the Assembly, and at the *coup d'état* was imprisoned. Upon his release he resigned his chair. In 1871 he entered the Assembly at Bordeaux and supported Thiers. In 1876 the Assembly elected him life-member of the Senate, and in 1880–1 he held the portfolio of Foreign Affairs. His greatest service to philosophy is a French translation of Aristotle's works. He contributed much to Western knowledge of Indian philosophy by his works on the Vedas, on Buddhism, and on Buddha and his Religion.

Basal Ganglia : see BRAIN (Glossary).

Basedow, Johann Bernhard (originally Johann Berend Bassedau). (1723–90.) A famous German educational reformer or revolutionist. Born in Hamburg ; educated at Leipzig ; professor in the Academy at Soröe, Denmark, 1753. Transferred to the Gymnasium at Altona in 1761. Rousseau's *Émile* suggested certain improvements in textbooks, and, soliciting aid from interested friends, he published his *Elementarwerk* with 100 copper-plate illustrations. 'Everything according to nature' might be said to be his watchword. In 1771 he was called to Dessau by Prince Leopold, and in 1774 took charge of the famous Philanthropinum. Manual training, gymnastics, the conversational language-method, the free use of pictures for illustration, the dialogue form of textbooks, &c., were introductions of his. Owing to lack of tact, he was forced to retire from the school in 1776, and lived an irregular life afterwards.

Basel (Confession of): Ger. *Baseler Konfession* ; Fr. *Confession de Bâle* ; Ital. *Confessione di Basilea*. A Confession belonging to the Zwinglian branch of the reformed theology, first drafted by John Oecolampadius in 1531 ; further elaborated by Oswald Myconius in 1532 ; and promulgated in 1534. The Confession is remarkable for its simplicity, for its freedom from influences due to dogmatic disputes (except that with the Anabaptists), and for its comparative subordination of Protestant bibliolatry.

Literature: SCHAFF, Creeds of Christendom, i. 385. (R.M.W.)

Bashfulness [ME. *bashen*, for *abashen*, to abash]: Ger. *Schüchternheit* ; Fr. *timidité spontanée* (or *instinctive*) ; Ital. *timidità istintiva*. Those mental and physical attitudes of instinctive and spontaneous timidity shown by young children in the presence of persons more or less strange.

Bashfulness characterizes the attitudes of the child before the sense of self is sufficiently developed to arouse reflective attitudes of MODESTY (q. v.). Cf. COYNESS, SHAME, TIMIDITY.

Literature: see under SHYNESS. (J.M.B.–G.F.S.)

Basil, or Basilius, Saint. (cir. 329–79 A.D.) One of the 'three lights of the church of Cappadocia,' called Basil the Great. He was a follower and great admirer of Origen. Born in Caesarea, Cappadocia, he studied in Athens, 351–5. After extensive travels, he spent seven years in monastic retirement in Pontus. In 370 he became bishop of Caesarea, and held the office until his ascetic habits brought on death. He was the brother of Gregory of Nyssa, and an intimate friend of Gregory Nazianzen.

Basilides. The events of his life are unknown. He lived in Egypt in the reigns of Trajan and Hadrian, from about 100 to about 140 A.D. He was a Gnostic, and founded the sect of Basilidians. See GNOSTICISM.

Bathmism [Gr. $\beta\alpha\theta\mu\acute{o}s$, a step] (not in use in other languages). 'All the mechanisms necessary to the mature life of the individual are constructed by the activity of a special form of energy known as growth-energy or bathmism.'—E. D. Cope (*Primary Factors of Organic Evolution*, 1896). Hence bathmogenesis, bathmic energy, &c.

It is one of the newer attempts to designate VITALISM (q.v.), of which 'self-adaptation' (Henslow) and 'genetic energy' (Williams) are others ; they seem, however, to lose nothing of the essential obscureness of the vitalistic conception. (C.LL.M.–J.M.B.)

Bauer, Bruno. (1809–82.) A German rationalistic, theological, and historical writer. He belonged to the younger group of Hegelians, the Hegelians of the 'left' (Strauss), who taught that immortality is merely the eternity of the universal reason ; that the God-man is simply humanity ; that the Godhead attains self-consciousness first in human spirits. After 1834 he devoted himself to the scientific 'criticism' of the Bible.

Baumgarten, Alexander Gottlieb. (1714–62.) A German philosopher, born and schooled in Berlin. At the Orphanage in Halle, he was much influenced by A. H. Francke, Breithaupt, and Lange. He early began writing poetry. A strong prejudice against Wolff, received in Halle, led him to carefully study the system, and he became an adherent in his twenty-first year. He lectured in Halle, 1735–40. He then became, and remained until his death, professor of philosophy in Frankfort-on-the-Oder. His writings constitute a sort of completion of the work which Wolff began—an encyclopaedic review of all the sciences. He made numerous contributions to the modern German philosophical vocabulary, as e.g. the expression *an und für sich* (a modification of Wolff's *vor und an sich*) and the term Aesthetics, denoting both the science of the lower forms of knowledge and the science of the beautiful.

Baur, Ferdinand Christian. (1792–1860.) A German Protestant theologian, Bible critic, and historian. Studied theology at Blaubeuren Theological Seminary and at the University at Tübingen. In 1817 he became professor of theology in the former institution and in 1826 in the latter. He is the founder of the 'Tübingen school' of Bible critics and Hegelian thinkers. A profound scholar and a strong constructive critic, he is chiefly known for his bold views in biblical criticism.

Bayle, Pierre. (1647–1706.) A French sceptical philosopher and critic. The son of a Protestant minister, he studied at the college at Toulouse, and was for several years a private tutor at Geneva and Rouen. Professor of philosophy in the Protestant College of Sedan after 1675; professor of philosophy and history at Rotterdam after 1681; editor of a critical monthly review, 1684–87. Deprived of his professorship in 1693 on account of his religious views.

Baynes, Thomas Spencer. (1823–87.) An English philosophical writer. He studied at a private school, at Bristol College, and at the University of Edinburgh. He was professor of logic at Edinburgh, 1851–55, and professor of logic, rhetoric, and metaphysics in the University of St. Andrews after 1864. He was assistant editor of the London *Daily News*, 1857–64, and editor of the 9th ed. of the *Encyclopaedia Britannica*.

Beasley, Frederick. (1777–1845.) An American clergyman in the Protestant Episcopal Church. Educated at Princeton College, he became professor of mental and moral philosophy in the University of Pennsylvania and Provost of the University, 1813–28.

Beats [AS. *betan*]: Ger. *Schwebungen, Tonstösse*; Fr. *battements*; Ital. *battimenti*. When two or more tones are sounded simultaneously their sound-waves interfere; and the result, when the difference between their vibration rates is slight, is a rhythmical intensive variation in the total impression. This is termed 'beating.'

Their rapidity depends on the difference of the vibration rates of the tones. The limits of distinguishable beats seem to be about thirty per second for the deepest, and sixty for the highest tones of the musical scale.

Beats have been divided by König into lower and upper, on the following formula: n_1 is the vibration rate of the lower, n_2 that of the higher tone. N is a whole number. Then the vibration rates are:

Lower beats, $n_2 - N \cdot n_1$;

Upper beats, $(N + 1) n_1 - n_2$.

Literature: WUNDT, Physiol. Psychol. (4th ed.), i. 466 ff.; SANFORD, Course in Exper. Psychol., expts. 79–81; EBBINGHAUS, Psychol., i. 301. See also works cited under ACOUSTICS, especially KÖNIG, Quelques Expériences d'Acoustique (1882), chaps. ix, x. (E.B.T.)

Also KÖNIG, Poggendorff's Annalen, clvii. 177 ff.; STUMPF, Tonpsychologie, ii; KÜLPE, Outlines of Psychol., § 45; HELMHOLTZ, Tonempfindungen, 4. Aufl.; HENSEN in Hermann's Handb. d. Physiol., iii; NUEL, art. Audition, in Richet's Dict. de Physiol. (with extensive bibliography). See *Literature* under HEARING. On the questions of subjective and central localization involved see WUNDT, loc. cit.; K. L. SCHÄFER, Pflüger's Arch., lxi. 544, and Wiedermann's Annalen, lviii. 785; MEINONG and WITASEK, Zeitsch. f. Psychol., xv. (1897), 189 ff.; M. MEYER and EBBINGHAUS, ibid., xvi. (1897), i. 152; STUMPF, ibid., xv. (1897), 289; M. MEYER, ibid., xvii. (1898), 401; xvi. (1898), 196; (with STUMPF), ibid., xviii. (1898), 274, 294, 302; Beitr. z. Ak. u. Musikwiss., ii. (1898), 25; STUMPF, ibid., i. (1898), 1. (J.M.B.)

Beattie, James. (1735–1803.) A Scottish poet and philosophical writer. He was born at Laurencekirk, and educated at Marischal College, Aberdeen. He became schoolmaster of Fordoun in 1753, and under-master in the grammar school at Aberdeen, 1758. He was appointed professor of moral philosophy in Marischal College in 1760, and entered into intimate philosophical intercourse with Reid, Campbell, Gerard, and others. In 1770 he published his famous *Essay on the Nature and Immutability of Truth*, attacking Helvetius and Hume and advocating what was afterwards called the doctrine of Common Sense.

Beat tone: Ger. *Stosston*; Fr. *son résultant*; Ital. *suono* (or *tono*) *di battimento*. At a certain rapidity of succession, beats may themselves form a tone—the beat tone. These are 'upper' and 'lower.'

If N is 1 (see BEATS), the first lower beat tone is the difference tone of the first order $(n_2 - n_1)$. No other beat tones coincide, in cases of simple tones, with audible combination tones; in cases of compound tones there may be coincidence. The beat tones are heard most clearly in dissonances. (E.B.T.)

Literature: WUNDT, Physiol. Psychol. (4th ed.), i. 471; SANFORD, Course in Exper. Psychol., expt. 82; EBBINGHAUS, Psychol., i. 312. Also the citations under BEATS, especially the references to KÖNIG, and under ACOUSTICS. (E.B.T.—J.M.B.)

Beauty and **The Beautiful** [Lat. *bellus*, pretty, charming]: Ger. *Schönheit, das Schöne*, (*schön* as adj. is broader than 'beautiful'; rather = 'fine'); Fr. *beauté, le beau*; Ital. *bellezza, il bello*. (1) That quality which is apprehended as a specific value, the marks or characteristics of which are discussed under AESTHETIC and FEELING (aesthetic). In this broad sense it is used as a generic term including, as subordinate species, the sublime, the beautiful in narrower senses, the graceful, comic, tragic, &c.

(2) Various narrower senses of which the most important are: (*a*) That portion of aesthetic value which excludes the predominant aspect of magnitude or power (the Sublime) and the mingled unpleasant features of the tragic, comic, pathetic, &c., while including the pleasure derived from expression, as well as that from form or colouring. (*b*) That portion of aesthetic value which depends solely on form, or on form and sensuous elements combined, as contrasted with the value derived from the idea or characteristic expressed. Other shades of meaning are indicated below. Cf. EXPRESSION, CHARACTERISTIC, SUBLIME, FITNESS, and ART (II and III).

The three main points of view from which the subject has been treated have been stated under the title AESTHETIC (q. v.) as (1) that of the psychology of beauty, which considers especially the nature and origin of aesthetic experience; (2) that of an analysis (*a*) of the form and content of objects judged beautiful,

and (*b*) of the nature of the aesthetic judgment itself, in order to find the distinguishing marks or categories of beauty; (3) that of the metaphysics of beauty, i. e. the relation of beauty to ultimate reality. Discussions of beauty may be roughly grouped as follows: I. Ancient writers, who deal mainly with problems (2, *a*) and (3), above; II. Modern writers prior to Kant, dealing especially with (1) and (2, *a*); III. Kant, who investigated (2, *b*); IV. German writers following Kant and developing various lines, especially (3); V. Recent investigation, dealing especially with (1).

I. The Greek term for beauty (τὸ καλόν) seems to have been applied at first to objects of sight (so in Russian until very recently), especially to the human form (Hesiod uses it of the female, not of the male). In consequence of the religious associations of the word which was applied to many of the gods and goddesses, and more especially because of the prominence in Greek life of manly beauty and of artistic creation in nearly every form, the term came to embody for the Greek nearly all that was of highest value. It represented not an abstract quality nor an occasional pleasure, but the real value of life, in which he measured the various 'goods.' As, however, intellectual and moral life gained in importance the concept 'beautiful' came to widen its scope to include these, and finally to give them the pre-eminence. This made the constant interchange of aesthetic, moral, and metaphysical points of view a natural occurrence. Finally, the laws of tectonics and of plastic art emphasized the characteristics of symmetry, and of unity in variety, as the essential marks of beautiful forms.

Socrates, according to Xenophon, examined the conception of *kalokagathia*, 'fair and good,' in which the Greek ideal of the 'best people' found expression, decided that no such connection between beauty of outward form and goodness of inner character as the popular view implied could be verified, and concluded that the concept, if true at all, must apply as a whole to the inner life. He also urged that the beautiful, like the good, must be useful and fit for its end, and refused to regard as adequate any abstract criterion, such as the 'well-proportioned.'

Plato, although dealing with beauty only incidentally (except in the dialogue *Hippias Major*, of doubtful authenticity), brought out nearly all aspects of the Greek aesthetic consciousness. Under (1), psychological aesthetics, he names as aesthetic senses vision, hearing, and, in a lesser degree, smell. These senses yield 'pure pleasures,' unmixed with any pain or want. More specifically, these pure pleasures are given by beauty of colour and form, and by sounds which are smooth and clear and have a single pure tone. Tragedy and comedy excite a feeling less purely aesthetic, because it contains a mixture of pain with pleasure. As to (2), the characteristics of beauty, Plato in the *Gorgias* advances the view that objects are beautiful in proportion as they either (a) are useful, or (b) give delight when contemplated (ἐν τῷ θεωρεῖσθαι χαίρειν). In the *Philebus* he distinguishes from things which are relatively beautiful (πρός τε καλά) those which are intrinsically and absolutely beautiful (καλὰ καθ' αὑτά). As to the marks of this latter class he seems to adopt two attitudes. At one time he specifies a number of characteristic marks, e. g. beautiful forms are 'straight lines, circles, and figures formed out of them by rulers,' &c. (where measure or symmetry seems to be the essential feature), or sounds smooth and clear (simplicity ? purity ?). 'Measure and symmetry,' he declares, 'are beauty,' a doctrine forced upon him no doubt by the whole development of Greek art, and by the experimental and theoretical considerations of the Pythagoreans. The Greek word from which we derive the two different terms 'cosmos' (cosmic) and 'cosmetic' shows the two ideas 'order' and 'decoration' fused. Variety is also an aesthetic element. At another time, he seems to reject these considerations, regards it as confusing and illogical to say that colour or form or any such thing is the source of beauty (i. e. to explain a single concept by several various marks), and falls back on the statement that it is the presence of beauty which makes things beautiful. This would naturally force a modern to conclude that beauty must be defined in terms of subjective value, but it leads with Plato to (3), his metaphysics of beauty. For beauty is thus identified with the Platonic Ideas. It is distinguished from wisdom in that it is visible, perceptible by sense. It 'shines.' It is easiest seen in the human form. From this the seeker of beauty may pass on to beauty of all forms, then to beauty of soul, then to beauty of institutions and laws, then to beauty of science, until finally the vision of beauty absolute, separate, and eternal is reached. Plato's depreciatory view of poetry did not affect the value which he set upon beauty. The lover of beauty is of the same class with the philosopher.

Aristotle treats beauty only incidentally. Its main characteristics are said to be 'order, symmetry, definite limitation,' and hence it is not alien to mathematics. A certain magnitude is also a condition of beauty, especially in the human form. 'Small men may be well proportioned, but cannot be called beautiful.' Subjective definitions are also given: 'the beautiful is chosen for itself and is worthy of praise (like the good)'; or, 'that good which is pleasant because good.' The virtues, or rather the excellences or admired qualities, are said to be beautiful,—especially the crowning quality of 'nobility of soul,' which is a kind of lustre of beauty. Real beauty is also distinguished from a beauty which has reference only to desire, as manifested in sexual preference.

Cicero rendered a twofold service in the definition of beauty. He distinguished clearly the concept of beauty from that of adaptation or fitness to an end ; and secondly he noted the division of beauty (*pulchritudo*), as a generic term, into its species, dignity (*dignitas*) and grace or loveliness (*venustas*), the masculine and womanly aspects. Plato had prepared the way for this by distinguishing two classes of the beautiful, the manly or energetic (ὀξύς), and the calm or modulated or well-ordered (κόσμιος). But the Latin 'dignitas' is a more adequate expression than the Greek ὀξύς. A similar distinction was made by Vitruvius in his characterization of the three styles of architecture. The Doric is strong and severe, the Corinthian ornate and graceful, the Ionic between the two. A great number of aesthetic terms were developed by the rhetoricians, especially Quintilian, to describe the three main styles, and it was in this connection that the concept of the SUBLIME (q. v.) received its treatment in the treatise ascribed to Longinus.

The most important contribution of Plotinus to the theory of beauty was his sharp delimitation of beauty from the good. Using a suggestion of Plato, he characterizes the good as awakening desire (a) for its possession, and (b) for possession of it as reality. The beautiful on the contrary (a) belongs not to the observer but to itself; and (b) it is enough to have the seeming or appearance of beauty. Beauty is therefore objective, disinterested, and is thus essentially an appearance, i. e. a sensuously apprehended quality. In aesthetic enjoyment, we do not distinguish reality from semblance.

Beauty in its ultimate or metaphysical character is an expression, a shining forth, of spirit in some particular form or shape. The ground of aesthetic pleasure is that the soul perceives in the beautiful object a trace of its own nature as rational, participating in 'form' or 'idea.' Unity in variety is thus pleasing because the soul is such a unity. Bodily beauty is, however, inferior to beauty of soul, and this in turn receives its charm from reason (*νοῦς*). Hence symmetry is quite inadequate as explanation of beauty. Beauty consists rather in the light, the life, that streams forth in connection with the symmetry; and this in turn derives its value from its ultimate source, the good.

This general conception of beauty as a manifestation of the good under sensuous conditions was influential with mediaeval writers. Thomas Aquinas names as its objective characteristics, 'clearness or brightness of colour' and 'symmetry'; 'brilliance of form' (*resplendentia formae*), in addition to materials proportionally divided, or to diverse powers or actions; harmony in diversity. The beautiful is distinguished from the good in that whereas, in the case of the good, desire is satisfied by the possession of its object; in the case of the beautiful, desire is satisfied, not by the possession, but by the aspect or cognition of the object. Vision and hearing are the aesthetic senses because they are the cognitive senses.

II. The influence of Greek conceptions is also manifest in the earliest modern writers on beauty in England and France. In France beauty was usually discussed incidentally to the treatment of art. But in art the authoritative canon was held to be 'imitation of nature'; hence the beauty of a work of art was its truth—'rien n'est beau que le vrai' (Boileau). In England, Shaftesbury, like Plotinus, distinguishes successive grades of beauty, from dead forms up to God. Beauty is in the form, not in the matter. More specifically, 'all beauty is truth'; 'what is beautiful is harmonious and proportionable.' Its essence is to be found in the study of 'inward numbers and proportions.'

A more systematic attempt to define the psychological basis of aesthetic feeling was made by Hutcheson (1725), who anticipated most of the categories later elaborated by Kant. Beauty is apprehended by a 'sense,' i. e. it is immediately perceived, and does not arise from any knowledge of principles or of the usefulness of the object, nor can it be altered by it. The categories of the aesthetic are subjective; it is (1) not a quality in the object, 'without relation to any mind which perceives it'; it denotes a perception. (2) Beauty may be original, or comparative. The formal law of original beauty is uniformity in variety. Comparative, or relative, beauty is felt on the comparison of some object with its original, which may be either some object in nature (as in imitative arts), or some idea or intention (beauty of purposiveness). The suggestion that there is a harmony between reason, which seeks regularity or uniformity, and the 'sense' which finds beauty in the same, is another anticipation of Kant's theory.

Hogarth, in his *Analysis of Beauty* (1753), named as the principles which make objects beautiful, 'fitness, variety, uniformity, simplicity, intricacy, and quantity.' Of these it is variety which is the cause of pleasure in the 'line of beauty,' or in the still more intricately curving serpentine 'line of grace,' which are asserted to be at the basis of beauty in art.

Burke's *Essay on the Sublime and Beautiful* (1756) marks an attempt to find a physiological explanation of aesthetic feeling. Discarding the more usually accepted principles of proportion, fitness and perfection, he names as the elements of beauty (1) smallness of size, (2) smoothness of surface, (3) gradual variation of parts, (4) delicacy, (5) brightness and mildness of colour. Discarding also the usual restriction of beauty to vision and hearing, and seeking for a common mark of aesthetic feeling in all senses, he fixes on smoothness as most important. This produces a 'relaxing' or softening effect on the body, and this in turn produces the passion of love in the mind, which is the psychological counterpart of beauty in the object. Cf. SUBLIME.

Home (*Elements of Criticism*, 1762) is noteworthy as developing the analytic method of treating beauty which had been suggested in Hutcheson and was later elaborated by Kant. He seeks, that is, to analyse beauty or determine its essential characteristics. First he notes that while undoubtedly subjective it is yet perceived as 'spread upon the object'; hence its restriction to vision and hearing, which do not locate the feeling in the organism. Beauty is either 'intrinsic' or 'of relation' (to some external object). Intrinsic beauty may be of colour, of figure, or of motion; and the beauty of figure has, as elements, regularity, simplicity, uniformity, proportion, and order.

Hume discussed aesthetic TASTE (q. v.), and Adam Smith incidentally called attention to the effect of custom and fashion on our ideas of beauty—a line of thought developed by Alison and Jeffrey (see ASSOCIATION, aesthetic) and, with modifications, by Stewart.

III. In Germany, Baumgarten had written the first systematic treatise on Aesthetics (*Aesthetica*, 1750–8). While finding the essence of beauty in the familiar principle of 'perfection,' he yet made a psychological advance by treating it as perfection 'felt' rather than intellectually apprehended. This distinction, emphasized by Mendelssohn's accentuation of feelings as a distinct class of mental states, seems to have stated for Kant the problem of distinguishing definitely the judgments as to the beautiful, which are based on feeling, from those of science and ethics, based on intellect and will. Kant's treatment of beauty is thus distinguished from the Greek in that it is not a metaphysics of beauty—beauty is 'subjective'; nor an attempt to find its formal elements in beautiful objects. Nor does he, like the contemporary British psychologists, seek the physiological or psychological sources of aesthetic feelings. Kant examines the judgment, 'This is beautiful,' to consider its presuppositions and distinctive character as compared with other judgments. This gives the following: (1) The beautiful, as contrasted with both the good and the agreeable, is the object of a disinterested satisfaction. (2) The beautiful is regarded as a quality of a thing, and hence as pleasing universally, not as pleasing me alone. In this it differs from the merely agreeable, which is not necessarily regarded as more than a subjective gratification. (3) The beautiful is 'purposive,' i.e. adapted to our mental powers, but is not judged as to its conformity to any definite end, subjective or objective. It differs in this from the perfect. (4) The beautiful is judged as pleasing, necessarily; we think it ought to be approved by others. Disinterestedness, objectivity, and purposiveness without consciously conceived end, are thus the essential marks. A free beauty (as of a flower), and a dependent beauty (as of a human being, which must conform to some concept of what the thing is intended to be), are also distinguished. This latter kind of beauty leads to an increased satisfaction by its addition of perfection to beauty; intellectual content and characteristic, to form.

IV. The immediate successors of Kant in Germany were influenced in their treatment of beauty (*a*) by the great contemporaneous interest in art, and (*b*) by metaphysical motives. The former factor made the beauty of art the primary object of consideration, whereas Kant had emphasized the free beauty of nature. But consideration of the beauty of art, especially in connection with the newly awakened historic interest, brought to the fore the conception of the 'ideal' embodied in the art, and this in turn lent itself readily to metaphysical definitions of beauty in terms of the idea or ideal. Cf. IDEAL, IDEALISM (Schelling, Hegel). So Schelling defined beauty as 'the infinite represented in finite form'; Hegel, as 'the ideal as it shows itself to sense'; Schopenhauer, as an objectification of will, considered not as a particular, but as representative of the Idea. Jouffroy represented a similar standpoint in France. This 'idealism' may be either abstract, if the tendency is to regard the 'idea' by itself or in isolation from sensuous form, as the highest or true beauty (so with Schelling, Schopenhauer, Solger, Weisse, Lotze, according to Hartmann); or concrete, in which the unity of idea and sensuous form is insisted upon as essential (Hegel, Trahndorf, Schleiermacher, Deutinger, Ersted, Vischer, Zeising, Carriere, Schasler). The chief importance of all this group is in connection with art. Their most important contribution to the theory of beauty was their emphasis upon the element of the significant or CHARACTERISTIC (q. v.). The emotional element received less attention.

In contrast with idealism, which he rejected as 'mystical' aesthetics, Herbart considered it a more scientific procedure to study the formal elements in beauty, and this was carried out systematically by his disciple Zimmermann. Not the 'what' but the 'how' is the proper object of aesthetic inquiry. Cf. FORM, and FORMALISM.

V. Recent writers have followed, in the main, one of two general lines, attempting either (*a*) to define more sharply and accurately the exact nature of the beautiful; and this generally by examining especially the subjective condition—the line marked out by Kant; or (*b*) to find the psychological and physiological causes of specific aesthetic pleasures. Of the first class, Bergmann (*Über das Schöne*, 1887) emphasizes the contemplative attitude as the essential factor; Siebeck (*Das Wesen der ästhetischen Anschauung*, 1875) deduces the beautiful from the Herbartian theory of apperception, as the interpenetration of sensuous and spiritual presented as illusion in the process of apperception, where there is a seeming appearance of personality beneath the form. Lotze (*Ueber den Begriff der Schönheit*, 1845; *Outlines of Aesth.*, 1884, trans. 1886) maintains that the beautiful is not to be sharply separated from the agreeable, but is one of a continuous series of higher and higher values. From another standpoint beauty is the appearance to immediate intuition of a unity underlying ideal, means, and necessary laws— a unity which cannot be discovered completely by cognition.

Begg (*The Devel. of Taste*, 1887) considers the question of the subjective or objective character of beauty, and criticizes the association theory. Dimetresco (*Der Schönheitsbegriff*, 1877) argues for a recognition that there is both a beauty of form alone, and a higher composite beauty of ideal content added to form. Guyau (*Les problèmes de l'esthétique contemporaine*, 1884) urges a broadening of the field accorded to beauty, and its closer affiliation with other pleasurable feelings, rather than its delimitation from them. He insists (against the 'play theory') that 'all that is serious and useful, real and living, may become beautiful.' 'The beautiful is a perception or an action which stimulates life within us under its three forms simultaneously (i. e. sensibility, intelligence, and will), and produces pleasure by the swift consciousness of this general stimulation ; as contrasted with a sensuous or intellectual object, which stimulates only part.' Köstlin (*Aesth.*, 1869 ; *Ueber den Schönheitsbegriff*, 1878 ; *Prolegomena z. Aesth.*, 1889) has discriminated in great detail the various aspects and manifestations of the beautiful and its allied concepts. Von Hartmann (*Philos. des Schönen*, 1887) asks, what is the object to which we attribute beauty ?—and declares it to be neither things objective in ordinary sense, nor subjective feeling, but rather a middle something which he calls 'der aesthetische Schein,' aesthetic SEMBLANCE (q. v.), or appearance. This may be of the eye, of the ear, or, as in the beauty of poetry, of the fancy. Grades of formal and concrete beauty are set forth in great detail, and the related aesthetic concepts analysed. Groos (*Einleitung in die Aesth.*) adopts the conception of 'aesthetischer Schein,' and defines it as 'inner imitation' of outer data. This has also been called 'illusion' and 'make-believe.' Semblance is recommended in this work. It is the product of the imagination.

When now a sensuously agreeable datum is taken up into the aesthetic image, illusion, or semblance, we have the beautiful ; when a sensuously disagreeable, the ugly. The conception of semblance or illusion is further developed by Konrad Lange (*Die bewusste Selbsttäuschung als Kern des aesthetischen Genusses*, 1895) into the conception of 'conscious self-illusion.'

Marshall (*Pain, Pleasure, and Aesthetics*, 1894) discusses rather aesthetic feeling (see FEELING, aesthetic) than the beautiful. He finds aesthetic pleasures to be those which are relatively permanent in revival. Santayana (*The Sense of Beauty*, 1896) defines beauty as 'value positive, intrinsic, and objectified,' or 'pleasure regarded as the quality of a thing,' and distinguishes beauty of material, beauty of form, and beauty of expression.

The writers last named in many cases might be properly included also in the second class of recent writers, as defined above, viz. those who seek not merely to define the concept of the beautiful, but to find psychological or physiological explanations of specific beauties, or more broadly of aesthetic feeling in general. Typical examples only of this second class can be named. Darwin treated of the sense of beauty in connection with sexual selection. Spencer and Allen give a biological explanation of various aesthetic pleasures (Spencer, *Psychol.*, ii ; *Essays*, ii ; Allen, *Physiol. Aesth.*, 1877 ; *The Colour Sense*, 1878). Allen defines the beautiful as 'that which affords the maximum of stimulation with the minimum of fatigue or waste.' Colour is beautiful, because our frugivorous ancestors lived on bright coloured fruits, and so naturally learned to be attracted by colour.

Helmholtz (*Sensations o' Tone*, 1863), Stumpf (*Tonpsychologie*, 1883), Edmund Gurney (*The Power of Sound*, 1880), J. Sully (*Sensation and Intuition*, 1874), have treated especially the problems of tones and of harmony and beauty in MUSIC (q.v.). Fechner (*Zur experimentalen Aesth.*, 1871 ; *Vorschule d. Aesth.*, 1876) made a notable attempt to define methods for an experimental determination of pleasing figures, and emphasized again the importance of ASSOCIATION (q. v.). He found the rectangle whose sides bore the ratio of the GOLDEN SECTION (q. v.) to be regarded as the most beautiful by the largest number of persons experimented upon. Similar experiments have been made by Witmer (Wundt's *Philos. Stud.*, ix) and discussed by Helwig (*Eine Theorie des Schönen*, 1897), who holds that the maximum of beauty is a mean between extremes.

Vernon Lee and Anstruther-Thomson (*Contemp. Rev.*, 1897) seek a physiological basis for beauty in the furtherance of equilibrium, respiration, and circulation produced by the contemplation of beautiful forms. The general standpoint of this class of investigations is stated by Souriau (*L'esthétique du mouve-*

ment, 1889). The beautiful is something so complex that it is impossible to determine its nature *a priori.* Aesthetics will become a science only when the experimental method is applied to it. Biological science has made it possible to explain many of the simpler instances of beauty by showing their relation either to the welfare of the organism as a whole, to the mechanism of the special senses, or to the sex instincts. Cf. the topics SUBLIME, COMIC, TRAGIC, PATHOS, UGLY, ASSOCIATION, ART, AESTHETICS, FEELING (aesthetic).

Literature: KNIGHT, Philos. of the Beautiful, i. (1891; a brief but comprehensive outline of the history of theories); BOSANQUET (Hist. of Aesth., 1892) emphasizes rather theories of art than of beauty; J. SULLY, art. Aesthetics, in Encyc. Brit.; WALTER, Gesch. d. Aesth. im Alterthum (1893; very complete); SCHASLER, Krit. Gesch. d. Aesth. (1872; the most thorough general work); ZIMMERMANN, Gesch. d. Aesth. (1858; a valuable supplement to the preceding); LOTZE, Gesch. d. Aesth. in Deutschland (1868; critical and suggestive); VON HARTMANN, Die deutsche Aesth. seit Kant (1886; fuller on recent writers); C. HERMANN, Die Aesth. in ihrer Gesch. u. als wiss. Syst. (1876); H. STEIN, Die Entstehung d. neueren Aesth. (1886; 17th and 18th centuries); SOMMER, Grundzüge einer Gesch. d. deutschen Psychol. u. Aesth. (1892; Baumgarten to Schiller); CHAIGNET, Les Principes de la Science du Beau (1860); LEVÊQUE, La Science du Beau (1862; contains historical sketches); D. STEWART, Essays (Works, ed. Hamilton, v); MARSHALL, Pain, Pleasure, and Aesth. (1894); NEUDECKER, Stud. z. Gesch. d. deutsch. Aesth. seit Kant (1878). The last three have historical discussions. See also recent Psychologies, especially those of VOLKMANN, WUNDT, SULLY, BAIN, LADD, and BALDWIN, the literature under the topics referred to, and BIBLIOG. D. (J.H.T.)

Beck, Jacob Sigismund. (1761–1840.) An important German Kantian; an opponent of Reinhold. He was born near Danzig, in Lissau, and educated at Königsberg. He read at Halle (1791–9), and was professor of philosophy at Rostock in the later years of his life. As a pupil, he stood in the closest proximity to Kant, and wrote a work on the philosophy of his master, which the Kantians used as a compendium.

Becoming [AS. *becuman*]: Ger. *Werden*; Fr. *devenir*; Ital. (*il*) *divenire.* (1) Any process by which a definite new stage, form, or condition is reached.

It is opposed to mere change, which is a more general notion, and involves no notion of a limiting condition to be reached; and to growth, which implies that the new stage is an advance.

(2) In a more general sense for any change or flux. Thus being is contrasted with Becoming in characterizing the Eleatics and Heraclitus (cf. Weber's *Hist. of Philos.*). See CHANGE. (R.H.S.)

Begging the Question: see PETITIO PRINCIPII.

Being [AS. *beon*]: Ger. *Sein*; Fr. (*l'*)*être*; Ital. (*l'*) *essere, Ente.* (1) The most general predicate possible and to be affirmed of anything whatever. So in Hegel's 'being equals nothing' (*Sein gleich Nichts*): cf. HEGEL's TERMINOLOGY, Glossary, *Sein.*

(2) Affirmed of that which exists or may exist or have reality. This meaning always involves some unity and determinateness in the existent. So in Aristotle's 'Esse in Potentia' and 'Esse in Actu.'

(3) Existence in time or space (*ens,* entity) as opposed to idea or representation. From this point of view the question may be raised whether any being corresponds to a certain idea, i. e. whether the idea has being or not.

As a fundamental conception in every philosophy, the word has had as many specific definitions as there are philosophers. The materialists make being equivalent to matter; the idealists make it equivalent to mind. For Herbart, relations have no place in being; for Lotze, to be is to be in relations. Cf. REALITY AND EXISTENCE, and see the extensive citations given in Eisler, *Wörterb. d. philos. Begriffe,* Sein. (R.H.S.)

Belgic Confession: Ger. *Belgische Konfession*; Fr. *Confession belge*; Ital. *Confessione belgica.* The doctrinal standard of the Dutch and Belgian Reformed Churches, and of the Dutch Reformed Church in the United States.

It was drafted, in 1561, by Guido de Brès and others; adopted by the Synods of Antwerp, Wesel, Emden, Dort, and Middelburg (1566–81); purged of Arminian 'corruptions' and readopted by the Synod of Dort, 1619. In formal construction it is like the Gallican Confession, but is less dogmatic on important points such as the Incarnation and Trinity, the Church and the Sacraments. It is important, historically, as the most representative of the moderate Calvinistic Confessions.

Literature: SCHAFF, Creeds of Christendom, i. 502, iii. 383; DERMOVT, Geschiedenissen d. Nederlandsche Hervormde. (R.M.W.)

Belief [ME. *beleve*]: Ger. *Glaube*; Fr. *croyance*; Ital. *credenza*. Mental endorsement or acceptance of something thought of, as real.

It is one of the conquests of modern psychology that it has marked off the field of belief, and so brought to an end the historical controversies which turned upon differences of definition. There have been two great ways of distinguishing belief from other mental states: (1) The term has been used to include all states of mind in which the object presented was not explicitly declared unreal. This made it possible to say that we believe in our sensations as well as in our reasoned conclusions, in our intuitions as well as in our pictured hopes. Under this definition the uncritical attitude of the child, in not rejecting anything, is called belief or credulity. (2) Belief is considered by another school of thinkers as a positive endorsement, not merely a negative acceptance, of something as real; that is, it is an attitude over and above the uncritical consciousness of bare experience itself. On the basis of these two forms of definition theories of belief have fallen into two great classes. On the first usage belief attaches to what is psychologically immediate; on the second it does not. Cf. IMMEDIACY (psychological).

According to the first class of theories, belief is considered a spontaneous and immediate attribute of consciousness, a 'first intention,' and as such it has been considered a form of feeling (Hume's *Enquiry*, Ladd), of will (Bain's first view in *Emotions and Will*, 'Belief'), or of intelligence (James Mill, Herbart). Opposed to this general way of looking at belief is the second class of theories which consider it a matter of reflection, a 'second intention,' a new phenomenon added to mere presence in presentative consciousness. According to this view belief proper is only present when a certain complexity of the mental life affords the requisite conditions. This line of distinction is rapidly gaining ground. It is well to recognize the difference of fact between the lower form of acceptance of experience, on the one hand, called by Bain 'primitive credulity,' and described by the present writer under the term 'reality feeling,' and, on the other hand, the higher attitude of mind which accompanies the weighing of evidence, the attaining of conviction, and the asserting of a reflective judgment. If the former be called belief, the distinction might be marked by an anti-

thesis between implicit or unformulated belief, and explicit or formulated belief. The more explicit belief, or belief proper, is marked in the German by the term Anerkennen (-ung), meaning 'acceptance as true' (Für-wahr-halten). It is belief as function of the Co-EFFICIENT (q. v.) of reality or truth (nach Merkmalen, &c., Platner, *Philos. Aphor.*, i. § 44, quoted by Eisler) distinctly recognized as objective. See below. Anerkennung, however, means the recognition of or acceptance of a thing for what it claims to be, as the recognition of another self as a self.

As thus defined, belief is explained in various ways by different authorities. It is held (1) that belief is a sentiment, an 'emotion of conviction' (Bagehot), aroused by a complex interplay of presentations and ideas, or a feeling of 'vividness' and intensity in ideas (Hume's *Treatise*, Taine, Dugald Stewart); or (2) it is an intellectual fact (Bain's second view, in *Ment. and Mor. Sci.*, Appendix, 100), an 'irresistible or inseparable association' (James Mill); or (3) it is an active determination, either voluntary or spontaneous, a personal attitude toward the play of presentations. Bain's first view was one of the earliest statements. This view, as supported to-day, takes either the form of the postulate of an ultimate principle of 'assent' (J. S. Mill; Brentano's 'Judgment'; James' 'Attention' and 'Will to Believe'), or of making the attitude of belief the result of an assimilation of new elements into the group of motor processes, by which mental activity is realized, and to which it is limited. This view as held by the present writers is more fully developed below.

There are certain great departments of experience in which belief arises, and in these several departments we may look for the special marks or signs upon which the belief-attitude goes out. These marks are called 'criteria' of belief, when looked at as belonging to or adhering in the facts or objects which stimulate belief (that is, considered logically and metaphysically), and 'coefficients of reality,' when considered as guiding indications to consciousness in its attribution of reality (that is, considered psychologically and genetically). Cf. JUDGMENT, and Co-EFFICIENT. We have the spheres of judgment or beliefs in fact or truth, divided into (1) belief in the external world of fact on the basis of 'sensational' and 'memory' coefficients, and (2) belief in truth, on the basis of the 'intellectual' coefficient, or evidence.

With these goes the other sphere of beliefs or judgments of worth or appreciation proceeding on (3) the 'ethical' coefficients, and (4) the 'aesthetic' coefficient. The last two named characterize what is called aesthetic and ethical WORTH (q.v.).

The coefficients on the basis of which belief in the reality of the external world arises have been much in dispute. The view that the external world consists in 'the permanent possibility of sensation' (J. S. Mill), has been developed (Pikler) into the statement that the test or coefficient of external reality is 'voluntary control,' i. e. the means through voluntary action of securing the sensations which are, according to Mill, a permanent possibility. On the other hand, the view (Spencer) that the belief in the external world arises through 'sensations of resistance' (Widerstandsgefühl) has been correspondingly generalized into the view that the primary coefficient of external reality is 'limitation of mental activity.'

A third view (Lipps, Stout, Baldwin) suggests that these two criteria have reference respectively to two equally necessary, though not co-ordinate, elements in external reality, i. e. (1) present fact, which involves mainly a 'limitation of activity,' presenting the coefficient of 'incontrollableness,' and (2) persistence, or possibility of sensational repetition, which proceeds mainly upon the coefficient of the 'voluntary control' through memory, of the series which a second time terminates in the resistance or limitation. To which may be added the fact that memory also includes limitation; and that present fact has a controllable or 'get-able' aspect. For the possibility of sensational repetition is an indication of external reality only in so far as the repetition depends on conditions which are incontrollable, viz. which do not depend merely on our free movements in space.

In other words, there is belief in external reality only if and so far as voluntary control involves adaptation to the incontrollable. This incontrollableness is present both in the primary perception and in the ideal representation: it is because we perceive things as existing, persisting, and changing independently of our free movements that we ideally represent them as existing, persisting, and changing independently of our position relatively to them in space, including our presence or absence. *Mutatis mutandis*, these remarks apply to thought-reality. Ideally represented connections are believed in, therefore, just in so far as they are for us conditions to which we must adapt ourselves in the pursuit of ends, whatever these ends may be. Thus voluntary control is bound up with belief just because belief presents us with the conditions to which voluntary control must adapt itself if it is to be effective. Belief is a condition of activity, and activity a condition of belief. The two statements express different aspects of the same fact.

If we call the former the 'sensational' and the latter the 'memory' coefficient of external reality, the two necessary factors are recognized. It is possible that in lower forms of life the sensational coefficient is all; and in these the element of persistence, or ground of possible recurrence of stimulation, is presumably wanting.

The consideration of the coefficient of thought-reality, i. e. the 'criteria of truth,' raises a similar question. Only that aspect which concerns the psychological recognition of truth as having reality is in place, however, in this connection. Of the criteria established in logic, 'consistency' or 'non-contradiction' would seem to correspond to the coefficient of 'voluntary control.' It involves, when progressively applied, the repetition and refining, by the voluntary pursuit of truth of relationships already established. The other logical criterion, 'the inconceivability of the opposite' (Spencer), appeals to the criterion of 'limitation of activity,' or 'incontrollableness' (Zwangsgefühl, Lipps).

It is through the 'memory coefficient' of reality of all sorts that the state of mind called EXPECTATION (q. v.) arises. These coefficients of reality, of both sorts, bear relation to the active attitudes of the mind, and would seem to support the view that belief is an affair of activity. On the other hand, it is possible to recognize purely sensory and affective criteria, such as sensations of resistance (Spencer), 'vividness' of memory (Taine, Rabier), as coefficients of external reality; or only cognitive criteria, such as 'inherent consistency and non-contradiction,' 'contradictory representation,' 'inhibition among ideas,' 'irresistible or indissoluble association,' as coefficients of truth. This would be to support the view that belief is an affective, or again a cognitive phenomenon. The decision between these two opposed ways of looking at the matter would seem to require a genetic examination of the concepts of REALITY and TRUTH (see those terms).

The relation of belief to WILL (q. v.)

would also seem to turn upon the way we view the coefficients of reality ; if we recognize only 'voluntariness' or 'control' as ground of belief, then it is very hard to distinguish between the two ; so we have belief determined by 'the passional life' (James), by 'authority' (Balfour). On the other hand, if we find 'restriction of activity' in any of its forms (e. g. 'resistance,' 'consistency,' 'indissoluble association,' 'motor adaptation') an element in the coefficient, then belief cannot be the same as volition. Volition would represent work against limitations, belief activity within limitations and adapting itself to limitations ; for the limitations are not mere negations, but positive conditions—a point of view developed further under TRUTH.

According to Baldwin, 'There is a distinct difference in consciousness between the consent of belief and the consent of will. The consent of belief is in a measure a forced consent : it attaches to what is—to what stands in the order of things whether I consent or no. The consent of will is a forceful consent—a consent to what shall be through me. Further, in cases in which belief is brought about by desire and will, there is a subtle consciousness of inadequate evidence, until by repetition the item desired and willed no longer needs volition to give it a place in the series deemed objective : then it is for the first time belief, but then it is no longer will' (Handb. of Psychol., Feeling and Will, 1891, 171).

Those who hold this view would say, however, that the influence of will on belief is nevertheless real, inasmuch as the volition or control factor in the coefficient is also present, though secondary. It works by the voluntary reinstatement of motives, reasons, &c., in which personal preference and interest serve to set the attention on some data and to exclude others.

In disbelief we have a state of belief in a contrary truth. It involves the same sort of reflective determination as positive belief, and so does not differ psychologically from it. Logically expressed, disbelief is the same as 'negative judgment' based on a contrary positive judgment. The contrary of belief is accordingly not disbelief, but DOUBT (q. v.).

Conviction is a loose term whose connotation, so far as exact, is near to that here given to belief. Making up one's mind, being convinced, weighing evidence, &c., are phrases describing the complex play of ideas preparatory to belief.

As compared with the term judgment we may say that belief is the psychological, and judgment the logical or formal, side of the same state of mind, called succinctly by Stout the 'Yes-No' consciousness. See also FAITH.

Literature : HUME, Treatise on Human Nature, §§ 7 ff., and Enquiry, § 5, Pt. II ; JAMES MILL, Analysis of the Phenomena of the Human Mind (ed. J. S. Mill) ; J. S. MILL, notes in preceding, i. 412 f.; Dissertations, iii ; Exam. of Hamilton, chap. xi ; DUGALD STEWART, Philos. of the Human Mind, Pt. I. chap. iii ; FECHNER, Drei Motive u. Gründe des Glaubens ; ULRICI, Glauben u. Wissen ; NEWMAN, Grammar of Assent ; BAIN, Emotions and Will, 'Belief,' and Ment. and Mor. Sci., Appendix ; WARD, Encyc. Brit. (9th ed.), art. Psychology ; BRENTANO, Psychol., ii. chap. vii ; LIPPS, Grundthatsachen des Seelenlebens, chap. xvii ; JAMES, Princ. of Psychol., ii. chap. xxi ; The Will to Believe ; STOUT, Analytic Psychol., Bk. I. chap. v, and Bk. II. chap. xi ; BALDWIN, Handb. of Psychol., Feeling and Will, chap. vii ; BALFOUR, The Foundations of Belief ; ADAMSON, Encyc. Brit., art. Belief ; VORBRODT, Die Psychol. des Glaubens ; BAGEHOT, Lit. Stud., i. 412 f.; ROYCE, Religious Aspect of Philos., chaps. ix, x ; HÖFFDING, Outlines of Psychol., V. D. See also the references given under JUDGMENT and in BIBLIOG. C, 2, l. Cf. the following topic. (J.M.B., G.F.S.)

Belief (in theology and religion): Ger. *Glaube*; Fr. *foi*; Ital. *credenza, fede*. This word has always been loosely used. Before proceeding to consider its theological and religious meaning, two other senses of the term, which are involved in the religious usage, are to be distinguished.

(1) The term is employed in a *quasi*-logical sense to denote the kind of judgment which is based not on purely intellectual grounds of affirmation, but on sentiment or will, especially in their reference to practical life. This may be illustrated by the common usage of the words 'make believe,' where, on the basis of an artificial universe, inclusions and exclusions are made according to the practical necessities of the occasion. Belief here implies an organization, which carries the subject of it beyond mere apprehension of objects or mere understanding of propositions in the direction of what has been called 'will to believe.' It has been made the basis of more or less important views classed together under the term FAITH-PHILOSOPHY (q. v.).

(2) In contrast with this is the psychological meaning of BELIEF (q. v.) given above.

(3) The theological employment of the term coincides most closely with customary usage. The theologian distinguishes two meanings: (1) probability, giving a more or less tenable opinion; (2) certainty, either (*a*) of a general nature, and having no very specific grounds, or (*b*) of a special nature, and dependent either upon the report of witnesses or upon remembered facts. Roman Catholic theologians further distinguish between explicit and implicit belief. When a man believes a truth which he knows, the belief is said to be explicit; when he extends this belief to consequences involved in this truth, which he does not know, it becomes implicit. Thus there are dogmas which all Christians ought to believe explicitly—e.g. Creation, the Trinity, the authority of the Church. On the other hand, all that flows from divine revelation—which the Church interprets—ought to be believed implicitly.

(4) In philosophy of religion, the implications and problems referred to under (1) and (2) have an essential place. Here belief means definite statement that a portion of human experience is of such and such a character, and that particular occurrences are explicable in such and such a manner. This belief in the nature and value of experience, or experiences, has two pivotal principles. First, the doctrine that the divine, or supernatural, can, and does, enter into relation with man. Second, the universally diffused conviction that for every effect a cause can be found. Belief consists essentially in an application of the conception of divine causality to cases where no natural cause can be traced, or to which natural causation appears to be inapplicable. In the history of religions, perception of this divine causality usually originates in the superior insight of individuals who are—or are supposed to be—specially gifted. This, in turn, may be translated into modern phraseology by saying that some men, simply on account of their superior power of attention, organize their experience differently from others. Cf. FAITH, MYTH.

Literature: BRENTANO, Psychol., Bk. II. chap. vii; W. JAMES, Princ. of Psychol., ii. chap. xxi, and The Will to Believe; STOUT, Analytic Psychol., i. chap. v, ii. chap. xi; J. KÖSTLIN, Der Glaube, sein Wesen, Grund und Gegenstand; O. PFLEIDERER, Grundriss d. christl. Glaubens- u. Sittenlehre; J. CAIRD, Philos. of Religion; J. ROYCE, Religious Aspect of Philos., chap. xi; F. B. JEVONS, Introd. to the Hist. of Religion, chap. xxvi;

NEWMAN, Grammar of Assent. See also references given under BELIEF above. (R.M.W.)

Bell and Lancaster (monitorial system): A monitorial system whereby one pupil teaches to other pupils what he himself has been taught.

This system, used by Bell in Madras, India, and begun at the same time in England by Joseph Lancaster about the beginning of the 19th century, was of great importance in introducing and furthering the cause of universal elementary education in Great Britain.

Literature: J. M. D. MEIKLEJOHN, Life of Bell (1881); Sketch of Lancaster, Encyc. Brit. (9th ed.). (C.DE G.)

Belligerency [Lat. *bellum*, war]: Ger. *Kriegszustand*; Fr. *l'état de guerre*; Ital. *stato di guerra, belligeranza* (little used). The state, relatively to each other, of nations at war. Rebels may come to occupy this state, in relation to the government to which they refuse allegiance, if the rebellion assumes the proportions of a civil war.

The term war (*bellum*) is used to indicate *non actio, sed status* (Grotius, *De Iure Belli et Pacis*, i. 2). It is a *status* affecting neutral powers, as well as the immediate parties to the hostilities. Belligerency is the *status* of one enemy with respect to the other.

Literature: The Prize Cases, 2 Black's United States Reports, 673; WHARTON, Int. Law Digest, § 69; HOLLAND, Stud. in Int. Law (1898), Pt. I. vi, II. viii. (S.E.B.)

Benedictines: Ger. *Benedictiner*; Fr. *Bénédictins*; Ital. *Benedettini*. A monastic order, founded by Benedict of Nursia (480–543), at Monte Casino, in Campania, in 528. His rules, which for some centuries governed the monastic orders of the Western Church, were set forth in 529.

The Benedictines have passed through many vicissitudes. In 580, on the destruction of their buildings by the Lombards, they were scattered and fled to Rome. In the 8th century riches and social exclusiveness had seriously corrupted them till, in 817, Benedict of Aniane reinforced the original rules. In the 10th century, like reforms again became necessary. The Order passed through numerous trials till the Reformation, when it was seriously threatened by the Jesuits. It gained new life in the 17th century, when its members were the most distinguished scholars of the Roman Catholic Church. This is the connection in which it is important for philosophy. The editions of the Fathers and Doctors then superintended, chiefly by the Congregation of

St. Maur, have become classical; the same Congregation also made extensive contributions to the scientific study of history. At present the Order is most active in Austria.

Literature: MABILLON, Acta Sanct. Ord. St. Bened. and Annales Ordinis S. B.; MONTALEMBERT, Les Moines de l'Occident (Eng. trans., 1860); TASSIN, Hist. de la Congrégation de St. Maur. (R.M.W.)

Beneke, Friedrich Eduard. (1798–1854.) A German philosopher, born and educated in Berlin. He disappeared March 1, 1854, and his body was found in a canal in June. He had met his death by drowning. He was a follower of Fries in basing philosophy on psychology. While Docent in Berlin University his lectures were prohibited in consequence of a work on ethics (1822). He taught in Göttingen, 1824–7, but returned to Berlin to become professor extraordinary (1832). He held this position until his death.

Benevolence [Lat. *benevolentia*]: Ger. *Wohlthätigkeit*; Fr. *bienfaisance*; Ital. *benevolenza*. The habit of voluntary activity (or virtue) which is shown in the effort to promote the good of others.

The definite recognition of benevolence as a virtue which should be placed alongside of the cardinal virtues of the ancients is a result of Christian influence: although, in the early Christian and mediaeval writers, it was usually, under the name of love or charity, added to the four CARDINAL VIRTUES (q.v.), as a 'theologic' virtue.

In Plato and Aristotle the love of, or desire for the good of, man as man found no place: the substitute for the modern virtue of benevolence was partly the minor virtue of liberality, partly the sentiment of friendship. In Aristotle's view of friendship, in which the good of one's friend is held to be identical with one's own good, the essence of benevolence may be seen. But friendship is restricted in application to one or a few; and they must bear some similarity in condition and sentiments to their friend. A wider view entered Greek philosophy with the cosmopolitanism of the Stoics and the 'philanthropy' of Xenocrates and the Academic. Benevolence may be said to be a due regard for the needs of others, as JUSTICE (q. v.) is a due regard for their rights. The difficulties connected with benevolence are chiefly: (1) the difficulty urged by Kant, of making the feeling of love a duty; beneficence but not benevolence may be commanded: the solution of which lies in the tendency of the sentiment to follow the principle of action.

(2) The question whether benevolence is due to some (relatives, benefactors, &c.) rather than others, as Butler asserts, or to all men equally. To some extent the difficulty may be due to the intermixture of the claims of justice with the call for benevolence. Practically, the difficulty arises when a man has to decide between the different groups to which he belongs, e. g. family, country, humanity. There has been in history a gradual extension of the unity of feeling between man and man, which has made for the widening of benevolence, but which at the same time carries with it the danger that the extension of the sphere of benevolence may interfere with its intensity. (3) A third difficulty is connected with the dispute as to the quality of the good which is to be sought for others. Kant asserts that it is simply their happiness, not because this is the true or unconditioned good, but on the ground that their true goodness or virtue is purely personal and cannot be affected by others: a view, however, which results from a too absolute separation of the rational from the sensitive nature of man.

The question of the 'disinterestedness' of benevolence was a constant subject of controversy with the British moralists. By Hobbes it was reduced to love of power, by Mandeville characterized as self-love under a veil of hypocrisy, while Shaftesbury, Hutcheson, Butler, and Hume defended its 'disinterestedness.' By modern writers of the psychologico-hedonistic school (e. g. J. S. Mill, G. Grote), sympathy, which may be said to be the impulsive basis of benevolence, is made the bridge between desire for personal pleasure and the altruistic sentiment of benevolence.

Literature: HOBBES, Elements of Law, chap. i. 9, and Leviathan, i. 14, 15; MANDEVILLE, Fable of the Bees; BUTLER, Sermons, and Diss. on Virtue, apud fin.; HUME, Princ. of Mor., App. ii; KANT, Met. d. Sitten.; SIDGWICK, Meth. of Eth., III. iv; PAULSEN, Syst. d. Ethik, iii. 7, 9. (W.R.S.)

Bentham, Jeremy. (1748–1832.) An English jurist and moral philosopher, born in London and died in Westminster. He was educated at Queen's College, Oxford, and first studied law, but later abandoned the profession without practising. In 1785–86 he travelled, visiting Paris, Constantinople, Smyrna, and White Russia. His aim in life was the reform of legislation. His standard of ethical judgment he expressed in a phrase probably first used by Cumberland, viz. 'the greatest happiness of the greatest number.' He makes the science of Ethics include public ethics, or jurisprudence and private ethics, or morality.

Benthamism: the ethical theory which makes the ethical end the 'GREATEST HAPPINESS (q. v.) of the greatest number,' as advocated by Jeremy Bentham. (J.M.B.)

Berengarius (Berenger) of Tours. (998–1088.) A mediaeval theologian born at Tours; he died on the island of St. Cosme. He was educated at the school of Chartres as a pupil of Fulbert, 'the Socrates of the Franks.' In 1031 he became director of the Catholic school in Tours, and in 1040 archdeacon of Angers. He was doubtless influenced by the writings of Erigena: was of a rationalistic turn of mind, and was twice forced by the Synod in Rome to recant, viz. in 1059 and in 1079.

Berger, Johann Erich von. (cir. 1772–1833.) A German philosopher, who was professor at Kiel. He learned the philosophy of Kant through Reinhold, but sympathized with Fichte, and later with Schelling, whose follower he is considered.

Berkeley, George. (1685–1753.) He was born at Killcrin, Ireland, and died in Oxford. He was educated at Trinity College, Dublin, becoming a Fellow there in 1707. While a student he formed a friendship with Dean Swift. In 1710 he published his celebrated system of idealism. In 1713 he removed to London, but went as chaplain with Lord Peterborough to Italy. He returned to London in 1720, and to Ireland in 1721. In 1724 he became dean of Derry, and in 1728 married Anna, the daughter of John Forster, Speaker of the Irish House of Commons. In the same year (1728) he sailed for Rhode Island, for the purpose of founding a college in America for the education of missionaries to work among the Indians of America. While in Rhode Island he officiated in Trinity Church, Newport. When he left for England in 1732, his plans having been frustrated, he made valuable contributions to the library and to the beneficiary resources of Yale College. Returning to London he was made bishop of Cloyne in 1735.

Berkleianism: the form of IDEALISM (q. v.) advocated by Bishop Berkeley.

Bernard of Chartres. A mediaeval Platonic philosopher and theologian, the contemporary of William of Champeaux, born about 1070–80. His second name, Sylvester, is usually omitted, his name being based on the place of his labours. An enthusiastic Platonist and realist, he sought to avoid any antagonism to Aristotle, whose authority he respected.

Bernard, Saint. (1091–1153.) Abbot of Clairvaux, mediaeval philosopher and theologian, and a Doctor of the Western Church. He was born in his father's castle at Fontaines, near Dijon, and died in Clairvaux. He entered the monastery of Citeaux in 1113, and in 1115 established the Order of Citeaux at Clairvaux in Champagne, becoming the first abbot of the community. Ascetic and eloquent, pious and mystical in his convictions, he was the relentless persecutor of Abelard, of his pupil Arnold of Brescia, of the Cathari, and of Gilbert of Poitiers. He drew up the rule for the Order of Knights Templars, then in its infancy, in 1128. In 1146 he stimulated Europe to the second crusade. He was canonized in 1173 by Pope Alexander III. He wrote several beautiful Latin hymns, English versions of which are found in every hymnal.

Bible [Gr. βιβλίον, a book]: Ger. *Bibel*; Fr. *Bible*; Ital. *Bibbia*. The name given to the collection of canonical sacred books of the Jews and Christians. See CANON.

Used also, in the plural, of the sacred books of the ethnic religions—the Bibles of religion; and, by analogy, of the greatest works of genius in literature—Homer, Dante, Shakespere, and Goethe are the Bibles of literature.

The Bible may be discussed from two points of view, the second of which is of primary importance for philosophy of religion. (1) It may be discussed in and for itself. Here the original languages, the division and arrangement of the constituent books, the canon, the text, and the translations, form the chief objects of inquiry. (2) It may be viewed in its relation to other literature of a similar kind. Here comparative problems, and the questions of inspiration and revelation, constitute the main subjects of study.

Literature: see the arts. in any of the great Encyclopaedias, e. g. Encyc. Brit.; Herzog (German); Lichtenberger (French); Hastings' Dict. of the Bible; CHEYNE, Encyc. Biblica (arts. on the several books). Also the titles cited under BIBLICAL CRITICISM. (R.M.W.)

Biblical Criticism: Ger. *Bibelkritik*; Fr. *critique biblique*; Ital. *critica biblica*. The theological discipline which lays the foundations for a satisfactory exegesis.

It naturally falls into three parts, from all of which preconceived and dogmatic opinions are to be rigidly excluded. (1) Investigation of the formative conception, historical constitution, nature, and authority of the collection of books known as the Canon. This discipline is usually termed Biblical Canonics. (2) Textual criticism, or investigation of the MSS., of the received text, and generally of all questions that bear upon the construction of a satisfactory text. This is often called the Lower Criticism. (3) Literary and historical criticism of single books, or of groups, usually known as the Higher Criticism. On the basis of a satisfactory text, this discipline proceeds to the investigation of questions of authorship; circumstances of historical origin, including audience, design, and peculiar character; relation of the work under consideration to others which may be fittingly classed with it. Another important office of higher criticism is investigation of the sources employed by an author and his credibility in the use of them. The key-note of higher criticism lies in its complete independence of traditional or dogmatic opinions. In this respect, like Canonics, it is of special value and interest for philosophy of religion.

Literature: on the Canon of the O. T. see the relative works of F. Buhl, Wildeboer (Eng. trans.), W. H. Green, and Ryle (Introd.); of the N. T., Reuss, S. Davidson, and Westcott. On Textual Criticism of O. T. see Strack, Prolegomena Critica, in V. T. Hebraicum; of the N. T., Scrivener's Introd., Schaff's Companion, and Green, Higher Criticism of the Book of Genesis. On Higher Criticism of O. T. see Cheyne, Founders of Criticism; Robertson Smith, O.T. in the Jewish Church; Wellhausen, Hist. of Israel (Eng. trans.); of the N. T., Bleek, Introd. to N. T. (Eng. trans., 2 vols.); Sanday, Gospels in the Second Century; Abbot, Authorship of the Fourth Gospel; Green (as cited above). (R.M.W.)

Biblical Psychology: Ger. *biblische Psychologie*; Fr. *psychologie biblique*; Ital. *psicologia biblica*. An integral portion of theological anthropology. It consists essentially of a discussion of man's entire constitution on the basis of Scripture declarations.

Two main problems occur in it: (1) Is man composed of spirit ($\pi\nu\epsilon\hat{v}\mu a$), soul ($\psi v\chi\acute{\eta}$), and body?—or (2) Is he composed of soul and body? The Greek Fathers, taken as a whole, adopted the former view; while the Latin Fathers, thanks partly to the emergence of Gnostic and other heresies, and partly to the poverty of the Latin language (*spiritus* and *anima* hardly conveying the sense of the Greek terms),

tended to the latter view, or to a discreet silence. In the course of history, Biblical psychology has been rather elbowed out by dogmatics in the Western Church. The mystics raise the question of $\pi\nu\epsilon\hat{v}\mu a$ and $\psi v\chi\acute{\eta}$ once more; and during the last 150 years more attention has been paid to it, especially in Germany, though systematic works are few.

Literature: Melanchthon, Liber de Anima (1552); Servetus, Christianismi Restitutio (1553); Jacob Böhme, De Triplici Vita (1620); Bonnet, Palingénésie philos. (1767); J. F. v. Meyer, Blätter f. höhere Wahrheit (1818–32); Olshausen, Opuscula (cir. 1825); H. Schubert, Gesch. d. Seele (1830); K. F. Göschel, Von d. Beweisen d. Unsterblichkeit d. menschl. Seele (1835); T. J. van Griethuyzen, Diss. de notion. vocab. $\sigma\hat{\omega}\mu a$ et $\sigma\acute{a}\rho\xi$ (1846); M. F. Roos, Fundamenta Psychol. Sacrae (1857); J. Froschammer, Ueber d. Ursprung d. menschl. Seele (1854); H. Schultz, Die Voraussetzungen d. christl. Lehre v. d. Unsterblichkeit (1861). More recent works are: Rudloff, Lehre v. Menschen; Beck, Umriss d. bibl. Seelenlehre (Eng. trans.); Franz Delitzsch, Syst. d. bibl. Psychol. (Eng. trans.); I. Taylor, Physical Theory of Another Life; J. B. Heard, The Tripartite Nature of Man; Bishop Ellicott, Destiny of the Creature; J. Laidlaw, Bible Doctrine of Man. See, too, art. Geist in Herzog's Real-Encyc.; Hoekstra, in Jaarb. f. w. Th., vii; Van den Ham, ibid., v; Lotze, Microcosmus, Bks. II, III, V (Eng. trans.). (R.M.W.)

Biblical Theology: Ger. *biblische Theologie*; Fr. *théologie biblique*; Ital. *teologia biblica*. One of the more recent theological disciplines which grew out of the effort, made at the close of the 18th century, to throw aside traditional interpretations in order to arrive at the doctrines really contained in the Bible itself. It consists essentially in a species of higher exegesis which attempts to shake itself free from dogmatics. Accordingly, it may be defined as that department of theology which systematizes the doctrines contained in the sacred books of the Jews and Christians with special regard to their historical formation.

It is of the highest importance for philosophy of religion on account of the historical and ethical spirit in which it has been conducted. Biblical theology dates from the works of Zacharia (supernaturalist, 1792) and Ammon (rationalist, 1801). J. F. Gabler (1802) was the first to mark it off as a distinct discipline and to insist on its historical and non-dogmatic character. Schmidt, of Tübingen (1838), was the pioneer in pointing out its character as a higher kind of exegesis. In the history of the study, New Testament theology developed first. Ewald's *Lehre der Bibel* (1871–6) is the earliest satisfactory discussion of the entire field, the Old Testament included. But till the higher criticism had done its work, the Old Testament portions could not be satisfactorily treated either in the historical or ethical spirit. Recent investigations have tended to detailed presentation of parts of the entire subject, e. g. the Pauline theology; and a complete work from a single hand, covering the whole field from a single standpoint, is still lacking.

Literature: of great historical importance are: GABLER, Bib. Theol. d. N. T. (1800–2); VATKE, Rel. d. A. T.'s nach den kanonischen Büchern entwickelt (1835); SCHMIDT, in Tübinger Zeitsch. f. Theol., Heft 4 (1838); EWALD, Lehre d. Bibel v. Gott, oder Theol. d. A. u. N. Bundes (1871–6). On the O. T.: H. SCHULTZ, O. T. Theol. (Eng. trans., 2 vols.); ED. RIEHM, Alttestamentliche Theol. (1889); B. STADE, in Zeitsch. f. Theol. u. Kirche, Heft 1 (1893). On the N. T.: B. WEISS, Bib. Theol. of the N. T. (Eng. trans., 2 vols.); W. BEYSCHLAG, N. T. Theol. (Eng. trans., 2 vols.). (R.M.W.)

Biel or **Byll, Gabriel.** Born in Speyer, Germany; date uncertain. Died in Tübingen, 1495. A German theologian and philosopher. Educated at Heidelberg and Erfurt; became cathedral preacher at Mainz. In 1477 he was made provost of Urach. He was an adviser in the establishment of the University of Tübingen, and became professor of theology in the University in 1484. He followed William of Occam and opposed the scholastic doctrine of sensible and intelligible species; was a Nominalist.

Bill [Lat. *billa*]: Ger. (1) *Gesetzvorschlag, Gesetzentwurf*; (2) in commerce, *Wechsel*; Fr. (1) *projet de loi*; (2) in commerce, *une lettre de change*; Ital. *progetto di legge*. (1) In parliamentary law, a proposed statute, reduced to form, but not yet finally enacted. A bill for an Act becomes an Act when approved by the executive. (2) In commercial law, a bill of exchange. (3) In the law of procedure, bill or bill in equity, a written petition to a court of equity; bill of indictment, a written charge of crime made by a grand jury; it is prepared by the public prosecutor, and the jury endorse it as 'a true bill.' (S.E.B.)

Binaural Hearing: Ger. *binaurales Hören*; Fr. *audition binauriculaire*; Ital. *udizione binauricolare*. Normal hearing with both ears.

(1) There is great individual difference in the apprehension of a given pitch by the two ears separately. In many cases the difference of hearing may amount to a musical quarter-tone. This phenomenon, diplacusis, may be induced by pathological conditions and take on a pathological import. See Stumpf, *Tonpsychologie*, i. 266, 274. 424; ii. 109, 221, 459, 551; Külpe, *Outlines of Psychol.*, 299.

(2) The binaural hearing of beats, and of difference and beat tones, is of importance for the theory of audition in general; but the facts are not yet satisfactorily made out. See Wundt, *Physiol. Psychol.* (4th ed.), i. 478, and the citations given under BEATS. Cf. LOCALIZATION OF SOUNDS. (E.B.T.)

Binocular Vision: Ger. *binoculares Sehen*; Fr. *vision binoculaire*; Ital. *vista binoculare*. Normal vision with the two eyes.

The united function of the eyes has been made the object of extended study, owing to its importance for theories of the perception of visual SPACE (q. v.). Experiments have been made on: (1) The mapping of the retina into points. See CONGRUENT, CORRESPONDING, and IDENTICAL POINTS; also DOUBLE IMAGES, HOROPTER. (2) The facts of CONVERGENCE (q. v.); also see ASYMMETRY, DEPTH (visual), PRIMARY POSITION, STEREOSCOPIC VISION. (3) Binocular COLOUR MIXTURE, AFTER-IMAGES, and CONTRAST. See these terms.

Literature: SANFORD, Course in Exper. Psychol., chap. vii; also under topics referred to. (E.B.T.)

Biogenesis [Gr. βίος, life, + γένεσις, origin]: Ger. *biologische Continuität*; Fr. *biogenèse* (not in use), *continuité biologique*; Ital. *biogenesi*. The law of biogenesis gives expression to the fact that every living being (animal or plant) is derived from a living parent or parents.

The doctrine of the continuity of living substance has been firmly established, and is expressed in the aphorism *omne vivum e vivo*. The opposed and now discredited doctrine of abiogenesis asserted that, in certain cases, living beings arise by spontaneous generation from dead matter. Bastian is the most important recent advocate of abiogenesis.

The term Biogenesis was first proposed by Huxley in 1870. The names of Francesco Redi, Spallanzani, Pasteur, Tyndall, Roberts, and Dallinger are associated with the gradual establishment of the doctrine.

Literature: HUXLEY, Pres. Addr. Brit. Assoc. (1870), reprinted in Essays, viii; also art. Biology, Encyc. Brit. (9th ed.), iii; M. VERWORN, Gen. Physiol. (Eng. trans., 1899); H. C. BASTIAN, The Beginnings of Life (1872). (C.LL.M.–E.S.G.)

Biogenetic: Ger. *biogenetisch*; Fr. *biogénétique*; Ital. *biogenetico*. Pertaining to the origin and evolution of life; applied also to the origin and evolution of other things, such as mind, society, &c., when interpreted in terms of life or investigated by a biological method. (J.M.B.)

The form biontogenetic is used by Morselli (*Antropologia generale*) with especial reference to the origin and differentiation of the special forms of life.

Biogenetic Law: Ger. *biogenetisches Grundgesetz*; Fr. *loi biogénétique, loi phylogénétique* (more used); Ital. *legge biontogenetica*. 'The organism recapitulates in the short and rapid course of its individual development (ontogeny) the most important of the form-modifications undergone by the successive ancestors of the species, in the course of their long and slow historic evolution (phylogeny), and the causal relation of the two histories is to be explained in terms of heredity and adaptation. When these are thoroughly analysed, it will be possible to say that the phylogeny is the mechanical cause of the ontogeny' (Haeckel).

This 'fundamental law of development,' formulated by Fritz Müller (1864) and developed by Haeckel (1866), carries further v. BAER'S LAW (q. v.), and has in turn served as basis for later formulations of the principle of RECAPITULATION (q. v.) The law has been criticized by many zoologists. (C.LL.M.)

The recapitulative characters which appear in ontogeny are distinguished by Haeckel as 'palingenetic' (their production, 'palingenesis'), from the 'cenogenetic' characters due to new adaptations ('cenogenesis'). (E.S.G.)

Literature: F. MÜLLER, Für Darwin; HAECKEL, Gen. Morphol. (1866); A. MILNES MARSHALL, The Recapitulation Theory, Brit. Assoc. Lects. and Addr. (1890), xiii; A. SEDGWICK, On the Law of Development, Quart. J. Microsc. Sci., xxxvi; C. H. HURST, Nat. Sci. (March and May, 1893), 350, 421. (C.LL.M.–J.M.B.)

Biological Analogy (in sociology). Analogy set up between society and a biological organism.

Such an analogy has been urged as affording an explanation of social organization, mainly under the lead of Herbert Spencer, who works it out in physiological detail. Recent writers who uphold the view are Schäffle, Novikow, Worms, v. Lilienfeld, Fouillée. It has been somewhat severely criticized by writers of the 'psychological' school (Tarde, Barth, Giddings, Baldwin) and others (Mackenzie, de Greef, Lacombe). Many writers preserve the word organism as applicable to society, but refuse to interpret organism by the biological analogy; others prefer to use the term ORGANIZATION (q. v.). Cf. ORGANISM.

The arguments for and against the biological conception are usually equally analogical, points of resemblance being matched with points of difference. A real explanation would involve problems both of function, or method of growth, and of matter; such as (*a*) that of the essential social phenomenon, stated in its lowest terms. Is this the same as the essential biological phenomenon, stated in its lowest terms? This is the question of matter or of analysis; and the simple statement of it seems to forbid a biological view of society in strictness: for the biologists find the cell, on the whole, the lowest form of life; and to read into the cell the properties necessary for social organization is extravagant, to say the least. And (*b*) the method of social growth and progress presents an equally essential problem, that of genesis. Does society grow by cell-division, propagation, and heredity? Here, again, biological conceptions are strained to breaking in the presence of such facts as imitation, invention, tradition, ethical and religious sentiments, with their sanctions.

Moreover, the step from the point of view of social activity to that of vital activity or function is questionable, considered merely as scientific procedure. In order simply to ask a question about society intelligently, the investigator has to imagine and enter into a social, i. e. a psychological, situation, in which he takes the point of view of mental changes, functions, activities, &c., and not that of biological, i. e. physiological, functions. The distinction made between FORCE AND CONDITION (q. v.) has application here. See also SOCIAL FORCES, and SOCIONOMIC FORCES.

Literature: see under SOCIOLOGY and SOCIAL PSYCHOLOGY (especially the works of the authors cited above). BARTH, Philos. d. Gesch. als Sociol. (1897), and WORMS, Organisme et Société (1897), may be cited as representative writers respectively for and against the analogy. (J.M.B.)

Biological Sciences. The sciences which deal with the phenomena manifested by living organisms and by living matter. (C.LL.M.)

The following table presents a general scheme of the biological sciences :—

Philos. zool. avant Darwin (1886); H. F. OSBORN, From the Greeks to Darwin (1894); J. V. CARUS, Gesch. d. Zool. (1872), and Bibliotheca Zool., i. (1861), ii. (1887); works of Buffon, de Maupertuis, Robinet, Bonnet, Harvey, Oken, Lamarck, Erasmus Darwin, Charles Darwin, Agassiz. (J.M.B.—E.S.G.)

I. GENERAL.

Biology: 1. GENETIC Animal Plant — i. Evolution (older Natural History)

a. Origin and Descent : Phylogeny—
   Biogenesis
   Origin of Species
   Factors of Evolution
   Phyletic Relationships and Classification
   Heredity and Variation
b. Bionomics : Ontogeny—
   Relationships *inter se*—
      Protective Resemblance, Mimicry, Sexual Selection, &c.
   Relations to Environment—
      Developmental Mechanics
c. Distribution of Plants (flora) and Animals (fauna, faunistic)—
      (Isolation, &c.)

ii. Theory of Life { Vitalism and other theories

iii. Mental Evolution { Psychology (genetic)

2. COMPARATIVE Animal Plant — Comparative {
Morphology (Anatomy)
Physiology
Cytology
Embryology (and Development)

II. SPECIAL.

Zoology (Animals)
Botany (Plants)

Morphology (Anatomy)
Physiology
Embryology
Cytology

Descriptive or Taxonomic (of species)
Quantitative
   (statistical : bearing on problems of i. *a, c,* above)
   (experimental : bearing on problems of i. *b,* above)

(J.M.B.—E.B.P.)

Literature : see references under ZOOLOGY (special subdivisions) and BOTANY. For particular questions, see under the various topics in the table above. Also DELAGE, Structure du Protoplasma (1895); Année Biol. (from 1895); Zool. Rec. (from 1864, also for list of journals); Zool. Jahrb. (from 1829); BAILEY, Survival of the Unlike (1896); WILSON, The Cell in Devel. and Inheritance (1896); BROOKS, The Foundations of Zool. (1899); T. H. HUXLEY, Collected Essays, ii, vii, viii, ix (1893–4); H. SPENCER, Princ. of Biol. (1863–7); M. VERWORN, Gen. Physiol.(Eng. trans., 1899); E. HAECKEL, Anthropogenie, 4. Aufl. (1891), and Natürliche Schaffungsgesch., 4. Aufl. (1892); O. HERTWIG, Zeit- u. Streitfragen d. Biol., Pt. I (1894), Pt. II (1897); GEOFFROY SAINT-HILAIRE, Hist. Nat. Gén. des Règnes Organiques (1844–62); ST. GEORGE MIVART, Genesis of Species (1871); E. PERRIER, La

Biology [Gr. βίος, life, + λόγος, discourse] : Ger. *Biologie*; Fr. *biologie*; Ital. *biologia*. The general science of life, including both plants and animals. (J.M.B.)

The term was first introduced by Lamarck (1801). Also used by Treviranus and Bichat. As now used, it comprises the more general problems of life, while more special problems fall under Zoology and Botany. Huxley claims that anthropology, sociology, and psychology are by right subdivisions of biology. Cf. the table given under the topic BIOLOGICAL SCIENCES.

Literature : E. R. LANKESTER, The Adv. of Sci.; and art. Zoology, in Encyc. Brit. (9th ed.); T. H. HUXLEY, art. Biology, in Encyc. Brit. (9th ed.). See under ZOOLOGY, BOTANY, and the topics (with literature) given under BIOLOGICAL SCIENCES. (C.LL.M.—J.M.B.)

Bionomic Forces: Ger. *bionomische Kräfte*; Fr. *forces bionomiques*; Ital. *forze bionomiche.*

Forces not themselves belonging to life which yet condition or limit the development and evolution of life.

Such are the mechanical, chemical, and other forces of the environment in which the organism develops. Mechanical strain and gravitation direct vital growth, but are not themselves vital forces. It is the action of such extra-vital forces as well as that of the properly vital forces that natural selection formulates. It has often been pointed out (see Cope, *Primary Factors of Evolution*, chap. vii ; Cattell, *Science*, N.S., iii. 668 ; Baldwin, *Psychol. Rev.*, iv. 1897, 219) that natural selection in biological evolution is not a force or cause, but a condition. Spencer's phrase, 'survival of the fittest,' itself analyses natural selection. The fitness is assumed. It is due to earlier real causes ; the survival or selection which 'natural selection' formulates is an *ex post facto* statement of results of the interaction of vital and bionomic forces. Cf. FORCES AND CONDITIONS, and SOCIONOMIC FORCES. (J.M.B.)

Bionomics [Gr. βίος, life, + νόμος, law]: Ger. *Bionomie, (Lehre der) bionomischen Verhältnisse*; Fr. *bionomie*; Ital. *bionomia*. That branch of biological study which deals with the relations of organisms among themselves, and with their environment, throughout their life-history. Cf. BIONOMIC FORCES. (C.LL.M.–J.M.B.)

E. Ray Lankester, by whom the term was suggested (*Adv. of Sci.*; also art. Zoology, in *Encyc. Brit.*, 9th ed., xxiv), says that Buffon (1707–88) alone, among the greater writers of the last three centuries, emphasized this way of studying organic nature. Darwin's work brought bionomics into the field of scientific inquiry, and led to a recognition of its true value. Sprengel, Wallace, Poulton, Fritz and Hermann Müller, Weismann, and others have paid special attention to this branch of biology.

Literature: see BIOLOGICAL SCIENCES. (C.LL.M.)

Biophores [Gr. βίος, life, + φορός, bearing]: Ger. *Biophoren*; Fr. *biophores*; Ital. *biofori*. The hypothetical vital units.

First used by Weismann (*Germ-Plasm*, 1893; cf. also his essay 'Amphimixis' in *Essays on Heredity*, Eng. trans., ii, and Spencer, *Princ. of Biol.*, 2nd ed.). More or less equivalent to the physiological units of Spencer, the gemmules of Darwin, the pangens of De Vries, the plasomes of Wiesner, the micellae of Nägeli, the plastidules of Haeckel, the bio-

blasts of Beale, the somacules of Foster, the idioblasts of Hertwig, the idiosomes of Whitman, the biogens of Verworn, and the gemmae of Haacke. They must not be identified with the molecules of which they are composed. In Weismann's scheme of nomenclature they combine to form DETERMINANTS (q.v.), these to form ids, and these again to form IDANTS (q. v.), which are the hypothetical equivalents of the observable CHROMOSOMES (q. v.). (C.LL.M.)

The simplest known units, capable of exhibiting the essential phenomena of life, are the lower unicellular organisms. The hypothetical units are merely molecular aggregates, capable of forming one of the links in the metabolism of living matter. (E.S.G.)

Blackstone, Sir William. (1723–80.) An eminent English jurist, best known for his commentaries on law. Admitted to the bar 1746 ; became Vinerian professor of law in 1758 at Oxford, where he had been educated. He was elected to Parliament in 1761, made solicitor-general in 1763, and became justice of the court of common pleas 1770.

Blank Experiment : see PUZZLE EXPERIMENT.

Blasphemy [Gr. βλασφημεῖν, to speak impiously]: Ger. *Gotteslästerung*; Fr. *blasphème*; Ital. *bestemmia*. Blasphemy in the restricted sense means speaking irreverently of God or of divine things; in the more general sense it is applied to profane swearing of any sort.

In Scripture the *loci classici* are Matt. xii. 31, Mark iii. 29, and Luke xii. 10; the widest divergence of opinion exists as to interpretation of these passages. In the early and mediaeval Church the term was employed to denote definite ecclesiastical offences. *Blasphematici*, in the early days of Christianity, were those who recanted under stress of persecution. The term was also applied to those who spoke slightingly of God, Christ, and the Virgin; and to those guilty of heresy. During the ages when the Church was supreme, torture and other forms of punishment, including death, were inflicted. In modern times, heresy and blasphemy have been viewed as essentially distinct offences. Formerly both were ecclesiastical, and punishable by ecclesiastical courts. Now the latter is, in some places, an offence at common law; it is a misdemeanour to speak, write, or publish any profane words vilifying or ridiculing God, Jesus Christ, the Holy Ghost, the Old or New Testament, or Christianity in general.

if done with intent to corrupt public morals, to mock and insult believers, or to bring religion into hatred or contempt. See *The Mod. Rev.* (1883), 586 ff., and Blackstone, *Comm.*, iv. 59. (R.M.W.)

Blastocoele [Gr. βλαστός, germ, + κοῖλος, hollow]: Ger. *Dotterhöhle, Furchungshöhle*; Fr. *blastocèle*; Ital. *blastocele*. A cavity which, in the development of many animals, forms in the midst of the group of cells produced by the cleavage of the ovum.

A term suggested by Huxley for the segmentation cavity of von Baer. It gives origin, in some cases, to the enteron or digestive cavity of the coelenterates, and is regarded on the PLANULA THEORY (q. v.) as the primitive gut. Where the enteron arises by invagination it must be carefully distinguished from the blastocoele. See EMBRYO (with figure). (C.LL.M.)

Blastoderm [Gr. βλαστός, germ, + δέρμα, skin]: Ger. *Keimhaut, Blastoderm*; Fr. *blastoderme*; Ital. *blastoderma*. The layer of cells overlying the yolk, forming the germinal membrane from which the embryo animal is developed. (C.LL.M.—E.S.G.)

The term is due to Pander (1817), who observed the blastoderm of the fowl, and traced its differentiation into an outer or serous layer, a middle or vascular layer, and an inner or mucous layer. Remak (1850–5) showed that the middle layer splits or cleaves into two. Thus four layers result, the relations of which have been in the light of more recent inquiry tabulated by Allen Thomson as follows:—

Primitive Blastoderm	Ectoderm	Epiblast	Body wall (Somatopleure)	Secondary Blastoderm
	Mesoderm.	Mesoblast		
	Endoderm	Hypoblast	Visceral wall (Splanchnopleure)	

In holoblastic or complete segmentation the primitive blastoderm forms a continuous vesicle; in meroblastic or incomplete segmentation it forms a layer resting upon the uncleaved or unsegmented yolk-mass. See OVUM, and CLEAVAGE.

Literature: F. M. BALFOUR, Compar. Embryol. (1880–81); ALLEN THOMSON, art. Embryology, Encyc. Brit. (9th ed.). (C.LL.M.)

Blastomere [Gr. βλαστός, germ, + μέρος, part]: Ger. *Furchungskugel*; Fr. *blastomère*; Ital. *blastomero*. Any one of the cells produced by the cleavage of the animal ovum. See EMBRYO. (C.LL.M.)

Blastopore [Gr. βλαστός, germ, + πόρος, passage]: Ger. *Urmund*; Fr. *blastopore*; Ital. *blastoporo*. The orifice of the two-layered invaginate embryo or gastrula of many animals.

The term was introduced by Lankester in 1875. Regarded by Haeckel as the primitive mouth, and yet considered by many as the homologue of the anus of Rusconi in the frog, this opening has been the subject of much discussion by zoologists. The term blastopore, as descriptive, avoids theoretical implications as to its ultimate fate. It seems, in some cases, to mark the position of the future mouth; in others of the future anus; and in some, by becoming slit-like and closing along the middle line, of both. See EMBRYO (with figure).

Literature: E. R. LANKESTER, Quart. J. Microsc. Sci., xv. (1875) 163; MINOT, Embryology. For its relations to the primitive streak in vertebrates, see BALFOUR, Compar. Embryol.; also HERTWIG, Embryol. of Vertebrates (Man and Mammals). (C.LL.M.)

Blastosphere [Gr. βλαστός, germ, + σφαῖρα, sphere]: Ger. *Blastula*; Fr. *blastosphère*; Ital. *blastosfero*. The spherical mass of cells enclosing the blastocoele, the product of the holoblastic segmentation or cleavage of the ovum. See EMBRYO. (C.LL.M.)

Blastula [Gr. βλαστός, germ]: Ger. *Blastula*; Fr. *blastula*; Ital. *blastula*. A term applied to the (blastula) stage at which the segmented ovum consists of the BLASTOSPHERE (q. v.). (C.LL.M.)

Blending [M. E. *blenden*, to mix]: Ger. *Verschmelzung*; Fr. *fusion*; Ital. *fusione.* An alternative rendering of the German Verschmelzung. See FUSION, which is preferred. (E.B.T., J.M.B.)

Blind Spot [Lat. *punctum caecum*]: Ger. *blinder Fleck*; Fr. *tache aveugle*; Ital. *punto cieco*. A spot in each retina insensitive to light.

Fig. 1. Blind spot in right eye. After Helmholtz. One may plot one's own blind spot for oneself (by enlarging the blank space from a centre with a pen) on a paper. (J.M.B.)

It is situated at the place of entry of the optic nerve. It is figured, e. g., by Helmholtz (right eye: *Physiol. Optik*, 2nd ed., 252). (See Fig. 1.)

The question of its filling out—so that the field of vision of the single eye seems continuous—is of some importance for the theory of visual space. The facts are: (1) that at the blind spot we see nothing; (2) that in binocular vision, the blind spot of each retina is covered by a sensitive portion of the other; (3) that the blind spot may easily be filled out by association (central processes), whose nature is determined by the stimulus of the surrounding retinal region. Whether or not this supplementing is materially assisted by (4) eye movements or motor tendencies, which serve as local signs for the insensitive region, may also be discussed.

The existence of the blind spot was first

a class form a considerable element in the community, for whose education and occupation special provisions have been made in all civilized communities. The literature concerning the blind is mainly educational in character, and gives an account of the treatment of the blind in past times, of statistics of the frequency, causes, and kinds of blindness, of the methods and appliances used in their education, of the management of institutions for the blind, of noteworthy blind persons, and the like. A much more limited, but in this connection more pertinent, series of studies relates to the psychology of the blind as a class (Heller, two arts. in *Philos. Stud.*, 1895, 130, &c.). The problems include the effect of the

Fig. 2. Close the right eye, and keeping the left fixed on the upper asterisk on the diagram (Fig. 2), move the latter toward the eye and away from it till a point is found at which the black oval disappears. For the blind spot of the right eye, turn the diagram upside down and close the left eye. (After Sanford.)

Fig. 3. The blind spot is demonstrated simultaneously in both eyes by Fig. 3. Look at the asterisk while holding a card in the median plane of the head (to prevent either eye seeing the other's part of the diagram). (After Sanford.)

demonstrated by Mariotte, 1668. It is easily demonstrated by Figs. 2, 3.

Literature: HELMHOLTZ, Physiol. Optik (2nd ed.), 717; WUNDT, Physiol. Psychol. (4th ed.), ii. 103; SANFORD, Course in Exper. Psychol., expts. 113, 114. The general works on physiological psychology. (E.B.T.—C.L.F.)

Blindness (and the blind): Ger. *Blindheit*; Fr. *cécité*; Ital. *cecità*. The term blindness is a most general one designating any distinct lack of the power to respond to the stimuli which give rise to vision. It may be partial or total, and may be due to injuries or deficiencies in any part of the optical mechanism accessory to the retina, in the retina itself, in the optic nerves, in the cortical or subcortical centres for vision, or in the connections between these. Cf. VISION (defects of). The blind as

deprivation of sight upon the use and training of the other senses; the precise directions in which the hearing and touch of the blind excel those of the seeing; the mental peculiarities of imagination and association, memory and attention; the influence of blindness upon emotional temperaments, and the like. Persons who have been both blind and deaf (and dumb) have naturally attracted considerable attention, and the methods used in their education have furnished valuable illustrations of psychological principles (see BRIDGMAN, LAURA, AND KELLER, HELEN). Some special studies have also been made on the dreams of the blind (Jastrow, *Princeton Rev.*, Jan. 1888). (J.J.)

Literature (general): W. H. LEVY, Blindness and the Blind (1872); KITTO, The Lost

Senses (1860); DE LA SIZERANE, Les Aveugles; NORRIS and OLIVER, Syst. of Dis. of the Eye (1897), ii; H. S. PEARCE, A Study of the Blind, Int. Med. Mag., vii. 167–79 (1898); J. SOURY, Cécité corticale: Vision des Couleurs, Mémoire des Lieux, Idée d'Espace, Rev. Philos. (1896). (J.J.–L.M.)

Blindness (mental, or psychic): Ger. *Seelenblindheit*; Fr. *cécité mentale* (or *psychique*); Ital. *cecità psichica*. This condition, known also as mind- or object-blindness, involves a failure to recognize objects by their visual properties, although the objects themselves are seen.

It appears to depend upon a loss or disintegration of the cluster of associations and memory images which group themselves about an object or idea and constitute for each individual his apperceptive content of such object or idea. Briefly, knowledge of things, though conditioned by sense impressions, proceeds by more or less elaborate perceptive interpretation. In mental blindness the object is seen, but it is not recognized by the seer, and fails to arouse its cluster of associations. The classic case described by Charcot, of a gentleman who was normally possessed of an unusually vivid power of visual imagination — picturing clearly the physiognomies of absent friends, the scenes of travel, &c.—and who through mental anxiety almost entirely lost his visual memory, so that he failed to recognize his own image in a mirror, illustrates one form of mental blindness. The condition produced by Munk in dogs, by extirpating portions of the occipital cortex, is analogous. Such dogs see, for they avoid obstacles; but they fail to recognize the individual character of objects, save through the other senses. Such dogs if deprived of smell are unable to distinguish meat from anything else. If they had been taught to perform certain movements in response to visual signals, these signals would no longer be correctly interpreted, e. g. the sight of a whip inspires no terror; just as in human cases familiar objects are not recognized (Elder, *Aphasia*, 170). Word blindness is a specific defect of similar nature, but limited to the recognition of the conventional written and printed symbols called words (see SPEECH AND ITS DEFECTS); while mental deafness is the name for a similar defect regarding auditory recognition. The relations of mental blindness to other cerebral and optical disturbances have been minutely studied, but no simple formulation of these is possible; the tendency of this defect to be associated with HEMIANOPSIA

(q.v.), as well as other evidence, indicates its connection with a region in the occipital cortex, mainly on the left side, which extends also into the angular and supramarginal gyri of the parietal lobe. (J.J.)

Literature: WILBRAND, Die Seelenblindheit (1881); detailed references cited in article 'Mind Blindness' in Tuke's Dict. of Psychol. Med.; BASTIAN, Aphasia, 210–13; ELDER, Aphasia, 175; WYLLIE, Disorders of Speech, 274; COLLINS, The Faculty of Speech, 302; HUYS, in Norris and Oliver's Syst. of Dis. of the Eye; LUCIANI and SEPPILLI, Localizzazioni cerebrali (1885); SEPPILLI, in Riv. di Freniat, passim. See also under SPEECH AND ITS DEFECTS. (J.J.–E.M.)

Blood [AS. *blōd*]: Ger. *Blut*; Fr. *sang*; Ital. *sangue*. The circulating medium of the body, exclusive of lymph. It is contained within the system of tubes—the blood-vessels —consisting of the heart, arteries, capillaries, and veins.

Blood is composed of a fluid portion, the plasma, and a formed portion, the corpuscles, which are of three kinds, the red and white corpuscles or leucocytes, and the blood-plates or blood-platelets. Cf. LYMPH. (C.F.H.)

Blues: Ger. *Niedergeschlagenheit*; Fr. *dépression*; Ital. *umor nero*. A popular name for moods or periods of mental depression. See MELANCHOLIA. (J.J.)

Bluntschli, Johann Kaspar. (1808–81.) An eminent Swiss jurist, born and educated at Zurich. Educated also at Berlin under Savigny. In 1833 he was appointed professor of law at Zurich, and at Heidelberg in 1859. He took an active part in politics in both Switzerland and Baden, and enjoyed a world-wide reputation for his historical and juristic writings.

Blush [AS. *blysa*, a glow]: Ger. *Erröthen*; Fr. *rougeur*; Ital. *rossore*. The reddening appearance, due to vaso-motor changes, which appears on the skin, especially of the face and neck, during emotions of SHYNESS (q. v.) and SHAME (q. v.).

Literature: DARWIN, Expression of the Emotions, 331 ff.; MANTAGAZZA, Physiognomy and Expression; MOSSO, Fear; BALDWIN, Social and Eth. Interpret., 203 ff. (J.M.B.)

Bocardo: see MOOD (in logic).

Bodin, Jean. (1530–96.) A French political philosopher. He was a teacher of law at Toulouse, an advocate in Paris, and royal officer at Laon. In his great political work, the State is defined as a group of families regulated by authority and reason, and the relation of the natural differences of nations to differences in their forms of government is discussed.

Body [AS. *bodig*, a body]: Ger. *Körper*; Fr. *corps*; Ital. *corpo*. The being which has its existence as an individual in space and time; the material thing.

In physics, a body is a space-occupying being exercising certain forces. In mathematics, a body is simply filled space. In physiology and psychology the word is used to mark the contrast between mind and matter; Locke (e.g.) opposes 'spirit' to 'body' (in general), and we commonly speak of mind and body (the physical person). (R.H.S.)

Body and **Flesh** (in theology). (1) The 'psychological' or 'natural' body (σῶμα ψυχικόν). Sensation, passion, and impulse are the leading features of this body. (2) The 'spiritual' body (σῶμα πνευματικόν). This body is the organization of the spirit, and is only less corporeal; many have identified it with the 'resurrection body.' (3) The social or mystical body of the Church, inspired with life by faith in Jesus Christ. This sense of the term is referable specially to the Pauline theology. Cf. 1 Cor. xii. 27; Eph. i. 23; ii. 16; iv. 4, 12, 16; v. 23, 30; Col. i. 18, 24; ii. 19; iii. 15.

Closely connected with body is the term Flesh (σάρξ). Flesh, which is the material element of body, is characteristically human, and as such is the subject of corruption, contingency, and weakness which leads to sin. It is the matter of which body is the form.

Literature: see under BIBLICAL PSYCHOLOGY; also HOLSTEN, Die Bedeutung d. Wortes σάρξ im Lehrbegriff d. Paulus; WENDT, Die Begriffe Fleisch u. Geist; MÜLLER, Die christl. Lehre d. Sünde (Eng. trans.); DICKSON, St. Paul's Use of the Terms Flesh and Spirit; THOLUCK, in Stud. u. Krit. (1855). (R.M.W.)

Boethius (or **Boetius**), **Anicius Manlius Torquatus Severinus.** (cir. 475–525 A.D.) A Roman philosopher and statesman. Born in Rome, he received a liberal education, becoming a good Greek scholar. He was chosen consul in 510, and appointed *magister officiorum* by Theodoric, king of the Goths, who reigned at Rome. His probity brought upon him the enmity of courtiers whose corrupt practices he opposed. He was finally imprisoned and executed. During his imprisonment he wrote his famous *Consolations of Philosophy*. A passage from his commentary on the *Isagoge* of Porphyry gave rise to

the prolonged discussion between the Realists and Nominalists of later Scholasticism.

Bohme, Jakob, also **Böhm** and **Behmen.** (1575–1624.) A German mystic, who was born, lived, and died near Görlitz, in Upper Lusatia. He was a shoemaker by trade, and a member of the Lutheran Church. Cf. MYSTICISM.

Bolzano, Bernhard. (1781–1848.) A German Catholic who sought to represent the doctrines of the Church as a complete system. Educated in philosophy and theology in Prague, he took holy orders, and in 1805 was appointed to the chair of philosophy of religion in the University of Prague. He stood in philosophical connection with Kant and Zimmermann. He was deposed in 1820, and suspended from priestly functions on account of his views.

Bona fides [Lat.]. Good faith; absence of unfair intent. Bona-fide purchaser: one who acquires title, without notice of any claim adverse to his vendor's right of transfer, and upon the faith that no such claims exist, and who has therefore parted with some valuable consideration, or otherwise altered his legal condition for the worse.

Roman law first marked out definitely the effect of an unexpressed but unfair intention upon contractual acts (cf. Sohm's *Instit. of Roman Law*, § 15). It came largely as part of their law of procedure (cf. *Instit. of Just.*, iv. 6, *de Actionibus*, 28 ff.). Good faith was of little importance in legal proceedings, as distinguished from equitable ones. English law developed in the same way. The chancellor was the first judge to decide causes according to the conscientious duty of the party, and so condemn all departures from honesty and uprightness to the injury of another (cf. Pomeroy on *Equity Jurisprudence*, i. § 56). In its application to prescriptive titles, good faith on the part of the possessor is of less importance in Anglo-American than in Roman law. (S.E.B.)

Bonaventura, Saint Giovanni Fidanza. (1221–74.) An eminent scholastic theologian called the Seraphic Doctor. Born in Bagnorea, States of the Church, he became a Franciscan monk, was educated in theology in Paris, was made general of the Franciscan Order in 1256, and cardinal in 1273. He died at Lyons, was canonized 1482, and made sixth Doctor of the Church 1587. Cf. SCHOLASTICISM.

Bonnet, Charles. (1720–93.) A Swiss naturalist and philosopher. He very early wrote on insects and plants, and became correspondent of the French Academy before he was thirty. Having weakened his eyes with the microscope, he devoted himself to more general subjects: to psychology and philosophy. He was one of the pioneers of physiological psychology cf. Külpe, *Einl. in die Philos.*, 63).

Bonum [Lat.]: see GOOD.

Boole, George. (1815–64.) An English mathematician and logician, professor of mathematics in Queen's College, Cork. His work, *An Investigation into the Laws of Thought*, was the first elaborate treatise in mathematical or symbolic logic.

Botany. The special division of the BIOLOGICAL SCIENCES (q.v.) which deals with plants. (J.M.B.)

Literature: CH. DARWIN, Variations in Plants and Animals under Domestication; SACHS, Lehrb. d. Botanik (1873), and Hist. of Botany (1890); A. P. DE CANDOLLE, Physiol. Végétale (1832); A. DE CANDOLLE, Origin of Cultivated Plants (1884); G. HENSLOW, Origin of Floral Structures (1888); BAILEY, The Survival of the Unlike (1896); S. VINES, Textbook of Botany (1895). (E.S.G.)

Bounty [Lat. *bonitas*, goodness]: Ger. *Prämie*; Fr. *prime*; Ital. *premio*. A sum paid by the Government to the producers of some particular commodity or service; presumably one which they would not be prepared to undertake for the sake of its probable commercial results, in the absence of some special inducement of this kind.

In England, the line of industry most systematically encouraged by bounties has been the production of wheat. For the effects of this policy, see Smith, *Wealth of Nations*, Bk. IV. chap. v. In most other countries, and especially in recent years, the sugar bounties have formed the most conspicuous application of this method of encouraging industry. For bounties to shipping, see SUBSIDY. There is no sharp line of distinction between the terms Bounty and Subsidy. The former is the more general; the latter is mainly applied to bounties in aid of transportation enterprises of various kinds. (A.T.H.)

Bourignon, Antoinette. (1616–80.) A Flemish mystical missionary who professed to receive divine revelations, and exerted a marked influence over the French mystics, especially over Pierre Poiret.

Bouterwek, Friedrich. (1766–1828.) A German philosopher. Educated as jurist and littérateur in Göttingen, he began lecturing

there in 1791 upon the Kantian philosophy. He was made assistant professor in Göttingen in 1797, and full professor in 1802. Besides philosophical works he wrote poetry and a much-praised *History of Poetry and Eloquence.*

Bowen, Francis. (1811–90.) An American writer in philosophy, history, and economics. Born in Charlestown, Mass., he was educated at Harvard University. Editor of *The North American Review*, 1843–54. Became Alford professor of natural religion, moral philosophy, and civil polity in Harvard University in 1853.

Boyle, Robert. (1627–91.) A celebrated Irish chemist and natural philosopher; son of Richard, the first earl of Cork. He was educated as an investigator in natural philosophy at Eton and Geneva. He later mastered Hebrew and Greek in order the better to defend Christianity. He was one of the founders of the Royal Society; improved the air-pump, and made important discoveries in pneumatics. He repeatedly declined a peerage. Through his liberality and effort Eliot's Indian Bible was published, and the Society for the Propagation of the Gospel in New England established. He endowed the Boyle Lectures.

Brachy- [Gr. βραχύς, short]: Ger. *kurz-*; Fr. *brachy-*; Ital. *brachi-*. A prefix used in combination with various terms to indicate shortness or smallness of the part denoted; thus a brachycephalic skull is a relatively broad and short one; brachydactilia indicates shortness in the fingers; brachyrrhinia, a short nose, &c.

For illustration see INDEX (cephalic), and CRANIOMETRY. The opposite of Brachy- is Dolicho-, as in DOLICHOCEPHALIC (q.v.). Used first by G. Retzius. (E.M., J.J.)

Brahma and **Brahmanism.** The principal deity of the Hindu pantheon. As originally conceived, Brahma may be compared to Spinoza's Substance. He was the one self-created and self-subsisting being.

This conception being, in its purity, too remote and abstract for the people, the older gods of the Vedic pantheon, especially Vishnu and Siva, took their places alongside of Brahma, thereby constituting a triad of deities relatively coequal; cf. ORIENTAL PHILOSOPHY (India).

Literature: MONIER WILLIAMS, Hinduism and Indian Wisdom; BARTH, Religions of India; MAX MÜLLER, Hibbert Lectures; and art. Brahmanism in Encyc. Brit., 9th ed. (R.M.W.)

Braidism: see HYPNOTISM.

Brain [AS. *bregen*]: Ger. *Gehirn, Hirn* (chiefly in compounds); Fr. *cerveau encéphale*; Ital. *encefalo, cervello* (in broad sense). That part of the central or axial nervous system which (in higher vertebrates) is enclosed within the skull; the expanded cephalic portion of the neural tube, including the centres of origin of the twelve cranial nerves, when present.

[This article consists of the following paragraphs: I. Historical; II. Embryology; III. Anatomy; IV. Comparative Anatomy; and V. Functions. A full bibliography of general works follows, and a glossary is added supplying brief definitions of more important organs.]

I. HISTORICAL.—That the brain is in some way connected with thought was recognized very early, and this view prevailed among the Greek physicians in spite of the fact that Aristotle described the brain as the most bloodless and inert organ of the body. The Pythagoreans, Hippocrates, and Plato clearly recognized the head as the seat of the intellect and will. Descartes was the first to elaborate a consistent theory of brain functioning (cf. LOCALIZATION).

During the 17th century great advances were made in the purely anatomical study of the brain, yet Leuwenhoeck was the first to employ the microscope in its investigation. Reil introduced hardening and preservative processes. Rolando and Stilling may be said to have founded the new technique by introducing a method of preparing sections, though this process would have been relatively fruitless but for Gerlach's discovery of the possibility of staining the sections (cf. NEUROLOGY). Experimental neurology dates from Flourens, 1824; but its fruition began in 1870 with Fritsch and Hitzig.

II. EMBRYOLOGY.—[In this and the following sections free use should be made of the glossary at the close of the article.] The brain, in common with the entire nervous and sensory apparatus, arises from modifications of the ectoderm. In higher animals the central nervous system appears as a plate extending down the dorsal axis of the ectoderm, and it is very early supplemented by accessory cephalic plates or bands composed of cells which are to be employed in the elaboration of the higher organs of special sense. The first stage in differentiation is the appearance of the medullary groove, which soon deepens and becomes closed dorsally to form the neural or medullary tube, out of whose substance the entire central nervous system is plastically constructed. At or near the suture formed by the closing of the neural tube arise the rudiments (Anlagen) of the sensory ganglia. Cf. NERVOUS SYSTEM (Histogenesis), and Plate A (BRAIN).

The tube becomes inflated at three points toward the cephalic extremity, thus forming three embryonic vesicles representing the primary fore-brain, mid-brain, and hind-brain, respectively.

The cephalic vesicle soon evaginates on either side, forming pouches (the primary optic vesicles) which project towards the skin, where they meet the in-growing rudiments of the lenses. In the course of their being moulded about the lens the original cavity is obliterated by the invagination of the lateral aspects forming double walls, or the retina and pigment layer of the choroid respectively. The cephalic portion of the primary fore-brain also expands, and, in all but the lowest vertebrates, divides into two hemispheres, whose ventricles remain connected by a median portion (the aula) via two apertures (the portae).

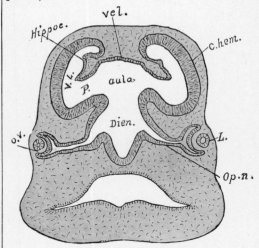

Fig. 1. Cross-section of head of embryo, showing relations of lateral ventricles (*V.L.*) to diacoele (*Dien.*), via the portae (*P.*) and aula; *vel.*, velum; *Hippoc.*, rudiment of hippocampus; *op.n.*, optic nerve; *L.*, lens of eye; *O.V.*, secondary optic vesicle.

The second or mid-brain vesicle remains undivided, its roof forming the optic tecta in which are situated the primary centres for vision. From the dorsal aspect of the roof arise the four eminences, collectively constituting the corpora quadrigemina. The base

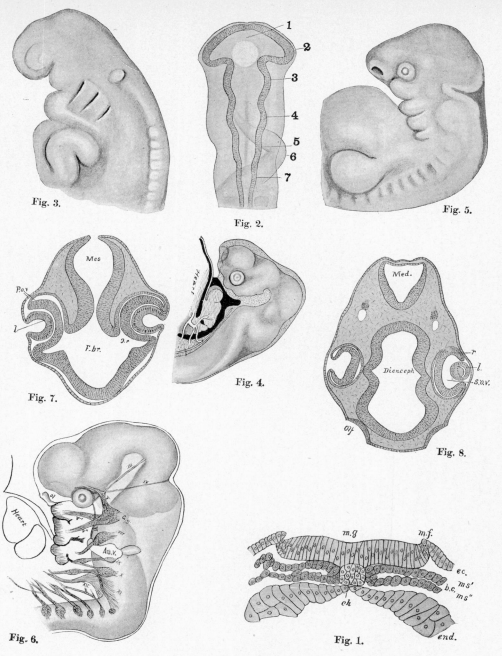

Plate A (Brain)

Fig. 1. — Cross-section of dorsal region of vertebrate embryo at stage of medullary plate (Hertwig). *m.g.*, medullary groove; *m.f.*, medullary folds; *ec.*, adjacent ectoderm; *ch.*, notochord; *b.c.*, somatic cavity; *ms′* and *ms″*, the two layers of mesoderm; *end.*, endoderm.

Fig. 2. — Chick at 58 hours (Mihalcovics). 1, primitive fore-brain; 2, primary optic vesicles; 3, mesencephalic vesicle; 4 and 5, metencephalic vesicle; 6, heart; 7, spinal cord.

Fig. 3. — Human embryo, 4 mm. long (His). The auditory vesicle and three gill clefts are present; also the faint indication of the optic vesicle.

Fig. 4. — Brain of a later human embryo (His). The flexures in the mid-brain and pons region are begun. The eye, lens, nasal sac, and hemispheres appear.

Fig. 5. — Still later human embryo, superficial view (His). Lower jaw and arm appear.

Fig. 6. — Brain of human embryo, 10.2 mm. long (His). Nerve roots are indicated by Roman numerals.

Fig. 7. — Frontal section through head of snake embryo (Herrick). Formation of secondary eye vesicles and lenses. *F.br.*, primary fore-brain; *l.*, lens; *Mes.*, mesencephalon; *o.r.*, optic pouch; *P.o.v.*, primary optic vesicle.

Fig. 8. — Later stage of same (Herrick). Formation of olfactory pits and lens-capsule. *Dienceph.*, diencephalon; *l.*, lens; *Med.*, medulla; *olf.*, nasal sack; *r.*, retina; *s.o.v.*, secondary optic vesicle.

of this segment is largely occupied by bands of fibres connecting higher regions with the medulla oblongata and cord, and constitutes the crus. The cavity of the mid-brain (mesencephalon) is gradually almost obliterated (in mammals), leaving only the aqueduct of Sylvius.

The third vesicle subdivides to form the cephalic (metencephalic) and caudal (myelencephalic) portion, the former being bounded by the pons and isthmus region and cerebellum, and the latter by the walls of the medulla oblongata proper. In this way the five most important divisions of the brain are marked out.

Scarcely less important than the vesicles in the architectonic of the brain are the flexures. The cephalic vesicle is flexed ventrad at an early stage, making room for the dorsal growth of the hemispheres and producing the cranial flexure. As though in compensation, the pons region is also flexed ventrad, affording room for the cerebellum, and, at a still later period, the cervical flexure marks the lower level of the medulla. By such means the axis of the brain is crumpled to accommodate the inequalities of growth.

As one result of these distortions, the actual cephalic terminus of the neural tube is obscure. Comparative researches indicate that the tube is, at an early stage, connected with the surface by a neuropore, whose position is supposed to be in some point of the lamina terminalis. See Plate A (NERVOUS SYSTEM).

The two hemispheres are probably discrete from the first, being separate evaginations from the primary fore-brain vesicle. In some cases they are represented simply by solid thickenings of the walls of the vesicle. In other cases the roof of the two hemispheres expands to form the mantle or pallium, which is at first membranous, and this, in turn, produces the dorsal walls of the cerebral hemispheres and their cortex, as well as a vascular membrane which, under the name of paraplexus and preplexus (plexus choroideus anterior), is folded into the cavities.

From this secondary fore-brain (prosencephalon) an evagination is thrust out from the ventro-cephalic extremity of each hemisphere to form the olfactory bulbs (containing the rhinocoele), and, after receiving accretions from the olfactory mucous membrane, these form the first central stations of the olfactory nerves. These, and the stalk connecting them with the hemispheres (crura), and the eminence in which they are inserted (lobi olf.), together with the entire median and ventral parts of the cerebrum, including the hippocampus and part of the gyrus fornicatus of higher brains, have been grouped together as rhinencephalon, from their association with the olfactory function.

The median unaltered part of the primary fore-brain becomes the diencephalon, including the thalamus and its appendages. The cavity is reduced to a narrow slit (the third ventricle or diacoele). This extends ventrally into the infundibulum and optic recesses.

Within the walls of the diencephalon there arise a variety of nuclei of great importance in the physiology of the brain. Of these the mammillaria are associated with smell, the geniculata with vision, and the subthalmicus, and perhaps the ruber, with general and somatic sensation.

The second embryonic vesicle is less profoundly modified, though its ventral aspect is largely reinforced by fibres to and from the higher regions, thus forming the pes pedunculi.

The metencephalon and myelencephalon are formed from the walls of the third vesicle, which collectively constitute the rhombencephalon. The roof of the entire region is primarily membranous (tela-form), and so remains in some lower animals. It is partly transformed into a complicated plexiform organ which, with outgrowths of the pia, constitutes the metaplexus. In various portions of the rhombencephalon lateral outgrowths of cellular matter encroach upon the roof, forming more or less complete roofs over the fourth ventricle. The most constant of these outgrowths is the cerebellum or epencephalon. The cellular materials of which the cerebellum is largely composed arise from rudiments in the lateral walls of the tube, and are pushed dorsad, forming two lateral hemispheres which coalesce dorsally, though a centre of proliferation also exists at the caudal extremity. See NERVOUS SYSTEM (Histogenesis).

A special group of nuclei (n. dentatum, &c.) is developed in the ventral aspects of the cerebellum by proliferations of ventricular epithelium, and similar bodies (the olives) are formed by diverticles of ventricular epithelium in the base of the medulla oblongata. The floor of the medulla, otherwise, is largely occupied with fibres from the myelon and the root nuclei of the cranial nerves, whose development obeys similar laws to those of the cord.

The entire length of the brain has been laid off into embryonic zones, each with its intrinsic peculiarities. (1) The basal plate, occupying the ventral median line; (2) laterally the fundamental plates, containing the root zones of the motor nerves; (3) alar plates, with the root zones of the sensory nerves; (4)

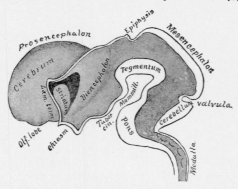

Fig. 2. Diagrammatic hemisected embryonic brain. Modified from His.

dorsal plate forming the roof. (1) and (4) are primarily membranous, and, as the most conservative portions of the nerve-tube, are especially valuable in determining relation-ships. Cf. NERVOUS SYSTEM (Comparative Anatomy).

III. ANATOMY. Recalling the fact that all the structures of the adult brain are derived from plicated and thickened modifications of the medullary tube, the essential relations are best seen in a hemisection of the entire brain, especially that of an embryo. See Fig. 2; cf. also Plate A (NERVOUS SYSTEM).

In the adult the front of the original fore-brain (lamina terminalis) occupies a position well toward the middle of the brain. Ventrally it terminates in the recessus preopticus, cephalad of the chiasm.

The two great prosencephalic commissures originally lie in the lamina terminalis, though this relation is obscured in adult life. Of these commissures the ventral one (precommissure) connects the ventral portion of the prosencephalon, while the dorsal one (callosum) is the commissure of the pallium proper. The great arch which this commissure makes over the portae and aula leaves a space closed only by the thin septum lucidum. The membranous part of the roof next following is the invaginated vascular preplexus; then the evaginated preparaphysis and the velum, finally the post-paraphysis (Zirbelpolster) and the supra-commissure.

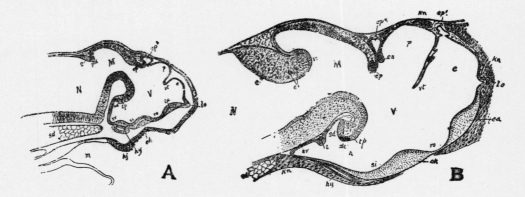

Fig. 3. *A*, sturgeon larva three days old. *B*, similar larva four weeks old. Median longitudinal sections. After Kupffer.

c., Cerebellum; *ca.*, precommissure; *cc.*, commissura cerebelli; *cd.*, chorda dorsalis; *ch.*, chiasm and commissura post-opticae; *cp.*, post-commissure; *cs.*, supra-commissure; *de.*, commissura mollis; *e.*, secondary fore-brain (prosencephalon); *en.*, entoderm; *ep*[1]., paraphysis; *ep*[2]., epiphysis; *h.*, infundibular region; *hf.*, sucking disk; *hy.*, hypophysis; *kn.*, cartilage; *lo.*, recessus neuroporicus; *M.*, mesencephalon; *m.*, mouth; *N.*, metencephalon; *P.*, praepineal roof of diencephalon (parencephalon); *pd.*, plica dorsalis; *ro.*, recessus opticus; *sd.*, sinus dorsalis; *si.*, sinus post-opticus; *sv.*, saccus vasculosus; *t.*, commissura terminalis; *tp.*, tuberculum posterius; *V.*, primary fore-brain (diencephalon); *vt.*, velum transversum of the fore-brain.

In the higher brains the mesal and caudal part of the hemispheres, viz. the hippocampal region with its olfactory centres, is connected with its fellow of the opposite side and the base of the thalamus by a transverse band (the hippocampal or fornix commissure). In man the fornix is appressed upon the callosum lying ventrad of it, but leaving a triangular interval, the lyra Davidis. The corpus fornicis receives fibre bands (crura) from the hippocampus, and sends others (columnae) towards the mammillaries.

The roof behind the supra-commissure is produced dorsad to form an organ of variable size and structure which, in lower animals, stands in intimate relation with a median PARIETAL ORGAN (q.v.). This epiphysis (sensu stricto) is vascular, membranous, or absorbed in various groups. Near the point where the epiphysis unites with the roof of the thalamus are the cellular habenulae with their commissure. Then follows (passing caudad) the short lamina intercalaris and the post-commissure at the cephalic limit of the mesencephalon.

The ventral aspect of the thalamus exhibits the post-optic recess, infundibulum, and mammillary recess; while a vascular outgrowth from a point caudad of the infundibulum occurs in various aquatic animals, and constitutes the saccus vasculosus. These are all diverticula of the third ventricle. The mammillaries are cellular masses caudad of the tuber cinereum (see Glossary), and are end-stations for the fornix fibre columns. The ventral part of the thalamus, or hypothalamus, contains at least four commissures beside the chiasm of the optic nerves.

The floor of the mesencephalon is composed of the massive pes pedunculi, a strong tract of motor fibres from the cortex to the pyramidal tracts of the spinal cord. This is the chief efferent path from the brain to the trunk. Lying dorsally of it is the tegmentum. It contains the afferent nuclei (ruber and niger), whose relations seem to be with the motor systems especially, serving as shunting stations for the cerebellum. The tegmentum also contains the lemniscus fibres, which are the great conductors of sensory impressions to the brain. They associate the sensory nerve roots of the medulla oblongata and cord with the caudal portion of the mesencephalic roof. The dorsal walls of the mesencephalon contain optic centres (tectum, &c.), as well as stations for the communication with the co-ordinating motor nuclei; and, accordingly, in the caudal portions lie the nuclei of the third and fourth nerves.

The medulla oblongata and cerebellum constitute a single region (rhombencephalon). The medulla oblongata is that part of the brain which forms the transition to the spinal cord, and, accordingly, it departs less than the rest of the brain from the type of structure exhibited by it. The embryonic third vesicle is greatly enlarged to form the metacoele, and its roof is largely membranous. In the massive part of the embryonic medulla oblongata there may be distinguished a basal plate, two fundamental plates, and two alae. It is by complications and proliferations from the epithelium of the latter that the lateral and dorsal outgrowths, including the olives (His) and the cerebellum (Herrick), are developed.

Ventrally the surface exhibits the ventral columns and pyramids which are crossed transversely by the pons fibres from the middle cerebellar peduncle and the trapezoides fibres from the roots of the eighth nerve. Dorsally, after removing the cerebellum, the dorsal columns (funiculi gracilis et cuneatus) of each side unite to form the restiformia, and these pass into the post-peduncles of the cerebellum. The dorsal fibres of the cord (Goll's and Burdach's columns) terminate in the nuclei of the funiculi gracilis et cuneatus, and are continued cephalad into the lemniscus by bundles arising in these cell clusters. These soon decussate and take their place in the ventro-lateral region laterally from the pyramid fibres, which also cross at this level. This more or less continuous decussation in the medial line forms the raphe.

We may follow this general review by a more detailed description of the major divisions.

Cerebrum. In the development, after separation of the hemispheres, a thickening in the base of each projects into the ventricle and constitutes the striatum, an intermediary station through which pass nearly all the fibres connecting the cortex with lower parts of the system. The striatum is divided by the fibres of the corona radiata or internal capsule into the nucleus lentiformis and the n. caudatus, each with subordinate portions. As the development proceeds the hemispheres become flexed about an axis terminating in the fossa Sylvii of either side, and the result of this and analogous alterations is expressed by dividing the external aspect into lobes (l. frontalis, parietalis, occipitalis, temporalis, insula, &c.). The internal concomitant of this process is expressed by the subdivision of the lateral ventricles into the cephalic, caudal, and ventral cornua. At the same time the rapid expansion of the surface, due to formation of the cortex, results in irregularities of the cortex constituting gyri or convolutions separated by fissures or sulci. The most mesal and caudal portion of the cortex is strongly conduplicated, forming a reverse curve in section,

The transection in Plate B (BRAIN), Fig. 1, conveys a good idea of the general relations. The topography of the cortex may be gathered from Figs. 5, 6, and 7. Cf. LOCALIZATION (cerebral).

The superficial layer of grey matter of the cerebrum, containing the highest centres for sensation and voluntary motion (cortex in

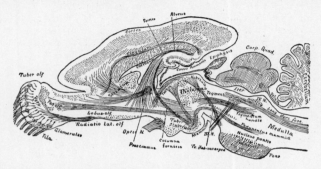

Fig. 4. Generalized longitudinal section of mammalian (rodent) brain. Modified from Edinger.

and giving rise to the hippocampal region or cornu Ammonis, with the gyrus hippocampi, whose section is S-shaped, and the gyrus un-

strict sense), is usually regarded also as the seat of consciousness. Ontogenetically the cortex is derived from the pallium, and in-

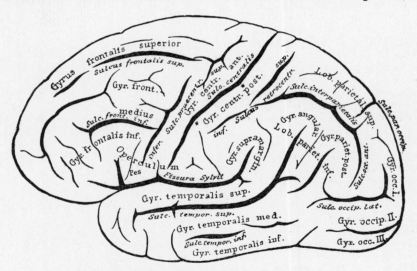

Fig. 5. Lateral view of the human brain. After Edinger.

cinatus, which is folded in the reverse sense into the inner limb of the S. The fibres collected on the ventricular aspect of this region form the alveus, while the tangential ectal fibres pass through the fimbria into the fornix. See Fig. 4.

cludes the outer cellular part as contrasted with the inner fibrous parts of the hemisphere's walls. In the ventral and mesal regions the cortical layers merge into ventricular grey matter, with which they have a common origin from the proliferating ventricular epithelium.

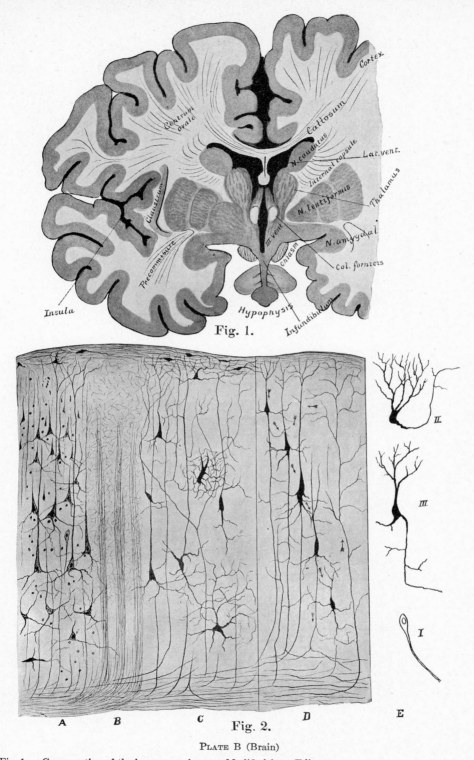

Fig. 1.

Fig. 2.

PLATE B (Brain)

Fig. 1. — Cross-section of the human cerebrum. Modified from Edinger.
Fig. 2. — Combined drawings from sections of the cortex prepared by various methods. Mainly after
Cajal. *A*, section stained with haematoxylin; *B*, prepared by Weigert's method, showing fibre
bundles; *C*, prepared by the Golgi method; *D*, diagram showing supposed path of stimuli; *E*, stages
in the development of neurocytes.

Although the arrangement and distribution of cortical elements varies in different regions, they may be conveniently included in four layers outside of the white matter. The most superficial zone is sparsely provided with cells in which ramify the dendrites of the deeper nerve cells. In this layer also originate the tangential fibres connecting with other regions. This is the tangential fibre zone (also molecular, neuroglia, or Cajal-cell layer). The second layer is filled with small pyramidal cells, which tend to increase in size in deeper portions, forming a transition to the third layer of large pyramids. Beneath the latter is a zone of variously placed polymorphic cells.

The relations between the cells of these layers are seen in Plate B (BRAIN), Fig. 2.

to the lower centres, collecting in the corona radiata, and afterwards constituting the internal capsule, are there segregated somewhat in accordance with their sources; and, accordingly, various parts of the capsule contain fibres with different functions. See LOCALIZATION.

The speech centre (Broca's region) contributes a special tract to the pyramids. The parietal motor zones are also represented by more or less distinct bands in the internal capsule. The optic radiations connect the optic centres of the thalamus with the occipital cortex, and it is probable that each sensory area has its reflex tract connecting with the appropriate lower centres. Special tracts from the striatum pass to the tegmental nuclei.

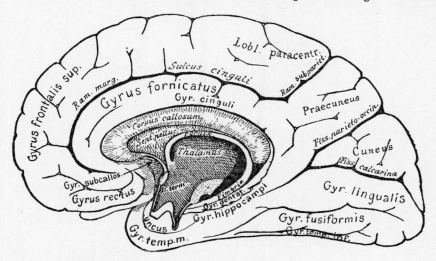

Fig. 6. Median longitudinal section through the human brain. After Edinger.

The pyramidal cells give rise to strong neurites, which extend into projection-tract fibres and which occasionally give off strong collaterals, passing via the callosum to homologous regions of the opposite hemisphere. Other cells send their neurites into the tangential zone outward: see ASSOCIATION FIBRES.

The framework of the cortex is originally supplied by the spongioblasts of the endyma (see NERVOUS SYSTEM, Histogenesis), and, in the adults of the lower animals, these cells continue to span the entire thickness of the cortex. In the massive cerebrum of higher animals the so-called neuroglia cells supplement the primitive spongioblastic framework.

The neurites of the cortical cells destined

Cerebellum. Although derived from outgrowths of the lateral walls of the metacoele, the cerebellum in mammals consists of a median vermis and two lateral hemispheres, with two or more smaller paired bodies (flocculi). The surface is marked by convolutions and depressions analogous to the gyri and fissures of the cerebrum. The cortex of the cerebellum (Fig. 8) is extraordinarily complex, and beautifully illustrates the apparatus for nervous discharge by contiguity rather than by structure continuity. Three layers may be distinguished above the white fibre zone. Of these the middle layer, composed of the cells of Purkinje, is most important. These large pyramidal cells are in a single layer, and their very numerous dendrites ramify in mazy arborizations within the ectal or molecular layer (Fig. 9). The neurites from the bases of the cells of Purkinje pass in regular order into the ental white layer, but give off, in their course, numerous collaterals which enter into close relations with other similar cells. In the ectal layer, or zona molecularis, the dendrites of the Purkinje cells are intimately associated with the terminal ramifications of the scandent fibres, which, arising in unknown (probably extra-cerebellar) cells, ascend between the

resemble the cells of Purkinje, but their neurites ramify in the same layer.

The external connections of these cells are problematical. Of the three pairs of cerebellar peduncles, the cephalic pair (superior brachia) connect the cerebellum with the tegmental nuclei and with Gower's ascending tract of the spinal cord. The middle peduncles consist, chiefly at least, of fibres from the pons, which pass to the lateral cerebellar hemispheres (pilea). These fibres are in part neurites from the Purkinje cells of the cerebellar cortex, ter-

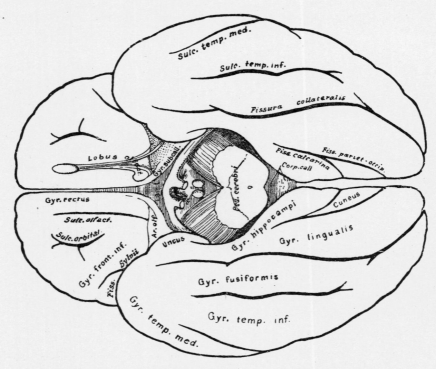

Fig. 7. Ventral view of the human brain. After Edinger.

Purkinje cells and ramify among their dendrites. Other cells within the molecular layer give off tangential fibres, from which arise collaterals which descend and surround with their fine ramifications the bodies of the Purkinje cells, thus effecting a co-ordination with the latter. Beneath the Purkinje layer is the zona granulosa, composed essentially of small polygonal cells having large nuclei whose dendrites soon subdivide, while their neurites enter into the molecular layer and there bifurcate. Other cells of the granular layer

minating about the cells of the nuclei pontis of the same and the opposite side, and also going an unknown distance cephalad in the pyramids; in part they are neurites of the cells of the nuclei pontis, terminating probably as the scandent fibres of the molecular zone of the cerebellar cortex. The cells of the nuclei pontis are in communication not only with the terminal arborizations of the Purkinje cells, but with collaterals from the underlying pyramidal fibres. We clearly have here provision for both ascending and descending fibres connecting the cerebellar cortex with the great motor and sensory tracts leading down from the cerebral cortex. The caudal peduncles enter the corpora restiformia and contain fibres to the fleece and vermis. They receive the ascending direct cerebellar tract of the spinal cord, fibres from the great lemniscus system (nuclei funiculi gracilis et cuneatus), and, directly or indirectly, fibres from the auditory nerve, and others less thoroughly known.

The Membranes (meninges). The membranous envelopes of the central nervous system are three in number, the innermost or pia belonging strictly to the nervous organ, tween the two cerebral hemispheres dorsally of the callosum, forming the falx and enclosing the great longitudinal blood sinus. The membranes are subject to various diseases, often of a serious character. Leptomeningitis is a purulent inflammation of the pia and adjacent parts of the brain. It is an infectious and often epidemic disease due to a diplococcus. Primary meningitis originates at the base of the brain; minute hemorrhages in the brain substance and distension of the ventricles are frequent concomitants. The prognosis is grave, and recovery in any event usually but partial. Tubercular meningitis is apparently due to infection from other organs. Pachy-

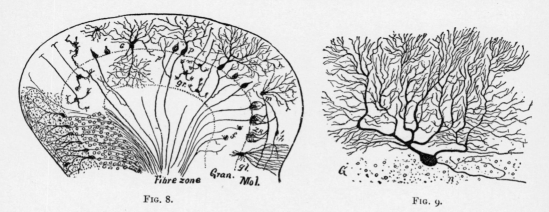

FIG. 8.   FIG. 9.

Fig. 8. Diagrammatic section of a convolution of the cerebellum.
Gran., granular layer; *Mol.*, molecular layer ectally of Purkinje cells; *P*, Purkinje cells; *G*, cell of Golgi type, with finely divided neurite in granular layer; *gr.*, granule cell with bifid neurite in molecular layer; *m*, basket cell, whose collaterals, *zk*, form arborizations about the cells of Purkinje; *f*, dendrite cells; *gl.*, glia cells.

Fig. 9. A single Purkinje cell (by Golgi's method). *n*, axis-cylinder process, passing into the granular layer (*G*).

while the outer one, the dura, is more closely associated with the bony walls. The middle membrane, or arachnoid, is variable in its relations. Sometimes the outer envelope is called pachymenix, and the inner leptomenix, though these terms appear more often in combinations, such as pachymeningitis. The dura within the cranium is apparently simple, but within the spinal cavity it is cleft into an inner layer, or theca, and an outer one closely attached to the vertebrae. The interval between these is the epidural space. The space between the cerebellum and cerebrum is occupied by a fold of dura (sometimes ossified) constituting the tentorium. From the middle of the tentorium a similar fold extends be- meningitis is an inflammation of the dura, and is an accompaniment of various diseases, especially chronic diseases of the brain itself. The meninges are freely supplied with sensory cerebro-spinal and vaso-motor sympathetic nerves.

Circulation in the Brain. The circulation within the brain is chiefly provided for by the vessels of the meninges, and those of the intrusions of the brain walls forming apparently intra-ventricular plexuses. Although Mendel has found that the pressure in the cortical arteries is less than that in the carotids, it is true that any serious alteration in the vascular pressure is attended with functional disturbance. The intra-cranial arteries fall into two systems. (1) The meningeal, or dural, which ramify upon the dura and diploi of the cranium. Nearly the whole dura is supplied by branches of the external carotid, of which the medi-dural is the largest. The internal carotid supplies the hypophysis and Gasser's ganglion. The vertebral gives rise to the post-dural, which supplies the dura of the postcranial fossa, especially the falx. (2) Intrinsic arteries are such as supply the brain substance. Four arteries supply this system, the paired carotids and the vertebrals. These primary vessels combine to form the circle of Willis in the brain base, and from this polygonal vessel arise all the cerebral arteries. Intra-vascular pressure is less in the grey than in the white matter. The veins likewise are divided into dural and intrinsic veins, and all of the dural and most of the intrinsic veins open into sinuses or spaces with non-collapsible walls. The largest sinus is the longitudinal, parallel to the sagittal suture, and is the vessel presenting most difficulty to intra-cranial operation. The lymphatic system of the brain, though obscure, is not wholly absent. Its most rudimentary form is seen in the peri-cellular spaces. The lymph canals collect and pass out in company with the veins. The endyma and hypophysis are closely associated with the lymph-vascular systems.

IV. FUNCTIONS OF THE BRAIN. Two general theories of brain function may be distinguished. According to the earlier, more mechanical theory, the brain is a collection of different organs which, while more or less connected serially by nervous paths, are nevertheless distinct in nature and function. This anatomical survey of the psychological concept of discrete faculties received strong support from the data of localization, although there have always been advocates of the doctrine of cerebral unity. Modern histological researches have reinforced the argument for the essential unity of the brain by showing that not only are all parts derived from the homogeneous brain-tube, but that the cellular elements have a homologous origin from the ventricular epithelium. Furthermore, the discovery of communication by contiguity rather than actual continuity of structure, indicates that the intercommunication may be much more complicated and extensive than was formerly supposed possible. The vast complexity of the fibrous processes from the various cells, and the systems of collaterals and association fibres, reveal in the brain a degree of solidarity inconsistent with a rigid localization. The conditions seen in brains of Amphibia, where

an almost undifferentiated zone of cells adjacent to the ventricles serves for all the various and diverse functions, and where chains of associated cells mark the course of tracts of the highest importance, forcibly impress the

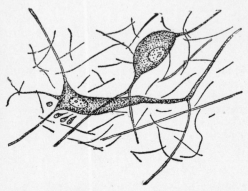

Fig. 10. Switch cell from pes (tegmentum) region of the fish.

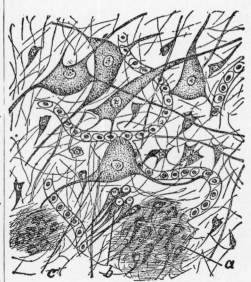

Fig. 11. Portion of nucleus ruber (rotundatus) of the fish. *a*, Gelatinous glomerule; *b*, clustered cells; *c*, a ganglion cell.

idea that it is rather the relations than the structure of the cells which determine the function, and that the nervous or physical resultant is, in a sense, the algebraic sum of the activities—an equation of function.

The neurocytes may be roughly classed as centripetal, centrifugal, and intercalary, with respect to the central organ or stations; though, strictly speaking, each neurocyte is simply a node in a path, the cellipetal parts being dendrites; the cellifugal, the neurite. The third class seems to serve to divide a tract or to switch stimuli from the direct to an indirect route, as in the tegmental nuclei. See Figs. 9, 10, 11.

There is much reason to believe that within, as well as outside the central system, many neurocytes may be merged in a single long circuit or tract. In some cases the cell body is thrown out of circuit and remains a mere appendage with a nutritive function only, while in others the impulse passes through the cell, and is there probably reinforced or modified. Good illustrations of the complicated paths pursued by a stimulus are afforded by the special senses. For example, an irritation in the nasal epithelium passes via a neurite, or from cell to cell to a neurite whose fine arborizations enter a glomerule and communicate with one of the dendrites of one of the mitral cells of the pero. See Fig. 6 (Nervous System). Thence the stimulus may pass via a neurite or chain of cells to the hippocampus, and there a similar communication is effected with the dendrites of the long pyramids of the hippocampal cortex, in the bodies of which we may suppose an excitation is established, the effect of which upon the total equilibrium of the sensorium constitutes a sensation of smell. But, at the same time, other neurites convey stimuli via the fimbria and fornix to the thalamus, where reflex associations of the most complicated sort are effected. In fact the whole infra-cortical tone is perhaps modified, and profound changes in circulation and the relative receptivity of various sense organs may result. Nor are these sub-conscious changes devoid of their secondary influence on consciousness.

The theory of consciousness which seems best to conform to the conditions of brain structure and its observed unity is that each conscious state is an expression of the total equilibrium of the conscious mechanism, and that intercurrent stimuli are continually shifting the equilibrium from one to another class of activities. In other words, the sensation accompanying a given colour presentation is not due to the vibrations in the visual centre in the occipital lobe, but to the state of cortical equilibrium or the equation of cortical excitement when that colour stimulus predominates. Previous vestigial excitements and co-ordinations with the data from other cortical centres

all enter into the conscious presentation. As the wave of excitation passes from the visual centre to other parts, the proportional participation of other centres increases, producing a composite containing more distantly related elements.

What the exact nature of the infra-conscious processes in the thalamus, &c., is, may never become wholly clear. The stimuli from the organ of sense are said to be organized for presentation to the cortical centres. A very important function also is the proper provision for the complex reflex co-ordinations. Removal of any centre or area impairs the equilibrium, and so, aside from suppressing the function of the destroyed organ, alters the 'tone' of consciousness.

The existence of non-functioning cells or portions from which new neurocytes may develop on occasion, is rendered probable by the data of histogenesis and by the occurrence of functional substitution.

That the cerebellum does not participate in the psychical, emotional, or generative functions has been made probable by recent experiments. That it has no direct relation to the fifth or eighth nerve roots seems likely, although some connection with the vestibular apparatus is conceded.

The direct effect of injury to or disease of the entire cerebellum is disturbance of motor equilibrium and co-ordination evidenced by imperfect station and locomotion without notable reduction of motor power. Astasia, or unsteadiness of head, trunk, and limbs, is permanent. Injury confined to the median lobe produces similar symptoms, but less pronounced, while unilateral injury affects the equilibration of the same side. Section of the peduncles of one side produces essentially the same effects as destruction of the corresponding lateral lobe of the cerebellum. Section of the middle peduncles results in atrophy of the nucleus pontis of the opposite side and the connecting pons fibres. There is evidence that removal of one half of the cerebellum increases the excitability of the opposite cerebral hemisphere.

The medulla oblongata participates largely in the reflex functions of the spinal cord, but is pre-eminently the locus of the primary centres of special sense. Here, too, the centres of the vagus nerve provide for vital co-ordinations. The term 'vital node,' though perhaps an anatomical fiction, expresses the intimate co-ordinations between the centres for vascular, respiratory, and digestive functions in centres immediately adjacent to the floor of the metacoele. The psychical importance of these centres lies in their intimate, though obscure, relation to the emotions. The anatomical basis for this connection is, as yet, wholly unknown.

For discussion of the phylogeny of the Brain, see Nervous System.

V. Comparative Anatomy.—Comparisons of the human brain with that of brutes are made in various ways, the relations of mere volume or weight being untrustworthy. In general, it is obvious that the extent to which consciousness has been interpolated in the cycle of nervous processes increases as we ascend the scale. The area of cortex devoted to the immediate spheres of the sense organs is surprisingly great in lower vertebrates. The lowest of the special senses (smell) is found to occupy a relatively enormous proportion of the cortex in reptilia, and even in marsupials such a disproportion is conspicuous. It is only in higher mammals that a large proportion of the cortex seems to have been reserved for correlations of higher orders. The apparent absence of a callosum in marsupials, &c., has a morphological rather than functional bearing, for the associational fibres proper to the callosum pass via the precommissure. In the estimation of the position of a brain type in the scale, use is made of certain indices. The occipital and parietal indices are the distances along the mesal margin of the hemisphere intercepted by the intersection of the external parieto-occipital fissure and the central Rolandic fissure respectively, measuring from the occipital pole in the first case, and from the occipito-parietal intersection in the other; the measurements being in hundredths of the entire length along the dorsal margin of the hemisphere. A table of such measurements is given as follows:—

Human.

5½–6½ months	O. index,	18·8 ;	P. index,	28·5
6½–7½ ,,	,,	18·6	,,	24·7
7½–8½ ,,	,,	20·7	,,	24·1
At term	,,	20·8	,,	25·7
4–5 years	,,	23·2	,,	24·2
Adults	,,	21·2	,,	25·5

Apes.

Orang	,,	23·2	,,	21·3
Chimpanzee	,,	24·2	,,	19·9
Hamadryas	,,	29·5	,,	20·5
Cynocephalus	,,	29·7	,,	22·6
Macaque	,,	31·0	,,	19·0
Cebus	,,	33·1	,,	20·6

In low apes there is an enormous increase in the occipital portion of the border, whereas in high apes the amount of increase is smaller. Only Primates, which alone possess well-developed occipital lobes, exhibit transitory fissures of the cerebrum. The cuneus in certain abnormal conditions of the human brain resembles that of apes.

The insula is larger in the male than in the female, and in the European than in lower races. In the relations of the insula and its opercula the embryonic conditions in man resemble those of apes. Cf. Index (cephalic), and Anthropoid.

Literature: Excellent literature lists will be found in Schwalbe's Neurologie, in Quain's Anatomy, in Amer. Textbook of Physiol. (Philadelphia, 1896), and in most of the other general works cited below. Edinger's Berichte published in Schmidt's Jahrb. and Merkel und Bonnet's Ergebnisse give comprehensive annual summaries. L. F. Barker, The Nerv. Syst. and its Constituent Neurones (New York, 1899; 1122 pp., 683 figs.), is an excellent and comprehensive digest of the literature, especially the most recent, on nerve-cells and their relations. H. C. Bastian, The Brain as an Organ of Mind (London, 1880); Über das specifische Gewicht des Gehirns, Arch. f. Heilk. (1886). W. v. Bechterew, Die Leitungsbahnen im Gehirn und Rückenmark (Leipzig, 1884). L. Bianchi, Functions of the Frontal Lobes, Brain, xviii (1895). Th. L. W. v. Bischoff, Das Hirngewicht des Menschen (1880). E. Brissaud, Anatomie du cerveau de l'homme (Paris, 1893). A. Broca, Anatomie descriptive des circonvolutions cérébrales, Gaz. hebdom., xxxviii (1891). T. E. Clark, Comparative Anatomy of the Insula, J. of Compar. Neurol. vi (1896). D. J. Cunningham, The Complete Fissures of the Human Cerebrum and their Significance in connection with the Growth of the Hemisphere, J. of Anat. and Physiol., xxiv (1890); The Surface Anatomy of the Cerebral Hemispheres, Cunningham Mem. of the Roy. Irish Soc., No. vii (1892). B. Davis, Contributions toward determining the Weight of the Brain in different Races of Men, Philos. Trans. (1869). C. Debierre, Sur les anomalies des circonvolutions du cerveau de l'homme, C. R. Soc. de Biol., iii (1891). Déjerine, Anatomie des centres nerveux, i (Paris, 1895). H. H. Donaldson, Anatomical Observations on the Brain and Sense Organs of the Blind Deafmute, Laura Bridgman, Amer. J. of Psychol., iii, iv (1890-1); The Growth of the Brain (London and New York, 1895). T. Dwight, Remarks on the Brain of a Distinguished Man, Proc. Amer. Acad. Sci., xiii (1887). L. Edinger, Vorlesungen über die nervösen Centralorgane des Menschen und der Thiere, 5th ed. (1896, trans., 1899). Exner, Zur Kenntniss vom feineren Baue der Grosshirnrinde, Wien. Sitzungsb., III Abth., lxxxiii (1881). Ferrier, The Functions of the Brain, 2nd ed. (London, 1886). E. Flatau, Atlas of the Human Brain and Description of the Course of the Nerve Fibres, trans. by Nathan and Carslaw (Glasgow, 1894). P. Flechsig, Die Leitungsbahnen im Gehirne und Rückenmarke des Menschen (Leipzig, 1876); Gehirn und Seele: Rectoratsrede (Leipzig, 1894). M. Foster, A Textbook of Physiol., 7th ed. (London and New York, 1891). Ganser, Gehirn des Maulwurfs, Morphol. Jahrb., vii (1882). A. v. Gehuchten, Anatomie du système nerveux de l'homme, 2nd ed. (Louvain, 1897). C. GOLGI, Untersuchungen über den feineren Bau des centralen und peripherischen Nervensystems, trans. from the Italian (Jena, 1894). B. v. GUDDEN, Gesammelte und hinterlassene Abhandlungen (Wiesbaden, 1889). D. J. HAMILTON, On the Corpus Callosum in the Adult Human Brain, J. of Anat. and Physiol., xix (1885); On the Corpus Callosum in the Embryo, Brain, viii (1885). H. HELD, Die centrale Gehörleitung, Arch. f. Anat. u. Physiol.—Anat. Abth. (1893); other papers on the medulla and the quadrigemina, same periodical (1891–3), in Neurol. Centralbl. (1890), and in Abhandl. d. kgl. sächs. Gesell. d. Wiss. (1892). J. HENLE, Handbuch der Nervenlehre des Menschen, 2nd ed. (Braunschweig, 1879). HERMANN, Handb. d. Physiol. (1879). C. L. HERRICK, Illustrations of the Architectonic of the Cerebellum, J. of Compar. Neurol., i (1891), and The Histogenesis of the Cerebellum, ibid., v (1895); numerous other papers in the same journal (1891–9). HERVÉ, La circonvolution de Broca, Thèse (Paris, 1888). A. HILL, The Plan of the Central Nervous System (Cambridge, 1885). W. HIS, Zur allgemeinen Morphologie des Gehirns, Arch. f. Anat. u. Physiol.—Anat. Abth. (1892). S. HONEGGER, Vergleichend-anatomische Untersuchungen über den Fornix (Zürich, 1891). T. H. HUXLEY, On the Brain of Ateles paniscus, Proc. Zool. Soc. (1861). A. v. KÖLLIKER, Handb. d. Gewebelehre des Menschen, ii (Leipzig, 1896). W. KRAUSE, Über Gehirngewichte, Allg. Wien. med. Zeit. (1888); and Int. Monatssch. f. Anat. u. Physiol., v (1888). LANGLEY AND GRÜNBAUM, On the Degenerations resulting from Removal of the Cerebral Cortex and Corpora Striata in the Dog, J. of Physiol., xi (1890). LUYS, Nouvelles recherches sur la structure du cerveau et l'agencement des fibres blanches cérébrales: L'Encéphale (1884). J. MARSHALL, Relations between the Weight of the Brain and its Parts and the Stature and Mass of the Body in Man, J. of Anat. and Physiol., xxvi (1892); The Brain of the late George Grote, with Comments and Observations on the Human Brain and its Parts generally, J. of Anat. and Physiol., xxvii (1892). TH. MEYNERT, Psychiatry, trans. by Sachs (1885); also art. Brain, in Stricker's Histol. (1872); Das Gesammtgewicht und die Teilgewichte des Gehirnes, &c., Vtljsch. f. Psychol. (1867). G. MINGAZZINI, Il Cervello in relazione con i Fenomeni psichici; Studio sulla Morfologia degli Emisferi cerebrali dell' Uomo (Turin, 1895). MONAKOW, several works bearing especially on the optic connections in Arch. f. Psychol. (1889, 1892, 1895). H. MUNK, Über den Hund ohne Grosshirn, Arch. f. Anat. u. Physiol.—Physiol. Abth. (1894). H. OBERSTEINER, Anleitung beim Studium des Baues der nervösen Centralorgane im gesunden und kranken Zustande, 3rd ed. (Leipzig, 1896), Eng. trans. of earlier ed., Philadelphia (1890); Die neueren Forschungen auf dem Gebiet des Centralnervensystems, kritisch beleuchtet, Wien. med. Wochen., xlv (1895). H. F. OSBORN, The Origin of the Corpus Callosum; a Contribution upon the Cerebral Commissures of the Vertebrata, Morphol. Jahrb., xii (1887). E. PUSATERI, Sulla fine Anatomia del Ponte di Varolio nell' Uomo, nota prelim., Riv. di Patol. Nerv. e Ment., i (1896). A. RAUBER, Lehrb. d. Anat. des Menschen, 4th ed., ii. Abth. II (Leipzig, 1894). Reference Hand-Book of the Medical Sciences, Wm. Wood & Co., articles by Browning, Wilder, Spitzka, Baker, Herrick, and others. G. RETZIUS, Biol. Untersuch. (Stockholm, 1875–95); Atlas of the

Brain. J. V. ROHON, Zur Anatomie der Hirnwindungen bei den Primaten (München, 1884). H. SACHS, Vorträge über den Bau und die Thätigkeit des Grosshirns (1894). E. A. SCHAEFER, Spinal Cord and Brain, iii, Part I of Quain's Anatomy, 10th ed. (London and New York, 1893). SCHIFF, Lehrb. d. Physiol. G. SCHWALBE, Lehrb. d. Neurol. (Erlangen, 1881). SHERRINGTON, Nerve Tracts degenerating secondarily to Lesions of the Cortex Cerebri, J. of Physiol., xi (1890); Further Note on Degenerations following Lesions of the Cerebral Cortex, J. of Physiol., xi (1890). O. SNELL, Die Abhängigkeit des Hirngewichtes von dem Körpergewicht und den geistigen Fähigkeiten, Arch. f. Psychiat., xxiii (1891); Das Gewicht des Gehirnes, Münch. med. Wochensch. (1892). E. C. SPITZKA, Architecture and Mechanism of the Brain, J. of Nerv. and Ment. Dis. (1878 f.). TOPINARD, Le Poids de l'Encéphale, Mém. Soc. de l'Anthropol., iii (1888). W. TURNER, The Convolutions of the Human Cerebrum (Edinburgh, 1866); The Convolutions of the Brain, Verh. d. int. Congresses (Berlin, 1890), ii, and J. of Anat. and Physiol., xxv (1890). VULPIAN, Leçons sur la physiologie du système nerveux (Paris, 1866). W. WALDEYER, Die Hirnwindungen des Menschen, Verh. d. int. Congresses (Berlin, 1890); Das Gibbon-Hirn, Virchow-Festschrift, iii (1891). MAX WEBER, Vorstudien über das Hirngewicht der Säugethiere, Festschrift f. Gegenbaur, iii (Leipzig, 1896). CARL WEIGERT, Beiträge zur Kenntniss der normalen menschlichen Neuroglia, Abh. d. Senckenberg'schen Naturf.-Ges. in Frankfurt a. M., xix. 1 (1895). C. WERNICKE, Lehrb. d. Gehirnkrankheiten, i (1881); Grundriss der Psychiatrie in klinischen Vorlesungen, Theil I, Psycho-physiologische Einleitung (Leipzig, 1894). B. G. WILDER, The Outer Cerebral Fissures of Mammalia, especially of the Carnivora, and the Limits of their Homologies, Proc. Amer. Assoc., xxii (1873); On the Removal and Preservation of the Human Brain, Trans. Amer. Neurol. Assoc. (1883); J. of Nerv. and Ment. Dis., N.S., viii (1883); Methods of Studying the Brain, The 'Cartwright Lectures' for 1884, N. Y. Med. J., xxxix–xl (1884); The Cerebral Fissures of Two Philosophers, Chauncey Wright and James Edward Oliver, J. of Compar. Neurol., v (1895), and J. of Nerv. and Ment. Dis., N.S., xx. (1895). W. WUNDT, Gehirn und Seele, in 'Essays' (Leipzig, 1885); Grundzüge d. physiol. Psychol. (4th ed.), Erster Bd., Erster Abs. (Leipzig, 1893).

GLOSSARY OF BRAIN ANATOMY.

[The cross-references in SMALL CAPITALS refer to other topics in the Dictionary, those in Roman type to other terms in this glossary.]

Afterbrain. The medulla oblongata.

Ala Cinerea. The thin dorsal wall of the metacoele where it joins the velum caudale.

Alar Plate. One of the regions of the medullary tube. The longitudinal zone on either side near the base from which arise the sensory nerve roots.

Alveus. The fibrous layer of the ventricular surface of the gyrus hippocampus.

Ammonshorn: see Hippocampus.

Ansa Lentiformis. Fibres from the putamen of the nucleus lentiformis which, instead of passing through the internal capsule, pass near the brain base on their way to the thalamus.

Ansa Peduncularis. Fibres forming an arch

superficially to the cerebral peduncles and ventrad of the nucleus lentiformis; the 'substantia innominata.'

Aquaeductus Sylvii : see Iter.

Arachnoidea. The middle one of the three membranes investing the brain. See BRAIN (Meninges).

Arbor Vitae. The peculiar ramose appearance presented by a section of the cerebellum, which is due to the distribution of the white and grey matter.

Area Olfactoria. The region on the ventral aspect of the hemispheres through which the olfactory radiations pass on their way to the hippocampus.

Area Parolfactoria. The median aspect of the hemispheres cephalad of the lamina terminalis and ventrad of the free cortex [Edinger].

Area Post-perforata : see Perforata.

Area Preperforata : see Perforata.

Aula. The remnant of the first embryonic vesicle which connects the third ventricle by way of the portae with the lateral ventricles.

Axial Lobes. The solid masses of grey matter forming the massive part of the hemispheres in some low vertebrates. They contain the homologues of the striata and some additional undifferentiated structures.

Axis, Cerebro-spinal : see Neuraxis.

Basal Ganglia. The masses of grey matter below the cortex forming the terminal stations of the lower projection systems. The corpora striata [Edinger], or these bodies together with the nuclei of the thalamus [many authors].

Basal Plate. One of the regions of the medullary tube. The longitudinal zone forming the median ventral portion (primarily membranous).

Brachium Coniunctivum Cerebelli. The prepeduncle. See Pedunculi Cerebelli.

Brachium Inferius Cerebelli. The postpeduncle. See Pedunculi Cerebelli.

Brachium Opticum. The central prolongation of the optic tracts, together with fibres from the cortex.

Brachium Pontis. The medi-peduncle. See Pedunculi Cerebelli.

Brachium Quadrigeminum : see Brachium Opticum.

Brachium Superius Cerebelli. The prepeduncle. See Pedunculi Cerebelli.

Broca's Region. The cortical region near the Sylvian fissure associated with the function of speech.

Bulb. The medulla oblongata, especially in compounds, as bulbar paralysis; a term the use of which is not to be commended.

Bulbus Olfactorius. The protuberance from the hemisphere which receives the olfactory 'nerve' (more properly radix: see Radix Olfactorius). It consists of an external part, or pero, and an axial portion, the pes.

Burdach's Column. The more lateral of the two dorsal fibre columns of the cord. In the medulla it becomes the funiculus cuneatus.

Calamus Scriptorius. The most caudal tip of the fourth ventricle.

Calcar [Avis]. A protuberance into the caudal cornu of the lateral ventricle due to the invagination of the cortex in the region of the fissura calcarina; the hippocampus minor.

Canalis Centralis. The remnant of the cavity of the medullary tube of the embryo and the continuation within the spinal cord of the ventricles, or coelia, of the brain.

Capsules. The internal and external capsules are white bands between the nuclei lentiformis and caudatus (capsula interna) and ectally of the latter (capsula externa). The motor fibres from the parietal regions of the cortex are more or less segregated within the internal capsule in accordance with their distribution in the cortex. See Corpus Striatum.

Cauda Equina. The brush-like divergent cluster of fibres springing from near the caudal extremity of the spinal cord.

Caudate Nucleus : see Corpus Striatum.

Central Grey. Relatively undifferentiated grey matter which retains its primitive position near the ventricular surface.

Centrum Semiovale. The oval mass of white matter in the dorsal region of the hemisphere dorsad of the insula.

Cerebellum. The massive organ developed in the roof of the medulla by the concrescence of lateral masses. In man it is corrugated, lobed, and plicated in such a way as to increase enormously its cortical layers. It is intimately connected with equilibration, in which function it is associated with the labyrinthine nerve from the internal ear.

Cerebrum. The paired body developed from the thickened parietes of the embryonic fore-brain, consisting of two hemispheres connected by commissural fibres. The organ *par excellence* of intelligence, volition, and consciousness.

Chiasma [Opticum]. The crossing (partial decussation) of the optic nerves ventrally of the brain. See NERVOUS SYSTEM (Cranial Nerves).

Cingulum. A band of fibres in the gyrus fornicatus connecting the latter with the olfactory lobes.

Circle of Willis. The polygonally arranged trunk of blood-vessels near the base of the brain (and within it), from which arise the more important arteries of the brain. See BRAIN (Circulation).

Choroid Plexus. An invagination into the brain ventricles of the pia, together with ependymal lining. Cf. Tela : see PLEXUS.

Clark's Column. A cellular column in the dorso-lateral region of the spinal cord connected by fibres with the cerebellum (= columna vesicularis).

Claustrum. A small layer of nerve cells embedded in the external capsule entally of the insula.

Clava. A protuberance in the higher part of the funiculus gracilis containing the nucleus of the funiculus gracilis.

Coelia. Cavities formed by the dilation of the original cavity of the medullary tube; the brain ventricles. See VENTRICLE.

Colliculi. A pair of protuberances into the mesocoele in some lower animals.

Columnae Fornicis. The two columnar masses of fibres from the corpus fornicis, leading thence to the thalamus and corpora mammillaria via tractus cortico-mammillaris.

Columns : see special article on this topic.

Commissure : see special article on this topic.

Conarium : see Epiphysis.

Conus Terminalis. The conical caudal portion of the spinal cord, extending into the filum terminale.

Convolution : see Gyrus.

Corona Radiata. The sum of the fibres connecting the cortex with lower centres and passing through the capsules of the corpus striatum. The name refers to the appearance presented by the fibres as they radiate from the striatum.

Cornu Ammonis : see Hippocampus.

Cornu Ventriculare. One of the horn-like projections from the lateral ventricles. These are distinguished as the cephalic (or anterior), caudal (or posterior), and ventral (or median or descending) cornua.

[Corpora] Quadrigemina. The four paired

eminences upon the roof of the mammalian mesencephalon. The cephalic pair (pregeminum) are in the position of the tectum opticum of lower vertebrates.

[Corpus] Callosum. The dorsal band of commissural fibres connecting the cortex of the two hemispheres, especially (it is claimed) the regions supplying the corona radiata.

[Corpus] Candicans: see Corpus Mammillare.

[Corpus] Dentatum: see Nucleus Dentatus.

Corpus or Nucleus Ectomammillaris. That part of the mammillary lying laterad of the central cell cluster.

Corpus Fornicis. The median (azygos) body formed by the fusion of the crura fornicis. It gives rise to the columnae fornicis ventrally.

[Corpus] Geniculatum. A cell cluster on the lateral aspect of the thalamus connected with the optic fibre system. Two parts (laterale and mediale) are recognized.

Corpus or 'Ganglion' or Nucleus Habenulae. A paired mass of cells in the dorsal part of the thalamus (epithalamus) near the insertion of the epiphysis.

Corpus or Nucleus Interpeduncularis. A cell cluster on the median ventral aspect of the brain base cephalad of the pons within the trigonum interpedunculare; the terminus of Meynert's bundle.

Corpus or Nucleus Mammillaris. A cluster of cells caudad of the infundibulum and within the tuber cinereum. The inferior terminus of the columnae fornicis.

[Corpus] Pineale: see Epiphysis.

[Corpus] Restiforme. One of the caudal peduncles (post-pedunculi) of the cerebellum, forming a protuberance on the dorso-lateral aspect of the medulla.

[Corpus] Striatum. The principal cell aggregate in the base of the hemisphere (see Basal Ganglia). The striata are composed of the caudate and lentiform nuclei, which are separated by the internal capsule (q. v.). The striata are represented in the axial lobes of lower animals.

Corpus Subthalamicum or Corpus Luysi: see Nucleus Subthalamicus.

[Corpus] Trapezoideum. Transverse decussating fibres of the ventral part of the medulla connecting the auditory nuclei of the one side with the lemniscus tract of the other.

Cortex Cerebelli. The superficial layers of grey matter of the cerebellum.

Cortex Cerebri. The external layer of the mantle part of the hemisphere, composed chiefly of cells and their processes, and containing the centres for the voluntary motions and sensations. The organ of consciousness.

Crura Cerebri: see Pedunculi Cerebri.

Crura Fornicis. The fibres of the fornix which connect the hippocampal region with the median corpus fornicis.

Crusta: see Pes Pedunculi.

Culmen. One of the lobules of the vermis cerebelli on the dorsal aspect.

Cuneus. A triangular lobe of the mesal cortex bounded by the fissura parieto-occipitalis and the fissura calcarina.

Decussatio Cerebelli Ventralis. Fibres which cross in the middle line near the ventral aspect of the cerebellum. The exact components of this decussation remain to be made out.

Decussation. The number of decussations is very great. See special article on this topic.

Deiter's Cells. The constituent elements of the neuroglia.

Deiter's Nucleus. A cell cluster dorsally of the acustic nucleus in the lateral part of the medulla.

Diacoele. The third VENTRICLE (q.v.).

Diencephalon. The thalamus.

Dorsal Plate. One of the regions of the medullary tube. That longitudinal zone forming the dorsal region, usually membranous and in some segments plexiform.

Dorsal Sac: see Paraphysis.

Dorso-median Fasciculus: see Fasciculus Longitudinalis Dorsalis.

Dura [Mater]. The outer membrane of the brain. See BRAIN (Meninges).

Embolus. A mass of grey matter in the cerebellum mesally of the nucleus dentatus.

Encephalon. The brain.

Endyma: see Ependyma.

Epencephalon. The cerebellum.

Ependyma. The (originally ciliated) lining membrane of the coelia.

Epiphysis. The median projection from the dorsal wall of the epithalamus caudad of the supra-commissure. Cf. PARIETAL ORGAN.

Epistriatum. One of the parts of the axial lobe of some low vertebrates.

Epithalamus. The dorsal part of the thalamus containing the nucleus habenulae and other cell groups.

Falx [Cerebri]. A vertical projection of the dura occupying the longitudinal fissure between the cerebral hemispheres.

Fascia Dentata. The gyrus dentatus.

Fasciculus Communis. A longitudinal fibre system of the medulla of the lower vertebrates, contributing one of the sensory components to the cranial nerves. Probably represented by the fasc. solitarius of the mammals. See NERVOUS SYSTEM (Cranial Nerves).

Fasciculus Longitudinalis Dorsalis. A tract of longitudinal fibres collected ventrally of the ventricle, appearing near the region of the nuclei of the third and fourth nerves and extending through the medulla into the spinal cord.

Fasciculus Retroflexus: see Tractus Habenulo-interpeduncularis = Meynert's bundle.

Fasciculus Solitarius: see Tractus Solitarius.

Fibrae Arcuatae. Transverse fibres in the medulla. Two portions are recognized—the externae, lying ectally of the trapezoideum near the ventral surface, and the internae, more deeply situated than the trapezoideum.

Fillet: see Lemniscus.

Filum Olfactorium. One of the fibre bundles of the radix olfactorius (q. v.).

Filum Terminale. The slender caudal prolongation of the spinal cord.

Fimbria. The fibrous zone at the ventral edge of the hippocampus.

Fissura. A furrow of the cortex. Frequently used interchangeably with sulcus. The German Nomenclature Commission propose to limit the term fissure to the more deeply incised sulci of the cerebrum or cerebellum. This distinction is inconstant and leads to confusion. A more satisfactory distinction would be to restrict the term fissure to the cerebrum, and sulcus to the cerebellum, thus embodying in the name a locative index. For the terminology of the fissures see the figures.

Flechsig's Tract. The direct cerebellar tract, or dorso-lateral tract of the cord; an ascending tract lying dorsally of Gower's Tract (q. v.).

Flocculus. One of the lateral projections of the cerebellum. A subordinate portion forms the paraflocculus.

Fluid, Cerebro-spinal. A clear fluid, somewhat resembling lymph, filling the brain ventricles and the subarachnoid space.

Folium Vermis. One of the lobuli of the median lobe of the cerebellum, lying on its dorsal surface. A modern usage applies the term folium generically for gyri of the cerebellum, limiting the application of gyrus to the cerebrum.

Foramen of Magendi. An opening through the dorsal roof of the medulla communicating with the subarachnoid space.

Foramen of Monro: see Portae.

Forceps. That portion of the callosal fibres clothing the caudal cornu of the lateral ventricles.

Fore-brain: see Prosencephalon.

Fornix. A complicated fibre system connecting the hippocampus with other parts of the brain. See Columnae, Corpus and Crura Fornicis, and Fimbria.

Fossa Sylvii. The depression in the lateral aspect of the cortex cerebri in which the insula is situated.

Fovea Limbica. A depressed line separating the olfactory region of the ventral aspect of the hemisphere from the pallium proper.

Fundamental Plate. One of the regions of the medullary tube. A longitudinal zone on either side of the basal plate containing the origins of the motor nerves.

Funiculus Cuneatus. The medullary continuation of the column of Burdach of the spinal cord.

Funiculus Gracilis. The medullary continuation of the column of Goll of the spinal cord. A terete fibre bundle immediately adjacent to the dorso-median line of the medulla.

Ganglion: see special article on this topic. For many current descriptive terms beginning with ganglion see Nucleus.

Gasser's Ganglion. The ganglion on the root of the fifth cranial nerve.

Genu. A purely descriptive term indicating the abrupt flexure of an organ or tract, as the genu of the root fibres of the seventh nerve, or the genu corporis callosi.

Glomerulus Olfactorius. One of the aggregates of fibres formed by the intermingling of the terminal arborizations of the olfactory radices ('nerves') with the dendrites of the mitral cells of the olfactory bulb (pero). See Radix Olfactorius.

Goll's Column. The median dorsal bundle of the cord which is continued into the medulla as the funiculus gracilis.

Gower's Tract. A tract from the spinal cord to the cerebellum; the ascending antero-lateral tract of the cord. By some authors regarded as going to the cerebrum as well as to the cerebellum.

Gyrus. One of the folds or convolutions between the fissures of the cerebral cortex. A gyrus of the cerebellum may conveniently be distinguished as a folium. For the terminology of the gyri see the figures.

Habenula or **Habena:** see Nucleus Habenulae.

Hemisphere. One of the lateral halves of the cerebrum. Also applied to the lateral lobes of the cerebellum, except the vermis.

Hind-brain. The cerebellum or the cerebellum and pons; sometimes also applied to the cerebellum and medulla or to the medulla alone.

Hippocampus. The cornu ammonis or caudo-median portion of the cerebral cortex, which is curiously conduplicate and partly rolled by a reverse curve into the ventricle. The osmotic cortical region.

Hippocampus minor: see Calcar.

Horn: see Cornu.

Hypophysis. A composite body formed by the union of an outgrowth of the mucous membrane of the fauces with a process from the infundibulum.

Hypothalamus. The ventral portion of the thalamus, including the infundibulum. Contrasted with the epithalamus.

Infundibulum. The ventral projection of the hypothalamus with the corresponding portion of the diacoele. The hypophysis comes into relation with the brain at this point.

Insula [Reili]. A submerged gyrus lying in the Sylvian fossa, and protected (in man) by the opercula.

Isthmus. The constricted part of the brain immediately cephalad of the cerebellum.

Iter. The tube-like remnant of the second embryonic vesicle; the cavity of the mesencephalon, or mesocoele; the aquaeductus Sylvii.

Lamina Terminalis. That part of the median wall of the fore-brain which extends from the preoptic recess to the paraphysis. It is supposed to contain the morphological front, or cephalic extremity, of the nerve tube. See Neuropore.

Laqueus: see Lemniscus.

Lemniscus. The fillet; a bundle of sensory fibres extending from the lateral aspects of the medulla to the mesencephalon. It contains ascending tracts from the several sensory nuclei of the medulla and spinal cord.

Limbic Lobe. The mesal part of the pallium and the ventral structures of the hemispheres, including the hippocampus, septum, gyrus fornicatus, parolfactory region, &c. All of these, except possibly the gyrus fornicatus, seem to be associated with the olfactory function.

Lingula. One of the lobes of the vermis cerebelli.

Lobus. A term applied to poorly defined areas of the cerebrum; a more extensive term than gyrus, as frontal, temporal, occipital lobes.

Lobus Olfactorius. The protuberance of the cerebrum, from which arises the pes olfactorius.

Luys' Body: see Nucleus Subthalamicus.

Lyra [Davidis]. A triangular median area between the callosum and the corpus fornicis.

Mantle: see Pallium.

Mauthner's Fibres. Large fibres in the spinal cord arising in cells connected with the roots of the eighth nerve. They are found in tailed amphibia and fishes, and are probably associated with the power of equilibrium in a fluid medium.

Medulla Oblongata. The prolongation of the spinal cord cephalad which surrounds the metacoele, or chamber formed from the third embryonic vesicle, with the exception of the cerebellum. The pons is sometimes excluded. The medulla and cerebellum together constitute the rhombencephalon. The medulla is primarily the seat of the nerve centres connected with the vital somatic processes.

Medullary tube. The embryonic nervous system at a very early period of its development, immediately after its invagination from the ectoderm, and while still preserving its primitive character of an undifferentiated epithelial tube.

Meninges: see BRAIN.

Mesencephalon. The mid-brain, comprising the corpora quadrigemina tegmentum and pes pedunculi.

Mesocoele: see Iter.

Mesostriatum. One of the parts into which the axial lobe of some vertebrates has been divided.

Metacoele. The fourth VENTRICLE (q. v.)

Metathalamus. That part of the diencephalon forming the transition into the mesencephalon.

Metencephalon. The cerebellum and pons; sometimes also applied to the medulla or to both the cerebellum and the medulla.

Meynert's Bundle: see Tractus Habenulo-interpeduncularis.

Mid-brain. The mesencephalon.

Myelencephalon: see Neuraxis; also applied to the medulla oblongata alone.

Neuraxis. The brain and spinal cord, or cerebrospinal axis.

Neuroblast. An immature nerve cell. Cf. Neurocyte.

Neurocyte. The mature nerve cell. See special article on this topic.

Neuroglia. The supporting tissue of the neuraxis. See special article on this topic.

Neuron: see Neurocyte.

Neuropore. The point where the medullary tube communicates with the outer body surface at the cephalic extremity. A point in the lamina terminalis, supposed to indicate the position of the neuropore, is termed the recessus neuroporicus (= lobus olfactorius impar, Kupffer).

Nidulus: see NUCLEUS.

Nidus [Avis]. A depression on the ventral surface of the cerebellum. Nidus is also used as a synonym for NUCLEUS (q. v.).

Nodulus. One of the ventro-mesal projections of the cerebellum.

Nucleus: see special article on this topic.

Nucleus Ambiguus. The ventral motor nucleus of the vagus nerve.

Nucleus Amygdalae. A mass of cells at the union of the parietal lobe of the hemisphere with the thalamus; probably associated with the olfactory apparatus.

Nucleus Arcuatus. A cell cluster associated with the fibrae arcuatae of the medulla.

Nucleus Caudatus: see Corpus Striatum.

Nucleus Dentatus. A cluster of nerve cells in the ventro-lateral parts of the vermis cerebelli.

Nucleus Funiculi Cuneati. The terminal nucleus of the column of Burdach.

Nucleus Funiculi Gracilis. The terminal nucleus of the column of Goll.

Nucleus Globosus. A mass of nerve cells in the ventral part of the cerebellum mesally of the embolus.

Nucleus Habenulae. A cell cluster near the roof of the diacoele (third ventricle) near the origin of the epiphysis.

Nucleus Lentiformis or **Nucleus Lenticularis:** see Corpus Striatum.

Nucleus Niger. A cellular stratum of the mesencephalon between the pes pedunculi and the tegmentum; the substantia nigra Sömmeringi.

Nucleus Pontis. A cell cluster in the pons dorsally of the pyramids and serving as a switch-station between the latter and the cerebellum.

Nucleus Ruber. An important cell cluster in the cephalic part of the tegmentum (mesencephalon).

Nucleus Subthalamicus or **Corpus Luysi.** A mass of nerve cells in the caudal part of the thalamus near the nucleus ruber and closely associated with the nucleus niger, which replaces it in the pes region.

Nucleus Tegmenti. A cell cluster in the mesoventral part of the cerebellum.

Nucleus Trapezoideus. Cells in the corpus trapezoideum.

Oblongata: see Medulla.

Olfactory Lobe: see Lobus Olfactorius; sometimes also applied to the olfactory bulb.

Olives. A series of corrugated layers of gray matter in the ventral part of the medulla connected with the fillet and cerebellum. They are derived from evaginations of the walls of the primitive medullary tube.

Opercula. Lip-like folds of cortex walling in the Sylvian fossa and covering the insula.

Optic Lobes. The homologues of the cephalic pair of corpora quadrigemina as seen in various lower vertebrates.

Pallium. The brain mantle, or roof of the prosencephalon; it contains the cortex in higher brains, but is membranous in some fishes.

Paracoele. The lateral VENTRICLE (q.v.).

Paraphysis. An evagination of the membranous roof of the fore-brain cephalad of the velum transversum. Some recent writers denominate this the 'preparaphysis' to distinguish it from a similar evagination of the tela between the velum transversum and the supra-commissure, the 'post-paraphysis.' The latter is more properly termed 'dorsal sac'; it is the Zirbelpolster of the Germans. The morphological significance of these structures is intimately bound up with that of the epiphysis and PARIETAL ORGAN (q.v.).

Pedunculi Cerebelli. Three pairs of fibre bundles connecting the cerebellum with the other parts of the brain. The cephalic pair (prepeduncles, or brachia conjunctiva cerebelli anterior) can be followed cephalad to the tegmentum; the medi-pedunculi (brachia pontis, or processi cerebelli ad pontem) decussate ventrally, forming the pons; while the post-pedunculi (brachia conjunctiva cerebelli posterior) form the corpora restiformia.

Pedunculi Cerebri. The compact fibre bundles connecting the hemispheres with the lower centres and appearing as convergent prominences on the ventral surfaces of the mesencephalon. See Pes Pedunculi.

Perforata or **Perforated Space.** An area in which numerous blood-vessels enter the brain. The two most important are the preperforata in the area olfactoria and the post-perforata in the trigonum interpedunculare.

Pero Olfactorius. The ectal portion of the olfactory bulb, including the glomerules and mitral cell zone; the formatio bulbaris of some authors.

Pes Olfactorius. The ental part of the olfactory bulb.

Pes Pedunculi. The pedunculi cerebri in their course through the mesencephalon where they appear on the ventral aspect leaving between them the trigonum interpedunculi.

Pia [Mater]. The inner membrane of the brain. See BRAIN (Meninges).

Pillars of the Fornix: see Columnae Fornicis.

Pineal: see Epiphysis.

Pituitary: see Hypophysis.

Plexus. An anastomosis of nerves outside the brain. See special article on this topic.

Plexus Choroideus: see Choroid Plexus.

Pons [Varolii]. The bundle of transverse fibres crossing the ventral aspect of the medulla near its cephalic end and composed largely of the middle peduncle fibres of the cerebellum.

Portae. The two openings from the aula into the lateral ventricles.

Post-geminum. The caudal pair of corpora quadrigemina.

Pregeminum. The cephalic pair of corpora quadrigemina.

Prosencephalon. The secondary fore-brain, including the striata.

Psalterium. The commissura hippocampi.

Pseudocoele. A remnant of the original cleft separating the two cerebral hemispheres included between the two laminae of the septum, the fifth ventricle.

Pulvinar. A tuberosity of the dorso-lateral aspect of the thalamus belonging to the optic system and associated with the geniculatum.

Purkinje's Cells. Large, globose cells characteristic of the cerebellar cortex.

Putamen. A distinct part of the nucleus lentiformis.

Pyramids : see Tractus Cortico-spinalis.

Radiatio Strio-thalamica. Fibres connecting the striatum (caudate nucleus) and the thalamic and mesencephalic nuclei.

Radiatio Thalamo-occipitalis (= **Optic Radiation** or **Gratiolet's Bundle**). A tract from the primary optic centres (geniculata, &c.) to the cortex about the cuneus.

Radix : see special article on this topic.

Radix Olfactorius. The so-called olfactory nerve, which is now supposed by some to consist of the root portion only, the ganglion being scattered in the mucous membrane of the nose ; formerly, however, often applied to the tractus olfactorius.

Raphe. A continuous decussation in the median plane of the medulla.

Recessus Infundibularis. The cavity of the infundibulum ; a part of the diacoele.

Recessus Mammillaris. The projection of the diacoele into the mammillary region of the thalamus.

Recessi Post- and Pre-optici. The projections of the diacoele caudad and cephalad of the chiasm.

Rhinencephalon. The olfactory bulb and tractus ; sometimes also extended to include the lobus olfactorius.

Rhombencephalon. The medulla, pons, and cerebellum.

Saccus Vasculosus. A vascular plexiform protrusion of the ventro-mesal wall of the thalamus, in some animals caudad of the hypophysis and between that body and the mammillaria.

Septum [**Pellucidum**]. The thin median partition separating the hemispheres cephalad of the aula. It contains the pseudocoele.

Spongioblast. One of the epithelium cells which constitute the embryonic nerve tube and give rise to the ependyma and neuroglia of the adult.

Stem. All of the brain except the pallium and the cerebellum.

Stratum Lucidum. The middle zone of the gyrus hippocampi.

Stratum Zonale [**Thalami**]. The superficial fibre layer on the dorsal aspect of the thalamus.

Striae Acusticae. Transverse fibres connecting the accessory acustic nucleus of one side with the lemniscus of the other.

Striae Lancisii. Fibres which connect the hippocampus with the lobus olfactorius by way of the dorsal surface of the callosum.

Striae Medullares : see Striae Acusticae.

Subarachnoid Space. The space between the arachnoid and the pia and in communication with the brain ventricles through the foramen of Magendi.

Substantia Gelatinosa [**Rolandi**]. An area of the spinal cord near the apex of the dorsal cornu and in the path of the root fibres.

Substantia Nigra [**Sömmeringi**]: see Nucleus Niger.

Substantia Perforata : see Perforata.

Substantia Recticularis. The region beginning in the tegmentum at the level of the nucleus ruber and extending caudad into the medulla ventrally of the ventricle.

Sulcus : see Fissura.

Sylvian Fossa : see Fossa Sylvii.

Taenia Thalami. A slender band of fibres connecting the hippocampus with the habenulae.

Tapetum. Fibres clothing the caudal and ventral cornua of the lateral ventricles.

Tectum Opticum. The roof of the mesencephalic ventricle in lower vertebrates. Its place is largely occupied by the cephalic pair of the corpora quadrigemina in mammals.

Tegmentum. The infra-ventricular region of the mesencephalon dorsad of the pes pedunculi.

Tela [**Choroidea**]. A membranous part of the roof of the brain, especially the roof of the thalamus and parts adjacent, from which the choroid plexus is developed. See PLEXUS.

Telencephalon : see Prosencephalon.

Tentorium [**Cerebelli**]. A transverse projection of the dura lying between the cerebrum and the cerebellum.

Terma : see Lamina Terminalis.

Thalamus. The walls of the diencephalon. Divided into hypo-, meta-, and epi-thalamus. The thalamus contains many important primary sensory centres.

Tonsilla. Lobes on the ventral aspect of the cerebellum laterally of the uvula.

Torus Longitudinalis. A paired ridge on either side of the medial line of the tectum, projecting into the mesencephalic ventricle, in fishes.

Torus Semicircularis. Lateral projections from the walls of the mesencephalic ventricle in fishes.

Tracts. Bundles of fibres with a common origin and destination. The list below is incomplete, and where the name contains the termini no description is added.

Tractus Acustico-spinalis. Mauthner's fibres.

Tractus Acustico-tectalis. Part of lemniscus.

Tractus Bulbo-corticalis. Olfactory radiation.

Tractus Bulbo-epistriaticus. Olfactory radiation.

Tractus Cerebello-olivaris.

Tractus Cerebello-spinalis. Flechsig's tract.

Tractus Cerebello-tegmentalis.

Tractus Cortico-epistriaticus.

Tractus Cortico-habenularis. Taenia thalami in part.

Tractus Cortico-habenulo-peduncularis.

Tractus Cortico-mammillaris : see Columnae Fornicis.

Tractus Cortico-spinalis. The great motor paths from the cerebrum to the spinal cord and appearing as pyramidal elevations on the ventral surface of the medulla ; the pyramids.

Tractus Cortico-tegmentalis.

Tractus Cortico-thalamicus.

Tractus Habenulo-interpeduncularis. Meynert's bundle.

Tractus Intermedio-lateralis. The lateral cornu of the cord.

Tractus Mammillo-peduncularis.

Tractus Nucleo-cerebellaris.

Tractus Occipito-mesencephalicus. Optic radiations.

Tractus Olfacto-habenularis. Taenia thalami in part.

Tractus Olfactorius.

Tractus Olfactorius Lateralis.

Tractus Olfactorius Septi.

Tractus Opticus. The fibres of the optic nerve as they spread out over the lateral aspect of the thalamus.

Tractus Peduncularis Transversus.

Tractus Septo-mesencephalicus.

Tractus Solitarius. The common descending root of the vagus and glossopharyngeal nerves. Cf. Fasciculus Communis.

Tractus Strio-lobaris.

Tractus Tecto-bulbaris.

Tractus Tecto- et Thalamo-spinalis. Part of lemniscus.

Tractus Tecto-nuclearis.

Tractus Tecto-spinalis. Part of lemniscus.

Tractus Tecto-thalamicus.

Tractus Tegmento-cerebellaris.

Tractus Thalamo-bulbaris et -spinalis. Part of lemniscus.

Tractus Thalamo-mammillaris. Vicq d'Azyr's bundle.

Tractus Vago-cerebellaris. Secondary vagus bundle.

Trigonum Interpedunculare. The triangular space between the pes pedunculi.

Tuber Cinereum. An excrescence on the ventral aspect of the thalamus caudad of the infundibulum.

Tuber Olfactorium : see Bulbus Olfactorius.

Uncus. A protuberant part of the hippocampus ; the gyrus uncinatus.

Uvula. One of the lobules on the ventral aspect of the median lobe of the cerebellum.

Valvula. A valve-like projection from the cephalic edge of the cerebellum at its union with the velum medullare cephale.

Velum. A thin membranous state of the dorsal part of the walls of the medullary tube : cf. Tela. Especially Velum Medullare Cephale, the thin roof of the metacoele cephalad of the cerebellum ; Velum Medullare Caudale, the thin roof of the metacoele caudad of the cerebellum ; and Velum Transversum, a transverse fold of the tela extending into the diacoele. The latter is commonly assumed as the arbitrary boundary between the prosencephalon and the diencephalon.

Ventricles : see special article on this topic.

Ventriculus Septi [Pellucidi] : see Pseudocoele.

Vermis Cerebelli. The large median lobe of the cerebellum.

Vicq d'Azyr's Bundle : see Tractus Thalamo-mammillaria.

Volvula. A massive projection of the cerebellum thrust within the mesencephalic ventricle of fishes. (Also called Valvula.)

Worm : see Vermis.

Zona Granulosa [Cort. Cerebelli]. The deeper layer of the cerebellum below the cells of Purkinje.

Zona Molecularis [Cort. Cerebelli]. The peripheral layer of the cortex of the cerebellum in which the dendrites of the cells of Purkinje ramify.

Zona Spongiosa. That part of the dorsal cornu of the cord between the zona terminalis and the substantia gelatinosa.

Zona Terminalis. That region of the dorsal cornua of the spinal cord where the sensory nerve fibres enter. (H.H.)

Bramantip : see MOOD (in logic).

Brandis, Christian August. (1790–1867.) German philosophical historian and author. The son of a celebrated physician of the same name, he was born in Hanover, and died at Bonn ; co-operated with Emmanuel Bekker in editing a critical edition of Aristotle's works ; was secretary to King Otho in Greece. He was made professor of philosophy in Bonn University. His chief contributions to philosophy were historical works on Greek and Roman philosophy.

Bravery : see COURAGE.

Breathing [ME. *brethen*, to blow] : see RESPIRATION.

Bridgewater Treatises. A series of eight monographs in Natural Theology, published between 1833 and 1840.

Francis Henry, eighth earl of Bridgewater, who died in 1829, bequeathed £8,000 to the President of the Royal Society of London, which was to be paid to authors, selected by him, who should produce treatises on the Power, Wisdom, and Goodness of God as manifested in creation. The works appended, though now of comparatively slight value, are of great interest as revealing the scope of Natural Theology before the enunciation of the doctrine of Evolution.

The treatises are : Thomas Chalmers, *The Adaptation of External Nature to the Moral and Intellectual Condition of Man* ; John Kidd, *The Adaptation of External Nature to the Physical Condition of Man* ; William Whewell, *Astronomy and General Physics considered with reference to Natural Theology* ; Charles Bell, *The Hand, its Mechanism and Vital Endowments as evincing Design* ; P. M. Roget, *Animal and Vegetable Physiology considered with reference to Natural Theology* ; William Buckland, *Geology and Mineralogy considered with reference to Natural Theology* ; William Kirby, *The Habits and Instincts of Animals with reference to Natural Theology* ; William Prout, *Chemistry, Meteorology, and the Function of Digestion considered with reference to Natural Theology* ; Babbage's so-called *Ninth Bridgewater Treatise* is associated with these. (R.M.W.)

Bridgman, Laura, and **Keller, Helen.** Two blind deaf-mutes born and educated in the United States.

A psychological study of the blind deaf-mute may contribute largely to an understanding of the relations of the senses to one another, and of the relation of sense endowment to intellectual achievement and general mental development. For all such development language is of fundamental importance, serving as it does as the most effective channel of communication, and as an aid to and medium of rational operations and of human sympathy. For the blind the oral forms of communication and the direct appreciation of sounds, supplemented by the significant experiences of touch and movement, furnish the materials for the elaboration of a psychic life differentiated from that of the seeing only by limitations of experience, the effects of which are not easy to describe or detect. For the deaf, even if dumb, the same service is as successfully, though very differently, performed by the world of letters and of art and by the visual interpretation of expression and conduct. In both, imitation, though restricted, is still a potent and comprehensive instructor. When both defects concur in the same individual the psychological status is decidedly altered. Such persons are dependent for all possibilities of communication and education upon the tactual-motor group of sensibilities and modes of expression; for it is legitimate in this connection to ignore, not wholly, but nearly so, the sense avenues of taste and smell. That the tactual-motor senses may successfully and adequately serve as avenues of approach to a rich intellectual life is proven by what has been accomplished in the instruction of blind deaf-mutes. Of such Laura Bridgman and Helen Keller form the most notable instances.

The significant facts regarding Laura Bridgman are as follows. She was born in possession of the full quota of senses on December 21, 1829, into a farmer's family at Hanover, New Hampshire. She is described as a precocious child who had acquired a considerable stock of words, when just after her second birthday she was stricken by a serious attack of scarlet fever. She remained for two years in a feeble condition; her hearing was totally gone, and though slight traces of vision remained for a time, these had disappeared when her education was begun by S. G. Howe in 1837. Taste and smell were also markedly blunted. During the years preceding her education she had used a very limited number of rudimentary natural signs to indicate her most pressing wants, and had been taught to knit and to sew, and to perform simple household duties. Howe began her instruction by pasting raised letters upon simple objects, such as a key, a spoon, a fork, a mug, and establishing by repeated feeling of the letters and the objects an associa-

tion between them; from the word symbol he passed to letter symbols, using the raised letters on a movable board. Words could thus be formed, e.g. p-i-n for pin, and p-e-n for pen, and the objects corresponding to the name be produced and felt, the shapes and uses of the object being already familiar. It was only after weeks of persistent practice at this puzzle or game-like performance that his pupil grasped the idea that the letters could be used as the names or symbols to stand for and in place of the objects. Then followed more easily, but still slowly, the signs of the manual alphabet (the signs being made in the child's palm, and followed and repeated by her fingers), then writing, and reading raised print and ordinary writing; and the path of education thus opened, though necessarily a slow one, was limited only by the general mental endowment and persistency of the pupil. At first nouns, then simple verbs and adjectives, were acquired, until a considerable vocabulary had been formed; each addition at first requiring to be illustrated or interpreted directly or indirectly into tactual-motor terms. 'Door open' and 'door shut,' 'light' and 'heavy,' 'large' and 'small,' 'rough' and 'smooth,' 'cold' and 'warm,' 'stand' and 'sit,' 'walk' and 'run,' 'in' and 'out,' 'above' and 'below,' and so on, were taught by associating the action or position or contrast of sensible qualities in the objects with the words as formed by the shapes of the component letters. When once reading was begun, the possibilities of information were extensively widened, and her mental processes participated more largely in the steps of normal acquisition.

Miss Bridgman lived to be sixty years old, passing her days uneventfully, but in the enjoyment of a moderately full intellectual, emotional, and moral life. Her tastes were simple and domestic, and needlework occupation filled much of her time. Quite naturally, for one largely dependent upon literature for language forms, her language, both spoken and written, reflected its book origin, and was rarely of a conversational type; her early stages of language acquisition were particularly significant as illustrations of thought processes in blind deaf-mutes and of their development. Neither brilliant nor markedly original, she acquired a fair acquaintance with literature, and aspired to some attempts at authorship; these are dominated in the main by a conventional religious sentiment. She conducted an extensive correspondence, and prepared autobiographical accounts of her experiences before instruction, and an interesting diary. She was never taught to speak, although she constantly made noises and attempted to develop her power of utterance. Her brain was made the subject of a detailed examination, (see the paper by Donaldson, as cited below).

Helen Keller was born June 27, 1880, at Tuscumbia, Alabama. Her ancestry on both sides is not without distinction; her father, Major A. H. Keller, held responsible political offices. Born with all her senses intact, she was deprived of sight and hearing, and totally so, by a serious illness which befell her at the age of eighteen months. Her other senses remained unimpaired. She has the enjoyment and advantage of a keen sense of taste and smell, and her physical health has always been excellent. Her education was begun in February, 1887; during her first seven years she had acquired a considerable knowledge of objects and their uses, but the only means of influencing her or interpreting her wants was by a limited group of natural signs and gestures. The precocity, persistency, and general mental alertness which she has continued to exhibit to a remarkable degree were probably influential throughout her early childhood. The first steps in language taken by her able teacher, Miss Sullivan, were similar to those used with Laura Bridgman, but the alacrity of her pupil, the readiness with which she grasped the notion that all things had names, and that these names could be indicated by movements of the fingers, rendered unnecessary many intermediate stages. Progress which in the case of Laura Bridgman was measured by days and weeks, was made by Helen Keller after hours, or at most within a few days. Thus she had soon acquired a considerable vocabulary, and was able to form simple sentences and to receive and transmit communications. In 1890, in response to her repeated requests, she was taught to speak orally, the method consisting in allowing her to feel the lips and throat of the speaker, and in directing her to place her own organs in the same position and to utter the sounds. By the guidance of this muscular sense she has acquired a facility and clearness of utterance that compares favourably with that of the seeing deaf. Within three weeks after her first lesson in oral speech (March 26, 1890), she gave clearly, in an audible voice, an account of her visit to the poet Holmes. Since then she has evidenced an unusual linguistic and literary ability; she reads raised print fluently, writes and reads the Braille point for the blind; has a creditable knowledge of French and German, as well as of Latin and Greek. Besides writing in ordinary script, she uses a typewriter skilfully, and even one fitted with Greek characters. Her knowledge of literature is extensive, and her memory for what she has read unusually retentive. She is quick in apprehending, most tenacious in remembering, and assimilates with ease and insight; her imagination is active, and expresses itself with aptness and originality. An acquaintance with her extensive correspondence, with the accounts of her doings and studies, and her original stories is necessary to appreciate the significance of these characterizations. Her studies at the present time include the full curriculum required for entrance to Radcliffe College (Cambridge, Mass.); and in a portion of these studies (elementary and advanced German, elementary French, Latin, Ancient History, English) she passed the examinations in 1897, and took honours in English and German. While her talents are largely in the direction of language and literature, and while she confesses to a considerable difficulty with mathematics, her ability estimated without regard to the inherent difficulties of her acquisition is more than creditable to her years, and gives promise of an unusual intellectual career.

It would be premature to attempt any general or final deductions from the facts thus outlined; but it may be of value to illustrate the nature of the psychological principles which they suggest. The most comprehensive principle is that the mental training and culture resulting from the assimilation and elaboration of ideas is measurably independent of the sensory means by which the materials for these are furnished: the edifice does not reveal the nature of the scaffolding. The processes of gaining information may be slow, circuitous, and awkward, but the acquisition once formed is normally complete and correct. And yet this is but moderately true; our senses are more than a scaffolding to knowledge, and the edifice manifests all the characteristics of a continuous organic growth. The mental canvas, though conveying a similar impression, is not suffused with the glow of vivid life-likeness, with the warm and rich reality of experience. The normality of the intellectual life of a gifted blind-deaf person is largely the resultant of the community of expression with that of the seeing and hearing. The same language is used, but the richness of the verbal associations, their colour and flavour, must inevitably be paler and more meagre, and in certain directions defective or false. The community of language conceals the differences of psychological processes, for which, however, we have no other adequate expression. This 'literary' tone of thought and memory, of imagination and application, is unmistakably reflected in the writings and conversation of Helen Keller.

One great advantage of sight in intellectual acquisitions is the relatively large horizon which it encompasses. Quite a numerous group of impressions are grasped at a glance, and in so far as necessary may be focussed for a longer period, and may be reseen and reread *ad libitum*. Appeals to the ear are momentary, and their renewal, though easy, requires a repetition of the entire process. This disadvantage is very much more emphasized for the tactual-motor senses. If one considers the difficulties of studying geometrical problems when the outlines of the figures can only be felt point by point, or of solving algebraic problems without constant recourse to the portion of the problem already worked, the significance of this distinction will be sufficiently manifest. For those with a full quota of senses the scope of 'mental arithmetic' is ordinarily ludicrously small as compared with their powers to manipulate with written symbols. The 'mental' nature of the processes in Helen Keller may in part account for the remarkable retentiveness and scope of her memory. In these and many other respects the study of the blind deaf contains possible contributions to our understanding of psychological processes both in the normal and in the defective.

Literature, on Laura Bridgman: LAMSON, Life and Educ. of Laura Bridgman (1881); S. G. HOWE, in the successive Reports of the Perkins Institute, Boston; Laura Bridgman (Boston, 1890); HALL, in Mind (1879), also in Aspects of German Culture (1881), 237–77; SANFORD, Writings of Laura Bridgman, Overland Mo. (1887); DONALDSON, Amer. J. of Psychol., iv; JERUSALEM, Laura Bridgman, Eine psychol. Stud. (1891). On Helen Keller: Helen Keller, a Souvenir, published by the Volta Bureau, Washington, 1892; second Souvenir, 1900; ANAGNOS, in Reports of the Perkins Institute, Boston, 1888, 78–107; 1889, 67–138; 1892, 52, 302; ANAGNOS, Helen Keller (Boston, 1889); GLENA,

Helen Keller (Genève, 1894). Among the large number of brief accounts the most noteworthy are: McFARLAND, Helen Keller, a Psychological Study, in Proc. of the Amer. Assoc. to Promote the Teaching of Speech to the Deaf (1894); SULLIVAN, The Instruction of Helen Keller, ibid. (1894); JASTROW, Psychological Notes on Helen Keller, Psychol. Rev. (1894), 356; CHAMBERLAIN, Helen Keller as she really is, Ladies' Home J. (1899), also in Ann. of the Deaf; FULLER, How Helen Keller learned to speak, Amer. Ann. of the Deaf (January, 1892); DANGER, Dreisinnige, in Die Kinderfehler (1899). (J.J.)

Brightness: Ger. (1) *Helligkeit Intensität der Lichtempfindung*; Fr. (1) *intensité d'éclairage* (or *lumineuse*); Ital. (1) *chiarezza, intensità luminosa*. (1) The intensity of any visual impression, whether of brightness in the sense below, or of colour, or of the two together. This is the common meaning. Cf SATURATION.

(2) The quality or component of visual sensation correlated, on the physical side, with light mixed in the proportion in which it comes to us from the sun, or with mixtures of homogeneous lights that are psychologically equivalent to this; the quality of black, grey, or white; the colourless quality. (E.B.T.–C.L.F.)

By a slight extension of the meaning of grey (so as to take in, in accordance with custom in the exact sciences, the end-members of the series, black and white) this quality may be called greyness, and thus confusion with the usual meaning of brightness may be avoided. (C.L.F., J.M.B.)

For 'brightness' in the qualitative sense the word 'light' is sometimes used. But light is the physical correlate of all visual sensations that are normally aroused; and, as the term 'intensity' is current in psychophysics, it is possible to employ 'brightness' for the black-white qualitative series (Ger. (2) *Helligkeit* and *Helligkeitsunterschiede, Schwarz-weiss-Reihe, neutrale Farbe*; Fr. (2) *sensation de la lumière*, or *sensation lumineuse* (*incolorée* or *achromatique*; opp. to *sensations des couleurs*); Ital. *sensazione di luce* (or *luminosa*) *acromatica*), and 'intensity' for the strength of brightnesses and of colours alike. See Visual Sensation under VISION. (E.B.T.)

Brown, Thomas. (1778–1820.) A Scotch metaphysician and physician. Educated at Edinburgh, he was a pupil of Dugald Stewart, and published a refutation of Erasmus Darwin's *Zoönomia* before receiving the degree of M.D. He practised medicine seven years. In 1810 he was made professor of moral philosophy in Edinburgh University.

Browne, Peter. Died 1735. Provost of Trinity College, and afterwards bishop of Cork. He made a reputation as an orthodox theologian by a treatise against Toland. Later he opposed Locke in two anonymous works.

Bruno, Giordano. (cir. 1548-1600). An Italian philosopher. He was born at Nola, in Naples, educated for the Church, and taken into the Dominican Order (1563). Of independent and speculative habit of mind, he found himself at variance with the orthodox doctrine. In 1576 he was forced to leave his monastery, and fled first to Geneva, then to Paris, and finally to England. He returned about 1592, to live in Venice. Accused of heresy, he was first imprisoned in Rome for seven years, and then burned as a heretic. In 1889 a monument to him was erected on the spot of his execution. He accepted the Copernican theory of the movements of the heavenly bodies.

Büchner, Friedrich Karl Christian Ludwig. (1824-99.) A German physiologist, physician, and philosopher, born at Darmstadt. He maintained materialistic, atheistic, and 'humanitarian' views. His best known work is entitled *Force and Matter* (*Kraft und Stoff*).

Buckle, Henry Thomas. (1821-62.) An English writer on the philosophy of history. His father, who was a merchant, bequeathed to him an ample fortune, enabling him to gather together a fine private library. He is best known for his *History of Civilization in Europe*, which attempts to establish a new and scientific method of studying history.

Buddeus (or Budde), Johann Franz. (1667-1729.) A Lutheran theologian and philosopher, born at Anclam, Pomerania, and died in Gotha. In 1692 he became professor of the Greek language in Coburg; in 1693, professor of moral philosophy in Halle; and in 1705, professor of theology in Jena.

Buddha: Ger. *Buddha*; Fr. *Bouddha*; Ital. *Budda*. Buddha (the knower, the enlightened one, the awakened) is not a person, as is so often supposed, but a name applied to a person who has achieved a certain spiritual and intellectual state. One who is delivered entirely from desire, who is a Jina, or conqueror of the needs arising in the sense-world, and who has overcome through knowledge of the 'eightfold path,' attains Buddhahood. A Buddha is also marked by his missionary activity in spreading *the* knowledge; this in contradistinction to such as possess the knowledge yet retain it for themselves (Pacceka buddhas).

According to the Buddhist teaching, there were Buddhas in the past and there will be Buddhas in the future; but so far as present knowledge goes, *the* Buddha was Siddhattha, of the family or tribe of the Sakyas (the powerful), who lived in the 6th century B.C. He is known also as Gotama Buddha, Gotama being a Vedic surname of the Sakya family; and as Sakya Muni, or the Sakya sage.

Literature: OLDENBERG, Buddha, s. Leben, s. Lehre, s. Gemeinde (Eng. trans.); SAINT-HILAIRE, Le Bouddha et sa Religion (Eng. trans.); T. W. RHYS DAVIDS, Buddhism (1880), Hibbert Lectures (1881), and Buddhism (American Lectures, 1896). Cf. ORIENTAL PHILOSOPHY (India). (R.M.W.)

Buddhism. See BUDDHA, and ORIENTAL PHILOSOPHY (India).

Buffon, Georges Louis Leclerc. (1707-88.) Philosopher and naturalist; born in Montbard, Burgundy, and liberally educated in France by his father. He travelled in Italy and England in company with Lord Kingston. In 1835 he translated Newton's *Treatise on Fluxions*. In 1839 he became a member of the Academy of Sciences and intendant of the royal garden in Paris. In 1753 he was admitted to the French Academy. In 1776 he received from the king the title Count de Buffon.

Bulb [Lat. *bulbus*, root]: Ger. *Bulbus*; Fr. *bulbe*; Ital. *bulbo*. A synonym for medulla oblongata. See BRAIN. Also used in combination, as bulbar paralysis, &c. (H.H.)

Butler, Joseph. (1692-1752.) An English prelate and philosophical writer. Born at Wantage in Berkshire, he entered the grammar school there, then attended an academy at Gloucestershire, and entered Oriel College, Oxford. He was admitted into holy orders in 1716 or 1717, and became rector of Haughton. In 1725 he obtained the living at Stanhope. In 1733 he became chaplain to Lord Chancellor Talbot, and in 1736, clerk of the closet to the queen. In 1738 he was promoted to the see of Bristol, and two years after was made dean of St. Paul's. In 1750 he was translated to the bishopric of Durham. He died at Bath, and was buried at Bristol. His reputation rests chiefly on his *Analogy of Religion, Natural and Revealed, to the Constitution and Course of Nature*.

Butler, William Archer. (1814-48.) An Irish writer and teacher of philosophy.

Educated at Trinity College, Dublin, he became professor of moral philosophy there in 1837. He was ordained in 1837, and in 1842 became rector of Raymoghy in addition to being professor. He is best known for his *Lectures on the History of Ancient Philosophy.*

Byzantine : Ger. *Byzantin* ; Fr. *Byzantin* ; Ital. *Bizantino.* From Byzantium, the name of the older city on the site of which Constantine founded Constantinople ; the name applied to the Roman Empire of the East (330 or 395–1453 A.D.).

Notable in the early history of Christian doctrine, in connection with the Arian controversy. Thereafter, Julian ‘the Apostate,’ Chrysostom, and Justinian are among its most prominent names in the history of religion and thought. It is also important, as concerns aesthetics, for its influence upon Roman art. Thanks mainly to Gibbon, the Byzantine Empire has long been misprized, but more recent researches have revealed its true importance.

Literature : GIBBON, Decline and Fall of the Roman Empire (in Bury's ed.); G. Finlay, Hist. of Greece (ii and iii); J. B. BURY, Later Roman Empire ; C. W. C. OMAN, Byzantine Empire ; BAYET, L'Art Byzantin. (R.M.W.)

C

Cabala [Heb. *gabbâlâh*, tradition]: Ger. *Kabbala*; Fr. *cabale*; Ital. *cabala*. This word has two distinct meanings. (1) In Hebrew it means originally 'to receive,' hence it came to signify a 'doctrine received by tradition.' In this sense it was applied to Jewish sacred literature, the Pentateuch excepted, and to the oral traditions which came to be collected in the *Mishnah*. (2) The restricted meaning, alone important for philosophy, came into vogue during the middle ages, most probably in the 11th century. In this sense the term is applied to the semi-philosophical, semi-theological, or theosophical system which, although a product of mediaeval Judaism, purports to have been traditionally transmitted from the earliest times—from Adam in Paradise, as the *Sohar* states.

The Cabala is essentially an esoteric system, which claims to render explicit doctrines contained implicitly in the Jewish sacred books. It deals with the original God, who, being boundless and incomprehensible, proceeds to acts of creation in order to reveal himself; with the emanations (*Sephiroth*) from God; with the creation and nature of man and angels; with the constitution of the material universe; with the meaning of revelation, particularly as given in the law.

The sources of the Cabala are two. (1) The *Sepher Yetzira*, or Book of Creation—a short gnomic treatise containing a mystical theory of numbers; it purports to have been written by the Rabbi Akiba, who died in 120 A.D., but is probably referable to the close of the 9th century. (2) Of much greater importance is the *Sepher Hazohar* (usually referred to as the *Sohar* or *Zohar*), or Book of Splendour. This is an esoteric commentary on the Pentateuch, purporting to have been composed by Simon ben Yochi towards the end of the 1st century A.D. Modern investigators now hold that it was composed by Moses de Leon, a Spanish Jew, who died in 1305 A.D. In making the compilation he of course reduced to something like order a mass of floating material, the age of which cannot be determined. Cf. JUDAISM.

Literature: this is summarized in UEBERWEG, Hist. of Philos., i. 419 ff. (Eng. trans.). See also art. Kabbalah, in Encyc. Brit.; A. FRANCK, Syst. de la Kabbale; H. GRÄTZ, Gnosticismus u. Judenthum; GINSBURG, The Kabbalah, its Doctrines, Development, and Literature. (R.M.W.)

Cabanis (or **Kabanis**), **Pierre Jean George**. (1757–1808.) French philosopher and physician. Born at Conac, he studied medicine at Dubreuil and settled at Auteuil in the vicinity of Paris. He became an intimate friend of Diderot, d'Alembert, Condorcet, and Franklin in Paris, and the friend and political supporter of Mirabeau. In 1796 he became a member of the Institute, and in 1797 professor of clinical medicine in Paris.

Cacodemonia or **Cacodemonomania** [Gr. κακός, evil, + δαίμων, demon, + μανία, madness]: Ger. *Kakodämonie*; Fr. *démonomanie*; Ital. *cacodemonia*. A delusional belief on the part of an insane subject that he is possessed by or under the influence of an evil spirit. In opposition to Agathodemonia, the influence of a good spirit. Cf. DEMON POSSESSION. (J.J.)

Cadence [Lat. *cadere*, to fall]: Ger. *Schluss* (*Ganzschluss*, *Halbschluss*, *Plagalschluss*); Fr. *cadence*; Ital. *cadenza*. A musical close in which the dominant passes into the tonic chord is a complete cadence ; that in which the subdominant passes into the tonic is an imperfect or plagal cadence.

Literature: HELMHOLTZ, Sensations of Tone, 293 ; SANFORD, Course in Exper. Psychol., expt. 96 ; PARRY, art. Cadence, in Grove's Dict. of Music and Musicians, i. 290 (1879). (E.B.T.)

Caird, John. (1820–98.) Born at Greenock on the Clyde, he died at Dungourney. Educated in the Greenock schools. At the University of Glasgow, 1840–5 ; he received the M.A. degree in 1845, and was soon after ordained at Newton-on-Ayr. Elected to the Chair of Theology in the University of Glasgow in 1862, he taught with great success, influencing his countrymen in the direction of a more philosophical theology. He was profoundly influenced by the philosophy of Hegel. In 1873 he was appointed Principal of Glasgow University, and continued in that position until his death. Delivered the Gifford Lectures in 1892–3, and again in 1895–6.

Calculus (in mathematics) [Lat. *calculus*, a pebble]: Ger. (*Differential- und Integral-*) *Rechnung* ; Fr. *calcul* (*infinitésimal*) ; Ital. *calcolo* (*infinitesimale*). A distinctive or well-defined system or method of reasoning by the aid of algebraic symbols.

The term is most familiarly applied to the *infinitesimal calculus*, in which the laws of continuously varying quantities are investigated by supposing the variations to be made up of an infinite number of infinitesimal parts, called *differentials*. The aggregate of an infinite number of differentials, making a finite quantity, is called an *integral*. Cf. INFINITE, INFINITESIMAL, and LIMITS. (S.N.)

Callisthenes. A Macedonian historian and philosopher who died about 328 B.C. He was a cousin and pupil of Aristotle, and the companion of Alexander the Great in Asia. Fragments of his writings remain.

Calorie : see UNITS OF MEASUREMENT.

Calvin, John. (1509–64.) An eminent Protestant reformer and philosophical theologian. Born at Noyon, Picardy, in France, and educated at Paris, Bourges, and Orleans. When twelve years of age he was tonsured, but was afterwards won away from the Church by relatives and friends, who showed him contradictions between the Bible and Roman doctrines. He enlisted in the Reformation about his nineteenth year. In 1533 he was forced to leave Paris, and retired to Angoulême. He fled from France to Strassburg in 1534,

to Basel in 1535, to Bern, Zurich, Basel again, and Strassburg again in 1538, and to Geneva in 1541. At Geneva he came to be ruler of the city. There he completed his famous *Institutes*, fought all heretics, was implicated in the burning of Servetus, and died. See CALVINISM.

Calvinism: Ger. *Calvinismus* ; Fr. *Calvinisme* ; Ital. *Calvinismo*. Calvinism is the name of the theological system promulgated by John Calvin, and is summed up chiefly in his *Christianae Religionis Institutio*.

Calvinism had its historical and logical predecessor in AUGUSTINIANISM (q.v.), and, from a philosophical standpoint, possesses similar merits and defects. Calvin treats of predestination, sin, and grace in the spirit of Augustine ; but, owing to the intervention of Reformation principles, diverges on such problems as the Church, faith, and justification.

Although, on the whole, Calvin was a practical rather than a speculative genius, his system, just because it is a system, possesses definite philosophical characteristics. It may be described as an account of human life set in the framework of a divine teleology. As such, it leans upon well-marked premises, and if they be granted, the resultant conclusions follow with great force. These premises may be summarized thus : (1) God, who is a self-conscious Spirit, has created the world, and being all-powerful, is able to interfere supernaturally in his universe. (2) He created the world in order to manifest therein his own 'glorious perfections.' The final cause of creation must therefore agree with this original purpose. (3) As concerns mankind, this final cause implies an ultimate division into the 'elect' and the 'non-elect.' The very idea of election, in other words, implies reprobation also. God foreordained 'whom he would admit to salvation and whom he would condemn to destruction.' (4) The eternal destiny of an individual is predestined by God's original purpose, which is one with final cause.

It is important to observe that, in elaborating the details of this system, Calvin was swayed, unconsciously, by the dead hand of Scholasticism. He was essentially a Realist. Adam, made in God's image, constituted the original human type ; human nature as a whole was contained in him. By his own act he apostatized, thereby falling from fellowship, or 'concurrence,' with God, and coming under condemnation to death and moral corruption. Adam being in this way the archetypal man, all subsequent human nature was involved in his fall, and tainted by his apostasy. Hence men are not condemned for the sin of another, but on account of a taint which is inherent in their very nature, and which renders them hateful to God. Yet God is gracious ; not only just, but benevolent. So, to accomplish the redemption of man, he became incarnate in Jesus Christ, who, by his life, passion, and death, merited for man the free gift of salvation. In order to share in this benefit, men must become one with Christ, must be 'members of his body.' This they accomplish through faith, which in turn produces repentance and justification—justification implying that the righteousness of Christ is imputed to men. But God in his justice has predestined some to reprobation as well as to salvation. Those who refuse to accept the opportunity offered by the plan of salvation will be damned eternally; those who share it with living faith and a godly sorrow for sin will be saved by God's effectual calling, the 'concurrence' of his Spirit preserving them in ever-increasing holiness. The Church and the Sacraments are the supports which God has furnished for aiding the Christian on earth.

It is obvious that, in this scheme, a central position is occupied by the relation of the divine will to man's will. On this subject Calvin himself is not invariably decisive, and it has occasioned much discussion among his followers and opponents. The problem is: 'Whether did God predestinate man to sin, and therefore many to hopeless condemnation; or did man lapse by his own free will, which was in no way affected by God's predestination?' On the whole, so far as Calvin is concerned, the evidence seems to me to be decisive in favour of the former alternative. In other words, the *system* implies that, in order to the realization of the final cause of the universe, the Fall was eternally decreed. No doubt Calvin resiles from this in such a document as the 'Agreement by the Genoese Pastors'; but this is primarily of a mediating nature, and forms no part of the system as a whole. It is to be remembered, however, that as time passed, and scholastic influence weakened, Calvinists commonly adopted the latter or permissive alternative.

Calvinism long exercised profound influence in Great Britain, especially in Scotland, in Holland, in the French Protestant Church, in Switzerland, Hungary, Bohemia, and in the United States, particularly in New England. In some of these, like England and Holland, it has long ceased to possess control; while in others, like Scotland, its influence has been seriously undermined.

Literature: BAUM and REUSS, Calvin. Opera quae supersunt Omnia (Eng. trans.); DE BÈZE, Hist. de la Vie et de la Mort de J.-C.; HENRY, Leben C.s (Eng. trans.); FROTHINGHAM, Studies of Religious Hist. and Crit.; LOBSTEIN, Die Ethik C.s in ihren Grundzügen entworfen; JON. EDWARDS, Works; NEANDER, HARNACK, Hist. of Dogma (Eng. trans.), v, vii; CUNNINGHAM, The Reformers and the Theol. of the Reformation; MOZLEY, Augustinian Doctrine of Predestination; CHANNING, Moral Argument against Calvinism; McCOSH, Method of Divine Government; COPINGER, Treatise on Predestination, Election, and Grace; KUYPER, Calvinism; art. in Herzog's Real-Encyc.; HODGE, System. Theol. (R.M.W.)

Cambridge Platonists. A school of religio-philosophical thinkers who flourished, chiefly at the University of Cambridge, from the third quarter of the 17th century.

The principal exponents of the movement are noted below under *Literature*. The school is in essentials one of the several examples of the reaction of Gnosis against Scholasticism. But peculiar elements belonged to the contemporary English environment, and variously determined the direction of the speculations of members of the group. The majority, being clergymen, were familiar with, and repelled by, the two leading types among their contemporaries—the Obscurantist Sectarians, and the Laudian Sacerdotalists. But antagonism to Hobbes played a potent part. The reconciliation of reason with religion, broad toleration, contemplation of things spiritual, often in a mystical manner, were their chief characteristics. Plato and the Neo-Platonists, especially Proclus and Plotinus, Descartes, Malebranche, and Böhme, were their principal authorities; although Cudworth, Culverwel, More, and Smith possessed a wealth of learning, extending over many other fields. In some respects, their learning proved a snare, for they had little or no conception of accurate investigation, and they did not approach their sources in a trained historical spirit; hence a distinct tendency to run into extravagance. Cudworth's hypothesis of the 'plastic nature,' and his proofs of the being of God; Culverwel's harmony of faith and reason; More's subtle mysticism; Norris' presentation of Malebranche to the English mind; Patrick's 'latitudinarianism'; Smith's interpretation of religion; Glanvill's conception and use of scepticism; and the ultimacy of moral distinction between right and wrong, common to several of the group, are probably the most important contributions of the school. It should be noted that the movement was in the air, and that Glanvill, Hales, and Norris were Oxford men, while others, like Gale and Pordage, were in no sense members of the inner circle, though evincing affinities with some of the salient tendencies. The school has never received the attention which it deserves, as the most concerted attempt ever made in England to furnish forth a satisfactory philosophy of religion. This is traceable mainly to the tradition that English thought is largely empirical. The Cambridge Platonists really represent a spiritualized Puritanism; an element which, on the whole, has never been absent from English thought, although its most marked influence is to be traced in literature rather than in philosophy.

Literature: TULLOCH, Rational Theol. and Christ. Philos. in England in the 17th century; HUNT, Religious Thought in England; ROBERTSON, Hobbes; HALLAM, Literature of Europe (chapter on the Hist. of Spec. Philosophy from 1650 to 1700); LECKY, Rise and Influence of Rationalism in Europe, i. 110 f.; FISHER, Hist. of Christ. Doctrine, 366 f.; ERDMANN, Gesch. d. Philos. (Eng. trans.), ii. 99 f.; LOWREY, Philos. of Ralph Cudworth; v. STEIN, Sieben Bücher z. Gesch. d. Platonismus; METCALFE, The Natural Truth of Christianity (selections from Smith); POWICKE, John Norris; BROWN and CAIRNS, Culverwel's Light of Nature; arts. Cudworth and Henry More in Encyc. Brit.; COOPER, Annals of Cambridge, iii. (For full literature on separate members of the school see the following articles in the Dictionary of National Biography:—Ralph Cudworth, Nathaniel Culverwel, Richard Cumberland, Edward Fowler, Theophilus Gale, Joseph Glanvill, John Hales, John Howe, Henry More, John Norris, Simon Patrick, John Pordage, George Rust, John Smith, Benjamin Whichcote, John Worthington.) (R.M.W.)

Campanella, Tommaso. (1568–1639.) An Italian monk and philosopher. Born at Stilo, Calabria, he entered the Dominican order. His work, *Philosophy demonstrated by the Senses* (1591), was opposed by the Aristo-

telians. Imprisoned by the Government in 1599, he remained confined for twenty-six years, during which he published his most important philosophical works. Pope Urban VIII released him, and he moved to Rome, 1626. In 1634 he removed to France for greater security, and was befriended by Richelieu and pensioned by the king. He died in Paris. He took his starting-point in philosophy from Telesio, but developed independent views.

Campimeter: see LABORATORY AND APPARATUS, III, B (*a*).

Canon [Gr. κανών, a straight rod, a measure]: Ger. *Kanon*; Fr. *canon*; Ital. *canone*. This word has two meanings: (1) in logic, ethics, aesthetic and historical criticism, &c.: a rule, a fundamental principle, a standard of excellence, a norm. Mill (*Logic*, Bk. VI. chap. iv. § 2, end) speaks of 'the true canons of inductive philosophy.'

In aesthetics the canon is a rule or law which must be observed if certain results are to be achieved; hence a rule for aesthetic CRITICISM (q. v.). Such, e.g., were held to be for the Greek drama the 'three unities' of time, place, and action, which it was attempted at one time to apply to all drama. They were not consistently carried out, however, in the practice of the Greek dramatists, nor did Aristotle fully maintain them. (J.H.T.–H.S.)

In law the canon is generally a rule of usage, not of regulation. Canons of interpretation: the recognized rules for construing documents. Canons of descent: the recognized rules of inheritance. Canons of the Church: the rules of Canon Law. (S.E.B.)

(2) In theology: a collection of books which are fundamental and authoritative. The latter is the important signification for philosophy of religion, as it applies specially to the 'scriptures' of the Old and New Testaments. The second meaning is derived metaphorically from (1), probably through the custom of calling the Greek classical writers κανόνες.

Scholars trace the O. T. canon through several stages, which may be summarized as (1) Ezra (see 2 Esdras xiv. 44); (2) Nehemiah; (3) Prologue to the Wisdom of Sirach; (4) the Synod of Jamnia (90 A. D.). The history of the formation after Nehemiah is very complex. The O. T. canon really consists of three 'canons':—(1) The Pentateuch; (2) the Prophetic Books, and the semi-prophetic, semi-historical writings like Judges and Joshua; (3) the HAGIOGRAPHA (q. v.).

Notwithstanding the wide use made of the N. T. books before that time, no formal canon of the N. T. antedates the organization of the Latin Church, and the occasion for according higher authority to some writings proceeded from the disturbance caused by the Gnostic and other 'heresies.' By the end of the 2nd century, the N. T., as we know it, was finally endorsed, but as some books still remained in dispute no canon, in the strict sense, can be said to have existed. Indeed, the first formal use of the term is by Athanasius (d. 373). Before his time there was merely a consensus of opinion as to 'the Gospel' and 'the Apostle.' The Council of Laodicea (363) forbade the reading of 'non-canonical' books, but the list of canonical writings purporting to proceed from it is unhistorical. The Council or Synod of Hippo Regius (393) gave a list of the canonical books of the N. T. which is identical with that now recognized. There are also canons of the Abyssinian, the Armenian, and the Greek Churches.

Literature: see also BIBLICAL CRITICISM; arts. in Herzog's Real-Encyc. and Encyc. Brit.; also for Scripture usage Hastings' Dict. of the Bible; BLEEK, Introd. to O. T.; DIESTEL, Gesch. d. A. T. in d. christl. Kirche; HOLTZMANN, Kanon u. Tradition; S. DAVIDSON, Canon of the Bible. (R.M.W.)

Canon Law [Lat. *ius canonicum*]: Ger. *kanonisches Recht*; Fr. *droit canon*; Ital. *diritto canonico*. The rules of faith and order prescribed for any body of churches and their members by the competent ecclesiastical authority; most often used for those of the Church of Rome.

The regulations constituting the Canon Law of the Latin Church, which governed its corporate administration, and ruled its relations to the civil authority, consisted in (1) the 'canons' of the Councils of the Church, which are distinguished from 'dogmas' and from civil 'laws'; (2) the judgments of the Fathers; (3) the Decretals of the Popes. The whole subject is of the utmost importance in relation to the organization of religion in early and mediaeval Europe.

At the beginning of the English Reformation, Parliament provided for a national version of the Canon Law, and in the *interim* kept in force all decrees of English national or provincial synods, not repugnant to the general law of the land. No such version has ever been made, but a body of canons for the regulation of the clergy was compiled in 1604.

Literature: RICHTER, Corpus Iuris Canonici; HAASSEN, Gesch. d. Quellen u. d. Lit. canonischen Rechts; PHILLIMORE, Eccles. Law of the Church of England; MAITLAND, Canon Law in the Church of England. For full literature, see arts. in Herzog's Real-Encyc. and the Encyc. Brit. (S.E.B.—R.M.W.)

Canonization [Mod. Lat. *canonizare* (Gr. κανών), to put into catalogue]: Ger. *Kanonisation, Heiligsprechung*; Fr. *canonisation*; Ital. *canonizzazione*. The ceremony by which, in the Roman Catholic Church, eminent deceased believers are raised to the rank of saints.

The custom of canonization had its origin in the commemoration of martyrs, but when it took its present formal shape we do not know. The first express use of the term occurs as late as the 12th century. The person canonized is 'honoured by the Church with public worship'; and the decree of canonization is viewed as an 'exercise of the infallible authority of the Church.' The judicial process of investigating claims is held to prove that miracles continue to be of common occurrence in the Church. No one can be canonized till a century after death.

Literature: POPE BENEDICT XIV, De Canonizatione; Decrees of POPE URBAN VIII; FABER, Essay on Beatification. Cf. HAGIOLOGY. (R.M.W.)

Canthus [Gr. κανθός, the corner of the eye]: Ger. *Augenwinkel*; Fr. *coin* (or *angle*) *de l'œil, grand canthus, petit canthus*; Ital. *angolo dell' occhio*. Point of union of the upper and lower eyelids at the temporal (canthus minor) and nasal (canthus major) angles of the eye. (C.F.H.)

Capacity [Lat. *capax*, able to contain]: Ger. *Kapazität, Fähigkeit*; Fr. *capacité*; Ital. *capacità*. (1) The power of receiving impressions or ideas, or of acting upon them; frequently in reference to passive receptivity only. (2) Physical power of any sort.

The term is used, particularly in anthropometrical studies, in reference to the amount of innate or acquired endowment in a given direction; e. g. the capacity of the muscles to endure strain, the visual capacity of the eyes as tested by the greatest distance at which an object can be seen, or in general the extent or comprehensiveness of the mind, mental capacity. The spacial capacity of the skull is termed the Cranial Capacity (see the next topic). (J.J.)

Capacity (cranial): Ger. *Schädelkapazität*; Fr. *capacité cranienne*; Ital. *capacità cubica* *del cranio*. This is measured by determining how much shot, sand, peas, millet, or mustard seed, &c., the skull will hold; different skulls (of men and women, highly developed races, and poorly developed ones) vary in moderate cases from about 1,200 to 1,600, in extreme cases from 1,000 to 1,800 cubic centimetres in capacity; with an average in all races of 1,400 cubic centimetres (85 cubic inches).

Skulls whose capacity is 1,350 to 1,450 cubic centimetres are termed mesocephalic, those smaller than 1,350 cubic centimetres microcephalic, and those larger than 1,450 cubic centimetres megacephalic. Cranial capacity in cubic centimetres when multiplied by a fraction differing (according to size) a little from ·9 gives the approximate brain weight in grammes. The volume of the skull naturally exceeds the skull capacity, and is measured by the amount of water displaced by the skull when immersed, or better, when held inverted and partly immersed to a definite point, the rest being calculated by empirically determined formulae. Cf. CRANIOMETRY, and the literature there given.   (J.J.)

Capacity (in physics). Capacity for heat, or thermal capacity, is the amount of heat required to raise the temperature of unit mass of a substance 1° centigrade. Capacity for electricity of a conductor is the quantity of electricity required to produce unit of potential. Cf. UNITS OF MEASUREMENT.   (S.N.)

Capital [Lat. *caput*, head]: Ger. *Kapital*; Fr. *capital*; Ital. *capitale*. A stock of goods or rights which may be used to produce income.

No word in the whole range of economic terminology has given rise to more controversies and misunderstandings. There are two main questions whose settlement gives trouble: (1) Shall we regard capital from the social standpoint, as consisting of useful things, or from the individual standpoint, as consisting of property rights? (2) Shall we regard it as a mode of measurement of wealth, and contrast it with income, or shall we regard it as a mode of use of wealth, and contrast it with goods for consumption? According to the answers given to these questions, we have four sets of definitions.

(1) From the individual's standpoint, wealth measured as capital means 'his possessions at any given point of time' (Cannan).

(2) From the individual's standpoint, wealth used as capital means 'that part of a man's stock which he expects to afford him revenue' (Smith).

(3) From the social standpoint, wealth measured as capital 'is to be regarded as a stock of goods left over from the satisfaction of present wants' (Kneis).

(4) From the social standpoint, wealth used as capital is 'that part of the wealth of a country which is employed in production' (Ricardo).

The fourth of these meanings is used by the great majority of economists; but it is one to which it is very difficult to give precision. How shall we determine what is capital and what is not, when in fact so many goods are employed partly to assist production, and partly at the same time to give enjoyment as articles of direct consumption? For instance, is the clothing woven by a loom capital or not, in this sense? Many answers have been given. Kleinwaechter says, 'The conception of capital should be limited to tools of production.' Jevons takes the other alternative, calls it 'the aggregate of those commodities which are employed for sustaining labourers.' Ricardo and Senior regarded it as wealth which is employed productively. MacCulloch extended it to include all wealth which may be thus employed—a much broader conception. Walras and Pareto count as capital all goods which 'serve more than one use'; a definition more curious than practical. Taussig, carrying out the same idea in better shape, considers capital as 'inchoate goods'— goods which are not ready for the final consumer. But this comes very near the third definition instead of the fourth; for until the very act of final consumption we cannot tell whether goods have reached their last use or not. As long as they exist at all, they are in a sense inchoate. Boehm-Bawerk's definition of capital as 'a group of intermediate products' is practically equivalent to Taussig's; only he introduces the idea of individual capital by making acquisition the purpose for which such goods exist. Marx is much more explicit in this direction: 'Means of production and subsistence become capital when they serve as means of exploitation.' Mill, despairing of any objective criterion, simply remits the distinction to the mind of the employer; while Clark goes a step further, and makes complete logical separation between the capital itself, which is an aggregate of value (compare Turgot's conception of *valeurs accumulées*), and the 'capital goods by which it may be at any moment represented.'

This uncertainty as to what should be included under the term capital gives rise to many controversies on the propositions concerning wealth (witness the endless battles over the wage-fund theory), and makes it almost useless for purposes of quantitative analysis. For this reason a small but increasing group of economists is now adopting the third definition in preference to the fourth, and regards stocks of goods as capital, independent of the use to which they are put. The chief difficulty to this use of the term is that it occupies ground covered by the traditional definition of wealth, 'utilities fixed and embodied in material objects.'

Courcelle-Seneuil and Fisher adopt a definition which covers both the first and the third senses : 'La somme des richesses existantes, à un moment donné, dans l'espace qu'on désigne ou dans la possession de la personne dont on parle.' Capital is here regarded as a mode of measuring wealth : a wealth-fund, contrasted with income, which is a wealth-flow : an integral of which income is the differential. It is justified primarily and chiefly because, in the hands of an analyst like Fisher, it solves brilliantly a whole series of quantitative problems with which the older conception was unable to deal.

Literature : FISHER on Capital, Econ. J. (1896-7) ; BOEHM-BAWERK, Kapital und Kapitalzins. (A.T.H.)

Captains of Industry : see EMPLOYER, and ENTREPRENEUR.

Cardinal Point and Value : Ger. *Kardinalpunkt u. -werth* ; Fr. *valeur (et point) cardinale* ; Ital. *valore* (and *punto*) *cardinale*. Introduced by Fechner for the point and the stimulus-value (Reizwert) of the 'relative maximum of sensation' (Fechner, *Elemente d. Psychophysik*, ii. 49). Cardinal value is defined by Külpe (*Outlines of Psychol.*, Eng. trans., 250) as 'the value at which sensation increases in direct proportion to stimulus intensity.' See FECHNER'S LAW, and WEBER'S LAW. (J.M.B.)

Cardinal Virtues : Ger. *Kardinaltugenden* ; Fr. *vertus cardinales* ; Ital. *virtù cardinali*. The principal or leading virtues upon which the other virtues depend or 'hinge.'

The term seems to have been first used by St. Ambrose, who adapted to Christian usage the Platonic classification as he found it in Cicero. The cardinal virtues are there enumerated as prudence, temperance, fortitude, and justice.

Literature : ZIEGLER, Gesch. d. chr. Eth.

(2nd ed.), 234 ff. ; SIDGWICK, Hist. of Eth. (3rd ed.), 44, 133, 143. (W.R.S.)

Cardiograph : see LABORATORY AND APPARATUS, III, B.

Caricature [Ital. *caricare*, to charge, overload] : Ger. *Karikatur* ; Fr. *caricature* ; Ital. *caricatura*. A species of characterization in which there is exaggeration of some feature with a view to producing a ludicrous effect, usually that of ridicule. It is thus related to those aspects of the comic in which there is a feeling of superiority, whereas the grotesque, in which there is often exaggeration, is allied to the humorous. See COMIC, and CHARACTERISTIC. (J.H.T.)

Carmelites : Ger. *Carmeliter* ; Fr. *Carmélites* ; Ital. *Carmelitani*. A monastic order, said to have been founded by one Berthold, on Mount Carmel, towards the close of the 12th century—although much earlier records purport to refer to its existence.

It was recognized formally by the Church in 1224. The Crusades being over, it spread to Europe in the 13th century, and assimilated itself to the mendicant orders. It is chiefly celebrated for its invention of the scapulary, said to have been brought from heaven by the Blessed Virgin Mary. The miraculous qualities of this woollen yoke gave the order great vogue, and it flourished till its fatal dispute with the Jesuits—brought to a close in 1698. Thereafter it tended to break up, there being at least four generals at one time. It is interesting as contributing a chapter to the history of religious emotion and belief in the 13th, 14th, and 15th centuries, and furnishes one of the classical cases of 'Aberglaube.'

Literature : HELYOT, Hist. des Ordres Monastiques ; MANNING, Life of St. Teresa ; ANON., Ordres Monastiques (Berlin, 1751, printed in Paris). (R.M.W.)

Carneades. (cir. 215–cir. 125 B.C.) A Greek sceptical philosopher. He founded the New Academy. Sent as an ambassador from Athens to Rome, his eloquent orations were greatly admired ; but Cato the Censor, to guard the youth from his sophistical teaching, had him dismissed from the city.

Caro, Elme Marie. (1826-87.) A French philosophical writer, born in Poitiers, and educated in Paris. Lecturer of the École Normale, Paris, 1857 ; professor in the Sorbonne, 1867 ; member of the French Academy, 1876. His best known works are devoted to the defence of Christianity and the philosophy of theism.

Carpenter, William Benjamin. (1813–

85.) Eminent English physiologist and pioneer in physiological psychology, born at Exeter, and educated in medicine at Edinburgh. About 1840 he settled in Bristol. He became professor of medical jurisprudence in University College, editor of *The British and Foreign Medico-Chirurgical Review*, Fellow of the Royal Society, and President of the British Association for the Advancement of Science (1872).

Carpocrates, or **Carpocras.** A heresiarch of Alexandria, and Alexandrian Gnostic, who probably lived in the 2nd century A.D. He had numerous followers called Carpocratians, who still existed in the 6th century. He belonged to the Paganizing, rather than the Judaizing, Agnostics.

Cartesianism (from Descartes): see PRE-ESTABLISHED HARMONY, and OCCASIONALISM.

Case (or **Instance**). The result of a single observation or experiment. See ERRORS (of observation). (J.M.B.)

Case (grammatical): see INFLECTION.

Case-law: Ger. *Processrecht*; Fr. *droit des causes*; Ital. *giurisprudenza*. Law stated in judicial decisions, published in the form of reported cases; particular judicial precedents, as distinguished from universal legal principles.

The opinions of courts of last resort, announcing their final determinations and stating their reasons for it, are now generally published by official reporters, as soon as there are enough of them to make up a volume. Similar publications are sometimes made of the opinions delivered in inferior courts, particularly in large cities. From the time of Henry VIII, when the 'Year-books' end, no official reports were published in England until 1865, their place being supplied by unofficial ones. The earlier American reports were also unofficial. Unofficial reports are generally called by the name of the compiler, e.g. Burrow's Reports, Johnson's Reports; official reports by the name of the Government, e.g. United States Reports, Virginia Reports; sometimes by that of the Court, e.g. Law Reports, Queen's Bench Division; Cour dé Cassation (with date). In England and the United States official law reports are an authoritative declaration of the law, as to every point necessarily involved in the determination of the cause. So far as an opinion goes beyond this, it is *obiter dictum*, and not of binding authority. *Obiter dicta* are discouraged in France, and when they amount to laying down rules which it is the appro-

priate province of the legislative power to prescribe, the judge may be prosecuted criminally (*Code Civil*, art. 5; *Code Pénal*, art. 127). Case-law on the continent of Europe is generally not recognized. Judicial decisions are regarded as instructive but not authoritative. 'Non exemplis sed legibus iudicandum sit' (*Code of Just.*, vii. 45, *de Sententiis*, &c., 13). Cf. LAW.

Literature: AUSTIN, Jurisprudence, lect. xxxix; HOLLAND, Jurisprudence, chap. v, iii; MERLIN, Répertoire de Jurisprudence, Arrêt, vii. (S.E.B.)

Caste [Lat. *castus*, pure]: Ger. *Kaste*; Fr. *caste*; Ital. *casta*. A class distinguished originally by marks of race, but later by occupation, or religious faith, or both, and perpetuated by descent and rigid limitation of social intercourse; a name given by the first European (Portuguese) settlers in India to divisions of the social system.

'Caste, at first, means "pure," and signifies that there is a moral barrier between the caste and the outcast. . . . The native word [varna] means "colour," and the first formal distinction was national, (white) Aryan and "black man"' (Washburn Hopkins, *The Religions of India*, 28). 'In societies of an archaic type, a particular craft or kind of knowledge becomes in time an hereditary profession of families, almost as a matter of course' (Maine, *Early Hist. of Institutions*, lect. viii. 245). 'The maintenance of those class-divisions which arise as political organization advances, implies the inheritance of a rank and a place in each class. The like happens with those subdivisions of classes, which in some societies constitute castes, and in other societies are exemplified by incorporated trades' (Spencer, *Princ. of Sociol.*, v. iii. § 444). (F.H.G.)

It commonly originates in usages which have become prescriptive, or have been stereotyped into duties; and where the division is most completely crystallized, religious sanction often plays a great formative part. Although the term is applied pre-eminently to the Brahmanic system of India, caste, or something like it, may be found in many civilizations, and at widely separated periods of time; e.g. in Iran (Persia), in pre-Brahmanic India, in Madagascar, among the North American Indians, in mediaeval Europe, and to-day in countries having nobility. Nevertheless, India remains the classic instance of the institution.

Literature: HAUG, Brahma u. d. Brahmanen; WEBER, Nachträge, 795; Indische Stud., x; LYALL, Asiatic Studies (1st ser.), chap. vii; MUIR, in the J. of the Roy. Asiatic Soc., N.S., ii. 217, and Old Sanskrit Texts, i. 454; SCHOEBEL, Étude sur le Rituel du Respect Social dans l'État Brahman; KERN, Ind. Theorieen over de Standenverdeeling; HOPKINS, Four Castes, and in J. of Amer. Oriental Soc., xiii; SCHLAGINTWEIT, in Zeitsch. d. deutschen Morgenländischen Gesell., xxxiii. 549. (R.M.W.)

Casual [Lat. *casus*, fall]: Ger. *zufällig*; Fr. *accidentel, fortuit*; Ital. *casuale*. Happening fortuitously or accidentally. See ACCIDENT. (J.M.B.)

Casuistry [Lat. *casus*, a case]: Ger. *Kasuistik*; Fr. *casuistique, arguments de casuiste*; Ital. *casistica*. (1) The systematic discussion of the application of moral law to particular cases (called 'cases of conscience') in which such application is not clear and certain.

(2) The over-subtle or verbal discussion of the moral quality of particular acts or sentiments, especially when tending toward greater moral laxity than is permitted by the dominant moral opinion of the time or by the unsophisticated individual conscience.

Ethical reflection begins with the discussion of difficult cases of conduct. Discussion of this kind becomes prominent when new ideas of life enter an established social order, as in the time of the Sophists or in early Christian times. In the New Testament there are many examples of such discussion; and these become more numerous and more systematically worked out in several of the Church Fathers (e. g. Justin, Athanasius, Augustine). But casuistry, as a distinct body of ethical teaching, is the result of additional causes: in particular, the elaboration of church creed and practice, which reached completeness in the great scholastics of the 13th century; the growing externality of moral doctrine, which tended to look on the moral law as an external rule, a mere aggregate of numerous cases of action, and on conduct as separable into distinct processes of motive, intention, and act; the separation of different orders of men, especially clergy and laity, learned and unlearned; and the attempt to assess exactly the merit or demerit of each particular action, and to assign to each sin its appropriate penance—an attempt in which the distinction, enforced by the later Stoics, of the morally indifferent from the obligatory and the forbidden, was further developed, and a classifica-

tion of sins (original and actual, mortal and venial) was carried out. In this way manuals of conduct were prepared chiefly as guides for the confessional (Summa Artesana, 1330; Summa Pisana, 1470; Summa Angelica, 1492; Summa Rosella, 1495; Summa Pacifica, 1574): at first arranged according to subject, afterwards with the cases in alphabetical order. These manuals entered into the minutest details of conduct, and the subtlest refinements of motive and intention.

A famous example of a casuistical discussion is the controversy concerning the murder of tyrants, occasioned by the assassination of the Duke of Orleans in 1407—an act which was defended by Jean Petit, of the University of Paris. The variety of opinions brought out in these discussions, coupled with the absence of a dominating moral principle to guide the discussion, led to many differences of opinion amongst the doctors of casuistry which were fitted to perplex the lay conscience. Hence arose the doctrine of PROBABILISM (q. v.), which was the logical outcome of the casuistical method. Casuistry has appeared in history when external law, as opposed to ethical principle, has been taken as the ultimate guide of conduct. Conspicuous instances are to be found in Judaism, of which the Talmud is the main casuistical authority. Although there were casuists among the Reformers, Ethics has for long shaken itself free from these discussions. (W.R.S.–R.M.W.)

Literature: AQUINAS, Secunda Secundae; RAIMUND DE PENNAFORTI, Summa de Casibus Poenitentialibus (1719); the Angelica (burnt by Luther); BUSENBAUM, Medulla casuum conscientiae; ESCOBAR, Theologia Moralis; PASCAL, Provincial Letters; PERRAULT, La Morale des Jésuites; W. PERKINS, Whole Treatise of Cases of Conscience; SANDERSON, De Obligatione Conscientiae, and Nine Cases of Conscience; ALSTED, Theologia Casuum; BALDWIN, Tractatus de Casibus Conscientiae; SPENER, Pia Desideria; STRAUCH, Theologia Moralis; BUDDEUS, Isagoge Historica; STAUDLIN, Gesch. d. Sittenlehre; H. MERZ, Das System d. christl. Sittenlehre; J. RICKABY, Mor. Philos., 152; MIELZINER, Introd. to the Talmud; STRACK, Einleitung in d. Talmud. JEREMY TAYLOR's Ductor Dubitantium (1660) is the chief manual of casuistry by a Protestant theologian. It is an examination of doubtful 'cases of conscience,' but is without the special characteristics, given above, of mediaeval casuistry. See also GASS, Gesch. d. chr. Eth., §§ 123–8. (R.M.W.–W.R.S.)

Catalepsy [Gr. κατά, down, + λῆψις, from λαμβάνειν, to seize]: Ger. *Katalepsie*; Fr. *catalepsie*; Ital. *catalessi*. A nervous disease characterized by intermittent attacks of powerlessness, and a peculiar form of muscular rigidity which is either absolute, the limbs remaining as if petrified, or of a form termed *flexibilitas cerea*.

In this condition the patient's limbs may be placed by another in any position of flexion or contraction, although the patient is helpless to contract the muscles voluntarily. The state is further characterized by an inability to speak, an almost trance-like unconsciousness, succeeded upon awakening by a total forgetfulness of what ensued during the attack, and frequently by total or partial insensibility. The attack is usually in the nature of a paroxysm of a few hours' (rarely days') duration, with intervals of relief. It may occur at any age, but is most common in early adult life, and soon after puberty. It is distinctly more common in women than in men. In most cases it is associated with HYSTERIA (q. v.), but may occur in the absence of true hysterical symptoms. It is frequently induced by nervous exhaustion, by emotional disturbances, religious excitement, sudden shock, fright, or injury. It occasionally occurs in the course of mental affections, e. g. melancholia and in hebephrenia or puberal insanity, as well as in the various forms of paranoia, acute hallucination, &c.

It is differentiated from ecstasy or trance by the peculiar behaviour of the muscles; by the loss of memory upon the cessation of the attack; by the complete immobility and the suddenness of the loss of sense-functions. The inspired expression of the ecstatic is in marked contrast to the vacant immobility of the cataleptic. Catalepsy is distinguished from tetanus by the suspension of the mental activities and the freedom from pain. The attempts to simulate this condition are usually detected by the failure of protracted and complete rigidity, and by the presence of reflex and other signs of sensibility.

The cause (or causes) of the state is not satisfactorily explained; the possibility of passively moving the limbs which do not respond to powerful electric irritation offers a point of special difficulty. The fact that the attack may be induced by mental excitement suggests a cortical origin, possibly an inhibition of the restraining influence of higher over lower centres. Artificial catalepsy occurs in the state of hypnosis, and is characterized by a similar muscular rigidity and pliability (flexibilitas cerea). Charcot and his followers regard it as a distinct state, the first of the three which they recognize (cf. HYPNOTISM). It is induced by a sudden light, loud sound, or strained fixation; and in addition to the characteristic posture of the limbs, presents superficial anaesthesia, but special sensibility with general suggestibility remain intact; the eyes open with a vacant stare, and reflex irritability is almost completely abolished. The state may also be induced (Charcot) by opening the eyes of a lethargic subject. Those who do not recognize the distinct forms or phases of hypnosis as distinguished by the Paris school, regard artificial catalepsy as a special state of muscular rigidity induced by suggestion through posture, unconscious contagion, or the like; and variable according to the nature of the suggestion.

Catalepsy has figured in mental EPIDEMICS (q. v.) and in religious ecstasy. The term owes its origin to the spiritualistic theory of disease which beheld in the paroxysm the seizure by some foreign agency or spirit. The tendency to use the term as including all forms of trance-like states is not to be approved. Cf. TRANCE. (J.J.)

Literature: CHARCOT, Maladies du système nerveux; A. BINET and CH. FÉRÉ, Animal Magnetism (Eng. trans.); BRIQUET, Traité de l'Hystérie (1889); PITRES, Leçons cliniques sur l'hystérie (1891); GILLES DE LA TOURETTE, Traité clinique et thérapeutique de l'hystérie (1891); P. JANET, L'État mental des Hystériques; RICHER, Études cliniques sur la grande hystérie (1885); LE MAITRE, Contribution à l'Étude des états cataleptiques (1895). (L.M.)

Also MILLS, art. Catalepsy, in Pepper's Med. Cyc.; Tuke's Dict. of Psychol. Med., and Wood's Ref. Handb. Med. Sci. (sub verbo). (E.M.–J.M.B.)

Cataphasia (or **Kata-**) [Gr. κατάφασις, assent]: Ger. *Kataphasie*; Fr. *cataphasie* (*acataphasie*); Ital. *catafasia*. A degeneration of speech, usually connected with serious nervous disease, in which the patient, either spontaneously or in answer to questions, constantly repeats the same word or phrases.

The word is also used (Kussmaul) to describe serious degeneration in the formation of sentences, the patient's language being reduced, like that of a child just beginning to speak, to the skeleton words of a sentence with little grammatical construction (hence also termed agrammatism) and much repetition. See SPEECH AND ITS DEFECTS. (J.J.)

Cataplexy (or **-is**) [Gr. κατά, down, + πλῆξις, from πλήσσειν, to strike]: Ger. *Kataplexie*; Fr. *cataplexie*; Ital. *cataplessia*. A word suggested by Preyer (*Die Kataplexie und der thierische Hypnotismus*, 1878) to describe the immobility and apparent paralysis induced by rigidly restraining the movements of an animal.

The experiment of holding a hen and making it stare at a chalk line and remain immovable was described by Kircher, 1646. Preyer has shown that the restraint is the essential factor, the chalk line or other method of fixing the attention being secondary. Such observations have been repeated upon pigeons and other birds, upon guinea-pigs, rabbits, lizards, crabs, frogs, and other animals. Almost all of these, after proper manipulations for a few seconds or minutes, cease to struggle, and may be made to assume, as if paralyzed, unusual positions, and to maintain them for a considerable period. The explanation of this state has wavered between the view that the cataplectic state is a form of hypnotic sleep (Danilewsky), and that it is a quasi-paralysis due to intensive shock or fright (Preyer). The latter view assimilates it to the natural fascination of animals by beasts of prey and to other forms of fright, and regards the instinct to feign death as a cognate phenomenon.

A more recent view (Verworn) regards the phenomenon as of the nature of a posture reflex (Lagereflex), the animal responding to the tactile stimulus of the manipulation by an attitude in some cases suggestive of the most suitable position for regaining its equilibrium. Although the fact cannot be satisfactorily explained, it is certainly the case that the tendency to assume certain positions is morbidly present in the animals subject to cataplexy. What is peculiar is the retention of the posture for so long a time. This is referred to the release of the inhibitory impulses sent down from the hemispheres to the lower centres; and this in turn is substantiated by the fact that frogs without their hemispheres retain such posture reflexes for a much longer time than the normal frog. Should this type of explanation be regarded as satisfactory, the term cataplexy would no longer be appropriate for the phenomenon in question.

The term is also used with reference to the similar paralyzing effects of shock or fright in men, and the effects of sudden and massive stimuli upon hypnotic subjects. Charcot's method of rendering subjects statuesquely immobile in the accidental position of the moment by the sudden sound of a gong or the flash of a light would be of this type; also the fact that sleep may be induced (in children—Baldwin) by a sudden flash of light in a dark room. Cf. CATALEPSY, and HYPNOTISM.

Literature: PREYER, as cited above (with illustrations); VERWORN, Die sogenannte Hypnose der Thiere (1898); E. GLEY, De quelques conditions favorisant l'hypnose chez les animaux, Année Psychol., ii. (J.J.)

Catechetical Method (in education) [Lat. *catechismus*, instruction by word of mouth]. A form of instruction by means of questions and answers, usually for purposes of examination; when used in inductive teaching, it is equivalent to the Socratic method. See METHOD, and SOCRATIC METHOD. (C.DE G.)

Categorematic (**Words**, &c.) [Gr. κατηγόρημα]: Ger. *kategorematisch*; Fr. *catégorématique*; Ital. *categorematico*. Such words as may by themselves form the expression of one term, subject or predicate, of a proposition. All others, e.g. prepositions, conjunctions, adverbs, are called Syncategorematic.

The term κατηγόρημα appears occasionally in Aristotle as equivalent to predicate. This meaning was definitely assigned to it by the Stoics, who, distinguishing noun and verb as the essential parts of a proposition, gave a foundation for the grammatical distinction of categorematic from syncategorematic. That distinction was taken over from the Latin grammarians (e.g. Priscian), and begins to appear in logic in the tract *de Generibus et Speciebus*, often assigned to Abelard.

Literature: PRANTL, Gesch. d. Logik, ii. 148, 191, 256, 266. (R.A.)

Categorical (**Judgment**, &c.) [Gr. κατηγορικός]: Ger. *kategorisch*; Fr. *catégorique*; Ital. *categorico*. A judgment in which the assertion is made *simpliciter*, as holding good without explicit reference to any condition. Kant connects the categorical judgment with the fundamental thought-relation of substance (thing), of attribute (quality), and so distinguishes it from other forms of assertion.

The term with Aristotle means always 'affirmative.' The current modern sense, in which it is contrasted with hypothetical or conditional, seems to have been directly derived from Boethius, though, as Prantl has shown, the new sense of the term had already appeared among the later Peripatetic commentators on Aristotle and in Galen, and may have been influenced by the Stoic usage.

Literature: PRANTL, Gesch. d. Logik, i. 554, 575, 691; KANT, Logik, § 24, and Krit. d. reinen Vernunft, 86.   (R.A.)

Categorical Imperative: Ger. *kategorischer Imperativ*; Fr. *impératif catégorique*; Ital. *imperativo categorico*. A moral law which admits of no condition or exception. The term is opposed to Hypothetical Imperative, which is a law relative to a further end.

The use of the term is due to Kant (*Grundl. d. Met. d. Sitten*, ii), who reduces the moral law to the single categorical imperative: ' Act only on that maxim whereby thou canst at the same time will that it should become a universal law.' This formula of the imperative gives its bare form or universality. It is followed by a second formula for the same law giving its end, and thus stated: ' So act as to treat humanity, whether in thine own person or in that of any other, in every case as an end withal, and never as means only.' By combining these two formulae, a ' complete characterization ' is reached, which gives the conception of a ' kingdom of ends.' This final formula of the absolutely good will is stated in the words: 'Act on maxims which can at the same time have for their object themselves as universal laws of nature.' These are, however, only different formulae of the same categorical imperative or law, and each of them involves the other two.

Literature: discussions are to be found in historical and systematic works on ethics, and in the textbooks to Kant.   (W.R.S.)

Category [Gr. κατηγορία, an accusation, charge]: Ger. *Kategorie*; Fr. *catégorie*; Ital. *categoria*. (1) One of the ten classes of Beings, or of typical forms of speech used to assert Being, or, finally, of typical judgments regarding Being, as Aristotle distinguished these ten classes in his table of categories. (2) One of the forms or classes of conceivable objects, or one of the forms of judgments about objects, or, finally, one of the fundamental concepts of the understanding, as Kant classified these fundamental forms, classes, or concepts, in his table of categories. (3) Any very extensive or fundamentally important class of objects or of conceptions, especially if this class is distinguished from other classes, either by the general form or character of the assertions that can be made about it, or by the general method of thinking that is applicable to its study. Thus one may say, ' mind and body belong to different categories,' although both of them would actually fall under the same Aristotelian category of substance. (4) Popularly, and sometimes in technical usage, category becomes simply equivalent to the term class or general idea. (5) In post-Kantian technical usage (e. g. Hegel) the categories are any or all of the fundamental philosophical conceptions, whether metaphysical, logical, or ethical.

The original purpose of Aristotle in defining the categories of his well-known table was a complex one, and his motives were not very clearly analysed by himself. In part the categories represent a grammatical classification of forms of speech. In part they stand for very general classes of objects, as these classes get distinguished by ordinary speech. In part they are names for fashions of being, or for various ways in which objects can be regarded as real; and in so far they mark the chief varieties of meaning that can be assigned to the ontological predicate in metaphysical discussion. The latter way of viewing the categories is frequent in the treatise called the *Metaphysics* of Aristotle, and the philosopher here often observes that ' Being is variously asserted according to the categories,' as the characteristic of a substance, a quality, &c.

The full list of the categories of Aristotle is: οὐσία (substance), πόσον (quantity), ποιόν (quality), πρός τι (relations, especially such as double, half, greater than, &c.), ποῦ (place), ποτέ (time), κεῖσθαι (situation or position, such as is expressed by to sit, or to lie), ἔχειν (possession or acquired character, such as dress or ornament), ποιεῖν (activity in the more special sense, such as is expressed by active verbs like to cut or to burn), πάσχειν (passivity or passion, such as is expressed by the passive voice of any active verb). The grammatical relation of these classes to parts of speech as such is obvious, especially in the case of the later categories of the list. The metaphysical contrast between the first category and all the others leads to the frequent reduction by Aristotle of the whole list to the two classes, substance and accident. The more exact classification into the three fundamental categories, substance, quality or character in general (πάθος), and relation, is also known to our philosopher. As to the principles that led to the statement of the list of ten categories, and as to the stress that Aristotle himself laid upon the precise classification in question, opinions differ. Prantl (in his *Gesch. d. Logik*, i) gives a statement of all the various forms which the table of categories takes in Aristotle's writings, and in his lengthy discussion in this volume maintains that Aristotle laid no stress upon the exhaustiveness or finality of the table of ten categories. Zeller regards the full table of ten as representing an essential thesis of Aristotle. But there should be no doubt of the actual union of various motives as determining Aristotle's classification.

The categories were often discussed by the later ancient philosophers, and both the Stoics and Plotinus undertook to give revised lists. Kant's discussion of the categories in the *Krit. d. reinen Vernunft* makes the list depend upon the forms of judgment. Forms of judgment, however, involve fundamental ways of thinking of objects, and Kant's table of categories is therefore explicitly a classification of the possible objects of human thought according to the fundamental ways in which we can think about objects.

The result is the well-known list:

1. Categories of Quantity: Unity (*Einheit*), Plurality (*Vielheit*), Universality (*Allheit*).

2. Categories of Quality: Reality (*Realität*), Negation (*Negation*), Limitation (*Limitation*).

3. Categories of Relation: Substantiality (*Substantialität*), Causality (*Causalität*), Reciprocity (*Wechselwirkung*).

4. Categories of Modality: Possibility (*Möglichkeit*), Actuality (*Wirklichkeit*), Necessity (*Nothwendigkeit*).

The four groups correspond respectively to the classifications of judgment: (1) as singular, particular, and universal; (2) as affirmative, negative, and 'infinite'; (3) as categorical, hypothetical, and disjunctive; (4) as problematic, assertory, and necessary. Kant is himself thoroughly convinced of the exhaustiveness of this list, and of its fundamental systematic value. The categories of relation he generally states in the dual form: *Causalität und Dependenz*, i.e. relation of cause to effect, relation of substance to accident, &c.

The lack of any principle sufficient to secure the exhaustiveness of the Kantian table of categories was, despite his own assertion, a matter of general comment among his critics from the very beginning; and the dissatisfaction with the list of the logical forms of judgment which Kant had used, led to numerous efforts to deduce a list of categories from some single principle constitutive of the thinking process. Fichte, Schelling, and Hegel were all much influenced both in terminology and in doctrine by such efforts.

Inevitably these efforts led to a somewhat more extended technical conception of the categories than Kant had recognized, since Kant's list of fundamental conceptions could not be sundered, in the development of the idealistic systems, from concepts of logical, metaphysical, ethical, and even cosmological character. In consequence, the term category, in post-Kantian philosophy, comes to mean any relatively fundamental philosophical conception.   (J.R.)

Categories are psychologically defined by Stout (*Manual of Psychol.*, Bk. III. Div. ii. chap. i) as 'forms of cognitive consciousness: they are universal principles or relations presupposed either in all cognition or in all cognition of a certain kind.' And he refers to Ferrier (Introduction to *Instit. of Met.*) as showing how categories may be operative when their existence is not consciously recognized.

Literature: Works on metaphysics generally. An important recent work is HARTMANN, Kategorienlehre. See extensive citation in EISLER, Wörterb. d. philos. Begriffe (sub verbo). Psychological treatment is to be found in JAMES, Princ. of Psychol., ii. fin.; SPENCER, Princ. of Psychol., ii; BALDWIN, Ment. Devel. in the Child and the Race, chap. xi, and Selective Thinking, in Psychol. Rev. (Jan., 1898); SIMMEL, Arch. f. syst. Philos., i. 34 ff.   (G.F.S.—J.M.B.)

Catharsis [Gr. κάθαρσις, purgation or purification]: Ger. *Katharsis*; Fr. *catharsis*; Ital. *catarsi*. A term used by Aristotle to express the effect produced by tragedy and certain kinds of music. Tragedy, by means of pity and fear, is said to effect a 'catharsis of such passions.'

The conception of Aristotle, as seems clear from the passage relative to music in the *Politics* (v. 7), is that of exciting by art certain passions already existing in the spectator, viz. pity, fear, enthusiasm, in order that, after this homeopathic treatment, the person may experience relief from them and return to the normal condition. The cure is not wrought by the mere excitement, but by an excitement produced by an artistic agency, which at the same time brings order, harmony, and wholeness to bear. In the case of tragedy there is the additional factor (though not explicitly stated in this connection by him), that the spectator is sympathizing with sufferings and heroism portrayed in their more universal aspects. Hence he is further freed from the morbid and selfish. The metaphor is primarily medical, but may quite possibly have reference also to religious purification, while in the actual psychical process there must be an aesthetic element as stated above.

The numerous interpretations of Aristotle's meaning, of which fifteen were enumerated at the end of the 15th century, may be divided into three groups according as they interpret the term to mean (1) purification in the sense of refining; (2) a religious expiation or lustration; (3) a medical purgation and healing. Lessing, in his *Hamburgische Dramaturgie*, was a typical representative of the first group, making the effect of tragedy to be the reducing of the passions to the mean. The Romanticists emphasized especially the thought that the soul is through art freed from all the contradictions and miseries of actual existence, and raised to the plane of divine IRONY (q. v.). The third and now generally accepted interpretation was suggested by Milton, E. Müller, and Weil, and presented convincingly by Bernays.

Literature: BUTCHER, Aristotle's Theory of Poetry and Fine Art (1895); ZELLER, Aristotle (trans. by Costelloe and Muirhead, 1897); WALTER, Gesch. d. Aesth. im Alterthum (1893); BERNAYS, Zwei Abhai.dl. ü. die Aristotelische Theorie des Dramas (1880); DÖRING, Die Kunstlehre des Aristoteles (1876); BÉNARD, L'Esthétique d'Aristote (1887); EGGER, La Critique chez les Grecs (1887), and La Poétique d'Aristote (1878); BAUMGART, Handb. d. Poetik (1887), 423 ff. The works of DÖRING, BÉNARD, and EGGER contain bibliographies. See also UEBERWEG-HEINZE, Gesch. d. Philos. (J.H.T.)

Catholic Church [Gr. κατά, according to, + ὅλος, the whole]: Ger. *katholische Kirche*; Fr. *Église catholique*; Ital. *Chiesa cattolica*. The all-embracing and hence only authoritative Church.

The word Catholic is found in early Christian writers with no reference to the Church. Justin Martyr (*Dial. c. Tryph.*, 81) speaks of the Catholic, that is, the general, resurrection. Tertullian (*Adv. Marcion*, 2, 17) writes of the Catholic, that is, the all-embracing, goodness of God. It is first applied to the Church in the Epistle of Ignatius to the Church in Smyrna, where we read that where Christ is, there the Christian Church is. In Eusebius (*Hist. Ecc.*, 4, 15) it is applied to the local religious associations which recognize themselves as parts of the Church universal. It was first generally em-

ployed in its present sense in contrast to the purely national religion of the Jews. Later, it was attached to the orthodox Christian Church as contrasted with the heretics, especially the DONATISTS (q. v.).

The Catholic Church is the community which holds, maintains, and expounds universally received Christian doctrine. The Roman Catholic Church regards itself as possessing exclusive right to the title 'Catholic,' chiefly on the ground of unbroken apostolic succession; it alone holds the doctrine, and therefore alone can maintain it. Protestant writers tend to view the phrase as indicating an ideal, which is better conveyed in the words 'the communion of saints,' meaning thereby that the Church is not restricted to any one Christian community, but will, in the end, become universal. Cf. ROMANISM.

Literature: AUGUSTINE, Epist. 53, 1; PERRONE, Praelectiones, Tr. de Locis, cap. 3; PEARSON, On the Creed, art. ix; FAIRBAIRN, Catholicism, Anglican and Roman. (R.M.W.)

Catholic Reaction: Ger. *katholische Gegenwirkung*; Fr. *réaction catholique*; Ital. *reazione cattolica*. Catholic Reaction, also commonly known as the Counter-Reformation, is the name given to the movement of reform and restatement of fundamental principles that took place in the Roman Catholic Church, mainly as a result of the stimulus imparted by the Reformation. It is associated chiefly with: (1) the activity of the Jesuits (recognized by the Church, 1540); (2) with the Decrees of the Council of Trent (1542–63); (3) with the rehabilitation of the Inquisition.

As a whole, the movement was partly reformatory, partly reactionary. It was reformatory in so far as it purged the Church of much of the laxity, and nearly all the positive immorality, that had grown up under the influence of the Renaissance spirit. It was reactionary in so far as it stiffened the traditional organization and dogmas, and emphasized what was Roman rather than Catholic, thus accentuating the breach with the Reforming parties, and suppressing the reformers within the Church itself.

As results, (1) the Inquisition stamped out incipient Protestantism in Italy and Spain; (2) the Jesuits checkmated the spread of Protestantism in Germany, and made Catholicism once more the paramount power in Austria, South Germany, Bohemia, Poland, Hungary, and France; (3) the recentralization of the ecclesiastical system, accomplished chiefly by the Council of Trent, rendered its policy so clear that the entire machinery could be set in motion for the accomplishment of the same ends in widely separated communities.

Literature: PHILIPSON, La Contre-Révolution Religieuse au 16me Siècle; WARD, The Counter-Reformation (Epochs of Church History series); RANKE, Hist. of the Popes in the 16th and 17th centuries (Eng. trans.); BELLESHEIM, Wilhelm Cardinal Allen u. die engl. Seminare auf dem Festlande. For full lists in literature, see G. P. FISHER, Hist. of the Reformation (1891), 509 ff. (R.M.W.)

Catholicity (in theology) [Gr. καθολικός, general, universal]: Ger. *Katholicismus*; Fr. *catholicité*; Ital. *cattolicità*. In ecclesiastical controversy, Catholicity is the quality of universality which the Roman Church claims as peculiar to itself on the grounds (1) that it is not confined to any single people or to any one language; (2) that, as a matter of accomplished fact, it is universal; (3) that its members greatly outnumber other Christian sects, and that even taking all the others together, Roman Catholics are more numerous. The properties of unity, holiness, apostolicity, catholicity, exist, therefore, in no Christian society except that which recognizes the supreme authority of the Roman pope. (R.M.W.)

Cato, Marcus Porcius. (95–46 B.C.) An important Roman patriot and statesman, who adopted the doctrines and the discipline of the Stoics.

Causa sui [Lat.]. Self-caused; that which has the ground of its being in itself; the absolute.

According to Spinoza, 'that the idea of whose essence involves existence' (*Ethica*, i. def. 1). Cf. citations in Eisler, *Wörterb. d. philos. Begriffe*, sub verbo. (J.M.B.)

Causality: Ger. *Causalität*; Fr. *causalité*; Ital. *causalità*. (1) The necessary connection of events in the time series.

Opposed to mere logical necessity, in which time is not involved, and to 'chance' or 'freedom,' in which the connection is not a necessary connection. See CAUSE AND EFFECT, and NECESSITY. (R.H.S.)

(2) Notion of: that by which a process is thought to take place in consequence of another process. See CAUSE (notion of). (J.M.B.)

Cause (in law) [Lat. *causa*]: Ger. *Rechtsfall*; Fr. *cause, procès*; Ital. *causa*. A lawsuit. *Cause of action*: that which gives a right of action. It must be the efficient and proximate cause: *Causa proxima, non remota spectatur*. (S.E.B.)

Cause (notion of): Ger. *Begriff der Causalität*; Fr. *notion de cause*; Ital. *nozione di causa*. Whatever may be included in the thought or perception of a process as taking place in consequence of another process. (G.F.S.—J.M.B.)

The psychological treatment of causation must be distinguished from the logical. The logician has to inquire what the essentials of the conception are as a structural principle either of knowledge in general, or of this or that special department of science. The psychologist has to determine the elements which have actually entered into the conception or perception of causal connection in the various stages and phases of mental development.

Both logic and psychology have to discuss the existence and nature of necessary connection in the causal sequence. But they differ in their point of view. The logician may be right in affirming that for scientific purposes all that need be assumed is the regular recurrence of the same process on the repetition of similar antecedent conditions. But the psychologist who accepts this view does not find his own special problems solved by it. He has to inquire how the belief in uniform recurrence arises, and through what stages it passes. He may follow Hume in tracing the belief to the actual recurrence of certain experiences of uniform sequence which create an habitual expectation. He may also follow Hume in tracing the conception or necessary connection to the experience of a tendency produced by custom, which compels us to pass in thought from the perception of the antecedent to the ideal representation of the consequent. But if he does so he recognizes an element, necessary to the psychical development of the consciousness of causal sequence, which is of no logical value. This, indeed, is the position occupied by Hume himself. He puts forward habit, and the compulsory anticipation based on habit, as affording a psychological explanation of the growth of the concept of necessary causal connection; but he couples this doctrine with the emphatical denial that any such considerations can explain or justify its validity.

The psychologist may regard actual repetition of similar experiences as an inadequate explanation. He may find it necessary to posit a congenital tendency to assume uniformity, and to search for it even when it is not obviously present. But this may be

M 2

only a psychological postulate. The existence of such an innate tendency cannot be taken, without fuller discussion, as a proof or explanation of its validity.

It may be that the psychologist consider both the custom-theory and the theory of innate mental tendency as inadequate or incorrect. He may find himself compelled to lay emphasis on something specific and characteristic in the nature of the causal process as it actually takes place on any particular occasion. Thus uniform recurrence would cease to be the essential point. Mere occurrence apart from recurrence would in some manner manifest its causal character by its own intrinsic nature. We may take as representatives of this point of view those who find the origin of the consciousness of causal necessity in the experience of subjective activity and regard its application to material phenomena as due in the first instance to anthropomorphic or ejective interpretation. Supposing this doctrine to be justified psychologically, it does not immediately follow that the logical conception must conform to it. The anthropomorphic element may have been an indispensable factor in the origin and growth of the concept, and yet it may now have become superfluous for its scientific application. Or it may be superfluous in the investigation of physical phenomena but necessary in the treatment of psychical processes, or in an ultimate philosophical account of the universe. Such questions are properly logical or epistemological.

Literature: psychological textbooks in general. HUME, Treatise of Human Nature, Pt. III. § 14; REID, Works, 177 ff., 523 ff., 626 ff.; T. BROWN, Inquiry; MAINE DE BIRAN, Nouvelles Considérations sur les Rapports du Physique et du Moral de l'Homme; TETENS, Philos. Versuche, 312 ff.; HERBART, Psychol. als Wiss., 2. Theil, 142; WAITZ, Lehrb. d. Psychol., § 52; MILL, Logic, Bk. III. chaps. iii and v; VENN, Empirical Logic, 124 ff.; SIGWART, Logic, ii. Pt. III. § 73; WUNDT, Logik, i. 525; Syst. d. Philos., 292 ff.; KÖNIG, Entwickelung des Causalproblems; RIEHL, Der philos. Krit., ii. 248 ff.; FOUILLÉE, Psychol. des Idées-forces, ii. 169 ff.; WARD, Encyc. Brit., art. Psychology, 82; Naturalism and Agnosticism; H. GRÜNBAUM, Zur Kritik der modernen Causalanschauungen, Arch. f. syst. Philos., v. Heft 3; LOTZE, Metaphysics; BRADLEY, Appearance and Reality. (G.F.S.–J.M.B.)

Cause and Effect: Ger. *Ursache und Wirkung*; Fr. *cause et effet*; Ital. *causa ed effetto*. (1) Cause and effect (αἰτία, αἴτιον; *causa, effectus*) are correlative terms denoting any two distinguishable things, phases, or aspects of reality, which are so related to each other, that whenever the first ceases to exist, the second comes into existence immediately after, and whenever the second comes into existence, the first has ceased to exist immediately before. They must possess in common some one existent property. Of any two such things, the one which exists first is called the cause of the second, and the one which exists immediately after is called the effect of the first.

It is not necessary that the cause should differ from its effect in any respect except that they occupy different moments in time; but the names are more commonly applied in cases where there is also some other difference, e.g. at least a change of position in space. From the above definition it follows that with regard to any two things which have this relation to one another, the prior or subsequent existence of the one may be always validly inferred from the existence of the other; and hence they are said to be necessarily connected. See NECESSITY.

(2) This necessary connection between two existent things, which thus forms part of the causal relation, is sometimes held to constitute the whole. See CAUSE (notion of).

But in such cases some kind of logical priority is commonly ascribed to the cause, in place of the temporal priority given to it in (1). In this sense things held to exist, but not in time, are often called causes; and priority, such as belongs to a reason or logical ground, is ascribed to them, so that (a) one cause is said to have many effects; (b) it is said to be capable of existing without its effects, though they could not exist without it; (c) it is said to be real, while they are said to be phenomenal. Further, it is often supposed that the necessary connection between cause and effect is not merely logical, but in some sense real; and it is then generally held to consist in the 'activity' of the cause, a notion drawn from psychological experience where it is felt to precede or accompany the production of certain effects. The chief ambiguity in the use of the terms cause and effect is, however, due to the fact that some complex thing or event, which for some reason attracts attention, is taken as a whole to be the effect of which we seek the cause, or the cause of which we seek the effect; and thus the demands that a cause should immediately precede its effect, that it should cease to exist upon the occurrence of its effect, and that their relation should be absolutely invariable, are sacrificed.

There is no regular correlative to the Greek words αἰτία, αἴτιον. The term which comes nearest in meaning to effect is ἀποβαῖνον; but συμβαῖνον or ἑπόμενον, which also signify consequence, are more commonly used as correlatives. Αἰτία itself is used from the beginning in all the three senses afterwards distinguished by Aristotle as 'efficient,' 'final,' and 'formal' causes. It thus includes somewhat more of the meaning of reason than commonly belongs to the Latin and modern terms, being used in answer to the four different questions : What existed previously from which we might have inferred that this would happen? (efficient cause); With what purpose was this done? or, What good result does this produce? (final cause); What are the properties which make this thing what it is? (formal cause). All these meanings have in common the implications (a) that from a knowledge of the fact called cause, the existence of a fact, having the nature denoted by this, might have been inferred ; (b) that the cause itself is capable of existence, being thus distinguished from a mere reason or ground; but one or other of the additional meanings, which distinguish the above questions, seems in general to have been vaguely included under the term. Before Aristotle, the chief points worthy of notice are (a) that the pre-Socratic philosophers made little use of the term, chiefly using the word ἀρχή, in a sense most nearly analogous to Aristotle's material cause, to denote an existent thing, generally conceived as prior in time to all others, but also existing along with them, and such that its existence was necessary to theirs, but not vice versa ; (b) that in Plato strong emphasis is laid on those two meanings of αἰτία, in which it denotes either the reason why a thing is what it is, i.e. the qualities whose presence justifies us in calling it by the same name as other things, or the reason why a thing ought to exist. It was the method of Socrates which drew attention to these two questions. Aristotle distinguished by name four different kinds of cause, for each of which he has several synonyms, of which the following are perhaps the most important : (a) ὕλη or ἐξ οὗ γίγνεται, material cause ; (b) εἶδος, λόγος, τὸ τί ἦν εἶναι, formal cause ; (c) ἀρχὴ τῆς κινήσεως, efficient cause ; (d) τέλος, τὸ οὗ ἕνεκα, final cause. (i) The first of these conceptions is derived from the popular distinction of the material, out of which a thing is made as one of its causes. This does, of course, generally exist unshaped, before a thing is made out of it ; and it is this fact of its priority in time which allows it to acquire the name of cause. But to philosophical analysis it soon became doubtful whether such priority can be ascribed to it universally ; and hence in Aristotle it rather denotes one of the elements of an actually existing thing, without any prominent implication that it existed before the thing in question. It is distinguished from the other three causes in that, from a knowledge of its existence, you could not infer the existence of any particular thing, although it could not exist, unless some particular thing existed. (ii) The εἶδος, meaning originally the visible qualities, particularly the shape, and hence also the other qualities, which distinguish one kind of thing from another kind, was conceived by Plato as existing eternally, separately from the things resembling it, which from time to time came into existence ; and though he distinguishes eternity from everlasting duration, he does undoubtedly commonly regard the εἶδος as prior in time to that which it 'informs.' Aristotle denies its separate existence ; and with this its priority in time is also strictly destroyed, so that it becomes the mere correlative of ὕλη, denoting that one of the two elements composing an actually existing thing from which the existence of that thing could be inferred. Neither Plato nor Aristotle clearly distinguish the two meanings covered by this phrase, both of which they seem to affirm : (a) that the combination in the εἶδος of certain properties is the reason why those properties are combined in things resembling it ; (b) that the existence of the εἶδος is the reason of the existence of things resembling it. (iii) The efficient or 'moving' cause is a thing which existed in time before that of which it is the cause. It thus corresponds to cause as now used, and defined above. (iv) In the conception of 'final' cause are mingled the three different senses which may be conveyed by the two questions given above. A final cause is (a) that for the sake of which a thing ought to exist, i.e. either the good qualities which the thing itself possesses (εἶδος), or some other good thing of which it is the efficient cause ; (b) that for the sake of which a given thing was produced by some intelligence ; (c) the design, considered as a mental fact, which was the efficient cause of its production. It is only the failure to distinguish (c) from (b) which explains why the final cause was thought to be a cause at all, and why Aristotle regarded his ultimate final cause as also the ultimate cause of all motion. On the other hand, both Plato and Aristotle do generally regard that which is desired, and not our desire of it, as both final and efficient cause of the actions which lead to its attainment. It is through this confusion of (c) with (b) that (a) also comes to be regarded as capable of being an efficient cause, since (a) is identified with (b) both by Plato and Aristotle, on the ground that no one ever desires anything but what he at least thinks to be good. A further identification of the formal with the final cause, of which the grounds are to be found both in (a) and (b), leads to the curious paradox that both formal and efficient cause may be sometimes regarded as not prior but subsequent in time to that of which they are the cause. Partly as uniting the functions of formal and efficient cause, and partly in virtue of its own importance as defined by (a), the final cause was supposed to be more truly a cause than any other; and this position was generally maintained by the Stoics, as well as by the schools of Plato and Aristotle. The Epicureans, on the other hand, tended to restrict the term cause to things which could be observed regularly to precede in time. And some of the later sceptics, also in opposition to the Stoics, pointed out that cause and effect (under the names αἴτιον and πάσχον) are mutually dependent, thus denying to cause that logical priority which belongs to it in most of the Aristotelian senses. The Aristotelian tradition, however, remained substantially unaltered throughout the middle ages; but with the Renaissance and the growth of natural science important modifications began to appear. The material cause, as such, soon drops entirely out of sight, its place being taken by the notion of substance, which is not indeed generally denied to be a cause, but is regarded as contributing nothing to the definition of the term, since a cause must be an explanation why different things exist, in spite of their having one substance in common. This search for a cause, in the sense of something which accounts for differences, and will thus enable you to predict future changes, naturally throws the emphasis on cause in the sense of efficient cause. Accordingly we find that Bacon, though insisting on the importance of the search for forms or formal causes, regards this rather as an inquiry into the exact nature of efficient causes, by means of which you will be able to recognize each when you see it; and with regard to final causes, while not denying their existence, he strongly insists on their uselessness for the purpose of prediction, by which he must be understood to imply that we are incapable of discovering what the final causes of things are, not that, if known, inferences could not be drawn from them. As Bacon had ceased to use formal cause to denote one existent thing from which the existence of another could be inferred, so this term, like material cause, soon dropped out of use; and throughout modern philosophy only efficient and final causes have continued to be discussed. The meaning of the former has grown increasingly definite in the direction of definition (1); and the word cause, if used alone, is always to be understood as efficient cause.

The modern history of final and efficient causes may be conveniently divided as follows:—(i) Final cause was most exactly defined by Leibnitz. He held that every real change is caused by a desire for the best possible—either by God's desire for what is actually so, or by a finite spirit's desire for what it thinks to be so. But he seems to have considered that any desire, even if not for the best, would deserve the name of cause, though none such actually exist. That every change must be caused by a desire, and that in this world all changes are caused by a desire for the best possible, are propositions both included by him under the name 'law of SUFFICIENT REASON' (q.v.). He thus professes to have reduced all apparently efficient to final causation, but he is even less clear than Aristotle as to whether the object desired or the desire of it is to be regarded as final cause. The latter, the desire, he treats as an efficient cause, with this peculiarity—that he denies its effect to follow from it necessarily. Since, however, he insists that a like desire always will produce a like effect, he preserves freedom only in name. This reservation he made in opposition to Spinoza, who denied final causes only in the sense in which they contradict necessity. Since Kant, the term end, which is more commonly used than final cause, has had a still vaguer meaning. The ambiguity as to whether it denotes part of the mental fact called desire, or the object of desire, still continues, and to this is added the further ambiguity that it is used to imply that the object of the desire is good, although it is now recognized that we do not always desire even what we think good. It is often used also to cover a mere good effect, without the express condition that this was either an effect or an object of desire. Some hold, with Leibnitz, that teleological causation is not incompatible with, but only more true than, mechanical, although they recognize, with Spinoza, that mechanical causation involves necessity ; others deny the possibility of prediction in the case of actions determined by ends. See TELEOLOGY. (ii) The first prominent question raised in modern philosophy with regard to efficient causes was that connected with 'occasional causes.' The growth of the mechanical sciences had emphasized the fact that the causes and effects there dealt with might be regarded as equal quantities of some one quality, namely, that belonging to extended things as such. Descartes regarded the quality which was common to cause and effect in all such cases as one substance, and postulated that the causal relation could only hold between things which had such a common quality. This postulate, however, plainly did not hold between body and mind ; and yet the more fundamental proposition, that a cause was that from the prior existence of which you could certainly infer the subsequent existence of something else, and vice versa, just as plainly did apply to the relation between impressions on the sense-organs and sensations on the one hand, and between the will and bodily movements on the other. Accordingly Descartes' followers, most prominently Geulincx, regarded mental and bodily states, in relation to each other, as a different kind of cause—occasional as distinguished from efficient—and they further postulated God as actually efficient in bringing about the invariable correspondence between occasional causes and their effects. This discussion renders it obvious that the possibility of reciprocal inference between two existents, i.e. their necessary connection, is not sufficient to define cause and effect ; for since such inference is possible between simultaneous states of body and mind, it is necessary, in order to distinguish cause from effect, that we should include in our definition not only succession in time, but also identity in substance. The necessity for a new name to denote the relation between body and mind, and of a cause to account for their correspondence, is not equally obvious. Leibnitz also held that substances could not interact, but he also excepts God from the rule, in order to provide a cause for the correspondence of finite substances. A new question with regard to causality was raised by Hume, who declared effect to mean simply what habit led us to expect. He thus denied a necessary connection, i.e. the possibility of inference, between any two existent things ; but since he himself assumes this relation to hold between habit and the expectations it produces, his discussion is rather to be regarded as an inquiry into what reasons we have for supposing particular things to be causes and effects, than an inquiry into the meaning of the terms. Such inquiries have been very frequent since. For our purpose the chief importance of Hume's results lies in the fact that they led Kant to make a detailed investigation of causality, from which it appeared not only that states of one substance, not substances themselves, could alone be causes and effects, but also that the necessary connection between these is itself necessary, in a sense in which the invariable correspondence of bodily and mental states is not necessary, since the validity of the former is implied in the truth of ordinary judgments of perception.

Since Kant, speculations on the subject have chiefly taken the two following directions :— (a) The attempt to show that succession in time is not necessarily involved in any valid inference from existent to existent, but that, on the contrary, the true cause is, as Spinoza thought, an existent reason or ground of all other things. To this view Kant gave countenance by his inconsistent application of the term to things-in-themselves and to reason. (b) The discussion as to whether complex things or their states are causes, and, if the former, whether their causality is 'transeunt' or 'immanent,' i.e. whether they can or cannot produce effects on other things. With this question is closely connected the distinction between cause and 'necessary condition' ; the question with regard to plurality of causes for one effect, and the plurality of effects from one cause ; the question whether the whole state of the universe at any one moment must not be regarded as the only complete cause of any particular effect at the next ; and the question whether a quantitative equality between cause and effect is necessary. On none of these points has any general agreement been attained. (G.E.M.)

In the usage of science we find three ways of locating a cause with reference to its effect, distinguished by Wundt (*Logik*).

(i) The cause is a thing; (ii) it is a force; (iii) cause and effect are regularly connected processes or changes. For example, the cause of the fall of a stone is (i) the earth, (ii) the force of gravitation, (iii) the earlier process of raising the stone to the position from which it falls. (K.G.)

Literature: ARISTOTLE, Metaphysics; HUME, Treatise on Human Nature, Bk. I; KANT, Krit. d. reinen Vernunft; LOTZE, Metaphysik, Bk. I; SIGWART, Logik. See also BIBLIOG. B, 1, *c*; 2, *c*. (G.E.M.)

Cause Theory (of mind and body): Ger. *Theorie der Wechselwirkung*; Fr. *doctrine de l'influx (physique)*, or *de l'influence naturelle*; Ital. *teoria dell' interazione*. The theory that the conscious processes and the nervous processes which arise in immediate connection with each other are in some way causally related. Either they are supposed to be relatively independent agencies in mutual interaction, or one of them is supposed to act causally upon the other. Cf. MIND AND BODY. (G.F.S., J.M.B.)

Celarent: see MOOD (in logic).

Celibacy [Lat. *caelebs*, single]: Ger. *Cölibat, Ehelosigkeit*; Fr. *célibat*; Ital. *celibato*. Voluntary renunciation of marriage.

In general usage celibacy still retains its original Latin meaning; but in practice, owing to historical occurrences, it has come to be specially associated with the priests of the Roman Catholic Church.

Celibacy is conceived to be purer than the married state. This idea is very ancient, and, so far as Christianity is concerned, is doubtless connected with the dogma of the Fall. Had Adam not fallen, Paradise might have been peopled by a pure race propagated in some 'non-carnal' way. In 1 Cor. vii. 38 the superior sanctity of the single state is indicated; and so early as Ignatius and Polycarp the same idea had currency, while voluntary vows of virginity were common among ascetics. By the 5th century marriage was not permitted to priests after ordination. The Latin Church, in contradistinction to the Greek, went much further than this. And ecclesiastical politicians, like Hildebrand (Gregory VII), perceiving the value of priestly celibacy to the Church organization, succeeded ultimately in making it obligatory. The Council of Trent maintained the rule, and it still remains one of the principal points of difference between the Roman and the Reformed churches. It is worthy of note that investigators who view life from a normal standpoint (sociologists, physiologists, philosophers) condemn the practice; those who break life up into separable parts (mystics and priests) favour the usage. While celibacy strengthens ecclesiastical organizations, it works irreparable wrong upon individuals, especially upon women; such at least is the record of history. Its central idea is essentially ascetic, and it must be estimated ethically as such. Cf. ASCETICISM.

Literature: KLITSCHE, Gesch. d. Cölibats, Der Cölibat; LEA, Sacerdotal Celibacy in the Christian Church; LAURIN, Der Coelibat d. Geistlichen. (R.M.W.)

Cell [Lat. *cella*]: Ger. *Zelle*; Fr. *cellule*; Ital. *cellula*. (1) In biology: the fundamental unit of structure of organized bodies; as Virchow defined it, 'the elementary vital unit.'

A cell typically consists of cell-wall or membrane and protoplasmic contents, composed of nucleus, protoplasm proper, or cytoplasm, and often nucleolus and centrosome. These latter may be absent, and the membrane is lacking from many animal cells.

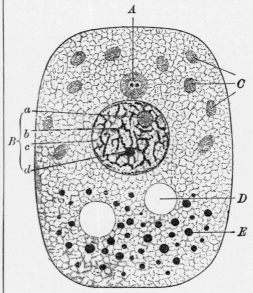

Diagram of a cell (after Wilson). Its basis consists of a thread-work (mitome or reticulum) composed of minute granules (microsomes) and traversing a transparent ground-substance. *A*, attraction-sphere, enclosing two centrosomes. *B*, nucleus (*a*, plasmosome or true nucleus; *b*, chromatin-network; *c*, linin-network; *d*, karyosome or net-knot). *C*, plastids, lying in the cytoplasm. *D*, vacuole. *E*, lifeless bodies (metaplasm) suspended in the cytoplasmic reticulum.

Sometimes vacuoles and other structures living (Plastids) and lifeless are present. Cf. the figure. See CELL THEORY, AMITOSIS, and MITOSIS. (C.F.H.)

(2) In neurology : by nerve-cell (Schäfer) is meant the whole unit of structure of the nervous system, i. e. the cell-body, the portion containing the nucleus (perikaryon of Foster and Sherrington), and all the processes which grow out from it: protoplasmic processes or DENDRITES (q. v.), and axis-cylinder processes or NEURITES (q. v.) or axones. Equivalent to NEURONE (q. v.) of European writers. (C.F.H.–H.H.)

Cell-division : see MITOSIS and AMITOSIS.

Cell Theory : Ger. *Zellenlehre* ; Fr. *théorie cellulaire* ; Ital. *teoria cellulare*. The doctrine that all organisms are composed either of individual cells (unicellular organisms) or of a compound aggregate of cells (the higher plants and animals) with certain cell-products ; and that every cell, no matter how differentiated in structure or function, is derived from a pre-existing cell.

Some of the stages of the cell theory are, in briefest possible outline, as follows :—(1) Observation by Malpighi and Grew, at the end of the 17th century, that under low powers of the microscope, plant structure appeared as (*a*) small spaces with firm walls and filled with fluid ('cells'), and (*b*) long tubes. (2) Proof by Treviranus (1808) that the tubes develop from cells, arranged end to end, by the breaking down of their partition walls. (3) The discovery of nuclei by Brown (*Trans. Linn. Soc. London,* 1833, in orchids), extended by Schleiden (*Müller's Archiv,* 1838, 137, plants generally). (4) The application by Schwann (*Mikrosk. Untersuchungen,* 1839), utilizing the observations of Henle and others, of the results reached in the microscopic study of plants to the analysis of animal tissues. So far, though the nucleus had been recognized, the cell-wall was regarded as an essential feature. Meanwhile the study of the structure and movements of protoplasm, begun by Bonaventura Corti (1772), led up to (5) the recognition by von Mohl (1846) and Remak (1852) of this living substance as the essential constituent of the cell in both plants and animals. (6) The proof by de Bary and Max Schultze (1859–61) that the protoplasm of animal cells and plant cells is of similar nature. (7) The conception, developed for plants by von Mohl (1846) and Nägeli and for animals set forth by Virchow (1858) in

his general law *omnis cellula e cellulâ,* that cells are genetically connected by an uninterrupted series of cell-divisions. (8) The discovery by Schneider (1873) of complex and orderly changes in the nucleus during cell-division, termed karyokinesis (Schleicher, 1878) or mitosis (Flemming, 1879). Cf. FERTILIZATION, HEREDITY, MITOSIS. (C.LL.M.)

Literature : O. HERTWIG, The Cell (Eng. trans. by Campbell, 1895) ; E. B. WILSON, The Cell in Devel. and Inheritance (1896), and the literature there quoted ; C. O. WHITMAN, The Inadequacy of the Cell Theory, J. of Morphol., viii. (1893) ; A. SEDGWICK, On the Inadequacy of the Cellular Theory of Development, Quart. J. Microsc. Sci., xxxvii. (1894) ; M. VERWORN, Gen. Physiol. (Eng. trans., 1899). (C.LL.M.–E.S.G.)

Cellifugal [Lat. *cella,* cell, + *fugere,* to flee] : Ger. *cellulifugal* ; Fr. *cellulifuge* ; Ital. *cellulifugo.* Passing in a direction away from a cell.

Said of a nervous impulse with reference to the cells from which the conducting axis cylinders arise. Opposed to cellipetal. There is usually an obvious morphological difference between the cellifugal and the cellipetal processes of a nerve-cell. Cf. NEUROCYTE. (H.H.)

Cellipetal : see CELLIFUGAL.

Cenogenesis : see PALINGENESIS.

Cenogenetic Characters : see BIOGENETIC LAW.

Central [Lat. *centrum,* a centre] : Ger. *central* ; Fr. *central* ; Ital. *centrale.* Pertaining to nervous centres or cells, as contrasted with peripheral, which means pertaining to nerve-courses or end-organs. (J.M.B.)

Centre [Lat. *centrum*] : Ger. *Centrum* ; Fr. *centre* ; Ital. *centro.* A collection of nerve-cells which act together for the performance of some more or less definite function.

Such are the various cortical centres, the respiratory centre of the medulla, the reflex centres of the medulla and cord, the various visceral centres of the sympathetic plexuses, &c. (H.H.)

Centre of Mass or **Gravity :** Ger. *Schwerpunkt, Massenmittelpunkt* ; Fr. *centre de masse, de gravité* ; Ital. *centro di gravità.* ('Centre of mass' is the more correct term, though the other is more familiar.) A point in a body or system of bodies such that, if the body or system were suspended by that point, it would be balanced in all positions when acted on by gravity. (S N.)

Centre of Rotation : Ger. *Drehpunkt (des Auges)* ; Fr. *centre de rotation (de l'œil)* ; Ital. *centro di rotazione (del globo oculare)*. The point at which the sagittal, frontal, and vertical axes of the eye intersect at right angles.

Literature : HELMHOLTZ, Physiol. Optik (2nd ed.), 614, 656 ; SANFORD, Course in Exper. Psychol., 119. (E.B.T.)

Centrifugal Force and **Centripetal Force** [Lat. *centrum*, centre, + *fugere*, to flee from ; and *centrum* + *petere*, to move toward, to seek] : Ger. *Fliehkraft oder Centrifugalkraft, und Centripetalkraft* ; Fr. *force centrifuge et centripète* ; Ital. *forza centrifuga e centripeta*. Centripetal force is any force drawing a body toward a centre of motion, as the planets are drawn toward the sun ; familiarly, a force continually deflecting the motion of a body, so that it shall move in a closed curve around a centre. The most familiar example of the force is seen in the case of a sling. The tendency of a body being always to continue its motion in a straight line, a force is required to keep the stone in the sling moving around in a circle. This force is exerted by the string of the sling.

Centrifugal force is, properly speaking, only the reaction of a body to a centripetal force. In the case of the sling, the latter is the pull of the holder's hand upon the string, while the former is the pull of the string upon the hand. In the case of a fly-wheel the centripetal force is exerted by the spokes to keep the parts of the rim in place, while the centrifugal force is a corresponding pull of the rim upon the spokes. The forces in question increase as the square of the angular velocity ; and if the latter becomes so rapid that the spokes are not strong enough to keep the rim in its place, they break, and the rim flies to pieces. In this case the pieces of the

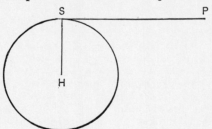

rim fly off in the direction in which they were moving at the moment of rupture, and not radially from the centre, as is commonly thought. So, in the case of the sling, if H is

the position of the hand, and S that of the stone at the moment of release, then both the centrifugal and the centripetal forces cease at this moment, and the stone flies off in the direction of the tangent SP. (S.N.)

Centrosome [Gr. κέντρον, centre, + σῶμα, body] : Ger. *Centrosoma* ; Fr. *centrosome, sphère attractive* (in botany) ; Ital. *centrosoma*. That specialized part of a cell which is regarded as the active centre in the process of division.

The term was proposed by Boveri (1887). The centrosome is now regarded by many observers as an essential and relatively permanent feature of the cell. It generally lies outside but near the nucleus. In its passive condition it is a minute speck in the cell ; but in its active phase it becomes the centre of an 'attraction sphere,' with radiating fibres, constituting the aster (Fol, 1877). Along these fibres the split CHROMOSOMES (q. v.) travel in cell-division to the opposite poles of the achromatic spindle. The question of its existence in the higher plants (angiosperms) is still under discussion.

Literature : TH. BOVERI, Ueber die Befruchtung der Eier von *Ascaris megalocephala*, Sitzber. Ges. Morph. Phys. (München, 1887) ; E. B. WILSON, The Cell in Devel. and Inheritance (1896). (C.LL.M.–E.S.G.)

Cephalic Index : see INDEX.

Cerebral Vesicles : Ger. *Hirnbläschen* ; Fr. *vésicules cérébrales* ; Ital. *vescicole cerebrali*. Embryonic expansions of the medullary tube giving rise to the several major divisions of the brain. See BRAIN (Embryology).

They form the embryonic structures, from which arise the fore-, mid-, and hind-brain. Though the ventricles are derived from the cavities of the vesicles, they do not correspond to them in number or form. (H.H.)

Cerinthus. Probably lived during the reign of Trajan, 98–117 (Eusebius). Founder of one of the heretical sects, called Cerinthians. Irenaeus regards him as a consistent Gnostic, stating that St. John wrote his gospel to weaken the influence of the sect.

Certainty (logical) [Lat. *certus*, sure, through Fr. *certain*] : Ger. *Gewissheit* ; Fr. *certitude* ; Ital. *certezza*. Complete CERTITUDE (q. v.) with reference to a logical assertion or judgment.

It keeps in view (1) the content of the assertion made, and (2) the attitude of the asserting mind. In both cases certainty attaches to the feature of objective validity. An assertion is certain when its content is taken to be such that it must be asserted by all intelligences, i. e. when its truth is taken to be assured by universally valid grounds. Logical certainty thus names only the representation of the universal or common character of certainty, that which does not depend on the special kind of content involved.

Historically, the problem may be said to begin in those discussions which preceded Aristotle's definite statement of the distinction between mediate and immediate truths (see *Anal. Post.*, i). From that time onwards the problem has been (1) to determine the nature of the assumed immediate truths in such a manner as to make the objective value claimed for them conceivable; (2) to clear up the relation in which mediate stands to immediate truth, and therewith, it may be said, to determine the worth of the highly metaphorical relation in which they are generally assumed to stand.

Literature: JAVARY, De la Certitude (1847); GRUNG, Das Problem der Gewissheit (1886); MILHAUD, Certitude Logique (2nd ed., 1898), and Le Rationnel (1897). (R.A.)

Certitude or **Certainty** (psychological) [Lat. *certitudo*, from *certus*, certain]: Ger. *Gewissheit*; Fr. *certitude*; Ital. *certezza*. The degree of assurance felt with reference to something presented to the mind.

This term is employed to express degrees of (1) conviction or belief. It is then applied to all cases from the slight tendency to accept a proposition or fact (characterized by the transition from the phrases 'I think,' 'I fancy,' to 'I presume,' 'I begin to be convinced') up to so-called 'complete certitude,' or knowledge. Certain authorities limit certitude to the highest degrees of assurance, where the possibility of doubt is excluded (e. g. Newman, *Grammar of Assent*). It also applies (2) to degrees of reality-feeling or 'realizing-sense,' in cases which do not involve argument, doubt, or explicit belief in any sort of assertion.

Like other terms of epistemological value, certitude is often carried over from the mind to its object and made a property of the latter; we say a proposition has certitude. In logic this is legitimate as a shorthand way of saying that a proposition is fitted to arouse certitude, or has a certain degree of PROBABILITY (q.v.).

Literature: see BELIEF, and CERTAINTY (logical). (J.M.B.–G.F.S.)

Cervical Region: see NERVOUS SYSTEM.

Cesare: see MOOD (in logic)

Chain Syllogism: Ger. *Schlusskette*, *Kettenschluss*; Fr. *sorite*; Ital. *sorite*. German logicians have named by cognate terms two forms of compound syllogism: (1) that in which the final syllogism has for its premises the conclusions of preceding syllogisms, Schlusskette, when the former is called Epi-syllogism, the latter Pro-syllogism; (2) when the conclusion is drawn from a series of more than two premises, SORITES (q.v.) or Kettenschluss.

Literature: UEBERWEG, Logik, §§ 124–5. (R.A.)

Chalybäus, Heinrich Moritz. (1796–1862.) A German philosopher, born and died in Saxony. In 1839 he became professor in Kiel. His best known works are on the history of modern philosophy and on ethics.

Champeaux, Guillaume de. A French philosopher, died in 1121. He taught rhetoric and logic in Paris. Abelard was first his pupil, then his rival, and afterwards his superior in fame and learning. In 1113 he became bishop of Châlons-sur-Marne.

Chance [Lat. *cadere*, to fall]: Ger. *Zufall*; Fr. *chance, hazard*; Ital. *caso accidente*. (1) An occurrence due to chance is one which has no assignable cause, and hence popularly supposed to have no cause. Chance itself was then hypostatized (the Greek τυχή) as a source of uncaused events.

The theory of absolute chance, or pure accidentalism, has been given up—only remaining as a metaphysical speculation, called TYCHISM (q. v.), in favour of the following meaning, for which the term should be reserved.

(2) A chance event is one that can be accounted for after it has happened, or predicted before it happens, by the law of PROBABILITY (q.v.). The same law provides a statement of the degree of probability, called 'the chance,' of an event's happening, on the basis of what is already known. Cf. VARIATIONS. (J.M.B.)

Change [Lat. *cambire*, to barter; through Fr.]: Ger. *Veränderung*; Fr. *changement*; Ital. *cambiamento, mutazione*. The occurrence of any difference or variation, whether any identity is involved or not. A general term which includes movement, modification, becoming, growth, &c. (R.H.S.)

The meaning of change (μεταβολή, *mutatio*) may be defined under two different heads, according as (1) a change is said to have occurred, or (2) a thing is said to have undergone a change.

(1) The occurrence of a change denotes

that there exists at some one moment of time a distinguishable thing which either did not exist at the immediately preceding moment or does not exist at the immediately succeeding moment. The term thus covers the transition (*a*) from the existence of nothing but time to the existence of something in time; (*b*) from the existence of something in time to the existence of nothing but time; (*c*) from the existence of something in time to the existence of something else in time, different from the first in some other respect than mere position in time.

(2) This sense is narrower than (1) in that it will not include (*a*) and (*b*), but wider in that it will include one case excluded by (*c*), namely, the fact (*a*) that what exists at two immediately successive moments, though differing in no distinguishable respect except position in time, may be said to have changed its position in time. In this sense every position in space may be said to change its position in time at every moment. This use only arises because any two things which differ from one another in no respect except that they occupy immediately successive moments of time, are said to be one thing. Thus a position in space which differs from another in no respect except its position in time, is said to be one and the same position as this other. If 'same position in space' be understood in this sense, then, further (*β*), if contiguous positions in space be occupied at immediately successive moments by things which differ in no distinguishable respect except their position both in time and space, these two things are also said to be one thing, and that thing is said to have changed its position in space. This change constitutes motion, and this and all following meanings are also covered by (1 *c*). It is recognized that motion, but not mere change of position in time, is one of the most important forms of change. But (*γ*) a thing which merely moves is not said itself to change, in the sense of being changed; and hence we get a third meaning of change, in which it can be applied to nothing less complex than a system of moving things, whose relative positions are changed in such a way that the configuration of the system is different at one moment from what it was in the last. Such a system is said to be one thing and to change, but only on condition that each of the elements composing it is one thing in the narrower sense defined under (*β*). This is the simplest sense in which a thing that occupies space may be said to change in quality. (*δ*) Further meanings of change in an extended thing are less definite, although it is to these that the term is most commonly applied. The thing can now only be defined as one thing by the condition that most of its parts, but not all, are the same in the sense defined under (*β*) at any two successive moments of time. In this sense, for the first time, a thing may be said to change in quantity. It changes in quantity alone if, while its figure is mathematically similar at two successive moments, some parts belong to it in the one which did not, or do not, belong to it in the other. It changes both in quantity and quality if its figure be also dissimilar at two successive moments, it being always understood that most of its parts remain the same as defined under (*β*). (*ε*) A still further difficulty in the way of exact definition of change in a physical thing, is introduced, if a thing be understood to include its 'secondary qualities,' as is usually the case. It is in this sense that a change of quality is most commonly predicated of a thing; and this denotes that a thing, defined as one and the same thing under (*δ*), besides its changes in quantity and figure, possesses also different secondary qualities at successive moments. The difference in its secondary qualities may consist either in the absence at one moment of one or more qualities present at the other, or in a difference in intensity or extension, or in both, of one or more qualities present at both moments. (*ζ*) A mental change may be defined as denoting the existence, at successive moments, of different qualities, or different quantities of the same quality, in one and the same mind; and a mind may be defined as one and the same, either, if it is self-conscious, by the feeling of the self that it is the same and that all its states belong to it, or, if it is not self-conscious, by the correlation of its states with one brain or part of a brain, defined as one under (*ε*). (*η*) A thing cannot be said to undergo a change from better to worse unless it also changes in some one of the senses above enumerated, and it is most commonly said to do so when this change is a change in quality.

It is plain that all senses of change under (2) imply that an identical element of content continues to exist in the thing changed, throughout the change, since this, combined with continuity in space in the case of physical things, and with continuity in time in all cases, is necessary to constitute it one thing, i. e. to constitute its material identity. Under sense (1) no such persistence of identical content is necessarily implied.

One thing is said to change another when it contains the cause of some change which occurs in the other.

Heraclitus, who emphasized the perpetual occurrence of change under the name of becoming (γίγνεσθαι), seems to have understood the term chiefly as denoting change in one thing's secondary qualities, this one thing being supposed by him to be fire. Plato, who makes much use of the same term, seems also to have meant chiefly change in a thing's qualities; and he would seem to have excluded motion, since he ascribes this to what is real, whereas γιγνόμενα is only used by him to denote what is phenomenal. Aristotle often identifies motion and change (μεταβολή), distinguishing four kinds of both: (1) change in essence (κατ᾽ οὐσίαν), (2) in quality, (3) in quantity, (4) in place; but elsewhere he distinguishes them, e. g. excluding (1) from the conception of motion. Similarly, he seems sometimes to affirm and sometimes to deny that becoming (γένεσις) and its correlative destruction (φθορά) fall under the conception of motion. After him no noteworthy advance towards a clearer conception of the terms seems to have been made till the growth of the mechanical sciences at the Renaissance, and the consequent distinction of 'primary' and 'secondary' qualities. This distinction brought into a clearer light that between motion and change of figure on the one hand, and change in qualities other than figure on the other. Hegel appears to have used becoming to include the logical relation between one proposition and that which may be inferred from it. This use is the more appropriate in him, since he conceives the truth of some propositions to be actually absorbed in that of others, so that they cease to be true. This supposed change of things not existing in time into one another, especially of opposites into opposites, has, whether meant metaphorically or not, become a characteristic doctrine with many who are influenced by him. Similarly, they talk of the dialectic 'movement' and of the 'self-development' of an Idea or Universal. It is generally held that change implies some persistent identical element, whether it be change of logical or existent entities; but it is not commonly distinguished

whether that which is identical in the latter case must itself always exist or not.

Literature: LOTZE, Metaphysics; SIGWART, Logic; see also BIBLIOG. B, 1, c.   (G.E.M.)

Channing, William Ellery. (1780–1842.) An eminent American Unitarian preacher and writer. Graduated at Harvard University, 1798, and studied theology at Cambridge and Newport. Ordained in 1803.

Chaos: see COSMOS, COSMOGONY, and NATURE (philosophy of).

Character [Gr. χαρακτήρ, a letter]: Ger. *Charakter*; Fr. *caractère*; Ital. *carattere*. An individual mind has a character, so far as its modes of feeling, thinking, and acting show unity, consistency, and distinctive individuality.   (G.F.S.–J.M.B.)

The term is applied to the mental life as a whole, but also to phases of it, as mental or moral character. Individual psychology is the science of character; important special topics being TEMPERAMENT and TYPE (see these terms).   (J.M.B.)

Character (in biology). Any anatomical or functional mark by which individuals are distinguished. It is entirely a relative term, that at one time being a character which at another time is a group of characters; a source of much confusion in discussions of ACQUIRED AND CONGENITAL CHARACTERS, CORRELATION, &c. See these terms.

The much-discussed question of specific characters is that concerning the congenital marks common to the individuals of a species, and of such a distinctive sort as to serve to distinguish one SPECIES (q. v.) from others.   (J.M.B.)

Characteristic: Ger. *Characteristik*; Fr. *caractéristique*; Ital. *caratteristica*. (1) A distinctive trait or quality, which marks or characterizes an individual as such in distinction from those qualities which he may have in common with family, race, &c.; called 'individual characteristic,' and also used adjectively. Applied also to natural objects and to races, peoples, &c., when considered as classes or unities. The substantive 'character' is preferred, however, as 'racial,' 'generic,' &c. characters. See CHARACTER (in biology).   (J.M.B.)

(2) In art and aesthetic criticism: a representation which brings out clearly and truthfully the elements which are most important in the object or action, as distinguishing it from others. This has a threefold aesthetic value: (*a*) through the recognition of

the truthfulness of the reproduction : this may be largely negative, for falsity or distortion is a source of displeasure ; (*b*) through its satisfaction of the interest in variety (as against monotony) ; (*c*) often also the demand to be oneself, and the feeling of interest in one's own peculiar personality, are strengthened and gratified by the recognition of marked individuality in what is portrayed. For the history of the characteristic in art theories, see ART, and EXPRESSION.

The discussion of the characteristic has not always been distinguished from that of expression. Properly, however, it is only one phase of expression. It has frequently been treated as an element outside of beauty ; 'Beauty is perfection of form unmodified by any predominant characteristic' (Hare). Yet it is now generally regarded as one of the important elements of aesthetic value.

Literature : BOSANQUET, Hist. of Aesth. (1892) ; FECHNER, Vorschule d. Aesth. (1876), chap. xxiii ; KÖSTLIN, Aesth. (1869) ; VON HARTMANN, Aesth., ii (1887). See also under EXPRESSION, and ART.   (J.H.T.)

Charity [Lat. *caritas*]: Ger. *Charitas, Menschenliebe* ; Fr. *charité* ; Ital. *carità*. (1) Benevolent love of others : commonly, in modern usage, it refers also (2) to the almsgiving in which that love is manifested.

It is not possible to distinguish charity in its first and more general signification from BENEVOLENCE (q.v.). But the place given to it by Paul (1 Cor. xiii), as the highest virtue of Christian character, and its connection in his exposition with Christian faith and hope, coupled with the absence of any equivalent conception in the pagan or classical list of cardinal virtues, led to Augustine's re-interpretation of the virtues as depending on love to God and one's neighbour, and to the subsequent classifications of Aquinas and the mediaeval moralists generally. In these classifications the triad, faith, hope, and charity, were distinguished as 'theologic virtues' from the four cardinal virtues of classical tradition, and were held to be implanted in man by the supernatural grace of God. Of the three, faith was held by Aquinas to be first in order of origin, charity to be highest in order of perfection. Charity is said to be the mother and root of the other virtues, since it is through it that they attain the perfection of virtue (*Summa*, II. i. Q. 62). A modern Roman Catholic writer (Father Rickaby) defines charity as 'the love that we bear to ourselves and our neighbours in view of our coming from God and going to God,' and says, 'Charity differs from philanthropy in looking beyond the present life and above creatures. A materialist or atheist may possess philanthropy, but not charity' (*Mor. Philos.*, 238–9).

The love or charity which characterized the early Christian society was from the first exhibited in provision for the poor by means of voluntary offerings. Charity, in this sense, was distinguished from mere liberality, because due to the love of man to man, in virtue of their common spiritual relationship to God and Christ. It was accordingly encouraged, and to a large extent organized, by the Church. The uncertain benefits of indiscriminate almsgiving, and its frequent evil effects on the recipients, have led to various systematic attempts at the organization of charity (partly in connection with the Church, partly by extra-ecclesiastical organizations)— these efforts being directed towards combating the causes of pauperism instead of merely mitigating its results.

The use of the term charity for favourable judgment upon the motives and character of others is connected with Paul's encomium upon it as 'thinking no evil.' This usage is as much justified by the original meaning of the term as the special signification of almsgiving.

Literature : LECKY, Hist. of European Morals, iv ; T. MACKAY, The State and Charity (1898).   (W.R.S.)

Charm [Lat. *carmen*, song] : Ger. (1) *Zauber*, (2) *bezaubern* ; Fr. (1) *charme*, (2) *charmer* ; Ital. (1) *incanto*, (2) *incantare*. (1) Noun : an object, saying, or formula, supposed to have peculiar virtue, and hence looked upon with veneration. Sometimes the influence is regarded as purely intrinsic to the object, as in certain verbal formulae, and at other times it is regarded as more or less derivative from connection with something else, usually a person.

(2) Verb : to exercise a peculiar or fascinating influence.

Usage (1) has been current in discussions of primitive religion (see FETICH, AMULET, IDOL) and superstition. Usage (2) is largely employed in descriptions of so-called FASCINATION, TRANCE, and HYPNOSIS, and in the practice of MAGIC (see these terms and the literature cited under them).   (J.M.B.–G.F.S.)

Charron, Pierre. (1541–1603.) An eminent French preacher and philosophical writer, follower of Montaigne, whose expressions he tried to systematize. He was born, and died, in Paris. His most famous treatise is *On Wisdom*.

Charter [Lat. *charta*]: Ger. *Freibrief*; Fr. *charte, lettres patentes* ; Ital. *patente*. A written grant made by public authority, conferring or securing rights; as the Great Charter, *Magna Charta*.

Formerly used for any written evidence of things done between man and man (Cowell's *Interpreter*, in verbo). (S.E.B.)

Chastity [Lat. *castus*, pure]: Ger. *Keusch-heit*; Fr. *chasteté*; Ital. *castità*. Purity of life in sexual relations.

As a virtue of character, chastity is closely related to, or is a special case of, temperance. Its connection with respect for the marriage-bond is obvious; but the latter is more dependent on the law and custom of particular times and communities, and belongs accordingly, as Sidgwick remarks, to the virtue of order rather than to that of purity. The exact nature of chastity has been discussed in great detail by some Roman Catholic moralists, largely in the interest of the Confessional. A short discussion is given by Sidgwick, *Meth. of Eth.*, III. xi. 7. (W.R.S.)

Chemical Synthesis: Ger. *chemische Synthese*; Fr. *synthèse chimique*; Ital. *sintesi chimica*. The union of chemical elements according to what is variously known as 'Dalton's law,' 'law of atomic weight,' 'law of chemical affinity,' &c.

Dalton's law, according to Armstrong (*Encyc. Brit.*, 9th ed., art. Chemistry), assumed 'the ultimate particles of matter to be incapable of further division ; atoms, possessing definite weights, the ratios of which could be denoted by numbers, the ratio of an atom of hydrogen being taken as unity. . . . Those which unite have affinity.' (J.M.B.)

Child Psychology: Ger. *Psychologie des Kindes*; Fr. *psychologie de l'enfant*; Ital. *psicologia della fanciullezza* (or *del bambino*). That department of PSYCHOLOGY (q.v.) which investigates the mind of the child.

Literature: L. N. WILSON, Bibliog. of Child-Study (also in Pedag. Sem., 1898; an alphabetical list of authors, with journals and works of reference, and classified subject-index); PREYER, The Mind of the Child (Die Seele des Kindes, 4th ed.); WARNER, The Study of Children; MOORE, Mental Development of a Child, Mo. Supp. iii to the Psychol. Rev.; OPPENHEIM, The Devel. of the Child; TRACY, The Devel. of the Child;

SHINN, Notes on the Devel. of a Child; SULLY, Studies of Childhood; COMPAYRÉ, Intellectual and Moral Devel. of the Child ; ZIEHEN, Ideenassociation des Kindes (1899); BALDWIN, Ment. Devel. in the Child and the Race, and Social and Eth. Interpret.; L. FERRI, Studio sullo Sviluppo mentale di un Bambino (1890); P. LOMBROSO, Psicol. del Bambino (1894); A. GARBINI, Colour-sense of Children, in Arch. per Antropol., XXIV. i. 72, ii. 193; HOLDEN and BOSSE, Arch. of Ophthal., xxix, 1900, No. 3. (J.M.B.–E.M.)

Chiliasm [Gr. χιλιάς, a thousand]: Ger. *Chiliasmus*; Fr. *chiliasme* (*millénium*); Ital. *chiliasmo*. The name applied to the apocalyptic ideas with regard to Christ's second coming, which flourished in the early Christian communities. The title is hardly accurate, because it refers to but one of the apocalyptic doctrines, viz. that the duration of the kingdom of Christ upon earth will be one thousand years (cf. MONTANISM).

The early years of Christianity were marked by deep unrest, spread over the civilized world. Incident to this were the semi-spiritual, semi-material ideals that a new and better state of things was soon destined to be realized on earth. These conceptions, though first crystallized in the late Jewish apocalyptic literature, were so characteristic of the times that they formed an integral part of the Christian consciousness. They were not dogmas, because dogma had not then appeared; they were naïve, or unsystematized, expectations. In short, they formed the mystic element which is always inseparably bound up with every great religious movement. Such writers as Papias, Irenaeus, the Montanists, Tertullian, Barnabas, and Justin Martyr gave expression to them; and so long as Christianity was struggling to gain a foothold they remained integral to its teaching. Although the Apocalypse of John—which is the classical Christian source for this expectation—is sharply differentiated from similar Jewish writings, sub-apostolic Christian writers adopted Jewish ideas on the subject without hesitation. As Christianity grew in power, Chiliasm waned correspondingly, and, after the Montanist controversy (165–220), it came to be viewed less and less as an essential element in the traditions of the Church. Augustine gave Chiliasm its death-blow by identifying the anticipated New Jerusalem with the Christian Church—which is already the City of God upon earth. The apocalyptic conceptions thus failed to find place in the formulated dogmas of the ecclesiastical organization; but when spiritual movements have reasserted themselves within the bosom of Christianity, Chiliastic tendencies have often reappeared, as e. g. in Joachim of Floris, and the pre-Reformation mystics; in the Anabaptism of the 15th and 16th centuries; and in various forms of Pietism till the present time.

Literature: CORRODI, Krit. Gesch. d. Chiliasmus; VOLK, Der Chiliasmus; SPENER, Die Hoffnung besserer Zeit; SCHÜRER, Hist. of the Jewish People in the Time of Christ (Eng. trans.); HILGENFELD, Die jüdische Apokalyptik; AUBERLEN, Daniel u. d. Offenbarung Johannis; HÖLEMANN, Die Stellung St. Pauli z. d. Frage ü. d. Wiederkunft Christi; HELLWAG, in the Theol. Jahrb. (Baur), 1848; JOËL, Blicke in d. Religionsgesch. zu Anfang d. 2. christl. Jahrhunderts; CUNNINGHAM, The Second Coming of Christ; RENAN, L'Antéchrist; DORNER, Person of Christ (Eng. trans.), i. 408 f.; BRIGGS, Pre-millenarianism. (R.M.W.)

China (religion in): see ORIENTAL PHILOSOPHY (China).

Chiromancy (or **Chei-**) [Gr. χείρ, hand, + μαντεία, divination]: Ger. *Chiromantik*; Fr. *chiromancie*; Ital. *chiromanzia*. A system of interpretation of the lines, lineaments, prominences, and general characteristics of the hand, with the usual purpose of reading therefrom the personal characteristics of the individual, or his fortunes and experiences in the future.

As an actual science or practice it merits little or no recognition in this work. It is interesting historically as a phase in the antecedents of modern science (such as alchemy or phrenology), and also anthropologically as a form of belief, or an attempt to read the future by the symbolic interpretation of accidental details (cf. DIVINATION, and MAGIC), akin in motive though not in practice to other forms of divination.

Literature: typical works which attempt a modern revival or restoration of this practice, usually under the term Palmistry, are E. H. ALLEN, Science of the Hand (1889, with bibliog.); H. FRITH, Pract. Palmistry (1895); EASTER HENDERSON, Guide to Palmistry (1894); A. R. CRAIG, Science of Modern Palmistry (1884); H. GERMAIN, Pract. Palmistry (1897). (J.J.)

Choice [Fr. *choix*]: Ger. *Wahl*; Fr. *choix*; Ital. *scelta*. The volition to perform an act, issuing out of comparison of this act with other alternative acts, or with the state of

remaining inactive. See MOTIVE, and VOLITION. (G.F.S.–J.M.B.)

This view represents choice as in all cases a function of some deliberation, and as always directed toward a conceived end. The question as between choice of means and choice of end (immediate and remote ends respectively) is really that of the determination of the end; seeing that if the means do not enter as part of the chosen end, a new act of choice follows for the adoption of means, and it then becomes end in its turn. The interesting case in which the chosen end is really a compromise to secure the relative satisfaction of a desire represented in the alternatives, but not directly realizable, has been covered by the distinction between 'potential' and 'final' choice; the former attaching to the larger whole of desire, and the latter to the compromise-end adopted to advance it. Most choices are thus final elements, or means, in a larger system of desire. (J.M.B.)

An ethical choice is a voluntary decision between two alternatives which are contrasted as morally good and bad, or relatively better and worse. (W.R.S.–J.M.B.)

Literature: see the general works on psychology, and BIBLIOG. G, 2, *w*. (J.M.B.)

Chord [Gr. χορδή, the string of a musical instrument]: Ger. *Klang, Zusammenklang, Accord*; Fr. *accord*; Ital. *accordo*. A harmonic, consonant or dissonant, combination of two or more simple, or more often compound, tones. A consonant chord is termed a concord, a dissonant chord a discord.

Literature: HELMHOLTZ, Sensations of Tone, 211; STUMPF, Tonpsychologie, ii. (E.B.T.)

Chorea [Gr. χορεία, dance]: Ger. *Veitstanz*; Fr. *chorée, danse de Saint-Guy*; Ital. *corea*. Functional disturbance of the motor centres resulting in spasmodic involuntary movements which persist for a longer or shorter time, but are interrupted by sleep (St. Vitus's dance).

The cause of the disease is unknown, though it is suggestively associated with rheumatism. It occurs chiefly in ill-nourished female children, and the prognosis is not necessarily unfavourable. (H.H.)

Christ [Gr. χριστός, anointed; ὁ Χριστός, the Anointed—a translation of the Hebrew 'Messiah']: Ger. *Christus*; Fr. *Christ*; Ital. *Cristo*. Originally not the name of a person, as is so often supposed, but of an office, that of Deliverer. Jesus of Nazareth came to be identified with the completely successful fulfilment of this office so soon after his death—perhaps during his life—that the office came to be wrapped up in the Person, as it never was in regard to Buddha. Cf. CHRISTOLOGY, INCARNATION, KENOSIS, TRINITY.

Stripping off later theological accretions, there seems to be little or no doubt that this identification was already an accomplished fact with the first generation of Christians. It reposed upon three considerations—crystallized propositions had not been formulated then: (1) The divinity, (2) the death, (3) the exaltation, of Jesus. To the earliest Christians the divinity of Jesus was synonymous with his fulfilment of the Messianic office as verified by his conception of the divine revelation, and by the fact that he stood in a unique relation to God. His death was a necessary incident in his Messianic work, for it opened the gate to that new kingdom of God, in which man would be delivered from sin for ever. His exaltation was the indispensable prelude to his return in glory at no distant period. Other beliefs about Christ belong to the realm of theology rather than of history, and fall properly under CHRISTOLOGY (q. v.). At the same time, several essential features of the earliest beliefs about Christ contain the germs of those which were to follow. In so far as they are Messianic, they differ from Jewish expectations in being non-political and of a spiritual, even eschatological, nature. The expectation of the second coming of Messiah is entirely non-Jewish, and affords the basis for the doctrine of the kingdom of God. Further, and in strong contrast with what might be anticipated in a Jewish environment, there is evidence for the very early use of the Trinitarian formula.

Literature: this is enormous. See arts. in Encyc. Brit. and Herzog's Real-Encyc., also in WEISS, Bib. Theol. of New Testament (Eng. trans.). Later works are HARNACK, Hist. of Dogma, i (Eng. trans.); SCHÜRER, The Jewish People (Eng. trans.), and Die Predigt Jesu in ihrem Verhältniss z. A. T. u. z. Judenthum; BALDENSPERGER, Das Selbstbewusstsein Jesu im Licht d. messianischen Hoffnungen s. Zeit; WENDT, Die Lehre Jesu (Eng. trans. of ii); WEIZSÄCKER, Apostolic Age (Eng. trans.); BOUSSET, Jesu Predigt in ihrem Gegensatz z. Judenthum; BEYSCHLAG, Bib. Theol. of the New Testament (Eng. trans.); GUNKEL, in Theol. Lit.-zeit. (1893); C. HOLTZMANN, in Zeitsch. f. Theol. u. Kirche, i. 367 f. On the early presence of the Trinitarian formula see RESCH, Aussercanonische Paralleltexte z. d. Evangelien, ii. Heft (Paralleltexte z. Matthaeus u. Marcus). (R.M.W.)

Christian Consciousness: Ger. *christliches Bewusstsein*; Fr. *conscience chrétienne*; Ital. *coscienza cristiana*. A variant on the Hegelian phrase 'universal consciousness,' meaning, technically, consciousness of Christian doctrine—in the sense of the Christian point of view—as diffused among men, and this with special reference to its unitary movement. The Christian consciousness is the Ethos, or self-determining expression, of Christendom.

Literature: BRACE, Gesta Christi; SCHMIDT, The Social Results of Early Christianity (Eng. trans.). Cf. ETHICS (Christian). (R.M.W.)

Christian Science: see FAITH-CURE.

Christianity [Lat. *Christianus*, partisan of *Christus*]: Ger. *Christenthum*; Fr. *Christianisme*; Ital. *Cristianesimo*. The name of the religion founded by Jesus Christ.

Although based upon the entire career of Jesus, and issuing from his Person, Christianity involved other elements even at the outset, and in the course of history it absorbed and assimilated several movements originally quite alien. On analysis, the constituent parts may be stated as follows: (1) Jesus Christ, in his life, death, and abiding personal influence. (2) The Jewish environment of Jesus and the earliest Christians—with special reference to the Old Testament conceptions of God, Man, the Messiah, and to the Jewish Law. On a broad survey of the history of Christianity, it may be said that, whenever personal religion and personal conviction of sin have predominated, or when a reaction against dogmatic theology and the domination of ecclesiastical organization has taken place, a tendency to emphasize the Jewish factor of personal relation to God, or to return to God's revelation of himself in Jesus, or to cling to both of these, has manifested itself. (3) Greek, Graeco-Jewish, and Neo-Platonic philosophy. During periods of theological controversy, especially controversy concerning the person of Christ (cf. CHRISTOLOGY), or concerning God's relation to the world and man, this element has commonly exercised sway. (4) Roman polity. The Latin, Greek, and Anglican Churches are organizations modelled upon the Roman empire. In pre-Reformation history the influence of the Roman or quasi-political element determined the external organization of the Church, and furnished an ideal, the realization of which was expected to result in the erection of the kingdom of God upon earth. (5) The peculiar national consciousness, or racial tendency, of the various people who came to be Christianized. This has expressed itself mainly by evincing strong affinity for one or other of the elements already noted; e. g. Latins and Celts for the Roman element; Teutons for the Jewish element; mystics—who appeared chiefly among the Teutonic stock—for the Greek element, which allows free play for personal and intellectual preferences. At the present time a new movement is in progress, particularly among the peoples of the Teutonic stock. They are deserting the individualism which has characterized them since the Reformation, and are beginning to emphasize the social side of Christianity—which, in the course of history, has been associated with the Roman element—yet without using the Roman polity, and drawing for motive force, not so much upon ecclesiastical organization, as upon the conviction of personal relation to Jesus, and the necessity for living his life here and now.

Literature: see CHRIST, CHRISTOLOGY; GORE (editor), Lux Mundi; E. CAIRD, Evolution of Religion; JULIA WEDGWOOD, The Moral Ideal; O. PFLEIDERER, Philos. and Devel. of Religion; ULLMANN, Reformers before the Reformation (Eng. trans.); WENLEY, Preparation for Christianity (an elementary outline). (R.M.W.)

Christology [Gr. χριστός, anointed, + λόγος, discourse]: Ger. *Christologie*; Fr. *Christologie*; Ital. *Cristologia*. The name given to the various doctrines, for the most part systematic or theologico-philosophical, concerning the Person of Christ. The subject is dominated by the problems which necessarily arise in connection with the coexistence of two natures in a single personality.

Christology in the strict sense cannot be said to have existed till after the formulation of the doctrine of Christ's exaltation to the right hand of God. And, notwithstanding its general harmoniousness, the teaching of the New Testament on the subject implies important questions not yet capable of clear statement, and therefore still unanswerable. They are connected chiefly with the part played in the minds of the earliest disciples and of the New Testament writers by the Jewish conception of Messiah. At the same time, it is undeniable that, if taken for what they bear on the face of them, the New Testament declarations, particularly those of the Pauline epistles, contain the suggestions, and even the formulated propositions, which later writers have no more than elaborated from different points of view and with additional aids.

After the 1st century Christology follows certain lines of development, which can be traced with sufficient clearness, notwithstanding the extraordinary clash of opinions prior to the great Councils of the Church.

(1) The period prior to the Arian controversy, say 100–325 A. D. Leading theories of this stage are: (*a*) EBIONISM (q.v.); a Jewish theory, exclusively humanitarian in doctrine, and denying the Virgin birth, and, therefore, the Incarnation. (*b*) GNOSTICISM (q.v.); a pagan and theosophical theory, characterized by evaporation of the human element in Christ's nature, which was treated as a phantasm; hence the name DOCETISM (q.v.) often applied to this doctrine. Variations of the theory are to be found in the speculations of the Basilidians, to whom Christ became divine at the moment of baptism; and of the Valentinians, who viewed the Virgin merely as Christ's means of entrance into the world. (*c*) The Alogi and the followers of Artemon, who are essentially Unitarians, or who at the most admit no more than the energizing of a divine principle or power in Christ. (*d*) The Patripassians of the Western and the Sabellians of the Eastern Roman world. The former merged the divinity of Christ in God by teaching that the 'same God is at once Father and Son,' a view which led to the inference that God himself had been crucified. The Sabellians taught a triple aspect theory; Father, Son, and Holy Ghost are modes in which the original divine substance is manifested. The characteristic result is a denial of Christ's personality, and this is summed up in the theory of Paul of Samosata, which leads to a sharp distinction between the Logos and the man Jesus. In all these schemes the influence of Greek, particularly Neo-Platonic, speculations operated powerfully. (*e*) The same may be said of the Christological speculations of the Apostolic Fathers: Justin Martyr, Clement of Alexandria, Origen, Irenaeus, Tertullian, and Dionysius. Of these Origen is the most important. Although he holds the eternal generation of the Son from the substance of the Father, he is affected by Docetism, and also by the tendency to subordinate Christ to God. Although he is the first to employ the term 'God-man,' there can be no doubt that the problems—even the 'heresies'—raised by the Arian controversy lie embedded in his teaching. Cf. PATRISTIC PHILOSOPHY.

(2) The Christology which resulted in the

Nicene Symbol, 325–81 A.D. The principal theory of this period is that associated with the name of Arius, who held the presence of both natures in Christ. Christ, although he existed before the world, was created at a definite time by a specific act of God's will. Consequently he must be subordinate to God, and of a different substance or essence. The semi-Arians, while denying unity of essence, and not going so far as to inculcate the Arian HETERO-OUSIA (q.v.), proposed the doctrine of similarity of substance, a theory that at least possessed the advantage of adaptability. The orthodox Christology, formulated in opposition to these 'heresies,' is summed up in the Nicene Creed, which teaches that Christ is begotten, not made, and that he is of one substance with the Father.

(3) The Christology which resulted in the Symbol of Chalcedon, 381–451 A.D. The issues of the Arian controversy retained vitality for years, and new departures from the conciliar dogmas emerged. These are chiefly: (a) APOLLINARIANISM (q.v.), which taught that, while Christ possessed a human body, he had no rational soul, the place of this being occupied by the Logos. Not being truly human, his whole redemptive work was held by this teaching to be vitiated. (b) NESTORIANISM (q.v.), by which the two natures are placed side by side in external juxtaposition, and without vital intercommunion. This has proved one of the most persistent views. (c) EUTYCHIANISM (q.v.), according to which the human nature is submerged or completely informed and transformed by the divine. The fully elaborated Christology of the Church was formulated by the Council of Chalcedon in opposition to these 'heretical' views; and, as this creed is not so well known, it may be worth while to quote the essential part: 'We all with one voice confess our Lord Jesus Christ one and the same Son, the same perfect in Godhead, the same perfect in Manhood, very God and very Man, the same consisting of a reasonable soul and a body, of one substance with the Father as touching the Godhead, the same of one substance with us as touching the Manhood, like us in all things, sin except; begotten of the Father before the worlds as touching the Godhead, the same in these last days, for us and our salvation, born of the Virgin Mary, the Mother of God, as touching the Manhood, one and the same Christ, Son, Lord, Only-begotten, to be acknowledged of two natures, without confusion, without conversion, without division, never to be separated; the distinction of natures being in no wise done away because of the union, but rather the characteristic property of each nature being preserved, and concurring into one person and one substance, not as if Christ were parted or divided into two persons, but one and the same Son and only-begotten God, Word, Lord, Jesus Christ.'

(4) Christology till the Third Council of Constantinople, 689 A.D. (a) The Monophysitic 'heresy' in the Eastern Church. This was a recrudescence of Eutychianism. Christ has but one nature in which the human element is a contingent quality of the divine. The watchword of the MONOPHYSITES (q.v.) —God has been crucified—led to their being called also Theopaschites. This Christology still obtains to-day in some of the smaller Christian Churches, notably the Abyssinian and Armenian. (b) MONOTHELITISM (q.v.), in which the controversy shifted from Neo-Platonic to semi-psychological ground. The Monothelites maintained that, as Christ is one person, so he must have but one will; this, as against the doctrine of the Church, that he has two co-operating wills—a human and a divine. The Third Council of Constantinople re-affirmed the formula of Chalcedon, and added a supplementary article 'preaching two natural wills and two natural operations.' From this time till the Reformation Christology practically stood fast on conciliar foundations; and it is worthy of note that the conciliar deliverances constitute the official Christology to-day in all the main branches of Christendom. A factual incarnation; two natures, supernaturally joined in one person, and this for the execution of a definite aim, otherwise impracticable; these sum up the teaching.

(5) Christology of Protestantism. Seeing that the Reformation was much more an ecclesiastico-political than a doctrinal change, Christology remained unaltered in essentials. Nevertheless, the new freedom and the spirit of the age let loose inquiry. (a) On the whole, Lutheran Christology exhibits some tendencies divergent from those of the Reformed Churches. The former lead to the emphasis of the divine nature of Christ rather than the human; the latter tend to separation of the two natures. The problem of the relation between the divine and the human element in Christ was thus raised once more, and a fresh discussion of the COMMUNICATIO IDIOMATUM (q.v.) took place. (b) Early in the 17th century the famous Kenosis *versus*

Krypsis controversy arose between the theologians of Giessen and Tübingen, and with this Protestant Christology, strictly so called, may be said to close. This discussion related essentially to Christ's use of his divine powers during the period of his HUMILIATION (q.v.). Both schools agreed in attributing the possession of these powers to him. The Giessen Kenotists held that he abstained from exercising them. The Tübingen Kryptics urged that he employed them secretly. Although it had little influence at the time, this controversy, especially on the Kenotic side, still exists.

(6) Recent and contemporary Christology. In the 19th century Christology has been profoundly affected by philosophical considerations, and particularly by the great German systems of the Kantian school. (a) Kant himself, so far as he retained elements of the 18th century rationalism, favoured a Unitarian standpoint, according to which Christ's divinity is an effect, not a precondition, of his life. (b) According to the Hegelian teaching, the divine and the human are different, not in kind, but only in degree; and therefore Christ differs in degree from other men; there is a greater fullness of the divine in him. (c) Schleiermacher, who approached the problem from the theological rather than the philosophical side, still retains humanitarian tendencies derived from the philosophical theologians, but finds in Christ's sinlessness a peculiar manifestation of deity, one not to be found in any other human being. (d) The most enlivening view of the middle of the 19th century was that of Richard Rothe, who departed from the formula of Chalcedon, and emphasized, as against Christ's two natures, his ethical personality. Christ came to be God by his life, passion, and death. This doctrine is, on the whole, possibly the most consonant with modern speculative thought. In the United States, Horace Bushnell adopted a view not very dissimilar. (e) More recently the Kenotic theory has had many representatives, of whom Delitzsch, Kahnis, Martensen, Lange, Godet, and Howard Crosby are the best known. The essential features of this Christology lie in the abandonment of the double will theory, approved by the Third Constantinople Council, and the substitution of a single will. Christ is held to have given up his divine attributes in the period between birth and resurrection. In other words, the human nature communicates its attributes to the divine; as to the precise extent of this

communication there is, of course, much divergence of opinion between the various Kenotists. (f) Dorner, who, like some of the Calvinists, has criticized the Kenotists severely, promulgates the idea of a progressive divinization of Christ, a conception which several of the Christocentric theologians accept. Christ became more and more divine as his humanity expanded, for only as his humanity grew could he be the vehicle of the Logos. For the last few years attention has been directed more to the investigation of the historical circumstances of Christ's life than to systematic theorizing about his nature. This is consonant with certain dominant theological tendencies, especially those formulated by the school of Ritschl.

Literature: see CHRIST. The authoritative work for the whole subject is DORNER, Doctrine of the Person of Christ (Eng. trans.). WEIZSÄCKER, Apostolic Age (Eng. trans.); BEYSCHLAG, Christ. d. N. T., and New Testament Theol. (Eng. trans.); F. C. BAUR, Die christl. Lehre v. d. Dreieinigkeit u. Menschwerdung Gottes in ihrer geschichtl. Entwickelung; HARNACK, Hist. of Dogma (Eng. trans.); NITZSCH, Dogmengeschichte; SCHNECKENBURGER, Zur kirchlichen Christol.; H. SCHULTZ, Die Lehre v. d. Gottheit Christi; art. Kenotiker u. Kryptiker in Herzog's Real-Encyc.; KANT, Religion within the Limits of Pure Reason (Eng. trans.); A. COQUEREL, Christologie; MARTINEAU, Seat of Authority in Religion; BIEDERMANN, Christl. Dogmatik; MATHESON, Aids to the Study of German Theology (for Hegelian view of Trinity); SCHLEIERMACHER, Der christl. Glaube; R. ROTHE, Dogmatik; DELITZSCH, Bib. Psychol. (Eng. trans.); MARTENSEN, Christl. Dogmatik; BRUCE, The Humiliation of Christ; F. J. HALL, The Kenotic Theory. For a recent destructive view of the early history see BRANDT, Die evangelische Gesch. u. d. Ursprung d. Christenthums; *contra* see SWETE, The Apostles' Creed; FAIRBAIRN, Christ in Modern Theol.; and in the Expositor, 1895 (with special reference to philosophy of religion); and his forthcoming work, The Person of Christ and Philos. of Religion; POWELL, The Principle of the Incarnation.　　　　　(R.M.W.)

Christophany [Gr. ὁ Χριστός, the anointed, + φαίνειν, to appear]: Ger. *Christophania*; Fr. *Christophanie*; Ital. *Apparizioni di Cristo*. The name given to the appearances of Christ to men after the Resurrection.

Setting faith aside, the narratives of the

Gospel writers and of Paul raise two problems: (1) What are the historical facts now ascertainable? (2) Were the appearances of a perfectly natural or physical character, or were they in marked ways abnormal or spiritual?

(1) The evidence warrants these historical conclusions: (*a*) As Schenkel points out, Christ appeared only to his faithful followers, none of his persecutors saw him. (*b*) Devoted disciples were persuaded that he had appeared to them soon after the Crucifixion. (*c*) The precise order of these incidents and their exact number cannot now be known historically. (*d*) The incidents connected with the recorded manifestations show that Christ appeared in his 'heavenly,' not in his 'earthly' body. (*e*) The manifestation to Paul was 'heavenly.' These conclusions lead to the following:—

(2) The Christophanies do not require, but, on the contrary, tend to exclude a conception of the Resurrection as a physical reanimation of the fleshly body. In a word, history cannot help faith to a bodily Christophany.

No doubt, the question may be considered from the standpoint of system rather than of history. In this case the problem may be put thus: Were the appearances subjective hallucinations, as Strauss, Renan, and Holsten hold; or were they objectively real, as Ewald, Weisse, and Hanne contend? But a decision as between these views would seem to involve an appeal to history.

Literature: HASE, Gesch. Jesu; the Lives of Jesus, by STRAUSS, NEANDER, SCHENKEL (all Eng. trans.), WITTICHEN, EWALD, PRESSENSÉ; MILLIGAN, The Resurrection; KEIM, Jesus of Nazareth, vi (Eng. trans.); v. HOFMANN, Die Lehre v. d. Person Christi; HARNACK, Hist. of Dogma, i. 85 *n*. (Eng. trans.); WEIZSÄCKER, Apostolic Age, i. 7 f. (Eng. trans.). (R.M.W.)

Chroma [Gr. χρῶμα, colour]: Ger. (1) *Vorzeichen*; (2) *Halbton, halber Ton*; (3) *Achtel*; Fr. (1) *signe de dièse* (*de bémol*, flat; *de bécarre*, sharp). (2) *demi-ton*, (3) *croche*; Ital. (1) *croma* (*diesis*, sharp; *bemolle*, flat), (2) *semituono*, (3) *croma*. (1) The sign (or) which denotes the raising or lowering of a note by a musical semitone. (2) A semitone. (3) An eighth note or quaver (more usually spelled *croma*). Cf. Stainer and Barrett, *Dict. of Musical Terms*, 22. (E.B.T.)

Chromaesthesia: [χρῶμα, colour, + αἴσθησις, perception]: Ger. *Chromaesthesie*; Fr. *chromesthésie, audition colorée*; Ital. *cromestesia*. A vivid association of colours with words, letters, sounds, &c.

These colours are thought of, or even seen, in space, when the letters are seen or the sounds heard. It forms one important instance of SYNAESTHESIA (q. v.). (J.J.)

Chromatic Aberration: see ABERRATION.

Chromatics [Gr. χρωματικός, relating to colour]: Ger. (1) *Farbenlehre*, (2) *chromatische Tonlehre*; Fr. *chromatique*; Ital. *cromatica*. (1) The science of colour. The term should properly be limited to colour as a function of light, but it is often applied to colour-sensation effects. Cf. VISION. (J.M.B.)

(2) Scales or series of notes including the black keys of the piano, or sharps and flats on the staff; they run in the scale of twelve semitones. Cf. Parry, art. Chromatic, in Grove's *Dict. of Music and Musicians*, i. 355 (1879). (E.B.T.)

Chromatopseudopsis [Gr. χρῶμα, colour, + ψευδής, false, + ὄψις, vision]: Ger. *Chromatopseudopsis*; Fr. *achromatopsie*; Ital. *cromatopseudopsia*. Abnormal colour perception; COLOUR-BLINDNESS (q. v.). (J.J.)

Chromatopsia [Gr. χρῶμα, colour, + ὄψις, vision]: Ger. *Chromatopsie*; Fr. *sensation anormale de couleur*; Ital. *cromatopsia*. An abnormal colour sensation; such as the yellow appearance of objects after a dose of santonin; also called Chromopsia, Chroöpsia. See VISION (defects of). (J.J.)

Chromatoscope: see LABORATORY AND APPARATUS, B, (*a*), (3).

Chromosome [Gr. χρῶμα, colour, + σῶμα, body]: Ger. *Schleifen*; Fr. *chromosome* (preferred), *bâtonnet*; Ital. *cromosoma*. One of the deeply staining bodies in the nucleus of the cell during the process of division.

The term was first used by Waldeyer in 1888. The chromosomes are of special interest as the biological units which, as observation shows, play an important part in the division of cells, and especially in FERTILIZATION (q. v.) and the changes which follow thereon. They originate from the nuclear network of the cell, and vary in number from 2 to 168. Every species of animal and plant has a fixed number; in all organisms which arise by sexual reproduction the number is even; and in the majority of observed cases, in the cells which unite in fertilization, the number of chromosomes is one-half that which is characteristic of the tissue-cells of the species. In division they split longitudinally, half of each passing into each of the two daughter nuclei. In the later stages of the development of ova and spermatozoa they in some cases give rise to tetrads and dyads. (C.LL.M.)

Literature: VAN BENEDEN, Recherches sur la maturation de l'œuf, Arch. de Biol., iv (1883); E. B. WILSON, The Cell in Devel. and Inheritance (1896); M. FLEMMING, Beiträge zur Kenntniss der Zelle, Arch. f. mikr. Anat. (1879–82).　　　　　　(C.LL.M.–E.S.G.)

Chronic (1), and **Acute** (2) [Gr. χρονικός, relating to time; Lat. *acutus*, sharp]: Ger. (1) *chronisch*, (2) *akut*; Fr. (1) *chronique*, (2) *aigu*; Ital. (1) *cronico*, (2) *acuto*. These terms are used in reference to diseases to distinguish those which are of long duration, slow progress, and gradual onset, from those which appear somewhat suddenly, progress rapidly, and continue for only a brief time.

No definite period applicable to all cases can be assigned to differentiate the one from the other, but in many cases the differentiation is easily made (compare the distinctions between chronic and acute mania under MANIA). The term subacute is used to refer to diseases intermediate in character between the chronic and the acute, and is more akin to the latter. Acute is also used with reference to symptoms, such as pain, of an extreme and pronounced character.　　　　　　(J.J.)

Chronometry (mental): see MEASUREMENT, and REACTION TIME.

Chronoscope, Chronograph, and **Chronometer**: see LABORATORY AND APPARATUS, III, C (1).

Chrysalis [Gr. χρυσός, gold]: Ger. *Puppe, Goldpuppe*; Fr. *chrysalide*; Ital. *ninfa, crisalide*. A term introduced by Lamarck for the complete or obtected pupa of flies, butterflies, and moths; so called from the golden glance on the pupae of many species of butterflies. The term was used by Aristotle.

Literature: PACKARD, Textbook of Entomol.; SCUDDER, Butterflies of New England; KIRBY and SPENCE, Entomol.; D. SHARP, Cambridge Nat. Hist., Insects, Pts. I, II (1895–9).　　　　　　(C.S.M.–E.B.P.)

Chrysippus. (cir. 280–207 B.C.) Born in Cilicia and died at Athens. A Greek follower of Cleanthes, the Stoic. He is said to have died laughing at seeing an ass eating his own supper of figs.

Chubb, Thomas. (1679–1747.) An English glove-maker and tallow-chandler, who taught himself with remarkable success, and wrote several valuable works from a deistic point of view.

Church [Gr. τὸ κυριακόν, the Lord's House]: Ger. *Kirche*; Fr. *église*; Ital. *Chiesa*. Church has several meanings. (1) The root-meaning: a place of worship, a building. (2) A local congregation. (3) An organization of local congregations, either territorial (like the Presbyterian Church of the South in the United States); or national (like the Church of Scotland); or imperial (like the Anglican Church); or international (like the Roman Catholic Church). (4) The ideal church, or church universal; the church to whose members, whether in ecclesiastical connection or not, the saying 'theirs is the kingdom of heaven' may be applied.

For philosophy of religion, the principal subject of interest is the relation of the church, in this last sense, to the KINGDOM OF GOD (q. v.).

Literature: SOHM, Kirchenrecht; the Church Histories of NEANDER, BAUR, THIERSCH, and MÖLLER (all in Eng. trans.); HORT, Christian Ecclesia; McGIFFERT, Apostolic Age; HARNACK, Hist. of Dogma (Eng. trans.); PFLEIDERER, Philos. of Religion, iii. chap. iv. (Eng. trans.). For the recent Ritschlian view of the kingdom of God, see A. RITSCHL, Die christl. Lehre v. d. Rechtfertigung u. Versöhnung; KAFTAN, Truth of the Christian Religion (Eng. trans.); J. WEISS, Die Predigt Jesu v. Reiche Gottes; H. H. WENDT, The Teaching of Jesus (Eng. trans.); WAGENER, A. Ritschl's Idee d. Reiches Gottes im Lichte d. Gesch.; GARVIE, The Ritschlian Theol.　　　　　　(R.M.W.)

Church and State: Ger. *Kirche und Staat*; Fr. *l'église et l'état*; Ital. *Chiesa e Stato*. The relation between a state and the church, or churches, to which its people belong.

Until modern times, some kind of religious establishment has been deemed an essential part of the constitution of every sovereign state. The constitution of the United States forbids such an establishment for the United States, but not for the states. Connecticut retained one until 1818.

That the United States are to be regarded as a Christian nation, see Church of the Holy Trinity *v.* United States, 143 United States Reports, 437, 471. The Church of England is not a corporation by itself, but a part of the government of England; its Thirty-Nine Articles of faith having for its adherents the authority of law, and the civil courts having the ultimate decision of cases of ecclesiastical discipline for heresy.

Literature: MONTESQUIEU, Esprit des Lois, iii., Liv. 24 and 25; W. E. GLADSTONE, The State in its Relations with the Church (1838–41), and The Irish Church (1869).　　(S.E.B.)

Church Philosophy (Roman Catholic): see St. Thomas (philosophy of).

Cicero, Marcus Tullius. (106–43 B.C.) A distinguished orator, statesman, and philosopher of Rome, born at Arpinum, and murdered near Formiae, in Italy. He was liberally educated, studying Greek under Archias, the poet. He took deep interest in Greek literature and philosophy. About 90 B.C. he began the study of law under Mucius Scaevola. After travelling through Asia Minor, he returned to Rome in 77 B.C., in restored health. In 75 B.C. he became quaestor and was assigned to Sicily; in 69, aedile; in 66, praetor; in 63, consul with C. Antonius; in 62 he declined the governorship of a province and returned to the senate as a private individual; in 58 he went into exile, and his elegant house on the Palatine Hill was burned by Clodius; in 55 he was restored by the senate and people, being received with every demonstration of popular favour; in 52 he acted as proconsul of Cilicia and Pisidia for one year. He joined the army of Pompey against Caesar, but was kindly treated afterwards by Caesar at Rome.

Cicero approved the assassination of Caesar and denounced Mark Antony. The republican cause was lost in the coalition of Octavius with Antony and Lepidus. Cicero was proscribed, and killed by soldiers of Octavius.

Circular [Lat. *circulus*, a circle]: Ger. *circulär, kreisförmig*; Fr. *circulaire*; Ital. *circolare*. Used in certain connections in neurology and pathology to mean self-sustaining or self-repeating: e.g. 'circular process,' as respiration; 'circular reaction,' one whose muscular movement is itself a stimulus, through sight or another sense, to its own repetition; 'circular insanity.'

The theory of the 'circular reaction' has been developed in connection with Imitation (q.v.).

Literature: Pflüger, Teleol. Mechanik d. leben. Natur, in Pflüger's Arch., xv (1877); Baldwin, Ment. Devel. in the Child and the Race, chap. ii; Groos, The Play of Animals (Eng. trans.), Index. (J.M.B.)

Circulating Capital: Ger. *flüssiges Kapital*; Fr. *capitaux circulants*; Ital. *capitale circolante*. (1) 'That portion of stock employed with a view to profit which does not yield such profit till it is parted with' (Malthus). (2) 'That which fulfils the whole of its office in the production in which it is engaged by a single use' (Mill). In general, subsistence and materials, as distinct from tools and buildings.

Malthus, following Adam Smith, defined circulating capital by its private relations to the owner. Mill, following Ricardo, defined it by its relations to the technique of production. The latter method is now in general use. Cf. Fixed Capital. (A.T.H.)

Circulation: Ger. *Geldumlauf*; Fr. *circulation*; Ital. *circolazione*. (1) The total amount of means of exchange circulating from hand to hand—coin and notes, but not cheques—better known as Currency (q.v.). (2) The total volume of transactions effected directly or indirectly by the use of money in a given period.

The development of the second and more important meaning is due to Newcomb. Economic quantities, says Newcomb (*Principles of Political Economy*), are of two kinds: funds and flows. A fund is a quantity or value pure and simple; a flow is so many dollars per hour, day, or year. The volume of the currency is a fund; the monetary circulation is a flow. If V represents the volume of currency, R the rapidity of its movements (i.e. the average number of times a dollar changes hands in the course of a year), and F the year's flow of currency, or monetary circulation, then $F = V \times R$. Newcomb further points out that this flow of money from buyers to sellers is compensated by an equivalent flow of goods from sellers to buyers, which he calls the industrial circulation, and draws important consequences from the necessary equality of the two. (A.T.H.)

Circulus in Probando [Lat.]: Ger. *Cirkelbeweis*; Fr. (Lat. form), *cercle vicieux*; Ital. *circolo vizioso*. Otherwise called *circular reasoning*, or *argument in a circle*; a form of the Fallacy of *Petitio Principii*, generally exhibited in a chain of consecutive reasonings, and consisting in the use as a premise of either the final conclusion to be established or of a proposition which is logically dependent for justification on that conclusion.

Literature: Whately, Logic, Bk. III. § 13; Mill, Logic, Bk. V. chap. vii. § 2. (R.A.)

Cistercian: Ger. *Cisterzienser*; Fr. *Cistercien*; Ital. *Cistercensi*. One of the monastic orders; founded by St. Bernard at Citeaux, in Burgundy, in 1098.

The Cistercian order is important in the history of Scholasticism (q.v.) and Mysticism (q.v.), on account of St. Bernard's connection with it. It becomes prominent again in the later history of thought, because Port Royal was one of its offshoots.

Literature: de Burgen, Annales Cistercienses; NEWMAN, Hist. of the Cistercian Order; JANAUSCHEK, Origines Cistercienses. See JANSENISM, MYSTICISM, SCHOLASTICISM.

(R.M.W.)

Citizen [ME. *citezein*, from Lat. *civitas*, a state]: Ger. *Bürger*; Fr. *citoyen*; Ital. *borghese*, *cittadino*. Originally any person enjoying municipal rights in a city; subsequently used to signify (1) a mere inhabitant of a city, or (2) a person enjoying political rights in a sovereign STATE (q. v.) (F.C.M.)

Civil (in law) [Lat. *civilis*]: Ger. *bürgerlich*; Fr. *civil*; Ital. *civile*. (1) Pertaining to the state. (2) Pertaining to the ordinary dealings of a state with its citizens, as distinguished from its dealings with them as to military, naval, criminal, or ecclesiastical affairs. (3) Pertaining to a state with respect to its citizens, as distinguished from its relations to foreign powers; as in civil war. Civil death, death in the eye of the law; terminating a man's existence, so far as the recognition and protection of the state is concerned, in the relation of the citizen. It may result from a sentence to imprisonment for life, or from taking perpetual monastic vows, under the laws of some states. (S.E.B.)

Civil Law: Ger. *Civilrecht*, *bürgerliches Recht*, *Römisches Recht*; Fr. *droit civil*; Ital. *diritto civile*. (1) The law of a particular state. (2) That part of the law of a particular state pertaining to civil affairs. (3) The law of ancient Rome (see CODE). (4) The law of modern Europe built upon the Roman civil law, as distinguished from that based on local customary law.

'Quod quisque populus ipse sibi ius constituit, id ipsius proprium civitatis est, vocaturque ius civile' (Just., *Instit.*, I. ii. 1). (S.E.B.)

Clairvoyance: Ger. *Hellsichtigkeit*, *Hellsehkunst*, to see across; Fr. *clairvoyance*, *lucidité*; Ital. *chiaroveggenza*. The alleged ability, by use of a peculiar faculty, to see things not normally visible at all, or things at a great distance.

Belief in this or in similar powers has existed from ancient times (cf. MAGIC), but has become specially prominent in several connections. Of modern instances may be mentioned (1) its connection with the doctrine revived by the successors of Mesmer, early in the present century, that persons in the mesmeric state, called somnambules, were able to see the internal structure of diseased organs and thus prescribe remedies. The doctrine was soon extended to the ability to read with closed eyes, to see events happening at a distance,

and the like. In this connection it was taken up (2) by modern phrenology, and especially by modern spiritualism, mediums frequently claiming clairvoyant power. It may also be mentioned that as a conjuring performance (second-sight), clairvoyance depends upon the rapid and skilful interpretation of an ingenious system of signals. When submitted to rigid scientific tests, no evidence of the reality of such a power is obtainable. A similar alleged power, in which the ear is the medium, is termed clairaudience. The further history of clairvoyance may be traced in the histories of spiritualism, hypnotism, and mesmerism, and the older forms of divination. (J.J.)

Literature: OCHOROWICZ, De la suggestion mentale (1887, Eng. trans.); A. LANG, Cock Lane and Common Sense, and The Making of Religion; the Proc. Soc. Psych. Res., vii. 30, 356 ff., and Ann. d. Sci. Psych., i. ff. (L.M.)

Clan [Gael. *clann*, offspring, family, stock]: Ger. *Sippe* (*Stamm*, given in dictionaries as equivalent to clan, is inaccurate); Fr. *clan*; Ital. *clan*. A body of kindred larger than a household and smaller than a tribe, and recognizing relationship in one line of descent —through the father or through the mother, but never through both.

Largely through the influence of J. W. Powell and the *Reports of the U. S. Bureau of Ethnology*, the word 'clan,' which originally, in English usage, meant specifically the kinship organizations of the Scotch Highlanders, has by general consent been adopted in ethnology and sociology as the generic name for all kinship organizations, metronymic or patronymic—special names for special examples of which are the Greek γένος, the Roman *gens*, the Arabic *hayy*, the Irish *sept*, and the North American (Algonkin) *otem* (*totem*). (F.H.G.)

Clanberg, Johann. (1622–65.) A German Cartesian, born in Westphalia, and educated at Gröningen under Andreae, and at Leyden under Raey. He taught at Herborn and Duisburg. In one of his works he defends his master against Revius and Lentulus. He anticipates in his writings some of the later developed doctrines of the Cartesian school.

Clang [Gr. κλαγγή]: Ger. *Klang*; Fr. *son*; Ital. *suono*. (1) The simple clang is often identified with the simple TONE (q. v.). Strictly, the term designates a musical note or compound tone; the complex of fundamental tone and overtones.

(2) A compound clang is a mixture of simple clangs, i. e. a concord or a discord.

(3) Both these uses are to be distinguished from the popular use, which restricts the word 'clang' to the metallic clangs of cymbals, trumpet, &c.　　　　(E.B.T.)

Although the substitution of the term clang is favoured by E.B.T. and C.L.F., the other psychologists of the DICTIONARY favour keeping the established term tone (simple and compound), the term compound tone being equivalent to clang as defined above. If the term clang is to be both 'simple' and 'compound,' there seems to be no gain in substituting it for simple and compound tone. It is just as easy to say compound tone as simple clang, when a musical note of tone and overtones is meant. The text of this work therefore follows the established usage.　　(J.M.B., E.C.S., J.MᶜK.C., G.F.S., J.J.)

Clarke, Samuel. (1675–1729.) An English theologian and philosopher, born at Norwich and educated at Cambridge. Delivered the Boyle Lectures in 1704 and 1705. In 1706 he became chaplain to Queen Anne, and in 1709 rector of St. James', Westminster, London. In correspondence with Leibnitz he defended the Newtonian philosophy.

Class [Lat. *classis*]: Ger. *Klasse*; Fr. *classe*; Ital. *classe*. The indefinite number of individual objects or cases characterized by the possession by each of a certain quantum of definite marks. The class, for logical purposes, is a wider and more arbitrary notion than the class as recognized in special scientific researches.　　　　(R.A.)

Class (social): Ger. (*sociale*) *Klasse*; Fr. *classe* (*sociale*); Ital. (1) *classe* (*sociale*), (2) *ceto* (*medio*, &c.). (1) A group distinguished from other groups by personal or social differences of a permanent sort, which produce variations in social intercourse; e. g. the criminal class, the working, leisure, professional, &c., classes. This meaning alone has value for social science, as it does not stop with mere logical classification, but indicates actual social results following upon the differences.

(2) Social distinctions of higher and lower, the differences between classes being those of colour, birth, wealth, education, or other quality, which is recognized as socially desirable, as in the expressions 'class distinctions,' 'classes and masses,' and as is seen in the classes produced by CASTE (q. v.). (J.M.B.)

Classic and **Classicism**: see STYLE, and ROMANTICISM.

Classification [Lat. *classis*, class, +

facere, to make]: Ger. *Klassifikation*; Fr. *classification*; Ital. *classificazione*. The process of arranging the objects of some province of experience into kinds or groups, characterized by the possession of common marks.

As ordinarily defined, it involves more than logical DIVISION (q. v.), the rules of which furnish the minimal conditions of the process. In addition, classification takes into account (1) either the specific purpose of the arrangement, or (2) the natural conjunctions of marks which are of most importance. In either case, the aim of classification is to render possible the greatest number of general propositions regarding the objects, and so to facilitate the complete and systematic survey of them. The ideal of a classification that is not determined by special, human ends, as e. g. in classification of occupations in a census return, is to copy in its systematic arrangement the real order of interdependence in the things themselves. What is called 'artificial,' as opposed to natural classification, differs in degree only, not in kind.

Literature: MILL, Logic, Bk. IV. chaps. vii, viii; VENN, Empirical Logic, chap. xxx; JEVONS, Princ. of Sci., chap. xxx.　　(R.A.)

Classification (in biology): Ger. *Taxonomie*; Fr. *taxonomie*; Ital. *biotassi*. That branch of biological study which deals with the arrangement of living beings into groups. The term Taxonomy is also used. (C.LL.M.–J.M.B.)

The aim of modern classification is to group living organisms according to their phylogenetic affinities. A number of species having certain characters in common, presumably derived from an ancestral form, are grouped together into a genus; similarly, genera are grouped into families, families into orders, orders into classes, and classes into phyla. Each phylum represents one of the main branches of the animal or vegetable kingdom. The distinctive differences between these various groups (generic, family, ordinal characters, &c.) are of increasing magnitude; but according to evolutionary doctrine, they are all of essentially the same nature, and due to the accumulation of what were originally individual differences. Cf. SPECIES, and VARIETY.　　　　(E.C.S.)

Literature: an able account of the systems of classification of animals from Aristotle, through Linnaeus, to modern times is given by E. RAY LANKESTER in the 9th ed. of the Encyc. Brit., xxiv. 804 ff., further developed in The Adv. of Sci. (1890). See also

AGASSIZ, Essay on Classification; HUXLEY, art. Animal Kingdom, in Encyc. Brit. (9th ed.), ii; KÖRNER, Die logischen Grundlagen d. System. d. Organismen (1883, with the references there given to works in biological science). For botanical classification see J. REYNOLDS GREEN, Manual of Botany (based on that of BENTLEY), 1896. (C.LL.M.)

Classification (in education). The simplest form of generalization; the grouping of objects according to common characteristics. See FORMAL STEPS, ABSTRACTION, and METHOD (in education). (C.DE G.)

Classification (of the fine arts). A grouping or division of the fine arts.

Attempted on various principles. The more important are: (1) End, giving a division into free and dependent, or non-serviceable and serviceable (Aristotle). This, however, groups under the second class, not merely the 'fine art' architecture, but also most of the minor and industrial arts. (2) Form, according as the arts are those of space or of time, or appeal to eye or ear. This gives (a) arts of repose, or 'shaping,' formative (bildende) arts, and (b) arts of motion, or speaking (redende) arts (Lessing, Schasler, et al.). To (a) are usually assigned architecture, sculpture, painting; to (b) music, the mimic dance or acting, and poetry. Or a triple division gives (a) arts of the resting eye (same as above); (b) of ear only (music, poetry); (c) of motion in space appealing to eye, or to eye and ear (mimic dance, acted drama, &c.; Hartmann). (3) Relation of material employed to the ideal expressed, giving the ascending series: architecture, sculpture, painting, music, poetry. (4) Historic development, involving also the relation of content to material, giving (a) symbolic, (b) classic, and (c) romantic, whose respective characteristic arts are (a) architecture, (b) sculpture, (c) painting, music, and poetry (Hegel). (5) Relation to nature, giving imitative (painting, sculpture, epic, drama, mimic dance) and non-imitative (lyric, most music, architecture). Similar to this is Gurney's division into 'presentative' (music, architecture) and 'representative' (sculpture, painting, poetry), whereas Spencer by the same terms indicates a division into arts appealing (a) mainly to sensation and perception, and (b) to the imagination (literature). (6) Psychological motive or origin. Viewing the arts as derived from expression through cry or gesture gives a grouping like that of (2) above (Véron). A derivation from instincts of (a) imitation, (b) decoration, (c) self-exhibition, gives (a) imitative arts as under (5)

above; (b) decorative (architecture, landscape gardening, many minor arts); (c) self-exhibiting (lyric poetry, bodily decoration, the dance, as arousing or appealing to sexual or martial emotions, &c.; Gross). Some (Lange, Baldwin) would combine (b) and (c); others add still further instincts, as that of 'monument making' (Brown).

Aristotle's conception of 'imitation' (see ART AND ART THEORIES) as the essential characteristic of art excluded architecture from the list of arts whose function is to minister to enjoyment (as contrasted with the useful arts). The imitative arts (viz. poetry, music, the dance, sculpture, and painting) he characterizes as imitating (i. e. representing) either actions or character and feelings. As further principles of division, he mentions: (a) means (as colour, the voice, measure, rhythm, harmony); (b) objects represented (as superior or inferior persons in tragedy or comedy); (c) manner (as narration, &c.). Lessing, starting from the distinction of arts employing coexisting materials from those employing successive tones, distinguished the province of painting and formative art from that of poetry. Kant, using the principle of expression which is accomplished by man through word, mien or gesture, and tone, divides the arts into (a) arts of speech, viz. rhetoric and poetry; (b) formative arts, subdivided into arts of sensible truth (sculpture and architecture) and arts of sensible illusion (painting and landscape gardening); (c) arts of the play of sensations (music) and the art of colour. Herder made a genetic series, viz. building, gardening, dress, manly exercises and contests, language—corresponding to the progress of civilization. Schiller distinguishes the fine arts (arts of taste or intelligence) from the 'moving' or 'touching' (rührenden) arts (arts of the heart and sentiment), but does not assign the specific arts under these heads.

Schelling set up a 'real' and an 'ideal' series of arts. He regarded music as the 'most real' and painting as the 'most ideal' of the first series, and sculpture as the unity of these; while to the 'ideal series' belong the lyric, the epic, and the unity of these, viz. the drama.

Schleiermacher made three classes: (a) accompanying arts (the mimic dance, music); (b) formative arts; (c) poetry. Weisse took music, formative art, and poetry, and subdivided each into three. Hegel attempts to find a basis for the division into arts of form, sound, and speech, by referring these to eye, ear, and sensuous representation; but lays more stress on the division into symbolic, classic, and romantic art, in which the ideal of beauty is respectively 'striven for, attained, and transcended.' Herbart separates arts 'which display themselves on all sides,' viz. architecture, sculpture, church music, and classic poetry, from those which 'present something in half-obscure light,' viz. landscape gardening, painting, entertaining music, romantic poetry. Schopenhauer grades the arts according to the kinds of ideas which are objectified. The lowest grade objectifies only ideas belonging to inorganic nature, i. e. weight, rigidity, &c., giving architecture as its chief art. Ideas of vegetative nature give landscape gardening and landscape painting. Ideas of higher grades give successively painting of still life, historical painting, sculpture, and poetry. Music, as being 'the copy or expression, not of the ideas, but of the will itself,' is assigned a unique position as 'telling of essence, not of shadows.' Vischer's classification is similar to the first of Hegel's.

Schasler uses the antithesis between rest and motion as his principle of division, regarding it as fundamental to the other antitheses of 'material and form.'

Hartmann has an elaborate scheme based on several principles. Aside from certain lower activities not properly art, though anticipations of it, he distinguishes (a) unfree, and (b) simple and complex free arts. Both the unfree and the simple free arts are next subdivided as belonging either to perception or reproductive fancy, and those of perception again into those of the resting eye, of the ear alone, and of motion apprehended by the eye, or by eye and ear. This gives: (a) as unfree arts of the resting eye, architecture and other constructive arts (gardening and cosmetic); as unfree arts of the eye in motion, games, gymnastics, social dance, &c.; and as unfree arts of reproductive fancy, or speech, eloquence in all its forms. (b) The simple free arts of perception: (1) of space (sculpture and painting); (2) of time (instrumental music, songs without words); (3) space-time arts (various kinds of mimic dance, acting, &c.). Poetry is the simple free art of reproductive imagination, but numerous subdivisions are made. Finally, binary, ternary, and quaternary combinations give the complex arts, such as the ballet, opera, &c.

Other writers attempt a classification based on psychological motives, like (6) above, of which the threefold division is that given by Groos, carrying out his classifications of plays. Lange offers a division into (a) arts on a purely instinctive basis growing out of movement and building plays and self-decoration, viz. dance, lyric music, architecture, ornamentation; (b) arts on the basis of conscious semblance or 'make-believe,' growing out of make-believe and imitative plays, viz. acting, the drama, epic, sculpture, painting.

In France Lévêque adopted the series given under (3) above, adding eloquence as a sixth, though not in the strict sense a fine art. Véron groups the six arts as under (2) and (3) above, deriving the two groups from the two modes of expression, cry and gesture, the production of sounds and of forms. All arts are thus differentiations of spoken or written (sign) language, the one group characterized by motion and rhythm, the other by order and proportion.

English writers have given little attention to classifications of the arts. Spencer suggests a division, on the basis of the nature of the states of consciousness involved, into presentative arts (appealing to sensation and perception chiefly) and representative art—the latter term reserved for literature of the imagination. Gurney uses the same terms 'presentative' and 'representative' for his main division, but gives to 'representative' the meaning 'imitative,' and classes music and architecture under the first; sculpture, painting, and poetry under the second. Further distinguishing marks are specified under the heads of subject-matter, material, and form. Colvin (in *Encyc. Brit.*, art. Fine Arts) considers each of the above divisions (1), (2), and (5) as useful for certain purposes. G. Baldwin Brown, while dealing only with 'arts of form,' traces them to a greater number of psychological springs than others, and emphasizes especially their festal origin. J. Mark Baldwin would correlate the decorative and imitative arts respectively with the self-exhibiting and imitative instincts, giving the same division as Lange.

Literature: SCHASLER, Syst. d. Künste, (2nd ed., 1884), and more fully in Krit. Gesch. d. Aesth. (1872); VON HARTMANN, chapter on Die Eintheilung d. Künste, in Bk. II. Pt. I of his Aesthetik (1886); BOSANQUET, Hist. of Aesth. (1892); KNIGHT, Philos. of the Beautiful (1891–3); COLVIN, in Encyc. Brit., art. Fine Arts; GURNEY, The Power of Sound (1880); GROSSE, Die Anfänge d. Kunst (1894, Eng. trans. 1897); GROOS, The Play of Animals (1896, Eng.

trans. 1898); LANGE, in Zeitsch. f. Psychol., xiv. 242; BALDWIN BROWN, The Fine Arts (1891); BALDWIN, Social and Eth. Interpret. (1897).   (J.H.T.)

Classification (of the mental functions). Distinction of the fundamental constituents of every concrete state of consciousness.   (G.F.S.–J.M.B.)

Aristotle distinguishes between intellection and conation (νοῦς and ὄρεξις) as ultimate mental functions. This dual division is retained by psychological writers up to the time of Tetens and Mendelssohn. With these writers a threefold division begins—cognition, feeling, and conation or will. Feeling is here used in the sense of affective consciousness (cf. Tetens, *Ueber die menschliche Natur*, i. Versuch X. § 625, published 1777). The new classification was adopted by Kant. It has been prevalent ever since, and is very generally current at the present time. It was first clearly expounded and defined in English by Hamilton.

Of late there has been a tendency to revert to a dual division, but the functions regarded as ultimate are cognition and feeling, not cognition and conation. Brentano brings feeling under conation, thus going back to the Aristotelian point of view. But he adds as another ultimate function judgment or belief. He proposes, as a principle of division, the different modes in which consciousness may refer to an object, as being pleased with it, desiring it, remembering it. He urges that if we do not formulate the problem in this manner, we are compelled to treat as ultimate all contents of consciousness which have an unanalysable specific quality, and that it is an endless and useless task to enumerate and distinguish elements which are ultimate in this sense. But this difficulty seems to be met by treating as ultimate only those general modes which are necessary to constitute any and every concrete conscious state. At the same time it seems to the present writer that Brentano's method of formulating the problem supplies by far the most convenient starting-point for the psychologist. The drawback is that in it there is no allowance for the possibility of conscious experience without objective reference.

Literature: besides the authors mentioned, see textbooks generally; also JAMES WARD, art. Psychology, Encyc. Brit. (9th ed.), xx. 39–44; J. SULLY, The Human Mind, ii. Appendix I; STOUT, Analytic Psychol., i. Bk. I; HÖFFDING, Psychology, chap. iv; FOUILLÉE, La psychol. des idées-forces, Introd.;

LOTZE, Microcosmus (3rd ed.), i. Bk. II. chap. ii. §§ 1–5. For history see BRENTANO, Psychologie, Bk. II. chap. v; HAMILTON, Metaphysics, Lects. XI and XX; DROBISCH, Psychologie, §§ 123–38.   (G.F.S.)

Classification (of the sciences). The systematic arrangement of the various branches of knowledge or of positive science (cf. SCIENCE) in order to fix their definitions, determine their boundaries, bring to light their interrelations, and ascertain how much of the task of science has been accomplished and what remains to be done. The value of such a classification depends not merely on the encyclopaedic or didactic uses to which a survey of the sciences may be put, but also on its utility as an instrument of intellectual progress. Cf. PHILOSOPHY, BIOLOGICAL SCIENCES, MORAL SCIENCES, ANTHROPOLOGY, SOCIAL SCIENCES, PHYSICAL SCIENCE.

The most celebrated classifications of the sciences proposed in modern times have been those suggested by Bacon, Comte, and Spencer. Bacon adopted a subjective principle of division, the psychological analysis of the intellectual faculties concerned in the various sciences: history, natural and civil, the latter including ecclesiastical and literary history, 'has reference' to the memory; poesy, 'feigned history or fables,' to the imagination; philosophy, divine, natural, human, to the reason. Divinity or revealed theology is other than divine philosophy or natural theology, and superior to it. The Baconian scheme was utilized in the preparation of the French *Encyclopaedia* (see also ENCYCLOPAEDISTS). Comte, on the other hand, followed the objective method of classification 'from the study of the things to be classified' in view of their 'real affinity and natural connections.' After excluding theology and metaphysics, he divides the positive sciences into two classes, abstract and concrete. According to the decreasing simplicity and generality of the phenomena to which they relate, the former arrange themselves in the following order of dependence: mathematics, astronomy, physics, chemistry, physiology or biology (of which psychology is a branch), and sociology. This, in Comte's view, is also the order in which the sciences have developed historically, and expresses their relative positions in the scale of 'positive' character. Spencer denies the possibility of arranging the sciences in serial order to represent either their logical or their historical dependence, and substitutes for the

Comtean 'hierarchy' a classification of his own. Using the terms abstract and concrete in a different sense from Comte, he makes three principal divisions: abstract science, 'which treats of the forms in which phenomena are known to us,' and includes logic and mathematics; abstract-concrete science, 'which treats of the phenomena themselves in their elements,' as mechanics, physics, chemistry, &c.; concrete science, 'which treats of the phenomena themselves in their totalities,' astronomy, geology, biology, psychology, sociology, &c. The issue between Comte and Spencer, and the subject at large, have been discussed further by Littré, J. S. Mill, Bain, Fiske, and others.

Literature: BACON, Adv. of Learning, ii, and De Augmentis Scientiarum, ii–ix; J. D'ALEMBERT, Encyc., Discours préliminaire; A. COMTE, Cours de Philos. Positive, i. 1–2; H. SPENCER, Essays on the Genesis of Science and the Classification of the Sciences (3rd ed., 1871); E. LITTRÉ, Auguste Comte et la Philos. Positive, ii. 6; J. S. MILL, Auguste Comte and Positivism, 32 ff.; A. BAIN, Logic, i. App. A; C. W. SHIELDS, Philos. Ultima, ii. 52–79; J. FISKE, Cosmic Philosophy. (A.C.A.Jr.)

Cleanthes. A Stoic philosopher, born in Assos, Asia Minor (cir. 300 B.C.). He moved to Athens and became the pupil of Zeno, at whose death he became head of the Stoic school. A hymn to Jupiter has survived, out of numerous works. Chrysippus was his pupil and successor.

Clear and Distinct (and **Clearness and Distinctness**) [Lat. *clarus et distinctus*]: Ger. *klar und deutlich*; Fr. *clair et distinct*; Ital. *chiaro e distinto*. The Cartesian test of truth; criticized and developed by Leibnitz. Cf. TESTS OF TRUTH. (A.C.A.Jr.)

Clearing-up: see ENLIGHTENMENT.

Clearness (in education) [OE. *cler, cleer,* clear]: Ger. *Klarheit*; Fr. *clarté*; Ital. *chiarezza*. That stage of method in which the mind of the pupil apprehends the presented facts with clearness of mental vision; the first formal step in method according to Herbart's terminology. See ABSORPTION, and METHOD (in education).

Literature: HERBART, Sci. of Educ. (trans. by Falkin), 126. (C.DE G.)

Cleavage [OE. *cleofan*]: Ger. *Eintheilung, Furchung*; Fr. *segmentation*; Ital. *segmentazione*. (1) Of the ovum. The process of segmentation or cell-division, by which the single cell from which multicellular animals and plants are developed becomes divided into an aggregate of cells, generally termed blastomeres.

First definitely described in the case of the frog's ovum by Prévost and Dumas (1824); observed even earlier, its true meaning was not clearly perceived till twenty years later by Bergmann, Kölliker, and others. The nature of the cleavage or segmentation of the ovum depends upon the amount of food-yolk present. Where there is little or none (alecithal), and the small amount present is equally distributed (homolecithal), the cleavage is total (holoblastic segmentation); where there is much and unequally distributed (heterolecithal, telolecithal), the cleavage is partial and usually affects only a patch of protoplasm, the blastodermic area (meroblastic segmentation); where it is centrally disposed (centrolecithal), and the formative protoplasm is arranged around the whole surface, cleavage affects the surface layer (peripheral segmentation).

(2) Of the mesoderm or mesoblast. The process by which the mid layer of many animals splits so as to give rise to the body-cavity or coelom of the schizocoel type. Cf. COELOM.

First clearly established by Remak (1850–4).

Literature: ALLEN THOMSON, art. Embryology, Encyc. Brit. (9th ed.). For other works see EMBRYOLOGY. (C.LL.M.–E.S.G.)

Clement of Alexandria, Titus Flavius. (cir. 150–cir. 213.) An eminent Father in the Patristic Church, born probably in Athens. He studied various pagan thinkers, and became the disciple of Pantaenus, the Christian philosopher in Alexandria. Clement succeeded him as head of the catechetical school. Origen was one of his pupils. Ordained presbyter in 202 A.D., he retired to Palestine. See ALEXANDRIAN SCHOOL, and PATRISTIC PHILOSOPHY.

Cleptomania (also **Kl-**) [Gr. κλέπτειν, to steal, + μανία, madness]: Ger. *Stehlsucht*; Fr. *monomanie du vol, cleptomanie*; Ital. *cleptomania, impulso al furto*. An irresistible impulse or morbid tendency to steal.

It was formerly regarded as a separate form of monomania or insanity in which the tendency to steal was the marked characteristic. It is now viewed as one of a series of morbid impulses appearing both in persons of apparent normal health but frequently of neurotic temperament, and also as a symptom in cases of mental defect and disease. Cases of persons, particularly women, of good social position and without any real motives for theft, yielding to the impulse to appropriate small and often useless articles, frequently occur, and are difficult to explain as criminal or insane. Their elucidation in special cases can only be gained in the light of a detailed personal history; that in many cases such actions are the result of distinctly morbid conditions cannot be questioned. The impulse to steal and appropriate also manifests itself in idiocy and imbecility, in epilepsy, and in the initial stages of general paralysis, in which cases the theft is often performed automatically and as if to satisfy an inborn instinct. A special tendency to this defect in pregnant women has been noted.

This form of impulse obviously has important legal relations, and is conspicuous in discussions of moral insanity and responsibility. The tendency to look upon criminals largely as persons of unsound mental constitution brings with it the view that professional thieves are to a greater or less extent subject to impulses which may be properly spoken of in many instances as cleptomaniacal. (J.J.)

Literature: BUCKNILL and TUKE, Psychol. Med. (1873); TAYLOR, Med. Jurisprudence (1894); CLEVENGER, Med. Jurisprudence (2 vols., 1898); SHATTUCK, Atlantic Med. Weekly (1896), vi. 401; V. MAGNAN, Leçons cliniques sur les Maladies mentales (1893), and Recherches sur les Centres nerveux (2e série); H. SAURY, Étude clinique sur la Folie héréditaire; LEGRAIN, Délire de dégénérés. (J.J.–L.M.)

Clifford, William Kingdon. (1845–79.) An English mathematician, born in Exeter, and educated at King's College, London, and at Trinity College, Cambridge. He was professor of mathematics and mechanics in University College, London.

Clonus and **Clonic** [Gr. κλόνος, a violent, confused motion]: Ger. *Zuckkrampf* (*klonisch*); Fr. *spasme* or *convulsion clonique*; Ital. *convulsione clonica, clono*. Alternating contractions and relaxations of muscles, not so rapid as in trembling or shivering. See ANKLE CLONUS, a spasmodic contraction of the muscles of the calf (5–7 per second).

Opposed to TONUS (q. v.) and tonic, which apply to short, sharp contractions. (C.F.H.)

Co-adaptation [Lat. *co + adaptare*, to adapt]: Ger. *gegenseitige oder complicirte Anpassung*; Fr. *coadaptations. (variations) coadaptives*; Ital *correlazione d' adattamento*. Complex as contrasted with simple adaptation, in which several structures by modification or variation are involved in a common adaptation. In cases of co-adaptation due to variation, the latter are called correlated VARIATIONS (q. v.). See also CORRELATION (in biology).

The supposed necessity for many structures to vary simultaneously so as to give rise to complex adaptation has been brought forward by Herbert Spencer, G. J. Romanes, and others as an objection to the application of Natural Selection in such cases. Wallace meets the difficulty by denying that the several component adaptations are necessarily simultaneous. Weismann meets it by suggesting that much of the adaptation is temporarily acquired by individual modification (INTRA-SELECTION, q. v.) and more recently by the hypothesis of GERMINAL SELECTION. The use of Intraselection—in this connection—has been carried further by the theory of ORGANIC SELECTION, according to which such modifications are gradually replaced by congenital variations.

Literature: HERBERT SPENCER, Princ. of Biol. (2nd ed.), 1898; also Contemp. Rev., Feb., March, and Dec., 1893; G. J. ROMANES, Darwin and after Darwin, ii. 64; A. R. WALLACE, Darwinism, 418; A. WEISMANN, Contemp. Rev., lxiv, 1893; Effect of External Influences upon Development, Romanes Lecture, 1894; BALDWIN, Science, N.S., iii, 1896, 438 ff., 558 ff., and Psychol. Rev., 1897, 393 ff.; LLOYD MORGAN, Habit and Instinct (1896). (C.LL.M.–J.M.B.)

Code (in law) [Lat. *codex*, a tablet]: Ger. *Gesetzbuch, Gesetzsammlung*; Fr. *code*; Ital. *codice*. A written statement of the law on one or more subjects, arranged in systematic and orderly form. A code may be a private and unofficial work, like David Dudley Field's *Draft Outlines of an International Code*. It may be an official work, sanctioned and promulgated by the government, and having the force of law. In such case, it is a substitute for the pre-existing law on the same subject.

Ordinarily, private codes precede and pave the way for public ones. Thus the codes of imperial constitutions compiled by Gregorianus and Hermogenianus came to be received as authoritative in the Roman courts, and served as models for the later Theodosian and Justinian codes (Smith's *Dict. of Greek and Roman Antiq.*, sub verbo).

The criminal code of Draco for Athens was promulgated about 624 B.C., and soon supplanted by the more general, and milder, code of Solon. From the latter, part of the Twelve Tables of Rome were probably copied, in the middle of the 5th century B.C. The Indian code, or *Institutes of Menu*, was probably a later production. The Theodosian code of the edicts and general imperial constitutions from the time of Constantine was compiled by a commission of sixteen jurists, appointed by Theodosius II, and promulgated by him as the law of the Eastern empire, A.D. 438. It was soon afterwards confirmed as law for the Western empire by the Roman senate, at the instance of Valentinian III. It is in sixteen books, and most of it is still extant. The term 'Justinian Code' is commonly, but inaccurately, used to designate the compilation made about a hundred years later, under direction of the Emperor Justinian, more properly known as the *Corpus Iuris Civilis*. This consists of four distinct works. One is an elementary treatise or statement of the leading rules of Roman law, in four books, designed especially for the education of law students, and called the *Institutes*. Another is a more detailed statement of the general principles and rules of Roman law, in fifty books, known as the *Digest* or *Pandects*. Another is a collection of the imperial rescripts, edicts, and constitutions down to Justinian's time, in twelve books, called the *Code*. Finally, comes a compilation, made later, of Justinian's new constitutions (*Novellae constitutiones*), promulgated after the compilation of his *Code*, during the residue of his reign, known as the *Novels*. It is probable that the *Novels* were not officially collated and published until after Justinian's death.

Numerous codes have since been published in different states. Those of the continental nations in the dark and middle ages may be found in the *Corpus Iuris Germanici* of Heineccius. Louis XIV codified important titles of French law. The *Code Napoléon* was one of the greatest works of Napoleon I. Though commonly spoken of as one code, it really consists of eight. The principal one is the *Code Civil*, completed in 1804, which with comparatively slight alterations remains the law of France on the subject of private rights. It has been substantially adopted in Belgium and Louisiana, and had an important influence in shaping that of Italy. Germany has had a succession of partial codes beginning with that of Frederick the Great in 1751, and culminating in the Imperial Civil Code in 1896.

England has codified only a few titles of her law, notably that of Bills and Notes. In the United States a large number of the states have codes of civil procedure; and a few, Georgia being the first (1860), have general civil codes. Japan has adopted a penal and also a civil code. A *penal code* is one defining and declaring the punishment of crimes, such as the *Code Pénal* of Napoleon, or the German *Strafgesetzbuch*.

All the public statutes of each of the United States are at times compiled or revised by public authority, the product being known as a compilation or revision, or the Revised General or Public Statutes, as the case may be. Such a publication is a substitute for the former laws, but as they do not assume to cover the entire field of rights or remedies, and rest on the foundation of an unwritten common law, they are not customarily designated as codes. Private compilations of a similar kind are often called Digests. Such was Brightly's *Digest of the Laws of the United States*, which was in common use by the courts until the publication of the *Revised Statutes of the United States* (1873). (S.E.B.)

Literature: THIBAUT, Ueber die Notwendigkeit eines allg. bürgerlichen Rechts f. Deutschland (1814); SAVIGNY, Vom Beruf unserer Zeit f. Gesetzgebung u. Rechtswiss. (1814); BENTHAM, Papers relative to Codification, &c. (1817); MAINE, Ancient Law, chap. i (1861); T. J. SEMMES, The Civil Law and Codification, Rep. of the Amer. Bar Assoc., ix. 189 (1886); J. C. CARTER, The Provinces of the Written and the Unwritten Law (1889); J. DOVE WILSON, The Recent Progress of Codification, Juridical Rev. (April, 1891), and the Proposed Imperial Code of Commercial Law, ibid. (Oct., 1896).

Codification : see CODE.

Coefficient (in psychology) [Lat. co- + *efficiens*, efficient] : Ger. *Koefficient, Merkmal* (in compounds), *Qualität* (in compounds); Fr. *coefficient, propriété* ; Ital. *coefficiente*. 'An essential peculiarity or distinguishing mark' for consciousness.

Suggested, as defined above, in the present writer's *Handbook of Psychology, Feeling and Will* (1891), chap. vii. § 3, in connection with BELIEF (q.v.), the coefficient of reality in different spheres being the marks, of whatever kind, attaching to mental contents, by which consciousness attains its beliefs. So in other cases; e.g. the coefficient of recognition is what Höffding calls Bekanntheitsqualität.

Literature : STOUT, Analytic Psychol., 'Belief'; JERUSALEM, Die Urtheilsfunction; BALDWIN, loc. cit. ; Mind, July, 1891; and Elements of Psychol., Glossary. (J.M.B., G.F.S.)

Coelentera [Gr. κοῖλος, hollow, + ἔντερον, intestine]: Ger. *Pflanzenthiere*; Fr. *cœlentérés*; Ital. *celenterati*. That group or subgrade of Enterozoa or Metazoa which remains possessed of a single enteric cavity, without formation of a separate body-cavity or coelom, and possesses only two definite cell-layers. Cf. COELOMATA.

The term was proposed by Leuckart (1848) to include the classes Polypi and Acalephae; adopted by Huxley (1869) to comprise the Hydrozoa and Actinozoa; subsequently, owing largely to the work of Haeckel, taken to include also the Sponges or Porifera, which are now, however, often given an independent position.

Literature: E. RAY LANKESTER, art. Zoology, Encyc. Brit. (9th ed.). (C.LL.M.—E.S.G.)

Coelom [Gr. κοίλωμα, a cavity]: Ger. *Leibeshöhle*; Fr. *cœlome, cavité du corps*; Ital. *celomati*. A cavity or series of cavities found in the mesoderm of many animals (hence termed COELOMATA, q. v.). It is surrounded by mesodermic walls, which frequently form a perivisceral sac or sacs enclosing the heart, and in many cases the alimentary canal. From its epithelial walls are derived the reproductive cells; and from them too are developed tubes or tubules for the excretion of nitrogenous waste.

First suggested as a technical term by Haeckel in his monograph on *Calc. Sponges* (1872), the term has since undergone further delimitation. According to mode of origin Huxley (1875) subdivided it into Enterocoel (having origin as pouches from the enteric cavity) and Schizocoel (by subsequent cleavage of the mesoderm). To these he added Epicoel (having origin from the outer wall of the body, as in the atrium of Amphioxus); but this is not a homologous cavity. The Hertwigs presented in 1881 a coelom theory in Embryology. Lankester and most modern zoologists utilize the coelom in classification.

Literature: HAECKEL, Die Kalkschwämme (1872); HUXLEY, Quart. J. Microsc. Sci., xv. 54 (1875); LANKESTER, ibid., xvii. 441 (1877); HERTWIG, Coelomtheorie (1881). (C.LL.M.)

Coelomata: Ger. *Coelomaten*; Fr. *cœlomata*; Ital. *celomate, celomarii*. That group or subgrade of Enterozoa or Metazoa which is characterized by the presence of a coelom in a distinct middle or mesodermal cell-layer.

The term was introduced by E. Ray Lankester (1877). Excepting the Porifera and Coelentera, all the great groups of the Metazoa are included in the Coelomata, although the coelom is quite rudimentary in the lower (Platyhelmia), and almost obliterated in others (Mollusca, Arthropoda) (E. R. Lankester, *Quart. J. Microsc. Sci.*, N.S., xvii. 441). (C.LL.M.—E.S.G.)

Coenaesthesis [Gr. κοινός, common, + αἴσθησις, feeling]: Ger. *Gemeinempfindung*; Fr. *cénesthésie*; Ital. *cenestesi*. See COMMON SENSATION. The word Coenaesthesis appears to have been first used in English by Sir W. Hamilton in 1837 (*Lects. on Met.*, II. xxvii. 157). (E.B.T.)

Coexistence [Lat co- + existens, being]: Ger. *Koexistenz*; Fr. *coexistence*; Ital. *coesistenza*. (1) Togetherness in TIME (q.v.). (2) Law of coexistence: see ASSOCIATION OF IDEAS. (J.M.B.)

Cogitate and **Cogitation** [Lat. *cogitare*, to think]: Ger. *nachdenken*; Fr. *méditer, méditation*; Ital. *cogitazione* (noun). Used popularly for think and thinking of the more meditative and reflective sort. Cf. REFLECTION. (J.M.B.)

Cogito ergo sum [Lat.]. 'I think, therefore I am.'

The motto of Descartes and of modern philosophy; the appeal to the inner life as the final source of knowledge of the real. See the various emendations and explanations offered by many thinkers cited in Eisler, *Wörterb. d. philos. Begriffe*, sub verbo. (J.M.B.)

Cognition [Lat. *cognoscere*, to know]: Ger. *Erkenntniss (-Vermögen)*; Fr. *connaissance*; Ital. *cognizione*. The being aware of an OBJECT (q. v.). (G.F.S., J.M.B.)

As above defined, cognition is an ultimate mode of consciousness co-ordinate with conation and affection. Cf. CLASSIFICATION (of mental functions). It may well be questioned, however, whether in current usage cognition does not imply judgment, at least in a rudimentary form, as well as presentation of object. It is not natural to speak of presentations as cognitions unless these objects are attended to in the sense of being noted and distinguished, and this may be said to involve judgment. The same difficulty arises with conation and affection, i. e. of finding 'pure' cases; but this does not render unnecessary the distinction of these rudimentary modes. The alternative term intellection is open to a similar objection to a greater degree (e. g. as used by Ward to include the logical processes). Knowledge is practically synonymous, but lacks an adjective form. (G.F.S.—J.M.B.)

Coincidence [Lat. *co-* + *incidere*, to happen]: Ger. *Koincidenz*; Fr. *coïncidence*;

Ital. *coincidenza*. (1) Agreement in general; in space (Mathematics), two outlines coincide when either superposed upon the other completely hides it; in time, two events coincide when they coexist.

(2) An event which, while seeming to be due to another or connected with it, can be accounted for nevertheless independently of it. Such a juxtaposition of terms in two mutually independent causal series, suggesting cause and effect between the terms themselves, is also called coincidence (in the abstract).

The doctrine of coincidence belongs to the theory of PROBABILITY (q.v.). Popularly such a conjunction of events is said to be 'due to CHANCE' (q. v.). A current psychological instance is found in the discussion of coincidence in connection with so-called VERIDICAL HALLUCINATIONS (q. v.) and apparitions of all kinds. Cf. VARIATION. (J.M.B.)

Coincident Variations: Ger. *übereinstimmende oder koincidirende Variationen* (Ortmann); Fr. *variations coïncidentes* (Y.D.); Ital. *variazioni di coincidenza* (E.M.). Those congenital variations which are similar in character and direction to particular acquired modifications, with which they are said to 'coincide.'

A term suggested by Lloyd Morgan, who contends that such variations, since they are shielded from the incidence of natural selection by the modifications with which they are coincident, will escape elimination. Thus fostered, they may appear to be acquired characters transmitted through inheritance, gradually increase and supersede the modifications (see ORGANIC SELECTION), and so give rise to evolution along definite lines illustrating ORTHOPLASY (q.v.).

Literature: LL. MORGAN, Habit and Instinct (1896); BALDWIN, Nature, lv. (1897) 558; and the references to OSBORN and POULTON given under ORGANIC SELECTION. (C.LL.M.–J.M.B.)

Cold-blooded Animals: Ger. *kaltblütige Thiere*; Fr. *animaux à sang froid, animaux à température variable*; Ital. *animali a sangue freddo*. Animals whose body temperature varies with the medium in which they live: the hematocrya, reptiles, amphibia, fishes. See ANIMAL HEAT. (C.F.H.)

Cold Sensation: see TEMPERATURE SENSATION.

Cold Spot: Ger. *Kältepunkt*; Fr. *point froid*; Ital. *punto di freddo*. A current term for one of the smallest spots on the skin which respond to the stimulus of cold. See TEMPERATURE SPOT. (J.M.B.)

Collapse [Lat. *collapsus*, from *con-* + *labi*, *laps-*, to fall]: Ger. *Kollaps*; Fr. *collapsus*; Ital. *collasso*. A sinking and partial abeyance of the vital powers; a condition of extreme nervous and general asthenia. Collapse may be due to shock, but occurs as well from other causes. Cf. SHOCK. (J.J.)

Collaterals [M. Lat. *collateralis*]: Ger. *Collateralen*; Fr. *collatérales*; Ital. *collaterali*. Fibres branching from the NEURITES or DENDRITES of a NEUROCYTE, and forming means of communication with other nervous elements. See those terms, and cf. SPINAL CORD. (H.H.)

Collective (in logic): Ger. *Sammel-* (in compounds, e. g. *Sammelwort*); Fr. *collectif*; Ital. *collettivo*. A collective term is, in logic, the word or complex of words expressing the thought of a number of objects or a group, taken and treated together as a whole. A proposition is collective when the predicate is asserted of a number of individuals on the ground or assumption that it has been found to attach to them severally. A peculiar type of collective term is that which contains the thought of a series, or coexistent plurality, as a whole or unit. Such terms are fruitful sources of fallacy. (R.A.)

Collective Psychology: see SOCIAL PSYCHOLOGY.

Collectivism [Lat. *colligere*, to collect]: Ger. *Kollektivismus* (Barth); Fr. *collectivisme*; Ital. *collettivismo*. Theoretical SOCIALISM (q. v.). The policy of public ownership of land and capital, and public management of industry. (A.T.H.–F.H.G.)

Specifically, Socialism and Communism as manifested in France since 1850; loosely used as a convenient synonym for either Socialism or Communism.

'The collectivists are French socialists and social democrats, who have adopted the views of the Germans, chiefly Marx and Lassalle' (Richard T. Ely, *French and German Socialism in Modern Times*, 149). 'Dans l'individualisme, l'homme est abandonné à lui-même, son action est portée à un maximum, et celle de l'État à un minimum. Dans le collectivisme, ses moindres actions sont dirigées par l'État, c'est-à-dire, par la collectivité' (Gustave Le Bon, *Psychol. du Socialisme*, Liv. I. chap. iii). (F.H.G.)

'Collectivism is a favourite word, especially affected by those theoretical French socialists who, while demanding a public ownership of the instruments of production and a collective organization of labour, are still content to leave private property intact, so far as objects of consumption are concerned, and even take the extreme view which allows of their transmission from father to son, and in general by testamentary disposition' (Cossa). (A.T.H.)

Literature: P. LEROY-BEAULIEU, Le Collectivisme: Examen critique du Nouveau Socialisme (1884); BARTH, Philos. d. Gesch. als Sociol., i. 214 ff. (and references there given; works cited above). (A.T.H.–J.M.B.)

Collier, Arthur. (1680–1732.) An English philosopher and clergyman, who was born and died at Langford Magna, Wiltshire. He became rector of Langford Magna, 1704. In his best known work, *Clavis Universalis*, he seeks to demonstrate the 'non-existence or impossibility of an external world.' He was in substantial agreement with his contemporary, Bishop Berkeley.

Colligation [Lat. *con-* + *ligare*, to bind]: Ger. *Colligation*; Fr. *colligation* (suggested); Ital. *collegazione* (suggested). The union of qualitatively like elements in consciousness.

Opposed to the union of the disparate as in Complication and Association. Drobisch (*Neue Darstellung der Logik* (5th ed.), § 29) makes the union one of like objects in a (logical) class or Colligationsbegriff (cf. Eisler, *Wörterb. d. philos. Begriffe*, sub verbo). This is opposed to the usage of the translator of Külpe's *Outlines of Psychology*, who assigns to colligation the meaning we give to INTEGRATION (q. v.). (J.M.B., G.F.S.)

Colligation (in logic). A term introduced by Whewell to indicate the function which an appropriate or illuminating conception discharges in binding together a group of facts. It is not easy, perhaps it is hardly desirable or necessary, to make a distinction between colligation and the general process which finds expression in the formation of hypotheses.

Literature: WHEWELL, Nov. Organ. Renov., 61–96; MILL, Logic, Bk. III. chap. ii, and Bk. IV. chap. ii. (R.A.)

Collins, Anthony. (1676–1729.) An able English deistical writer on theological themes. Born near Hounslow, in Middlesex, educated at Cambridge, he was an intimate friend of John Locke. He studied, but did not practise, law. In 1718 he became treasurer of the county of Essex.

Colony [Lat. *colonus*, farmer]: Ger. *Kolonie*; Fr. *colonie*; Ital. *colonia*. (1) In sociology and social psychology: used loosely for COMPANY (q.v.), especially where differences of locality are influential in determining an aggregation (sense not recommended).

(2) In biology: a biologically determined group of units; as in the phrases, 'colony of cells,' 'colonies' of Protozoa, of parasites, of insects, &c.; and in the phrase 'colonial animal,' for an animal whose organization does not extinguish the relatively separate mode of existence and physiological function of its component units. See Perrier, *Les colonies animales* (2nd ed., 1899). (J.M.B.–G.F.S.)

(3) In political philosophy: a community of emigrants who have settled territory at a distance from their mother land, and who remain under the protection, and in general policy under the government, of the mother country. Also, a group of permanently settled emigrants forming a distinct self-governing community.

Literature: the first great theoretical writer on social and political colonies was ADAM SMITH, Wealth of Nations, Bk. IV. chap. vii. The exhaustive modern authority on the history and policy of colonization is PAUL LEROY-BEAULIEU, De la Colonisation chez les Peuples modernes. (F.H.G.)

Colour: see VISION (headings Light and Colour Sensation).

Colour (in aesthetics) [Lat. *color*]: Ger. *Farbe*; Fr. *couleur*; Ital. *colore*. (1) The pigment used in painting. (2) The general colour tone or scheme of a natural object, or a work of art. (3) Metaphorically, the characteristics giving individuality to a work of art.

The aesthetic significance of colour was, like that of symmetry, recognized at an early date among the Greeks. This is brought out by Socrates' conversation with Parrhasius, as reported by Xenophon in the *Memorabilia*. Plato finds the beauty of colour in its intrinsic significance and symbolism, admitting also its pure sensuous agreeableness. Plotinus criticizes the doctrine that beauty is adequately described in terms of colour and symmetry. We do not until the present century, however, meet with any radically novel treatment of the aesthetic principles involved. Darwin, Spencer, Fechner, Allen, Groos, have sought to account for the aesthetic value of colour through the principle of association, and the various factors making for the conservation of the individual and the species in the evolution of the race. Aside from such considerations, the import of colour, as distinct from the principles of technique in its use in painting, has not constituted a topic apart from general aesthetic theories. Cf. BEAUTY, and ASSOCIATION (aesthetic).

Literature: KÖSTLIN, Aesthetik (1869); FECHNER, Vorschule d. Aesth. (1876); DARWIN, Descent of Man (1871); GRANT ALLEN, Physiol. Aesth. (1877), and The Colour-Sense (London, 1879); ROOD, Textbook of Colour (1881); GROOS, The Play of Animals, 'Sexual Selection.'　(J.R.A.)

Colour (of tones): Ger. *Klangfarbe, Klang-färbung*; Fr. *couleur du son, timbre*; Ital. *colore del suono, timbro*. A figurative synonym of TIMBRE (q.v.). E.B.T. uses ' clang tint,' which is not recommended (cf. CLANG).　(J.M.B.)

Colour (primary): Ger. *Grundfarbe*; Fr. *couleur fondamentale*; Ital. *colore fondamentale*. See Visual Sensation under VISION.

(E.B.T.)

Colour-blindness: Ger. *Farbenblindheit*; Fr. *achromatopsie, achropsie, dyschromatopsie*; Ital. *discromatopsia, cecità dei colori*. The name given to certain anomalies of vision characterized by the absence of particular colour tones, and in some cases by the shifting of the point of maximal brightness in the solar spectrum. See VISION (also defects of).

Hering's theory and classification are the most satisfactory. We have (1) partial colour-blindness, including (*a*) the two types of red-green blindness. In both the spectrum falls into a blue half and a yellow half, with a central neutral band. But the one type places the maximal brightness in (normal) yellow, the other in (normal) yellow-green; hence to the former the long-wave end of the spectrum is relatively bright, to the latter relatively dark. (*b*) Blue-yellow blindness. The short-wave end of the spectrum is very dark and little coloured; yellow is confused with white; red and green are distinguished (or rather blue-green; see König, *Sitzber. d. Berl. Akad.*, 1897, 718, for the only monocular cases). (2) Total colour-blindness. No colour tone is seen; the maximal spectral brightness lies in (normal) green.

Observations of colour-blindness have been greatly influenced by preconceived theory. All cases of partial colour-blindness were at first regarded by Helmholtz as due simply to the lack of the red, green, or violet substance. Since the facts contradict this view, a shift of excitability in the three sets of fibres has been assumed, and the terms ' trichromates,' ' dichromates,' ' monochromates,' retained; but the auxiliary hypotheses are extremely improbable. Wundt's theory makes

him ready to accept the absence of any sensation or group of sensations from the visual series. Hering's theory of antagonistic processes forbids the isolated abrogation of any principal sensation. The two types of red-green blindness he explains as due to difference of macular pigmentation. Blue-yellow blindness may be due to failure of the blue-yellow substance, or to a yellowish colouration of the lens. The rare cases of monocular colour-blindness are of very great importance for theory.

The methods of testing for colour-blindness are as follows:—

(1) Seebeck's and Holmgren's method. Coloured papers or worsteds are sorted and matched by the patient, without naming. This is the best rough method.

(2) Equations of mixed colours (with black and white sectors) are obtained by means of rotating disks, to be identified and matched. An exact method.

(3) Stilling's method. Numerals, made up of blotches of colour, are printed on a page dotted over with blotches of a different colour. Confusion is supposed to denote colour-blindness. Of little value.

(4) Spectroscopic examination: direct comparison of spectral colours, or mixture of different colours in colour equations. Essential.

(5) Leucoscopic method of equalizing complementaries. Not much used.

(6) Hering's special apparatus for partial colour-blindness. Excellent.　(E.B.T.)

Colour-blindness is a frequent defect, being found in from 3·5 to 5 per cent. of males, and 2 to 4 per cent. of females; it may be either congenital or acquired, is frequently hereditary, and when congenital is always incurable. Although a few important cases of monocular colour-blindness have been described, the defect usually exists in both eyes. Its cause has not been satisfactorily determined; the theories which attempt to account for the varieties of its occurrences are considered under VISION (q. v.).

Considered descriptively, as a visual defect, there may be distinguished (*a*) total lack of colour sense, and (*b*) an abnormal form of colour sense, or partial colour-blindness. (*a*) Total colour-blindness is rare; only about fifty cases have been described. All objects are seen simply in shades of gray, and the spectrum appears like ' a delicately executed pencil drawing,' lighter in the centre (the region of green) and becoming gradually darker at both (somewhat shortened) ends.

(b) Partial colour-blindness is the typical prevailing form upon which statistics are based. All persons who are partially colour-blind are able to make a considerable number of colour distinctions. These have been differently described by different investigators. Sir John Herschell said, ' What the sensations of the colour-blind really are we shall never know.' But the existence of cases of monocular dichromasy has proved (what was in fact definitely made out long before by William Pole from the study of his own case) that in all the ordinary instances the defective person sees all degrees of saturation of yellow and of blue, together with black and white, and sees nothing else. These individuals are nevertheless of two types, with no intermediate forms: for one set the spectrum is shortened at the red end (these were formerly called red-blind), and for the other it is not (green-blind). The occurrence and nature of blue-yellow blindness (Hering) or (blue) violet-blindness (Helmholtz) are not clearly determined. Acquired colour-blindness occurs in case of degenerated diseases of the eye, and the perception for form, which is independent of the colour sense in congenital colour-blindness, is frequently also affected. Such defect in typical cases begins in the peripheral portions, and as the disease proceeds, extends into the fovea; and furthermore the perception of green is apt to be disturbed first, then red, while yellow, and most of all blue, is retained to the end. Exceptional cases of hysterical, traumatic, and psychical colour-blindness have been described. It is also said to be more common among epileptics, criminals, and lunatics—classed by the Italian criminologists as degenerates. (J.J.–C.L.F.)

Literature: HELMHOLTZ, Physiol. Optik (2nd ed.), 371; WUNDT, Physiol. Psychol. (4th ed.), i. 507; HERING, Arch. f. Ophthal., xxxvi; NUEL, in Richet's Dict. de Physiol., i. 98; GOUBERT, De l'Achromatopsie (1867); GALEZOWSKI, Chromatopsie rétinienne (1869); DE WECKER and LANDOLT, Traité complet d'Ophthal., 566; LANDOLT, Arch. d'Ophthal. (1881, 114; 1891, 202); CH. FÉRÉ, Boîtes chromatoscopiques pour l'exploration et l'exercice de la vision des couleurs, C. R. Soc. de Biol. (1897), iv. 877 ff.; KIRSCHMANN, Philos. Stud., viii. 173 f., 407 f.; SACHS, Arch. f. Ophthal., xxxix. 108; G. LUCCIOLA, Guida all' esame funzionale dell' occhio (1896). Cf. Visual Sensation under VISION. (E.B.T.–L.M.)

Colour Circle: Ger. *Farbenkreis, Farbentafel*; Fr. *table des couleurs, cercle chromatique*; Ital. *disco di Newton, circolo cromatico.* A figure designed by Sir I. Newton to represent the laws of colour mixture. On the periphery of the circle are arranged the seven saturated colours of Newton, and also purple; at the centre is white; the mixed colours lie upon the surface of the disk. Cf. COLOUR MIXTURE, and COLOUR TRIANGLE.

Literature: NEWTON, Optics, I. ii. prop. 6; HELMHOLTZ, Physiol. Optik (2nd ed.), 325; HESS, Arch. f. Ophthal., xxxv; ZINDLER, in Zeitsch. f. Psychol., xx. 225. (E.B.T.)

Colour Mixture: Ger. *Farbenmischung*; Fr. *mélange des couleurs*; Ital. *mescolanza dei colori.* Colour mixture consists in the bringing of rays of different wave-length upon the same point of the retina.

Laws of colour mixture: (1) For every colour tone there is a correlated tone which, mixed with it in the right proportion, produces grey or white. See COMPLEMENTARY COLOUR, and Visual Sensation under VISION. (2) If two non-complementary terms of the closed colour series are mixed, there results an intermediate colour, whose tone depends on the relative amount of the two primaries taken, and whose saturation (provided those amounts are somewhat nearly equal) is determined by the distance that separates them in the colour series. (3) Mixture of similarly appearing colours gives similarly appearing colours, provided that the conditions of retinal ADAPTATION (q. v.) are approximately maintained.

Corollaries: (1) Any unsaturated colour may be produced by mixing the saturated colour with white, or black, or grey. (2) The series of colour tones can be produced by the mixture, in right proportions, of three colour tones, each pair of which would make, if mixed, the complementary of the third. The mixture of red, green, and blue-violet gives the most saturated colours and the best white. (3) The mixture of all colour tones, in right proportions, gives grey or white. (4) Until the Purkinje phenomenon begins to be effective, colour equations, of whatever physical composition their terms may be, are independent of objective light intensity. See VISION.

Methods of colour mixture: (1) Lambert's method of mixture by the reflection of different colours upon a common surface (good). (2) Projection of two spectra, partially coincident; or bringing of parts of the same spectrum to coincidence (essential). (3) By means of rotating disks: Maxwell's method (essential, but requires care and knowledge). (4) By irradiation through the juxtaposition of very small coloured surfaces (used in oil-painting, tapestry, &c.). (5) By double refraction (good for demonstration). (6) By actual mixture of pigments.

Literature: HELMHOLTZ, Physiol. Optik (2nd ed.), 312; EBBINGHAUS, Psychologie, 209; KÜLPE, Outlines of Psychol., 115; SANFORD, Course in Exper. Psychol., expts. 148–50; AUBERT, Physiol. d. Netzhaut, 154; HERING, Ueber Newton's Gesetz d. Farbenmischung, in Lotos, vii. (1887). Cf. COLOUR TRIANGLE, and COLOUR MIXTURE (binocular). (E.B.T.)

Colour Mixture (binocular): Ger. *binoculare Farbenmischung*; Fr. *mélange binoculaire des couleurs*; Ital. *mescolanza binoculare*. Under certain favourable conditions the presentation of different colours to the two eyes results in a mixture of the colours. There are, however, many sources of error in the experiments, and (in all probability) great individual differences between observers. Cf. RETINAL RIVALRY.

Literature: HELMHOLTZ, Physiol. Optik (2nd ed.), 926; SANFORD, Course in Exper. Psychol., expt. 167. (E.B.T.)

Colour Sensation: Ger. *Farbenempfindung*; Fr. *sensation de couleur*; Ital. *sensazione di colore*. See Visual Sensation under VISION.

Colour Tone or **Tint** or **Hue:** Ger. *Farbenton, Nuance*; Fr. *teinte, couleur, ton coloré*; Ital. *colore, tinta*. The visual quality which is correlated on the physical side primarily with wave-length (but, in the case of the purples, only with a mixture of light of different wave-lengths), and which, when mixed with a brightness quality, constitutes the sensation of colour. See Visual Sensation under VISION. It has recently been proposed to reserve the term Tint for the lighter, and to use Shade for the darker degrees of saturation.

Since tone suggests a definite vibration-period, and is hence not particularly applicable to the various purples, some other word would be better; in English writings, Hue is commonly used. It would be well to distinguish between colour tone (using that for a homogeneous light) and hue or nuance (to mean a mixed light, e.g. the purples). (C.L.F.)

Literature: WUNDT, Physiol. Psychol. (4th ed.), i. 482; EBBINGHAUS, Psychologie, 186, 198 f.; KÜLPE, Outlines of Psychol., 112;

FICK, in Hermann's Handb. d. Physiol., III. i. 183 (1879). (E.B.T.—C.L.F.)

Colour Triangle: Ger. *Farbendreieck*; Fr. *triangle des couleurs*; Ital. *triangolo dei colori*. A graphic representation of the laws of colour mixture, more exact and explicit than Newton's COLOUR CIRCLE (q.v.). Mayer (*Göttinger Anzeiger*, 1758) seems to have been the first to construct a colour triangle.

Literature: HELMHOLTZ, Physiol. Optik (2nd ed.), 326, 340; WUNDT, Physiol. Psychol. (4th ed.), i. 491; ROOD, Textbook of Colour, 221, 224 ff.; HERING, in Pflüger's Arch., xlvii. 417; FICK, in Hermann's Handb. d. Physiol., III. i. 184 (1879); ZINDLER, in Zeitsch. f. Psychol., xx. 225. (E.B.T.)

Colour Wheel: see COLOUR MIXTURE, and LABORATORY AND APPARATUS, III. B, (a), (4).

Column [Lat. *columna*]: Ger. *Säule, Strang*; Fr. *cordon, colonne*; Ital. *cordone, colonna*. A group of nervous elements (particularly fibres or tracts) extending a longer or shorter distance in an axial direction within the central nervous system, and preserving a more or less constant relative position and structure. Particularly the longitudinal fibre groups within the spinal cord, which are visibly distinguishable in cross-section. Aside from the columns of the SPINAL CORD (q.v.) the columnae fornicis may be noted as anatomically discrete tracts from the fornix to the thalamus. (H.H.)

Combination (chemical): see CHEMICAL SYNTHESIS.

Combination (economic) [Lat. *combinare*, to join]: Ger. *Vereinigung*; Fr. *coalition*; Ital. *coalizione, combinazione*. Organized economic action for a common end, especially in the case of persons who might otherwise be rivals; the reverse of competition.

Early economic thought on this subject deals chiefly with labour combination. It is but recently that combinations of capital have assumed co-ordinate importance. Combinations, whether of labour or of capital, have two distinct objects: economy of production and monopoly of sale. Where they do not make it their object to include all competitors, the former is generally the motive, and the results are likely to be salutary. Where they insist on the inclusion of all competitors, the alleged economy or improvement in quality is likely to be a pretext, and the hope of securing a monopoly price for their products is almost certain to be a dominant motive. Under such conditions, most of the gain which is due to COMPETITION

(q. v.) is abandoned, and a régime of high price, low efficiency, and conflict of class interests is likely to follow. If the management of the combination is intelligent enough, these evils will not ensue; but experience proves that we cannot rely on the existence of such intelligence. (A.T.H.)

Combination (in psychology): Ger. *Verbindung*; Fr. *combinaison*; Ital. *combinazione*. A general term for the union of elements in consciousness.

Cf. FUSION, INTEGRATION, SYNTHESIS, COMPLICATION, COLLIGATION, all of which are particular cases of combination. This usage is sanctioned by priority (Rabier, 1888; Baldwin, 1891), and is preferable to Connection (suggested as a translation of Verbindung by the translator of Külpe's *Outlines of Psychology*, 1895, 189). It is in use in the phrases 'combining property,' 'combining function,' of consciousness, &c., where 'connection' would not be so appropriate. This usage is established also in 'combination of visual images,' 'colour combination,' 'combination tone,' &c. (J.M.B., G.F.S.)

Combination (social). (1) Any uniting of individuals to effect a consciously apprehended purpose.

Combination implies forethought and deliberation, and is thereby distinguished from other forms of concerted action which are impulsive, as in a panic.

'All combination is compromise: it is the sacrifice of some portion of individual will for a common purpose' (J. S. Mill, *Dissertations and Discussions*, i. 191). It is too general and indefinite a term to have much technical value. The psychological factors involved are better covered by the term CO-OPERATION (q. v.).

Combination Tone: Ger. *Combinationston*; Fr. *ton de combinaison*; Ital. *suono di combinazione*. A tone (SUMMATION or DIFFERENCE TONE, q. v.) which arises when two tones are loudly sounded at the same time. It is clearest in the case of CONSONANCES (q.v.): cf. BEAT TONES.

Literature: HELMHOLTZ, Sensations of Tone, 152; STUMPF, Tonpsychologie, II. iii. 243, 450. (E.B.T.)

Comenius, Johann Amos. (1592–1671.) A noted German philologist, best known for his reforms in methods of teaching languages. His work *Janua Linguarum reserata* gave him a well-deserved fame as a pedagogical reformer. He was summoned to foreign countries to reform the methods of public instruction. He is regarded as the founder of pedagogical method.

Comic [Gr. κωμικός, comic, from κῶμος, a festal procession or revel]: Ger. *komisch*; Fr. *comique*; Ital. *comico*. That portion of the laughable which has an AESTHETIC (q.v.) or semi-aesthetic character. This excludes delight in cruelty (Schadenfreude), although some species of the comic (e. g. satire, ridicule) are complicated with refined forms of that emotion.

Objectively, as a species of the aesthetic, it has usually a predominating element of incongruity or contrast, which is, however (as against the tragic), not serious or irreconcilable. Subjectively, there are usually elements of shock, of tension suddenly released, and of the emotional seizure of laughter. Aside from the metaphysics of the comic, there are, as in the case of beauty, two main problems: (1) an analysis of the character of the comic, which may be (*a*) of comic objects, situations, or actions, or (*b*) of the subjective state of feeling; (2) an explanation on psychological, physiological, or biological grounds of why we laugh at given objects. Typical analyses of the object are those of Aristotle, Richter, Schopenhauer, and von Hartmann, who find some form of error or incongruity. Subjective analyses by Plato and Hobbes emphasize the feeling of superiority or 'sudden glory,' which becomes the freedom or caprice of subjectivity with Schlegel, Schelling, and Hegel. The relation of the comic to the beautiful was elaborated by Weisse, Vischer, and Bohts. The successive stages of the comic process were analysed by Zeising as those of tension, discharge, and recovery of poise as we free ourselves. This analysis is utilized by many recent writers, but with less metaphysical and more psychological interpretations (Hartmann, Groos). Lipps treats the comic as a special case of association. Kant and Spencer have sought physiological explanations of laughter. Darwin investigated in detail its physiological expression. Hall and Allin 'are convinced that all current theories are utterly inadequate,' and seek especially for genetic explanations.

The word ludicrous has been used fully as much as comic in English; but preference is given to the latter term here, both on account of its less special (intensive) connotation, and also because it is in use in all the other languages. (J.M.B.)

Literature: HARTMANN, Aesthetik (1886, gives history); KÖSTLIN, Aesthetik (1869); KRAEPELIN, in Philos. Stud., ii; LIPPS, in Philos. Monatsh., xxiv, xxv; also Komik und Humor (1898); MÜLLER, Das Wesen des Humors; MÉLINAUD, Rev. des deux Mondes, cxxvii; BAUMGART, Handb. d. Poetik (1887), 659 ff.; DEWEY, Psychol. Rev., i. 556 ff.; BERGSON, Le Rire (1900); HALL and ALLIN, in Amer. J. of Psychol., ix; Psychologies of BAIN, LADD, HÖFFDING, SULLY. (J.H.T.)

Comity (judicial) [Lat. *comitas*, friendliness]: Ger. *Höflichkeit*; Fr. *droit de convenance*; Ital. *cortesia*. The deference commonly paid by the courts of one jurisdiction to the laws or proceedings of another, in causes affecting rights claimed under such laws or proceedings. 'What is termed the *comity of nations* is the formal expression and ultimate result of that mutual respect accorded throughout the civilized world by the representatives of each sovereign power to those of every other, in considering the effects of their official acts. Its source is a sentiment of reciprocal regard, founded on identity of position and similarity of institutions' (Fisher *v.* Fielding, 67 Connecticut Reports, 108). (S.E.B.)

Commissure [Lat. *commissura*, a joint]: Ger. *Commissur*; Fr. *commissure*; Ital. *commessura*. A band of nerve-fibres connecting homologous centres of the central nervous system lying on opposite sides of the median plane. The tract commonly becomes compact and well differentiated at the median line (cf. DECUSSATION). Strictly speaking, all commissural fibres decussate, for the two ends connect elements not fully homologous. The term acquired its present use before the details of fibre terminations were known.

The commissures constitute important landmarks in neural anatomy. We may reduce them for the most part to isolated and greatly modified remnants of a double system connecting the dorsal and ventral segments of the nerve tube, and still seen in least modified form in the dorsal and ventral systems of the spinal cord. Cf. BRAIN, and SPINAL CORD. (H.H.)

Commodity [Fr. *commodité*, convenience; Med. Lat. *commoditia*, merchandise]: Ger. *wirthschaftliches Gut*; Fr. *bien*; Ital. *mercanzia*. (1) The singular of 'goods.' (2) Sometimes used in a broader sense to apply to things immaterial as well as material, to services as well as goods.

The singular substantive 'good' has in common life a very different meaning from the plural 'goods'; and the effort to use the singular 'good' in a special scientific sense is fraught with difficulty. Hence the employment of the term commodity.

As long as economists confined their use of the term wealth to material goods, the question whether a service was a commodity did not arise. But when the conception of wealth was extended to include services, the meaning of the term commodity was correspondingly widened; implicitly by some economists, explicitly by others (e. g. Marshall). It would be desirable to have some special term like 'benefit' to apply to goods and service both; and then subdivide benefits according as the labour of conferring and the pleasure of utilization are or are not coincident in time. In the former case production and consumption are simultaneous, and the benefit takes the form of a service. In the latter case there are material objects produced, and not at once consumed, and the benefit takes the form of a material commodity. In measuring wealth as a fund, we should consider only commodities. In measuring it as a flow, we should include both commodities and services. (A.T.H.)

Common (term, noun, &c.): Ger. *gemein* (in compounds); Fr. *commun*; Ital. *comune*. A name which may be applied to any one of an indefinite number of objects in the same sense, on the ground of their possessing severally the same definite marks. (R.A.)

Common Law: Ger. *gemeines Recht*; Fr. *droit commun, droit coutumier*; Ital. *diritto di consuetudine*. (1) The unwritten law of England.

(2) The unwritten law of English-speaking peoples, founded on that of England as it existed when the respective settlements were made, out of which these peoples sprang.

(3) The rules of right and remedy enforced by the ordinary courts of justice among English-speaking peoples generally, as distinguished from those enforced by courts of equity or admiralty.

Except in Louisiana, the bulk of the law in every American state is its common law, or else a codified statement of what was its common law. The United States have no national common law, but their courts sitting in each state ordinarily are bound to apply the common law of the state to which the parties are subject. See Holmes, *The Common Law* (1881). (S.E.B.)

Common Sensation: Ger. *Gemeinempfindung*; Fr. *sensation générale, sens du corps* (Bertrand); Ital. *sensazione (organica) generale*. A name originally given to the whole undifferentiated mass of ORGANIC SENSATION (q.v.), as forming the sense basis of the common feeling of the bodily organism, the feeling of health, comfort, briskness, fatigue, &c. COENESTHESIS (q. v.) is a synonym. As the separate qualities of the organic sensations have become known, the term has been restricted to such senses as pressure and pain, whose sensations are 'common' to several sense organs, or to such still unanalysed sense complexes as 'tickling,' 'pins-and-needles,' 'stuffiness,' &c.

Literature: WEBER, in Wagner's Handwörterb. d. Physiol., III. ii. 495; KÜLPE, Outlines of Psychol., 146; BEAUNIS, Les sensations internes (1889); FUNKE, Hermann's Handb. d. Physiol., III. ii. 289; KROENER, Das körperliche Gefühl (1887); SIR W. HAMILTON, Lects. on Met., ii. 157, 492; BERTRAND, L'Aperception du corps humain (1879); COLSENET, La Vie inconsciente (1880); RIBOT, Les Maladies de la Personnalité; SCHIFF, Dizion. ital. di scienze mediche, i. (1869); MORSELLI, Semej. malat. ment. (1898), i. (E.B.T.—L.M.—E.M.)

Common Sense: Ger. *Gemeinsinn*; Fr. *sens commun*; Ital. *senso comune*. (1) A term applied to opinions or facts which are the property of all men, as contrasted with the teachings of a conscious philosophy.

(2) A term of the Scottish School designating the intuitions which all men have in common. (R.H.S.)

(3) Used for the seat of the supposed 'common' or general sensation or perception in which various senses were thought to be united; κοινὴ αἴσθησις of Aristotle, *sensus communis*. Cf. Eisler, *Wörterb. d. philos. Begriffe*, Gemeinsinn. (J.M.B.)

Communicatio idiomatum [Lat.]. A term in dogmatic theology meaning 'communication of attributes,' and technically referring to the communication of attributes by the divine to the human nature in Christ, or vice versa.

Although early writers, like John Damascene, treat of this subject, it does not occupy a position of vital importance, because the doctrine of two natures in one person was assured by the creeds of the Church. Later, in scholastic times, the subject still continues of secondary interest, because the assumed fact of Christ's divinity obscured his humanity. The question became acute only after the Reformation, and then in the Lutheran Church. This in connection with the doctrine of Real Presence in the Eucharist. It is obvious that, unless the divine nature communicates its attribute of omnipresence to the human nature

of Christ, the Real Presence in the Eucharist is not possible. This 'ubiquity' controversy gave rise to much speculation on the subject; for, given two natures in one person, either (1) the attributes of one of the natures can be communicated to the whole person; or (2) personal functions may be carried out by one of the natures; or (3) the attributes of the divine nature may be communicated to the human nature; or (4) the attributes of the human nature may be communicated to the divine nature. The Lutheran interest centred mainly round (3). Similar speculations survive to-day in the KENOSIS (q.v.) controversy, and refer specially to (4).

Literature: see CHRISTOLOGY. SCHAFF, Creeds of Christendom, i. 285–94, 318–28; THOMASIUS, Christi Person u. Werk; DORNER, Hist. of the Doctrine of the Person of Christ (Eng. trans., particularly Div. 2, vol. ii); art. in Herzog's Real-Encyc., also art. Ubiquität in the same. (R.M.W.)

Communism [Lat. *communis*, common]: Ger. *Kommunismus*; Fr. *communisme*; Ital. *comunismo*. Extreme Socialism: specifically (1) the organization by village communities, which prevailed so extensively before the introduction of the system of private property, and of which many survivals are seen in Russia, India, &c. (2) The doctrines propounded, and policy advocated, in the 'Communistic Manifesto' of Marx and Engels.

This manifesto was composed in 1847, and had much to do with the Revolution of 1848. It spoke of the exploitation of the labourer, and of the measures necessary for his relief; among which it included abolition of landed property, and of inheritance; state credit to be given to people without capital; state ownership of means of transportation and production; compulsory obligation of all men to joint labour in industrial armies. The *International* (1864) was based on these same ideas, which however fell into great discredit in connection with the excesses of the Paris Communists in 1871; and the term has since been generally one of reproach. Cf. SOCIALISM. (A.T.H.)

Community (in philosophy) [Lat. *communis*, common]: Ger. *Gemeinheit*; Fr. *communauté*; Ital. *comunità*. Used loosely to describe conjoint action or co-operation, as in the phrase 'community of cause.' (J.M.B.)

Community (political): see STATE.

Community (social): Ger. (1) *Gemeinde*, (2) *Gemeinschaft*; Fr. *communauté*; Ital. (1) *comune, comunità*, (2) *comunanza*. (1) Used somewhat loosely for a particular human GROUP or SOCIETY (see those terms). (2) Used (also somewhat loosely) for any sort of relationship which is common to two or more individuals; as in the expressions 'community of interests,' 'hopes,' &c.

No technical use of this term is recommended. (J.M.B.)

Company [Lat. con- + panis, bread]: Ger. (1) *Gemeinschaft*, (2) *Gesellschaft*; Fr. (1) (2) *compagnie*; Ital. (1) *convivenza*, (2) *compagnia*. (1) A group of individuals without formal organization; a troop or band. See GROUP. (2) An association incorporated or chartered to do a particular kind of business, e.g. the East India Company.

(1) The history of definition (1) only is of much significance for scientific theory. Baldwin (*Social and Eth. Interpret.*, Pt. VI. chap. xii. § 2, 320) has proposed to give a technical meaning to 'company' in this sense, to designate swarms, troops, and herds of animals, and groupings of human beings that are formed by sympathy, instinct, or impulse, rather than by thought, and thereby to distinguish all instinctive or emotional groupings of individuals from the SOCIETY (q.v.) properly so called. Tönnies makes a partially coincident distinction between Gemeinschaft and Gesellschaft ('society'), basing it, however, on a distinction between racial will (Gattungswille or -wesen) and social will (socialer Wille). Cf. GENERAL WILL. Durkheim has developed a corresponding distinction between compagnie and société in the French. (F.H.G.)

The more exact criterion of the company belongs to social psychology, where the psychological determination of the acts of the members of a company places them under the headings respectively of instinctive and unreflective (or spontaneous).

Literature: DURKHEIM, La Division du Travail social; TÖNNIES, Gemeinschaft u. Gesell. (1887); WUNDT, Logik, ii. cap. iv. 4 a (esp. 599 f., note). (J.M.B.)

(2) Unincorporated associations of this kind were formerly common, but have become less so since the general extension of the privilege of incorporation which has marked the 19th century.

Small associations for similar purposes are usually known as copartnerships, the common name containing one or more of the names of the individual copartners, e.g. Doe & Roe, John Doe & Co. 'Co.' as thus used may indicate one or more unnamed associates.

Company is the term oftenest used in England (but not in the United States) to describe a private business CORPORATION (q.v.). (S.E.B.)

Comparative Jurisprudence: Ger. *vergleichende Rechtswissenschaft*; Fr. *jurisprudence comparée*; Ital. *diritto comparato*. The study of jurisprudence by comparing that of different peoples. Also termed Comparative Law.

The *ius gentium* of the Romans may be said to have been the product of comparative jurisprudence (Just., *Inst.*, I. ii. 1).

Literature: no English author has achieved more in this department than SIR HENRY SUMNER MAINE, Ancient Law, Village Communities, Early History of Institutions, Popular Government. (S.E.B.)

Comparative Philology: see PHILOLOGY.

Comparative Psychology: Ger. *vergleichende Psychologie*; Fr. *psychologie comparée*; Ital. *psicologia comparata*. The department of psychology which proceeds by the comparison of the minds of different animal forms.

It properly includes man as compared with the lower animals, although as commonly used it is synonymous with Animal Psychology. Its principal interest is in connection with genetic problems.

Literature: important recent books and essays are by DARWIN, ROMANES, LL. MORGAN, GROOS, WASMANN, BETHE, MILLS, THORNDIKE, as cited with others in the Psychological Index (1894 ff.), and in BIBLIOG. G, 1, f. A bibliography of older works may be found in GROOS, Spiele der Thiere (original). (J.M.B.)

Comparative Religion: Ger. *vergleichende Religionswissenschaft*; Fr. *science des religions comparées*; Ital. *scienza comparata delle religioni*. The name of that branch of inquiry which investigates religious phenomena by use of the comparative and historical methods.

In science generally the comparative method consists essentially in comparing groups of phenomena (linguistic, anatomical, religious, &c.), which occur in different lands, or periods, or forms, for the purpose of discovering their mutual similarities and differences. The spirit in which it is applied is pre-eminently historical. At the present time, this study of religious phenomena implies so much more than application of the comparative method merely that it has come to be designated Science of Religions by many scholars. This investigation differs from philosophy principally in that it takes the religious consciousness for granted, and considers its manifestations.

Comparative religion had its beginnings in the science of comparative grammar, known as philology. It was thrown out by a great movement with which the names of Bopp, G. Hermann, Lachmann, A. Kuhn, Benfey, Roth, Böhtlingk, Weber, Lassen, Burnouf, and Max Müller must always be indissolubly linked. Historically, then, comparative religion originated in an attempt to show that the same relationships subsisted between the gods—e. g. of India and Greece—as between words—e.g. Sanskrit and Greek verbs. Ahana (dawn) was Athene; Saranjus (the hurrying one) was prototype of the Erinyes; Sarama (the dog who tracks the red cows of the gods) was Hermes; and so on. Later it was discovered that some of these affiliations were brilliant guesswork, with little foundation in reality. This, coupled with the organization of ethnological and anthropological research, signalled the entry of new considerations into the field of comparative religion. The investigations of Tylor, Mannhardt, and A. Lang tended to prove that there was a universal primitive stage of civilization, marked by the presence of ubiquitous practices and ideas. This must needs be studied, not from the standpoint of philology, but from that of psychology, sociology, and so forth, in order that religious phenomena may be interpreted. The philologico-religious researches reveal at most a secondary, not a primitive stage; and new methods must be adopted. This line of investigation has been followed with great success of late years. Cf. ANIMISM.

Literature: the works of the writers mentioned above, and of RÉVILLE, TIELE, ROBERTSON SMITH, J. G. FRAZER, RATZEL, DE QUATREFAGES, WAITZ, GERLAND, PESCHEL, F. B. JEVONS. TIELE's Gifford Lectures and F. B. JEVONS' Introduction to the History of Religion are recent authoritative works. MISS KINGSLEY's West African Studies contains much important matter, tending to show that the animistic theory is not a complete explanation. See, too, Rev. de l'Hist. des Religions.   (R.M.W.)

Comparison [Lat. *comparare*, to compare]: Ger. *Vergleichung*; Fr. *comparaison*; Ital. *comparazione*. Attention directed to the discernment of likeness and difference between two or more objects constitutes comparison.   (G.F.S.–J.M.B.)

There may be apprehension of likeness and difference without comparison. Comparison is the process of searching for likeness in difference, or difference in likeness. In its fully developed form it seems to involve a transition of attention to and fro between the objects compared. It is an interesting question how far, and in what sense, both objects must be copresented in the act of comparing. In many cases it seems necessary to have both before consciousness, in the way of ideal representation by means of the memory-image of one of them. But this is by no means always so. Thus, in comparing two successive sounds, we can immediately judge the second to be the louder without retaining or reproducing a memory-image of the first. See Schumann in *Zeitsch. f. Psychol.*, xvii. 113 f. It is doubtful, however, whether this is really an act of comparison, and not a direct consciousness of difference; the experiments on threshold of difference seem to involve such a direct consciousness rather than an act of judgment.   (G.F.S.–J.M.B.)

Compassion: see PITY.

Compatible [Lat. *con-* + *patior*, to suffer]: Ger. *zusammenbestehend*; Fr. *compatible*; Ital. *compatibile*. Notions are said to be compatible, when the marks constituting their content can be represented as combined in, or as jointly possessed by, an individual subject. The spheres of such notions must at least intersect.   (R.A.)

Compensation [Lat. *compensatio*]: Ger. *Gegenforderung, Kompensation*; Fr. *compensation*; Ital. *compenso*. In the civil law and in Scotch law: payment by a set-off. It is the exercise of the right of a defendant in an action, to whom the plaintiff is indebted, to offer to set his demand off against the plaintiff's demand, submitting to judgment only for the difference, if any, in favour of the plaintiff.

'Compensatio necessaria est, quia interest nostra potius non solvere quam solutum repetere' (*Dig.*, xvi. 2, *De Compensationibus*, 3).   (S.E.B.)

Competition: see RIVALRY, and the following topics.

Competition (in biology): see EXISTENCE (struggle for).

Competition (in economics) [Lat. *competitio*]: Ger. *Konkurrenz*; Fr. *concurrence*; Ital. *concorrenza*. The effort of different individuals engaged in the same line of activity each to benefit himself, generally at the other's expense, by rendering increased service to outside parties.

Important as the term competition is, there have been few attempts to define it. It is not taken up in Malthus' *Definitions*. Mill lays down important propositions about its action, but seems to assume the fundamental meaning of the term as self-evident. Walker defines it by antithesis, as opposed to combination, custom, and sentiment. Marshall says: 'The strict meaning of competition seems to be the racing of one person against another with special reference to the bidding for the sale or purchase of anything.' Beauregard, in the *Nouveau Dictionnaire*, takes substantially the same ground. Neumann, in Schönberg's *Handbuch*, comes a little nearer the definition in this article. Wagner has gone into more detail than any other standard authority in defining the conditions which affect success in competitive enterprise; while Effertz has done more to analyse the nature of the competitive process itself. According to Effertz, struggles for EXISTENCE (q.v.) are of two kinds : struggles for domination, and struggles for annihilation. The struggle between buyer and seller in a bargain is of the former sort ; each tries to make the other serve him as fully as possible, but does not desire his abolition. The struggle between different buyers, or between different sellers, is of the latter class ; each is desiring to get rid of the others so far as he can. Competition, then, is the legalized form of the struggle for annihilation in modern life. What Effertz fails to note is the reason why it is legalized, as indicated in the last clause of our definition : because of its tendency to benefit an indefinite number of third parties, and thus become a means of collective economy of force and of general benefit to society. We cannot speak of the competition of two contestants in a fight ; we cannot even, under a proper use of terms, speak of the competition of different nations of Europe in increasing their standing armies : but we speak of their competition in furnishing their goods to outside nations, and thus trying to drive one another out of neutral markets, to the advantage of the neutral quite as much as to that of the successful competitor.

The benefits of competition are of three kinds : (1) As a regulator of prices. This is the one on which greatest stress has been laid in the past ; but the great increase of fixed capital in the present day renders this effect, in the case of industrial competition, slow and uncertain. (2) As a stimulus to productive efficiency, and especially to the introduction of new methods. (3) As a means of educating the community in rational egoism ; teaching its members that they must seek their industrial success, not in giving as little as possible to those with whom they deal, but as much as possible. The evil effects of competition are to be sought in the prominence which it gives to purely commercial powers of service to the public, at the expense, it may be, of other powers which are more necessary but less marketable. (A.T.H.)

To these advantages may be added (4) that competition acts, in many cases, as a stimulus to demand, and is thus both a determining and a producing factor in economic value and well-being. From the psychological point of view competition leads to the devising of new ways of inciting desire and of commending products not otherwise or not so greatly in demand ; and the increased demand in this or that direction—not compensated for by the withdrawal of demand in other directions— creates and establishes increased economic well-being and economic value. This, in turn, benefits many or possibly all of the producing competitors, notably in cases of the consumption of luxuries. Cf. RIVALRY, especially for remarks upon the use of the notion of struggle for EXISTENCE (q.v.) in connection with economic competition. (J.M.B.–H.S.)

Literature: A. WAGNER, Polit. Oekonomie, i ; EFFERTZ, Arbeit u. Boden. (A.T.H.)

Competition (mental) : see INHIBITION (mental).

Complementary Colour [Ger. *Complementärfarbe*; Fr. *couleur complémentaire*; Ital. *colore complementare*. Any two colours whose mixture (physical mixture of light waves) results in the destruction of colour tone, and the production of white or grey, in sensation, are termed complementaries ; so green and purple, orange and green-blue, blue and yellow.

But according to Hering green and red are complementary. On his theory of vision, complementariness is a case of ANTAGONISTIC COLOUR (q.v.). See COLOUR MIXTURE, and Visual Sensation under VISION.

Literature: HELMHOLTZ, Physiol. Optik (2nd ed.), 316, 375 ; FICK, Hermann's Handb. d. Physiol., III. i. 188 (1879). (E.B.T.)

Complex [Lat. *con-* + *plicare*, to fold] : Ger. *complicirt, Zusammen* (Herbart) ; Fr. *complexe*; Ital. *complesso*. Not SIMPLE (q.v.). More positively, as a substantive, a whole constituted of relatively distinguishable but still organically united parts or elements. Opposed to AGGREGATE (q.v.) in this latter respect. Sometimes used as a translation of Herbart's Zusammen (Herbart, *Metaphysik*). (J.M.B.)

Complex (in logic): Ger. *zusammengesetzt*; Fr. *complexe, composé*; Ital. *complesso, composto*. A whole is complex when the relation of its parts is such as to involve super- and sub-ordination, or interdependence of the parts. In this respect it is distinguished either from what is simple or from what is composite (compound). The word is used generally, however, with little attention to the distinction between complex and compound. Complex propositions are those in which subject or predicate, or both, involve a number of simple terms, and which cannot be resolved into a corresponding number of independent assertions. (R.A.)

Complication : Ger. *Complication*; Fr. *complication* (suggested); Ital. *complicazione*. The combination of partial presentations in a single simultaneous whole, whether perception or idea.

This definition is very similar to that of Ward (*Encyc. Brit.*, 9th ed., 57), who attributes the same meaning to Herbart (but without reference). Ward differs from Külpe (*Outlines of Psychol.*, Eng. trans., 278, 317), who (also without reference) claims the authority of Herbart as well, in that Ward makes Complication a matter of perceptual SYNTHESIS (q.v.) generally, in which our definition follows him, while Külpe seems to limit it to the union of lower and more simple elements. Wundt, on the contrary, defines complication as a form of simultaneous association (*Outlines of Psychol.*, Eng. trans., 234; also *Physiol. Psychol.*, 4th ed., ii. 448) between elements of unlike compounds in contrast with 'assimilations,' which are 'simultaneous associations between elements of like compounds.' Wundt's usage thus implicates his own special terminology. If the word be used at all, and cover a distinction not already marked by other terms, it would seem to be best to adopt Ward's usage, which marks the distinction between complication (a fusion or synthesis of the elements of a single presentation) and association (the union of relatively independent presentations). See FUSION, SYNTHESIS, INTEGRATION, and COLLIGATION. The differentia in these several definitions are those of (1) lower and higher (genetic), and (2) of closeness of union (functional), rather than of qualitative character (as Herbart's and Lipps' procedure). As a matter of fact, however, complication, as we define it, is probably coterminous with the other. Yet we suggest 'disparate complication' for Lipps' (and Wundt's) Verbindung disparater Vorstellung-sinhalte on the level of presentation. Stout (*Analytic Psychol.*, ii. 27) adopts this usage, except that he would subsume complication under association with the special qualification made in the phrase 'impressional association.' See his later treatment (*Manual of Psychol.*, 91 ff.), in which he contrasts complication with 'free reproduction.' (J.M.B., G.F.S.)

Complication Experiments. The name given to experiments upon the temporal displacement (by direction of attention) of simultaneous disparate stimuli.

Literature: WUNDT, Physiol. Psychol. (4th ed.), ii. 393; v. TSCHISCH, Philos. Stud., ii. 603; JAMES, Princ. of Psychol., i. 414; PIERCE and ANGELL, Amer. J. of Psychol., iv. 529; JASTROW, Amer. J. of Psychol., v. 239; PFLAUM, Philos. Stud., xv. 139. (E.B.T.)

Component Society : see SOCIOLOGY.

Compos mentis and **Non compos mentis** [Lat., also *compos sui*]: Ger. *dispositions-fähig*; Fr. (Lat. form); Ital. (Lat. form), *integrità, infermità di mente*. The former is a legal term for the possession of sound faculties of mind, sufficient to conduct one's affairs; and the latter denotes a condition of mental deficiency, as in idiocy, or of disorders, as in insanity, which would incapacitate an individual from so acting. See also SANITY, and INSANITY. (J.J.)

Composite (**Idea,** &c.): Ger. *zusammen-gesetzte* (*Idee*); Fr. (*idée*) *composée*; Ital. (*idea*) *composta*. Any idea, &c., resulting from the union of elements in consciousness; the result of COMBINATION (q. v.). A composite idea is a mental COMPOUND (q. v.) of the intellectual order. So of composite feelings and conations, in their respective orders. (J.M.B.)

Composition (linguistic). The uniting of two or more sentence elements into a syntactical complex representing a single idea, and in which, through modification of use or meaning in the whole or the parts, the components become more or less isolated from their value in the simplex; the result is called a compound.

The partial or entire surrender of individuality on the part of the component becomes therefore the test of a compound. It represents a psychological, and not merely a formal or grammatical, phenomenon. Note the difference between *nobleman* and *noble man, blackberry* and *black berry, goldfish* and *gold fish*. Isolation through modification of meaning or use in the compound is illustrated, e.g., by *great-heart, redbreast,* &c. The form of writing or printing is no test of a real compound. The following are, for instance, compounds: high priest, black art, old bachelor, Red Sea, through and through, far and wide, great and small, all at once, none the less.

Literature: H. PAUL, Principien d. Sprachgesch. (3rd ed., 1898), §§ 228 ff.; H. SWEET, New English Grammar, §§ 1545 ff. (B.I.W.)

Composition and Division (fallacies of): Ger. *Verbindung und Einteilung*; Fr. *composition et division*; Ital. *composizione e divisione*. The FALLACIES (q.v.) of composition and division (*sensus compositus*), for it is impossible to sever the treatment of them, depend upon the illegitimate identification in meaning of the relations in which whole and parts may stand, e. g. that of an aggregate to its units, of a universal to its particulars, of an organic whole to its members. They illustrate CONFUSION (q. v.) of thought.

In Aristotle's mode of treating Composition and Division, they are fallacies dependent upon grammatical structure, and are rightly described by him as in the language (cf. Poste's ed. of the *Soph. Elen.*, 106–7). In the more extended sense given to the fallacies by modern writers (Whately, *Logic*, Bk. III. § 11; Mill, *Logic*, Bk. V. chap. vii), they are *extra dictionem*, and altogether distinct from the verbal confusions signalized by Aristotle, which are all instances of AMPHIBOLOGY (q. v.). (R.A.)

Composition of Forces: Ger. *Vereinigung der Kräfte*; Fr. *composition des forces*; Ital. *composizione delle forze*. The composition of forces, all acting on or passing through a point, is the operation of determining a single force, called *the resultant*, which shall produce the same mechanical effect as do the several forces. The resolution of a force is the determination of three forces, acting in given directions, which shall be the equivalent of the given force. Since a point can only move in one direction, all the forces that can act upon it may be compounded into a single one. But in the case of a solid body, when the lines in which the forces act do not pass through any one point, all possible forces may be compounded into two resultants, one of translation, impelling the body in a certain direction, the other of rotation, a COUPLE (q.v.), tending to make it rotate round an axis having this same direction. The combination of the two motions is that of a screw, which rotates and moves forward at the same time.

Such a pair of forces may again be resolved into six, three of translation in the direction of three given axes of co-ordinates, and three of rotation around these same axes. (S.N.)

Composition Theory: Ger. *Compositionstheorie*; Fr. *théorie de la composition de l'esprit*; Ital. *teoria della composizione (mentale)*. The hypothesis that our mental states are the resultant of the varied combinations of certain primitive elements. In its extreme form it assumes that the ultimate units of composition are all of one kind. Cf. ATOMISM (in psychology).

Literature: for exposition of the most noted form of the theory see SPENCER, Princ. of Psychol., i. Pt. II. chaps. i, ii, and for criticism JAMES, Princ. of Psychol., i. chap. vi. Also RABIER, Psychologie, Pt. XI; BALDWIN, Handb. of Psychol., Senses and Intellect (1898); FOUILLÉE, Psychol. des Idées-forces, 21 ff. (G.F.S.)

Compound (in logic): see COMPLEX (in logic).

Compound (mental) [Lat. *con-* + *ponere*, to place]: Ger. (*psychisches*) *Gebilde* (Wundt); Fr. *composé (mental)*; Ital. *composto (mentale)*. A relatively independent composite mental content.

The term is suggested by Judd, the translator of Wundt, whom we follow in the main features of the definition (Wundt, *Grundriss d. Psychol.*, 3. Aufl., 107). (J.M.B.)

Compound Tone: Ger. *Klang*; Fr. *son*; Ital. *suono (composto)*. (1) A musical note, the complex of fundamental tone and overtones; contrasted with simple tone. (E.B.T.)

Compound tone is preferred to clang as translation of the German *Klang*, with this meaning. Cf. the remarks under CLANG.

(J.M.B.)

(2) A concord or discord. See CHORD.

The problem which the compound tone sets to psychology has been formulated in the question: Is the tone simple or complex, as apprehended in direct perception? Various answers have been given, and various explanations offered. The arguments in favour of its being simple are: (1) Verdict of the unmusical. The perception of complexity is due to practice. (2) 'Multiplicity' is predicable only of temporal and spatial complexes.

In favour of its complexity: (1) Verdict of musicians. Simplicity is an illusion due to lack of practice. (2) Analysis is possible with unknown instruments. (3) Overtones are always pure in tempered-scale compound tones. Cf. FUSION.

Literature: STUMPF, Tonpsychologie, ii. 17-22; KÜLPE, Outlines of Psychol., 289; SANFORD, Course in Exper. Psychol., expts.

85, 86, 92 ; TAINE, L'Intelligence, i. 175; MÜLLER, Zur Theorie d. sinnlichen Aufmerksamkeit (1873) ; LOTZE, Med. Psychol., 267 ; HELMHOLTZ, Sensations of Tone, 63. (E.B.T.)

Comprehension [Lat. *comprehendere*, to grasp]: Ger. *Begreifen* ; Fr. *compréhension, savoir*; Ital. *comprensione*. Knowledge of the relational or apperceptive type—'knowledge about'—as contrasted with that of the immediate or intuitive type—'acquaintance with.' Cf. KNOWLEDGE. (J.M.B., G.F.S.)

Comprehension (in logic): Ger. *Inhalt* ; Fr. *compréhension* ; Ital. *comprensione*. The mark or marks represented as common to a plurality of objects or cases; what is taken as constituting the general characteristics of a class.

The comprehension or content of a notion is therefore always relative to the EXTENSION (q.v.), or representation of a plurality of instances in which these common features are realized. The relation springs from the ultimate nature of thinking, as a process at once abstractive and at the same time having constant reference to reality.

The distinction is to be found in substance in Aristotle. It received a prominence in logic which it hardly merits in the *Port Royal Logic*, and has since become the cardinal doctrine in the strictly formal logic of Kant and Hamilton.

Literature: for historical notices, see BAYNES, in his translation of the Port Royal Logic, and in his New Analytic of Logical Forms (1850) ; HAMILTON, Lects. on Logic ; MILL, Exam. of Hamilton, chap. xvii. (R.A.)

Compromise [Lat. *compromissum*]: Ger. *Compromiss* ; Fr. *compromis* ; Ital. *compromesso*. In civil law, an agreement to refer a controversy to arbitration at common law ; a voluntary settlement of a controversy by accepting something less or other than the original demand.

'Compromissum ad similitudinem iudiciorum redigitur et ad finiendas lites pertinet' (*Dig.*, iv. 8, *De Receptis qui Arbitrium receperunt*, 1). (S.E.B.)

Comte, Isidore Auguste Marie-François Xavier. (1798–1857.) An eminent French philosopher and mathematician, who founded the school of positive philosophy. In 1814 he entered the Polytechnic School in Paris, and about 1820 became a disciple of St. Simon. The latter relation continued six years, and then terminated in mutual loss of esteem. He was tutor in mathematics and examiner of candidates at the Polytechnic School (1832–52). His best known work is *Cours de Philosophie Positive*. See POSITIVISM.

Comtism [from Auguste Comte]: see POSITIVISM.

Conation [Lat. *conatus*, from *conare*, to attempt]: Ger. *Streben* ; Fr. *volonté* ; Ital. *conato, facoltà conativa* (E.M.). The theoretical active element of consciousness, showing itself in tendencies, impulses, desires, and acts of volition. Stated in the most general form, conation is unrest. It exists when and so far as a present state of consciousness tends by its intrinsic nature to develop into something else. (J.M.B.–G.F.S.)

Used by Hamilton to include desires and volitions (*Lects. on Met.*, xi). Hamilton's editors (Mansel and Veitch) point out that the adjective Conative was used by Cudworth (*Treatise on Free Will*, ed. Allen, 1838, 31). In concrete cases conation is indicated by the special terms (q. v.) given in the definition. The term will is often used (corresponding to the German Wille) in the same sense, but it is impossible to keep it free from confusion with volition, and it is, perhaps, better to have the term conation set aside with this general meaning.

In German, Streben is the best equivalent on the whole, although the usage in German writers is conflicting. The principal question is between Begehren (Kant, Wundt, Höfler, notably in compounds) and Streben (Lipps, Beneke, Höffding, Jodl, and many others, who devote Begehren to DESIRE, q. v.). Wundt's use of Streben, in narrow contrast with Widerstreben (both as subheads under Trieb), has nothing to commend it; nor has Titchener's (*Amer. J. of Psychol.*, vii., 1895, 84) translation of Streben by Effort, the recognized German word for Effort being Anstrengung. The principal German terms for conative processes as recommended in this work are: Antrieb (conatus), tendency (of bodies); Anstrengung, effort ; Begehren (Begehrung, Begehrungsvermögen), desire ; Begierde, sensuous conations ; Gemüths- (in compounds: Kant's Begehrungsvermögen), conative-affective; Streben, conation; Trieb, impulse ; Wahl, choice ; Wille, will ; Willens- (in compounds), volitional ; Willkür- (in compounds), voluntary ; Wollen, volition.

Literature (using the term) : WARD, Encyc. Brit., art. Psychology, 42 f.; LADD, Psychol., Descrip. and Explan., chap. xi ; STOUT, Analytic Psychol., and Manual of Psychol.; HAMILTON and CUDWORTH, as cited above;

Morselli, Semej. malat. ment., ii. Of the thing, the general treatises on psychology. See also literature under Will, and Bibliog. G, 2, ε. For literature from 1894, see also the Psychological Index. (J.M.B., G.F.S.)

Conatus [Lat.]: Ger. *Antrieb, streben* (as verb); Fr. *tendance*; Ital. *tendenza*. The analogue of conation attributed to bodies and to nature generally.

The term is much used by Spinoza (*Ethics*), and its equivalent by those, notably in Germany, whose philosophy of nature is animistic and voluntaristic, e. g. Schopenhauer and Hartmann (Wille), Wundt, Paulsen (Trieb, Antrieb). The more neutral word Tendency (q.v.) is free from this animistic implication, but the German Tendenz seems to have it. (J.M.B.)

Concatenation(neural)[Lat. *con-* + *catena*, chain]: no foreign equivalents in use. Ital. *concatenazione* suggested (E.M.). The serial association of a number of nervous elements to form a single path or tract.

The term has been suggested to cover those cases where nervous impulses are translated from element to element without the necessity of a continuous fibre. It is becoming more and more evident that a large number of impulses are conveyed by this method, and it appears that in lower forms and embryos the concatenation is less complete than in higher or adult types. The simplest form of neural concatenation is seen in those cases where a series of neurocytes is formed with the terminal arborizations of a neurite from one cell communicating by contiguity with those of the dendrite of a second, and so on. Cf. the figures under Spinal Cord and Fig. 6 under Nervous System. The extreme case is seen in those peripheral nerves which are formed by the fusion of a moniliform series of proliferating cells (cf. Proliferation), while their nuclei become detached and remain in the wall in a state of latency until called upon to repair injuries or assist in metabolism. Yet it should be noted that this method of nerve formation is denied by some authorities. The original method by which various segments of the cord become united into paths of nervous translation is doubtless that which receives the above name.

Literature: C. L. Herrick, Development of Medullated Nerve Fibres, J. of Compar. Neurol., iii. No. 1 (1893); Julia B. Platt, Ontogenetic Differentiations of the Ectoderm in Necturus, Study ii, Quart. J. Microsc. Sci., N.S., xxxviii. (1896) 536–40. (H.H.)

Conceit: see Pride.

Conceivability and **Inconceivability**: see Tests of Truth.

Concentration [Lat. *con-* + *centrum*, centre]: Ger. *Konzentration*; Fr. *concentration*; Ital. *concentrazione*. A state of exclusive and persistent attention.

The term is also used of consciousness or the mind generally, but in all cases during concentration of mind or of consciousness the attention is being used as the vehicle of it. In concentration the attention is restricted to certain definite elements of content, which are thus much reinforced, while the inhibiting result of attention upon the presentations not attended to is also very marked. This two-fold result is called by Wundt 'narrowing of consciousness' (Engerung des Bewusstseins); both aspects of it are seen in Absent-minded-ness (q. v.). The other results of attention are likewise present in different degrees according to the amount of concentration, which thus becomes a statement of the degree of attention.

Literature: see Attention. (J.M.B.–G.F.S.)

Concentration (of studies). The adjustment of certain studies regarded as subordinate to others conceived to be principal.

Ziller is the father of the doctrine of concentration. He regarded history, religion, and literature as the central core of a proper curriculum of studies, the sequence of their topics to be determined in accordance with his doctrine of Culture Epochs (q.v.). The subject-matter having been selected, he proposed that the topics in the remaining studies, such as natural science, geography, mathematics, &c., should be selected in accordance with the intimacy of their relations to those of the central core. The ground for such an arrangement he found in the supposed psychical needs of the child, rather than in any rational correlation of the subject-matter itself. For similar reasons, others have proposed like schemes of instruction, but with different central cores, such as natural science and geography. Cf. Correlation, and Co-ordination.

Literature: F. McMurry, First Year-Book of Herbart Soc.; Parker, Talks on Pedagogics, or Theory of Concentration; C. A. McMurry, Gen. Meth., 69–89; De Garmo, Herbart and the Herbartians; Rein, Outline of Pedagogics, 101–35; Harris, Report of the Committee of Fifteen. (C. De G.)

Concept (in logic): see Term (logical).

Conception, with (1) **Concept**, and (2)

Universal [Lat. *concipere*, to take together]: Ger. *Begriffsbildung*, with (1) *Begriff*, and (2) *Allgemeinbegriff* (cf. NOTION); Fr. *conception*, with (1) *concept*, and (2) *conception universelle*; Ital. *concezione*, with (1) *concetto*, and (2) *concetto universale*. (1) Cognition of a universal as distinguished from the particulars which it unifies. The universal apprehended in this way is called a Concept.

(2) The term Universal stands for any mode in which particular experiences are unified so as to form a single whole which is identified as the same throughout the variety of its parts, phases, or aspects.

The individual marked by a proper name is a universal. Any individual man, John Jones or Richard Roe, is the unity of manifold states, qualities, activities, and relations. He remains the same man whether he is eating or sleeping, sitting or standing, struggling or triumphant, &c. The proper name marks the connecting unity as distinguished from the multiform ways in which it is particularized. Hence the proper name stands for a universal. Generality (see GENERALIZATION) is one kind, but only one kind, of universality. It consists in the repetition of like characters in numerically distinct examples or instances. So far as a plurality of otherwise distinct existences have a like nature, the likeness is a connecting unity, and from this point of view they can be apprehended as a single object of consciousness. Universals of this kind are called general concepts, and the mode of thinking by which they are cognized is called general conception.

Every general conception is a conception of what is general, i.e. of a like nature actually or possibly repeated in a plurality of particular cases. But besides this, each general conception also involves another kind of universal, inasmuch as in each case comprehended by it there is a distinction between the connecting unity and the particulars unified by it. The concept triangle comprehends an indefinite multiplicity of actual or possible triangles which are the particulars combined in it as examples or instances. But the like nature which is repeated in these several instances is itself a universal—a universal which is expressed in the form of combination or rule of construction given in the definition of a triangle. The particulars unified by this universal are not particular triangles, but the general constituents of any triangle—lines, angles, &c. We thus see that the general concept includes, besides its mere generality, a kind of universal analogous to that of the individual concept. On the other hand, it is equally true that the individual concept presupposes and includes general concepts. The various states, activities, relations, &c., which are connected in the unity of a continuous individual existence, are severally cases coming under general classes of states, activities, relations, &c. John is at present walking: his walking is a particular phase in the unity of his total existence, and so comes under the individual concept as such. But the present act is also an instance of a general kind of activity. Other people may walk as well as John, and he himself may repeat the act at various times.

There is one point in our definition of conception which requires to be specially emphasized. Conception is the 'cognition of a universal as distinguished from the particulars which it unifies.' The words ' as distinguished from' are of essential importance. The mere presence of a universal element in cognition does not constitute a concept. Otherwise all cognition would be conceptual. The simplest perception includes a universal. In perceiving the colour red I recognize it as the same in various moments of its appearance. In order to conceive red, I must do more than this; I must draw a distinction between its general nature and its particular appearances. The universal must be apprehended in antithesis to the particulars which it unifies. This is a process which probably cannot take place except in a very rudimentary form without the aid of language.

This is the best use in psychology. For the psychologist the term Conception implies a distinction between the universal and the particular. But in philosophy it is common to apply the word more widely, so as to cover the universal element in knowledge under all its forms, whether it is consciously disengaged from its particular embodiment or not. Thus the Kantian categories, considered merely as universal formative principles, are called in philosophical terminology concepts, even when they are not supposed to be distinguished by reflective analysis. Cf. ABSTRACTION, and GENERALIZATION. (G.F.S.–J.M.B.)

Literature: the textbooks of psychology, and BIBLIOG. C, 2, *g*.

Conceptual: Ger. *begrifflich*; Fr. *conceptuel*; Ital. *concettuale*. The adjective corresponding to concept, denoting a process in which concepts are co-operating factors;

and also the adjective of Conception, denoting the process of conceiving, i.e. by which a concept is reached. (J.M.B.)

Conceptualism: see GENERAL IDEA, NOMINALISM, and REALISM (1).

Conclusion [Lat. *con-* + *cludere*, to close]: Ger. *Schlussssatz*; Fr. *conclusion*; Ital. *conclusione*. A relative term, designating a judgment viewed in relation to the premises or asserted truths on which it is rested or from which it follows. (R.A.)

Concomitance (logical) [Lat. *con-* + *comes*, companion]: Ger. *Funktionsverhältniss*; Fr. *concomitance*; Ital. *concomitanza*. The relation among facts, events, or qualities of objects, expressed by their definite conjunction, and specially by their covariation. In the logic of induction the method of concomitant variations is founded on the general principle that if two facts are found constantly to vary together they are constantly connected. In practice the study of such conjoint variation is serviceable (1) as suggesting a law of connection, (2) as enabling a hypothetical law of connection to be tested, and, if valid, to be expressed in quantitative form. This method is theoretically a series of applications of the METHOD OF DIFFERENCE (q. v.), and is correspondingly more effective. (R.A.)

Concomitance (in theology): Ger. *Konkomitanz*; Fr. *concomitance, consubstantiation*; Ital. *concomitanza*. The doctrine according to which (1) the presence of Christ's body in the Eucharist implies the presence of his blood also, and (2), Christ being both God and man, he as both God and man is present in the Eucharist when either his body or his blood are there.

This doctrine forms the basis for the communion in one kind (the withholding of the cup) as concerns the laity in the Roman Catholic Church. (R.M.W.)

Concomitant Sensation: Ger. *Mitempfindung*; Fr. *sensation associée*; Ital. *sensazione concomitante* (or *associata*). (1) In general, any sensation that accompanies another adequately stimulated sensation, in the absence of its own adequate stimulus; another name for SYNAESTHESIA (q. v.), which is to be preferred. Special meanings are:—

(2) A sensation set up at one part of the skin by stimulation of another part; characterized by brief duration, and by the intermixture of the pain quality. See Wundt, *Physiol. Psychol.* (4th ed.), i. 140, 179.

(3) Sensations set up through stimulation (Miterregung) by way of the centrifugal paths in the opticus and acusticus nerves, after stimulation of the peripheral organ (Wundt, *Physiol. Psychol.* (4th ed.), i. 517). (E.B.T.)

Concrete [Lat. *concrescere*, to grow together]: Ger. *concret*; Fr. *concret*; Ital. *concreto*. A relative term, varying in sense with the conception formed of the nature of real existence and in degree with the range of thought about existence. To think concretely is to represent general relations as embodied in particular instances; and so to delineate the object thought of after the fashion and with the determining details of immediate perceptive experience. A concrete term is often defined as the name of a thing. (R.A.)

Concupiscence [Lat. *concupiscentia*, from *concupiscere*]: Ger. *sinnliche Begierde, Sinnenlust*; Fr. *concupiscence*; Ital. *concupiscenza*. Excessive or passionate desire; desire for an object which appeals to the senses.

It is found in Tertullian, who also uses *concupiscentivus* as a translation of ἐπιθυμητικός. In agreement with this usage, the term became a technical term in the scholastic psychology and ethics. Aquinas distinguishes the affections or emotions of man (*passiones*) into *concupiscibiles* and *irascibiles*— following the Platonic distinction of ἐπιθυμητικόν and θυμοειδές. Of the former, love (*amor*) is placed first. But *concupiscentia*, in its special signification, is distinct from love. Love, regarded strictly, is *amor amicitiae*, and seeks the good of its object. It is thus distinguished from *amor concupiscentiae*, in which an object of desire is sought by us for our own sake. In this special sense, *concupiscentia* is held to be a distinct emotion (*passio*), and to be always connected with sensitive appetite. Accordingly it was said to be the material cause of original sin, as want of original righteousness was its formal cause.

Literature: AQUINAS, Summa, II. 1, Q. 23, art. 1; Q. 52, art. 2; Q. 26, art. 4; Q. 30; Q. 82, art. 3. Cf. ZIEGLER, Gesch. d. chr. Eth., 286 ff. (W.R.S.)

Concurrence (divine). Rendering of the Latin phrase *concursus dei*. See ASSISTANCE.

Concurrence (in theology) [Lat. *con-* + *currere*, to run]: Ger. *Mitwirkung*; Fr. *coopération*; Ital. *concorrenza*. The doctrine, descending from Augustine and adopted by Calvin, that prior to man's 'apostasy,' in the Fall, his spiritual life and moral wholeness were maintained by the support, or concurrence, of the Divine Spirit. When by the plan of salvation this support is restored to men, for the purpose of renewing their moral and spiritual life, the concurrence under the changed circumstances is called GRACE (q. v.). (R.M.W.)

Condillac, Étienne Bonnot de Mably de. (1715-80.) French philosopher. Born at Grenoble, he was the early associate and friend of Rousseau and Diderot. He became abbé of Mureaux. In 1768 he was chosen a member of the French Academy. He introduced Locke to his fellow countrymen.

Condition and **Conditional** (in logic) [Lat. con- + dare, to give]: Ger. Voraussetzung; Fr. condition; Ital. condizione. A condition is the content of an assertion which is put forward by way of supposition, or hypothetically. The conditions are those represented circumstances which, did they hold good in any sense of that term, would establish the holding good in like manner of what is called, relatively, the conditioned or consequent. Any proposition which asserts the relation between a supposed content and that which is dependent thereon is conditional in form, and any reasoning which turns upon the same relation is conditional; although the assertion of the relation is categorical.

From the time of Boethius and his Latin predecessors (cf. Prantl, Gesch. d. Logik, i. 580, 678, 691 ff.) there has been confusion in the use of the terms conditional and hypothetical. These have been now identified, now distinguished, and that either by making the genus conditional and the species hypothetical, or vice versa (see Hamilton, Discussions, 150 ff.), or by defining each as having a distinct province and principle (see Keynes, Formal Logic, Bk. II. chap. viii). The variation points to the real difficulty of determining the precise import of the hypothetical or conditional assertion, a point on which logicians are still distractingly at variance. (R.A.)

Condition and **Conditioned**: Ger. Bedingung, bedingt; Fr. condition, conditionné; Ital. condizione. A condition is (1) a sine qua non, an 'essential' thing or event without which another (conditioned) cannot be, or (2) that which is 'sufficient' but not essential to the being of the other. See NECESSARY AND SUFFICIENT CONDITION. (J.M.B.)

The conception is more negative than cause, which is looked on as an active principle, while a condition is often a limiting and defining principle. J. S. Mill defines the conditions of a thing as the entire setting in which the thing exists. Kant speaks of

experience as conditioned by time and space. With Schelling and Hegel to be conditioned is equivalent to existing as a finite being. Cf. FINITE AND INFINITE, and FORCE AND CONDITION. (R.H.S.)

Hamilton called Philosophy of the Unconditioned the work in which he developed his view that 'to think is to condition. He means by this that we determine everything we are able to conceive and comprehend by its relation to something else by which it is conditioned and limited. Our knowledge deals with the conditionally limited' (Höffding, Hist. of Mod. Philos., Eng. trans., ii. 386 f.). (J.M.B.)

Conditional Immortality: Ger. konditionale Unsterblichkeit; Fr. immortalité conditionnelle; Ital. immortalità condizionale. The doctrine according to which man is not naturally immortal. The conception of natural immortality of the soul is an error due to uncritical acceptance of Greek, especially Platonic, philosophical ideas. On the contrary, man was created subject to death.

There is a possibility of rising above this mortality, and if he either can or will not take advantage of this possibility, he will pass to extinction either at the moment of physical death, or after judgment at a subsequent period. This doctrine may be called the 'aristocratic' idea of immortality, in the sense that only the fit survive to endless life. It has affinities with some modern idealistic systems—witness the adherence of Richard Rothe—but the entire weight of theological authority is against it. Cf. ANNIHILATION.

Literature: see ANNIHILATION; R. ROTHE, Dogmatik, iii. 133-69, 291-336; Theol. Ethik, §§ 471, 596; KABISCH, Die Eschatologie d. Paulus; SALMOND, Christian Doctrine of Immortality, 599 f.; PETAVEL, L'Immortalité conditionnelle. (R.M.W.)

Conditional Morality: see ABSOLUTE ETHICS, and ETHICAL THEORIES.

Condorcet, Marie Jean Antoine Nicolas Caritat, Marquis de. (1743-94.) French mathematician and philosopher. Born at Ribemont; educated at the College of Navarre. In 1769 was admitted to the Academy of Sciences. In 1777 he became permanent secretary of the Academy of Sciences, and five years later was admitted to the French Academy. He was a friend of d'Alembert, and had a large share in the Encyclopédie. Elected to the National Convention, 1792, he voted usually with the Girondists. In May, 1793, he was prescribed by the Jacobins, and concealed himself for eight months in the house of a friend, where he wrote his greatest work. He left his prison early in 1794 to enjoy a country outing, was arrested, and thrown into the Bourgla-Reine, where he was soon afterwards found dead, supposedly from self-poisoning. Lamartine calls him the Seneca of modern times.

Conduct [Lat. *conductus*, lead] : Ger. *Handlung*; Fr. *action morale*; Ital. *azione morale, condotta* (pathological—E.M.). The sum of an individual's ethical actions, either generally or in relation to some special circumstance.

According to the different tendencies of their thought moralists sometimes regard conduct or moral actions, sometimes character or motives, as the subject-matter with which ethics deals. Bentham is an example of the former; Kant, T. H. Green, and Martineau are examples of the latter method. But as conduct both proceeds from and tends to form character, both conceptions are required. Even by Utilitarian writers the actions which go to make up moral or immoral conduct are held to be not external results but intentions (J. S. Mill, *Utilitarianism*, 27). Thus 'conduct' is said by S. Alexander to be 'a state of mind' and not 'a mere outward act.' 'Conduct and character are in reality identical. A good character cannot exist except in its conduct, nor are there any actions approved by morality which do not proceed from a character which wills them.' (W.R.S.)

Conduct is popularly used also for action of any sort, but its restriction, as a technical term, to moral action is recommended. (J.M.B.)

Literature: H. SPENCER, Princ. of Eth., Part I ('Data'), chap. i; ALEXANDER, Moral Order and Progress, Bk. I. chap. ii.; treatises on ethics generally. (W.R.S.)

Conduction (nervous) : see NERVE STIMULATION AND CONDUCTION.

Confession [Lat. *con-* + *fateri*, to own] : Ger. *Beichte*; Fr. *confession*; Ital. *confessione*. This term is used in several senses: (1) in relation to faith, as 'confession of faith,' when it means profession (see CREED); (2) in relation to sin, which is the customary usage. In this connection it is of two kinds: (*a*) Public confession, or confession before the whole congregation or meeting. This was a usage of the early Christian Church, and was closely connected with repentance and turning from ungodly ways of life. It now survives under the name of Penance in ecclesiastical circles; and in times of religious (pietistic) revival, it is frequently employed much as it was in the early Church—parties who are converted or repentant relating their 'experiences.' (*b*) Private, or auricular, confession. In the Roman Catholic Church this is a part of the Sacrament of Penance. As a legalized practice it dates from the time of Leo the Great. Confession, practically of this kind, has been retained by some of the Reformed churches as a preliminary to admission to communion.

Literature: BINTERIM, Denkwürdigkeiten; KLEE, Die Beichte; SIEMERS, Die Sacrament-Beichte; DALLAEUS, De Sacramentalis Auric. Confessione. (R.M.W.)

Confirmation [Lat. *con-* + *firmare*, to strengthen] : Ger. *Firmelung, Confirmation*; Fr. *confirmation*; Ital. *cresima*. In the Roman Catholic Church, the second of the seven sacraments; in the Reformed churches which retain the practice, a renewal of the baptismal vows, usually in preparation for a first communion.

In the practice of the Reformed churches the principal element in confirmation is catechetical. In the Roman Catholic Church the anointment of the candidate by the bishop with the chrism or holy oil is the essential feature. This custom grew out of historical conflicts concerning the nature and implications of confirmation and baptism, which at last resulted in reservation of the confirmation ceremony (laying on of hands and anointing) to the hierarchy, while baptism could be celebrated by any priest. (R.M.W.)

Conflict (mental) : see INHIBITION (mental).

Conflict of Laws (*Conflictus legum* was Huber's phrase in his *Praelectiones iuris Romani*) : Ger. *Collision der Privatrechtsgesetze verschiedener Staaten*; Fr. *droit international privé, droit civil international*; Ital. *conflitto di leggi*. That branch of law declaring the rules for determining the selection of the law to be applied in cases directly affecting private interests, where there is a question between domestic or foreign law, or different foreign laws (see Holland, *Jurisprudence*, chap. xviii. 353 ff.). Among the leading subjects are marriage, divorce, contracts by persons under some legal disability, foreign judgments, and succession.

This head of law is the work of the last two centuries, and mainly of the nineteenth. So far as any state accepts any rules upon this subject, they become part of its municipal law.

Literature: WHARTON, on the Conflict of Laws; STORY, on the same; DICEY, on the

Laws of England, with reference to the same; SAVIGNY, on the same (trans. by Guthrie, 1880). (S.E.B.)

Conflict of Motives: see MOTIVE.

Confucianism: see CONFUCIUS, and ORIENTAL PHILOSOPHY (China).

Confucius. (551–478 B.C.) A Chinese teacher and philosopher. After his eighteenth year he held two subordinate posts in the government. At twenty-two he became a public teacher, and came to have, it is said, 3,000 disciples. Owing to the political disorders of the time, he devoted much attention to the principles of good government. In 500 B.C. he was made chief magistrate of Chung-tu. Owing to his marked success he was made assistant superintendent of public works, and afterwards minister of crime in Lu. The jealousy and fears of neighbouring states necessitated his retirement from office. For thirteen years he travelled from one state to another, usually honoured, but nowhere followed, by the rulers with whom he conversed. From 483 to 478 he was occupied with literary work.

Confusion (logical) [Lat. *confundere*, to confound]: Ger. *Verworrenheit*; Fr. *confusion*; Ital. *confusione*. Confusion in thinking indicates two conditions: (*a*) a lack of adequate determination of the contents of the several thoughts (i.e. notions or judgments) constituting the total apprehension; (*b*) specially, the lack of adequate determination of the all-important relation of order in these contents. As a result of (*a*), confused thinking is characterized by its capacity for identifying or distinguishing without sufficient grounds, a weakness to which the ambiguity of words contributes. As a result mainly of (*b*), confusion in thought exhibits itself in the various fallacies which rest upon an imperfect apprehension of the bearing of evidence upon a conclusion, e.g. PETITIO PRINCIPII and IGNORATIO ELENCHI (see those terms).

The definitions of clear, distinct, confused, &c., as quantities of notions, first laid down in Leibnitz' tract (*Meditat. de Cognitione, Virtute et Ideis*, 1684, trans. by Baynes, in App. to *Port Royal Logic*), found their way into all the textbooks of the Kantian school, and thence through Hamilton (*Logic*, §§ 9–10) into English philosophy.

Literature: good remarks, which supplement usefully Leibnitz' rather scholastic definitions, are in LOCKE, Essay, Bk. II. chap. xxix. See also MILL, Logic, Bk. V. chap. vii. (R.A.)

Confusion (mental): Ger. *Verwirrtheit*; Fr. *confusion mentale*; Ital. *confusione mentale*. (1) As a symptom: a condition of embarrassment, distraction, or lack of clearness of thought and appropriateness of action.

As a momentary condition it occurs frequently and normally in the transition from sleep to wakefulness, in recovery from faintness, or as an effect of anaesthetics. In weakened conditions of the nervous system, as in neurasthenia, a sense of confusion in mental orientation may be a recurrent symptom; while as a more or less serious and chronic condition with intervening lucid intervals it characterizes various forms of insanity, particularly those which involve dementia (cf. KATATONIA). See Schüle, *Klinische Psychiatrie* (1886). (J.J.)

(2) A form of mental disease, clinically and nosologically distinguished by modern German, Italian, and French alienists (see the works of Kraepelin, Chaslin, Ballet, Morselli). It is a variety of 'amentia' described by Meynert, called also 'confusional amentia.' Another variety is stupidity, or *amentia stupida* (*dementia acuta*). A third variety is hallucinatory acute insanity, or the 'hallucinatorischer Wahnsinn' of the German authors. (E.M.)

Congenital [Lat. *con-* + *genitus*, born]: Ger. *angeboren*; Fr. *congénital*; Ital. *congenito*. Congenital characters are those which are directly due to heredity, as contrasted with those which are acquired in the course of individual life. They need not be CONNATE (q. v.), i. e. manifested at birth, but may often be 'deferred' to a comparatively late stage of development, as in the case of the secondary sexual characters. See ACQUIRED AND CONGENITAL CHARACTERS (also for literature).

The clear distinction between congenital and acquired has been rendered of importance in view of the question whether acquired characters are inherited. If, as the Lamarckian school contend, this takes place, the acquired characters of one generation may become the congenital characters of the next.

Literature: A. WEISMANN, Essays upon Heredity, and Contemp. Rev., lxiv (1893); H. SPENCER, Princ. of Biol., and Contemp. Rev., lxiii (1893); LLOYD MORGAN, Habit and Instinct (1896). (C.LL.M.)

Congestion [Lat. *con-* + *gerere*, to crowd together]: Ger. *Congestion*; Fr. *congestion*; Ital. *congestione*. An abnormal accumulation of blood in an organ or part; hyperaemia. (C.F.H.)

Congruent [Lat. *congruere*, to come together]: Ger. *Deckbild, Deckpunkte*; Fr. *image de recouvrement, points de recouvrement*; Ital. *immagine da congruenza*. A congruent or total image is an image which rests upon a number of congruent points. Congruent points are points whose impressions are, in the given case, referred to a single point of external space.

Literature: WUNDT, Physiol. Psychol. (4th ed.), ii. 173; HELMHOLTZ (identifies CORRESPONDING POINTS, q.v., and congruent points), Physiol. Optik, 2nd ed., 844. See also IDENTICAL POINTS. (E.B.T.)

Congruity [Lat. *congruere*, to agree]: Ger. *Kongruenz*; Fr. *congruence*; Ital. *congruenza*. The property or quality of agreement among the parts of an aesthetic whole, involving, as compared with harmony, relatively greater emphasis upon the mere absence of the inappropriate, and relatively less emphasis upon the presence of factors mutually complementary. Cf. HARMONY. (J.R.A.)

Congruity and **Condignity** [Lat. *meritum de congruo*, merit on account of agreement with; *meritum de condigno*, merit on account of likeness to]. These are scholastic phrases, belonging to the period subsequent to Thomas Aquinas, and employed for the purpose of expressing with point and brevity the whole doctrine of grace. Congruity implies that, of its own natural constitution, human nature has the power to be obedient to God, and to originate certain lower acts of obedience which tend to draw it in the direction of divine grace. Condignity means that, after God has given his grace to men, they possess power to perform works of obedience of a kind so much higher as to be pleasing to God. (R.M.W.)

Conjugate Deviation: see DEVIATION.

Conjugation (in biology) [Lat. *coniugatio*]: Ger. *Conjugation*; Fr. *conjugaison*; Ital. *conjugazione*. The temporary union or permanent fusion of two unicellular organisms, a process which is usually followed by increased multiplication by fission.

The chief biological interest of this process lies in its relation to reproduction. It is accompanied by a partial or complete mixture of nuclear matter, and is regarded by many as foreshadowing the union of spermatozoon and ovum in the higher many-celled organisms.

Literature: WEISMANN, Essays upon Heredity; MAUPAS, Le rajeunissement karyogamique chez les Ciliés, Arch. Zool. expér. et gén., 2ᵉ sér., vii. No. 12, 13 (1889). (C.LL.M.)

Conjugation (linguistic). The union under a connected scheme of all the inflectional forms of a given verb.

The Latin word *conjugatio* is merely a direct translation of the Greek συζυγία (*syzygy*), a term applied by the Greek grammarians, first, to any systematic collection of related grammatical forms, then to a systematic collection of verb-forms, and especially to a classification uniting verbs of like inflection; thus, in Latin, the ' four conjugations.'

Verb-forms are primarily classified in conjugation according to voice, mood, tense. Distinctions of *voice* refer to the attitude or relation which the action of the verb set forth through the subject bears to that subject. The assertion of a *man-striking*, for instance, i. e. of the act of striking displayed in the case of a man, may mean (1) that the man does the striking, either without further information concerning the object struck, leaving that to inference, or passing it by as not involved in the matter to be stated, as in *the man strikes*, —or with statement of the object, as in *the man strikes a dog*; this is called the active voice. (2) That the man himself is the object upon which the action completes itself, as in *the man is struck*, the subject being left unstated. If it is necessary to state it, a phrase is added, as in *the man is struck by somebody*. This is called the passive voice, and is a linguistic device for avoiding a statement of the subject or for throwing the object into prominence. (3) That the man does the striking, i. e. that the action of striking is exemplified in him, and that he also represents the sphere in which the action is satisfied or comes to its effect. This is called the middle voice, in imitation of the helplessness of the old Greek terminology (μεσότης). It is closely allied to the passive, being in language-history generally the category out of which the passive is gradually isolated into an independent existence. The subject may be the sphere in which the action is satisfied in the sense (*a*) that the action returns upon the subject, as *he strikes himself*; (*b*) that the action returns upon something associated with the subject in its sphere, as Gr. ἐκόψατο τὴν κεφαλήν, he strikes himself in the head; λούομαι τοὺς πόδας, I wash my feet; but λούω τοὺς πόδας, I wash the feet (of some one else); (*c*) that the action returns upon the subject as a participant, as in διαδικάζεται, he becomes a party to a law-suit; as against δικάζει, he passes judgment; (*d*) that the action returns upon the subject as an interested party: thus δανείζει (act.), he lends; but δανείζεται, he borrows; (e) that the action returns upon the subject in the sense that it is kept within the subjective sphere, involving an intenser participation of the subject in its operation : thus ὁρῶ, I see (of the objective 'seeing'); but ὁρῶμαι, I see, appreciate, and feel. This is common in verbs expressing the sensuous and spiritual activities.

The Mood of a verb concerns the tone of the assertion. The predicate may be asserted of the subject in various attitudes, tones, or moods. The earlier attempts, led by Gottfried Hermann (1772–1848), to identify the moods with the Kantian categories have, with the displacing of logic by psychology as a guide in grammatical study, been entirely discontinued. The inflectional mechanism of the different languages variously adapts itself to the few simple and often vaguely defined modal distinctions seeking expression in the folk-mind. The Indo-European languages recognize the following :—The indicative is the mood which presents the assertion in the guise of reality. The subjunctive is originally the mood of the willed idea, i. e. it involves assurance, promise, and a consciousness of personal control, and is distinguished thus from the future indicative, which states a foresight of fact, a prophecy. In Latin grammar the term subjunctive is used in a much wider sense. Here it designates a class of grammatical forms in which the subjunctive and optative, and probably also future uses, have nearly blended. It is therefore in Latin the mood of the non-real. It introduces the assertion as a conception of the mind. The optative mood originally represented the predicate as a desire. The imperative, originally not a mood in the proper sense, used a form of the verb for the expression of a demand, without reference to a subject.

The moods were originally independent of the tenses, and the creation of orderly paradigms, in which forms have both mood and tense, is apparently a secondary development. The optative appears first only as a present, i. e. without tense; the subjunctive in the earliest record is limited to present and aorist. The development of moods for perfect and future is relatively late.

The Tense of a verb concerns the relation of the verbal action to the matter of time. Tense may express (1) the date of action, i. e. its location in time relatively to the time of speaking, as past, present, future; (2) various aspects of the action relative to its use of time : thus an action may be presented as going on in time present, past, or future; as completed in present, past, or future; as simply occurring; as consisting of repeated actions, &c. The inflectional languages have generally an insufficient supply of forms to serve for all the conceptions which might demand expression; hence two or more are frequently quartered upon a single form. The paradigm is a resultant of compromises between supply and demand.

Literature : B. DELBRÜCK, Vergleichende Syntax der Indogermanischen Sprachen (2 vols., 1893–7); references under PHILOLOGY. (B.I.W.)

Conjugation (logical). An obsolete term used by Apuleius (*De Doct. Platonis*, Bk. III. 208, ed. Bipont, 1788) to indicate the connection of propositions with a common term as premises of a syllogism. The term is evidently coined from the Greek συζυγία. (R.A.)

Conjunctive (in logic) : see DISJUNCTIVE.

Connate [Lat. *con-* + *natus*, born] : Ger. (1) *verwachsen*, (2) *angeboren*; Fr. (1) *conné*, (2) *inné*; Ital. *innato*, *connato* (suggested—E.M.). (1) In botany : congenitally united, e. g. of leaves united at the base. (2) In zoology : applied to congenital characters which appear at or shortly after birth.

The word connate is frequently used in zoology as synonymous with congenital. It has been suggested that the meaning should be restricted, as in definition (2), in which case those characters or modes of instinctive response which are congenital fall into two classes, (a) connate, (b) deferred. See Lloyd Morgan, *Habit and Instinct* (1896). (C.LL.M.)

Connection [Lat. *connectio*] : Ger. *Verbindung*; Fr. *connexion*; Ital. *connessione*. Used in psychology for different sorts of COMBINATION (q. v.). The latter term is preferred. (J.M.B., G.F.S.)

Connotation [Lat. *con-* + *notare*, to mark] : Ger. *Miteinbegreifen, Mitbezeichnung, connotativ* (adj.); Fr. *connotation*; Ital. *connotazione* (suggested—E.M.). The term is open to more than one interpretation. (1) The scholastic logicians, from the time of Occam, and perhaps a little earlier, used the word to indicate an aspect of terms opposed to absolute.

Homo stood *simpliciter* or absolutely for *man*; *iustus* stood primarily for a quality; secondarily, or *connotatively*, for the subject of that quality.

(2) Modern logicians, following J. S. Mill, have so far reversed this. Looking to the

function of general terms, they define connotation as the attributes making up the meaning of the term, what is implied; and contrast with that the denotative aspect, the sphere of application of the term. The distinction is clear and important, so far as class terms or common nouns are concerned. See MEANING, and SIGNIFICATIVE. (R.A.)

Conscience [Lat. *con- + scientia*, knowledge]: Ger. *Gewissen*; Fr. *conscience* (consciousness, for *conscience morale*); Ital. *coscienza*. The consciousness of moral worth or its opposite as manifested in character or conduct, together with the consciousness of personal obligation to act in accordance with morality and the consciousness of merit or guilt in acting. More precisely defined as the recognition by the individual of the moral value of character or conduct, or the recognition of the ultimate moral laws or principles upon which moral judgments concerning character or conduct rest, together with the attendant consciousness of personal obligation and of merit or guilt.

The term conscience, like its Greek equivalent συνείδησις, and Latin equivalent *conscientia*, means literally 'knowledge with'; but it has a specifically ethical significance which the Greek and Latin terms only gradually acquired. The French term *conscience*, though also used as an equivalent of the English 'conscience,' commonly means simply 'consciousness.' In the New Testament the term συνείδησις is frequently used in the ethical sense, i. e. not merely for 'consciousness of one's own state or acts,' but for 'consciousness of their moral worth or value.'

But the term is not used as a technical term of ethics by the classical philosophers. In Aristotle's *Ethics* the conception which approaches most nearly to the modern English use of 'conscience' is φρόνησις, often translated 'prudence,' but usually, in the *Ethics*, more nearly equivalent to 'moral insight.' It was in connection with the greater stress laid, especially by the Stoic philosophers, upon the rational nature of moral law that special prominence came to be attached to the subjective witness to morality in the individual's consciousness. Thus the self-dependent Wise Man of the Stoics is distinguished by a consciousness of his rational and moral worth. But his consciousness of the moral law is designated simply as reason, or the ruling part of the soul. The elaboration of the doctrine of conscience is due to the scholastic writers, who made dominant in their ethics

the conception of moral laws as laws of God revealed by him in the soul of man, for the regulation of human conduct. Two characteristics distinguished the scholastic doctrine of conscience. In the first place, a distinction was drawn between (*a*) the consciousness of the universally binding rules of conduct, to which the name SYNDERESIS (q. v.) was given; and (*b*) the relation to this general rule of the particular case: the latter being called specifically *conscientia*. This distinction is, in essence, adopted by leading modern moralists of the Intuitional school. But the terminology is changed. The term synderesis has fallen out of use; and the term conscience includes (if it is not always restricted to) the consciousness of the universal law or laws of morality, while the term 'moral judgment' is sometimes used for the application of the general rule to the particular case. In the second place, conscience was interpreted as an intellectual power. The moral quality of an action was said to be recognized by subsuming the act under the general rule formulated by conscience. In this way rules of conduct came to be systematized after a juridical pattern. Actions (whether real or possible) were classified and referred to their appropriate principles or moral rules. In carrying out this systematization difficulties arose as to the rules under which certain actions should be subsumed; and thus conflicts of opinion were brought to light concerning the moral worth of such actions. These came to be known as 'cases of conscience.' The difficulty of applying the formal principles to the details of conduct, and the differences of moral judgment which arose in this way, gave rise to the science of CASUISTRY (q. v.).

Both the above characteristics may be traced in the view of conscience held by the writers described by Sidgwick (*Meth. of Eth.*, I. viii. 3) as dogmatic intuitionists. But the doctrine of conscience elaborated by the English moralists has a different origin. Adam Smith remarks (*Mor. Sent.*, VII. iii. 3) that 'the word conscience does not immediately denote any moral faculty by which we approve or disapprove. Conscience supports, indeed, the existence of some such faculty, and properly signifies our consciousness of having acted agreeably or contrary to its directions'—a statement which harmonizes with the forgotten scholastic usage. In Hobbes, and even in Shaftesbury, the word cannot be said to have been used as a technical term ; and it is noticeable that, when used, it has commonly (if not always) the signification of a consciousness of wrong-doing, not of right (cf. Shaftesbury, *Inquiry*, II. ii. 1). But it was through the prominence given by Shaftesbury to the 'moral sense' that the doctrine of conscience, as held by the English moralists, arose. This doctrine was first elaborated by Butler. According to him, conscience does not, of itself and immediately, tend to action : it is the 'principle in man by which he approves or disapproves his heart, temper, and actions'; 'to preside and govern, from the very economy and constitution of man, belong to it;' and it is from this supremacy of conscience that we get the idea of human nature as a system or constitution—and a constitution adapted to virtue.

In two respects at least Butler's account is imperfect : as regards the relation of the subjective principle, called conscience, to the objective moral law, and as regards the constitution of the principle itself. In the first respect Butler asserts strongly (though not quite uniformly, when he speaks of its relation to self-love) the supremacy of conscience—assuming, therefore, that the individual conscience is in harmony with objective moral law : 'he hath the rule of right within, what is wanting is only that he honestly attend to it.'

A negative answer would thus seem to be required to the question of the schools : ' can conscience be educated ?' This negative answer is expressly given by Kant (*Werke*, ed. Hartenstein, vii. 204 ; Abbot's trans., 310), although he allows that ' it is possible to err in the judgment whether something is a duty or not'; conscience being thus distinguished from particular moral judgments and identified with the ultimate principle of PRACTICAL REASON (q. v.). Subsequent ethical analysis has been largely occupied with the endeavour to bring out in detail the relation of this inner response of conscience to the external order of the social environment. Hence the attempts to trace the gradual evolution of conscience, made by J. S. Mill, A. Bain, H. Spencer, and many others. From this point of view conscience is held (with many differences in detail) to be a social consciousness gradually built up in the individual by the influence of his environment: the specifically moral element entering, according to Spencer, when a less evolved feeling is controlled by a more evolved feeling.

This psychological view is accompanied by a modification of the doctrine to which Butler tended concerning the rational constitution of conscience. The rational or reflective element, it is held, comes last in the synthesis. It is preceded by an emotional and active response to surrounding conditions, exhibiting itself in a variety of moral and quasi-moral sentiments, only at a later stage rounded off and reduced to a formula by intellectual reflection. This account succeeds in giving an explanation of the historical and individual divergences of ' conscientious judgments'; it needs to be supplemented in order to explain the universal authority claimed by conscience—what Butler called its 'supremacy.' The social influence which determines the development of conscience almost entirely in its earlier stages is itself transcended in the rational or self-conscious organization of the moral life; so that conscience becomes not merely a social self, but an ideal self.

Literature: JOSEPH BUTLER, Sermons, and Diss. on Virtue ; J. S. MILL, Utilitarianism, chap. iii ; A. BAIN, Emotions (3rd ed.), 285 ff.; H. SPENCER, Princ. of Eth., Pt. I (' Data'), chap. vii ; T. H. GREEN, Proleg. to Eth., Bk. IV. chap. ii ; ELSENHAUS, Wesen und Entstehung des Gewissens. Also literature cited under ETHICS. (W.R.S.)

Conscious Illusion Theory (in aesthetics) : see ART AND ART THEORIES, and SEMBLANCE.

Consciousness : Ger. *Bewusstsein* ; Fr. *conscience* ; Ital. *coscienza*. The distinctive character of whatever may be called mental life.

'It is the point of division between mind and not mind ' (Baldwin, *Elements of Psychol.*, 57). Wherever there is not total unconsciousness, in the sense in which we attribute unconsciousness to a table or a log of wood, the existence of some form of mind we denote by the word consciousness. ' Whatever we are when we are awake, as contrasted with what we are when we sink into a profound and dreamless sleep, that it is to be conscious. What we are less and less, as we sink gradually down into dreamless sleep, or as we swoon slowly away ; and what we are more and more, as the noise of the crowd outside tardily arouses us from our after-dinner nap, or as we come out of the midnight of the typhoid fever crisis,' that is consciousness (Ladd, *Psychol., Descrip. and Explan.*, 30).

In the earlier English psychologists the word signifies the mind's direct cognizance of its own states and processes. Thus Locke: 'Consciousness is the perception of what passes in a man's own mind' (*Essay*, Bk. II. chap. i. 19); Reid: 'That immediate knowledge which we have of all the present operations of our mind' (*Works*, Hamilton's ed., i. 222). The wider usage which is now generally adopted is due to the Associationist School.

Literature: BAIN, Appendix to Emotions and Will; HAMILTON, Metaphysics, Lects. ix, xi–xiii; SIGWART, Logic (Eng. trans.), ii. 130–4; WUNDT, Grundriss, 238; BENEKE, Die neue Psychol., 171–206; LEWES, Physical Basis of Mind, 353 ff. (G.F.S., J.M.B.)

Consciousness of Kind: Ger. (1) *Artsinn* or *Artbewusstsein* (suggested. Analogies: *Artbegriff* in logic, *der Art Leute, Leute aller Art* (J.M.B.), *Gattungsbewusstsein* (Barth)), (2) *Bewusstsein der Gleichheit*; Fr. (1) *conscience de classe* (J.M.B.), *esprit de corps*, (2) *conscience de similitude*; Ital. (1) *coscienza di classe* (J.M.B.), *spirito di corpo*, (2) *coscienza della similitudine* (*della rassomiglianza*). (1) Consciousness of self, however vague, as having something in common with another.

This definition is preferred to that below (2), inasmuch as it does not attempt detailed analysis of this form of SOCIAL CONSCIOUSNESS (q. v.). See also SOCIUS. The French term *esprit de corps* has been used in the three languages for the phenomenon in this broad sense, but with emphasis on the side of action, and on some special bond of union; so that it is well to have a recognized English equivalent. This definition, moreover, is not incompatible with the second (2), since it leaves to further discussion the various psychological factors involved, and permits disagreement in regard to them. The French and German equivalents (2) recommended by F.H.G. seem psychologically ambiguous and unavailable, for each of them is equivalent to 'consciousness of resemblance,' which means quite another thing in current discussion. (J.M.B., G.F.S.)

(2) A complex state of mind combining (*a*) organic sympathy, (*b*) perception of resemblances and classification, (*c*) reflective sympathy, (*d*) affection, (*e*) desire for recognition and for affection or sympathy; and awakened by the presence or the thought of an individual who, in important respects, resembles oneself.

Introduced by Giddings (*Princ. of Sociol.*, 1896), and by him made the fundamental postulate of sociology. More fully analysed, described, and applied in *Elements of Sociol.*

(1898). The phenomenon, though not called by this name, was recognized by Aristotle, *Nic. Eth.*, Bk. VIII. chap. ii; Dante, *Il Convito*, Treatise III, chap. i; Spinoza, *Ethics*, Part III, props. xxvii, xxxiii, xlvi, lix, def. xviii; Spencer, *Princ. of Psychol.*, § 504; Baldwin, *Handb. of Psychol.*, Feeling and Will (1891), 193, and *Social and Eth. Interpret.* (1897), chap. xii and App. D. Spinoza's propositions are particularly clear.

Literature: titles cited above. See also SOCIAL CONSCIOUSNESS, and SOCIUS. (F.H.G.)

Consensual Actions and **Movements** [Lat. *consensus*, agreement]: Ger. (2) *Mitbewegung*; Fr. (2) *mouvements associés, syncinésie* (P.J.); Ital. (2) *movimenti consentanei*. (1) In psychology: reflex and instinctive actions which are stimulated by clearly conscious sensations. In this sense there are no exact foreign equivalents in use; those given for SENSORIMOTOR are nearest.

(2) In physiology: involuntary movements correlated with or accompanying a voluntary movement. See ACCOMPANYING MOVEMENTS.

(1) Used by Carpenter (*Ment. Physiol.*, 82 f.), who contrasts such actions, as to their seat in the nervous system (above the spinal cord but beneath the cerebrum), with the spinal reflexes. Shadworth Hodgson (*Met. of Experience*, iii. 134, iv. 150) uses the term in the wider sense, although quoting Carpenter, of actions which are themselves clearly known, and whose end is foreseen, but which involve no inhibition, effort, or volition (largely Hartley's 'secondarily automatic' actions). That is, Hodgson seems to include 'idiomotor' actions, while Carpenter uses 'sensorimotor' as equivalent to consensual. Cf. Conscious Reflex under REFLEX. As these latter terms are more exact, 'consensual' is not needed. The Latin form *consensus* was early used for the union or 'harmony' of parts of the animal organism: cf. Baumerus, *De consensu partium humani corporis* (Amstelodami, 1556). (J.M.B.)

Consensus gentium [Lat.]. Universal consent, common consent, or catholicity, considered a proof or test of certain principles. See TESTS OF TRUTH. (J.M.B.)

Consent [Lat. *con-* + *sentire*, to feel]: Ger. *Einwilligung*; Fr. *consentement*; Ital. *consenso*. The volition to allow something to take place. I consent to an action; I assent to a proposition: a distinction involving that between belief and will. Cf. BELIEF. (G.F.S.–J.M.B.)

Consentience [Lat. *con-* + *sentire*, to feel]: Ger. *Gesammtempfindung, niedriges Ichgefühl*; Fr. *sentiment du moi primitif ou organique*; Ital. *sentimento fondamentale dell' io organico*. The felt unity of consciousness considered as arising on the basis of sensation, apart from all intellectual processes.

Mivart speaks of consentience as 'a feeling resulting from the unobserved synthesis of our sensations' (*Proc. Zool. Soc.*, London, 1884, 463; quoted in *Century Dict.*), and as an 'unintellectual sense of self.' The term was also used by Lewes, but is not in general use. It might conveniently be adopted, seeing that it denotes the condition of unity of which other writers describe particular phases by such phrases (q.v.) as 'Anoetic Unity of Consciousness' (Stout), 'Passive consciousness,' 'Passivity' of consciousness (Bradley, Baldwin), 'Consensual' (Carpenter, S. Hodgson), 'Organic Self' (Ribot, Mackensie). (J.M.B., G.F.S.)

Consequence [Lat. *con-* + *sequere*, to follow]: Ger. (*nothwendige*) *Folge*; Fr. *conséquence*; Ital. *conseguenza*. A general term for different forms of conditioning or resulting. See CAUSE AND EFFECT, and CONSEQUENCE (logical). It is contrasted with sequence, in that it includes the idea of necessary connection, which the latter does not. We speak of a 'mere sequence' which is not a consequence. Cf. also FORCE AND CONDITION. (J.M.B.)

Consequence (in ethics). The results of an action, so far as they are distinguishable from the action itself.

The line between an action and its consequences can only be drawn in a more or less arbitrary way. The clearest distinction might seem to be to limit the term consequences to those results which are not foreseen or intended by the agent; but this definition is excluded by the familiar usage of the term, especially by Utilitarian writers. One set of consequences can be with tolerable clearness distinguished in (though hardly from) the action: namely, its effects upon the feelings of other conscious persons. The Utilitarian morality, inasmuch as it makes the worth of conduct depend upon its effects, is frequently called a 'morality of consequences.' In this sense the term is used by Bentham. 'The general tendency of an act is more or less pernicious according to the sum-total of its consequences. . . . Among the consequences of an act . . . such only, by one who views them in the capacity of a legislator, can be said to be material, as either consist of pain or plea-sure, or have an influence in the production of pain or pleasure.' See Bentham, *Princ. of Mor. and Legisl.*, chap. vii. (W.R.S.)

Consequent and **Consequence** (logical): Ger. *logische Folge, Consequenz*; Fr. *conséquent*; Ital. *conseguente*. A relative term, designating a judgment, the context of which is asserted to hold good, as following from the assumption that the context asserted in another judgment, called relatively the ANTECEDENT (q. v.), holds good. To the relation between propositions, so connected that the position of the one carries with it the position of another, the abstract name Consequence may be given, and evidently the abstract name may be used in application to all cases in which the truth of one judgment is asserted on supposal of the truth of one or more other judgments.

On the term *consequentia* and the scholastic elaboration of the doctrine connected with it, see Prantl, *Gesch. d. Logik*, iii. 137 ff. (R.A.)

Conservation (in psychology) [Lat. *con-* + *servare*, to keep]: Ger. *Erhaltungsvermögen*; Fr. *conservation*; Ital. *conservazione dei ricordi*. An older term for what is now called RETENTION (q. v.).

Used to describe the group of functions by which mental experiences are 'conserved.' Hamilton (*Lects. on Met.*, xxx) treats of the 'Conservative or Retentive Faculty' as 'Memory proper' (see his learned notes on earlier usage). Cf. Rabier, *Leçons de Psychol.*, chap. xiv. The term retention is now used by most psychologists; the abstract form retentiveness (Bain) being also available and convenient. (J.M.B.)

Conservation of Energy or **Conservation of Force**: Ger. *Erhaltung der Kraft* (*der Energie*); Fr. *conservation des forces* (*de l'énergie*); Ital. *conservazione delle forze* (*dell' energia*). The general law that, in a system of bodies neither acted upon by, nor acting upon, anything outside of itself, the total energy of the system remains invariable, only changing from one form into another. See ENERGY.

The system of bodies under consideration may be a swinging pendulum, the whole earth with everything on it, the solar system, or the entire universe. It should be said that no system of bodies less than the entire universe can be wholly isolated from outside action, because, do what we will, heat will be conducted or radiated away. The most we can do is to make the amount of heat received equal to that radiated, and then the law will hold. Intimations of this law are to be found very early. It first attained the dignity of a scientific doctrine through the investigations of Meyer (1842) and Joule (1843). (S.N.–H.B.F.)

Literature: discussed from a philosophical point of view by SPENCER, First Princ.; LOTZE, Metaphysics; WUNDT, Syst. d. Philos.; WARD, Naturalism and Agnosticism, ii. (J.M.B.)

Conservatism: Ger. *Conservatismus*; Fr. *conservatisme*; Ital. *conservatismo*. (1) The strong love of what is old, customary, and familiar, in opinion, social life and organization, religion, morals, &c. (2) In sociology: habitual opposition to change in social institutions, usages, or manners.

'We scruple not to express the belief that a truer spirit of conservatism, as to everything good in the principles and professed objects of our old institutions, lives in many who are determined enemies of those institutions in their present state, than in most of those who are themselves conservatives' (J. S. Mill, *Dissertations and Discussions*, i. 202). See LIBERALISM.

Literature: see under SOCIAL PSYCHOLOGY, and SOCIOLOGY. (F.H.G., J.M.B.)

Consideration (in law) [Lat. *consideratio*]: Ger. *Gegenleistung*; Fr. *cause*; Ital. *considerazione*. The material cause of an obligatory contract; that which a promiser considers, and the law admits to be, a sufficient equivalent for what he promises to do or forbear. The law requires it to have some value, but it need not be an adequate compensation.

Its legal value is measured by the detriment which it works to the promisee. See Smith on *Right and Law*, § 184. Natural love and affection is a sufficient consideration to make an executed gift of land, by deed, fully effectual, and is termed a 'good' consideration. Under most governments certain legal forms may supply the want of a consideration. By the common law, such an effect is produced by executing a contract under seal.

The obligation of a contract, in early society, comes from its form. A consideration is not admitted to be sufficient to support a contract to be performed in the future, until a somewhat advanced stage of civilization.

Literature: MAINE, Ancient Law; HOLMES, The Common Law, sects. 7, 8. (S.E.B.)

Consistency (topical) [Lat. *con-* + *stare*, to stand]: Ger. *Uebereinstimmung, Folgerichtigkeit*; Fr. *consistance*; Ital. *congruenza*.

A relative term, applicable to a series or group of connected propositions, and expressing the fact that their connection conforms to the general logical laws of inference. It implies more than compossibility, and it is evidently one condition, at least, of truth. The logic of consistency, or Formal Logic, is a statement of the general rules to which a group or series of propositions must conform, if it is to secure the first and simplest condition of truth. (R.A.)

Consonance [Lat. *con-* + *sonare*, to sound]: Ger. *Consonanz*; Fr. *consonance*; Ital. *accordi consonanti*. The relative unitariness or diversity of the total impression produced by a compound tone or chord is called respectively Consonance or Dissonance. They are popularly distinguished as being pleasant and unpleasant. (C.L.F.–J.M.B.)

The INTERVALS (q. v.) allowed by the laws of musical harmony are of three kinds: perfect consonances, imperfect consonances, and dissonances. Perfectly consonant are octave ($1:2$), fifth ($2:3$), and fourth ($3:4$); imperfectly consonant, major third ($4:5$), minor third ($5:6$), major sixth ($3:5$), minor sixth ($5:8$); all the rest are dissonant.

Consonance and dissonance have been explained: (1) by an unconscious apprehension of, and conscious satisfaction and dissatisfaction with, simple and complex vibration ratios (Lipps); (2) by presence or absence of BEATS (q. v.) (Helmholtz); (3) by degree of direct tone relationship (Wundt); (4) by degree of fusion of constituent tones (Stumpf, Külpe).

Literature: STUMPF, Tonpsychologie, ii. 231 f.; Beitr. z. Ak. u. Musikwiss.; KÜLPE, Outlines of Psychol., 304; WUNDT, Physiol. Psychol. (4th ed.), ii. 71; HELMHOLTZ, Sensations of Tone, 226; LIPPS, Grundthatsachen d. Seelenlebens, 269 f.; Psych. Stud. (1885), 92; Zeitsch. f. Psychol., xix. 1; SANFORD, Course in Exper. Psychol., expts. 83, 93, 94. (E.B.T.)

Consonant (vocal): see ALPHABET, and PHONETIC.

Constant Error: Ger. *konstanter Fehler*; Fr. *erreur constante*; Ital. *errore costante*. See ERRORS OF OBSERVATION.

Constant Quantity: see VARIABLE.

Constant Return: see INCREASING RETURN.

Constituent Society: see SOCIOLOGY.

Constitution [Lat. *constituere*, to establish]: Ger. *Constitution*; Fr. *constitution*; Ital. *costituzione*. The entire group of determining factors of a thing in so far as they are internal or organic to it. Cf. ORGANISM.

The limiting cases are illustrated (1) in biology, in that a new-born organism is said to inherit its entire constitution, and (2) in e.g. a drove of sheep, herded by dogs, which has no constitution at all. The conception is illustrated also in theories of knowledge which distinguish principles that are 'constitutive' from those that are 'regulative.' The new-born organism inherits its constitutive principles, but adds regulative ones when it comes into contact with an environment; the flock of sheep has in the dogs its regulative principles, but gets a constitutive one as soon as the individual sheep begin to follow the bell-wether. In various sorts of ORGANIZATION (q. v.) the regulative is emphasized, while in a true organism it is the constitutive. Cf. the remarks made under FORCE AND CONDITION. (J.M.B.)

Constitution (in law): Ger. *Staatsverfassung, Staatsgrundgesetz, Grundverfassung*; Fr. *constitution*; Ital. *costituzione*. The fundamental and supreme law, or laws and institutions, constituting the rule of organization and government of some particular association of persons; e.g. a state, or kingdom, or a private society. It may be written or unwritten; arranged in systematic form, as in the American plan, or made up of certain historic documents and national usages and traditions, as in the case of Great Britain. The term is also used, with less accuracy, to signify the terms of association by which a confederacy of sovereign powers is established.

In Roman law, a *constitutio* was that which the emperor had constituted by a decree, edict, or epistle; also an interlocutory praetorian edict (Gaius, i. 5).

The constitution of the United States is the supreme law of the land, and overrides any Act of Congress, treaty, state constitution, or state statute, which is in conflict with it, but only to the extent of such conflict. Each of the United States has a constitution of its own.

The office of a written constitution cannot properly be extended beyond drawing the outlines of the government, and laying down the main rules of administration. 'A constitution, to contain an accurate detail of all the subdivisions of which its great powers will admit, and of all the means by which they may be carried into execution, would partake of the prolixity of a legal code, and could scarcely be embraced by the human mind. It would probably never be understood by the public. Its nature, therefore, requires that only its great outlines should be marked, its important objects designated, and the minor ingredients which compose those objects be deduced from the nature of the objects themselves.' See McCulloch *v.* Maryland, 4 Wheaton's United States Reports, 316.

The first written constitution in history is that adopted by the planters of Connecticut in 1639. They did not, however, possess, and hardly claimed, political independence. The first written constitution framed for themselves by a people asserting their own sovereignty was that of the state of Virginia, adopted June 29, 1776. (S.E.B.)

Literature: POMEROY, Constitutional Law, Instructions (1875); SCHOULER, Constitutional Studies (1897); BURGESS, Polit. Sci. and Constitutional Law (1890); S. E. BALDWIN, Mod. Polit. Instit., chaps. i and iv (1898); GNEIST, Hist. of the English Constitution (Eng. trans.) (1886); TUCKER, The Constitution of the United States: a critical Discussion of its Genesis, Development, and Interpretation, i. chaps. iv and v (1899); TAMBARO, Le Relazioni fra la Costituzione e l'Amministrazione (1898).

Constitutional Law: Ger. *Staatsrecht*; Fr. *droit public, loi constitutionnelle, loi organique* (a law of a constitutional nature); Ital. *diritto costituzionale*. The law prescribed for a political society by its organic constitution: the law applicable to questions of constitutional right and duty.

In Great Britain the constitution is made up of certain historic usages, traditions, and documents; of the latter, Magna Charta, the Petition of Right assented to by Charles I, and the Bill of Rights of 1688, being the chief. It can virtually be altered by Act of Parliament. In the United States, constitutional law is derived from the written constitutions of the several states, and of the United States; and their provisions can only be altered by constitutional amendments, adopted in the manner provided in each constitution for itself, or by a constitutional convention, duly called, in which the whole people are represented by their delegates. 'Constitutional law, in the form which it has taken in the United States, is an American graft on English jurisprudence. Its principles and rules are mainly the work of the present (19th) century. They rest on the fundamental conception of a supreme law, expressed in written form, in accordance with which all private rights must be determined, and all public authority administered' (State *v.* Main, 69 Connecticut Reports).

The construction of every written document is a matter for the judges, not for the jury, in the trial of a cause. That of a constitution, therefore, always presents a judicial question, and as no statute can be valid if in conflict with the constitution, it is in the power of the judiciary to refuse to enforce or respect any statute which is contrary to the constitution, as they construe it.

Some of the Presidents of the United States have asserted that, so far as their official duty is concerned, they have a right to construe the constitution of the United States for themselves, with no regard to any construction which the Supreme Court of the United States may have placed upon it, except such as the reasoning of the court may demand. This doctrine is most explicitly set forth in President Jackson's Veto Message, on the occasion of the passage of the Bill to re-charter the United States Bank, in 1832.

Judges will not decide that a statute is unconstitutional, unless the case is plain.

The conception of a law restraining the legislature, and capable of enforcement by executive or judicial officers, in contravention of an act of legislation, is essentially an American one. Constitutional law can only exist in a state where the powers of sovereignty are divided between different departments, each possessing a certain independence of the others. (S.E.B.)

Literature: BLACKSTONE, Commentaries on the Law of England, i. chap. ii ; POLLOCK, First Book of Jurisprudence, Part II. chap. iii ; ROSSI, Cours de Droit Constitutionnel (1866) ; COOLEY, Constitutional Limitations (1890) ; COXE, Judicial Power and Unconstitutional Legislature (1893) ; DICEY, Law of the Constitution (1889) ; THAYER, Cases in Constitutional Law, i. chap. i. (1894).

Constraint: see RESTRAINT AND CONSTRAINT.

Constraint (social): Ger. *Zwang* ; Fr. *contrainte* ; Ital. *coercizione*. The direct compelling influence of one personality or of the social environment upon another personality, considered as a source, or the only source, of SOCIAL ORGANIZATION (q. v.).

The constraint theory is usually traced to Hegel's 'master and slave' doctrine. Its principal and ablest advocate is Durkheim.

Literature: HEGEL, Encyclopädie, Part III. §§ 431-3 (Philosophy of Mind, Wallace's trans., 55 f.) ; DURKHEIM, De la division du travail social, and Le Suicide ; BARTH (critical), Die Philos. d. Gesch., i. 289 ff.; BALDWIN (critical), Social and Eth. Interpret., § 317. (J.M.B.)

Construct [Lat. *construere*, to heap up]: no foreign equivalents in use. A word used by Lloyd Morgan (*Animal Life and Intelligence*) to indicate the fact that in the familiar objects of experience the mind supplements what is directly presented to sense by the addition of representative elements integrated therewith through association ; such a product is called a Construct.

When for example a man sees a sheep on a distant slope of down, the word sheep stands for a construct formed through the suggestive force of a retinal stimulus under certain given circumstances. The word was not proposed as a technical term, but was used for purposes of exposition. (C.LL.M.)

Constructive Imagination : see IMAGINATION.

Constructiveness : Ger. *productive* or *schöpferische Thätigkeit* ; Fr. *fonction constructive ou créatrice* ; Ital. *funzione costruttrice, facultà di costruzione (mentale)*. Mental constructiveness exists if, and so far as, the ideas and conceptions which enter into a train of thought become systematically modified or newly combined in the process of thinking. (G.F.S.—J.M.B.)

Consumer [Lat. *con-* + *sumere*, to take]: Ger. *Consument* ; Fr. *consommateur* ; Ital. *consumatore*. Man in his capacity as a recipient of the services of others. Cf. the second of the definitions of CONSUMPTION.

There is no class of consumers to be sharply distinguished *in extenso* from a corresponding class of producers. Nearly all men are producers and consumers by turns ; but so many economic events affect men, in their capacity as consumers, in a different manner from that in which they affect their capacity as producers, that it is often convenient to make an abstraction of the former relation, and study a group of men in this light solely. Such study is specially needed in dealing with problems of practical economics, many of which have suffered from a neglect of this aspect. (A.T.H.)

Consumer's Rent : the English term is generally used in the other languages without translation. The excess of the price which a person would be willing to pay for a thing, rather than go without it, over that which he actually does pay (Marshall).

It has long been obvious that, if the same article represents different costs of production to different sellers, those who can produce more cheaply will enjoy a gain corresponding to their advantage over their competitors. This gain, so far as it is due to advantage of location, was recognized by Ricardo under the name of economic rent; and the Ricardian conception was extended by Mangoldt, and by Walker, to cover the results of other advantages besides those of location. But it was reserved for Marshall to emphasize the fact that the same article may represent different degrees of utility to different buyers; and that those who consume with greater pleasure or advantage enjoy a gain in utility as consumers, which bears a striking analogy to the saving in cost to certain producers. Marshall therefore extended the term rent to cover consumer's gains of this kind. It may be doubted whether the extension is a wise one. Rent represents differences in expense of production rather than in cost of production; and utility, which is in some sense the converse of cost, is in no sense the converse of expense. Consumer's Gain or Surplus seems a better term than Consumer's Rent (and is also used by Marshall). (A.T.H.)

Consumption: Ger. *Consumption*; Fr. *consommation*; Ital. *consumo*. The destruction, wholly or in part, of any portion of wealth (Malthus).

Consumption may be regarded as negative production. Just as man can produce only utilities, so he can consume nothing more. He can produce services and other immaterial products, and he can consume them (Marshall).

The study of consumption of wealth is much more recent and less developed than the study of production. It dates from Malthus as a beginner; it was somewhat developed by the French economists in the early part of the 19th century; but its modern scientific form was first indicated by Gossen (1854) and Jevons (1871). In its theoretical aspects, it has been carefully studied by the Austrian school of economists (Menger, Wieser), and by Clark; its practical bearings have been developed by Marshall, Smart, and Patten. It is not fully settled whether the application of the term should be confined to material goods, as in the first of the definitions given, or extended to things immaterial, as in the second. Modern practice tends towards the latter usage.

Literature: MARSHALL, Princ. of Econ., Bk. III. (A.T.H.)

Contact Sensation [Lat. *contactus*, from con- + *tangere*, to touch]: Ger. *Berührungs-empfindung*; Fr. *sensation de contact*; Ital. *sensazione di contatto*. A sensation made up probably (Dessoir) of TOUCH SENSATION (q.v.) and PRESSURE SENSATION (q. v.).

Literature: DESSOIR, Du Bois-Reymond's Arch. (1892); SANFORD, Course in Exper. Psychol., expt. 22; SERGI, Psychol. physiol. (1888), 82. (J.M.B.)

Contagion (social and mental) [Lat. con- + *tangere*, to touch]: Ger. (*sociale und psychische*) *Ansteckung*; Fr. *contagion* (*sociale et mentale*); Ital. *contagio* (*sociale e psichico*). (1) In sociology: the imitative repetition of mental states, generally of impulsive or emotional sorts, from person to person, when exhibited on a large scale. While contagion thus understood is a social phenomenon of mimetic RESEMBLANCE (q. v.), the marks by which it may be more closely defined must be taken from psychology.

(2) In psychology: a form of imitative suggestion; a point of view which explains the character of being widespread which is essential to contagion considered as a sociological fact (see above). Both meanings are based on the pathological analogy of the contagion of disease.

Literature: see under CROWD, SOCIAL PSYCHOLOGY, SUGGESTION; also the manuals of mental pathology; VIERKANDT, Die psychische Ansteckung, in Naturvölker und Culturvölker, 89. (J.M.B.–G.F.S.)

(3) In psychiatry: a form of immediate imitation of delusions, erroneous conceptions, and pathological feelings. Generally this contagion is the product of family life, or of identical moral and social conditions. (E.M.)

The impulse which develops into contagion may be regarded as the common and fundamental impulse of IMITATION (q. v.). In its lowest form, to which there is also a morbid analogue, imitation is mechanical, and consists in the blind and unreflective repetition of what is presented to the senses. In a more developed and less direct form, it is represented by the moulding, in greater or less part, of one's actions and beliefs in accordance with the actions performed and the beliefs held by those among whom we live and move. Amongst movements in which mental contagion plays a prominent part, some are merely amusing as illustrating the vagaries to which the spell of contagion renders mankind liable; such as the tulipomania of the 17th century, the wild speculations of the Mississippi scheme and of the South Sea Bubble, and the endless fashions in dress and manners; while others have a serious and sad import for the history of culture. The various epidemics of witchcraft, the dancing mania, the Flagellants, the search for the philosopher's stone and the elixir of life, and in part the Crusades, represent instances in which it is not always clear what is normal and what abnormal.

On the strictly abnormal side, mental contagion, as exaggerated imitation, may appear in idiocy in the form of a senseless imitation of all acts and sounds (see ECHOLALIA). It appears in persons of a susceptible and neurotic temperament, in their tendency to be unduly affected by the actions of others, particularly actions which present an element of novelty or bizarrerie, or involve emotional excitement. Religious excitement offers many instances of this kind (see EPIDEMICS, mental), while the fact that suicides, murders, or any unusual forms of crime tend to be imitated is well known. Another class of extreme cases are those in which distinct insanity is communicated by contagion. Cases are known in which constant association with an insane person brings on a similar form of insanity, or in which the shock, which arises from witnessing insanity in another, produces insanity. Likewise, the simultaneous affection of two or more persons—called by the French *folie à deux*—may be cited as instances of contagion, acting probably on a predisposed nature. In certain mental disorders, particularly HYSTERIA (q. v.), morbid contagion is a most prominent and complicated factor of the disease.

Literature: arts. Communicated Insanity, and Imitation, in Tuke's Dict. of Psychol. Med. (and references there given); also references under IMITATION and SUGGESTION; HIRSCH, Epidemics of Hysteria, in Pop. Sci. Mo. (1896), 544; MACKAY, Hist. of extraordinary Popular Delusions (1852); E. KRÖNER, Die Folie à deux, Allg. Zeitsch. f. Psychiat., xl. 634; ARNAUD, La Folie à deux, &c., Ann. Méd.-Psychol. (1893); PROUST, Étude sur la Folie à deux, Thèse de Paris (1893); BAB-COCK, Communicated Insanity, Amer. J. of Insan., li. 518; IRELAND, The Blot on the Brain (1893), 206, and elsewhere; SIDIS, Psychol. of Suggestion (1898), also Century Mag. (1896), 849; LEHMANN, Aberglaube u. Zauberei (1898); A. D. WHITE, A Hist. of the Warfare of Sci. with Theol., chap. xvi, and elsewhere; FIGUIER, Les Mystères de la Sci.; P. REGNARD, Les maladies épidémiques de l'esprit (1887).   (J.J.)

Also CH. FÉRÉ, La Famille névropathique

(1894, on predispositions to the same mental derangements); H. MARION, La Solidarité morale; LARÈQUE and FALRET, La Folie à deux, ou Folie communiquée, Ann. Méd.-Psychol. (1877); RÉGIS, La Folie à deux, ou Folie simultanée (1880). On psychic epidemics see CALMEIL, De la Folie, ii (1856); also SIGHELE, Folla delinquente, 'Delinquenza settaria.'   (L.M.–E.M.)

Contemplation [Lat. *contemplare*, to contemplate]: Ger. *Contemplation*; Fr. *contemplation*; Ital. *contemplazione*. (1) A state of intuition of the divine, or of absorption in one's own mental life, as in MYSTICISM (q. v.).

(2) Used loosely for more or less persistent meditation and introspection. In this sense the contemplative life is contrasted with the active; and certain modes of experience (e.g. the aesthetic) are said to be contemplative, as not apparently involving conation.   (J.M.B.)

Content [Lat. *contentus*, contained]: Ger. *Inhalt*; Fr. *matière, contenu*; Ital. *contenuto*. (1) Whatever in any way forms part of a total consciousness considered in abstraction from its form, its relations, and all of its implications; or the whole together with its constituents. Yet the form or relations, considered as a whole, may be a content.

(2) A constituent of any kind of presented whole.

(3) An object meant or intended by the subject (Bradley, Bosanquet). See INTENT for this meaning, content being reserved for sense (1).

(1) This is a term which has recently come to be used to secure a neutral way of referring to what is in the mind, without designating its elements (whether cognitive, affective, or conative), and without raising the question as to the mind's ultimate relation to the matter and to its form. Content may thus be characterized as 'felt,' 'presented,' 'willed' content in this case or that. It is convenient, as allowing the question as to whether this or that aspect of experience is a content or, in some way, only an attribute of a content; as in the discussion as to whether 'mental activity' is a content, and, if so, of what sort. So also in questions of mental functional process or procedure (as in argumentation), we may distinguish conveniently the presented content (argued about), and the process (the arguing), going on to ask whether the latter is also found in consciousness as a content. The utility of the term may also be seen in the question as to how changes, development, &c., in content are possible.

(2) There has been a tendency to restrict the term content to what is called above presented content, i. e. the matter of cognitive and intellectual processes (Münsterberg). This has arisen possibly from the distinction between 'revived' and 'presented' or 'original' content, where the revival is understood to be intellectual revival, by images. It is advisable, however, it would seem, to leave open the possibility that experiences not cognitive may be intellectually revived (e. g. 'felt content' revived as 'represented content'), and also that all sorts of content may be revived in other than intellectual (e. g. affective in form). (J.M.B.–G.F.S.)

Literature (rather on topics involving the conception of content than on the term itself): Münsterberg, Die Willenshandlung; Ward, Encyc. Brit., art. Psychology; Stout, Analytic Psychol., i. 143 f.; Baldwin, Elements of Psychol., Glossary. Also literature under Activity (mental). (G.F.S.–J.M.B.)

Contiguity (law of) [Lat. *con-* + *tangere*, to touch]: Ger. *Gesetz der Berührungsassociation*; Fr. *loi d'association par contiguïté*; Ital. *legge dell' associazione di contiguità*. This law may be stated as follows: when presentations, or other associable contents of consciousness, occur simultaneously or in immediate sequence, the corresponding mental dispositions become associated. Cf. Association (of ideas). (G.F.S., J.M.B.)

Contingent [Lat. *con-* + *tangere*, to touch]: Ger. (1) *abhängig*, (2) *zufällig*; Fr. *contingent*; Ital. *contingente*. (1) Conditioned (q. v.). Also (2) synonymous with the adjectives Chance (q. v., first meaning) and fortuitous (see Probability).

It is recommended that contingent be confined to meaning (1), which includes the conception of chance (second meaning only), as defined in the theory of probability. The substantives contingence (abstract) and contingency are then synonymous with chance in its scientific meaning. (J.M.B.)

Contingent (logical): see Modality.

Continuity [Lat. *continuare*, to join together]: Ger. *Continuität, Stetigkeit*; Fr. *continuité*; Ital. *continuità*. Relative sameness through a series of changes, stages, or positions: in so far as any of the determining conditions of an aspect of reality remain unchanged, in so far that aspect is said to be continuous.

More special cases of the notion of continuity in mathematics and biology are given under the following topics, and in psychology under the term Continuum (q. v.). In philosophy the term uniformity has served in the doctrines of Uniformity of Nature (q. v.) and Uniformitarianism (q. v.) to express this meaning. Cf. literary citations in Eisler, *Wörterb. d. philos. Begriffe*, Stetigkeit. (J.M.B.)

Continuity (in biology): (1) Of life. The doctrine of Biogenesis (q.v.) summed up in the dictum, *omne vivum e vivo*.

(2) Of cells. The doctrine that every living cell is derived from a living cell: *omnis cellula e cellula* (see Cell Theory).

(3) Of germ-plasm. The doctrine that any cell, or group of cells, capable of developing into a complete organism, contains nuclear matter directly continuous with that from which the organism of which they are the products was developed. This doctrine is the basis of Weismann's studies of heredity (*Die Kontinuität des Keimplasma*, 1885; *Germ-Plasm*, 1893), to which it owes much of its currency. Cf. Heredity. Or, more particularly, as applied to the germ-cells, the doctrine that the germ-plasm in the offspring is not formed anew, but derived directly through cell-division from the germ-plasm of the germ-cells of the parent or parents. (C.Ll.M.–E.S.G.)

(4) Of variation. The doctrine that the sort of variation which is effective in producing evolution is by small and continued increments in the same direction, as opposed to the view that it is by sudden well-marked leaps (so-called 'discontinuous variation,' on which see Bateson, *Materials for the Study of Variation*, 1895). Cf. Variation. (C.Ll.M.–J.M.B.)

Continuity (in geometry): the points of a right line constitute an ordinal assemblage of points, which is called continuous because it possesses the following attributes :—

(1) Between any two points of the line there are other points of the line.

(2) If all the points of the line are distributed in accordance with any given law into two assemblages, A and B, so related that each point in A lies to the left of every point in B, either the assemblage A will possess a last point to the right, or the assemblage B a first point to the left.

In other words, it is not only the case, as Aristotle would have said, and as follows from (1), that there cannot be both a last point, P, in A, limiting A to the right, and a first point, Q, in B, distinct from P, limiting B to the left; but also that either A or B must have a limiting point, that a definite point exists at which the separation of the points of the line into the assemblages A and B occurs, and at which the line itself is separated into two distinct parts.

Every other ordinal assemblage which possesses these or analogous attributes is also called continuous. Thus the points of a line segment, the points of an unbroken curved line, the totality of the real numbers, both rational and irrational, all constitute continuous assemblages.

The significance of the first attribute is at once apparent. It is equivalent to the infinite divisibility of a line segment, which Aristotle maintained and Epicurus denied, and which Kant made the definition of continuity.

But this attribute alone is not sufficient for continuity. Thus the assemblage of the rational numbers—or of those points of a right line by which they may be represented—possesses it, but is evidently discontinuous. This assemblage does not possess the attribute (2).

Thus since there is no rational number whose cube is 2, we may distribute all the rational numbers into an assemblage A, consisting of those whose cubes are less than 2, and an assemblage B, consisting of those whose cubes are greater than 2. Evidently each number in A is less than every number in B. But there is no greatest number in A; for when any rational number has been assigned whose cube is less than 2, it is always possible to find a greater rational whose cube is also less than 2. And, in like manner, there is no least number in B.

We obtain an assemblage of numbers which possesses the attribute (2), and is therefore continuous, only when to the rationals we add the number $\sqrt[3]{2}$ and all other irrational numbers; and, in like manner, a continuous assemblage of points, when to the points which represent the rational numbers we add a point for every irrational number.

This subtle attribute (2) of continuity escaped notice until very recently. It was first brought to light independently in the early seventies by G. Cantor and Dedekind.

The extension of this analysis of continuity to two and three dimensional space is obvious. Thus the assemblage of all the right lines in a plane which pass through one and the same point is ordinal, and possesses attributes analogous to (1) and (2). And every point of the plane lies on one or other of these lines. The points of the plane may, therefore, in a variety of ways, be distributed among the elements of a continuous assemblage of one dimension—assemblages which are themselves continuous. See SPACE, and CONTINUUM.

Literature: DEDEKIND, Stetigkeit u. Irrationale Zahlen ; G. CANTOR, Grundlagen einer allg. Mannichfaltigkeitslehre. (H.B.F.)

Continuous Quantity: see CONTINUITY, and CONTINUUM.

Continuum [Lat.]. That which has the property of CONTINUITY (q. v.).

In psychology the conception of continuum has been developed mainly by Ward (*Encyc. Brit.*, 9th ed., art. Psychology), who maintains that there is in all mental change or development a progressive differentiation of that which was before less differentiated back to a theoretical state, before specific experience, in which there was an undifferentiated field ; a sensory or presentation continuum, and a motor continuum. 'Working backward,' says Ward (loc. cit., 35), ' we are led ... to the conception of a *totum obiectivum*, or objective continuum, which is gradually differentiated. ... Actual presentation consists in this continuum being differentiated.' The meaning of this position is seen in its opposition to the so-called atomistic view represented by Condillac and the Associationists, which depicts mental growth and change as a progressive uniting of elements before separate and discontinuous. See MIND-STUFF THEORY. The conception of a continuum is also extended to each of the qualitative sense-fields—an auditory, a visual, a touch, a colour, &c. continuum, each of them being conceived as having a continuous field of its own, not broken in upon by events from other fields— within which the presentations of the same quality or class, while differentiated, are nevertheless held together by continuous gradation. With Ward's view it is interesting to compare that contained in Cornelius's *Psychol. als Erfahrungswissenschaft*. Cornelius does not use the word continuum ; but he gives a view of mental development essentially analogous to Ward's, except that he denies subconsciousness, and identifies all differentiation with conscious distinction.

Literature: WARD and CORNELIUS (as cited above); JAMES, Princ. of Psychol., i. chap. xiii. (J.M.B.–G.F.S.)

Contra-conative: see ACTION, and INVOLUNTARY.

Contract [Lat. *contractus*, from *con-* + *trahere*, to draw]: Ger. *Vertrag* ; Fr. *contrat* ; Ital. *contratto*. (1) A coincident expression of will by two or more persons, intended by all, or naturally calculated and by some of them intended, to alter the legal relations of all to each other; an agreement between two or more parties to do or not to do a certain thing (Sturges *v.* Crowninshield, 4 Wheaton's U. S. Reports, 117).

The act of agreeing is the contract; the consequent change of relations expresses the obligation which proceeds from it.

(2) A written document executed by the contracting parties, setting forth the terms of their agreement.

In the Roman law there could be no contract without a consequent obligation. An obligation was of the essence of every contract. Agreements without an obligation, which would support an action, were styled conventions (*conventio*) or pacts (*pactum, pactio*). They might have a defensive force, in case of an action by one of the parties against the other. An agreement expressed with certain forms, or founded upon certain transactions, became a *contractus*. ' Sed cum nulla subest causa propter conventionem, hic constat non posse constitui obligationem. Igitur nuda pactio obligationem non parit, sed parit exceptionem' (*Dig.*, ii. 14, *de Pactis*, 7, § 4). Our definition of contract corresponds to the Roman definition of a convention, and may be compared with Savigny's definition of an agreement (Vertrag) as 'the union of several persons in one concurrent declaration of will, whereby their legal relations are determined.' In English and American law, while a contract not founded on a sufficient consideration, unless expressed in writing under seal, cannot support an action, it is none the less a contract. We recognize illegal contracts, and void contracts, as contracts (cf. Anson, *Principles of Contract*). Cf. CONSIDERATION. (S.E.B.)

Contract involves not a mere promise (*nudum pactum*), but an obligation at law (*obligatio*). It involves a relation of free persons. To Roman law and to Kant, marriage was a contract, and to Hobbes and other philosophers the union of men in states or even societies is founded on contract. See SOCIAL CONTRACT. Wherever there has been law there has been contract, but the present exactness of the notion of contract is due to Roman law (of *nexum*, later *contractus*). Scottish law and the Code Napoleon follow Roman law more closely than does the English.

Literature: SAVIGNY, Das neuere Römische Recht; MARKBY, Elements of Law; MAINE, Ancient Law; MACKENZIE, Roman Law; JUSTINIAN, Institutes, III. Tit. xiv., De Ob-

ligationibus, treating of oblig. ex contractu, quasi ex contractu, ex maleficio, quasi ex maleficio—or express and implied contracts, intentional and unintentional injuries; HOLMES, Common Law, Lects. 7, 8, 9. (J.B.–S.E.B.)

Contractility (muscular) [Lat. *con-* + *trahere*, to draw together]: Ger. *Contractionsfähigkeit*; Fr. *contractilité*; Ital. *contrattilità*. The property or function of living tissues to react in some way when a proper stimulus is applied. See VITAL PROPERTIES, and MUSCLE. (C.F.H.)

Contraction (muscular) and **Contracture**: Ger. *Zusammenziehung*, (more exactly) *Verkürzung*; Fr. *contraction*; Ital. *contrazione*. Action of a muscle by which its ends are brought closer together. Contracture is a condition in which the muscle fails to elongate normally after a contraction; also called 'contraction-remainder' (Hermann). See MUSCLE. (C.F.H.)

Contradiction (law, principle, or axiom of, in logic) [Lat. *contra* + *dicere*, to speak]: Ger. *Grundsatz des Widerspruchs*; Fr. *principe de contradiction*; Ital. *legge di contraddizione*. The Principle of Contradiction is but the explicit statement of a simple condition under which thinking can claim to attain its end, truth; or, negatively, without which thinking may not attain its end. To any assertion in which it is declared that some thought-content holds good, there is conceivable an opposed assertion, which does no more than declare that such thought-content does not hold good. Assertions so opposed are called technically Contradictories; and the Principle of Contradiction only expresses in generalized fashion their relation to truth by the formula: Contradictory judgments cannot both be true. The simplicity of the condition to be expressed, and the variety of ways of approaching its determination, account for differences of formulation. See also PROPOSITION.

All discussions of the principle lead backwards to the first formal and elaborate statement of it in Aristotle, whose method of treatment keeps wonderfully clear from both the strictly formal and subjective view and the ontological and objective. The best accounts of his view are in Prantl, *Gesch. d. Logik*, i. 119, 130 ff.; Grote, *Aristotle* (2nd ed.), App. iii; Maier, *Die Syllogistik des Arist.*, Pt. I. (1896), 41–73. A full notion of the various ways in which it has been expressed, with references to the main discussions concerning its scope, will be found in Ueberweg's *Logik*, § 77. On the difference between the Aristotelian point of view and that of formal logic, which takes its origin in the Kantian work, see Sigwart (*Logik*, § 23); on the principle in empirical logic, see Mill (*Exam. of Hamilton*, 471) and Venn (*Empirical Logic*). Bain (*Ded. Logic*, 14–17) tends to lay needless stress on consistency in language. (R.A.)

Contradictory (in logic): see OPPOSITION.

Contradictory Representation: see INHIBITION (mental).

Contraposition [Lat. *contra + ponere*, to place]: Ger. *Kontraposition*; Fr. *contraposition*; Ital. *contraposizione*. The process by which there is inferred from a given judgment, called the Contraponend, another judgment, called the Contrapositive, having for its subject the contradictory or negative of the original predicate, and for its predicate the negative of the original subject. (R.A.–C.L.F.)

It may be regarded, though it is a process of immediate inference, as involving two distinct steps: (1) the OBVERSION (q. v.) of the original proposition, (2) the CONVERSION (q. v.) of the obverted original. As involving conversion, the process is inapplicable to the particular affirmative proposition, the obverted form of which is the inconvertible particular negative. The contrapositions thus obtained may themselves be obverted, and the name contrapositive is often given to the form so expressed. See Keynes, *Formal Logic*, Pt. II. chap. iii.

The name has come into the traditional logic from Boethius (see Prantl, *Gesch. d. Logik*, i. 698), though the type of conversion had been recognized earlier. There has been no fixity of usage in regard to it, although the variations of opinion have been of slight importance. The name contraposition has been employed in a wider and in a narrower sense, and the process described has been designated by a variety of technical terms. (R.A.)

Contrary (in logic): see OPPOSITION.

Contrast [Lat. *contra + stare*, to stand]: Ger. *Kontrast*; Fr. *contraste*; Ital. *contrasto*. The juxtaposition of different and especially of opposite qualities or quantities, with a resulting emphasis of the characteristics of one or both the elements involved.

In sculpture and architecture applied most frequently to the disposition of masses and the arrangement of their limiting lines. In painting it is somewhat similarly, but also and especially, applied to the grouping of figures and the treatment of light, shade, and colour. In music it is applied widely either to the sequence of successive tones and chords, to the arrangement of crescendo and diminuendo, to the relations of piano and forte, to changes in tempo, to the differences in pitch and quality as between bass and soprano, and to the distinctions in timbre and quality in general. In literature it is applied very loosely to the treatment of scenes, characters, &c. (J.R.A.)

Literature: GROOS, Einleitung in die Aesth.; MARSHALL, Pain, Pleasure, and Aesth., and Aesth. Princ.; KIRSCHMANN, Psychol.-aesth. Bedeutung des Lichts- und Farbencontrastes, Philos. Stud. (1892); the general treatises on AESTHETICS (q. v.), notably v. HARTMANN, and on psychology, notably HÖFFDING. (J.R.A.–W.M.U.)

Contrast (affective). (1) The modifying, due to an affective state, of simultaneous or succeeding affective states. (2) The production of opposed or so-called contrary emotional states in connection with changes in the stimulating conditions; hope and fear, joy and sorrow, are pairs illustrating this form of contrast.

(1) The contrast effects extend to all phases of emotion—quality, excitement, hedonic tone. It has been much discussed under the term relativity, especially with reference to pleasure and pain, since Plato's theory of the relativity of pleasure, which may be called hedonic contrast. See PAIN AND PLEASURE. The qualitative contrast effects, usually called 'emotional contrast,' are either 'successive'—the after-effects of one emotional state upon succeeding emotional states, or 'simultaneous'—the modification of one relatively distinguishable element in an emotional state by another. The fluctuations of hope and fear are often cited to illustrate all these sorts of contrast. It is recommended that the term affective contrast be confined to this first meaning.

(2) In normal cases, under the second definition, the changed conditions reflect new information, knowledge, &c.; changes in the cognitive contents which stimulate the emotion. In many pathological instances, however, obscure organic or subjective changes produce very marked oscillations of emotion. The effects of contrast in sense (1) are present also in these cases.

Two special forms of contrast in this sense are distinguished and illustrated with the figure under HOPE AND DESPAIR: (*a*) the form due to dwelling in turn upon the varying possibilities of outcome of a given situation (such as the mingled hope and fear of a partisan spectator at a closely contested athletic contest), and (*b*) the form due to actual changes in the exciting situation (as the national joy and sorrow attending the fortunes of an army at war). It is recommended that the phrase 'contrasted emotion' be used for all cases corresponding to this second meaning.

Literature: the textbooks of psychology; the citations given under EMOTION, and under PAIN AND PLEASURE. See also BIBLIOG. G, 2, *k*. (J.M.B., G.F.S.)

Contrast (binocular): Ger. *binocularer Kontrast*; Fr. *contraste binoculaire*; Ital. *contrasto binoculare*. The collective name for contrast effects occurring between the images in the two eyes.

The classical instance of such contrast is the SIDE WINDOW EXPERIMENT (q. v.). A simple case is this: lay a white square of card on a black ground, bring a grey glass before the one and a blue before the other eye, and obtain double images. The one of these is, of course, blue; the other, however, is not grey, but yellowish.

Literature: FECHNER, Abhandl. d. kgl. sächs. Gesell. d. Wiss., vii. (1860) 511 ff.; HERING, in Hermann's Handb. d. Physiol., III. i. 600 f.; WUNDT, Physiol. Psychol. (4th ed.), ii. 209 ff.; HELMHOLTZ, Physiol. Optik (2nd ed.), 936 ff.; TITCHENER, Philos. Stud., viii. 231 ff.; BRÜCKE, Pogg. Ann., lxxxiv. 420 ff.; CHAUVEAU, C. R. Soc. de Biol., cxiii. 394 ff.; AUBERT, Physiol. Optik, 549. (E.B.T.)

Contrast (colour, simultaneous): Ger. *simultaner Farbenkontrast* (*Helligkeitskontrast*); Fr. *contraste simultané des couleurs*; Ital. *contrasto dei colori*. The mutual effects, in respect to colour and brightness, which simultaneously seen but separated visual areas have upon each other. (J.M.B.)

The general law of contrast is that the colour and brightness of a given object are affected by the colour and brightness of other, and especially of neighbouring, objects in the visual field, which they in turn affect in a corresponding way.

The special laws of simultaneous colour contrast are as follows: (1) the contrast effect is maximal along the line of contact (marginal contrast); (2) the increase of brightness in a bright field on dark ground is directly proportional to the brightness-difference of field and ground; (3) the more saturated the inducing ground, the more saturated the induced (contrast) colour; (4) contrast always takes the direction of greatest opposition, i. e. every colour induces its complementary (or antagonistic) colour—black white, and white black.

Helmholtz regarded contrast as due to a 'deception of judgment.' Wundt translates this phrase into 'an instance of the law of relativity,' thus bringing contrast into line with Weber's law, &c. Opposed to these central theories is Hering's peripheral theory, according to which contrast depends upon the interaction of retinal excitations; the retina functions always as a whole, however limited the area of a given stimulation. The latter hypothesis is gaining ground. See MEYER'S EXPERIMENT. According to Marillier, the phenomena of contrast were first pointed out by Chevreul. (E.B.T.)

Hering's device for obtaining different simultaneous contrast for the two eyes proves conclusively that the phenomenon is retinal (unless one could assume a right-handed and a left-handed judgment). Cf. Hering, *Zeitsch. f. Psychol.*, i. 18, and Sanford, *Course in Exper. Psychol.*, § 165. But there is no reason that the principle of relativity, which holds for sensation in general, should be suspended here, and hence it is without doubt a contributing cause to the total effect of contrast. (C.L.F.)

Literature: EBBINGHAUS, Psychologie, 217 (with refs. to Hering); HELMHOLTZ, Physiol. Optik (2nd ed.), 542; WUNDT, Physiol. Psychol. (4th ed.), i. 521; SANFORD, Course in Exper. Psychol., expts. 152–8; HERING, Zur Lehre vom Lichtsinn (1875). (E.B.T.)

Contrast (successive colour): Ger. *successiver Farbenkontrast* (*Helligkeitskontrast*); Fr. *contraste successif des couleurs*; Ital. *contrasto successivo dei colori*. The apparent alteration of a grey or of a coloured surface by the previous stimulation of the same retinal area by some other sort of light. In other words, it is merely the effect of the AFTER-IMAGE (q.v.) when projected upon a fresh stimulating surface. (E.C.S.–C.L.F.)

After-images may be so strong as to afford especially good instances of simultaneous contrast. It is clear that, unless precautions are taken, successive contrast may interfere with the results of experiments on simultaneous contrast.

Literature: WUNDT, Physiol. Psychol. (4th ed.), i. 514; HELMHOLTZ, Physiol. Optik (2nd ed.), 538; SANFORD, Course in Exper. Psychol., expts. 151–3; HERING, Zur Lehre vom Lichtsinn (1875); EBBINGHAUS, Psychologie, 230, 241 (other refs. to Hering). (E.B.T.)

Contrast (law of): Ger. *Gesetz der Association durch Kontrast*; Fr. *loi d'association par contraste*; Ital. *legge dell' associazione* *di contrasto.* The disputed law that there is a tendency of the presentations of contrasted objects, as such, to reinstate each other in consciousness. See ASSOCIATION (of ideas). (G.F.S.)

Contrast (visual space): Ger. *optischer Raumkontrast, optischer Kontrast von Raumgrössen*; Fr. *contraste spacial optique*; Ital. *contrasto visivo spaziale.* By an easy transference of the meaning of the term, certain phenomena of OPTICAL ILLUSIONS (q. v.), and of the estimation of spacial area, have been referred to the effect of a 'space contrast.'

Literature: MÜLLER - LYER, Zeitsch. f. Psychol., ix. 1; LOEB, Pflüger's Arch., x. 509, and Zeitsch. f. Psychol., xvi. 298; HEYMANS, Zeitsch. f. Psychol., ix. 248, and Philos. Stud., xiii. 613; WUNDT, Abhandl. d. kgl. sächs. Gesell. d. Wiss., xxiv. (1898) 55, and Philos. Stud., xiv. 1; BALDWIN, Psychol. Rev., ii. 244; WARREN and SHAW, Psychol. Rev., ii. 239. (E.B.T.)

Contra - volitional: for foreign equivalents see INVOLUNTARY. Opposed to volition; applied to movements, thoughts, &c., which resist voluntary control or direction.

Equivalent to contra-conative or involuntary as contrasted with aconative or nonvoluntary, in the scheme of terminology for the active functions recommended under ACTION (in psychology). (J.M.B.)

Contrition : see REPENTANCE.

Control [M.Lat. *contra* + *rotellum*, a roll]: Ger. *Kontrolle*; Fr. *contrôle*; Ital. *controllo* (*governo di sè*). Voluntary command of mind and body. As concerned with conduct in its ethical relations, see SELF-CONTROL.

The psychological questions involved in control turn about (1) control of muscular movement; (2) control of the attention; (3) control of emotion.

(1) By muscular control is meant the voluntary performance, inhibition, or modification of muscular movement in accordance with one's intention and volition. See MOVEMENT (control of).

(2) A question which is very important, both in education and in ethics, concerns the control of the attention. How far and by what means can we keep our attention under control? Of course this question can be asked only of voluntary attention; for attention which is drawn without our preparatory knowledge and intention is quite outside of our control. Of voluntary attention, one theory holds that it is also outside of our control, being a purely reflex thing, dictated by the strength of the influences which arise to call the attention in this direction or that. Admitting the fact that we seem to have a moderate degree of control or management of the direction of the attention, we may distinguish two sorts of possible control or management : first, 'direct,' and second, 'indirect' control of the attention. Under the head of direct control, those who hold that the attention is a mental principle of absolute power of mental initiation, urge the case in which we deliberate, and then choose what we will attend to. They say that all voluntary movement of the body involves attention of this sort; so also all voluntary direction of the train of thought. In this latter case, they hold that we can, by turning attention to this or that one of our moves, so reinforce it as to make it the controlling one, and thus determine our choice. In current discussion, the possibility of the mind's exercising any real initiation of changes in the flow of the mental life is put here, i. e. in the possibility of 'direct' control of the attention.

By 'indirect' control of the attention is meant the view that the mind cannot direct attention, interfere with or control the stream of thought, without preliminary motives, reasons, &c.; that its control is always indirect, or through earlier states of mind. In indirect control we proceed upon motives—the reasons on the ground of which we wish to give the train a turn in this or that direction. That is, we are under preliminary motives, interests, preferences, even when by attention we reinforce one of a set of possible alternatives. It is true, say the advocates of this theory, that we choose by attending; but it is also true that the attention itself is determined by an earlier choice, and so on. This preceding choice sets the elements which are really operative, and it is by identifying ourselves with these elements that we get control. This indirect control is certainly a fact, whether it explains all the cases of seeming control or not. It is shown in interesting pathological cases. Patients are reduced to complete inability to move a limb, simply because they cannot attend to it, and the reason that they cannot attend to it is that, through injury to the brain, they have no images to represent the movement. This shows that the attention, so far from being a self-sufficient activity, depends upon the presence of certain equivalents of what is to be attended to, through which the controlling or setting of the direction of the mental flow takes place. No acts can be voluntarily carried out, whether by sensorial or by intellectual attention, unless the elements of earlier acts of attention in the same direction can be brought up in mind.

These elements are held to be the indirect means by which a particular case of attention is realized and held under control. Put in general psychological terms, the attention is always a function of some content in consciousness, and to carry out an act of attention this content, or something equivalent to it, must be present first. The lack of the requisites of control is also seen in cases of fixed ideas, obsessions, &c., in which the patient finds it impossible to get his attention fixed upon other ideas requisite to the inhibition of the former. Cf. KINAESTHETIC SENSATIONS, and EQUIVALENTS.

Literature, on (1) and (2): see under MOVEMENT, and ATTENTION; also PICK, Zeitsch. f. Psychol., iv. (1892), 161; IRELAND, J. of Ment. Sci. (January, 1893), 130; BALDWIN, Ment. Devel. in the Child and the Race, chap. xv. On the physical basis of control and its impairment: CARPENTER, Ment. Physiol., Bk. I. chap. ix; Bk. II. chap. xvii; RIBOT, Diseases of the Will, chaps. i, ii; E. MORSELLI, Semej. malat. ment. (1895), ii.

(3) Control of emotion is admitted by all to be a phenomenon of voluntary effort, and the two possibilities, called direct and indirect, would seem to be open here. The indirect theory has the balance of authority, however, since the two influences which are evidently strong in this sort of control are both indirect, i. e. giving the attention to something other than the object which causes the emotion (though the movement of the attention itself might then be taken to illustrate direct control), and the suppression of the physical expression of the emotion.

Literature: JAMES, Princ. of Psychol., ii. chap. xxv. (J.M.B., G.F.S.)

Control Experiment: Ger. *Kontrollversuch*; Fr. *expérience de contrôle*; Ital. *esperimento di controllo* (or *di verifica*). An experiment conducted under conditions under which the operation of a supposed cause is known to be impossible, in order to discover whether the supposed effect of that cause still occurs. A check is thus put upon inference from experiments by use of the method of DIFFERENCE (q. v.). (J.M.B.)

Control Series: see CONTROL.

Convention (social) [Lat. *convenire*, to come together]: Ger. (1-4) *Convention*, (1) *Ueber-einkommen, Versammlung*, (2) *stillschweigendes Uebereinkommen*; Fr. *convention*; Ital. *convenzione*. (1) A formal or informal meeting of individuals, delegates, or representatives for a specific object. (2) An informal recognition of usage or custom. (3) A formal agreement of individuals reached after formal debate, stated in a social rule or usage, sanctioned by disapproval or social boycotting of offenders. (4) An international agreement, less formal than a treaty.

The essential meaning of convention is given in definition (2), and is best expressed by Hume (*Essays and Treatises*, ii. 344): 'Thus two men pull the oars of a boat by common *convention* for common interest, without any promise or contract. Thus gold and silver are made the measures of exchange; thus speech and words and language are fixed by human *convention* and agreement.' 'It has been asserted by some that justice arises from human *conventions*, and proceeds from the voluntary choice, consent, or combination of mankind. If by *convention* be here meant a *promise* (which is the most usual sense of the word), nothing can be more absurd than this position. . . . But if by convention be meant a sense of common interest, which sense each man feels in his own breast, which he remarks in his fellows, and which carries him, in concurrence with others, into a general plan or system of actions which tends to public utility, it must be owned that, in this sense, justice arises from human *conventions*' (ibid. 344). The tendency of usage, therefore, is to the emphasis of the informal side, i.e. to definition (2), as in the phrase 'recognized convention,' and in the use of the adjective 'conventional.' (F.H.G.–J.M.B.)

Convergence [Lat. *convergere*, to turn]: Ger. *Convergenz*; Fr. *convergence*; Ital. *convergenza*. A position (or movement) of the two lines of regard, in (or by) which they meet in a single fixation point.

Movements of the eyes in general are: (1) parallel movements, in which the lines of regard of the two eyes remain constantly parallel with each other; (2) convergent movements, in which they intersect at some point of objective space before the eyes; and (3) divergent movements (exceptional or pathological), in which they intersect at some point behind the eyes. Under the general heading of Convergent Movements we have, further, (*a*) convergent movements in convergence, realized in passing from a more remote to a nearer fixation point, and (*b*) divergent movements in convergence, realized in passing from a nearer point to a more remote. Cf. ASYMMETRY, and EYE-MOVEMENTS. (E.B.T.)

Convergence (in biology). A term used to express the development of similar structures and forms independently of affinity.

The course of evolution which leads to such resemblances, in two or more distinct lines, is spoken of as 'parallelism.' The extreme supporters of a mechanically caused evolution have assumed convergence to be of very high importance, and have even supposed that it may lead to a true and real approximation, so that the descendant species of distinct lines may coalesce into a single genus, perhaps even into a single species. A species or genus supposed to be thus formed by coalescence is said to have a 'polyphyletic' origin. The great example which has been relied upon is the gradual evolution of the horse from a far less specialized mammalian type, which has been supposed to have gone on independently throughout the whole of the Tertiary Period in the Old World and in the New, finally arriving at two species separated by only minor structural features. Such a theory requires continuous geographical isolation to prevent the eastward and westward drift of swift and wandering animals; and yet the whole fauna and flora of North America proclaim it as a part of the great Northern Belt, and prove beyond doubt that land continuity has been a far more prevalent feature than discontinuity. Such extreme views upon convergence were the natural outcome of a theory which looked upon animal form and structure as the expression of the direct influence of environing forces—a process referred to above as 'mechanically caused evolution.' Assume this theory and that acquired characters are hereditary, and it follows that lines of evolution, however distinct and separate at the start, will be made to approximate and even to fuse when subjected to the direct action of similar forces for a prolonged period. Those who have belief in the all-importance of natural selection, recognize the significance of convergence in producing resemblances in single parts, or even in combinations of important systems, such as the nervous, muscular, and skeletal, but they hold that the likenesses are invariably superficial, and, however striking, can always be disentangled from the results due to true affinity. The phenomena of convergence, so far as they are correctly interpreted, receive their complete explanation as the 'analogical' or 'adaptive' characters fully interpreted by Darwin in the first edition of the *Origin of Species* (1859). Thus, in chap. xiii. 427, he speaks of 'the very important distinction between real affinities and analogical or adaptive resemblances. . . . On my view of characters being of real importance for classification, only in so far as they reveal descent, we can clearly understand why analogical or adaptive characters, although of the utmost importance to the welfare of the being, are almost valueless to the systematist. For animals, belonging to two most distinct lines of descent, may readily become adapted to similar conditions, and thus assume a close external resemblance; but such resemblances will not reveal—will rather tend to conceal—their blood-relationship to their proper lines of descent.' A good example is given on p. 430, where Darwin, alluding to the striking resemblance of the marsupial wombat (*Phascolomys*) to a rodent, says, 'It may be strongly suspected that the resemblance is only analogical, owing to the *Phascolomys* having become adapted to habits like those of a rodent.' Darwin fully recognized that convergence, so far as it is correctly interpreted, was only his earlier principle. Thus, writing to Neumayr in 1877, he says, 'He [Hyatt] insists that closely similar forms may be derived from distinct lines of descent; and this is what I formerly called analogical variation.' The cases of convergence cited by W. B. Scott—the parallel development of the Tylopoda in the New World with the Pecora and Tragulina of the Old, and the evolution of a remarkable horse-like, and yet non-perissodactyle, form in Patagonia—would appear to be excellent examples of adaptive resemblances, the superficially similar forms taking each other's place, and undergoing corresponding adaptations to corresponding needs. It must be remembered that the paleontologist sees only the skeletal framework, and that the inferences from it to the other systems are limited. At the same time the scope of his inquiry presents a combination of systems peculiarly liable to be affected by, and thus to register, such convergent adaptations. It is probably for this reason that paleontologists have tended to magnify the importance of the principle. The zoologist with the whole animal anatomy before him sees these resemblances in their due relationship and proportion. There is no better example of convergence than that presented by the Marsupialia in relation to the higher Mammalia—far better than any examples to be cited from the Ungulata, because the blood-relationship is so infinitely more remote. In spite of this remoteness, we find the marsupial order, having the Australian continent almost to itself, becoming split up into forms which superficially resemble the most diverse dominant types of the higher mammals. Not only is there the rodent-like wombat (*Phascolomys*) alluded to by Darwin, but the dog-like *Thylacinus*, while a remarkable marsupial mole (*Notoryctes*) has recently been discovered. And all these resemblances, and many more, correspond precisely to parallelism in habits. If all these animals were extinct, and we only knew them through their skeletons, there can be no doubt that the resemblances would be far more misleading. As it is, we have the other anatomical systems by which to correct the bias unconsciously given by the strongly convergent osseous framework. But however corrected and limited, 'parallelism and convergence of development are,' as W. B. Scott maintains, 'very real phenomena, and on this account, as well as others, we must recognize the importance of giving due weight to geographical considerations in dealing with phylogenetic and taxonomic problems.'

E. Ray Lankester distinguished between the homologies or correspondences in structure which are due to blood-relationship (homogeny) and those which are due to adaptation (homoplasy). It is here maintained that the resemblances due to convergence are homoplastic. The convergences which are here described and illustrated are also briefly mentioned under Mimicry (q.v.), where it is suggested that the term Syntechnic may be conveniently applied to them. Other convergences of a different kind, but equally due to adaptation (homoplastic), are also described under the same head. (E.B.P.)

The operation of Organic Selection (q.v.) is also well illustrated in these phenomena, the converging lines of descent showing the directing influence of individual accommodations which are common to two species. These accommodations shield and foster congenital variations coincident with them, and therefore also coincident with one another in the two animal forms. In such cases convergence illustrates orthoplasy, as this directing influence of organic or indirect selection has been called by two of its original advocates, Osborn and Baldwin, both of whom have also

indicated its application in paleontology (Osborn, 'The Limits of Organic Selection,' *Amer. Naturalist*, xxxi. 944 ff.; Baldwin, 'Determinate Evolution,' *Psychol. Rev.*, iv., 1897, 393 ff.). (J.M.B., E.B.P.)

Literature: C. Darwin, Origin of Species, chapter on 'Classification,' and Life and Letters; Carl Vogt, The Nat. Hist. of Animals (Eng. trans., 1887); Oscar Schmidt, The Mammalia, Int. Sci. Ser. (1885); W. B. Scott, in Wood's Holl Biol. Lectures, 1898 (1899); E. D. Cope, The Origin of the Fittest (1887); E. Ray Lankester, Ann. and Mag. Nat. Hist. (1870). (E.B.P.)

Converse: see Conversion (in logic).

Conversion (in Christian theology) [Lat. *con-* + *vertere*, to turn about]: Ger. *Bekehrung*; Fr. *conversion*; Ital. *conversione*. Conversion may be defined in the words of Acts xx. 21: 'Repentance toward God, and faith toward our Lord Jesus Christ.' Cf. Grace.

In its ordinary acceptance, it implies divine grace and human desire, that is, both elements enter into the process. The problem lies in their relation. Lutherans teach that the Scriptures and the sacraments are the means of grace; but they may be, and often are, entirely resisted. Calvinists, on the contrary, tend to hold that grace is irresistible, and so to overpower the human element by the divine. Possibly, from the point of view of theology, the former lies nearer the truth; for conversion is to be distinguished from regeneration. In the former, the human element predominates; in the latter, the divine. At the same time, the Lutheran doctrine of means may easily be pushed too far; they are secondary at best.

In Roman Catholic usage, conversion is applied to the transubstantiation which takes place in the Eucharistic elements, one substance being converted into another, while the accidents of the original substance remain. (R.M.W.)

Conversion (in logic). The process by which, from a given proposition, called the Convertend, there is educed or inferred another proposition, called the Converse, in quality the same as the original proposition, and having for its subject the predicate, and for its predicate the subject, of the original proposition.

Essentially, conversion is the mere transposition of the terms, subject and predicate, of the given proposition to be converted. When the quantity of the given proposition is taken into account, the rule that the converse cannot contain more than the convertend leads to the special results, that the universal negative and particular affirmative can be converted without change of quantity, by simple conversion, as it is called; that the universal affirmative can only be converted into a particular affirmative by conversion *per accidens* or by limitation; and that the particular negative cannot be converted by either method.

The process and rules of conversion are dealt with fully by Aristotle. The term *conversio per accidens* comes from Boethius, whose confused chapter (*Introd. ad Syllog. Cat.*, chap. vii) throws little light on the designation. See Baynes, *New Analytic*, 28-9.

Literature: UEBERWEG, Logik, §§ 84-8; KEYNES, Formal Logic, Pt. II. §§ 62-5, 130, 133, 143. (R.A.)

Convertend: see CONVERSION (in logic).

Conviction (in psychology) [Lat. *convincere*, to overcome]: Ger. *Ueberzeugung*; Fr. *conviction*; Ital. *convinzione*. Belief of which the grounds are relatively conscious and obvious. See BELIEF. (J.M.B.)

Conviction (in theology): Ger. (*Sünden-*)*Zerknirschung*; Fr. *conviction*; Ital. *convinzione*. A word used in a semi-theological, semi-ethical sense, and principally in connection with sin: conviction of sin. It means self-consciousness, generally of an overwhelming sort, that one is, or has been, in the wrong. Moral blame is registered against oneself, and this leads to renewed effort after truer belief and better conduct. The term is essentially of Calvinistic origin in this sense. (R.M.W.)

Convulsion [Lat. *convulsio*, cramp]: Ger. *Krampf*; Fr. *convulsion*; Ital. *convulsione*. A violent and purposeless contraction or paroxysm of a group of muscles.

A succession of convulsions is known as a fit; a more localized involuntary contraction is termed a spasm. Eclampsia is also used as synonymous with convulsions, although usually referring to recurring convulsions, due to other causes than primary abnormalities of the brain (Gowers). Both spasms and convulsions are either tonic (continuous, cramp-like) or clonic (short, and alternating with relaxations).

The study of convulsions has been directed by two interests, the clinical and the physiological. The clinical interest is concerned with a description of the form of the convulsions and the muscle groups involved; with their occurrence as the primary or essential symptom of the disease, or as accompanying, or sequential to, other diseases; with their occurrence at special times or occasions of life—infantile, puerperal, traumatic, &c. The physiological interest is centred in the interpretation of the nature and dissemination of the convulsion as an index of the nerve 'discharge,' or 'explosion,' from special motor centres in the brain cortex. This has been most extensively studied in connection with the convulsions of EPILEPSY (q. v.), and is there considered.

Further general characteristics of convulsions are the order in which the muscle groups are affected; whether confined to one side of the body, whether involving loss of consciousness, whether preceded by premonitory symptoms or abrupt, whether isolated or one of a series of attacks, how far associated with other diseases (such as hysteria), and the like. These characteristics serve to differentiate the different forms of convulsion, and form an essential portion of the diagnosis of those diseases (epilepsy, general paralysis, cerebral lesions, eclampsia, chorea, stridulus, tetanus, hydrophobia) in which convulsive symptoms are prominent. Cf. EPILEPSY, and CHOREA. (J.J.)

Literature: MONAKOW, Gehirnpathologie (1897), 341 f.; FRANÇOIS FRANCK, Leçons sur les Fonctions motrices du Cerveau (1883); CH. FÉRÉ, Les Epilepsies et les Epileptiques (1890), with full bibliography. (L.M.)

Co-operation (in economics) [Lat. *co-* + *operari*, to work]: Ger. *Genossenschaftswesen*; Fr. *coopération*; Ital. *cooperazione*. (1) Profit-sharing: a system under which the labourer receives a dividend from profits, in addition to his wages, in case business results warrant it.

(2) Management of industry by the labourers themselves—producers' co-operation.

(3) Management of industry by those who expect to use its products—consumers' co-operation; frequently, but inaccurately, known as distributive co-operation.

(1) Conforms to popular usage, but is hardly countenanced by the best authorities at the present day; (2) is relatively unimportant. The advantages gained in the way of zeal rarely offset the loss in speculative foresight. (3) Seems by far the most promising in the way of future development. If the co-operators are really producing for themselves, they eliminate the speculative element altogether; so that the loss of foresight felt under (2) hardly counts in (3). Producing for themselves, they can educate themselves to use those things whose utility is great in proportion to their cost; and can subject

themselves to rules which conserve the public interest, but which the consumers would not tolerate if imposed by any other authority than their own. It is this educational possibility which has most contributed to the success of co-operative banks, co-operative purchasing agencies, and other forms of successful consumers' enterprise. (A.T.H.)

Co-operation (social): Ger. *Kooperation*; Fr *coopération*; Ital. *cooperazione*. Any grouping of individuals which is psychologically determined in the mind of each.

Social co-operation is characterized by what Ward calls 'inter-subjective intercourse'; it rests upon any sort of internal bond which is psychical—from mere herding from instinct, or collecting guided by smell or touch, up to deliberate pursuit of common social ends. The term is suggested for the broad meaning indicated as somewhat current under the term ASSOCIATION (social), when the emphasis is laid on the psychological bond which holds the group in question together. As psychologically determined it is contrasted with AGGREGATION (q.v.), which characterizes groups considered as sociologically and biologically determined. The method of psychological determination is conveniently discussed under the headings: (1) 'instinctive co-operation,' giving the COMPANY (q. v.); (2) 'spontaneous or imitative co-operation,' giving the CROWD (q. v.); and (3) 'intelligent or reflective co-operation,' giving the SOCIETY (q. v.).

Literature: see the terms referred to. (J.M.B.)

Co-ordinates : see CURVE.

Co-ordination (in logic) [Lat. *co-* + *ordo*, order]: Ger. *Coordination*; Fr. *coordination*; Ital. *coordinazione*. The relation between two notions which are contained within the sphere of a third notion, and are distinguished therefrom by difference in respect to one and the same feature, mark, or group of marks. The relation is that between constituent species of one and the same genus. (R.A.)

Co-ordination (of studies). The arrangement of studies as mutually related in their parts, yet essentially independent as branches of knowledge.

By concentration some studies are subordinated to others; by co-ordination they are put in relation to one another. It does not, however, forbid a grouping of subjects in accordance with their nature. Thus, the school studies may be grouped into humanistic, scientific, and economic. Cf. CORRELATION, and CONCENTRATION.

Literature: HARRIS, Five Co-ordinate

Groups of Studies in Schools, Educ. Rev. (April, 1896). (C.DE G.)

Cope, Edward Drinker. (1840–97.) An eminent American naturalist; educated in the University of Pennsylvania, and in Europe. Professor of natural science in Haverford College, 1864–7. He entered the employ of the Geological Survey of Ohio in 1868, and conducted an expedition into Kansas in 1891. In 1872–3 he served in the field in Wyoming and Colorado, and in 1879 entered the employ of the U. S. Geological Survey. He became professor of geology and paleontology in the University of Pennsylvania in 1891. He was the leader of the Neo-Lamarckian school of biologists in America.

Copernican Theory (after Copernicus): Ger. *Copernicanische Lehre*; Fr. *théorie de Copernic*; Ital. *teoria di Copernico*. The theory that the apparent diurnal revolution of the heavenly bodies is due to a rotation of the earth, and that the apparent motion of the planets around circles on the celestial sphere is an actual motion round the sun, in which the earth itself participates. The two last propositions lead to the term 'heliocentric theory.'

So much of the theory as asserts the rotation of the earth was propounded by some of the ancients, as we know from Ptolemy's *Almagest*, but its attempted refutation by Ptolemy led to its being ignored by astronomers before Copernicus. It is alleged that the heliocentric theory was taught by Pythagoras, but on very vague evidence. (S.N.)

Ekphantos the Pythagorean taught the rotation of the earth on its axis, and Aristarchus of Samos, called the 'Copernicus of the ancient world,' taught the heliocentric theory (see Gomperz, *Die griechischen Denker*, i. 98 f.). (K.G.)

Copernicus (or Polish **Kopernigk**), **Nicholas.** (1493–1543.) A celebrated astronomer, born in Thorn, Poland, after whom the COPERNICAN THEORY (q. v.) is named.

Coprolalia [Gr. κόπρος, filth, + λαλιά, speech]: Ger. *Koprolalie*; Fr. *coprolalie*; Ital. *coprolalia*. The involuntary, and perhaps unconscious, use of obscene words, occurring as a symptom of mental disorder in hysteria and other diseases; it seems to be of the nature of a spasm or tic. Cf. HYSTERIA. (J.J.)

Copula [Lat.]: Ger. *Copula*; Fr. *copule*; Ital. *copula*. The term whereby the fundamental relation of assertion, as affirmation or negation, is expressed.

In the categorical proposition, the simplest form of assertion, the unit of judgment, this expression is given through the verbs *is* and *is not*, which are therefore defined as the copula, and viewed as connecting the subject and predicate terms. It is only for the convenience of technical analysis that the verbs *is* and *is not* are employed exclusively as copula, and, apart from the ambiguity attaching to the verb *to be*, an ambiguity of which Aristotle shows himself fully aware, the method of technical treatment tends to obscure the real nature of the thought expressed in a judgment or proposition.

The name copula, in its accepted sense, Prantl (*Gesch. d. Logik*, ii. 196) finds first in Abelard, though with traces of earlier usage. From Psellus and Petrus Hispanus, the name passed into the technical vocabulary of logic (Prantl, ibid., iii. 42).

Literature: recent discussions regarding its true function will be found in HAMILTON, Lects. on Logic, lect. xiv; SIGWART, Logik, § 17; LOTZE, Logik, §§ 50–5; B. ERDMANN, Logik, §§ 201, 250. See also the heading Judgment in the textbooks of psychology. (R.A.)

Copy [ME. *copy*]: Ger. (1, 2) *Copie, Muster*, (2) *Exemplar*; Fr. (1, 2) *copie*, (2) *exemplaire*; Ital. *copia*. (1) Anything imitated or liable to imitation, whether intentionally set for imitation or not. (J.M.B.–G.F.S.)

(2) Something made by imitation of something else; as a verb, to imitate.

(1) As in the expressions 'copy for imitation,' 'printer's copy,' 'copy-book,' &c. The ambiguity arising from the two usages makes it desirable to use (1) altogether as the proper psychological term in all discussions of the imitative functions, model being reserved for a copy which is consciously set or held up for imitation. Under usage (2) we have the further turn that the word sometimes means a sample or specimen, as a 'copy' of a book. This, however, need not be reflected in psychological terminology. To secure clearness, the phrases 'copy-made' and 'copy-result' are recommended when the result of imitation is intended. The phrase 'the original' is often used (in Eng., Ger., and Fr.) for what is imitated when a direct comparison is made with the imitative result. See IMITATION (also for *Literature*), and MODEL. (J.M.B., G.F.S.)

Cornu [Lat.]: Ger. *Horn*; Fr. *corne*; Ital. *corno* (pl. *corna*). A purely descriptive term, indicating the horn-like form of an organ or cavity; especially applied to the cornua of the lateral ventricles, the cornua of the grey matter in the spinal cord, and the protuberant

curved portion of the hippocampus or *cornu Ammonis*. (H.H.)

Cornutus, L. Annaeus. Stoic philosopher of Septis, Africa, who lived in Rome under Nero; the teacher and friend of Persius, whose *Satires* he edited. Banished by Nero. A manual entitled *De Natura Deorum* is his only extant work.

Corollary [Lat. *corollarium*, from *corolla*, a little crown]: Ger. *Corollar, Corollarium* (math.); Fr. *corollaire*; Ital. *corollario*. A proposition, relatively of less scope or importance, seen to follow from, or to be implied in, a more extensive or important assertion which has already been established. (R.A.)

Corporation [Lat. *corpus*, through Fr.]: Ger. *Körperschaft, Corporation*; Fr. *corporation, communauté, société anonyme*; Ital. *corporazione*. An artificial person generally composed of an association of several natural persons, under a descriptive name, for certain particular purposes, who have or claim legal authority so to associate. It is its legal *status* as an artificial person which distinguishes it from an unincorporated association.

A *public corporation* is one formed for public purposes; a *private corporation* is one formed wholly or partly for private purposes.

Every independent sovereignty is a public corporation, and so is every corporation formed by its authority out of part of its citizens or subjects, or for part of its territory, for governmental purposes, e. g. a country, city, borough, town.

A private corporation may be formed partly for public purposes, e. g. a railroad company, a water company, a national bank. It may be formed by the association of public officers, e. g. an eleemosynary corporation, composed of the mayor, recorder, and other officers of a city, *ex officio*, to administer a charity.

The state grants authority for corporate associations, either by special charters or by the enactment of general laws, under which incorporation may be had by any who desire it, under specified conditions, and upon signing and filing certain papers for record.

Public corporations may exist independently of any agreement of association. They are agencies of governmental administration, and may be created and changed from time to time at the sole pleasure of the state, without the consent of the persons composing them.

Private corporations can only be formed by a voluntary agreement to associate. The state simply sanctions this agreement. It may, however, grant this sanction, or confer the corporate franchise, on such terms as it sees fit to impose. The acceptance of the franchise is an assent to its terms.

The state has also a certain control over private corporations, after their incorporation, by virtue of its general powers of government, to which all within its jurisdiction are subject. It cannot make any radical or fundamental change in the terms of the charter or nature of the franchise, without the consent of each of the individual corporators, for each can say : *Non haec in foedera veni.*

A corporation continues in an unbroken course of existence, notwithstanding the death of all its members, unless the charter be such as to make such continuance legally impossible. If a moneyed corporation, not of a charitable or public kind, the members have a property right in its assets, which each can transfer to another person at will, unless the charter otherwise provides.

A corporation can hold any property, real or personal, necessary for its corporate purposes, unless there are restrictions against this in the charter or general laws. Such restrictions are common, particularly as to real estate (by mortmain laws).

A corporation cannot legally act outside of the purposes of its incorporation : but, practically, it often may, and does.

A corporation *de iure* is one organized under and according to law.

A corporation *de facto* is one organized under a law, but not according to law ; or organized without any legal authority, but under a claim of such authority, and during the existence of a law under which a similar kind of organization might have been effected.

The corporations above described are 'corporations aggregate,' being composed of several persons. A 'corporation sole' is one composed of a single person, e. g. the bishop of an English diocese.

Every corporation has a right to a common seal, but may exist without one.

A *quasi-corporation* is an association recognized by law as an artificial person, capable of suing and being sued as such, but not having the full powers ordinarily incident to corporations.

'Neque societas, neque collegium, neque huiusmodi corpus passim omnibus habere conceditur ; nam et legibus et senatus consultis et principalibus constitutionibus ea res coercetur' (*Dig.*, iii. 4, *quod cuiuscumque universitatis nomine vel contra eam agatur*, 1). (S.E.B.)

Literature : THOMPSON, Commentaries on the Law of Private Corporations (1895), chaps. i, ii, iii ; DILLON, Treatise on the Law of Municipal Corporations, chaps. i, ii ; KYD, on Corporations, Introd. ; TAYLOR, Private Corporations (1894), chaps. i, ii, iii ; S. E. BALDWIN, Mod. Polit. Instit. (1898), chap. vi ; MOMMSEN, De Collegiis et Sodaliciis Romanorum (1843).

Corporeal [Lat. *corpus*, body]. Pertaining to the BODY (q. v.). (J.M.B.)

Corpus [Lat.]: Ger. *Körper* ; Fr. *corps* ; Ital. *corpo*. Body or organ.

Used in combination in many anatomical terms (e. g. *corpus callosum*). See BRAIN (Glossary). Most American and many European neurologists drop the substantive in many such cases, and write e. g. *callosum*. Where various nouns are compounded with the same descriptive adjective (e. g. *corpus fornicis* as contrasted with *crus fornicis*), *corpus* must be retained ; but it should never be applied to replace 'nucleus' for an histological aggregate, as it properly refers to a part anatomically discrete. (H.H.)

Corpus (in law): foreign equivalents the same. (1) The whole body of a certain thing, e. g. the *corpus* of the water in a lake, as distinguished from (a right to use) the power supplied by the outflow.

(2) The main body of a certain thing, as the *corpus* of the estate of an insolvent debtor. *Corpus delicti*: the body of, or most essential fact in, a crime, e. g. the slaying, upon a prosecution for murder. *Corpus iuris*: the *Corpus Iuris Civilis*. Cf. CODE. (S.E.B.)

Corpuscle [Lat. *corpusculum*, dim. of *corpus*, body]: Ger. *Körperchen* ; Fr. *corpuscule* ; Ital. *corpuscolo*. (1) A term applied to small units of structure in the body, often equivalent to CELL (q. v.). 'The *cells*, or *bone corpuscles*, are branched corpuscles' (Landois). See BLOOD, and LYMPH.

(2) Compound structures, the end-organs of certain sensory nerves. These are small oval or spherical bodies composed of connective tissue, in which end one or more nerve-fibres. Corpuscles of Vater and Pacini ; touch, or tactile, or palpation corpuscles ; corpuscles of Meissner, Krause, and Wagner. See SENSE ORGANS, and SKIN. (C.F.H.)

Correlation (in biology) [Lat. *co-* + *relatus*, related]: Ger. *Correlation* ; Fr. *corrélation* ; Ital. *correlazione*. (1) Physiological Correlation. The union of special organs and functions in a larger general function, e. g. the correlation of many functions with digestion, the rôle of internal secretions in many organic processes, &c. See Geoffroy-Saint-Hilaire, 'Balance des Organes,' *Des Anomalies de l'Organisation.*

(2) **Developmental correlation.** The development of organs and functions together for the accomplishment of a function which depends upon the union of them all, e. g. the development of the secondary sexual characters, with the mental changes of adolescence, &c. See Clouston, *Neuroses of Development.*

(3) **Correlation of characters.** The appearance of characters by variation, or growth, in vital connection with one another.

This form of correlation has separate statement in evolution theory, on account of the somewhat artificial conception of a character as something relatively independent in the organism, and so liable to separate variation and growth. So the need arises of accounting for the correlation or union of such characters. One of the most strongly urged objections to natural selection as a general law of evolution is that it requires simultaneous variation of many characters, in such a way that they support and further one another.

The difficulty is largely removed when we note that correlation, or functional and anatomical union, is the law, not the exception, and a character is a relative term; the character of any particular observation being an abstraction made for purposes of classification, statistics, or logic. See CO-ADAPTATION, and VARIATION. That is, characters do not vary as units separately. (J.M.B.)

Literature: see the analysis of literature under Correlation, by GLEY, in Année Biol., i. 13, and later vols. Also DELAGE, Structure du Protoplasma, in loc.; DARWIN, Origin of Species; K. PEARSON, Chances of Death, chaps. i, iii; and Math. Contrib. to the Theory of Evolution, in Proc. Roy. Soc. (1894 ff.); W. F. R. WELDON, Certain Correlated Variations in *Crangon vulgaris*, Proc. Roy. Soc., v. 51 (1892); On Certain Correlated Variations in *Carcinus maenas*, ibid. 54 (1893); F. GALTON, Co-relations and their Measurement, ibid. 45 (1888); ROMANES, Darwin and after Darwin, Pt. II; references under VARIATION. (J.M.B.—E.S.G.)

Correlation (in psychology). (1) The act of APPERCEPTION (q. v.) considered as resulting in the formation of explicit relationships among the parts of a mental whole.

(2) A law generalizing the special laws of ASSOCIATION (q. v.) in the statement that any relation between elements of content suffices to associate them in future experience.

It was used by McCosh (*Cognitive Powers*) to denote the more essential and necessary relationships, such as cause, logical ground, &c., in opposition to coexistence, contrast, &c., which are usually emphasized as acting in association. It proceeds upon an earlier act of correlation in sense (1). Cf. Baldwin, *Senses and Intellect*, 201. (J.M.B.)

Correlation (of studies). Primarily, the arrangement of studies and topics in accordance with their reciprocal relations; secondarily, the natural static relations that exist among the various branches of knowledge.

The correlation of topics in a given study naturally depends upon two things: (1) their relation to each other as component parts of a subject of instruction, as in mathematics; and (2) their relation to topics of other related subjects, as in geography and history. The sequence of topics in a given study. Cf. CONCENTRATION, and CO-ORDINATION.

Literature: HARRIS, Report of the Committee of Fifteen, Proc. of the Natnl. (U.S.) Educ. Assoc. for 1895, 87, 309, 343, 347, 349, 714; First Year-Book of the Herbart Society; McMURRY, Gen. Meth., 69–89; DE GARMO, Herbart and the Herbartians. (C.DE G.)

Correspondence (in mathematics): see NUMBER.

Corresponding Points : Ger. *correspondirende Punkte*; Fr. *points correspondants*; Ital. *punti corrispondenti.* Corresponding points are retinal points whose impressions unite in the great majority of cases to give a single spatially undifferentiated perception, and which therefore normally give single vision.

According to Helmholtz (*Physiol. Optik*, 2nd ed., 844), corresponding points (or Deckpunkte) are the points of the two fields of vision which appear to occupy the same position relatively to the point of fixation, and therefore coincide in the common visual field (Wundt's CONGRUENT POINTS, q. v.). Points which do not correspond he calls disparate points, following Fechner, who distinguishes further between homogeneous and heterogeneous correspondents, according as the impressions are alike or different in character.

Literature: WUNDT, Physiol. Psychol. (4th ed.), ii. 173; FECHNER, Abhandl. d. kgl. sächs. Gesell. d. Wiss., vii. (1860), 340; HERING, Hermann's Handb. d. Physiol., III. i. 351 (1879); HELMHOLTZ, as cited. (E.B.T.)

Cosmogony [Gr. κόσμος, the world, + γονή, generation]: Ger. *Kosmogonie*; Fr. *cosmogonie*; Ital. *cosmogonia.* A theory, or, as is more usual, a pictorial account of the genesis of the world (and often of living beings). Cf. CREATION, COSMOS, THEOGONY, and NATURE (philosophy of).

Among the most primitive civilizations known, nothing in the nature of a real cosmogony can be traced; and even when the scale of civilization rises a little higher, the myths are so simple and naïve that they can hardly be dignified with the name. But the great races of mankind—the Semites, Egyptians, and Aryans—all originated cosmogonies properly so called.

Literature: TYLOR, Early Hist. of Mankind; WAITZ and GERLAND, Anthropol. d. Naturvölker; GREY, Polynesian Mythol.; GILL, Myths and Songs of the South Pacific; BRINTON, Myths of the New World; BANCROFT, Native Races of North America; BASTIAN, Geographische Bilder; BAUDISSIN, Stud. z. semit. Religionsgeschichte; JENSEN, Die Kosmologie d. Babylonier; BUDGE, Egyptian Book of the Dead; WIEDEMANN, Religion of the Ancient Egyptians (Eng. trans.); BRUGSCH, Religion u. Mythol. d. alten Aegypter; SPIEGEL, Avesta; DARMSTETER, Ormazd et Ahriman; MUIR, Ancient Sanskrit Texts, iv; MAX MÜLLER, Ancient Sanskrit Literature; Sacred Books of the East; KRAUSE, Tuisko-Land, d. arischen Stämme u. Götter Urheimat; SHIVA SAMHITA, Esoteric Sci. and Philos. of Tantras; DEUSSEN, Allg. Gesch. d. Philos., I. i. Abth.; OLDENBERG, Die Religion d. Vedas; COX, Aryan Mythol.; WINDISCHMANN, Ursagen d. arischen Völker; POTT, Vedic and Orphic Cosmic Egg, in Kühn's Zeitsch. f. vergleichende Sprachforschung; v. BRADKE, in Zeitsch. d. Deutsch. Morgenländischen Gesell., xl. 347. (R.M.W.)

Cosmological Argument: see THEISM.

Cosmology: see COSMOS, NATURE (philosophy of), and METAPHYSICS.

Cosmos [Gr. κόσμος, world]. Used also in the other languages, as well as the equivalents for WORLD (q.v.). The universe conceived as an orderly system.

It is opposed in this sense to chaos, a mythological or hypothetical state of complete disorder, absolute lawlessness, or pure chance, against which the order and rationality which actually characterize the universe are thrown into relief. Frequently the term is used simply to denote the universe or the all of existence—always, however, with the implication of order or system in the background (as in A. Humboldt's *cosmos*); at other times it is used predicatively to assert expressly the fact of orderliness. Thus the scientific belief in the uniformity of nature might be described as a faith that we are living in a cosmos, not a chaos. The term is also used occasionally in a more limited reference to emphasize the presence of order or system in some particular department of experience. Thus we find writers speaking of 'the ethical cosmos' or 'the cosmos of ethical experience.'

The term κόσμος originally means order, and according to tradition was first applied to 'the world' by Pythagoras, whose mathematical and musical studies impressed upon him the idea of order and regularity in natural phenomena. The term is used by Heraclitus also in the sense of the world order. Later, it took the place of the earlier term οὐρανός to signify the 'world'; but even in Xenophon's time it was not in current use in this sense, for Xenophon speaks (*Memorabilia*, I. i. 11) of 'what the sophists call the Cosmos.' Κόσμος was used, moreover, it must be observed, as οὐρανός had also been, not for the universe in the modern sense—τὸ πᾶν, the All—but for the visible system of the earth and the heavens, the latter being generally regarded as a spherical enclosing envelope. There is also, as in the earlier term, more prominent reference to the phenomena of the heavens than to the earth. Anaximander speaks of ἄπειροι οὐρανοί, and later writers speak similarly of innumerable κόσμοι or world-systems. See MUNDUS. (A.S.P.P.)

Cosmothetic Idealism. A term suggested by Sir William Hamilton, who contrasted it, as Representationism, with Presentationism or Natural Realism. See IDEALISM. (J.M.B.)

Cost [ME. *cost*]: Ger. *Kosten*; Fr. *frais de production*; Ital. *costo*. The amount of wealth rendered unavailable in any economic process, or group of processes.

(1) If we measure wealth as property, cost will take the form of *expense*.

(2) If we measure wealth as accumulated resources, cost will take the form of *waste*.

(3) If we measure wealth as utility, or source of pleasure, cost will take the form of disutility—*pain*.

The physiocrats adopted a sense of cost analogous to (2): the cost of an article was measured by the amount of food embodied in its production. Smith distinguished (1) and (3): the former he called money cost or price; the latter, real cost or price. Malthus and Ricardo fell back on the Aristotelian conception of quantities of labour as the only measure of cost—a crude use of the third conception under forms borrowed from (1). Marx took Ricardo's conception, and showed the contradictions in which careless use of terms had involved the orthodox economists, but was not equally successful in establishing better forms for himself. Jevons, in this as in many other points, laid the foundations of more philosophic treatment; and the theory of pain-cost which he outlined has been superbly developed by Marshall. But pain-cost alone gives a somewhat incomplete explanation of price; and some writers (Patten), following out a half-forgotten conception of Ricardo, supplement it by a study of a fourth sense of cost in the form of *lapse of opportunity*. In recent years there has been a tendency in several quarters to go back to the sense of *waste* as the fundamental meaning of cost. The analysis based on this meaning seems to furnish a solution of several problems where old methods failed (compare the treatment of Wages in Hadley's *Economics*). On Prime Cost, Supplementary Cost, see Marshall, *Princ. of Econ.*, Bk. V. chap. iv. The old distinction between cost of production and cost of reproduction has lost its importance under modern analysis. (A.T.H.)

Counter-irritation : Ger. *Gegenreizung*; Fr. *contre-stimulus* or *contre-irritation*; Ital. *contro-stimolo*. A stimulation, irritation, or congestion, produced artificially in order to relieve inflammation in another part. See IRRITATION. (C.F.H.)

Couple [Lat. *copula*, a band, a bond]: Ger. *Kräftepaar*; Fr. *couple*; Ital. *coppia*. A force or resultant which tends to make a body rotate, without giving it any movement of translation. A couple may always

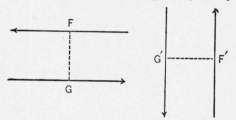

be represented by a pair of equal and parallel forces, F and G, acting in opposite directions. The moment of the couple is the product of either force into the perpendicular distance, FG, between the lines of action. The axis of a couple is any line perpendicular to the plane containing the forces; it is therefore only a direction in space.

The value of this conception arises from the theorem that, in their action on a rigid body, all couples, having the same moment and the same direction of axis, are equivalent. For example, the couple $F'\,G'$ will produce the same effect as $F\,G$, if $F' \times F'\,G' = F \times F\,G$. Hence, to define a couple, we need specify only its moment, and the direction of its axis.

Introduced into mechanics by Poinsot shortly after the middle of the first half of the century. (S.N.)

Courage [OF. *corage*, from Lat. *cor*, heart]: Ger. *Muth*; Fr. *courage*; Ital. *coraggio*. The habit of voluntary activity (or virtue) which is shown both in the control of pain and of the fear of pain, and in the due exercise and regulation of the active and combative impulses.

In the latter terms courage is defined by Plato in the *Republic*, while the former and more fundamental aspect is brought out by Aristotle. Aristotle treats courage as a MEAN (q. v.) or moderate state in respect of the feelings of fear and confidence, and distinguishes it from a double system of extreme states: excess of fear and defect of confidence, which constitute cowardice; and excess of confidence, which is rashness, and defect of fear (an unnamed quality).

Like all the personal virtues, courage is built upon an impulsive and organic basis; and in courage the impulsive basis is more obvious than in the case of the other virtues. Yet it is not entirely a matter of inherited constitution; and the courage of deliberate purpose, which is a moral virtue, may be distinguished from the courage of physical constitution, which is an inherited quality. Further, a distinction may be drawn between the passive courage which endures pain (the *fortitudo* of mediaeval ethics), and the active courage which prompts to enterprise in spite of danger.

What is popularly called 'moral courage' does not indicate a more moral, or more voluntary, quality than courage generally; it applies to the control of the fear of social evils (disgrace or ridicule from those who determine the opinion of the community), whereas the ordinary application of courage is to the control of the fear of physical evils.

Literature: PLATO, Laches, and Republic, iv; ARISTOTLE, Ethics, iii; SIDGWICK, Meth. of Eth., III. x; GREEN, Proleg. to Eth., iv. (W.R.S.)

Court (in law) [Fr. *cour*]: Ger. *Gerichtshof*; Fr. *cour*; Ital. *corte*. A tribunal for the administration of remedial justice, having, or acting under a claim of having, legal authority for its proceedings. If it have such authority, it is a *de iure* court; otherwise a *de facto* one.

Phrases. *Civil court*: (1) an ordinary court, as distinguished from a military, naval, martial, or ecclesiastical court; (2) a court having cognizance of civil actions, as distinguished from one having cognizance of criminal prosecutions, i. e. a *criminal court*. *Military court*: one having cognizance of offences by those in military service. *Naval court*: one having cognizance of offences by those in naval service. *Court martial*: (1) a court organized during war, in a place that is the seat of war, to dispense justice by martial law; (2) a military or naval court. *Day in court*: due opportunity to be heard in one's defence before an adverse judgment is pronounced in court. *The court* is often used to describe the judge as distinguished from the jury. (S.E.B.)

Cousin, Victor. (1792–1867.) French philosopher. He received a philosophic impulse under the tutelage of Laromiguière, Royer-Collard, and Maine de Biran. In 1815 he began to lecture in the Sorbonne, Paris, continuing the teaching of Scottish philosophy. He was an important factor in the reaction against Condillac and other sensualistic thinkers of the 18th century. In 1820 he was suspended for political reasons, and in 1827 again replaced in his chair. Cf. ECLECTICISM.

Covenants (doctrine of) [Lat. *con-* + *venire*, to come]: Ger. *Bundestheologie*; Fr. *doctrine des alliances*; Ital. *teoria dell' alleanza* (*di grazia*, &c.). Another name for the 'Federal Theology' of Cocceius (1603–69), professor at Leyden.

In contrast to the Scholastics, whose methods had been adopted by many of the Reformers (e. g. Calvin), Cocceius appealed to the Bible. The Bible is the history of the 'covenant of grace' made by God with man. This in contrast to the 'covenant of works' which subsisted before the Fall. According to the 'covenant of works,' God promised man everlasting felicity, on condition of obedience during the life on earth. According to the 'covenant of grace,' man needed to receive again what he had lost by the Fall, in order to be able to render obedience; and this fresh gift, due to the grace of God, has been transmitted by the Incarnation of Jesus Christ.

Literature: FISHER, Hist. of Christ. Doctrine, 347 f.; DORNER, Hist. of Protestant Theol., ii. 31 f. (Eng. trans.); WEISSMANN, Introd. in Memorabilia Eccl. Hist. Sacrae, ii. 698 f., 1103 f.; OWEN, The Doctrine of Justification; A. A. HODGE, Outlines of Theol., chap. xxi; C. HODGE, System. Theol., ii. 192 f.; KRAETZSCHMAR, Die Bundesvorstellung im Alt. Test.; T. M. LINDSAY, in Brit. and For. Evang. Rev. (1879). (R.M.W.)

Coyness [ME. *coy*, quiet, secret]: Ger. *Scheu, Sprödigkeit* (sexual); Fr. *coquetterie*; Ital. *civetteria* (sexual). The form of shyness, with its bodily reaction, due to consciousness of the presence of the other sex. Cf. SHYNESS, BASHFULNESS, SHAME, and MODESTY.

On the mental side coyness includes the form of so-called 'self-consciousness,' which is stimulated by the other sex; 'coquetry' and 'flirtation' when these are not deliberate; 'showing-off' or SELF-EXHIBITION (q. v.), and 'make-believe.' On the physical side, it involves attitudes of 'courting,' e. g. play, self-exhibition, advance and retreat, with the characteristic organic changes. The term 'self-consciousness,' when employed for coyness, is very inexact and confusing, and should be discontinued. The difference between coyness and modesty (when the latter relates to sex) is that the former does not involve reflective self-consciousness, while the latter does.

Literature: titles given under SHYNESS, especially GROOS, Die Spiele d. Thiere (Eng. trans.). (J.M.B.)

Craniology and **Craniometry** [Craniology: Gr. κρανίον, skull, + λόγος, discourse. Craniometry: κρανίον + μέτρον, measure]: Ger. *Craniologie, Craniometrie*; Fr. *craniologie, craniométrie*; Ital. *craniologia, craniometria*. In its most general sense craniology designates the accumulated systematic knowledge of the skull; thus including the anatomical, morphological, and pathological aspects, as well as the comparative study of the skull in different animals. The term, however, is apt to be used in reference to the study of the human cranium, with special regard to the ethnological conclusions as to race and origin which such study may yield.

The term seems to have originated with Gall's phrenological correlations; was established in the ethnological sense mainly by the efforts of Broca, and under recent developments has assumed a somewhat broader, as well as more scientific, character. The most practical subdivision of the topic seems to be that adopted by Török, who refers to cranioscopy the description of the anatomical and morphological characteristics of the skull (general form, position of distinctive points, shape of bones, sutures, &c.), and to craniometry the geometrical characteristics capable of precise measurement. Craniography refers to the study of the skull by means of charts, photographs, and projections, which in turn yield craniometric details not readily obtainable on the skull itself. The systematic and explanatory exposition of all such results belongs to craniology. The descriptions and measurements of cranial characteristics have been developed with great detail and precision, although a much-desired consensus of method of taking such measurements has not as yet been reached. Among the scores, if not hundreds, of such characteristics which have been proposed as significant for ethnological distinctions, the four most important are the maximum length and the maximum breadth of the skull (the relation of which leads to one INDEX, q. v., of several), the facial angle, and the cranial capacity (see CAPACITY, cranial) or cubic contents of the skull. In all these respects there are minor differences of measurement which prevent a general description from being precisely accurate. See also DIAMETER, and FACIAL ANGLE.

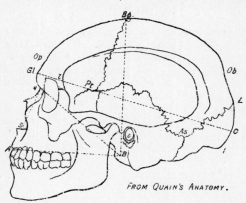

FROM QUAIN'S ANATOMY.

A is the alveolar point at the edge of the jaw between the incisors ; *As*, the asterion, or point of junction of the parietal, temporal, and occipital bones ; *C* is the auricular point, or centre of opening of the auditory meatus ; *B* is the basion, or middle point of the anterior margin of the foramen magnum ; *Bg* is the bregma, or junction of the coronal and sagittal sutures ; *I* is the inion, or occipital protuberance ; *N*, the nasion, at the root of the nose ; *S*, the sub-nasal, also spinal point, at the base of the sub-nasal spine.

Many important measurements may also be made on the living head (Cephalometry). Instruments for cranial measurements are termed Craniometers ; those for the head, Cephalometers.

As a partial guide to the points and proportions of the cranium, of importance in craniometry, the above illustration may be consulted.

With reference to the points fixed in the figure certain lines are drawn, which in turn give rise to diameters, angles, and indices. The various facial angles, and the lines determining them, are given under the topic FACIAL ANGLE (q. v.) ; and the other chief diameters are noted under DIAMETER.

Literature : TOPINARD, Anthropology, 31–51, 227–97 ; art. Craniologie, in Dict. des Sci. Anthropol. ; BROCA, Mém. d'Anthropol., 5 vols. ; and particularly, Instructions Craniologiques (1875) ; TÖRÖK, Reform d. Kraniologie, Int. Monatsch. f. Anat. u. Physiol., xi. 297, 360. (J.J.)

Also RIEGER, Eine exakte Methode der Kraniographie (1885) ; TÖRÖK, Ueber ein Universalkraniometer (1888) ; LOMBROSO, art. Cranio, in Encic. med. Italiana ; E. SCHMIDT, Anthropol. Meth. ; MORSELLI, Semej. malat. ment. (1st and 2nd ed., 1898) ; Année Psychol., v (1899) : Historique des Recherches sur la Céphalométrie ; MANOUVRIER, Aperçu de Céphalométrie anthropologique. (S.E.–L.M.–E.M.)

Crantor. A Greek academic philosopher, who lived about 300 B.C., and wrote a treatise on *Affliction*.

Crates of Thebes. A Greek cynic, a disciple of Diogenes of Athens, who lived in the 4th century B.C.

Cratylus. A Greek philosopher, who lived in the 5th century B.C. He was one of Plato's teachers. He maintained the doctrines of Heraclitus.

Crazy [Fr. *écraser*, to crush] : Ger. *verrückt* ; Fr. *fou* ; Ital. *matto, folle*. A popular term meaning insane, or of unsound mind. It is especially characteristic of a chronic broken-down or demented condition. (J.J.)

Creation (in biology) : see SPECIAL CREATION THEORY.

Creation (in theology) [Sansk. *kri*, to make ; Lat. *creare*, to bring forth] : Ger. *Schöpfung* ; Fr. *création* ; Ital. *creazione*. The genesis of the world, and the things therein, by a divine act. The conceptions by which it is characterized are less pictorial than those of COSMOGONY (q. v.), proceeding, as they usually do, from a more advanced civilization.

The term is usually associated with the Hebrew-Semitic doctrines to be found in the first and second chapters of Genesis. These doctrines have a philosophical aspect in that they are strictly dualistic, and so stand contrasted with the more or less monistic conceptions characteristic of Greek thought. In the history of Christian thought, the Old Testament account, adopted by the Church, has undergone various modifications. (R.M.W.)

'Immediate' creation, in which the divine act takes direct effect, is contrasted with 'remote' creation, by so-called 'second' or 'proximate' causes, in which the divine purpose is realized indirectly through the ordinary operations of nature. Cf. the philosophical conceptions of OCCASIONALISM and PRE-ESTABLISHED HARMONY. (R.M.W.–J.M.B.)

Literature: for the Jewish view, HOLZINGER, Hexateuch, 335 f.; WEBER, Syst. d. Altsynag. Paläst. Theol., 197 f. For history of modifications of doctrine in the Christian Church, TERTULLIAN, Adv. Hermogenem; ORIGEN, De Principiis, and Adv. Celsum; AUGUSTINE, De Genesi contra Manichaeos; Confessiones, xi–xiii; De Civ. Dei, xx; PETRUS LOMBARDUS, Libri Sententiarum; HUGH MILLER, Footsteps of the Creator; see also literature on MANICHAEISM. Modern works: ZÖCKLER, Theol. u. Naturwiss.; GUNKEL, Schöpfung u. Chaos; art. Schöpfung in Herzog's Real-Encyc.; REUSCH, Nature and the Bible (Eng. trans.). See also literature under COSMOGONY, and RELIGION (philosophy of). (R.M.W.)

Creationism: Ger. *Theorie der Schöpfung*; Fr. *théorie de la création*; Ital. *dottrina della creazione*. The form of Deism which teaches that the creative act by which the world arose did not, and does not, identify the Creator with the universe in an essential or substantial sense.

Creation by a single act, or 'continuous' creation (by a series of acts), alike hold the theory of transcendence as opposed to that of complete immanence. Theism vibrates between this form of Deism and Pantheism, attempting to hold a form of divine immanence which is still not pantheistic. Cf. DEISM, THEISM, and PANTHEISM (also for *Literature*). (J.M.B.)

Creationism (in theology): Ger. *Creationismus*; Fr. *créationisme*; Ital. *creazionismo*. The doctrine according to which the human spirit (*anima*) is created separately in each individual case, and infused from an external source into the foetus so as to vitalize it.

This doctrine is opposed to PRE-EXISTENCE (q.v.), and to TRADUCIANISM (q.v.), the two competing theories.

While Pre-existence (e. g. with Origen) and Traducianism (e. g. with Tertullian) were held in the earlier history of Christian thought, Creationism came to be the accepted doctrine later, as with Anselm, Thomas Aquinas, and Petrus Lombardus.

Literature: see BIBLICAL PSYCHOLOGY. (R.M.W.)

Credible (1) and **Incredible** (2) [Lat. *credere*, to believe]: Ger. (*un*)*glaublich*; Fr. (*in*)-*croyable*; Ital. (*in*)*credibile*. (1) Believable. (2) Unbelievable. See BELIEF. (J.M.B.–G.F.S.)

Credit [Lat. *creditum*, a thing entrusted, a loan]: Ger. *Kredit*; Fr. *crédit*; Ital. *credito*. The power to use a promise to pay as a means of present payment.

The advantages of credit are of two kinds: (1) It allows a man to extend his business activity to the range of his proved capacity, instead of limiting it by his accumulations. (2) It economizes the use of money, and makes it possible to extend business without feeling scarcity of coin.

The economists of the German Historical school distinguish three stages of industry: *Natural-, Geld-,* and *Kredit-Wirthschaft*. But it is an error to suppose that there is a direct substitution of credit for money in modern life. The tendency is rather towards a substitution of cash for credit in old fields, and a use of credit in relatively new ones.

The function of a banking system has been aptly described as the insurance of credit. (A.T.H.)

Credulity (1) and **Incredulity** (2) [Lat. *credere*, to believe]: Ger. (1) *Leichtgläubigkeit*, (2) *Ungläubigkeit*; Fr. (*in*)*crédulité*, Ital. (*in*)*credulità*. (1) Over-readiness to believe: the tendency to form a belief on slight objective grounds. The slighter the objective ground, as distinguished from the subjective interest or bias, the greater is the credulity.

(2) Under-readiness to believe: the tendency to withhold belief when the objective grounds are strong. It is also a matter of subjective bias.

These terms are not of sufficient exactness for scientific use. Bain has used the phrase 'primitive credulity' for the child's early uncritical attitude of acceptance toward things generally, on which see REALITY-FEELING, and BELIEF. (J.M.B.)

Creed [Lat. *credere*, to believe]: Ger. *Glaubensbekenntniss*; Fr. *confession, symbole*; Ital. *credo*. A systematic, authoritative, and dogmatic (in the sense of giving no reasons) statement of a body of doctrine, which constitutes a profession of faith.

Usually in written form, though this is by no means necessary. It may originate in various ways; e.g. sporadically, like the 'Apostles' Creed'; in a council of the entire Church, like the Creed of Chalcedon; in a special communion, like the Augsburg Confession; in a commission *ad hoc*, like the Westminster Confession, and so on. As matter of history, Christian creeds proceed (1) from the original and still united Church; (2) from one or other of the chief divisions of the Christian Church—the Latin, the Greek, the Lutheran, the Reformed.

As a matter of usage, the term Creed is specially applied to the 'Apostles',' the Nicene, and the Athanasian formulae.

Much attention has been paid recently to the historical investigation of the Creeds, especially the 'Apostles'.'

Literature: SCHAFF, Creeds of Christendom; SWAINSON, Apostolic and Nicene Creeds; HEURTLEY, Harmonia Symbolica; CASPARI, Quellen z. Gesch. d. Taufsymbols u. d. Glaubensregel; LUMBY, Hist. of the Creeds; ZAHN, Apost. Symb.; HAHN, Biblioth. d. Symb. u. Glaubensreg. d. alt. Kirche, iii; GEBHARDT, HARNACK, and ZAHN, Patr. Apost. Op., Bd. i, Heft 2; HARNACK, Apost. Glaubensbek.; SWETE, Apostles' Creed; OMMANNEY, Athanasian Creed. For further literature on Ritschlian school, see F. NIPPOLD, Die theol. Einzelschule; and on the recent Apostolicum controversy see arts. in Zeitsch. f. Theol. u. Kirche, and in Die christl. Welt. (R.M.W.)

Cretinism [Fr. *crétin*]: Ger. *Cretinismus*; Fr. *crétinisme*; Ital. *cretinismo*. A peculiar form of lack of development associated with disease of the thyroid gland, and presenting, as a prominent characteristic, a mental enfeeblement or idiocy.

The disease seems to be endemic, and largely confined to valleys of mountainous regions. It prevails in Switzerland. The cause of the disease is obscure, but recent research points to the interference with the function of the thyroid gland as the determining pathological change. Local, climatic, and hereditary predisposing conditions are important factors in its aetiology, but it may appear in a spasmodic form (sporadic cretinism). The disease seems almost invariably congenital, although it may fail to develop until early or late in childhood. Severe cases of cretinism are very short-lived. In typical cases the bodily abnormalities are a general failure of development, the adult rarely exceeding five feet in height, and presenting the general appearance of a child; the skull is broad and short, the bones thick, and the sutures may give place to the Wormian bone; the nose is broad and flat, the eyes widely separated, the face but slightly developed; the skin is apt to be rough, insensitive, and dark; the teeth are defective, the mouth large, the lips thick; the lower limbs are frequently emaciated, and the muscles poorly developed. One of the most characteristic physical signs is goitre, or enlargement of the thyroid gland, although other affections of this organ may also be present. Physiological activity is weak, involving a low temperature, slow respiration and circulation, irregular digestion, flabby muscles. If cretinism appears in early childhood (usually about the fifth year), the change from a normal bright child to a stunted cretin can be readily observed as years go by. Cretins may be simply weak-minded, understanding a few common words and directions, and capable of simple occupations; or they may be completely idiotic, speechless, and helpless. Hearing is apt to be affected, but the senses are usually fairly normal. The emotional development is low, but fear, affection, and the like may be shown.

Literature: art. Cretinism in Tuke's Dict. of Psychol. Med. (with references); GLEY, in Année Biol., i. 320 ff.; ALLARA, Sul Cretinismo (Ger. trans., 1894); LOMBROSO, art. Cretinismo in Encic. med. Italiana. (J.J.)

Creuz, Friedrich Casimir Carl von. (1724–70.) A German psychologist who was born and lived, as Geheimrath in his later life, at Homburg v.d. Höhe. He insisted that psychology should be based on experience alone.

Crime (in law) [Lat. *crimen*]: Ger. *Verbrechen*; Fr. *crime* (abstract), *délit*; Ital. *delitto*. (1) Any offence against the state by a breach of public rights and duties affecting the interests of the whole community. (S.E.B.)

An act declared by the state to be offensive to the state (in distinction from a *tort*, an act of wrong to an individual), forbidden by the state, and punished by the state. (F.H.G.)

(2) Any grave offence of such a character. Petty offences are known in law as misdemeanours. Every violation of law is a wrong, and in the early stages of civilization little account has generally been taken of the difference between wrongs to individuals and wrongs to the public. Hence, imprisonment for debt, and civic degradation as a consequence of (and punishment for) bankruptcy. As law develops, public remedies are confined to acts of public wrong, and individuals are left to seek a remedy by private actions for wrongs personal to themselves (*torts*).

Literature: BENTHAM, Mor. and Legisl., ii. chap. xvi; and BECCARIA, Dei Delitti e delle Pene, which led the way to a general mitigation of penalties for crime all over the civilized world; PHILLIMORE, Maxims and Princ. of Jurisprudence (1856), xiii; IHERING, Zweck im Recht, i; STEPHEN, Hist. of Criminal Law in England. (S.E.B.)

Crime (in sociology). (1) An act which awakens the passion of vengeance in the community, in distinction from a wrong which awakens the passion of revenge in an individual only.

(2) An act which public opinion pronounces hostile to social integrity and public welfare.

Maine (*Ancient Law*, chap. **x**) shows that in early Aryan communities crime was not differentiated from *torts* and sins. Crime is first clearly recognized when the community perceives the distinction between acts that individuals and their relatives seek to avenge, and acts which the whole community is moved to avenge, as e. g. by lynching. In the present century public opinion, influenced greatly by Jeremy Bentham (*Princ. of Mor. and Legisl.*, and *Theory of Penalties and Rewards*), has tended strongly to discountenance vengeance, and therefore to cease to conceive of crime as that which provokes vengeance, and to substitute for the older notions a conception of crime as that which is fundamentally contrary to public utility. The conflict of these ideas is well presented by Oliver Wendell Holmes, *Lectures on the Common Law*. The psychological ground of the newer views is clearly set forth by Baldwin, *Social and Eth. Interpret.*, Bk. I. chaps. ii and x. Cf. JUSTICE. (F.H.G.)

Criminal (in law): Ger. (1) *verbrecherisch*, (2) *Verbrecher*; Fr. (1, 2) *criminel*; Ital. (1) *criminale, penale*, (2) (*uomo*) *delinquente*. (1) Relating to crime. The term is used with reference both to crimes and misdemeanours, without discrimination. *Criminal conversation*: adultery (often abbreviated to *crim. con.*). *Criminal law*, the law defining (substantive) or punishing (adjective) criminal offences. (2) A person convicted of having committed a crime in the legal sense. See CRIME (in law). (S.E.B.)

Criminal (in sociology). (1) A person whose instincts or acquired habits incline him to conduct inimical to the integrity and wellbeing of society. See CRIME (in sociology). (2) Relating to the character or conduct of such a person.

Various types of criminals have been distinguished in recent anthropological literature (see especially Ferri, as below) :—

(*a*) *Criminal by Instinct*, or instinctive criminal, or criminal by nature, or congenital criminal, or criminal-born: terms of recent origin, designating those whose inherited qualities predispose them to crime.

A prominent class of cases are those which show physical characters of the atavistic or reversionary type. See ATAVISM.

(*b*) *Occasional Criminal*: one whose instincts are ethically and socially sound, but whose passions (of anger, cupidity, sexuality, or other) are so strong that he may commit crime under peculiar provocation.

(*c*) *Professional Criminal*: one who, whether sound in body and mind or not, deliberately follows crime as a business.

(*d*) *Criminal Reformer*: one who actively protests against social opinions and regulations, to the extent of violating convention or law. The commonest class are so-called *political criminals*, exemplified in the deeds of violence done by anarchists. Less marked instances are cases where the protest takes an ethical or strictly social form, as violations of marriage laws, &c.

Various subdivisions of the general subject are recognized :—

(*a*) *Criminal Anthropology*: the scientific study of the criminal in his various types, as revealed in his anatomical, physiological, and psychological characters.

(*b*) *Criminal Sociology*: the scientific study of crime and criminals, as DEMOGRAPHIC (q.v.) or social phenomena. Cf. CRIMINOLOGY.

The distinction between the legal and the anthropological or sociological criminal is of recent origin. Criminal anthropology is a product of medical jurisprudence, which, in turn, was developed from the legal and medical analysis of insanity as a defence in criminal cases.

Literature: the distinctions made above, inclusive, we owe largely to a group of Italian writers: LOMBROSO, *L'Uomo Delinquente* (1874–87), and (with FERRERO) *La Donna Delinquente* (1889); MARRO, *I Caratteri dei Delinquenti* (1887); GAROFALO, *Criminologia* (1890); SIGHELE, *La Foule Criminelle* (Fr. trans.; orig. 1892); FERRI, *Sociologia Criminale* (1880). See also BENEDIKT, *Anatomische Studien an Verbrecher-Gehirnen für Anthropologen, Mediziner, Juristen und Psychologen* (1879); TARDE, *La Criminalité comparée* (1890); PROAL, *Le Crime et la Peine*; FÉRÉ, *Dégénérescence et Criminalité* (1888); CORRE, *Les Criminels: Caractères physiques et psychologiques* (1889). See also under CRIMINOLOGY. (F.H.G.–J.M.B.)

Criminal Anthropology: see CRIMINAL, and CRIMINOLOGY.

Criminal Psychology: see CRIMINOLOGY.

Criminal Sociology: see CRIMINAL, and CRIMINOLOGY.

Criminal-born: see CRIMINAL.

Criminology: Ger. *Criminologie*; Fr. *criminologie*; Ital. *criminologia*. The science of crime and criminals.

The criminal has been studied mainly from the physical side, giving a natural history or Criminal Anthropology. It deals with two main questions: (1) the differentiation of criminal-types (as distinct from crime-types), which might be called Criminography, or Descriptive Criminology; and (2) the theory of the criminal as a racial phenomenon, for which Criminogenesis or Genetic Criminology might serve. A similar study of crime divides itself into two main inquiries: (1) the psychology both of crime and its types, giving Criminal Psychology, and also of criminal tendencies (a branch of Abnormal Psychology); (2) Criminal Sociology, dealing both with crime considered as a phenomenon, involving social relationships, variations, &c., being Criminal Sociology in a narrow sense, or Criminal Psychonomics (after analogy with bionomics); and also crimes studied singly, as to distribution, frequency, &c., by mathematical methods (Criminal Statistics). The psychological and sociological sides of the study of crime are as yet very undeveloped.

Literature: on criminal anthropology, see under CRIMINAL; on particular crimes, see under ANARCHISM, SUICIDE, &c.; on the social and psychological aspects, see under SOCIAL PSYCHOLOGY, and SOCIOLOGY. See also MACDONALD, *Bibliog. of Criminol.*; BILLINGS, *Index Catalogue* (sub verbis); and the literature under MORAL STATISTICS. (J.M.B.)

Crisis [Gr. κρίσις, decisive point]: Ger. *Krisis*; Fr. *crise*; Ital. *crisi* (in opposition to *lisi*). Crisis refers to the tendency of certain diseases, notably fevers, suddenly to decrease after a somewhat definite duration; the time or manner of such change being regarded as significant for recovery or death.

The conception was carried over to mental diseases, and was much used by Esquirol. The French usage of the term is more nearly equivalent to 'an attack' or 'spell,' and in an allied sense the notion formed an essential feature in the earlier doctrines of Mesmer; the purpose of his 'magnetic' treatment being to aid nature in calling out the crisis, and thus to quicken recovery. The symptoms induced by Mesmer were those usually observable in crisis; and the room in which the 'baquet' was set up and the cures performed was called the 'salle des crises.' (J.J.)

Criterion [Gr. κριτήριον]: Ger. *Kriterium, Kennzeichen*; Fr. *critérium*; Ital. *criterio*. Literally, a test, or standard of judgment. The criterion, in a logical reference, is the possible rule or body of rules by which a final decision may be given on the truth or falsity of judgments.

Since the time of Kant, it has been customary to distinguish a formal from a material criterion, to point out that a material criterion in the sense above defined is impossible, and that the formal criterion is to be found in the body of rules defining logical CONSISTENCY (q.v.), that is, in form, absence of contradiction and conformity to the requirements of logical consequence. The distinction is sound, though in the Kantian formulation it is made too absolute. See Kant, *Logik*, Introd., § vii; Hamilton, *Logic*, Lect. 27.

In the history of the discussions regarding a criterion of truth, the most important place is occupied by the attempts of the Stoics to establish a universal and practical standard, in face of the arguments urged against their view by the academics and sceptics. Many of the real points of interest in modern controversies are there anticipated. Modern philosophy has had the task of redefining the issue, and reducing the problem, so far as possible, to a manageable form. Cf. TESTS OF TRUTH, and see the references under CERTAINTY. (R.A.)

Criterion (aesthetic): Ger. *Massstab*; Fr. *critérium esthétique*; Ital. *criterio, canone*. See AESTHETIC STANDARD, and CRITICISM (aesthetic). (J.H.T.)

Criterion (ethical). The test or standard by reference to which the moral worth of character, or the rightness or wrongness of conduct, is determined.

The ethical criterion used for determining moral validity is commonly identical with the ultimate moral ideal, whether that be the moral law revealed in conscience or some conception of the *summum bonum*. But they are not necessarily identical. Thus, according to Spencer (*Princ. of Eth.*, Pt. I, 'Data,' chap. iv), happiness is the 'ultimately supreme end'; but owing to the indefiniteness of the conception itself, and of the means required to reach the ideal, he holds that it is imperfect, though perhaps not useless, as an ethical criterion of conduct. Cf. ETHICAL THEORIES. (W.R.S.)

Criticism [Gr. κριτικός, from κριτής, a judge]: Ger. *Kriticismus*; Fr. *criticisme*; Ital. *criticismo*. The system of philosophy of Immanuel Kant; so called from the titles of his three works, called *Critiques* (*Kritiken*). See KANTIANISM, KANTIAN TERMINOLOGY, NEO-KANTIANISM, and IDEALISM.

Literature: works of KANT; ADECKES, Kant Bibliography, Suppl. to the Philos. Rev.; Hist. of Mod. Philos. (with references, notably UEBERWEG-HEINZE); CAIRD, The Crit. Philos. of Im. Kant. Also references under topics cited, and in EISLER, Wörterb. d. philos. Begriffe (sub verbis). (J.M.B.)

Criticism (aesthetic). The appreciation or estimation of works of art. This presupposes some standard or criterion (see AESTHETIC STANDARD), which must be found ultimately in the end sought by ART (q. v.); but certain rules or canons, found embodied in works of art generally recognized as successful, may be used for the examination of supposedly similar productions. This, however, must always be subject to revision, if it appears that the work in question is seeking a new method. Otherwise criticism becomes merely formal, and is a hindrance to progress.

Aristotle was the founder of aesthetic criticism, and in his *Poetics* analysed Greek tragedy and formulated its rules. Horace and Quintilian criticized poetry and eloquence. The close of the 17th century saw a revival of criticism, especially in France and England (Boileau, Dryden, Pope), which, however, tended to be formal, and to see, in its rules derived from Greek art, the principles for all art whatever, e. g. Shakespere was condemned for 'irregularity.' Lessing and Winckelmann led the way in a truer appreciation of the antique.

The romantic movement (see ROMANTICISM) was in part a protest against the attempt to fetter art by supposed canons. Finally Goethe, the Schlegels, Schiller, Hegel, Coleridge, brought forward and applied the principles that rules are to be judged by the work of genius, not vice versa, and that the supreme tests of a work of art are (1) its interpretation and expression of the life and interests of the people and age in which it arose, and (2) the embodiment of these in forms which give aesthetic delight. These two principles, which may be called the historical and the aesthetic or psychological, are fundamental to modern criticism. In accordance with them a work of art should be judged both by its historical significance and by its relation to general laws of human nature.

Literature: CARRIERE, Die Kunst im Zusammenhang der Kulturentwickelung (3rd ed., 1885); ARNOLD, The Function of Criticism, in Essays on Criticism; SYMONDS, Essays, Speculative and Suggestive; J. M. ROBERTSON, New Essays toward a Critical Method (1897); WORSFOLD, The Princ. of Criticism (1897); MOULTON, Shakespere as Dramatic Artist (Int. Plea for an Inductive Science of Criticism), (3rd ed., 1893); SAINTSBURY, Essays in Eng. Lit. (1891); DOWDEN, New Studies in Literature (1895); L. J. WYLIE, Studies in the Evolution of Eng. Crit. (1894); E. HENNÉQUIN, La Critique Scient. (2nd ed., 1890); F. BRUNETIÈRE, L'Évolution des Genres dans l'Histoire de la Littérature (1890); Questions de Critique (1889); art. Critique Littéraire, in La Grande Encyc.; E. TISSOT, L'Évolution de la Critique Française (1890); A. RICARDOU, La Critique Littéraire, Étude Philos. (1896); BRAITMAIER, Gesch. d. poet. Theorie u. Krit. (1888); BOECKH, Encyklopädie u. Methodologie d. phil. Wissenschaften (2nd ed., 1886), 169–754; J. E. SPINGARN, A Hist. of Literary Criticism in the Renaissance (1899); GAYLEY and SCOTT, An Introd. to the Methods and Materials of Literary Criticism, i (1899); WINCHESTER, Some Principles of Literary Criticism (1899); E. ROD, in Int. Monthly (Jan., 1900); H. PAUL, Grundr. d. germ. Philol. (2nd ed., 1896), 221–47. (J.H.T.)

Critique: see CRITICISM.

Crowd [AS. *croda*]: Ger. *Menge, Haufe*; Fr. *foule*; Ital. *folla*. (1) In sociology: an incidental aggregation, held together by a relatively extrinsic and temporary bond. (2) In psychology: a group whose co-operation is relatively occasional and temporary, as opposed to that which is either instinctively or reflectively determined.

A crowd whose performances are particularly capricious and violent is called a mob.

Literature: SIGHELE, La Folla delinquente (1891 ; Fr. trans., La Foule criminelle); G. LE BON, Psychol. des Foules (1895), (Eng. trans., The Crowd); TARDE, Études de Psychol. Sociale (1898); P. ROSSI, L'Animo della Folla (1898), and Psicologia collettiva (1900); BALDWIN, Social and Eth. Interpret. (1897), § 151 ff. See also under SOCIOLOGY, SOCIAL PSYCHOLOGY, and IMITATION. (J.M.B.–G.F.S.)

Crusius, Christian August. (1715–75.) A German theologian, born near Merseburg, who became senior professor of the theological faculty and professor of philosophy at Leipzig. He zealously opposed the philosophy of Wolff and his followers. Crusius was strongly influenced by Rüdiger, through one of the latter's pupils.

Crystal Vision: Ger. *Krystallsehen* (?); Fr. *cristalloscopie, vision au cristal*; Ital. *cristalloscopia*. The awaking of visual perceptions of a more or less hallucinatory character by visual attention concentrated upon a crystal or other polished surface.

No theories of this phenomenon are as yet sufficiently mature to merit citation. It is generally looked upon, however, as in some way illustrating subconscious processes, as opposed to the older theory of supernatural influence.

Literature: NEWBOLD, Psychol. Rev., ii. (1895), 348; 'MISS X,' Proc. Soc. Psych. Res., v. 486 (with bibliography), and vi. 358; MYERS, ibid. viii. 436; HYSLOP, ibid. xii. 259; MORTON PRINCE, Brain (Winter, 1898). (J.M.B., G.F.S.)

Ctetology: see USE-INHERITANCE.

Cudworth, Ralph. (1617–88.) Born at Aller, Somersetshire; educated at Cambridge. He became master of Clare Hall in 1645; professor of Hebrew at Cambridge, 1645; master of Christ's College, 1654; prebendary of Gloucester, 1678. See NEO-PLATONISM.

Culpa [Lat.]: Ger. *Fahrlässigkeit* (?); Fr. *faute* (*coulpe* is used only for breaches of religious duty); Ital. *colpa*. A want of due care, whether intentional or unintentional; negligence.

Grotius uses the term as including an active wrong. 'Maleficium hic appellamus culpam omnem, sive in faciendo, sive in non faciendo, pugnantem cum eo quod aut homines com-muniter aut pro ratione certae qualitatis facere debent. Ex tali culpa obligatio naturaliter oritur, si damnum datum est, nempe ut id resarciatur' (*De Iure Belli et Pacis*, ii. 17. 1). Cf. Holtzendorff's discrimination between *culpa* considered as a violation of civil right, and as an infraction of criminal law, in his *Encyclopädie der Rechtswissenschaft* (sub verbis).

The essential characteristic of *culpa* is an omission of duty. This duty is that of *diligentia*. It is not owed to all the world, but is to those with whom we are brought in contact in a certain manner, and as to them may vary in degree. The greater the diligence required, the greater the *culpa* for its omission. A master's liability for the act of his slave might be so slight as to amount to *levissima culpa* (*Dig.*, ix. 2, *Ad Legem Aquiliam*, 44). 'Latae culpae finis est non intellegere id quod omnes intellegunt' (*Dig.*, l. 16, *De Verborum Significatione*, 223). The omission of duty may be so gross, that *lata culpa* will be tantamount to fraud or malice (*dolus*).

Literature: HESSE, Die Culpa des Römischen Rechts; PHILLIMORE, Maxims and Princ. of Jurisprudence (1856), xxviii.

Culpability [Lat. *culpabilitas*, blameworthiness]: Ger. *Schuld*; Fr. *culpabilité*; Ital. *colpevolezza*. The condition of deserving moral blame.

Moral culpability has to be distinguished from legal responsibility, which may exist without moral blame (as in a man's responsibility for injury done by his agent), and which does not extend to the inward sources of action, or to certain external actions. Culpability implies that the wrong action was performed by the agent, and that he knew or might have known what he was doing. The degree or extent to which constraint or ignorance may limit or annul culpability is discussed by Aristotle (*Ethics*, III. i.) and by almost every succeeding moralist. See ACCOUNTABLE, RESPONSIBILITY, and PUNISHMENT. (W.R.S.)

Culture [Lat. *cultus*, from *colere*, to cultivate]: Ger. *Kultur*; Fr. *culture, civilisation*; Ital. *cultura*, (more properly) *civiltà*. Culture refers to the comprehensive changes in individual and social life, due to the continued and systematic influences of mental improvement and refinement. Considered from a strictly sociological point of view, it is called civilization, but anthropologists make culture the broader term. In the individual it is EDUCATION (q. v.).

Whatever affects the intellectual status of man, whether directly or indirectly, may be said to be an element in culture. Arts and sciences, language and literature, education and government, social customs, ethics and religion, contribute directly to the culture of a people; but practical industries, means of transportation and communication, and the physical comforts of life exercise, particularly in modern times, no less profound, though more indirect, an influence upon the totality of human culture. The study of the development of these varied activities belongs alike to history and to anthropology. That special phase of historical study which is devoted to this end, as distinguished from that which deals rather with the sequence of events, is termed the history of culture (Cultur-geschichte), and is constantly gaining in scope and significance. Anthropology likewise recognizes the all-important influence which the factors of culture exercise in the status of primitive man, as well as in the various forms of civilization, historic and prehistoric, which that science considers. Cf. ANTHROPOLOGY.

It is customary in discussing the unfolding of culture in certain peoples, or in the human race at large, to speak of culture stages or epochs more or less distinctly marked off. The Stone Age and the age of bronze, or of iron, are suggestive of certain limits of development in primitive times, while such terms as 'mediaeval' suggest forms of life and civilization quite as strongly as a definite period of history. The eighteenth-century division into 'wild,' 'barbarous,' and 'civilized' periods was revived by Morgan.

The psychologist finds in the material furnished by history, and by anthropology, abundant material for the illustration of the principles with which his science deals, as well as of the complexity and variability of personal psychological traits. This field of investigation, however, is so extremely comprehensive, and requires for its successful pursuit such specialized methods, that it cannot be included in the science of psychology as ordinarily interpreted.　(J.J.)

The term Humanity is used as nearly synonomous with culture, and the culture-bringing influences and institutions (studies, art creations, &c.) are called 'the humanities,' or said to be 'humanizing.'　(J.M.B.)

Literature: much of the literature of general anthropology. As works illustrative of certain aspects of culture: LECKY, Hist. of European Morals; A. D. WHITE, Hist. of the Warfare between Science and Theology; HOLLAND, Rise of Intellectual Liberty; CROZIER, Hist. of Intellectual Development, i. (1897). Works devoted to culture history are: LIPPERT, Culturgeschichte (1886-7); NIKEL, Culturgeschichte (1895); MORGAN, Ancient Society. French writers prefer the title 'Histoire de la Civilisation' (see SEIGNOBOS, 1887, J. DE CROZALS, 1887). For historical matter and notes on the terms Culture and Civilization, with literary expositions, see BARTH, Philos. d. Gesch. als Sociologie, i. 251 ff., and 144 note. See also FOLK PSYCHOLOGY.　(J.J.–J.M.B.)

Culture Epochs (theory of, in education): Ger. *kultur-historische Stufen*; Fr. *époques de culture*; Ital. *epoche della civiltà*. The term 'culture epochs,' as used in educational theory, involves the idea that there is a parallelism between the development of each child and the historical development of the people or the race, and that in this parallelism we find a guiding principle for the sequence of subjects or, at least, topics of instruction. Ziller employs this principle in connection with his theory of concentration.

The culture material found in religion, history, and literature forms the core, or backbone, of the curriculum; the sequence of this subject-matter is determined by the ascertained parallelism between the stages in the child's development and the corresponding nodes, or stages, or 'epochs' in the history of culture or civilization, through which the people to which the child belongs has passed. See CULTURE, and CONCENTRATION.

Literature: ZILLER, Allg. Päd., 1890-98; REIN, Outlines of Pedagogics (trans. by Van Liew), 101-16; McMURRY, Gen. Meth., 90-105; DE GARMO, Herbart and the Herbartians; LUKENS, SEELEY, BROWN, DEWEY, McMURRY, GALBRAITH, HINSDALE, FILMLEY, and VAN LIEW in Second Year-Book of the National Herbart Society, 56-140; BALDWIN, Ment. Devel. in the Child and the Race, and Social and Eth. Interpret.; STEINMETZ, Année sociologique (1900).　(C.DE G.)

Cultus [Lat.]: Ger. *Kultus*; Fr. *culte*; Ital. *culto*. The external manifestation of the religious consciousness in rites, ceremonies, customs, &c. This as contrasted with doctrine, or religious thought and speculation. Cultus always implies acts.

The investigation of cultus belongs to the phenomenological section of the science and history of religions. The systematic elucidation of its pervading principles belongs to the portion of philosophy of religion which deals with the contents of the religious consciousness and their manifestation. The importance of both these investigations lies in the psychological reference which they imply, thus lifting the question even of ritual out of the sphere of barren antiquarianism, and explaining it from its vital causes.

In semi-popular usage the term cultus is frequently employed to designate an early, or rudely idolatrous, form of worship as contrasted with a later and more spiritual, to which the name worship is referred; it is also used to designate a semi-private usage rather than a national or universal one. See IDOLATRY, MYSTERIES, and WORSHIP.

Literature: PFLEIDERER, Philos. of Religion, iv. 182 f. (Eng. trans.); TYLOR, Primitive Culture; ROSKOFF, Das Religionswesen d. rohesten Naturvölker; FR. SCHULTZE, Der Fetischismus. For further literature see DE LA SAUSSAYE, Lehrb. d. Religionsgeschichte. See also FOLK PSYCHOLOGY. (R.M.W.)

Cumberland, Richard. (1632–1718.) Born at London, educated at Cambridge; rector of Brampton, 1658; of Allhallows, Stamford, 1667; bishop of Peterborough in 1691. His reputation was made by a work in moral philosophy, a refutation of Hobbes' system, called *Philosophic Inquiry into the Laws of Nature.*

Curiosity: Ger. *Neugier, Wissbegier*; Fr. *curiosité*; Ital. *curiosità*. The disposition to give attention, so far as it has for its motive the mere increase of knowledge, apart from practical interest. (G.F.S.–J.M.B.)

The two cases often distinguished (as in the German terms) are those respectively of curiosity and interest in novelty (Neugier), and the disposition to learn or to know for the sake of information (Wissbegier; cf. Groos, *Die Spiele d. Menschen*), the latter being, however, usually motived by the somewhat trivial reason which characterizes curiosity in general.

Literature: GROOS, loc. cit., 184 ff., also Die Spiele d. Thiere (Eng. trans.); JAMES, Princ. of Psychol., ii. 430. See the topic 'Interest' in the textbooks of psychology. (J.M.B.)

Currency [Lat. *currens*, running]: Ger. *Zahlungsmittel*; Fr. *monnaie* (in the broader sense); Ital. *circolazione*. The sum total of the means of payment which circulate or pass current from hand to hand—coin, government notes, and bank-notes, but not bank cheques.

The terms money and currency have not been sharply distinguished in practice; but currency is the broader of the two. Smith in one or two passages seems to use the term to denote the whole medium of exchange actually in use, as distinct from the officially accredited coinage. Mill habitually speaks of money when dealing with instruments that have an intrinsic value, like gold and silver coins, and of currency when he wishes to include government notes or bank-notes. Walker uses money for the distributive, currency for the collective, sense: paper money, a currency composed of paper. It has sometimes been proposed to extend the term currency to include such means of exchange as bank cheques, or to enumerate bank deposits in estimating its volume; but this is hardly sanctioned by the best authorities. (A.T.H.)

Curve [Lat. *curvus*, crooked]: Ger. *Curve*; Fr. *courbe*; Ital. *curva*. A line described according to a law.

Following the method of Descartes (*Géométrie*, 1637), a curve and its equation are represented by a relation between the co-ordinates of a point of the curve. The axes of co-ordinates are two lines $x\,x_1$, $y\,y_1$, usually at right angles to each other, intersecting at

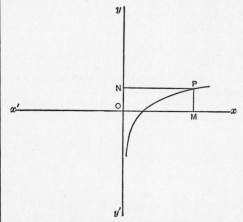

the point O, called the origin. The position of a point P is determined by its distances from the two axes, OM or NP (x) and ON or MP (y), x being the abscissa, and y the ordinate of the point P; x is positive when to the right of O, and negative when to the left; y is positive when above O, and negative when below. Cf. GRAPHIC METHOD (1).

The curve shown in the figure has for its

equation $y = \log x$, expressing the relations believed by Fechner and others to obtain between sensation and stimulus. See FECHNER'S LAW. (J.McK.C.)

Custom (in law) [Lat. *consuetudo*]: Ger. *Gewohnheit, Usus*; Fr. *usage*; Ital. *uso* (or *diritto usuale*). A usage so public, peaceable, uniform, general, long-continued, reasonable and certain, that it has acquired the force of law.

It is for the courts to determine when these conditions are satisfied. A custom becomes law, for practical purposes, when the courts recognize it as such, by applying it, as a rule of decision, in a particular case. They, however, treat it as having been law at the time when the cause of action arose. *Local* or *particular customs* are such as grow up in particular places or occupations.

Custom is the child of morals and the mother of law. Customary law is 'ius moribus constitutum' (*Dig.*, i. 3, *De Legibus*, &c., 32, §1). It is created for each people by themselves and their ancestors, as an unconscious adaptation of life to its environment, and comes to constitute their unwritten law. Before the French Revolution, France was largely dependent on local customs for her law, as the Custom of Normandy, the Custom of Paris. 'Common law, then, is founded on popular custom, and when the judges declare it, they merely discover and declare what they find existing in the life of the people, as the rule of their relations' (Effinger *v.* Lewis, 32 Pennsylvania State Reports, 367). 'As customs change, the unwritten law dependent upon them may change also' (ibid.). (S.E.B)

Literature: MAINE, Ancient Law, chap. i; HOLLAND, Elements of Jurisprudence, chap. v; POLLOCK, First Book of Jurisprudence, Part II. chap. iv; FELIX, Der Einfluss der Sitten und Gebräuche auf die Entwickelung des Eigenthums (1885).

Custom (in social psychology and sociology): Ger. *Sitte(n)*; Fr. *coutume, usage*; Ital. *costumi* (usually plural). A manner of acting somewhat widespread and habitual in a society, but not physically inherited.

Custom, in the individual, is the mother of morals and the daughter of law; for customs are enforced upon the individual, and he becomes accustomed to being moral—both before he is competent to judge for himself. Custom in society rests upon acquired HABIT (q.v.) in individuals. If a custom should be physically inherited, it would then be an instinct. Customs which are relatively less intrinsic to

social organization are called, at the time when most operative, fashions. The equivalent of human custom in animal companies is sometimes termed habit—used usually in the plural—and this for the evident reason that the notions of social custom and private habit merge into one in so far as, in the animals, both are covered by the organization of animal instinct. It is better, however, in animals as in man, to restrict habit to the individually acquired acts which, when generally current, become customs. Custom considered as socially transmitted from generation to generation is called TRADITION (q.v.). (J.M.B.-G.F.S.)

Originally, both morality and law are indistinguished from the custom of the community. They are only gradually differentiated from it, perhaps through the contact of different societies with divergent customs, and through the more urgent need of conformity to certain customs rather than others, leading to their more effectual enforcement by extreme penalties; these causes being accompanied by a growth of conscious reflection.

In civilized communities custom continues (for the most part) to protect morality and law, and at the same time to shape itself into a variety of forms determining the conduct of individuals and of groups of individuals. (W.R.S.)

Literature: HUME, Treatise on Human Nature (ed. Green and Grose), i. 403 ff., ii. 201; ADAM SMITH, Mor. Sent.; S. ALEXANDER, Moral Order and Progress; TARDE, Les Lois de l'Imitation; SIMMEL, Einleitung in die Moral-Wissenschaft, i; BALDWIN, Social and Eth. Interpret., chap. ii; WUNDT, Ethik, Part I. chap. iii; STEPHEN, Science of Eth., 137 ff.; POLLOCK, First Book of Jurisprudence, 10. (W.R.S.-J.M.B.)

Cutaneous Sensation [Lat. *cutis*, skin]: Ger. *Hautempfindung*; Fr. *sensation de la peau, sensation cutanée*; Ital. *sensazione cutanea*. A sensation set up by adequate stimulation of a point of the skin, without concomitant stimulation of joint, tendon, muscle (voluntary or involuntary), or other deeper-lying sense-organ.

In strictness, the adjective 'cutaneous' (or 'dermal') refers only to *cutis* (or *derma*), the true skin. Hence if pain (von Frey) is an epidermal sensation, it can be termed 'cutaneous' or 'dermal' only by an extension of the meaning of these words. (E.B.T.)

The typical cutaneous sensations, therefore, are those of touch and temperature. It is possible that pressure is also epidermal. (L.M.-J.M.B.)

Literature: WUNDT, Physiol. Psychol. (4th ed.), i. 413; VON FREY, Abhandl. d. kgl. sächs. Gesell. d. Wiss., xxiii. (1896); DESSOIR, Du Bois-Reymond's Arch. (1892); FUNKE and HERING, Hermann's Handb. d. Physiol., iii. 2; GOLDSCHEIDER, Gesamm. Abhandl. (1898); WEBER, Wagner's Handwörterb. d. Physiol., iii. 2. (E.B.T.)

Cuticle [Lat. *cuticula*, dim. of *cutis*, skin]: Ger. *Oberhäutchen*; Fr. *cuticule*; Ital. *cuticola*. Outermost layer of the skin; the epidermis. See SKIN. (C.F.H.)

Cyclopean Eye [Gr. κύκλωψ, a giant with one eye in the middle of the forehead]: Ger. *cyklopisches Auge*; Fr. *œil cyclopéen*; Ital. *occhio ciclopico*. All objects are referred to points in space exactly as they would be if, instead of two eyes, we had one eye in the middle of the forehead.

This fact was first made out by Hering, and this imaginary eye was well named by him the cyclopean eye. The best account of all the consequences of this mode of reference is given by Le Conte, *Amer. J. of Sci.*, 3 ser., i. 33, and *Sight*, 216. (C.L.F.)

Cyclosis (in botany) [Gr. κύκλωσις, a surrounding]: Ger. *Kreisen*; Fr. *cyclose*; Ital. *circolazione*. (1) The circulation of the latex (milky juice) in the vessels of plants. In this sense the term was applied by Max Schultze in 1831. (2) The rotational and circulatory movements of the endoplasm of the vegetable cell.

The movements of the endoplasm, to which the term is now commonly applied, were first observed by Bonaventura Corti (1772), and later by Treviranus (1807). They are: (*a*) Circulation, when the streaming takes place to and fro along the strands which join a more or less centrally placed mass of protoplasm, surrounding the nucleus, to the peripheral layer, in which streaming also takes place, but not in a direction common to all parts of it. (*b*) Rotation, when a peripheral layer of protoplasm surrounds a central vacuole. The endoplasm shows streaming movements in one direction within the ectoplasmic layer. Around the poles of rotation there is an indifferent band where the protoplasm is unaffected.

Literature: D. H. SCOTT, Introd. to Structural Botany (Flowering Plants, 1894); M. VERWORN, Gen. Physiol. (1899). (C.LL.M.)

Cynics: see SCHOOLS OF GREECE (Post-Socratic).

Cyrenaics: see SCHOOLS OF GREECE (Post-Socratic).

Cytology [Gr. κύτος, hollow, + λόγος, science]: Ger. *Cytologie, Zellenlehre*; Fr. *cytologie*; Ital. *citologia*. Science of the individual cell, as distinguished from Histology, which deals chiefly with the cells, and their relations to one another, in the formation of tissues and organs. See CELL. (C.F.H.)

Cytoplasm [Gr. κύτος, hollow, + πλάσμα, anything formed]: Ger. *Zellkörper*; Fr. *cytoplasme*; Ital. *citoplasma*. The protoplasmic substance of the cell-body as contrasted with that of the nucleus (karyoplasm). A term proposed by Strasburger in 1882. See E. B. Wilson, *The Cell in Devel. and Inheritance*, 1896. (C.LL.M.)

Czolbe, Heinrich. (1819–73.) A German medical man and philosopher, described by Höffding (*Hist. of Mod. Philos.*, Eng. trans., ii. 504 f.) as at first a 'consistent materialist.' He afterwards 'came very near Spinoza's fundamental ideas, which he attempted to develop empirically.' Cf. Vaihinger, 'Die drei Phasen des Czolbe'schen Naturalismus,' *Philos. Monatsh.*, xii. He was born near Danzig, educated at Berlin, lived and died at Königsberg.

D

Dabitis: see MOOD (in logic).

d'Ailly, Pierre: see D'AILLY under A.

d'Alembert, Jean Baptiste le Rond: see D'ALEMBERT under A.

Daltonism: Ger. *Daltonismus*; Fr. *daltonisme*; Ital. *daltonismo*. Partial colour-blindness: so called from John Dalton (1766-1844), the founder of atomic chemistry, who published an account of the phenomenon in 1794. See COLOUR-BLINDNESS, and VISION.

Literature: HELMHOLTZ, Physiol. Optik (2nd ed.), 359; DALTON, Mem. of Lit. and Philos. Soc. of Manchester, v. 1 (Oct. 31, 1794). The literature of colour-blindness begins with Tuberville, 1684. (E.B.T.)

Damiron, Jean Philibert. (1794-1862.) Born at Belleville on the Rhone, and studied under Victor Cousin in Paris. Befriended by Jouffroy, he taught various subjects in Paris, finally philosophy at the Sorbonne. He became an Academician before his death.

Damnation (eternal): see JUDGMENT.

Damnum absque Iniuria [Lat.]: Damage not due to wrong. One who suffers such damage has no cause of action. A man is not liable for any unintended, consequential injury, resulting from a lawful act, where he is chargeable neither with negligence nor folly (Morris *v.* Platt, 32 Connecticut Law Reports, 84). Nor is he liable for any loss which he may cause to another, by force of an inevitable accident: as in case he were blown through a shop window by a sudden gust of wind.

The Roman law gave an action for *damnum iniuria datum*, and *iniuria* included both wilfulness and negligence as a cause of damage (*Dig.*, ix. 2, *Ad Legem Aquiliam*, 5, § 1; 30, § 3). *Iniuria* in its most general sense embraced '*omne quod non iure fit*.' It included, as grounds of action, *contumelia, culpa, iniquitas, iniustitia*, and, of course, *dolus* (Just., *Instit.*, iv. 4, *De Iniuriis*).

Literature: SOHM, Instit. of Roman Law, § 72; PHILLIMORE, Princ. and Maxims of Jurisprudence (1856), xii, xlii. (S.E.B.)

Dancing Mania: Ger. *Tanzwuth*; Fr. *chorée saltatoire*; Ital. *mania saltatoria, coreomania*. An abnormal and excessive tendency to rhythmic movements, especially to dancing, manifested under special circumstances as the result of nervous contagion.

While some affected may be predisposed by temperament to such affections, the extension of the mania at certain periods has been so vast that it must have included normal individuals as well. Two marked epidemics, characterized by the dancing mania, occurred in the 14th and 15th centuries in Germany. See CONTAGION (mental). The manifestations are of a choreic nature, and are sometimes spoken of as choremania (also choreo- or choromania). In extreme cases the dancing, which is often of a violent spasmodic nature, continues until the subjects sink from exhaustion; their senses seem dazed, they become victims of hallucinations, and seem driven by an uncontrollable impulse to continue the contortions and saltations. Cf. Hecker, *Dancing Mania* (trans. 1885). Similar observations have been made by Lasnet among the Sakalanes in Madagascar. See CHOREA. (J.J.)

Dante (or **Durante**), **Allighieri** (or **Alighieri**). (1265-1321.) Born at Florence, and died in Ravenna. The greatest of Italian, and one of the greatest of all poets. He received a liberal education under the tutelage of Brunetto Latini, becoming skilful in music and painting, as well as verse-making. An early love gave him the poetic impulse, and the death of the object of his affection became a deep and abiding sorrow in life. He devoted himself to philosophy, studying in Paris, Padua, and Bologna. The Thomist, Siger, attracted him most. In 1302 he was exiled, for political reasons, from his native city. He became the guest of Can (Grande) della Scala, and later of Guido of Ravenna. His philosophy follows Albert (in physics) and Thomas (in politics and theology) very closely.

Darapti: see MOOD (in logic).

Darii: see MOOD (in logic).

Darwin, Charles Robert. (1809-82.) An eminent English naturalist. Born at Shrewsbury, England, he was educated in the grammar school at that place, at the University of Edinburgh, and at Christ's College, Cambridge. In 1831 he received the Bachelor's degree, and sailed with Captain Fitzroy in H.M.S. *Beagle*, to survey the coast of South America. He himself went as a volunteer naturalist. The voyage extended round the world, 1831-6. In 1842 he took up his residence in the village of Down, Kent, where he prosecuted his studies and researches. His work *On the Origin of Species by Means of Natural Selection* is most famous: it expounds the principle of NATURAL SELECTION (q.v.)—discovered also by Wallace—which has revolutionized the biological sciences. See also DARWINISM, NEO-DARWINISM, and EVOLUTION.

Darwinism [from Charles Darwin]: Ger. *Darwinismus*; Fr. *Darwinisme*; Ital. *Darwinismo*. The distinctive features of the theory of organic evolution proposed by Charles Darwin.

In popular speech the word Darwinism is used as equivalent to organic evolution in general, and the 'descent of man' in particular. In the works of evolutionists it is applied either (1) to the views set forth in Darwin's works, which lay the main stress on natural selection, but allow of the inheritance of acquired characters as subsidiary thereto; or (2) to the view which was distinctive of Charles Darwin: the theory of Natural Selection. The latter usage is preferable. See NEO-DARWINISM, NATURAL SELECTION, EVOLUTION, and EXISTENCE (struggle for).

Literature: CH. DARWIN, Origin of Species; A. R. WALLACE, Darwinism; ROMANES, Darwin and after Darwin; POULTON, Charles Darwin and the Theory of Natural Selection; F. DARWIN, Life and Letters of Charles Darwin. See also under EVOLUTION. (C.LL.M.)

Datisi: see MOOD (in logic).

Datum: see GIVEN (in logic).

Daub, Carl. (1765-1836.) A German theologian, the friend and follower of Hegel, with whom he stood in close agreement. He is 'the founder of Protestant speculative theology.'

David of Dinant. A Christian Aristotelian of the latter part of the 12th and early part of the 13th centuries. His doctrines were condemned in 1209, and again in 1215, by the Church. He probably received his philosophic impulse from Moorish commentators on Aristotle's works. His followers are called Davidists.

Davidson, Thomas. (1840-1900.) Born at Deer, Aberdeenshire, Scotland; educated at Aberdeen University; taught in schools in Great Britain, Canada, and St. Louis, Missouri. In 1875 he settled in Cambridge, Mass. He founded the Glenmore School for philosophical study at Keene, New Hampshire.

Day-blindness: Ger. *Tagblindheit*; Fr. *nyctalopie*; Ital. *cecità diurna, emeralopia*. A symptom rather than a distinct disorder, characterized by an inability to see clearly in strong light. Nyctalopia is also used.

It may be due to hyperaesthesia of the retina, and result in a clearer vision by dim light or at night, than in full daylight. In suddenly passing from darkness to bright light a transient form of normal day-blindness may be said to exist. The opposite condition is Night-blindness. See Fuchs, *Textbook of Ophthalmia* (trans. 1899), 496. (J.J.)

Day-dreaming: see REVERY.

Daymare [AS. *day* + Ger. *Mahr*, a spectre]: Ger. *Oppressionsanfall*; Fr. *dépression (neurasthénique, &c.)*; Ital. *incubo della veglia*. A feeling of temporary distress or terror, similar to nightmare, but occurring in a period of wakefulness. It is difficult to assign a cause for the feeling, but it may be connected with a disorder of the cerebral circulation. See NIGHTMARE. (J.J.)

De Facto: see DE IURE.

De Iure [Latin]. Of right; authorized by law. The term is correlative to *de facto*, which is used to describe what exists in fact, but not of right. See CORPORATION. (S.E.B.)

The antithesis currently implies the ground or justification upon which a consideration rests. *De facto* indicates 'a condition, not a theory'; a situation which has the sanction of actual existence as opposed to that which has the sanction of law, morality, or theory, though not realized in fact. (J.M.B.)

Deaf-mutism [AS. *deaf* + ME. *mewet*, akin to Gr. μυ, uttered with closed lips]: Ger. *Taubstummheit*; Fr. *surdi-mutité*; Ital. *sordo-mutismo*. Deaf-mutism, while signifying the combined presence of a defect in hearing and an inability to speak, more precisely refers to the condition in which defective hearing, congenital or acquired in early childhood, hinders or retards the development of speech.

The deaf-mute in typical cases is of normal intelligence, and has no abnormality of the vocal organs. It should be noted, however, that nervous and other defects are more than normally frequent in cases of deaf-mutism, owing to the fact that the condition which induced the deafness is apt to induce other defects. Cf. DEAFNESS AND THE DEAF.

The special relation that obtains between deafness and mutism is in accordance with the general principle that motor or expressive functions are developed under the guidance of sensory or receptive functions. The motor tendency comes from within, but the result of the co-ordinated activity is guided by some one of the sensory processes; we hear when we speak or sing, we see when we write or draw. See CONTROL SERIES. The natural stimulus which keeps active the vocal instincts of the child is the hearing of its own voice and the voices of others. The deprivation of this normal sensory guide brings with it, by mere inertia, a failure of development of the impulses to articulate. But we both feel and hear what we speak, just as we both feel and see what we write. We can write, though imperfectly, with the eyes closed, or learn to write in the absence of sight, and we can learn to speak in the absence of hearing. The mutism is therefore not absolute, but capable of moderate cultivation. See DEAFNESS AND THE DEAF. In the determination of mutism, the most important factor is the age at which deafness occurs. Mutism always ensues (unless corrected by training as just indicated) in cases in which the deafness is congenital or occurs in early infancy. The precise age has not been determined—although a specially directed statistical investigation is capable of determining it—at which the occurrence of deafness will entail mutism; but it is likely that if deafness occurs not earlier than the fifth to seventh year, speech will continue without special efforts; while if special efforts are made to encourage the speech faculties which are developed at a still earlier age (say from the second year onward), there is reason to believe that mutism could be avoided. However, in persons who have been long deaf, but who speak fluently, there is frequently an imperfection of articulation, and especially of modulation, which indicates the absence of the corrective tendencies of the ear. The degree of the deafness is likewise a most important factor in the determination of mutism. Even those with partial hearing may become mute, but on the other hand even a slight amount of hearing is an advantage in the acquisition of speech. Before modern methods of education were established almost all the deaf were mute, but the possibility of replacing the ear by the muscle-sense has been satisfactorily established, and thus has modified the relation between deafness and mutism. Many writers speak of the semi-mute in reference to those who have acquired a partial control of speech in the absence of hearing.

Literature: see under DEAFNESS AND THE DEAF. (J.J.)

Deafness and the Deaf [AS. *deaf*]: Ger. *Taubheit* (*ein Tauber*); Fr. *surdité* (*un sourd*); Ital. *sordità* (*un sordo*). Any impairment in the perception of auditory stimuli, sufficient to deprive the individual of the benefits of ordinary conversation and the sounds of daily life, is termed deafness. See HEARING (defects of).

It varies from a slight difficulty in hearing the ordinary tone of voice, to absolute insensibility to sounds. Those whose defect requires special modes of education are commonly spoken of as the deaf. The most important fact in regard to deafness is its association with dumbness or mutism, persons thus affected being termed the deaf-and-dumb, or deaf-mutes. The special nature of this connection is considered under DEAF-MUTISM (q. v.); but its existence must be constantly borne in mind in considering the status of the deaf, as must also the great tendency of deafness to be congenital (about sixty per cent.), with its further considerable tendency, when acquired, to occur in early childhood.

As in the case of the blind the two dominant interests in the study of the deaf are the educational and the psychological. The former (which is largely represented in the literature) is concerned mainly with the accounts of provisions maintained in various countries for the education of the deaf, the methods of instruction employed, and the status of the deaf as a class. The psychological interest is centred in the determination of the effects upon the other senses, the intelligence, and the general mental and emotional development which is brought about by the deprivation of this sense.

Inasmuch as an overwhelming portion of significant sounds are those of language, the modes of communication adopted by the deaf are at once an important psychological and educational factor. The realm of sound covered by music is lost to the deaf as colour is to the blind. These forms of communication are: (1) gesture language, (2) manual sign (and alphabetic) language, and (3) oral speech. The gesture language as used by deaf-mutes is an elaboration of the primitive and natural sign language, in which things and ideas are referred to by pantomime, imitation or suggestion of their distinctive characteristics, supplemented by a considerable number of conventional signs. While such language is in part individual, it is remarkable how well deaf-mutes and primitive people using sign-language can understand one another (Tylor), and how extensively and rapidly it can be employed by those skilled in the art. The finger-alphabet consists of an artificial series of positions of either one or two hands (the former far more usual and preferable), each position answering to a letter. These letters are rapidly formed, and with equal rapidity interpreted by the eye of the one addressed. In case of blind deaf-mutes, such letters can be formed in the palm of the hand and thus interpreted, but of course much more slowly. This language is thus a manual equivalent of articulate words in terms of movements instead of sounds. The oral method attempts to induce on the part of the deaf-mute the movements of the lips and voice by imitation of these movements as seen in speaking, and to cultivate the practice of reading the movements of the lips in others—lip-reading. The capacity for training in this direction varies in different deaf-mutes, but the success of the method, especially when applied to young children, is unquestionable. When employed along with the manual alphabet it is called the combined method. Of the two parts of the process concerned, lip-reading is simply an interpretation of the visual accompaniments of articulation, of which many persons of defective hearing but normal articulation avail themselves in following a conversation. The speaking is guided by the muscle sensations induced by the position of the vocal organs, but this guidance is far inferior to that of the ear; hence the articulation of the deaf-mute, even in the best cases, is only approximately correct, while the defective intonation and modulation produces a harsh and somewhat unpleasant effect. In the case of Helen Keller, who is completely blind and deaf, it has even been possible to educate the articulation without the aid of the sight of the lips, by means of the muscle sensations conveyed to her hands, which are placed upon the throat and lips of the speaker. See BRIDGMAN, LAURA, AND KELLER, HELEN.

In all respects, both psychological and educational, the age at which deafness occurs is highly important. The earlier the age the more serious the defect; while of course those who lose their hearing in late childhood or later retain their articulation. The degree of deafness is also important; the retention of even slight hearing constituting a considerable advantage.

As regards intellectual and emotional effects of deafness, it is often maintained, although without adequate investigation, that while in respect to ordinary occupations the deaf person is almost normal (more so than the blind), his lack of a ready communication with his fellow men is apt to induce a relative isolation, and a tendency to a morose, unsocial disposition. (J.J.)

Literature: MYGIND, Deaf-mutism (trans., 1881); T. ARNOLD, Education of Deaf-mutes (1888); A. G. BELL, Facts and Opinions relating to the Deaf (1888); J. HEIDSICK, Der Taubstumme und seine Sprache (1889); J. KITTO, The Lost Senses (1860); BELL, Methods of Instructing the Deaf (1898); E. A. FAY, Marriages of the Deaf in America (1898, with bibliography); H. H. HUBBARD, Deaf-mutism (1894); GELLI, Audition (1898); URBANTSCHITSCH, Ueber Hörübungen bei Taubstummheit und bei Ertaubung im späteren Lebensalter (1895); J. K. LOVE and H. ADDISON, Deaf-mutism (1896); E. WALTHER, Handb. d. Taubstummbildung (1895). (J.J.—L.M.)

Deafness (mental or psychic): Ger. *psychische Taubheit*; Fr. *surdité mentale* (or *psychique*); Ital. *sordità mentale* (or *psichica*). A condition analogous to MENTAL BLINDNESS (q. v.), affecting the understanding and interpretation of sounds.

It is distinguished from ordinary deafness by the retention of the power to hear sounds; what is lost is the power to appreciate the significance of the sounds. Inasmuch as by far the largest part of auditory interpretation lies in the realm of words and music, mental deafness (also known as mind-deafness) assumes the forms of word-deafness and musical deafness, or TONE-DEAFNESS (q. v., also AMUSIA). These defects often involve defects of MEMORY (q. v.). Cf. SPEECH AND ITS DEFECTS. (J.J.)

Deanthropomorphism [Lat. *de*, and Gr. ἄνθρωπος, man, + μορφή, shape]: Ger. *Deanthropomorphismus*; Fr. and Ital. not in use. 'A progressive purification of theism' (Romanes) by an elimination from the idea of God of human attributes: the opposite of ANTHROPOMORPHISM (q. v.). The term is used by Fiske, *Cosmic Philosophy*, and Romanes, *Contemp. Rev.*, July, 1886. (J.M.B.)

Death (physiological) [OE.]: Ger. *Tod*; Fr. *mort*; Ital. *morte*. Final cessation of the vital functions. Death of the body (somatic death) occurs when one or more functions (respiration, circulation, excretion, nervous co-ordination) become disturbed to such an extent as to render the harmonious working of the various organs impossible.

A tissue is said to die when it loses permanently its power of responding to its appropriate stimuli. The brain and nervous system die, in man and warm-blooded animals, at the moment of somatic death; gland tissue dies very soon after. Smooth muscle retains its irritability 45 minutes, skeletal muscle some hours, after death. (C.F.H.)

If by 'natural' death is meant the cessation of the existence of an individual organism as such, then death occurs universally among organized beings, since sooner or later they all cease to live as individuals, either themselves undergoing dissolution, or giving rise by some method of reproduction to other individuals. But by death is more generally meant the cessation of the processes of life, transforming a living being into a corpse. The question then arises, whether such death is an inherent property of living substance, or has been gradually evolved in the course of evolution. Weismann urges that, since in the lower unicellular plants and animals reproduction takes place by simple fission, generations following each other without the formation of any corpse, death does not here occur, and these organisms are, in a limited sense of the word, immortal. In the higher forms, where differentiation takes place between reproductive and somatic or body cells, the former only are perpetuated, and the latter sooner or later after reproduction cease to live, and so give rise to a corpse. Weismann holds that death has been developed by natural selection, because long-continued life of the individual, subject to injuries from its environment, would no longer be of use to a species capable of sexual reproduction. Other observers, like Minot in the case of the higher organisms, and Maupas in the case of the unicellular infusoria, argue that senile decay or atrophy occurs in the life of all individuals or asexually reproduced generations, and would always ultimately lead to death, were it not for the rejuvenating influence of amphimixis. That this is the case with the majority of multicellular organisms can hardly be doubted. Whether this view is true of all unicellular organisms is still uncertain. It must be remembered that the potato has been reproduced by cuttings since its first discovery, and that sexual reproduction is unknown among many fungi and the bacteria. See AMPHIMIXIS, AGAMOGENESIS, SEX, and GERM-CELLS.

Literature: A. WEISMANN, Essays upon Heredity, &c. (trans. 1892), ii; M. VERWORN, Gen. Physiol. (trans. 1899); Y. DELAGE, Structure du Protoplasma, &c. (1895); E. MAUPAS, Recherches expérimentales sur la Multiplication des Infusoires ciliés, Arch. Zool. expér. et gén., vi (1888). (E.S.G.)

Death (spiritual): Ger. *geistiger Tod*; Fr. *mort spirituelle*; Ital. *morte spirituale*. (1) A condition of alienation from God, such as is noticed in several passages of the New Testament.

(2) Often taken to imply annihilation, when considered from a theological point of view, but spiritual death means more correctly the second, or 'intensified,' death, which is the ultimate doom of the deliberately godless, or grace-rejecting. As such, it includes the conceptions of eternal perdition, without hope of resurrection, and of eternal loss of happiness, with all the horror consequent thereupon. See ESCHATOLOGY.

On the whole, the probability is that the conception is originally Jewish.

Literature: WEBER and SCHNEDERMANN, Jüdische Theol.; GEBHARDT, Doctrine of the Apocalypse, 291 (Eng. trans.); ALGER, Doctrine of a Future Life; SALMOND, Christian Doctrine of Immortality. (R.M.W.)

Decadence (social): Ger. *Verfall*; Fr. *décadence*; Ital. *decadenza*. See SOCIAL RETROGRESSION. (F.H.G.)

Decalogue [Gr. δέκα, ten, + λόγος, word, reason]: Ger. *Dekalog*; Fr. *décalogue*; Ital. *Decalogo*. The law of the Ten Words, otherwise called the Testimony (Exod. xxv. 21), the Covenant (Deut. ix. 9), and the Ten Commandments. It is given in two versions (Exod. xx. 2–17; Deut. v. 6–21).

The miraculous details connected with

the accounts of its promulgation, and the extremely composite nature of the texts containing them, have given rise to numerous critical problems, which cannot yet be regarded as solved by any means. It may be said, however, that, of the two versions, the former is esteemed the older and more authoritative, although Wellhausen dissents, and much weight is given to his view by Meisner. Some critics hold that the Decalogue could not have been formulated prior to the conception of religion developed by the prophets, and that, therefore, it is not earlier than the 8th century (Vatke, Wellhausen, Nöldeke, Smend, &c.); others that it has a Mosaic substratum, to which additions were afterwards made (Kuenen, Montefiore, Kittel, &c.); others that it is substantially Mosaic, but that interpolations, in the way of amplifications, have been made (Ewald, &c.).

The Decalogue is of the highest importance for the history of ethics and religion. It brings prominently forward, almost for the first time, the characteristically social nature of both. The community (Allgemeinheit), which plays so prominent a part in modern discussions of these subjects, is here emphasized. Its limitation lies, of course, in its predominatingly negative character, which is probably traceable to the fact that it was intended, in the first instance, as a condemnation of practices rife among the Semitic tribes at the time of its promulgation.

Literature: articles in the Encyc. Brit., and in Herzog's Real-Encyc.; Ewald, Hist. of Israel (Eng. trans.), ii. 18 f., 158 f.; Kuenen, Rel. of Israel (Eng. trans.), i. 285 f.; Wellhausen, Comp. d. Hex., 331 f.; Smend, Lehrb. d. alttest. Religionsgesch., 139 f.; Baentsch, Das Bundesbuch, 92 f.; Meisner, Der Dekalog; Driver, Literature of the O. T., and Deuteronomy; Schultz, O. T. Theol. (Eng. trans.); Kittel, Hist. of the Hebrews (Eng. trans.); Geffken, Ueber d. verschiedenen Eintheilungen d. Decalogus u. d. Einfluss derselben auf d. Cultus; B. Bauer, in Zeitsch. f. specul. Theol. (1838); Lemme, Die religionsgeschichtliche Bedeutung d. Decalogs. (R.M.W.)

Decay (in biology): see Degeneration (in biology), and Development.

Deceit: see Lie, and Equivocation.

Deceptive Reasoning: see Reasoning.

Decision [Lat. *de + caedere*, to cut]: Ger. *Entschliessung, Entschluss*; Fr. *décision*; Ital. *decisione*. The selective Determination (q. v.) of an end for action by choice between alternatives. Cf. Höfler, *Psychologie*, 518.

Wundt distinguishes between Decision, as a function of selective choice (Wahlhandlung), and Resolution (q.v.) made for future voluntary action (Willkürhandlung). Judd (trans. of Wundt's *Elements of Psychol.*) uses decision as equivalent to Entschliessung. (J.M.B.)

Declarative: see Predication, and Proposition.

Declension [Lat. *declinatio*, a bending aside]: Ger. *Declination, Wortbeugung*; Fr. *déclinaison*; Ital. *declinazione*. Modification of form in nouns, adjectives, and pronouns, by which they are enabled to express the relations of case. In the so-called inflectional languages the noun-forms serve not only to name the objects of thought, but also, chiefly through their endings, to denote the relations they bear in the sentence to the nucleus of the thought or statement, i. e. the verb.

The term had its origin in the grammatical system of the Greeks; κλίσις, from κλίνειν, to lean, was translated into Latin as *declinatio*. The various inflections were regarded as deflections from the upright as represented in the leading form. Thus the nominative was called the 'upright' case (εὐθεῖα, *casus rectus*), the others 'oblique' (πλάγιοι). The cases are so many 'fallings' (πτώσεις, *casus*, from *cadere*, to fall). The Indo-European mother-speech was provided with seven different groups of noun-forms for the conventional expression of the most important relations within the sentence. Thus the nominative indicated the substantive idea, in connection with which the action of the sentence as expressed in the verb was concretely set forth, and received its psychological shape. The accusative served as the complement of the verb by giving its action direction and a point of application. The genitive indicated a whole, of which a part was affected by or involved in the governing word. It was the case of the genus or greater whole, and was hence named by the Greeks ἡ γενικὴ πτῶσις. The ablative indicated the source of the action of the verb. The dative indicated that which the action concerned. The locative indicated the place or the sphere within which the action took place. The instrumental expressed accompaniment, and hence means. In the separate languages the number of cases was generally reduced, a single case-form often assuming the functions of two or more. Such syncretisms are generally due to confusion of the case-functions in use, rather than to a blending of form.

Literature: B. DELBRÜCK, Vergleichende Syntax, i. 181 ff. (B.I.W.)

Decorative Art [Lat. *decoratus*, from *decus*, ornament]: Ger. *decorative Kunst, Zierkunst*; Fr. *art décoratif*; Ital. *arte decorativa*. (1) Art which aims rather to heighten the aesthetic value of some aspect of a larger whole than to embody aesthetic value in an independent construction. It includes personal adornment (cosmetic) and ornamentation, especially that of architecture and utensils, by drawing, painting, or carving. Its canons are 'adaptation, significance, and abstraction or conventionalization' (Collingwood). (2) Used by Véron as equivalent to formally beautiful art, as opposed to expressive art. This is not to be recommended, as the other usage has been constant.

Literature: COLLINGWOOD, The Philos. of Ornament (1883); MORRIS, The Lesser Arts of Life (1882); GROSSE, The Beginnings of Art (1897); VÉRON, Aesthetics, vii; BALDWIN, Social and Eth. Interpret., § 100; HADDON, The Evolution of Art (1895); SEMPER, Der Stil in den technischen und tektonischen Künsten (1878–9). See also CLASSIFICATION (of the fine arts). (J.H.T.)

Decrees (divine): see FOREORDINATION.

Decretum salutis. One of the 'Divine Decrees' according to the system of Calvin. It is closely connected with the dogma of election, and with the *decretum reprobationis*; all are intimately bound up with the dogma of original sin, the consequent 'plan of salvation,' and they played a leading part in the controversy on SUPRALAPSARIANISM (q. v.).

Literature: CALVIN, Institutes, iii. chaps. xxi f. See CALVINISM. (R.M.W.)

Decurtate Syllogism: see SYLLOGISM.

Decussation [Lat. *decussatio*]: Ger. *Faserkreuzung*; Fr. *décussation*; Ital. *incrociamento*. The crossing of fibre-tracts of the central nervous system at the median plane in such a way that the terminations of a given tract are in centres of different orders, while the crossing tracts are bilaterally symmetrical (see COMMISSURE). A decussation differs from a commissure, in that commissural fibres are supposed to connect homologous centres; but strictly, all commissural fibres appear to decussate, for, if the fibres are neurites, one end originates in a cell and the other terminates in a free arborization about a cell of a different layer.

In practice a decussating fibre is one which obviously connects centres of different orders on opposite sides. See BRAIN, and SPINAL CORD. (H.H.)

Deductio: see DEDUCTION, and METHOD (logical).

Deduction [Lat. *de* + *ducere*, to lead]: Ger. *Deduction*; Fr. *déduction*; Ital. *deduzione*. The type of mediate inference in which a conclusion is put forward as being implied in the propositions which are taken as data.

The essential mark is the necessity wherewith the conclusion is taken to follow from the understanding of the data and the combination of their contents. The name is applied either to the process of developing in thought and combining data, or to the represented relation between data and conclusion, or to the conclusion itself. The kind of relation involved leads naturally to the common definitions of deduction as reasoning from the general to the particular, or from the containing whole to the contained parts, neither of which is sufficiently accurate. For Deductive Method, see METHOD.

It is only in modern times, mainly among English logicians, that the term has been employed to name one distinctive form of reasoning, contrasted from the outset with induction. *Deductio*, in its first technical use, was a translation of Aristotle's term ἀπαγωγή, and somewhat in this sense it still keeps a place in modern logical terminology in the phrase *Reductio per deductionem ad impossibile*. The ancient, mediaeval, and most commonly used terms to indicate what is now called deduction were syllogism and demonstration. (R.A.)

Deduction (in education). In instruction, deduction is a less rigorous process than in science, being used chiefly to form anticipations of further experience; or, as with Herbartian writers, who use the term loosely, to imply a wide application of derived generalizations to appropriate new particulars. See METHOD (in education).

Literature: HARRIS, Psychologic Foundations of Education, 62–89; DE GARMO, Essentials of Method, chap. v; JEVONS, Princ. of Sci. (C.DE G.)

Defect (ethical): see FAULT, and VICE.

Defect and **Defective** (mental) [Lat. *defectivus*, imperfect]: Ger. *Defekt (psychischer)*; Fr. *défectuosité (mentale)*; Ital. *deficienza (mentale)*. The term defective refers to classes of persons who lack some of the sensory or mental or moral capabilities which are characteristic of normal individuals. Such a lack is a defect.

The class would thus include (*a*) those with marked sensory defects, sufficient to characterize the individual as abnormal, i. e. mainly the blind and the deaf; (*b*) individuals hereditarily lacking in normal mental capacity, imbeciles and idiots; and (*c*) those lacking in moral or social endowment to such an extent as to constitute them abnormal members of society. The criminal classes are thus cited as defectives. In this latter sense the term includes those called degenerates. See DEGENERATION ; also ATTENTION (defects of), HEARING, MEMORY, SPEECH, VISION, WILL. (J.J.)

Defective Syllogism: see SYLLOGISM.

Deferred (Instinct, Character, &c.): see INSTINCT, and ACQUIRED AND CONGENITAL CHARACTERS.

Deficient (in logic): see QUANTITY (logical).

Definite and **Indefinite** (in biology): see DETERMINATE (in biology).

Definite Term: see QUANTITY (logical).

Definition [Lat. *de + finis*, end]: Ger. *Definition, Begriffsbestimmung*; Fr. *définition*; Ital. *definizione*. The term definition is applied either to the process of fixing the limits of a notion, and so explaining it, or clearing it up; or to the proposition in which the result of the process is expressed, and there, again, it is sometimes confined to the predicate of the proposition.

The process starts from the content or comprehension of the thought to be defined, but would be inadequately expressed as an ' explication of the comprehension.' The explication comes about only by reference to the extensions, which are determined by the various marks making up the comprehension. Such reference, according to the logical doctrine, is said to be ' adequate,' if there be determined the genus, by preference the proximate genus, and the specific difference, the objects represented in the thought to be defined being thus distinguished from all others. The component parts of the definition, the genus and specific difference or species, may be, and have been, interpreted in the history of logic from a more objective, or from a more subjective, point of view.

The generic and specific marks constitute the *essence* (logical) of the *definiendum*, and there are thus excluded from the definition derivative and accidental marks. Individual objects and *summa genera* are logically indefinable. The test of a definition is the exact equivalence of the spheres of its subject and predicate. Definitions have been distinguished as (*a*) nominal, the explanation of the meaning of a word, and real, the explanation of the nature of the thing defined ; (*b*) analytic, which starts with the notion as given, and synthetic, in which the notion is put together; of synthetic definitions, the most important is the genetic, the statement of the rule of operation by which the objects defined are represented as constructed, applicable in mathematics, and in practical sciences and arts; (*c*) rational, when the notion is determined from within, by thought, and empirical, when the notion is formed by selection from what is given in experience. These distinctions are not all happily expressed, nor free from difficulty. The term nominal definition, if retained at all, should be restricted to the explanations, given in any dictionary, of the accepted usage of language, explanations rendered necessary by the natural conditions of language. The thing defined is always that which is represented in our thought and sought to be expressed in our language ; the mode of existence assigned to it is not determined by the definition, and falls outside of that. The other distinctions point to problems, partly of theoretical importance, partly of practice.

The doctrine of definition, beginning in the controversies between Plato and Antisthenes, received complete formulation in Aristotle, of whose logical analysis it is the culmination. The technical rules which he laid down have kept their place as the accepted, traditional logic, though the special interpretation of them by Aristotle has long been given up. In the scholastic disputes regarding universals, particularly in the school of Occam, there may be traced the beginnings of the larger questions regarding the function of definition in knowledge, the possibility and limits of it, which play the most important part in modern treatment of the subject. The Kantian philosophy, by its distinction of formal logic from theory of knowledge, separated the technique of definition as a formal process from the theoretical questions regarding the nature and scope of definition. From the empirical point of view, Mill emphasized the distinction between definitions which postulate, and those which do not postulate, the existence of objects corresponding to the definitions given.

Literature: for Aristotle's doctrine, see especially PRANTL, Gesch. d. Logik, i. 321–40. For the distinctions of kinds among definitions, see UEBERWEG, Logik, § 61. The modern problems are discussed in LOTZE, Logik, Bk. II.

chaps. i, ii ; VENN, Empirical Logic, chap. xi ; RICKERT, Lehre v. d. Definition (1888), and Die Grenzen der naturwiss. Begriffsbildung (1896). See also E. C. BENECKE, in Mind, vi. 530 ff. (R.A.)

Definitive : see METHOD (logical), WHOLE, and PROPOSITION.

Deformity (1) and (2) **Deformation** [Lat. *de + forma*, shape]: Ger. *Deformität, Missgestalt* ; Fr. *difformité, déformation* ; Ital. *deformità, deformazione*. (1) A lack of proper form or symmetry in the development of a part of the body ; irregularity of features ; disproportionate or unnatural deviation in structure from the usual. Somatic deformities are designated stigmata ; see STIGMA.

(2) Artificial deformations are intentional distortions. The tendency to divert some portion of the human anatomy from its normal shape is very widespread. The custom at times acquires a special religious or ceremonial significance, but seems more frequently due to a crude aesthetic instinct. Flattening of the skull, constraining of the foot, piercing of the ears, nose, or lips to attach thereto ornaments of various types, separating and notching the teeth, twisting, curling, and knotting the hair, tattooing and painting the skin, illustrate various forms of development of this tendency. See Flower, *Fashion in Deformity*, 1881.

The term deformity is sometimes used figuratively to refer to mental defect or distortion, and is then equivalent to mental abnormality. (J.J.)

Literature : DELISLE, Contrib. à l'Étude des Déformations (1880) ; GOSSE, Essai sur les Déformations du Crâne (1858) ; LAGNEAU, in Gaz. heb. de Méd. (1879), 5, 6. (L.M.)

Degeneration [Lat. *de + genus*, race] : Ger. *Entartung* ; Fr. *dégénérescence* ; Ital. *degenerazione*. Decay or retrogression from the point of view of evolution. (J.M.B., G.F.S.)

While degeneration is a term applicable to biological processes in general, its psychological significance is limited to mental degeneration in man. As such it expresses a retrograde tendency in human evolution.

The conception of a class of degenerates was formed by Morel (1857). It includes a variety of types with the common factor of a nervous diathesis, and the presence of certain more or less definite abnormalities. In the lowest forms of degenerates hereditary influences are most prominent, and the defects of body and mind most marked ; e. g. idiocy and cretinism complicated with such disorders as rachitis.

The highest stage would be represented by persons of apparent normal intelligence, and even of an unusual development in certain directions. Such persons are apt to be enthusiastic and ambitious, with vivid imagination and impulsive temperaments ; but their brilliancy of conception is not supported by industry and persistence. Moreover, they are apt to exhibit a want of balance in certain directions, which may develop into pronounced insanity. They form part of the borderland between sanity and insanity, in which marked eccentricity in certain directions is still entirely compatible with high ability, and the occupation of a worthy place in society. Between these extremes an indefinite number of types and classes may be interposed.

In the social sense, criminals of various grades—the immoral and the outcast—represent forms of degeneration. How far these can be described by characteristic physical symptoms is doubtful ; but the occurrence of bodily abnormalities in such persons to a much larger extent than in normal individuals, though not in all cases (Magnan), has been clearly substantiated. Marked asymmetry, a misshapen skull, a peculiar form of ear, irregular teeth, rachitis, abnormal sexual development, are some of the characteristics noted as significant in this connection ; while mentally, instability, violent excess, or again deficiency, of emotional sensibility, defective speech, mental dullness, or idiosyncrasies, may be mentioned. A most important factor is heredity ; the families of the degenerate are apt to be afflicted with various forms of nervous disorder, such as alcoholism, insanity, idiocy, paralysis, or epilepsy accompanied often by immorality, and diseases of infancy both before and after birth. The frequency with which alcoholism and sexual excess appear in the history of degenerates is constantly noted ; as is also the tendency of the degenerate to become the victim of such habits as indulgence in opium, hasheesh, and other psychical poisons. The doctrine of mental degeneration may readily be carried too far, but the term serves a useful function in describing a real but somewhat vague and heterogeneous class of abnormal individuals and tendencies.

Degenerative Insanity (*Folie des dégénérés*) refers to distinctive types of insanity to which degenerates are liable ; such insanity is of strongly marked hereditary origin, and presents more or less morbid mental weakness, impulsiveness of will, and monomania. See DIATHESIS.

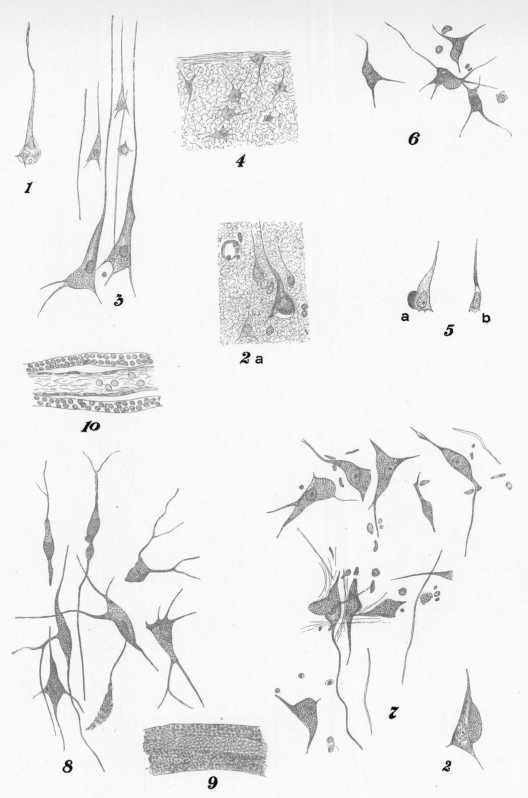

PLATE A (Degeneration)

Pathological conditions in nervous structures in a case of general paralysis. Degenerated portions in yellow. Fig. 1, Cell vacuolated and apex process varicose. Figs. 2 and 2a, Degenerate cells from Broca's region. Fig. 3, Large pyramidal cells from precentral convolution. Fig. 4, So-called scavenger cells from the temporal lobe, tangential fibres near the top of the section. Fig. 5, a, b, Deep and superficial pyramid of frontal lobe. Fig. 6, Thalamus cells above the peduncular bundle. Fig. 7, Cells from the forward extension of the nucleus niger. Fig. 8, Cells from the niger further back. Figs. 9 and 10, Two stages in the alteration of the blood vessels. — From a ' Report upon a Case of General Paralysis,' *J. of Compar. Neur. III.*

Literature: MOREL, Traité des Dégénérescences (1857), and Études cliniques, Du Délire chez les dégénérés (1886); LEGRAIN, MAUDSLEY, Pathol. of Mind (1880); MAGNAN, Des héréditaires dégénérés, in Recherches sur les Centres nerveux (2ᵉ série, 1893), 109–426; KOCH, Die psychopathischen Minderwerthigkeiten (1891); DALLEMAGNE, Dégénérés et Déséquilibrés (1894); FÉRÉ, Dégénérescence et Criminalité (1895), La Famille névropathique (2nd ed., 1898); TALBOT, Degeneracy (1898); A. MEYER, Signs of Degeneration, Amer. J. of Insan., v. 52, 344–63; PETERSON, N. Y. State Hosp. Bull. (1896); KRAUS, Amer. J. of Insan. (1898), iv. 655 ff.; SOLLIER, Psychol. de l'Idiot et de l'Imbécile; MEIGE, Les possédés noirs (1894). (J.J.)

Also KRAFFT-EBING, Lehrb. d. Psychiatrie; SCHÜLE, Lehrb. d. Psychiatrie (3rd ed. Klinische Psychiatrie); ARNDT, Lehrb. d. Psychiatrie, and Die Entartung (1896); MORSELLI-BALLET, Le Psicosi, in Trattato di Medicina di Charcot (trad. italiana); MAGNAN, Dégénérescence mentale, C. R. Soc. d. Biol., ix. (1894); LOMBROSO (and his pupils), *opera omnia*. (E.M.)

Degeneration (in biology). Retrogression from the more complex to the less complex, from a relatively elaborate and complete structure in earlier forms to a relatively simple or incomplete structure in later forms.

E. Ray Lankester (lecture on Degeneration before the British Association, 1879) says: 'It is clearly enough possible for a set of forces, such as we sum up under the head "Natural Selection," so to act on the structures of an organism as to produce one of three results, namely these: to keep it *in statu quo*; to increase the complexity of its structure; or, lastly, to diminish the complexity of its structure. We have as possibilities either Balance, or Elaboration, or Degeneration.' Animals which acquire a sedentary and fixed mode of life (Ascidians, Cirripedes, &c.) and parasitic animals often undergo degeneration; the former losing locomotory and sensory organs, the latter often losing digestive organs as well (Tapeworms, &c.). The phylogenetic degeneration of the species (or organ) is often recapitulated in the ontogenetic degeneration of the individual, which in the course of its life-history is seen actually to pass from a higher to a lower type of structure (Ascidians).

Literature: ANTON DOHRN, Der Ursprung d. Wirbelthiere (1875); E. R. LANKESTER, Degeneration, in Adv. of Sci. (1890); Discourse before Brit. Assoc., Sheffield meeting (1879); and Degeneration (in Nature series); DEMOOR, MASSART, and VANDERVELDE, Evolution by Atrophy (Eng. trans., 1899). (C.LL.M.–E.S.G.)

Degeneration (nervous). Destruction or morbid alteration of the tissue of an organ as a result of injury or disease. Cf. ATROPHY, and APLASY.

Even normal functioning of the nervous tissue produces destructive alteration in the substance, and such changes carried beyond the point where they are readily restored may be termed morbid. Histological changes due to fatigue have been demonstrated (Hodge, Tuke, Mann, Lugaro, and others). See FATIGUE. The initial symptoms of degeneration may be active inflammations (neuritis, encephalitis, myelitis), or they may be of a more chronic and metabolic nature. In the central system circulatory changes (hyperaemia or vascular stasis) are among the earliest symptoms, though direct intoxications due to irritative poisons (alcohol or ptomaines) may also occur. The characteristic changes in nervous tissue proper are always accompanied by alterations in the sustentive (neuroglia) and nutritive apparatus.

Among all forms of nervous degeneration, that due to alcoholic poisoning is most instructive, as affording most conclusive evidence of the relation between structural and mental changes. The psychical symptoms are such as amnesia, diminished power of attention, insomnia, impairment of the will, and disturbances of the muscular and co-ordinating power, as well as a blunting of the moral perceptions. These are followed by hallucinations, delusions, and various chronic insanities. In many respects the disease is analogous to general paralysis of the insane. Corresponding to these functional changes are two sorts of structural alterations, viz.: (1) the impairment of the means of communication between neurocytes, showing itself in the destruction of the fine root-like processes of the dendrites, and afterwards in the formation of moniliform varicosities of the dendrites themselves as a result of decomposition; (2) changes in the cell-body itself, such as vacuolation, degeneration of protoplasm (pigmentation), and the results of imperfect or exaggerated nutrition. The capillaries are shrunken and irregular. See Plate A (DEGENERATION).

Experimental administration of alcohol to animals (Berkley) has resulted in changes entirely similar to those found in the human subject suffering from alcoholism. Pathological dementia results from the interruption of communication between cell and cell because of the loss of the gemmulae and tumefaction of the dendrites, so that co-ordination of the psychical centres becomes impossible. See PARALYSIS (general).

Degenerations due to peripheral lesions are well illustrated by the results of injury to the sense-organs. Thus, in case of destruction of the bulb of the eye, the anterior pair of the corpora quadrigemina are reduced in size, by reason of the degeneration of some nerve-cells

A group of cortical cells illustrating the degenerative processes due to ingestion of alcohol. Shrinkage of the body of the cell, tumefaction of the processes, and loss of the gemmulae, are seen, both in the human subject suffering from alcoholism, and in animals to whom alcohol has been experimentally administered. (After Berkley.)

and the atrophy of others, together with the disappearance of the fibres of the optic tracts and reticular substance. The external geniculatum is also greatly reduced in size, but this is due to the degeneration of fibres from the optic tract and the gelatinous substance, rather than of the neurocytes. There is a similar loss of substance in the pulvinar. The so-called Forel's commissure is the only one affected.

In congenital anophthalmia and atrophy of the bulb, a special layer of cells in the occipital cortex of the cerebrum is atrophied. These cells near the calcarine fissure, constituting the specific cortical centre for vision, are connected, via the optic radiations, with the geniculata.

Destruction of isolated areas in the cerebral cortex results not only in degeneration of the coronal fibres and pes pedunculi well into the cord, but in secondary degeneration of collaterals passing via the callosum to corresponding areas of the opposite side, and also of the arcuate or associational fibres of the corresponding hemispheres. In case of unilateral injury to the cortex, the callosal fibres degenerate as far as to the corresponding cortex of the opposite side. The number of degenerate fibres is proportional to the extent of the injury. In case of bilateral injury the amount of degeneration is greater. The associational (arcuate) fibres degenerate only on the side of the lesion. These phenomena explain the fact that the removal of a small cortical area diminishes the total psychical efficiency, for it is plain that the secondary degeneration must affect the larger circle of associations. Degeneration of nerve-fibres (neuritis) may result from peripheral irritation, or from disease of the cells of origin, whether gangliocytes in spinal ganglia, or neurocytes of the central system. In spite of great diversity in the details of such degeneration, all cases exhibit, according to Klippel, three stages: tumefaction of the myelin sheath, granular disintegration and fragmentation of the axis cylinder, with liquefaction of the myelin, and, finally, resorption of the whole. In acute cases the initial tumefaction is greater.

After complete separation from the nervous centres, the peripheral part of a nerve suffers degeneration throughout its whole extent, even in those cases where continuity is eventually re-established. The changes in the latter case are as follows: (1) Segmentation of the myelin and axis cylinder at the intersegmental lines. (2) Proliferation and migration of the nuclei. (3) Fragmentation and resorption of myelin and axis cylinder. (4) Increase of protoplasm about the nuclei, which migrate to the axis of the nerve-tube; then follows the formation of a new axis cylinder. (5) Formation of a new sheath surrounding the embryonic fibre. (6) Union of the peripheral end with the stump, in which similar changes have taken place. (7) Formation of myelin—a process which proceeds from the wound towards the distal end.

For details of Gudden's and Marchi's methods of employing experimental degeneration in research, see NEUROLOGY. (H.H.)

Literature: H. J. BERKLEY, Studies on the Lesions produced by the Action of certain Poisons on the Cortical Nerve Cell, (1)

Alcohol, Brain, xviii (1895); E. BERGMANN, Ueber experimentelle aufsteigende Degeneration motorischer und sensibler Hirnnerven (Vienna, 1892); FOREL, Ueber das Verhältniss der experimentellen Atrophie und Degenerationsmethode zur Anatomie und Histologie des Centralnervensystems, Festschrift f. Nägeli und Kölliker (Zürich, 1891); v. GUDDEN, Experimentaluntersuchungen über das peripherische und centrale Nervensystem, Arch. f. Psychiatrie, ii (1870); G. C. HUBER, A Study of the Operative Treatment for Loss of Nerve Substance in Peripheral Nerves, J. of Morphol. (1895; accompanied by a good bibliography); HOWELL and HUBER, A Physiological, Histological, and Clinical Study of the Degeneration and Regeneration in Peripheral Nerve Fibres after Severance of their Connections with the Nerve Centres, J. of Physiol., xiii (1892), and xiv (1893); M. KLIPPEL, Comment débutent les dégénérescences spinales? Arch. de Névrol., 2e série, i (1896); STROEBE, Experimentelle Untersuchungen über die Degeneration und reparatorischen Vorgänge, in Ziegler's Beitr. z. pathol. Anat. u. z. allgem. Pathologie, xv (1894); G. B. VALENZA, Sui cambiamenti delle cellule nervose, in Mem. R. Accad. Sci., Napoli (1896); L. F. BARKER, The Nervous System and its Constituent Neurones, chap. xx (1899; full bibliography, with good digests of most recent work); F. NISSL, Ueber eine neue Untersuchungsmethode des Centralorgans speciell zur Feststellung der Localisation der Nervenzellen, Centralbl. f. Nervenh. u. Psychiat. (1894); H. STROEBE, Die allgemeine Histologie der degenerativen und regenerativen Processe im centralen und peripheren Nervensystem, nach den neuesten Forschungen. Zusammenfassendes Referat. Centralbl. f. allg. Pathol. u. pathol. Anat. (1895; digest of literature up to 1895); H. H. TOOTH, The Gulstonian Lectures on Secondary Degenerations of the Spinal Cord (London, 1889), and Brit. Med. J. (1889); A. WALLER, Experiments on the Section of the Glossopharyngeal and Hypoglossal Nerves of the Frog, and Observations of the Alterations produced thereby in the Structure of their primitive Fibres, London, Edinburgh, and Dublin Philos. Mag., 1850; also in Philos. Trans. (London, 1850), and in Edinburgh Med. and Surg. J. (1851). (H.H.)

Dégérando, Joseph Marie, Baron de. (1772–1842.) Born in Lyons, he was imprisoned by the republicans in 1794, during the siege of Lyons. He escaped to Switzerland and into the kingdom of Naples, re-turning to Paris in 1796. In 1797 he took part in the march against Italy.

Degree [Lat. *de* + *gradus*, step, through the Fr.]: Ger. *Grad*; Fr. *degré*; Ital. *grado*. See QUANTITY, INTENSITY (mental), and KIND AND DEGREE.

Degree of Consciousness: see SUBCONSCIOUS.

Deification: see APOTHEOSIS.

Deism [Lat. *deus*, God]: Ger. *Deismus*; Fr. *déisme*; Ital. *deismo*. The form of THEISM (q. v.) which separates God from the world, in the sense of denying that the concept of God includes in whole or part the concept of the world. (J.M.B.)

Deity: see GOD, THEISM, and RELIGION (psychology of).

Dejection [Lat. *de* + *iacere*, to cast or throw]: Ger. *Niedergeschlagenheit*; Fr. *abattement*; Ital. *tristezza, mestizia*. A state of mental depression or despondency. It is especially characteristic of weakened states of body and mind, such as neurasthenia; and is prominent most of all as a chronic characteristic of MELANCHOLIA (q. v.). The lowness of spirits in dejection, characteristic of individuals who are apt to take a gloomy view of the ordinary events of human life, led to the delineation of the melancholic temperament as one of the typical varieties. See TEMPERAMENT, and DEPRESSION. (J.J.)

Delamination [Lat. *de* + *lamina*, fold]: Ger. *Spaltung*; Fr. *délamination*; Ital. *delaminazione*. The splitting off of one cell-layer from another by means of cell-proliferation, e. g. of the mesoblast or of the PLANULA (q. v.). See also EMBRYO. (E.S.G.)

Delbrück, Johann Friedrich Ferdinand. (1772–1848.) He was born in Magdeburg, and studied in Halle under the Kantian Jacob and the anti-Kantian Eberhard. For several years he was a private tutor, then continued his studies, and in 1797 became an instructor in the gymnasium of the Grey Cloister in Berlin. In 1809 he became councillor to the East Prussian Government and professor of the theory, criticism, and literature of the fine arts; in 1816, councillor to the government and to the schools in Düsseldorf. He moved in 1818 to Bonn as professor of aesthetic literature and philosophy.

Deliberation [Lat. *de* + *librare*, to balance]: Ger. *Ueberlegung*; Fr. *délibération*; Ital. *deliberazione*. The comparison of alternative courses of action which precedes and issues in choice. The basis of comparison is to a very large extent the relation of the alternative courses and their consequences to the self as a whole. (G.F.S.–J.M.B.)

Delirium [Lat. *delirium*, madness, raving]: Ger. *Delirium*; Fr. *délire*; Ital. *delirio*. A temporary, disordered mental condition occurring particularly in fevers, and presenting excitement, wild, irregular, and incoherent thought, and a confused consciousness. There may also be hallucinations and illusions, ravings and violent actions. That form in which the patient is relatively inactive and maintains a low muttering is termed 'quiet' delirium, while that accompanied by violence and loud ravings is termed 'active' delirium. Although the symptoms presented by delirium are those typical of insanity, the two conditions are quite distinct; the insanity following a severe fever is also entirely distinct from the delirium of the fever itself.

Delirium is not confined to cases of fever, as other diseases may produce the cerebral conditions upon which the delirium depends. Particularly in affections of the brain and spinal cord, or their surrounding membranes, is delirium apt to be a prominent symptom. The nature of the mental wanderings is quite variable and individual, past experiences or fanciful ones occupying the patient's attention to the exclusion of the present. Although he can be momentarily aroused, and may respond to simple questions, he soon drifts back to the delirious state. From a clinical point of view delirium is characteristic of the special fevers (typhoid, scarlet fever, yellow fever, influenza, &c.); of inflammatory conditions of special organs (pneumonia, peritonitis, sunstroke, dysentery); of certain brain affections (meningitis, epilepsy, hydrophobia, lead poisoning, concussion); of such chronic diseases as Bright's disease; of the result of brain inanition (lack of food, exposure, loss of blood). In addition, the delirium caused by the action of drugs, or mental poisons, is especially significant, and of these the delirium of alcohol has been most extensively described. Opium, hasheesh, chloroform, ether, nitrous oxide, all produce more or less prolonged and characteristic forms of mental wanderings. See INTOXICATION, and PSYCHIC EFFECTS OF DRUGS. For Delirium Tremens, see ALCOHOLISM.

The term delirium is also used in reference to any marked and somewhat systematic delusion symptomatic of cases of insanity; thus the delirium of persecution, the delirium of grandeur; and it is similarly used with reference to such delusions in connection with the diseases of which they are symptomatic; as the delirium of epilepsy, of hysteria, of alcoholism, or mania sine delirio, and the like. See HALLUCINATION, and ILLUSION.

Literature: CHASLIN, La Confusion mentale, also Rêve et Delirium (1887); BIANCHI, La Frenosi sensoria (1895); MENDEL, art. Delirium in Eulenburg's Real-Encyk. der ges. Heilkunde; textbooks of mental diseases. (J.J.)

Delusion [Lat. *delusio*, from *de + ludere*, to play]: Ger. *Wahnvorstellung*; Fr. *illusion, idée fausse ou fixe*; Ital. *illusione (psichica), delirio*. A false belief or perception determined by belief; typically it is of a somewhat persistent nature, and involves more or less elaborate reasoning processes.

It differs from an illusion (when these words are precisely used), in that the illusion is a direct mental construction in which the element of logical inference is slight; and from an hallucination, in that the hallucination is a false perception arising from within, largely independent of an external stimulus. See HALLUCINATION, and ILLUSION. (J.J.–J.M.B.)

When used popularly, delusion may refer to a false belief, due to ignorance, imperfect education, or bias; when used in reference to abnormal mental states, a delusion is due to a perverted or morbid mental action which prevents the subject from realizing the falsity of his belief, either by the evidence of his senses or otherwise. Such fixed and elaborate delusions are almost always evidences of insanity. In rather rare cases they constitute the sole disorder, which is then termed delusional insanity. When limited, as they usually are, to a few topics, they form the monomanias which contribute so largely to the popular conception of insanity, and give distinctiveness and individuality to the inmates of insane asylums. PARANOIA (q.v.) is an allied condition, of which delusion is the most characteristic symptom.

The types and varieties of delusion are almost endless in scope. They may be distinguished according to their mode of affecting the subject as elevating or exciting, or as depressing, or again as modifying the personality. Another classification is based upon the form of the delusion, whether of grandeur, of suspicion, of persecution, of unseen agency, &c. Clouston gives a list of nearly a hundred special delusions, such as the unreasonable belief in being poisoned, defrauded, of being pregnant, having no body or no stomach, that it is wrong to take food, of being in relation with the devil, of letters being written about one, of having committed murder or other crimes, of being called names, of being a king, being God or Christ, &c. Many of these delusions become systematized and enlarged, and may involve hallucinations and illusions; while others remain purely in the delusional realm of false beliefs. For further details see HALLUCINATION, ILLUSION, INSANITY AND SANITY, MANIA, MELANCHOLIA, and DEMENTIA.

Literature: EMMINGHAUS, Allgemein. Psychopath.; MORSELLI, Semej. malat. ment., ii; FRIEDMANN, Ueber den Wahn (1894); KRAEPELIN, Psychiatrie, i. 159–77; DE JONG, La Psychologie des Idées fausses des Aliénés, Verh. d. 3ten int. Congr. f. Psychol., Munich (1896); KOCH, Die überwertigen Ideen, Centralbl. f. Nervenh., xix; HIRSCH, Physical Mechanism of Delusion, J. of Nerv. and Ment. Dis. (1898), 157 ff. (J.J.)

Demand [Lat. *de + mandare*, to entrust]: Ger. *Nachfrage*; Fr. *demande*; Ital. *domanda*. (1) The quantity of a given commodity, which the buyers in a given market are ready to purchase at a given price. (2) The rate at which buyers are ready to carry off the commodity at a given price, i. e. the quantity they will take per unit of time. (3) The quantity of purchasing power offered, at a given price relation, in exchange for the article demanded.

Demand is a quantity; desire, a feeling. This radical difference was not at first perceived. Smith distinguished absolute demand (quantity desired) from effectual demand (quantity which the buyer was both willing and able to purchase at the natural price). Ricardo, Malthus, and Mill gradually advanced to the conception given in (1): a sliding scale, or series of relations between quantity and price. This idea was given exactitude by Cournot and Dupuit.

The development of the mathematical theory of consumption has led most modern writers to substitute the conception (2), of a rate of demand for a pure quantity, and to make the problem of market price a kinetic rather than a static one. Cf. SUPPLY AND DEMAND.

Malthus noted two senses of demand, corresponding roughly to the distinction between (1) and (3). The last named meaning was emphasized by Walras and by Cairnes. Marshall says that there is no fundamental difference between (1) and (3), because, when the price is introduced, the two expressions reduce to the same pecuniary value; but he fails to see that when we take demand as a series of relations, the price is usually an unknown quantity to be determined; and that Cairnes'

method of determination differs fundamentally from Mill's. (A.T.H.)

Dementia [Lat. *de + mens*, mind]: Ger. *Schwachsinn*; Fr. *démence*; Ital. *demenza*. One of the main types of mental disorder, characterized by acquired (not congenital) enfeeblement of mental power.

Persons so afflicted are sometimes called 'dements.'

There may be no excitement, depression, or aberration, but only a more or less pronounced inactivity, and loss of mental receptivity and capacity. It is impossible to fix any particular degree of mental impairment as constituting dementia, as it may vary from a slight failing of the mental powers to a condition of utter helplessness of body and mind. It has been characterized as 'a general weakening of the mental power, comprising usually a lack of reasoning capacity, a diminution of feeling, a lessened volitional and inhibitory power, a failure of memory, and a want of attention, interest, and curiosity.' Lack of initiative is marked; even when once aroused, the mental powers are fairly normal.

The commonly described forms of dementia are the following: (1) Primary dementia is really a form of STUPOR (q. v.), which many prefer to describe under this head or with katatonia. It usually comes on during adolescence as a form of extreme inactivity and abeyance of mental faculties, and may be only temporary. It is akin to deep amentia.

Several writers (Kraepelin, *Psychiatrie*, 6th ed., ii. 137–214; and *Zeitsch. f. Psychol.*, 56, 254; Christian, *Ann. Méd.-Psychol.*, 1898, 1899) describe as *dementia praecox* a primary tendency to decline into dementia, with marked apathy, automatisms, recurring short periods of depression and excitement, &c., but without the concomitant symptoms with which such traits are connected in mania, melancholia, or paranoia.

(2) Secondary dementia, the ordinary form, is often termed sequential or terminal dementia, as it represents the final stages of other forms of insanity, mania, melancholia, &c. Here again degrees are important, and depend largely on the duration, nature, and severity of the former insanities. Many dements are practically reduced to an animal existence, losing all sensibility and refinement, becoming unclean in habit and idiotic in appearance. They seem almost dead to their own past, no longer recognize their friends, and if unaided by those about them would quickly perish. Less severe cases are more active physically,

are able to occupy themselves with simple household duties, and frequently live long, dying of other causes than the brain degeneration. In some cases dements are liable to sudden outbursts of excitement and violence; and destructive tendencies are common amongst them. The anatomical changes are very obscure, perhaps more marked in the internal organs than in the nervous system. Kraepelin holds that the cases of secondary dementia present not a dementia following mania or melancholia, but from the start are characteristic processes of deterioration. See PSYCHOSES.

(3) Senile dementia is an exaggerated form of normal senescence, in which the mental enfeeblement proceeds more rapidly and to a greater extent than usual. Bodily decrepitude accompanies the loss of memory and other faculties. In certain cases hallucinations and delusions occur. Distinct pathological changes in the brain and its membranes have been substantiated.

(4) Paralytic dementia is a term which is used as synonymous with the dementia or final stage of general PARALYSIS (q.v.). In addition, some writers distinguish alcoholic or drug dementia, and organic dementia, which results from gross brain disease.

Literature: CLOUSTON, Ment. Diseases (4th ed., 1896), lects. vii, viii, and x; RIEGER, Beschreibung der Intelligenzstörungen (1888); ZIEHEN, Allgem. Path. des Intelligenzdefects, in Lubasch and Ostertag's Ergebnisse der Allg. Pathol. (1899); all systematic works on mental diseases. (J.J.)

Demerit [Lat. *de* + *merere*, to deserve]: Ger. *Unverdienst*; Fr. *démérite*; Ital. *demerito*. (1) Ethical: see MERIT.

(2) Theological: the condition of inability on man's part to achieve more than a certain modicum of righteousness, and absence of power to remain on a moral level satisfying to God. It is a consequence of the view of human nature issuing from the dogma of original sin. (R.M.W.)

Demesne [OF. *demaine*, possession]: Ger. *Domäne*; Fr. *domaine*; Ital. *dominio*. That portion of a mediaeval manor which the lord retained in his own possession and cultivated by means of his serfs, or that portion of a mediaeval kingdom of which the king remained immediate lord. (F.C.M.)

Demiurge: see GNOSTICISM, and SOCRATICS (Plato).

Democracy [Gr. δῆμος, people, + κράτος, power]: Ger. *Demokratie*; Fr. *démocratie*;

Ital. *democrazia*. By derivation simply 'rule of the people.' Specifically: (1) A form of government in which the control lies with the mass of the people, without respect of fortune. (2) Sometimes loosely: the great mass of the people themselves. (3) Sometimes in the United States: the Democratic party, supposed to represent the rights of the people in some peculiar sense.

The typical democracies are: in ancient times the Greek (Athens), in mediaeval the Italian (Florence), in modern Switzerland and the United States.

Plato unhistorically represents democracy as growing out of oligarchy (plutocracy) and passing into tyranny (*Republic*, viii). Aristotle agrees with Plato that it is the rule of the poor (*Pol.*, III. v), but sees more virtue in it than Plato. The presence of slavery in ancient democracies detracts from their democratic character. The device of representation enables modern democracies to embrace much larger bodies of men than the ancient, though Rousseau counts democracy best suited for small states, monarchy for large (*Contrat Social*, iii). Lewis points out that the division of governments into monarchies, oligarchies, and democracies is as old as Herodotus (Bk. III). It probably became current in his time (5th century B.C.), though he represents it as older. (J.B.)

Literature: for the aspects of modern democracy see MONTESQUIEU, ROUSSEAU, and DE TOCQUEVILLE. Cf. CORNEWALL LEWIS, Political Terms, chap. ix, Democracy, and the authors there quoted; also chap. v, Sovereignty.

Democritus. (cir. 460–cir. 357 B.C.) A Greek philosopher, born at Abdera, Thrace. Called 'The Laughing Philosopher,' for his cheerful disposition. He was rich by inheritance, and devoted himself to travel and learning. He was probably the greatest of the followers of Leucippus. See PRE-SOCRATIC PHILOSOPHY (Atomists).

Demography [Gr. δῆμος, people, + γράφειν, to write]: Ger. *Demographie*; Fr. *démographie*; Ital. *demografia*. The statistical description of human populations in their physical, rather than in their social and moral aspects.

The term is of recent origin. 'Il y a toutefois une étude qui constitue assurément une science et qui est si étroitement liée avec la statistique, qu'on l'a confondue souvent avec elle; c'est la démographie. . . . La démographie est la science de la population; elle en constate l'état, elle en étudie les mouvements, principalement dans la naissance, le mariage, la mort et dans les migrations, et elle s'efforce de parvenir jusqu'à la connaissance des lois qui la régissent' (E. Levasseur, *La Population Française*, i. 18). (F.H.G.)

Demon [Gr. δαίμων, a god, an evil spirit]: Ger. *Dämon*; Fr. *démon, diable*; Ital. *demonio, diavolo*. Supernatural beings less than divine, which may be (1) either good or bad, or (2) only bad.

Philosophically viewed, demons are connected (1) with man's tendency to regard unknown, or imperfectly known, phenomena from an anthropomorphic or anthropopathic standpoint. This accounts for the wide differences in the connotation of the term to be found, as matter of history, in various civilizations. The personification of cosmic phenomena (animism) must be cited as the origin of all such conceptions. Viewed in this, the more general, way, demons are supernatural beings who may be good or bad. The conception is preserved in our modern phrase 'good or evil genius.' (2) More specifically, demons are directly connected with man's ideas of the origin of evil and of the causes of misfortune. They are external causes, causes contrasted with those to be found in man's own spirit or in his bodily weaknesses. In this regard, they are specially characterized by the fact that, unlike wood-sprites, fairies, and similar beings, they interest themselves in human affairs. They cannot be treated as non-moral or unmoral. They are baleful agencies as a rule. Although, according to the older views, their activity may be for good (as often in the *Arabian Nights*), since the Christian era they have been deemed essentially evil, in contrast to good spirits—angels. This alteration of standpoint is due to the dogma of the Fall; and although distinct traces of its influence are to be found in pre-Christian culture (e.g. Isa. xiv. 12 f.), the almost exclusive stress laid upon this idea by the Christian consciousness is absent. See DEMONOLOGY (also for *Literature*). (R.M.W.)

Demonolatry [Gr. δαίμων + λατρεία, service]: Ger. *Dämonolatrie*; Fr. *démono'atrie*; Ital. *demonolatria*. The worship of spirits—good or, as is more usual, evil.

Generally it may be said that, till distinctively theological conceptions have matured—and this is specially true of Christian theology —no deliberate choice is made of an evil being as an object of worship. Hence, demonolatry is usually a simple propitiation of spirits that might do harm were they to be slighted. MAGIC (q.v.), in its various forms, may be taken as expressive of this propitiation. Worship, in the sense of adoration, plays a minor part, and, when it does take place, incantation rather than prayer figures prominently. See DEMONOLOGY (also for *Literature*). (R.M.W.)

Demonology [Gr. δαίμων, a demon, + λόγος, discourse]: Ger. *Dämonologie*; Fr. *démonologie*; Ital. *demonologia*. In the most general anthropological sense, demonology treats of systems of beings intermediate in rank between gods and men.

Under the dominance of Christian influence the demons became the spirits of evil, while the angels became the spirits of good. Like all such doctrines, the conception of the demon has a long history and development, in which are reflected the culture stages of the believers in the demon's acts and powers. In savage peoples the demon is hardly more than a human soul under new conditions of existence; the doctrine thus becomes closely related to the general views of the nature of the soul and of life after death (see ANIMISM). The most influential field of the demons, whether viewed as the ghosts of the dead or as separate and superhuman beings, was in the production of disease; and to a lesser extent they were summoned to account for the failure of crops, and the various good and ill fortunes of a primitive existence. The patient was seized or possessed by the demon (hence the term epilepsy), and in case of nervous attacks (trance, mania, epilepsy, &c.) the foreign spirit might be heard speaking through the mouth of the possessed body. The specific nature of the belief in the demon is usually well shown by the arts practised to banish or to exorcize it (see EXORCISM), such practices being frequently of the nature of magical or religious charms. Dreams and nightmares were also explained as the result of demon possession. In more developed civilizations the demon notions change their character, and are strongly influenced by the prevalent religious systems and observances. But practices closely akin to those derived from immediate belief in demon possession remain as survivals to the present day. The detailed history of the beliefs in demons, with their elaboration into hierarchies with specific and individual functions, forms a most important chapter in the history of the development of religion. See also DEMONOMANIA, and WITCHCRAFT.

Literature: art. Demonology in Encyc. Brit. (9th ed.), and references there given; NEVIUS, Demon Possession (1895); A. D.

WHITE, Hist. of the Warfare of Science with Theology, chaps. xv, xvi ; LEHMANN, Aberglaube u. Zauberei (1898) ; also references under ANIMISM and EXORCISM. (J.J.)

Demonology (religious). The department of science and history of religions which deals with the belief in demons, taking this phrase in its widest acceptation. The main problems are : (1) to give an authentic account of demons in all the phases of religious culture, from the lowest nature-religions to Christianity ; (2) to show how the definite demon-system of one religion or people (e.g. Persia, Babylonia-Assyria) has influenced the development of another (e.g. the Jews after the Exile). Philosophically, the problem is to determine how, at different times and under various conditions, men have conceived of their relation to demons, especially as regards the ethical implications of this relationship.

Literature: ROSKOFF, Gesch. d. Teufels; TYLOR, Primitive Culture ; H. SPENCER, Princ. of Sociol., i ; A. BASTIAN, Der Mensch in d. Gesch., and Beitr. z. vergleichenden Psychol.; WELCKER, Griech. Götterlehre, i. 731 f.; DOUGHTY, Arabia Deserta; KING, Babylonian Magic and Sorcery; TIELE, Babylon.-Assyr. Gesch., 548 f.; BAUDISSIN, Stud. z. Semit. Religionsgesch.; ROBERTSON SMITH, Religion of the Semites ; WEBER and SCHNEDERMANN, Syst. d. altsynagog. Palästin. Theol.; EISENMENGER, Entdecktes Judenthum ; EVERLING, Die Paulinische Angel. u. Dämonologie; CONYBEARE, in Jewish Quart. Rev. (1896); art. Exorcismus in Herzog's Real-Encyc.; CONWAY, Demonology and Devil Lore; PFLEIDERER, Philos. of Religion (Eng. trans.), iii. 307 f. See DEVIL. (R.M.W.)

Demonomania or **Demon Possession** [Gr. δαίμων, a demon, + μανία, madness]: Ger. *Dämonomanie, Besessenheit*; Fr. *démonomanie*; Ital. *demonomania*. Demonomania is a morbid mental condition, in which the patient believes himself, more usually herself, possessed by a demon. The term demon possession may be applied either to this condition or to the prevalent belief that certain forms of disease or manifestations are caused by demons. Possession and spirit possession are also used, to give a wider field for interpretation.

The condition may be considered either as a type of insanity, or in its historical aspects. As the former it is often akin to a religious melancholia, the patient believing himself eternally damned, suffering from agonies of self-accusation, and exhibiting many of the characteristics of melancholiacs. Another type of demonomania is the hysterical one, characterized by convulsions, and thus giving rise to the term Convulsionaires. Such demonomaniacs are subject to attacks of violence and fury, accompanied by starts and choreic jerks, and loud shouting, in which the central idea of possession by a demon is prominent. In extreme cases this crisis, which lasts from ten minutes to half an hour, may be accompanied by assaults on the bystanders, destruction of property, beating of their own bodies. A very constant symptom of the attack is anaesthesia. Ecstasy, catalepsy, and somnambulism may be noted ; and most characteristic is the tendency of such attacks to be contagious and lead to epidemics (see CONTAGION). A person so affected may be termed a demoniac or demonomaniac. It is especially significant as a symptom of the delirium of degeneracy.

On the historic side, demon possession is important as a stage in the development of medical theory of disease, and as suggesting a rational explanation in terms of modern psychiatry of the actions and influences of abnormal individuals in former ages. In this connection it has an equal significance for the history of religion. Cf. DEMONOLOGY (with literature there cited). (J.J.)

Literature: V. MAGNAN, Leçons cliniques (1893, 2e série 1897); and Recherches sur les centres nerveux (2e série 1893); MAGNAN and LEGRAIN, Les Dégénérés ; MAGNAN and SERIEUX, Le Délire chronique; MICHLA, Nouv. Dict. de Méd. (1872), sub verbo ; BONFIGLI, Riv. sper. fren., 1893; also the titles cited under CATALEPSY. (L.M.)

Demonstration [Lat. *de* + *monstrare*, to show]: Ger. *Demonstration, Beweisführung durch Schlussfolgerung*; Fr. *démonstration*; Ital. *dimostrazione*. A reasoning in which the conclusion has at once the logical necessity which expresses its relation to the premises as grounds from which it follows, and the material necessity which expresses the assumption that the premises are themselves judgments of objective worth. All demonstration therefore implies that the premises from which the conclusion proceeds are ultimate truths, the validity of which admits of no question, and the certainty of which requires no evidence. The problems which such a description of demonstration suggests—viz. (1) what is the kind of certainty attaching to judgments of objective worth ? (2) within what spheres are such judgments possible ? (3) on what does the possibility of such judgments rest?—form the main topic of the theory of knowledge.

Demonstration is the latinized equivalent for Aristotle's term ἀπόδειξις, and all definitions of it are more or less transcripts of his definition of ἀπόδειξις (*Anal. Post.*, i. 2). The term demonstration does not appear to have become the current, accepted equivalent till the period of the Arabic writers on logic, who translated ἀπόδειξις by it. The earlier Latin use, as in Boethius, does not go beyond the etymological sense, of showing, bringing before the mind as if pointed to, which the term still retains even in its specialized acceptation. For it is the peculiarity of demonstration that it claims for the conclusion reached by a mediating process the same simple absolute certainty that we incline to allow, without question, to the direct apprehension of a fact. The fundamental problems regarding demonstration begin in English philosophy with Locke's assignment of relations among abstract ideas to demonstration, and contrast of those with propositions about matters of fact. Locke's view was developed further by Hume, and Hume's mode of treatment reappears in J. S. Mill (*Logic*, Bk. II. chaps. v–vii); cf. excellent remarks in D. Stewart (*Philos. of Hum. Mind*, Pt. II. chaps. iv, v). The critical philosophy has brought the problem to the issue as to the exact character of judgments that are synthetic and at the same time claim to be self-evident. See Kant, *Critique of Pure Reason*, Doctrine of Method, chap. i.

Literature: MANSEL, Limits of Demonstrative Science, in Letters, &c., 79 ff.; LOTZE, Logik, Bk. III. chap. v; SPENCER, First Principles, Pt. II. chap. ii; KROMANN, Unsere Naturerkenntniss; JAMES, Princ. of Psychol., chap. xxviii; DELBŒUF, Essai de Log. scient. (R.A.)

Demonstrative: see DEMONSTRATION, and REASONING.

Demoralization [Lat. *de + moralis*, moral]: Ger. *Demoralisation*; Fr. *démoralisation*; Ital. *demoralizzazione*. The introduction of moral or mental disorder. See DISORDER (moral), and ORDER (moral). (J.M.B.)

De Morgan, Augustus. (1806–71.) An English mathematician, who contributed much to formal logic. He was professor of mathematics in University College, London.

Dendrite [Gr. δενδρίτης]: Ger. *Dendrit, Protoplasmafortsätze*; Fr. *dendrite*; Ital. *dendrito*. One of the protoplasmic or cellipetal processes of a neurocyte or nerve-cell. See NEUROCYTE (or NEURONE).

The term protoplasmic process, still in use, implies the older view that these projections served a nutritive function solely. It seems to be abundantly indicated that they receive nervous stimuli. The dendrite is commonly provided with root-like gemmulae, which are said to be the first to be attacked in nervous degeneration. (H.H.)

Denomination (logical) [Lat. *de + nomen*, a name]: Ger. *Benennung*; Fr. *dénomination*; Ital. *denominazione*. Denomination, in the scholastic logic, was a characteristic of terms, dependent on the relation of primary and derivative, especially in the case of an abstract term and the derived concrete.

Iustus, albus, e. g., were said to be predicated denominatively, because they referred to the possession of certain marks, i. e. were derived from *iustitia, albitudo*, possessed by the subject. In this sense the term is no longer used. Nor has the only other employment of it, as the process by which a name is selected for the common attributes recognized in the process of generalization and imposed on the class, acquired general acceptance. Cf. Thomson, *Laws of Thought*, § 48. (R.A.)

Denominative: see NAME AND NAMING, and TERM.

Denotation [Lat. *de + notare*]: Ger. *Bezeichnung*; Fr. *dénotation*; Ital. *notazione* (on the foreign equivalents compare CONNOTATION). Denotation, as a technical term, is used in a narrower and in a wider sense. In the former it is expressly relative to CONNOTATION (q.v.), and applicable within the range of the distinction between concretes and their attributes. In this sense it indicates one function of every concrete general name, that whereby a number of individuals (things, persons, cases) are marked off as possessing the attributes which constitute the meaning of the name. From this point of view, denotation might be said to march with connotation up to and exclusive of the lower limit (the proper name) and of the higher limit (the abstract term). In the wider sense, which connects with the vague untechnical use of the word 'denote,' denotation would include also the function of names where the connotative reference is absent, and from this point of view the proper name and the strictly abstract term would be said to have denotation; the one denoting a concrete individual without reference to attributes possessed in common with others; the second denoting an attribute or group of attributes conceived *in abstracto*, i. e. without reference to concrete exemplification of them.

Historically, the technical use of denotation seems to be due to J. S. Mill, whose account has been followed in the definition given. The obscurity which results from the conjunction of a wider and a narrower sense of the term has given rise to a number of disputes, of no great importance. Denotation, in the narrower sense, is equivalent to logical EXTENSION (q.v.).

Literature: MILL, Logic, Bk. I. chap. ii ; KEYNES, Formal Logic, Pt. I. chap. iii.   (R.A.)

Density [Lat. *densitas*, thickness]: Ger. *Dichtigkeit* ; Fr. *densité* ; Ital. *densità*. Familiarly, specific gravity. The quantity of matter, or mass, contained in unit volume of a body.

At any given place it is proportional to the ratio of the weight of a body to its volume, whence the old term specific gravity. The concept being independent of gravity, the term density is now that most used in physics. (S.N.)

Denumeral: see MULTITUDE.

Deontology [Gr. δέοντα, duties, + λόγος, discourse]: Ger. *Pflichtenlehre*; Fr. *déontologie, théorie des devoirs* ; Ital. *dottrina dei doveri, deontologia*. The theory of duty or obligation.

The term is sometimes used to describe ethical science. It indicates a view of ethics in which the conception of duty, rather than those of right, virtue, or goodness, is made fundamental in morality.

The term was used by Bentham as the title of one of his late works (first published by Bowring), although, on his view, as expressed in the *Principles of Morals and Legislation*, duty was a social or political conception, and room was not found for it in the region of ' private ethics.'   (W.R.S.)

Dependence [Lat. *de* + *pendere*, to hang]: for foreign equivalents see INDEPENDENCE. Any relation of CONDITION (q. v.), or CAUSE (q.v.).

Dependence (consciousness of): see RELIGION (psychology of).

Dependence and **Dependent** (in logic): see RELATION.

Depreciation [Lat. *depretiare*, to depreciate]: Ger. *Entwertung* ; Fr. *dépréciation* ; Ital. *deprezzamento*. Loss of value : commonly applied to the currency only, in which case it means decrease in the quantity of commodities which a monetary unit will purchase.

The cause of depreciation may be either increase in the supply of money or diminution in the demand for money. The former is the more common. Among its most frequent causes are (1) increased production of the precious metals ; (2) emission of paper money by governments. The chief causes of diminu-

tion in demand are (1) substitution of credit for money as a means of exchange; (2) distrust in the money authorized by the government, and substitution of some other basis of contract.

Depreciation manifests itself by a rise in prices ; see INDEX NUMBER. This results in a loss to creditors and to those who have fixed incomes, and in gain to debtors and those who have contracts to pay fixed sums. For the former can buy less goods with the money they receive, while the latter can discharge their debts or fulfil their contracts with fewer commodities or less labour.

The opposite of depreciation, both in its causes and effects, is appreciation.   (A.T.H.)

Depression [Lat. *de* + *premere*, to press] : Ger. *Traurigkeit, Depression* ; Fr. *dépression* ; Ital. *depressione*. A condition characterized by a sinking of spirits, lack of courage or initiative, and tendency to gloomy thoughts.

The symptom occurs in weakened conditions of the nervous system, such as neurasthenia, and is especially characteristic of melancholia. Dejection and depression are practically used synonymously ; depression refers more definitely to the lowered vitality of physical and mental life, dejection to the despondency of the mental mood. See DEJECTION, and MELANCHOLIA.   (J.J.)

De primo ad ultimo: see SORITES.

Depth (in logic). A term generally used as synonymous with COMPREHENSION (q.v.). Cf. Hamilton, *Logic*, i. 141.   (R.A.)

Depth or **Distance, Visual** (perception of): Ger. *optische Wahrnehmung der Tiefe* ; Fr. *perception visuelle de la profondeur* (*du relief, de la distance*—L.M.) ; Ital. *percezione della profondità* (*distanza*). The visual perception of depth or of the third dimension may be either a monocular or a binocular perception. (1) Monocularly, the perception may be mediated by degree of accommodation, by dispersion images, or by the apparent motion of one object in front of another which is caused by movements of the head or of the body. Mathematical perspective, aërial perspective, overlapping of figures, cross shadows, are all monocular criteria also, though secondary. No one of these criteria is very reliable ; so that (except in so far as it is aided by associated binocular habits or ideas) monocular vision is characterized by lack of fine discrimination of depth.   (E.B.T.—E.C.S.—C.L.F.)

(2) Binocularly, the perception may be mediated by disparate images or by the movements of convergence and accommodation. The part

played by the two possible factors in actual perception is still a matter of dispute (see Hillebrand, *Zeitsch. f. Psychol.*, xvi. 71; Arrer, *Philos. Stud.*, xiii. 116, 222, and references there quoted). Secondary criteria, in binocular perception, are the relative clearness of the object fixated, its size, the distribution of light and shade upon it, the number of objects lying between it and the body of the observing subject, its relative speed of movement across the field of vision, &c. Cf. ABERRATION (chromatic). (E.B.T.)

Literature: Physiological Psychologies of WUNDT and LADD; Psychologies of JAMES (especially) and KÜLPE; for references to literature see also Psychologies of DEWEY, LADD, and BALDWIN; recent *résumé* by BOURDON, Année Psychol., iv. 390 ff. (J.M.B.—L.M.)

Derangement [Fr. *de + ranger*, to put in order]: Ger. *Geistesstörung*; Fr. *dérangement d'esprit*; Ital. *disordine*. As applied to mental conditions, the term indicates any form of insanity, or divergence from normal soundness of reason. The mind, or the person, is said to be deranged when a distinct form of insanity, or an irresponsible condition, is present. See SANITY AND INSANITY. (J.J.)

Derivation (linguistic) [Lat. *derivatio*?]: Ger. *Ableitung, Derivation*; Fr. *dérivation*; Ital. *derivazione*. The history of a word in terms of its formation from a shorter basal element or word called the root. Words formed from other words or from roots by the addition of suffixes are called derivatives.

Thus *friendliness* is said to be derived from *friend*; *friend* itself from the root *frij*, 'to love'; *holy* from *whole*, &c. But such statements, while serving an immediate practical purpose, by misrepresenting the historical facts usually lack scientific exactness. See ETYMOLOGY. (B.I.W.)

Dermal Sensation [Gr. δέρμα, the skin]: Ger. *Hautempfindung*; Fr. *sensation de la peau, sensation cutanée*; Ital. *sensazione cutanea*. A synonym (used, e. g., by Sanford, *Course in Exper. Psychol.*, chap. i) for CUTANEOUS SENSATION (q.v.). (E.B.T.)

Descartes (or **Des Cartes**), **René.** (1596–1650.) A French philosopher and mathematician, born at La Haye, who entered upon his education at the college of La Flèche. In 1612 he left school, dissatisfied with scholastic methods and doctrines. In 1616 he joined the Dutch army; in 1619 that of the duke of Bavaria. In 1621 he renounced his military profession, and began again the pursuit

of knowledge, travelling in Italy, France, and other countries. In 1629 he settled in Holland. In 1647 the French court granted him a pension. Invited to the Swedish court by Queen Christina, he went to Stockholm, where he died. He is properly called the 'father of modern philosophy.' See MIND AND BODY, OCCASIONALISM, and PRE-ESTABLISHED HARMONY.

Descent (doctrine of): Ger. *Abstammungslehre, Descendenzlehre*; Fr. *théorie de la descendance*; Ital. *teoria della discendenza* (or *dell' evoluzione*). The theory that all the diverse forms of organic life are the descendants, through the ordinary processes of reproduction, of previously existing forms. Descent of man is the origin of man in accordance with this theory. (E.S.G.—J.M.B.)

This theory, that animals and plants are in all cases genetically related to earlier forms, is the doctrine of continuity in evolution as applied to the organic world. Its general acceptance among biologists may be said to be due to the publication of the *Origin of Species*. Darwin used the phrase 'descent with modifications' to characterize the theory of evolution. It should be noted, however, that the term MODIFICATION (q.v.) has since been used by some authors with a specialized meaning.

Literature: C. DARWIN, Origin of Species; E. HAECKEL, History of Creation; O. SCHMIDT, Doctrine of Descent. See the literature of EVOLUTION. For the influence of the theory of descent upon classification see E. R. LANKESTER, art. Zoology in Encyc. Brit. (9th ed.), xxiv. (C.LL.M.—J.M.B.)

Descent (in logic): see QUANTITY (logical).

Description [Lat. *de + scribere*, to write]: Ger. *Beschreibung*; Fr. *description*; Ital. *descrizione*. The statement of the distinctive marks of an object, the marks being of such a kind as can be presented in direct perceptive experience.

Descriptions, accordingly, may be more or less complete, according as the purpose, the distinction of the object, may be effected by more or less enumeration of detail. It is an accepted doctrine of logic that the concrete individual object can be described, not defined. Empirical theory of knowledge tends to regard detailed, complete description as identical with explanation. See SCIENCE, and cf. APPRECIATION. (R.A.)

Desert [Lat. *de + servire*, to serve]: Ger. *Verdienst*; Fr. *mérite*; Ital. *merito*. What is due to a man in the way of praise or reward, blame or penalty, in respect of the usual quality of his conduct.

From the moral point of view, a man's desert depends on his personal attitude to morality, and not merely on the social utility of his achievements. See MERIT. (W.R.S.)

Design (in philosophy) [Lat. *designare*, to mark out]: Ger. *Zweck*; Fr. *dessein*; Ital. *disegno*. The attribution of cases of adaptation in nature to conscious design.

A form of TELEOLOGY (q. v.), in which the concept of finality is anthropomorphic and is carried into the details of nature. It is the ground for the argument from design for the existence of God. It is characteristic of the more deistic forms of THEISM (q. v.). (J.M.B.)

Design (in psychology): Ger. *Ziel* (*Absicht*); Fr. *dessein*; Ital. *disegno*. A conscious and deliberate plan of action. Cf. PROJECT, PLAN, INTENTION, and PURPOSE.

A design is an END (q. v.) which is more or less remote, and for whose attainment the means are more or less clearly understood and within control. It carries the idea also of some preliminary deliberation. We will to move a limb, or to taste of a dish, but we design to take a walk, or to eat a dinner. This is the tendency of usage, but it might be more consistent than it is. (J.M.B., G.F.S.)

Designate and **Designation**: see TERM (logical).

Desire [Lat. *desiderare*, to wish for]: Ger. *Begehrung, Begehren* (abstract); Fr. *désir*; Ital. *desiderio*. Appetence, in which the attainment of an end is represented by means of a train of ideas.

Our definition restricts the application of the term to a special form of conation or appetence, arising only at a certain level of mental development. This usage is modern. The earlier psychologists, such as Wolf and Locke, apply the word to the conative side of our nature in general. But it does not appear that the connotation which they attached to the word differs essentially from that which we have assigned to it. They made it co-existent with conation in general, only because they failed to distinguish more primitive and simple from more developed and complex modes of the conative attitude. 'The cases in which the subject is incited to action by ideas, as distinct from perceptions, are cases of desire. . . . By the time that ideas are sufficiently self-sustaining, they form trains that are not wholly shaped by the circumstances of the present; entirely new possibilities of action are opened up. We can desire to live again

through experiences of which there is nothing actually present to remind us; and we can desire a new experience which as yet we only imagine' (Ward, as cited below, 73–4).

Literature: WARD, art. Psychology, Encyc. Brit., Pt. XX; GREEN, Prolegomena to Ethics, Bk. II. chap. ii; BALDWIN, Handb. of Psychol., Feeling and Will, 320–30; LADD, Psychol., Descrip. and Explan., 601–8; SIDG-WICK, Meth. of Eth., Bk. I. chap. iv; HÖFFDING, Psychologie, 325; JODL, Lehrb. d. Psychol., 426. For desire, in the general sense of conation, see CONATION; also the citations made by EISLER, Wörterb. d. philos. Begriffe, 'Begehren.' (G.F.S., J.M.B.)

Despair: see HOPE AND DESPAIR.

Despotism [Gr. δεσπότης, master, lord]: Ger. *Despotismus*; Fr. *despotisme*; Ital. *despotismo*. (1) As a form of government, despotism is the sovereign and arbitrary rule of a single person. (2) It is frequently applied to arbitrary rule, even of a subordinate ruler.

Despot is in Greek originally the master of a slave, and is very properly applied by Herodotus to the Persian kings. To Aristotle (*Pol.*, III. ix; *Ethics*, VIII. x) despotic government (nearly convertible with tyrannical) is that of a single ruler that rules, not for the public good, but for his own. In our own time we should feel that despotism would be a less harsh term than tyranny to apply to a rule like that of the czar of Russia, which, though arbitrary, is not without laws, nor entirely for the ruler's personal advantage. The use of 'despot,' in the later Byzantine empire (see Murray's *Eng. Dict.*, and Gibbon, *Decline and Fall*, chap. liii), for the first of the princes of the blood under the emperor, was of course not warranted, either by derivation or history. See AUTOCRACY, and AB-SOLUTISM. (J.B.)

Destiny: see FATE, PROVIDENCE, ESCHA-TOLOGY, and IMMORTALITY.

Destutt, Antoine Louis Claude, Comte de Tracy. (1754–1836.) Born of an ancient and noble family of France, he joined the army, and, after brilliant service, the party of the Revolution. He sat in the Constitutional Assembly beside Lafayette, and during the Reign of Terror was imprisoned. Two days before his trial the Reign of Terror ended, and he was released. It was during his imprisonment that he conceived the plan of his greatest work. During the Consulate the Society of Ideologists met at his house in Auteuil near Paris, among them Dabains and Benjamin

Constant. He has been called the logician and metaphysician of the school of Condillac.

Desuetude (in law) [Lat. *desuetudo*]: Ger. *Abkommen, ausser Gebrauch treten*; Fr. *désuétude*; Ital. *disuso*. Discontinuance of use; especially of the use of some part of the unwritten law.

The term is correlative with custom (*consuetudo*). What law custom creates, disuse may eventually abrogate (Effinger *v.* Lewis, 32 Pennsylvania State Reports, 367). 'Rectissime etiam illud receptum est ut leges non solum suffragio legislatoris, sed etiam tacito consensu omnium per desuetudinem abrogentur' (*Dig.*, i. 3, *De Legibus*, &c., 32, § 1).

By the law of England and the United States, no legislative enactment is abrogated by desuetude. Statutes may be treated as 'dead letters' by the public, but never are by the courts, except as juries in criminal cases may virtually disregard them, by acquitting a person charged with their violation, not because the act was not proved, but because they consider them as obsolete, and so of no force. (S.E.B.)

Determinants [Lat. *determinare*, to limit]: Ger. *Determinanten*; Fr. *déterminants*; Ital. *determinanti*. The hypothetical group of hypothetical units or biophores, by the distribution of which during development the differentiations of the multicellular organism are determined.

The determinant takes its place in the elaborate scheme of heredity developed by Weismann. Admittedly hypothetical, it none the less serves to make clear a definite conception. See A. Weismann, *The Germ-Plasm* (1893). (C.LL.M.)

Determinate (in biology) [Lat. *determinatus*, from *determinare*, to limit]: Ger. *bestimmt, bestimmt gerichtet*; Fr. *déterminé, (variation) orientée* (Y.D.); Ital. *determinato*. (1) Congenital variations in definite directions, due to some specific cause, and not conforming to the law of probability, are said to be determinate, as contrasted with indeterminate, indefinite, or fortuitous. (C.LL.M.–J.M.B.)

(2) Evolution resulting from the continued action of some cause by which its course is directed is said to be determinate. See ORTHOGENESIS, and ORTHOPLASY. (J.M.B., C.LL.M.)

(1) According to some biologists, individual modifications of structure, due to use or the action of the environment, in one generation, determine congenital variations of a similar kind in the next generation. According to others, the survival, under natural selection, and interbreeding of those which vary congenitally in certain directions produces further variability in these directions, simply by shifting the mean, and evolution becomes determinate (sense 2), although variations are really not so. According to still others, variations are determined by an inner tendency, at present unexplained by science.

(2) According to some, for whom determinate variations do not exist, the course of evolution is determined solely by the action of the environment, direct or indirect (extrinsic determination, extreme Neo-Darwinism); according to others, it is mainly determined by the inherent nature of organic life, producing determinate variations (intrinsic determination, Neo-Lamarckism, orthogenesis); and according to still others, it is due to the supplementing of natural selection by the screening influence of individual accommodations upon indeterminate variations (organic selection, orthoplasy). See MODIFICATION, VARIATION, and ACQUIRED CHARACTERS. (C.LL.M.–J.M.B.)

Determination (logical) [Lat. *determinatio*]: Ger. *Determination, Bestimmung*; Fr. *détermination*; Ital. *determinazione*. The form of definition which restricts the generality of a notion by adding marks to its meaning, that is, by increasing its comprehension or depth.

So the πρόσθεσις of Aristotle (*Anal. Post.*, i. 27, 87 *a*). Spinoza (*Epist.* 59) made a metaphysical application in denying all determination to the absolute, since *omnis determinatio est negatio*, the denial of the contrary of the marks which are added. Similarly Schelling. Among modern logicians, determination has come to mean the process of restricting the generality by definition (Ueberweg, *Logik*, 4th ed., § 52). See additional citations in Eisler, *Wörterb. d. philos. Begriffe*, sub verbo. (R.A.)

Determination (psychical or mental). The co-operation of all the factors which adequately condition and issue in a mental END-STATE (q. v.). See also END (meaning 2).

The essential matters are progress towards an end-state, generally involving a series of changes, and the inclusion of no elements extraneous to the state whose determination is in question. The conception of determination in the individual mind is analogous to that of psychological and biological determination in evolution. Cf. the other forms of DETERMINATION. (J.M.B., G.F.S.)

The distinctive use of 'psychical' or 'mental' (in contrast with 'psychological'

DETERMINATION; see next topic) should be noted. The former indicates the individual's own consciousness of a process, the latter the observation of a process by another observer. This general contrast of points of view is recommended under PSYCHICAL AND PSYCHOLOGICAL. (J.M.B.–G.F.S.)

The subject has been discussed under various terms, the principal question being as to the relative share of subjective factors, such as associations, dispositions, &c., on the one hand, and objective, nervous or stimulating, factors on the other hand, in the several typical modes of mental determination, especially those of mental objects, and of volitions. The adaptive determination of thought progressively has been called, by Stout, RELATIVE SUGGESTION (q.v.); and the theory that volition is always a case of determination, in the sense of the definition, has been called DETERMINISM (q.v.), as opposed to INDETERMINISM (q.v.). The present writer has applied the phrase systematic determination to the series of progressive determinations—each from the platform of the earlier system—which make up the development of knowledge as a whole. An interesting case is indicated by the phrase 'decision or determination to act' thus, or so; it is really a predetermination of an end for action, being an end-state resulting from the earlier determination known as deliberation.

Literature: STOUT, Analytic Psychol.; SIMMEL, Arch. f. syst. Philos., i; URBAN, Psychol. Rev., July, 1892; BALDWIN, Social and Eth. Interpret., §§ 55–7, 78, and in Psychol. Rev., Jan., 1898. (J.M.B.)

Determination (psychological). The evolution of mind considered as showing a series of forms progressively determined towards greater complexity. It is correlative to the biological determination seen in 'determinate evolution,' and analogous—as a problem—to the mental or psychic determination of the individual's 'stream of thought.'

Literature: see titles under DETERMINATION (mental). Also JAMES, Princ. of Psychol., ii, *ad fin.* (J.M.B.)

Determinism [Lat. *de + terminus*, end]: Ger. *Determinismus*; Fr. *déterminisme*; Ital. *determinismo*. The theory according to which choice between alternative courses of conduct can, in all cases, be fully accounted for by psychological and other conditions. See FREE WILL CONTROVERSIES, and DETERMINATION (mental). (G.F.S.–J.M.B.)

Determinism (in biology). The doctrine that all organic phenomena have efficient causes or antecedents, in terms of which they are explicable.

Biological determinism asserts that, no matter what psychological phenomena may or may not accompany organic changes, these changes in themselves are determined by antecedent vital changes. See EVOLUTION (cosmic). (C.LL.M.–J.M.B.)

Determinism (theological): see FORE-ORDINATION.

Deus ex Machina [Lat.]. Divine agency considered as apart from nature, and modifying or interfering with it on occasion.

This view was developed in its philosophical form in what is known as DEISM (q.v.). The expression is often used as setting into relief an artificial and extreme dualistic vein in theistic discussion. (J.M.B.)

Deuteranopia [Gr. δεύτερος, second, + ἀ + ὄψομαι, to see]: Ger. *Deuteranopie*; Fr. and Ital. not in use. The name proposed by v. Kries for what was formerly called green-blindness. See PROTANOPIA. (C.L.F.)

Deutoplasm [Gr. δεύτερος, second, + πλάσμα, substance]: Ger. *Nahrungsdotter*; Fr. *deutoplasme, lécithe*; Ital. *deutoplasma*. That portion of the egg which affords nourishment to the formative protoplasm; commonly called the yolk. Proposed by Van Beneden (1870). (C.LL.M.)

Development (biological) [Lat. *devolutus*, through the Fr.]: Ger. *Entwicklung*; Fr. *développement*; Ital. *sviluppo*. The entire series of vital changes normal to the individual organism, from its origin from the parent cell or cells until death.

Development refers to the individual (ONTO-GENESIS), evolution to the race (PHYLOGENESIS), a distinction of terms (q.v.) made by Haeckel. In most organisms there are well-marked stages in development, characterized by structural changes. For the law of such changes during the prenatal or embryological period see RECAPITULATION; on changes in the subsequent periods see DEVELOPMENTAL INSANITIES, ADOLESCENCE, SENESCENCE. Cope and Hyatt have formulated a law of decay, according to which the individual's retrograde development, or decline after maturity, anticipates the future degeneration of the species to which it belongs, giving a sort of reverse recapitulation.

For the distinction between development and growth see GROWTH, and GROWTH (psychic); if made in biology, it would mean that development applies to what is constitutional and characteristic of the species, growth to what is acquired by the individual—development

274

to adaptation, growth to ACCOMMODATION (q. v.). In addition to the topics referred to, see EMBRYOLOGY.

Literature: see topics mentioned above; HYATT, Science, N.S., Jan. 27, 1897; HAECKEL, Gen. Morphol. (1866). (J.M.B., E.B.P.)

Development (mental): see MENTAL DEVELOPMENT, and EVOLUTION (mental).

Development Formula: see SYMBOLIC LOGIC.

Developmental Insanities: Ger. *Entwicklungspsychosen*; Fr. *psychoses du développement*; Ital. *psicosi dello sviluppo* (e.g. *della pubertà*). Those nervous disorders which tend to appear at certain periods in the growth and development of the brain.

The bringing to complete fruitage of the highest evolution in nature is a most delicate process, subject to dangers of many kinds, and incident to different periods. While these may be aggravated by unhygienic conditions, the determining factor is heredity. 'A bad or a good heredity means more during development than after.' Most of the disorders of development are accordingly regarded as manifestations of nervous instability, or of a neurotic diathesis. Such taint may be so slight that, under ordinary circumstances, the individual would pass through his normal span of years without mental disorder or marked abnormality; but under the influence of misfortune or excitement, particularly if it occur at critical periods in his life, he is apt to exhibit pathological symptoms. Those bearing upon them the marks or stigmata of DEGENERATION (q. v.) are specially prone to developmental neuroses.

Developmental disorders in children are apt to take the form of convulsions, delirium, night-terrors, somnambulism, and the like. During dentition, convulsion is the typical form of manifestation of an unstable brain. The delirium may be connected with a distinct fever, but the high temperature does not of itself lead to delirium except in the predisposed brain.

The developmental neuroses incident to puberty and adolescence are of supreme importance; for these periods are recognized as the ones when breakdown is most imminent, when the tyranny of heredity is most apt to make itself felt, when the decadence of the unfit begins to appear. Epilepsy and, especially, hysteria are apt to appear in the years following puberty.

The ages from twenty to twenty-five are most liable to mania and neurasthenia; and the percentage of cases of insanity which occur at this period, in which hereditary influences can be traced, is unusually large. Many of the forms of mental disturbance incident to this period, while not technically insanities, are yet significant. A characteristic form of minor psychosis may appear as an exaggerated self-will: the youth or maiden becomes ungovernable, breaks out into attacks of violence, becomes lazy, may be prone to deceit and lying, may leave home without reason, or create scandal. In all this there is a characteristic periodicity, periods of abandonment and excess giving way to periods of propriety and self-restraint. It would be misleading to regard such attacks as insanity, but they are closely related causally to the influences which produce true insanity. The form of insanity usually described as the insanity of adolescence is characterized by a maniacal tendency (seventy-eight per cent.) and a motor restlessness. 'The maniac is, in the male sex, restless, boisterous, full of mock-heroic pseudo-manliness, obtrusive pugnaciousness, with often a morbid sentimentality; while in the female sex we find also restlessness, with lack of self-control, intolerance of control by others, impulsiveness, hysterical obtrusiveness, and emotional perversion. In both sexes we naturally find strong and perverted sexual ideas and practices.' Periodicity of attack and remission is particularly characteristic, and is related, in women especially, to the periodicity of sexual functions. In about one-third of all cases the ending is secondary dementia—a severe decay of mental functions, comparable to extreme idiocy. Such dementia, however, may be consistent in some cases with the spasmodic, but transitory, display of latent mental powers. Some cases recover once or twice with years of sanity, but in the end pass into true dementia. Less frequently the adolescent insanity is of a melancholic type, still showing remissions, but not so definitely as in maniacal cases; there is apt to be hypochondria and extreme concentration upon one's self. Suicidal tendencies may occur; religious depression and delusions are frequent. Such cases when persistent develop into forms of stupor—more common in females than in males. Masturbation in males, and hysterical symptoms in females, are the chief complications.

Akin to adolescent insanities are those connected with childbirth, with the climacteric, and with senility. All these relate to periods of development in the progress from birth to death, and are dominated by hereditary influences and endowments. For description of these in relation to development see Clouston, *Ment. Diseases*.

A different view of this subject is taken by Kraepelin, who recognizes the occurrence of several distinct disease-processes of characteristic course and outcome. See PSYCHOSIS.

Literature: T. S. CLOUSTON, Ment. Diseases (4th ed., 1883); The Neuroses of Development (1891); and Developmental Insanities, in Tuke's Dict. of Psychol. Med.; EMMINGHAUS, Die psychol. Störungen des Kindesalters (1887); J. LANGDON DOWN, Mental Affections of Childhood (1889); MARRO, La Pubertà (1896–8); KAHLBAUM, Die Hebephrenie; SACHS, Nervous Diseases of Children (1895); MORGAN, Der Irrsinn im Kindesalter (1889); ZIEHEN, MARRO, and VOISIN, Proc. XIII internat. Med. Cong., 1900. See also under ADOLESCENCE. (J.J.)

Developmental Mechanics: Ger. *Entwicklungsmechanik*; Fr. *biomécanique* (Delage; see, however, Roux, as below, viii. 362); Ital. (not in use). The department of biology which investigates by experimental methods the development of the individual organism, conceived as consisting in more or less mechanical reaction to the stimulating conditions of the environment.

The term was suggested and the department of research was much furthered by Roux, who founded the *Archiv f. Entwicklungsmechanik*. Cf. BIOLOGICAL SCIENCES. (J.M.B.)

Deviation [Lat. *deviare*, deviate]: Ger. *Ablenkung, Deviation*; Fr. *déviation*; Ital. *deviazione*. In general, a turning from, as the deviation of a ray of light in passing through a prism, or the turning aside of the eye from a given position.

An abnormal and somewhat persistent turning of the eyes (and head) to one side is termed conjugate deviation, and may result from a lesion in one hemisphere. Such conjugate deviation is thus a symptom of hemiplegia; the (head and) eyes cannot be turned towards the affected side, or the unopposed antagonistic muscles may turn the eyes towards the unparalyzed side.

Besides conjugate deviation, primary and secondary deviation are distinguished. If the lateral muscle of one eye be paralyzed, then the deviation of the axis of the paralyzed eye is the primary deviation. Such deviation may be convergent or divergent, according as the external or internal rectus is affected. If the patient is required to fixate an object with his affected eye, while the sound eye is prevented from seeing the object, the sound eye will move still further in one direction, and the deviation of the visual axes is increased; this increased deviation is the secondary deviation. These results follow from the innervation mechanism of binocular vision (see also VISION, defects of). Deviation may produce double vision or DIPLOPIA (q. v.). Cf. Norris and Oliver, *System of Diseases of the Eye*, iv. (J.J.)

Deviation of the Retinal Meridians: Ger. *scheinbare verticale Meridiane der Sehfelder*; Fr. *déviation des méridiens verticaux apparents*; Ital. *deviazione dei meridiani, ecc.* The name given to a slight normal irregularity in the arrangement of CORRESPONDING POINTS (q. v.), most evident in the case of the apparent retinal vertical.

Literature: VOLKMANN, Physiol. Untersuchungen im Gebiete d. Optik (1864); SANFORD, Course in Exper. Psychol., expt. 209; used in explanation of certain optical illusions by ZEHENDER, Zeitsch. f. Psychol., xx. 65 (1899). (E.B.T.)

Devil [Gr. ὁ διάβολος, the slanderer]: Ger. *Teufel*; Fr. *diable*; Ital. *diavolo*. In the language of religion, the name given to an apostate angel, who is the instigator of evil, and the 'ruler of the kingdom of darkness.' The term diabolism is applied to actions which are devilish, as those attributed to the victims of demon possession. See DEMONOMANIA. (R.M.W.–J.M.B.)

This conception, which gradually became personified in Christian theology, can be traced in the earliest and rudest religious conceptions of man, and probably had source in the double nature of humanity. The contrast between body and spirit, between self and not-self, is responsible for the growth of the contrasted feelings of a will to do and an opposing power. In the lowest nature-religions, where there are no moralized deities, we find conceptions of destructive demons who must be propitiated. Mischief, rather than evil, is originated by such beings. Higher in the scale, we come upon such 'adversaries' as Typhon, the Titans, Ahriman, Moloch, Siva. And, sometimes, as in the case of Phoebus Apollo, the same divinity is worshipped under two aspects—as the patron of good, and as the author of vengeance. All this lies within the realm of myth; that is to say, it belongs to the pictorial representation of certain broad facts in human experience. With the rise of apocalyptic ideas, in the first century, the Jewish conception of Satan began to be personalized; this process was completed, thanks to the intervention of the later Greek conceptions of angels and demons, and to the direction taken by the Christian consciousness during the years of the formation of the Church. By the 6th century the personification is so complete that the devil is able to appear disguised as Christ, and to employ this ruse for the destruction of souls. Its persistence and domination is attested by the prosecutions for witchcraft, which continued till near the close of the 18th century, and attained their height in the 17th.

It is noticeable, from the philosophical standpoint, that theology has always treated the devil from a psychological or ethical standpoint. The problem involved is really ontological, and as a consequence of philosophical criticism, coupled with the modern explanation of the myth by way of historical development, the idea is now without vital influence. The whole matter belongs to the sphere of metaphysics, and particularly to the problems surrounding the origin, meaning, and nature of evil.

Literature: ROSKOFF, Gesch. des Teufels; HÖLEMANN, Reden d. Satan; OOSTERZEE, Christ. Dogmatics, 413 f.; SCHULTZ, Old Test. Theol. (Eng. trans.), ii. 269 f. The best account, in brief, is A. RÉVILLE, in Rev. des Deux Mondes, Jan. 1870 (Eng. trans., The Devil, 1877). (R.M.W.)

Dextrality [Lat. *dexter*, right]: Ger. *Recht-* (*und Link-*) *händigkeit*; Fr. *dextralité* (E. Nourry), *droitier* (*et gaucher*) (right and left-handed persons; no abstract terms in use); Ital. *destrismo* (*e mancinismo*) (right and left-handed persons). (1) The supremacy of the right hand, right-handedness.

(2) The fact of asymmetry of the hands, right- and left-handedness being special cases of it. (J.J.–J.M.B.)

For left-handedness, sinistrality is the corresponding word. The general bilateral symmetry of structure and function of the body is not complete; the most pronounced variation is in the superior development of the right side, particularly the hand. There is very generally a preferred foot as well as hand, and persons walking with their eyes closed are apt to manifest a tendency to circle quite constantly, some to the right, others to the left. There can be no doubt that left-handedness has always been exceptional, and right-handedness the normal. Even the relics of palaeolithic man indicate a predominant right-handedness, while historic records of the most ancient date give evidence of the recognition of the unusualness of left-handedness. Left-handedness however never fails to occur, although in varying proportions; it is sometimes stated as affecting about two persons in a hundred. Persons with equal facility in the use of either hand are termed ambidextrous; but even they prefer one or the other hand for the most accurate and delicate manipulations. In a striking number of cases ambidextrous persons are originally left-handed, but have acquired right-handed skill as well.

Of theories attempting to explain right-handedness, some refer it to the difference in position of the viscera, which favours a greater development of one side. Others regard it as determined mechanically by muscular advantage. Some emphasize the importance of education and acquired habit in the propagation of right-handedness; others regard it as an inborn difference. Amidst this diversity of opinion the best substantiated fact is this: that right-handedness and superiority of development of the left cerebral hemisphere are the rule. Such superiority is evidenced by the fact that our speech faculties are more usually localized in the left hemisphere (see SPEECH AND ITS DEFECTS); while in a few exceptional cases of aphasia in left-handed persons the disease has been located in the right hemisphere. Brain weight is not a satisfactory test, but on the whole confirms the advantage of the left hemisphere; while a few cases of exceptional left-handedness, with greater weight of the right hemisphere, are on record. As to the explanation of the greater development of the left hemisphere, as determined by a better blood-supply, or by a general advantage of the left side in nutrition, &c., little that is definite can be offered. It is likely that the initial tendency to right-handedness is present in most persons, but in a slight degree, and that this slight tendency is so emphasized by education, and the social and industrial consensus, that in the end it is well marked. Some persons have a decided right-handed tendency, others an equally pronounced left-handed tendency, which resists all efforts to be corrected or brought into accord with the usual. Experiments on children as to original right- or left-handed tendencies are not sufficient to show positive results, but in some cases reveal a decided congenital right-handedness developing at a well-marked period. That animals are capable of preferential training for one side or the other has been demonstrated. (J.J.)

Literature: DANIEL WILSON, Left-handedness (1891); BALDWIN, Ment. Devel. in the Child and the Race, chap. iv; LOMBROSO, *opera omnia*, and the works of his school, on dextrality compared with left-handedness in normals, lunatics, degenerates, epileptics, criminals, &c. (cited under CRIMINOLOGY). See also ASYMMETRY. (J.J.—E.M.)

Diabolism: see DEVIL.

Diacoustics [Gr. διά + ἀκουστικός, pertaining to hearing]: Ger. *Diakustik*; Fr. *diacoustique*; Ital. *diacustica*. The science of refracted sounds; also called diaphonics. See HEARING (refraction). (E.B.T.)

Diagnosis [Gr. διά + γιγνώσκειν, to know]: Ger. *Diagnose*; Fr. *diagnostic*; Ital. *diagnosi*. The determination of the nature of a disease from its symptoms. Differential diagnosis refers to the comparative groupings of symptoms, whereby closely related conditions may be distinguished from one another.

Diagnosis forms one of the principal factors of practical medicine, and is no less important in regard to mental than to physical diseases. Symptoms of mental disorder, however, are particularly difficult to describe and explain, since the normal variation of mental traits is both large and indefinite. For examples of diagnosis, compare what is said of the diagnosis of insanity (under SANITY AND INSANITY), and the differential diagnosis of the different forms of aphasia (under SPEECH AND ITS DEFECTS). (J.J.)

Diagoras. Lived in the 5th century B.C. A Greek poet and philosopher, who followed Democritus of Abdera; he was born on the island of Melos, and became a citizen of Athens. He was called an atheist, because he rejected the popular religion, polytheism. He left Athens 411 B.C., possibly banished for impiety. Died at Corinth.

Diagram (logical): see LOGICAL DIAGRAM.

Diagrammatic Reasoning: see REASONING.

Dialectic [Gr. διαλεκτική]: Ger. *Dialektik, dialektisch*; Fr. *dialectique*; Ital. *dialettico, dialettica*. (1) In ancient philosophy and logic: pertaining to reasoning or argument, and (as a noun) a system or course of reasoning or argument; (2) Kantian sense: see KANT'S TERMINOLOGY; (3) Hegelian sense: see HEGEL'S TERMINOLOGY, III, IV; (4) an extension of Hegel's usage: the logical statement of a thought or other process, considered as realizing itself in recurrent symbols or material forms. Cf. the writings of the Neo-Hegelian school (Wallace, Caird, Watson), to whom the respective definitions are per-

sonal interpretations of Kantian and Hegelian thought.

Literature: see extensive citations in EISLER, Wörterb. d. philos. Begriffe, 'Dialektik'; McTAGGERT, The Hegelian Dialectic. (J.M.B.)

Dialectics (in education). The art of teaching by means of discussion, as seen in Plato's dialogues, and involving, as with Socrates, inductive appeals to special instances. See METHOD (in education).

Literature: McMURRY, The Method of the Recitation, 221–32; XENOPHON, Memorabilia, Bk. IV. chap. ii; ROSENKRANZ, Philos. of Educ., 101–4. (C.DE G.)

Diallelon: see DIALLELUS, and TAUTOLOGY.

Diallelus [Gr. διάλληλος, through one another]: CIRCULUS IN PROBANDO (q.v.). (J.M.B.)

Dialogic Method: see SOCRATIC METHOD.

Dialogism: see INFERENCE.

Diameter [Gr. διά + μέτρον, a measure]: Ger. *Durchmesser*; Fr. *diamètre*; Ital. *diametro*. In craniometry several of the important maximal distances of the skull are termed diameters.

Certain of the most important of the cranial diameters are (*a*) the anterior-posterior, or maximum length from the most prominent point of the glabella to the occipital point (*Gl, O* of the illustration under CRANIOLOGY); (*b*) the transverse maximum, i.e. the greatest transverse diameter of the cranium wherever found; (*c*) the frontal, or width of forehead; (*d*) the maximum occipital, or greatest width of back of the head; (*e*) the vertical, giving height of the skull, or distance from the top or culminating point of the vertex (or by some, from the bregma) to the basion or middle of the anterior region of the foramen magnum (line *Bg, B* of the illustration under CRANIOLOGY). Many other diameters have been proposed as significant, some in the living head, as well as on the skull (see Gould's Dict. of Med., art. Diameter). The relations of *a* to *b* and others give rise to indices. See CRANIOLOGY, FACIAL ANGLE, and INDEX (also for *Literature*). (J.J.)

Dianoetic [Gr. διά + νοεῖν, to think]: Ger. *Dianoetik, dianoetisch*; Fr. *dianoétique*; Ital. *dianoetico* (suggested.—E.M.). (1) Pertaining to the intellectual or reasoning function and processes. (2) Made by Hamilton to apply strictly to the discursive or elaborative faculty, in contrast with NOETIC (q.v.), which denoted cognitions (*Lects. on Met.*, xxxviii). (J.M.B.)

In the first sense, Aristotle distinguished between the dianoetic and the ethical virtues. (K.G.)

278

Diaphonics : see DIACOUSTICS.

Diaspora [Gr. διασπορά, dispersion]. The name given to the Jews dispersed throughout the Roman empire ; also applied, by analogy, to a work carried on by Moravian missionaries, with the object of 'evangelizing' the state churches of the continent of Europe (Jas. i. 1 ; 1 Pet. i. 1).

Literature: SCHÜRER, The Jewish People in the Time of our Lord (Eng. trans.); KUENEN, Religion of Israel (Eng. trans.), iii. chap. xi ; EWALD, Hist. of Israel (Eng. trans.), vi. 81 f.; GRAETZ, Hist. of the Jews (Eng. trans.), ii. chap. viii ; HAUSRATH, New Testament Times : The Times of the Apostles, I. div. ii. (Eng. trans.) ; MOMMSEN, Hist. of Rome (Eng. trans.), iv. 538 f.; MORRISON, The Jews under Roman Rule ; HAVET, Le Christianisme et ses Origines, iii. (R.M.W.)

Diathesis [Gr. δ.ά + τιθέναι, to place]: Ger. *Diathese* ; Fr. *diathèse* ; Ital. *diatesi*. A constitutional predisposition of the body, whereby it is rendered specially liable to a certain disease; thus there may be a gouty, a diabetic, a phthisical, or an insane diathesis. The term has been extensively used with reference to mental conditions, and in this sense acquires much the same meaning as degeneration.

Persons with such a degenerate diathesis have a brain deterioration, which exposes them to insanity as the result of shock, of serious disturbance with the ordinary current of life, or at the critical periods of change of life—dentition, puberty, childbirth, climacteric. Such persons are also characterized by unusual mental traits, a tendency to instability of character and action, as well as by bodily 'stigmata.' See DEGENERATION. In a somewhat different sense, the term is employed to indicate the milder forms of mental irregularity not amounting to distinct insanity.

Literature: MAUDSLEY, Pathol. of Mind (1895); CLOUSTON, Ment. Diseases (5th ed., 1898); KOCH, Die psychopathologischen Minderwertigkeiten (1891) ; MOREL, FÉRÉ, MAGNAN, as cited under MENTAL PATHOLOGY. (J.J.)

Dibatis, Dimaris, or **Dimatis:** see MOOD (in logic).

Dicaearchus. A Greek philosopher and writer of the 4th century B.C., who followed Aristotle. His history of the Greek people is extant, and one of the most important sources of biographical data.

Dichotomy [Gr. δίχα, apart, + τέμνειν, to cut]: Ger. *Zweitheilung* ; Fr. *dichotomie* ; Ital. *dicotomia*. A form of logical division in which, at each step, the genus is separated into two species, determined by the possession and non-possession, the presence and absence, of a mark or attribute. The species so determined satisfy the rules of division : they exclude one another, and they exhaust the extent of the genus divided. As the process depends only on the formal relation between positive and negative terms, it has been called formal, and also exhaustive division.

Division by dichotomy first received recognition from Plato (especially in the dialogues *Sophistes* and *Politicus*), who, however, did not handle it from the purely formal point of view. His method is open to the objections urged against it by Aristotle (especially *De Partib. Animal.*, i. chap. iii), and is certainly of no value for the practical ends of classification. The principle of the method lies at the foundation of Jevons', and indeed of all symbolic logic, for it is not dependent on the relation of genus and species, but expresses the fundamental distinction in thought between position and negation. (R.A.)

Dichromatism [Gr. δίς, twice, + χρῶμα, colour]: Ger. *Dichromatismus* (*Rothblindheit*, *Grünblindheit*, *Blaublindheit*); Fr. *dichromatopsie* (*anérythropsie*, &c.); Ital. *cecità parziale pei colori*. That deviation from normal colour vision, in which the colour distinctions of the spectrum are practically reduced to two ; or, again, accepting as full and normal colour vision a range of colour which may be regarded as composable of three fundamental colours (trichromatic, Helmholtz) or four (Hering), the colour vision of a dichromatic eye would be composable out of two fundamental colours only. See COLOUR-BLINDNESS, VISION (visual sensation), and VISION (defects of). The term is used by Helmholtz. (J.J.–E.B.T.)

Dicta probantia [Scholastic Lat.]. A prominent phrase in the 'Biblical' section of the old dogmatic theology. It is used there of the 'proof texts,' so called; the *dicta probantia* furnish answer to the question, 'What does God's word teach us in Holy Scripture?'

Since the rise of the historical method, and the parallel development of historical theology and Biblical theology, this problem has come to be viewed and treated in a wholly new way.

Literature: ERNESTI, Institutio Interpretis Novi Testamenti. (R.M.W.)

Dictum: see MODALITY.

Dictum de Omni et Nullo: see ARISTOTLE'S DICTUM.

Didactics [Gr. διδακτικός, taught]: Ger. *Didaktik* ; Fr. *didactique* ; Ital. *didattica*.

The science and art of teaching. See PEDA-GOGICS, INSTRUCTION, and METHOD (in education). (J.M.B.)

Didactics (in theology). One of the sections of paedeutics which, in turn, is one of the main divisions of practical theology. Didactics is to be distinguished from catechetics. The former is the more extended use, and presupposes larger stores of knowledge. Religious education, as given by oral lecture to adults and to theological students, may be said to constitute the field of didactics. (R.M.W.)

Didascalic Syllogism: see SYLLOGISM.

Diderot, Denis. (1713–84.) French philosopher, born at Langres, educated by Jesuits, and intended first for the Church, and later for the law. He eagerly embraced the study of literature. He became joint editor of the *Encyclopédie* with d'Alembert. He is considered chief of the sceptical philosophers called the ENCYCLOPEDISTS (q.v.). He died in Paris.

Difference [Lat. *dis*, apart, + *ferre*, to bear]: Ger. *Unterschied*; Fr. *différence*; Ital. *differenza*. The property of being distinguishable; that is, two mental objects or contents are said to be different, in certain features, for consciousness when in respect to those features one could not be taken for the other. Cf. LIKENESS, and INDIVIDUAL. The production of new differences is called Differentiation.

The case of numerical difference represents this criterion most plainly; for here the identification of the two contents as the same is prevented only by the fact of actual duplication of experience, as in the sight, handling, &c., of both objects at once, or by variations in the context. The absence of the experience of duplication—together with all other 'features' within our definition—would leave no room for difference. This is the psychological justification of Leibnitz' theory of the 'sameness of INDISCERNIBLES' (q.v.). (J.M.B.)

Difference (consciousness of): Ger. *Unterschiedsempfindlichkeit*; Fr. *sentiment de différence*; Ital. *senso (sentimento) di differenza*. Awareness of the presence of distinguishable aspects in a total experience either with or without singling out special constituents; it thus includes both DISCERNMENT (q.v.) and DISCRIMINATION (q.v.).

The use of the word Sense in this connection, with its foreign equivalents, is not to be commended. It would be better to say Apprehension of Difference (with proper foreign equivalents). (G.F.S.–J.M.B.)

Difference (method of): Ger. *Methode der Differenz*; Fr. *méthode des différences*; Ital. *metodo delle differenze*. The method of difference may be applied either in investigation, i.e. discovery, or in criticism of evidence, i.e. proof. In both cases the basis is the comparison of two complexes of circumstances differing only by the presence and absence of the phenomenon under consideration.

As conformity to this condition of exclusive difference is practically unattainable in observation, the method is pre-eminently that available in experiment where the exclusive difference can, so far, be introduced. Reasoning from the difference proceeds on the ground that for the change from presence to absence of the given phenomenon the explanation cannot be found in antecedent or conjoined circumstances which remain unaltered, but must be sought in those attendant, antecedent, or conjoined circumstances which exhibit the same change from presence to absence. The principle of this reasoning is the canon of the method as formulated by Mill: 'If an instance in which the phenomenon under investigation occurs, and an instance in which it does not occur, have every circumstance in common save one, that one occurring only in the former, the circumstance in which alone the two instances differ is the effect, or the cause, or an indispensable part of the cause, of the phenomenon' (*Logic*, Bk. III. chap. viii. § 2).

Literature: the term Method of Difference is due to J. S. MILL, Logic. The method and its principle had been recognized, and its general function defined, by FRANCIS BACON, Nov. Org., ii. Aph. 12; by HUME, Treat. of Human Nature, Bk. I. Pt. III. § 15; by HERSCHEL, Study of Nat. Philos., §§ 145, 156. On the limitations to the inference from the method of difference, see JEVONS, Pure Logic and Minor Logic, Works, 295 ff.; SIGWART, Logik, § 95; VENN, Empirical Logic, chap. xvii. (R.A.)

Difference (method of least noticeable): Ger. *Methode der eben merklichen Unterschiede*; Fr. *méthode des modifications minima* (Rouvier), or *des différences à peine perceptible*; Ital. *metodo delle variazioni minime* (Villa). See PSYCHOPHYSICAL METHODS.

It is recommended that the word 'noticeable' be retained in preference to 'perceptible' and 'distinguishable' (or the use of the phrase 'judgments of difference'), as being free from theoretical implications. (J.M.B.)

Difference Tone : Ger. *Differenzton* ; Fr. *son différentiel* ; Ital. *suono di differenza, fenomeno del Tartini.* The difference tone, or Tartini's tone, is the stronger of the two COMBINATION TONES (q. v.). It is usually defined as a tone whose vibration rate corresponds to the difference between the vibration rates of the primaries (Helmholtz, *Sensations of Tone*, 153). The work of König makes it probable that there are two difference tones : the one of the vibration rate $b-a$ (where a is the vibration rate of the lower, and b that of the higher generator), and the other of the vibration rate $2a-b$ (König, *Quelques Expériences d'Acoustique*, ix, x, 1882); and that the one or other of these is audible, according to conditions (Ebbinghaus, *Psychologie*, 308).

It is producible: (1) by two tones ; (2) by fundamental with overtone ; (3) by overtone with overtone ; (4) by tone and difference tone, &c. The difference tones from (4) onwards are difference tones of the second, third, &c., order. See BEAT TONES.

Literature : WUNDT, Physiol. Psychol. (4th ed.), i. 464 ; HELMHOLTZ, Sensations of Tone, 152 ; MEYER, Criticism of Current Theories and New Facts, Zeitsch. f. Psychol., xi. 177, xvi. 1 ; STUMPF, Tonpsychologie, ii. 229, 243 ff. ; citations under SUMMATION TONE and BEAT TONE. (E.B.T.)

Differential: see CALCULUS.

Differentiation: see DIFFERENCE.

Differentiation (in biology) [Lat. *differentia*]: Ger. *Differenzierung* ; Fr. *différenciation* ; Ital. *differenziamento.* (1) The process by which the various parts of one cell acquire structural differences corresponding to a physiological division of labour. Seen more especially in the Protozoa. (2) The process by which the apparently similar, or undifferentiated, cells become different in structure and function. The latter is often spoken of as the physiological division of labour, and is necessarily accompanied by morphological differentiation. (3) The state reached by the above process, most strikingly exhibited in the development of the embryo into the adult organism. The differentiation of the tissues in ontogeny is termed histogenesis. For theories see EPIGENESIS, and PREFORMATION ; see also DETERMINANT. On nervous differentiation see NERVOUS SYSTEM (II).

Literature : F. M. BALFOUR, Compar. Embryol. ; OSCAR HERTWIG, Embryol. of Vertebrates (man and mammals), and The Cell (trans., 1895); KORSCHELT and HEIDER, Embryol. of Invertebrates ; MINOT, Embryology. (C.LL.M.—E.S.G.)

Differentiation (in mathematics): the principle of the differential CALCULUS (q. v.).

Dignitas : see MAXIM.

Dignity : see WORTH.

Dilemma [Gr. δίς, twice, + λῆμμα, something taken]: Ger. *Dilemma* ; Fr. *dilemme* ; Ital. *dilemma.* A composite form of conditional syllogism, sometimes called hypothetico-disjunctive, from combining the features of the hypothetical and the disjunctive syllogism ; it is best defined as a syllogism having a hypothetical major premise with more than one antecedent and a disjunctive minor.

The dilemma in the earliest forms was regarded more as a rhetorical device than as a distinct type of logical reasoning. In this sense the alternative conditions were generally taken as two—a positive and its negative—one of which must be true, and which therefore could be laid down as alternatives in the minor premise ; both entailed the same unpleasing consequent, which was then affirmed in the conclusion. The popular use of the word dilemma conforms to this first sense, but is reconcilable with the more elaborate analysis which has been given. There are considerable divergencies among modern writers as to the best mode of defining it (cf. Keynes, *Formal Logic*, Pt. III. chap. vi). (R.A.)

Dilemmatic : see PROPOSITION, and SYLLOGISM.

Dimaris : see DIBATIS.

Dimatis : see DIBATIS.

Dimension : see QUANTITY, and SPACE.

Diminishing (and **Increasing**) **Return :** Ger. *fallende Produktivität, abnehmender (und zunehmender) Gewinn* ; Fr. *loi de la culture, bénéfice diminuant (et croissant)* ; Ital. *produttività decrescente* or *profitto decrescente.* (1) The obvious fact in agricultural production that, when a certain point of cultivation has been reached, increased application of labour and capital per acre does not produce correspondingly increased crops. (2) Any phenomenon in the relations between cost and return which has, or is supposed to have, some resemblance to the one just noted.

A comparison of return with cost will take various forms, according as we take different senses of the word COST (q.v.). We may compare either (1) income with expense ; (2) utility with pain; or (3) production with waste.

If we spend more and more money in applying labour and capital to a given piece of land, we have at first an increasing return ;

then for a moment perhaps a constant return; and finally a diminishing return, as instanced in definition (1). The development of this principle is due to Turgot, Anderson, and Ricardo.

If we spend more and more minutes per day upon our work, we have up to a certain point increased efficiency, and increased surplus of pleasure over pain. Beyond that point, the utility of our consumption diminishes, and the pain of our labour increases; until finally a time comes when the added pleasure from what we can produce no longer balances the added pain of production. It is by an operation of this kind that the hours of labour are often determined. This analysis is due to Jevons. But it is not improbable that the actual determination of hours is based on waste rather than on pain. (A.T.H.)

Dimorphism [Gr. δίς + μορφή, shape]: Ger. *Dimorphismus*; Fr. *dimorphisme*; Ital. *dimorfismo*. The differentiation of the individuals of a species of animal or plant into two more or less divergent forms. (C.LL.M.)

The most familiar case is that of sexual dimorphism, where the males and females are divergent in form and character. In hymenopterous insects, such as ants and bees, the females are frequently dimorphic; the so-called queens being fully developed sexually, while the workers (so-called 'neuters') are imperfectly developed females—the whole insect in each case showing structural differentiation. In butterflies we find seasonal dimorphism. When there are more than two forms the term polymorphism is employed, as in many animal colonies (Siphonophora and other coelenterates) and groups.

Literature: AUGUST WEISMANN, Studies in the Doctrine of Descent (trans. by Meldola), and Germ-Plasm; E. B. POULTON, The Colours of Animals; E. HAECKEL, Natürliche Schöpfungsgeschichte (9th ed., 1898); D. SHARP, Insects, in Cambridge Nat. Hist.
(C.LL.M.—E.S.G.)

Ding an sich [Ger.]; Fr. *chose en soi*; Ital. *cosa in sè*. A Kantian phrase for 'thing-in-itself' or 'noumenal' thing—thing considered in opposition to the phenomenon or appearance by which it is manifested. See THING, and NOUMENON. (J.M.B.)

Dioecious [Gr. δίς + οἶκος, a house]: Ger. *zweihäusig*; Fr. *dioïque*; Ital. *dioico*. A term applied to those plants, and often extended to animals, in which the sexes are distinct; as opposed to monoecious, where male and female organs are found in the same indi-

vidual. The terms unisexual and hermaphrodite are more frequently used in zoology.

Linnaeus placed in his twenty-second class of Dioecia those plants which have the staminiferous and pistiliferous flowers on separate individuals. (C.LL.M.)

Diogenes. A Cynic philosopher, born in Asia Minor about 412 B.C. He was a pupil of Antisthenes, the founder of the Cynic school, and faithfully practised such tenets as 'that it is god-like to have no needs.' His heroic virtue and apathy to pleasures and pains have become world-famous. In his old age he is said to have been taken by pirates on a voyage to Aegina, where he was sold as a slave. Purchased by Xeniades, a Corinthian, he was first liberated and then hired as a tutor by his former master. Died at Corinth, 324.

Diogenes Laertius. A name connected with a fragmentary work entitled *Lives and Doctrines of Famous Philosophers*. Nothing is known of the author. But the work contains many biographies and stories, of more or less doubtful trustworthiness, together with many and valuable extracts. He probably lived in the 2nd century A. D.

Diogenes of Apollonia. A Greek philosopher, who lived in the 5th century B.C., and taught philosophy in Athens. Disciple of Anaximenes, he took air to be the first principle of things. See PRE-SOCRATIC PHILOSOPHY (Ionica).

Dion (or Dio) Chrysostomus. Born about 50 A.D. at Prusa, Bithynia. Greek philosopher and rhetorician. His surname (signifying 'golden mouth' or 'speech') was given him because of his eloquence. He shares to some extent the superficiality and insincerity of the Greek Renaissance, in which he lived.

Dionysius, Saint, called **The Great.** Born at Alexandria, latter part of 2nd century A.D.; died there 265. He was the assistant of Origen in the catechetical school in 233; bishop of Alexandria in 248; driven out of the city by persecution, 250; banished to Libya in 257; restored, 260. He was the most distinguished convert and pupil of Origen's school.

Diopter: see DIOPTRICS.

Dioptrics [Gr. διοπτρικός, pertaining to the use of the διόπτρα]: Ger. *Dioptrik*; Fr. *dioptrique*; Ital. *diottrica*. That part of the science of optics which treats of the refraction of light; opposed to Catoptrics. See VISION (light).

Diopter: the power of a lens with a focal distance of 1 m., the unit of measurement of lenses. For convex lenses it is written $+D$; for concave, $-D$ (Helmholtz, *Physiol. Optik*, 2nd ed., 122). A lens of n diopters is one that has a focal distance of $\frac{1}{n}$ metres.

(E.B.T.–C.L.F.)

Literature: HELMHOLTZ, Physiol. Optik (2nd ed.), 53 ff.; FICK, in Hermann's Handb. d. Physiol., iii. 1 ff.; AUBERT, Physiol. Optik, 393 ff. See KÖNIG's Bibliography in Helmholtz's Physiol. Optik, 2nd ed. (E.B.T.)

Diplogenesis [Gr. διπλόος, twofold, + γένεσις, production]: Ger. (not in use); Fr. *diplogenèse* (rare); Ital. *diplogenesi*. An hypothesis according to which any influence which modifies the bodily tissues impresses on the germ-plasm of the individual a similar change, which is thus transmitted to offspring and rendered hereditary. The term was proposed by Cope in 1890 (see *The Primary Factors of Organic Evolution*, 1896). (C.Ll.M.)

Diplopia [Gr. διπλόος, double, + ὤψ, eye]: Ger. *Doppelsehen*; Fr. *diplopie*; Ital. *diplopia*. Double vision; the condition in which an object is seen by one eye, or more usually by the two eyes, as two objects, and not as a single one. Monocular diplopia may be due to an imperfection of the media of the eye, or to retinal disease, resulting in dispersion of the rays of light; it can readily be produced artificially by holding a prism so that part of the rays reach the retina directly, and the others indirectly, through refraction.

The important forms of diplopia are binocular, which may be regarded as normal or physiological when it is experimentally produced by observing an object beyond or within the distance for which the eyes are converged, or by displacement of one eye, &c.; and it is pathological when due to a disturbance of the normal balance between muscles, by reason of paralysis or other cause. Such diplopia may be crossed (heteronymous), or direct (homonymous). As the image of the object seen falls in the fovea of the sound eye, it is distinctly seen by this eye; but as it falls in a peripheric region of the affected eye, it is there more or less indistinctly perceived. The former is called the true, the latter the false image. If the false image is on the same side of the true image as the affected eye is of the sound eye, the diplopia is homonymous; if on the other side, heteronymous. Either of these may be complicated by vertical diplopia, in which one image appears above or below the other, or the vertical diplopia may exist alone. According to the particular muscles affected, the diplopia assumes a special character, for the details of which consult the literature given below. It may be further noted that diplopia when slight may remain undetected, and the distinct image alone be attended to; and that false projection of objects in space may result from diplopia. See VISION (defects of).

Literature: GOWERS, Diseases of the Nervous Syst., ii. 169–80; NOYES, Diseases of the Eye, 140–3; PARINAUD, La Vision (1899); NORRIS and OLIVER, Syst. of Diseases of the Eye, iv. 3–167; BERRY, Diseases of the Eye (1893), 587. (J.J.)

Dipsomania [Gr. δίψα, thirst, + μανία, madness]: Ger. *Dipsomanie*; Fr. *dipsomanie*; Ital. *dipsomania, alcoolofilia* (E.M.). An uncontrollable craving for alcoholic liquors, together with the abnormal mental symptoms which result from alcoholic excess. See ALCOHOLISM. (J.J.)

Direct and **Indirect**: see PREDICATION, PROOF, and INDIRECT VISION.

Direction [Lat. *dirigere*, to make straight]: Ger. *Richtung*; Fr. *direction*; Ital. *direzione*. That property of space whereby right lines from a common point of origin are differentiated from one another; applied figuratively also to other continua. (J.M.B.)

Direction (sense of). The more or less perfect and immediate localization of the regions of the external world with reference to oneself.

It is a special case of ORIENTATION (q.v.), the word 'sense' being used to cover that direct apprehension of direction which approaches the immediate character of a sensation. Its most marked development is in certain animals, e.g. homing pigeons, domestic dogs, &c., which are supposed to have such a sense, acting independently of the other senses. It is, however, becoming more widely the opinion that in these cases the animals follow either certain indications of sight, &c., or act reflexly upon organic stimulations such as temperature, humidity, and movements of air, as is the case with the migrating instinct in birds. Before adopting any general view, the actual performances of animals, under each type, should be treated statistically, with calculations of the number of failures or trials with error, with which the successes may be compared. With man, judgment of direction seems to be largely a matter of education and experience, resting, however, like all other functions, upon individual differences in aptness to learn. This would seem to be supported by the cases in which, as with the present writer, the ordinates of direction, lettered as points of the compass, are fixed by long custom at one's birthplace, and remain as a sort of mental scheme to impose themselves upon every new environment.

Literature: see the citations under ORIENTATION, and many of those given under INSTINCT; H. E. ZIEGLER, Zoolog. Jahrbücher, x. (1897) 254. (J.M.B.)

Direction (in optics): see LINE OF DIRECTION.

Disagreeableness: see PLEASANTNESS AND UNPLEASANTNESS.

Disamis: see MOOD (in logic).

Disbelief: see BELIEF.

Discernment [Lat. *discernere*, to separate]: Ger. *Merken*; Fr. *discernement*; Ital. *discernimento*. Separate attention to a part of some kind of whole, simultaneous or successive, involving an elementary judgment of difference between the part singled out and the whole to which it belongs.

Discernment as here defined implies distinction of an object from its total context in experience, but not from another special object which is also singled out in like manner. See DISCRIMINATION.

Literature: CLAY, The Alternative, A Study in Psychology, 21. (G.F.S.–J.M.B.)

Discipline (in education) [Lat. *disciplina*]: Ger. (1) *Erziehung*, (2, 3) *Disciplin*; Fr. *discipline*; Ital. *disciplina*. (1) Primarily, and in the large sense, systematic training through education. (2) Secondarily, and in the restricted sense, the maintenance of authority by means of rewards and punishments. (3) A particular branch of study. See FORMAL CULTURE. (C.DE G.)

Discontinuity (in biology). The view held by those who deny CONTINUITY (in biology) in any one of the four meanings enumerated under that topic. (J.M.B.)

Discontinuity (in logic): see MULTITUDE.

Discord [Lat. *dis*, apart, + *cor*, heart]: Ger. *Missklang*, *Dissonanz*; Fr. *dissonance*; Ital. *dissonanza*. See CHORD. (E.B.T.)

Discount [OF. *disconter*; Lat. *dis*, away, + *computare*, to count]: Ger. *Disconto*; Fr. *escompte*; Ital. *sconto*. The difference in value between the right to receive a thing at once and the right to receive it at some future time.

The difference between discount and interest is one of form rather than of substance. If A buys of B for $95 the right to receive $100 a year hence, the transaction takes the shape of a discount. If A loans B $95 with the provision that he shall receive at the end of the year $5 more than the original $95, the transaction takes the form of an investment with interest. But the legal and economic relations of the parties are exactly the same in the two cases. The ethical and philosophical questions involved in the transaction are discussed under INTEREST. (A.T.H.)

Discourse: an older term for the DISCURSIVE (q.v.) process. See also UNIVERSE (in logic). (J.M.B.)

Discovery [Lat. *dis* + *cooperire*]: Ger. *Entdeckung*; Fr. *découverte*; Ital. *scoperta*. The process (or result of the process) of attaining to a new truth, a fact or relation of facts not forming part of already established knowledge.

The term has a twofold implication: (1) of an ideal antecedent, a suggestion, preconception, or hypothesis; (2) of the establishment of the ideal antecedent as objectively true. Discovery is therefore most intimately connected with proof. It is often contrasted with INVENTION (q.v.).

Literature: WHEWELL, Philos. of Discovery (1860); G. GORE, Art of Scientific Discovery (1878). (R.A.)

Discrepancy: see HARMONY, and INCONSISTENCY (in logic).

Discrete [Lat. *discretus*, separate]: Ger. *discret*; Fr. *discret*; Ital. *discreto*. (1) Discontinuous (see CONTINUITY, and CONTINUUM).

(2) In logic: specifically but not generically different. Discrete notions are those which are co-ordinated under a more general notion. (J.M.B.)

Discrimination [Lat. *discrimen*, that which separates]: Ger. *Unterscheidung*, *Distinction*; Fr. *discrimination*, *distinction*; Ital. *distinzione*, *discriminazione* (Buccola). (1) A judgment of difference between two or more objects, each of which is discerned from the total context of experience at the time.

(2) Used for Consciousness of DIFFERENCE (q.v.) in cases of successive sensation, especially under experimental conditions, the full expression being SENSE DISCRIMINATION (q.v.). (G.F.S.–J.M.B.)

As between Discrimination (1) and Distinction, for which the foreign terms are common, there seems to be a subtle variation in the character of the judgment involved. Distinction has become a logical term, to indicate a more formal and verbal judgment of difference, in extreme instances resting on verbal identity, logical consistency, &c.—'a distinction without a difference'—while judgment of discrimination has a more real or material reference, and with it a certain psychological appreciation. For example, it is more appropriate to say that I make a distinction between these two terms, than that I discriminate between them. The scholastics worked out many refinements in their *distinctio essentialis, realis, formalis quidditatis,* &c., for which special histories should be consulted. (J.M.B.)

Discursive [Lat. *discurrere,* to run about]: Ger. *discursiv*; Fr. (*pensée*) *discursive*; Ital. (*facoltà*) *discorsiva*. Pertaining to the reasoning or logical function of the mind.

Discursive process is one which attains a result through a series of distinct steps, each logically depending on those which precede. It is used in opposition to INTUITIVE (q. v.), as applicable to knowledge which is not immediately apprehended. The discursive faculty is an early designation of the reasoning function. Hamilton speaks of the elaborative or discursive faculty (*Metaphysics,* Lect. xx. v). Cf. Kant, *Pure Reason,* trans. Micklejohn, 43. Ward uses the word intellection somewhat in this sense (*Encyc. Brit.,* art. Psychology). Cf. INTELLECT. (J.M.B.–G.F.S.)

Disease [Ital. *disagio,* trouble]: Ger. *Krankheit*; Fr. *maladie*; Ital. *malattia.* While disease refers to any morbid deviation from normal health—a disease of mind or body—it refers specifically to a group of morbid conditions which affect the same part of the body and exhibit similar symptoms, such as a disease of the lungs, a disease of the brain, Bright's disease, a disease of the will.

An important distinction is drawn between organic or structural diseases, in which there is a lesion or pathological condition of some part of the body; and functional diseases, in which there is an irregular action of a part, but without any organic abnormality. Any malformation of a part of the body, or lack or excess of development, would form the basis of organic disease; while interferences with the circulation or digestion or the nervous processes would form the basis of a functional disease. Diseases are further considered as to their course, their classification, their symptoms, their diagnosis, their usual course or duration, their prognosis, and their treatment. These aspects are equally of importance in nervous and mental as in bodily diseases, and are in the main of medical rather than psychological interest. Illustrations of one or

more of these terms in connection with mental diseases is given in the topics SANITY AND INSANITY, and SPEECH (defects of). The general scope of mental diseases is indicated in the topic MENTAL PATHOLOGY; see also ABNORMAL PSYCHOLOGY. (J.J.)

The great progress of mental pathology of to-day has been just that it has established distinct inherent diseases which have their regular evolution and their distinct existence. The great alienists of the past—Pinel, Esquirol, &c.—dealt mainly with symptoms. (L.M.)

Disharmony [Lat. *dis* + Gr. ἁρμονία]: Ger. *Disharmonie*; Fr. *désharmonie*; Ital. *disarmonia.* See HARMONY. (E.B.T.)

Disintegration [Lat. *dis* + *integer,* whole]: Ger. *Desintegration*; Fr. *désintégration*; Ital. *disintegrazione.* (1) A general word for all sorts of decay, decomposition, demoralization, the thought being that of a positive decline from a previous state to relative organization. (2) Spencer's use: see INTEGRATION AND DISINTEGRATION. (J.M.B.)

Disinterested Action: Ger. *uneigennützige Handlung*; Fr. *action désintéressée*; Ital. *azione disinteressata.* Action which is not determined by a view to personal pleasure or private interest.

The question concerning the nature and reality of disinterested action dominated the controversies of the English moralists. The discussion was started by Hobbes, who held that self-preservation, and the desire of power as a means to self-preservation, were the source of all human 'passions' or tendencies to action. The controversy centred round the 'disinterestedness' of benevolence, which Hobbes explained as due to desire of power, and Mandeville afterwards declared to be simply self-love in disguise. The chief opponents of Hobbes' view were Shaftesbury, Hutcheson, and Butler. Butler contended that 'disinterestedness' belonged not to benevolence only, but to all the primary impulses or 'particular passions'; these, he held, tend directly to an object, and not to the (personal or 'interested') pleasure of enjoying the object. This view was also adopted by Hume. Cf. ALTRUISM, BENEVOLENCE.

Literature: HOBBES, Elements of Law; BUTLER, Sermons; MANDEVILLE, Fable of the Bees; HUME, Princ. of Morals, App. ii. (W.R.S.)

Disjunct and **Conjunct:** see MODALITY.

Disjunct Species: see SPECIES (in logic).

Disjunction: see DISJUNCTIVE.

Disjunctive [Lat. *dis+iungere*, to join]: Ger. *disjunctiv*; Fr. *disjonctif*; Ital. *disgiuntivo*. Disjunction, taken generally, is the name for the relation obtaining among the co-ordinate species of a genus; a disjunctive judgment, therefore, is one in which the assertion made is of such a relation. The relation may affect either the predicate (*S* is either *P* or *Q*) or the subject (either *X* or *Y* is *Q*), or a number of propositions (either *A* is true or *B* is true). The second type is either disjunctive in verbal expression only, or does not require to be distinguished from the third. The essential feature of the judgment is the presence of an expressed alternative. Probably it is desirable to recognize in the disjunctive, as in other types of assertion, a gradation from propositions which are highly concrete, of a kind often called divisive, to propositions of a highly abstract character. A disjunctive syllogism is generally defined as one in which the major is a disjunctive proposition and the minor a categorical proposition, restricting the indeterminateness of the alternation stated in the major.

Disjunctive judgments and syllogisms seem first to have been recognized by the peripatetic followers of Aristotle, who regarded them as forms of conditional argument. From the mere formal or grammatical point of view they were handled by the Stoic logicians, who tended towards placing them on a level with the hypothetical syllogism as a distinct genus. In modern logic, discussions regarding the disjunctive have concerned three points mainly: (1) whether and in what sense the disjunctive involves a special and independent general principle, e.g. as Kant maintained, the law of excluded middle; (2) whether the disjunctive assertion shall be interpreted as implying the exclusive character of the alternants stated; (3) how the disjunctive stands related to the conception of the contents of knowledge as a systematic whole.

Literature: PRANTL, Gesch. d. Logik, i. 386 ff., 446 ff.; KANT, Logik, §§ 27–9, 77–8; HAMILTON, Logic, i. 326 ff., ii. 369 ff.; KEYNES, Formal Logic, Pt. II. chap. ix, Pt. III. chap. vi; BRADLEY, Princ. of Logic, Bk. I. chap. iv; LOTZE, Logik, §§ 69, 71–4; BOSANQUET, Logic, Bk. I. chap. viii; LANGE, Logische Stud., chap. v. (R.A.)

Disorder (moral) [Lat. *dis+ordo*, order]: Ger. *Immoralität, moralische Verdorbenheit*; Fr. *désordre moral*; Ital. *disordine morale*. The state of man as possessing impulses to conduct inconsistent with morality.

The technical use of this term is mainly restricted to theologians, who regard this moral disorder as the effect of the Fall. The Fall, they hold, has made all mankind subject to evil, and (according to Calvinistic theologians) of themselves altogether incapable of any good. In this view the moral disorder amounts to total depravity. Goodness comes only from the supernatural grace of God; even the natural virtues (or what are called virtues) displayed by the spiritually unregenerate are not recognized as exceptions to this doctrine of total depravity.

The presence of moral disorder (in the sense of tendencies to evil) in human nature is a fact of universal experience. But the theory of the fact above given is only rendered necessary by the assumption that man was originally created perfect, and thereafter lost all power of well-doing. A history of human development has to show both how anti-moral tendencies have arisen and persisted, and also the gradual process of moralization. Cf. MORAL ORDER. (W.R.S.)

Disparate [Lat. *dis + par*, equal]: Ger. *disparat, verschiedenartig*; Fr. *disparate, (sensations ou notions) hétérogènes* (L.M.); Ital. *disparato*. 'Qualitatively distinct, as sensations of the different senses' (Herbart).

Wundt (*Physiol. Psychol.*, 4th ed., i. 286) gives as criterion of disparate (or verschiedenartige) sensations the lack of intermediate stages or of continuous transition from one to the other, which occurs only in sensations of different senses; they are opposed to qualitatively similar (gleichartige) sensations, between which such a continuous transition is possible by variations in the stimulus (cf. Külpe, *Outlines of Psychol.*, 278).

Disparate retinal points are points that are not 'identical.' See CORRESPONDING POINTS, and IDENTICAL POINTS. Cf. Wundt, *Physiol. Psychol.* (4th ed.), ii. 174. (J.M.B.–E.B.T.)

Disparate (in logic). A term applied to notions which do not fall within the sphere of any common notion (except of great generality), which have therefore no common elements of comprehension, though capable, at the same time, of having portions of their spheres common.

There has never been a fixed doctrine regarding the term disparate or its use. Cicero defines disparate as 'quod ab aliqua re per oppositionem negationis separatur, ut sapere, non sapere.' Boethius (cf. Prantl, *Gesch. d. Logik*, i. 686) begins the more modern tendency by defining 'disparata, quae tantum a se diversa sunt nulla contrarietate pugnantia.' The Aristotelian tradition is represented by Burgersdyk's definition, 'disparata sunt, quorum unum pluribus opponitur, eodem modo' (*Inst. Log.*, i. 95; cf. Prantl, *Gesch. d. Logik*, iv. 52, 133). The definition here given corresponds to Leibnitz' treatment (*Nouv. Essais*, iv. 2, § 1), from whom it has found its way into the modern logics.

Literature: HAMILTON, Logic, i. 209–24; UEBERWEG, Logic, § 53; BRADLEY, in Mind, N.S., iv. (R.A.)

Disparity (logical): see DISPARATE (in logic).

Dispensation [Lat. *dis* + *pensare*, to ponder, requite]: Ger. *Dispensation, Erlassung*; Fr. *dispensation, dispense*; Ital. *dispensa*. Employed, in connection with religion, in two distinct senses: (1) An *ethos* or generally diffused set of ethico-religious circumstances under which humanity, or a portion of it, is said to live; e.g. the Mosaic dispensation—ruled by the law; the 'gospel' dispensation—ruled by GRACE (q. v.).

(2) After the Church had evolved its organization, a member who broke its rules or customs could be restored to fellowship only by repenting and penance. The latter became so severe in the course of time, that it could not well be enforced in all cases. The relaxation allowed by the Church is called a dispensation. It is now applied to any departure from established law or custom of the ecclesiastical organization, duly permitted by the recognized authorities. Theoretically, dispensation can be granted only in affairs relating to law recognized as 'human' by the Church. (R.M.W.)

Dispersal [Lat. *dispersus*, scattered]: Ger. *Verbreitung, Ausbreitung*; Fr. *dissémination*; Ital. *disseminazione*. The means by which the seeds, eggs, or embryos of sedentary plants or animals are distributed over a more or less wide area.

Dispersal forms an interesting and important subject of study in botany. It is effected by the wind, by water currents, and by animals. In many cases the seeds are provided with secondary structures, flattened expansions, plumes, hooks, spines, &c., by which dispersal may be furthered. In animals (such as molluscs and coelenterates) dispersal is generally effected by currents. In some river forms means are provided to check dispersal, which would entail the sweeping of the young out to sea. In some Protozoa the spores are dispersed by the wind.

Literature: CH. DARWIN, Origin of Species (1859); A. R. WALLACE, Island Life (1880); A. KERNER, Nat. Hist. of Plants; W. J. SOLLAS, On the Origin of Fresh-water Faunas, Trans. Roy. Soc. Dublin, ii, iii (1884). (C.LL.M.–E.S.G.)

Dispersion Circle: see PHYSIOLOGICAL DISPERSION CIRCLE.

Disposition [Lat. *disponere*, to dispose]: Ger. *Disposition*; Fr. *disposition*; Ital. *disposizione*. (1) An effect of previous mental process, or an element of original endowment, capable of entering as a co-operative factor into subsequent mental process. (2) A PREDISPOSITION (q. v.). Sense (1) is recommended. (G.F.S.–J.M.B.)

(3) Hering uses the term for the after-effect of general ADAPTATION (visual). (E.B.T.)

The term is applied both to consciousness and to nervous action (see the next topic). Dispositions are both congenital (as impulse or native tendency = PREDISPOSITION) and acquired (acquired tendency). In recent discussion (Lipps, Stout, Höfler, &c.) disposition has this broad meaning, while Einstellung applies to acquired tendencies, as in the 'setting' of the attention (Külpe, *Outlines of Psychol.*, § 74, 4). On the mental side, the characteristic thing about disposition is its preparatory influence in the determination of subsequent states of mind. It represents impulse or habit under arrest. Considered with reference to the event towards which its determining influence is directed, it enters into expectation. In psychophysical experiments it shows itself in so-called ANTICIPATION (q.v.). The typical rise and gradual growth of an acquired disposition is a function of accommodation through a series of exercises. HABITUATION (q.v.) is applied to this process—a translation of the German Einübung.

Literature: LIPPS, Grundthatsachen des Seelenlebens; STOUT, Analytic Psychol., i, and Manual of Psychol.; HÖFLER, Psychologie; WITASEK, Arch. f. sys. Philos., III, 1897, 273. (J.M.B.–G.F.S.)

Disposition (nervous). The tendency of a nervous centre, system, or element to function in a particular manner, either from native endowment or from previous functioning.

German physiologists use the word Bahnung, which includes the actual canalization (Waller) or anatomical path-making which results from continued nervous discharges in the same direction. Disposition has functional reference, and the English term FACILITATION (q.v.) has been suggested for Bahnung. (J.M.B., G.F.S.)

According to Wundt, this functional disposition constitutes the physiological basis of ideational association (*Physiol. Psychol.*, 4th ed., ii. 473), and therefore of retention. Inherited dispositions (see PREDISPOSITION) are the basis of instinctive actions.   (E.B.T.)

Disputation: see OBLIGATIONS (in logic).

Dissent: see OBJECTION; and cf. ASSENT, and CONSENT.

Dissimilar (and **-ity**): see RESEMBLANCE AND SIMILARITY, WHOLE (logical).

Dissociation [Lat. *dis* + *socius*, a companion]: Ger. *Dissoziation*; Fr. *dissociation*; Ital. *dissociazione*. The process by which we come to discriminate within a whole components which have not been discriminated in previous experiences of this whole.   (G.F.S., J.M.B.)

Dissociation (law of). When *a* and *b* have occurred together as parts of the same total object, without being discriminated, the occurrence of one of them, *a*, in a new combination, *ax*, favours the discrimination of *a*, *b*, and *x* from each other. 'What is associated now with one thing and now with another, tends to become dissociated from either, and to grow into an object of abstract contemplation by the mind. One might call this the law of "dissociation by varying concomitants"' (James, *Princ. of Psychol.*, i. 506). See also Stumpf, *Ueber den psychologischen Ursprung der Raumvorstellung*, 130–4 (*Unterschieden wird nur, was getrennt wahrgenommen worden ist*, 132).   (G.F.S., J.M.B.)

Dissociation (and **Disaggregation**, pathological): Ger. *Dissoziation* (*Auflösung*); Fr. *dissociation* (*désagrégation*); Ital. *dissociazione* (*disgregazione*). In general, dissociation refers to the converse of the processes of evolution or building up of functions of which life so largely consists.

Dissolution or degeneration exhibits the breaking down of more highly developed structures into simpler ones, the retrogression from a more highly complex and elaborate stage to a less developed one. Dissociation more specifically refers to special forms of mental abnormality of the type thus outlined.

Such abnormalities may be very slight in character, representing merely the momentary lapse of the most completely developed functions of the mind. When more grave they are frequently termed Disaggregation. In connection with the study of ATTENTION (q.v.), of HALLUCINATIONS (q.v.) and ILLUSIONS (q.v.), of disorders of PERSONALITY (q.v.), and of CONSCIOUSNESS (q.v.), states of dissociation and disaggregation are constantly met with. The main trend of conscious thought is apparently disintegrated, and a portion of the stream is dissociated from the rest; so that the subject, while in his normal state, is unaware of what has taken place in the abnormal or dissociated state; and in turn in the latter state seems but dimly conscious of his surroundings and his normal personality. From the momentary interruption of collected thought, known as abstraction or reverie, to actual hallucinations; from somnambulism and artificially induced states of hypnosis to hysteria and mania, the rôle of dissociation may be clearly recognized. What the nature of the process in the central nervous system may be, which brings about these changes, has been the subject of theoretical interpretation, which may be profitably considered in connection with the doctrine of personality and of hallucinations.

Literature: titles cited under the topics referred to above, especially the works of JAMES, PIERRE JANET, BINET, RIBOT; also PARISH, Hallucinations and Illusions (1897).   (J.J.)

Dissonance [Lat. *dis* + *sonare*, to sound]: Ger. *Dissonanz*; Fr. *dissonance*; Ital. *dissonanza*. See CONSONANCE.   (E.B.T.)

Distance: see EXTENSION, and SPACE.

Distance (visual perception of): see DEPTH.

Distinct and **Distinctness**: see CLEAR AND DISTINCT.

Distinct Term: see QUANTITY (logical).

Distinction: see DISCRIMINATION.

Distinguish: see DISCRIMINATION.

Distraction [Lat. *dis* + *tractus*, drawn]: Ger. *Zerstreutheit*; Fr. *distraction*; Ital. *distrazione*. (1) A state of distraction exists when a plurality of disconnected objects tend simultaneously to occupy attention, so that it cannot be effectively exercised upon any one of them. See ATTENTION (and defects of).   (G.F.S.—J.M.B.)

(2) Pathological. There are several irreducible cases: (*a*) from ABSENT-MINDEDNESS (q.v.), from excessive concentration or preoccupation, possibly delusional; (*b*) from incapacity to concentrate steadily; (*c*) from too few or too many excitations badly systematized or in conflict among themselves. See Pierre Janet, *Automatisme psychologique* (1889), and *État mental des Hystériques* (1893).   (L.M.)

Distraction of Attention (experimental): Ger. *Ablenkung der Aufmerksamkeit*; Fr. *distraction de l'attention*; Ital. *distrazione dell' attenzione*. A state of inattention artificially produced by positive stimulation of the attention to something else.   (J.M.B.)

The state of inattention may be induced most easily by the supervention of a distracting stimulus upon an already existent state of attention. It is theoretically important that the state of inattention should be examined, since we wish to know what are the attributes of the simple processes given in that state, and what results the measurement of sensibility and sense discrimination yields during inattention as compared with the results gained during attention. The problem is, however, still very far from solution. It seems that only the error methods can be employed (see PSYCHOPHYSICAL METHODS), that the distraction must be continuous and must have a strong affective tone, and that scents fulfil the required conditions better than any other form of distracting stimulus hitherto tried. (E.B.T.)

In this article (and others) the terms 'sensibility' and 'sense discrimination' are substituted for SENSITIVITY (q. v.) and SENSIBLE DISCRIMINATION (q. v.) used by the writer. (J.M.B.)

Literature: BERTELS, Diss. (Dorpat, 1889); Papers in the Amer. J. of Psychol., by DANIELS, HAMLIN, MOYER, BIRCH, DARLINGTON, &c.; MÜNSTERBERG, Psychol. Rev., i; BINET, Rev. Philos., xxix. 138, xxx. 136; DE SANCTIS, Patol. dell' attenzione (1898). (E.B.T.)

Distribution (in biology) [Lat. *distribuere*]: Ger. *Verbreitung, Verteilung*; Fr. *distribution géographique*; Ital. *distribuzione, bio-corologia*. That branch of biology which deals with the distribution of animals or plants in space (chorology) and in time (chronology). In 1857 Sclater established six great zoological regions.

Literature: DE CANDOLLE, Géographie botanique (1855); ORTMANN, Marinengeographie; the works of SCLATER (1857 and 1899), A. MURRAY (1866), A. R. WALLACE (1876–80), A. HEILPRIN (1887), and F. E. BEDDARD (1897), on the Distribution of Animals; BAKER, Elementary Lessons in Botanical Geography (for the Distribution of Plants). (C.LL.M.–E.S.G.)

Distribution (in economics): Ger. *Distribution*; Fr. *distribution*; Ital. *distribuzione*. The economic process by which the shares of the product which go to labour, capital, natural agents, &c., are determined.

The analysis of price into rent, wages, and profits is very old, and is fully developed in Smith's *Wealth of Nations*. Ricardo showed the existence of certain peculiarities in regard to rent, and anticipated the form of modern analysis on this subject. J. B. Say (1803) made distribution a 'department' of political economy, co-ordinate with production and consumption. Most English writers have made a fourth department—exchange.

According to the theory currently held, of which Marshall is the acknowledged exponent, there is in each year a net income or 'national dividend,' which is divided into component parts by economic laws, and which is capable of statical analysis. According to another theory, first developed by Newcomb, that which is distributed is essentially a flow rather than a quantity, and the attempt to analyse it by static methods involves great danger of fallacy.

Literature: MARSHALL, Princ. of Econ., i. (A.T.H.)

Distribution (in logic): Ger. *Vertheilung, Distribution*; Fr. *distribution*; Ital. *distribuzione*. The abstract name distribution now signifies in logic the state of a term in a proposition, in regard to its quantity. A term is said to be distributed, when it is taken universally; to be undistributed, when it is taken particularly.

The modern sense of the word distribution seems first to have been fixed by Petrus Hispanus (see Prantl, *Gesch. d. Logik*, iii. 60 f.), who defines it as 'multiplicatio termini communis per signum universale facta, ut cum dicitur " omnis homo," iste terminus "homo" distribuitur,' and thus restricts the application to terms taken universally. The earlier usage, from Cicero onwards, regarded distribution as the process of considering the effect of the quantifying additions by which a term was made universal in application. (R.A.)

Distribution of Errors: see ERRORS, and cf. VARIATION (statistical treatment of).

Distributive Principle: see SYMBOLIC LOGIC.

Disutility [Lat. *dis* + *utilitas*]: Ger. *subjektive Kosten*; Fr. *perte d'utilité*; Ital. *inutilità* (rare—E.M.). The sum of the motives which tend to counterbalance the estimated utility of a line of conduct, and which, at the economic margin (see MARGINAL INCREMENT), are just equal to that utility.

The early writers on utility treated it as nearly synonymous with pleasure, and used pain as its antithesis. But utility can probably not be treated as equivalent to pleasure; and even if it could be, there is need of a word to express the counterbalancing motives more fully than pain does. For instance, in Jevons' *Theory of Political Economy*, we are led to infer that a man continues to work as long as the pleasure from the earnings is in excess of the pain involved; and that he stops at a point of indifference. But a number of other causes besides actual pain may lead him to stop; in other words, he may have an excess of pleasure in work at the stopping point. The pain *plus* these other motives—in case they can be logically superadded—constitutes the disutility; or, as Marshall calls it, 'discommodity.' (A.T.H.)

Diverse and **Diversity**: see RESEMBLANCE AND SIMILARITY, and cf. DIFFERENCE.

Divided Proposition, &c. (in logic): see MODALITY.

Divination: see MAGIC.

Divine Government: see GOVERNMENT (divine).

Divine Right: Ger. *göttliches Recht*; Fr. *droit divin*; Ital. *diritto divino*. Right conferred by God. The phrase is chiefly used to express the theory that kings hold their authority, not from the choice or consent of their subjects, but from God himself.

It has been the policy of nearly all rulers to represent their office as sacred: 'There's such divinity doth hedge a king' (*Hamlet*, iv. 5); hence their frequent alliance with religion. But the idea of divine right came most to the front in England in the 17th century, during the disputes of the Stuarts with the people. At the Restoration, 1660, it was the accepted Royalist doctrine. Sir Robert Filmer (in various writings from 1648 to 1680) based it on the patriarchal authority of Adam as father of the human family. His conclusion was that constitutional liberties were not rights of the people, but gracious concessions of the king. Filmer was answered by Algernon Sidney and Locke, the latter as champion of the Revolution of 1688. By 1760 the Tory doctrine had passed into an acquiescence in a *de facto* government. The older doctrine had an ephemeral revival at the time of the Holy Alliance, 1814, and it seems to be held by the present emperor of Germany. Cf. ABSOLUTISM, PASSIVE OBEDIENCE, MONARCHY. (J.B.)

Divine Type: Ger. *göttlicher Typus*; Fr. *type divin*; Ital. *tipo divino*. A quality or character of material things, which is regarded as expressing the divine character.

While the general thought is that of symbolism (see SYMBOL), it has been elaborated in detail by Ruskin (*Mod. Painters*, ii), by whom infinity is treated as the type of divine incomprehensibleness; repose as that of divine permanence; symmetry, of divine justice &c. (J.H.T.)

Divinity: see GOD.

Divisibility [Lat. *divisus*, from *dividere* to divide]: Ger. *Theilbarkeit*; Fr. *divisibilité*; Ital. *divisibilità*. The property according to which any quantity or whole is resolvable into parts, which remain parts of this whole.

The differentiae of the concept of divisibility consist (1) in actual resolution, not mere distinction, of parts. Many cases of QUANTITY (q. v.) admit, as quantities, of distinction of parts, while they cannot be resolved into these parts: such is a biological organism. (2) in resolution into parts which retain their quantitative relation to the whole. Chemical analysis, for example, does not illustrate divisibility—except on the purely quantitative theory of atomic weights. So a mental whole or object is not divisible. Indivisibility is usually used not to cover all cases to which divisibility does not apply, but only cases of minimum, including infinitely small, quantities. Cf. the cross-references made under ATOM (various topics).

The problem of the divisibility of matter early arose to plague philosophers: cf. MONAD. That of finite and infinite divisibility constitutes one of the antinomies (cosmological) of Kant (*Critique of Pure Reason*, in loc.).

Literature: see the extensive citations given by EISLER, Wörterb. d. philos. Begriffe, 'Teilbarkeit.' (J.M.B.)

Division (logical) [Lat. *dividere*, to divide]: Ger. *Eintheilung*; Fr. *division*; Ital. *divisione*. The resolution of a genus into its constituent species, or the analysis of the extent of a general notion.

So defined, the process of division finds its theoretical lower limit at classes not presenting features, variation in which determines classes of less extent. Such classes were called *infima species*; they were the indivisibles or *atoms* in the Aristotelian scheme, and were regarded as natural kinds, types fixed in nature. In a less objective way the Aristotelian logic defines the superior limit, or *summa genera*—classes of widest extent, in which therefore the determining marks are at a minimum. The process implies the rules: that the constituent species or dividing members in each division shall be determined by variation in respect to one and the same feature of the generic marks, called the *fundamentum divisionis*; that the constituent species shall exclude one another; that the species shall exhaust the genus or divided whole. In a continuous series of divisions and subdivisions, it is also advisable to secure that the successive *fundamenta divisionis* selected should stand in a regularly descending scale of specification, *ne fiat divisio per saltum.* Cf. GENUS (in logic). (R.A.)

Division of Labour: Ger. *Arbeitstheilung*; Fr. *division du travail*; Ital. *divisione del lavoro.* The system under which different individuals, instead of labouring to supply each his own wants, specialize their production, and rely on the products of others for a large part of their consumption.

The system is described by Greek writers (Xenophon and Aristotle), and its workings were elucidated by Beccaria and Turgot. The name, 'division of labour,' is due to Adam Smith. Wakefield, Mill, and others have shown that division of labour is simply the most obvious among many forms of labour co-operation; and Wakefield went so far as to oppose the current use of the term as incorrect and misleading. In this last particular his ideas have not found acceptance. For the effects of division of labour see Smith, *Wealth of Nations*, Bk. I. chap. i. (A.T.H.)

Dizziness [AS. *dysig*, foolish, stupid]: Ger. *Schwindelgefühl, Drehschwindel*; Fr. *vertige*; Ital. *vertigine.* An organic sensation of whirling, lack of balance, and confusion primarily spacial. (J.M.B.)

It is set up by rotation of the body, sharp jerking of the head, the movement of a boat at sea, elevation above level ground, &c.; to which may be added organic or functional troubles of the auditory apparatus (*vertige de Ménière*). There is also dizziness from stomachic and toxic causes—from alcohol and poisons of many kinds. It is to be distinguished from the oesophageal sensation of nausea or sickness, which often accompanies it. Its seat is in doubt, but in some cases it is probably the ampullae of the semicircular canals.

The mode of origin of the sensation has been studied (1) by way of experiment upon deaf-mutes, controlled by autopsy, and (2) by rotation experiments made with the normal human subject. Vivisectional experiments upon birds and fishes (3) sustain the general conclusion that the canals constitute an organ for orientation, but furnish no evidence as to the presence or absence of sensation. See ORIENTATION, ILLUSIONS OF MOTION (2), and STATIC SENSE (also for *Literature*). (E.B.T.–L.M.)

Docetism [Gr. δοκεῖν, to imagine, appear]: Ger. *Doketismus*; Fr. *docétisme*; Ital. *Docetismo.* The doctrine of the Docetae—that during his earthly life Christ possessed a phenomenal or phantom body, not a real or natural one.

This 'heresy' was an early result of the many difficulties connected with the problem of two natures in a single personality. Christian apologists, like Clemens Alexandrinus, regarded the Docetae as a regularly constituted sect, founded by Julius Cassianus. The truth rather is that Docetism was an inevitable accompaniment of the peculiar speculations of the Manichaeans and Gnostics, the former taking a more extreme view than the latter, and extending their phenomenalism, not only to Christ's body, but practically to all occurrences connected with his life as a man (the crucifixion, resurrection, &c.). Some of the later mystics, like Boehme, have displayed Docetic leanings. Cf. GNOSTICISM, and MANICHAEISM. (R.M.W.)

Documentary Hypothesis: Ger. *Urevangeliumshypothese*; Fr. *hypothèse de l'évangile primitif*; Ital. *ipotesi documentaria.* A hypothesis regarding the composition of the books of the Bible out of which the HIGHER CRITICISM (q. v.) may be said to have sprung. It consisted essentially in the theory that discrepancies were to be reconciled by the recognition of a plurality of documents, and of an editor who used these documents. It was originated by Du Pin and Witsius, at the end of the 17th century, and reached its zenith with Eichhorn and his school in the last quarter of the 18th century.

Literature: DU PIN, A New Hist. of Eccles. Writers (Eng. trans.), 1 f.; WITSIUS, Misc. Sacra, 103 f.; LOWTH, Preliminary Diss. and Trans. of the Prophecies of Isaiah; EICHHORN, Einleit. ins Alt. Test.; and Urgeschichte (in Repertorium f. Biblische u. Morgenländische Litt.), iv, and espec. v. 187 f. (R.M.W.)

Dogma [Gr. δόγμα, a thing thought]: Ger. *Dogma*; Fr. *dogme*; Ital. *dogma.* (1) Any expression or embodiment of an opinion or belief; a teaching or doctrine explicitly stated. This is the primary sense of the term, and is relatively neutral as compared with other usages.

(2) A formula authorized by the official representatives, or by the finally decisive expounders, of the faith of the Christian Church, or of any branch of that church whose teaching may be in question, such formula being expressive of what this religious body not only holds to be the truth, but officially requires its followers to accept. In a similar sense, the term dogma may be used to name the explicit

or official teaching of any religious body whatever, whether Christian or not, although historical usage connects the word dogma most frequently with the Christian Church, as represented by the decisions and formulations of the General Councils, or of the popes, respecting the faith, and also, especially in more modern discussion, with the various formulated creeds of the bodies into which Christendom has come to be divided.

(3) An expression of a more or less fundamental and universal conviction, without any statement of the grounds for such conviction, or with an explicit refusal to attempt to give such grounds, or with an insufficient or uncritical statement of these reasons.

In this sense the term is often used as a term of reproach, and in polemic philosophical writing frequently implies that the teaching called a dogma is held by the opponent upon insufficient grounds. In this sense one speaks of a 'mere dogma.' In this sense too Kant regards earlier philosophy, and especially the Leibnitz-Wolffian philosophy, as dogmatism, and so calls it because of its failure to meet his own critical requirements. In order, however, to give this polemic sense of the term dogma a more precise formulation, Kant himself (*Krit. d. reinen Vernunft*, 2nd ed., 765) distinguishes dogmas from mathematical theorems, as well as from principles of the understanding, and proposes, as the technical definition of dogma, the following :—

(4) 'A direct synthetic proposition upon the basis of mere conceptions'; i. e. an assertion that, without the aid of mathematical construction, or of appeal to the general conditions which make our experience possible, asserts of a subject what is not involved in the mere definition of that subject.   (J.R.)

Philosophy is interested rather in the problem regarding the sources of dogma than in dogma itself. Historically, very varied views have been held on this question. Roman Catholics derive dogma from revelation as given in the Scriptures, and from tradition, that is, authority. Theoretically, the early Protestants quarried dogma from the Scriptures; but, practically, a great deal of Roman Catholic dogma passed into their schemes through the medium of the Christian consciousness as a whole. This latter fact began to become plain early in the 19th century, especially when the historico-genetic method was articulated. Hence, the question was consciously put: From what source other than the Scripture is dogma derived, seeing that there is another source ?

Here great divergence of opinion became manifest. Some, like Schleiermacher, J. T. Beck, Schenkel, and Plitt, relied on a subjective source—'pious self-consciousness,' 'conscience,' and the like. Others, like Martensen, founded on a quasi-objective source—'the perfect mediation between the ideas of the Scriptures and the ideas of modern civilization.' The problem has recently attracted fresh attention in philosophical circles, thanks to the attitude towards authority taken by A. J. Balfour in *The Foundations of Belief*, and the similar tendencies of Benjamin Kidd in *Social Evolution*. The fundamental fallacy attaching to the several discussions of this second source, regarded from a philosophical standpoint, is that they fail to analyse the process of thought of which dogma is a result.

Literature : this is enormous, and is fully given in Herzog's Real-Encyc., art. Dogmatik; HARNACK, Hist. of Dogma (Eng. trans.), i. 15 f., 359 f., vi. 33 f.; BALFOUR, The Foundations of Belief, 185 f.; WALLACE, Lectures and Essays on Nat. Theol. and Ethics, 73 f.; RITCHIE, in the Int. J. of Ethics, v. 107 f.   (R.M.W.)

Dogmatics : Ger. *Dogmatik*; Fr. *dogmatique*; Ital. *dogmatica*. The name given to that section of systematic theology which deals logically with doctrine; it is otherwise called doctrinal theology.

Dogmatics has for its field all doctrinal questions connected with God; those relating to man as a religious being, and the subject of God's care; and those arising from the essential relationship between God and man following from the conclusions reached in the previous sections. The entire subject is bound up with the history of dogma, as a preliminary apparatus; and with speculative philosophy as an indispensable organon.

Literature: articles in the various theological encyclopedias, e.g. HERZOG; ROTHE, Theol. Encyc., 100 f.; SCHLEIERMACHER, Der christl. Glaube; LIPSIUS, Lehrb. d. Dogmatik; DORNER, Syst. of Christ. Doctrine (Eng. trans.); FRANK, Syst. d. christl. Gewissheit; KÄHLER, Die Wiss. d. christl. Lehre, ii ; H. SCHULTZ, Grundr. d. evang. Dogmatik.   (R.M.W.)

Dogmatism : Ger. *Dogmatismus*; Fr. *dogmatisme*; Ital. *dogmatismo*. (1) A form of philosophy which assumes a certain system of principles as its starting-point. Opposed to dogmatism are SCEPTICISM (q. v.) and CRITICISM (q. v.).

In the strict sense, any philosophy is dogmatic which avoids the Pyrrhonic scepticism. Every discipline must start with certain unproved assumptions. In the broader sense, an uncritical philosophy which makes unnecessary assumptions is called dogmatic. So the philosophy of the middle ages, which in the main took the teaching of the Church as a starting-point, is dogmatic.

The current distinction between dogmatism as a principle and dogmatism as a method is not well founded. Since dogmatism is simply the positing of unproved principles, any dogmatism involves a dogmatic method, and any dogmatic method involves dogmatism. (R.H.S.)

(2) Applied specifically to the philosophy of Christian Wolff, in whom the dogmatic tendencies of pre-Kantian philosophy, and notably of Leibnitz, are said to culminate. Kant himself was a disciple of Wolff in his 'dogmatic' or pre-critical period (see the histories of philosophy). For Fichte's use, see IDEALISM. Cf. DOGMA (3). (J.M.B.)

Dolichocephalic [Gr. δολιχός, long, + κεφαλή, head]: Ger. *dolichocephal, langköpfig*; Fr. *dolichocéphale*; Ital. *dolicocefalo*. Long-headed; the opposite of BRACHYCEPHALIC; having a cephalic index (ratio of maximum transverse diameter of skull or head to maximum anterior-posterior diameter) of considerably less than the normal; usually less than 75 : 100. If a further distinction is made between sub-dolichocephalic and true dolichocephalic, the former would include skulls with a cephalic index of 75·01–77·77 : 100, and the latter, of less than 75 : 100. Among dolichocephalic races may be cited West African negroes, Arabs, Kaffirs, &c. See INDEX (with illustration), and CRANIOMETRY. (J.J.)

Dolour [Lat. *dolor*, pain]: Ger. *Schmerz*; Fr. *douleur*; Ital. *dolore*. Bodily or mental pain or suffering, but particularly mental. It is characteristic of MELANCHOLIA (q.v.). (J.J.)

Dolus [Gr. δόλος]: Ger. *Dolus*; Fr. *dol*; Ital. *dolo*. (1) A crafty act, intended to mislead another, and do him damage.

(2) A wrongful act of the above description. This is more precisely styled *dolus malus* (*Dig.*, iv. 3, *De Dolo Malo*, 1, § 2).

Dolus, in the primary sense, was often justifiable or meritorious; as if the object of the craft and injury were a public enemy, or a robber. It was then *dolus bonus* (*Dig.*, iv. 3, *De Dolo Malo*, 1, § 3). When there was no such excuse, it was *dolus malus*, and *dolus* is ordinarily used in Roman law in the meaning of *dolus malus*. Gross negligence was treated

as tantamount to *dolus* (*Dig.*, xvi. 3, *Depositi vel Contra*, 32); but only in determining civil remedies (*Dig.*, xviii. 8, *Ad Legem Corneliam*, &c., 7). A special action lay for *dolus*, and it was the foundation also of a defensive exception. See Phillimore's *Princ. and Maxims of Jurisprudence*, xxviii; Sohm's *Instit. of Roman Law*, §§ 29, 72. Fraud, malice, or bad faith, does not seem to be an indispensable element in *dolus malus* (*Dig.*, iv. 3, 18, § 5). 'Dolum ex indiciis perspicuis probari convenit' (*Code*, ii. 21, *De Dolo Malo*, 6). (S.E.B.)

Domestic [Lat. *domesticus*, belonging to the household]: Ger. (1) *Haus-(Industrie)*, (2) *heimisch*; Fr. *domestique*; Ital. *domestico*. (1) Conducted within the home; thus the domestic system of manufacture is contrasted with the factory system. (2) Confined to the home country; thus domestic trade is contrasted with foreign trade.

In the development of modern manufactures, it is customary to mark three periods: that of the guild system, when the workmen controlled the capital; that of the domestic system, when the capitalist employed labour in the labourer's house; and that of the factory system, when he employs labour with buildings and machines of his own. The sweating system is a survival of the domestic system. (A.T.H.)

Domesticated Animals: Ger. *Hausthiere*; Fr. *animaux domestiques*; Ital. *animali domestici*. Those which are kept for the service of man, or for his pleasure. It is not improbable that the choice of animals for domestication was originally limited to those which freely breed under the conditions imposed by man. (C.LL.M.)

The principal importance attaching to domestication, from the biological point of view, arises from the great and permanent change brought about in the animals' general conditions of life, e.g. of shelter, abundant food, artificial protection, limited breeding, &c., most of which result from artificial selection and afford scope for natural selection. The changes of a bodily kind are very great—amounting in many cases to the production of morphological differences far exceeding those which separate the majority of allied species. Yet the absence of sterility *inter se*, as Huxley early insisted, separates such strongly marked races from true species (cf. Huxley and Poulton, as cited below).

Darwin points out that, as said above, the environmental changes are usually assisted by artificial selection or weeding-out carried to an extremely severe degree. And this consideration, it would seem, applies notably to the mental characters, e. g. temperament, intelligence, gentleness, cleanliness, &c., which are essential in the choice of house and yard animals; while physical characters, such as colour, shape, &c., are often of aesthetic, rather than of utilitarian, value. Domestication offers extraordinary opportunities for the experimental study of heredity, variation, modification, hybridism, &c., and also for that of comparative psychology. (J.M.B.–E.B.P.)

Literature: DARWIN, in his Animals and Plants under Domestication (1868), has given a vast array of facts with regard to the origin of, and changes undergone through, domestication; HUXLEY, Darwiniana (1893); POULTON, Charles Darwin, 126, 129, 138. (C.LL.M.–E.B.P.)

Domicile (also written **Domicil**) [Lat. *domicilium*]: Ger. *Wohnsitz, Domizil*; Fr. *domicile*; Ital. *domicilio*. The place where one resides, with the intent to make it his home.

The domicile of a married man is ordinarily presumed to be the home of his family. Temporary absences do not affect a domicile; nor even a long residence elsewhere, when there is a continuing intent to return. 'Domicile of origin' is that existing at birth. It is that of the father or, in case of an illegitimate child, of the mother. A man's domicile, as it exists from time to time, is ordinarily that of his wife and minor children. 'Forensic domicile' is that which one has in view of the law, with reference to determining the forum before which he may sue or be sued. A domicile, under some systems of law, may be chosen for such a purpose, without disturbing the general domicile. An 'election of domicile' may also extend to a choice between two permanent and rightful domiciles, as in the case of a child, born in a country where his mother is temporarily sojourning, who at his majority can elect between his domicile of birth and his domicile of nationality. See French *Code Civil*, Art. 9.

'Et in eodem loco singulis domicilium non ambigitur, ubi quis larem, rerumque ac fortunarum suarum summam constituit, unde rursus non sit discessurus, si nihil avocet; unde cum profectus est, peregrinari videtur; quo si rediit, peregrinari iam destitit' (*Code*, x. 39, *De Incolis*, &c., 7). (S.E.B.)

Dominicans: Ger. *Dominikaner*; Fr. *Dominicains*; Ital. *Domenicani*. The name given to the brethren of the Order of St. Dominic.

The society was founded in 1216. It was one of the mendicant orders, the members taking the vows of mendicancy, as well as those of chastity, poverty, and obedience. It soon made rapid progress, and is of importance to philosophy because Albertus Magnus and Thomas Aquinas sprang from its ranks. Later, some of the 'reformers before the Reformation,' like Tauler, Suso, Eckhart, and Savonarola, also belonged to it. It is usually understood that the promulgation of the dogma of the Immaculate Conception, by Pius IX, was a severe blow to the order.

Literature: HELYOT, Hist. des Ordres monastiques; CARO, St. Dominique et les Dominicains; KLEINERMANN, Der dritte Orden v. d. Busse d. heiligen Dominicus. (R.M.W.)

Donation [Lat. *donare*, to give]: Ger. *Schenkung*; Fr. *donation*; Ital. *donazione*. The technical name given to the edict (324) by which Constantine the Great is alleged to have made a portion of Italy over to the Papacy as a gift. The matter belongs to the larger discussion of the temporal power. The edict was not known till the 8th century, and it was exposed by Laurentius Valla.

Literature: DANTE, Inferno, xix. 112 f.; MÜNCH, Ueber d. erdichtete Schenkung Constantins d. Grossen; MACK, De Donatione a C. M. sedi Apost. oblata. (R.M.W.)

Donatists: Ger. *Donatisten*; Fr. *Donatistes*; Ital. *Donatisti*. The name given to a sect of the Christian Church in Roman Africa early in the 4th century.

It was probably derived from Donatus Magnus, bishop of Carthage. During the Diocletian persecution, a wave of enthusiasm led Christians to suffer every extremity for their faith. Consequently, any one who gave up his Bible to the civil authorities came to be called a *traditor*, and incurred much odium. The Donatists held that no *traditor* could effectively fulfil the functions of the priesthood, and especially of bishop. This view led to an open schism over the election of a bishop of Carthage in 311; the controversy continued for a century, and caused serious disorders till, in 411, a conference was held at Carthage between the Donatist and Catholic parties—the latter being championed by Augustine. As a result, the Catholic view was affirmed; but the Donatist party, despite the rigours of civil persecution, maintained itself till the 7th century, when it was submerged, with the rest of the Christian community, by the Saracen invasion. The controversy is interesting for philosophy of religion, as having elicited some of Augustine's most effective work on the relation between God and man, and on the meaning of Catholicity.

Literature: OPTATUS MILEVITANUS, De Schismate Donatistarum; RIBBEK, Donatus u. Augustinus; DEUTSCH, Drei Actenstücke z. Gesch. d. Donatismus; VÖLTER, Der Ursprung d. Donatismus; HARNACK, Hist. of Dogma (Eng. trans.), v. 38 f., 140 f.　　(R.M.W.)

Donders' Law: Ger. *Donders'sches Gesetz* (*der Augenbewegungen*); Fr. *loi des mouvements des yeux, de Donders*; Ital. *legge di Donders*. With parallel lines of regard 'every position of the line of regard in relation to the head corresponds to a definite and invariable torsion value.' In Helmholtz' language: 'With parallel lines of regard the angle of torsion in both eyes is a function only of the angles of vertical and lateral displacement.'

Donders' law is important (1) for sure and easy recognition of direction in the field of regard, and (2) for the apprehension of the movement of objects in the field when the eye itself has moved. It was named after Donders by Helmholtz. See ORIENTATION (law of constant).

Literature: DONDERS, Nederlandsch Lancet (Aug., 1846), and Holl. Beitr. zu d. anat. u. physiol. Wissenschaften (1848), i. 105, 384; HELMHOLTZ, Physiol. Optik (2nd ed.), 619; WUNDT, Physiol. Psychol. (4th ed.), ii. 119; HERING, in Hermann's Handb. d. Physiol., III. i. 474; AUBERT, Physiol. Optik, 653; SANFORD, Course in Exper. Psychol., expt. 131.　　(E.B.T.)

Donum superadditum [Lat.]. A phrase which has occurred in the controversies concerning the question, 'What did Adam lose when he fell — was his loss of something natural to him, or of something bestowed upon him supernaturally (*donum superadditum*)?'

Protestants tend to hold that Adam lost something which was a part of his proper nature as human. Roman Catholic theologians hold that he lost divine grace, and that this was a *donum superadditum*, i.e. it formed no part of Adam's essence, but was an accident— something bestowed by divine power. The question is of no importance for philosophy of religion, except in so far as it involves the question of the possibility of man's natural knowledge of God, a denial of which would be easy from the standpoint of the *donum superadditum* theory.　　(R.M.W.)

Double Aspect Theory: Ger. *psychophysischer Parallelismus* (not an adequate equivalent, unless connected with the identity theory of mind and body—K.G.); Fr. *théorie de l'unité à deux faces*; Ital. *teoria del doppio aspetto*. The theory of the relation of mind and body, which teaches that mental and bodily facts are parallel manifestations of a single underlying unity.

The double aspect theory acknowledges the incomparability of material and conscious processes, and maintains the impossibility of reducing the one to the other, in terms either of materialism or idealism (spiritualism). It professes to overcome the onesidedness of these two theories by regarding both series as only different aspects of the same reality, like the convex and the concave views of a curve (G. H. Lewes); or, according to another favourite metaphor, the bodily and the mental facts are really the same facts expressed in different language. The most characteristic feature of the theory is its strenuous denial of the possibility of causal interaction between body and mind, or vice versa, in deference to the supposed necessities of the law of the conservation of energy. For interaction it substitutes parallelism or concomitance. Each side seems to 'get along by itself,' or rather, as Bain puts it, 'we have always a two-sided cause. The line of causal sequence is not mind causing body, and body causing mind, but mind-body giving birth to mind-body' (*Mind and Body*, 132). This doctrine of 'a double-faced unity,' as Bain calls it, has more recently appropriated to itself the name of MONISM (q. v.). In stating the theory, the main stress is frequently laid upon the unbroken sequence of the material facts; in that case the theory approximates the doctrine of conscious automatism, and the position becomes practically indistinguishable from the more 'guarded and qualified materialism' with which Bain, indeed, in the volume referred to, appears to identify it (cf. *Mind and Body*, 140). Wundt, on the other hand, while accepting the principle of psychophysical parallelism in an empirico-psychological reference, gives it ultimately a metaphysical interpretation which brings it nearer to an idealistic position. The theory, therefore, while professing to harmonize materialism and spiritualism, occupies a position of somewhat unstable equilibrium between the two, and shows a tendency in different expositors to relapse into the one or the other.

The doctrine of parallelism appears as a metaphysical theory in Spinoza, for whom thought and extension are parallel and co-ordinate attributes of the one substance. 'Ordo et connexio idearum idem est ac ordo et connexio rerum' (*Ethica*, ii. 7). 'Obiectum ideae humanam mentem constituentis est corpus, sive certus extensionis modus actu existens, et nihil aliud' (ii. 13, with its Scholion, 'omnia, quamvis diversis gradibus, tamen animata sunt'). As revived in this century, it owes its currency (1) to the advance of physiological psychology, which demonstrates the closeness of the connection between the material and the mental; (2) to a perception of the crudity of pure materialism; (3) to the formulation of the doctrine of the conservation of energy, which is sometimes understood as implying that the physical universe is a closed cycle of energy-transformations. W. H. Clifford, Romanes, and perhaps Spencer, together with Wundt, Höffding, and Paulsen, may be mentioned as representatives of the theory in one or other of its forms. The position of Shadworth Hodgson and Professor Huxley is rather to be described as AUTOMATISM (q. v.).

Literature: see MIND AND BODY. (A.S.P.P.)

Double Images: Ger. *Doppelbilder*; Fr. *images doubles, diplopie*; Ital. *diplopia, vista doppia*. The images of a luminous point that stimulates retinal points situated beyond the limits of binocular correspondence (see CORRESPONDING POINTS), and is therefore seen double by the two eyes. For the general phenomena of 'seeing double,' see DIPLOPIA.

Literature: HELMHOLTZ, Physiol. Optik (2nd ed.), 841; AUBERT, Physiol. Optik, 605; HERING, in Hermann's Handb. d. Physiol., III. i. 397, 424; SANFORD, Course in Exper. Psychol., expts. 208, 211, 220. (E.B.T.)

Double or Multiple Personality: see PERSONALITY (disorders of). (J.J.)

Double (Negation, &c.): see MOOD (in logic).

Doubt [Lat. *dubius*, uncertain, prob. from *duo*, two]: Ger. *Zweifel*; Fr. *doute*; Ital. *dubbio*. Lack of belief under circumstances in which belief is felt to be possible.

In the article on BELIEF (q.v.), it is seen that certain complex intellectual conditions are preliminary to it. When these conditions are consciously present, but the assurance or consent of belief is not yet secured, there is doubt. Positively, this state of mind is due to a certain lack of harmony (seen in the derivation of doubt and Zweifel) among presentations, variously described as contradiction, contradictory representation, inconsistency; and negatively, as lack of evidence, unreality, both of which points of view are considered under BELIEF.

Literature: see under BELIEF. (J.M.B., G.F.S.)

Doubt (in logic). Primarily the state of mind relative to a proposition requiring evidence but not having, for either its truth or its falsity, evidence that is sufficient. The implied reference is always psychological, and the state is definable in relation to belief and disbelief, not in relation to knowledge *pro* or *con*. (R.A.)

Doubt (insanity of): see DOUBTING MANIA.

Doubting Mania: Ger. *Zweifelsucht, Grübelsucht*; Fr. *folie du doute*; Ital. *follia* (or *monomania*) *del dubbio*. This disorder, which has received various names (see art. Doubt, Insanity of, in Tuke's *Dict. of Psychol. Med.*), may be most naturally described as an abnormal self-consciousness in the direction of great hesitation and doubt, combined with more or less impairment of the will. The main symptom, haunting doubt, may be regarded as a form of fixed imperative idea from which the patient finds no escape.

Sufficient cases have been described, in which this symptom is apparently the only divergence from normal mental action, as to lead to their classification as cases of insanity of doubt. The disease seems to affect frequently, but not invariably, those hereditarily disposed to mental disorders; it progresses usually with periods of intermission, and as a rule remains incurable. The patient often maintains a long struggle against his morbid ruminations, and is perfectly aware of their unreasonable character; he retains, as long as he can, his place as a useful working member of society, but in the end withdraws more and more within himself, and frequently voluntarily seeks admission in an asylum. The cases vary considerably; a few types may be described. A characteristic form of the mania is of a metaphysical character; the subject doubts his own existence, questions the evidence of his senses, speculates as to the precise and ultimate causes of every detail and trifle, and recurs unceasingly to the same topic, repeating the same arguments *pro* and *con*, and with all forms of subtleties and hair-splitting considerations. This form of mental rumination may be confined to one special topic; frequently it is numbers (cf. ARITHMOMANIA), such as an irresistible impulse to count everything. Another class are morbidly scrupulous and conscientious, fearing lest they may have done wrong, may have failed to do their precise and literal duty; they dwell upon the most trifling and improbable circumstances, and often come to a standstill in their actions by reason of such fear. Others are constantly anticipating accidents, are in dread that somebody may fall out of a window at his or her feet, may speculate as to what should be done, and so on. Somewhat different, but frequently mentioned in the same connection, is the fear of contact with objects. The patient lives in a constant dread of contamination, and regulates his action, and allows his thoughts to dwell unnecessarily upon these considerations. Some of these forms have received special designations, such as metaphysical mania, reasoning mania, arithmomania, &c.

Transitory and slight tendencies to almost all these habits may be recognized by all as normal at certain periods. The abnormality consists in their persistence and absorption of the intelligence to the exclusion of normal thought and action. See INSISTENT IDEAS, and WILL (defects of).

Literature: LEGRAND DU SAULLE, La Folie du Doute (1875); RITTI, Gaz. Hebdomadaire, No. 42 (1877); GRIESINGER, Arch. f. Psychiat. (1868-9), i. 626 ff.; BERGER, Arch. f. Psychiat. (1876), 237; B. BALL, art. Doubt, Insanity of, in Tuke's Dict. of Psychol. Med.; MAGNAN, Recherches sur les Centres nerveux (2e sér.); BALLET-MORSELLI, Le Psicosi (1896). Also works cited under DEGENERATION. (J.J.)

Drama: see CLASSIFICATION (of the fine arts).

Dream [ME. *dreme*]: Ger. *Traum*; Fr. *rêve*; Ital. *sogno*. Conscious process during sleep.

Theories of dreaming are still unconvincing; even the description of the facts is incomplete. There is doubt (1) as to the condition of the attention (is it absent, or is it fixed, as in hypnotic somnambulism?); (2) as to movement (do we tend to carry out our images in movement less or more than in waking life?); (3) how much mental control is there in dreams? (4) what are the physical conditions of dreaming (anaemia or hyperaemia of the brain?—dissociation over a large area, or lack of inhibition from a particular centre? —how is dreaming related to the physical recovery due to sleep?); (5) as to sleeping without dreams (is it possible?). The discussion of these questions waits upon an adequate theory of SLEEP (q. v.).

Literature: see under SLEEP. Possibly the best general work is S. DE SANCTIS, I Sogni (1899). (J.M.B., G.F.S.)

Dream (anthropological). The phenomena of dreams played an important part in primitive culture. The so-called Dream-theory holds that from them, in part, arose the notion of a soul separate from the body, and surviving the dissolution of the body; for the visions of the dreamer were readily interpreted as the excursions of his soul into other regions, and the report back to his waking soul of what had been there experienced. As the dead were frequently dreamt of, such excursions were located in the after-life into which the soul went, when it no longer returned to the body; while the phenomena of trance, and delirium, and madness were looked upon as the possession of the affected persons by the souls of others. Dreams also were regarded as significant for, or prophetic of, the future; and thus arose more or less elaborate systems of dream-interpretation (Oneiromancy), which became part of the craft of the wise man, or magician. See ONEIROLOGY, DEMONOLOGY, and MAGIC. (J.J.)

Literature: TYLOR, Primitive Culture; SPENCER, Princ. of Sociol., i. (L.M.)

Drill: see HABITUATION.

Drobisch, Moritz Wilhelm. (1802-96.) Born and educated at Leipzig, where he became professor of mathematics (1826) and philosophy (1842). He was the first to bring the writings of Herbart into prominent notice.

Drugs and Poisons (effects of): see INTOXICATION, and PSYCHIC EFFECTS OF DRUGS. (J.J.)

Drunkenness [from *drink*, AS. *drincan*]: Ger. *Betrunkenheit*; Fr. *ivresse*; Ital. *ubbriachezza*. A state of alcoholic intoxication. See ALCOHOLISM, and DIPSOMANIA. (J.J.)

Druses [probably from Ismail Darazi or Durzi]: Ger. *Maroniten*; Fr. *Druses*; Ital. *Drusi*. A Syrian people, whose religious history is well known, but whose ethnology and religion are still obscure. They are agnostic theists.

Their doctrine of a supreme and unknowable deity is accompanied by many fantastic elaborations. God was incarnated ten times, on the last and final occasion in the person of Hakim, the sixth of the Fatimite caliphs (1016 A.D.). The Universal Intelligence is the greatest of God's creatures, and alone can hold intercourse with him. Below this are numerous ranks of subordinate spirits. The doctrine of metempsychosis is held. The religion is closely connected with the aberrations of some Mohammedan sects, particularly the Batinya branch of the SHI'ITES (q. v.). The Druse doctrine of incarnation, however, separates them entirely from the essential principles of Islam.

Literature: DE SACY, Exposé de la Religion des Druses; CHURCHILL, Ten Years' Residence in Mount Lebanon; CARNARVON, Recollections of the Druses; GUYS, La Théogonie des Druses; arts. in Eucyc. Brit. and in Herzog's Real-Encyc. (R.M.W.)

Dual (Relative, &c.): see LOGIC (exact).

Dualism (in art) [Lat. *duo*, two]: Ger. *Dualismus*; Fr. *dualisme*; Ital. *dualismo*. The view which holds to an actual external beauty, apart from the perception of it. See REALISM (aesthetic). (J.M.B.)

Dualism (in philosophy). (1) A general tendency to divide any genus of objects of philosophical thought into two widely separate categories, as saints and sinners, truth and falsehood, &c.; opposed to the tendency to look for gradations intermediate between contraries. Especially (2) any theory which explains the facts of the universe by referring them to the action of two independent and eternally coexistent principles. Cf. PLURALISM. (C.S.P.–A.S.P.P.)

Dualism appears as a religious theory in connection with the question of good and evil; and Zoroastrianism, with its opposition of Ahriman, the principle of darkness and evil, to Ormuzd, the principle of light and goodness, is usually cited as typical. But in so far as the system teaches the ultimate triumph of Ormuzd, even Zoroastrianism hardly abides by an ultimate dualism, and later sects sought to rise to a higher unity by representing Ormuzd and Ahriman as twin sons of a more fundamental principle called Zrvana Akarana, or limitless time. The dualism of Zoroaster reappeared within the Christian Church as the Manichaean heresy. Within the present century J. S. Mill, in his posthumous *Essay on Religion*, expressed the view that a dualistic theory was, on the whole, most in accordance with the facts to be explained.

In a purely metaphysical reference, dualism is connected with the opposition of matter and spirit, and signifies the assertion of the two as independent, co-eternal, and equally necessary principles. In ancient philosophy, the conception of spirit as consistently immaterial was first realized by Plato. Plato regards the ideas as alone truly existent, but he finds it impossible to explain the world of phenomena without a second principle of non-being or necessity, the so-called Platonic matter, as the groundwork of sensuous existence and the explanation of imperfection and evil. In the ethical turn given to the meta-physical opposition, the strong bent of Plato's own mind may be recognized, and perhaps also the influence of Oriental ideas. Aristotle's philosophy is essentially an attempt to overcome the Platonic dualism by a profound application of the notion of development, the Aristotelian πρώτη ὕλη being defined as mere possibility. But, as a matter of fact, says Zeller, 'matter acquires in Aristotle a meaning which goes far beyond the concept of simple possibility. From it arise natural necessity (ἀνάγκη) and accident (αὐτόματον and τύχη), which limit and encroach upon the power which nature and man have of realizing their aims. It is due to the resistance of matter to form that nature can only rise by degrees from lower forms to higher; and it is only from matter that Aristotle can explain that the lowest special concepts diverge into a number of individuals. It is obvious that matter thus becomes a second principle besides form, endowed with a power of its own' (*Outlines of Greek Philos.*, § 56).

In Neo-Platonism, the notion of emanation is employed to bridge over the gulf between matter and the supra-essential Deity, while in Christian thought the knot is cut by making God the Creator of the material world. The influence of the Platonic dualism on the Christian consciousness may be traced practically in the tendency to asceticism, and, generally, in what has been termed 'other-worldliness.' Typical thinkers of the Renascence period, on the other hand, like Paracelsus and Bruno, in their revolt against mediaeval thought, proclaimed the unity of spirit and matter in all that exists, and thus preluded to the doctrine of Leibnitz or more modern scientific monism. Meanwhile, the advance of science, by clarifying the conception of matter, emphasized the contrast between the inner world of consciousness and the outer world of extended mechanically moving things. Modern philosophy opened accordingly, in Descartes, with a reassertion in its extremest form of a dualism between the *res cogitans* and the *res extensa*, which thus became a problem for his successors. Spinoza reached a speculative monism by reducing both thought and extension to attributes or aspects of the *unica substantia*, while Leibnitz, emphasizing activity as the essence of substance, conceived the universe as a harmonious system of spiritual or quasi-spiritual forces. But this monistic idealism was abandoned by the Wolffians, and their dualism reappears in the various unreconciled oppositions of the Kantian philosophy

—between understanding and sense, phenomena and noumena, practical reason and desire. The chief post-Kantian systems are attempts to reach a doctrine of speculative monism which shall transcend and embrace the dualistic elements of the Kantian philosophy.

If the relation between mind and body be treated as a special question, to be solved without prejudice to the ultimate metaphysical issue, the term dualism may be used in a more specific sense—as opposed alike to subjective idealism, materialism, and so-called monism (the double aspect theory)—to denote a theory which represents the relation between the material world (acting through the body) and the mind as one of causal interaction between real things. The further question then remains whether these interacting and relatively independent substances can be harmoniously included in a single system or life. Cf. CAUSE THEORY, and MONISM.

The term dualism appears to have been first used by Thomas Hyde in his *De Religione veterum Persarum* (1700). It was used by him in a religious reference, and Bayle in his article on Zoroaster gave currency to it in the same sense. Wolff was the first to use it as applied to the opposition of mind and matter. Wolff frequently divides philosophers into dogmatists and sceptics, the former being subdivided into monists and dualists, the monists being again divisible into idealists and materialists, and the idealists, finally, into egoists and pluralists. Hamilton uses the term much in the Wolffian sense with special reference to the theory of perception. Natural dualism, or NATURAL REALISM (q.v.), is the name he gives to the doctrine of Reid and the Scottish school, which asserts 'an immediate knowledge by mind of an object different from any modification of its own.' 'The Ego and the Non-Ego are thus given in an original synthesis, as conjoined in the unity of knowledge, and in an original antithesis, as opposed in the contrariety of existence. In other words, we are conscious of them in an indivisible act of knowledge together and at once, but we are conscious of them as, in themselves, different and exclusive of each other' (*Lects. on Met.*, i. 292). The term Hypothetical Dualist is applied by Hamilton to 'the great majority of modern philosophers,' because, while maintaining the existence of an independent external world, they deny 'an immediate and intuitive knowledge' of it.

Literature: see PHILOSOPHY, and METAPHYSICS. (A.S.P.P.)

Dualism (in theology). Dualism has appeared sporadically in theological inquiries, and can hardly be said to be a determining standpoint constantly, as has so often been the case in philosophy ; it is a consequence, not a presupposition. Its appearances may be classified under four heads : (1) The theological, strictly so called. Here dualism leads to the dogma of two deities—a good and an evil, as in the old Persian religion. This point of view usually crystallizes when the oppositions, obviously present in the world, assume the guise of enigmas, and when, as a result, unreason must be forced to bear its part in furnishing a hypothesis. Christian theology, taken as a whole, has been comparatively free from such lapses : whether it has won its freedom logically is another affair. It has been forced to deal with the problem of evil in its most acute form, that is to say, after the evil in the world—which so pressed on the old Celtic religion—and moral evil—which affected the old Persian religion—had both been fully set forth. Its dualism has been permissive: the devil being a creature of God, and not an independent power. (2) Anthropological. In its conception of man, theology is thoroughly dualistic. Body is sharply distinguished from soul ; and the latter is conceived to be destined to existence in some sort of independence of the former, that is, the two possess separate reality. The doctrine of trichotomy—according to which man is divided into body, soul, and spirit —does not affect this fundamental dualism ; for, on this plan, soul really becomes identical with vitality, a characteristic shared by man with the animals, and spirit takes the place of soul on the ordinary division of dichotomy. (3) Soteriological. Here, too, theology is fundamentally dualistic. It posits a God separate from the universe, and especially from man—a God who has certain self-conscious purposes in regard to salvation, which he is working out on the human race. It may be said that it is difficult to see how the anthropological and soteriological points of view can be reconciled with the results of modern inquiry, especially as these are systematized by prevailing types of monistic philosophy. (4) (*a*) Social (with regard to the constitution of society as a whole). This dualism is purely historical, and finds its most eminent illustration in the dualism between the church and the world, the religious and the civil life, so characteristic in the centuries lying between the complete formation of the organization of the Latin Church and the Reformation. (*b*) Social (with regard to the individual man). Here we come once more upon a question that still retains vitality. The dualism between faith and knowledge marks this division. It is closely connected with the principle of authority. See FAITH. (R.M.W.)

Dullness [ME. *dull*]: Ger. *Dummheit, Stumpfsinnigkeit*; Fr. *stupidité, lenteur*; Ital. *torpore*. Lowered or sluggish activity.

Dullness in a sense organ appears as a relative insensibility, in that a given stimulus makes a much slighter impression than would normally be the case; or the impression may be ill-defined and vague, or develop slowly, such defect in extreme degrees amounting to ANAESTHESIA (q. v.). In regard to mental operations, dullness refers particularly to slowness, though also to limited scope of mental powers. Persons who come entirely within the normal range of variation of mental ability might be called dull; if still more deficient, they might be termed weak-minded. Dullness may also refer to special forms of mental deficiency, as dullness of the emotions, or of the moral sensibilities. (J.J.)

Dumbness: see DEAF-MUTISM, and SPEECH (defects of).

Dumbness (psychic or mental) [AS. *dumb*]: Ger. *psychische Stummheit*; Fr. *mutisme psychique*; Ital. *mutismo psichico*. Inability to frame one's meaning in the customary words; an aphasic defect.

'A distinction is legitimate between psychic and cortical dumbness, corresponding to the current distinction on the sensory side. Just as there is a distinction between being unable to hear words (cortical deafness) and being unable to understand the meaning of words we hear (psychic deafness), so there is a distinction, shown pathologically, between being unable to speak words and being unable to express our meaning in words' (modified from the writer's *Ment. Devel. in the Child and the Race*, 1st ed., 437; the term was first suggested in the *Philos. Rev.*, ii., 1893, 389). Cf. BLINDNESS (psychic), and DEAFNESS (psychic). It is a narrower case of paraphasia or of 'inco-ordinate amnesia' (Bastian), the ground of the defect being, in contrast with other cases, in the higher motor or expressive functions. Séglas calls a special case of it 'mutisme hystérique' (*Les Troubles du Langage*, 97 f.). It illustrates the general motor defect called Psychic Paralysis under LOCALIZATION (cerebral) (q. v.). (J.M.B.)

Dunamis [Gr.]: see GREEK TERMINOLOGY (Glossary, δύναμις), and POWER.

Duns Scotus, Joannes. (cir. 1265–1308.) A scholastic theologian and philosopher, surnamed the 'Subtle Doctor.' The English, Irish, and Scots, all claim him as countryman. Said to be of gentle rank, and to have studied at Oxford. Became a Franciscan friar, and in 1301 professor of theology at Oxford. Moved to Paris in 1304, and taught theology with great success. A realist in philosophy, he opposed Thomas Aquinas, and founded the school of Scotists who for centuries opposed the Thomists.

Duration: see TIME, and TIME SENSE.

Duration, Least (experiments on) [Lat. *durare*, to continue]: Ger. *kleinste Dauer*; Fr. *durée minimale*; Ital. *durata minima*. The least time in which a given mental event may occur with normal distinctness; that is, without fusion, or confusion, with earlier or later events.

For example, the duration of a series of sounds at the maximum rapidity at which they are clearly distinguished from one another, divided by the number of intervals between the successive sounds, gives the 'duration' of one. It is necessary that the term duration, with this meaning, should be qualified by the word 'least' (or 'lower limit of'), seeing that the determination of duration in other connections (in reaction-time and time-sense experiments) concerns the 'normal' or the 'maximum' time taken up, and not the 'least' time. (J.M.B.)

Experiments on duration have been made upon certain mental processes (cf. Külpe, *Outlines of Psychol.*, 30, 238, 382 ff.; Wundt, *Outlines of Psychol.*, 143). The duration of a sensation varies with the conditions of stimulation. Pressures of moderate intensity appear to last about $\frac{1}{20}$ to $\frac{1}{30}$ sec., deep tones last about $\frac{1}{25}$ sec., mid-region tones $\frac{1}{45}$ to $\frac{1}{70}$ sec., high tones $\frac{1}{100}$ to $\frac{1}{200}$ sec.; visual sensations (direct vision, without after-image) last from $\frac{1}{20}$ sec. upwards. The duration of the idea in the 'train of ideas' has been estimated at about $\frac{3}{4}$ sec. See TIME SENSE, and REACTION TIME.

Literature: HELMHOLTZ, Physiol. Optik (2nd ed.), 480 ff.; MARBE, Philos. Stud., ix. 384; HENRY, Compt. Rend. (1896), cxxiii. 604; v. KRIES, Zeitsch. f. Psychol., xii. 81; KUNKEL, Pflüger's Arch., ix. 197, xv. 27; EXNER, Wien. Akad. Ber. (1868); Pflüger's Arch., xiii. 234; URBANTSCHITSCH, Pflüger's Arch., xxv. 323; STUMPF, Tonpsychologie, i. 211, &c.; MAYER, Amer. J. of

Sci. and Arts (Oct. 1874, Apr. 1875); R. SCHULZE, Philos. Stud., xiv. 471; ABRAHAM and BRÜHL, Zeitsch. f. Psychol., xviii. 177; SCHWANER, Diss. (Marburg, 1890), 37; SERGI, Zeitsch. f. Psychol., iii. 175; v. WITTICH, Pflüger's Arch., ii. 329; TRAUTSCHOLDT, Philos. Stud., i. 213; KRAEPELIN, Tagebl. d. Naturforscherversammlung z. Strassburg (1885); GALTON, Brain (1879), 149; MÜNSTERBERG, Beiträge, i.   (E.B.T.)

Duty [OF. *deuté*, from Lat. *debere*, to owe]: Ger. *Pflicht*; Fr. *devoir*; Ital. *dovere*. Literally, a debt; what is required of a man by the moral law; or, more strictly, the relation of the moral law to a moral person, whose will can be swayed by other motives than the consciousness of the law.

The conception of duty, in the form which it takes in modern ethical thought, has been formed by a variety of causes : chiefly (1) the analysis of moral conceptions—including that of τὸ δέον, what is necessary or required—by Plato and Aristotle; (2) the influence of the Stoic writers, by whom τὸ καθῆκον, the fitting, was held to be determined by reason, apart from the emotional nature of man; (3) the Jewish and Christian conceptions of the moral law as declared and enforced by God. Under these influences, and that of the Roman jurists, who were themselves under the influence of the Stoic philosophy, morality came to be expounded as a system of laws, obedience to which constituted the 'duty' of a moral agent.

Even when this juridical aspect is less prominent in the conception of morality generally, it always belongs to the conception of duty. In this way, however, the range of the conception is often narrowed. Bentham and the Utilitarian school regard duty as applying, not to everything which is in accordance with their ethical standard, but only to that portion of right conduct which is protected by an adequate sanction—political, social, or religious (to which J. S. Mill would add personal or 'conscientious'). The presence of the sense of duty, or feeling of obligation, in the individual consciousness is explained as due to the pressure of these sanctions demanding obedience, and their conflict with anti-ethical tendencies : so that with the moralization of human nature the feeling of duty or obligation may be expected to disappear (cf. H. Spencer, *Data of Ethics*, chap. vii).

On the other hand, Kant and the moralists of the Intuitional school commonly regard duty as the fundamental conception of morals. With Kant it is the moral law or dictum of practical reason, in its bearing on a will which is subject to other than moral or rational motives.   (W.R.S.)

Duty (in law): Ger. *Verpflichtung, Verbindlichkeit*; Fr. *obligation, devoir*; Ital. *dovere*. That active or passive furtherance of the rights of others which is enforced by law. See Holland on *Jurisprudence*, chap. vii. 74. Legal duty is correlative to legal right. To enforce a duty is to vindicate a right, whether it be a duty owed to the state as a whole, or to particular individuals. A duty of the latter class is a duty *in personam*. A duty owed to all our fellow-citizens, or to a large class of them, is a duty *in rem*, or an impersonal one. See Pollock's *First Book of Jurisprudence*, chap. iv. 81.

Literature: WOLFF, Instit. of the Law of Nature and of Nations, i. chaps. iv, v.
                                  (S.E.B.)

Dwarf [ME.]: Ger. *Zwerg*; Fr. *nain*; Ital. *nano*. A person of complete physical development, but of unusually small dimensions.

While such persons are sometimes well formed, there is usually a greater or less amount of either a lack of proportionality of the several parts of the body, or a decided malformation. In certain forms of idiocy, particularly cretinism, a stunted, dwarfish growth is frequent. It is frequently a stigma of degeneration. In common with giants, dwarfs have figured considerably in legendary lore, and are often the subject of much attention among primitive peoples; while the custom of retaining dwarfs at court to furnish amusement appears from Roman to modern English times. Anthropometrically and biologically, such cases are as interesting as extreme variation in height. See FREAK, and SPORT.

Literature: art. Dwarf in Encyc. Brit. (9th ed.); DE QUATREFAGES, The Pygmies (Eng. trans., 1895).   (J.J.)

Dyad: see MONAD, and cf. Pythagoreanism under SCHOOLS OF GREECE.

Dynamic: see FORCE, POWER, DYNAMICS, and TERMINOLOGY (Greek, δύναμις).

Dynamic Economics: Ger. *dynamische Oekonomik*; Fr. *économie dynamique*; Ital. *economia dinamica*. (1) That part of the science which deals with flows instead of funds—with rates of supply, demand, or income, instead of quantities pure and simple. (2) Popular, but less correct : that part of the science which deals with changes in the state of society, and therefore with shifting data instead of permanent ones.

Patten, who has written much on this subject, uses the second distinction. The practical evil attending its use is, that it implies that problems regarding rates of income are not dynamic, and can be solved by methods analogous to those of statical mechanics. Almost every economist except Newcomb has, at one time or another, been influenced by this fallacy. Even Marshall, who discusses clearly the limitations of statical analysis, often fails to abide by those limitations in practice. (A.T.H.)

Dynamic (Relation, &c.): see RELATION, and SYNTHESIS.

Dynamic Theory (of matter): see MATTER.

Dynamics [Gr. δυναμικός, pertaining to forces]: Ger. *Dynamik*; Fr. *dynamique*; Ital. *dinamica*. The science which treats of the laws of motion of bodies, as produced by the action of forces. Now proposed to be extended so as to include both branches of theoretical MECHANICS (q. v.). (S.N.)

Dynamogenesis [Gr. δύναμις, force, + γένεσις, production]: Ger. *Dynamogenesis, ideomotorisches Grundgesetz* (K.G.); Fr. *dynamogénie* (*dynamogénique*); Ital. *dinamogenesi*. The principle according to which changes in the conditions of sensory stimulation of the nervous system always show themselves in corresponding changes in muscular tension or movement.

The term 'dynamogeny' is used for the fact (cf. James, *Princ. of Psychol.*, ii. 379) covered by the principle of dynamogenesis. The adjective DYNAMOGENIC (q.v.) was earlier applied (Féré, *Sensation et Mouvement*) to slight differences of stimulation, considered as producing increased motor effects. The facts have been generalized as in the definition above, dynamogenesis being a sensori-motor principle of genetic value. The present writer (*Feeling and Will*, 281; as also Ladd, *Psychol., Descrip. and Explan.*, 229) uses the phrase 'mental dynamogenesis' to express the psychologically equivalent principle, that every change in sensory consciousness tends to be followed by change in motor consciousness.

Stumpf holds, on the contrary, that the generalization is not justified, since a threshold of stimulation must be recognized, below which sensory changes are ineffectual. Yet the finer work in suggestion, and in the recording of motor effects, seems to show that the threshold is entirely relative. Moreover, the theory of threshold takes no account of dispositions, contrast effects, &c., which do not come clearly into consciousness, but which represent so-called subliminal stimulations. The conception of the brain in analogy with a storage battery for potential energy is possibly less reasonable than that which treats the entire nervous system in analogy with a highly charged electric system, in which all changes are equalized throughout all the parts.

Literature: BROWN-SÉQUARD, Physiol. and Pathol. of the Central Nerv. Syst. (1860), and Princ. Actions des Centres nerveux (1879); STUMPF, Ueber den Begriff der Gemüthsbewegung, Zeitsch. f. Psychol. xxi; also special citations given in the works referred to above, especially in JAMES, Princ. of Psychol., ii. chap. xxii, and titles under DYNAMOGENIC. (J.M.B., G.F.S.)

Dynamogenic. Any stimulus or influence which increases the available muscular power is termed dynamogenic. Thus if, while under the stimulus of music, one can exert a stronger pressure upon the dynamometer than normally, such influences would be termed dynamogenic. The term is also used in a more general sense in regard to the tendency of a stimulus to call out a motor response. See DYNAMOGENESIS.

Literature: BALDWIN, Ment. Devel. in the Child and the Race (1895), 165 f.; TRIPLETT, Dynamogenetic Factors in Pacemaking and Competition, Amer. J. of Psychol., ix. 501 ff. (J.J.)

Care should be taken to distinguish this form from the passive form dynamogenetic, which characterizes the motor change or result of the dynamogenic process. See GENESIS AND GENETIC. (J.M.B.)

Dynamometer and **Dynamograph**: see LABORATORY AND APPARATUS, III, A.

Dyne: see UNIT (of physical measurement).

Dyophysites [Gr. δύο, two, + φύσις, nature]: Ger. *Dyophysiten*; Fr. *Dyophysites*; Ital. *Diofisiti*. The name applied to that party in ancient Christological controversy who held that the God-man had two natures.

The problem, 'How can the complete God and the complete man be united in one being?' naturally produced many conflicting solutions. The dyophysitic answer was as follows:—The godhead of the Logos in Christ must be distinguished from the mortal body. The former is uncreate, the latter created. Birth, temptation, suffering, death, belong to the human nature,

Dynamism =
[Stone Luck - 1930

not to the divine. Mary was not the 'mother of God,' but bore the humanity of Christ. Nevertheless, there was one Person only; for the Logos, without transformation of self, took up into its substance the humanity, and this by an act of grace.

Literature: writings of PAUL of Samosata, DIODORUS of Tarsus, THEODORE of Mopsuestia, NESTORIUS of Constantinople, CYRIL of Alexandria; HEFELE, Conciliengesch. See APOLLINARIANISM, MONOPHYSITES, and NESTORIANS.   (R.M.W.)

Dyotheletism [Gr. δύο, two, + ἐθελητός, voluntary]: Ger. *Dyotheletismus, Zweiwillenlehre*; Fr. *dyothélisme*; Ital. *diotelismo*. The name given to one of the conclusions deduced from the doctrine that Christ had two natures.

Martin I and the Lateran Synod (449 A.D.) lay special stress on the necessity for attributing two wills to the two natures. He who denies the two wills—who is a Monothelite— denies the reality of the Incarnation. The problem is fundamental to the widely different development of Christological speculation in the West as contrasted with the East.

Literature: DORNER, Hist. of the Devel. of the Doctrine of the Person of Christ (Eng. trans.), Div. II. i. 164 f.; HARNACK, Hist. of Dogma (Eng. trans.), iv. 255 f.   (R.M.W.)

Dys- [Gr. δυς, hard, bad]: Ger. *Dys-*; Fr. *dys-*; Ital. *dis-*. The use of this prefix indicates an imperfect, defective, or difficult form of the activity to which it applies. It is used (1) in a most general sense to imply any and all forms of imperfect action; and (2) in a specialized sense to denote a perverted or difficult form of action as opposed to absence of capability (prefix *a-, ab-*), or to unusual presence (prefix *hyper-*). If distinguished from the prefix *para-*, it refers to difficulty of action, while *para-* refers to a perverted or false action. Examples: Dysphasia denotes either a general defect of speech of any kind, or difficulty in speaking. Dysboulia is an impairment of will action. Dysarthria is a defective articulation; Dyspepsia, impaired digestion, &c.   (J.J.)

E

E : (1) In logic, the symbol of the universal negative judgment—no men are monkeys.

(2) In experimental psychology, the symbol of excitation or stimulus ; a varying quantity, as ounces of pressure, units of sound, light, &c.

(3) E-values (Ger. *E-Werthe*). One of the most important of the special symbols of Avenarius' EMPIRIO-CRITICISM (q. v.). Cf. also INTROJECTION. (J.M.B.)

Earnings [AS. *earnung*]: Ger. *Erwerb*; Fr. *gain, salaire*; Ital. *guadagni*. Property rights acquired by economic service, whether on the part of an individual or a corporation.

Earnings is a narrower term than income, which includes property acquired by any method whatsoever. Thus taxes form part of the public income, but not of the public earnings ; the latter being confined to receipts from mails, water-works, and other forms of economic activity on the part of the state. (A.T.H.)

Eberhard, Johann August. (1739–1809.) German philosopher, born at Halberstadt, Prussia, and died at Halle. He was educated in theology at Halle, and in 1778 became professor of philosophy there. In theology he was rationalistic.

Ebionites [Heb. pl. *'ebjonim*, the poor]: Ger. *Ebioniten*; Fr. *Ébionites*; Ital. *Ebioniti*. Although unsolved or partially solved problems still surround this name, one may say that it has been used in three distinct senses : (1) It was applied at first to all Christians, on account of their poverty ; (2) it was used of the Jewish Christians exclusively, as by Origen ; (3) by the time of Epiphanius and Jerome it designated a distinct sect among the Jewish Christians—one contrasted with the Nazarenes. The Ebionites, in all prob-ability, had their rise in the Pharisaic influences naturally incident to Palestinian Christianity. This can be gathered from the doctrines in which they always agreed. They were Christians because they accepted Jesus as Messiah. But they were Jews, because they (1) denied Jesus' divinity, (2) enforced the obligation of the law, (3) rejected and anathematized St. Paul. Latterly, however, these Jewish elements were transformed by doctrines derived from the ESSENES (q. v.), as is proved by the *Book of Elchaisai* ; while later still (by the beginning of the 3rd century) important GNOSTIC (q. v.) factors became prevalent. These are to be seen in Alcibiades of Apamea (219 A.D.).

Literature: GIESELER, in Arch. f. Kirchengesch., iv. 279 f. ; SCHLIEMANN, Clement, 449 f. (for the primary sources) ; RITSCHL, in Nieder's Zeitsch., iv. 573 f. ; BAUR, De Ebion. orig. et doctrina ; HILGENFELD, Nov. Test. extra Canonem receptum, fasc. iii. 153 f. ; LIGHTFOOT, Ep. to the Galatians, 306 f., and Ep. of Ignatius, i. 319 f. ; STANTON, The Jewish Messiah, 166 f. ; CAMPBELL, Critical Studies in St. Luke, 169 f. (R.M.W.)

Eccentric Projection : Ger. *excentrische Projection* ; Fr. *extériorisation des sensations* (L.M.) ; Ital. *projezione (o localizzazione) eccentrica (delle sensazioni)*—(E.M.). The fact that when a stimulus works not upon the nerve-ending, but upon the nerve-tract, the corresponding sensation is regularly referred to the peripheral ending of the nerve. Cf. PROJECTION, and PROJECTION (nervous). (TH.Z.)

Eccentric projection, which is a phenomenon of nervous projection, should be carefully distinguished from projection as misused for localization in space. Cf. Ladd, *Physiol.*

Psychol., 385 ff., and James, *Princ. of Psychol.*, ii. 31 ff. (with numerous references). See Höfler, *Psychol.*, 343 f., for the restriction as in the definition. (J.M.B.)

Eccentricity [Gr. ἐκ + κέντρον, the centre]: Ger. *Eccentricität*; Fr. *excentricité*; Ital. *eccentricità, bizzarria*. An oddity or peculiarity of behaviour or manner.

Insane persons are frequently eccentric, but eccentricity alone is by no means a conclusive symptom of insanity. It is obvious that what is unusual in one age or in one group of surroundings may be quite usual in another, and that unusual or eccentric behaviour may be expressive of very different motives and influences in different cases. As a rule the eccentric is indifferent to the world's blame or criticism, and pursues his own methods with little reference to the sanctions of society. The term is thus popular rather than scientific, and frequently occurs in discussions of the borderland that separates sanity from insanity (Maudsley, *Mental Pathol.*, 297-8). In the discussion of the possible relations between genius and insanity, the question of morbid eccentricity is again prominent (see art. Eccentricity in Tuke's *Dict. of Psychol. Med.*; see also Moreau de Tours, *Les Eccentriques*, 1894). (J.J.)

Ecclesia: see Church.

Echolalia (also **Echophasia**) [Gr. ἠχώ, echo, + λαλιά, prattle]: Ger. *Echosprache*, or *Echolalie*; Fr. *écholalie*; Ital. *ecolalia, lalomimesi*. The thoughtless and somewhat automatic repetition by the subject of the words and tones addressed to him.

It occurs as a symptom in degenerative nervous disorders (imbecility, dementia, Guinon's disease) and also in disturbances of speech (see Bateman, *Aphasia*). The word is due to Romberg, 1853. Gilles de la Tourette (*Arch. de Neurol.*, 1885, 19) notes an allied symptom in the nervous malady of Siberia, termed myriachit. (J.J.)

Eckhart, Meister (Master). (cir. 1260–1327.) 'The greatest of the German mystics.' Born in Thuringia, he became vicar of the Dominican order at Erfurt, vicar-general in Bohemia, teacher at Paris, 1311–2, teacher of theology at Strassburg, and in 1327 provincial in Cologne. A reformer of monasteries, an eloquent and scholarly preacher, a free spirit, he has been called 'the father of modern pantheism.' A papal bull after his death denounced twenty-eight sentences in his sermons.

Éclaircissement: see Enlightenment.

Eclampsia [Gr. ἐκ + λάμπειν, to shine]:

Ger. *Eclampsie*; Fr. *éclampsie*; Ital. *eclampsia*. A form of Convulsion (q.v.). (J.J.)

Eclecticism [Gr. ἐκ + λέγειν, to gather]: Ger. *Eklekticismus*; Fr. *éclectisme*; Ital. *eclettismo*. A system of philosophy which strives to incorporate the truth of all systems. The best known example is the Alexandrian Neo-Platonic school, usually known as the Eclectic school. See Alexandrian School. Among modern eclectics, Leibnitz and Cousin are best known.

Since a more or less arbitrary choice is apt to be a mosaic rather than an organized philosophy, the method is rather in disfavour and the term often a reproach. (H.R.S.)

Eclecticism (in theology). As in philosophy, so in theology, a name given to the tendency to borrow doctrines from different sources and the attempt to retain them side by side.

The first outburst of eclecticism in theology occurs at Alexandria with Clement, Origen, and Synesius, who draw upon Pagan, classical, and Christian sources. Here, however, there are distinct traces of syncretism—that is, the fusion of elements which eclecticism, strictly so called, does not allow to modify one another. In modern times the term has been applied to theologians who attempt to mediate between the faith of the Church and the results of scientific, critical, or philosophical inquiry, without, however, possessing a fundamental or unitary system. Such are I. A. Dorner, Martensen, J. P. Lange, Chr. v. Hofmann, Lipsius, and others. Schleiermacher might be classed in the same group. It is represented among British-American writers by such a thinker as A. B. Bruce. Indeed, this tendency may be ascribed to nearly all 'liberal' theologians belonging to the 'Evangelical' churches of Great Britain and the United States. It is to be remembered, in this connection, that eclecticism has a wider legitimate field in theology than in philosophy, and so cannot be applied fairly in a derogatory sense exclusively. O. Pfleiderer's classification of A. Ritschl as an eclectic can hardly be maintained.

Literature: O. Pfleiderer, Devel. of Theol., Bk. II. chap. iv; A. B. Bruce, Apologetics; I. A. Dorner, Syst. d. christl. Glaubenslehre (Eng. trans.). (R.M.W.)

Economic Freedom: Ger. *Rechtszweck des Staats*; Fr. *liberté économique*; Ital. *libertà economica*. The absence of any legal restrictions upon rights of property or contract, except such as are necessary for preserving similar rights of property or contract to different individuals.

The idea of economic freedom was the result of a protest against the 'mercantile system' of international trade restraints on the one hand, and the system of internal police restrictions adopted by the Wohlfahrtsstaat on the other. The idea expressed in the definition has been perhaps most fully developed by W. v. Humboldt.

The development of these ideas, both in theory and in practice, has been checked by the growth of democracy and the ideals of equality connected with it. As Lassalle so well showed, equal rights under unequal conditions mean assured inequality. Hence the pressure for factory acts, for laws governing the prices and profits of large corporations, for progressive taxation, and for extension of government activity. (A.T.H.)

Economic Harmonies: Ger. *Interessen-Harmonien*; Fr. *harmonies économiques*; Ital. *armonie economiche*. A series of coincidences between the self-interest of individuals and the general interest of society in matters relating to wealth.

The agreement between the results of egoism and altruism is perhaps no closer in economic life than in other departments of human activity; but it is, at any rate, more verifiable. As a natural consequence, the relations between self-interest and public interest have been more clearly recognized in this field than in any other; and there has been a tendency to assume the existence of such a harmony in all cases where it is not specifically disproved. The *laissez-faire* principle of the PHYSIOCRATS (q. v.), urging non-interference with industry, was the natural result of this assumption, which was afterwards carried to an extreme by Bastiat in France and Prince-Smith in Germany.

Literature: BASTIAT, Harmonies économiques. Among the most active critics of the views represented by Bastiat may be mentioned the names of PROUDHON, LASSALLE, MARLO, and MARX. (A.T.H.)

Economic Law: Ger. *Gesetz des menschlichen Verkehrs, ökonomisches Gesetz*; Fr. *loi économique*; Ital. *legge economica*. A universal proposition relating to wealth: e. g. law of diminishing return; law of supply and demand.

The earliest students of political economy regarded their subject as an art, and often thought of economic laws as matters of human enactment. The economists of the early part of the present century went to the other extreme. Having discovered certain sequences of cause and effect, they thought that these sequences applied to a wider range of places and times than was actually the case. In other words, they overlooked the conditional character of these laws. They are universal in the sense that they are not subject to exceptions; but they are to be stated in narrowly defined terms rather than in loose or broad ones. In the view now generally held, the conditions of their applicability are determined by natural selection. The struggle for existence between different groups creates economic types; and so far as an economic law involves an assumption as to human motives, its application may be limited by the extent of the conditions which create and perpetuate the type to which a certain motive belongs.

Literature: BAGEHOT, Postulates of Eng. Polit. Econ. (A.T.H.)

Economic Mean: see ECONOMIC MOTIVE.

Economic Method: Ger. *ökonomische Methode*; Fr. *méthode économique*; Ital. *metodo economico*. The logical processes habitually employed by an investigator for the discovery or development of laws relating to wealth. These processes fall into two groups—deductive methods, which start from generalizations as to the conduct of individuals; and historical methods, which start from observation of the conduct of masses.

Down to the end of the last century the dominant methods were historical, though the French and English economists both made much use of deduction when it suited their purpose. Ricardo's work, on the other hand, was rigorously deductive, and so was that of Malthus. Deductive methods were carried to an almost absurd extreme by the 'orthodox' writers of the first half of the 19th century. John Stuart Mill showed a healthful reaction from this extreme; and Mill's use of historical method was carried yet further by a group of German writers of the third quarter of the century (Knies, Roscher, Brentano, Schmoller, Cohn, &c.), who called themselves by the distinctive name 'Historical school.' About 1870 a counter-reaction toward deductive methods made itself felt, headed by Menger in Austria, and by the MATHEMATICAL ECONOMISTS (q. v.) of all countries of Europe. At present the leading economists make use of both deductive and historical methods, being guided in their choice by the character of the problems under investigation.

Literature: KEYNES, Scope and Method of Polit. Econ. (A.T.H.)

Economic Motive: Ger. *ökonomisches Motiv*; Fr. *motif économique*; Ital. *motivo economico*. A motive connected with a line of conduct or feeling whose results are capable of quantitative analysis.

No term in the whole range of philosophic discussion has been more loosely used. Under one set of conceptions of the term, an economic motive is equivalent to a hedonistic motive. Another conception is derived from the abstraction of an 'economic man,' of which the English economists about the middle of the 19th century made some use. 'Political economy,' says Mill, 'is concerned with man solely as a being who desires to possess wealth, and who is capable of judging of the comparative efficacy of means to that end.' A more precise and more useful meaning of the term can be developed on lines like this: social services, in their objective or impersonal aspect, tend to take the form of wealth. When they do this, they become capable of measurement. So far, therefore, as wealth forms the basis of motives, the balance of such motives can be compared with impersonally measurable causes or effects, or both. To motives whose balance can be studied in this way, we give the name 'economic.' (A.T.H.)

Economic Science, or Economics, or Political Economy [Gr. τὰ οἰκονομικά, matters of the household]: Ger. *Oekonomie, National-Oekonomik*; Fr. *économie politique*; Ital. *economia politica*. The science which deals with the phenomena of wealth.

Economics, as conceived by the Greeks (e. g. Xenophon, Aristotle), dealt with the questions involved in the ordering of a household, as distinct from politics, which dealt with the questions involved in the ordering of a state. In the middle ages the separate study of wealth fell into abeyance. Economic questions were handled only as part of a system of morals (Aquinas), or in connection with some disputed points of law—especially those involved in the taking of interest or usury.

About the beginning of the 16th century we see attempts to develop an art of political economy, which should guide the statesman in his attempts to promote public wealth, in the same way that the art of domestic economy guides the householder in his attempts to promote private wealth. The first economists who took this view are known as Cameralists, because they dealt almost entirely with the conduct of the *cameralia* or goods belonging to the exchequer. It is hardly necessary to say that this conception, which identified public wealth with government property, was a very narrow one. It was the outgrowth of a conception of the state which made the ruler stand *in loco parentis* towards his subjects. Though the phenomena of government property must always form an important field of economic investigation, they now constitute the domain of the special science of finance rather than of the more general science of economics.

In the 17th century another school arose, generally known as the Mercantilists. This school remained dominant until after the middle of the 18th century, nor is its influence wholly lost at the present day. The most noted practical exponent of mercantile principles was the great French financier, Colbert; the best known writers who advocated them were perhaps Thomas Mun, William Petty, and, later, James Stuart. The name given to this school is derived from the conception, prominent in its writings and practice, that a nation makes money in the same manner as an individual merchant, by selling more than he buys—i. e. by exporting more than the nation imports. In the hands of all but its most able advocates, this mercantile system tended to become a miserly system—to lay too much stress on the hoarding of the precious metals, and too little on wise purchases of outside commodities.

The reaction against the errors of the mercantile system led to the development of the French school of Physiocrats, who laid stress on natural resources as a measure of wealth. Quesnay (1694-1774) was the most original writer of this school, Turgot its most eminent statesman. The physiocrats laid stress on the agricultural produce of the community as the basis of its prosperity, and counted the value of the manufactures as limited by the surplus of food which the farmers had left over beyond their own wants. From the over-valuation of money and manufactures, which was characteristic of the mercantilists, they passed to an under-valuation.

This error was corrected by Adam Smith (1723-90), whose *Wealth of Nations*, published in 1776, is usually counted as the starting-point of modern political economy. In its general basis the work of the English school, from Smith to Mill, is nevertheless essentially physiocratic; and its most serious errors, like the wage-fund theory, have resulted from carrying over to its broader definitions of capital and wealth, certain propositions which were quite true when capital was identified with food supply alone. The great positive contribution of the English school to economic science was its theory of free competition; and in developing this theory, it may be said to have passed from the old art of political economy to the modern science of economics. Among the many notable names which it includes, we may, without unfairness, select those of Ricardo, Malthus, and John Stuart Mill in England, and Say in France. Still greater precision was given to the theory of competition by the mathematical economists, of whom Cournot and Jevons have been the most influential, and later, by the Austrian school, of whom Boehm-Bawerk is perhaps the ablest exponent.

The study of the workings of free competition tended naturally (though not universally) to produce an economic optimism, which regarded free trade, among nations and among individuals, as a panacea for all social ills. In matters of international trade a reaction against this view is represented by the protectionists (see PROTECTION); in matters of individual trade, by the socialists, of whom Karl Marx is by far the most prominent (see SOCIALISM).

Both Individualism and Socialism, in their extreme forms, are essentially deductive in method, carrying certain assumed premises out to a logical conclusion. The opinion is gaining ground that more stress should be laid on the rest of the premises, and less on the subsequent logical process, if we are to make real progress in economic study. This is the avowed policy of the German historical school, founded by Knies and Roscher in the middle of the present century, and culminating in Wagner and Cohn; it was less loudly preached, but quite as successfully practised, by most of the English and French successors of Mill. The danger which beset the earlier exponents of the German school was a tendency to eclecticism, which sometimes went so far as to deprive their work of all claim to scientific character. The younger generation of writers, brought up under the influence of Darwin, are able to avoid this danger, while preserving the historical character of their investigations.

One or two examples will illustrate this point. In the older generation, the orthodox economists were inclined to treat interest and rent as necessary consequences of the existence of capital and land as factors in production; while their opponents, like Lassalle or George, seeing in history certain cases where interest or rent did not exist, argued that these things were the result of arbitrary enactment, and might be abolished. But the modern historical economist is able to show in actual experience why the present institutions of private capital and private landholding were adopted, and to deduce the consequences of these institutions. He is not compelled to regard them as part of the order of nature, or adjust their results to his conceptions of natural right. He admits their institutional character, but he does not admit that their enactment was arbitrary. On the contrary, he can prove that they were a result of a struggle for existence between different peoples; he can show why they were necessary at the time of their adoption, and can judge with a high degree of accuracy what changes must take place before they become unnecessary to retain. Again, look at the theory of population. Malthus deduced certain consequences from a tendency of population to increase faster than food supply, and argued for 'preventive checks.' His opponents said that there was no such general pressure —only a local one—and that preventive checks were therefore unnecessary. The historical economist is able to show that this localization of the pressure of poverty is the result of the instituting of the family and inheritance, in themselves most powerful preventive checks; and that while Malthus may have been technically wrong in certain details, his opponents are practically wrong in far greater measure.

As a result of these methods, the conception of the relation of economics to ethics has changed radically. They are no longer regarded as independent sciences. The ethics of a people is at once the basis and the consequence of its economic activity. The balance and play of economic motives is the result of the people's ethics; but the future development of that ethics depends largely, and sometimes almost exclusively, upon the economic results of the public morality. The attempt to study either of these sciences without reference to the other is practically a thing of the past.

Literature: for a general bibliography see RAND, Bibliog. of Economics (1895). The great book on the subject is still ADAM SMITH, Wealth of Nations (excellent edition, with notes by Thorold Rogers, Clarendon Press, Oxford; good abridgment by Ashley, in Macmillan's Economic Classics); next to it stands J. S. MILL, Principles of Political Economy. A brief bibliography of some of the more modern writings will be found at the beginning of the successive chapters of HADLEY's Economics (N. Y. and London, 1896); a fuller one in ANDREWS' Institutes of Economics (Boston, 1889); a very complete and good one in COSSA's Introduction to the Study of Political Economy (trans. by Dyer; London, 1893). (A.T.H.)

Economy (in aesthetics): Ger. *Oekonomie-princip*; Fr. *principe d'économie*; Ital. *principio dell' economia*. The principle or law which asserts that the aesthetic value of any object, as a statue, or act, as dancing, depends upon the absence of all superfluous features or elements, and upon the presence of the essentials only.

The brothers Weber (Mechanik d. mensch. Gehwerkzeuge, in *Pogg. Ann.*, 1837) appear to have been the first to maintain, on the basis of experimental observations, that the physiologically correct, that which involves no wasted energy, is synonymous with the aesthetically beautiful. Spencer (*Essays, Scientific*, &c., ii., 1892) has developed the principle of economy in a somewhat similar manner as applied to literary style and to physical grace. Avenarius, under the title Princip des kleinsten Kraftmasses (*Philos. als Denken d. Welt*, 1876), employs essentially the same conception as a basal philosophic doctrine. Fechner also accords the principle distinct importance (*Vorschule d. Aesth.*, ii., 1876). It has been criticized by Bosanquet (*Aesthetics*, 1892) as essentially a restatement, with certain additions of a physiological character, of Aristotle's doctrine of the appropriate relations of the parts to the whole in a work of art. On this last point see HARMONY; for the bearings of the physiological considerations see RHYTHM. For applications of the principle of economy to painting and sculpture, see Hildebrand, *Problem d. Form* (1893). See also Ruskin, 'The Lamp of Sacrifice,' in *Seven Lamps of Architecture*. (J.R.A.)

Economy (logical principle of). A principle maintained by E. Mach that general concepts are merely an adaptation for the economy of mental process. That they have that effect was noticed by Locke. (C.S.P.)

Ecstasy: see MYSTICISM; and consult Eisler, *Wörterb. d. philos. Begriffe*, Ekstase.

Ecstasy (as a condition) [Gr. ἔκστασις, displacement]: Ger. *Ekstase*; Fr. *extase*; Ital. *estasi*. A condition of the nervous system and mind characterized by immobility, suspension of normal sensory and motor functions, and rapt concentration upon a limited group of ideas.

It is particularly characteristic of various forms of religious absorption. 'The symptoms are very much alike in all cases: after sustained concentration of the attention on the desire to attain an intimate communion with heavenly things, the self-absorption being aided perhaps by fixing the gaze intently upon some holy figure or upon the aspirant's own navel, the soul is supposed to be detached from the objects of earth, and to enter into direct converse with heaven; the limbs are then motionless, flaccid, or fixed in the maintenance of some attitude which has been assumed; general sensibility is blunted or extinguished, the special senses are unsusceptible to the impressions which usually affect them, the breathing is slow and feeble, the pulse is scarcely perceptible, the eyes are perhaps bright and animated, and the countenance may wear such a look of rapture, the fashion of it be so changed, that it seems to be transfigured and to shine with a celestial radiance' (Maudsley). Sensibility to external impressions is not always completely destroyed, but there seems an inability to break through the trance and respond to such impressions. At times there is nearly a complete forgetfulness of what has occurred during the ecstatic state, but usually the ecstatic can give some account of his vision and experiences; such reports have been influential in the shaping of religious doctrines both among primitive men and in historical religions.

The condition is closely related to HYPNOSIS (q. v.) and to CATALEPSY (q. v.), and as a rule ecstasy is not closely differentiated from trance except by the presence of a religious or supernatural absorption not found in TRANCE (q. v.). It is usually self-induced, and seems subject to contagion and the dominance of psychological motives. Ribot regards it as a typical form of extinction of the will. The insensibility to pain may be so diminished that severe tortures remain unfelt; martyrs dying at the stake may have been spared the anguish of their fate by the insensibility produced by religious ecstasy. Conditions of violence or of automatic movements connected with religious excitement are also described as cases of ecstasy; such are the 'jumpers,' 'shakers,' 'dancers,' 'flagellants,' &c. Cf. CONTAGION (mental), and also HYSTERIA, EPILEPSY, STIGMA.

Literature: MAUDSLEY, Pathol. of Mind, 70–3 and elsewhere; HAMMOND, Diseases of Nerv. Syst. (7th ed., 1881), 775–86. For cases see art. Ecstasy in Tuke's Dict. of Psychol. Med., and RIBOT, Diseases of the Will

(Eng. trans., 1884), of Personality (1887), and Psychol. of Attention (1890); MANTE-GAZZA, Estasi Umane (1887), and in French translation. (J.J.)

Ectoderm [Gr. ἐκτός, outside, + δέρμα, skin]: Ger. *äusseres Keimblatt*; Fr. *ectoderme*; Ital. *ectoderma*. The outer layer of cœlenterate animals. Also used to denote the outer of the two primitive cell-layers of the embryo animal, sometimes termed epiblast. See BLASTODERM, EMBRYO, and EPIBLAST. (C.LL.M.–E.S.G.)

Ectoplasm [Gr. ἐκτός, outside, + πλάσμα, substance]: Ger. *Ektoplasma*; Fr. *ectoplasme*; Ital. *ectoplasma*. The outer layer of the proto-plasm of certain animal and vegetable cells.

Long recognized in certain unicellular or-ganisms, and termed ectosarc. The observa-tion has been extended to the tissue cells of higher animals and plants.

Literature: C. KUPFFER, Ueber Differen-zierung des Protoplasma an den Zellen thieri-scher Gewebe., Zeitsch. naturw. Ver. Schles.-Holst. (1875); O. HERTWIG, The Cell (trans., 1895). (C.LL.M.)

Edelmann, Johann Christian. (1698–1767.) A German pietist converted by Bud-deus, who in later life became a believer in Spinoza's philosophy. He opposed the Wolffian philosophy throughout his life.

Educability: see EDUCATION, and PLAS-TICITY.

Education [Lat. *educatio*, from *educare*, to rear, nourish]: Ger. *Erziehung*; Fr. *éducation*; Ital. *educazione*. The science and art of human development; the training of the mind and body through instruction and exercise. See INSTRUCTION, TRAINING, DISCIPLINE, and CULTURE. (C.DE G.)

The capacity to profit by experience in such a way as to accommodate to conditions which recur has been called educability in psycho-logy and biology. The burnt child which dreads the fire is a more familiar case than the bird which, once misled by a bright-coloured distasteful insect, thereafter avoids insects of the same marking. The method in most of the instances is by trial and error, or EXPERIMENTATION (q. v.).

Literature: LLOYD MORGAN, Habit and Instinct; LANKESTER, Nature (April 28, 1900). (J.M.B.)

Educative Instruction: Ger., see below; other equivalents are not in use. Such instruc-tion, both as to matter and method, as directly promotes the development of moral character.

It is a watchword of the Herbartians (erziehender Unterricht). By it they mean that the entire subject-matter of instruction should be so selected and taught as to con-duce to the ethical upbuilding of the pupil, both as an individual and as a member of the various social, economic, and political groups to which he may belong. This idea lies at the foundation of Ziller's doctrine of CONCENTRA-TION (q. v.). See CULTURE EPOCHS.

Literature: ZILLER, Allg. Päd., 160–79; HERBART, Sci. of Educ. (trans. by Felkin), 135–42; McMURRY, Gen. Meth., 14–105; DE GARMO, Herbart and the Herbartians; ARDIGO, Sci. dell' educazione (1893). (C.DE G.)

Edwardeans (no foreign equivalents in use). The name given to a group of American theologians who, starting from the distinctive ideas of Jonathan Edwards, transformed the traditional Calvinism in some of its leading doctrines. Other names, such as New England Theology, Berkshire Divinity, &c., have been applied to the movement.

The 'governmental' theory of the atone-ment; choice as the characteristic embodiment of the moral nature of the will; man's 'ability' or freedom, yet dependence on a sovereign God; and a denial that original sin is 'im-puted,' are among the leading doctrines, though advocated, as was natural, in various ways by different members of the group. The whole movement is of undeniable importance with reference to the evolution of philosophical thought in the United States; an evolution which, in its early stages, was bound up with theological questions even more than that of Scottish thought.

Literature: JONATHAN EDWARDS, Works, i. 481 f.; G. P. FISHER, Discussions in Hist. and Theol. (the Essay on the Philosophy of Jonathan Edwards); and Hist. of Christ. Doctrine, 394 f.; EDWARDS A. PARK, in Schaff-Herzog's Religious Encyc., ii (the art. New England Theology, where the literature is fully given). (R.M.W.)

Edwards, Jonathan. (1703–58.) An American minister and metaphysician, born at East Windsor, Conn., and died at Princeton, N.J. Graduated from Yale College, 1720. Received the Master's degree from Yale, 1723. He was a tutor at Yale, 1724–6. In 1727 he became pastor of the church at Northamp-ton, Mass. In 1750 he was forced to give up his charge, after having attempted certain re-forms in the communion service. In 1751 he became missionary at Stockbridge among the Housatonic Indians, and pastor of the white church there. In 1757 he was elected President of Princeton College, N.J., but died soon after.

Effect: see CAUSE AND EFFECT.

Effectual Calling: Ger. *wirksame Berufung*; Fr. *grâce* (or *vocation*) *suffisante*; Ital. *grazia sufficiente*. In the language of Evangelical theology, 'calling' is the first indication of 'conversion.' God's grace working through the Word (usually as preached) effects the 'call.' In the Calvinistic theology, there is an 'external' call, which is extended to all equally; and an 'internal' call, which is addressed to the elect. The latter is known technically as effectual calling.

Literature: Westminster Shorter Catechism, 31. See CALVINISM, and GRACE. (R.M.W.)

Effeminacy [Lat. *ex + femina*, a woman]: Ger. *Feminismus, weibisches Wesen* (no exact equivalent); Fr. *féminisme*; Ital. *effeminatezza*. The presence of feminine characteristics of mind and character in the male. Effeminacy is mainly used in reference to the more delicate and conventional attributes of woman, while the term feminism refers to the appearance in the male of distinct physical and mental approximations to the female type. If excessive, this condition may be termed sexual inversion, and the subject so afflicted an invert. See SEXUAL CHARACTERS.

Literature: H. ELLIS, Sexual Inversion and references there given; H. MEIGE, in Nouv. Iconographie de la Salpêtrière, and Rev. d'Anthropol. (1895–6). (J.J.)

Efferent [Lat. *ex + ferre*, to bear]: Ger. *centrifugal*; Fr. *efférent*; Ital. *efferente*. The term applied to those nerves (also termed centrifugal) which carry impulses outward from the central nervous system; also to the impulses so transmitted. Suggested by W. B. Carpenter (1842), *Human Physiol.* (1st ed.), 83. It is opposed to AFFERENT, or CENTRIPETAL (see those terms). (C.LL.M.)

Efficacy; see GRACE.

Efficiency and **Efficient Cause:** see CAUSE AND EFFECT.

Efficiency (economic) [Lat. *efficiens*]: Ger. *Produktivität*; Fr. *productivité*; Ital. *produttività*. Power of producing wealth; especially power of rendering a surplus of product above cost.

The Continental economists, especially the Germans, have given precision to this idea of economic efficiency by discussing the difference between 'productivity'—an excess of product over the waste involved in production—and 'rentability'—an excess of earnings to the owner above the expenses involved in the ownership of a piece of property. (A.T.H.)

Efficient Series: see MOVEMENT.

Effluvium: see PERCEPTION.

Effort, Bodily (consciousness of): Ger. *Spannungsempfindung, Kraftempfindung*; Fr. *sentiment de l'effort moteur*; Ital. *sensazione* (or *sentimento*) *di sforzo* or *di tensione*. The experience which accompanies bodily movement, so far as it involves the overcoming or the attempt to overcome resistance. (G.F.S., J.M.B.)

It is a disputed point whether sense of motor effort is peripheral in its origin (KINAESTHETIC, q.v.), or a concomitant of the outgoing current (a sensation of INNERVATION, q.v.).

Literature: BAIN (Senses and Intellect, 4th ed., 79–80) represents the first view in its purest form. WUNDT held (Physiol. Psychol., 1st and 2nd eds.) that sensational consciousness of effort is correlated with the outgoing current; but, in his later works, he does not regard this sensational consciousness as an ultimate and undeniable fact. Its quality, he now thinks, is ultimately determined by prior experiences due to peripheral stimulation; cf. note by TITCHENER, Mind, N.S. ii. (1893) 143, on Innervationsempfindung in Wundt's Psychology. The outgoing current view is also supported by MACH, Die Bewegungsempfindungen, and by WALLER, The Sense of Effort, an objective Study, Brain, liv and lv. (1891) 179 ff. (cf. adverse criticisms by G. E. MÜLLER in Zeitsch. f. Psychol., iv. 122 ff., and by BALDWIN in Amer. J. of Psychol. v. (1892) 273; for a statement of the opposite view, see JAMES, The Sense of Effort, and Princ. of Psychol., ii. 189 ff., 480–518; BASTIAN, The Brain as an Organ of Mind (1880), 543; MÜNSTERBERG, Die Willenshandlung, 78 ff., and Beitr. z. exper. Psychol., i. 152 ff.; GLEY, Le Sens musculaire, Rev. Philos. (Dec. 1885); DELABARRE, Ueber Bewegungsempfindungen (1891); BALDWIN, Ment. Devel. in the Child and the Race; report of discussion of the subject following a paper by BASTIAN, in Brain (1887); LADD, Psychol., Descrip. and Explan.; BEAUNIS, Les Sensations internes, chap. xii; and a résumé by HAMLIN, Amer. J. of Psychol., viii. 13. (G.F.S.–J.M.B.)

Effort, Mental (consciousness of): Ger. *Anstrengung*; Fr. *sentiment de l'effort mental*; Ital. *sentimento dello sforzo mentale*. The intensification of mental activity which arises on the occurrence of any sort of obstruction.

About the same problem presents itself as in the case of bodily EFFORT (q. v.), except that the conditions of mental effort are still more obscure. (G.F.S.—J.M.B.)

The antithesis between effort and resistance has played an important rôle in the development of French psychology under the lead of Maine de Biran, to whom the experience of effort was fundamental. (L.M.)

Effort (in education). The doing of work through sheer force of will; contrasted with activity induced by amusement or other external allurement.

The place and function of effort in school work forms an important part of the doctrine of interest. The view is held by some that pure volitional effort on the part of the pupil, quite apart from any interest whatever, is the result most to be desired in school study. Others hold that we should esteem highly only the effort that arises from a genuine interest in the studies themselves. See under INTEREST.

Literature: DEWEY, Interest as related to Will, second supplement of the First Year-Book of the National Herbart Society. (C.DE G.)

Ego and **Alter** [Lat. terms for self and other]: Ger. same, or *das Selbst und das Andere*; Fr. same, or *le moi et l'autre*; Ital. same, or *il se-soggetto e il se-oggetto*. The object-self (the ego) of the individual consciousness as distinguished in the same individual's thought from another (the alter).

The antithesis of ego and alter necessarily restricts the meaning of ego to the object-self (see SELF for the distinction of object-self from subject-self), inasmuch as it is in relation to the alter, which is object of thought. The interpretation of the ego-alter relation has been variously attempted. For the intuitive theory there is immediate apprehension of both the self and the other. For many thinkers, the alter is a reading into another's body of the essential features of the object-ego; for which process the term 'ejection' was suggested by Clifford. See EJECT. Other writers have developed the thought that the ego is a re-production of traits first discovered in alter personalities. This latter view has been united with the theory of ejection by the present writer in what he calls the 'dialectic of personal growth,' which includes the two processes going on together and equally essential. The self-thought tends to a general form which includes two poles, one the ego and the other the alter. The elements of content, at first 'projective' in the social environment (i. e. cognized as objects but with no antithesis to subject), are taken up by imitation, thus becoming 'subjective' or part of the ego, and being then ejected into the other, constitute the alter. Apart from the use of terms a substantially similar view has been independently developed by Royce and adopted by Stout.

Literature: CLIFFORD, Seeing and Thinking; ROYCE, Studies of Good and Evil; STOUT, Manual of Psychol.; BALDWIN, Social and Eth. Interpret. (J.M.B.—G.F.S.)

Ego and **Non-Ego** [Lat. terms for self and non-self]. The self and the not-self of the individual's consciousness. See SELF, and NOT-SELF. (J.M.B.)

Egoism [Lat. *ego*, self]: Ger. *Egoismus*; Fr. *égoïsme*; Ital. *egoismo*. Attitudes or dispositions having as their conscious end the advantage of the personal self are termed egoistic, and constitute egoism. Egotism is also used in this sense. Cf. ALTRUISM, and SELFISHNESS. (J.M.B.)

Egoism (ethical). Exclusive interest in self: more precisely, it describes one or other of two theories, the former psychological (see the preceding topic), the latter ethical, i. e. that the standard for conduct is its tendency towards the preservation, interest, or pleasure of the individual agent.

Both theories are commonly accompanied by a hedonistic interpretation of the nature of the individual's interest or good; even when (as in Hobbes and in Spinoza) the notion of self-preservation is preferred to that of pleasure. The psychological and ethical theories were conjoined in the doctrine of Epicurus, and of most hedonistic moralists, before the rise of utilitarianism in the 18th century in Great Britain. More recently the two theories (hedonistically interpreted) have been combined by A. Barratt.

Literature: A. BARRATT, Physical Eth. (1869); SIDGWICK, Meth. of Eth., Bk. II; H. SPENCER, Princ. of Eth., Pt. I. chaps. xi-xiii; SORLEY, Eth. of Nature, chap. ii; general treatises on ethics. See also BIBLIOG. F, 2, *a*. (W.R.S.)

Egotism: see PRIDE, and EGOISM.

Egypt (religion in ancient): see ORIENTAL PHILOSOPHY (Egypt).

Eidolon: see PERCEPTION.

Einfühlung (Ger.): see TERMINOLOGY (German).

Eject and **Ejective** [Lat. *eiectum*, from *eiicere*, to throw out]: Ger. *Ejekt*; Fr. *éject*; Ital. *ejettivo* (ejective). Some one else thought of in terms of the thinker's own consciousness of himself. In its earlier stages it amounts to the interpretation of external phenomena, expressions, signs, &c., as involving experience analogous to that of the percipient or thinker.

Suggested by Clifford (*Seeing and Thinking*); employed by Romanes (*Matter, Mind, and Monism*), by whom the principle of ANTHROPOMORPHISM (q. v.) in theism is said to produce the 'world-eject'; by Morselli (*Semej. malat. ment.*, ii) in pathological conditions; and by Baldwin (*Social and Eth. Interpret.*), who makes the process of ejection a necessary and continuous factor in the development of the consciousness of PERSONALITY (q. v.). The adjective 'ejective' qualifies the matter or content which in a particular case constitutes the 'eject.' See also PERSONIFICATION.   (J.M.B.–G.F.S.)

Elaboration and **Elaborative Faculty** [Lat. *e* + *laborare*, to labour]: Ger. (1) *Denkvermögen*; Fr. *élaboration*; Ital. *elaborazione*. (1) The process and function of thinking or reasoning. Synonymous with DISCURSIVE FACULTY (under which see citations). See also REASONING.

(2) The formation of new mental products of any sort from given material. (J.M.B.–G.F.S.)

Eleatics: see PRE-SOCRATIC PHILOSOPHY (Eleatics).

Election: see FORE-ORDINATION.

Electric Organs: Ger. *elektrische Organe*; Fr. *organes électriques*; Ital. *organi elettrici*. Masses of peculiarly modified tissue found in certain fishes, which are capable of generating and discharging more or less severe electric shocks.

These organs are in most cases metamorphosed muscular masses, though, in the electric shad of the Nile, *Malopterurus*, they are developed from cutaneous structures, probably glands. They are under the control of the brain, and are supplied by nerves which, except in *Malopterurus*, correspond to motor nerves, and whose peculiarly developed terminal organs are modified motor end-plates. The electric nerves arise from special enlargements of the medulla or spinal cord which are variously placed in different species. These 'electric lobes' correspond to excessively developed and modified motor nuclei. In *Malopterurus*, however, there are two electric nerves, each arising from a single huge cell in the spinal cord and dividing into over a million branches.

Literature: GUSTAV FRITSCH, Die elektrischen Fische (Erste Abt., 1887; Zweite Abt., 1890), Leipzig (with bibliography);

E. DU BOIS-REYMOND, Gesammelte Abhandlungen, ii (Berlin); BABUCHIN, Uebersicht der neuen Untersuchungen über Entwickelung, Bau, und physiologische Verhältnisse der elektrischen und pseudo-elektrischen Organe, Arch. f. Anat. u. Physiol. (1876).   (H.H.)

Electricity: see ENERGY, and UNITS.

Electro-biology: Ger. *Elektrobiologie*; Fr. *électrobiologie*; Ital. *elettrobiologia*. A term under which the phenomena now known as hypnosis were described by certain exhibitors and writers in England and America (about 1850).

The term involves an extravagant hypothesis to the effect that the process by which the operator influenced his subject was in some way connected with electricity and the vital factor of animal existence. See W. B. Carpenter, *Mesmerism, Spiritualism*, &c. (1877).   (J.J.)

Element [Lat. *elementum*]: Ger. *Element*; Fr. *élément*; Ital. *elemento*. That which cannot be reduced to simpler terms under the conditions of the investigation.

In science the term refers to the different kinds of atoms, the sorts of material, of which the world is composed. See MATTER. During the ancient and mediaeval periods earth, air, fire, water constituted the elements. In logic the simplest idea which enters into a conception or system of conceptions is called an element of that conception or system.   (H.R.S.)

Element (material): see MATTER.

Element of Consciousness: Ger. *Bewusstseinselement*; Fr. *élément de la conscience*; Ital. *elemento della coscienza*. Any content of consciousness in which introspection fails to detect internal complexity is elementary, and for the psychical life an element.

This use of element is opposed to that which applies the term to the original mental functions from the point of view of psychological ANALYSIS. The element is such for psychical or mental ANALYSIS. See the distinction made under those terms. See also CLASSIFICATION (of the mental functions).   (J.M.B., G.F.S.)

Elenchus [Gr. ἔλεγχος]. Refutation by argument. See IGNORATIO ELENCHI. (J.M.B.)

Elimination [Lat. *eliminare*]: Ger. *Elimination, Ausschalten* (Groos); Fr. *élimination, sélection négative*; Ital. *eliminazione*. (1) By natural selection: the process by which, under nature, the weakly or anywise unfit are excluded, in the struggle for existence, in greater or less degree, from taking part in the propagation of their kind. See NATURAL SELECTION.   (C.LL.M.–J.M.B.)

Darwin, in the *Origin of Species*, laid great stress on the struggle for EXISTENCE (q. v.). Herbert Spencer applied to the result of the process the phrase 'survival of the fittest.' It is now generally recognized that the survival of the fittest as a result is due to the elimination of the unfit under the stress of the struggle for existence.

Literature: C. DARWIN, Origin of Species; H. SPENCER, Princ. of Biol.; works on evolution. (C.LL.M.)

(2) By conscious selection. A similar result to (1), secured by the intentional exclusion of certain individuals on the part of man.

This is best illustrated by the weeding-out practised by horticulturalists, and by other cases of ARTIFICIAL SELECTION; also seen in SOCIAL SELECTION and SOCIAL SUPPRESSION. See those terms.

In both these cases (1) and (2), the elimination may be complete or only partial, according as the individual has already been productive or not, while remaining still fertile. The result of partial or late elimination is the same as that of reduced fertility, and is subject to similar treatment to that given to relative fertility by the theory of REPRODUCTIVE (or GENETIC) SELECTION (q. v.). Until the work of Pearson on this latter subject biologists had done nothing towards establishing quantitative results in the matter of greater or less fertility, and the experimental investigation of the question by conscious elimination has never been undertaken. GALTON'S LAW (q. v.) of ancestral inheritance gives the contribution of each parent to the endowment of each child, &c., but does not determine the entire contribution of the individual to the subsequent generations in terms of his relative fertility. (J.M.B., E.B.P.)

Elimination (in logic): see REASONING.

Elis (school of): see PRE-SOCRATIC PHILOSOPHY.

Emanation [Lat. *e* + *manare*, to flow]: Ger. *Emanation, Ausstrahlung*; Fr. *émanation*; Ital. *emanazione*. A pantheistic conception of the being of the universe. The emanated being 'flows out' or 'proceeds' from the Godhead, so that all finite beings at different removes from the primitive essence are part and parcel of the Divine Being. It is one of the various devices for solving the problem of the one and the many. The plurality of the emanated beings was not supposed to affect the unity of the primitive Divine Being. (H.R.S.)

Emanation is essentially a cosmological, or rather a cosmogonic, process: series of beings, often in a descending scale, proceed from the original unknowable and unbroken unity till, at length, the present world with all its imperfections and evils is produced.

It has happened in the history of thought that God and the universe have been separated, either metaphysically—as reality and appearance, or morally—as good and evil. When this separation became very marked, the problem arose: How can the two be connected? One form of the answer was furnished by the theory of emanation. Technically, the theory may be said to involve a pluralism based on an abstract monism. For this reason it is utterly untenable. Its most characteristic examples are to be found in Indian philosophy (Vedânta), and particularly in the various Gnostic systems, also in Neo-Platonism (Plotinus, Proclus).

Literature: see ALEXANDRIAN SCHOOL, and GNOSTICISM. (R.M.W.)

Emancipation [Lat. *e* + *manus* + *capere*, to deliver out of one's hands]: Ger. *Emancipation, Freilassung*; Fr. *émancipation*; Ital. *emancipazione*. The act of setting free.

The term emancipation was originally applied to the act whereby a Roman parent or master conferred freedom upon a child or slave. In modern times the term has been applied to any change whereby a class of persons has been relieved from old disabilities or invested with new rights, e.g. the abolition of slavery in the United States, or of serfdom in Russia, the removal of disabilities imposed on Roman Catholics in the United Kingdom; the extension of the parliamentary franchise to classes hitherto without political power, &c. The term has also been applied to changes which increase personal liberty or independence in a less definite manner, e.g. the changes in the position of women which have taken place in our time are sometimes comprehensively described as the emancipation of women. (F.C.M.)

Embryo [Gr. ἔμβρυον]: Ger. *Embryo, (Keim-) Frucht*; Fr. *embryon*; Ital. *embrione*. The term applied to the developing animal prior to the stage at which the tissues and organs are fully differentiated; in phanerogamic botany, to the rudimentary plant in the seed.

Early writers distinguished between the mammalian embryo and the foetus—the former term being applied during the period of germination, the latter during the period of cherishing. But it is difficult to determine exactly when embryonic development is superseded by that which is post-embryonic.

The fertilized OVUM (q.v.) undergoes a process of cleavage or segmentation. This, in the case of alecithal and HOMOLECITHAL (q.v.) ova, affects the whole ovum, and is then termed holoblastic. When there is much food-yolk and the ova are markedly HETEROLECITHAL (q.v.), the cleavage only affects at first a portion of the ovum, and the segmentation is meroblastic. In the case of holoblastic segmentation the cell divides into two; these again divide, and so on, giving rise to a number of cleavage cells or blastomeres. To the group of cells thus formed, the term morula or polyblast is applied. In the midst of these a cavity, the segmentation cavity of von Baer, or blastocoel is formed. The hollow vesicle is called a blastosphere. Rarely, the blastosphere splitting by delamination into two layers, an outer epiblast or ectoderm, and an inner hypoblast or endoderm, the blastocoel becomes the digestive cavity or enteron.

In the majority of cases (among the Coelomata) the hollow blastosphere is invaginated so as to form a two-layer cup or gastrula (see figure), the inner layer being the

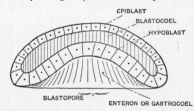

Stage in the formation of the Gastrula in *Amphioxus*.

hypoblast, and the outer the epiblast. The orifice of invagination is termed the blastopore (Lankester), the invaginated cavity the archenteron or gastrocoel. The primary layers may also be differentiated from the morula stage by an inner mass of cells (hypoblast) becoming overgrown by an outer layer of cells (epiblast); so-called epibolic invagination. A middle layer (mesoblast or mesoderm) is formed between the epiblast and hypoblast.

This is, or in time becomes, two-layered and segmented in segmented animals; the inner or splanchnic layer is associated with the hypoblast, and forms the muscular wall of the digestive tube; the outer somatic layer is associated with the epiblast, and forms the muscular body wall. The space between the

two walls is termed the coelom. It is of paired origin, and segmented in segmented animals. In meroblastic cleavage and in the blastodermic vesicle of the higher mammalia, the embryo is gradually folded off from the yolk mass or the umbilical sac, by which process the space beneath the hypoblast is gradually converted into the digestive tube. In reptiles, birds, and mammals certain accessory structures known as embryonic membranes (the amnion and the allantois) are formed. From the epiblast of the embryo are formed the epidermis, the epithelium of the mouth and vent, the central nervous system, the essential and some of the accessory structures of the organs of special sense. From the hypoblast are formed the epithelium of the true enteron, that of the lungs, liver, pancreas, &c., and the notochord. From the mesoblast are formed the muscles, bones, connective tissue, blood vascular system, renal organs, and genital organs. Cf. CLEAVAGE, and SEGMENTATION. For literature see EMBRYOLOGY. (C.LL.M.–E.S.G.)

Embryology [Gr. ἔμβρυον + λόγος]: Ger. *Embryologie, Entwicklungsgeschichte*; Fr. *embryologie*; Ital. *embriologia*. The study of the changes undergone by the animal in developing from the ovum to the stage where the tissues and organs are fully differentiated.

For the history of embryology see Allen Thomson's art. in the 9th ed. of the *Encyclopaedia Britannica*, iii. What Hutton and Lyell did respectively for geology, von Baer and F. M. Balfour did for embryology. The limits of the term are hard to set. Balfour says: 'The term embryology is now employed to cover the anatomy and physiology of the organism during the whole period included between its first coming into being and its attainment of the adult state.' The definition here given is somewhat narrower, and more closely accords with the scope of Balfour's own work.

Literature: ALLEN THOMSON, as above; F. M. BALFOUR, Compar. Embryol. (1880–1); O. HERTWIG, Textbook of Embryol.; Man and Mammals (Eng. trans. by Mark, 1892); KORSCHELT and HEIDER, Textbook of Embryol., Invertebrates, i (Eng. trans. by Mark and Woodworth, 1895); C. S. MINOT, Human Embryol.; E. SCHÄFER, in Quain's Elements of Anatomy, Part I, Embryology (1890); Bibliography of Vertebrate Embryology, Mem. of Brit. Soc. of Nat. Hist., iv, No. 11 (1893). (C.LL.M.–E.S.G.)

Emerson, Ralph Waldo. (1803–

82.) An American poet and essayist, who stimulated the philosophical movement in New England called Transcendentalism. Born in Boston, educated in a Boston public school and Harvard University, he taught school 1821–6, chiefly in Boston. In 1826 he was 'approbated to preach,' and in 1829 was ordained as the associate of Henry Ware in the second Unitarian Church in Boston. In 1832 he resigned his pastoral charge, announcing in a sermon that he could no longer conscientiously administer the Lord's Supper. The following year he spent in Europe, where he made the acquaintance of Carlyle, and remained a firm friend until the latter's death. After 1834 he devoted himself to literary work, writing and lecturing on a variety of themes. His lecturing began in Boston Mechanics' Institute, but continued in all parts of the United States and in England.

Emersonianism. TRANSCENDENTALISM (q. v.) as contained in the writings of R. W. Emerson. (J.M.B.)

Eminent Domain [Mod. Lat. *dominium eminens*]: Ger. *Oberhoheit über das Staatsgut*; Fr. *domaine éminent*; Ital. *dominio eminente*. (1) The right of the sovereign to take any private property for public use, in case of necessity. (2) The right of the sovereign to control those property rights of a public nature which pertain to the citizens generally, and to control or take any private property for public use, in case of necessity.

The sovereign's right to devote the persons and lives of his subjects to public use is styled 'eminent power,' and, added to eminent domain, constitutes 'eminent right' (Wolff on *The Law of Nature*, Lib. II. § 1065).

Eminent domain covers personal property as well as real, but is seldom exercised with regard to the former, since there is seldom any necessity for such action. To take land is often necessary, because no other land than that taken will answer the purpose. Compensation to the owner is generally required by modern legislation (see *Code Civil* of France, art. 545). It is invariably required by American constitutional law (see Cowley on *Constitutional Limitations*, chap. xv). When the legislature authorizes a taking for certain purposes, and declares them to be public ones, its judgment will be respected by the courts, unless they are palpably such that they cannot be brought under that description (United States *v.* Gettysburg Electric Railway, 160 United States Reports, 680).

Literature: VATTEL, on The Law of Nations, Lib. I. chap. xx. § 244; HEINECCIUS, Elementa Iuris Naturae, Lib. II. §§ 169–71. (S.E.B.)

Eminent Power: see EMINENT DOMAIN.

Eminenter [Lat.]. Beyond measure or degree. 'Eminenter est supra omnem mensuram, super omnes gradus. Deus causa ac principium eminenter' (Goclenius, *Lex. Philos.*, 146: quoted by Eisler; cf. his other citations, *Wörterb. d. philos. Begriffe*, sub verbo).

A scholastic term used by Descartes, Spinoza, Wolff, &c. (J.M.B.)

Emmetropism (or **-ia,** or **-y**) [Gr. ἐν + μέτρον, measure, + ὄψ, eye]; Ger. *Emmetropismus*; Fr. *emmétropie*; Ital. *emmetropismo*. Normal or perfect vision in regard to focal adjustment. When the shape and refractive media of an eye are such that without the aid of the muscles of accommodation parallel rays of light can be brought to the focus precisely on the retina, such an eye is termed emmetropic.

For practical tests rays of light from a point more than twenty feet away may be regarded as parallel. By some writers, emmetropism also includes the power to focus sharply for all distances, from 5 inches or over. An eye which cannot accomplish this is ametropic. See VISION (defects of). (J.J.)

Emotion: Ger. *Affekt* (see below); Fr. *émotion*; Ital. *emozione*. A total state of consciousness considered as involving a distinctive feeling-tone and a characteristic trend of activity aroused by a certain situation which is either perceived or ideally represented. (G.F.S.–J.M.B.)

The use of the word emotion in English psychology is comparatively modern. It is found in Hume, but even he speaks generally rather of passions or affections. When the word emotion did become current its application was very wide, covering all possible varieties of feeling, except those which are purely sensational in their origin. 'All' emotions 'agree in this respect, that they imply peculiar vividness of feeling, with this important circumstance to distinguish them from the vivid pleasures and pains of sense; that they do not arise immediately from the presence of external objects, but subsequently to the primary feelings which we term sensations or perceptions. Perhaps, if any definition of them be possible, they may be defined to be vivid feelings, arising immediately from the consideration of objects perceived or remembered, or imagined, or from other prior emotions' (Brown, *Philos. of the Human Mind*, i. 405). Bain's usage is equally wide.

It is common in defining emotion to assign as a distinctive characteristic a special degree of intensity or vividness. See EXCITEMENT. This introduces a certain vagueness and ambiguity into the conception. We have accordingly omitted reference to degree of intensity, and considered solely the characteristic nature of emotion. Otherwise our definition is an attempt to find a conception which will serve as common ground in the discussions which gather round the subject of emotion.

The subject of emotion has been much cleared up through the discussions stimulated by the so-called JAMES-LANGE THEORY (q. v.). The questions now receiving attention are the relation of emotion to the so-called 'expression'—the psychophysics of emotion; the distinction of 'coarser' from 'finer,' and of emotion proper from sentiment; the analysis of the emotional psychosis, leading to the recognition of separate qualities, besides the hedonic tone (as opposed to the older theory that emotion is only compounded pleasure and pain); and the origin of emotion, together with the 'expression'—the genetic question, as involved in the evolution of mind in general.

The German use of terms is as difficult as the English. Gefühl is used—as is the English feeling—for abstract emotion considered as mainly a modification of the affective life. Concrete states of emotion are designated Affekte. The fact, however, that emotion involves conation as well makes it a matter of Gemüth, and we have the phrases Gemüthszustand, Gemüthsbewegung, Gemüthserregung. The higher states of mind in which ideal representation is prominent, and for which the English 'sentiment' is used, are designated höhere Gefühle. The most useful and frequent single term, however, is Affekt for the cruder emotions, with which may well be used Gefühlsdisposition (Höfler). In French, émotion is fairly equivalent to emotion, sentiment having the broader connotation of the words feeling and Gefühl. (J.M.B., G.F.S.)

Literature: BALDWIN, Handb. of Psychol., Feeling and Will, 135-7, 174 ff. (important for definition), and Ment. Devel. in the Child and the Race, chap. viii; JAMES, Princ. of Psychol., chap. xxv, and Psychol. Rev., i. 516 f.; SHAND, Character and the Emotions, Mind, N.S., No. 18 (April, 1896); LANGE, Über Gemüthsbewegungen; D. IRONS, The Nature of Emotion, Philos. Rev. (1897), vi. 242-56, 471-96; STUMPF, in Zeitsch.

f. Psychol., xxi. (1899) 47; LEHMANN, Hauptgesetze des menschlichen Gefühlslebens, 56 ff.; STOUT, Manual of Psychol.; JODL, Lehrb. d. Psychol.; RIBOT, Psychol. des Sentiments (Eng. trans.); ZIEGLER, Das Gefühl; SERGI, Dolore e Piacere. See also BIBLIOG. G, 2, *e*; the lists in loc. in Psychol. Index, i. ff.; EISLER, Wörterb. d. philos. Begriffe, 'Affekt'; and textbooks of psychology. (G.F.S.)

Emotion (aesthetic). What has generally been meant by the emotional element in aesthetic psychoses is a condition of mental excitation, whether agreeable, disagreeable, or both, involving processes of a distinctly intellectual and spiritual character, and especially such processes in distinction from merely sensuous pleasures and pains. In this sense the idea is most closely represented by the present use of the term SENTIMENT (q. v.).

Literature: on the differentia of aesthetic emotion see BOSANQUET, Aesthetic Emotion, Mind (1894); MARSHALL, Pain, Pleasure, and Aesthetics (1894); BAIN, Emotions and Will (3rd ed., 1875); RIBOT, Psychol. of the Emotions (Eng. trans., 1897). (J.R.A.)

Emotion (ethical, social, and religious): see SENTIMENT, HONOUR, REVERENCE, REMORSE, REVENGE, REGRET, RESPECT, and RELIGION (psychology of).

Emotional Disposition: Ger. *Gefühlsdisposition* (Höfler); Fr. *disposition émotionnelle*; Ital. *disposizione all' emozione, emotività*. A permanent mental disposition giving rise to certain kinds of EMOTION (q. v.) on presentation of a certain object. The emotion varies according to the circumstances under which the object is presented. Cf. DISPOSITION. (G.F.S., J.M.B.)

Emotional Expression: Ger. *Ausdrucksbewegungen*; Fr. *expression émotionnelle*; Ital. *espressione emotiva*. The characteristic bodily changes which occur in connection with EMOTION (q. v.). (J.M.B.-G.F.S.)

The detailed determination of these changes for the separate emotions involving the facial muscles is called 'facial expression.' Since Darwin's book on the *Expression of the Emotions*, the theory is current that the grosser emotional expressions are survivals of reactions which were of utility to the animal when in the presence of the conditions which excited the emotion. To this law of 'utility,' called by Darwin that of 'serviceable associated habits,' he added others to account for other cases: the law of 'analogous feeling stimuli' (developed by later writers, especially James, from Darwin's suggestion), by which experiences which excited similar emotions are supposed to issue in the same expression; that of 'antithesis,' whereby opposite emotions show opposite expressions, although only one of the expressions may have utility; that of 'direct nervous discharge,' according to which stimulations, mainly of an excessive character, would discharge themselves in muscular activity. This principle has taken formulation in later writers in the principle of 'hedonic expression' (Spencer, Bain; the expression is from Baldwin), which recognizes the facts that pleasure increases muscular movement in certain muscles, and that pain lessens it; the same principle being used by the last-named writer to explain 'antithesis.' Darwin assumed that the state of emotion preceded the expression and caused the latter: the so-called CAUSE THEORY (q.v.) of emotion. Recently the theory has been advanced— called the 'James-Lange Theory'— that the emotion is the mental indication of the changes which constitute the so-called 'expression'; that is, the actions of utility or other take place, and these are reported in the brain, giving rise to the qualitative experiences which we call emotions. The recurrence of a certain emotion, or its artificial stimulation, in the absence of its appropriate object, is the incipient revival of the earlier expressions—an 'organic reverberation' (James). This, called variously the 'effect theory,' the 'peripheral theory,' &c., of emotion, is still under discussion, in opposition to the 'cause theory,' noted above.

Literature: see under EMOTION, also BIBLIOG. G, 2, *e*; DARWIN, Expression of the Emotions; BELL, Anatomy of Expression; LANGE, Die Gemüthsbewegungen; JAMES, Princ. of Psychol., ii. chap. xxv; and Psychol. Rev. (1894), i. 516; PIDERIT, La Mimique et la Physionomie (1888); MANTEGAZZA, Fisionomia e Mimica (1878); IRONS, arts. in Mind and Philos. Rev. (since 1893); DEWEY, The Theory of Emotion, Psychol. Rev., i. 553, ii. 13; STOUT, Manual of Psychol.; SOLLIER, Rev. Philos. xxxvii. (1894) 241; WORCESTER, Monist, iii. (1893) 285; LEHMANN, Hauptgesetze des Gefühlslebens; BALDWIN, Ment. Devel. in the Child and the Race, chap. viii; STUMPF, Begriff der Gemüthsbewegung, Zeitsch. f. Psychol., xxi. 47 ff.; the general works on psychology, especially those of WUNDT, LADD, JODL. (J.M.B., G.F.S.)

Empedocles. Greek philosopher, who lived in the 5th century B.C. Born at Agrigentum in Sicily. His talents and scientific attainments led his countrymen to offer him a crown,

which he refused, using his influence to found a republic in Sicily. Fragments of a poem on Nature remain from his works.

Empire: see GOVERNMENT.

Empirical [Gr. ἐμπειρία, experience]. Based upon (empirical views), guided by (empirical medicine), derived from (empirical knowledge) EXPERIENCE (q. v.). (J.M.B.)

Empirical Logic: Ger. *empirische Logik*; Fr. *logique empirique*; Ital. *logica empirica*. The treatment of logic on the basis or from the point of view of a sensationalist or other markedly empiricist theory of knowledge.

(R.A.–C.S.P.)

The latter term, however, is very indeterminate. The defining marks of an empiricist theory of knowledge can hardly be assigned with theoretical accuracy; and, on the historical side, theories of knowledge that are rightly described as empirical have not always exhibited the same features. In its extreme form, the empirical theory of knowledge identifies knowing with the immediate process of sense perception, and represents all connection in the content known as identical in kind with such connection as it is assumed may be apprehended in sense perception. From this point of view, the problem of empirical logic becomes the description of the ways in which a transition is made from the restricted, individualized basis of sense perception to the elaborated, generalized representation of experience constituting science, together with an explanation or justification of the admitted difference between the primary and the derived aspects of knowledge. It is easily seen that in such an inquiry the central question is that of the universal, whether in the form of the general notion, general idea, concept, or in that of the general proposition; for it is universality that stands most sharply in conflict with the features assigned to the primary, fundamental type of knowledge. One or other of these aspects of this universality may be the more prominent, as e. g. the rather psychological feature of generality, as in notions or terms, in the discussion of which empirical logic tends towards extreme nominalism; or the more comprehensive aspect of knowledge as involving truth, objective validity, in the treatment of which empirical logic becomes a theory of inductive inference. The questions entering into the fundamental discussion regarding knowledge are so varied, some being psychological, some metaphysical, and empiricism has been so much determined in scope and direction by the counter-theory to which it has been opposed, that historically empirical logic has been presented in many degrees of completeness. The distinguishing features of knowledge on which it proceeds— (1) rejection of the universal, or explanation of it by reference to the psychological mechanism of association and language; (2) restriction of necessity in thought to analytical connections; with (3) the correlated denial of any absolute value in matters of fact; (4) restriction of the import of judgments, i. e. of the kind of relations known, to such connections as are within the range of immediate perceptive experience, e. g. similarity, co-existence, sequence—may not all in conjunction be used as the basis of a logical theory. Historically, there have been combined views of a strictly rational character regarding mathematical knowledge with those strictly empirical regarding matters of fact. So, too, a thoroughly empirical logic in respect to physics may be combined, as by the Scottish philosophers, Reid and Stewart, with assumptions as to first principles altogether irreconcilable with strict empiricism.

Empirical logic may be said to begin with the first attempts to describe the rise and formation of knowledge from the basis of sense perceptions. In any such description there is involved something of the specifically logical question, the question as to the worth of a form or way of knowing, as to the justification of its obvious claim to give insight into objective reality. Even prior to the definite formulation of the logical problem by Aristotle, indications are to be found of the beginnings of an empirical logic. Probably nothing contributed more to determine the question as to the method by which we gather generalized knowledge from particular facts of experience than the rapid development of the one physical science in which the Greek mind holds the same place that it has assured for itself in philosophy and in the formal sciences of mathematics and astronomy, viz. medicine. Alcmaeon of Crotona, whose empirical description of knowledge is referred to in the *Phaedo* (96 B), was a physician, and in the works that can be assigned to Hippocrates there occur the first discussions as to method in relation to matters of experience (see Chauvet, *La Philos. des Médecins Grecs*, 1886, 8–42; Gomperz, *Griech. Denker*, i. Bk. III. chap. i; and Galen, *De Placitis Hippoc. et Platonis*, Bk. IX). Unmistakable traces of the empirical strain are to be found in the imperfectly recorded speculations of Antisthenes, who first definitely advanced some of the characteristic marks (v. sup.) of an empirical view of knowledge (cf. Dümmler, *Antisthenica*, and Gomperz, loc. cit. ii. Bk. IV. chap. ii. 7, 9). It is quite possible that from his acquaintance with and interest in medical work, Aristotle was led to formulate, as Hippocrates had already done, some of those very general precepts as to comparison of like and unlike cases, division of a problem into parts, ascent from particulars and descent thereto which make up his otherwise unimportant contribution to empirical logic (see Eucken, *Die Methode d. Aristot. Forschung*, 1872, esp. § iv). The Aristotelian logic is in itself dominated by a conception of nature so profoundly opposed to empiricism as above defined, that it may rather be taken as a typical representation of the rationalist doctrine. It proceeds under the guidance of an ideal of knowledge so definite, and it describes in such methodical detail the forms of knowing, that it determined for all later times the lines along which an empirical logic must be elaborated.

The Stoic logic, owing to the new point of view, that of monism, from which the Stoics worked over the Aristotelian material, presents in several of its features a pronounced empirical colouring. Their extreme nominalism, dependent on their metaphysical individualism—a doctrine in which they anticipate Leibnitz—involved as natural consequence an equally mechanical mode of explaining the formation of higher types of knowledge than simple sense apprehension. With individualism, however, which is the root-principle of all empirical theories of knowledge, the Stoics managed to combine the representation of a teleological connection of all things, and the influence of this counter-thought is reflected in their theory of knowledge, and forbids us to describe that as through and through empirical (see Nikolai, *De logic. Chrysippi libris*, 1859; Heinze, *Erkenntnisslehre der Stoiker*, 1880; Stein, *Erkenntnisslehre der Stoa*, 1868; Bonhöffer, *Epiktet u. die Stoa*, 1890). To induction and inductive methods, the Stoics contribute nothing; though Philodemus informs us that they were absolutely opposed to induction.

All the characteristic features of empiricism are represented, with perfect consciousness of their significance, though without due recognition of the problems they raise, in the unfortunately scanty remains of the Epicurean doctrine of knowledge. It is evident that the Epicureans did attempt to work out some general representation of the ways in which the mind passes from the immediately given, the isolated phenomena, which serve as signs, to the inferred realities underlying them and signified by them; and the dominating conception of nature under which they worked was adapted to a strictly empirical, almost mechanical, account of these processes. But we have only imperfect knowledge of their labours (see Gomperz, *Herkulanische Studien,* i, 1865; Bahnsch, *Des Epikureers Philodemus Schrift* περὶ σημείων καὶ σημειώσεων, 1879; Marquand, in *Johns Hopkins Studies in Logic,* 1883).

Undoubtedly the speculations of the academic and sceptical schools, particularly of Arcesilaus and of Carneades, the Hume of the Hellenic world, had the view of knowledge from which the only logic possible is that we have called empirical, but of their doctrine of probability we have very scanty information (see Brochard, *Les Sceptiques Grecs,* 1887). Galen's large work on scientific proof is lost (see J. Müller, *Galen's Werk v. wiss. Beweis,* 1896), but in his minor philosophical and in his medical works there is much to show how he strove to elaborate a general theory of method (cf. Chauvet, op. cit., 109–70). What he has to offer, however, is of much the same generality as the corresponding part of Aristotle's work. In truth the development of empirical logic from this time onward is dependent mainly on the advances made in detailed knowledge of nature, on the alteration gradually brought about in general conceptions of reality, and therewith on the changes introduced in human ideals of knowledge.

Within mediaeval times, it is to be said that there is little or no development of empirical logic. Some features of empiricism are of course to be detected wherever nominalism or mysticism is found, but for the most part they failed to produce effect on logical theory. The strong current in Renascence times towards first-hand knowledge of nature could not be without effect on doctrines of knowledge and so on portions, more or less extensive, of logic. Among the revived systems of antiquity, Epicureanism was not overlooked, and a new theory of induction was from Bacon's time a problem for the logician and philosopher. The philosophical basis of empirical logic in modern times was laid by Locke, who otherwise contributed little to the discussion of the more specifically logical questions. So far as knowledge of external nature is concerned, no theory of knowledge can be more empirical than that of Berkeley, whose nominalist views are pronounced, and who at the same time supplied, from another side of his speculative view, the universal factor otherwise wanting on the empirical theory of knowledge. In all essentials his view is that accepted by the Scottish school—Reid, Stewart, Brown—for as regards the logical problem, it is indifferent whether the external world be regarded as an orderly congeries of perceptions or as having a mode of independent existence.

A special and a more resolutely consistent strain of empiricism than Locke's takes its start in Hobbes, whose work, even more than that of Locke, finds continuation in Condillac, De Tracy, and the ideologists. Hume's strongly empirical interpretation of knowledge leads him to dismiss the logical problem as of small value. The omission was made good in J. S. Mill's *Logic* (1893), which, with some inconsistencies of language, may be said to present logic from the point of view of the empirical theory of knowledge. In essentials the same account of logic, but with much improvement in detail, and a deeper recognition of the philosophical interests involved, is given in Venn. The important works on method by Jevons, Wundt, Sigwart, though in no case founded on the strictly empirical interpretation of knowledge, agree in so many points of general principle with Mill that they might without injustice be reckoned among empirical logics. Finally, positivism, which emphasizes one characteristic of the empirical doctrine, and shares its ideal of knowledge, is, as regards its method or logic, strictly empirical.

Literature: as representing ways in which the new ideas of the Renascence were brought to bear upon logic, may be instanced VALLA (1415–65), VIVES (1492–1540), and particularly NIZOLIUS (1498–1576), whose remarkable attack on the notion of universality deserves notice. His work De veris Principiis et vera Ratione philosophandi (1553) was re-edited by Leibnitz (1670). See also BACON, Novum Organum (1620; best edition, with full commentary and introduction, by T. Fowler, 1878); Jos. GLANVILL, Vanity of Dogmatizing or Seipsis Scientifica (1661), Plus Ultra (1668); GASSENDI (1592–1655), De doctrina Epicuri (1647); Logica, in Opera, v. 1 (1655) (see THOMAS,

La Phil. de Gassendi, 1889); J. B. DUHA-MEL, De Mente Humana; MARRIOTTE, Essai de Logique, contenant les Principes de la Science (1678); HOBBES, Computatio sive Logica (1655); CONDILLAC, La Logique (1780), L'Art de Penser (1755), L'Art de Raisonner (1755), La Langue des Calculs (1798), forming vols. xxii, xxvi, xxviii, and xxiii of Condillac's Œuvres; DESTUTT DE TRACY, Él. d'Idéologie, Pt. III. La Logique (1805); DE GERANDO, Des Signes et de l'Art de Penser (4 vols., 1800); LEIDENFROST, De Mente Humana (1793); LOCKE, Human Understanding (1689); P. BROWNE, Procedure, Extent, and Limits of Human Understanding (1728); BERKELEY, Princ. of Human Knowledge (1710); HUME, Treatise (1739), Human Understanding (1748); BEDDOES, Obs. on the Nature of Demonstrative Evidence (1793); TH. BROWN, Inquiry into the Relation of Cause and Effect (1804; 3rd ed., 1818); HERSCHEL, Discourse on the Study of Nat. Philos. (1831); J. S. MILL, Syst. of Logic (1843); OPZOOMER, De Weg d. Wetenschap (1851); W. S. JEVONS, Princ. of Sci. (1873; 2nd ed., 1877); R. SHUTE, Discourse on Truth (1877); K. PEARSON, Grammar of Sci. (1892); L. T. HOBHOUSE, Theory of Knowledge (1896); VENN, Logic of Chance (1866; 2nd ed., 1876), Empirical Logic (1889); COMTE, Cours de Philos. Positive (1839), and Synthèse Subjective, i (1856).   (R.A.)

Empiricism: Ger. *Empirismus*; Fr. *empirisme*; Ital. *empirismo*. (1) The doctrine that truth is to be sought in immediate sense experience. Opposed to RATIONALISM (q.v.), and usually a reaction from extreme idealism.

(2) In EPISTEMOLOGY (q.v.) the opposite of nativism in any form. With the English empiricists the doctrine took the form of denying innate ideas. See NATIVISM AND EMPIRICISM.

The tendency shows all grades of radicalness, from a wholesome reaction against unbridled speculation to the purest SENSATIONALISM and MATERIALISM (see those terms). See also EXPERIENCE, and EMPIRICAL LOGIC.   (H.R.S.—J.M.B.)

Empirio-criticism: Ger. *Empiriokriticismus*; Fr. *empiriocriticisme*; Ital. *empiriocriticismo*. The philosophical system of Richard Avenarius. Besides the works of Avenarius, see Willy in *Vtljsch. f. wiss. Philos.*, xx. 57 ff.; and on the term, ibid., xxii. 53 ff. The system is criticized by Wundt in *Philos. Stud.*, xii, xiii (1896–7). A new exposition and further development of the system is J. Petzoldt's *Einführung in d. Philos. d. reinen Erfahrung* (1900–).   (J.M.B.)

Employer [Fr. *employeur*]: Ger. *Prinzipal, Brodherr*; Fr. *employeur, patron*; Ital. *padrone*. A man who pays wages from funds which he either owns or borrows, as distinct from a superintendent who hires labourers at others' expense; especially one who hires large bodies of workmen on these terms.

The root 'employ' in this word does not have the simple meaning 'use'; it has the more complex meaning, 'give employment to.' There is no force in Henry George's remark, 'It is not capital that employs labour, but labour that employs capital.'   (A.T.H.)

Emulation (in education): Ger. *Wetteifer*; Fr. *émulation*; Ital. *emulazione*. Desire and effort to equal or surpass another; imitative rivalry.

The Jesuits, who made the most extensive use of emulation as a principle of instruction, called it the 'whetstone of talent, the spur of industry.' In the lower schools they arranged the boys in pairs of rivals, each boy being constantly on the watch to catch his rival tripping, and instantly to correct him. Each class also was divided into two hostile camps called Rome and Carthage, which had frequent pitched battles (concertations) on set subjects. Remains of this system are still seen in competitive exercises between pupils, classes, and literary societies. Emulation as a principle should be much restricted, because of its powerful tendency to divert the mind from the real ends of study, and to direct it to unworthy personal ends.

Literature: HUGHES, Loyola and the Educ. Syst. of the Jesuits, 208–17; PAINTER, Hist. of Educ., 171–3; SCHMIDT, Gesch. d. Päd., 245.   (C.DE G.)

Enactment [Lat. *en* + *actus*, from *agere*, to do]: Ger. (1) *legislative Genehmigung einer Acte, Gesetzerlassung*, (2) *Verfügung, Verordnung*; Fr. (1) *action de passer une loi*, (2) *loi*; Ital. (1) *decretare una legge*, (2) *atto legislativo*. (1) The act of enacting a law. (2) The law enacted; a legislative act.

The form of English legislation is the preparation of a bill for an act, its approval by the Lords and Commons, and its presentation by them to the Crown for the royal assent. The American form is generally the same, the final act being the approval by the executive. The general style of the commencement of the bill is *Be it enacted*, that is, may it be enacted. The executive assent first makes it an enactment.   (S.E.B.)

Encephalon : see BRAIN.

Encyclopedia (philosophical): Ger. *Encyclopädie*; Fr. *encyclopédie*; Ital. *enciclopedia*. Applied to the entire round of philosophical studies, but varying with the particular writer's views of philosophy, from the Positivism of the French ENCYCLOPEDISTS (q.v.) to the Logicism of the NEO-HEGELIANS (q.v.). (J.M.B.)

Encyclopedists [Lat. *encyclopaedia*]: Ger. *Encyclopädisten*; Fr. *Encyclopédistes*; Ital. *Enciclopedisti*. The French thinkers who in the third quarter of the 18th century edited the *Encyclopédie ou Dictionnaire raisonné des Sciences, des Arts et des Métiers* (28 vols., 1751–72; *Supplément*, 5 vols., 1776–7; *Table analytique*, 2 vols., 1780), or contributed to the work.

Of the group, Diderot was editor-in-chief, d'Alembert his principal associate until the retirement of the latter in 1757. D'Alembert was the author of the *Discours préliminaire*, in which the plan of the work was defined on the basis of Bacon's division of the sciences and the Baconian method. Rousseau also ceased to write for the *Encyclopédie* in 1757, and thereafter manifested an active hostility to his former collaborators. Other notable contributors were Voltaire, Grimm, d'Holbach, Quesnai, Turgot, Marmontel, Duclos, de Jaucourt. Haller and Condorcet aided in the preparation of the supplementary volumes. Montesquieu at his death, in 1755, left an article partly finished. Buffon was early associated with the work, but it is not certain that anything from his pen was actually printed (Morley, *Diderot*, i. 129–30). Writers of lesser rank were numerous and from all classes in society. After the defection of d'Alembert, Diderot remained the sole principal editor, and by his unflagging energy and courage carried the enterprise through to its termination. Among the many difficulties which confronted him, not the least vexatious were the opposition of the orthodox party, and the interference of the authorities. For the *Encyclopédie* was more than a great 'dictionary of sciences, arts, and trades'; it was conceived in the spirit of the Illumination movement, and it carried the principles, as well as the results, of the new thinking into the culture of the time. Thus it became at once a storehouse of information and a revolutionary force.

Literature: DAMIRON, Mém. pour servir à l'Hist. de la Philos. au XVIIIᵉ Siècle, i. 3, especially 240–3, ii. 5, especially 10–12; K. ROSENKRANZ, Diderots Leben u. Werke, i. 147–253; JOHN MORLEY, Diderot and the Encyclopaedists. i. chap. v. Also the histories of philosophy (as WINDELBAND, Gesch. d. neueren Philos., i. § 44), and the histories of literature (as HETTNER, Litteraturgeschichte d. 18ten Jahrhunderts, ii. Absch. 2, especially Kap. 1). (A.C.A.Jr.)

End (ethical): for equivalents, see the following topic. The ultimate purpose which ought to be aimed at in conduct, and to which other purposes ought to be subordinated.

Ethics may be said to be a theory of the end or ends of conduct. This view was first made definite and prominent by Aristotle, whose whole doctrine is dominated by the conception of end (τέλος). Starting from the position that well-being (εὐδαιμονία) is by common consent the end, he seeks a more precise definition of this conception. And modern ethical controversy is largely concerned with the claims of rival conceptions (e. g. happiness, perfection, self-realization) to be regarded as the ethical end. This teleological view of ethics is contrasted with the quasi-jural view in which moral law is the ultimate conception (as in Kant and the intuitional school). (W.R.S.)

From one point of view the definition of ethical end in terms of actual psychic purpose is a mistaken one. Ends are—in so far as immediate to the individual, i. e. in so far as they are purpose—particular aspects of conation, and in their most generalized form still particular with reference to one another — general only with reference to the particular cases generalized or subsumed under each, and that in the peculiar sense of subordination in a system. If an end becomes really universal, just then it loses its ethical significance; since it is imposed upon the individual or upon the particular conative tendencies, not developed by their systematization, so that it is not the individual's psychic end. Further, the genetic point of view is quite ignored by this form of definition. As consciousness develops, the synthesis of conative processes becomes ever more complex and indefinitely varied, and the resulting psychic ends or ideals ever richer and more adequate to experience. The individual's concrete purpose—even his most general purpose or life-ideal—is therefore never universal. In so far as he treats it as universal, it is as a formal regulative demand, not a purpose; and just here arises the antinomy of good intention with reference to purpose, and bad performance with reference to law.

We come, therefore, to require a definition of ethical end from the point of view of the psychological rather than the psychic (see PSYCHIC AND PSYCHOLOGICAL)—an objective rather than a subjective determination of the end; hence the definition given: what 'ought to be the purpose' is the end. But, although this is the definition justified by history—despite much confusion between the two points of view—the question again leads us into a theoretical *cul de sac*. If we mean, What end, if fulfilled by all men, would be of most worth? that cannot be answered except on purely logical grounds; for to determine it as value or worth would be to attain the complete systematization of ends, which we have seen above is not only not actual, but genetically impossible. But to determine it on logical grounds is to determine a logical end, not one of worth; a situation in which the demands of logic primarily, not those of action or appreciation, would be completely satisfied. If, again, we mean, What end fulfilled would also fulfil the final world-end, would realize cosmic teleology?—that statement, just because it is in terms of the cosmic, not of the personal, can be answered only in terms of the cosmic, i.e. by science. What—the question becomes—what, as fact, is the end of cosmic, including human, evolution? This can find a formal answer, again, from the forms of knowledge, a logical answer; but such an answer cannot be made a regulative principle to determine the individual's ought; for the individual is under the lead of certain facts, not of all knowledge, and to say that he ought to act from the point of view of all knowledge—that is, from the point of view of the universal element in knowledge—is to mock him with logical tautologies, when he needs practical adjustments. That is to say, if all men gave up their practical adjustments to pursue what we tell them they ought to pursue in view of a universal teleology, the teleology would be the first thing to suffer.

The question of psychic end, therefore, is—in the more modest form in which it is capable of solution, and even of intelligible statement—the scientific question of (1) the systematization of individual concrete purposes in enlarging systems: the determination of voluntary conations; (2) the origin and development of the ethical consciousness in the social conditions under which the individual's voluntary life is lived. These are both psychic or mental determinations. If they be handed over to psychology, we have then left over for ethics the objective questions: (1) the ethnological and social forms which ethical strivings have taken on; and (2) the place of these in a general philosophy of reality, which shall include that of a general teleology.

The strictly ethical questions, then—making use of the psychology of the conative life in advance—are: (1) What ends have men pursued as good and bad? (2) What ends may they pursue as good and bad? (3) What significance does the category of good and bad, as thus filled in with instances, have in the make up of things? Cf. the remarks on the ethical end under ETHICS.

The last question is a metaphysical one, concerning the broad distinction between science of fact and appreciation of worth; and its problem is that of finding a category in which facts and worths are both subsumed in a profounder synthesis. Cf. ORIGIN *versus* NATURE, and METAPHYSICS.   (J.M.B.)

Literature: SIDGWICK, Meth. of Eth., I. vi; general works on ethics and psychology; and BIBLIOG. F, 2, *i*.   (W.R.S.)

End (in psychology) [AS. *ende*]: Ger. (1) *Zweck, Ziel* (most general, remote), *Beweggrund* (in cases of voluntary movement), (2) *Ende*; Fr. (1) *but*, (2) *fin*; Ital. (1) *scopo*, (2) *fine*. That which satisfies a conation. Cf. PROJECT (voluntary), PURPOSE, PLAN, INTENTION, and DESIGN.

But there are two points of view from which this satisfaction may be regarded. We may consider (1) the form in which the end appears to the striving subject before its attainment, or (2) the psychical state which arises when it is completely attained.

(1) Thus from the first point of view the end consists in some positive result as ideally represented or in some manner cognized before its achievement.

(2) From the second point of view, the end consists in that relative cessation of conative activity which depends on the fact that the activity has completed itself and has nothing further to accomplish. It will consist not in pleasure or relief but in satiety. If a conative process is allowed to develop freely without interruption or repression, it tends to go on until a certain result ensues, and when the result is attained it ceases of itself; this result is the termination, and in that sense the end of the process. It is desirable that these two meanings should be marked by some difference of terminology. We therefore propose to use 'end' for (1), and 'terminal end,' or simply TERMINUS (q. v.), for (2).   (G.F.S.–J.M.B.)

The desirableness of this appears from the confusion of the two meanings which one finds in ethical discussions, especially when the conception of terminus is generalized into what we are calling the END-STATE (q. v.) of mental process generally; the so-called ethical end being treated alternatively in one way and then in the other. The distinction between end and end-state has been suggested by various writers in different expressions, as e. g. distinctions between 'subjective and objective' end, 'conscious and unconscious' end, 'psychic' as opposed to psychological, 'biological,' and 'philosophical' end, the 'end' as distinguished from the 'object' of desire, &c. Writers on hedonism and utilitarianism revel in this confusion; and it takes on another of its many-headed forms in the idealists who make some universal or abstract conception still an 'end,' confusing or identifying the end-state of a cosmic or thought process, viewed objectively, with the individual's mental end. See END (ethical).

A further distinction should also be made between two forms of end in the first and proper sense—that between 'concrete' and 'ideal,' or between 'immediate' and 'remote' ends. The concrete or immediate end is usually incidental to a larger intention in which the ideal, or this ideal end, takes form—the so-called 'remote' or 'ultimate' end. See CHOICE (for a similar distinction). This larger determination includes a system of concrete ends, and may itself have an explicit conscious end or only an end-state as its goal. The grocer's remote end is to get rich; his end-state is vital satisfaction; his concrete ends are weighing sugar, buying tea, and collecting bills. Cf. TELEOLOGY. (J.M.B., G.F.S.)

Literature (in which the distinction of (1) and (2) is made): LIPPS, Grundthatsachen des Seelenlebens, 623 ff.; BALDWIN, Feeling and Will, chap. xvi; STOUT, Man. of Psychol., Index. See also the textbooks of psychology and ethics. (G.F.S.–J.M.B.)

End of the World: see ESCHATOLOGY.

Endoderm [Gr. ἔνδον, inner, + δέρμα, layer]: Ger. *inneres Keimblatt*; Fr. *endoderme*; Ital. *endoderma* or *entoderma*. The inner layer of coelenterate animals, or the inner of the two primitive cell-layers of the embryo mammal, often termed hypoblast. See BLASTODERM, EMBRYO, and HYPOBLAST. (C.LL.M.–E.S.G.)

Endomusia: see INTERNAL SPEECH AND SONG.

Endophasia: see INTERNAL SPEECH AND SONG.

End-organ: Ger. *Endorgan*; Fr. *organe nerveux périphérique* (Y.D.); Ital. *termina-zione nervosa*. (1) Any organ which forms a terminus of a path of nervous conduction. Its function may be to initiate or to receive the discharge.

(2) Usual meaning: the peripheral terminus. Most end-organs are so related that they clearly perform both of these functions. Even in the case of motor and other efferent nerves the peripheral end-organ seems to exert some sort of reactionary influence. It seems probable that every fibre is normally in a state of neural tension between its end-organs, and that the discharge is the rhythmical readjustment of the equilibrium which has been disturbed by the stimulus at one terminus. Cf. Brain Origin, by Sir William Broadbent, *Brain*, xviii (1895). See HEARING, VISION, MUSCLE, SENSE ORGAN, &c. (H.H.)

Endorsement: see BELIEF, and SYNKATHESIS.

Endothelium [Gr. ἔνδον, within, + θηλή, a papilla]: Ger. *Endothel*; Fr. *endothélium*; Ital. *endotelio*. A term widely used (His) to designate the cellular lining of cavities, blood-vascular, lymphatic or synovial, which do not open, directly or indirectly, to the exterior. It consists of a single layer of thin cells joined at their edges. Cf. EPITHELIUM. (C.F.H.)

End-plate: Ger. *Endplatte, Nervenhügel*; Fr. *plaque motrice*; Ital. *lama terminale*. The terminal organ of a motor nerve embedded in the muscular fibre. See NERVOUS SYSTEM (nerve). (H.H.)

End-state: Ger. *Endzustand*; Fr. *état final*; Ital. *stato finale*. (The foreign equivalents are suggested.) The goal or result of a concrete mental DETERMINATION (q. v.); that state in which any specific process in consciousness issues and completes itself. See END.

For example, belief is the end-state of argumentation, choice the end-state of deliberation, accomplished action that of effort, &c. In cases of conative process as such the word TERMINUS (q. v.) is suggested, seeing that here the end-state is one of satiety or real termination. (J.M.B., G.F.S.)

Endyma [Gr. ἔνδυμα, garment]: Ger. *Ependymium, Ependym*; Fr. *épendyme*; Ital. *ependima*. The epithelial lining of the entire medullary tube and the cavities formed from it. Synonym: Ependyma. See NERVOUS SYSTEM (embryology), and NEUROGLIA. (H.H.)

Energeia [Gr.]: see GREEK TERMINOLOGY (6), and POWER.

Energism [Gr. ἐν + ἔργειν, to work]: Ger. *Energismus*; Fr. *énergisme*; Ital. *energismo*. The view that the highest good consists in ethical activity, or the realization of objective rather than subjective life-conditions (Lebensinhalt). Used by Paulsen, *Einleitung in d. Philos.*, 432 (Eng. trans.). (J.M.B.)

Energy [Gr. ἐνέργεια]: Ger. *Energie*; Fr. *énergie*; Ital. *energia*. An ideal physical quantity manifesting itself under different forms which are so related that one form can never be increased except at the expense of an equal quantity in some other form.

The conception was first developed in mechanics in the two forms of kinetic and potential defined below, and the term force (Kraft) was applied to it. It was for a time supposed that all other forms could be reduced to one of these two, but this view now seems untenable.

The forms of energy hitherto recognized may be defined and measured as follows:—

(1) *Kinetic energy*, or energy of motion, is measured by, or equal to, the product of one-half the mass of a body into the square of its velocity, or, in algebraic language, $\frac{1}{2} mv^2 = E$. In the case of a system of bodies such a product may be formed for each body, and the sum of all the products is the kinetic energy of the system. If at any moment we could determine the velocity v of each particle of matter in the solar system, the sum of all the products $\frac{1}{2} mv^2$ would be the total kinetic energy of the solar system at that moment.

(2) *Potential energy*, or energy of position, is in mechanics an integral of which the differential is the product of a force acting between two bodies into the differential of the distance by which they are separated. In the common case of a heavy body it increases with the height of the body above the surface of the earth. In the case of a system of bodies attracting each other with a force inversely as the square of the distance, the potential energy is the sum of the quotients formed by dividing each product of the masses of every two of the bodies by their distance apart, and regarding the sum as algebraically negative. Thus if the masses are m_1, m_2, m_3, &c., and the distance of the mass m_1 from m_2 is $r_{1,2}$, and so with all the other pairs, the potential energy at any moment is

$$-\frac{m_1 m_2}{r_{1,2}} - \frac{m_1 m_3}{r_{1,3}} - \frac{m_2 m_3}{r_2 r_3} - \&c. = P.$$

The relation of kinetic and potential energy may be illustrated thus:—If P be a point at a height a above a level plane AB, and a body be dropped from P or thrown from it in any direction whatever with any velocity whatever, or suffered to slide without friction from P along an inclined plane PB or PC, the square of its velocity will increase by the same amount $2 ag$ (g being the acceleration of gravity) during the fall from P to AB, no matter by what path the fall takes place, or what part of the

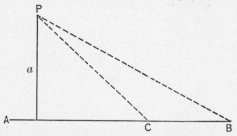

plane AB is reached. That is, if it leave P with the velocity v_0, and we call v the velocity with which it reaches AB, we shall always have

$$v^2 = v_0^2 + 2 ag,$$

and therefore, for the kinetic energy,

$$\tfrac{1}{2} mv^2 = \tfrac{1}{2} mv_0^2 + mag.$$

However a body is thrown, if we leave out resistance, its velocity and its varying height h above any arbitrary plane or level, say the earth's surface, during flight are such that the quantity

$$\tfrac{1}{2} mv^2 + mgh, \text{ or } E + P, \qquad (A)$$

is constant until it reaches the earth or is in some way interfered with, so that, if the kinetic energy $\frac{1}{2} mv^2$ increases, the potential energy mgh or P will diminish, and vice versa.

(3) *The energy of heat.* The theorem that $E + P$ remained constant during the motion of any system of bodies acted on only by their mutual attractions was proved by the mathematicians of the 18th century. But they had to couple this theorem with the important proviso that the bodies must never come into collision, because then some of the quantity $E + P$ would be lost through a diminution of the velocity of the colliding bodies, and hence of E. Then it was shown by Rumford and others that this loss of E was always accompanied by the generation of an amount of heat proportional to the loss of E. If we call H the amount of this heat, expressed in appropriate units, we should then have

$$E + P + H = \text{constant},$$

even when the bodies come into collision, or, in the case of a projectile, after it strikes the ground. Thus, by adding H to the equation (A), we have

$$\tfrac{1}{2} mv^2 + mgh = E + P + H,$$

which remains true after the fall of the body,

because the annihilation of velocity, and hence of E, is compensated by the generation of an equivalent amount H of heat, which raises the temperature both of the projectile and of the ground where it struck.

As an illustration, when a solid shot is fired from a modern rifled gun at an armour plate a flash of fire is seen, and plate and shot may both be partly melted by the heat.

(4) *Energy of molecular condition.* It is found that when bodies change their state, as when water freezes or evaporates, or when two substances combine to form a compound, heat may be generated or disappear, according to the character of the change. A general law is that if such bodies are restored to their original state, the loss of heat in the one process exactly balances its gain in the other; and this, however great the number of intermediate states the bodies may pass through. We may call the sum total of this energy C.

(5) *Radiant energy or radiance.* Every hot body radiates its heat through the space around it, thus imparting energy to the ether. The energy thus imparted is now believed to take a form of waves of electric energy, known as Maxwellian or Herzian waves, and its amount is exactly equal to that which the hot body loses. So, if we call R the total heat-energy of the ether, R will constantly gain as the body loses its heat-energy H, and vice versa.

(6) *Electrical energy.* The generation of electricity requires an expenditure of energy equal to half the product of the quantity of electricity generated into its potential. Thus, as electric energy L appears, energy in some other form disappears, and vice versa.

(7) *Magnetic energy*, which appears when a body is magnetized. We may call it M.

All known forms of energy may be included under one of these seven heads, so that the sum total of energy of all seven forms in the universe

$$E + P + H + C + R + L + M$$

remains for ever constant. This is the theorem of the 'Conservation of Energy.' But the values of the seven separate quantities are continually changing, and these changes may be conceived as transformations of some of the kinds into others. The usual rule of nature is that position energy P is being constantly converted into kinetic energy E, and this into heat H, which again is converted into radiance R, which is propagated indefinitely through the ether. The store of P in the beginning consisted in the diffusion in space, as nebulous matter, of

the materials now forming the stars and planets; and this store is being converted into E by the process of condensation produced by the mutual attraction of all the matter of the universe.

It is sometimes supposed that thought or mental action of some sort may be a distinct form of energy. This cannot be. Mental action may be, and doubtless always is, accompanied by an exhibition or transformation of energy, but the energy itself can be only that of the matter composing the brain and nervous system.

Literature: a very complete popular exposition of the theory of energy and its conservation is found in HELMHOLTZ, Ueber die Erhaltung der Kraft: Populäre wissenschaftliche Vorträge, Heft 2 (1876). Instructive and yet simpler are THOMSON's two addresses, On the Origin and Transformation of Motive Power, and On the Sources of Energy in Nature available to Man for the Production of Mechanical Effect (Popular Lectures and Addresses, ii). SPENCER's exposition in his First Principles is defective, through trying to extend the conception of energy into fields where no transformation of mechanical energy into the concepts of the field is possible. (S.N.)

The term energy is used also by the advocates of 'dynamic monism' to indicate the principle of real unity which underlies all phenomena. Cf. E. Morselli, Filosofia monistica in Italia, in *Riv. di Filos. Scient.* (1886); Fontana, *Monismo e Dinamismo* (2nd ed., 1897); Haeckel, *Der Monismus* and *Die Welträthsel* (1899). (E.M.)

Enfranchisement: see FRANCHISE.

Engel's Law: Ger. *Engel'sches Gesetz*; Fr. *loi d'Engel*; Ital. *legge di Engel*. A generalization with regard to the relative proportions of income spent for different purposes by workmen of different grades. The lower the income, the greater is the proportion spent for food.

First given definite shape by the Saxon statistician Engel in 1857. Subsequent observations in different countries have shown a surprising degree of constancy in the results of all careful statistics of family budgets. (A.T.H.)

Ἐν καὶ πᾶν [Gr.]. Literally, 'one and all': used to characterize the theory of PANTHEISM (q. v.). (J.M.B.)

Enlightenment [AS. *licht*, light]: Ger. *Aufklärung*; Fr. *libre-pensée*, *émancipation intellectuelle*; Ital. *secolo* (or *periodo*) *dei lumi*. A philosophical period of the 18th century characterized by an impetus to culture. The group comprises a large number of men of varying tendencies.

A striving toward freer, more independent thinking, emancipation from established dogmas, and an empirical or materialistic leaning characterized the period. Lessing, Mendelssohn, Reimarus, Tetens, Herder, Locke, Newton, Voltaire, Condillac, and Diderot are representatives of the movement, which affected Germany, England, and France. Cf. this topic in the histories of philosophy. (H.R.S.)

Ennui [Fr.]: Ger. *Langeweile*; Ital. *noia*. The unpleasant feeling which arises through persistence in more or less futile mental activity, or through the persistent presence of tendencies to mental activity which fail to find satisfying objects for their exercise. (G.F.S.)

Entelechy [Gr.]: see POWER.

Enterozoa [Gr. ἔντερον, gut, + ζῷον, animal]: Ger. *Eingeweidewürmer*; Fr. *entérozoaires* (suggested, not in use—Y.D.); Ital. *enterozoi*. That group or grade of animals characterized by the presence of a digestive cavity or enteron.

A term proposed by Lankester. Haeckel's term METAZOA (q. v.) is more frequently employed. Lankester divides the animal kingdom into two grades: (1) the Plastidozoa (= Protozoa), which consist either of single cells or colonies of equivalent cells, and (2) the Enterozoa (= Metazoa), in which two differentiated layers surround a primitive digestive cavity. The enteron in some rare cases originated directly from the BLASTOCOEL (q. v.), an orifice arising disruptively, and the hypoblast and epiblast originating by DELAMINATION (q. v.). More commonly it arises by INVAGINATION (q. v.). See GASTRAEA THEORY, and EMBRYO.

Literature: E. R. LANKESTER, Adv. of Sci. (1890), in which the art. Zoology, from the 9th ed. of Encyc. Brit., is reprinted with some modifications; F. BALFOUR, Compar. Embryol. (C.LL.M.)

Enthusiasts [Gr. ἐν + θεός, a god]: Ger. *Enthusiasten*; Fr. *enthousiastes*; Ital. *entusiasti*. The name given to a sect of Christian monachists, or monks, who began to flourish in Syria towards the close of the 4th century. They believed that, as a result of the Fall, every man was inhabited by an evil spirit, who ruled him. Asceticism, and especially inward prayer (hence their other common name, Euchites), could, notwithstanding this, so affect a man as to enable him to enter at length into direct communion with the Holy Spirit—hence the name Enthusiasts.

They were called also Messalians, Adelphians, Lampetians, Marcionists. Their doctrines are of some importance for ethics as illustrating the logical consequences of extreme asceticism, mysticism, and pure contemplation. Neander calls the Enthusiasts the first mendicant friars.

Literature: NEANDER, Church Hist. (Eng. trans.), iii. 341 f.; SALMON, in Smith and Wace's Dict. of Christ. Biog., 'Euchites.'
(R.M.W.)

Enthymeme [Gr. ἐν + θυμός, mind]: Ger. *Enthymem*; Fr. *enthymème*; Ital. *entimema*. A reasoning in which some part of the grounds for the conclusion (i. e. one or other of the premises) is suppressed in the statement.

According to Aristotle, the enthymeme is a syllogism from probabilities or signs, and he assigns to it in rhetoric a definite function as corresponding there, in the special field of rhetoric (i.e. persuasion), to syllogism in purely intellectual or scientific matter. It would not therefore have been, in Aristotle's view, essential to the enthymeme that its statement should be elliptical; but his expressions or illustrations lend themselves readily to that interpretation, which, after the distinction between apodictic and dialectical reasoning had been rejected from logic, was naturally adopted.

Literature: the fullest historical discussion of points relating to the Enthymeme is given by HAMILTON, Discussions, 154–7; Lects. on Logic, lect. xx. See also GROTE, Aristotle (2nd ed.), 202–3; COPE, Introd. to Arist. Rhetoric, 103 ff., and MANSEL's ed. of Aldrich (4th ed.), App. F, where (218) the correct explanation of the etymology of the term is given. (R.A.)

Entity and **Ens** [Lat.]: see LATIN TERMINOLOGY (5), BEING (3), and REALITY AND EXISTENCE.

Entoptic Phenomena [Gr. ἐντός + ὀπτικός, pertaining to sight]: Ger. *entoptische Erscheinungen* (or *Phänomene*); Fr. *phénomènes entoptiques*; Ital. *fenomeni endottici*. Visual appearances due to processes within the eye itself are called entoptic, and the processes entoptic phenomena. (E.B.T.–J.M.B.)

The principal entoptic phenomena, if we take the phrase in its widest meaning, are the following: (1) Under certain experimental conditions we may perceive the shadow of the iris, the presence of liquids on the surface of the cornea, corneal specks, lines and blotches from the front part of the lens and its membrane, as well as the figures termed MUSCAE VOLITANTES (q. v.), &c. Le Cat's experiment, well calculated to show these phenomena, is as follows:—Set up a short-focus lens at a distance from a source of light, and place in the focus of the lens a card with a hole made by a fine pin. The rays entering the eye are not focussed on the retina, but so refracted as to traverse the eye in a nearly parallel direction. Sharp shadows of objects in or on the eyeball are thus thrown on the retina. The objects seen on the outside of the corneal surface, since they are not really within the eye, are termed by Laqueur 'pseud-entoptic' phenomena.

(2) Move a candle to and fro, below and slightly to the side of the eyeball, and as close to the eye as is convenient. Shadows of the retinal blood-vessels, and indications of the borders of the fovea centralis, are discernible.

(3) Look through a pinhole, held close to the eye, at an illuminated surface. Move the pierced card quickly, in circular sweeps. Shadows of the retinal vessels in the neigh-bourhood of the fovea will be seen. The macular region shows granulations (possibly retinal cones).

(4) Look fixedly at a misty sky, or through a blue glass at a clear sky or uniformly white surface (cloud, &c.). Bright yellowish points, followed by shadowy darker specks, will be seen taking a rapid course in fairly constant directions. The phenomena are those of retinal circulation.

(5) Move the spread fingers quickly to and fro before the eyes, or look steadily at a FLICKER (q. v.) of a moon's disk of black and white sectors. The macula lutea becomes visible; streams of fine particles, possibly the lymph corpuscles, are seen; and, sometimes, elaborate patterns, the shadow-figures of Purkinje.

(6) Bergmann's experiment: look at the vertical lines of a fine grating; the lines are wavy and beaded in appearance. The phenomenon is supposed to be due to the mosaic arrangement of the cones.

(7) Appearance of the BLIND SPOT (q. v.).

(8) Pressure applied to the eyeball produces phosphenes (circular patterns of light and dark alternating colour-patches) and 'movement figures' (pulsing colour-figures). A jerk of the eyes gives a blue spot surrounded by a yellow band, due to mechanical retinal stimulation at the edge of the blind spot.

(9) Adaptation to dark: IDIORETINAL LIGHT (q. v.), in the form of light chaos, light dust, together with subjective black or grey. On Müller's theory the grey is of central origin. See Visual Sensation under VISION.

Literature: HELMHOLTZ, Physiol. Optik (2nd ed.), 184; SANFORD, Course in Exper. Psychol., expts. 110–21, 170. (E.B.T.)

Entozoa [Gr. ἐντός, within, + ζῶον, animal]: Ger. *Parasiten*; Fr. *entozoaires* (not in use); Ital. *entozoi*. A term formerly used for internal parasites

Since these do not form a natural group, the term is now discarded, though the word is still occasionally met with. It was introduced by Rudolphi. (C.LL.M.)

Entrepreneur [Fr.]: Ger. *Unternehmer*; Fr., see topic; Ital. *intraprenditore, impresario.* An employer who is also a speculator.

Introduced into current English usage by F. A. Walker. Down to a comparatively recent time it was the custom to speak of the man who takes the direction and risk of industrial enterprise as the 'capitalist'; of his return as 'profit'; and to analyse this profit into interest and wages of superintendence. Walker showed, as Mangoldt had done before him, that these two elements in profit are subject to distinct laws, and may be received by distinct persons. The capitalist receives interest; the man who furnishes the management receives true or net profit. This man Walker was at first inclined to call the undertaker, but he afterwards fell back on the French term entrepreneur. The entrepreneur's profit is due partly to his superior skill in organizing labour, but chiefly to foresight in predicting the wants of the market. George says: 'It is not as an employer of labour, but as a speculator in the products of labour, that the producer needs capital'—an overstatement, but with a basis of truth. (A.T.H.)

Environment [Fr. *environner*, to surround]: Ger. *Umgebung, Umwelt, Lebensverhältnisse*; Fr. *milieu, conditions ambiantes, ambiance*; Ital. *ambiente, mezzo, condizioni mesologiche* (E.M.). A term for the totality of external circumstances and conditions which affect the organism at any stage of its existence; also used of the organism as a whole in relation to its constituent parts or cells. (C.LL.M.–E.B.P.)

Rendered current as a technical term in biology by Herbert Spencer, who conceived the organism and its environment as constantly acting and reacting upon each other. It is applied in a figurative sense to the conditions of the mental life in the phrase 'moral,' 'social environment,' &c., for which the French term milieu is also much used by writers in English. The phrase 'bionomic conditions' (bionomische Verhältnisse) has recently come into use, together with the term BIONOMICS (q. v.). (C.LL.M.–J.M.B.)

Envy: see JEALOUSY AND ENVY.

Epagoge [Gr. ἐπί + ἄγειν, to bring]: Ger. *Epagoge*; Fr. *syllogisme épagogique*; Ital. *induzione.* Argument by INDUCTION (q.v.). (J.M.B.)

Epiblast [Gr. ἐπί + βλαστός]: Ger. *äusseres Keimblatt, Hornblatt*; Fr. *épiblaste*; Ital. *epiblasto.* The outer of the two primitive layers of the embryo animal, also termed ECTODERM (q. v.).

The term is due to Michael Foster. First published (1871) by Huxley (*Anatomy of Vertebrated Animals*), who considered the epiblast to be homologous with the ectoderm, or outer layer, of the coelenterates. The origin of the two primitive layers (epiblast and hypoblast) appears in some cases to be by INVAGINATION (q. v.), and in others by DELAMINATION (q. v.). Some biologists consider the one, some the other, as the more primitive method of origin. See GASTRAEA THEORY, ECTODERM, and EMBRYO. (C.LL.M.–E.S.G.)

Epicheirema [Gr. ἐπιχείρημα, an attempted proof—Aristotle]: Ger. *Epicherem*; Fr. *épichérème*; Ital. *epicherema.* A syllogism in which one or both of the premises is supported by a reason. (J.M.B.)

Epictetus. Stoic philosopher, born at Hierapolis, Phrygia, about 60 A. D. The slave of Epaphroditus in Rome; he was made free, and then banished, with other philosophers, in 89 A. D. by Domitian. He then began teaching and lecturing at Nicopolis in Epirus. He wrote little, remarks taken down by his pupil Arrian in two treatises, the 'Discourses' and the 'Manual,' being the source of our knowledge of him.

Epicureanism: Ger. *Epicurismus*; Fr. *Épicurisme*; Ital. *Epicureismo.* The theory of Epicurus: in particular, his ethical doctrine that pleasure is the chief good (the only thing worth having on its own account), and that each man's pleasure is his own chief good—in the pursuit and attainment of which his moral excellence consists.

The doctrine of Epicurus and his disciples was hardly so much a philosophy, in the sense in which Platonic, Aristotelian, and even Stoic doctrines were philosophies, as a plan for the conduct of life. Logic and natural science are in it subordinated to the moral doctrine. Ideas or conceptions must be derived from felt sensations; language must consist of terms each referring to a distinct and clear conception—this is the basis of his logic. His natural science is even less original, although it is more elaborate: all reality is material; and the play of the atoms accounts for the universe and all its contents. His only variation from Democritus is the assumption of a spontaneous swerving on the part of the atoms varying their downward motion, to account for the formation of aggregates, and so of life and mind. The whole theory of reality, like the theory of knowledge, is, however, a mere preliminary to clear the way to the peaceful and happy life, which Epicurus puts forward as resulting from the abolition of the fear of the supernatural. The gods exist in intermundane spaces, but have no concern with or influence upon human affairs. And with the fear of the gods disappears the fear of death. 'Good and evil are only where they are felt, and death is the absence of all feeling.' The affairs of the state are equally disturbers of the happy life, and from them Epicurus counsels withdrawal; their place being taken by the more flexible bonds of friendship. Health of body and tranquillity of mind are the sum and substance of this happy life. Pleasure is the first good; but, if all pains were removed, pleasure could be varied only, not increased in amount.

Pleasure is always desirable in itself from its correspondence with our nature; but it is not always to be chosen, for it may lead to pains greater than itself. Some desires are not even natural; and some natural desires are not necessary; and of the necessary desires, the satisfaction of some is necessary for happiness, of others for an unperturbed frame of body, of others for life itself. 'If thou wilt make a man happy,' he is reported to have said, 'add not unto his riches, but take away from his desires.' Desire should be regulated by prudence, from which all the other virtues follow. 'We cannot live a life of pleasure which is not also a life of prudence, honour, and justice; nor lead a life of prudence, honour, and justice which is not also a life of pleasure.'

This theory of life Epicurus himself illustrated in the midst of a circle of friends—men and women—who frequented his garden at Athens. Abjuring the conventional bonds of society, he became the centre of a quasi-religious community, and the founder of a school which received and perpetuated his teachings with devotion, and without venturing on any important variation of opinion. The doctrine soon spread not only in Greece and Italy, but also in the barbarian world; the school also encountered persecution, mainly on account of its anti-political and anti-religious views.

The greatest literary representative of Epicureanism is Lucretius (*De Natura Rerum*, 54 B.C.). Atticus and others of the friends of Cicero belonged to the sect; and the writings of Philodemus, an Epicurean of the same period, have been disentombed from the ruins of Herculaneum. Epicureanism was one of the four philosophical schools endowed by the Emperor Marcus Aurelius about 176 A.D.; but, in the end of the 4th century, the Emperor Julian records the disappearance of the creed. The Renaissance led to the revival of the tendency towards a natural life and its enjoyment, which characterized Epicureanism. As a system it was resuscitated by Gassendi (1592–1655), who was not without followers at the time. The fundamental doctrine of Epicurus—that pleasure is the end of life—has perhaps never been without adherents. But the modern greatest happiness theory, as presented, for example, by Bentham, has many points of divergence from, as well as of similarity to, Epicureanism. In particular, it does not reaffirm the doctrine that the control of desire, rather than its satisfaction, is the means to a happy life; and it is largely a political theory.

Our knowledge of Epicurean doctrine depends chiefly on the fragments of Epicurus and his followers preserved by Diogenes Laertius and Stobaeus; on the discoveries at Herculaneum; on the writings of Cicero, and on the poem of Lucretius.

Literature: Histories of Philosophy; GUYAU, La Morale d'Épicure (1878); W. WALLACE, Epicureanism (1880). (W.R.S.)

Epicurus. (337 or 341–270 B.C.) Born on Samos, he professed to be self-taught, but was probably a pupil of Xenocrates in youth. In 319 or 323 B.C. he visited Athens, travelled in Ionia, and opened a school in Mytilene. In 306 he returned to Athens, bought a garden, and founded the Epicurean School of Philosophy. He wrote much, but only a few letters, preserved by Diogenes Laertius, have come down to us. See EPICUREANISM.

Epidemic (mental): Ger. *geistige Epidemie*; Fr. *épidémie mentale*; Ital. *epidemia psichica*. See CONTAGION (mental).

Epigenesis [Gr. ἐπί + γένεσις, production]: Ger. *Epigenese*; Fr. *épigenèse*; Ital. *epigenesi*. The hypothesis that in the differentiation of structure during embryological development all characters are produced, not having been present before; as opposed to the hypothesis of PREFORMATION (q. v.), i.e. that such differ-

entiation is an unfolding of characters already preformed in the germ.

Harvey (1651) somewhat prophetically gave expression to this view. F. C. Wolff in 1759 championed it in opposition to the preformationist Haller. Modern researches on the cell and the changes of the chromatin matter of the nucleus have placed the two hypotheses in a new light. Weismann at first supported strongly, and now opposes it; O. Hertwig supports it in a modified form.

Literature: J. HARVEY, Exercitationes de Generatione; F. C. WOLFF, Theoria Generationis; A. WEISMANN, Germ-Plasm (1893); O. HERTWIG, The Biol. Problem of To-day (trans. by P. C. Mitchell, 1896); WHITMAN, Evolution and Epigenesis, Wood's Holl Biol. Lects. (1894); DRIESCH, Analytische Theorie d. organischen Entwicklung (1895); DELAGE, La Structure du Protoplasma et l'Hérédité (1895). For a summary of recent views see E. B. WILSON, The Cell in Devel. and Inheritance, where full reference to the literature of the subject will be found. (C.LL.M.–E.B.P.)

Epiglottis [Gr. ἐπί + γλωττίς, mouth of windpipe]: Ger. *Kehldeckel*; Fr. *épiglotte*; Ital. *epiglottide*. A plate of yellow elastic cartilage, in man shaped like an obovate leaf, attached in front of the superior opening of the larynx.

Ordinarily it stands up behind the base of the tongue; but in the act of swallowing, it probably falls back over the vocal cords and assists in preventing the entrance of solids or liquids into the trachea. Swallowing, however, may be performed normally with the epiglottis absent, the sphincter muscles of the larynx being sufficient to protect its aperture. According to some an important function of the epiglottis consists in toning the voice, raising the pitch by pressing down upon, and thus shortening, the vocal cords (Ellis), at the same time acting as a reinforcing vibration. Cf. SPEECH AND ITS DEFECTS. (C.F.H.)

Epilepsy [Gr. ἐπί + λαμβάνειν, to take, seize]: Ger. *Fallsucht, Epilepsie*; Fr. *épilepsie, haut mal, petit mal*; Ital. *epilessia, mal caduco*. In its most general sense epilepsy denotes discharging lesions of the nervous system, which are paroxysmal in character, and accompanied by more or less serious disturbances of consciousness; specifically it denotes the most distinctive form of such neuroses, known as true, genuine, or idiopathic epilepsy.

History. Epilepsy was well known in ancient times, and was regarded as an infliction of the gods; hence the term *morbus sacer*, *morbus divus*. The term *morbus comitialis* is connected with the custom of adjourning the forum whenever any of its members was seized with an epileptic attack. Other terms suggestive of demoniac or astral origin were also used. The name 'falling sickness' was applied to epilepsy within recent times.

Nature. The contributions of Hughlings-Jackson have established the conception (first suggested by Todd) of epilepsy as the explosion or discharge of nervous energy mainly from centres in the motor area of the brain. The study of epileptic convulsions thus contributes to the knowledge of the localization of brain functions. Such evidence is most clearly obtained in cases of epileptiform seizures, or Jacksonian epilepsy, in which the convulsions always begin in the same part of one side of the body, extending from this in a definite order of progression, first to other groups of muscles on the same side, and then to the opposite side (see below). The view which regards epilepsy as a central motor discharge with ultimate relations to the several layers of nerve-cells in the cortex, to the several levels of evolution of motor faculty, to the loss of consciousness, to the nature and order of the aurae, &c., does not deny the existence of epilepsy as the result of a discharge in the medulla and pons, and the possibility of a convulsive centre (in the medulla), stimulation of which in animals may produce convulsions; but it subordinates these phenomena to the chief and typical ones which in man are of cortical origin.

Cause. Many and various conditions are influential in the production of epileptic fits. Hereditary disposition is regarded as most important, the epileptic tendency being not so much a specific disease as the mark of an unstable condition of the brain. An hereditary taint may be discovered in more than one-third of all cases. Such taint may appear in one member of a family as insanity, in another as a nervous disorder, in a third as hysteria, and in a fourth as epilepsy. The epileptic tendency is thus recognized as a significant mark of degeneration, and its prevalence among criminals (see CRIMINOLOGY) has been frequently noted. Age is an important factor, nearly one-half of all cases appearing between the 10th and 20th year, and nearly 30 per cent. before the 10th year. Of specific exciting causes may be cited: injury to the brain by concussion, exposure to the sun, acute diseases, digestive derangements, alcoholism,

menstrual disorders, sudden fright or similar emotional disturbance, and the like; but in a third or a half of all cases no definite exciting cause may be assigned. The disorder is thus mainly a functional one, brought about by a general instability of the nervous system and, possibly, more immediately connected with an irritation in the motor area, such as that produced by a tumour, depressed bone, anaemia, disturbance of circulation, or definite injury.

Morbid anatomy. A great variety of pathological changes have been found in cases of epilepsy, many of which are also common in other diseases. Negative cases presenting no serious pathological changes are quite common. Most frequent and characteristic are degenerative changes in the brain cortex, morbid changes in the skull and membranes, a simple type of convolution, asymmetry of the hemisphere. A special tendency to disease of the cornu Ammonis has been emphasized by some writers. None of these changes are sufficiently common to be regarded as essential, and all of them have been regarded as secondary or resultant; thus again bringing into prominence the theory of a functional instability accompanied frequently by degenerative changes, as the essential cause of the epileptic attacks.

Varieties. It is customary to distinguish the major attacks (grand mal), in which there is a loss of consciousness, and prolonged and severe muscular spasm, from the minor attacks (petit mal), in which there is brief loss of consciousness without or with slight muscular spasm. In Jacksonian epilepsy there is no loss of consciousness, but a definite 'march' of convulsive symptoms. In masked epilepsy (épilepsie larvée) the convulsions are replaced by mental symptoms, of which automatism is the most usual. A large number of varieties are also recognized, according to the diseases which accompany the epilepsy (gastric, spinal, &c.); according to the time when the fits appear (diurnal, nocturnal); according to the members involved in the fits (partial, monospasm, &c.); according to the supposed cause (vasomotor, cortical); and so on. Hystero-epilepsy is specially considered under HYSTERIA (q. v.).

Symptoms. These may be considered (Ross) as (1) those preceding the paroxysm, (2) those of the paroxysm itself, and (3) those observable in the intervals between the attacks. (1) One class of premonitory symptoms may appear hours, or even days, in advance in the form of headache, dizziness, depression, excitement, mental confusion, or the like. But the more constant premonitory symptoms, called aurae, immediately precede the attack, and may be said to be the subjective feelings aroused by the changes in the brain which bring on the attack. Such aurae are limited to the period before unconsciousness ensues; hence those who rapidly pass into unconsciousness (about half of all cases) will be unable to describe the aura. Such aurae are extremely variable in type, although often quite constant in the successive attacks of the same individual. The aura may be motor (twitching of the thumb, rotation of the eyes, jerking of the muscles); sensory (tingling, numbness, flashes of light, sharp noises, bad odours or tastes); vasomotor (dizziness, flushing, choking); secretory (salivation); psychical (fear, feeling of confusion or strangeness, hallucinations of forms or voices). The unilateral or bilateral location of the motor and sensory aurae, the frequency with which they begin in small muscles, the order in which they spread to other muscles, have been interpreted as indicative of the portion of the cortex at which the discharge begins, and of the direction in which it proceeds; thus, when the attack begins in the head, the order is head, arm, leg; when in the hand, the order is hand, head, leg; when in the leg, the order is leg, arm, head; such order indicating an extension of the discharge into neighbouring cortical centres.

(2) In the minor attacks of epilepsy (*epilepsia mitior* or petit mal) there is momentary unconsciousness, a slight pallor or vertigo; possibly a contraction of the pupils, a fixed stare, a rolling of the tongue, chewing movements, and the like. The patient may be speaking, pause, exhibit the symptoms of the attack, and proceed as if nothing had happened. At the onset of major attacks (epilepsy in the special sense, *epilepsia gravior* or haut mal) there is loss of consciousness, sudden falling, great pallor, and (usually) a sharp cry. The patient then exhibits a brief stage of tonic but unequal contraction of all the muscles of the body. There may be distortions of all kinds, rotation of the head and neck, flexion of hand, arm, &c. This tonic stage gives way to a clonic stage, with spasms usually more marked on one side, and the face or tongue usually affected before the trunk or leg. The head may be drawn from side to side, the eyeballs rolled about, the face distorted, the jaws violently clinched; there may be frothing at the mouth, and excess of secretions in general. In this stage the pallor has been succeeded by venous hyperaemia, the face being dull-red, the veins of the head and neck distended and throbbing. Upon this succeeds a stage of relaxation, exhaustion, or coma with gradual returning consciousness. There is often a long period of diminished energy and mental confusion. In Jacksonian epilepsy (epileptiform seizures) there is slight or no loss of consciousness, and the spasm begins on one side and proceeds in definite order; i.e. if it begins in the hand, it goes up the arm and down the leg. The more sudden the onset of the spasm the more rapidly it spreads, and the shorter the seizure. The seizures may be very frequent. In masked epilepsy the symptoms are of a totally different type, the convulsion being replaced by an abnormal psychosis of which the patient may be entirely ignorant upon returning to consciousness. Anger or violence may be the prevailing symptom, and severe injury may be inflicted on others by an epileptic in this state; or there may be an altered speech or personality, or a series of automatic acts.

(3) In the interval between the seizures many epileptics are perfectly normal in every respect; and noted historical cases of men of ability subject to epilepsy belong to this class. In many cases there is impairment of memory, especially in regard to recent events; in others there may be a dullness or mental deficiency, differing in amount from slight stupidity to imbecility. The moral nature is often perverted, and the temperament morose, suspicious, and irritable. Such mental impairment is quite as common in the minor as in the major forms of epilepsy, and, while related to the frequency of the seizures, it is also related to the prevalence of mental rather than motor symptoms during the attacks.

Epilepsy and Insanity. While epilepsy is entirely compatible with normal mental action, the tendency of frequent fits, extending over many years, to impair the faculties, to dull the finer feelings, and to change the character is a most potent one. Apart from the decay of faculty and dementia to which epileptics are subject, there are recognized distinct relations between epilepsy and insanity. The two may be viewed as effects of a common cause; or the brain degeneration which the explosive discharges bring about may be regarded as the exciting cause of the insanity. Epileptic insanity is apt to assume the form of mania, characterized by irritability and impulsiveness; in such states crimes and assaults have frequently been committed, and have given rise to serious discussions regarding mental responsibility (Maudsley, *Responsibility in Mental Disease*). The mania may occur just after the paroxysm, or it may occur between paroxysms, or take the place of the paroxysm, as in masked epilepsy. The term *furor epilepticus* was often used in connection with these violent outbreaks of epileptics. Periods of automatism and unconscious action in epileptics may also be regarded as significant in this connection.

Literature : BINSWANGER, Die Epilepsie, in Nothnagel's Spec. Pathol. u. Ther., xii (1899); GOWERS, Epilepsy (1881); FÉRÉ, Les Épilepsies et les Épileptiques (1890); Ross, Nerv. Diseases, ii. 885–920; J. HUGHLINGS-JACKSON, Epileptiform Convulsions, &c., Trans. Int. Med. Cong. (1881), ii. 6, and Croonian Lectures on Evolution and Dissolution of the Nervous System, Brit. Med. J. (Mar. 29, Apr. 5 and 12, 1884); RONCOVONI, L'Epilessia (1895); GÉLINEAU, Les Épilepsies (1900). See also BIBLIOG. G, 1, *g*. (J.J.)

Epiphany [Gr. ἐπί + φαίνειν, to bring to light]: Ger. *Epiphania (Erscheinung Christi)*; Fr. *Épiphanie*; Ital. *Epifania*. The festival of the manifestation of God through Christ to mankind. It was first observed by the Eastern Church, which maintained that the manifestation took place at baptism, not at birth. The festival was celebrated on January 6. In the Western Church, Epiphany was never connected with the baptism, but with the manifestation of Christ to the Wise Men from the East, who were regarded as the 'firstfruits of heathendom' for Christ.

Literature : BINGHAM, Origines, Bk. XX. chap. iv; AUGUSTI, Handb. d. christl. Archäol., i. 542 f.; BINTERIM, Denkwürdigkeiten, v. Pt. I. 310 f. (R.M.W.)

Epiphenomenon [Gr. ἐπί + φαίνομαι, to appear]: Ger. *Beiprodukt, Begleiterscheinung*; Fr. *épiphénomène, (quelque chose) surajouté*; Ital. *epifenomeno*. A secondary or added accompaniment to a process, considered as merely incidental, and having no part in the further development of the process.

The term is in use mainly to characterize the Epiphenomenon Theory of the relation of mind to body, which makes the former an incidental effect of brain processes—'a spark thrown off by the engine'—having no effect upon the brain changes which constitute a closed system. See MIND AND BODY. (J.M.B.)

'The addition of consciousness to living bodies affords no ground for supposing that consciousness has a causality of its own, or reacts upon the organism in which it appears' (Hodgson, *Theory of Practice*, i. 425). According to the same writer, the theory conceives consciousness 'in some such way as the foam thrown up by and floating on a wave'— 'a mere foam, aura or melody, arising from the brain, but without reaction upon it' (*Time and Space*, 279). An early psychological statement is by Maudsley, *Physiol. and Pathol. of Mind*. (A.S.P.P.–J.M.B.)

Epiphysis [Gr. ἐπί + φύσις, a growth]: Ger. *Zirbeldrüse*; Fr. *épiphyse, glande pinéale*; Ital. *epifisi, ghiandola pineale*. See BRAIN, and cf. PARIETAL ORGAN. Synonyms: Pineal gland, Conarium. (H.H.)

Epistemology [Gr. ἐπιστήμη, knowledge, + λόγος, discourse]: Ger. *Erkenntnisstheorie*; Fr. *épistémologie*; Ital. *gnoseologia, dottrina della conoscenza*. (1) Theory of the origin, nature, and limits of knowledge. Cf. GNOSIOLOGY. (H.R.S.–J.M.B.)

(2) The systematic analysis of the conceptions employed by ordinary and scientific thought in interpreting the world, and including an investigation of the act of knowledge, or the nature of knowledge as such, with a view to determine its ontological significance; otherwise known as Theory of Knowledge.

The first definition of epistemology, commonly spoken of as the relation of knowledge to reality, has hitherto been most prominent, and epistemological inquiry has generally been undertaken in view of doubts which have been raised as to the trustworthiness of the knowing process, and the validity of its results. It is thus, as Paulsen well points out, a secondary, not a primary product of thought. 'Philosophy began everywhere with metaphysics; questions as to the form and origin of the universe, the nature and source of existence, the essence of the soul and its relation to the body, form the first subject of philosophical reflection. Only after long occupation with such questions does the question arise of the nature of knowledge and its possibility. It is raised by the divergent views to which meditation on physical and metaphysical questions leads. This divergence raises the question : Is it at all possible for the human understanding to solve these problems ? Epistemology develops as critical reflection upon metaphysics' (*Einleitung in die Philos.*, 2nd ed., 349). Thus, in ancient philosophy, the Sophists may be said to be the first definitely to raise the epistemological question, by their sceptical impeachment of the possibility of truth or universally valid statement.

This is the epistemological issue which is mainly discussed by Plato and Aristotle, but it is found (cf. for example the *Theaetetus*) to involve the question of the constitution of knowledge, as debated between sensationalists and rationalists, empiricists and transcendentalists. But such questions are discussed by Plato and Aristotle in the context of their metaphysical and more purely logical inquiries. The epistemological problem comes more into the foreground as a separate investigation, in consequence of the systematic attack on the possibility of knowledge by the Sceptics. The discussion of 'the criterion of truth' by the Stoics and Epicureans is a conscious and deliberate attempt to arrive at a theory of knowledge, as a preliminary to metaphysical construction. The theory of Probabilism, developed by the Sceptics of the later Academy, is an outcome of the same discussions.

In modern times, epistemology first steps into the foreground with Locke, whose *Essay*, according to its author's own account, had its origin in 'the difficulties that rose on every side' in the course of a metaphysical discussion. Whereupon, says Locke, 'it came into my thoughts that we took a wrong course, and that, before we set ourselves upon inquiries of that nature, it was necessary to examine our own abilities, and see what objects our understandings were or were not fitted to deal with' (Epistle to the Reader). In the introductory chapter he emphasizes in similar language the necessity of a theory of knowledge as a preliminary to metaphysical inquiry. 'Till that was done,' he continues, 'I suspected we began at the wrong end. . . . Extending their inquiries beyond their capacities, and letting their thoughts wander into those depths where they can find no sure footing, it is no wonder that men raise questions and multiply disputes which, never coming to any clear resolution, are proper only to continue and increase these doubts, and to confirm them at last in perfect scepticism. Whereas, were the capacities of our understandings well considered, the extent of our knowledge once discovered, and the horizon found which sets the bounds between the enlightened and the dark parts of things—between what is and what is not comprehensible by us—men would perhaps with less scruple acquiesce in the avowed ignorance of the one, and employ their thoughts and discourse with more advantage and satisfaction in the other' (I. i. 7). The design of the *Essay* is, accordingly, in his own words, to inquire into 'the certainty, evidence, and extent' of our knowledge, and at the same time 'to search out the bounds between opinion and knowledge, and examine by what measures, in things whereof we have no certain knowledge, we ought to regulate our assent and moderate our persuasions' (I. i. 3). In these and other similar passages Locke impressed upon succeeding English philosophy its predominantly epistemological character. It will also be noted that they express the epistemological question in its characteristically modern form, as referring to the limits of human knowledge—the form in which it meets us in Hume and Kant, Comte and Spencer. Kant's description of dogmatic metaphysics as the arena of endless contests, comparable to the shadow-fights of the heroes in Walhalla, and his idea of 'criticism' as the science which is to determine 'the extent, validity, and worth' of our *a priori* cognitions, and thus to settle the question as to the possibility or impossibility of 'metaphysics,' repeat almost verbally Locke's conception of his own enterprise, though the execution in the two cases is of course different. Repeating Locke's metaphor, Kant blames Hume for declaring certain questions to lie beyond the 'horizon' of human knowledge, without determining where that horizon falls. 'He (Hume) merely declared the understanding to be limited, instead of showing what its limits were; he created a general distrust of the power of our faculties, without giving us any determinate knowledge of the bounds of our unavoidable ignorance.' As contrasted with scepticism, criticism does not 'examine the *facta* of reason, but reason itself in the whole extent of its powers, and in regard to its capacity of *a priori* cognition; and thus we determine, not merely the empirical and ever-shifting bounds of our knowledge, but its necessary and eternal limits' (see *Critique of Pure Reason*, Preface to First Edition, Introduction, and Transcendental Doctrine of Method, chap. i).

This way of stating the epistemological question entirely disappears in Kant's idealistic successors. The philosophy of Fichte and Hegel (especially in the *Wissenschaftslehre* and the *Logik*) may be said to consist largely of an analysis of cognition and the categories of thought, but no distinction is drawn between theory of knowledge and metaphysics. After the philosophical interregnum, however, which followed the collapse of the Hegelian school in Germany, the 'return to

Kant' which began between 1860 and 1870 once more placed Erkenntnisstheorie in the centre of philosophical interest. The multiplication of Neo-Kantian treatises on this subject had proceeded so far, in 1878, as to call forth Lotze's protest against 'the constant whetting of the knife,' which, he says, 'becomes tedious if it is not proposed to cut anything with it.'

The conception of epistemology which is thus traceable directly to Locke and Kant is open to certain fundamental objections. Locke himself errs by supposing that the first objects of knowledge are the subjective states of the individual mind. He conceives the problem to be : How is the passage legitimated from states of consciousness to external or trans-subjective reality? But this is to invert the real process of knowledge. States of consciousness are not known as objects, except to the psychologist, and, when so known, they are known as elements in a real world, and in contrast to the world of external or physical reality. The notion of reality or of object is, therefore, prior to the distinction between external and internal, i. e. between objective and subjective in the popular use of these terms. Accordingly, a start cannot be made in the analysis of knowledge from the individual knower, conceived as enclosed and isolated within the circle of his own mental states. Then, again, it is impossible to criticize the validity of knowledge, as it were *ab extra*, in the Kantian manner. It is obvious that we cannot sit in judgment upon our cognitive faculties without employing those very faculties, and thereby implying their trustworthiness. The validity of knowledge as such is an ultimate and inevitable assumption, and Hegel's well-known comparison of Kant's procedure to the resolve of Scholasticus not to enter the water till he had learned to swim, crystallizes in an epigram the contradiction involved in the attempt to determine whether the world of knowledge is merely subjective (phenomenal), or gives us things as they are. Kant's results. in this reference, really rest upon his attribution of certain elements in knowledge—the universal elements of time, space and the categories— to the subject, and certain others—the particularity of sense—to the object : and this in turn rests upon the confusion between epistemology and psychology which still disturbs his treatment, and leads him to identify *a priori*, or necessary in knowledge, with what is subjective or innate in the individual mind.

But if criticism of knowledge in the Lockian and Kantian sense must be abandoned, the need of a theory of knowledge still remains. Its use is, in the first instance, polemical, in answer to the challenge of scepticism, subjectivism, agnosticism, relativism. In this regard, it is the province of epistemology to investigate the nature of the cognitive relation as such, in order to discover its essential conditions, and so to determine whether the circumstances of human knowledge are such as to invalidate its claim to be a true account of reality. An agnostic relativism condemns knowledge because it does not satisfy certain conditions. By exposing the inherently contradictory nature of the demands made, epistemological analysis deprives such criticism of its basis, and restores us to the original confidence of reason in itself. Till scepticism and agnosticism cease from the land, this polemic will necessarily continue to be prominent in epistemological literature, whichever side may win the greater body of adherents. As matter of history, the questions of epistemology in this reference are conveniently tabulated by Külpe (*Einleitung in die Philos.*, 119–20) as follows :—

(1) The question of the origin of knowledge, giving rise to the opposing views of the rationalists and empiricists (or sensationalists), and the mediating position of Kantian criticism; (2) the question of the validity and the limits of knowledge, giving rise to the variety of positions expressed by such terms as dogmatism, scepticism, relativism, positivism ; and (3) the question of the nature of the objects of knowledge, as subjective or trans-subjective, giving rise to the opposition of idealism and realism. But the three questions merge into one another.

Apart from such controversial issues, epistemology is sometimes held to include, as indicated in the second definition, an analysis of knowledge in the widest sense—a critical analysis of all the conceptions by which we endeavour to interpret the world. This 'criticism of categories,' as it has been called, does not involve the larger enterprise of Kant. It is an objective or, as Hegel called it, a disinterested analysis, which, by making clear the precise significance of each conception and the sphere of its application, allows the one, as it were, to judge and supersede the other. The result of the analysis is consequently the recognition of 'degrees of truth' (or conversely, degrees of 'abstraction') in the representations of the world which arise from the application of different conceptions. Kant's table of the categories and Hegel's *Logik* are contributions to such a Kategorienlehre, or immanent criticism of thought. In more recent times, epistemology finds perhaps its most important function in a criticism of the assumptions involved in the methods and fundamental conceptions of the different sciences. Ward has more than once urged that this is 'the chief business of philosophy' (cf. *Mind*, O.S., viii. 153 and xv. 213). The general result of such a philosophical criticism of science must necessarily be to show that the accounts given of the world by the different sciences are essentially dependent on the abstractions or assumptions on which these sciences proceed. And in proportion as this insight is reached, these accounts are forced to surrender their pretensions to final or absolute truth; they are seen to be only aspects of experience, possessing relative truth in a greater or less degree.

[Such procedure was made explicitly the method of metaphysics by Herbart — his 'rectification of conceptions'—and was employed with great force by Lotze. Cf. HER-BARTIANISM. (J.M.B.)]

Epistemology requires to be distinguished from the psychology of cognition, and it is also commonly distinguished from metaphysics or ontology and from logic. A few words on these distinctions may serve to give greater precision to the foregoing account of the scope and function of epistemology.

The distinction between psychology and epistemology is embodied in the Cartesian distinction between the *esse formale seu proprium* of an idea, regarded only as a specific mode of consciousness, and its *esse obiectivum sive vicarium*, when it is taken in its representative capacity, as standing for some object thought of. The psychologist deals with psychical events merely as such—as facts connected with and dependent on other facts. The interconnections of this factual world— the laws of the happening of psychical events— are what the psychologist has to investigate. In perception, for example, he is concerned, as Sully puts it, 'with the genesis and development of our perceptions as subjective or psychical processes having certain physiological concomitants,' but not with 'the objective import and validity of the result.' Croom Robertson suggested (*Mind*, O.S., viii. 15) that, in view of this difference of standpoint, the word knowledge might be conveniently banished from psychology, and

its place taken by the more colourless term intellection; just as Ward says that the traditional 'Cartesio-Lockian idea,' which is essentially an epistemological term, might be replaced in psychology by the phrase state of consciousness. In brief, psychology, although dealing in popular parlance with the subjective, treats these subjective facts, like any natural science, as an objective world in which it traces causal connections, concomitances, or sequences, and the evolution of the more complex from simpler formations. But it does not analyse the subject-object relation which constitutes knowledge as such, and which is the presupposition of psychology as well as of every other science. To analyse this relation and its implications is the specific task of epistemology.

Epistemology is usually distinguished from ontology or metaphysics in the narrower sense of that term. Philosophy, in other words, is defined as 'a theory of knowing and being,' and epistemology and ontology are regarded as the two complementary inquiries into which it falls. The two inquiries are, however, so closely allied that it is impossible to carry on either independently and (for example) to treat epistemology, as Locke apparently intended, as entirely 'preliminary' to metaphysics. Some, accordingly, have refused to make any distinction between the two. But the analysis of knowledge, though involving fundamental ontological conclusions, cannot give us all that is included under metaphysics or ontology, regarded as a synthetic statement in ultimate terms of the nature of reality. This statement must be based not only upon the structure of knowledge, but upon ethical and aesthetic considerations, upon our notions of value, and the relation of our ideals to the ultimate ground of reality.

The variations of current usage in regard to the scope of logic make it difficult to formulate any generally recognized distinction between logic and epistemology. Some would identify the two, while others would prefer to include epistemology as a branch of logic in a generalized sense. It is certainly true that the best logical treatises of the present day, such as those of Sigwart, Lotze, Bradley, Bosanquet, Wundt, contain a great deal of properly epistemological matter. But although the traditional logic of the textbooks cannot claim the unity of an independent science—being, in fact, an amalgam of elements from different sources, such as grammar,

336

psychology, and metaphysics—still, the usage which defines logic as the science of the formal principles of thought—the exposition of the laws of formal consistency in passing from one statement to another—appears too firmly established to make successful innovation probable. Cf. LOGIC, and EMPIRICAL LOGIC.

Literature: the term epistemology appears to have been first made current by FERRIER in his Institutes of Metaphysics(1854). Works on philosophy, and BIBLIOG. B, i, *d*. In German there is a department of literature devoted to Erkenntnisstheorie. (A.S.P.P.)

Episyllogism: Ger. *Episyllogismus*; Fr. *épisyllogisme*; Ital. *episillogismo*. A syllogism of which one (or both) of the premises is stated as the conclusion of another syllogism. The latter is called technically a prosyllogism. See CHAIN ARGUMENT, and SYLLOGISM. (R.A.)

Epithelium [Gr. ἐπί + θηλή, a nipple or papilla]: Ger. *Epithel*; Fr. *épithélium*; Ital. *epitelio*. Cellular covering of free surfaces of the body and of all natural cavities which open, either temporarily or permanently, to the exterior; also applied to lining of serous, lymphatic, and vascular channels and cavities which do not open to the exterior. Cf. ENDOTHELIUM.

The term was originally used of the mucous membrane of the lips and mouth, where the etymological significance of the word is plain. (C.F.H.)

Equality [Lat. *aequus*, equal]: Ger. *Gleichheit*; Fr. *égalité*; Ital. *eguaglianza*. (1) Consciousness of: the discernment of lack of difference between two experiences in respect to QUANTITY (q. v.) or NUMBER (q. v.). (2) Notion or concept of: the thought of lack of difference in quantity or number in general.

The meaning given first is genetically earlier, and arises probably with the treatment of things in groups of greater or less size, either (*a*) by reaction upon the groups as wholes, with varying results, (*b*) by establishing one to one correspondence among the parts, or (*c*) by measurement: the three processes occurring genetically in the order given. When by any of these processes disparity or difference is discovered, the consciousness of equality arises over against that of difference. It is this antithesis with difference or inequality that distinguishes equality from identity. After the number concept is further developed—this consciousness of equality and inequality being its first stage (see NUMBER CONCEPT)—the numerical distinctness of the

two or more experiences is consciously recognized, and the direct comparison is made. This use of comparison with ABSTRACTION (q. v.) gives the second meaning, in which equality is an abstract idea.

In mathematics and symbolic logic the symbol of equality is ($=$), and the formula of equality ($A = A$) is called an equation. (J.M.B.)

Equality (social). (1) Practical equivalence of social rank, consideration, and enjoyment of opportunities that are created by society or the state. (2) A social shibboleth of revolutionary origin in France—'Liberty, Equality, Fraternity.'

Matthew Arnold, essay on *Equality*, gives credit to Menander for the first serious advocacy of equality as a social condition. It was Rousseau, however (*Du Contrat Social* and *Émile*), who created a popular enthusiasm for equality as an ideal. William Godwin (*Political Justice*) and Jeremy Bentham (*Morals and Legislation*) were the first serious advocates of equality in English political literature. Fitzjames Stephen's *Liberty, Equality, and Fraternity* is a destructive criticism. Matthew Arnold's essay is a plea for social equality. W. C. Brownell's *French Traits* is a psychological study of actual social equality in France. Giddings (*Elements of Sociology*) has argued that liberty presupposes fraternity, and fraternity a practical equality. (F.H.G.)

Equation: see EQUALITY.

Equilibrium: see ORIENTATION (1).

Equilibrium (in aesthetics): see BALANCE.

Equilibrium (illusions of): see ILLUSIONS OF MOTION AND MOVEMENT.

Equilibrium (in biology): see ACCOMMODATION.

Equilibrium (in economics) [Lat. *aequus*, equal, + *libra*, a balance]: Ger. *Gleichgewicht*; Fr. *équilibre, indifférence*; Ital. *equilibrio economico*. Such a set of conditions with regard to the amount and distribution of wealth, that the motives for an increase of any particular kind of wealth exactly balance the motives against such an increase.

Thus a market price establishes itself at a point of equilibrium where the demands of those who are willing to buy at that price or a higher one exactly equal the supplies offered by those who are ready to sell at that price or any lower one. If the price is higher, the supply exceeds the demand, and tends to drive the price down; if it is lower, the demand exceeds the supply, and tends to force the price up.

The equilibrium here described is a static

one; it deals with quantities and not with rates. The attempt to establish a point of dynamic equilibrium or normal price, where rates of production and consumption shall be equal, is far more complex and uncertain. (A.T.H.)

Equilibrium (in physics): Ger. *Gleichgewicht*; Fr. *équilibre*; Ital. *equilibrio*. The state of a body which is free to move, and acted on by forces so related that they neutralize each other, so that the body has no tendency to move. In order that a system of forces may produce equilibrium, the resultants of the forces, both that of translation and that of rotation, must vanish.

If the forces producing equilibrium are such that when the body acted on is slightly displaced it tends to return to its place, the equilibrium is called stable; if it tends to move still further from the position, it is called unstable; if the equilibrium remains undisturbed, it is called indifferent or mobile. If a wheel free to turn on a horizontal axis has a weight attached to its rim, it is in stable equilibrium when the weight is directly below the axis; in unstable, when the weight is vertically above the axis. (S.N.)

Equilibrium (sensation of): Ger. *Empfindung des Gleichgewichts*; Fr. *sensation d'équilibre, sens de l'équilibre*; Ital. *senso dell' equilibrio*. The sensation arising from the erect balancing of the body. Its existence is in evidence principally when it is disturbed. (J.M.B.)

The 'sense' of equilibrium is apparently built up from the muscular, cutaneous, and pressure senses, and from visual perception. At the same time there seems to be no doubt that the semicircular canals of the ear (see STATIC SENSE, also for literature) arouse and sustain a permanent muscular tone, which contributes greatly to the maintenance of equilibrium. The growth of the necessary associations may be observed in the child learning to hold the head erect. Cf. DIZZINESS. (E.B.T.–J.M.B.)

Equipollence or **-cy** [Lat. *aequus*, equal, +*pollere*, to be able]: Ger. *Aequipollenz*; Fr. *équipollence*; Ital. *equipollenza*. The relation between two propositional forms which represent the same fact. It translates the Gr. ἰσοδυναμῶν. (C.S.P.)

There has been a twofold tradition on the nature of equipollence: one, as stated above, restricting it to the qualitative; the other extending it to all cases in which two propositions, formally different, must be true or false together. The one tradition goes back to Apuleius (see Prantl, *Gesch. d. Logik*, i. 583), the other to Galen (see id., i. 568–9). As illustrating the one, see Wallis, *Logica*, Lib. II. cap. vi; for the other, see Crackanthorpe, *Logica*, Lib. III. cap. iv. Cf. Ueberweg, *Logik*, § 96. Recently the term has fallen into desuetude, and its place tends to be taken by Obversion. (R.A.)

Equity (in law) [Lat. *aequitas*]: Ger. (1) *Billigkeit*, (2) *Gerechtigkeit*; Fr. (1) *équité*; Ital. *equità*. (1) Justice; that which is *ex aequo et bono*. (2) The system of remedial justice administered by courts of Equity, or (what is synonymous) courts of Chancery. (3) The kind of remedy afforded by that system. It is one circumscribed by precedent, and not always identical with natural equity.

The rigid forms in which legal remedies are encased, and by which legal rights are practically determined, in early societies, gradually give way to methods of procedure based more on reason and leaning more to substance of right. Strict law is thus harmonized with or modified into equity. The Roman praetors, at the instance of the Roman lawyers, by the annual praetorian edict, brought about this change at Rome. In England it was initiated by the lord chancellor, as the keeper of the king's 'conscience,' and soon produced a system of judicial procedure known as chancery, administered by separate courts of Chancery. These courts often interposed to prevent the use of a legal advantage gained in the ordinary law courts, as by enjoining a judgment creditor against enforcing a judgment which he had obtained under such circumstances as to make it inequitable for him to use it. They also gave a remedy, when there was no adequate one, at law. In the United States a similar division of lawsuits, between actions at law and actions in equity, formerly existed in most states, and now exists in the Federal courts. In England, and in many of the United States, the distinction was abolished during the latter half of the 19th century. Cf. CODE.

Literature: POMEROY, Equity Jurisprudence, i. chap. i; SOHM, Instit. of Roman Law, § 13; MAINE, Ancient Law, chaps. ii, iii. (S.E.B.)

Equivalence (law of): see CONSERVATION OF ENERGY, for which it is sometimes used. (J.M.B.)

Equivocal [Lat. *aequus*, equal, +*vox*, voice]: Ger. *mehrdeutig, zweideutig*; Fr. *équivoque*; Ital. *equivoco*. Terms are 'equivocal' when with identity of verbal expression there is difference of meaning, and they may therefore stand for wholly distinct notions or things. (R.A.)

Equivocation : Ger. *Zweideutigkeit* ; Fr. *équivoque* ; Ital. *equivoco*. The use of an expression capable of two meanings, one false and the other true, for the purpose of suggesting the false meaning to the hearer without committing the speaker to that meaning.

On the morality of equivocation there is no little diversity between common opinion and moral principle. In a lie or falsehood it is common to distinguish (1) the objective discrepancy between the statement and the facts, called material falsehood ; and (2) the intention to deceive, called formal falsehood. The moralist, who looks to the intention of the agent as determining right and wrong, is accordingly led to regard the formal falsehood as that, and that only, which is essentially contrary to morality. And formal falsehood is present in the equivocation as much as in the lie—from which equivocation is only distinguished by the absence of material falsehood. See, however, the further distinction between 'positive' and 'negative' misrepresentation under LIE.

On the other hand, the external treatment of morality which distinguished the casuistical moralists (see CASUISTRY) made it easy to defend equivocation and to distinguish it from lying. Thus Sanchez, quoted by Pascal (*Lett. prov.*, ix), says : 'It is permitted to use ambiguous terms so that they may be understood in a different sense from that in which one understands them oneself.' On the same ground permission is given to mental reservation (restriction mentale): 'One may swear that one has not done a thing which one has really done, by saying within oneself that one did not do it on a certain day, or before one was born,' or even 'after having said aloud "I swear," one may add to oneself "that I say," and then continue aloud "that I did not do that."' 'And this is very convenient in many circumstances, and always quite correct when necessary or useful for health, honour, or happiness.' (W.R.S.)

Erastianism : Ger. *Erastianismus* ; Fr. *Érastianisme* ; Ital. *Erastianismo*. Generally stated, Erastianism means the supremacy of the civil authority in ecclesiastical as well as in civil causes.

This politico-ecclesiastical doctrine derived its name, though not its entire contents, from Thomas Erastus, professor of medicine at Basel

in 1580. He was opposed to anything in the nature of a theocratic church. His doctrine was espoused by such members of the Westminster Assembly as Selden, Coleman, and Lightfoot.

Literature : THOMAS ERASTUS, Explicatio quaestionis gravissimae utrum excommunicatio, &c. (Eng. trans. by Lee) ; Subordinate Standards of the Free Church of Scotland (the Claim of Right and Protest) ; BUCHANAN, Ten Years' Conflict ; HANNA, Life of Chalmers ; WALKER, Dr. Robert Buchanan ; Free Church of Scotland, Annals of the Disruption. (R.M.W.)

Erasure : see METHOD OF ERASURE.

Eratosthenes. (276–194 B.C.) A Greek philosopher and astronomer, noted for his learning. Bunsen ranks him next to Aristotle, adding that he is 'as far superior to him [Aristotle] in extent of learning as inferior in grasp of intellect.' He was a pupil of Callimachus, and librarian in the great Alexandrian library.

Erdmann, Johann Eduard. (1805–92.) Born at Wolmar, Livonia ; studied at Dorpat and Berlin ; became professor of philosophy at Halle in 1836, and died at Halle.

Erethism [Gr. ἐρεθισμός, irritation] : Ger. *Erregungszustand* ; Fr. *éréthisme* ; Ital. *eretismo*. An exaggerated degree of irritability in a part of the body ; applied frequently to an irritable condition of the brain and nervous system. (J.J.)

Eretria (school of) : see PRE-SOCRATIC PHILOSOPHY.

Erg : see UNIT (of physical measurement).

Ergograph : see LABORATORY AND APPARATUS, III, A.

Erhard, Johann Benjamin. (1766–1827.) A Berlin physician, who wrote on psychology, mental pathology, ethics, and jurisprudence. In his education he was much influenced by Shaftesbury, Moses Mendelssohn, J. H. Lambert, and, later, by Kant.

Erhardt, Simon. (1776–1829.) After 1809 a teacher at Schweinfurt, Ansbach, and Nürnberg ; in 1811 professor of philosophy at Erlangen, and, later, at Freiburg ; in 1823 professor of philosophy at Heidelberg. He belonged to the school of Schelling.

Erigena, Johannes Scotus. Born in Ireland between 800 and 815 ; died in the latter half of the 9th century—place unknown. He was probably the keenest and most profound thinker of the 9th century. In 843 probably he went to France, where he enjoyed the patronage of Charles the Bald. He was the forerunner of scholasticism. He advocated the supremacy of reason, and maintained a vague Pantheism. Condemned as a heretic at Paris in 1209 for his writings on predestination and transubstantiation.

Eristic: see Megarians, under SCHOOLS OF GREECE (Post-Socratic).

Eros [Gr.]. The principle of love in NEO-PLATONISM (q. v.) and MYSTICISM (q. v.).

Erotomania or **Eroticomania** [Gr. ἔρως, love, + μανία, madness] : Ger. *Erotomanie*; Fr. *érotomanie*; Ital. *erotomania*. A symptom of various mental troubles, characterized by a morbid and intense passion for the opposite sex; the sexual feeling is imaginative and emotional rather than carnal.

The term is also used to express excessive sexual passion, and thus becomes synonymous with nymphomania in women, and satyriasis in men. (J.J.)

Error: see TRUTH AND ERROR.

Error of Mean Square: see ERRORS OF OBSERVATION.

Errors of Observation (theory of): Ger. *Ausgleichungs - Rechnung*; Fr. *théorie des erreurs*; Ital. *teoria degli errori*. A department of the theory of probability treating of the adjustment of measurements and quantitative estimates; called also method of least squares (Ger. *Methode der kleinsten Quadrate*; Fr. *méthode des moindres carrés*). The method was first used by Gauss (about 1795) and was first described by Legendre (1806).

When a magnitude is measured a number of times the determinations will differ, and when all the measurements are equally valid, their average is likely to be more nearly the true magnitude than any single measurement. The departures of the separate measurements from the true value are called errors, and their departures from the average are called residuals. As, however, errors and residuals will coincide theoretically when the number of experiments is large, the term error is often used to include residuals. There will be more small errors than large ones, and they will be distributed in a definite fashion given by the equation

$$y = ce^{-n^2 x^2},$$

and represented by the bell-shaped curve *VYU*.

In this curve the size of an error is represented by the abscissae *OP*, *OU'*, &c., and its frequency by the ordinates *OY*, *PQ*, &c. The number of errors less than a given size is represented by the area of the curve above the abscissa. Thus one-half of all errors will be smaller than *OP*. This error is called the probable error. The mean of all the errors—the mean error—will be a little larger, *ON*; the error of mean square, where there is an inflection point on the curve, and where a few experiments give the most accurate results, is *OS*. The modulus is *OL*. If the probable error be 1·00, the mean error is 1·18, the error of mean square 1·48, and the modulus 2·10. The reliability of the average is inversely proportional to these errors, and proportional to the square root of the number of observations.

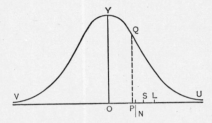

The theory of errors of observation is based on the assumption that each error is the result of a great number of small causes independent of each other and equally likely to make the measurement too small or too large. The theory as applied in physical science is not concerned with constant errors which it cannot eliminate. In psychology, however, the real magnitude is known in some cases, and the perception or judgment may tend to be on the average too large or too small. The difference between the true magnitude and the average of the measurements is the constant error, which may be positive or negative. The average departure from the true magnitude is called the average error in psychophysical work, while the average departure from the average is called the variable error. In certain time measurements the term ' mean variation' (M. V.) has been used by psychologists. This is identical with the mean error of physical science or the variable error of the psychophysical methods. This error or variation is found by taking the difference between each separate measurement and the average of them, and taking the average of these differences without reference to the signs.

These distinctions are important for the statistical treatment of VARIATION (q. v.) and for the study of the PSYCHOPHYSICAL METHODS (q. v.).

Literature: treatises on the subject were published in the same year, 1812, by GAUSS and LAPLACE. Useful works in English are AIRY, Theory of Errors of Observation (1861), and MERRIMAN, Method of Least Squares (6th ed., 1893). See also under VARIATION (statistical treatment of). (J.MᶜK.C.)

Eschatology [Gr. ἔσχατος, last, + λόγος, word, reason]: Ger. *Eschatologie*; Fr. *eschatologie*; Ital. not in use. The section of dogmatic theology which—as compared with theology proper, anthropology, and soteriology—deals with the 'doctrine of the last things'; that is, with death, the future life, and the end of the world.

Jewish eschatology was essentially connected with the Messianic hope in its various developments, early Christian with the apocalyptic expectation of the Second Coming. Dogmatic eschatology, having direct reference to the conduct of the present life, was formulated during the supremacy of the mediaeval church. See CHILIASM, IMMORTALITY, and MESSIANIC HOPE.

Literature: LUTHARDT, Die Lehre v. d. letzten Dingen; ALGER, Doctrine of a Future Life (with very full literature); OXENHAM, Catholic Eschatology and Universalism; SPLITTGEBER, Tod, Fortleben u. Auferstehung; DAVIDSON, The Doctrine of Last Things; SALMOND, The Christ. Doctrine of Immortality; CHARLES, Hist. of the Doctrine of a Future Life in Israel, Judaism, and Christianity. (R.M.W.)

Esoteric and **Exoteric** [Gr. ἐσωτερικός, ἐξωτερικός]: Ger. *esoterisch, exoterisch*; Fr. *ésotérique, exotérique*; Ital. *esoterico*. Terms used to characterize two different presentations of doctrine with the Pythagoreans, Plato, and Aristotle. What was taught to their most advanced disciples was denominated esoteric; what was given to the pupils not in the inmost circle and to the outside world was called exoteric. The term exoteric is used by Aristotle to denote a treatment of a subject fitted to the ordinary reader; a meaning very close to that of our word 'popular.' (H.R.S.)

Esprit de Corps [Fr.]: Ger. *Korpsgeist* (Barth); Ital. *spirito di corpo*. The consciousness, on the part of a member of a social group, of the interests common to the group.

Defined sociologically, the effects or external evidences of this consciousness are meant. In either case the term interest is to be understood in the widest sense. The esprit de corps is a function of the social consciousness —of consciousness having social interests— and is to be accounted for in terms of the general principles according to which social life is reflected in consciousness. Cf. CONSCIOUSNESS OF KIND, SOCIUS, and (for literature) SOCIAL PSYCHOLOGY. (J.M.B.)

Essence [Lat. *essentia*, from *esse*, to be]: Ger. *Wesen*; Fr. *essence*; Ital. *essenza*. The constant and necessary nature of a thing as contrasted with its accidents. (H.R.S.—J.M.B.)

Aristotle uses the word for (1) the form, (2) the matter or substratum, (3) the concrete being, the individual. See FORM AND MATTER. But the scholastics defined the word more precisely in contrast with substance: essence is the nature of the individual thing, substance is the indeterminate substratum, which, united to the form, makes up the individual thing. Descartes follows the scholastic usage, but since his time the word essence has usually had the same meaning as substance. Kant defines essence as determined by an idea; hence it may be false to reality, while the nature of a thing is actually experienced and cannot be false. Cf. SUBSTANCE, NATURE, ATTRIBUTE, ACCIDENT. For citations see Eisler, *Wörterb. d. philos. Begriffe*, 'Wesen.' (H.R.S.)

Essenes [possibly Gr. ὁσιότης, holiness; possibly Heb. *Chassidim*, the pious]: Ger. *Essener*; Fr. *Esséniens*; Ital. *Esseni*. A Jewish sect.

Our knowledge of the origin, customs, and tenets of this sect is very imperfect. As a result, much conflicting conjecture has arisen. The primary sources are few and scanty; references, usually less rather than more extended, being made only by Philo of Alexandria, Pliny the Elder, Eusebius of Caesarea, and Josephus. On the whole, it seems probable that the Essenes were one of the many phenomena which resulted from the introduction of foreign, especially Hellenic, culture into Palestine. They were fanatics in their strict observance of the Mosaic law of ceremonial purity; yet they adored the sun, held non-Jewish beliefs about the soul, entertained Greek views regarding the future life, and advocated a doctrine of pre-existence not widely different from that of the Pythagoreans. Their points of contact with doctrines distinctive of the early Christian community have given rise to many conjectures, some having gone so far as to allege that John the Baptist and Jesus were Essenes. Yet they are not even mentioned in the Gospels.

Literature: the best brief account in English is that of F. C. CONYBEARE, in Hastings' Dict. of the Bible, art. Essenes; SCHÜRER, Hist. of the Jewish People in the Time of Christ, Div. II. ii. 188 f. (gives the literature fully); GINSBURG, The Essenes, their History and Doctrines; THOMSON, Books which influenced our Lord, 75 f.; MORRISON, The Jews under Roman Rule, 323 f.; CHEYNE, Origin of the Psalter, 418 f., 446 f.; COHN, in the Jewish Quart. Rev. (1892), 38 f.; FRIEDLÄNDER, Zur Entstehungsgesch. d. Christenthums, 98 f.; CONYBEARE, Philo about the Contemplative Life, 278 f.; HARNACK, Hist. of Dogma (Eng. trans.), i. 68 f., 243.   (R.M.W.)

Essential (in logic): see QUANTITY, and TERM.

Essential Attribute: see ESSENCE.

Essential Co-ordination (of Avenarius): see INTROJECTION (passim), and for literature EMPIRIO-CRITICISM.

Esthesiogenic: see AESTHESIOGEN.

Esthesiometer (or **Aesth-**): see LABORATORY AND APPARATUS, II. B. (c), (3).

Eternal Generation [Lat. *aeternus*, perpetual, +*genus*, race]: Ger. *ewige Schöpfung*; Fr. *génération éternelle*; Ital. *generazione eterna*. Eternal generation is a phrase indicating a certain view of the relation between the Father and the Son. Origen, in particular, contends for the eternal generation of the Son, as against Gnostic emanation and the like. According to this doctrine, the generation of the Son is a process that always continues. 'The Father did not beget his Son and let him go from himself, but always begets him.'

After the middle of the 2nd century, Christian thinkers began to employ the forms of the Alexandrian philosophy when they attempted to systematize the doctrines of their faith. The relation between the Deity and the Logos which the Alexandrians had pondered, offered some parallels, throwing light upon the difficult questions connected with the Trinity. The view is otherwise known as circumincession— that is, mutual interpenetration. The subject is of philosophical interest as illustrating the influence of Graeco-oriental conceptions upon the statement of Christian dogma.   (R.M.W.)

Eternity [Lat. *aeternus*, perpetual]: Ger. *Ewigkeit*; Fr. *éternité*; Ital. *eternità*. (1) Indefinite or endless duration in time; hence (2), as transcending the limits of temporal duration, that of which the conception includes timeless reality.

'Per eternitatem intelligo ipsam existentiam, quatenus ex sola rei aeternae definitione necessario sequi concipitur' (Spinoza, *Ethica*, i. def. 8). Schelling defines eternity as 'Sein in keiner Zeit' (*Vom Ich*, 105), and Hegel as 'absolute Zeitlosigkeit': 'nur das Natürliche ist der Zeit unterthan, insofern es endlich ist; das Wahre dagegen, die Idee, der Geist, ist ewig' (*Encyk.*, § 258). Cf.

many citations in Eisler, *Wörterb. d. philos. Begriffe*, 'Ewigkeit.'   (J.M.B.)

(3) In theology: this term is commonly used as the relative of TIME (q. v.), and therefore as implying the absence of limits which time imposes, or the transcendence of these limits.

The word has been predicated of creation. The problem of the eternity of creation raises all the fundamental questions connected with theism, especially those concerning the relation of God to the world. As the matter is not made the subject of special declarations in Scripture, it has ordinarily been set forth in a purely dogmatic manner. In other words, it has involved the adoption of fundamental and positive metaphysical positions, which usually have not been criticized, as philosophy understands this process. Theology, which posits Deity, may be said to solve the difficulty by asserting that time is eternally in God. Accordingly, everything is simultaneous as concerns God himself, but parts are so separable from each other that they can be 'revealed' in the succession which time implies.

Literature: DORNER, Syst. of Christ. Doctrine (Eng. trans.), ii. 21 f.   (R.M.W.)

Eternity of God: Ger. *Ewigkeit Gottes*; Fr. *éternité de Dieu*; Ital. *eternità di Dio*. One of the attributes of God, deduced by some theologians from the ontological argument.

Philosophically, this subject raises the entire problem of transcendency and immanency; as, for example, in the question whether, although eternal, God can stand in the same relation to every event in time. Positing God, as theology does, it is possible to reply that he bears a different relation to different 'aeons,' and yet to maintain his unity with himself. But this solution is not open to philosophy, which must set out from the differences indicated, and, after pushing them to their extremest limits, attempt to reconcile them by strict speculative or rational methods.

Literature: DORNER, Syst. of Christ. Doctrine (Eng. trans.), i. 243 f.   (R.M.W.)

Ether [Gr. αἰθήρ, the upper, purer air]: Ger. *Aether*; Fr. *éther*; Ital. *etere*. A medium or substance which, so far as we can yet determine, fills all space, and whose existence is inferred from the phenomena of radiance and electricity, the former being attributed to waves of the ether, the latter to a condition of it.

That ether penetrates transparent bodies is

shown by the passage of light through them ; it may therefore be supposed to penetrate and fill all bodies. No mechanical action has been detected between the ether and ordinary matter, since the rarest comets move through the ether without experiencing any appreciable resistance. Yet the heat-energy of bodies is communicated to the ether as radiance, a term which includes light and radiant heat ; and if heat be a mode of molecular motion, the latter is communicated from matter to ether, though molar motion is not. Owing to these limitations of the action between matter and ether, the substance of the latter almost eludes investigation. (s.n.)

Ethical Emotion : see FEELING (ethical), and cf. SENTIMENT.

Ethical Judgment : see MORAL JUDG-MENT.

Ethical Sense : see MORAL SENSE.

Ethical Theories : Ger. *ethische Theorien* ; Fr. *théories de morale* ; Ital. *teorie morali* (or *di morale*). Theories concerning the moral value of character and conduct ; especially theories which attempt an explanation of ultimate practical worth.

There are two main sources from which ethical theories are derived : (1) direct reflection on actual conduct and its perplexities ; (2) application to conduct of general philosophical theory. Ethical doctrine is almost always drawn from both sources ; but the predominance of one or other may determine the nature of an ethical theory. In any society the earliest ethical doctrine is usually derived from the former source. This is seen in the early ethical speculation of Greece. The ethical reflections of the Pre-Socratic philosophers have usually the slightest, if any, connection with their speculations concerning the ultimate nature of reality (Heraclitus and Pythagoras being partial exceptions) ; and the beginning of scientific morality in Socrates is expressly dissociated from any theory of the nature of the world. On the other hand, the new view of God and man introduced by Christianity, the Kantian analysis of experience, and the Darwinian theory of natural selection are instances of theoretical views which have had profound consequences for ethical doctrine. But this distinction of the two different sources of ethical doctrine does not adequately characterize (as Ziegler thinks) the difference between the great movements of ethical thought. Greek ethics, for example, becomes a metaphysical theory with Plato ; and, in general,

the great philosophical thinkers have elaborated their ethical and theoretical doctrines in close connection.

It thus happens that the distinctive marks of the leading ethical theories cannot be given apart from an explanation of the general philosophical position to which they belong. This is specially the case with such writers as Plato, and in modern times Kant, Fichte, Hegel, Schopenhauer, and Spencer.

The main grounds of distinction between ethical theories are : (1) Their different modes of conceiving the moral ideal or *summum bonum*. (2) Different views concerning the way in which the human consciousness apprehends the bindingness of moral rules or the intrinsic worth of moral ideals—whether by some kind of immediate knowledge (Intuitionism) or by experience of the tendency of actions to bring about results judged to be good (Empiricism, and, when the continuity of the experience of the race is emphasized, Evolutionism). Both intuitionism and, to some extent, evolutionism are frequently understood as signifying special views of the ideal or end. (3) Differences concerning the nature of moral obligation, or the relation of the moral principle to man's will, lead to the distinction of autonomous and heteronomous systems. The former find the moral law, as well as the motive for conforming to it, in man's own nature—generally in his nature as rational ; the latter derive the law, as distinct from the motive for conforming to it, from some external authority, such as the will of God, or the law of society ; while Kant includes as heteronomous all theories which admit as moral motives any other inducements than pure reverence for the moral law, which is at the same time practical reason. (4) This last point indicates, however, a further ground of distinction—regarding the motives which can be recognized in the moral life. Morality may be so defined, as it was by the Stoics and by Kant, as to dissociate entirely the moral or rational from the emotional life : to this view the term Rigorism may appropriately be applied. On the other hand, the character of an ethical doctrine may be determined by the emphasis laid on a special aspect of the emotional life, or a special kind of motives, as in the position given to sympathy in the moral theory of Adam Smith, and afterwards of Schopenhauer. Other grounds of distinction between ethical theories sometimes given, as that of the kind of objects to which moral action has regard (whether oneself simply, or other persons, or communities), may be better dealt with in subordination to the first ground of distinction.

Premising that the ethical theories of the great systematic thinkers (idealistic or naturalistic) fit but badly into any independent classification, and restricting attention to the two first grounds of distinction given above, as the most important, we may distinguish (1) theories which depend chiefly on a special view of the ideal, end, or *summum bonum*: (*a*) the various forms of Hedonism, which agree in maintaining that pleasant feeling is the ultimate standard of moral value; (*b*) the doctrines of perfection and SELF-REALIZATION (q.v.), according to which the moral ideal is a perfection of character, or the complete and harmonious development of personal capacities; (2) theories which start from the mode in which morality is apprehended or realized: (*c*) the various forms of Intuitionism, aesthetic or perceptional and rational; (*d*) the various forms of Empiricism, which when not simply hedonistic, and when it does not accept its rules of duty from some external authority (as Hobbes proposes to accept them from the sovereign), usually connects itself with some theory of evolution.

(*a*) According to hedonism, the moral value of conduct depends upon its tendency to increase pleasure and diminish pain. This is common to all forms of the theory from Aristippus of Cyrene, the 'imperfect Socratic,' onwards. The most important advocate and systematizer of this doctrine was Epicurus, who emphasized the value not of momentary feelings, but of a pleasant or happy life, and the necessity therefore of a mind free from disturbance and care (see EPICUREANISM). For him the ideal life is one of tranquillity— of quiet living and freedom from pain. But it has to be pointed out that a life of excitement—of many and varied pleasures, sufficiently numerous and intense to make up for considerable pains—is an equally legitimate ideal for the hedonist. And only a calculus of pleasures and pains and of the probabilities of life could decide which ideal is more desirable, hedonistically, for any individual agent. In modern times hedonism has divided into two opposed theories, egoistic and universalistic, according as the moral end is held to be the agent's own greatest pleasure, or that of mankind (or even sentient beings) generally (see GREATEST HAPPINESS, EGOISM, and UTILITARIANISM). To the latter the

name Utilitarianism was given by J. S. Mill. The term ALTRUISM (q.v.), used by Comte, emphasizes the reference to other individuals rather than to communities; but as only individuals are conscious of pleasure and pain, this does not distinguish the theory from utilitarianism. The real distinction (using both terms hedonistically) is that altruism does, and utilitarianism does not, deny moral value to the pleasure of self. Mill's important modifications of the hedonistic doctrine are, first, his emphasis on the importance of permanent sources of interest over disconnected pleasures — a point further elaborated by Sidgwick; and, secondly, his distinction of pleasures in kind or quality, and contention that (e.g.) intellectual pleasures are of higher moral value than sensuous pleasures, quite independently of any superior intensity, purity, fruitfulness, or other quantitative distinctions. But this clearly makes not pleasure itself, but that which distinguishes the higher pleasure from the lower the ultimate standard of value, and is accordingly inconsistent with the hedonistic principle.

(*b*) The doctrines of PERFECTION (q.v.), and SELF-REALIZATION (q.v.), in so far as they are distinct from the more purely rationalistic or intuitional forms of idealistic ethics, may be said to date from Aristotle, who maintained that the chief good consisted in an activity in accordance with the highest virtue (see EUDAIMONIA). The theories which may be grouped under this head are much more divergent from one another in nature, and often less clear in statement, than are the different hedonistic theories. The nature of the perfection which is to be attained, or of the self which is to be realized, can only be expounded after a philosophical inquiry; and the ethical doctrines of Spinoza and Leibnitz, Fichte and Hegel, might all be included under this head. The form in which the notion of self-realization appears in contemporary ethics is largely due to T. H. Green, who lays special stress both on the spiritual or rational and on the social nature of the self.

(*c*) According to the intuitional view of ethics the end of conduct consists in the correspondence of voluntary activity with certain intuitively recognized moral rules. This view has its historical antecedent in the Stoic doctrine of laws of nature, belonging to the reason of the universe and apprehended by the consubstantial reason of man. The same doctrine formulated in theological terms led to the dominant systems of mediaeval ethics and their related doctrines of SYNDERESIS (q. v.) and CONSCIENCE (q. v.). In the beginning of English philosophy these moral first principles were regarded as principles of the *sensus communis* by Herbert of Cherbury; and he may accordingly be held to be the founder of the English school of intuitional or common-sense morality. But in the English moralists of the 18th century this immediate apprehension of moral value was interpreted as aesthetic or perceptional rather than rational by Shaftesbury and Hutcheson. Hutcheson elaborated the doctrine (derived from Shaftesbury) of a moral sense—'a natural and immediate determination to approve certain affections, and actions consequent upon them, or a natural sense of immediate excellence in them'—and combined this view with the utilitarian criterion of the distinction between right and wrong. On the other hand, the rational or 'dogmatic' interpretation of the moral faculty was worked out anew by Samuel Clarke, Price, and Reid. The 'philosophical' intuitionism of Kant reaches a complete synthesis of moral law founded upon a criticism of the reason. The speculative theories of ethics which have resulted from Kant's criticism tend rather to the perfectionist than to the traditional intuitional ideal.

(*d*) The theory of evolution, which traces the development both of moral conduct and of moral ideas, was, when first applied to ethics, associated with the hedonistic theory, but was soon found to lead to modifications of that theory (as by Spencer); while other writers (of whom L. Stephen was one of the earliest) have attempted a more specifically evolutionist ethics. By these writers some such conception as social vitality has often been taken as the ethical ideal; but the most valuable part of the work done by the evolutionist moralists has been (as was natural) in tracing the genesis and progress of morality both historically and in the individual, rather than in independent contributions towards the solution of the question of the ultimate conditions of moral value (however, cf. WORTH).

Literature: hedonistic theories are chiefly represented by GASSENDI, De vita, moribus et doctrina Epicuri (1647); HOBBES, Elements of Law, Human Nature (1640), and Leviathan (1651); LOCKE, Essay concerning Human Understanding (1690); HUTCHESON, Syst. of Mor. Philos. (1755) (who adopts greatest happiness as the moral standard); HUME, Human Nature, Bk. III (1740), and Princ. of Mor. (1751); LAMETTRIE, L'art de jouir (1751); HELVETIUS, De l'esprit (1758); HOLBACH, Syst. de la Nature (1770), and Éléments de la morale universelle (1776); PALEY, Mor. and Polit. Philos. (1785); BENTHAM, Princ. of Mor. and Legisl. (1789); J. S. MILL, Utilitarianism (1861); H. SIDGWICK, Meth. of Ethics (1874); SPENCER, Princ. of Ethics (1879–93); GIŻYCKI, Grundzüge d. Mor. (1883), and Mor. Philos. (1888). Cf. J. WATSON, Hedonistic Theories (1895).

Divergent expressions of the perfectionist ideal, combined with hedonistic factors, are to be found in CUMBERLAND, De legibus naturae (1672); SPINOZA, Ethica (1677); LEIBNITZ, Théodicée (1710), Nouveaux Essais (written 1704), and Principes de la Nature et de la Grâce (1714). Modern theories of self-realization influenced by FICHTE (Syst. d. Sittenlehre, 1798), and more precisely by HEGEL (Philos. des Rechts, 1821), are represented in English chiefly by F. H. BRADLEY (Ethical Studies, 1876) and T. H. GREEN (Prolegomena to Ethics, 1882).

The chief moral sense writers were SHAFTESBURY, Inquiry concerning Virtue and Merit (1699); HUTCHESON, Inquiry into the Original of our Ideas of Beauty and Virtue (1729); Essay on the Passions, with Illustrations on the Moral Sense (1728); and Syst. of Mor. Philos. (1755). The ethics of sympathy was set forth by ADAM SMITH, Mor. Sent. (1759), and in more recent times by SCHOPENHAUER, Die beiden Grundprobleme d. Moral (1841). The intellectualist tradition of intuitionism is represented by CUDWORTH, Eternal and Immutable Morality (publ. posthumously, 1731); S. CLARKE, Boyle Lectures (1705); J. BUTLER, the ethical doctrine of whose Sermons (1726) is allied to that of Shaftesbury, and who approaches the intellectualist view in his Diss. on Virtue (1736); R. PRICE, Principal Questions and Difficulties of Morals (1757); T. REID, Active Powers (1788). Modern intuitional ethics has been modified by KANT, Grundlegung d. Met. d. Sitten (1785); Krit. d. prakt. Vernunft (1788). It is represented chiefly by WHEWELL, Elements of Morality (1841); CALDERWOOD, Handb. of Mor. Philos. (1874); RICKABY, Mor. Philos. (1889). MARTINEAU'S Types of Ethical Theory (1885) is the most brilliant and original outcome of recent intuitional doctrine.

The influence of the theory of evolution upon

ethics is shown chiefly in SIMCOX, Natural Law (1877); SPENCER, Princ. of Ethics (1879–93); L. STEPHEN, Science of Ethics (1882); ROLPH, Biologische Probleme (1882); HÖFFDING, Grundlage d. human. Ethik (Ger. trans., 1880), and Ethik (Ger. trans., 1888); S. ALEXANDER, Moral Order and Progress (1889); WUNDT, Ethik (1886); SIMMEL, Einleit. in die Moralwissenschaft (1892–3); BALDWIN, Social and Eth. Interpret. (1897). SORLEY, Ethics of Naturalism (1885), and HUXLEY, Evolution and Ethics (Romanes Lecture, 1893), are criticisms of the evolution theory of ethics. (W.R.S., H.S.)

Ethics [Gr. τὰ ἠθικά, from ἦθος, used by Aristotle in the sense of character and disposition, but having originally the same reference to the externals of custom or usage as ἔθος, of which it is a lengthened form. The term *moralis* was introduced by Cicero as an equivalent of Aristotle's ἠθικός]: Ger. *Ethik* (*Sittenlehre*); Fr. *morale, éthique*; Ital. *etica*. The science of the ideal in human character and conduct.

The terms ethics, moral science, and moral philosophy are used almost synonymously. No distinction can be drawn between 'ethical' and 'moral,' except that the latter term is somewhat more commonly used of the facts and judgments with which the science deals. Ethics has sometimes been defined as the 'art' of conduct, just as logic has been called the art of thinking. But the former definition can be defended as little as the latter. According to the older use of the terms, an art has to do with production, not with practice or conduct. Further, ethics does not teach the doing of good, but knowledge of the nature and conditions of goodness. This knowledge may be applied to practice, but it does not necessarily imply the condition of will required for good conduct. Ethics has, however, to do not merely with actual conduct, but with right or good conduct, and accordingly with an ideal from which rules may be laid down for actual conduct, so that it may be called a normative science.

Whether it should be regarded as a science or as a branch of philosophy is a more difficult question: partly owing to the uncertainty which attaches to the distinction between science and philosophy, partly owing to the nature of ethical inquiry itself. It has to do with the facts of conduct as displayed in individual experience and in the social order and development, and thus deals with a more or less well-defined group of phenomena.

But it is concerned not merely with the order of occurrence of these facts, but with their relation to norms or rules, in virtue of which relation the facts of conduct are judged good or bad, right or wrong. These norms or rules, which may appear almost disconnectedly in ordinary consciousness, admit of inner relation and justification when shown to result from an ideal which has validity as a standard of moral goodness or moral value.

It is in determining the ideal or moral end that ethics requires a philosophical rather than a merely scientific mode of treatment. The attempts to decide this question independently of general philosophy or of metaphysics are chiefly the following: (*a*) testing the applicability to conduct of the various ends which are *prima facie* reasonable— a method which may leave the inquirer with two or more competing systems, and which besides seems to attribute too great importance to the precise applicability of the end to the complex and varying conditions of life, while the reasonable ends to be considered can hardly be exhaustively discovered without an inquiry into the conditions of self-conscious activity and its relation to reality; (*b*) appealing to the individual consciousness of what is desired, as was done by J. S. Mill in the interests of his happiness-theory; (*c*) testing the fitness of conduct to promote social order and progress. At any given stage of social development the conditions of social order may be laid down from an analysis of that order and examination of the conduct fitted to maintain it; but the social order is itself in constant process of development, the direction of which is partly determined by the moral ideals of the members of the society. And at any given stage of the development of an individual consciousness, its content may be systematically elaborated so as to give an account of the duties it holds binding, or of the ends regarded by it as desirable; but this content also is variable. And a standard is needed to justify the obligatoriness of these duties or the value of these ends. Thus neither the sociological nor the psychological method seems sufficient to determine the ideal of goodness for conduct. Cf. END (moral).

We accordingly find that, in nearly all cases, ethical doctrines are closely connected with the general philosophical point of view of a thinker. This does not hold true of many of the English moralists of the 18th century, nor, among systematic philosophers, of Herbart; but the contemporary moralists who treat ethics simply as a science are often influenced by a naturalistic or an agnostic interpretation of the world and of life.

The fundamental conceptions of ethics are: (1) the ideal or end, which is the standard of goodness in character and conduct. The terms right, duty, virtue, value are sometimes used in place of this; but, more correctly, they signify respectively the agreement of conduct with the rule or law resulting from this standard, the relation of the law as authoritative for a will which may nevertheless disobey the law, the organization of right conduct into habits of acting, the degree of approximation to the ideal. (2) Freedom, or the power of conforming to the law or realizing the ideal belonging to human conscious activity. It is only because man is able not only to apprehend a moral law or ideal, but consciously to guide his conduct by it, in presence of competing inducements, that he is a moral being. Ethics has accordingly to investigate the meaning and possibility, as well as the implications and applications of these conceptions. And in this department of its inquiry it is not independent of metaphysics. But these questions are connected with other ethical questions of a more specifically scientific character: e.g. the psychological nature of moral motives, moral ideas, and moral habits (or virtues); the system of duties and of virtues, and their connection with social institutions and customs. With regard to these questions, the theory of evolution has had a most important bearing upon ethics, bringing out the history of moral conduct and moral ideas in connection with one another and with social institutions. Cf. ETHICAL THEORIES.

Literature: in addition to the works cited under ETHICAL THEORIES, the following may be cited: SCHLEIERMACHER, Syst. d. Sittenlehre (1835); RENOUVIER, Sci. de la morale (1869); HERBART, Prakt. Philos. (1808); STEINTHAL, Ethik (1885); NAHLOWSKY, Allg. Ethik (1885); E. VON HARTMANN, Das sittliche Bewusstsein (1879); PAULSEN, Syst. of Ethics (Eng. trans., 1899); GUYAU, Esquisse d'une Morale sans Obligation (1885); S. H. HODGSON, Met. of Experience, iii (1899); the important elaborations of ethics as the theory of values by MEINONG, Psychologisch-ethische Untersuchungen z. Werttheorie (1894), and v. EHRENFELS, Syst. d. Wert-

theorie (1897–8); and the introductory works: J. H. MUIRHEAD, Elements of Ethics (1892); J. DEWEY, Outlines of Ethics (1891); J. S. MACKENZIE, Manual of Ethics (1893); J. SETH, Study of Ethical Principles (1894). Among the more important histories of ethics are SCHLEIERMACHER, Krit. d. bisherigen Sittenlehre (1803); VORLÄNDER, Gesch. d. Moral-, Rechts- u. Staats-Lehre (1885); I. H. FICHTE, Syst. d. Ethik (1850); SCHMIDT, Ethik d. alten Griechen (1882); ZIEGLER, Ethik d. alten Griechen u. Römer (1881), and Christl. Ethik (2nd ed., 1892); GASS, Gesch. d. christl. Ethik (1881); JODL, Gesch. d. Ethik in d. neuern Philos. (1882–9); FOUILLÉE, Syst. de Mor. contemporains (1883); GUYAU, Mor. anglaise contemporaine (2nd ed., 1885); and the admirable short Outlines of the History of Ethics by H. SIDGWICK (3rd ed., 1892). See also ETHICS (Christian). (W.R.S., H.S.)

Ethics (Christian). (1) A systematic scientific ingathering and articulation of the doctrines of Christianity in their bearing upon individual conduct; and (2) an exposition of the Christian *ethos* or general Christian attitude towards life and society.

In its root sense, the term ethics does not refer merely to conduct, but also to a community or agreement amongst larger or smaller groups of men in approving and appropriating or disapproving certain modes of life and ideals of character. This is best indicated, possibly, in the contrasts presented by different modern nationalities, or by different sections of the Christian community, or even between different ranks of society in the same state. Theologically viewed, Christian ethics is the practical aspect of the considerations which dogmatics sets forth theoretically.

A due and full statement of the contents of Christian ethics would consist of the following: (1) an account of the relation of Christian ethics to other disciplines—to metaphysics, ethics proper and moral philosophy, psychology, theology, sociology, and the like; (2) a discussion of the Christian ideal in its religio-historical, formal, and material aspects; (3) an outline of Christian duties directly deducible from the foregoing; (4) following from all these, what might be called a Christian sociology—dealing with marriage and the family, the state, and so on. Some would add to this a discussion of the Church, viewed as the Christian community.

Literature: DORNER, Syst. of Christ. Ethics (Eng. trans.), where the literature of special

347

topics is fully given; NEWMAN SMYTH, Christ. Ethics; MAURICE, The Epistles of St. John; KNIGHT, The Christ. Ethic; KÖSTLIN, Christl. Ethik. (R.M.W.)

Ethnography (1), **Ethnology** (2) [(1) Gr. ἔθνος, a people, + γράφειν, to write; (2) ἔθνος, people, + λόγος, discourse]: Ger. *Ethnographie, Ethnologie* (*Völkerkunde*); Fr. *ethnographie, ethnologie*; Ital. *etnografia, etnologia*. Ethnography and ethnology form two large divisions of ANTHROPOLOGY (q. v.), and relate to the study of human groups and organizations—hordes, clans, races, peoples, nations.

In distinction from one another, ethnography includes the descriptive, external account of particular groups of men and their status, occupations, and institutions; while ethnology presents the explanatory and investigative study of such racial and cultural relations in general. The two divisions thus deal largely with the same materials, many investigations contributing almost equally to both; and differ mainly as the preparatory collection, arrangement, and description of the nature and occurrence of any phenomena differ from the systematic and interpretative study of the causes and influences affecting it and its correlated phenomena.

Of prime importance to these sciences is everything that relates to the determination of origins, migrations, distributions, variations, and correlations of the several races and peoples. Apart from the problems which concern the descent of man and his antiquity, the fundamental ethnological problems relate (*a*) to the specific unity of the human species, whether originally derived from one single parent stock (the monogenistic view) or from several (the polygenistic view); (*b*) to the varietal diversity of man, i. e. the fundamental type varieties of the human race (Hominidae); (*c*) to the classification of these in suitable ethnical groups (Mongolian, Caucasian, American, Ethiopian, or similar classification); (*d*) to the determination of the migrations and distribution of such races and their relation to one another. In this investigation the distinction between prehistoric and historic is of prime importance; prehistoric evidence being largely of the form of skeletal remains of man and relics of primitive industries, while in historic times these are in themselves more complete, and are supplemented by written and oral traditions and a wealth of suggestive details in regard to institutions and organizations. The unity and fundamental varieties of the human race must be largely

decided upon the evidence of the physical character of human remains—i. e. such evidence is somatological or physical, while the further history of human groups, although both physical and mental, is largely the latter. It is to be derived from the evidence of man's sociological institutions, the direction and nature of his psychological development, his language, his arts and sciences, his religion. The detailed problems of ethnology thus relate to the racial history, the distribution and evolution of special physical traits (colour of skin, proportion of head, &c.), or of particular groups of customs and institutions. This latter division is particularly fertile, and constitutes a large portion of ethnological literature. Language, written and spoken, groups of customs and traditions, myths and beliefs, family relationships and tribal organizations, music and the dance, the arts of the field and the loom, of the worker in wood, in metal, or in stone; the history of human habitations, and transportation by land and sea; these and many more may be cited to indicate the scope of special ethnological studies. Such descriptive details, when collected in regard to a single people or group, as well as the comprehensive description in all these respects of the physical and mental status of a special people or group, may properly be spoken of as ethnographic. Such ethnographic literature, particularly as accumulated by travellers in modern times, is most extensive.

Literature: general introductory works to the study of Ethnology are: KEANE, Ethnology (1897), 442; TOPINARD, Anthropology (1878), 548; QUATREFAGES, The Human Species (1879), 498; BRINTON, Races and Peoples (1890), 313; MORSELLI, Antropol. generale (1889–91). Also see ANTHROPOLOGY. Consult in regard to the status of special literature the article Ethnography in Encyc. Brit. (9th ed.), ad fin. (J.J.)

Ethology [Gr. ἔθος, custom, + λόγος, discourse]: Ger. *Ethologie, Charakterologie* (Bahnsen); Fr. *éthologie*; Ital. *etologia*. The science of the formation of human character, whether of individuals or of groups of men.

The term is used by J. S. Mill, who regards ethology as a deductive science, whose 'principles are properly the middle principles, the *axiomata media* (as Bacon would have said) of the science of mind; as distinguished, on the one hand, from the empirical laws resulting from simple observation, and, on the other, from the highest generalizations.' He calls it 'the Exact Science of Human Nature;

for its truths are not, like the empirical laws which depend on them, approximate generalizations, but real laws '—although ' hypothetical only,' and affirming ' tendencies, not facts.' Other usages are those of Wundt and Bailey.

Literature: J. S. MILL, Syst. of Logic, Bk. VI. chap. v; WUNDT, Logik (2nd ed.), ii. 2. 369; J. WARD, in Int. J. of Ethics, i. 446 ff.; T. P. BAILEY, Ethology (1899), and Bibliog. Refs. in Ethology (1899). (W.R.S.–J.M.B.)

Ethos [Gr.]: Ger. *Ethos*; Fr. *mœurs*; Ital. *costume morale*. Moral disposition or character; especially the prevalent moral disposition of a community, as shown in its customary behaviour.

The reference to the internal traits of disposition, instead of to external results, distinguishes ethos from CUSTOM (q. v.), although the Greek term ἦθος (of which it is a transliteration) had originally the same reference to external conditions as the related term ἔθος. Cf. Wundt, *Ethik*, Pt. I. chap. i. (W.R.S.)

Etiology [Gr. αἰτία, cause, + λόγος, discourse]: Ger. *Ätiologie*; Fr. *étiologie*; Ital. *etiologia*. (1) In philosophy: the science of CAUSE AND EFFECT (q. v.).

(2) In medicine: the science of the causes of organic and mental disease. (E.M.)

In biology: that branch of biology which deals with the origin and mode of development of organic beings.

Introduced by Huxley (*Anatomy of Invertebrate Animals*, Introd. 35, 1877), but not in general use. (C.LL.M.–J.M.B.)

Etymology [Gr. ἔτυμος, true, + λόγος, discourse]: Ger. *Etymologie*; Fr. *étymologie*; Ital. *etimologia*. The history of a word, so far as it can be traced towards its origin, as regards both its form and its signification; that department of scientific grammar which concerns itself with the determination of such word-history.

Among the ancient Greeks, etymology was used of the search for the ἔτυμον, the real and essential meaning of a word, a search conducted in the belief that words, as necessarily connected with the things they denoted, held within them the secret of the inner nature of things and ideas. The etymology of modern scientific grammar seeks to discover the earlier history of the forms and values of words, using the comparison of cognate languages and dialects where direct tradition fails. It includes the cases where a word can be followed back into the territory of another language from which it has been borrowed. The etymology of a word is not directly applicable in determining the proper form or use of that word in current speech. The earlier meaning is no ' truer' than the later. It shows, however, how the word has come to be what it is, and affords a basis of judgment in estimating the orbit and axis of its value.

The best illustration of modern etymological work will be found in Murray's *New English Dictionary* (1884–), and Kluge's *Etymol. Wörterbuch der deutschen Sprache* (6th ed., 1898–). (B.I.W.)

Eubulides. Lived in the 4th century B.C. Born at Miletus, he became the pupil of Euclid of Megara, and a member of the Megarian school. He and Alexinus are mentioned as inventors of new fallacies in the school. They opposed Aristotle.

Eucharist [Gr. εὖ, well, + χάρις, favour, grace]: Ger. *heiliges Abendmahl, Eucharistie*; Fr. *sainte cène, eucharistie*; Ital. *Eucaristia*. One of the several names given to the sacrament of the Lord's Supper.

The sacrament of the Eucharist did not reach its complete development in the Latin Church till the 6th century; and after the Reformation very divergent views emerged with regard to it. Without going into the numerous details connected with the subject, these positions may be very briefly summarized as follows: (1) The doctrine of the real presence. The whole substance of the bread is converted into the body, and the whole substance of the wine into the blood, of Christ, as the Council of Trent decreed. This, and the Lutheran doctrine, raise the curious problem of the ubiquity of Christ. (2) The doctrine of the virtual presence, which implies that the Eucharist is the only medium through which Christ confers the benefits of his atonement upon men. (3) The doctrine of the figurative presence, according to which the rite and the elements are memorials of Christ's death till he come. Philosophy of religion would distinguish between the rite and the elements, while a distinctively Christian philosophy of religion would contend for the spiritual presence of Christ in the former, but hold the latter for mere symbols. Obviously, the meaning of the spiritual presence here advocated admits of widely divergent interpretations.

Literature: DORNER, Syst. of Christ. Doctrine (Eng. trans.), iv. 305 f., where the literature is fully given. (R.M.W.)

Euclid of Alexandria. Lived about

300 B.C. in Alexandria, and taught mathematics there in the reign of Ptolemy I (Soter), who died about 282 B.C. His *Elements of Geometry* is the only ancient system of geometry extant. It was a standard work for 2,000 years. He is called 'the father of geometry,' which is termed 'Euclidian' from him.

Euclid of Megara. Greek philosopher, who lived about 400 B.C. Pupil of Socrates, and said to have seen him die. After that event (399 B.C.) he returned to Megara and founded a famous school of Megarians, taking his doctrine in part from both the Eleatics and Socrates.

Euclidian Space. The 'ordinary' or tri-dimensional SPACE (q. v.) of the Euclidian geometry. (J.M.B.)

Eudaemonism [Gr. εὐδαιμονία, happiness]: Ger. *Eudämonismus*; Fr. *eudémonisme*; Ital. *eudemonismo*. The theory that happiness is the chief good for man, or the ethical END (q. v.) for his conduct.

The term is derived from EUDAIMONIA (q.v.), which was first used as the leading conception of ethics by Aristotle. The eudaemonism of Aristotle was a theory which placed the chief good in an active life in accordance with the highest excellence or virtue. But a different view, which found the essential element of this highest life in the feeling of pleasure, found its way into the school of Aristotle as early as the *Eudemian Ethics* formerly ascribed to Aristotle himself, and included in the *Corpus Aristotelicum*. The hedonistic interpretation of what constitutes eudaimonia, or happy life, was urged with confidence by Epicurus and his followers; and the traditional renderings of the word into other languages have encouraged this meaning. Thus the term eudaemonism, in modern philosophy, is almost universally used for the ethical theory which puts forward happiness (in the sense of pleasure and freedom from pain) as the end of life. The term eudaemonism (happiness-theory) becomes in this way indistinguishable in meaning from hedonism (pleasure-theory). The distinction drawn by Külpe (*Einleitung in die Philos.*, § 14) that hedonism takes corporeal pleasure for the end, and eudaemonism mental pleasure, is not in accordance with historical usage, and would leave no important theories to be described as hedonistic.

The character and practical value of the theory vary greatly according to the sources (sensuous, intellectual, aesthetic, social, or conscientious feelings) to which happiness is regarded as mainly due, and according to whether the agent is bidden to regard his own happiness only or to promote that of others. Kant is thus mistaken in asserting that 'the eudaemonist is he who sets the highest determinant of his will in utility and his own happiness. All eudaemonists are therefore practical egoists' (*Anthrop.*, init.). The vast difference between the egoistic and universalistic forms of theory has been set forth, especially, by J. S. Mill (*Utilitarianism*) and H. Sidgwick (*Meth. of Ethics*). Owing to the variance between the Aristotelian meaning of eudaimonia and the modern 'happiness,' stricter writers prefer the term hedonism to eudaemonism, e. g. Sidgwick (as above); on the other side, see Pfleiderer, *Zur Ehrenrettung des Eudämonismus* (1879). The term is used in its Aristotelian sense by J. Seth, *Ethical Principles* (1894). (W.R.S.)

Eudaimonia [Gr. εὐδαιμονία, commonly rendered happiness]: Ger. *Glückseligkeit*; Fr. *bonheur*; Ital. *felicità*. Well-being or welfare. See EUDAEMONISM.

The word means literally the condition of being guided or favoured by a good genius, and hence good fortune or happiness. Plato speaks of εὐδαιμονία as the end or goal of the political art (*Euthyd.*, 291 B); and the term is adopted by Aristotle as used both by thinkers and by plain men as an expression for the highest attainable good of man. As such it becomes the central conception of his ethical system, and receives a special meaning as the result of his analysis. He holds it to be an active condition which cannot be analysed into any succession or sum of pleasures, though pleasure accompanies its realization. It is a well-being which consists in well-doing—an activity (ἐνέργεια) in accordance with the highest excellence (ἀρετή, or virtue) attainable by man (*Eth. N.*, I. iv. 2, &c.); and his highest conception of this activity was a life of pure speculation, although he did not maintain that such a life was attainable by man. The Aristotelian or Peripatetic school, however, soon tended to an interpretation of eudaimonia in terms of pleasure (ἡδονή), and Epicurus enforced the doctrine that eudaimonia was pleasure. In this way the Latin equivalent of εὐδαιμονία (*felicitas*), as well as its traditional renderings in modern languages, have a hedonistic meaning which is alien to the Aristotelian conception of eudaimonia. (W.R.S.)

Eudemus. A Greek, native of Rhodes, pupil of Aristotle. He is signalized by the *Eudemian Ethics*, formerly attributed to

Aristotle. Other fragments of his are extant. See PERIPATETICS.

Eusebians: Ger. *Eusebianer*; Fr. *Eusébiens*; Ital. *Eusebiani*. One of the great parties at the Council of Nicaea. They were so called from their leader, Eusebius, bishop of Caesarea. The Lucianists (Arians) and the Alexandrians were the other parties. The Eusebians occupied the middle position, but stood much nearer to the Lucianists than to the Alexandrians; and they might easily have turned the scale in favour of Arian views, had their tactics been more adroit.

Literature: GWATKIN, Studies of Arianism; HARNACK, Hist. of Dogma (Eng. trans.), iv. 51 f. (R.M.W.)

Eutychianism: Ger. *Eutychianismus*; Fr. *Eutychianisme*; Ital. *Eutichianismo*. So called from Eutyches, who was head of a monastery near Constantinople. His doctrine was fully formulated 448–51 A.D. It is another of the many attempts to solve the problem of the two natures—divine and human—in a single person, Christ. It consists essentially in an emphasis upon the unity of personality to the obliteration of the distinction of natures. The human nature is deified by being absorbed into the divine. Hence, in opposition to NESTORIANISM (q. v.), Eutychianism teaches that God was born, was tempted, suffered, and died.

Literature: MANSI, Sacrorum Conciliorum nova et amplissima Collectio, ix. 674 f.; MARTIN, Le Pseudo-Synode d'Éphèse; HARNACK, Hist. of Dogma (Eng. trans.), iv. 197 f. (R.M.W.)

Evangel: see GOSPEL.

Event [Lat. *eventus*, from *evenire*, to happen]: Ger. *Ereigniss*; Fr. *évènement*; Ital. *evento, avvenimento*. Any change in the world of FACT (q. v.).

The notion of event covers objective phenomenal changes and sequences of all sorts. The common usage makes the event a matter of time; and this is emphasized by the usage according to which events are the subject-matter of history, that is, each event is in relation to a series of happenings in time. Whether events may take place out of time would seem to depend upon one's general theory of time in relation to reality. (J.M.B.)

Everett, Charles Carroll. (1829–1900.) American writer on philosophy and theology. Born at Brunswick, Maine, and died at Cambridge, Mass. Graduated from Bowdoin College in 1850, studied at Harvard and Berlin Universities, was Unitarian clergyman, became professor of theology in Harvard

Divinity School in 1859, and dean of that institution in 1878.

Evidence and **Evident** [Lat. *e + videre*, to see]: Ger. *Evidenz, evident, einleuchtend*; Fr. *évidence, évident*; Ital. *evidenza, evidente*. As used in logic, the term signifies the propositions or assertions of fact from which a conclusion is taken to follow. Distinctions in such evidence concern the matter involved, for evidence is equivalent to the reasons, not the causes, of a judgment, and thus has always an objective or universal significance.

The common division of evidence resolves itself into (*a*) the intuitive and demonstrative, and (*b*) the empirical or moral, and is far from satisfactory. Systematic treatments of evidence are generally of three kinds: (1) logical, the most general, and embracing as one of its topics the discussion of the kinds of evidence; (2) historical; (3) legal. It is questionable whether the points of divergence between the legal and the logical treatments of evidence do not outweigh the resemblances. The logical treatment is identical with Methodology at large. See METHOD, and REASONING.

Literature: of historical evidence good treatments are DAUNOU, Cours d'Études historiques; G. CORNEWALL LEWIS, Methods of Observation and Reasoning in Politics. On legal evidence, see FITZJAMES STEPHEN, Digest of the Law of Evidence. (R.A.)

The adjective evident applies to propositions for which the evidence is adequate; but its use in philosophy is rather to describe those truths which are self-evident, or which need no evidence. The transition from one of these meanings to the other appears in the theory of intuitive or innate knowledge, which the mind is said to recognize without evidence, thus making empirical or demonstrative proof unnecessary. See Self-evidence under TESTS OF TRUTH; also CLEAR AND DISTINCT. (J.M.B.)

Evidence (in law): Ger. *Evidenz, Beweismittel*; Fr. *évidence*; Ital. *prova*. The means of proof; facts or means of ascertaining facts, from which other facts may properly be inferred. Any probative matter serving as a legitimate basis of inference as to the existence of a fact. See Thayer's *Cases on Evidence*, 2.

No matter can constitute a legitimate basis of inference, unless it is relevant to the fact to be inferred, and of a kind which the law permits to be adduced.

In the trial of causes, the best evidence of which the nature and circumstances of the case admit is ordinarily required. If the best evidence cannot be had, secondary evidence may be introduced, that is, evidence of a less direct and convincing character. Direct testimony, sometimes called direct evidence, is that by which a fact in issue can be established without resort to inference, except the usual inference that the testimony of witnesses having personal knowledge of the thing in question is true. It consists of such testimony; which is itself a fact.

Circumstantial evidence is evidence of circumstances from which inferences as to the matter in controversy may legitimately be drawn.

Evidence from witnesses is given orally, or by written depositions over their signature, taken on due notice to the adverse party.

Evidence in chief is the evidence with which the *actor* or plaintiff opens his case. Evidence in defence is that next introduced by the *reus* or defendant. Evidence in rebuttal is that which may then be introduced by the *actor* or plaintiff, to meet the evidence in defence.

Literature: GREENLEAF, on Evidence, i. chap. iii; THAYER, Preliminary Treatise on Evidence at the Common Law (1898). (S.E.B.)

Evidence (internal and external): Ger. *Evidenz* (*innere und äussere*); Fr. *preuve* (*interne et externe*); Ital. *evidenza*. The name applied to the main principles by which the higher CRITICISM (q. v.) is guided.

They may be briefly summarized as follows: (1) Internal: (*a*) a document must consort, as to time, place, and circumstances, with what it purports to be historically; (*b*) style has many differences, and these may indicate various stages in the career of a single author, or they may imply differences of authorship and of period; (*c*) differences of opinion and of point of view indicate differences of authorship and of period; (*d*) the citations made in a document throw important light upon its time and place, and upon its relation to the authorities cited. This is the most difficult of the internal principles to apply in practice. (2) External: (*a*) definite testimony to a document by other genuine and authoritative writings is of great value for assignment of its period; (*b*) contrariwise, the silence of writers, who might reasonably be expected to advert to a document, furnishes important evidence of a negative kind. This is much the more difficult of the external principles to apply in practice. It has acquired greater influence and importance in the present century than it had in previous times.

Literature: DU PIN, New Hist. of Ecclesiastical Writers (Eng. trans.), vii f.; H. P. SMITH, in the Presb. Rev. (1882); C. A.

BRIGGS, in the Journal of the Society of Biblical Literature and Exegesis (1884). (R.M.W.)

Evident: see EVIDENCE AND EVIDENT.

Evil [ME. *evel*]: Ger. *Übel*; Fr. *mal*; Ital. *male*. That which is contrary to good or well-being.

The classification of evils commonly follows the classification of goods; as into mental, corporeal and external, or, by a more radical division, into natural and moral, i. e. those independent of, and those dependent upon, human volition. It is with the latter that ethics is concerned: the distinction of moral evil from moral good; its ultimate ground and the conditions by which the evil may be overcome and the good attained. Other questions concerning evil have to do with its psychological nature—whether or not it is identical with pain or tendency to pain; and its ultimate essence—whether it is something positive, or a mere negation of reality (which is good), or, equally with good, an appearance merely, transcended in the absolute. In the latter reference we have the theological problem of the compatibility of the existence (and origin) of evil with a moral government of the world. See THEODICY, and ORIGIN OF EVIL (also for literature). These questions bring to light the controversy of OPTIMISM and PESSIMISM (q. v.), with which not only scientific ethics, but all reflection upon life, is full. (W.R.S.)

Leibnitz distinguishes three forms of evil: (1) metaphysical (the necessary limitation of the Creator); (2) physical (suffering, lawful penalties, &c.); (3) moral (sin).

Great confusion prevails in the discussion of evil, its origin and nature, from the failure to distinguish moral and natural evils. The theory of pain as a natural or biological fact having its legitimate place and evident utility in the genesis of the organism and in the development of the mind should be kept apart from that of moral evil or sin. The question of mental and moral suffering also should be discussed psychologically and its precise nature determined before it is classed either with physical pain or with moral evil. Dogmatic theology has darkened counsel on the subject by classing all pains together as evils, making them incidents of sin or results of the 'Fall,' and finding it necessary to 'apologize' for their presence in the economy of things. To this is added the further confusion of placing in the same category those external 'evils' which consist in misfortune simply—the destruction of crops or the spread of the plague—and are quite apart from the psychologically conditioned 'evils.' Cf. THEODICY, and SIN. (J.M.B.–K.G.)

Evil Eye: Ger. *böser Blick*; Fr. *mauvais œil*; Ital. *mal' occhio, fascino, jettatura*. The term refers to a widespread belief in the power of certain persons, gifted with the 'evil eye,' to work ill on those upon whom they direct their gaze. It forms one of a large number of practices connected with so-called magic or SORCERY (q. v.). The history of this belief is rather obscure; while its distribution and variations are very wide.

Literature: ELWORTHY, The Evil Eye (1895). See also under MAGIC. (J.J.)

Evocation [Lat. *e + vocare*, to call out]: Ger. *Evocation* (suggested); Fr. *évocation*; Ital. *evocazione* (suggested). The calling up of a memory by another person, through suggestion, normal or pathological.

The term, in use in French, is recommended for adoption in English (on the suggestion of P. Janet), with the technical use also of the verb to 'evoke.' It is useful in French, and would be also in English, mainly in cases of hypnotic and other alterations of memory in which suggestibility and artificial control of the subject, in some degree, is relatively common. But it is difficult to draw a line between such cases and the normal awakening of memories, by verbal or other suggestions. Cf. Janet, *Automatisme psychol.* (J.M.B.)

Evolution (in biology) [Lat. *evolutus*, from *evolvere*, to unfold]: Ger. *Evolution, Entwicklung* (development); Fr. *évolution*; Ital. *evoluzione*. (1) The continued production of life in accordance with the theory of DESCENT (q. v.). It is opposed to SPECIAL CREATION (q. v.). (J.M.B. E.B.P.)

(2) The theory that individual development is an unfolding of that which already exists preformed in the germ-cells; as opposed to EPIGENESIS. Cf. EVOLUTION (mental).

(1) Setting aside early speculations, based on deduction from assumed general principles, rather than on induction from observed facts and phenomena, a necessary preliminary to organic evolution as a scientific generalization was: (i) the establishment of approximate conclusions as to the age and evolution of the earth, and (ii) a body of evidence as to the succession of organic forms based on a study of fossils. Hence it has been truly said that Lyell was the necessary precursor of Darwin. Such investigation served to establish the fact of progress, but at the same time it emphasized that of apparent discontinuity.

There was at first little evidence of fossil species shading continuously one into another; in fact, the very conception of species was opposed to such a view. Darwin, however, by a study of a vast mass of data collected from many sources, and dealing with domesticated animals and plants, species under nature, distribution in space, embryological and paleontological evidences, showed (*a*) that existing and fossil species are only more or less isolated forms on what are really continuous lines of development: he accounted for apparent discontinuity by the imperfection of the record; (*b*) that Natural Selection affords good reason that adapted organisms should survive and transmit their adaptations progressively, and gives an intelligible explanation of the facts of geographical distribution, classification, morphology, embryology, and rudimentary organs; (*c*) that the elimination of intermediate forms between successive relatively stable adapted forms may account for the apparent isolation of these forms along the varied and divergent lines of continuous evolution; (*d*) that divergence once established would be emphasized, and give rise to independent lines of descent; and (*e*) that man has produced great results in his domesticated breeds by this very principle of selection working through heredity upon variations. Cf. DOMESTICATION.

In natural selection, of which there had been previous hints, notably in the writings of Herbert Spencer (see Clodd, *Pioneers of Evolution from Thales to Huxley*), and which was also independently discovered by A. R. Wallace, students of organic nature found a working hypothesis, in accordance with which the theory of evolution could be fruitfully applied. See NATURAL SELECTION, and MALTHUSIANISM. Since the publication of Darwin's *Origin of Species*, the further development of the CELL THEORY (q.v.) has placed the doctrine of continuity beyond question for existing forms of life, and rendered it in the highest degree probable for all life in the past. The chief problems now under discussion are: (1) the range of natural selection; (2) the nature and limits of hereditary transmission; (3) the theory of variation (the origin, character, amount, and direction or distribution of variations); and (4) whether the theory of evolution as it stands, with all the factors (see FACTORS OF EVOLUTION) now recognized, suffices to account for (i) all forms of adaptation, (ii) specific differences, and (iii) the apparent breaches of continuity between specific forms, present and past. Fuller discussions are given under HEREDITY, and VARIATION.

A recent attempt to treat biological phenomena by mathematical methods has met with great success in the hands of Galton, Pearson, Weldon, and others. Pearson considers quantitative determinations necessary in three great fields before an exact theory of evolution is possible : i. e. (1) variation, (2) selection, and (3) heredity. His own papers have dealt with all of these on the basis of statistical data (Mathematical Contributions to the Theory of Evolution, *Proc. Roy. Soc.*, London, 1894 ff.). For results and methods see (1) VARIATION (different topics), (2) REPRODUCTIVE SELECTION, NATURAL SELECTION, and SELECTION (with the topics mentioned under that head), (3) GALTON'S LAW (of ancestral inheritance), and HEREDITY. These methods apply also to many of the other problems of general biology, such as CORRELATION (q. v.), REGRESSION (q. v.), collateral inheritance, &c.

The distinction between progressive evolution along one line and divergent evolution along different lines has been covered by Romanes by the terms monotypic and polytypic evolution respectively (*Darwin and after Darwin*, iii).

(2) See PREFORMATION. The general recommendations are made that the term evolution be strictly limited to the first meaning (1), and that Preformation be used for the second (2). Also that the distinction made by Huxley between evolution and DEVELOPMENT (q. v.) be carefully observed. The corresponding German terms are respectively Evolution and Entwicklung ; a usage which does away with the ambiguity hitherto arising from using Entwicklung for both evolution and development. The term development will then cover the entire ontogeny of an organism, including the second meaning above (2).

Literature : LYELL, Princ. of Geol.; HERBERT SPENCER, First Princ., and Princ. of Biol.; DARWIN, Origin of Species, Descent of Man, and Life and Letters (by F. DARWIN); WALLACE, Contributions to the Theory of Natural Selection, and Darwinism ; HUXLEY, Essays ; WEISMANN, Essays, and Germ-Plasm ; COPE, Origin of the Fittest, and The Primary Factors of Organic Evolution; OSBORN, From the Greeks to Darwin ; LANKESTER, Adv. of Sci.; POULTON, Charles Darwin ; HAECKEL, Generelle Morphologie. General expositions are ROMANES, Darwin and after Darwin ; CONN, The Method of Evolution (1900). Cf. also the topics mentioned in the article BIOLOGICAL SCIENCES (1). (C.LL.M.–J.M.B.–E.B.P.)

Evolution (mental): Ger. *geistige Evolution* (or *Entwicklung*) ; Fr. *évolution* (or *développement*) *mentale* ; Ital. *evoluzione* (or *sviluppo*) *mentale*. The theory of DESCENT (q. v.), as accounting for the series of minds in the animal forms, including man. It is contrasted with mental development, which is the progress of the individual mind from birth to death.

As in biology, it is well to distinguish the words evolution and development in this way, the one designating the phylogenetic, the other the ontogenetic problem. We are suggesting the same distinction in the foreign equivalents, although in the other languages, as in English, development is often used to cover both.

The hypothesis of mental evolution has very much the place in genetic psychology that the general theory of 'descent' has in biology; in each it is opposed to the well-known 'special creation' theory. And it is becoming more and more evident, as the question of mental evolution is more adequately discussed, that the problem is common to biology and psychology, and must be treated as one broad topic. Biological evolution has to take account of the mental processes at different stages in the life forms, and mental evolution has to make a similar recognition of the evolution of the physiological organism at each stage. The future evolution theory, in other words, will undoubtedly be a psychophysical theory.

That it is already, in some degree, is seen in the establishment, as factors of evolution, of Darwin's sexual selection, Wallace's recognition markings, and in the working out of a theory of MIMICRY (q.v.) and warning colours. The hypothesis of ORGANIC OR INDIRECT SELECTION (q. v.) also gives, as no other hypothesis has, scope for the effective exercise of the mental faculties in the determination of lines of evolution of both body and mind.

Accordingly, we find that the great problems of mental evolution are the same, and can generally be put under the same headings as the problems of biological evolution ; i. e. the problems of INHERITANCE, or other means of transmission, of acquired mental characters ; of the RECAPITULATION of mental evolution in individual development ; of mental VARIATIONS and their significance ; of SELECTION applied both to minds and to thoughts ; of ADAPTATION and ACCOMMODATION (see those terms).

Besides these questions, which the theory of mental descent shares with biology, it has certain problems of its own which biology cannot itself deal with, but which constitute a series of considerations to be carried over from genetic psychology to biology ; the questions arising from the facts of social co-operation of all kinds. Under the topic SOCIAL PROGRESS the problem is indicated in more detail ; here it may suffice to say that the adaptations and transmissions due to social life, in its widest meaning, in animals and man, are important factors, not only in mental, but also in biological evolution.

The further distinction of mental evolution from social evolution has been attempted, but there is great difference of opinion as to how far it is successful. Mental development in the individual cannot be explained without the recognition both of the social influences which enter into it directly, and also of the strain of individual heredity which indicates the social conditions of the individual's ancestors. Cf. MENTAL DEVELOPMENT, and SOCIAL EVOLUTION AND PROGRESS. Many of the problems of mental evolution centre in the theory of INSTINCT (q. v.).

Literature : DARWIN, Descent of Man ; WALLACE, Darwinism ; SPENCER, Princ. of Psychol.; SCHNEIDER, Menschlicher Wille, and Thierischer Wille ; ROMANES, Mental Evolution in Animals and Man ; WUNDT, Hum. and An. Psychol. (Eng. trans.); JAMES, Princ. of Psychol., ii. chap. xxviii ; JODL, Lehrb. d. Psychol. ; STANLEY, Evolutionary Psychol. of Feeling ; LLOYD MORGAN, Habit and Instinct, and Animal Life and Intelligence ; GROOS, The Play of Animals (Die Spiele der Thiere, 1896), and The Play of Man (Die Spiele der Menschen, 1899) ; BALDWIN, Ment. Devel. in the Child and the Race, and Social and Eth. Interpret. See also INSTINCT. (J.M.B., G.F.S.)

Also DE DOMINICIS, La Dottrina dell' Evoluzione (1880) ; ANGIULLI, La Filosofia e la Scuola (1888) ; GRASSI-BERTAZZI, I Fenomeni psichici e la Selezione (1898). (E.M.)

Evolution of Religion : see RELIGION (evolution of).

Ex post facto [Lat.]. After the fact.

Applied to opinions or arguments constructed to suit, derive, or justify the facts after they are known. It is associated with intellectual pretence. (J.M.B.)

Exact Logic : see LOGIC (exact).

Exact Science : see SCIENCE.

Exaltation [Lat. *exaltare*, to lift up] : Ger. *Exaltation, Aufregungszustand* ; Fr. *exaltation* ; Ital. *esaltazione*. Exaltation, as contrasted with depression, refers to a condition of mind in which the mental processes are quickened, and the imagination is active and directed to lofty aspirations. It is also used in a wider sense as synonymous with mental excitement.

Mental exaltation up to a certain degree is normal and physiological, and is particularly natural in childhood and youth, as also among groups or individuals of lively, emotional temperament. It may exceed normal bounds as the result of excessive excitement, of intoxication, or fever, or of distinct brain disease. Considered pathologically, it characterizes a large group of mental disorders (mania and general paralysis chiefly), which take their tone from the excessive excitement and action of brain functions. It refers more specifically in this connection to the delusions of grandeur and vanity, of unusual strength, importance, or wealth, &c., which so frequently accompany mental disease. Such exaltation may affect only a limited range of ideas, or may infuse the entire personality and sequence of thought. Patients believe themselves to be the Lord of lords, Jesus Christ, the king of England, the strongest or wealthiest of men, describe their feats of prowess or skill, their vast possessions, their claims to reverence and greatness. See MEGALOMANIA. Such delusions of exaltation may be accompanied by actual hallucinations, which fortify the subject in his beliefs. Insane exaltation of this type may ensue as a primary mental disorder, the exaggeration of a temperamental disposition; it more usually appears as a symptom or sequel of mania (occasionally of melancholia) or of other specific forms of insanity (insanity of masturbation, epileptic insanity, general paralysis).

Literature : CLOUSTON, Ment. Diseases, particularly lect. iv ; general textbooks of mental diseases (KRAFFT-EBING, MENDEL, MORSELLI), and monographs on mania. (J.J.)

Example : see REASONING.

Excellence [Lat. *excellens*, high] : Ger. *Vortrefflichkeit* ; Fr. *excellence* ; Ital. *eccellenza*. A high degree of WORTH (q.v.) or value, of whatever kind ; not a technical term.

The excellences of character which are shown in a man's habitual conduct are called virtues. Virtue is thus excellence which is human, voluntary, and established as a habit of character. The Greek term ἀρετή meant excellence, especially of manly quality. In the writings of Plato, and still more definitely of Aristotle, it gradually acquired the special and technical signification of VIRTUE (q.v.). The term excellence has preserved the wider and less technical signification. (W.R.S.)

Excess or **Overproduction :** Ger. *Ueberschuss* ; Fr. *excès* ; Ital. *sopraproduzione*. The principle that results analogous to those of conscious choice or determinate variation are secured by the excessive or over-production of variations, giving materials for the survival of the fittest. It is part of the conception of NATURAL SELECTION (q. v.).

Special applications of it have been made in GERMINAL SELECTION (q. v.) and in the theory of the acquisition of voluntary movement by the production of excess movements through a diffused nervous discharge (Spencer), imitative effort, &c. According to this latter theory the individual proceeds by trial and error, and gradually secures the adaptive combinations. Spencer (*Princ. of Psychol.*) and Bain (*Emotion and Will*, 4th ed.) gave currency to this view of the acquisition of movements; it has been called by the present writer (*Ment. Devel. in the Child and the Race*, 2nd ed., 1896) 'Functional Selection.' Cf. also Lloyd Morgan, *Habit and Instinct.* (J.M.B., C.LL.M.)

Exchange [Lat. *ex + cambiare*, to change]: Ger. *Wechsel*; Fr. *échange*; Ital. *scambio.* (1) The transfer of rights to wealth from one individual to another. (2) In commercial, as distinct from theoretical usage, the means employed for the transfer of rights and credits from one locality to another, especially (foreign exchange) when those localities are situated in different countries.

Exchange, in its first or broader sense, was first made one of the main divisions of economic science by James Mill, and has since ranked in many standard textbooks as one of four co-ordinate 'departments' of political economy—production, distribution, and consumption being the other three. (A.T.H.)

Excitability [Lat. *excitare*, to call forth, to wake up]: Ger. *Reizbarkeit*; Fr. *excitabilité*; Ital. *irritabilità.* Power of responding with an appropriate reaction to normal stimulus. See NERVE STIMULATION, and LIVING MATTER. (C.F.H.)

Excitation: Ger. *Erregung*; Fr. *excitation*; Ital. *eccitazione.* The vital change set up by the action of a STIMULUS (q. v.).

Literature: see the psychological and physiological textbooks, especially KÜLPE, Outlines of Psychol., 81; WALLER, Human Physiol. (1891), 291. (E.B.T.)

Excitement: Ger. *Aufregung*; Fr. *excitation*; Ital. *eccitazione, eccitamento.* Heightened condition of consciousness, especially in its conative and affective aspects.

The term 'excitement' is the psychological counterpart of the physiological term 'excitation.' Both words presuppose something which is excited or 'called into action.' On the physiological side this is nervous tissue, and excitation is a process taking place in nervous tissue. On the psychological side, what is excited is regarded as a condition of conscious process—a psychical disposition or predisposition. According to the current hypothesis of psychophysical parallelism, psychical dispositions, &c., are throughout correlated with physiological; permanent possibilities of conscious process involve permanent possibilities of nervous process. It is open to the psychologist to consider the physiological side of the total psycho-physiological occurrence so far as he finds it useful to do so.

Under this definition excitement may be looked upon as variation in the quantity, considered apart from the hedonic tone, of emotion. Very high excitement may be supposed to be present with relatively neutral or mixed pleasure-pain tone.

Literature: BAIN, Emotion and Will; STOUT, Manual of Psychol.; BALDWIN, Feeling and Will, chap. x. § 1. (G.F.S.–J.M.B.)

Excluded Middle (principle of): Ger. *Grundsatz des ausgeschlossenen Dritten* (*oder Mitte*); Fr. *principe du tiers* (*milieu ou moyen*) *exclus*; Ital. *principio del terzo escluso.* The principle or axiom of excluded middle (or third) formulates one aspect of the simple and universal condition of knowledge—that every judgment must be either true or false.

Between the assertions, then, which express the truth and the falsity of any significant judgment (for the meaningless has no right to recognition as judgment), there is no medium; one or other must be true. Obviously it is necessary, in order to avoid confusion regarding the scope and nature of this principle, to exercise the greatest care to secure that the assertions do no more than express the truth or falsity of some relation represented in thought, a condition not easily satisfied if there be any ambiguity in the subject of the assertions considered. Cf. LAWS OF THOUGHT.

Literature: for history, see UEBERWEG, Logik, § 78; HAMILTON, Lects. on Logic, lect. v; DELBŒUF, Essai de Logique scientifique, 165 ff.; SIGWART, Logik, § 25. (R.A.)

Exclusi tertii principium (in logic) [Lat.]. The principle of EXCLUDED MIDDLE (q. v.). (J.M.B.)

Exclusion: see LAWS OF THOUGHT.

Exclusion (method of): Ger. *Methode der Exclusion*; Fr. *méthode d'exclusion*; Ital. *metodo di esclusione.* That portion of Bacon's general view of induction which consists in eliminating by comparison of cases, particularly of negative cases, all that is non-essential—the residue, if the exclusions be made adequately, being necessarily the real cause involved. 'Whenever Bacon speaks of ordinary induction and of his own method he always remarks that the former proceeds *per enumerationem simplicem*, that is, by a mere enumeration of particular cases, while the latter makes use of exclusions and rejections' (Ellis, in Bacon's *Works*, i. 34).

On the conditions of the method, its limitations and character, as conceived by Bacon, cf. Ellis, loc. cit., 35-9, and Fowler's ed. of the *Nov. Org.*, Introd., § 9. The general nature of inductive processes as methods of exclusion or elimination of the non-essential is well stated in Bain, *Induc. Logic*, chap. v. (R.A.)

Excommunication [Lat. *ex* + *communicatio*, partnership]: Ger. *Excommunikation*; Fr. *excommunication*; Ital. *scomunica*. This word means strictly the ban of the Church, although it is sometimes applied, figuratively, to expulsion from other associations.

After the Council of Nicaea, and during the centuries in which the Church was supreme, excommunication took two forms. *Excommunicatio minor* deprived the condemned of the sacraments; *excommunicatio major* deprived him of all religious consolations—even of burial in consecrated ground —and barred him from all intercourse with Christian people. Necessarily, the state has to be called upon to enforce the second part of this ferocious penalty, and by the beginning of the 13th century we find it co-operating with the ecclesiastical authority. After the Reformation the greater excommunication was abolished, in Protestant realms, as a civil punishment, but the lesser was often enforced, as in Scotland, as a necessary part of ecclesiastical discipline. In these circumstances, the position of the Roman Catholic Church towards the greater excommunication has become largely theoretical.

Literature: KOBER, Der Kirchenbann; GOESCHEN, Doctrina de discp. ecc. ex ordinationibus; RÜETSCHI, Bann bei den Hebräern, in Herzog's Real-Encyc.; any history of mediaeval society and times. (R.M.W.)

Executive (in law) [Fr. *exécutif*]: Ger. *Executiv, Staatsgewalt* (executive power); Fr. (see above); Ital. *esecutivo* (*potere*). Pertaining to the execution of laws; or the supreme magistrate or magistracy charged with the execution of the laws. Executive requisition: a demand by the executive of one state upon the executive of another, for the surrender of a fugitive from justice.

It was the doctrine of Montesquieu in his *Esprit des Lois*, and the belief of many American statesmen in the 18th century, that the executive power could be separated by clear lines from the legislative and judicial. Experience has shown the contrary. A large field of governmental action, known as administrative, while lying mainly in the control of the legislature, may be committed by it, in great part, to the executive magistracy (Story, on the *Constitution of the United States*, ii. 524; Pomeroy's *Constitutional Law*, § 173).

Literature: WOOLSEY, on Polit. Sci., ii. chap. ix. (S.E.B.)

Exegesis [Gr. ἐκ + ἡγέομαι, to lead]: Ger. *Exegese*; Fr. *exégèse*; Ital. *esegesi*. The object of one of the four main departments of theology—exegetical theology (the others being historical, systematic, and practical theology).

The object is the interpretation of the, and any, authoritative sacred books. In the scheme of Christian theology it is usually divided into two parts—Old Testament and New Testament exegesis. Historically viewed, it may be divided into periods, in each of which contrasted methods and presuppositions prevailed. Thus we have rabbinical exegesis, patristic exegesis, mediaeval exegesis, modern exegesis. The apparatus employed in the last is vastly more extended and much more scientifically applied than in the others.

Literature: this is enormous, and is fully given in Herzog's Real-Encyc., arts. Exegese, Hermeneutik; REUSS, Hist. of the New Testament (Eng. trans.); WOGUE, Hist. de la Bible et de l'Exégèse jusqu'à nos Jours. (R.M.W.)

Exercise [Lat. *ex* + *arcere*, to enclose, through Fr.]: Ger. (1) *Einüben* (*-ung*), (2) *Ausüben* (*-ung*); Fr. *exercice*; Ital. *esercizio*. (1) Learning or training through doing or practice; also the function or task which is the means of it. See HABITUATION, and cf. PREPARATION.

(2) The performance of a function or task in which the performer is more or less competent; also the function or task in question.

Exercise is in one case practice into a function—an ACCOMMODATION (q. v.) process; in the other it is the practice of a function —an expressive or keeping-up process, a giving scope to what has already been acquired. See TERMINOLOGY (German), 'Übung.' The second meaning is recommended. (J.M.B.)

Exhaustion : see LAWS OF THOUGHT.

Existence [Lat. *existens*, existent]: see REALITY AND EXISTENCE, and cf. BEING.

Existence (struggle for): Ger. *Kampf ums Dasein*; Fr. *lutte pour la vie, concurrence vitale*; Ital. *lotta per l' esistenza* (or *per la vita*). The attempt to remain alive, or technically to survive, on the part of organisms. As a necessary factor in Darwinism, the conception involves the further restrictions : (1) that the organism which survives is already or still capable of propagating in the manner normal to its species; and (2) that it finds opportunity to do so : failing either of these conditions, the case would not be one of successful struggle for existence, from the point of view of evolution.

Three clearly distinguishable forms of struggle for existence may be distinguished.

(1) The competition for food, &c., that arises among organic beings through overproduction.

(2) Competition in any form of active contest in which individuals are pitted against one another.

(3) Survival due to greater fitness for life in a given environment, whether combined with direct competition with other organisms or not.

The second case (2) is that in which animals (*a*) fight with, or (*b*) prey upon, one another, only the former of these having any analogy to the form of competition due to a limited supply of food, &c., and then only in the case in which the strife results from the circumstances of getting a living— not in the case of mere combativeness, in which the stronger animal kills from aggressiveness. In case (*b*) one animal feeds upon members of another group as his natural prey—as the eating of insects by birds, leading to special adaptations for concealment, warning, &c., in the species preyed upon. This has nothing to do with overproduction in the sense given in (1), except in so far as the species preyed upon overproduce to compensate for the constant drain upon it (a very different thing).

A case of (2 *a*), important for its effects upon the next generation, is that of the struggle of males for the female, occurring irrespective of the number of available females. Cf. SEXUAL SELECTION.

The third case of 'struggle' (3) is that in which individuals struggle against fate—the inorganic environment — not against one another. This is really a 'struggle to accommodate,' to reach a state of adjustment or balance under which continued living is possible; as the other forms are respectively 'struggle to eat' (in a large sense), and

'struggle to win,' so this is 'struggle to accommodate.' The distinction between cases (2) and (3) disappears in instances in which the animal accommodates actively to meet his enemies, which then become part of his environment in the sense of case (3).

The relation of large productiveness to this form (3) of the struggle would seem to be but indirect. It would not matter how many individuals perished provided some lived; and any amount of overproduction would not help matters if none of the individuals could cope with the environment. Yet the theory of indeterminate, or indefinite, variation makes the chances—under the law of probability— of the occurrence of any required variation a definite quantity, and these chances are of course increased, i. e. for so many more variations another chance of one that is fit— with increased production. No better case in point could be cited than Dallinger's experiments on the effects of changes of temperature on infusoria.

In recent evolution theory the doctrine of natural selection has come to rest more and more on the second and third sorts of struggle (2 and 3), and less on the Malthusian conception (1). Experimental studies which support the selection view (e. g. Weldon on Crabs, Poulton on Chrysalides) show the eliminative effect of the environment, and the preying of some animals upon others, rather than direct competition *inter se*, among individuals of the same species, for food or other necessities of life. It is these forms of the struggle, too, that we find nature especially providing to meet through concealing and warning colours, mimicry, &c., in the one case, and high plasticity and intelligent action in the other.

The result common to all the sorts of struggle for existence, however, is the survival of an adequate number of the fittest individuals; and this justifies the use of the term in the theory of evolution to cover the wide variety of instances. Cf. NATURAL SELECTION, INTRASELECTION, GERMINAL SELECTION, and GROUP SELECTION. (J.M.B., E.B.P.)

Darwin on reading Malthus, *On Population*, conceived the idea that over-population would be a universal fact in organic nature, were there no process by which the numbers were constantly reduced. He was thus led to lay stress on the struggle for existence, and the elimination of those individuals which were unsuccessful. Combining this conception of elimination in the struggle with that of variation, he reached the hypothesis of natural selection. A similar relation to Malthus is true of Wallace (see Poulton, *Charles Darwin*). In this case the competition arises from common wants and an inadequate supply for all, the competition being either direct rivalry of one animal with another, or mere lack of something necessary to some.

Literature: MALTHUS, On Population (1798); CHARLES DARWIN, Origin of Species (1859); F. DARWIN, Life and Letters of Charles Darwin (1887). (C.LL.M.–J.M.B., E.B.P.)

Existence of God: see THEISM.

Existential Judgment: Ger. *Existential-satz*; Fr. *jugement d'existence*; Ital. *giudizio di esistenza*. A judgment in which the existence of the subject is explicitly predicated. See JUDGMENT, and PROPOSITION. (G.F.S.)

Exner, Franz. (1802–53.) Born and educated in philosophy and jurisprudence at Vienna. In 1827 he taught philosophy in the same place, and in 1831 became professor of philosophy at Prague. In 1848 he was called to Vienna to enter the ministry, and died as ministerial commissary to Padua.

Exogamy [Gr. ἔξω, outside, + γάμος, marriage]: Ger. *Exogamie*; Fr. *exogamie*; Ital. *esogamia*. Marrying out: a term (proposed by McLennan) for the custom which requires a man to take a wife from some other clan or tribe than his own.

The custom in various forms is most widely distributed, both amongst savages and in all stages of civilization. Its origin has formed the subject of much discussion, from which no consensus of opinion has as yet resulted. The institution was, in many instances, a sacred one, its violation being punishable with death; and it was evidently connected with the recognized degrees of relationship, particularly whether tribal, paternal, or maternal, which marriage brought about. Its discussion thus involves the general question of the history of human marriage and kinship, and the evolution of the family, clan, and tribe. Apart from minor factors and supplementary causes of exogamy in special cases, the two dominant factors assigned for its dissemination are: (1) the noxious and weakening effects which result from too close inbreeding of families, which in turn leads to a psychical lack of sexual attractiveness among those who have grown up closely together, and who are usually of near kin (the view of Westermarck, &c.); and (2) the scarcity of women in primitive communities owing to the practice of female infanticide, and the consequent tendency to marriage by capture from other tribes (the view of McLennan). The opposite of exogamy is endogamy, or the prohibition of marriage outside of the tribe. The relation in evolution of one to the other is not very clearly established.

Literature: MCLENNAN, Stud. in Amer. Hist. (1st and 2nd series, new ed., 1886 and 1896); WESTERMARCK, The Hist. of Human Marriage (1891); LETOURNEAU, The Evolution of Marriage (1895); STARCKE, The Primitive Family (1889). (J.J.)

Exorcism [Gr. ἐξορκισμός, administration of an oath]: Ger. *Beschwörung, Exorcismus*; Fr. *exorcisme*; Ital. *esorcismo*. The act of expelling evil spirits from persons or places by the pronouncing of formulas, or the observance of prescribed rites.

The process, under various forms, is almost as widespread as mankind, and derives its origin from the conception that disease and ill-fortune are produced by some evil spirit or demon. The cure of the disease or the removal of the misfortune can be accomplished only by the exorcism, or at times by appeasing the possessing spirit through offerings. Among primitive peoples the ceremonies of exorcism are often extremely crude, such as the frightening of the spirit by beating of drums and the cries of bystanders; while in more advanced civilizations which inherit traditional religious systems, the formulas and rites assume a very elaborate and specialized form. It was naturally the priest's function to deal with spirits, and it equally became his function to act as physician and effect cures, by driving out the spirits. Almost every nation of history has recorded some formulas and magical proceedings which custom and authority brought into use for the exorcism of the various ills that flesh is heir to; while survivals of these, frequently in a broken-down and weakened form, are current to the present day. It received special recognition in Christian rituals, especially that of Baptism. Similar processes were applied to haunted houses, or ill-fated places. Cf. ANIMISM, DEMONOLOGY, and MAGIC, and consult the references there given. (J.J.)

Exoteric: see ESOTERIC.

Expectation [Lat. *ex* + *spectare*, to look]: Ger. *Erwartung*; Fr. *attente, expectation*; Ital. *aspettazione, attesa*. Belief that future experience will be of a definite sort, based upon past experience. 'Any man knows that he will die, and may make a variety of arrangements in anticipation of death, but he cannot with propriety be said to be expecting it unless he has actually present to his mind a series of ideas ending in that of death, such series being due to previous associations, and unless, further, this series owes its representation at this moment to the actual recurrence of some experience to which that series succeeded before' (Ward, *Encyc. Brit.*, art. Psychology, 63).

Expectation arises from the so-called 'memory-coefficient' of reality (see BELIEF); that is, it is aroused by those marks of memory-images which serve to bring the assurance that they represent a former real series of experiences capable of being tested either by voluntary activity, as in going to the corner which I am expecting to find, or by submission to the series of events which lead up to the one expected and condition my activity, as in keeping my eyes open at the panorama until the expected portrait of Washington comes on. Expectation is the word for that attitude towards reality in general which concerns itself with what Mill expressed, in the case of the external world, as 'the permanent possibility of sensation,' and which has been more adequately formulated as voluntary control of a memory series, in such a way as to bring back the original evidence of reality or truth under conditions of limitation of activity. Expectation has been made use of by Hume in his theory of causation, and by Mill in his discussion of the uniformity of nature, and its degrees—or rather how much right we have to expect—are given mathematical expression in the theory of PROBABILITY (q. v.). (J.M.B., G.F.S.)

Expediency [Lat. *expedire*, to hasten]: Ger. *Nützlichkeit*; Fr. *utilité*; Ital. *utilità*. The quality of being advantageous for, or adapted to promote, the interest in view. See UTILITY.

The expedient in this sense is often contrasted with the right—the latter being determined by an absolute rule or law, whereas the former seeks its interest independently of the law. But when the interest or end of conduct is widened so as to include not merely individual but general happiness, and when this is regarded (as by the utilitarians) as the rule of right, the contrast disappears. Thus Paley says: '"Whatever is expedient is right." But then it must be expedient on the whole, at the long run, in all its effects collateral and remote, as well as in those which are immediate and direct.'

Literature: PALEY, Mor. and Polit. Philos.,
Bk. II. chaps. vi–viii; J. S. MILL, Utilitarianism, chap. ii. (W.R.S.)

Expense [Lat. *expensum*, money spent]: Ger. *Selbstkosten, Ausgaben*; Fr. *dépense, prix de revient*; Ital. *spesa*. Cost measured in money.

In the production of any article or service there are usually two kinds of expense: the special expense connected with the production of that particular article, which will be saved if the article in question is not made; and an indeterminate share in the general expenses connected with the maintenance of the factory, or other industrial enterprise—expenses which go on with little or no diminution, even if the particular article in question ceases to be made. Expenses of the former class are called direct, distributed, prime, or operating expense; those of the latter are called indirect, undistributed, supplementary expenses, or fixed charges. (A.T.H.)

Experience [Lat. *experientia*, from *experior*, to try : Ger. *Erfahrung*; Fr. *expérience*; Ital. *esperienza*. (1) Psychological: consciousness considered as a process taking place in time. We can speak of an experience, meaning a specific phase or mode of conscious change, or of experience as a whole, meaning the events of the mental life in general. (G.F.S.—J.M.B.)

The word is used so vaguely and ambiguously by writers on philosophy that definition is difficult. We find for instance such writers as Royce and Bradley speaking of an 'absolute experience' which is not subject to time conditions. This usage seems to deprive the term of all distinctive meaning. An experience in the historical and ordinary application of the term is a phase of conscious life which some individual 'passes through' or 'undergoes.' This does not imply mere passivity on the part of the individual. On the contrary he may, and does, anticipate or search for many of his own experiences. So far as this is the case experience includes 'experiment' in the widest sense, and involves a process of trial and error. (G.F.S.)

(2) Psychic or mental: the entire process of phenomena, of present data considered in their raw immediacy, before reflective thought has analysed them into subjective and objective aspects or ingredients. It is the summum genus of which everything must have been a part before we can speak of it at all.

In this neutrality of signification it is exactly correlative to the word PHENOMENON (q. v.), meaning (4). If philosophy insists on keeping this term indeterminate, she can refer to her subject-matter without committing herself as to certain questions in dispute. But if experience be used with either an objective or a subjective shade of meaning, then question-begging occurs, and discussion grows impossible. (w.j.)

The distinction between the meanings (1) and (2) is that between the two points of view of PSYCHIC (or MENTAL) AND PSYCHOLOGICAL (q. v.), as made in many places in this work. The neutrality and immediacy of meaning (1) is psychic, i. e. neutrality with reference to the subject which may be having the experience. When philosophy uses this meaning it is by abstraction from the content of the experience as thought in which the experience defined as neutrality has its place. That is, this neutrality can be postulated only of phenomena having some sort of psychic phase to which the phenomena are immediate. To make the term synonymous with raw unexperienced process, from the objective point of view, would be to go over to another extreme of interpretation. (j.m.b.–g.f.s.)

Locke's polemic against innate ideas supplies an excellent illustration of the use of the term. His position on this point is in reality a special form of protest against blind submission to authority, as contrasted with the method of finding out for ourselves by direct contact with reality. For Locke an 'innate idea' implied a belief thrust upon the mind from a foreign source, instead of arising in the normal course of the development of consciousness in relation to its objects. Since the starting-point of this development is in sense-experience, Locke insists that we cannot have ideas prior to or independent of sensations.

A distinction is frequently drawn between 'internal' and 'external' experience. But there is great confusion in the use of these terms. A thing may, in the same sense of the word, be in one place and therefore not in, i. e. out of, another; but we express no intelligible relation if we speak of two things as being, one in a given room and the other in last week. Yet evident as it seems that the correlatives in and not-in must both apply to the same category, whether space or time, presentation (or non-presentation) to a given subject, and so forth, we still find psychologists more or less consciously confused between 'internal,' meaning presented in the psychological sense, and 'external,' meaning not 'not-presented,' but corporeal or oftener extra-corporeal (Ward). If we insist on logical stringency, it would seem that no distinction between inner and outer experience is tenable. Suppose that 'inner' is taken to mean inside, and 'outer' outside the body. When we speak of experience as inside the body, we can only mean 'arising in connection with certain material processes which occur within the body'; but in this sense all experience is equally internal.

Suppose, next, that 'outer' is taken to mean 'having a spatial character and relation,' and 'inner' to mean non-spatial. On this view, again, all experience is equally internal. Feeling, thinking, and willing are not spatial processes; they have no shape or position : it is true that spatial relations are presented to consciousness; but the presentation of them is not an event in space. Suppose, in the third place, that 'inner' is taken to mean whatever forms a part or phase in the stream of processes constituting the existence of an individual consciousness, and 'outer' whatever is distinct in existence from this stream of processes. Here it is evident that the definition of 'internal' experience coincides with the definition of experience in general.

It thus appears that the attempt to distinguish two kinds of experience, one of which is 'external' and the other 'internal,' breaks down hopelessly. None the less the use of such phraseology is so persistent and widespread that we must assume it to be founded on some real distinction. The actual state of the case appears to be as follows. All experience is internal, in the sense of being inside or constituting part of the existence of an individual consciousness. But this statement implies nothing as regards the nature of the object to which experience refers— the object of which it is an experience. My thinking is always a conscious process; but I am not always thinking about conscious process. When I think of the moon, I mean something distinct in existence from my own stream of consciousness or any part of it; the object, as I at the moment understand it, is by its intrinsic nature something which would have existed if I had never been born. On the other hand, I may think of an emotion of disappointment or anger which I remember feeling yesterday, or am feeling now, or am likely to feel to-morrow. Here, not only is the process of thinking an experience of mine, but the object thought of is also an experience of mine. Now the phrase 'internal experience' seems to refer especially to cases in which an experience has other experiences of the same subject for its object; or to cases, if such there be, in which an experience is immediately aware of itself as such. External experiences, on the other hand, are experiences which have for their object whatever is taken to be distinct in existence from the stream of individual consciousness or any part of it.

The two sorts of experience are, however, largely correlative. We cannot reflect on our own states without taking account of their objects in some measure. It is a disputed question, how far it is possible to know other things without at the same time having some apprehension of the self and its processes. But it seems that ordinarily in the developed human consciousness some such self-awareness is present, though it may be relatively dim and vague. On the various interpretations of experience see IDEALISM, EPISTEMOLOGY, and NATIVISM AND EMPIRICISM. For literature, see BIBLIOG. B, i, *d*. (G.F.S.)

Experiment [Lat. *experimentum*, a trial]: Ger. *Versuch, Experiment*; Fr. *expérience*; Ital. *esperimento*. The alteration of phenomena or of the methods of observing phenomena, in order to obtain knowledge regarding them.

Wundt defines an experiment as 'observation connected with an intentional interference on the part of the observer, in the rise and course of the phenomena observed,' which definition follows Mill and other writers. Common usage, however, would call an observation made under artificial conditions, as with instruments, an experiment. Mill remarked that experiments have a very limited range in mental philosophy, whereas Wundt holds that observation having to do with objects, and experiment with processes, the experimental method alone is valid in individual psychology, and that there is no fundamental psychical process to which it cannot be applied. (J.MᶜK.C.)

Experiment in the general sense then is not opposed to observation, but is a special type of it, and where applicable at all, adds immensely to the information which might be yielded by observation, while at the same time enabling much to be known that would never fall within the compass of observation. Experiment is the most potent instrument for effecting that elimination of the accidental which is the necessary preliminary to the establishment of a law of fact, and has an equally important function in the indispensable work of verifying or testing any generalization by comparing it with fact. Like observation, it is a directed and controlled process,

and is therefore always in the service of a varying mass of already acquired knowledge. The general principle regulating inference from experiment is formulated in the canon of the method of DIFFERENCE (q. v.). For Crucial Experiment see EXPERIMENTUM CRUCIS. (R.A.)

Experimental Science: see SCIENCE.

Experimentation or **Experimenting** (as a mental process): Ger. *Experimentiren*; Fr. *expérimentation*; Ital. *(lo) sperimentare*. The process of 'trial and error,' or 'try-try-again,' considered as a natural method of securing results for which no direct way of attainment is known.

Animals and children proceed by experimenting in many instances. In cases of motor accommodation it is aided by the process of EXCESS (q.v.) or overproduction.

Literature: GROOS, Die Spiele d. Thiere (Eng. trans.), also Die Spiele d. Menschen (Eng. trans.); LLOYD MORGAN, Habit and Instinct. (J.M.B.)

Experimentum crucis [Lat.]. An EXPERIMENT (q.v.) so arranged that its results will be final or crucial in solving a problem: as the introduction of a flame into a jar to determine whether one of a group of inflammable gases is present or not. (J.M.B.)

Expiation: see ATONEMENT.

Explanation [Lat. *ex + planus*, smooth]: Ger. *Erklärung*; Fr. *explication*; Ital. *esplicazione*. Any relative clearing up of a perception or notion in terms of judgments or notions already assented to.

There has been much discussion as to what constitutes real or ultimate explanation, the matter of dispute being the final terms to which the thing explained may be reduced— to axioms, to self-evident or *a priori* truths, to invariable sequence, to descriptive or analytical judgments. Explanation in positive science means the reduction of a phenomenon to the terms of a general principle, whatever that principle be; it may be reached by empirical and experimental methods, and is then called (following Platner) empirical explanation. The deductive derivation of a fact or notion from universal truths may be called in contrast logical explanation, which becomes metaphysical when the universal is one to which metaphysical validity is attributed.

Explanation is often made synonymous with DEFINITION (q.v.), but definition is a more restricted term. Definition follows upon explanation, and consists in the statement of the explanation in its lowest terms, and in certain forms which satisfy logical tests. Moreover, the logical demand of definition may be filled from the point of view of formal precision within the limits of knowledge, while the psychological demand for explanation may be unsatisfied. Further knowledge in this case may furnish an explanation which in turn may result in a new definition. Cf. REASONING.

Literature: the general works on logic, especially MILL, SIGWART, ERDMANN, BOSANQUET, and WUNDT; VENN, Empirical Logic; JEVONS, Princ. of Sci.; PEARSON, Grammar of Sci. (2nd ed.). (J.M.B.)

Explicative Judgment: see ANALYTIC AND SYNTHETIC JUDGMENT.

Explicite: see IMPLICITE.

Exponible: see PARVA LOGICALIA.

Expression: see LANGUAGE FUNCTION, SPEECH, GESTURE LANGUAGE, and EMOTIONAL EXPRESSION.

Expression (aesthetic) [Lat. *exprimere*, to press out]: Ger. *Ausdruck*; Fr. *expression*; Ital. *espressione*. (1) The act of expressing or conveying meaning. Often with the connotation of clear, forceful, penetrating, and emotionally appropriate manner. (2) The meaning itself of an object or work of art, as distinct from the act or manner of conveying it. (3) The manner in which any part or the whole of an object or work of art imparts its peculiar significance, and in the latter case more specifically the mode in which the artist reveals ideas and emotions, whether in interpretation of nature and mankind, or as embodying his own immediate subjective experience as such. For the relation of expression to beauty, see BEAUTY (II and III).

Expression as a constituent element of aesthetic value appears to have been explicitly recognized by Socrates. It is somewhat incidentally treated by Aristotle, who mentions it, in the sense in which it indicates expression of character, as a feature in good painting, and a matter of distinct importance in tragedy. He also compares to their disadvantage in this respect the formative arts with music. Plotinus recognizes it indirectly, but it does not become a principle of fundamental significance until its development by Winckelmann. The subsequent history of art shows in many directions reflections of the principle under the influence of the larger spirit of Romanticism. The emphasis upon the expression of individuality and the characteristic, together with the tendency to break from slavish adherence to classicism and the accepted models of art, is illustrated in poetry by Goethe, Schiller, and Byron; in the treatment of the novel by Victor Hugo; in painting by the cultivation of landscape, as exemplified by Corot and Turner, and in the development of genre by such men as Millet and Bréton. Wagner may fairly represent this trend as affecting music. In sculpture and architecture the influence of the principle is no less truly felt, but it is mingled with other influences. Schwanthaler and Lassus may, however, serve as illustrations. Cf. CHARACTERISTIC, and ART THEORIES.

Literature: BOSANQUET, Hist. of Aesthetic (1892); VAN DYKE, Princ. of Art (1887); VÉRON, Aesthetics (1879); TAINE, Lects. on Art (1896, 2nd ed.); SANTAYANA, The Sense of Beauty (1896); SULLY PRUDHOMME, L'Expression dans les Beaux-Arts (1898); GURNEY, Power of Sound (1880); v. HANSEGGER, Die Musik als Ausdruck (2nd ed., 1887). (J.R.A.)

Expression (facial): see PHYSIOGNOMY, and EMOTIONAL EXPRESSION.

Extension [Lat. *ex + tendere*, to stretch]: Ger. *Ausdehnung*; Fr. *extension*; Ital. *estensione*. A continuous, coexistent, manifold of positions, in which the distance and direction of the constituent parts are not qualitatively determined. Cf. SPACE.

There are many kinds of serial arrangement. Extension is distinguished from time series, because its constituent parts are coexistent, not successive. It is distinguished from qualitative and intensive series, such as the scale of pitch, because the order of its parts is not dependent on the intrinsic nature of each part. The reason why one tone is placed between two other tones in the scale of pitch, is that comparison shows it to be higher than one of them, and lower than the other. The relative position of the parts of extension is not fixed in this way by qualitative comparison.

Psychological theories of the perception of extension have been roughly divided into two classes: (1) the nativist; (2) the genetic. The purely nativist theory maintains that all perception of extension is due to original endowment, so that it can no more be accounted for by psychological conditions than the sensations of colour or sound. The purely empirical form of the genetic theory wholly denies both that the perception itself is a matter of original endowment, or that it contains any constituent factor exclusively belonging to it which is due to original endowment, and so incapable of psychological derivation or explanation. As an example of the purely empirical view, we may refer to the attempt of Bain, J. S. Mill, and others to reduce the whole perception of extension to series of motor sensations combined in certain ways, and occurring in a time series. Unreflective common sense resorts to the form of nativism which makes space a matter of psychologically immediate perception. Older writers, such as Hobbes and Locke, never seem to have thought of doubting it. Berkeley is a nativist as regards the tactual perception of extension in all its forms, and also as regards the visual perception of the second dimension. But he was the first to call in question the possibility of directly perceiving the third dimension by sight. He made the perception of distance from the eye a result of the association of visual with tactual experiences. In modern times it is difficult to find any competent authority for a purely nativist position such as would support the Kantian view of SPACE (q. v.) as an *a priori* form. Nativist writers, while affirming an original perception of extension both by sight and touch, usually regard this perception as at the outset vague and rudimentary; its further development is regarded by them as due to experience, and capable of psychological explanation (Stumpf, Hering, &c.). Others, who have been called 'nativists of process' (Lotze, Wundt), hold that extension is reached by a functional synthesis of unextensive data (intensive and qualitative) which are called LOCAL SIGNS (q. v.). These writers consider their theory genetic, though not empirical. A third view current at the present time cannot properly be called either nativist or empirical. It is empirical as regards the form of extension; but it is nativist as regards the matter which is arranged in this form, although on this distinction its two main advocates, Ward and James, do not seem to be in complete agreement. It regards the serial order of positions, distances, &c., as the result of mental processes which are traceable by the psychologist. But it maintains at the same time that the matter which assumes this form is, in part at least, of a peculiar kind distinctively belonging to the perception of extension, and due to an original and irreducible kind of sense-experience. This ultimate sense-experience is called extensity (Ward), or extensiveness (James). See EXTENSITY. Discussion is now very largely between the genetic nativism (of process) and this sensational or 'original quality' view.

Locke uses the term 'expansion' instead of extension. It is obvious that according to the definition sounds, (smells, &c.), are not extended. There are no audible positions coexistent with each other, and separated and connected by audible distances. It would seem to be a legitimate problem to ask why there are not, i. e. what local signs they lack, or why their extensity (if they have it) does not develop into extension.

Literature: HERBART, Psychol. als Wiss., §§ 109–15; VOLKMANN, Lehrb. d. Psychol., §§ 90–9; LOTZE, Metaphysik, §§ 543–73; Medicin. Psychol., §§ 325–435; Grundzüge d. Psychol. (4th ed.), §§ 31–43; BAIN, Senses and Intellect (4th ed.), 196–204; T. K. ABBOT, Sight and Touch; STUMPF, Die Raumvorstellungen; WUNDT, Physiol. Psychol. (3rd ed.), ii. 28 f. and 189 ff.; Logik, ii. 457–60; LIPPS, Grundthatsachen, 475–587; WARD, Encyc. Brit. (9th ed.), art. Psychology; JAMES, Princ. of Psychol., ii. 132–282; STOUT, Manual of Psychol., 330 ff.; VICTOR HENRI, Die Raumwahrnehmungen des Tastsinnes, §§ 159–214; the Psychologies of LADD and BALDWIN contain many literary references. (G.F.S.–J.M.B.)

Extension (in physics). That property of matter in virtue of which it seems to occupy space. It is intimately associated with IMPENETRABILITY (q. v.).

In mathematics: the property of occupying space in one or more dimensions. (S.N.)

Extension (logical): Ger. *Umfang*; Fr. *extension*; Ital. *estensione*. The extension or extent of a general notion is the whole range of concrete objects, lower classes, cases or instances in which are found the distinctive characters making up the COMPREHENSION (q.v.) of the said notion. See also QUANTITY (in logic).

The distinction between the two aspects of all generalizing thought, the reference to the concrete instances on the one hand, and the relatively abstract marks or meaning on the other, is so fundamental that it could not but make itself felt in the earliest scientific analysis of thought, in the Aristotelian logic, though it did not then receive any special denomination. The same lack of definite naming is traceable in the whole scholastic logic. It is only in the 15th century that some indications of the distinction as having logical significance began to appear, and in modern logic recognition of its value dates from the *Port Royal Logic*, 1662. Leibnitz, Wolff, and Kant, with their followers, as they tried to make the notion the unit of logical thought, naturally assign greatest importance to a distinction which is most clearly evidenced in notions. Sir W. Hamilton is the latest exponent of this view.

Literature: historical notions of this distinction in HAMILTON, Discussions, App. II, and Logic, lect. viii; BAYNES, New Analytic of Logical Forms. All the larger treatises on logic, such as those of LOTZE and SIGWART, discuss the distinction. On the relative merits of extension and comprehension as basis of logical relations, see MILL, Exam. of Hamilton, chap. xxii; LANGE, Logische Stud. (1877); VENN, Symbolic Logic (2nd ed.), chap. xix; HUSSERL, in Vtljsch. f. wiss. Philos. (1891). (R.A.)

Extensity or **Extensiveness** (no fixed foreign equivalents, but those for EXTENSION; see below). An original spacial property supposed to attach to some or all sensations; also called voluminousness. (J.M.B., G.F.S.)

Stumpf uses Raum, räumliches (raumähnliches) Moment, Verbreitung des Eindrucks, Tongrösse, as well as (immanente) Ausdehnung. Stumpf, Ebbinghaus, and others use the adjectives massig, breit, uns rings umflutend, dünn, stechend, fein, spitzig, dick, voll, &c., to denote opposites of this 'extensity.' In Ital. estensività is suggested (E.M.).

Literature: JAMES (a 'feeling of crude extensity,' 'discernible in each and every sensation, though more developed in some than in others, is the original sensation of space.' It is clearest in sensations of 'hearing, touch, sight, and pain'), Princ. of Psychol., ii. 134–5; WARD, Encyc. Brit. (9th ed.), art. Psychology, 46; BAIN, Senses and Intellect (1868), 111, 199, 227; STUMPF, Raumvorstellung, 272, and Tonpsychologie, ii. 51; KÜLPE (a given attribute of sensations of sight and pressure; an areal extension, Ausgedehntheit), Outlines of Psychol., 30; J. MÜLLER (connate areal vision), Physiol. d. Gesichtssinnes, 56, 71. (E.B.T.)

Also H. TAINE, De l'Intelligence, ii. 81 ff. and 128 f. (Eng. trans., On the Intelligence); CH. DUNAN, Théorie psychologique de l'espace, (1895). (L.M.)

Extensor Muscles: see FLEXOR AND EXTENSOR.

External and **Internal:** see EXTERNAL OBJECTS, and EXPERIENCE.

External Objects: Ger. *Dinge* (*und Ereignisse*) *der Aussenwelt*; Fr. *objets extérieurs*; Ital. *oggetti esterni*. Things and events presented in sense-perception considered as existing independently of the process by which they are perceived. As thus existing they are said to have externality. (G.F.S.–J.M.B.)

One of the oldest psychological theories of our perception of an external object is that of Hobbes. According to him, sensation and sense-perception are due to the resistance offered by the organism to change produced by an external impression. 'Seeing, therefore, there is in the whole organ, by reason of its own internal natural motion, some resistance or reaction against the motion which is propagated from the object to the innermost part of the organ, there is also in the same organ an endeavour opposite to the endeavour which proceeds from the object, so that when that endeavour inwards is the last action in the act of sense, then from the reaction, how little soever the duration of it be, a phantasm or idea hath its being, which by reason that the endeavour is now outwards, doth always appear as something situate within the organ' (*Works*, Molesworth's ed., i. 391). This may be regarded as the germ of theories such as those of Maine de Biran, Bain, and others, which lay main stress on the experience of resistance to motor activity. Berkeley, following Locke, insisted on the relative uncontrollableness of sensations as compared with the flow of ideas. He also brought into prominence the essential part played by fixity and uniformity in the order of occurrence of sensation. This line of thought was afterwards followed up by J. S. Mill in his celebrated chapter in the *Examination of Hamilton*, entitled 'Psychological Theory of the Perception of External Reality.' A suggestive restatement of this doctrine is given by H. Cornelius in his *Psychologie als Erfahrungswissenschaft*, 99–114 (1897). Cf. BELIEF, and EXTERNAL WORLD.

Literature: PIKLER, Psychol. of the Belief in Objective Existence, Pt. I; Objectiva capable of Presentation, 4 (1890); STOUT, Manual of Psychol.; CROOM ROBERTSON, in Mind, O.S., xvi. 100, republished in Philos. Remains, 465 ff. (1894). Other notable references are WARD, Encyc. Brit., art. Psychology, 55–7; BALDWIN, Feeling and Will, 160 ff., and art. in Mind, O.S. (1891); SPENCER, Princ. of Psychol., ii. Pt. VII. chaps. xvi–xviii; LIPPS, Seelenleben, chap. xix; JAMES, Princ. of Psychol., chap. xxi; ROYCE, Studies of Good and Evil, viii. 198 ff. (G.F.S.)

External World (cognition of): Ger. *Erkenntniss einer Aussenwelt*; Fr. *connaissance du monde extérieur*; Ital. *percezione del mondo esterno*. Cognition of external objects and events as interconnected in a unified system.

Merely perceptual consciousness is concerned only with isolated objects or groups of objects. The cognition of an external world develops gradually by a process of ideal construction; and this ideal construction is essentially a social function involving co-operative thinking and willing. For belief in the external, see BELIEF, and EXTERNAL OBJECTS.

Literature: see the titles under EXTERNAL OBJECTS; and especially HUME, Treatise, Pt. IV. § 2; MILL, Exam. of Hamilton; LIPPS, Grundthatsachen, §§ 410–51; ROYCE, Studies of Good and Evil, 198 f.; STOUT, Manual of Psychol. (G.F.S., J.M.B.)

Externality: see EXTERNAL OBJECTS.

Extirpation [Lat. *extirpatio*]: Ger. *Abtragung, Extirpation*; Fr. *extirpation* or *avulsion* (according to the case—(Y.D.)); Ital. *estirpazione*. The experimental removal of some part of an organ (as of the brain) for the purpose of ascertaining the nature of the changes in function resulting from its removal. Cf. LOCALIZATION (cerebral). (H.H.)

Extra-mundane: see MUNDUS.

Extreme Cases: see SCIENTIFIC METHOD.

Extrinsic: see INTRINSIC AND EXTRINSIC.

Eye-measurement. Sometimes used as translation of the German Augenmass. Measurement, &c., of VISUAL AREA (q.v.) is recommended in its stead. (J.M.B., H.M.)

Eye-movements: Ger. *Augenbewegungen*; Fr. *mouvements de l'œil*; Ital. *movimenti dell' occhio*. The normal movements of the two eyes together under control of certain muscles. Cf. Eye under VISION. (J.M.B.)

Eye-movements are of psychological importance in certain connections. (1) Free movements are supposed, on Wundt's genetic theory of space-perception, to account for the general form of the monocular field of vision, and the perception of the position of objects within it (Wundt, *Physiol. Psychol.*, 4th ed., ii. 130, 131). (2) Free movements along the compared lines are our chief means of measurement of visual areas, the phenomena of which accordingly fall under Weber's law: the measurement being, probably, in terms of the intensity of muscular and tendinous, perhaps of pseudo-articular, sensations (Wundt, op. cit., 131). See KINAESTHETIC SENSATION. (3) Normal asymmetry of movement in the horizontal and vertical directions is thought to explain certain optical illusions, e.g. the greater apparent height, as compared with the breadth, of a square, &c. (cf. Wundt, op. cit., 137, and *Abhandl. d. kgl. sächs. Gesell. d. Wiss.*, xxiv. 2). (4) The movements of CONVERGENCE (q. v.) and ACCOMMODATION (q. v.) apparently constitute the primary basis of our judgment of depth or binocular perception of DISTANCE (q.v.) (Wundt, *Physiol. Psychol.*, 197, 215; cf. Arrer, in *Philos. Stud.*, xiii. 116; Hillebrand, in *Zeitsch. f. Psychol.*, vii. 97, xvi. 71; Dixon, in *Mind*, N.S., iv. 195). (5) Eye-movements do not assist us to estimate extent of movement when there is no possibility of reference to a fixed point. In themselves, that is, they are little noticed; their function has become symbolic. Illusions of movement may arise from this fact (see Külpe, *Outlines of Psychol.*, 362). (6) Involuntary eye-movements are disturbing factors in many optical investigations, e.g. in the determination of the sensibility of the fovea to colour. They are, further, the condition of Purkinje's dizziness.

The physiological investigation of eye-movements began with J. Müller (cf. Helmholtz, *Physiol. Optik*, 2nd ed., 668); the psychological with Herbart and Lotze (Helmholtz, op. cit., 739, 740). It should be noted that the psychological importance of eye-movements is still a matter of keen dispute.

Literature: see the titles given above, and under SPACE (perception of), and LOCAL SIGN. (E.B.T.)

F

Facial Angle: Ger. *Gesichtswinkel*; Fr. *angle facial*; Ital. *angolo facciale*. In a general way the facial angle is the angle made by the axis of the face with the axis of the skull.

Since the first-suggested facial angle (that of Camper, 1786), many others have been proposed which differ in the selection both of the horizontal and of the particular points selected for the determination of the oblique facial line, as is indicated by the accompanying figure. The main purpose of the facial

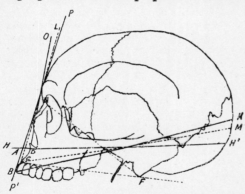

The facial angle of Camper is the angle formed by the lines *HH'* and *PP'*. The angle *PBK* is the facial angle of Geoffroy-Saint-Hilaire and Cuvier, its vertex at the edge of the incisors; *LCM* the angle of Jules Cloquet, its vertex at the alveolar border; *ODH'* the angle of Jacquart at the subnasal point. (Modified from Topinard.)

angle was to indicate the amount of gnathism or projection of the upper jaw, this being regarded as significant in zoological evolution, and also in the evolution of the higher races. For this distinctive purpose the ordinary facial angle is by some (Topinard) regarded as unsatisfactory, and the inferior facial or subfacial angle (formed at the alveolar point *C* by lines to the subnasal point *D* and the occipital condyle *F*) is regarded as a better index of prognathism. The significant difference in shape between an orthognathous and prognathous skull is shown in the topic PROGNATHISM (q.v.). For the subnasal facial angle Topinard gives for white races $89°$ to $51·3°$, yellow races $76°$ to $68·5°$, and black races (prognathous) $69°$ to $59·5°$. Camper's angle varies in man from about $70°$ to $80°$. Goniometers and craniometers are used for measuring facial angles.

Literature: arts. Angles craniométriques, and Prognathisme, in Dict. des Sci. Anthropol.; TOPINARD, Anthropology; KEANE, Ethnology; QUAIN, Anatomy, new ed., Appendix; and references given under CRANIOMETRY. (J.J.)

Facilitation [Lat. *facilis*, easy]: Ger. *Bahnung*; Fr. *facilitation*; Ital. *facilitazione, agevolezza*. Increased ease of function, or of disposition for it, resulting from stimulation of any sort. It is one of the marks of the growth of HABIT (q. v., also for literature).

The term has been given technical meaning as a translation of the German Bahnung (in neurology), which latter carries the idea of the preferential determination of a function, relatively to other functions, as to its pathway of discharge. Cf. TITCHENER, Amer. J. of Psychol., vii. 80. For cognate terms in psychology, see EXERCISE, HABITUATION, and PREPARATION. (J.M.B.–G.F.S.)

Fact [Lat. *factum,* made]: Ger. *Thatsache*; Fr. *fait*; Ital. *fatto*. An objective datum of experience.

Fact is distinguished from TRUTH (q. v.) in that (1) it is immediate, a datum carrying the belief on the part of the observer that it is independent of him; and also in that (2) it is immediately objective, a matter of presentation in time or space. Such expressions as the 'universe,' or 'world,' or 'thing of fact,' all emphasize one or other of these two characters, in contrast with the spheres of desire, value, discourse, &c., which implicate attitudes or constructions on the part of the observer. Fact might be defined thus: datum of experience considered as abstracted from the experience of which it is a datum. The notion of fact includes abstraction even from the experience by which the fact is reached or asserted. And inasmuch as it is just this sort of abstraction which the notion of actuality—or of the so-called 'trans-subjective'—covers, we may say that a fact is anything which is found to be actual. The fact is, however, not absolute, but always relative to some experience.

Literature: see EPISTEMOLOGY, and TRUTH AND ERROR. (J.M.B., G.F.S.)

Leibnitz distinguished 'truths of fact' (vérités de fait) from 'truths of reason' (vérités de raisonnement); the first being guaranteed by the 'law of sufficient reason,' the second by the 'law of contradiction.' (K.G.)

Fact (in law). Whatever has occurred; an act or event by which a thing has been brought into relation with a person. Investitive fact: one by which a right comes into existence. Divestitive fact: one by which a right is divested. Translative fact: one by which a right is transferred.

Literature: POLLOCK, First Book of Jurisprudence, chap. vi. 132; HOLLAND, Jurisprudence, chap. x. 2. (S.E.B.)

Factitious: see INTRINSIC AND EXTRINSIC.

Factor [Lat. *facere*, to make]: Ger. *Factor*; Fr. *facteur*; Ital. *fattore*. Any one of a plurality of causes or conditions which together determine a thing or event.

Technical uses of the term are in mathematics, biology, aesthetics, &c.: see FACTORS OF EVOLUTION. (J.M.B.)

Factors of Evolution: Ger. *Factoren der Evolution*; Fr. *facteurs de l'évolution*; Ital. *fattori dell' evoluzione*. The agencies or conditions of whatever character which determine organic evolution.

The word factor is made to cover both terms of the distinction between FORCE AND CONDITION made under that topic. The causes of organic evolution must themselves be phenomena of an organic or vital sort—the subject-matter of biology. But, as in other sciences, we find the operation of these properly biological forces or causes conditioned, limited, and interfered with by extra-biological conditions. The greatest of all these is natural selection, which is a restriction set upon mating, not a biological cause or even a positive force of any sort. So isolation, artificial selection, &c.; these are all conditions of evolution, and factors of a real but in a sense negative value. On the other hand, the vital functions of reproduction, variation, accommodation, direct competition, preying, &c., are biological forces, the motive principles belonging distinctively to life. These are causes or factors of a positive sort, in the determination of evolution. (J.M.B.)

This distinction roughly corresponds to that between (1) originative, and (2) directive factors, the latter being the conditions, the former the causes. Prior to Darwin, the chief factor recognized in evolution as progressive was that which is now associated with the name of Lamarck, the transmission to offspring of that which the organism gained by individual effort, together with that indicated by Buffon, the transmission of that which is impressed on the organism by the environment. Darwin and Wallace suggested natural selection as the chief directive factor in progress. Wallace and Weismann regard natural selection as the all-sufficient directive factor of progressive evolution. Mivart, Nägeli, and others believe in an inherent tendency to progress in certain directions. Natural selection as a directive factor is universally recognized, though its range is still open to discussion. Sexual selection by selective mating was regarded by Darwin as a supplementary directive factor in evolution. The ORGANIC SELECTION (q.v.) of Baldwin, Morgan, and Osborn, and Karl Pearson's REPRODUCTIVE OR GENETIC SELECTION (q.v.) have also been added to the list of factors of organic evolution.

The importance of ISOLATION (q.v.) as a factor was recognized by Moritz Wagner (1868), and has been emphasized by Gulick and Romanes. The PHYSIOLOGICAL SELECTION (q.v.) of the latter author is now generally regarded as an isolation factor.

Literature: see EVOLUTION, ISOLATION, NATURAL SELECTION, and the references given under the special topics mentioned. (C.LL.M.)

Factors of Production: Ger. *Factoren der Produktion*; Fr. *facteurs de la production*; Ital. *fattori della produzione*. Agencies of different character, whose combination is essential for the production of wealth.

Following the usage laid down (though not very explicitly) by Adam Smith, most economists have recognized three such factors—land, labour, and capital. The French economists have, as a rule, recognized but two—labour and capital; land being included under capital. George recognizes only land and labour; capital being stored-up labour. On the other hand, Walker and Marshall recognize four factors—land, labour, capital, and business ability. (A.T.H.)

Faculty [Lat. *facultas*]: Ger. *Seelenvermögen*; Fr. *faculté*; Ital. *facoltà*. Capability for a certain kind of mental process.

To say that an individual mind possesses a certain faculty is merely to say that it is capable of certain states or processes. But we find in many of the earlier psychologists a tendency to treat faculties as if they were causes, or real conditions, of the states or processes in which they are manifested, and to speak of them as positive agencies interacting with each other. Thus persistence in voluntary decision is said to be due to extraordinary strength of will, or to will-power, or to the faculty of will. Certain mental processes in man are said to have their source in the faculty of reason, and certain other processes in lower animals are explained by the existence of a faculty of instinct. This mode of pretended explanation has received the name of Faculty Psychology. Locke, in criticizing the phrase 'freedom of the will,' has brought out very clearly the nature of the fallacy involved. 'We may as properly say that the singing faculty sings, and the dancing faculty dances, as that the will chooses, or that the understanding conceives; or, as is usual, that the will directs the understanding, or the understanding obeys, or obeys not, the will; it being altogether as proper and intelligible to say that the power of speaking directs the power of singing, or the power of singing obeys or disobeys the power of speaking' (*Essay on Human Understanding*, Bk. II. chap. xxi. § 17).

Literature: HERBART, Lehrb. d. Psychol.; LOTZE, Microcosmus, Bk. II. chap. ii; STOUT, Manual of Psychol., Bk. I. chap. iii; citations in EISLER, Wörterb. d. philos. Begriffe, 'Seelenvermögen.' (G.F.S., J.M.B.)

Faintness [ME. *faynt*, weak, feeble]: Ger. *Ohnmacht, Schwächegefühl*; Fr. *faiblesse*; Ital. *languore, (senso di) mancamento*. More or less loss of consciousness. (J.M.B.)

The feeling of faintness or loss of consciousness shows itself externally in pallor of countenance, loss of muscular power, and difficulty in breathing. It may be due to excessive exertion, to emotional shock, or may ensue as the result of obscure central changes. The faint itself—more precisely termed SYNCOPE (q.v.)—is the result of more or less severe disturbance of heart action, and is characterized by suspended animation and unconsciousness. Cf. UNCONSCIOUS STATE. (J.J.)

Faith [Lat. *fides*, trust]: Ger. *Glaube*; Fr. *foi*; Ital. *fede*. Faith is practically identical with BELIEF (q.v.), and may be defined as the personal acceptance of something as true or real, but—the distinguishing mark—on grounds that, in whole or part, are different from those of theoretic certitude.

The moment of will enters into the assent of faith in the form of some subjective interest or consideration of value. Some faith-judgments are translatable into judgments of knowledge; but we cannot say that all are. There may be content in the *pistis* that will resist the processes of the *gnosis*. In that case the final test of validity would have to be sought in the sphere of the practical rather than in that of theoretical truth.

Literature: the titles cited under BELIEF, and WILL TO BELIEVE; also ORMOND, Foundations of Knowledge, Pt. III. chaps. i, iii. (A.T.O.)

Faith (saving). A distinction has been drawn between 'historical' faith and 'saving' faith. The former, as its name implies, leans upon institutions, customs, and the like, which have developed in the course of the evolution of the Christian consciousness. The latter is primarily subjective, that is to say, it implies pre-eminently a process proceeding within the individual man. As was natural, it acquired great importance from the principles of the Reformers, and it is delineated very fully, in its various phases and stages, in the writings of the early Protestant theologians, and of those who have since followed them more or less closely. Saving faith, as Martensen has pointed out in another connection, does not imply present perfection; it is 'a living commencement which contains within itself the possibility of a progressive development and a fulfilment of the vocation of man.' So far as it can be treated philosophically, the matter belongs to the sphere of religious psychology. Cf. CALVINISM.

Literature: SCHLATTER, Der Glaube im N. T.; CUNNINGHAM, Historical Theol., ii. 56 f.; BUCHANAN, Doctrine of Justification, its History and Exposition; NEWMAN, Lects.

on Justification; COPINGER, Treatise on Predestination, Election, and Grace (with literature); DORNER, Syst. of Christ. Doctrine (Eng. trans.), ii. 318 f. (R.M.W.)

Faith and **Knowledge** (in theology). In the history of human experience, particularly on its moral and religious sides, periods have tended to recur in which the dualism, or even opposition, between faith and knowledge has constituted a prominent, sometimes a determining, characteristic; and one may add that, in every age, individuals or associations exist whose tendency is to emphasize it. Thanks to the distinctive teaching of the Ritschlian school, it has again acquired prominence within the last twenty years. It is easy to see that, during a time of deep religious feeling, faith in some mysterious process or object, conceived to be of the last importance for man's welfare, may lead towards an elimination or disparagement of the intellectual features usually associated with knowledge. At such a time, disposition of heart (will) is abstracted from knowledge, set over against it, and regarded as essentially superior. The process may go so far as to result in a settled conviction that blind assent to certain propositions, which cannot be construed rationally, constitutes the mark of moral and religious attainment. Tendencies of this kind may often be detected in so-called 'evangelical' circles and movements. On the contrary, periods and persons have been dominated by a desire to exalt knowledge at the expense of faith. Here insistence has been laid upon reason, especially in its analytic processes, to such an extent that everything in the nature of faith has been extruded. Eighteenth-century 'rationalism,' and its legitimate successor in the 19th century—'free-thought'—are typical of this. The truth is that both views are based upon a false abstraction. Faith and knowledge cannot be separated in this way, because no part of man's psychological nature can be torn from the rest, and treated as if it were wholly uninfluenced by the other elements. Faith is itself a kind of knowledge, because it depends for its distinctive content upon the nature of the object to which it is directed. Knowledge is itself a kind of faith, for it depends upon the unrealized ideal of more perfect knowledge still, which supplies the immanent principle of all intellectual progress. The fact that the various elements in man's psychological constitution (intellect, will, &c.) can be separately named, does not sever them; they can be viewed in separation only on account of their prior unity. And, similarly, the fact that the individual and the social consciousness are inseparable, points to a necessary teleological unity (in which faith predominates) with past experience and present practice (in which knowledge predominates). Faith has objective as well as subjective aspects, and so cannot be divorced from knowledge. Knowledge has ideal as well as sensuous aspects, and so cannot be divorced from faith. In other words, the real problem of the relation between faith and knowledge lies not in their differences, but in the principle of their unity. Cf. FREEDOM (in theology), RATIONALISM, and FAITH PHILOSOPHY.

Literature: KÖSTLIN, Der Glaube, sein Wesen, Grund u. Gegenstand; and Der Glaube u. seine Bedeutung f. Erkenntniss u. Kirche; KÖNIG, Der Glaubensact d. Christen; J. CAIRD, The Fundamental Ideas of Christianity, i. 31 f.; and Philos. of Religion, 160 f.; KAFTAN, The Truth of the Christian Religion (Eng. trans.), i. 14 f., 116 f., 403, ii. 408 f.; ORR, The Ritschlian Theol., chaps. iii, vii; WENLEY, Contemp. Theol. and Theism, 85 f., 135 f.; GARVIE, The Ritschlian Theol.; HERRMANN, The Communion of the Christian with God (Eng. trans.), Bk. III. (R.M.W.)

Faith Cure: see MIND CURE.

Faith Philosophy: Ger. *Glaubensphilosophie*; Fr. *fidéisme*; Ital. *fideismo, filosofia della fede*. The philosophy which bases fundamental truth upon immediate (ideal) apprehension.

In some of its forms the faith philosophy includes both theoretical and practical principles among the truths thus maintained; more often it seeks support in such conviction for the postulates of ethics and religion. 'Faith,' again, is used in different senses: it may mean a direct apprehension of reality or a source of ideas (a special 'spiritual faculty'), in particular of ideas concerning the absolute and the transcendent world held to be free from the finite limitations of intellectual cognition; or it may mean the instrument of assent, conviction, assurance of truth, especially in relation to principles incapable of theoretical demonstration. The second of these interpretations commonly implies the third, and appears in connection with it; the third is much the most important.

Historically, the faith philosophy is often a product of reaction. Sometimes it makes its appearance in reaction from a prevalent intellectualism in favour of more spiritual views of the world and life; in this sense, particularly, it is akin to mysticism, and easily passes over into it (cf. the mediaeval mysticism, especially in its earlier phases, over against the scholastic rationalism). More frequently it takes its origin in opposition to negative or sceptical speculation, or is framed as a means of escape from such, either by the sceptic himself or by the defender of fundamental truth in opposition to particular negative systems, or to the spirit of the age. In this form it is a characteristic phenomenon of periods of Aufklärung, or of transition from one stage of culture to another, and is scarcely to be distinguished from the philosophy of feeling. The second half of the 18th century and the 19th have been especially prolific of movements of this type. The reaction against the enlightenment in France was headed by Rousseau with his 'sentimental Deism.' At the close of the same period in Germany appeared Hamann, Herder, and Jacobi, to whose thinking in the history of opinion the term faith philosophy (Glaubensphilosophie) most specifically applies. Chief among these was Jacobi, who opposed the witness of faith alike to the pantheistic (Spinozistic) and the phenomenalistic (Kantian) view of the world. Jacobi was severely criticized by Kant, the practical side of whose own system was based upon 'moral' or 'practical faith,' but faith in a sharply defined sense as bound up with the necessary implications of practical reason, and articulating into the ideal demands of pure reason, which the latter of itself alone was unable to satisfy. Since Kant the philosophy of religion has made large use of the principle of faith or feeling, sometimes in close dependence on the Kantian analysis, sometimes independently or in divergence from it. In Germany at the present time one chief school of theologians, the Ritschlian, takes its departure from Neo-Kantian positions. In Britain, France, and America the doctrine of faith has reappeared in various quarters, often under the pressure of the perplexities of the time in regard to the truths of morals and religion (Hamilton, Mansel, Romanes, Renouvier, James). The principle has peculiar attractions also for minds of the literary or artistic order. (A.C.A.Jr.)

Literature: J. J. ROUSSEAU (1762), Profession de Foi du Vicaire Savoyard, iv; JACOBI, Ueber die Lehre des Spinoza (1785); David Hume ü. den Glauben, oder Idealismus u. Realismus (1787); Von den göttlichen Dingen (1811); KANT, Was heisst sich im Denken orientiren? (1786), Werke (2nd ed.), Harten-

stein, iii; Krit. d. reinen Vernunft, 22–7, 87–92, 316–22, 370–85, 400–34, 526–47; Krit. d. prakt. Vernunft, 1–8, 53–60, 125–52; Krit. d. Urtheilskraft, 450–500; HAMILTON, On the Philos. of the Unconditioned (1829); Metaphysics, Appendix, Letter to Calderwood; MANSELL, Limits of Religious Thought (1858); ROMANES, Thoughts on Religion (1895); JAMES, The Will to Believe (1897). (A.C.A.Jr.–J.M.B.)

Faithfulness of God: see ATTRIBUTES (of God).

Fall (the) [Gr. σφάλλειν, to trip up]: Ger. *Sündenfall*; Fr. *chute*; Ital. *caduta*. The theological doctrine of the first human sin and its consequences.

This subject is connected so universally with the statements made in Genesis (ii–iv), that some reference must be made to them. Many hold that these statements are nothing more than the Hebrew form of a legend that was widely current among the people who inhabited the Mesopotamian valley centuries before we know anything of Jewish civilization; and although there is no historical evidence as yet (there seems to be archaeological) that the Hebrews derived this legend, say, from the Assyrians, striking parallelisms have been brought to light. Further, myths of a more or less similar character are to be found in India, Thibet, Persia, China, Tahiti, and Greece; while, as is well known, the conception of a lost 'Golden Age' was very widely prevalent. It ought to be emphasized, however, that the Hebrew form of the legend bears marks of the religious genius of the Jews, in that many of the grosser and more purely materialistic characteristics of other accounts have been eliminated. The story in Genesis is probably unhistorical; that is to say, no such events as are narrated there ever occurred. On the other hand, its affinities for similar tales in widely varying civilizations preclude us from viewing it as merely allegorical. It is a pictorial or mythological presentation of a truth incident to the constitution of human nature and to the progress of the race. As Wellhausen says, ' it is the yearning cry that goes through all the peoples; as they advance in civilization, they feel the value of the goods they have sacrificed for it.' Man leads a double life—of aspiration (purpose) and of accomplishment (means). But in all the important or permanent things of life, the distance between the two proves so great that it seems incapable of being bridged. Hence arises a profound consciousness of defect, and an attempt to explain its origin. At this point the problem passes over to philosophy of religion.

As a result of inspecting various religions, philosophy of religion distinguishes three theories of the 'Fall.' (1) God may be defective in himself—the theory supported to-day by Schopenhauer and v. Hartmann. (2) There may be a power opposed to God—possibly responsible along with him for the creation, and continuing, with him, joint-governor of the universe; this is the theory exemplified classically in the old Persian religion. (3) There may be a fault in nature itself, or in a portion of nature, such as man—in this case, the result of deterioration in some way from a primitive condition or perfection, or of sin. Another form of this theory is to be found in the legend of Prometheus, for whose transgression mankind suffers. This presents a curious parallel to 'Adam's guilt.' The theological view of the entire problem may be said to be of a mediating, or not fully reasoned, character. It is so drawn as to render belief in God accordant with an acceptance of evil as fact. It is ingenious, but not ultimate. Philosophically, the question belongs to metaphysics, and demands exhaustive treatment of the problem of evil. At present this problem awaits such elucidation as can be given only after an adequate critical appreciation of the principles involved in the much misunderstood conception of evolution. Cf. ANTHROPOLOGY (in theology), THEODICY, MANICHAEISM, and SIN.

Literature: PFLEIDERER, Philos. of Religion (Eng. trans.), iv. 1 f.; MARTENSEN, Christ. Dogmatics (Eng. trans.), § 78; HEGEL, Philos. of Religion (Eng. trans.), i. 271 f., ii. 200 f.; WEDGWOOD, The Moral Ideal, chaps. vii, viii; J. CAIRD, The Fundamental Ideas of Christianity, i. 196 f., ii. 1 f.; Evil and Evolution (anonymous); A. MOORE, Evolution and Christianity; MATHESON, Can the Old Faith live with the New? 219 f.; DILLMANN, Commentary on Genesis (Eng. trans.); RYLE, Early Narratives of Genesis; SCHRADER, Cuneiform Inscriptions and the Old Test. (Eng. trans.), i. 37 f.; DELITZSCH, Wo lag d. Paradies?; SCHILLER, Ueber d. erste Menschengesellschaft nach d. Leitfaden d. mosaischen Urkunde; MÜLLER, Christ. Doctrine of Sin (Eng. trans.); ORR, The Christ. View of God and the World; any treatise on dogmatic or systematic theology.   (R.M.W.)

Fall of God: see MANICHAEISM.

Fallacy [Lat. *fallere*, to deceive]: Ger. *Beweis-Fehler, Schluss-Fehler, Fallacie*; Fr. *sophisme*; Ital. *sofisma*. Fallacy is any violation of the conditions of proof, any failure to conform to the laws of valid reasoning.

As each condition of proof may be violated, the only complete description of fallacy would be given as an enumeration of the forms assumed by such violations. Concrete reasoning, involving generally a complex of such conditions, does not adapt itself readily to such detailed scrutiny; but the attempts to classify systematically the varieties of fallacy in concrete reasoning have not been very successful, and have generally involved a certain confusion between two distinct principles of division: (1) the nature of the circumstances inducing fallacy; (2) the logical condition violated. In the traditional treatment, which is an inheritance from Aristotle's logic, the former principle appears mainly in the case of so-called verbal fallacies. The discussion of fallacy having mainly a practical end, a classification which assigns a place to the more common and important types of fallacy is the most useful. The main groups in such a classification seem to be:—

(1) *Formal Fallacies*, violations of conditions which are stated in terms of non-significant symbols—such, e. g., are the errors which arise from misinterpretation of the relation between a positive and a negative proposition, especially when the terms are complex, or confusion between contraries and contradictories; violation of the rules of conversion and contraposition; violation of the syllogistic rules, the most important being *undistributed middle* and *illicit process*; violation of the rules of hypothetical syllogism, of which Aristotle's *fallacy of the consequent* is the best known.

(2) *Verbal Fallacies*, those which depend on, or involve a double interpretation of, the parts of the reasoning, and which are possible by reason of the ambiguity of words or verbal expressions. Under this class come Aristotle's fallacies *in dictione*, though it has to be noted that what he called composition and division are really verbal or grammatical fallacies, and do not correspond to what modern logicians include under that term.

(3) *Real Fallacies*, those which arise from a confused conception either of the contents of the evidence put forward, or of the relation between that evidence and the conclusion taken to be proved by it, or of the bearing of the conclusion reached on some thesis or issue contemplated. Such confusion of thought may conveniently be further specified as in

deductive or in inductive reasoning. Of the deductive, the main types are: (*a*) what may be called *composition* and *division*, for the error involved is a confusion of thought regarding the different relations of whole and part, of which the numerical is only one, though perhaps the most important; (*b*) what may bear the Aristotelian title *fallacies of accident*, resting on confusion of thought regarding the true relation of absolute and relative, abstract and concrete, general and specific or individual, unqualified and qualified, whether in terms or assertions; (*c*) *petitio principii*, begging the question; assuming as ground of proof what is in fact the *probandum*, or what is itself only to be proved from the *probandum*, or what can only be proved jointly with the *probandum*. *Circulus in probando* or *in demonstrando*, argument in a circle, a form of this fallacy, is generally characterized and facilitated by the interpolation of several intermediate steps between the identical assertions. *Hysteron proteron* (ὕστερον πρότερον) is a name for one variety of such a circle. To this head may also be referred that frequent source of fallacy in indirect reasoning on concrete matters—*incomplete disjunction*, or inadequate enumeration of alternative possibilities.

(4) *Ignoratio elenchi*, irrelevant reasoning, where the argument, sound, it may be, in itself, is supposed to establish a conclusion which is not that drawn from the premises used. Of this a number of special forms have received special names: *argumentum ad hominem, ad populum, ad verecundiam, ad baculum*, involving identification of the truth of a thesis with the character or consistency of its supporter, with its conformity to popular prejudice, with the moral elevation and purity of purpose of its advocates, or with the power of overcoming its antagonists by physical force. More subtle forms are those of *shifting ground, objections, partial refutation, proving too little or too much*.

Inductive fallacies, being violations of the conditions of inductive proof, can best be arranged as attaching to the several steps whereby a universal relating to concrete fact is formed, applied in explanation, and tested. Such fallacies have a considerable resemblance to those of deductive reasoning. There are few current technical designations of them. The most important varieties are: *neglect of negative instances* (including all types of non-observation); *undue simplification*, depending on neglect of points of differ-

ence and on intrusion of the subjective into the objective, and involving as cases oversight of plurality of causes and of the multiformity or complexity of both causes and effects; *post hoc ergo propter hoc*, the substitution of coexistence or mere temporal sequence for cause and effect; *insufficient enumeration* of conditions operative, of successive stages in a process, or of alternative possibilities of explanation; *insufficient verification*; *false analogy*.

Literature: the epoch-making treatments of fallacy have been: (1) that of ARISTOTLE, in the Sophistici Elenchi (cf. ed. by E. Poste, with full notes and translation, 1866); (2) BACON's survey of the Idola, in Nov. Org., Bk. I; (3) WHATELY's, in Bk. III of his Logic; (4) MILL's, in Bk. V of his Logic. The Aristotelian doctrine is well stated and illustrated in DE MORGAN, Formal Logic (1847), and in N. K. DAVIS, Theory of Thought (1880). An excellent treatment of the whole subject from the practical view of logic, as a preservative against error, is given in A. SIDGWICK, Fallacies (1883). A very elaborate classification and helpful treatment is in WELTON, Manual of Logic, ii (1896). There are also excellent remarks, though confined to fallacy in one special field, in BENTHAM, Book of Fallacies (1824).   (R.A.)

Falsity (1) and **False** (2) [Lat. *falsus*]: Ger. *Falschheit* and *falsch*; Fr. *fausseté* and *faux*; Ital. *falsità* and *falso*. (1) The property of positively violating in some respect the requirements of truth. (2) Not true. See TRUTH.   (J.M.B., G.F.S.)

Familiarity ('sense' or consciousness of): see RECOGNITION.

Family [Lat. *familia*, household]: Ger. *Familie*; Fr. *famille*; Ital. *famiglia*. (1) A natural group of persons consisting of father, mother, and children. (2) A larger natural group including grandparents, grandchildren, and collateral relatives. (3) A household: a group partly natural, partly artificial (including servants).

Definition (3) most nearly approximates the original meaning of the word, which etymologically signifies the servants or slaves of a household. The word was extended to mean the group partly natural, partly artificial, held together under the *patria potestas*. The investigations of modern ethnologists have brought into familiar use the terms *polyandrian family*, a woman with more than one husband, and their children; *polygynous family*, a man with more than one wife, and their children; *punaluan family,* a group of brothers jointly married to a group of sisters, and their children; *monogamous family,* one man with one wife, and their children. On the origin and significance of the family see MARRIAGE; also on the forms of animal families, and for literature. (F.H.G.)

Family: see CLASSIFICATION (in biology).

Fanaticism [Lat. *fanaticus,* inspired]: Ger. *Fanatismus;* Fr. *fanatisme;* Ital. *fanatismo.* The word anglicized as fanaticism was used in classical times of priests who were supposed to be the intermediaries of revelations or of oracles; in particular, it was applied to those of them whose actions were wild or noisy. The word has now come to be used in a disparaging sense. We say that, in the middle ages, extreme ascetic practices, such as scourging, branding, and the like, were products of fanaticism. The term implies credulity in religious or other matters, accompanied by a vehemence which expresses itself in hatred or violence towards opponents.

As Taylor says, fanaticism is enthusiasm inflamed by hatred. That is, it is a perversion of enthusiasm caused by excess or lack of balance. So far as it can be treated scientifically, fanaticism belongs to the province of psychology. It is often considered to be a form of abnormal brain action affecting persons predisposed to mental disease. It is very susceptible to the influences of contagion, and may certainly be regarded as belonging to the borderland between sanity and insanity. The history of persecution for religious belief, and of witchcraft, affords abundant illustrations of fanaticism which may be considered in part pathological. Cf. CONTAGION (mental), and references there cited.

Literature: ISAAC TAYLOR, Fanaticism, and The Nat. Hist. of Enthusiasm; LECKY, Hist. of Rationalism. (R.M.W.–J.J.)

Fancy [Gr. φαντασία]: Ger. *Phantasie;* Fr. *fantaisie;* Ital. *fantasia.* IMAGINATION (q. v.) in cases in which the process is not controlled by subjective selection, according to a systematic plan, but proceeds according to the more temporary and accidental affinities of the ideas themselves.

Fancy is often called 'passive imagination,' and treated under imagination in the textbooks of psychology (which should be consulted for literature). (G.F.S.–J.M.B.)

In aesthetics fancy applies to quaint, airy, capricious, or even grotesque products of imagination; therefore particularly to the lighter and less serious aesthetic creations. (J.R.A.)

Fantastic [Gr. φαντασία, fancy]: Ger. *phantastisch;* Fr. *fantastique;* Ital. *fantastico.* Belonging to or descriptive of FANCY (q.v.).

As applied to aesthetic objects, the fantastic is that quality which springs from the capricious and arbitrary play of imagination, especially when engaged with its lighter and more airy creations; applied to natural objects (e. g. cliffs) when characterized by very unusual and bizarre features; distinguished from the peculiar quality in caricature, in so far as the latter involves intentional over-emphasis of certain characteristics in order to give them prominence, whereas the fantastic involves a less definitely purposive playfulness of the imagination; distinguished from the grotesque in art, in so far as this involves, intentionally or otherwise, the same element of explicit and quasi-humorous over-emphasis of certain features, as found in caricature. In the case of natural objects the grotesque and the fantastic are often nearly synonymous, the latter applying more appropriately to the more delicate and less violent effects. Cf. CARICATURE, FANCY, and GROTESQUE. (J.R.A.)

Fapesmo, Faresmo: see MOOD (in logic).

Fashion: see CUSTOM.

Fate and **Fatalism**: see NECESSITY, and IDEALISM (Plato's ἀναγκή).

Fathers (of the Church): see PATRISTIC PHILOSOPHY, and SCHOLASTICISM.

Fatigue (mental) [Lat. *fatigare,* to fatigue]: Ger. *Ermüdung;* Fr. *fatigue;* Ital. *fatica, strapazzo* (exhaustion). A qualitative state following upon continued mental activity.

Fatigue varies with different functions, and with the degree of mental concentration. A distinction is made (cf. MacDougall, *Psychol. Rev.,* Mar., 1899) between fatigue (Ermüdung) and weariness (Müdigkeit). (J.M.B.)

In experimentation, it is directly dependent upon the number of observations taken in a single series, and is indicated by a steady decrease in delicacy of perception and readiness of judgment. It is characterized by (1) a weakening of attention, (2) a diminished capacity of reproduction, and (3) the prominence in consciousness of certain organic sensations. Cf. MUSCULAR SENSATION. (E.B.T.)

Literature: (mental and muscular) A. Mosso, La Fatica (1891, also in Fr.); A. BINET and V. HENRI, La Fatigue intellectuelle (1898); KÜLPE, Outlines of Psychol., 43. References on aspects of fatigue will be found further in many experimental monographs: e. g. BURGERSTEIN, Die Arbeitskurve einer Schulstunde (1891); EB-

BINGHAUS, Ueber eine neue Methode z. Prüfung geistiger Fähigkeiten und ihre Anwendung bei Schulkindern, 3rd Int. Cong. of Psychol. (1897), 134; Zeitsch. f. Psychol., xiii. 401; FRIEDRICH, in Zeitsch. f. Psychol. (1896), xiii. 1; GRIESBACH, in Arch. f. Hygiene (1895), xxiv. 124; LEUBA, in Psychol. Rev. (1899), vi. 573; GERMANN, ibid., 599. See also MACDOUGALL (as cited above), résumé and criticism; JOTEYKO, extensive résumé and bibliog. (to 1899) of muscular fatigue, &c., Année Psychol. (1898), v; HENRI (ibid.) on muscular sense. See also citations under MUSCULAR SENSATION. (E.B.T.—L.M.—J.M.B.)

Fatigue (physical). (1) Nervous: those changes observed in the nerve cell due to excessive functioning.

Recent experiments have shown that excessive or long-continued activity in nerve

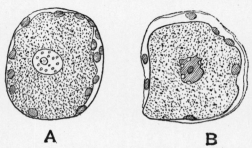

A and B   Resting and Fatigued Ganglion
Cells.   (After Hodge.)

cells produces changes in their size and histological appearance. The activity of a nerve-cell is at first accompanied by turgescence of the protoplasm, but prolonged activity causes diminution of the size and changes the histological appearance. The nucleus suffers analogous changes. The nucleolus at first increases and then diminishes in size. An excitation continued for six hours produced in one case a shrinkage of 16·50 per cent. in ganglion cells. See the figure. Consult especially the works of Hodge, Tuke, Mann, Lugaro, Sadovski, Whitwell, Roth, cited in the list given below.

Literature: A. MOSSO, Les Phénomènes psychiques et la Température du Cerveau (Turin, 1892), and Arch. Ital. de Biol., xviii (1892), Eng. trans. in Philos. Trans. Roy. Soc., clxxxiii (1893); La Fatica (trans. into Fr. and Ger.); C. F. HODGE, Study of Changes due to Functional Activity in Nerve Cells, J. of Morphol., vii (1892) (contains a good bibliography); Die Nervenzellen bei der Geburt und beim Tode an Altersschwäche, Anat. Anz., xi (1894); VAS, Studien über den Bau des Chromatins in der sympathischen Ganglienzelle, Arch. f. mikr. Anat., xl (1892); P. VEJAS, Ein Beitr. z. Anat. u. Physiol. d. Spinalganglien (Munich, 1883); G. MANN, Histological Changes induced in Sympathetic, Motor, and Sensory Nerve Cells by Functional Activity, J. of Anat. and Physiol., xxix (1894); E. LUGARO, Sulle Modificazioni delle Cellule, Lo Sperimentale, xlix (1895), also in Arch. Ital. de Biol. (1895-6), xxiv; G. LEVI, Contributo alla Fisiologia della Cellula nervosa, Riv. di Patol. Nerv. e Ment., i (1896); G. B. VALENZA, I Cambiamenti microscopici delle Cellule nervose nella loro Attività funzionale, &c., Mem. R. Accad. delle Sci. di Napoli (1896); FRANZ NISSL, Die Beziehungen d. Nervenzellensubstanzen zu den thätigen ruhenden u. ermüdeten Zellzuständen, Neurol. Centralbl. (1896), xv. 20; HODGE, Changes in Ganglion Cells from Birth to Senile Death, J. of Physiol. (1894), xvii; A Microsc. Study of the Nerve Cell during Electr. Stimulation, J. of Morphol. (1894), ix; M. LAMBERT, Note sur les modifications produites par l'excitation électrique dans les cellules nerveuses des ganglions sympathiques, C. R. Soc. de Biol. (Paris, 1893), v; F. C. EVE, Sympathetic Nerve Cells and their Basophile Constituents in Prolonged Activity and Repose, J. of Physiol. (1896), xx; C. A. PUGNAT, Sur les modifications histologiques des cellules nerveuses dans l'état de fatigue, C. R. de l'Acad. d. Sci. (Paris, 1896), cxxx; L. JACOBSOHN, Ueber das Aussehen d. motorischen Zellen im Vorderhorn des Rückenmarks nach Ruhe u. Hunger, Neurol. Centralbl. (1897), xvi. (H.H.)

(2) Muscular: see FATIGUE (mental), MUSCLE, and MUSCULAR SENSATION (3).

Fault (moral) [Lat. *fallere*, to deceive]: Ger. *Fehler*, *Schuld* (guilt); Fr. *faute*; Ital. *fallo*. Used without precise definition for (1) a less serious moral defect; (2) a less important morally wrong or theologically sinful act; (3) the fact of responsibility for moral or other evil consequences.

Rousseau says in *Émile*, 'it is better to commit a fault (sense 2) than to contract a vice.' The expression, 'it is his fault,' illustrates meaning (3); cf. also the distinction among sins as venial, heinous, &c. See SIN, WRONG, and VICE. (J.M.B.)

Fear [AS. *fær*]: Ger. *Furcht*; Fr. *peur*, *crainte* (higher forms); Ital. *paura*, *timore* (higher). (1) An emotion, arising in a situation demanding practical adjustment; but of such a nature as to disable and disconcert either by its strangeness or by the threat of approaching evil. In intense fear no form of adjustment may be possible except evasion or escape; and in extreme cases even these are impossible. (G.F.S., J.M.B.)

(2) The emotion arising from the EXPECTATION (q. v.) of what is disagreeable. In this sense fear is contrasted with hope, as in the expression 'hopes and fears.' See HOPE AND DESPAIR. (J.M.B., G.F.S.)

(1) Fear belongs to the primary emotions, i.e. to those which are found at every level of mental development above the mere sense reflex. It may have its source either in the disconcerting strangeness or obtrusiveness of an occurrence, or in previous painful experiences connected with the object which occasions it. Some writers (e. g. Spencer and H. M. Stanley) have laid one-sided emphasis on the second mode of origin. Spencer seems to identify fear (at least in its primitive form) with the revival of past painful experiences with connected motor activities. 'To have in a slight degree such psychical states as accompany the reception of wounds, and are experienced during flight, is to be in a state of what we call fear' (*Psychology*, viii. 213). H. M. Stanley agrees in affirming that 'we can only have the pain of fear so far as we have experienced pain.' But he denies, with good reason, that the pain of fear is merely a reoccurrence of the previous painful experiences on which it depends. Yet he goes to the other extreme in emphasizing a supposed 'pain at pain.' Both Stanley and Spencer seem to neglect the other possible occasion of fear—the startling and disconcerting effect of a strange, sudden, or violently obtrusive occurrence. But this is an undoubted condition of great importance, even in primitive forms of the emotion. The contrast between meanings (1) and (2) is that between lower or organic and higher or intellectual EMOTION (q.v.).

Literature: DARWIN, Expression of Emotions, 290 ff.; MOSSO, Fear (Eng. trans.); SPENCER, Princ. of Psychol., viii. 213; H. M. STANLEY, Evolutionary Psychol., chap. vii; W. JAMES, Principles, ii. 396, 415, 446; STOUT, Manual of Psychol. On the genetic relation between fears of the two sorts, see SCHNEIDER, Der thierische Wille, and BALDWIN, Social and Eth. Interpret., chap. vi. (G.F.S.–J.M.B.)

Fear (in religion). (1) A self-regarding emotion which had widespread influence on the character of religious thought and practices, especially in the higher animistic stage when sacrifices, magic, &c., became prevalent.

At the same time, it should be noted that this influence may be easily exaggerated. For it has to be remembered that, after ceremonies had crystallized sufficiently, their due observance often transformed fear into confidence—confidence born of the realized propitiation of the cause of terror. It is customary to trace this phase of fear to the feeling of DEPENDENCE (q.v.): hence such a famous phrase as 'Primus in orbe deos fecit timor' (Statius, *Theb.*, iii. 661).

(2) In religions which contain a strong moral infusion, representing a much higher stage than that alluded to above, fear commonly implies conviction of misdeed. Here 'conscience doth make cowards of us all.'

The self-regarding emotion gives place to an altruistic tendency caused by the connection which 'conscience' forms with the object of worship. Such phrases as 'Perfect love casteth out fear' (1 John iv. 18), and 'The fear of the Lord is the beginning of wisdom' (Ps. cxi. 10), point to a devotion which obliterates mere self, and by this very fact lifts man to the highest religious level. Cf. RELIGION (psychology of).

Literature: A. RÉVILLE, Prolegomena to the Hist. of Religions (Eng. trans.), 30 f., 67 f.; TEICHMÜLLER, Religionsphilosophie, 32 f. The subject is treated incidentally in all competent works on primitive civilization. (R.M.W.)

Fechner, Gustav Theodor. (1801–87.) A German scientist, educated at Sorau, Dresden, and Leipzig (in medicine), where he became professor of physics, 1834–9. He wrote on a wide range of subjects, and contributed much to aesthetics, psychophysics, ethics, and the theory of electricity. See the next topic.

Fechner's Law: Ger. *das Fechner'sche Gesetz*; Fr. *loi de Fechner*; Ital. *legge di Fechner*. A deduction made by Fechner from WEBER'S LAW (q. v.), and called by him 'law of intensity' (Massgesetz), stating that the intensity of sensation increases as the logarithm of the stimulus.

Expressed as an equation, called the 'measurement formula' (Massformel), it is
$$I = C \log S,$$
in which I is the intensity of sensation, S the stimulus, and C a constant to be determined for different senses, different individuals, &c. If just noticeable differences in sensation are proportional parts of the stimulus (Weber's law), and if the just noticeable difference, including the threshold, may be used as a

unit for measuring sensation, Fechner's law is valid, but these assumptions are questioned by many authorities. Wundt and other writers do not distinguish the law of Fechner from Weber's law. See the literature cited under PSYCHOPHYSICS and WEBER'S LAW, and in BIBLIOG. G, I, *d*. (J.MᶜK.C.)

Feder, Johann Georg Heinrich. (1740–1825.) A German who became professor of philosophy at Göttingen, 1768–97, and then director of the Georgianum at Hanover until his death.

Federation [Lat. *foederare*, to league together]: Ger. *Bundesstaat, Staatenbund*; Fr. *état fédéral*; Ital. (*con-*)*federazione*. A political community formed by the combination of a number of smaller communities which remain distinct, although united.

The only statement which can be made about all federations is that they have their origin in a pact or treaty. In other respects, they differ very widely among themselves. Some federations have been little more than leagues of sovereign states. The federal pact has differed from an ordinary alliance chiefly in its greater permanence. (F.C.M.)

Feeble-mindedness: Ger. *Schwachsinnigkeit, Beschränktheit*; Fr. *faiblesse mentale*; Ital. *semplicità di spirito*. A minor degree of defective intelligence. Cf. IDIOCY, and IMBECILITY. (J.J.)

Feeling [AS. *felan*]: Ger. *Gefühl*; Fr. *sentiment*; Ital. *sentimento* (an imperfect rendering of feeling and Gefühl. The Latin-Italian forms fail to reflect the shades of meaning of feeling and sentiment in the abstract—E.M.). Consciousness as experiencing modifications abstracted from (1) the determination of objects, and (2) the determination of action.

Despite the current controversies about feeling and the wide differences of usage—both of which are equally embarrassing in the other modern languages—and indeed because of them, a certain disposition has sprung up to adopt a wide sense of the term as against the narrower usages. The above definition aims (1) to recognize what is historically common in the usages of the languages having the equivalent terms. This excludes a variety of special definitions. (2) It aims to mark off a phase of mental life which current psychology recognizes with great unanimity, and more or less adequately expresses in various statements of the so-called 'threefold classification,' knowledge, feeling, and will, and which is fixed also in popular speech. (3) It allows unre-

stricted analysis looking toward further determination of feeling and its characters—pleasure, pain, excitement, &c.—and also of its psychophysical explanation by 'incoming' or 'outgoing' currents, by central processes, or what not. (4) It also admits free genetic inquiry into the stages of feeling, from the simplest, where object and action-determination may be held to be absent or to have any degree of conscious presence, up to the highest emotions, where these determinations may be so prominent that feeling can be assumed only by abstraction. (5) It allows both the analytic and the genetic discussion of the hedonic problem, making no preliminary decision on such matters as indifference, inhibition, fusion, summation, &c.

The growing demand for such a broad definition shows itself in the currency attained by the word affection, with its adjective form affective; and the fact that the adjective is more widely used than the noun indicates, in so far, that feeling is an abstraction from a concrete state of mind. (The use of the adjective affective seems to have come into English through the French.) Moreover, the noun affection is applied to the abstraction itself considered as a hypothetical element in the mental life. This has the danger of leading to the misuse of the abstraction—a danger pointed out as real also in the case of CONATION (q.v.)—and the failure to start out from the concrete. The recommendation accordingly is (1) that Feeling be used for this phase of experience in its combination, with knowledge and will, in a concrete state of mind, i.e. as a consciously made abstraction from a richer whole; (2) that Affective be employed as synonymous with feeling used adjectively; and (3) that Affection be used for the purely hypothetical element which underlies the concrete manifestations of feeling. This is carried out in the definitions of AFFECT, AFFECTIVE (or FEELING) TONE, and AFFECTION (see those terms).

Literature: the general works on psychology, and also the works cited in BIBLIOG. G, 2, *e*—especially the discussions of HAMILTON, WUNDT, LEHMANN, LADD, WARD, STOUT, BALDWIN. JAMES' usage is erratic here, as in other cases. Special questions concerning feeling are noted under PAIN AND PLEASURE, EMOTION, and CLASSIFICATION (of the mental functions). (J.M.B., G.F.S.)

Feeling (aesthetic). (1) The affective thrill arising upon the contemplation of beautiful or impressive objects; the capacity of response to aesthetic stimuli. (2) The atmosphere or emotional tone characterizing the whole or any part of an aesthetic object.

The history of the analysis of aesthetic feeling as such is intimately bound up with the development of psychology. Plato and Aristotle both developed theories of pleasure and pain, and subsequent philosophic writers elaborate more or less upon their views. But it is not until the time of Kant and his immediate predecessors that we meet with a really serious attempt to differentiate feeling as an element of aesthetic experiences, and submit it to critical examination. Sulzer, writing under the influence of Leibnitz, may be mentioned as the first to carry out such a systematic analysis. He finds in feeling the essential characteristic of primitive consciousness. The pleasure actually felt in the beautiful, he insists, is to be referred to the increased feeling of mental activity—a doctrine closely related to Aristotle's theory of pleasure—although he admits with the Wolffians that the nature of beauty itself rests upon perfect unity in plurality. Tetens and Kant are largely responsible for the adoption of the term feeling (Gefühl) to designate the agreeable and disagreeable aspect of conscious processes, the term sensation (Empfindung) having generally been used before. Kant's development of the principle of aesthetic judgment involves a recognition of the significance on the one hand of aesthetic feeling merely as such, and on the other hand an elaboration of the more distinctly intellectual factors entering into aesthetic experiences. For him the act in which beauty is perceived constitutes essentially an implicit judgment in terms of feeling. This judgment rests ultimately upon the adaptation of the perceived object to our mental capacities. Under the influence of interests which were more distinctly ethical, Home, Hutcheson, Shaftesbury, Burke, and other English writers developed an analysis of feeling which, despite its shortcomings, marks a distinct advance in the attempts to unravel the complexities of aesthetic experience. Thus Shaftesbury reduces the moral sense and the sense for beauty to a fundamental regard in the mind for harmony and proportion wherever found. Hutcheson goes further, and maintains that we possess an 'internal sense,' through which we perceive beauty. This, too, is apparently much what Burke means, when he speaks of 'taste' as a name for the faculty with which we judge works of art. Coming to more recent treatments, we may mention the

tendency shown by certain aestheticians toward the recognition of feeling as the basal aesthetic category, from which aesthetic theory should proceed. This movement is in somewhat definite antithesis to the logical, ethical, and metaphysical trend of those writers who emphasize more particularly form and content as the fundamental aesthetic elements. Köstlin, Carrière, and Bosanquet may serve as illustrations of the latter trend; Kirchmann, Horwicz, and Marshall of the former. Cf. SENTIMENT.

Literature: for general treatises, see AESTHETICS; indications under FEELING; NAHLOWSKY, Das Gefühlsleben (1884); LEHMANN, Hauptgesetze des menschlichen Gefühlslebens (1892); GROOS, Einleitung in d. Aesthetik; HARTMANN, Aesthetik (1886-7); MARSHALL, Pain, Pleasure, and Aesthetics (1894). (J.R.A.)

Feigning (in biology): see MAKE-BELIEVE (3).

Felapton: see MOOD (in logic).

Felicific [Lat. *felix*, happy, + *facere*, to make]: Ger. *glückbringend*; Fr. *agréable, qui donne le bonheur, visant au bonheur*; Ital. *felicitare* (verb). Tending to produce happiness.

That the morality of conduct depends upon its felicific consequences is the thesis of EUDAEMONISM and of HEDONISM. See those terms. (W.R.S.)

Felicity: Ger. *Glück*; Fr. *félicité, bonheur*; Ital. *felicità*. See HAPPINESS, and FELICIFIC.

Female [Lat. *femina*, a woman]: Ger. *weibliches Wesen*; Fr. *femelle*; Ital. *femmina*. That organism which produces ova or ovules.

The differentiation of the sexes forms an interesting subject of study both in botany and zoology. The theory of evolution has given it prominence. Associated with the differentiation of sex there has been a differentiation in the sexual individuals giving rise to the secondary SEXUAL CHARACTERS (q. v.).

Literature: O. HERTWIG, Die Zelle u. die Gewebe (1893); Y. DELAGE, Structure du Protoplasma et l'Hérédité (1895); GEDDES and THOMSON, Evolution of Sex (1889). (C.LL.M.)

Feminism: see EFFEMINACY.

Fénelon, François de Salignac de la Mothe. (1651-1715.) Born at Périgord, France, he went to the University of Cahors in 1663; afterwards, to the college of Plessis. He began preaching in 1666, went to the seminary of St. Sulpice, and received holy orders about 1675. In 1678 he became superior of the order of Nouvelles Catholiques, and in 1686 was sent by Louis XIV to Poitou to convert Protestants. He became preceptor to the duke of Burgundy in 1689; tutor to the duke of Anjou in 1690, and to the duke of Berri in 1693; member of the French Academy the same year; archbishop of Cambray in 1695. He died at Cambray.

Ferguson, Adam. (1723–1816.) A Scottish philosopher and historian, educated at St. Andrews and Edinburgh. He was ordained in 1745. He was professor of natural philosophy at Edinburgh, 1759–64; professor of moral philosophy, 1764–85. He was one of the commissioners sent from England to the United States to effect peace in 1778.

Ferio, Ferison: see MOOD (in logic).

Ferrari, Giuseppe. (1811–76.) Italian historian and philosopher. Born at Milan, and educated in law at Pavia. He devoted himself to literature. In 1840 he was chosen professor of philosophy at Rochefort, and later at Strassburg. He was removed from the latter position on account of his communistic ideas. In 1848 he was reinstated at Strassburg, but again removed. In 1859 he returned to Italy, and became professor of philosophy first at Turin, then at Milan, and finally at Florence.

Ferri, Luigi. (1826–95.) Born at Bologna; studied at the Paris Normal School. He was made professor of history in the Istituto di Perfezionamento at Florence in 1863, and in 1871 became professor of theoretical philosophy at the University of Rome. On the death of Mamiani in 1885, he became editor of *Filosofia delle Scuole italiane*, the title of which he altered to *Rivista italiana di Filosofia*. He was eclectic, showing chiefly the influence of his French training and of Mamiani and the Italian metaphysicians.

Ferrier, James Frederick. (1808–64.) A Scottish moral philosopher, born at Edinburgh and educated at Magdalen College, Oxford. In 1842 he became professor of history at Edinburgh, and in 1845 professor of moral philosophy at St. Andrews. His fame rests on his *Institutes of Metaphysics*.

Ferrier's Experiment: Ger. *Ferrier'scher Versuch*; Fr. *expérience de Ferrier*; Ital. *esperimento di Ferrier*. An experiment, devised by D. Ferrier, in disproof of 'innervation sensations' supposed to arise from efferent nervous processes.

The effort experienced when there is vigorous thought of a movement, but no execution of it, is shown by Ferrier's experiment (as e.g. holding the finger on the trigger of a gun and making the usual effort, while the finger is held still) to consist of respiratory sensations and sensations from actual movement of other muscles.

Literature: D. FERRIER, Functions of the Brain (2nd ed.), 386; SANFORD, Course in Exper. Psychol., expt. 38.　　(E.B.T.–J.M.B.)

Fertility [Lat. *fertilis*, fruitful, from *ferre*, to bear]: Ger. *Fruchtbarkeit, Zeugungsfähigkeit*; Fr. *fertilité* (*fécondité*); Ital. *fertilità* (*fecondità*). The power of producing a relatively large number of young by sexual reproduction.

It is a somewhat vague term, since such fertility may be due to several distinct causes. The 'gross fertility' of a species is the ratio of the number of parents to the number of fertilized germ-cells, which is approximately the number of ova matured. Species differ widely in this respect; in some cases thousands of eggs are produced, as in many fish, in other cases only a few, or even one at a time, as in man.

The 'net' (or 'effective,' see below) fertility of a species is the ratio between the number of parents and the number of offspring which reach sexual maturity. Owing to the destruction of large numbers of young, it does not by any means follow that a species will numerically increase because its gross fertility is very great. See NATURAL SELECTION.

Fertility is, of course, subject to individual variation and modification. See STERILITY. That fertility is inherited has recently been shown by Karl Pearson, to whom the distinction between 'gross' and 'net' fertility is due. As a rule species which differ considerably in structure are not fertile *inter se*. See HYBRID.　　(E.S.G.)

The term 'effective' fertility is suggested to bring out the evolutionary significance of Pearson's distinction: only those individuals of the offspring which live to exercise the reproductive capacity are 'effective' or significant as representing the fertility of their parents. The idea that fertility is correlated with other characters—taken with the idea that fertility is inherited—lies at the foundation of Pearson's theory of REPRODUCTIVE (or GENETIC) SELECTION (q. v.).　　(J.M.B.)

Literature: CH. DARWIN, Origin of Species (1859), and Animals and Plants under Domestication; K. PEARSON, The Chances of Death, i (1897); Mathematical Contrib. to the Theory of Evolution, vi, Philos. Trans. Roy. Soc., v. 192 (1899); and Grammar of Science (2nd ed.), chap. **xii**; see also under the topics referred to.　　(E.S.G.)

Fertilization [Lat. *fertilis*, fruitful]: Ger. *Befruchtung*; Fr. *fécondation*; Ital. *fecondazione*. Of animals: the process which occurs in all cases of sexual reproduction, consisting essentially in the union of two cells, derived generally from different parents, and termed respectively in animals the OVUM (q. v.) and the SPERMATOZOON (q. v.).

Of plants: the process by which the pollen is conveyed to the stigma.

Modern views of fertilization or fecundation are intimately associated with the later developments of the CELL THEORY (q. v.). Newport in 1854 observed the penetration of the ovum by the spermatozoon in the case of the frog. O. Hertwig showed in 1875 that in an egg fertilized by a spermatozoon there are two nuclei: one due to the spermatozoon; the other that of the ovum itself. Later research has shown that the essential feature of fertilization is the union of a sperm-nucleus of paternal origin with a germ-nucleus of maternal origin. The meaning of the process is still *sub judice*. According to some (Bütchli, 1876), its purpose is to afford an impetus to the cell-divisions necessary for development. According to others (Weismann, 1891), its purpose is to secure a sharing of those nuclear elements (chromosomes), which are perhaps the bearers of heredity, and which, according to some recent observers, remain separate throughout all cell-divisions, so that each cell contains chromosomes derived genetically both from those of the sperm and from those of the ovum. Weismann regards the process as productive of variation; Haeckel as a means of checking variation. Another view (Boveri, 1887) to some extent combines the theory of impetus with that of hereditary sharing. The spermatozoon is by many held to supply the CENTROSOME (q. v.) which is effective in the division or cleavage of the ovum, the chromosomes being the hereditary substance which is thus divided, while the ovum supplies the cell-substance which surrounds the dividing nuclei. Artificial chemical fertilization has recently been experimentally produced by Loeb (Amer. J. Physiol., iii, Oct. 1889; iv, Jan. 1901). See PARTHENOGENESIS.

Literature: see EMBRYOLOGY, and CELL THEORY. (C.LL.M.)

Fesapo, Festino: see MOOD (in logic).

Fetich (or -ish) and **Fetichism** (or -shism, or -cism) [derivation, see below]: Ger. *Fetisch, Fetischismus*; Fr. *fétiche, fétichisme*; Ital. *feticcio, feticismo*. Any object to which peculiar potency is attached by reason (1) of the supposed indwelling of a deity or spirit; (2) of its being regarded as a sign, token, or representation of such spirit; or (3) of some intrinsic peculiarity in structure, origin, &c.

The term was applied by the Portuguese in West Africa to the small objects, sticks and stones, claws, plants, &c., venerated by the natives, which they interpreted as charms. The French and English adopted the meaning from the Portuguese, although both languages already had the word: ' And French she spak ful faire and fetysly ' (Chaucer). The term was first used in a scholarly sense by de Brosses, 1760, and its modern use is due to Tylor, Lubbock, and Schulze.

Fetichism is an important factor in the natural religions of primitive peoples. Any object may become a fetich, but there is a natural tendency to select, for the embodiment of hidden power, odd and unusual bits of stone, twigs, bark, root, corn, claws of bird or beast, teeth, skin, feathers, human and animal remains, and a host of curious trifles that chance discovers. The fetich becomes a charm which may be worshipped, prayed to, or petted, and thus may become the means of securing the good things and avoiding the ills of life. If disaster ensue the fetich may be trodden on and beaten until a change of luck produces apologies and promise of future regard. The fetich need not be the actual abiding-place of the spirit, but may be connected with it in some symbolic or mystic manner. Likewise, too, injury worked upon the representative or effigy may redound by sympathetic magic upon the original. It thus may become a form of witchcraft, which in turn leads to counter-charms and magical preventives. The doctrine is closely related to the spirit theory of disease, and to the general animistic conceptions (see ANIMISM) of both nature and religion which are so closely merged in primitive thought.

Literature: TYLOR, Primitive Culture, ii. 143 ff., and elsewhere; SCHULTZE, Der Fetichismus (Eng. trans. in Humboldt Library), and references there given. Also references under RELIGION (evolution of). (J.J.)

Fetich (in pathology). In certain perversions of the sexual instinct, the person, part of the body, or particular object belonging to the person by whom the impulse is excited, is called the fetich of the patient. So used by Lombroso and Binet (*Fétichisme dans l'Amour*). Cf. PERVERSION (sexual). (E.M.)

Feudal System: see TENURE.

Feuerbach, Ludwig Andreas. (1804–72.) A German philosophical writer. Born at Landshut, educated at Heidelberg and Berlin in theology and philosophy. Became a Docent in Erlangen, 1828–32, but injured his chance of promotion by a public denial of immortality.

He lived for a long time on his own property at Ansbach, writing prolifically. In 1860 he moved to Rochenberg, near Nuremberg, where he died.

Fiat (of will) [Lat.]: Ger. *Willensentschluss*; Fr. *décision volontaire*; Ital. *decisione*. The state of consciousness which exists in the moment of deciding between alternative courses of action. The negative form of fiat, i. e. the fiat to stop, check, inhibit, &c., has been called 'veto' or 'negat.'

Literature: (fiat) JAMES, Princ. of Psychol., ii. 501, 526, 561, 568; (veto) BALDWIN, Feeling and Will, chap. xv.   (G.F.S.–J.M.B.)

Fibre and **Fibril**: see NERVOUS SYSTEM, III.

Fichte, Immanuel Hermann von. (1797–1879.) German philosopher, son of Johann Gottlieb Fichte. Educated in philology in Berlin, his father's system of philosophy attracted him, and he devoted himself to it. He opposed Hegel, and in 1836 became professor of philosophy at Bonn; 1842–63 at Tübingen. After 1863 he lived in private life at Stuttgart.

Fichte, Johann Gottlieb. (1762–1814.) A German philosopher. Baron von Miltitz placed the lad successively in the family of a clergyman at Niederau, at the town school at Meissen, and at the Princes' School of Pforta, where he read Goethe, Wieland, and Lessing. Studied theology at Jena and Leipzig. He read Spinoza and Wolff, and became a fatalist. After several years spent as private tutor in Zurich, he returned to Leipzig (1790) and studied the Kantian critiques. In 1794 he became professor of philosophy at Jena, where he met Goethe, Schiller, Wieland, Herder, Humboldt, and Jacobi. He also fell into correspondence with Reinhold, whom he had succeeded at Jena, the Schlegels, Tieck, Schelling, and Novalis. In 1799, charged with atheism, disclaimed as an exponent of the critical philosophy by Kant, and criticized severely for a work on the French Revolution, he resigned his position and withdrew to Berlin, where he became rector of the new University of Berlin. Fichte's system is often designated Ethical Idealism. He died at Berlin.

Ficino (**Ficinus**), **Marsiglio** (**Marsiglius**). (1433–99.) Celebrated Italian scholar and philosopher. He was carefully educated by Cosimo de' Medici for a position at the head of an academy of Platonism, which was afterwards founded (1460). The art of printing was invented, and Ficino translated into Latin the entire works of Plato and Plotinus, adding commentaries to each. He claimed to harmonize Platonism with Christianity, and founded a school of mystics which included Reuchlin, Agrippa of Nettesheim, Ramus, Telesino, and others. He with others opposed Pomponatius.

Fidelity of Reproduction: Ger. *Reproduktionstreue*; Fr. *fidélité de reproduction*; Ital. *fedeltà di riproduzione*. A phrase introduced by Müller and Külpe for the relative accuracy of memory.

Its investigation is theoretically important, as bearing upon the older associationist theory that memory, recognition, &c., imply the comparison of a given impression with its memory image. The method of 'reproduction' (see MEMORY, experiments on) aims to secure its quantitative measurement.   (E.B.T.–J.M.B.)

Literature: KÜLPE, Outlines of Psychol., 197, 207; KENNEDY, Psychol. Rev., v. (1898) 477 (with bibliog.); BENTLEY, Amer. J. of Psychol., xi. 1 ff.; ANGELL and HARWOOD, ibid., 67 ff.; citations under MEMORY (experiments on).

Fides: see BONA FIDES.

Field of Consciousness: Ger. *Umfang des Bewusstseins*; Fr. *champ de la conscience*; Ital. *campo della coscienza*. Consciousness, with all that is in it at any one time, considered as a spread-out area.

The 'field' is analogous with field of vision in many details, attention being likened to fixation, inattention to indirect vision, the movements of attention to the exploration of the field of regard. 'Area of consciousness' is often employed to translate Umfang des Bewusstseins, especially when the German phrase is used to denote the apprehension of the maximum number of successive stimulations (sounds, &c.) in a single pulse of attention without readjustment; but 'span of consciousness' is better in this latter sense.   (J.M.B.)

The field of consciousness varies with individuals, with conditions of attention, with states of health or disease. Remarkable narrowing of the field occurs in states of distraction, in certain anaesthesias, in suggestive (notably hypnotic) states, in the psychoses of fixed ideas. For the distinctions of parts of the field with respect to vividness or degree, see SUBCONSCIOUS.   (P.J.–J.M.B.)

Literature: the psychologies generally, especially WUNDT and JAMES. Experimental studies have been made principally on the SPAN OF CONSCIOUSNESS (q. v.).   (J.M.B.)

Field of Regard: Ger. *Blickfeld*; Fr. *champ de regard*; Ital. *campo di sguardo*. The space which can be traversed by the regard of the moving eye; the fixation field of the eye when moved. Where only distant objects come into consideration, it stands to the field of vision as the projection of an unchanging retinal image stands to the projection of the retina itself.

Literature: HELMHOLTZ, Physiol. Optik (2nd ed.), 617, 677, 680; SANFORD, Course in Exper. Psychol., 119, 434; AUBERT, Physiol. Optik, 593, 646, 663 f.; HERING, in Hermann's Handb. d. Physiol., iii. 1, 442 ff.; WUNDT, Physiol. Psychol. (4th ed.), ii. 125 f. See also FIELD OF VISION. (E.B.T.–E.C.S.)

Field of Touch: Ger. *Tastfeld*; Fr. *champ tactile* (rarely used, ambiguous—L.M.); Ital. *campo tattile*. A phrase formed after the analogy of 'field of vision,' to denote the sum-total of tactile sensations aroused by stimuli acting upon the skin at any one time. It is thus, so to speak, the 'projection' of the skin, as the field of vision is the projection of the retina. (E.B.T.–J.M.B.)

Field of Vision: Ger. *Sehfeld, Gesichtsfeld* (*Gesichtskreis*); Fr. *champ visuel*; Ital. *campo visivo*. The sum-total of visual sensations aroused by stimuli acting on the unmoved retina at any given time.

'The field of vision is, so to speak, the outward projection of the retina, with all its images and other peculiarities' (Helmholtz, *Physiol. Optik*, 2nd ed., 679). The field of vision moves, therefore, with movement of the eyes. It may be conceived of, in general, as a hollow hemisphere, shifted concentrically upon a similar hemisphere of slightly different radius—the FIELD OF REGARD (q.v.).

Literature: SANFORD, Course in Exper. Psychol., 119; WUNDT, Physiol. Psychol. (4th ed.), ii. 108, 126; AUBERT, Physiol. Optik, 591, 609; HERING, in Hermann's Handb. d. Physiol., iii. 1, 351; HELMHOLTZ, Physiol. Optik (2nd ed.), 678, 680. (E.B.T.–E.C.S.)

Figure (and **Figurative**) (in aesthetics) [Lat. *figura*, from *fingere*, to form]: Ger. (1) *Figur*, (2) *Bild* (*bildlich*); Fr. *figure*, *figuré*; Ital. *figura, figurativo*. (1) Form or shape, considered with especial reference to outline. (2) A form or image. (3) A word or words used in a sense other than their usual meaning, especially when a concrete sensuous image is used to convey an abstract concept or relation.

The aesthetic value of figurative language seems to reside mainly in (1) the thrill or resonance of feeling which is attendant upon the sensuous image; whereas in dealing with abstract terms the image is relatively vague, and the feeling element correspondingly lacking; (2) pleasurable elements or values of any sort attaching to our experiences suggested by the image and transferred by association to the thought presented; (3) the recognition of an analogy or underlying unity between various objects or parts of experience, having the aesthetic value of unity in variety. Cf. SYMBOL, and UNITY IN VARIETY. (J.H.T.)

Figure (syllogistic): Ger. *Schlussfigur*; Fr. *figure du syllogisme*; Ital. *figure del sillogismo*. Figure is the modification of the categorical syllogism, consequent on the relation in which the middle term stands to the major and minor terms in the premises.

Each of the possible relations, which—position only being taken into account—are four in number, determines a special figure or type of syllogism. For each figure there may be formulated special rules, embodying the particular conditions required in order that reasoning of that type shall conform to the fundamental general rules of syllogism. Practically, the special rules state the conditions necessary to secure for each position of the middle term that the middle term shall be once distributed, and that no term shall be distributed in the conclusion which was not distributed in the premises.

Only three figures, those commonly reckoned as I, II, and III, were recognized by Aristotle, whose grounds for the limitation are not explicit and have been matter of dispute. What was afterwards recognized as a IV figure was not indeed ignored by Aristotle, and its varieties or moods were elaborately worked out by the earlier Peripatetics, who still regarded them as indirect modifications of the I figure. By whom the IV figure was explicitly constituted, we do not know. Galen, on the authority of Averroes, has the credit of it, but the matter is doubtful. Cf. MOOD (in logic).

Literature: UEBERWEG, Logik, § 103; HAMILTON, Lect. on Logic, App. X, and Discussions, App. II. A. In modern logic, discussion as to the grounds and value of the distinctions of figure was revived by KANT (see especially his tract, False Subtlety of the Four Syll. Figures, 1762, trans. by T. K. ABBOT, in Kant's Introd. to Logic, 1885), and had some importance assigned to it by Hamilton, mainly in connection with his doctrine of unfigured syllogism. See REDUCTION, and QUANTIFICATION OF THE PREDICATE. In LAMBERT's Neues Organon (i. Pt. IV, especially § 232) an attempt is made to recognize a distinct function for each figure, and to formulate for each a principle or dictum. HERBART (Lehrbuch, § 68) contrasts the I and II figures as subsumptive, with the III figure as substitutive, a distinction which is partially adopted, though without expressive reference to the figure, in LOTZE's view of the types of reasoning (Logik, §§ 97 ff.). (R.A.)

Filioque [Lat.]. The Nicene Creed as said in the churches of the West (Roman Catholic, Anglican, Protestant Episcopal in the United States) contains the following passage: 'I believe in the Holy Ghost, the Lord and Giver of life, Who proceedeth from the Father *and the Son*' (*filioque*). The italicized words were not in the original creed, and emerged first at the third Council of Toledo (589). Continued controversy with the ARIAN (q.v.) party doubtless caused their insertion, which was not approved till Charlemagne's Council of Aix-la-Chapelle (809). Even thereafter Leo III does not recommend their usage, which, so far as the popes are concerned, dates as late as Benedict VIII (1014).

The insertion of the word raised the influential dogmatic controversy concerning the 'single and double procession of the Holy Spirit,' over which the final separation between the Eastern and the Western churches took place. It involves the whole question of the nature of the Trinity—'in essence' and 'in revelation.' The Bonn Conference of 1875 (Old Catholic) proposed as a substitute the reading, 'I believe in the Holy Ghost, Who proceeds from the Father *through* the Son.'

Literature: FFOULKES, Historical Account of the Addition of the Word 'Filioque' to the Creed; LANGEN, Die trinitar. Lehrdifferenz zw. d. abendl. u. d. morgenl. Kirche; SCHAFF, Creeds of Christendom, ii. 545 f.; HOWARD, The Schism between the Oriental and Western Churches. (R.M.W.)

Final and **Finality**: see TELEOLOGY.

Final Cause: see CAUSE AND EFFECT, and TELEOLOGY.

Final Utility (abbreviation for 'final degree of utility'): Ger. *Grenznutzen*; Fr. *ophélimité*; Ital. *utilità finale*. The intensity of desire satisfied by the last increment of a commodity purchased or consumed. See MARGINAL INCREMENT.

About 1870, Jevons made an independent discovery of Weber's law in certain new aspects, of which the most important was this: that the value of any stimulus is the degree of satisfaction obtained from its last repetition, and therefore varies inversely with the amount

(or rather with the rate) at which the stimulus is furnished. This was expressed by Jevons in the proposition that value depends not on 'total' utility, but on 'final' degree of utility. Further developments of this matter have been made by Say and Pareto. (A.T.H.)

Finance [OF. *finance*; Med. Lat. *finantia*, money payment]: Ger. *Finanz*; Fr. *finances*; Ital. *finanza*. (1) An orderly arrangement of receipts and expenditures. (2) Especially applied to the receipts and expenses of public corporations. (3) A scientific investigation of the laws governing these receipts and expenses.

A very large part of the early literature of political economy dealt with public finance. In fact one of the early German names for the science was Cameral-Wissenschaft (science of the exchequer). (A.T.H.)

Literature: ADAM SMITH, Wealth of Nations, ii; E. DE PARIEU, Traité des Impôts (1862); P. LEROY-BEAULIEU, Traité de la Sci. des Finances (1877); A. WAGNER, Finanzwiss. (1876 ff.); G. COHN, Finanzwiss. (1889); H. C. ADAMS, The Sci. of Finance (1898).

Fine Art: see ART AND ART THEORIES, and CLASSIFICATION (of the fine arts).

Finite (in mathematics) [Lat. *finis*, end]: A quantity conceived to have some definite value or boundary, as a finite straight line which is bounded by two points between which it lies. (S.N.)

Finite (notion of): Ger. *endlich, begrenzt*; Fr. *fini*; Ital. (*il*) *finito*. The conception of any sort of mental object as being limited or of exhaustible quantity.

The notion of the finite is an abstraction which arises in opposition to INFINITE (notion of, q.v.). The normal object is in a context or setting of which it is a definite or limited part, and normal experience thus makes the assumption of limits without explicit recognition of them as such. When, however, reflection arises upon the fact of limitation or upon the possibility of inexhaustible quantity, the notions of the finite and the infinite arise together. (J.M.B.)

Fire-worship: Ger. *Feueranbetung* (-*cult*); Fr. *culte du feu*; Ital. *culto del fuoco*. Religious observances directed toward fire.

Although we know numerous facts relating to fire-worship, which testify to its wide prevalence among different peoples in various stages of culture, it cannot be said that a complete or even systematic account of the subject is possible as yet. In the lower ranges of culture, fire-worship pertains to

ANIMISM (q.v.) and FETICHISM (q.v.). Fire possesses a spirit which must be propitiated. For while its influence for good is great, man knows but too well, from sad experience, its terrible possibilities for evil. Forest-fires, hut-fires, and the like must have taught those who possessed no means of fighting the flames many a stern lesson. At this stage, either the fire is worshipped itself, being invested with qualities animistically and anthropopathically, or a fire-spirit receives adoration and gifts, the particular fire used in the worship being, as seems most probable, identified at the moment with this spirit. On a still higher level of culture, this fire-spirit is abstracted from all particular fires, and therefore becomes a god— usually one god among others, as in Mexico, among the Semites, in the early nature-worship of India and Persia. (The later religion of eastern Iran, systematized by Zoroaster, is to be distinguished carefully from this last. Here fire gradually became more symbolical and less personal.) At this stage fire is sometimes a theophany (Exod. iii. 2). The main difficulties in dealing with fire-worship, apart from the abounding obscurity of the transition from the animistic to the polytheistic stage, arise from (1) the use of fire in numerous sacrifices unconnected with fire-worship; (2) the fact that worship of fire produced many observances which, although analogous to those connected with sun-worship, do not belong to the latter; and (3) the fact that there is sometimes fire-mythology without a development of fire-worship, as in Polynesia. Cf. ORIENTAL PHILOSOPHY (Persia, India).

Literature: TYLOR, Primitive Culture, ii. 277 f. (where much literature is cited); JEVONS, Introd. to the Hist. of Religion, 229 f.; LUBBOCK, Origin of Civilization, 312. The subject is treated incidentally in many works on primitive society, civilization, and religion. (R.M.W.)

Fission [Lat. *fissus*, a cleft]: Ger. *Theilung*; Fr. *scissiparité*; Ital. *scissiparità*. A method of asexual reproduction among unicellular organisms, the lower Metozoa and the unicellular elements of Metozoa, in which the parent divides into two, often unequal parts. Each half subsequently grows into a complete organism similar to the parent. This process of reproduction is called schizogamy. In the elements of Metozoa the resulting daughter-cells rarely entirely separate. Cf. AGAMOGENESIS and CELL DIVISION. (C.LL.M.—E.S.G.)

Fissure [Lat. *fissura*]: Ger. *Fissur, Furche*;

Fr. *scissure*; Ital. *scissura*. See BRAIN (Glossary).

Fit [ME. *fit*, a fight]: Ger. *Anfall*; Fr. *attaque*; Ital. *attacco* (*di male*, &c.). A popular term applied to any sudden paroxysm or convulsive attack, but particularly to attacks of EPILEPSY, PARALYSIS, or APOPLEXY: see these terms. (J.J.)

Fitness (consciousness of): Ger. *Gefühl der Uebereinstimmung*; Fr. *sentiment de la congruence* (or *d'accord*); Ital. *sentimento di congruità*. A general awareness of congruity or incongruity, not involving any definite recognition of what the congruity or incongruity consists in. It is thought to be an important factor in the constructive processes of IMAGINATION (q. v.).

Literature: the definition follows BALDWIN, Senses and Intellect, 232–4; Feeling and Will, 202. (G.F.S.)

Fitness (in aesthetics): Ger. *Zweckmässigkeit*; Fr. *convenance, finalité*; Ital. *convenienza*. Adaptation of means to end.

As an aesthetic principle this takes two distinct forms, according as the end in question is external or internal. The former gives the principle of utility, as the fitness of a house for a given use conceived as a separate matter from the house itself; the latter gives the principle of intrinsic fitness, as of the parts of the house to the whole. If, however, in the first case we introduce the conception of 'home' as that whole of which the house is a part, we may think of the fitness of the house to realize the idea or purpose of the home, and so the fitness becomes intrinsic. This ambiguity may explain why some have regarded fitness as an aesthetic principle, while others decidedly reject it.

Socrates apparently made fitness, in the sense of usefulness, the supreme aesthetic principle, and Plato allowed it to stand as one element, while recognizing, also, an intrinsic beauty. Cicero distinguished sharply the use from the beauty of objects, though he pointed out that the same form may be at once the most useful and the most beautiful; and Vitruvius agreed with him in holding the two to be independent, though both enter into perfect architecture, which involves 'firmitas,' 'utilitas,' and 'venustas.'

In modern writing, Hutcheson's 'comparative beauty' is nearly the same as intrinsic fitness, while Home's 'beauty of relation' is fitness for some external end. Burke rejects the identification of fitness, which satisfies the understanding, with beauty, which appeals to feeling, although each has its place in a work of art. Kant gave the problem a new turn. He rejected entirely fitness in the sense of utility, admitted intrinsic fitness as a constituent of dependent beauty, and finally made adaptation, not to any objective end, but to our mental powers, an essential characteristic of the beautiful of any sort. With this, fitness easily passes from a formal to a metaphysical principle.

In recent aesthetics the principle of utility has been discussed chiefly in connection with the requirements of architecture, where Ruskin sets it beside 'skill' and 'beauty' as an essential factor; Fechner (*Vorschule der Aesthetik*, i. 203 ff.) gives it an aesthetic value (1) by association, (2) as exemplifying the general aesthetic principle of harmonious co-operation of the parts of a whole, (3) as showing a task or idea successfully met or carried out. Hartmann (*Aesthetik*, ii. 1887) gives extended consideration to the conception of intrinsic fitness or adaptation to an immanent end, as it appears in organic nature, and further makes usefulness an indispensable prerequisite to the beauty of all tools and structures which belong to man's working life. Santayana (*Sense of Beauty*, 1896) considers fitness in the sense of adaptation to environment, and gives it indirect aesthetic value (1) through its establishment of permanent forms, which then become for us the normal or typical; (2) through association. In the third place, it is the principle of organization in the arts (determining the styles of building that shall be permanent), and thus, as in (1), plays a part in beauty. The conception of intrinsic fitness has not received special treatment under that term in recent writing, having passed over apparently into the more definite terms of proportion and harmony, or, in its aspect of conformity to an ideal, into certain aspects of the conception of expression. Carriere, however, makes Zweckmässigkeit, in the sense of immanent purposiveness, the essence of beauty. 'Beauty is perceived purposiveness in a pleasing form.' Cf. BEAUTY, EXPRESSION, HARMONY, PROPORTION, and UTILITY. (J.H.T.)

Fitness (in biology): see FITTEST (survival of the).

Fitness (in philosophy and ethics): Ger. *Angemessenheit*; Fr. *convenance, conformité*; Ital. *convenienza, conformità*. Being adapted or suitable (1) to the nature of things, or (2) to the constitution of man.

In both senses, fitness has been taken by certain moralists as the standard of right conduct. In opposition to Hobbes' doctrine of the dependence of morality upon social institutions, Samuel Clarke laid stress upon 'eternal and necessary differences of things, from which follows the "fitness" of certain actions antecedently to all positive command and irrespective of reward or advantage.' This conception of 'fitness' is common to many of the English moralists. It was made clearest by R. Price, who distinguished two meanings of the word, viz. 'aptitude of any means to an end,' and 'rectitude.' In the latter sense he spoke of 'fitness or duty.' In both of its meanings he held the term to be indefinable—'a simple perception of the understanding.' A less intellectual and more aesthetic view of this fitness had been previously put forward by Shaftesbury and Hutcheson; the latter referring to the 'peculiar perception of decency, dignity, and suitableness of certain actions.' Butler, while expressing assent to the views of Clarke, lays stress himself upon suitability to the constitution of man rather than to the nature of things. Paley, on the other hand, turns the phrase to his own purposes by regarding it as meaning 'fitness to produce happiness,' while Bentham criticizes it as worthless and capable of meaning 'whatever a man likes.'

Literature: S. CLARKE, Boyle Lectures (1706); PRICE, Principal Questions, &c., in Morals (1758). (W.R.S.)

Fittest (survival of the): Ger. *Ueberleben der Passendsten*; Fr. *survivance du plus apte*; Ital. *sopravvivenza del più adatto*. A phrase used to express the effective result of the process of natural selection, during the struggle for EXISTENCE (q. v.), involving survival among (1) individual organisms, (2) groups of organisms.

Suggested by Herbert Spencer shortly after the publication of Darwin's *Origin of Species*, it is sometimes used as equivalent to natural selection ('natural selection or the survival of the fittest'). But natural selection is the process from which the survival of the fittest follows as a result. The term 'fittest' is ambiguous, from its generality. It suggests the question, fittest for what? To which the answer is, fittest for the particular environment of the organism to which the term is applied, environment being used in its widest sense as including other organisms, and as forming a stage on which may be waged any of the forms of 'struggle for existence.' Critics forgetful of this have sometimes objected that those which survive are not the fittest, e. g., in human evolution it is not always the intellectually or morally fittest or highest which survive. The criticism is based on a misapprehension as to the meaning of the term fitness in biology. Fitness indicates any sort of endowment or acquirement by which the animal escapes elimination in the struggle for existence. His survival is *ipso facto* proof of his fitness.

Literature: DARWIN, Origin of Species (1859); SPENCER, Princ. of Biol. (1863–4); works cited under EVOLUTION. (C.LL.M.–J.M.B.)

Fixation of Memories: Ger. *Fixiren der Erinnerungen* (suggested); Fr. *fixation des souvenirs*; Ital. *(il) fissarsi dei ricordi* (E.M.). This term designates all of the conditions under which sense impressions which modify consciousness leave traces or residuals capable of revival in the form of images. (P.J.)

Fixation Point: Ger. *Fixationspunkt, Blickpunkt*; Fr. *point de fixation, point de regard*; Ital. *punto di mira*. 'In normal vision both eyes are so set that they fixate one and the same external point,' which is therefore termed the fixation point or point of regard (Helmholtz, *Physiol. Optik*, 2nd ed., 617). It is the point of the field of regard which corresponds to the stimulation of the centre of the fovea centralis (cf. Wundt, *Physiol. Psychol.*, 4th ed., ii. 99). The primary fixation point is the fixation point in the primary position for CONVERGENCE (q. v.).

Literature: WUNDT, as cited; HERING, in Hermann's Handb. d. Physiol., III. i. 350, 441; AUBERT, Physiol. Optik, 589. (E.B.T.)

Fixed Capital: Ger. *stehendes Kapital*; Fr. *capitaux fixes*; Ital. *capitale fisso*. Permanent investments; instruments of production which are not directly transformed into articles of sale, nor even consumed in production except by a gradual process of attrition or deterioration.

Adam Smith defined fixed capital as consisting of goods which yield a profit without changing masters; and this is substantially Malthus' definition. Ricardo said that it consisted of goods 'of slow consumption.' Mill defines it as capital which exists in a durable shape, and the return to which is spread over a period of corresponding duration, as distinct from circulating capital, which fulfils the whole of its office in the production in which it is engaged by a single use. (A.T.H.)

Fixed Charges: see EXPENSE.

Fixed Idea: Ger. *fixe Idee*; Fr. *idée fixe, obsession*; Ital. *idea fissa, fissazione* (E.M.). The term fixed idea, when used in the sense of a delusion, refers to a morbid or false conception which dominates the reasoning processes of the patient, and forms an integral part of his insanity. The various forms of MONOMANIA (q. v.) may be cited as cases of fixed ideas in this sense. It is also used in the sense of an IMPERATIVE IDEA (q. v., with literature). (J.J.)

Flesh: see BODY.

Flexor and **Extensor Muscles** [Lat. *flectere*, to bend, and *extendere*, to stretch out]: Ger. *Beugmuskel, Streckmuskel*; Fr. *muscle fléchisseur, muscle extenseur*; Ital. *muscolo flessore ed estensore*. Muscles that either bend (flexor) or straighten out (extensor) a joint.

A pair of muscles, one flexor and the other extensor, are called antagonistic muscles. Cf. ANTAGONISM. A common German expression is 'Beuger und Strecker.' For a list of flexor and extensor muscles see Quain's *Anatomy*. (C.F.H.)

Flexure [Lat. *flexura*, a bending]: Ger. *Krümmung*; Fr. *courbure*; Ital. *flessione*. (1) The deviation from a straight line in the axis of a body, especially of the medullary tube. (2) The regions of such bending in the embryonic brain; cf. BRAIN (Embryology).

The future configuration of the brain is largely determined by these flexures, which are necessitated by inequalities in the development of the different segments of the medullary tube, especially in the lateral zones. (H.H.)

Flicker [AS. *flicerian*, to flutter]: Ger. *Flimmern (Flackern, Flattern)*; Fr. *papillotement*; Ital. *scintillio, scintillamento*. A visual perception whose condition is intermittence or intensive alternation of stimuli, within certain time limits.

The limit of flicker, according to Helmholtz, on rotating disks is passed, in diffuse daylight or intense lamplight, at a speed of 40–50 rotations in one sec.; in moonlight or candlelight, at a speed of 20. Other authorities, however (e. g. Cattell), consider these figures incorrect. Flicker has auditory and tactual analogues in beating and tickle, and, like them, is unpleasant. Cf. PHOTOMETRY (methods of). (E.B.T.–J.M.B.)

Literature: HELMHOLTZ, Physiol. Optik (2nd ed.), 489; EBBINGHAUS, Psychol., 243; KÜLPE, Outlines of Psychol., 250; SANFORD, Course in Exper. Psychol., expt. 161; FICK, in Hermann's Handb. d. Physiol., III. i. 215; BELLARMINOW, Arch. f. Ophthal., XXXV. i. 25 ff.; MARBE, Philos. Stud., ix. 384 ff., &c.; SZILI, Zeitsch. f. Psychol., iii. 359 ff.; SCHAPRINGER, ibid., v. 385 ff.; SCHENCK, Pflüger's Arch., lxiv ff.

Fluctuations of Attention [Lat. *fluctuare*, to move to and fro]: Ger. *Schwankungen der Aufmerksamkeit*; Fr. *oscillations de l'attention*; Ital. *oscillazioni dell' attenzione*. If a stimulus of minimal intensity (watch-tick at some distance, flow of sand, tuning-fork tone, liminal smell, &c.) or of minimal difference from its surroundings (light grey on white, dark on black) is steadily attended to, the sensation is found to disappear and reappear at irregular intervals; this is attributed to variations or 'fluctuations' of the attention.

Attempts have been made to give a peripheral explanation of the phenomenon (fatigue and recuperation of the sense organ); but differential experiments have supported the hypothesis that the fluctuations are of central origin. (E.B.T.)

Literature: SANFORD, Course in Exper. Psychol., expts. 61 b, 140 c; WUNDT, Physiol. Psychol. (4th ed.), ii. 295. The first investigation was made by URBANTSCHITSCH (cf. ATTENTION, experiments on). The first systematic tests were carried out by N. LANGE, Philos. Stud., iv. 390 ff. See also BUCCOLA, La legge del tempo nei fenomeni psichici (1883); DE SANCTIS, Atti Soc. Antropol. Roma (1897); H. ECKENER, Philos. Stud., viii. 343 ff.; K. MARBE, ibid., viii. 615 ff.; E. PACE, ibid., viii. 388 ff.; J. B. HYLAN, Psychol. Rev., iii. 56 ff., and Monog. Suppl., VI; H. O. COOK, Amer. J. of Psychol., xi. 119 ff.; H. MÜNSTERBERG, Beitr. z. exper. Psychol., ii. 69 ff. See also ATTENTION (experiments on). (E.B.T.—E.M.—L.M.)

Fluttering Heart: see ILLUSIONS OF MOTION AND MOVEMENT.

Folie [Fr.]: Ger. *Wahnsinn, Verrücktheit*; Fr. (as in topic); Ital. *follia, pazzia* (scientific). The French term for madness or insanity; but referring more particularly to the loss of reason involved in the disorder.

Alienation ('aliénation mentale') is a broader term which refers to all forms of mental changes, of whatever origin or nature. Many forms of mental disease have been first or chiefly described by the French; and for these the French terms are current. Of these may be mentioned folie circulaire, or recurrent or alternating insanity, characterized by the alternation of periods of excitement and depression; folie à deux, or communicated insanity, insanity affecting two or more persons, generally of the same family, at once; folie du doute, or DOUBTING MANIA (q.v.); folie épidémique, or epidemic insanity, &c. In addition many of the French equivalents for forms of mental disease are composed of the term folie with an appropriate context: folie des grandeurs, folie des ivrognes, folie épileptique, folie simulée, &c. (J.J.)

Folium [Lat. *folium*, leaf]: Ger. *Blatt*; Fr. *lamelle*; Ital. *lamella, foglietta* (embryol.). See BRAIN (Glossary).

Folk-lore (the English word is used in all the other languages). Folk-lore has been defined as 'the comparison and identification of the survivals, in modern ages, of archaic beliefs, customs, and traditions' (Gomme).

The word was invented by W. J. Thoms (1846), from folk + lore, after analogy with German compounds. In all civilizations there is a considerable part of the population whose habits of thought are relatively unaffected by the advances of culture, and who retain, by tradition and the conservatism of custom, something of the mental and material life of bygone periods of development. The collection of the customs, superstitions, myths, and lore of this 'unlearned and least advanced portion of the community,' and the systematic exposition and interpretation of these in the light of historical civilizations, of analogous primitive conditions among savages, and as an aid to the ethnology of races, is the object of the study of folk-lore. In one aspect folk-lore is not so much a special collection of facts, as a special mode of viewing them—namely, as survivals or mental relics of past ages, as things existing in our time, but not of it. It is thus a subdivision of anthropology, which considers similar material in its general aspects. The special material of folk-lore has been divided by Gomme into: (1) Superstitious beliefs and practice; (2) Traditional customs; (3) Traditional narratives; (4) Folk-sayings. Each of these in turn is much subdivided: the superstitions in regard to nature, plants, animals, goblins, witches, magic, &c.; festival, ceremonial, local customs and games; nursery tales, hero tales, creation, deluge, fire-myths; ballads, songs, place legends; jingles, nursery rhymes, riddles, proverbs, nicknames, place rhymes.

Literature: GOMME, The Handbook of Folk-lore (1890), and Ethnology in Folk-lore (1892); FRAZER, The Golden Bough; A. LANG, Custom and Myth; Publications of the Folk-lore Society; and more special references given in the works cited. (J.J.)

Folk Psychology: Ger. *Völkerpsychologie*; Fr. *psychologie des peuples*; Ital. *demopsicologia, psicologia etnica* (E.M.). The psychology of races, nations, or analogous social groups.

Folk psychology is specifically the study of the mental products in primitive peoples, and is thus closely related to anthropology and to folk-lore. The chapters of general anthropology which deal mainly with intellectual organizations, such as myth, legend, animism, religion, the beginnings of art and science, furnish much of the material. The effect of climate on mental endowments, the evolution of national characteristics, the analysis of mental processes in undeveloped peoples, and many other topics of similar import belong as definitely in this field as in any other. It is not possible to differentiate sharply the content of folk psychology from other parts of anthropology, and yet the term suggests a point of view and an interest which is important and readily intelligible.

Folk psychology is to be distinguished from SOCIAL PSYCHOLOGY (q.v.), which is concerned generally with the part played by the social factor in determining mental development. The term folk psychology is traceable to Steinthal and Lazarus, who planned and edited the *Zeitschrift für Völkerpsychologie und Sprachwissenschaft* (1860). They did not, however, distinguish clearly between folk psychology and social psychology. (G.F.S., J.M.B.)

It is desirable that the term folk psychology should be retained in this sense in preference to RACE PSYCHOLOGY (q.v.), since the latter has been given the different meaning—designating the science of the evolution of mind in the animals and man—by Spencer (*Princ. of Psychol.*), and since no other suitable term with this meaning has been suggested. (J.M.B., G.F.S.)

Literature: WAITZ, Völkerpsychol.; STEINTHAL and LAZARUS in Zeitsch. f. Völkerpsychol.; LE BON, Psychol. of Peoples (Eng. trans.); TOSTI, Psychol. Rev., v. 347; WUNDT, Völkerpsychol., I. i, ii (1900); SCHULTZE, Psychol. d. Naturvölker (1900). Much psychological material of this character is to be found in the general works cited under ANTHROPOLOGY; see particularly STEINTHAL, Grammatik, Logik, u. Psychol. (1855); LAZARUS, Das Leben d. Seele (3rd ed., 1883); BASTIAN, Der Mensch in d. Gesch. (3 vols., 1860), Beitr. z. Ethnol. (1871), Geographische u. ethnol. Bilder (1873), Der Völkergedanke (1881), Wie das Volk denkt (1892), Ethnol. Bilderbuch (1887), and Allerlei aus Volks- u. Menschenkunde (1888). (J.J.—J.M.B.)

Fool [Lat. *follis*, a bellows, a wind-bag]: Ger. *Narr*; Fr. *fol, fou*; Ital. *scemo, scimunito*. Used popularly as a term of disparagement in reference to mental ability; more exactly to refer to one defective in judgment and reasoning power, but not to a sufficient degree to merit the term imbecile or idiot. It implies low capacity for rational action, accompanied by a harmless, innocent disposition. See IDIOCY, and IMBECILITY. (J.J.)

Force [Lat. *fortis*, strong]: Ger. *Kraft*; Fr. *force*; Ital. *forza*. Specifically, in physics, the immediate cause of change of motion.

Left to itself, every particle of matter would move only in a straight line, with uniform velocity. Hence change of this uniform motion occurs only under the action of some cause, and this cause, and at the present time this alone, is, in physics, called force.

The matter of our own bodies is subject to its action, and through this fact, together with the muscular sense, do we become conscious of the action of force. If a weight is held in the hand, we are conscious of a cause acting on the muscles tending to overcome the muscular power we exert, and of an effort necessary to resist this action.

Fundamental laws of force are these :—(1) It acts only between bodies ; no body ever changes its motion except under the influence of some other body. (2) The action takes place in right lines ; in the case of each particle of a body this line is that in which the force acting on the particle impels it to move. (3) The action along every such line is mutual ; the line passes from the particle, *A*, acting to that acted on, *B*; and then *B* exerts an equal action on *A* along the same line, but in the opposite direction.

A ——————————————— B

If *A* and *B* are the acting particles, *A* can impel *B* only in the direction *AB* or *BA* ; and then *B* impels *A* equally in the opposite direction, *BA* or *AB*. If *A* attracts *B*, *B* attracts *A* equally ; if *A* repels *B*, *B* repels *A* equally ; if *A* presses against *B*, *B* presses equally against *A*. This law is that of action and reaction.

The ideal measure of a force is the change of velocity which it is competent to produce in a body acted on by no other force, and entirely free to move. The unit is the force which, acting on a unit-mass during a unit of time, will produce a unit of velocity. But as all bodies accessible to us are acted on by gravity, which causes them to fall when free to move, this measure is not the practical one. Practically a force is measured by the weight which it will balance. Cf. ENERGY, with which force is often confused. (S.N.)

Force (figurative meanings) and **Condition.** Used, as in SOCIAL FORCE (q. v.), moral force, economic force, &c., with much ambiguity. When so used the word should lose its physical connotation; and the fact of agency should be defined in terms of the material and changes peculiar to the sphere in which the force is said to work.

Force means that which produces a change of rest or motion; and the sorts of forces are those producers of change which manifest themselves under different but constant physical conditions. We speak of mental, sociological, &c., forces in the analogous case of change in phenomena of one of these several orders; and to give the term any intelligible meaning we must keep within the particular order of phenomena as strictly as does the physicist in defining his forces always in terms of motion in space which determines other motion in space. In other words, the force is intrinsic or internal to the movement in which it is said to be exerted.

Thus social forces are social grounds of social change; moral forces, moral grounds of moral change, &c. The real force in the particular case is often confused with the extraneous conditions which limit them or interfere with them. Variations in agricultural conditions which limit production are not economic forces; the farmer's changed expenditures, conditional upon agricultural variations, are economic forces. So also, brain-changes are not psychological forces. The President is not a political force, though his message to Congress is.

These figurative meanings given to the word force carry confusion throughout the borderlands of the sciences generally; we find such confusion between biological and BIONOMIC FORCES (q. v.); between social and SOCIONOMIC FORCES (q. v.); between psychological and PSYCHONOMIC FORCES (q. v.). We recommend the carrying out of the distinction suggested under the terms cited (ending in 'nomic,' Gr. νόμος) into the various spheres where the separation may be made between forces proper to the group of phenomena of a science and those of another group and science which limit or in any way condition the former. This preliminary distinction would go some way towards settling many of the disputed questions of the demarcation of the bounds of the sciences. (J.M.B.)

Force (political). (1) Compulsion exercised by the state. See SOVEREIGNTY, and GOVERNMENT; also FORCE (figurative meanings). (J.M.B.)

(2) When the opinions or aims of a part of the nation exert an influence on the action of the governing body, that part of the nation is said to be a force in politics, or a political force. More strictly, the expression should be 'a section of opinion, &c., has (not is) a political force,' i. e. exerts political influence.

The expression has become current only in recent times; but we find the germ of it in such passages of Bentham as the *Parliamentary Reform Catechism* (1818), 150, § 7 : ' The sense of the whole body of the people cannot be adequately conformed to by their representatives except in so far as the suffrage of each person has a force and effect' equal to that of every other. The meaning of 'a political force' was essentially conveyed by the *Times* (London) when it declared (Nov. 18, 1843) that the Anti-Corn-Law League was 'a great fact. He who frames laws must to some extent consult' it. (J.B.)

Foreign (in law) [Fr. *forain*]: Ger. *ausländisch*; Fr. *étranger*; Ital. *straniero*. Pertaining to a foreign sovereignty. 'The several states of the United States are, as respects their relations to each other, excepting only such of these as are regulated by the constitution of the United States, independent and foreign sovereignties' (Fisher *v.* Fielding, 67 Connecticut Reports, 105). A corporation chartered by one state is therefore a foreign corporation in every other. (S.E.B.)

Foreknowledge [AS. *for*, before, + *cnawan*, to know]: Ger. *Vorherwissen, Voraussicht*; Fr. *préscience*; Ital. *prescienza*. Full knowledge of the future.

If God, according to our idea, must be omniscient, as theology contends, then he must be as fully aware of the future as of the past, and therefore possesses foreknowledge. This conclusion has had great importance for religious thought on account of the manner in which it has been applied to 'the plan of salvation.' If God's foreknowledge be a determining element in the salvation of mankind, what room is left for spiritual freedom in men? This problem, running back to the writings of Plato, has produced endless discussion; for instance, as between Calvinists and Arminians. Philosophically, the questions connected with foreknowledge are secondary; that is to say, they depend upon the solution of the problem of omnipresence. According to the answer given to this will the speculative view of foreknowledge be. Cf. ATTRIBUTES (of God), CALVINISM, and GOD (in theology).

Literature: A. B. BRUCE, The Providential Order of the World, lect. x; K. MÜLLER, Die göttl. Zuvorersehung u. Erwählung; SCHLEIERMACHER, Glaubenslehre; SANDAY and HEADLAM, Commentary on Romans, 214 f., 310, 342 f.; BEYSCHLAG, Die paulin. Theodicee, Römer, ix–xi; and Theol. of the N. T. (Eng. trans.); JOWETT, St. Paul's Epistles, ii. 483 f.; DORNER, Syst. of Christ. Doctrine (Eng. trans.). (R.M.W.)

Forensic (in law) [Lat. *forensis*, belonging to the forum or market-place]: Ger. *gerichtlich*; Fr. *du barreau*; Ital. *forense, legale*. Pertaining to proceedings in the trial of causes.

Forensic domicile: a domicile assigned or selected for the purpose of investing a particular court with jurisdiction in a particular case. Forensic medicine: the application of medical science to aid in determining questions of legal right or responsibility; legal medicine or medical jurisprudence. (S.E.B.)

Foreordination [Sansk. *pra*, before, + Lat. *ordo*, order]: Ger. *Vorherbestimmung*; Fr. *prédestination*; Ital. *predestinazione*. God's eternal and unchangeable purpose with the universe.

Although the relation of God to the world and to man, implied in the term fore-ordination, has been argued oftener from the standpoint of theology than from that of philosophy, the problem belongs essentially in the philosophical field; that is, all theological replies involve philosophical presuppositions. The first striking feature of the question is its ubiquity. Under varying aspects, but with substantially identical implications, we find it in the oriental doctrine of metempsychosis, in Plato, in the Stoics, in the ALEXANDRIAN SCHOOL (q. v.); among the PHARISEES and ESSENES (q. v.); in the theology of Mohammedanism. Among Christians, it is systematized by Augustine, whose treatment is almost entirely theological. From him it passes over to the scholastic doctors, especially to Thomas Aquinas, who attempts to provide a philosophical basis for Augustine's conclusions by means of the doctrine of 'concurrence.' Here necessity is modified, as regards man, by enthroning the human will (voluntary) as the proximate cause of action, although this was determined originally by God. In post-Reformation times the theological aspect of the doctrine once more ousts the philosophical, and in Calvin we have a new Augustine. This theological interest has dominated till the present time.

Philosophy will be ready to attack the problem again only when, in the light of a constructive criticism of evolution, the abstract, external deity of the middle ages, which is still the God of much theology, has given place to a more worthy, not to say rational, conception. The failure of Kant, Schelling, and Schopenhauer to further the solution of the problem must be traced to their inability to advance beyond a shadowy verbal Theism, or an abstract agnostic Monism. See AUGUSTINIANISM, CALVINISM, and DETERMINISM.

Literature: PFLEIDERER, Philos. of Religion (Eng. trans.), iv. 29 f.; VATKE, Die menschl. Freiheit; A. SABATIER, L'Apôtre Paul, 347 f.; AQUINAS, Summa, Quaest. 29; MOZLEY, Augustinian Doctrine of Predestination; EDWARDS, Free Will; CHANNING, The Moral Argument against Calvinism; MÜLLER, Christ. Doctrine of Sin (Eng. trans.); McCOSH, Meth. of Divine Government; DORNER, Syst. of Christ. Doctrine (Eng. trans.), i. 188 f. (where full literature is given). (R.M.W.)

Forgetfulness [AS. *for*, away, + *getan*, to get]: Ger. *Vergesslichkeit*; Fr. *oubli*; Ital. *oblio*. Failure to reproduce the content of previous experience for any reason.

It may be due to decay of mental dispositions, or to other conditions. It is a normal limitation of memory, not such a defect as would illustrate AMNESIA (q. v.). See also MEMORY (defects of).

Literature: R. VERDON, in Mind, O.S., ii. 437; textbooks of psychology. (G.F.S.–J.M.B.)

Form: see MATTER AND FORM, and the topics below.

Form (as opposed to Matter) [Lat. *forma*]: Ger. *Form* (as opposed to *Inhalt*); Fr. *forme* (as opposed to *matière*); Ital. *forma*. See MATTER AND FORM, and cf. CONTENT.

Form and **Formalism** (in aesthetics): Ger. *Form, Formalismus*; Fr. *forme, formalisme*; Ital. *forma, formalismo*. A shape or figure, as in a painting or group of statuary; and hence the arrangement or disposition of the parts of an object or series, as contrasted with the matter or content, is its form.

There are three elements of which aesthetics takes account in estimating aesthetic value: (i) The sensuous impression, as the colour, or lustre, or sound (tone-colour); (ii) the form, viz. the arrangement of these elements; (iii) the ideal content or significance. Emphasis on either of these to the exclusion of the others gives respectively impressionism (colourists), formalism, idealism (as against formalism, but not in the sense in which it is opposed to realism). Form may be considered either in relations of quantity, under which fall rhythm, proportion, symmetry, greatness of extension or power, &c.; or in relations of quality, embracing harmony, variety, &c. In general, it may be said that the aesthetic value of the formal aspect of beauty is based upon two principles: (1) positive stimulation, or heightening of mental activity, as in the case of the sublime; (2) ease of apperception, which is furthered by a correspondence on the part of the object to the general characteristics of all mental activity, such as unity in variety, and the rhythmic nature of attention. Cf. FEELING, PLEASURE (aesthetic), and the specific topics cited above.

As indicated under the topic BEAUTY, the Greeks placed supreme value upon form, i.e. upon order, limit, measure, symmetry, harmony, in the conduct of life as well as in the products of art. This found recognition in Plato's preference for pure (geometrical) forms, and in his statements that every art and craft and organism is full of rhythm and harmony and grace, or beautiful form (εὐσχημοσύνη), and that tragedy is the arranging of its elements in a manner suitable to each other and to the whole. This last demand received more definite formulation in Aristotle's definition of tragedy as 'a whole action,' which has beginning, middle, and end.

Aristotle makes the general statement also that beauty depends on size and order; and again, that the main species of beauty are order, symmetry, definite limitation. The art and literary criticism of the 17th and 18th centuries laid great emphasis upon form, and the principle of unity in variety was frequently accepted as the adequate explanation of beauty. The admiration for Greek art, especially sculpture, furthered the tendency towards the emphasizing of formal beauty. Kant expressly excluded the sensuous element from a claim to aesthetic value, and while admitting the value of the ideal element, under the title of dependent beauty, still insisted that this was not in the proper sense aesthetic, but intellectual value. A 'pure judgment of taste' relates only to free beauty, and has as its determining ground merely the purposiveness of the form (i. e. the adaptation of the form to our mental powers). This gave the principle which was taken up by Herbart, and developed by Zimmermann, in opposition to the idealism of Schelling, Hegel, and Vischer. Herbart (e. g.) excluded from aesthetics the concepts of the charming, the noble, the pathetic, the touching, and others, as belonging not to the beautiful, but to the interesting. Zimmermann made this formalism more ab-

stract in connection with the general Herbartian theory of Vorstellungen, or presentations, and stated as the most general aesthetic laws: (i) Under the form of quantity: the stronger presentation is the more pleasing; (ii) quality: prevailing identity of the formal elements pleases, opposition is unpleasant. Köstlin has made the most complete analysis of the elements of beautiful forms and of their various concrete embodiments, but is hardly a formalist. Fechner also, while examining aesthetic forms experimentally, is careful to give other factors due recognition. Helwig and Herckenrath represent a recent formal theory: 'Beauty is a mean.' See also BEAUTY, ART, CHARACTERISTIC, and EXPRESSION.

Literature: ZIMMERMANN, Gesch. d. Aesthetik (1858); Aesthetik als Form-Wissenschaft (1865); VISCHER, Krit. Gänge, vi (1860); HARTMANN, Aesthetik, i. 267–303, 484–509 (1886); BOSANQUET, Hist. of Aesthetic (1892); FECHNER, Vorschule d. Aesthetik, xxi (1876); KÖSTLIN, Aesthetik (1869); HELWIG, Eine Theorie des Schönen (1897); HERCKENRATH, Problèmes d'Esthétique (1898); SANTAYANA, The Sense of Beauty (1896); A. HILLEBRAND, Das Problem d. Form in d. bildenden Kunst (2. Aufl., 1897); MARIO, L'Estetica (1896). (J.H.T.)

Form Quality: Ger. *Gestaltsqualität*; not in use in Fr. and Ital. That which characterizes a mental whole as being of a particular form, as being formed, or as having relations of parts.

The question of form qualities has been stated and discussed by the writers cited below. Gestaltsqualität was suggested by Ehrenfels. Meinong used the term 'funded content' (fundirte Inhalt) for the same 'quality of form' considered as common (or funded) to different (funding) contents; as the form of the same melody played in different keys. Stout uses the phrase 'form of combination' as the English rendering; it avoids the ambiguity of the term 'quality.'

Literature: EHRENFELS, Vtljsch. f. wiss. Philos. 1890, 249; MEINONG, Zeitsch. f. Psychol., ii. 245; CORNELIUS, ibid., xxii. 101; LIPPS, ibid., xxii. 385; STOUT, Analytic Psychol., i. Bk. I. chap. iii; HÖFLER, Psychologie, 153. (J.M.B., G.F.S.)

Form Studies: Ger. *Formaldisciplinen*; Fr. *études formelles*; Ital. *studii* (or *discipline*) *formali*. Studies in which formal predominate over thought aspects; opposed to concrete, or content studies.

Grammar is typical, since it considers

primarily the correct forms for the expression of thought, rather than the thought itself. For this reason, linguistic studies in their early or grammatical stages are called 'formal,' whereas such studies as history and geography are called concrete, since they deal chiefly with facts and their relations. In varying degree all studies have their formal as opposed to their concrete side; thus, mathematics is both pure and applied. Cf. INSTRUCTION. (C.DE G.)

Forma, Formalis, Formaliter [Lat.]: see LATIN AND SCHOLASTIC TERMINOLOGY, Glossary, sub verbis.

Formal Cause: see CAUSE AND EFFECT.

Formal Culture : Ger. *formale Bildung*; Fr. *éducation formelle*; Ital. *educazione formale*. The doctrine of the applicability of mental power, however gained, to any department of human activity.

This doctrine is used as a standing argument for so-called disciplinary education, especially that in pure mathematics and classical languages. The assumption is that if the student masters these, he will thereby acquire a mental power that can be applied almost equally well to any kind of practical or professional life. This gymnastic theory of education involves the idea that it does not matter upon what the mind is exercised, provided only the exercise be vigorous and long-continued. The inadequacy of the theory lies in the fact that it ignores or underestimates the importance of the choice of subjects, both for their gymnastic efficiency, and their ultimate worth in developing the individual. A life of crime develops acuteness of intellect, but it does not develop good citizens. Again, mental alertness in philology, or grammar, or higher algebra, does not insure corresponding alertness in those fields in which there is neither knowledge nor interest. The mind is never efficient in any department of endeavour in which either education or experience has not provided rich and abundant masses of apperceiving ideas.

Literature: HINSDALE, Disciplinary Studies, Proc. Natnl. Educ. Assoc. (1894), 625–35; TOMPKINS, The Philos. of Teaching, 265; BAKER, Educational Values, Proc. Natnl. Educ. Assoc. (1895), 197–203; ZILLER, Allg. Päd., 95–8. (C.DE G.)

Formal Logic : Ger. *formale Logik*; Fr. *logique formelle*; Ital. *logica formale*. Usually identified with the Aristotelian logic (see below), and contrasted with material and empirical logic. (J.M.B.)

The notion of formal logic can only be determined historically. All logic is, and is admitted to be, formal in one sense—as having to deal with the general laws and modes of thinking by which knowledge is constructed, and not with the special character which determines each type of concrete knowledge. On the recognition of such a distinction logic is based, and it constitutes the common element in all conceptions of logic. But so soon as it attempts to define more closely the object of logical treatment, and the method of treating it, differences of a fundamental kind appear, and only in reference to them is the notion of formal logic definable. In its modern significance, formal logic presents itself as of three distinct types.

(1) The first, which has perhaps obtained too readily a monopoly of the title, takes its origin in the Kantian philosophy, and in all its varieties bears more or less traces of Kant's way of distinguishing forms of thought from matter, and of isolating the function of thought. As this common, universal function of thought is identified, more or less closely, with the process of uniting diverse contents of consciousness through their partial agreement in a notion, or concept—that is, is identified with generalization or abstract classification—it follows that the laws of thought are contemplated as conditions involved in the formation of notions, and that the processes of thought, judgment, and reasoning are interpreted from the point of view of the notion as the unit involved. Historically this formal view found much with which it could amalgamate in the traditional, Aristotelian logic, which, though originally based on a different principle, gave great prominence to classification, and was indeed dominated by the ideal of knowledge as a completed classification. Of this first view, commonly called, in modern works, 'formal' or 'subjectively formal' logic, the best known representatives in English philosophy are Hamilton and Mansel. Hamilton's *New Analytic* is a development from the principle that all thinking is expression of the relations among notions, such relations being conceived as of classes to one another.

(2) A second type of formal logic is that expressed in Herbart's view of the logical treatment of thought, as isolating the content represented in thought, and viewing it in abstraction, either from the psychological processes by which thinking is produced, or from any metaphysical question as to real existence. It was natural that from this point of view

the relation of position and negation in thought contents should have been made prominent, and have been at least co-ordinated in importance with the relations of greater and less generality. Theoretically, Herbart's view is the transition stage from the Kantian to the third modern type of formal logic.

(3) According to this third type, the function of thought which is truly universal, and which alone is capable of complete isolation and perfectly abstract treatment, is that presented in the antithesis of positing and negating. Of all other relations in thought, however general, it may be said that they depend on the special content of the terms about which position and negation may be exercised. In this view, clearly, there is not involved any philosophical theory as to the nature of thought, nor is it dependent upon any psychology. It may be united with rationalism or with empiricism. It may work either with the mechanism of expression of thought contained in the Aristotelian logic, altering or modifying as is required, or by the adoption of some more or less symbolic method for representing its terms and the relations among them. Of this third type the representatives are Boole, Jevons, and generally modern exponents of SYMBOLIC LOGIC (q. v.), such as Venn and Schröder.

Literature: criticism and discussion of formal logic has generally had reference to the first type, that more or less Kantian in character. On it, pro and con, see MANSEL, Letters, &c., and Prolegomena Logica; UEBERWEG, Logik (passim; Ueberweg carries out a continuous critique of the way in which formal logic handles the main logical questions); TRENDELENBURG, Log. Untersuch., chap. ii; MILL, Exam. of Hamilton, chap. xx. (R.A.)

Formal Rightness. The characteristic of those actions in which the will or intention of the agent is ethically good. See RECTITUDE (also for foreign equivalents). Cf. RIGHT.

The distinctions between formal and material rightness, and between formal and material wrong or sin, are connected with a view of morality which takes into account, and treats as having a certain (at least relative) independence, both the external manifestation of the act and the internal volition or intention. The will or intention to do right constitutes formal rightness. But, owing to intellectual deception, or physical hindrance, formal rightness may not always issue in material rightness. Similarly,

material rightness may be present without formal. Cf. Rickaby, *Mor. Philos.*, 33. For an illustration, see EQUIVOCATION. (W.R.S.)

Formal Steps (in method): Ger. *formale Stufen*; Fr. *degrés formels*; Ital. (not in use). The essential stages of a rational method; so called, because these steps are conceived to be a sort of formula for correct methods of teaching.

Herbart conceived four such formal steps, which he named Clearness, Association, System, and Method. Ziller and his followers subdivide differently, using less technical terms, as follows: Preparation, Presentation, Association, Generalization, Application. Cf. METHOD.

Literature: HIWET, Die formalen Stufen des Unterrichts; McMURRY, Method of the Recitation; DE GARMO, Essentials of Method; HERBART, Sci. of Educ. (trans. by Felkin), 126–8. (C.DE G.)

Fortitude [Lat. *fortitudo*]: Ger. *Tapferkeit*; Fr. *courage*; Ital. *fortezza d' animo*. The name given (e. g. by Cicero) to the virtue of courage (ἀνδρεία); one of the four cardinal virtues of the traditional classification.

Owing largely to the influence of the Christian moralists, whose doctrine was affected by the social conditions of the Christians during the early centuries of the empire, *fortitudo*, as a Christian virtue, came to signify more especially the passive side of courage—that of bearing pain and injury—rather than the active courage shown in carrying out enterprises involving danger. See COURAGE. (W.R.S.)

Fortuitous: see ACCIDENT, and CHANCE.

Fortuitous (or **Accidental**) **Variation** (in biology): see VARIATION (in biology).

Fortune [Lat. *fortuna*]. A popular term meaning variously destiny, fate, future ill-fortune or welfare of any sort. Cf. NECESSITY, and PROVIDENCE. (J.M.B.)

Fortune physique (1), and **Fortune morale** (2). French expressions, used also in other languages, for the distinction between so-called objective or external (1), as contrasted with subjective or internal (2), fortune or experience. Generalized to apply to the contrast between the moral sphere, universe, or economy as a whole, and the physical.(J.M.B.)

Forum (in law) [Lat. *forum*, market-place]: Ger. *Gerichtsstand*, *Jurisdiction*; Fr. *ressort*, *juridiction*; Ital. *foro*, *giurisdizione*. (1) The tribunal having cognizance of a cause. (2) The territory of the sovereign having jurisdiction of a cause.

Lex fori: the law of that territory, applicable to the cause. This regulates the form of procedure.

Ordinarily personal actions are brought before a court, to the process of which the defendant is subject; *actor sequitur forum rei*. This is the court of his domicil, *forum domicilii*, or one within whose territorial jurisdiction he is found, and served with process. Real actions are brought in the *forum rei sitae*; criminal proceedings, commonly, in the *forum delicti* (*commissi*). (S.E.B.)

Fourier's Law: Ger. *Fourier'sches Gesetz*; Fr. *loi de Fourier*; Ital. *legge di Fourier*. A law of periodic vibration, formulated by the French mathematician Fourier (1768–1830), and reduced by Helmholtz to the following acoustical terms:—Any vibratory movement of the air, corresponding to a musical tone, may be always (and in the given case only in a particular manner) represented as the sum of a number of simple vibratory movements, corresponding to the partials of the musical tone.

Literature: HELMHOLTZ, Sensations of Tone (Eng. trans.), 3rd ed., 34. (E.B.T.)

Fovea centralis [Lat.]: Ger. *Netzhautgrube*; Fr. *fovea centralis*; Ital. *fovea centralis, fossa centrale*. The central depression of the macula lutea or yellow spot of the retina, which consists here of little more than a single layer of attenuated cones.

The fovea is also called the 'spot of clearest vision,' since visual discrimination falls off towards the periphery of the retina. Cf. INDIRECT VISION, and VISION.

Literature: WALLER, Human Physiol., 410, 411; HELMHOLTZ, Physiol. Optik (2nd ed.), 34; in general, any work on physiological optics; SANFORD, Course in Exper. Psychol., expts. 111, 117; see also YELLOW SPOT. On the question of the colouration and night-blindness of the fovea, see HERING, Pflüger's Arch., liv. 281, lix. 403; KÖNIG, Sitzber. d. Berl. Akad. (June, 1894); LADD FRANKLIN, Psychol. Rev., ii. 137; SHERMAN, Philos. Stud., xiii. 434; UHTHOFF, Zeitsch. f. Psychol., xx. 326; and references cited above. (E.B.T.)

Franchise [Fr.]: Ger. *Freiheit*; Fr. (as in topic); Ital. *franchigia, privilegio*. A privilege of a public nature, held by grant from the sovereign.

Corporate franchise: the rights granted by a charter of incorporation, or acquired by incorporation under general laws. Elective franchise: the right of suffrage. Formerly franchise was used also to denote the place within which the privilege enjoyed was to be exercised. Thus the franchises of churches were the church enclosures within which the right of asylum existed.

A franchise is (except by special authority from the government) a personal privilege, and incapable of assignment. (S.E.B.)

Franciscans: Ger. *Franziskaner*; Fr. *Franciscains*; Ital. *Francescani*. The name given to the brethren of the Order of St. Francis.

The Order was founded 1210–23; a century later it is said to have attained a membership of over 200,000, and it had received many privileges from the Holy See. It is of importance in the history of mediaeval philosophy, because its doctors were realists as opposed to the nominalism of the Dominicans; and again, Scotists as opposed to Dominican Thomism. The Order came to be torn by internal strife regarding the interpretation of the vow of poverty, a strife which in 1415, and again in 1517, gave rise to two specially recognized divisions—the Observants and the Conventuals. Among the distinguished thinkers of the Order have been Bonaventura, Alexander of Hales, William of Occam, and Roger Bacon.

Literature: the relative arts. in Herzog's Real-Encyc., and Encyc. Brit., 9th ed.; MORIN, St. François et les Franciscains; LITTLE, The Grey Friars in Oxford; HAURÉAU, De la Philos. scolastique, ii. 214 f. (R.M.W.)

Fraternity [Lat. *frater*, a brother]: Ger. (1) *Brüderlichkeit*, (2) *Brüderschaft*; Fr. *fraternité*; Ital. (1) *fraternità*, (2) *frateria*. (1) Brotherly feeling and conduct. (2) An organization supposed to be characterized in a high degree by brotherly feeling, e.g. Greek letter societies.

Some of the oldest words in every language express the idea and sentiment of fraternity, which was the attitude of mind peculiarly characteristic of the CLAN (q.v.). The notion of a fraternity of all men became possible only after gentile organization gave place to civil and imperial. It was because of this transition that Stoic philosophy and the Christian religion inculcated the duty of striving for universal brotherhood. Fraternity, with liberty and EQUALITY (q.v.), became a shibboleth of the French Revolution. (F.H.G.)

Fraternity may be distinguished from equality as positive from negative. It is the 'enthusiasm of humanity' not enforceable by law. The difficulties of reconciling it with liberty and equality are brought out by J. Fitzjames Stephen, *Liberty, Equality, Fraternity*, chap. vi. (J.B.)

Fraud (in law) [Lat. *fraus*]: Ger. *Betrug*; Fr. *tromperie, fraude*; Ital. *frode*. Wilfully causing or using the error of another to subject him to loss.

Loss must in fact result, before it is actionable, at law. In equity: any intentional act or omission involving a breach of confidence or good faith, and naturally resulting in loss to another. See Pomeroy's *Equity Jurisprudence*, § 873. Actual fraud always involves untruth, but in equity there need not always be moral culpability. Constructive fraud, in equity, is fraud imputed from reasons of public policy by the rules of equity, where there is no proof of actual fraud or wrongful intent ; as where a trustee buys the property which it is his duty to sell, although he may pay its full value. (S.E.B.)

Fraunhofer Lines : Ger. *Fraunhofer'sche Linien*; Fr. *raies de Fraunhofer*; Ital. *linee di Fraunhofer*. The colours of the solar SPECTRUM (q. v.) are not continuous; they are crossed vertically, at unequal intervals, by fine dark lines or bands. These lines, which mark the absence of certain degrees of refrangibility in the rays that reach us, are produced by the passage of light through incandescent vapours in the solar atmosphere. The chief Fraunhofer lines are a constant series of ten, named A, a, B, C, D, E, b, F, G, H. Helmholtz (*Physiol. Optik*, 2nd ed., 287) gives the following table of corresponding wave-lengths $(\mu\mu)$:—

A 760·400 extreme red.
B 686·853 red.
C 656·314 limit of red and orange.
D 589·625–589·023 golden yellow.
E 526·990 green.
F 486·164 cyan blue.
G 430·825 limit of indigo and violet.
H 386·879 limit of violet.

The lines were discovered by Wollaston in 1802 ; described by Fraunhofer in 1814 ; explained by Kirchhoff in 1859. They form the constants of all spectroscopic work. (E.B.T.)

Freak : see SPORT.

Free and **Freedom** [AS. *freo* and *freodom*]: Ger. *frei, Freiheit*; Fr. *libre, liberté*; Ital. *libero, libertà*. The conception 'freedom' seems to imply first, negatively, the absence of external constraint ; and second, positively, the power inherent in the object called 'free,' of following the laws of its own nature.

Further than this very general account, it is perhaps impossible to give an exact signification which will cover the allowable use of the term in all connections. The signification of the term tends to vary according to the kind of object called 'free.' (1) Movement is said to be free when unrestrained by any obstacle outside the moving body or its normal conditions ; e.g. the movement of the limbs of an animal when unparalyzed and unbound.

(2) As applied to voluntary action, especially in choosing between alternatives, the question of the meaning of freedom leads to the controversy concerning free-will. See FREE-WILL CONTROVERSIES.

Here three views may be distinguished : (*a*) that volition is free when, and in so far as, it is due to the character and motives of the individual —because it is his action (as distinguished from actions due to the application of external force, or to physiological reflex) ; (*b*) that the free volition is in some way and to some extent independent of motives—being due to a self not entirely accounted for by character, motives, and circumstances ; (*c*) that free action means action in accordance with reason, reason being thus regarded as a man's true self (Spinoza and Kant). See WILL.

(3) In political and ethico-political reasoning, different meanings of freedom may be distinguished : (*a*) a nation is said to be free when not under the rule of another nation, or when not subject to a tyrant who is above law ; (*b*) as referring to the relations of the citizens or people to the state. Freedom (*a*) sometimes implies full political rights : a man is free who has the 'franchise'; this signification is called political (or 'civil') freedom ; (*β*) sometimes it is used for what is called individual freedom. This is commonly interpreted as implying the absence (so far as possible or expedient) of interference with the individual by the government. And this meaning is connected with the political ideal of INDIVIDUALISM (q. v.) : that the liberty of any individual should be restrained by the government only in so far as necessary to prevent his interference with the like liberty of others (Kant, Spencer). According to another view, which also takes freedom as its ideal, this freedom must be not merely negative (freedom from interference), but positive, and therefore implying a social order which provides, for the individuals, opportunity for cultivating and exercising their capacities (cf. T. H. Green, *Works*, ii. 308 ff.). (W.R.S.)

Free (in economics): Ger. *frei*; Fr. *libre*; Ital. *libero*. Not subject to special acts of restrictive legislation, e.g. free labour, that which is not under a special status like that of the slave or apprentice ; free trade, trade which is either untaxed or at any rate not subject to discriminating taxes in favour of other trade. (A.T.H.)

Freedom (consciousness of): Ger. *Freiheitsgefühl*; Fr. *sentiment* or *expérience intime de la liberté*; Ital. *sentimento della libertà*. The consciousness that a decision arises from the self, and not from conditions in any way foreign to the self. See FREE AND FREEDOM, and WILL. (G.F.S.–J.M.B.)

Freedom (economic): see ECONOMIC FREEDOM.

Freedom (in theology). The condition, with reference to religious relationships, of the agent endowed with freedom of WILL (q. v.). See also FREE AND FREEDOM.

Freedom has been discussed by theologians in every age, and the subject is so large that it is impracticable to enter upon it historically here. It may be said, generally, that, when separated from 'moralism,' the theological treatment of freedom has been developed along two lines, a negative and a positive. (1) Negative: this aspect of the matter has consisted chiefly in criticism of metaphysical views, which imperil, or are supposed to imperil, the foundations of dogma, even although deterministic theologians, like Luther, have not been wanting. As a rule, Pantheism, naturalism, and evolutionary Agnosticism have been attacked in turn. (2) Positive: here the problem has been to reconcile the antinomy between God's overruling power, especially as regards man's salvation, and human freedom. It has been held that, while man is free, divine justice demands a restriction of the freedom of the lawless (sinful) will, a view which reappears in many guises. Again, the antinomy may be overcome by supposing that God is conditioned by free human causality, but that, at the same time, he is not passive in this process, because, being God, he mediates it. God's life and man's are distinct; and God's plan with man is to lift him from less to more complete freedom. In a word, man, though free in his own action, cannot be viewed as the author of his freedom, for God cannot but be the cause whence man's free causality proceeds. This is held to be shown by the growth in strength for the realization of ideals which the good man enjoys. Schleiermacher's psychological 'determinism' is a reaction against old dualistic views, and may be said to initiate modern tendencies. The conclusions still remain obscure or unsatisfactory, mainly because the relation of mankind and men to God and his plan has not been analysed sufficiently and without pre-possession. Humanity and individuals can hardly be regarded as free or unfree in precisely the same sense.

Literature: DORNER, Syst. of Christ. Doctrine (Eng. trans.), ii. 106 f., iii. 10. (R.M.W.)

Free-thought and **Freethinkers**: Ger. *Freidenken, Freidenker*; Fr. *libre pensée, libres penseurs*; Ital. *libero pensiero, liberi pensatori*. Untrammelled rational reflection on matters of religion, apart from, or in defiance of, dogmatic authority, together with the negative results of such reflection; and those who advocate it. Specifically, the rejection, on the basis of such reflection, of the distinctive doctrines of Christian revelation. The term is characteristically used in designation of 18th-century Deism. (A.C.A.Jr.)

Frenzy [Gr. φρένησις, inflammation of the brain]: Ger. *Raserei*; Fr. *fièvre chaude* (popular), *manie aiguë* (scientific); Ital. *frenesia*. An agitation of the brain, which renders the individual temporarily delirious or deranged.

It is used mainly in a popular sense for extreme maniacal excitement, aroused perhaps by anger, passion, and the like; but it also retains an older usage, in which it is regarded as equivalent to a temporary madness or derangement. (J.J.)

Frequency: see ERRORS OF OBSERVATION.

Fresison: see MOOD (in logic).

Friendship [AS. *freon*, to love]: Ger. *Freundschaft*; Fr. *amitié*; Ital. *amicizia*. The relation of mutual benevolence or love between two or more persons who desire one another's society.

Friendship was a specially prominent feature of Greek life. Philosophical schools, such as the Pythagorean and Epicurean, were constituted as societies of friends, and two books (viii, ix) of Aristotle's *Ethics* were devoted to the topic, which was afterwards discussed by Cicero and many other moralists. Its position in modern life is hardly so conspicuous, owing to the larger part played by domestic life, and perhaps also to the more varied organizations for different purposes entailed by the complexity of modern society. At the same time, the word is often used in a wide sense: sometimes it means little more than acquaintance; sometimes it is used with reference to any object of benevolent interest (where reciprocity is hardly possible)—thus men are called friends of the poor, of their country, of mankind, of art, of religion. The stricter sense of the word implies both some intensity, and also reciprocity, of sentiment. This does not necessarily involve (as in the Pythagorean and in the early Christian society) community of goods, but it does involve readiness to serve and benefit one another. Nor does it require equality of age, or of social position, or of business, or even of opinion, though, when these are absent, friendship is less commonly met with. But it does seem to require a certain harmony of sentiment or of character; though the harmony may be due not so much to any striking similarity, as to the two characters being complementary.

Aristotle's division of friends, according as they have pleasure, utility, or the good as their object, and his recognition of the last as the only true kind, serve to bring out the characteristic which gives to friendship its value in the moral life. (w.r.s.)

Fries, Jacob Friedrich. (1773–1843.) German philosopher. Born at Barby, educated at Magdeburg, Leipzig, and Jena. In 1801 he lectured in Jena. He travelled in Germany, Switzerland, France, and Italy. In 1805 he became professor of philosophy and elementary mathematics at Heidelberg, returning to Jena in 1816 as professor of theoretical philosophy. In 1819 he was, for political reasons, deposed, but restored in 1824. Died in Jena. He called his system 'philosophical anthropology,' making self-knowledge the basis of all other forms. His most important work is his *Neue Kritik der reinen Vernunft*.

Fringe: Ger. *Relationsfärbung* (Cornelius, *Psychologie als Erfahrungswissenschaft*, 168); Fr. (not in use); Ital. *frangia* (Ferrari, in trans. of James' *Princ. of Psychol.*). The notional awareness of the meaning or significance which accompanies mental images, e. g. words, as they succeed each other in a train of thought. See NOTION.

Literature: JAMES, Princ. of Psychol., i. 258, 281–2, 471–2, 478; STOUT, Analytic Psychol., i. 92. (G.F.S., J.M.B.)

Froebel, Friedrich. (1782–1852.) An important German educational reformer. A childhood saddened by the loss of his mother, the instruction of an affectionate brother, and deep religious impressions received in his first school, mark his early years. He studied at both Jena and Berlin. He visited Pestalozzi twice, and, in co-operation with a friend, started a school at Keilhau. He opened schools also in Switzerland—at Watersee, Burgdorf, and Willisau. He studied comparative philology in Göttingen. In 1840 he established the first Kindergarten in Brandenburg, and afterwards opened schools in various other German cities. His principle is that free creative activity is the means as well as the end of education, especially with children. His greatest work is *Die Menschenerziehung*.

Function [Lat. *functio*, from *fungor*, I execute]: Ger. *Funktion*; Fr. *fonction*; Ital. *funzione*. (1) In biology and physiology: any normal activity, process, or performance accomplished by an organism or an organ. (J.M.B.)

(2) In mathematics: a variable y is called a function of a second variable x when to each value of x there corresponds a definite value or a set of definite values of y. Cf. VARIABLE AND CONSTANT QUANTITY.

It should be observed that the relation between y and x is not necessarily one which admits of analytical expression. Thus the statement: '$y = 1$ for every rational value of x, and $y = 0$ for every irrational or imaginary value of x,' defines y as a function of x, although it would evidently be impossible to express the relation between y and x analytically. It is customary to indicate the fact that y is a function of x by the formula $y = f(x)$, and then to represent the value of y which corresponds to any particular value of x, say b, by the symbol $f(b)$. In like manner, y is called a function of the two variables x and z, $y = f(x, z)$, when to each pair of values of x and z there corresponds a definite value or set of values of y, &c. (H.B.F.)

Function (mental): Ger. *psychische Funktion*; Fr. *fonction mentale*; Ital. *funzione mentale*. (1) Any conscious process considered as taking part in a larger system of processes.

(2) Any one of the fundamental constituents entering into every concrete state of consciousness. Cf. CLASSIFICATION (of the mental functions). (G.F.S.–J.M.B.)

Functional Selection: see EXCESS, and SELECTION (in biology).

Fundament [Lat. *fundamentum*]. Used by certain neurologists as translation of the German Anlage. See RUDIMENT, and cf. PROTON, and DISPOSITION. (J.M.B.)

Fundamental Tone: Ger. *Grundton*; Fr. *son fondamental*; Ital. *suono fondamentale, tonica*. The lowest tone, or prime, in a compound tone.

Literature: WUNDT, Physiol. Psychol. (4th ed.), ii. 63; STUMPF, Tonpsychologie, ii. 2; HELMHOLTZ, Sensations of Tone (3rd ed.), 22. (E.B.T.)

Fundamental Truth: Ger. *Grundwahrheit*; Fr. *vérité fondamentale*; Ital. *verità fondamentale*. Ultimate or essential truth: the ultimate principle or principles of any department of thought or of knowledge as a whole. The term is characteristically employed to designate principles deemed indispensable to sound thinking and right action, e. g. by McCosh in the sub-title of his critique of the philosophy of J. S. Mill, *A Defence of Fundamental Truth*. (A.C.A.Jr.)

Fundamentum (in logic): (1) *Eintheilungsgrund* or *Eintheilungsprincip*, (2) *Beziehungsgrund*; Fr. (1) *principe de division*, (2) *fondement de relation*; Ital. *fondamento*. The term fundamentum is used in logic in two references: (1) *fundamentum divisionis*: the principle according to which the co-ordinate species of a genus are distinguished from one another; more exactly, then, the generalized attribute, variations in which constitute the species.

(2) *Fundamentum relationis*: the connecting circumstances taken into view, together with the objects or terms connected, and constituting part of the meaning of each correlative. (R.A.)

Funding [Lat. *fundus*, farm]: Ger. *Fundirung*; Fr. *consolidation, conversion*; Ital. *conversio (di debito)*. The conversion of a debt due on demand to one whose principal and interest can only be called for at stated dates.

If a corporation (private or public), or an individual, simply leaves bills unpaid, telling the creditors to get what security they can, the result is an unfunded, or floating, debt. If these bills are taken up by the issue of formal obligations to pay interest (and usually principal also) at dates distinctly specified, the debt is said to be funded. When these obligations set a date for payment of the principal (maturity), they are known as bonds. When the principal is paid by the issue of a new loan, whether at maturity or before it, the operation is known as refunding. (A.T.H.)

Furor [Lat. *furor*, a raging, madness]: Ger. *Wuthanfall (-ausbruch)*; Fr. *fureur*; Ital. *furore*. An excessive outburst of sudden maniacal excitement, passion or anger.

It may be caused by specific disorders (*furor uterinus, furor epilepticus*), may be directed towards a special object or person, and may be characterized for its special symptoms as *furor brevis, furor transitorius*, &c. It is mostly characteristic of MANIA, EPILEPSY, and HYSTERIA. (J.J.)

Fusion [Lat. *fundere*, to pour]: Ger. *Verschmelzung*; Fr. *fusion*; Ital. *fusione*. When partial constituents of a total experience, owing to their similarity or other intrinsic affinity, combine in such a way that it is difficult to discriminate or analyse them, they are said to be fused. The more difficult discrimination or analysis is, the greater is the degree of fusion. (G.F.S.–J.M.B.)

A term whose definition is still in the making. We may say provisionally, that fusion is either (1) a relation obtaining between certain sensory (or, perhaps, between these and affective) contents, whose occurrence implies an approximation of the fused processes towards sensational simplicity, or (2) the result of the realisation of such a relation, i. e. the fused mass itself.

The term has played a large part in recent systematic psychology, but it takes on a slightly different meaning in the hands of different psychological schools. We note the following usages: (1) Stumpf defines fusion as that union of two sensation-contents in which they form not a mere sum, but a more or less unitary whole (*Tonpsychologie*, ii. 128). He offers a psychophysical theory of fusion in which it is based on what he calls specific synergy (loc. cit., 214. Cf. Meinong, *Zeitsch. f. Psychol.*, vi. 429). Stumpf's views are more fully developed in the *Beitr. z. Ak. u. Musikwiss.*, 1, 'Konsonanz und Dissonanz' (cf. the notice by Pace in the *Psychol. Rev.*, Mar. 1900, 185). Külpe has extended the notion of fusion to non-sensational contents. For him there are only two forms of conscious combination, fusion and colligation: if the elements combined are temporally and spatially identical but differ in quality, their connection is termed fusion; if they differ in duration or extension, colligation (*Outlines of Psychol.*, 277). Müller deprecates the employment of the word as an explanatory concept (*Zeitsch. f. Psychol.*, x. 43). For the fusion of tones the term Blend is often used (Sanford).

(2) Wundt employs the term fusion throughout his treatment of perception, to denote the fundamental form of simultaneous association (*Physiol. Psychol.*, 4th ed., ii. 437), without laying stress, as Stumpf and Külpe do, upon the typical character of tonal fusion. He includes in the meaning of the word (i) the intimacy of the combination, and (ii) the novel character of the product (loc. cit., 38). The idea of space is the result of an 'extensive fusion' (233) (a fusion of different sensational elements—in this case movement sensations and tactual sensations); auditory ideas are 'intensive' fusions (fusions of like sensational elements).

(3) Certain logicians (e. g. Erdmann, *Logik*) use fusion (Verschmelzung) for the union of elements involved in abstraction.

The doctrine of fusion stands in close relation to that of 'funded contents' (*fundirter Inhalt*), elaborated with differences of emphasis and of terminology by Ehrenfels, Meinong, Witasek, Cornelius (*Zeitsch. f. Psychol.*, xii. 189 *n*.), which has its roots in Mach's discussion of tone sensations (*Analyse d. Empfindungen*, 128).   (E.B.T.–C.L.F.–J.M.B.)

The word COMBINATION (q. v.) is used in this article to translate Verbindung, rather than Connection, which is preferred by E. B. T.   (J.M.B.)

Literature: SANFORD, Course in Exper. Psychol. expt. 83; articles in the Zeitsch. f. Psychol., by FAIST, xv. 102; MEINONG and WITASEK, xv. 189; MEYER, xvii. 401, xviii. 274; LIPPS, xix. 1; STUMPF, xv. 280, 354, xvii. 422, xviii. 294; and in the Philos.

Stud. by SCHULZE, xiv. 471; BUCH, xv. 1, 183; HERBART, Psychol. als Wiss.; CORNELIUS, Ueber Verschmelzung u. Analyse, Vtljsch. f. wiss. Philos., xvi. 404 ff., xviii. 30 ff.; LIPPS, Der Begriff d. Verschmelzung u. damit Zusammenhängendes, in Stumpf's Tonpsychologie, ii, Philos. Monatsh., xxviii. (1892), 547 ff.; MEINONG, Beitr. z. Theorie d. psychischen Analyse, Zeitsch. f. Psychol., vi. 340, 417; ARDIGO, Opere filosofiche, vii, viii, and L'unità della coscienza (1898), who uses the word confluenza.   (E.B.T.–G.F.S.–E.M.)

Future (consciousness of) [Lat. *futurus*, about to be]: Ger. *Zukunftsgefühl*; Fr. *sentiment de l'avenir*; Ital. *sentimento del futuro*. The mode of time-consciousness which attaches to preadjustment to a coming impression or ideal representation of a coming event. See TIME (cognition of).   (G.F.S., J.M.B.)

Future Punishment: see JUDGMENT.
Future State: see ESCHATOLOGY.

G

Gabler, Georg Andreas. (1786–1853.) A German philosopher who, in 1835, succeeded Hegel at Berlin. He belongs, with Göschel, Hinrichs, Schaller, and others, to the so-called 'right' or orthodox wing of the Hegelian school. His best known work was expository of Hegel.

Galen (Galenus), Claudius. (130 to cir. 210 A. D.) An eminent Greek physician and philosopher. Born at Pergamus, Mysia, he studied both the Platonic and Peripatetic systems of philosophy. Satyrus instructed him in anatomy. He travelled extensively while young to perfect his education. About 165 A. D. he moved to Rome, and became very celebrated as a surgeon and practising physician, attending the family of Marcus Aurelius. He returned to Pergamus, but probably visited Rome three or four times afterwards. He wrote in philosophy, logic, and medicine. Many, probably most, of his works are lost. He was the one medical authority for thirteen centuries, and his services to logic and philosophy were also great.

Gallicanism [Lat. *Gallia*, Gaul, France]: Ger. *Gallikanismus*; Fr. *Gallicanisme*; Ital. *Gallicanismo*. The name given to the nationalizing, independent spirit that so long characterized the Roman Catholic Church in France.

It originated with Irenaeus so early as the 3rd century, and continued for generations, with various vicissitudes, till, under Louis IX (1226–70), the Church in France came to possess peculiar constitutional and ecclesiastical immunities with respect to Papal jurisdiction. The people were protected from the Church in civil affairs; the elections of bishops were to be made by the chapter and clergy of a diocese; and the Church in France had the right to call a council of its own membership. This naturally gave rise to many struggles with Rome, but the disputes usually ended in favour of the French. After the Revolution, the Ultramontane or Roman party gradually gained the upper hand.

Literature: F. HUET, Le Gallicanisme; DUPIN, Les Libertés de l'Église Gallicane; DE MAISTRE, Du Pape; LAMMENAIS, De la Religion dans ses Rapports avec l'Ordre politique. (R.M.W.)

Galluppi (or **Galupi**), **Pasquale.** (1770–1846.) An Italian philosopher, born in Tropea, Calabria. In 1831 he became professor of logic and metaphysics in the University at Naples, and later a member of the Institute of France. He wrote on logical and metaphysical themes; and died in Naples.

Galton's Law (of ancestral inheritance): no foreign equivalents in use. The law formulated by F. Galton to the effect that the distribution among his ancestors of what an individual inherits is as follows : the parents contribute, on the average, together $\frac{1}{2}$, the grandparents together $\frac{1}{4}$, the great-grandparents together $\frac{1}{8}$, &c. 'It may be popularly stated thus : each group of ancestry of the same grade contributes to the heritage of the average offspring double the quantity of the group of the grade above it' (Pearson).

The force of each individual's contribution to successive generations is seen to diminish rapidly when we remember that there are two parents, four grandparents, eight great-grandparents, &c. If we give Galton's formulation thus :

$$H = \tfrac{1}{2} + \tfrac{1}{4} + \tfrac{1}{8} + \dots, \&c.,$$

or $H = \left(\tfrac{1}{4}\right) 2 + \left(\tfrac{1}{16}\right) 4 + \left(\tfrac{1}{64}\right) 8 + \dots, \&c.,$ we see that a person contributes only $\frac{1}{64}$ to his great-grandchild's heredity. This serves to illustrate another principle which is also associated with Galton's name : that of Re- gression (q.v.). For it shows that single individuals of marked characters—called in extreme cases 'sports'—have little permanent influence in changing the stock. The ordinary individuals, representing the average or mean of the species, neutralize the hereditary force of the sport in succeeding generations.

This law has been confirmed by Galton, in the case of Bassett hounds (*Proc. Roy. Soc.*, London, lxi. 401, read June 3, 1897 ; see also *Nature*, July 8, 1897), and by Pearson, also n studies of statistical data. An abstract of Pearson's paper (*Proc. Roy. Soc.*, meeting of Jan. 27, 1898) by himself is printed in *Science* (Mar. 11, 1898), from which the following quotation is made :—

'When the writer of the present paper wrote his memoir on heredity, in 1895 (*Philos. Trans.*, clxxxvii. A, 253), the only available material was contained in Mr. Francis Galton's *Natural Inheritance*, and in the data and measure- ments in Mr. Galton's hands, which he at once placed, with his usual generosity, at the writer's disposal. The very suggestive theory of heredity developed in the *Natural Inheri- tance* has two main features : (*a*) a theory of regression, which states the average propor- tion of any character which will be inherited under any degree of relationship. This theory was very simple : if the average of the sons of any parent had w of the parent's deviation from the average parent, then the average grandson would have w^2 of the deviation, and so on. Collateral heredity was also deter- mined, and for two brothers was found equal to $2w$. Mr. Galton's value of w was $\frac{1}{3}$.

'(*b*) A law of ancestral heredity. Accord- ing to this law the two parents contribute $\frac{1}{4}$, the four grandparents $\frac{1}{8}$, the eight great- grandparents $\frac{1}{16}$, and so on, of the total heritage of the average offspring. Mr. Galton, in 1889 (*Natural Inheritance*, 136), considered this law to rest on a somewhat slender basis.

'In the *Philosophical Transactions* memoir of 1895 the writer started from the general theory of multiple correlation, and supposed the coefficient of heredity to be a quantity which had to be determined by observation for each pair of relatives and for each character. Mr. Galton's own data, when treated by the fuller mathematical theory developed in that memoir, seemed to demonstrate that fraternal could not possibly be twice filial inheritance. But if heredity be looked upon as a quantity to be determined by observation for each organ and each grade of kinship, e. g. if there be no numerical relationship between direct and collateral heredity, then Mr. Galton's law of ancestral heredity must fall to the ground. Accordingly the writer, in 1895, discarded (*b*) and endeavoured to develop (*a*) on the general basis of multiple correlation.

'The recent publication of Mr. Galton's remarkable paper on ancestral heredity in Bassett hounds has, however, led the writer to reconsider (*b*). If the law be true, then for every organ and for every grade of kinship the amount of heredity is numerically de- terminable. The solution of the problem of heredity is thrown back upon the solution of an infinite series of linear equations. Their solution gives results which seem to the writer in good agreement with all we at present know about the influence of heredity in various degrees of kinship. For example, fraternal is no longer *twice* filial regression, but has a value (0·3881) well in accord- ance with the writer's 1895 calculations on Mr. Galton's data. In short, if we discard Mr. Galton's relations between the regressions for various grades of kinship, and start solely from his law of ancestral heredity, the whole theory of heredity becomes simple, luminous, and well in accordance with such quantitative measurements as have so far been made. That it confutes one or two purely hypothetical and semi-metaphysical theories is no disadvantage.

'It is possible, and the writer believes de- sirable, to somewhat generalize the law of ancestral heredity. Modifying Mr. Galton's definition of midparent, a conception is formed of the mid-sth parent, a sort of mean of the ancestry in the sth generation, and the con- tribution of this mid-sth parent to the off- spring is assumed to have a constant ratio to that of the mid-$(s+1)$th parent, whatever be the value of s. With this simple law the whole of heredity is found to depend upon a single constant γ, termed the *coefficient of heredity*. γ may vary from organ to organ and from race to race. It may itself be sub- ject to selection, if heredity be not looked upon as *a priori* given and antecedent to any evolu- tion by natural selection. In Mr. Galton's statement of the law, $\gamma = 1$. This may really be the case, but it is not necessary to the theory, and it is not required by any facts as yet observed.

'Given this simple law of ancestral heredity, there flow from it the following results :—

'(1) The values of all the correlation and

regression coefficients between any pair of relations, i.e. heredity between any grade of individual kinship. The chief of these are actually calculated in the paper [of which this is an abstract].

'(2) The value of the stability that results from any long or short process of selective breeding, and the variability of the breed so established. A coefficient of stability is introduced in the paper and discussed at some length. . . .

'(3) The law of cross heredity, i.e. the degree of relationship between two *different* organs in kindred. It is shown that the coefficient of cross heredity for any pair of organs in any grade of kindred is equal to the product of the coefficient of direct heredity in that grade into the coefficient of organic correlation.

'(4) That simple panmixia without active reversal of natural selection does not lead to degeneration.

' It may be of interest to add that since the law of ancestral heredity allows for the variability of each individual ancestor from the ancestral type, giving that variability its share in the heritage of the offspring, it is inconsistent with Weismann's theory of the germ-plasma. It does not, of course, answer one way or the other the question as to the inheritance of acquired characters.

' To sum up, then, it seems to the present writer that Galton's law of ancestral heredity leads to, what has not hitherto existed, a rounded and comprehensive theory of heredity. It describes with surprising closeness all facts so far quantitatively determined, and opens up a wide range of conclusions which await testing by fresh data. Should those data be in agreement with its predictions, then the law of ancestral heredity will in the future play as large a part in the theory of evolution as the law of gravitation has played in planetary theory. It is the quantitative basis on which Darwinism, the evolution of species by natural selection *combined with heredity*, will then be placed; and at one stroke it will clear away a veritable jungle of semi-metaphysical speculations and hypotheses, and this for the simple reason that it is based upon quantitative observations and not on verbal subtleties. It will be difficult, perhaps, to make people realize that there is a science of heredity, simple and consistent, in existence; yet even at the present time it is the number of observers and experimenters, rather than the science, which needs to be strengthened.'

The law is illustrated in the accompanying figure given by Galton in *Nature*, Jan. 27, 1898, and taken by him from the *Horseman* (Chicago), Dec. 28, 1897; it was devised by A. J. Meston to illustrate Galton's law. Galton's article is quoted at some length.

'It is a property of the infinite series $\frac{1}{2} + \frac{1}{4} + \frac{1}{8} + \&c. \ldots$ that each term is equal to the sum of all those that follow. The prepotencies and subpotencies of particular ancestors, in any given pedigree, are eliminated by a law that deals only with *average* contributions, and the varying prepotencies of sex in respect to different qualities are also presumably eliminated. Corrections for these can of course be made in any particular pedigree, taking care that the corrected series still amounts to 1 exactly.

'It should be borne in mind that "heritage" has a more limited meaning than " nature," or the sum of the inborn qualities. Heritage is confined to that which is inherited, while nature also includes those individual variations that are due to other causes than heredity, and which act before birth. Now individual variation in a race that is stable must have a destructive as well as a constructive effect. Consequently its effects balance one another in *average* results, and disappear from a law which deals only with these.' Cf. VARIATION (statistical treatment of).

' The area of the square diagram represents the total heritage of any particular form or faculty that is bequeathed to any particular individual. It is divided into subsidiary squares bearing distinctive numbers, which severally refer to different ancestors. The size of these subsidiary squares shows the average proportion of the total heritage derived from the corresponding ancestors. . . . The subject of the pedigree is numbered 1. Thenceforward, whatever be the distinctive number of an ancestor, which we will call *n*, the number of its sire is 2 *n*, and that of its dam is 2 *n* + 1. All male numbers in the pedigree are therefore even, and all female numbers are odd. To take an example: 2 is the sire of 1, and 3 is the dam of 1; 6 is the sire of 3, and 7 is the dam of 3. Or working backwards, 14 is a male who is mated to 15; their offspring is 7, and a female, who is mated to 6; their offspring is 3, a female, who is mated to 2; and their offspring is 1, the subject. . . . The numbered squares could be continued indefinitely. In this small diagram they cease with the fourth generation, which contributes $\frac{1}{16}$ part to the total heritage, therefore the whole of the more distant ancestry, comprised in the blank column, contribute $\frac{1}{16}$ also.'

Literature: GALTON, as cited; PEARSON, as cited, also other papers in the series Contrib. to the Math. Theory of Evolution, Proc. Roy. Soc., meeting of Feb. 17, 1898 (abst. in Science, Apr. 22, 1898), and ibid., xlvi. (1900) 140; and Grammar of Sci. (2nd ed., 1900). (J.M.B., E.B.P.)

Gambling [AS. *gamen*, play]: Ger. *Glücks-* (or *Hazard-*)*spiel*; Fr. *jeu* (*de hasard*); Ital. *giuoco* (*d'azzardo*). Staking something of value on one alternative of an issue, the result of which cannot be foreseen or controlled; the play itself is known as 'game of chance.' See PLAY.

Gambling may be looked at both as a sport, a pastime, a recreation, and as a serious business, a passion. The distinction is important when we come to discuss the ethics of gambling. Viewed as sport, the various elements of PLAY (q.v.) are present; yet it is a question whether the staking of something of value does not interfere in all cases with the purity of the play impulse. Certainly in most cases the hope of gain and the fear of loss bring an element of reality into the situation which is opposed to the make-believe or SEMBLANCE (q.v.) of play. In so far as the play motive is pure or socially predominating, other considerations than those of the gambling itself—e.g. the right to play—must enter to give the indulgence ethical value.

The moral question, however, comes in as soon as we leave the play feature out; and various considerations may be advanced on either side. Negatively, it may be said that gambling is not ethically wrong: (1) because if a man stakes what is his own, he has the right to spend it as he please, and he has the right to take from another on the other's own terms. Furthermore, (2) it is just the form of risk which every business venture involves: the merchant buys silk hoping to sell it again before the market price falls below the figure he himself paid; this risk, however, he runs. (3) If we say his motive is not good, seeing that he hopes to make money without giving a fair equivalent either in value or in labour, this again confronts us in many other commercial situations: the unearned increment of land-value often arises from loss to some one else; 'bargains' of all kinds, notably at auctions, come from others' misfortune; taking a high rate of interest from the man whom the loan 'accommodates' is likewise getting return without equivalent. We do not ordinarily condemn a man who takes an unearned legacy. (4) If we shift the point of view and take that of society, saying that what is not of social utility is wrong, we have then to reply that it is the ethically right, not the socially useless, that is in question; and while much may be said to prove that the ethically wrong is always also socially useless, it is a very different thing to convert the proposition. This last point, however, brings us to a distinction which is most important, and on which the whole problem of the relation of social regulation and sanction to personal ethical obligation in large measure turns. To this we may return below.

On the other side it may be said—in addition to the points replied to above—that gambling is wrong: (1) because, and in so far as, it is serious—a passion, not a sport—and comes to supersede the regular forms of industry and business. But this, it is evident, is not an objection to gambling in itself, but to its excess or misuse, and consequently not an ethical objection at all. The man who gambles his time away as well as his money—taking both from his family—is ethically reprobate, not because he gambles, but because he is such a man; so also is he who rents a boat daily and goes fishing, catching nothing. The latter is taking risks; but we blame him for neglect, not for the form it takes—fishing. (2) It is wrong because, and in so far as, it is in a large sense dishonest—a point which, to the present writer, is a valid ethical objection, and the only one, to gambling. To pretend to know, to guess at an issue, to give the 'bluff' to fortune seriously—the money or any other value staked is the warrant of its seriousness, and so is the passion of gain—is the opposite of knowledge, of the careful estimation of evidence and probabilities, of the drawing of legitimate inferences, upon which all normal honestly acquired values rest. Action should proceed only from conviction, or from some deeper motive by which the possible inadequacy of the ground of conviction, and so the absence of conviction, must be or is justified. But in all forms of gambling it is just the point that the issue is known to be beyond calculation, the lack of knowledge is the explicit requirement of fair play; and the action proceeds upon the explicit and mutual will to gain by ignorance. In other words, the man who loses is the victim of this mutual pretence to know, and the man who gains is rewarded for it. They distribute values while doing violence to the relations upon which the values depend. They both act from negative ethical sanctions. If this type of conduct were made universal, it would work havoc with all moral conduct and social order. It is not 'will to believe,' nor 'will to deceive'—the gambler's resolution—but what is often taken for the former: will to ignore the whole system of values by which the moral life is regulated and held to its standards. For this reason, to gamble seriously is to rebel against moral law for a reward. For moral relationships are constituted by action which is reasonable, having motives of knowledge, grounds common to men who think; and to act from unreason, confessedly without ground adequate to the act, is to enter these relationships to destroy them.

From this last point of view we get some light upon the earlier pros and cons of the discussion. The merchant is not gambling, because he is acting on reasonable prospects of gain both in his business as a whole and on his particular ventures. So far as he does take risks on a single article, it is in the interest of his general business. The competitions of commercial life which result in loss to others are the exception to the general expectation, and show bad judgment or low capacity, or are incidental effects—except those which result from the real gambling or design of others, such as stock gambling or manipulation. The business ventures which are gambling are those in which money is staked on a risk whose issue is not foreseen.

Again, the cases of so-called gambling which take advantage of calculation of chances and knowledge of probabilities do not fall within our definition. The law of probabilities, so far as it is exact, is a reasonable resort; and the morality of the use of it rests upon grounds foreign to those of gambling. On certain of the grounds usually given for condemning gambling, it is difficult to see how INSURANCE (q.v.) of any sort is legitimate. In having his life insured a man secures gain indirectly for his family, or directly for himself in the increased ease and free expenditure it allows him, without giving an equivalent. And, moreover, his sole motive is to secure this result. But it is not gambling, for it makes use of knowledge—statistics and probability—which is open to all, and which is used by the insurance companies in their calculations.

Reverting to the question of social utility, we have now the point of view, that being ethically wrong—on the ground that it involves dishonesty—gambling is also socially condemnable; for dishonesty of the sort described is anti-social: it is getting the profit, the value, of a system of social relationships without right to it. Yet this does not exhaust the grounds for its social condemnation; that rests besides upon the general rules of social or governmental interference with individual conduct, and these may contemplate the suppression or regulation of the socially injurious or unproductive quite apart from its ethical character.

Literature: the works on ethics which contain sections on Applied Ethics; GROOS, Play of Man, Pt. II. i. 4 (Eng. trans.), with many references. For works on games see PLAY. (J.M.B.)

Games: see GAMBLING, and PLAY.

Gamogenesis [Gr. γάμος, marriage, + γένεσις, origin]: Ger. *geschlechtliche Fortpflanzung*; Fr. *gamogenèse, reproduction sexuelle* (more often used); Ital. *riproduzione sessuale*. Sexual reproduction, or that mode of reproduction which involves the union of OVUM (q.v.) and SPERMATOZOON (q.v.), or their equivalents. A synonym is Amphigony. See FERTILIZATION, CONJUGATION, and AGAMOGENESIS. (C.LL.M.)

Ganglioblast [Gr. γάγγλιον, tumour, + βλαστός, germ]: Ger. *Ganglioblast*; Fr. *névroblaste*; Ital. *ganglioblasto*. An undifferentiated nerve cell of the spinal or extra-axial ganglia; an immature GANGLIOCYTE (q.v.).

'Aesthesioblast' has been proposed as a name for this type of embryonic cell, but this term is sometimes ambiguous. A ganglio-

blast is simply a special variety of NEURO-
BLAST (q. v.). (H.H.)

Gangliocyte [Gr. γάγγλιον, tumour, +
κύτος, cell]: Ger. *periphere Ganglienzelle*; Fr.
cellule ganglionnaire; Ital. *ganglioceto*. One
of the nerve cells of a spinal or other extra-
axial GANGLION (q.v.). The term 'aesthesio-
cyte' has also been proposed.

The gangliocyte commonly gives rise to a
neurite which passes into the central nervous
system. Thus in the spinal ganglia such
fibres form the greater part of the dorsal or
sensory roots. (H.H.)

Ganglion [Gr. γάγγλιον, a tumour] : Ger.
Gangle; Fr. *ganglion*; Ital. *ganglio*. An
aggregate of nerve cells or GANGLIOCYTES not
contained within the central nervous system;
especially the centres of origin of the sensory
or centripetal nerves. See NERVOUS SYSTEM.

The use of the word 'ganglion' for cell
clusters within the central nervous system
is to be condemned as inaccurate and ambiguous, as well as unnecessary. The distinction between ganglion and plexus, when a
disperse or reticular cell cluster is meant,
is arbitrary. Instead of plexus, GANGLIO-
PLEXUS (q. v.) may be suggested in such
cases. Cf. GANGLIOCYTE, and PLEXUS. The
cells of the cerebrospinal ganglia are unipolar;
those of the sympathetic ganglia, as a rule,
multipolar. See the references given under
NEUROLOGY. (H.H.)

Ganglioplexus [Gr. γάγγλιον, tumour, +
πλέξις, mesh] : Ger. *gangliöses Geflecht, Gang-
lienplexus*; Fr. *plexus ganglionnaire*; Ital. *plesso
gangliare*. A disperse or loosely aggregated
ganglion in a meshwork of fibres (e. g. sympathetic visceral ganglia). See GANGLION, and
PLEXUS.

For convenience, a ganglioplexus is distinguished on the one hand from NEUROPLEXUS
(q. v.), where anastomosis of nerve trunks is
alone included (e.g. brachial plexus), and from
a neuro-reticulum, which refers to anastomosis
between ultimate nerve fibrils, as in the retina
(Dogiel). Cf. NEUROPILEM. (H.H.)

Gans, Eduard. (1798–1839.) Studied
law in Göttingen and in Heidelberg, where
he came to know Hegel. In Berlin he became a follower and intimate acquaintance of
Hegel. In 1820 he began teaching in Berlin,
after 1825 as ordinary professor of law. He
did much for the spread of Hegel's ideas.

Garve, Christian. (1742–98.) German
philosopher, born at Breslau, and educated
under A. G. Baumgarten at Frankfort, at
Halle, and at Leipzig. He was strongly in-

fluenced by Gellert, and especially by Engel,
with whom he became very intimate. In
1770 he succeeded Gellert as professor of
philosophy in Leipzig, but in 1772, on account of ill health, resigned his chair.

Gassendi, Pierre. (1592–1655.) Philosopher, born at Champtercier, Provence. A
precocious youth, he took, for a time, in 1612,
the professorship in theology at Digne. In
1616 he became professor of philosophy in
the university at Aix. He next took priestly
orders (1617), and became canon, and then
provost, of the diocese of Digne (1623). In
1645 he was made professor of mathematics in
Paris. He corresponded and enjoyed close
friendship with Kepler, Descartes, Galileo,
Hobbes. In some respects his philosophy
resembles Locke's.

Gastraea Theory : Ger. *Gastrulatheorie*;
Fr. *gastræa-théorie*; Ital. *teoria della gastrea*.
The theory that the ancestor of the Metazoa
was a two-layered sac or gastrula, formed of
an outer ectoderm and an inner endoderm,
which arose by invagination, and enclosed the
archenteron or primitive digestive cavity,
opening to the exterior by the primitive mouth
or blastopore. See GASTRULA, EMBRYO, and
INVAGINATION. (E.S.G.)

First suggested by Haeckel and summarized
by him in the *Quart. J. of Microsc. Sci.*, xiv.
(1874) 142 and 223, this view has been widely
accepted. Compare Lankester's PLANULA
THEORY (q.v.), according to which the primitive enteron originated by DELAMINATION
(q. v.).

Literature : HAECKEL, Quart. J. Microsc.
Sci. as above, and xvi. (1876) 51; LANKESTER,
Ann. and Mag. Nat. Hist., May, 1873, and
Quart. J. Microsc. Sci., Oct., 1877; F. M.
BALFOUR, Compar. Embryol. (1880). (C.LL.M.)

Gastrula : see GASTRAEA THEORY (also
for literature), and cf. EMBRYO. (C.LL.M.)

Gautama or **Gotama.** The founder of
Buddhism ; the name of Buddha as a person-
ality. See BUDDHA, and ORIENTAL PHILO-
SOPHY (India).

Gemmule [Lat. *gemmula*, a little bud]:
Ger. *Knöspchen*; Fr. *gemmule*; Ital. *gemmula*.
(1) A term sometimes applied to embryonic
stages in the development of the Sponges.

(2) The term applied by Darwin to the
ultra-microscopic organic particles given off
by cells. See PANGENESIS. (C.LL.M.)

Gender [OF. *gendrer*, from Lat. *generare*,
to beget]: Ger. *Geschlecht*; Fr. *genre*; Ital.
genere. A grammatical classification of nouns
connected either through meaning, or merely

through outward form, with the distinctions of sex.

The Indo-European and the Hamitic-Semitic groups of languages are the only ones in which discrimination of gender is fully observed. Some languages discriminate in the form of their nouns between objects as inanimate and animate, e. g. the Cherokee; others between objects as rational and irrational, noble and mean, &c. In most cases such discriminations are mere traditional superfluities, serving little or no purpose in identifying the object. In modern English they have in general been omitted, except as they serve such purpose. The origin of the gender distinctions has been commonly explained, since Adelung and Grimm, as a consequence of the primitive tendency to personify natural objects. Recently the view has been urged by Brugmann and others that the distinction is originally one of grammatical form, attached to the sex-discrimination, through the accident that some words of a class, now thought of as feminine, denoted female objects. Thus it is suggested that the Indo-European *gṇná*, lying behind, Greek γυνή, &c., may have originally been abstract or collective, like other words of this ending, and have denoted 'hearing,' then 'the animal that hears.' This noun, with perhaps others of its class, may then have led the whole group over into association with the notion of female sex. This theory is at present too imperfectly developed to warrant acceptance. Whatever the origin, it is evident that in the languages employing it the discrimination is chiefly one of grammatical form. This the linguistic consciousness attests. 'Der Kopf' is no more masculine to the German than 'la tête' is feminine to the Frenchman. Language is a conventional, rather than a purely practical, body of signs, and in acquiring a language the speaker learns and accepts the gender of nouns as he does the rest of their forms. In adopting new words a language generally assigns them to the gender groups according to the form of the ending.

Literature: J. GRIMM, Deutsche Grammatik, iii. 311 ff.; K. BRUGMANN, Das Nominalgeschlecht, Techmer's Int. Zeitsch., iv. 100 ff.; and The Nature and Origin of Noun Genders (1897); B. I. WHEELER, Grammatical Gender, Class. Rev., Nov. 1889, 390 ff.; and J. Germ. Philol., Oct. 1899; B. DELBRÜCK, Vergleichende Syntax, i. 89 ff. (1893). (B.I.W.)

General Concept, Idea, or **Notion**: Ger. *Allgemeinbegriff*; Fr. *notion générale*; Ital. *concetto (nozione) generale*. The thought of certain characters as found in, or representative of, a plurality of special cases or instances. See ABSTRACT IDEA, CONCEPTION, and GENERALIZATION.

The terms general concept, general idea, and general notion refer to the same kind of psychical state from somewhat different points of view. A general concept always includes two essential and essentially distinct constituents: (1) An 'image' which may be, and very frequently is, merely a 'word'; (2) the meaning of this image which is not itself present to consciousness in the form of an image or images. The term general idea emphasizes the presence of the image. The term general notion emphasizes the presence of consciousness of meaning.

Historical discussion of the general idea has mainly turned on the nature of the mental imagery which it involves. Verbal signs or their equivalent are generally recognized as playing a most important part. The generic image or percept may accompany the word or function instead of it. Ultimately the distinction between abstract and concrete thought is not a matter of imagery: it is rather notional (see NOTION). The controversy as to the nature of abstract ideas goes back to the time of the scholastic dispute concerning nominalism, realism, and conceptualism. Realism is not a psychological theory at all, as it relates to the nature of the reality apprehended in the abstract idea. But the issue as between nominalism and conceptualism remains one on which psychological writers have not come to complete clearness. Berkeley stands out as a typical representative of nominalism, holding that what we have in the mind when we conceive an abstract idea is either merely a word or an individual image, on part of which attention is concentrated, the rest being regarded as irrelevant. Certain modern writers hold that this is all that exists in consciousness, but add that there are unconscious mental modifications or physiological dispositions, which play an essential part in the process. This view is well represented by Lipps, Ribot, and von Kries. Others, with whom the present writer agrees, hold that unconscious dispositions are not sufficient, but that there is in consciousness another factor which nominalism omits. Baldwin states this in strictly motor terms, with which Royce seems to agree (see remarks by Havard, *Rev. de Mét. et de Mor.*, iv, 1896, 690). See NOMINALISM, and REALISM. (G.F.S.—J.M.B.)

General Consciousness: see SOCIAL CONSCIOUSNESS.

General Good: Ger. *allgemeines Wohl*; Fr. *bien général*; Ital. *bene generale*. The good of all mankind, or, in a more restricted sense, of the community referred to.

In the former sense the promotion of general good has often been taken as the ethical ideal for man's conduct, e.g. by Cumberland (*De Leg. Nat.*, 1672), under the name 'the common good of all rationals'; sometimes, in the more restricted sense, the general good of the members of a state or community is said to be the end of statecraft in that community. In working out either of these views, it is commonly assumed that a certain amount of evil befalling some members of the community may be counterbalanced by an equal amount of good accruing to an equal number of other persons; though the precise statement and development of this position are only carried out when 'good' is interpreted as equivalent to 'happiness' (see GREATEST HAPPINESS). The question as to the nature or constituents of good is fundamental for ethics. Hedonists maintain that it is reducible to happiness in the sense of pleasure and freedom from pain. But the conception, as originally put forward in English ethics by Cumberland, involves two constituents, happiness and perfection: and various attempts have been made so to interpret the latter notion as to give a satisfactory account of the good for man. See PERFECTION, and SELF-REALIZATION.

Literature: SIDGWICK, Meth. of Eth., Bk. III. chap. xiv; GREEN, Proleg. to Eth., Bk. III. (W.R.S.)

General Term: Ger. *allgemeiner Terminus*; Fr. *terme général*; Ital. *termine generale*. The verbal expression of a notion or concept; that is, of the representation of marks common to an indefinite number of individuals.

A general term may therefore be described as being the name of each and all of a number of individuals; or, better, as being applicable to each and all on the ground of, and with the implication of, their possessing in common definite marks. (R.A.)

General (or Social) Will: Ger. *Gesammtwille* (Wundt), *sozialer Wille* (Tönnies); Fr. *volonté générale* (Rousseau); Ital. *volontà sociale* (or *collettiva*). Used vaguely to indicate a supposed collective will in a community or group of individuals arising from their intercourse with one another, assented to, though not always privately endorsed, by all the individuals, and expressed or expressible through some common channel, such as the state, conventions, voting, &c.

Various attempts have been made to give exact psychological or metaphysical definition to the general will, distinguishing it from the individual's will, the 'will of all,' &c., but they all represent more or less personal points of view. The beginning of the discussion, and also the term, are to be found in Rousseau (cf. SOCIAL CONSCIOUSNESS). Tönnies makes a further distinction between the general will of a society or Gesellschaft, and that of a COMPANY (q. v.) or Gemeinschaft, calling the latter 'race-will' (Wesenwille). He thus finds a genetic opposition between the race-will resting on Trieb (instinctive Handlung) and the social or general will resting on intelligent choice (Willkürhandlung). So far as this is sound, as the present writer holds it to be (so also Wundt, *Logik*, II. ii. 600), it forbids the use of the term 'will' for both the two forms. Wundt justifies the use of the term in the interests of a theory of will which includes impulse, i. e. makes will synonymous with conation. This is more than questionable psychologically; and if conation is to be used at all, this is its fair opportunity. We then have two forms of general or common conation (Gesammtstreben): (1) the 'common impulse' of the company (e. g. of animals, crowds, &c.), with the German equivalent Gesammttrieb; and (2) general, social, or common will, with the equivalent Gesammtwille. Wundt would seem to be right in saying that the opposition between the two forms is that of higher and lower in evolution, and in pointing out that social impulse and instinct are always present as well in higher social organization, and essential to it (loc. cit., 600 n.). Cf. also Barth, *Geschichtsphilos. als Soziol.*, i. 382, who follows Tönnies.

The distinction to the effect that the individual pursues a general plan of action, while society only attains bit by bit without such a plan, seems to be valid.

Literature: ROUSSEAU, Contrat Social; BOSANQUET, Philos. Theory of the State (1899); NOVIKOW, Conscience et Volonté sociales (1899); TÖNNIES, Philosophical Terminology, Mind, N.S., No. 31 (July, 1899); and Gemeinschaft u. Gesell. (1887); WUNDT, Logik, II. ii. chap. iv. § 4 a; BALDWIN, Social and Eth. Interpret., chaps. xii, xiii; BARTH, as cited; also many of the references cited under SOCIAL PSYCHOLOGY. (J.M.B.–G.F.S.)

Generalization [Lat. *generalis*, from *genus*, kind]: Ger. *Verallgemeinerung*; Fr. *généralisation*; Ital. *facoltà* (*operazione*) *di generalizzare*. The act of recognizing a likeness of nature where it has not been recognized before, involving either the formation of a new GENERAL CONCEPT (q. v.) or the extension of an old one to cover a new class of instances. See also CONCEPTION.

All generalization involves abstraction; to generalize is to recognize likeness which had been previously masked by differences; to recognize the likeness is also therefore to recognize these differences as irrelevant, and to disregard them from the point of view of the general conception. Such recognition is abstraction.

Sigwart distinguishes between two kinds of generality. The first kind is 'merely numerical,' and comprehends like instances which are 'not conceptually distinguishable, but only separate in space and time': the proposition that oxygen and hydrogen combine to form water is given as an illustration. See EXTENSION (logical). The second kind of generality is that of a genus, to which are subordinated specific instances: this is illustrated by the proposition that 'all the elements combine chemically in certain proportions.' Sigwart apparently proposes to limit the term 'generalization' to the formation or extension of the second kind of general concept.

Literature: the textbooks of psychology and logic (e. g. SIGWART). (G.F.S.—J.M.B.)

Generation (spontaneous): Ger. *Zeugung*; Fr. *génération*; Ital. *generazione*. See Abiogenesis, under BIOGENESIS.

Generation of God. A phrase which refers to the relation of origination subsisting between God and Christ—directly or through the medium of the Logos—whereby the latter is the 'Son of God.'

Out of this question the christological conclusions of the 4th century grew, and were embodied in dogmas. The problem appears clearly with Justin Martyr, the first dogmatic theologian of Christianity, who was doubtless moved to systematic consideration of the matter by contemporary GNOSTICISM (q. v.) and DOCETISM (q. v.). Justin transferred the generation of Christ from God to the Logos. From all time the Logos was able to become man, and, by the will of God, did become human in Christ. Thus in Christ humanity was united with Deity. The discussion was taken up later by Origen and others, and thence passed over into the controversy over ARIANISM (q. v.). In its beginnings it is of interest as showing how Christianity early felt the pressure of Gnostic modes of thought and found it necessary to express itself by aid of Gnostic conceptions.

Literature: DORNER, The Devel. of the Doctrine of the Person of Christ (Eng. trans.), Div. I. i. 274 f., ii. 209 f., 270 f.; HARNACK, Hist. of Dogma (Eng. trans.), ii. 220 f. (R.M.W.)

Generic [Lat. *genus*, kind]: Ger. *generisch*; Fr. *générique*; Ital. *generico*. Generic applies to differences which distinguish species belonging to different genera, as e.g. isosceles triangle is specifically different from equilateral triangle, and generically different from a square; or to the points of agreement by possession of which numbers of distinct species would be referred to one and the same genus, as e.g. the mental life of a man and an ant might be said to be specifically different and generically alike.

In recent logical treatments, e.g. that of Lotze and Bosanquet, generic has been used as the designation of a judgment in which the predicate is asserted of the subject universally, but as attaching to or incompatible with the constitutive marks of the subject, therefore without explicit qualification of the subject, as e.g. man is fallible, rational, mortal, or the like. (R.A.)

Generic Image: Ger. *Gemeinbild* (not *Vorstellung*, which is given as the equivalent of Idea); Fr. *image composée*; Ital. *immagine composita*. A mental IMAGE (q. v.) possessing a distinct and salient centre or core corresponding to the common characters of a class, together with a vague and inconstant margin corresponding to the variable characters of the individuals composing the class.

The generic image is supposed to originate in the repeated presentation of like contents in varying combinations. An analogy is usually drawn from what is called 'composite photography.' The following description of the process is given by Huxley:—'When several complex impressions which are more or less different from one another—let us say that out of ten impressions in each, six are the same in all, and four are different from the rest—are successively presented to the mind, it is easy to see what must happen. The repetition of the six similar impressions will strengthen the six corresponding elements of the complex idea, which will therefore acquire greater vividness, while the four differing impressions of each will not only acquire no greater strength than they had at first, but in accordance with the law of association, they will all tend to appear at once, and will thus neutralize one another.'

Such an account of the genesis of the generic image is essentially defective, for it fails to bring out the part played by selective interest in emphasizing certain features of experience to the neglect of others. But it is noteworthy that those writers who have laid most stress on the importance of the generic image agree in this view of it as a merely passive product of the play of external impressions, e. g. Herbart, Beneke, and Galton. Herbart and Beneke do not use the term 'generic image' (Gemeinbild), but they describe what is meant by it with entire clearness and distinctness. Some writers (including those named above) have simply identified the generic image with the rudimentary conception, and have thought that in accounting for its origin they have accounted for the origin of conceptual thinking. But this view is rejected by most competent psychologists. A conception cannot be quite identified with an image of any kind. All depends on the meaning of the image, the representative value which it has for thought. On the other hand, it is usually held that the generic image plays a more or less important part in the genesis of concepts of a low order of generality. Though not in itself a conception, it is supposed to supply a kind of material peculiarly adapted to function as a vehicle of conceptual thinking. No doubt this is so to some extent, but the importance of the generic image, even from this point of view, has been frequently exaggerated.

Literature: psychological textbooks in general; HERBART, Psychol. als Wiss., &c., §§ 120–3; BENEKE, Logik, § 38 ff., and Psychol. Skizzen, ii. 158 ff.; WAITZ, Lehrb. d. Psychol., 518 ff.; VOLKMANN, Psychologie, ii. 243, 247; HUXLEY, Hume, 94 ff.; GALTON, Inquiries into Human Faculty, Appendix on Generic Images; STOUT, Analytic Psychol., 179 ff., 183 ff., 196. (G.F.S., J.M.B.)

Generosity [Lat. *generosus*, from *genus*, race]: Ger. *Edelsinn*; Fr. *générosité*; Ital. *generosità*. The disposition shown either in the favourable estimate of the good qualities of others, or in the bestowal of goods or favours upon others with more or less self-denial.

It is nearly equivalent to liberality, but indicates a more intense form of the same disposition and involves self-denial. Thus Adam Smith (*Mor. Sent.*, Pt. IV. chap. ii) distinguishes generosity from humanity : ' Humanity consists merely in the exquisite fellow-feeling which the spectator entertains with the sentiments of the persons principally concerned. . . . The most humane actions require no self-denial. . . . But it is otherwise with generosity. We never are generous except when in some respect we prefer some other person to ourselves, and sacrifice some great and important interest of our own to an equal interest of a friend or a superior.' (W.R.S.–J.M.B.)

Genesis (1) and **Genetic** (2) [Gr. γένεσις] : Ger. (1) *Genese* or *Ursprung* and (2) *genetisch*; Fr. (1) *genèse* or *origine* and (2) *génétique*; Ital. (1) *genesi*, (2) *genetico*. (1) Original production. (2) Pertaining to, exhibiting, exemplifying or dealing with genesis. Cf. ORIGIN *versus* NATURE.

As contrasted with origin, genesis has come to be the scientific term for the exhaustive statement of the essential factors and conditions in the production of phenomenal changes and complex products generally. It has the further advantage of supplying an adjective which may be used both actively and passively. Genetic science is science which deals with problems of origin and development; and the problems with which it deals are also described as genetic. Again, the forces at work to produce a result are described as genetic, as well as the results which these forces produce. In compounds, however, for the active sense 'genic' is more properly used, and genetic for the passive. In German the case is about the same, Ursprung being used as synonymous with Genese (as origin is with genesis in English); but as there is no adjective form from that stem to use both actively and passively, genetisch comes to supply the lack. So also with origine and genèse in French.

The problems and data of SCIENCE (q. v.) are often divided into two great headings, quantitative and genetic, either of which, however, may be either descriptive or explanatory (employing exact measurement). The ideal of science is to secure both quantitative and genetic statements of all phenomena.

Literature: see under EVOLUTION; also RITCHIE, Darwin and Hegel; ROYCE, Religious Aspect of Philos.; BALDWIN, The Origin of a Thing and its Nature, Psychol. Rev., ii. (1895) 551. (J.M.B., G.F.S.)

Genetic Method (in education): Ger. *genetische Methode*; Fr. *méthode génétique*; Ital. *metodo genetico*. The explanation of things, for purposes of instruction, according to their genesis, or manner of coming into being. See METHOD (in education). (C.DE G.)

Genetic Psychology: Ger. *genetische Psychologie*; Fr. *psychologie génétique*; Ital. *psicologia genetica, psicogenìa*. Psychology in so far as it concerns itself with questions of mental evolution, development, and growth.

The terms development and evolution suggest the two great departments of genetic psychology: the development of the individual mind, and the evolution of the mind in the history of the animal series and of man. For the former CHILD (or infant) PSYCHOLOGY (q. v.) is used. In the latter there are again two departments, as just indicated: mental evolution in the animals and man, treated by RACE PSYCHOLOGY, and its differential forms in the human species, treated by FOLK PSYCHOLOGY: see these terms, also for literature; and see PSYCHOLOGY. (J.M.B.)

Genetic Selection: see REPRODUCTIVE (or GENETIC) SELECTION.

Genius [Lat. *genius*, the tutelar spirit of a place]: Ger. *Genius, Genie*; Fr. *génie*; Ital. *genio*. A person whose mental or moral capacity or achievements are of extraordinarily high quality or value. As applied to the endowment or capacity which makes such a person successful as contrasted with the man, we have the distinction between Genius and Genie in the German. The generality of the term genius has been such, that various writers have proposed the most varying definitions of the distinguishing marks of the genius' endowment. (J.M.B.–G.F.S.)

There is great lack in English of an adjective corresponding to the French *génial*; the form 'genial' might be made technical; as genial idea, an idea of genius.

Genius refers to mental superiority in an unusual degree, and usually implies innate originality and individuality. Passing by the literary discussions of the nature of genius, and the appearance of men of genius, the scientific interest in recent years may be said to have been chiefly concerned with (1) the determination of a working conception of genius; (2) the investigation of the prominent characteristics of great men; (3) the hereditary character of unusual mental powers; (4) the possible relations between genius and insanity or degeneration.

(1) That the distribution of human faculty fairly well follows the laws of the general distribution of VARIATIONS (q. v.) has been shown by Galton, who thus develops the conception of genius or greatness as the few outlying members of an orderly series, the number in the group diminishing according to determined laws, as the degree of eminence or divergence from the average increases. This conception is useful in many ways, and is particularly helpful in the investigation of heredity. (2) The natural history of great men; what they derive from nature, and what from nurture, what influences favour and what hinder their growth; their possible peculiarities of physique, their precocity, their physiological and psychological characteristics— these and similar problems have been rediscussed in the light of recent science. While no conclusions of general validity can be readily cited, the scope of the literature suggests the aims and direction of such study. (3) The hereditary transmission of mental endowment has intrinsic interest, and is also of great importance in the formulation of general conceptions of heredity. Galton has conclusively exhibited the hereditary nature of greatness in the groups which he has studied, not only in general, but also in considerable detail. (4) The view that genius is an abnormal, as well as an unusual, phenomenon is an old one, and has been revived in connection with recent studies of morbid psychology (Moreau de Tours), and of degeneration (Lombroso). The general statement may be ventured that the special liability of men of unusual endowments to nervous and mental disorders has been fairly well established, but that the conception of any identity of nature between the phenomena that constitute insanity and genius is not proved. The point of greatest strain and achievement is naturally near to the danger line of accident and disaster. (J.J.)

Lombroso has revived the doctrine of Moreau de Tours, who had united, in 1859, the ideas of the French alienists, Lélut, Morel, and others, in his work *La Psychologie morbide dans ses Rapports avec la Philosophie et l'Histoire*. The revival of Moreau's theory by Lombroso and his pupils (e.g. Antonini, Patrizi, Sergi, Cognetti, &c.) consists in ingrafting the concept of the neurosis peculiar to genius upon the doctrine of degeneration held by Morel. Lombroso believes that genius is an epileptoid variety of degeneration, and bases his opinion upon certain characters (stigmates) of the men of genius. Max Nordau in his book, *Degeneration* (Eng. trans.), applied this doctrine as a method of criticism in modern arts and poetry. Against Lombroso and his exaggerated deductions in pathological and social psychology, Morselli, Venturi, and others have come forward, who think genius is a progressive or evolutionary variation of the human (and every other living) type, either general or partial. Morselli thinks genius consistent with some degeneration, since a profitable variation of intellect, sentiment, or will is capable of developing together with some degenerative characters. The Lombrosian view of the epilepsy of the genius is vigorously opposed as a useless appendage to what is otherwise a definite clinical conception. (E.M.)

A much discussed question is the relation of the great man—the genius, especially the greatest man—to the general course of history and to social evolution. On the one hand, the 'great-man theory' of history holds that the genius is himself not a product of the social movement, but a phenomenon—a variation or other positively new influence—which sets the direction of the historical and social movement subsequent to him. On this view history is a series of smaller movements, each carrying out the impulse given it by some great character. Opposed to this is the view that the great man is himself an index of the social movement anterior to him—he is a result of the deeper moving forces from which history issues. He is, therefore, only relatively, not absolutely, the centre of new influences : the indication rather than the initiator of social change. Besides these opposed views, each extreme, more moderate opinion recognizes the importance of the genius, but does not make him an unaccountable prodigy. It attempts to reach a philosophy of the social movement as a whole, which, while recognizing the implicit forces which produce the genius, still allows place for great variations and their influence ; not admitting either that the environment is altogether the cause of Cleopatra, or that the course of the world's political history would have been different— to quote Pascal's famous saying—if Cleopatra's nose had been shorter ! Cf. Comte, *Cours de Philos. positive*, ed. Littré (3rd ed., 1869), iv ; and for a judicious discussion of this question, with citation of literature, see Barth, *Philos. d. Gesch. als Sociol.*, i. 200 f. Statistical inquiries into the inheritance of unusual talent have been made by Galton (*Natural Inheritance*, 1889), and into the nature and distribution of men of genius by Odin (*Genèse des grands hommes*, 1895). (J.M.B.)

Literature : GALTON, Hereditary Genius, and English Men of Science (1874) ; JOLY,

Psychol. des grands hommes (1893) ; WEISE, Allg. Theorie des Genies ; RADESTOCK, Genie u. Wahnsinn (1889) ; SCHOPENHAUER, World as Will and Idea, i. Bk. III. § 36, and ii. chap. xxxi ; HIRSCH, Genius and Degeneration (1897) (contains full literary references) ; MOREAU (de Tours), La Psychol. morbide dans ses Rapports avec l'Hist. (1856) ; SPENCER, Study of Sociol. ; JAMES, The Will to Believe, 216 ff. ; LOMBROSO, L'Uomo di Genio (6th ed.), Genio e Follia, and The Man of Genius (1894) ; BRENTANO, Psychol. des Genies ; MALLOCK, Aristocracy and Progress ; NORDAU, Degeneration ; ALLEN and FISKE, Atlantic Mo., xlvii. 75 and 351 ; BALDWIN, Social and Eth. Interpret. ; MORSELLI, Genio e Nevrosi (1892), and Riv. di Filos. Scient., *passim* ; ALPH. DE CANDOLLE, Hist. des Sciences et des Savants (1873) ; NISBET, The Insanity of Genius (1891) ; TÜRCK, Der geniale Mensch (1897) ; ODIN, as above. (J.J.–J.M.B.–G.F.S.)

Genu [Lat. *genu*, knee] : Ger. *Knie* ; Fr. *genou* ; Ital. *ginocchio*. See BRAIN (glossary).

Genus (in biology) : see CLASSIFICATION (in biology).

Genus (in logic) [Lat. *genus*, birth] : Ger. *Genus* ; Fr. *genre* ; Ital. *genere*. A class which contains within its extension, or is divisible into, smaller classes, called relatively species.

The significance of the term has always shared the ambiguity which is discernible in classification. Genera have been distinguished partly by reason of the obvious differences in the larger types of natural forms, partly by reference to the relatively arbitrary process of arranging in accordance with selected marks. The first or empirical factor is predominant in the popular sense of the term, and in much of the Aristotelian and Scholastic logic ; the second has been insisted on in the more strictly formal logic. The divergence of the two views makes itself manifest at the limits of classification, at the conception of a *summum genus* and an *infima species*, which tend on the one view to be regarded as having a place *in rerum natura*, while on the other they are but ideal boundaries to an arbitrary process. (R.A.)

One of the Aristotelian rules of DIVISION (q. v.) in logic is that the differences of different genera are different, that is to say, cross-divisions are not to be made. This rule is signally violated in the modern classifications of chemistry, mathematics, and logic itself ; but in biology, owing to the common origin of species, the classification is hierarchical, as Aristotle required. Cf. PREDICABLES. (C.S.P.)

411

Geometrical Mean: see MEAN AND MEDIAN.

Geometry [Gr. γεωμετρία, measurement of the earth]: Ger. *Geometrie*; Fr. *géométrie*; Ital. *geometria*. The science of the relations growing out of extension in space, abstraction being made of all properties but those pertaining to space itself.

Its subject-matter is formed of ideal bodies, having mobility, rigidity, and extension, but no other properties of matter. The property of extension may be ideally limited to one or two dimensions, or reduced to no dimensions, as in the case of a point. Such bodies are in imagination moved about as if real, and the science is constructed by pure reasoning about their necessary properties. Cf. SPACE. (S.N.)

George, Leopold. (1811–73.) Born in Berlin, he became Privatdocent there, and then professor of philosophy at Greifswald, where he died. He attempted to synthesize the philosophical principles of Hegel and Schleiermacher. His *Metaphysics* and *Psychology* are his chief works. These were followed, much later, by *Logic as a Theory of Knowledge*.

Geotropism: see TROPISM.

Gérando, Joseph Marie de: see DÉGÉRANDO.

Germ [Lat. *germen*, a bud]: Ger. *Keim*; Fr. *germe*; Ital. *germe*. A word sometimes used for the organism in an early embryonic stage, or for the rudimentary beginnings of an organ. Now generally restricted to use in composition, e.g. germ-cell (see OVUM), GERMPLASM (q.v.), germ-layer (see EPIBLAST, and HYPOBLAST). (C.LL.M.)

Germinal Selection: Ger. *Germinalselektion*; Fr. *sélection germinale*; Ital. *selezione germinale*. The outcome of intra-germinal competition or 'struggle for existence,' as the result of which certain DETERMINANTS (q.v.) flourish rather than others. Cf. INTRASELECTION.

Suggested by Weismann (*Monist*, vi. No. 2, Jan. 1896, also *Ueber Germinalselektion*, 1896) as a supplementary hypothesis, in his scheme of hereditary transmission, to account for the hypertrophy and atrophy of some organs or structures, and for the appearance of variations in certain directions. He unwarrantably admits the position that variations appear 'when and where they are wanted,' and so seem to be DETERMINATE (q.v.); but by this hypothesis he is able to claim that natural selection has already been at work upon the germinal determinants. (C.LL.M.–J.M.B.)

The hypothesis of germinal selection is generally considered one of the most important recent suggestions looking to the supplementing of natural selection without resort to the Lamarckian FACTORS OF EVOLUTION (q. v.). It is the last possible application of the notion of struggle for existence, carrying that conception beyond the struggle of individuals and the struggle of parts to the struggle of germs in the single organism. It provides a purely hypothetical way of securing lines of determinate evolution.

Literature: THOMSON, The Problem of Life; CONN, The Method of Evolution; GROOS, The Play of Man (Eng. trans.), 373; and (more technical) DELAGE, Année biologique, 1 ff., Index; WEISMANN, as cited above. (J.M.B.)

Germinal Vesicle: Ger. *Keimbläschen*; Fr. *vésicule germinative*; Ital. *vescicola germinativa*. The nucleus of the ovum before the formation of the polar bodies.

The germinal vesicle was described by Purkinje in 1825, the germinal spot (nucleolus) by Wagner in 1836. The terms are now falling into disuse. See F. M. Balfour, *Compar. Embryol*. (C.LL.M.)

Germination (in botany) [Lat. *germen*, a bud]: Ger. *Keimen*; Fr. *germination*; Ital. *germinazione*. The resumption of the active processes of growth by seeds and spores after a time of quiescence or suspended animation. (E.S.G.)

Germ-plasm: Ger. *Keimplasma*; Fr. *plasma germinatif*; Ital. *germiplasma, plasma germinativo*. The substance which forms the physical basis of heredity. Employed by Weismann (*The Germ-Plasm*, 1893). Probably identical with IDIOPLASM (q.v.). Cf. SOMA. (C.LL.M.)

Gerson, Jean Charlier de. (1363–1429.) Born at Gerson, died at Lyons. A French theologian. In 1377 he entered the College of Navarra in Paris, and d'Ailly and Henry of Oyta taught him logic and theology. In 1397 he was made dean of Bourges; after 1401, pastor of St. Jean en Grève in Paris. He lectured on mysticism in 1404, and wrote a work on the subject in 1407. His denunciation of the murderer of the duke of Orleans necessitated his leaving Paris (1419) and remaining several years in Germany. His numerous works were among the first printed books. He is supposed by some to be the author of the *Imitation of Christ*. His work on the *Consolations of Theology* is also well known.

Gersonides. (cir. 1288–1344.) Born in Bagnol, Languedoc. A follower of Maimonides. He studied Aristotle in the works of Averroës, and was familiar with the Bible and Talmud.

He sought to show, as his master had begun to do, the agreement of Aristotle with the Bible, believing that the latter touches all fields of knowledge. He differed from Averroës in asserting personal immortality. He exercised great influence over Spinoza, as did also Maimonides.

Gestation (period of) [Lat. *gestare*, to carry]: Ger. *Tragzeit, Dauer der Schwangerschaft*; Fr. *gestation*; Ital. *gestazione, gravidanza*. The time which elapses between the conception and the birth of the young mammal.

The following are the periods of gestation in some of the commoner mammals, in days: elephant 593, giraffe 440, mare 330, cow 286, man 280, red deer 245, hippopotamus 234, monkey (cebus) 150, pig 120, dog 63, cat 56, kangaroo 38. Attempts have been made to find a definite relation between the average length of life and the period of gestation.

Literature: R. OWEN, Compar. Anat. and Physiol. of the Vertebrates; F. LATASTE, Des variations de durée de la gestation chez les mammifères, C. R. Soc. de Biol., Paris, 9e sér., iii. 21–162 (1891). (C.LL.M.)

Gesture Language [Med. Lat. *gestura*, a mode of action, from Lat. *gestus*, an act]: Ger. *Gebärdensprache*; Fr. *langage de gestes*; Ital. *linguaggio mimico*. The conventionalized use of mien and gesture for the expression of thoughts and feelings.

The facial movements and the gestures which to a greater or less extent accompany vocal speech, enforcing or supplementing it, and which notably play an important part in the expression of mood among, for instance, the peoples of Southern Europe—Greeks, Neapolitans, Sicilians, Portuguese—are closely allied in their psychological conditions to the phenomena of speech. The interpretation of such gestures as are handed down in the art of ancient peoples may be regarded as an auxiliary to hermeneutics. See K. Sittl, *Die Gebärden d. Griechen u. Römer*; A. Baumeister, *Gebärdensprache in d. Kunst*, Denkmäler, i. 586 ff. Among scattered tribes of savages the language of gesture, based in part on reflex movements, in part on directly significant movements, often becomes a conventional system, serving the purpose of communication without aid from vocal speech.

Literature: G. MALLERY, First Ann. Rep. Bureau of Ethnol. (Washington), 1879–80, and Sign Language, Techmer's Int. Zeitsch., i. 193 ff. (1884); CH. DARWIN, Expression of Emotion in Man and Animals (1872). (B.I.W.)

The artificial gesture language of the deaf shows the operation of such a system constructed from alphabetical elements. (J.M.B.)

Geulincx (or **Geulinks**), **Arnold**. (1625–69.) Cartesian philosopher, educated at the University of Louvain, where he later lectured. Moved to Leyden, and became a Protestant. See CARTESIANISM, and OCCASIONALISM.

Ghost [Sansk. *ghas*, spirit]: Ger. (1) *Gespenst*; Fr. (1) *spectre, fantôme*; Ital. (1) *ombra, anima*. (1) An apparition, usually of the sort taken to be a disembodied spirit, but applied also to any sort of apparent manifestation from a spirit world.

(2) An early word for SPIRIT (q.v.). (J.M.B.)

Ghost Theory. A name often given to Herbert Spencer's theory of the origin of religion.

The 'ghost theory' is affirmed in many places in Spencer's *Principles of Sociology*, where the evidence is also adduced. A brief statement of it in his own words is as follows:— 'While primitive men, regarding themselves as at the mercy of surrounding ghosts, try to defend themselves by the aid of the exorcist and the sorcerer, who deal with ghosts antagonistically, there is simultaneously adopted a contrary behaviour towards ghosts—a propitiation of them. . . . Out of this motive and these observances come all forms of worship. Awe of the ghost makes sacred the sheltering structure for the tomb, and this grows into the temple, while the tomb itself becomes the altar. From provisions placed for the dead, now habitually and now at fixed intervals, arise religious oblations, ordinary and extraordinary, daily and at festivals. Immolations and mutilations at the grave pass into sacrifices and offerings of blood at the altar of a deity. Abstinence from food for the benefit of the ghost develops into fasting as a pious practice; and journeys to the grave with gifts become pilgrimages to the shrine. Praises of the dead and prayers to them grow into religious praises and prayers. And so every holy rite is derived from a funeral rite' (*Princ. of Sociol.*, i. 416–7, 3rd ed.). Spencer's theory has been subjected to much criticism, not only by professional theologians, but by the first authorities on primitive man and culture. On the whole, the balance is against it, at least in the form in which he has stated the theory. It may be apposite to add that the problem of the origin of religion is really a philosophical and psychological one. See RELIGION (evolution of, and psychology of).

Literature: a large literature has grown up on this subject; the following works represent various points of view: KELLOGG, Genesis and Growth of Religion; KING, The Supernatural, its Origin, Nature, and Evolution; LIPPERT, Der Seelencult in seinen Beziehungen z. althebräischen Religion; Die Religionen d. europ. Culturvölker; and Christenthum, Volksglaube u. Volksbrauch; MAX MÜLLER, Gifford Lectures (4 vols.), and Hibbert Lectures; TIELE, Elements of the Science of Religion, i. 68 f., ii. 208 f.; RAUWENHOFF, Wijsbegeerte v. d. Godsdienst; v. SIEBECK, Lehrb. d. Religionsphilos.; the more literary works of ANDREW LANG contain many incidental suggestions; DE WETTE, Vorlesungen ü. d. Religion, 184 f. Cf. ANCESTOR WORSHIP, ANIMISM, MAGIC, and RELIGION (various topics). (R.M.W.)

Gilbert de la Porrée (Gilbertus Porretanus). (1070–1154.) A French theologian and scholastic philosopher. Educated under Bernard of Chartres, he taught in Chartres, Paris, and Poitiers. He became bishop of Poitiers in 1142. Celebrated as a dialectician, he was suspected and twice arraigned before the council by Bernard of Clairvaux and the pope.

Gioberti, Vincenzo. (1801–52.) An Italian patriot and philosopher. In 1817 he obtained a position in the ecclesiastical household of the king of Sardinia, and devoted himself to the study of the Bible, of church history, and the classic literature of Italy. Doctor of divinity in 1823, he took sacerdotal orders, 1825. In this year he became professor of theology at Turin, where he had graduated. In 1834 he became chaplain to the king, Charles Albert. Accused of favouring the liberal party, he left Turin and resided in Brussels, where he taught in a private institution, and wrote books. He returned to Turin in 1848, and was warmly welcomed. He became successively president of the Chamber of Deputies, minister of public instruction, and president of the council. He resigned, however, in 1849, and, moving to Paris, died there.

Given [AS. *gifan*]: Ger. (*das*) *Gegebene*; Fr. (*la*) *donnée*; Ital. (*il*) *dato*. One of the hypotheses of a problem; used also in the Latin form *datum* (of which it is a translation). In Greek mathematics, the corresponding word was also extended to whatever is determined in certain specified ways by a given hypothesis. The plural *data* is loosely applied to any unquestioned knowledge upon which a judgment is based, and in particular to our percepts, in the phrase 'data of experience.'

The English adjective, *given*, has an exceedingly convenient use to indicate that that which its noun denotes must be understood as specified (in the verification of what is said) previously to the specification of something mentioned before. Thus, 'Some woman is adored by any given man,' is said to avoid all possibility of understanding the statement as 'Some woman is adored by every man.' (C.S.P.)

Gland [Lat. *glans*, an acorn]: Ger. *Drüse*; Fr. *glande*; Ital. *glandula*. A secreting organ or part; an agglomeration of glandular epithelial cells, arranged in a great variety of ways, viz. in tubes—tubular glands, simple and compound; in sacs—'acinous,' 'racemose,' or 'saccular,' simple and compound; ductless glands. Cf. INTERNAL SECRETION.

Originally applied to oval bodies on the course of the lymphatics, and these are still referred to under the name 'lymphatic glands' (Quain, &c.). The tendency, however, is to restrict the term to collections of true secreting cells. As to 'lymph-glands.—It is a misnomer to call these structures glands, for they produce no secretion. A better term is lymph-nodes.' Cf. Dunham, *Histology* (1898), 114. See LYMPH. (C.F.H.)

Gnosiology [Gr. γνῶσις, knowledge, + λόγος, discourse]: Ger. *Gnosiologie*, *Erkenntnisslehre*; Fr. *gnosiologie* (suggested—TH.F.); Ital. *gnoseologia*. The science of knowledge, its origin, process, and validity. Cf. EPISTEMOLOGY, meaning (2), for which gnosiology is recommended, epistemology being used for the broader inquiry given under meaning (1) of that topic. (J.M.B.)

Gnosis, Gnostic, Gnosticism [Gr. γνῶσις, knowledge]: Ger. *Gnosis, gnostisch, Gnosticismus*; Fr. *gnose, gnostique, gnosticisme*; Ital. *gnosi, gnostico, Gnosticismo*. The philosophico-religious doctrine of a widely diffused sect or sects of (heretical) Christians in the 2nd and 3rd centuries of our era was called Gnosticism, the sect Gnostics, and the principle of their teaching Gnosis.

The Gnostics professed to advance beyond mere faith (πίστις) and to reach a knowledge (γνῶσις) concerning religious and philosophico-religious questions. In so doing, they sought to combine specifically Christian principles with elements of Jewish and heathen doctrine. The result was a mixture or amalgam of Christian, Jewish, Hellenic (especially Neo-Platonic), and oriental (Persian) conceptions. Among the chief speculative problems to which the Gnostics directed their attention were the nature of the Deity and his relation to the world (emanation doctrine), creation, matter, the nature and origin of evil, &c. Their method was imaginative rather than logical; their doctrine was mythological to a large degree, and differed widely with the various leaders and parties. They were looked upon as heretics by the Church, and their opinions condemned in favour of the growing Catholic dogma.

Literature: F. C. BAUR, Die christliche Gnosis (1835); LIPSIUS, Gnosticismus (re-printed, 1860, from Ersch and Gruber's En-cyclopädie, i. 71); SCHAFF, Hist. of the Christ. Church, and Ante-Nicene Christi-anity, chap. x. §§ 115–36; UEBERWEG-HEINZE, Gesch. d. Philos. (8th ed., 1898), ii. § 7. See also PATRISTIC PHILOSOPHY (2). (A.C.A.JR.)

Goclenius, Rudolf. (1547–1628.) Born at Corbach; studied (1568–70) philosophy and theology at Marburg and Wittenberg, and became Privatdocent in philosophy at Wit-tenberg in 1571. In 1575 he became rector of the Paedagogium at Cassel; in 1581 pro-fessor of physics at Marburg; and in 1589 professor of logic, ethics, and mathematics at the same place.

God: see the following topics; also THEISM, and the several topics RELIGION.

God (idea of) [AS. *God*]: Ger. *Idee Gottes*; Fr. *idée de Dieu*; Ital. *idea di Dio*. The notion of Deity or Supreme Being which is formed in the human consciousness, and which includes conceptions of the nature, essential attributes, and relations of this Being.

The question of the idea of God is both psychological and ontological, and involves considerations of origin, nature, and validity. The theories of origin may be classified (1) in relation to consciousness, as derivative and original; (2) in relation to the mode of appre-hension, as empirical or intuitional. Theories of nature are as numerous as the forms of theistic belief, and include MONOTHEISM, polytheism, PANTHEISM, HENOTHEISM, DEISM; see these terms, and especially THEISM, and RELIGION (psychology of). Theories of validity may be classified under the heads of subjective and objective; the former, while asserting various degrees of subjective validity for the idea, deny its ob-jective authority. The objective theories affirm the objective validity of the idea. On this basis the Anselmian and other ontological arguments for the existence of God are founded.

Literature: PFLEIDERER, Philos. of Re-

ligion; LEPSIUS, Philos. u. Religion (1885); MCCOSH, The Intuitions of the Mind; HARRIS, Philos. Basis of Theism. See THEISM. (A.T.O.)

God (in theology). The conception and being of God are usually treated in two ways from the theological standpoint. (1) Historic-ally: (*a*) the Old Testament doctrine of God; (*b*) the New Testament doctrine of God. (2) Systematically: (*a*) in his own proper nature, involving mainly the analysis of the ATTRI-BUTES (q.v.) of God, and all the problems neces-sarily connected therewith; (*b*) God's revela-tion of himself, involving his relation to the universe and especially to man; (*c*) proceed-ing from the last, and closely connected with questions of revelation, the aspects of God, or more exactly, problems connected with dis-tinctions within the Godhead (see GODHEAD, and TRINITY). The problems occurring under (2, *a* and *b*) obviously involve underlying phi-losophical principles, apart from which no progress can be made, and apart from atten-tion to which no consistent conclusions can be reached.

Literature: for (1 *a*), DAVIDSON, art. on the O.T. Teaching about God, in Hastings' Dict. of the Bible, with the literature there cited; (1 *b*), SANDAY, ibid., art. on the N.T. Teaching about God, with the literature there cited; any good work on N.T. Theology, e.g. WEISS (Eng. trans.), BEYSCHLAG (Eng. trans.); (2 *a*), see under ATTRIBUTES (of God); (2 *b*), see CHRISTOLOGY; any good History of Christian Doctrine, e.g. BAUR (Ger.), HAGEN-BACH (Eng. trans.), SHEDD (Eng.); ULRICI, Gott u. d. Natur; FLINT, Theism; PFLEI-DERER, Philos. of Religion (Eng. trans.), iii. 237 f.; (2 *c*), HEGEL, Philos. of Religion (Eng. trans.), ii. 25 f.; BAUR, Die christl. Lehre v. d. Dreieinigkeit u. Menschwerdung Gottes; MEIER, Die Lehre v. d. Trinität in ihrer historischen Entwickelung. (R.M.W.)

Godhead [AS. *God* + *hád*, office, dignity]: Ger. *Gottheit*; Fr. *divinité*; Ital. *divinità*. The name usually given by theologians to the completed conception of God as triune; the three Persons as one God constitute the God-head.

As the Athanasian Creed says: 'But the Godhead of the Father, of the Son, and of the Holy Ghost, is all one: the Glory equal, the Majesty co-eternal. Such as the Father is, such is the Son: and such is the Holy Ghost ... And yet they are not three Gods: but one God.' Accordingly, the term Godhead may be used also to indicate the essential divinity not only of God, but of

Christ and of the Holy Spirit. As the same Creed says, in another place : 'Equal to the Father, as touching his Godhead : and inferior to the Father, as touching his Manhood.' See ATTRIBUTES (of God), CHRISTO-LOGY, GOD, and TRINITY.

Literature: GRATRY, A Guide to the Knowledge of God (Eng. trans.), ii ; STEEN-STRA, The Being of God as Trinity in Unity. (R.M.W.)

Goetae [Gr. γόης, a wizard, sorcerer]. A name given to wandering Jewish magicians, thaumaturgists, or exorcists who flourished throughout the Roman empire during the early days of Christianity, and lived on the credulity of the masses.

Simon Magus may be mentioned as perhaps the most important representative of the class. Jesus may have referred to them (Matt. xxiv. 11, 24–8 ; Mark xiii. 22 ; John vi. 23, 24), and Paul was familiar with them (see Acts viii. 9 f., xiii. 6 f.).

Literature: JOSEPHUS, Ant. of Jews, viii. 2, 5 ; ORIGEN, Cont. Cel., i ; EWALD, Hist. of Israel (Eng. trans.), vii. 179, 317, 391, viii. 89, 123 ; ZELLER, Acts of the Apostles (Eng. trans.), i. 250 f. ; SCHOLZ, Götzendienst u. Zauberwesen bei d. Hebräern. (R.M.W.)

Golden Rule: Ger. *goldene Regel* ; Fr. *règle d'or* ; Ital. *regola d'oro*. The name given to the Gospel precept : 'Whatsoever ye would that men should do to you, do ye even so to them' (Matt. vii. 12 ; Luke vi. 31).

This rule has often been adopted as expressing the sum of social morality. The negative side of the same precept is sometimes given as its equivalent. Thus Hobbes summarizes the fundamental moral laws in the command : 'Do not that to another which thou wouldst not have done to thyself.' And he identifies this with the golden rule, from which, however, it differs in not enjoining active beneficence, and requiring only abstinence from evil. See Sidgwick, *Hist. of Eng. Eth.* (3rd ed.), 167. (W.R.S.)

Golden Section: Ger. *goldener Schnitt* ; Fr. *section d'or* ; Ital. *sezione aurea*. That division of a magnitude in which the smaller portion is to the larger, as the larger portion is to the whole.

Derived primarily on the mathematical side from the division of a line into extreme and mean ratio, but applied more widely to a similar relation between the dimensions of surfaces, e. g. the two adjacent sides of a rectangle and the sum of these sides, the parts of the human figure, &c. The relation involved has also been applied in explanation of musical harmony, the relation between the vibration rates of the various tones concerned being supposed to illustrate it. The supposed aesthetic value of the relation has been referred to its embodiment of a just proportion, expressing mediation between complete equality (1 : 1) and complete inequality (1 : 2). This value has been shown to be subject to numerous modifications. The most agreeable forms among parallelograms are the apparent squares and figures whose sides conform to the relations of the golden section. In the case of a line, whether horizontal or perpendicular, the golden section, although very agreeable, is not aesthetically the most satisfactory division.

The division of a line into extreme and mean ratio was accomplished by Euclid. The aesthetic value of the relation involved was first developed by Zeising, who gave it the widest application throughout the range of the beautiful in nature and in art. He saw in it the concrete embodiment of an ultimate aesthetic principle, i. e. the combination of a complete diversity in an harmonious unity. Fechner investigated experimentally the application of the principle to various simple geometrical forms, and found it subject to sundry modifications. Helwig, Witmer, and others have made further experiments, and have also discussed the theoretical bearings of the principle.

Literature: ZEISING, Neue Lehre von den Proportionen des menschlichen Körpers (1854), and Aesthetische Forschungen (1855); FECHNER, Zur experimentalen Aesthetik (1871), and Vorschule d. Aesthetik (1876); WITMER, Philos. Stud., ix ; HELWIG, Theorie des Schönen (1897). (J.R.A.)

Good [AS. *god*]: Ger. *Gut* ; Fr. *bien* (preferred), *bon* ; Ital. *bene*. Possessing WORTH (q. v.) of some sort. (W.R.S.–J.M.B.)

Anything which satisfies a desire has worth in that respect, and is called good for that purpose. At the same time, this same thing may yet be in other respects, and on the whole, bad. In a fuller, ethical sense the term 'good' is applied only to that whose worth cannot be thus inverted or changed, i. e. is intrinsic, sometimes with the distinctive adverb 'morally good.' Hence the assertion of Kant that the only unconditional good is a good will.

Good as a substantive means a thing possessing worth. An old classification, adopted by Aristotle, divides goods into external goods, goods of the body, and goods of the soul—from which the inquiry starts into the true human good; and this inquiry constitutes ethical science. Cf. Class, *Ideale u. Güter* (1886).　　　　　　　　(W.R.S.)

Goodness (ethical): Ger. *das Gute*; Fr. *bonté*; Ital. *bontà*. The possession of intrinsic worth.

The term has the same vagueness as GOOD (q. v.). Hence the distinction drawn by Shaftesbury (*Inquiry*, Bk. I. § 3), who says that goodness depends only on the affections, and may belong to any sensible creature; whereas 'virtue or merit' belongs to man only, since it implies the reflex or moral sense which makes the conception of worth and honesty an object of his affection.

Goodness is also used as an abstract expression for that which is morally highest, or of greatest worth—the GOOD, or the SUMMUM BONUM (q. v.). In this sense goodness or the-good-in-itself (αὐτὸ ἀγαθόν) is used in Plato's *Republic* to express the ultimate ground, not only of moral activity, but of all reality. It is thus raised from a purely human to a universal conception.　　(W.R.S.)

Goods: Ger. *Güter*; Fr. *biens*; Ital. *merci*. The elements that constitute wealth; objects capable of satisfying human desire.

It is a moot point whether immaterial wealth should be characterized as goods; and it is also doubtful whether non-transferable objects should be included under the term. Marshall adopts a very wide interpretation, including at once things external and internal, material and personal, transferable and non-transferable. But it seems questionable policy to depart so widely from current usage.　　　　　　　　(A.T.H.)

Gorgias, of Leontini. A Greek orator and sophist, a contemporary of Socrates and of Empedocles, who is sometimes said to have been his teacher. The influence of Zeno upon him was supreme. See PRE-SOCRATIC PHILOSOPHY (Sophists).

Göschel, Carl Friedrich. (1781–1861.) German philosopher, follower of Hegel; a jurist. Educated at Bonn, he was for some time counsellor of the provincial court in Naumburg; after 1845 first president of the Consistory for Saxony. Died in Naumburg. He sought to demonstrate the harmony of Hegel's philosophy with Christianity.

Gospel [AS. *God*, God, + *spell*, a narrative]: Ger. *Evangelium*; Fr. *évangile*; Ital. *evangelo*, *vangelo*. The term is used in three senses: (1)

The most general—good news of any kind; (2) that in which it is commonly employed throughout Christendom—the good news of redemption through the mediation of Jesus Christ; (3) by analogy from (2), the distinctive—possibly new—teaching peculiar to a man or school.

Gospels is the collective term used to denote the writings of the four Evangelists—Matthew, Mark, Luke, John. For obvious reasons, these writings have received closest attention from Christian and anti-Christian writers for centuries. Here it is possible only to indicate, and this with the utmost generality, the views of them generally entertained to-day. Every one recognizes that the writings attributed to Matthew, Mark, and Luke agree among themselves in very striking ways—hence their ordinary name the Synoptic Gospels, that is, the Gospels which 'see together'; similarly all agree that these Gospels differ in the most marked way from the writing attributed to John, often called the 'spiritual Gospel.' Hence two distinct problems have arisen — the synoptic problem, and the problem of the Fourth Gospel. Many would doubtless admit that, at the present time, the former is more completely understood, and is further on the way towards satisfactory solution than the latter. (1) After Eichhorn (1794), Gieseler (1818), Schleiermacher (1818), and Credner (1836) had initiated modern criticism by formulating the DOCUMENTARY HYPOTHESIS (q.v.), the greatest desideratum for a fuller elucidation of the synoptic problem was a more thorough examination of the relation between Matthew and Luke on the one hand, and Mark on the other. This was undertaken by Weiss and Wilke simultaneously (1838). They suggested that Mark came first in the order of time; that its writer presented more precisely than his companions an original document, accessible to all three; and that the writers of Matthew and Luke used a second document, one not employed by the writer of Mark, and known as the Logia of Matthew. With the exception of the adherents of the TÜBINGEN SCHOOL (q. v.), New Testament critics have in the main followed these lines of Weiss and Wilke till the present time. The view now generally approved, though with differences in detail, upon which it is impossible to enlarge here, is that the three synoptic writers all used an existing (earlier) source which is most faithfully presented by the writer of Mark; that the writers of Matthew and Luke used a second early source (consisting of Logia or sayings), excerpts from which constitute the main differences between their Gospels and that attributed to Mark; that possibly, though here there is dispute, the writer of Luke had these Logia before him in a collection which contrasted with that used by the writer of Matthew. As to dates: there is least evidence regarding Matthew, which possibly falls within the 1st century. Mark, too, cannot be dated with any certainty, and probably could not have been written before A.D. 68. Having regard to the evidence which the Pauline writings throw on the subject, Luke cannot well have been written after A.D. 80.

(2) The problem of the Fourth Gospel is admitted to be exceedingly difficult, even if on no other account than that it is not a historical document in the same sense as the synoptics. This obviously introduces sources of much perplexity. There are those who altogether deny its historical character, and point out the impossibility that John could have had a part in its authorship. Others, on the contrary, sharply contend for both these positions. It seems certain that this Gospel was well known by A.D. 185, and it seems problematical that it was quoted by Basilides in A.D. 125. It is practically certain that its author was a Jew. Little more, of a definite character, can be said. After all that has been done and written, one is forced to agree with Harnack, that 'the origin of the Johannine writings is, from the standpoint of a history of literature and dogma, the most marvellous enigma which the early history of Christianity presents' (*Hist. of Dogma*, i. 96, 97). The problem of the relation between the Logos, as used by the writer of John, and the Jewish-Alexandrian conception—the point where the entire discussion touches philosophy most closely—must, like the whole Johannine question, be regarded as still *sub iudice*.

Literature: REUSS, Hist. of the N. T. (Eng. trans.); HOLTZMANN, Einleitung in d. N. T.; WEIZSÄCKER, Untersuch. ü. d. evang. Gesch.; WENDT, Die Lehre Jesu (Eng. trans. of 2nd part); P. EWALD, Das Hauptproblem d. Evangelienfrage; KEIM, Jesus of Nazara (Eng. trans.), i; DAVIDSON, Introd. to the N. T.; the most handy summary in English (from an advanced standpoint) is CARPENTER, The First Three Gospels. For Fourth Gospel: WATKINS, Bampton Lects.; SCHENKEL, Characterbild Jesu; THOMA, Die Genesis d. Johan. Evangel.; BEYSCHLAG, N. T. Theol. (Eng.

trans.), i. 216 f.; WEISS, Life of Christ (Eng. trans.); SANDAY, in the Expositor (1891–2); HARNACK, in Zeitsch. f. Theol. u. Kirche, ii. 189 f.; WEIZSÄCKER, Apostolic Age (Eng. trans.), ii. 206 f. (R.M.W.)

Government (divine): Ger. *göttliche Regierung*; Fr. *gouvernement divin*; Ital. *governo divino*. (1) The name given to that view of God's relation to the world which is immediately deducible from his attribute of omnipotence.

(2) The term is also applied to the moral order of the world as indicated under THEODICY.

Because omnipotent, God governs the universe according to his will, that is, in conformity with his nature. This is the positive side. The negative appears in the fact that this conception of the universe (as cosmos) excludes, on the one hand, a mere determining fate and, on the other, mere blind chance. In dogmatic theology this idea of government refers rather to nature than to man, the relationship of the Deity to humanity being expressed more eminently in the scheme of salvation. See ATTRIBUTES (of God), GOD, GODHEAD, and THEODICY.

Literature: McCOSH, Method of Divine Government; FLÜGEL, Das Wunder u. d. Erkennbarkeit Gottes; DE MARGERIE, Théodicée; Herzog's Real-Encyc., art. Théodicée; LOTZE, Microcosmus (Eng. trans.); ORR, Christian View of God and the World; PFLEIDERER, Philos. of Religion (Eng. trans.), iv. 20 f.; REUSCH, Nature and the Bible (Eng. trans.). See also the citations under RELIGION (philosophy of), THEODICY, and in BIBLIOG. E, i, b. (R.M.W.)

Government (political). The ruling or directing of a community as a whole, and as organized into a STATE (q. v.).

The discussion of government, and forms of government, is at least as old as Greek philosophy. The distinction of state from society is vital here: a society with a common government is a state; a state without government would be a mere society. It is not essential that the ruling or directing power should be sovereign (in Austin's sense). It is not sovereign in subject communities (Mysore, Basutoland); but the two qualities are usually combined. See also ARISTOCRACY, DEMOCRACY, and STATE (philosophy of). (J.B.)

Grace [Lat. *gratia*]: Ger. *Anmuth*; Fr. *grâce*; Ital. *grazia, graziosità*. That species of the beautiful, or of aesthetic value, found primarily in ease and spontaneity of posture or motion, and, by analogy, in freely flowing curves and contours, in slender columns, in speech or conduct which suggests ease and spontaneousness rather than power.

It is thus contrasted with the sublime or majestic, but the element of smallness is not so prominent as in the pretty. Beauty with the element of dignity inspires respect, and keeps the observer at a distance; grace attracts—a factor still more prominent in the German Anmuth, which is nearly equivalent to 'grace and charm.' This distinction was suggested by Plato, made more explicit by Cicero, and elaborated by Schiller (*Anmuth u. Würde*). Hogarth distinguished from the waving line of beauty the more varied serpentine line of grace formed by winding a line about a cone.

Literature: SCHILLER, Grace and Dignity, in Essays, Aesth. and Philos.; HARTMANN, Aesth., ii. chap. iv; WALTER, Gesch. d. Aesth. im Alterthum; SPENCER, Essays, ii. (J.H.T.)

Grace (in theology): Ger. *Gnade*; Fr. *grâce*; Ital. *grazia*. The name given to the special attribute of God manifested to humanity in the plan of redemption. It involves the conception of favour, accompanied by spontaneity, mercy, and goodness, which the recipient has not merited.

It originates in God's 'eternal pleasure.' God's grace is held to establish a kingdom of grace; and here the controversies with which the subject is connected begin to emerge. To what extent does man, looking to his lost condition, co-operate with God in this kingdom of grace? The antagonism between AUGUSTINIANISM (q. v.) and PELAGIANISM (q. v.), as between CALVINISM (q. v.) and ARMINIANISM (q. v.), originated here. An antinomy between sin and freedom, between grace and works, displayed itself which had the greatest influence on thought, especially after the Reformation. It need hardly be added that these problems arise in a universe which is presupposed to be constructed, as regards man, on a definite plan. Man fell; hence God's grace, and all the difficulties which the conception has called up.

Literature: Lichtenberger's Encyc. des Sci. religieuses, art. Grâce Divine, by BOIS; CUNNINGHAM, Historical Theol.; SPENER, Von d. Natur u. Gnade; Herzog's Real-Encyc., art. Gnade, by LANGE, gives full literature; SCHLEIERMACHER, Glaubenslehre; any good work on Biblical theology—OEHLER, WEISS (Eng. trans.). (R.M.W.)

Graces (Christian). A term used, generally in Christian ethics or in homilies, to indicate the characteristic marks of the ethico-religious life in the Christian man. The graces are practical accompaniments of the main Christian virtues—faith or fidelity; love or steadfastness of good will; wisdom as displayed in cheerful hope. They reveal themselves principally in the unaffected or unconscious performance of duty as inspired by the Christian ideal.

Literature: see ETHICS (Christian). (R.M.W.)

Grade (of consciousness) [Lat. *gradus*, degree]: Ger. *Rang*; Fr. *grade, rang*; Ital. *ordine*. Relative position in the scale of animal minds.

Grade is the term recommended for the place of this or that consciousness from the point of view of psychological observation, as opposed to the relative 'degree' of consciousness of the same mind from time to time. See SUBCONSCIOUS for the further working out of this distinction. (J.M.B., G.F.S.)

Grammar [OF. *gramaire*, from Med. Lat. *grammaria*, improperly used for *grammatica*]: Ger. *Grammatik*; Fr. *grammaire*; Ital. *grammatica*. Orderly presentation of the material of language.

When the basis of arrangement is the form and relation which the phenomena exhibit in actual use, it is called descriptive grammar. Most school grammars belong to the descriptive class, though in recent days a tendency has shown itself to seek aid from historical grammar, so far as it can be done without compromising pedagogical clearness of statement. When the basis of arrangement is the relation to an order of historical development, it is called historical grammar. When the basis is relation to the general principles governing the psychological life of language, it is called general or philosophical grammar. Only two peoples have independently developed complete grammatical systems, the Hindus and the Greeks. The Hindu system, characterized by greater objectivity, gave the impulse, when opened up to Western scholars in the beginning of this century, to the development of modern scientific grammar. The Greek system originated in the service of philosophy, and later freed itself from the leading-strings of metaphysics, only as the accumulation of ordered facts compelled it. The little handbook of Greek Grammar prepared by Dionysius Thrax, probably in the 2nd century B. C., under the title Τέχνη Διονυσίου Γραμματικοῦ, became the basis for all the Greek and Latin grammars down to modern times, and determined the traditions of all descriptive grammar in the Western world.

Literature: H. STEINTHAL, Gesch. d. Sprachwiss. bei den Griechen u. Römern (1863; 2nd ed., 1890); TH. BENFEY, Gesch. d. Sprachwiss. (1869); B. DELBRÜCK, Einleitung in das Sprachstudium (2nd ed., 1885, Eng. trans.); G. UHLIG, Dionysii Thracis Ars Grammatica (1883). (B.I.W.)

Grandeur (delirium of): Ger. *Grössenwahn, Megalomanie*; Fr. *délire des grandeurs, mégalomanie*; Ital. *delirio di grandezza, megalomania*. The belief, on the part of an insane person, that he possesses unusual powers, riches, or other sorts of superiority: MEGALOMANIA (q. v.).

Delusions of grandeur accompany the excited or exalted forms of mania and central paralysis. In some cases this fixed delusion is the chief symptom of insanity, thus forming a monomania of grandeur, or pride. For literature see EXALTATION, MANIA, and MONOMANIA. (J.J.)

Graphic Method (of recording): see LABORATORY AND APPARATUS, II, *general*.

Graphic Method (of representation): Ger. *graphische Methode*; Fr. *méthode graphique, méthode des courbes*; Ital. *metodo grafico*. The presentation to the eye of the results of measurements or statistics by means of curves and other figures.

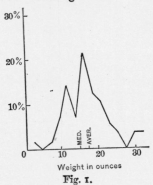

Fig. 1.

While an algebraical CURVE (q. v.) can but rarely represent the complex quantitative relations with which experimental psychology is concerned, it is an advantage to represent graphically to the eye the relations of quantities and even simple numerical results. Thus the subjoined curve (Fig. 1) shows the estimate from memory of the weight of a book (24 oz.) made by fifty-six students. The estimates (in ounces) are the abscissae, and the percentages of the whole numbers making the several estimates are the ordinates. It should be noted that in such curves the relations between ordinates and abscissae are arbitrary. Simple numerical results can sometimes be illustrated to advantage, as by rectangles or sectors. Thus if of every 100 associations 47 were classed as objective, 40 as logical, and 13 as verbal, the results might be represented in either of the two ways shown in Fig. 2. (J.McK.C.)

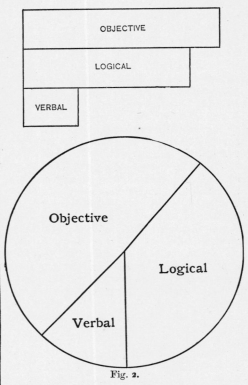

Fig. 2.

This method, as well as the curve, has been much used by Francis Galton for psychological and anthropological data, and owes much of its development to him. Cf. Galton, *Natural Inheritance*, and *Inquiries into Human Faculty*. (J.M.B.)

Graphology [Gr. γραφή, writing, + λόγος, lore]: Ger. *Graphologie, Handschriftenkunde*; Fr. *graphologie*; Ital. *grafologia*. The study or science of HANDWRITING (q. v.).

In the best French and German works, graphology views handwriting as a motor indication or expression, to be interpreted by the aid of and along with the other motor activities on the basis of psychological principles. As a practical art, attempting to interpret or read character in individuals from their handwriting, it has as little scientific basis as palmistry or phrenology. While both the principles and conclusions are frequently of doubtful validity, yet the study includes the legitimate factors in a possible science of handwriting.

From the practical point of view of identification of handwriting, graphology is also called into requisition, and the term graphologist becomes equivalent to handwriting expert.

The pathology of handwriting presents a further interesting aspect of the study. The study of the degeneration of handwriting in the insane (see article of this title in Tuke's *Dict. of Psychol. Med.*) has revealed characteristic divergences from the normal in cases of general paralysis, idiocy (see Piper, *Schriftproben von Schwachsinnigen*, 1893), mania, melancholia, as well as in hysteria, changes of personality, hypnotic states, &c. In all such cases, handwriting is viewed as only one among many of the significant forms of highly specialized motor expressions. Mirror writing (see Ireland, *Blot on the Brain*, 1893, 299) is a form of writing in which the letters are reversed as if seen in a mirror, and occurs sporadically in normal individuals (notably in children) as well as in connection with mental disorders, and offers special problems of interest in the development and dissolution of writing. Agraphia includes the inability to write or difficulty in writing resulting from disorder in the cerebral centre for writing. See AGRAPHIA, and SPEECH AND ITS DEFECTS.

Literature: J. CRÉPIEUX-JAMIN, L'Écriture et le Caractère (1895, also in Eng. trans.); P. HELOT, L'Écriture et le Caractère (1889); LOUIS DES CHAMPS, La Philos. de l'Écriture (1892); also the periodical La Graphologie, published in different forms since 1871. ERLENMEYER, Die Schrift (1879), and PREYER, Psychol. des Schreibens (1895), represent the most valuable attempts to interpret handwriting. (J.J.)

Gratification: see SATISFACTION.

Gratitude [Lat. *gratitudo*, from *gratus*, pleasing]: Ger. *Dankbarkeit*; Fr. *gratitude, reconnaissance*; Ital. *gratitudine, riconoscenza*. The sentiment on the part of the recipient of a favour towards its donor, involving a disposition to promote the good of the donor.

Gratitude, inasmuch as it is the disposition to promote the good of another, is a special case of BENEVOLENCE (q.v.); but seeing that this disposition to do good is in a manner due to the other in return for favour received, the quality is assimilated to JUSTICE (q.v.). The question whether gratitude can be disinterested, or is always founded on self-love, is frequently discussed by the English moralists.

Literature: HUTCHESON, Inquiry, § 2, vi; J. GAY, Prelim. Diss. to King's Origin of Evil, xlix; HUME, Princ. of Mor., App. ii. (W.R.S.)

Grave Harmonics. An erroneous term for COMBINATION TONES (q.v.). (E.B.T.)

Gravesande, Willem Jakob van's. (1688–1742.) Dutch philosopher and mathematician. Studied in Leyden. Began practising law (1707) at the Hague. In 1715 he accompanied an embassy to England as secretary, and became acquainted with Newton. He was chosen Fellow of the Royal Society. In 1717 he became professor of mathematics and astronomy at Leyden, and introduced the Newtonian philosophy to that institution. His works deal in part with Newton's philosophy.

Gravitation [Lat. *gravitare*, to gravitate]: Ger. *Schwerkraft, Gravitation*; Fr. *gravitation*; Ital. *gravitazione*. That seemingly universal tendency of every particle of matter to move towards every other particle with a force directly as the product of the masses of the particles, and inversely as the square of the distance (r) which separates them.

The fact that all bodies on the earth's surface tend to fall downwards was known from the beginning of human experience. That the force thus indicated tends towards the centre of the earth must have been dimly recognized since the time of Ptolemy. That the planets gravitate towards the sun was vaguely seen by Kepler, and more clearly by Huyghens and others. That the moon gravitates towards the earth was shown by Newton, who first propounded the law in all its generality. Gravitation differs from all other forces of nature in being, within the limits of human experience to the present time, absolutely incapable of increase, diminution, or modification by any agency whatever. Through all transmutations of the forms of matter, under the highest velocities in the planetary system, through all masses of extraneous matter that may intervene, every pair of atoms attract each other unceasingly according to the stated law.

Intimately associated with gravitation is the question whether it is really an *actio ad distans*—whether it takes place without any intervening medium or other agency. Leibnitz objected to the Newtonian theory that a body cannot act where it is not. This negation is accepted as an axiom by many physicists, who find support for their view by the apparently well-ascertained fact that electric and magnetic attraction and repulsion act through the agency of the ether, and conclude from analogy that gravitation may be due to the same or a similar cause.

Some astronomical phenomena have recently led to the suspicion that gravitation does not vary rigorously as the inverse square, but increases more rapidly towards the sun by an amount so minute as to make its establishment difficult, except by the most refined and elaborate researches. The simplest proposed form of the modified law is that instead of being inversely as r^2, it is inversely as r to the power $2+x$, where

$$x = 0.0000001612 = 1612 \div 10^{10} \quad \text{(S.N.)}$$

Greatest Happiness : Ger. *höchstes Glück* ; Fr. *bonheur suprême, suprême félicité* ; Ital. *felicità suprema*. The greatest possible surplus of pleasure over pain in the life or lives referred to ; the reference being either to an individual, a community, mankind at large, or sentient beings generally.

The ethical doctrine that greatest happiness is the ideal of conduct received formal statement in Western thought by Epicurus ; but the doctrine that the greatest happiness which the individual ought to pursue is not his own happiness, but that of the community, seems to have originated in political theory, and, in its precise formulation, to be mainly due to certain English writers of the 18th century. The social content of morality was undoubtedly no modern discovery. The conditions required for a quantitative estimate of happiness are laid down by Wollaston (*Religion of Nature*, 1722); and regard for the happiness of others was made the criterion of virtue by such writers as John Gay (*Prelim. Diss. to King's Origin of Evil*, 1731, xxxvi) and Hutcheson (*Syst. of Mor. Philos.*, 1755). Hutcheson makes their 'tendency to universal happiness' the criterion of the material goodness of actions (whereas their formal goodness consists in their flowing 'from good affections in a just proportion'), and this criterion is systematically applied by him.

One of the most distinct of early statements of this criterion is in Priestley's *Essay on the First Princ. of Government* (1768): 'The good and happiness of the members, that is, the majority of the members of any state, is the great standard by which everything relating to that state must finally be determined' (p. 17). The double phrase 'good and happiness' does not imply here that good is different from happiness, for it is immediately added that 'justice and veracity, for instance,' have 'nothing intrinsically excellent in them separate from their relation to the happiness of mankind' (p. 18). A similar view is found in Beccaria (*Dei delitti e delle pene*, originally published in 1764), who asserts that the only proper end for legislation is 'la massima felicità divisa nel maggior numero'—an expression rendered in the English translation (3rd ed., 1770) by the phrase to which Bentham afterwards gave currency, 'the greatest happiness of the greatest number.' The constituents of greatest happiness are enumerated by Bentham (*Princ. of Mor. and Legisl.*), and made the basis of a hedonistic calculus. The importance, as sources of happiness, of permanent objects of interest is brought out by J. S. Mill (*Utilitarianism*, chap. ii), and still more by Sidgwick (*Meth. of Eth.*, III. xiv).

Literature: the authors cited ; see also ETHICS, and ETHICAL THEORIES, and BIBLIOG. F, 2, *r*. (W.R.S.)

Greek Terminology (considered in relation to Greek philosophy).

(1) The vocabulary of European philosophy has its principal source in the technical language of Greek philosophers. Of this technical language, a portion has passed directly over into our modern philosophical usage, e. g. a number of the familiar terms of the traditional formal logic, such as syllogism, enthymeme, &c. A portion, however, and in fact a very large portion, has reached us in the form of Latin translations and imitations of Greek terms. Of this part, again, there are subdivisions. The classical Roman philosophical writers began the process of 'making the dialectic art speak in Latin' (see citations in Prantl, *Gesch. d. Logik*, i. 511, at the outset of an important discussion of the Roman terminology). The words *substantia* and *essentia*, as translations of οὐσία, belong, for instance, to this first stratum of Latin imitations of Greek terms. A second group of Latin terms and phrases, formed under the influence of Greek originals, is found in the theological terminology of the Latin Church. The scholastic philosophy constitutes a third period during which Latin imitations or translations of Greek originals entered philosophical language. And from time to time, in modern

philosophy, the coining of new compounds, of Greek origin, has gone on side by side with a continuation of the processes to which the scholastic vocabulary itself was due. The effective tendency to add to all these sources of philosophical terms the modern vernacular languages themselves has existed ever since Meister Eckhart, whose Middle German vocabulary contained many striking imitations of Greek and of scholastic terms by means of purely German words (e. g. Istigkeit for *essentia* = οὐσία). It will be seen, therefore, that the influence of Greek terminology has been manifold, and indirect as well as direct, since even the terms of vernacular origin are often more or less obviously modelled after Greek terms.

(2) The process whereby the Greek terminology of philosophy arose and became gradually more elaborate and more settled is, in outline, as follows.

First, the early thinkers, in the Pre-Socratic period, began by undertaking to discover general explanations of the origin and nature of things. In advancing their theories, they were from the start led to emphasize certain aspects of the physical world—aspects which they deemed of especial importance as furnishing, or as illustrating, their explanations. To these emphasized aspects they gave names, some of which were already familiar in popular language. So the early names of the elements, water, air, fire, were of course words in daily use. But in two ways the undertaking, thus begun, very soon led to new developments. First, certain of the aspects of the world, which the philosopher was led to emphasize, were less familiar to the popular mind, and required relatively new names, so that, before long, quite novel coinages began to appear in the technical vocabulary of philosophy, or else words before existing were given a prominence that at once, by taking them out of their more usual context, changed them into technical terms. Of the former tendency, present for instance in the Pythagorean vocabulary, the coinage of new abstract nouns by individual philosophers remains, even to the present time, a familiar example. Here is, in fact, a perennial accompaniment of abstract thought; and few systematic thinkers have failed to coin at least one or two abstract nouns. Of the words already existent, but turned into technical terms by the way in which they are isolated and emphasized, the ἄπειρον of Anaximander forms the first instance in the history of Greek philosophy. When Homer (*Od.* viii. 340 : see Schmidt's *Synony-*

mik d. griechischen Sprache, iv. 512) makes Hermes speak of δεσμοὶ ἀπείρονες, the meaning of the Homeric ἀπείρων, as 'numberless,' is clear. But what Anaximander meant by calling his elementary material the ἄπειρον (i. e. the *Infinite*, or as Burnet, in the work cited below, renders it, the *Boundless*) becomes something at once technical and obscure, about whose precise meaning there has been much discussion. The term presumably means (see Windelband, *Gesch. d. alten Philos.*, 25, and Schmidt's *Synonymik*, in the passage just cited) at once that which is *boundless in its power to originate* new products, and *boundless in its extent* ; and it is thus a typical example of an early and *undifferentiated* terminology, whose meanings and usages have indeed too much of the 'boundless' about them.

(3) But next, even when the early philosopher coins no new words, and does not consciously intend any unfamiliar usage of the already existent terms, still it is his fate to find his most familiar words *altering their meaning* as he uses them. For to him these familiar words soon come to name principles and ultimate processes, rather than the objects ordinarily in question when common sense employs the words. In vain then does the thinker, anywhere in his choice of fundamentally important terms, cling to the speech of the people. His thought transforms whatever it touches. The πῦρ ἀεὶ ζωόν (fire ever-living) of Heraclitus is so characterized by him that it soon loses much of the seeming of the merely sensuous 'fire' of the common-sense world with which he no doubt intends to identify it. For this world-fire is 'kindled and extinguished' according to 'fixed measure'; it is intelligent; it is 'want and satiety'; and so in many other ways fire, taken as the name of the world-principle, soon alters its significance, and can no longer be conceived as *mere* fire. Here again we deal with a tendency ever since important in the history of terminology. The later vocabulary of psychology, of ethics, and of metaphysics is full of instances of the way in which technical usage has again and again come to make the familiar seem strange. Thus everybody uses the verb *to be*, and distinguishes between existence and non-existence; but a discussion of the meaning of the terms for 'being' at once seems, to the popular mind, something extremely recondite; and the most common words soon appear utterly foreign and mysterious when once they are found, in such a discussion, as technical terms. From the Eleatic philosophers down, and very

notably in Plato's ontological dialogues, such as the *Parmenides*, the *Sophist*, and the *Philebus*, this is what happens to the terms used for being.

(4) The consequence to which these often unconscious transformations of the popular usage lead is that ere long, in early Greek philosophy, each thinker comes to employ, upon occasion, conscious devices for marking off his own peculiar usage of terms. To this end: (*a*) He sometimes *objects to the popular view*, because it does not sufficiently observe the meanings and distinctions of its own words. In calling attention to such popular confusions, the thinker indeed intends, so far, to clarify ideas without of necessity reforming vocabulary. But the effect upon terminology is inevitable, since the distinction, once emphasized, renders impossible the naïve usage. The attack of Parmenides upon the common opinions about the relation of being and non-being involves, for instance, just such an insistence upon the importance of a distinction already known to language, but, as Parmenides holds, neglected by common sense. You *cannot truly speak* of non-being; you *must not recognize* it. For it is absolutely *different from* being. The result of such observations becomes of importance for the future of terminology. Or again: (*b*) The thinker, in a somewhat different fashion, is led to express his own theory of things by consciously asserting that certain terms and phrases in common use are essentially *misleading*, so that for them there ought to be *substituted* such and such other words. To make observations of this kind is to aid in the formation of a definite terminology, in case the observations are themselves at all successful. Thus the early thinkers, after Parmenides, when attention has once been called to the deeper problems about the genesis of things, are found using such expressions as that of Empedocles : 'There is no *origination* (φύσις) of anything mortal, nor yet any end, . . . but only *mixture* and *separation* of what is mixed (μίξις and διάλλαξις). But amongst men it is *called* φύσις' (see Fairbanks, *First Philosophers of Greece*, 162). Or again, Anaxagoras declares that 'The Greeks do not rightly use the terms 'coming into being" and "perishing" (τὸ δὲ γίνεσθαι καὶ ἀπόλλυσθαι).' As a fact, he continues, one should use the terms συμμίσγεσθαι and διακρίνεσθαι, terms which again mean mixture and separation (Fairbanks, op. cit., 245). Efforts towards an establishment of usage which have reached this stage involve an intentional adjustment of terms to doctrines,

and herewith the history of terminology proper begins.

(5) The next higher stage is the one especially due, in Greek thought, to the influence of Socrates, and in part also of the Sophists. The undertaking to *define terms* now becomes a recognized part of the philosophical ideal. Defining terms and reflectively *clarifying ideas* are henceforth undertakings that progress side by side. The method involved becomes a very important portion of the dialectical art. The Platonic dialogues develop this art with great and conscious virtuosity. The elementary faults in definition are well recognized (see the often-quoted passages in Plato's *Theaetetus*, 146–7, 208 D ; in the *Meno*, 71 B ; and in the *Gorgias*, 448 B ; and cf. Zeller, *Philos. d. Griechen*, 3rd ed., Th. II. Abth. I. 617). In avoiding these faults, and in developing true definitions, one also undertakes to create a more precise terminology. By means of the processes of *classification and division* of terms and of ideas so extensively developed by Plato, one comes to arrange terms in more systematic groups, the hierarchy of classes in the case of the subdivisions of any largest class requiring *the selection of appropriate terms* for all the members of the hierarchy. Such systematic arrangements, however, often also require, for the filling out of the omissions in the scheme, the *coinage of new terms*, and this coinage is now guided by needs of which the method makes one definitely conscious. The direct influence of the art of classification upon the organization of philosophical terminology is thus from the start visible, and may be especially observed in the more technical Platonic dialogues, such as the *Parmenides, Theaetetus, Sophist*, and *Philebus*. The art in question also inevitably develops its own special terminology, whereby its various processes are themselves named (see, for a general survey of the Platonic use of classification, the monograph of Lukas, *Die Methode d. Eintheilung bei Plato*, Halle, 1888. In this monograph, special summaries of the terminology used by Plato for the art of classification are given, pp. 28, 54, 85, 110, 216). *To divide* a larger class into its subdivisions is expressed in Plato by the verbs τέμνειν and διαιρεῖσθαι. He uses, both for logical classes and subclasses, the terms γένος and εἶδος; but no definite distinction between these two terms, as *genus* and *species*, exists for Plato (see also Campbell, in Jowett and Campbell's ed. of the *Republic*, 300). Yet, despite this high development of the Platonic art of classifying and organizing

terms and meanings, Plato himself is led to no established system of philosophical terms, such as Aristotle undertook to develop. Plato's usage varies with the different dialogues, and in ways that have suggested to many investigators inquiries as to the chronology of the Platonic use of language in the various periods of his literary activity (Campbell, Lutoslawski, &c. See the literature in Lutoslawski's book (cited below), and the recent papers of Natorp, *Arch. f. d. Gesch. d. Philos.*, xii). These 'stylometric' investigations, to be sure, concern much more than matters of technical terminology. Campbell calls Plato's philosophical terminology 'incipient, tentative, transitional,' and points out that he regarded the sophistic efforts in this direction as pedantry. In fine, then, the *art* of defining terms is for Plato a favourite and highly elaborate art, but he applies it each time afresh; and he is never disposed to be bound by the usage involved in the results of his previous efforts.

(6) In Aristotle, terminology and the ideal of a philosophical system culminate together. At the outset of his various systematic discussions, Aristotle often engages in a more or less extended argument regarding what does, and what does not, fall within the precise scope of any particular branch of science. In such and such matters the physicist ($\phi\upsilon\sigma\iota\kappa\acute{o}s$) is interested; the metaphysician ($\acute{o}$ $\pi\rho\hat{\omega}\tau os$ $\phi\iota\lambda\acute{o}\sigma o\phi os$) is concerned with other aspects; and yet others are the affairs of the student of dialectics or of morals. The *boundaries of the sciences* thus stand as definitely named and conscious *limitations* of that freedom of the argument to wander wherever it will, upon which Plato, in the *Theaetetus*, had laid such stress, and of which Plato's most famous dialogues furnish so many instances. This new tendency in Aristotle is only one symptom of the general interest of that philosopher in technically distinguishing the various *aspects* of things, in fixing upon terms and expressions suited to each aspect, and in *solving fundamental problems by means of this method of distinctions*. For Aristotle's divisions of the sciences are not wholly due to the same interest which gets expressed in the modern 'division of labour,' since Aristotle himself covered the whole range of the various sciences, whose provinces he all the while divided, by their definitions, from one another. Nor yet is his interest *merely* that of the lover of system for its own sake; for Aristotle is no pedant. His use of the distinctions of a highly wrought terminology is, to a consider-

able extent, due to his effort to *harmonize the various points of view* of earlier thinkers, and *to solve apparent contradictions* by showing how, 'in a certain sense,' each of two apparently contradictory propositions can be true. Thus terminological organization and definiteness is, with Aristotle, *a conscious instrument of his many-sidedness*. In finding his various terms, Aristotle makes free use of the rich materials already prepared for him by the previous thinkers, especially by Plato. In the fifth book of the *Metaphysics* he gives us a specimen of his terminological method, in the form of a discussion of the various meanings of a series of philosophical terms and usages. This book was presumably written as a separate essay, and many of its distinctions are elsewhere more fully discussed, in their systematic places. But the device of *at once appealing to general usage*, while at the same time *consciously purifying and altering it*, is much more systematically used by Aristotle than by Plato, with the result that almost no terms pass through Aristotle's hand without, as Eucken says, retaining traces of the influence of his thought (Eucken, *Gesch. d. philos. Terminol.*, 26). Meanwhile, Aristotle freely *invents new terms*, in a way easily rendered possible by the facility of forming compounds in Greek. Eucken (loc. cit.) enumerates, as a mere specimen of Aristotle's construction of terminology, a list of some seventy-five new terms and expressions, but regards the philosopher's transformation and fixation of the earlier usages as of still more historical importance. A notable characteristic of the Aristotelian language, also dwelt upon by Eucken, is the setting into sharp antithesis of terms formerly either synonymous, or else less sharply distinguished. Thus $\gamma\acute{e}\nu os$ and $\epsilon\hat{i}\delta os$ with him first assume their well-known antithesis as *genus* and *species*. Another familiar Aristotelian antithesis is that of $\acute{\epsilon}\xi\iota s$ and $\delta\iota\acute{a}\theta\epsilon\sigma\iota s$ (*permanent condition* or *established habit* on the one hand, *temporary* or *changeable disposition* on the other hand). Still more important is the antithesis of $\delta\acute{\upsilon}\nu a\mu\iota s$ and $\acute{\epsilon}\nu\acute{\epsilon}\rho\gamma\epsilon\iota a$ (*capacity* or *potentiality* on the one hand, *attainment* or *actuality* on the other); and well known is also the characteristic contrast between $\pi\rho\acute{o}\tau\epsilon\rho o\nu$ $\tau\hat{\eta}$ $\phi\acute{\upsilon}\sigma\epsilon\iota$ and $\pi\rho\acute{o}\tau\epsilon\rho o\nu$ $\pi\rho\grave{o}s$ $\acute{\eta}\mu\hat{a}s$, which plays such a part in Aristotle's theory of knowledge (the former expression meaning the universal principle, or, as Prantl is fond of calling it, der schöpferische Begriff, the creative notion or form; while the latter expression refers to the individual, especially to the sensuous individual, which in *our knowledge* comes first, while in the *nature of things* the universal is prior to the individual). These are all classic instances of the *evolution of terminology in Aristotle through sharper differentiation of expressions and of meanings.*

(7) In consequence, philosophy owes to Aristotle a very large portion of its later technical terminology. In logic the debt is especially obvious and well known, since here, even where Aristotle uses expressions already employed by Plato or by other writers, their definitive meaning or usage is rightly most associated with Aristotle's name. The well-known table of Categories; the terms substance, accident, quality, quantity, relation, &c.; the classes of judgments; the names of the processes, or of the means, of inference, and of the modes and figures of the syllogism (apart from a few later additions or formal refinements of Aristotle's terminology); the names of the principal fallacies of the textbooks of formal logic; the well-known metaphysical distinction between form and matter (a distinction now very familiar even in popular language); the terminology of all the principal ontological problems—these, whether preserved to us in the original Greek terms, or represented by Latin translations, are some of the most characteristic of the Aristotelian contributions to the speech of later thought. It is true that, upon closer examination, the part played by Plato in the preparation of all these expressions appears greater than at first sight. Plato, for instance, in the *Theaetetus*, already gives what Lutoslawski ventures to call the first table of categories (*Theaet.* 185); and in the *Sophist* and the *Philebus* other efforts towards a systematic list of fundamental notions are present. In many other cases Plato has also prepared the way. But, as we have already found Eucken pointing out, Aristotle is even more important as a reformer and an establisher of previously suggested terminology, than as an inventor of wholly new terms. In the other branches of science, Aristotle's terminology is of great historical importance, although the growth of knowledge has in many regions tended to set beside his terms others of later date. Of permanent significance is his terminology, especially, in the philosophical portions of the philosophy of nature, in psychology, in ethics, and in such portion of political science as his own discussions have most affected.

(8) In later Greek philosophy the terminology of the Stoics is of the first importance. The most significant and characteristic advances of all the later Greek terminology have to do (i) with the *growth of a clearer consciousness as to the inner life, and as to the contrast between the objective and subjective aspects of reality* (see Eucken, op. cit., 31; and the terminological discussions in Siebeck's *Gesch. d. Psychol.*, Th. I, Abth. II, especially Siebeck's account of the later doctrine of the *emotions*, 222–41, and the summary of later doctrines as to the *practical aspect* of mental life, 241–61, as well as the chapter on the concept of *consciousness*, 331–42). The later Greek terminology is influenced (ii) *by the relations between philosophy, and the now more or less independent developments of the special sciences,* such as medicine. Here the *psychophysical problems* connected with psychology are of especial importance for terminology. The doctrine of the *pneuma,* or 'vital spirit,' is a typical instance where medical and philosophical speculations interacted, and influenced terminology (see Siebeck, op. cit., 130–60). Here, indeed, the theories in question had their basis in very early thinking, and their place in Aristotle. But the Stoics, and Galen (who died about 200 A.D.), extended and systematized both the empirical bases and the speculative applications of this doctrine of the pneuma, and the result, in one direction, influenced even the quite modern terminology of psychological theory (e.g. in case of the Cartesian doctrine of the 'animal spirits'); while, in another direction, through a contact with Jewish theology (in Philo and in the Jewish-Alexandrine speculation generally), the theory of the pneuma came to occupy a place of vast importance in the history of theology. The well-known popular distinction of 'body, soul, and spirit' becomes historically intelligible only in the light of this particular development of terminology; and the doctrine of the Trinity received expression in terms belonging partly to the same historical context. On the other hand, the development of the psychophysical terminology is also seen in the later doctrine of the *temperaments,* systematized by Galen, and since very widely popularized through psychological discussions (cf. Siebeck, op. cit., 278–90). Other instances of this type of terminological development are not lacking. But (iii) the later terminology expresses a constantly increasing interest in the *problems of theology,* viewed as such. Despite the growing sense

of the contrasts between inner and outer, subject and object, good and evil, divine and mundane, the Stoic philosophy, which is prevailingly monistic, recognizes such contrasts only in order to attempt to reduce them again to unity ; and the terminology of the theories here concerned became important for all later theology. Central in this development is the doctrine of the λόγος. The philosophical use of this term began indeed with Heraclitus, but as a metaphysical term, for the *objective reason* in things, it had gone into the background since that thinker, both Plato and Aristotle giving other terms the preference. The Stoics revived it, and developed, in connection with it, a considerable terminology, whose applications were at first pantheistic. Later, through Philo, as well as through the inner development of certain Stoical and eclectic tendencies, the term *logos* came into relations with theistic doctrines, and attained a very important place in Christian theology. The relations between the term *logos* and the before-mentioned πνεῦμα were from an early stage close, and the interpretation given to both became also of critical significance, in the discussions regarding the monistic and dualistic interpretations of the relations between God and world, and between the divine spirit and the individual soul. (Upon the *logos*, and the whole related terminology, see, in addition to the systematic histories of Greek philosophy, Heinze's *Lehre vom Logos in d. griechischen Philos.*, Oldenburg, 1872.) In close connection with the theological problem stands that regarding the *freedom of the will*, whose influence upon psychological terminology goes, together with the consequences of that advance, in a knowledge of the *inner life* above mentioned (cf. Siebeck, op. cit., 248 ff. ; Heinze, op. cit., 125 ff., 153 ff.). And next (iv) the later terminology is significant in its more purely *ethical aspects*. The Stoical definition of the highest good as *the concordant or consistent life*, or as the life *in accordance with nature* (ὁμολογουμένως ζῆν, or ὁμολογουμένως τῇ φύσει), is an instance of an expression that has since been in very general use (cf. Zeller, *Philos. d. Griechen*, Th. III, Abth. I, 211). The concept of the *indifferent*, which is neither good nor ill, but is a mere matter of fortune (the ἀδιάφορον in general), is expressed by another characteristic Stoic term. The Stoic theory of *virtue*, and of the various special *virtues*, involves a terminology that is, in part, modelled after Aristotle and Plato, in part independently expressed. The doctrine of the *absolute*

distinction between the wise and the foolish amongst men, and of *the absence of degrees in the possession of the virtues*, also affects the ethical terminology of the Stoics. These may serve merely as examples of Stoic usage. Less significant are the Epicurean additions to ethical terminology. (v) In the later, and especially, again, in the Stoic *logic*, there appear considerable alterations and elaborations of former terminology, as well as new expressions. (Here one may consult especially Prantl, *Gesch. d. Logik*, i. 412–96. More compendious is Zeller's account, *Philos. d. Griechen*, Th. III, Abth. I, 63–70, 86–114.) In the first place, here, the technical name *logic* is itself of Stoic origin, Aristotle having used the terms διαλεκτικός and ἀναλυτικός. The term dialectic survives, to be sure, as the usual one for the Stoics also. In the next place, the Stoics offer a revised table of categories, wherein, instead of the Aristotelian table, they offer a list of four categories, *substratum* (τὸ ὑποκείμενον), *quality* (τὸ ποιόν), *state or condition* (τό πως ἔχον), and *relation* or *relative state* (τὸ πρός τί πως ἔχον). They also pay considerable attention to the doctrine of the judgment, and in this region develop a complex and formal terminology, especially in case of the theory of the hypothetical judgment. A similar development of relatively new terminology exists in case of their theory of the hypothetical syllogism (see, in particular, Prantl, op. cit., 470). Finally, (vi) apart from the foregoing characteristics of the later terminology, there is to be noted a general alteration of the context and significance of the various conceptions of philosophy—an alteration which is due to the deepening religious consciousness of the centuries immediately following the Christian era, to the broadening of those interests in common humanity which grew with civilization, to the greater prominence given by later thought to the destiny of the individual soul, and, in general, to the richer, if also more problematic and confused, life of the Roman empire, and of early Christianity. From this point of view it has to be remembered that terms such as those for justice, for freedom, for the divine, for reason, and for humanity, necessarily tend to have a greater, although also vaguer, depth of meaning for later, ancient thinkers than for those whose world was a narrower one. That this greater depth of meaning also often implies a more obscure character, a tendency on the part of the thinkers to lose sight of the sharper definitions of their terms; and that the same progress in human experience leads, on the other hand, to an increasing temptation to seek escape from all these too-puzzling life-problems by means of formalism and pedantry: these are the inevitable mishaps of a more complex civilization. In general, moreover, it has to be remembered that, if the life of humanity, after the Christian era, faced problems of deeper meaning than those of the Greek cities, there was never again present, in the ancient world, the creative power that Plato and Aristotle had possessed, so that the later ancient philosophy was never adequate to its vastly enlarged task. In the work of the last great thinker of Greek philosophy, Plotinus, the older terminology was not notably reformed or increased; but the deepened insight into religious and ethical problems, and the vaster world in which Plotinus lived, tend to change the force and the implication of his terms in a way which Eucken has in general discussed (op. cit., 39 f.).

(9) The foregoing sketch of the history of Greek terminology is intended only as a rude outline, to suggest the general motives that appear to have determined the development of philosophical speech. Upon the subject, taken in its entirety, no adequate treatise exists. Materials bearing upon the topic have been collected in the most various ways, and lie scattered throughout the literature of ancient philosophy. While therefore no adequate bibliography of our topic can here be given, it is proper to add to the few foregoing literary references a more formal mention of a number of aids to a study of Greek terminology. Of the general histories bearing upon ancient thought, Zeller's *Philosophie der Griechen* contains, usually in the form of footnotes, a great many discussions of individual terms. These discussions are introduced at points of the text, determined by the general interests of Zeller's explanation of the various doctrines, so that here, as is usual throughout the whole literature of philosophy, the terminological interest is subordinated to the systematic and to the expository interests. The general index to Zeller's history, published as a supplement to the third edition (the first part only being referred to, in this index, in its fourth edition), is inadequate as a terminological index of the notes in question, so that for Zeller's best remarks the student must in general seek in their own places. Briefer are the discussions of terms to be found from time to time in Ueberweg's and Windelband's histories. The latter author, in his *General History of Philosophy*, treats of the development of concepts, rather than of the philosophers as individuals, or of their systems as separate wholes; but no very great space is given to the special history of terms, although many terms are incidentally treated. In Windelband's account of Greek philosophy in the *Handbuch der klassischen Alterthumswissenschaft*, there are also a good many brief statements of a terminological character. Prantl's *Geschichte der Logik* is decidedly full in its account of the development of the logical vocabulary; but once more, the material is widely scattered through Prantl's text, and is not easy to find for the purposes of the history of special terms. A valuable collection and comparison of all of the various enumerations which Aristotle gives of his categories (see the summary table in Prantl, i. 207) is a good example of the elaborateness of Prantl's work in this field. Specially upon terminology itself Eucken has written, in his admirable and compact *Geschichte der philosophischen Terminologie*, several times cited in the foregoing. Here pp. 8–47 are devoted to a sketch of the history of Greek terminology. The relations of the technical terminology of Greek philosophy to the language taken as a whole, and to the popular and literary usage, can be extensively studied by a use of J. H. Heinrich Schmidt's *Synonymik der griechischen Sprache* (Leipzig, 1876–86, 4 vols.), where, of necessity, the philosophical vocabulary is always treated, so to speak, as an episode in the general development of the language, but where a great mass of material bearing upon our subject has been collected, compared, and indexed. Examples of Schmidt's method, and of its relation to philosophical interests, are his article 13 (i. 282 ff.) on γιγνώσκειν; his series of articles 41–50, at the outset of Book II, on the Greek expressions for space and time relations; his article 81 (ii. 527–49) on εἶναι, the existential vocabulary, and the copula; and his article 147 (iii. 621–55) on νοῦς and its allied terms. Of no little interest for an understanding of the relations between the popular and the technical vocabulary of ethics is Leopold Schmidt's *Ethik der alten Griechen*. The terminology of Greek psychology receives much attention in Siebeck's *Geschichte der Psychologie* (Erster Theil).

(10) Passing from more general to more special works, the vocabulary of the early Greek philosophers has been discussed, with

much independence, although in the usual incidental way, by Burnet, in his *Early Greek Philosophy* (see, for example, his account of the term φύσις, p. 10; ἄπειρον, p. 59 ff.). Regarding the terminology of Plato, the material is indeed oppressively vast, but for that reason extremely hard to bring into order. Ast's *Lexikon Platonicum* (3 vols., Leipzig, 1853–8) is still the principal attempt at a complete account of the Platonic vocabulary. There exists also Mitchell's *Index Graecitatis Platonicae* (2 vols., Oxford, 1832). In the third volume of Jowett and Campbell's edition of the *Republic*, an essay by Campbell upon 'Plato's Use of Language' contains, as its second part, a study of the *Platonic diction*. Of this part of the essay one sub-section (pp. 291–340) is especially concerned with Plato's *philosophical expressions*. The Platonic vocabulary upon its ontological side has been very elaborately analysed, as a contribution to the 'history of concepts and of terms,' by Peipers, in his *Ontologia Platonica* (Leipzig, 1883). Plato's logical terms, not without much discussion of other sides of his vocabulary, find place in Lutoslawski's recent work upon *The Origin and Growth of Plato's Logic* (London, 1897). In this book, moreover, since the author is much concerned in attempts to fix the chronology of Plato's writings by means of stylometric criteria, an account is given of a long series of works that have been devoted to various aspects of Plato's style and language; and in consequence Lutoslawski's book, in addition to its intrinsic worth, is a valuable bibliographical aid to any one interested in a comparative study of the literature regarding Plato's language and usage of terms. In the case of Aristotle, the centre of all study of his vocabulary remains the great *Index* of Bonitz, which forms the concluding volume of the Berlin Academy edition of Aristotle's works. The recent *Aristoteles-Lexikon* of Kappes (Paderborn, 1894), founded upon the Bonitz *Index*, but put into an extremely compendious form, is a serviceable vocabulary of Aristotle's technical terms, intended for the use of the student who is finding his way into Aristotle. Wallace's *Aristotle* also contains brief definitions of a large number of Aristotelian terms. Aristotle himself, especially in the logical treatises, and in the *Metaphysics*, has done much to render definite the task of studying his terminology, by discussing extensively the various meanings of terms. He was in fact, as we have seen, the first writer upon terminology.

(11) To pass to still more special aids to terminological study, we may mention a few specimens of the literature dealing with particular terms, or groups of terms. Here the most prominent place will be given to examples of the literature of Aristotelian terms. The English editions of the individual dialogues of Plato often contain discussions of the terminology of the dialogue, or comparisons with other dialogues. To limit ourselves here to two very recent cases:—In an edition of the *Philebus*, by Bury (Cambridge University Press, 1897), there is an appendix upon 'τὸ ἄπειρον in Early Greek Thought,' followed at once by another upon 'τὸ ἄπειρον and τὸ πέρας in Plato' (see op. cit., 178–95). In a later appendix (201–11), Bury discusses the Platonic and, incidentally, the general Greek conception of truth (ἀλήθεια). In his edition of the *Timaeus* (London, 1888), Archer Hind, in his lengthy introduction, discusses a part of the Platonic ontological vocabulary, in various dialogues, as well as in particular in the *Timaeus* itself, and in his notes discusses also many points of Platonic terminology. On Aristotelian terminology, one may here first mention Brentano, *Von der mannigfachen Bedeutung des Seienden bei Aristoteles* (1862), an account of the Aristotelian ontological concepts and terms, with especial reference to the concepts of actual and possible being, and of the categories. Of standard importance is Trendelenburg's *Geschichte der Kategorienlehre* in his *Historische Beiträge zur Philosophie*, i. See also Newman's edition of the *Politics*.

Of the same subject Schuppe has treated in his little book *Die Aristotelischen Kategorien* (Berlin, 1871). The ontological vocabulary of Aristotle is dealt with in the two standard editions of the *Metaphysics*, that of Bonitz, and that of Schwegler. See also the dissertation of Bernard Weber, *De οὐσίας apud Aristotelem Notione eiusque Cognoscendae Ratione* (Bonn, 1887)—a very clearly stated account of all the principal fundamental concepts and terms in question. On the Aristotelian concept of ἀνάγκη there is a much older dissertation by Eug. Pappenheim (Berlin, 1856), entitled *De Necessitatis apud Aristotelem Notione*, which contains also a study of the terms τὸ δυνατόν and τὸ ἐνδεχόμενον, and of the related terminology. A Berlin dissertation of 1866, by Oscar Weissenfels, discusses *Chance* and *Matter* in their ontological relations, under the title *De Casu et Substantia Aristotelis*, but contains fewer terminological comparisons.

An important matter of Aristotelian usage is included in the topic of a dissertation by Johann Schmitz (Bonn, 1884), *De φύσεως apud Aristotelem Notione, eiusque ad Animam Ratione*. The terminology of Aristotle regarding the Intellect, active and passive, in its relation to all the much-debated problems of Aristotle's doctrine upon that subject, comes under consideration in Brentano's *Psychologie des Aristoteles* (Mainz, 1867); and the later history of the question (down to 1882) is summed up in an essay by Zeller, originally published in the Berlin Acad. *Sitzungsberichte* for 1882, under the title *Ueber die Lehre des Aristoteles von der Ewigkeit der Welt*. See also Eugen Eberhard, *Die Aristotelische Definition der Seele und ihr Werth für die Gegenwart* (Berlin, 1868). An important topic, both of Platonic and Aristotelian psychology, bearing upon the usage of a difficult term, is treated in the dissertation of Peter Meyer, *ὁ θυμός apud Aristotelem Platonemque* (Bonn, 1886). The same term, together with other psychological terms in Aristotelian usage, forms the topic of Dembowski's dissertation (Königsberg, 1881): (1) *De κοινοῦ αἰσθητηρίου Natura et Notione*; (2) *De Natura et Notione τοῦ θυμοῦ quatenus est Pars ὀρέξεως*. Another important psychological term is the subject of an essay by J. Freudenthal, *Ueber den Begriff des Wortes φαντασία* (Göttingen, 1863), who on p. 52 ff. compares the φαντασία with other related mental processes, and so discusses also, in a measure, the terminology of these processes. Both psychological and epistemological terms, especially, of course, the latter, receive treatment in Kampe's *Erkenntnisstheorie des Aristoteles* (Leipzig, 1870). Upon the systematic terminology of Aristotle's zoological writings there is a dissertation by Ludwig Heck (Leipzig, 1885), entitled *Die Hauptgruppen des Thiersystems bei Aristoteles und seinen Nachfolgern*, which also gives space to the classifications and terminology of Pliny and Albertus Magnus. The fundamental concept of Aristotle regarding the elements, together with this side of his terminology, is treated, in its relation to later thought, by Lorscheid, *Aristoteles' Einfluss auf die Entwickelung der Chemie* (Münster, 1872).

These form a few examples selected from the literature of the more difficult or less accessible portions of the Aristotelian terminology. The philosopher's ethical vocabulary has been very extensively discussed, but is perhaps sufficiently treated in various standard editions of the *Nicomachean Ethics*.

The need of a systematic treatment of the whole range of Greek terminology is made only the more obvious by these fragmentary notes of the literature; and it may be hoped that due attention will ere long be given to this need. (J.R.)

GLOSSARY.

The numerals refer to the paragraphs of the article.

ἀδιάφορον, 7.
ἀλήθεια, 11.
Ἄμεσα (immediate): in Aristotle, see HEGEL'S TERMINOLOGY, IV (*a*).
ἀνάγκη, 11.
ἀναλυτικός, 7.
ἄπειρον, 2, 10, 11.

γένος, 5, 6.
γιγνώσκειν, 9.

διάθεσις, 6.
διαλεκτικός, 8.
διαρεῖσθαι, 5.
δύναμις, 6, and see POWER.

εἶδος, 5, 6.
εἶναι, 9, and see BEING (2).
ἐνέργεια, 6, and see POWER.
ἕξις, 6.

κοινὸν αἰσθητήριον, 11.

λόγος, 8.

νοῦς, 9: see also NOUS.

ὁ θυμός, 11.
ὄρεξις, 11.
οὐσία, (1), see ESSENCE: cf. LATIN TERMINOLOGY, 7.

πνεῦμα, 8.
πρότερον (in phrases), 6.
πῦρ (of Heraclitus), 3.

τέμνειν, 5.
τὸ δυνατόν, 11.
τὸ ἐνδεχόμενον, 11.
τὸ πέρας, 11.
τὸ ποιόν, 7.
τὸ πρός τί πως ἔχον, 8.
τό πως ἔχον, 7.
τὸ ὑποκείμενον, 7.

φαντασία, 11.
φυσικός, 6.
φύσις, 4, 10, 11.

Green, Thomas Hill. (1836–82.) An English philosopher, born at Birkin, Yorkshire; died at Oxford. His father was rector of Birkin. He was educated at Rugby, and at Balliol College, Oxford. In 1860 he was elected Fellow of Balliol, and in 1862 won the Chancellor's prize for an essay on novels. In 1866 he became a tutor at Balliol. In 1872 he was re-elected Fellow, and in 1878 Whyte Professor of Moral Philosophy. He was the leader of the Neo-Hegelian movement in England.

Gregarious Instinct [Lat. *grex*, a flock]: Ger. *Herdeninstinkt*; Fr. *instinct grégaire*; Ital. *istinto d'aggregazione*. The instinct to go in companies. The alternative theories of this instinct are those of INSTINCT (q. v.) generally.

Literature: see titles given under COMPARATIVE PSYCHOLOGY, and SOCIAL PSYCHOLOGY. (J.M.B.)

Gregariousness: see GREGARIOUS INSTINCT, and SOCIALITY.

Gresham's Law: Ger. *Gresham'sches Gesetz*; Fr. *loi de Gresham*; Ital. *legge di Gresham*.

The principle that the worse currency drives out the better, so far as its quantity will permit.

Observed as long ago as Aristophanes, but more distinctly formulated by Sir Thomas Gresham in the 16th century. The proviso in the last clause of the definition was emphasized by Ricardo.

A man will tend to use light coin for paying his debts, and heavier coin for export or melting. If there is enough of the light coin to meet the demand for the former purpose, the heavier coin will disappear from circulation. (A.T.H.)

Grief [Fr. *grief*, grievance, from Lat. *gravis*, heavy]: Ger. *Kummer*, *Weh* (woe); Fr. *chagrin*, *peine*; Ital. *pena*, *dolore* (*morale*). Painful EMOTION (q. v.) accompanying consciousness of loss or other misfortune to self or others.

It is manifested in a relatively passive way, by disturbance and depression of organic functions, by cries, complaints, and movements which give relief by drawing off nervous energy, rather than by specific motor attitudes towards environing conditions such as characterize fear, anger, &c. Grief is the analogue on the perceptual and ideational level of mere physical suffering on the sensational level. Indeed, there are border cases in which it is difficult to draw a line between the two: the bodily expression is similar in both cases. This is true to a large extent of fear as well as of grief; but in fear there is a further complication, which gives the emotion its distinctive character: there is a more or less imperative demand for practical adjustment, in view of an emergency, together with more or less of felt incapacity to deal with the situation effectively. Extreme conditions of grief are distress and woe.

Literature: Grief has had little independent treatment. For its depressive effects on circulation, &c., see the experimental titles under EMOTION, and in BIBLIOG. G, 2, *k*. (G.F.S., J.M.B.)

Groot, Geert de, Gerhardus Magnus. (1340–84.) French philosopher, educated in Paris, who taught philosophy in Cologne with success. He suddenly decided to become a popular preacher, and founded the Brotherhood of the Common Life. He was a disciple of Ruysbroek, the great practical mystic. Thomas à Kempis was reared under the influence of the Brotherhood founded by Geert de Groot for the purpose (among others) of attracting the common people to a religious and church life,

by using the vulgar tongue in church and in translations of the Bible.

Groot (**Hugo de**): see GROTIUS.

Gross Earnings: Ger. *Brutto-einnahme*; Fr. *produit brut*; Ital. *guadagno lordo*. The total income from an industrial process, or group of processes, without deducting for things destroyed in the work.

Gross earnings may be measured, either by the means of satisfaction which a person receives in a certain time; or by the money which comes into his hands, as a result of things which he does for others. The aggregate of gross receipts of all members of the community constitutes the 'societary circulation' of Newcomb. See CIRCULATION, and cf. NET EARNINGS. (A.T.H.)

Grote, George. (1794–1871.) English historian and philosopher, born at Clay Hill, Kent, and died in London. He became vice-chancellor of London University, and later president of University College.

Grote, Nikolay Jakovlevič. (1852–99.) Educated at St. Petersburg. He was professor of philosophy at the Historical-Philological Institute of Niezhin (1876), and full professor at the universities of Odessa (1883) and Moscow (1889). Became president of the Psychological Association of Moscow (1889), and editor of the *Voprosi Philosophii* from its foundation (1889). He wrote in Russian and French.

Grotesque [Ital. *grotta*, an artificially made grotto]: Ger. *grotesk*; Fr. *grotesque*; Ital. *grottesco*. A species of the fantastic, including an element of caricature or humour, unconscious or intended. Cf. CARICATURE. (J.H.T.)

The grotesque seems to stand to the formal element in the requirement for beauty much as the comic does to the material or 'meaning' element. As the comic is the aesthetically distorted in respect to meaning, so the grotesque is the distorted in respect to form. In both cases the effect is possible psychologically only when the aesthetic is not only possible but is actually suggested. (J.M.B.)

Literature: SYMONDS, Essays Speculative and Suggestive; H. SCHNEEGANS, Gesch. d. grotesken Satire (1894), 1 ff.; the general works cited under AESTHETICS and BEAUTY; see also BIBLIOG. D, *d*. (J.H.T.)

Grotius, Hugo (**Hugo de Groot**). (1583–1645.) An eminent Dutch jurist and theologian, born at Delft, educated in Leyden. He accompanied the Dutch embassy to Paris in 1598. In 1613 he became pensionary of

Rotterdam, but in 1618, upon the defeat of the liberal party, he was imprisoned. Escaping from prison, he went to Paris, where he was well received, and in 1634 appointed Swedish ambassador by Oxenstiern. Died at Rostock on a journey. He is best known for his work *De Iure Belli et Pacis: Libri Tres*.

Ground [AS. *grund*]: Ger. *Grund*; Fr. *raison, fondement*; Ital. *ragione, evidenza*. Any objective condition of BELIEF (q.v.).

(G.F.S., J.M.B.)

Ground (in philosophy): see WORLD-GROUND.

Ground (logical): see REASON (sufficient).

Group [Fr. *groupe*]: Ger. *Gruppe*; Fr. (as above); Ital. *gruppo*. A plurality of individuals apprehended or treated together, yet with recognition of their individuality.

The second clause of the definition marks off the group-idea from the GENERAL CONCEPT (q.v.). The group-idea embraces all the individuals at once, with their peculiarities; so no single individual can represent or stand for the group. The recognition of likeness in the individuals is not necessary to the group, as it is to the general; nor is there of necessity any abstraction from their qualities. Yet both of these characterize some groups. For example, a horse, virtue, and a bag of diamonds may constitute a group; but the character of value may not (1), or may (2), be the reason for grouping them, and they may not (1), or may (2), be apprehended as a group of three. These two cases may be known as (1) the 'simple or concrete,' and (2) the 'numerical or abstract' group respectively.

The concrete group is probably first in the child's mind, and also in the mind of primitive man, before the rise of counting. Children and savages have groups which are only *these fingers, these stones*, &c., not these *objects* nor *so many* objects. Yet since the perception of likeness comes very early, and requires direct motor adaptation, the groups which are generalizations of like particulars are soon most important. And on the basis of this general sameness the idea of substitution arises, which is the nucleus of the notion of the numerical unit—the first stage in the evolution of the notion of NUMBER (q. v.). The numerical group, however, involves a further step, i. e. the dropping of all concrete marks in the units; the abstracting from all particularity. The unit must become not only liable to substitution for any other in the same group, but also for any other in any

other group. This is aided probably by the direct comparison of groups, by which a group of groups is secured. It is on account of this extreme abstractness, no doubt, that the idea of number is so late an achievement. The mathematical use of the numerical group is illustrated in connection with NUMBER (q.v.).

The grouping tendency seems to be fundamentally connected with activity. The need of treating things in groups creates a practical interest in their apprehension in groups. Furthermore, there is a direct resort to grouping in all rhythmical performances—a breaking up into three notably—which serves to create 'measure' and 'tempo' in music and dancing. The subjective accentuation of certain terms of a series—due possibly to adjustments of movement or of the attention—serves to make primitive groupings, and may possibly account for all of them. The subjective grouping of active impulses would seem to make the transition to the idea of the unit—both the unit of substitution, and the abstract numerical unit—easier, seeing that a unit of action is capable of direct manipulation, and is also free from the compelling characters attaching to concrete external objects.

Literature: apart from the topics RHYTHM and NUMBER (see those terms), the group has had little discussion from the psychological point of view. (J.M.B., G.F.S.)

Group (in mathematics): see MATHEMATICS, and NUMBER.

Group (social). Any specific collection of individuals, e. g. family, community, state, &c., considered as preserving concrete relationships. When the concrete relationships are abstracted from, we have an AGGREGATION (q. v.) of neutral units.

It is interesting to note that the social group illustrates the transition from the 'concrete' to the 'numerical' GROUP (see the distinction made under that term). It is based on likeness, and involves generalization with the possibility of substitution; but it has not reached the degree of abstractness in which the characters of individuals are subordinated to the notion of the numerical unit. Indeed, the older view of such a social unit or individual—extreme individualism based on 'natural law' and 'natural right'—is now exploded, and it is recognized that each social group has for its unit a social individual, of a definite character peculiar to the group, rather than a mere individual liable to substitution for a similar unit in another group.

For the purposes of a formal sociology which seeks to establish the modes of organization common to all social groups, the assumption of a social unit of a highly abstract sort, a quasi-numerical unit, is legitimate. The term AGGREGATION (q. v.) is suggested for such a group of groups, or for a group capable of substitution in the social whole for any other group. Any social group thus becomes, for purposes of investigation, an aggregation (or mathematical group). Such a formal treatment of social life results in a social logic, properly so called. Its most fruitful application, no doubt, is found in the statistical investigations of social life in which—as in similar problems of biology—sufficiently large aggregations of individuals are taken to get results true of the average individual or abstract unit. Such treatment is illustrated in Pearson's *Chances of Death* and Durkheim's *Suicide*, and put to practical use in Life Insurance. See UNIT, NUMBER, and VARIATION; and for literature, SOCIOLOGY. (J.M.B.)

Group Selection: Ger. *Gruppenselektion*, *Gruppenauslese*; Fr. *sélection des groupes*; Ital. *selezione di gruppo* (or *fra gruppi*). NATURAL SELECTION (q. v.) operative upon social groups. Cf. SELECTION.

The competition or struggle for existence is here between groups as such, not between individuals, except as individuals' success contributes to the success—stability, persistence, survival—of the group. It is seen in all sorts of tribal and national competition, brought about by migration, rival occupation of territory, &c.; and in war, and commercial and social rivalry, in which one form or type of social life is imposed by one group upon another, whose type thus tends to disappear.

Pearson distinguishes between 'extra-group' and 'intra-group' competition (*Chances of Death*, i. 113); and Gumplowicz, who finds the group the 'social unit,' uses the terms Rassenkampf and Classenkampf (*Sociol. u. Politik*, 37, 53; cf. Barth, *Philos. d. Gesch. als Sociol.*, i. 245).

Literature: BAGEHOT, Physics and Politics; ALEXANDER, Moral Order and Progress; BALDWIN, Social and Eth. Interpret., 1st ed. (where the term is suggested), § 120; 2nd ed., Appendix H. 2 (in French and German eds., § 313 a). (J.M.B.)

Growth (mental) [AS. *growan*, to be green]: Ger. *psychisches Wachsen* (*Wachsthum*); Fr. *croissance* (*développement*) *psychique*; Ital. *sviluppo psichico* (or *mentale*). The progressive differentiation and integration of experience in the individual, due to the persistence of the after-effects of previous mental process as conditions of subsequent mental process; that is, to the production of more or less permanent DISPOSITIONS (q. v.). (G.F.S.)

It is convenient to limit the terms growth and development to what takes place in the individual mind. EVOLUTION (q. v.) is the term recommended for the progressive emergence of higher mental stages from the phylogenetic point of view. A useful distinction between growth and development may be observed; development meaning the gradual unfolding of mental powers, only in so far as this is predetermined by congenital constitution. The term growth is then used distinctively to mark the part played in the process by the special circumstances and the connected experiences of the individual. Croom Robertson says this view is 'rendered much more definite when there is coupled with it a reference to the bodily conditions of mental life. In particular, we are thereby helped to conceive of the individual as endowed originally with definite mental capacities. . . . Organized, however, as the nervous system is at birth, it is then but imperfectly developed, responding with a small number of reactions to a few simple impressions, or expending its energy in random movements. . . . As the development of the system is then known to proceed, through childhood and youth, in dependence upon its inherent powers, more than upon (though not without) the presence of soliciting circumstances, we may more distinctly comprehend how new phases of mental life should from time to time manifest themselves, for which no explanation is to be sought in the foregoing conscious experience. While, again, the growth of the nervous system as a whole, and of its various parts, at each stage of development evidently proceeds in relation to the physical circumstances, naturally present or artificially supplied, so may we more clearly see how the mind will expand and acquire this disposition or that, according to the nature of the incidental experience or express instruction it receives.'

To this distinction may be added the one made under ANALYSIS between PSYCHIC (or MENTAL) AND PSYCHOLOGICAL (q. v.). The consciousness of the processes of change which determine growth is 'psychic' or mental experience; the changes to an outsider or theorist are psychological. (G.F.S.–J.M.B.)

Growth (physical). (1) The natural process of individual development.

(2) That part of individual development which is due to particular conditions, such as use and disuse, variations in nutrition, temperature, &c.

The first use is more general. We speak of the growth of a tree, the hair, a boy; of impeded or retarded growth. The distinction between development and growth, however, recommended under the preceding topic, has much to commend it in biology, growth being reserved for the variations in ontogenetic development due to changes in conditions of life, to use and function, &c. Cf. DEVELOPMENT (biological).

Literature: see the topics referred to under DEVELOPMENT. For observations on the growth of school children by BOWDITCH, BOAS, and others, see WILSON, Bibliog. of Child Study. (J.M.B.)

Guilt (ethical) [AS. *gyldan*, to pay]: Ger. *Schuld*; Fr. *culpabilité*; Ital. *colpa*. The state of having committed a crime, or consciously offended against moral law. The absence of guilt is innocence.

The view of guilt differs according as the standpoint is that of law or that of morality. From the former point of view guilt means transgression of a positive law, though this view is often modified in the judgment passed upon the act by taking into account the transgressor's knowledge or ignorance of the law, and even his temptations to transgress. From the moral point of view, consciousness of duty is of the essence of guilt. From this point of view it has been regarded as the contrary of merit. 'Merit is only present when the moral action is performed in opposition to a psychically present immoral tendency; guilt is present only when the immoral action is performed in spite of a psychically present moral consciousness.' See Simmel, *Einl. in d. Moralwissenschaft*, chap. iii. (W.R.S.)

Guilt (in law): see IGNORANCE, and INTENTION.

Guilt (in theology): Ger. *Schuld* (often *Sünde*); Fr. *culpabilité*; Ital. (*stato di*) *colpa*. Theologically, guilt is always associated with sin, particularly with original sin, but under certain limitations. These limitations appear so early as Paul, who distinguished sharply between ἁμαρτία and παράπτωμα. The former is the general condition of defect due to Adam's fall; the latter is actual transgression, and, as such, is accompanied by guilt. Or, again, the former is a state common to humanity; the latter implies acts of individual men.

Choice, then, is regarded as an essential antecedent of guilt; for guilt is possible only, not actual, under God's permission of the fall. Positive transgression of the law of righteousness involves guilt, which, in turn, is recognized by self-consciousness or by 'conscience.' Guilt, then, is a realized issue of the liability to sin; as such it stands on a different level from legal guilt, for it implies that man has put a false infinite (himself) over against the true infinite (God), and has chosen to serve the former. In other words, timeless issues are set in motion; hence the last importance of the question. See FALL, and SIN.

Literature: SACK, in Stud. u. Krit. (1869); ROTHE, Theol. Ethik, iii. 1 f.; Herzog's Real-Encyc., art. Sünde; any treatise on dogmatics. (R.M.W.)

Gustatory Sensation: see TASTE SENSATION.

Gyrus [Gr. γῦρος, circle]: Ger. *Windung*; Fr. *circonvolution*; Ital. *circonvoluzione*. See BRAIN (glossary).

H

HABEAS CORPUS — HABIT

Habeas Corpus [Lat.]. A form of writ designed to secure the speedy release of any one unlawfully confined. Its issue is a matter of right, and the procedure summary.

A similar remedy was afforded by the Roman praetor, by the interdict 'de homine libero exhibendo' (*Dig.*, xliii. 29). The English Habeas Corpus Act, 31 Car. II, chap. ii (given in full in Lieber's *Civil Liberty*, Appendix, 489), is the foundation of the statutes upon this subject of the United States and the several states. The writ is prayed out by, or in behalf of, the prisoner, and directed to the person who holds him in custody, who is required to produce him before the authority issuing the writ, within a time designated, together with a statement of the cause of his detention. If this cause is adjudged to be insufficient, the person will be forthwith discharged.

Literature: see also, with regard to the Roman law processes of this nature, Dig., xliii. 30, De liberis exhibendis, &c.; SOHM, Inst. of Roman Law, § 88; DEMELIUS, Die Exhibitionspflicht. (S.E.B.)

Habit [Lat. *habitus*, from *habere*, to have]: Ger. *Gewohnheit*; Fr. *habitude*; Ital. *abito*, *abitudine*. (1) In psychology: a mental function whose repeated performance results in progressively better accommodation, and is accompanied by a feeling of familiarity and increased facility. The function itself is called a habit.

The abstract term habit is applied to the increased accommodation, familiarity, and facility, as in the expression 'due to habit.' The law of habit in psychology is the generalization that any function becomes thus modified and organized with repeated efforts. The inquiry into the reasons for habit leads to an analysis in which the elements of conation are most marked as passing from the type represented by effort (volitional conation) through gradual modification to impulse (non-volitional conation). Habit thus denotes the progressive modification of the conditions which determine a function through a series of changes, and as such is considered a genetic principle of the first importance: the principle of formation and conservation of type in mental operations. Thus considered, it is in contrast with the genetic principle of ACCOMMODATION (q. v.), which generally requires the modification of habitual performances.

(2) In neurology and physiology: a function which has become relatively organized and fixed. The psychological character noted above, whereby the conation involved passes from the volitional gradually to the non-volitional stage, is revealed on the organic side by the principle of so-called 'downward growth' or FACILITATION (q. v.) in the nervous system.

(3) In biology: an individually acquired function. Habit is thus sharply distinguished from INSTINCT (q. v.). A different usage — mainly by descriptive zoologists — extends the term habit (Ger. Habitus; Fr. mœurs) to include all specific actions of animals, whether instinctive or acquired. This is not to be endorsed, since the only possible hypothesis on which the instincts of animals can be brought under the conception of habit as used in psychology and physiology is that of LAMARCKISM (q. v.), according to which the instincts have been acquired gradually as so-called 'race-habits.' Apart, however, from

the possible truth of that hypothesis, it is better, both for consistency and for clearness in discussion, to distinguish that which is individually acquired from that which is physically inherited. An extreme form of this usage is current among botanists, who speak of the habits—of growth, &c.—of plants. (J.M.B.–G.F.S.)

Literature: HAMILTON, Lects. on Met., XVIII. iii; REID, Active Powers, Essay III; HARTLEY, Observations on Man, Prop. XXI; LLOYD MORGAN, Habit and Instinct; GROOS, The Play of Animals, and The Play of Man (Eng. trans.); SCHNEIDER, Der thierische Wille, and Der menschliche Wille; BALDWIN, Ment. Devel. in the Child and the Race. Also general and genetic works on psychology, and BIBLIOG. G, 2, *m*. Further (in biology): HERBERT SPENCER, Principles of Psychology; A. WEISMANN, Essays on Heredity; H. EIMER, Organic Evolution; WALLACE, Darwinism; ROMANES, Mental Evolution in Animals. (C.LL.M.)

For references to the scholastic authorities, and on their usage, see EISLER, Wörterb. d. philos. Begriffe, 'Habitus.' (J.M.B.)

Habitat [Lat. *habitare*, to inhabit]: Ger. *Wohnsitz*; Fr. *habitat*; Ital. *abitato*. The local environment of an animal or plant. See ENVIRONMENT, and MILIEU. (C.LL.M.–J.M.B.)

Habituation: Ger. (1) *Einübung*, (1, 2) *Gewöhnung*; Fr. *accoutumance* (TH.F.); Ital. *assuefazione*, (*l'*) *abituarsi* (to habituate). (1) The becoming accommodated or habituated with respect to the performance of a given function. Cf. EXERCISE (1), PREPARATION, and TERMINOLOGY (German), 'Einübung.'

The term drill is also used, especially in cases in which an external authority imposes the exercise for purposes of training, &c. (J.M.B.)

(2) A tendency set up in the course of an experimental series, to judge of a given number of that series in the terms of foregone judgments. It is the 'becoming habituated to the expression of a given judgment.' Cf. HABIT, and see DISPOSITION. (E.B.T.)

Hades [Gr. Ἅιδης]. The name employed by the translators of the Septuagint, and by the writers of the New Testament, for the sphere where the souls of the departed dwell.

The term Hades is common in Greek, from Homer down. In dealing with the Hellenic conception, care must be taken to differentiate between Hades (otherwise Aïdes, Aïdoneus, and Plouton), the deity—brother of Zeus and Poseidon—and Hades, the underworld or abode of the dead. Here we are concerned with the latter only. In the poems attributed to Homer, Hades appears as the dwelling-place of shadows. On the whole, these shades continue there essentially the life from which they have departed, being engaged in similar or identical occupations; but this existence is, as it were, a species of trance—its unreality, bloodlessness, joylessness, comfortlessness form the striking characteristics (cf. *Odyssey*, xi). Its inhabitants are veritable ghosts that squeak and gibber. Or, as Achilles says, relating his vision of Patroclus' shade: 'So spake he, and stretched out his hands but grasped him not, for vapour-like the spirit vanished into the ground with squeaking, gibbering cry. . . . Ah me! truly then there is in the dwellings of Hades a phantom, but φρένες (i.e. passions, affections, emotions, will) it hath not at all' (cf. *Iliad*, xxiii. 66 f.). The pathos of loss would seem to be the idea which Homer most associated with the inhabitants of the nether world. In a word, the view of the future life represented by him is non-religious; that is to say, it offers a reply to the quasi-philosophical question, What becomes of the dead?—a reply, moreover, which, to this stage, has no special connection with religion, because not involving any ideal of a higher life. By the time of Pindar this has changed, and Hades sometimes appears as a place where rewards and punishments are meted out (cf. *Olymp.*, ii. 95 f.; *Fragm. Thren.*, ii and iii). Moral considerations make their appearance here, and, for reasons connected with the development of Greek culture, which we still know but imperfectly, this progressive expansion of ideas connected with Hades continues in the later writers, becoming more spiritualized, more distinctively religious, till, in the end, the squealing ghosts of Homer give place to the Justice of Sophocles, dwelling in the underworld, and ruling even men's lives; and to Plato's argument for the immortality of the soul. The movement is from a merely imaginative idea about the place of shades to a moral conception of the conditions which govern human life eternally on account of its very constitution.

In the Septuagint, Hades is, as a rule, the translation of the Hebrew word Sheol, which occurs frequently in the Old Testament.

The conceptions of Hades are, on the whole, negative. While souls continue to exist there, they are conceived of as stripped of the qualities which most characterize the living; and few positive traits are added.

The ideas of separation from the living, of cheerlessness, of absence of all the moral and social determinations that mark human life, predominate. In the Apocalyptic literature, the conceptions tend to become slightly more positive, as, for example, in the Book of Wisdom, where the idea of moral distinctions appears; while, in the still later Rabbinical literature, the doctrine of Hades as an intermediate state, which may be a preparation either for eternal bliss or for eternal misery, is formulated. A very notable fact is that the word is used only on ten distinct occasions in the New Testament. Here, once more, the negative tendencies of the Old Testament are maintained, to such an extent indeed that, if we except the ethical implications of the word as used by Jesus (e. g. Luke xvi. 23), little difference can be traced. In a word, no doctrinal use can be made of the term. Cf. ESCHATOLOGY.

Literature: SALMOND, Christ. Doctrine of Immortality; BÖTTICHER, De Inferis; WEBER and SCHNEDERMANN, Jüdische Theol. auf Grund d. Talmud; OERTEL, Hades; HAMBURGER, Real-Encyc. f. Bibel u. Talmud; E. RHODE, Die Psyche; HARTWIG, Die Darstellung d. Unterwelt. (R.M.W.)

Haecceitas [Schol. Lat.]. This-ness or thing-ness. See LATIN AND SCHOLASTIC TERMINOLOGY. (J.M.B.)

Hagiographa [Gr. ἅγιος, sacred, + γράφειν, to write]. One of the divisions of the Canon of the Old Testament: the Law, the Prophets, and the Writings or Hagiographa (sacred writings). Under the last are included the following books:—Psalms, Proverbs, Job, Song of Songs, Ruth, Lamentations, Ecclesiastes, Esther, Daniel, Ezra, Nehemiah, and Chronicles. Many important questions with regard to the formation of the Old Testament Canon are involved in this division and nomenclature. See CANON.

Literature: an excellent and most compact summary is ROBERTSON, The Old Testament and its Contents; GEIGER, Nachgelassene Werke, iv; REUSS, Hist. of the Canon of Holy Scripture (Eng. trans.); FRANCIS BROWN, in the J. of the Soc. of Bib. Lit. and Exegesis (1882), 95 f.; KAUTZSCH, Hist. of the Lit. of the O. T. (Eng. trans.); the relative arts. in Herzog's (German) and Lichtenberger's (French) Encycs.; Hastings' Dict. of the Bible; Cheyne's Encyc. Biblica. (R.M.W.)

Hagiology [Gr. ἅγιος, sacred, + λόγος, word, reason]: Ger. *Heiligenlegenden*; Fr. *hagio-logie*; Ital. *Agiologia*. The section of ecclesiastical history which deals with the saints of the Church—their lives, their achievements, the reasons for their CANONIZATION (q. v.).

Naturally, hagiology has received more attention from Roman Catholics than from Protestants. It may be usefully studied by those interested in philosophy of religion, from the historical and archaeological sides, and particularly for the light that it casts upon the psychology of religion.

Literature: this is enormous, and must be sought in bibliographies under specific names. The works on Anselm, Aquinas, Albertus Magnus, Francis, Bernard, Catherine of Siena, and Eckard are specially important from the side of philosophy of religion. (R.M.W.)

Halacha and **Haggada** [Heb.]. The two divisions of the Midrash.

Midrash denotes the exegesis, exposition, and illustration of the 'Law of Moses,' which, beginning after the return from the Exile, continued to occupy the attention of the Jewish ecclesiastical schools with increasing exclusiveness. Halacha is the name given to the interpretation of the sense of the Hebrew Scriptures; it was formulated chiefly in the Rabbinical schools, and was at once legal and highly casuistical. Haggada is the name given to the stories, legends, parables, and so forth which served to illustrate the Law. It was practical, rhetorical, and quasi-popular-homiletical, as a theologian would say. See TALMUD.

Literature: WÜNSCHE, Bibliotheca Rabbinica; WEBER and SCHNEDERMANN, Jüdische Theol. For the general atmosphere in which this interpretation grew up, see SCHÜRER, The Jewish People (Eng. trans.); HAUSRATH, New Testament Times (Eng. trans.). (R.M.W.)

Hallucination [Lat. *hallucinatio*]: Ger. *Hallucination*; Fr. *hallucination*; Ital. *allucinazione*. (1) The perceptual construction of an object which has in its construction no elements of external reality.

(2) The object thus perceived. (J.J.–J.M.B.)

Since the days of Esquirol (1838) an hallucination has been distinguished from an ILLUSION (q. v.) by the fact that in the latter a misinterpretation of an actually existent object is involved, while the true hallucination has no really external starting-point. This distinction, although practically valid, must not be drawn too rigidly, for in many cases the two approach one another closely. Illusions involve some elements of hallucination, and many hallucinations originate in a more remote external suggestion. See ILLUSION.

In medicine: the existence of hallucinations has been recognized from the time of Hippocrates; and their prevalence in insanity has always served as one of the popular characteristics of that state. The explanation of hallucinations and illusions was, until modern times, largely along the lines of possession or influence from the outside. Their subjective nature came into serious recognition towards the opening of the present century, and Esquirol (1772–1840) was influential in establishing their scientific importance. Historically, hallucinations have played an important part among all nations, especial significance being attached to appearances which presented themselves to great men at critical times.

Occurrence. Hallucinations, while specially characteristic of insanity, and of disturbed conditions of the nervous system, undoubtedly occur in perfectly normal persons; but the frequency with which they occur in states of fatigue, ill-health, or mental anxiety is most suggestive. The census of hallucinations gathered by the Society for Psychical Research indicates a wide dissemination of hallucinations in the sane; the numbers given, however (12 per cent. in all; 9·75 per cent. in men, 14·5 per cent. in women), are probably in excess of their actual occurrence. Hallucinations are most frequently met with in monomania (so-called delusional insanity), paranoia, and melancholia, but are not uncommon in mania. There is considerable diversity of statement in regard to the prevalence of hallucinations in mania and melancholia; this is largely due to differences of classification of these disorders, as well as to more minute differentiation between hallucinations and delusions in connection with these states (Parish, as below, 21 ff.). How far the vagaries and elaborate fancies of general paralysis are of the hallucinatory type is likewise variously stated (Parish, as below, 25–6); about one-third of all cases seem thus affected. Hallucinations may occur in the epileptic aura, in post-epileptic states, and in hysteria; and are characteristic of the action of various drugs (see PSYCHIC EFFECTS OF DRUGS). Acute bodily diseases, fevers, fasting, and exhaustion, dream-like states, certain forms of artificial hypnosis, and forms of heart trouble are also apt to induce hallucinations.

Varieties. Hallucinations are most fre-

quently divided according to the sense which is affected; if affecting only one sense they may be termed simple; if more than one sense, compound. In the case of the insane it is important to distinguish between those which are recurrent and reflect the dominant mental tone, and those which are sporadic and unrelated to the mental tone. The two senses which are far more commonly affected than any others are sight and hearing. Amongst the sane about 60 per cent. of hallucinations are visual, 33 per cent. auditory; but this may readily be interpreted to mean that visual hallucinations are the more striking and the more apt to be remembered. Amongst the insane, auditory hallucinations seem fully as frequent as visual, owing mainly to the prevalence of the hallucination of hearing voices. Smell and taste hallucinations may occur, but it is difficult to eliminate some organic basis of sensation for these. Tactile hallucinations, hallucinations of the muscular sense, and of the organic sensations likewise rarely appear as individual hallucinations, however important they may be in contributing or originating the elaborate delusions in which other senses co-operate. Amongst the sane there was recorded one case of hallucination of more than one sense, to seven cases confined to one sense; of these complex hallucinations two-thirds are visual and auditory. No adequate statistics on this point exist for the insane; but the relations are probably not very different. Another variety of hallucination is the negative hallucination, occurring mainly as the result of hypnotic suggestion (see HYPNOSIS). In this the subject fails to see what is actually present; he may thus ignore a piece of furniture, an individual, a certain word or letter on a page, &c. The psychological process here involved is very different from that of the ordinary positive hallucination, which may be similarly aroused by hypnotic suggestion. Other forms of hallucination commonly described are the hypnagogic hallucinations, which occur in the transitional states in going to sleep and in waking from sleep; motor hallucinations, in which the patient appears to move while really at rest (cf. ILLUSIONS), or feels that he is flying, walking in air, &c.; unilateral and hemiopic hallucinations, which appear to one eye or to one ear only; and so on.

Illustrations. Human faces and figures are a frequent form of visual hallucination, often assuming terrifying expressions; animal forms are common. Both frequently move and take part in dramatic action. Mysterious signs, flashes of fire, areas of colour may appear, as in the visions of religious ecstatics. The kaleidoscopic changing of forms that appears in opium and other drug intoxication is also characteristic. In the complex hallucinations (those of persecution particularly), what first appears as a voice may later assume a definite shape. The variety of such delusions is endless, being determined largely by the dominant emotional tone and the personal temperament. The mysterious voices of one age become communicated through an invisible telephone in another; or the magic action by witchcraft becomes a form of mesmerism or of electricity. In all such cases the starting-point and specific nature of the hallucination is of greatest significance; its development and elaborations are too variable for psychological interpretation. Voices are perhaps the most prevalent form of hallucination, and frequently dominate the patient's entire conduct. As already indicated, hallucinations of touch are apt to be of the form of paraesthesia. Abnormal sensations are misinterpreted; creeping sensations become the attacks of ants or vermin; anaesthesias lead to conceptions of the limbs as made of wood or glass, the absence of a stomach, and the like. Changes of personality may be similarly conditioned. Visceral disturbances may lead to the presence of olfactory hallucinations—bad odours. A perverted taste may lead the patient to detect imaginary poison in his food. This group of quasi-hallucinations seldom appear alone, but co-operate with other hallucinations in the formation of delusions under the dominance of the prevailing mental tone.

Theories. While the special senses are concerned in the origin of hallucinations, they afford no explanation of the hallucination itself. For hallucinations are not mainly of crude sensations like flashes of light and sudden noises, but of definite objects and scenes; moreover, persons who have become blind or deaf may be subject to hallucinations in the domain of the lost sense. While admitting that sensory changes may induce hallucinations (as in intoxication, &c.), these are secondary to the main phenomenon, which is of central origin. Theories (Ferrier, Tamburini) which ascribe the initial impulse of the hallucination to the highest cortical (ideational) centres may be termed centrifugal. Such views hold that when an irritation begins in the appropriate highest centre

(or, in another view, is brought to that highest centre from an irritation in the subcortical centre), and proceeds outward (under certain favourable but not clearly determined conditions), it causes an hallucination, just as the reverse process normally causes a true perception. This view, according to which the hallucination is projected outward and materialized by a process the reverse of normal sense-perception, seems to be favoured by the fact that certain persons can produce hallucinations by an action of the will, that hallucinations do not occur in states of severe mental defects (idiocy, dementia), that the same factors are important in actual life and in hallucinations, and further, in recent discussions, by the fact that such hallucinations are doubled when a prism is held in front of the eye, are coloured when seen through coloured glass, and so on. That this type of theory is inadequate can readily be shown. To begin with, the fundamental process involved cannot be regarded as plausible or physiological; the sporadic cases of voluntary hallucinations are far too few to be significant; the doubling and colouring of the hallucination is perhaps an inference (more or less unconscious) from what happens to normal objects.

An adequate theory can be formed only on the basis of a more exact knowledge of the relations of cerebral centres than we now possess. The most helpful theories (those of Meynert, James, Kandinsky, Parish, and others; see Parish, as below, 132–52) proceed on the basis of an identity of the sensory and reproductive centres, and exhibit the hallucination as a disturbance of the usual relation between the particular perceptive centre and its associative bonds. It is a state of dissociation, which is the common point of all hallucinatory states (Parish); it is the suppression of the activity of the highest cortical centres which makes possible the undue excitement of the subcortical centres, which in turn occasion hallucinations (Meynert); it is the over-accumulation of nerve-currents (owing to the absence of free communication with neighbouring cells) which acts like an explosion and produces an hallucination (James). While these theories are helpful, no one of them can be said to present an adequate account of what goes on in the hallucinated mind; such defect being the almost necessary result of our defective knowledge in regard to the physiological counterparts of normal perception, association, and reproduction.

It has been held (Baldwin) that hallucination, like illusion, arises from a disturbance of the normal relation which holds in all perception between central and peripheral elements. When for any reason the central factor is over-stimulated or the peripheral is ineffective, the normal interpretation of the objective is disturbed, and an assimilation of data takes place, in which central processes—images, schemes, beliefs—dominate. Cf. ILLUSION.

For the relation of hallucination to insanity see SANITY AND INSANITY, EPILEPSY, and HYSTERIA; see also ILLUSION, DELUSION, DREAM, INTOXICATION, HYPNOSIS, PSYCHIC RESEARCH, and VERIDICAL HALLUCINATION.

Literature: the most comprehensive study, from the normal point of view, is EDMUND PARISH, Hallucinations and Illusions (1897), especially chaps. i–iv (with full references). See also the Psychologies of JAMES, TAINE, BALDWIN. Pathological: SANDERS, art. Sinnestäuschungen, in Eulenburg's Real-Encyk., xviii; TAMBURINI, Riv. di Freniat. (1880); HOPPE, Erklärung d. Sinnestäuschungen bei Gesunden u. Kranken (4th ed., 1888); MORSELLI, Semej. malat. ment.; KANDINSKY, Krit. u. klin. Betrachtung im Gebiet d. Sinnestäuschung (1885); SNELL, Allg. Zeitsch. f. Psychiat., l. 534; BAILLARGER, Mém. de l'Acad. Roy. de Méd., xii; KRAEPELIN, Psychiatrie, and Vtljsch. f. wiss. Philos., v; KRAFFT-EBING, Die Sinnesdelirien (1864); A. MAYER, Die Sinnestäuschungen (1869); ZIEHEN, Psychiatrie (1894). Historical mainly: JOH. MÜLLER, Ueber phantastische Geisteserscheinungen (1826); ESQUIROL, Ment. Pathol. (Eng. trans., 1845); BRIERRE DE BOISMONT, Hallucinations (trans., 1859); GRIESINGER, Ment. Pathol. (Eng. trans., 1867). Many of the books on mental diseases contain interesting treatment of hallucinations, e. g. Twentieth Cent. Pract. of Med.,xii. 80–9. (J.J.)

Hamilton, Sir William. (1788–1856.) Eminent Scottish metaphysician, born at Glasgow, and educated at Glasgow and Oxford. Intended for a physician, he decided to study law. In 1817 and 1820 he travelled in Germany. Not succeeding eminently as an advocate, he applied for the chair of moral philosophy in Edinburgh, upon the death of Thomas Brown, but was not appointed (1820). In 1821 he was made professor of civil history at Edinburgh. In 1836 the chair of logic became vacant at Edinburgh, and Hamilton, after an exciting candidacy, was elected. He continued to lecture until his death, May 6, 1856.

Handwriting: Ger. *Handschrift*; Fr. *écriture*; Ital. *scrittura*. The material recording of thought by imitative or conventional signs, for purposes of social communication, through movements of the hand.

The transition from the purely imitative to the purely conventional, from the pictograph to true handwriting, was probably very slow. The essential fact that the sign, either imitative or conventional, records and communicates a meaning, is present to both; but the former no doubt illustrated a stage of mental progress having generalization without much abstraction. It is reasonable to suppose that the evolution of writing, following after that of speech, reacted to aid the evolution of abstract thought.

The psychological problem of handwriting deals with the acquisition of the necessary movements, together with the control and inhibition involved in the progressive execution of the series of movements. Theories from the purely psychological point of view have been developed by Goldscheider (*Zeitsch. f. Psychol.*, xxiv, 1892) and Baldwin (*Ment. Devel. in the Child and the Race*, chap. v. § 2). They agree in making handwriting an imitative function, taking its start in 'tracery imitation' (the malende Reproduction of Goldscheider), and developing by the gradual association of certain sensational series: a 'visual form' series, a 'kinaesthetic movement' series, and a remote 'optical' series; of which, however, Goldscheider recognizes only the two last. The two theories differ as to which of these is the original copy series (Goldscheider saying the 'optical' and Baldwin the 'visual form' series), and in the relative place of the various sensational elements in the acquisition of control. Goldscheider has shown (loc. cit.) by experiment that the 'kinaesthetic movement' series involves pressure sensations entering into the resistance of the plane written on. For troubles and variations in handwriting based on the preceding analysis see Goldscheider (loc. cit.), and the topics AGRAPHIA and MIRROR WRITING. Cf. also GRAPHOLOGY (q. v. for matters pertaining to handwriting as expressive of character, &c.).

Literature: as referred to; BROADBENT, on Handwriting of the Blind, Brit. Med. J. (1876), i. 435; the manuals of Psychiatry of ERLENMEYER, EMMINGHAUS, and MORSELLI. Also the titles given under the topics referred to. (J.M.B.)

Haploscope: see LABORATORY and APPARATUS, III, B, (a), (10).

Happen and **Happening** : see EVENT.

Happiness [ME. *hap*, chance]: Ger. *Glück*; Fr. *bonheur*; Ital. *felicità*. A desirable and, on the whole, pleasurable condition of life.

The definition of J. S. Mill (*Utilitarianism*, chap. ii)—'by happiness is intended pleasure and the absence of pain ; by unhappiness, pain and the absence of pleasure'—expresses the ordinary acceptation of the term in English, and of its equivalents in most modern languages.

As the traditional rendering of the Greek εὐδαιμονία, the term is sometimes used in a less precise sense for the most desirable—or for any desirable—condition of human life, whether that condition be, in ultimate analysis, reducible to terms of pleasure, or not. 'Blessedness' is an alternative rendering of εὐδαιμονία, not so constantly associated with a hedonistic interpretation ; and 'wellbeing' is also used. See GREATEST HAPPINESS, and EUDAEMONISM. (W.R.S.–J.M.B.)

Haptics [Gr. ἅπτειν, to touch]: Ger. *Haptik*; Fr. *haptique* (not generally used—L.M.); Ital. *teoria del tatto, aptica* (suggested—E.M.). The doctrine of touch with concomitant sensations and perceptions—as optics is the doctrine of sight, and acoustics that of hearing.

Suggested by Dessoir (Du Bois-Reymond's *Arch.*, 1892), who made two subdivisions of the subject: (1) contact sense, and (2) pselaphesia—corresponding roughly to passive and active touch; the term has since come into general use, though no universally accepted definition can be offered. It may cover (and this is probably its best use) the whole range of function of skin, muscle, tendon, and joint, and even of the static sense—thus including the senses of temperature and pain, and the perceptions of position, movement, &c.; or it may be restricted to cutaneous sensations and perceptions in the narrower sense. (E.B.T.)

Literature: SANFORD, Course in Exper. Psychol., chaps. i, ii, and bibliographies; HENRI, Raumwahrnehmung d. Tastsinnes (1898); DESSOIR, loc. cit.; FUNKE, in Hermann's Handb. d. Physiol., iii. 2; HERING, ibid.; WEBER, in Wagner's Handb. d. Physiol., iii. 2 (this paper may be said to represent the first step in the science); MACH, Bewegungsempfindungen (1875); FULLERTON and CATTELL, Perception of Small Differences (1892); VON FREY, Abhandl. d. k. sächs. Gesell. d. Wiss. (1896), and Berichte, 1894-7;

Zeitsch. f. Psychol., xx. 126; DELABARRE, Bewegungsempfindungen (1891); WUNDT, Physiol. Psychol. (4th ed.), i. 429; MÜNSTERBERG, Beitr. z. exper. Psychol., iv; MORSELLI, Semej. malat. ment. (1898), i; DRESSLAR, Amer. J. of Psychol., vi. 313 ff.; GRIFFING, Psychol. Rev., monograph, Suppl. i; M. F. WASHBURN, Philos. Stud., xi. 190 ff.; G. TAWNEY, Psychol. Rev., ii. 588 ff.; TAWNEY and HODGE, Psychol. Rev., iv. 591; F. KIESOW, Arch. Italiennes de Biol., xxvi. 417; Zeitsch. f. Psychol., xx. 126; BLIX, Upsala Läkare förenings Förhandlinger, xviii. 2, 7, 8; Zeitsch. f. Biol., xxi. 145; GOLDSCHEIDER, Gesammelte Abhandl., 1898; VIERORDT, Zeitsch. f. Biol., xii. 226, and Grundr. d. Physiol.; MÜLLER and SCHUMANN, Pflüger's Arch., xlv. 37; &c. (E.B.T.–L.M.)

Harmonics [Gr. ἁρμονική, the theory of sounds]: Ger. *harmonische Obertöne*; Fr. *harmoniques*; Ital. *armoniche*. A word often used loosely in the sense of OVERTONE (q.v.). Strictly, the harmonics of a tone are other tones of which the fundamentals are partials of the original tone. See Helmholtz, *Sensations of Tone* (3rd ed.), chap. xxv. (E.B.T.)

Harmony (in acoustics) [Gr. ἁρμονία]: Ger. *Harmonie*; Fr. *harmonie*; Ital. *armonia*. (1) That element of a musical whole which arises from the simultaneous or immediately successive sounding of tones, in distinction from MELODY (q.v.).

In musical theory and in instruction harmony is the department dealing with the composition of tones for the production of musical effects. Harmony thus includes both consonances and dissonances; disharmonies are the discords not allowed by musical practice. (J.M.B.–E.B.T.)

(2) The words harmony and disharmony are often used loosely as the equivalents of CONSONANCE and DISSONANCE (q.v.).

(3) The terms sometimes correspond to degrees of indirect tone relationship. So used by Wundt, *Physiol. Psychol.* (4th ed.), ii. 71. (E.B.T.)

Harmony (in aesthetics). Applied, apart from music, to indicate any agreeable arrangement of forms, colours, or other qualities in an aesthetic whole, with special reference to some criterion of CONGRUITY or FITNESS (q.v.), whether implicitly or explicitly recognized.

Harmony does not exclude either conflict or CONTRAST (q.v.). They are rather means of augmenting its agreeable effects, through emphasis upon the unification of diversities, which constitutes its basal characteristic. This is illustrated by the conflicts in comedy and tragedy, and by the contrasts involved in the increasing use of broken chords in modern music. Harmony is distinguished from SYMMETRY (q.v.) by the disposition of parts or qualities in accordance with their aesthetic values, as determined by their relations to one another and to the whole of which they form the parts, rather than in accordance with their exact quantitative and mathematical values. It is distinguished from BALANCE (q.v.) in so far as this emphasizes the fact of a certain opposition among the parts of an aesthetic whole, while harmony emphasizes their intrinsic unity. It is distinguished from PROPORTION (q. v.) in that the latter is applied to quantitative relations, whereas harmony applies more specifically to qualitative relations.

The principle of harmony in its essential intention is not only fundamental in the Greek aesthetic consciousness and the development of Greek aesthetic theory, but it may also be said to involve the basal interest of Greek reflective thought in its attempt to reconcile the one and the many. Of musical origin, the principle first comes to light among the Pythagoreans, who appear to have applied the term primarily to the relation involved in the octave. Thence, among other developments, they extended its significance to the orbits of the heavenly bodies, in the doctrine of the harmony of the spheres. With Plato and Aristotle the principle gains a wider aesthetic implication in the analysis of the appropriate relations which the parts should sustain to the whole in a work of art; less explicitly with Plato and with relatively greater emphasis upon the value of the simplicity of pure unity; more explicitly with Aristotle and with greater emphasis upon the unity of variety, as in his account of the drama. In the Platonic system of thought, and in some degree characterizing all philosophy developed under its influence, the ethical conception of the good as the complete, the sound, the whole, the tempered, that which lacks excess, makes itself felt in the realm of aesthetic considerations. In both morals and art, therefore, as well as in metaphysics, the principle of harmony appears as central. In modern thought the solutions reached of the Greek philosophic problem lead to a less explicit emphasis upon harmony. It is recognized as a somewhat self-evident principle, although it gains a richer and more positive content through the stress placed upon its complementary principle, contrast, which in its more

pronounced forms involves the extreme of permissible variety in the aesthetic unity. This enlargement of the principle in aesthetic theory is best reflected in art itself, by the enrichment of harmony through the increasing complexity of modern, as compared with ancient, music. For other aesthetic principles closely related see CONTRAST, EXPRESSION, and FORM.

Literature: for a typical instance of elaborate modern treatment see KÖSTLIN, Aesthetik (1869); BOSANQUET, Hist. of Aesthetic (1892); WALTER, Gesch. d. Aesthetik im Altertum (1893); SCHASLER, Gesch. d. Aesthetik (1872). See also HARMONY and MELODY. (J.R.A.)

Harmony (Cartesian): see PRE-ESTABLISHED HARMONY.

Harmony (in logic). Absence of all logical INCONSISTENCY (q. v.). (J.M.B.)

Harmony (Pythagorean): see Pythagoreans, under PRE-SOCRATIC PHILOSOPHY, and HARMONY (in aesthetics).

Harshness (of tone) [ME. *harsh*]: Ger. *Rauhigkeit*; Fr. *rudesse du son*; Ital. *asprezza del suono*. The terms harshness and roughness are predicated of musical sounds in several slightly different senses. (1) A stage in the perception of two simultaneously sounded tones intermediate between the discontinuity of beats and pure dissonance (Wundt, *Physiol. Psychol.*, 4th ed., i. 474). (2) A characteristic of certain intervals constructed upon the same lower note, due to beating partials (Helmholtz, *Sensations of Tone*, 192-3, and *Pop. wiss. Vortr.*, i. 88; Stumpf, *Tonpsychologie*, i. 203, ii. 521, 534). (3) A characteristic of deep tones in general, compared with which high tones are 'smooth' (Preyer, *Elemente d. r. Empfindungslehre*, 54; Stumpf, *Tonpsychologie*, i. 173). (4) The words point to the presence with tone of noise, or to the prominence in a compound tone of certain partials; as when we say that the tone of a string instrument or reed instrument is 'harsh' as compared with the tone of a tuning-fork or bottle-whistle. (E.B.T.)

Hartley, David. (cir. 1705-57.) An English philosopher, educated at Jesus College, Cambridge. He was educated for the Church; for conscientious reasons, however, he preferred medicine. He sought to explain mental facts by physiological.

Hate [AS. *hatian*, to hate]: Ger. *Hass*; Fr. *haine*; Ital. *odio*. An emotion characterized by the type of aversion (see APPETENCE) which aims to damage or destroy, under conditions of more or less permanent restraint, limitation, or powerlessness, and the feeling-tone of intense ANGER (q. v.).

The relation of hate to anger is very obscure, the essential impulse to destroy being present in each, and the emotional excitement being largely common. The difference appears to introspection to consist in the sense of thwarting, limitation, or powerlessness, which accompanies hate. It is sometimes held that hate is more intellectual in its character than anger. This intellectual character of hate is doubtless real, but it arises from the knowledge or belief which results in the consciousness of being thwarted. The emotion of hate seems, when the opportunity of damaging the hated object occurs, to pass into anger or rage. The firm setting of the jaws and shaking of the head appear to be more prominently characteristic of anger when it passes over into hate.

Hate is usually made the direct opposite of love, but the relation is not so simple; for the opposite of anger is not expressed in any single term, though covered by the term LOVE (q. v.).

The element of relative permanence attaching to hate possibly arises from the same condition of limitation or thwarting, which needs a certain grounding or more or less extended series of reasons. Whatever its cause, it certainly appears in such expressions as 'rankling' hate, 'suppressed,' 'smothered,' 'cherished' hate—expressions which are not usually applied to anger; on the contrary, anger is said to be in 'outbursts,' 'fits,' 'paroxysms,' &c.

Literature : see ANGER and EMOTION.

(J.ᴹ B., G.F.S.)

Haunted Swing : see ILLUSIONS OF MOTION AND MOVEMENT, II.

Hazard : see CHANCE.

Hearing [AS. *hyran*]: Ger. *Gehör* ; Fr. *ouïe, audition* ; Ital. *udito*. The special sense whose end-organ is the ear, whose nerve is the cochlear branch of the auditorius, and whose stimulus is sound.   (J.M.B.–E.B.T.)

I. THE EAR [AS. *eare*]: Ger. *Ohr* ; Fr. *oreille* ; Ital. *orecchio*. Organ of hearing, and an important organ for equilibration of the body. On the side of audition the ear is the mechanism that transforms vibrations of the medium into sensations of sound. On the side of EQUILIBRIUM (q. v.) it yields sensations, along with those from skin, muscles, and eyes, which indicate position of the body at rest and the direction of its movements of rotation

or translation. Recent investigations, notably those of Lee, have tended to demonstrate that these two distinct functions are associated with different parts of the auditory mechanism.

Comparative. Organs usually described as auditory are present in many jelly-fishes in the form of otocysts in the margin of the bell at the base of the tentacles. Lee's experiments with Ctenophores indicate that these are wholly organs of equilibration. Echinoderms present two kinds of organs, both probably for orientation of the body—the one a modified spine, a true balancer consisting of a calcareous knob supported on a pivot and covered with ciliated epithelium, the cilia being longest about the neck ; the other a true otocyst, found sometimes in great numbers in the cutis of the holothurians. Nearly all molluscs have a pair of otocysts, situated generally near the pedal ganglia (bivalves, lamellibranchs, and gastropods), but always innervated from the cerebral ganglia. In cephalopods these become highly developed organs of orientation with the so-called maculae and cristae acousticae, and are placed in the head close to the cerebral ganglia. From worms, as a class, specialized auditory organs are strangely absent. A very few genera of polychetes, however, have a pair of otocysts in one of the anterior segments. Arthropods are well provided with auditory organs. In the decapod crustacea they commonly occur in the basal joint of the antenules, but rarely they are placed, as in *Mysis,* in the endopodite of the last pair of swimming appendages. Auditory organs of insects consist of groups of peculiar cells, resembling ganglion cells, each provided with a sensory hair. These organs are situated most variously on the body — on the different segments, on the antennae or mouth parts, on the wings or legs. In some insects the sensory hairs project from the surface, but in most cases they lie just underneath the surface, the chitin over them being commonly modified to act as a tympanic membrane. In vertebrates, the auditory organs are uniformly situated within the skull on either side near its base. In addition to the auditory capsule proper in fishes, the end-organs of the auditory nerve are widely distributed over the surface of the head and body as lateral line organs.   (C.F.H.)

Structure. The ear has four parts: (1) the outer ear, comprising the auricle or pinna, and the auditory meatus for the collection and concentration of air-vibrations ;

443

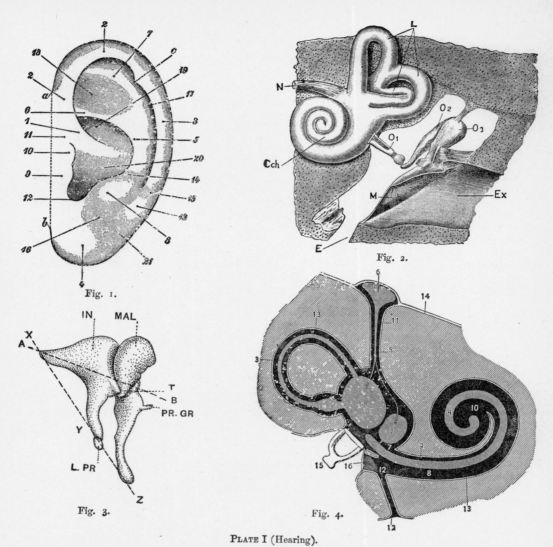

Fig. 1.

Fig. 2.

Fig. 3.

Fig. 4.

PLATE I (Hearing).

Fig. 1. **Auricle of man.** After Schwalbe, from Wood's *Reference Handbook of the Medical Sciences.* *a, b,* base of the auricle; *a, b, c,* triangle of the auricle; *c,* tubercle of Darwin; 1, crus helicis; 2, 2, ascending portion of helix; 3, descending portion of helix; 4, lobule; 5, main portion of the antihelix; 6, crus inferius anthelicis; 7, crus superius anthelicis; 8, antitragus; 9, tragus; 10, tuberculum supratragicum; 11, sulcus auris anterior (incisura trago-helicina); 12, incisura intertragica; 13, tuberculum retrolobulare of His; 14, sulcus auris posterior (incisura anthelicis); 15, sulcus helicolobularis; 14, 15, sulcus obliquus of His; 16, sulcus supralobularis; 17, fossa navicularis or scaphoidea; 18, fossa triangularis; 19, cymba conchae; 20, cavitas conchae; 21, sulcus retrolobularis.

Fig. 2. **The middle and internal ear (diagrammatic).** After Headly, from Parker and Haswell's *Zoology.* *Cch,* cochlea; *E,* Eustachian tube; *Ex,* external auditory meatus; *L,* labyrinth; *M,* tympanic membrane; *N,* auditory nerve; O_1, O_2, O_3, the three auditory ossicles (stapes, incus, malleus).

Fig. 3. After Helmholtz, illustrating the movements of the malleus and incus. The handle of the malleus near the point *Z* rests on the drum membrane, the long process of the incus is articulated with the stapes. The line *A, B* indicates the axis of rotation of the two bones; the line *X, Y, Z* joins this axis with the two ends of the crank lever which these bones form. *IN,* incus; *L. PR,* long process of the incus; *MAL,* head of the malleus; *PR. GR,* processus gracilis of the malleus; *T,* tooth of the malleus interlocking with a tooth of the incus.

Fig. 4. **Diagram indicating the perilymphatic and endolymphatic spaces of the internal ear.** After Testut, from Wood's *Reference Handbook of the Medical Sciences.* The endolymphatic spaces cross-hatched, the perilymphatic spaces black. 1, utriculus; 2, sacculus; 3, semicircular canals; 4, cochlear canal; 5, endolymphatic canal; 6, saccus endolymphaticus; 7, canalis reuniens, or canal of Hensen; 8, scala tympani; 9, scala vestibuli; 10, their point of union at the helocotrema; 11, aquaeductus vestibuli; 12, aquaeductus cochleae; 13, periosteum; 14, dura mater; 15, stapes in the fenestra ovalis; 16, fenestra rotunda.

444

(2) the middle ear, or tympanum, containing the auditory ossicles for transmitting and strengthening these vibrations; (3) the inner ear, or labyrinth, comprising the vestibule, semicircular canals, and cochlea, with their specific sensory nerve termini; (4) the auditory nerve and its end-stations within the brain.

The parts of the auricle are indicated in the accompanying Fig. 1. It is of relatively small significance to hearing in man, as compared with many of the lower animals, where it is not only large, but supplied with important muscles. This may be correlated with the well-known imperfection of our ability to discriminate the direction of sounds. The extreme variability of the auricle is due to its functional degradation, and this is doubtless the explanation of its anthropological importance in studies of degeneracy, &c.

are arranged to form a simple crank lever, so that the vibrations of the membrane are transmitted to the perilymph of the inner ear with diminution of amplitude, but increase of power (see Figs. 2, 3). The impulse is therefore transmitted through this chain of bones as mass motion, not as molecular or sonorous vibration. Two small muscles, the tensor tympani and the stapedius muscle, regulate respectively the tension of the tympanic membrane and of the stapes in the oval foramen, and are doubtless of importance psychologically in connection with the act of attention to auditory stimuli.

Most of the lower vertebrates (Ichthyopsida) lack the middle ear, their aquatic environment rendering unnecessary any mechanism for increasing the intensity of sonorous vibrations. But the air-breathing vertebrates, from the higher Amphibia onwards, exhibit

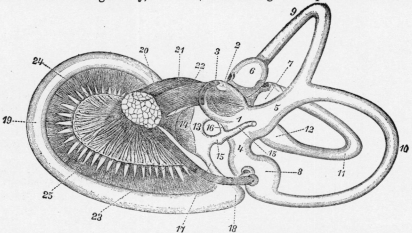

Fig. 5. The right membranous labyrinth of a human embryo at the fifth month, seen from the mesial side. After Retzius, from Barker's *Nerv. Syst.* 1–5, utriculus: 2, recessus utriculi; 3, macula utriculi; 4, sinus posterior; 5, sinus superior; 6, ampulla superior; 7, ampulla lateralis; 8, ampulla posterior; 9, ductus semicircularis superior; 10, ductus semicircularis posterior; 11, ductus semicircularis lateralis; 12, widened mouth of crus simplex of the lateral semicircular canal opening into the utriculus; 13, sacculus; 14, macula sacculi; 15, ductus endolymphaticus; 16, ductus utriculo-saccularis; 17, ductus reuniens; 18, caecum vestibulare of ductus cochlearis; 19, ductus cochlearis; 20, facial nerve; 21–4, N. acusticus; 21, N. vestibuli; 22, N. saccularis; 23, N. ampullaris inferior; 24, N. cochleae; 25, distribution of N. cochleae within the lamina spiralis ossea.

The middle ear is separated from the external auditory meatus by the tympanic or drum membrane. It is not, however, shut off completely from communication with the outside air, for the Eustachian tube connects its cavity with that of the mouth, and thus serves to equalize the air-pressure on the two sides of the tympanic membrane. The auditory ossicles (malleus, incus, and stapes), extending from the inner face of the tympanic membrane to the oval foramen and inner ear,

this mechanism in increasing complexity. The tympanic cavity and Eustachian tube are regarded as derivatives of the first, or spiracular, gill cleft of the lower fishes, while the auditory ossicles are apparently derived from bones of the facial skeleton of the fishes connected with the mandibular and hyoid arches.

The labyrinth is an intricate excavation in the temporal bone of the skull (the bony labyrinth), containing a closed membranous sac, the membranous labyrinth, fitting loosely the bony chamber, and separated from it by a lymph space, whose fluid, the perilymph, does not communicate with the similar fluid, or endolymph, within the membranous labyrinth. The parts of the membranous labyrinth are the utriculus, into which the semicircular canals open, each with an expansion or ampulla at one end, the sacculus, the recessus labyrinthi, and the cochlea. Their relations are shown by the accompanying Figs. 4 and 5. Each of these, except the recessus, contains a patch of sensory epithelium. The morphology and functions of these parts can be better understood after a rapid survey of their phylogenetic and embryological development.

In the fishes there is associated with the ear an elaborate system of cutaneous and subcutaneous sense organs, the lateral line organs, whose canals and patches of sensory epithelium resemble very closely the semicircular canals and their cristae in the internal ear. The ear of these animals, moreover, lacks the cochlea and organ of Corti, the corresponding part of the labyrinth (lagena) being provided with a simple sensory spot like the cristae of the semicircular canals. The ear and lateral line organs not only resemble each other in structure, but they arise embryologically from the same area of thickened ectoderm, and they have been shown experimentally to have similar functions, viz. the regulation of the bodily equilibrium. In these animals the sense of hearing is very feebly developed, some authors even going so far as to deny its presence altogether. It is obvious, however, that a structure adapted to perceive simple impulses in a fluid medium, such as must be mediated by an organ of equilibration, will also be able to respond to vibratory impulses of low frequency in the same medium. As a matter of fact, we know that fishes, though they may be deaf to sound-waves of the higher frequencies, are nevertheless very sensitive to mechanical shocks, such as passing footfalls. Now, the terrestrial animals require much less elaborate organs of bodily equilibrium than do the aquatic animals; but, on the other hand, they find themselves in an environment of aërial vibrations which are of great importance to their vital economy. Accordingly the lateral line organs disappear in vertebrates higher than the Amphibia, the semicircular canals alone being sufficient for the static sense, while a portion of the sacculus, the lagena, progressively increases in complexity until in the mammals it becomes the cochlea. Parallel with these changes the sound-conducting apparatus of the middle ear is gradually evolved. It thus appears that there are two distinct sense organs in the internal ear, organs which have had a common origin, and which, even in man, may be only incompletely differentiated from each other; viz. the vestibule and semicircular canals for the sense of equilibrium, and the cochlea, the organ of hearing.

In its embryological development, the human ear first appears as a thickened bit of ectoderm at the side of the medulla oblongata, which soon becomes depressed to form the 'auditory saucer.' At a later period this saucer is completely invaginated to form the 'auditory vesicle,' retaining, however, for a time its communication with the outer surface of the body. This condition is permanent in the sharks, the endolymph of the labyrinth communicating with the outer sea-water by the endolymphatic duct, just as the lateral line canals freely communicate with the surface by pores. In higher animals this connection is early lost, though the recessus labyrinthi is regarded as a vestige of that connection. The lining membrane of the auditory vesicle develops a patch of sensory epithelium, and as the vesicle becomes constricted into the several chambers comprising the labyrinth, an extension of this sensory patch grows into each chamber. These sensory areas then become separated by indifferent epithelium, and thus arise the three cristae in the ampullae, the macula utriculi, the macula sacculi, and the organ of Corti. The structure of all of these sensory organs except the organ of Corti is similar and very simple, the specific sensory cells being shorter than the indifferent cells, and provided with hairs which project into the endolymph. The base of these cells is embraced by the terminal arborizations of the corresponding nerve-fibres (see Fig. 6). This structure is essentially similar to that of the sensory organs in the lateral line canals of fishes.

The bony cochlea is formed somewhat like the interior of a snail-shell, with two and one-half turns of the spiral, and with a bony shelf or ledge, the lamina spiralis, extending outward from the axis, or modiolus. Within the spirals of the bony cochlea are three membranous canals: (1) The scala vestibuli communicates at its base with the perilymphatic space around the vestibule, whose fluid is caused to vibrate by the foot of the stapes, which plays in the fenestra ovalis between

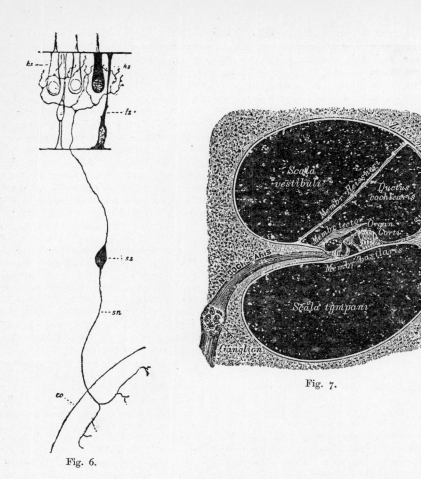

Fig. 7.

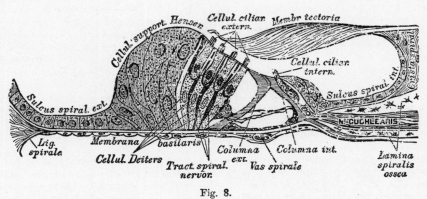

Fig. 6.

Fig. 8.

PLATE II (Hearing).

Fig. 6. Scheme of the peripheral termination of the N. vestibuli. After Retzius, from Barker's *Nervous System.* *co,* central nervous system; *fz,* indifferent supporting cells of the sensory epithelium; *hz,* hair cells, or specific sensory cells; *sn,* central nerve-fibre; *sz,* cell of the ganglion vestibulare.

Fig. 7. Semidiagrammatic section of a single turn of the cochlea. After Heitzmann.

Fig. 8. Semidiagrammatic section of the organ of Corti. After Retzius, from Heitzmann's *Anatomie des Menschen.*

the middle ear and this space. (2) The scala tympani communicates at the apex of the spiral with the scala vestibuli, and at its lower end terminates at the fenestra rotunda. Sonorous vibrations entering the perilymphatic space pass up the cochlear spire through the scala vestibuli and down through the scala tympani, terminating at the fenestra rotunda, by whose membrane they are deadened or passed back into the middle ear. (3) The scala media, which occupies a position in the spiral between the other two scalae, is the only part of the cochlea derived from the original auditory vesicle; accordingly it contains the specific sensory apparatus (organ of Corti), and its cavity does not communicate with those of the other scalae. From the free edge of the spiral lamina of the bony cochlea two membranes which bound the scala media are stretched to the outer wall of the spiral canal. One of these lies in the same plane as the spiral lamina, and constitutes the basilar membrane, or floor of the scala media, separating it from the scala tympani and supporting the organ of Corti; the other is Reissner's membrane, forming the roof of the scala media and separating it from the scala vestibuli.

The organ of Corti is an elaboration of the ectodermal epithelium which covers the basilar membrane (see Figs. 7 and 8). Rising up from the basilar membrane are two sets of firm rods, the rods of Corti, which incline toward each other, uniting at the apex to enclose a tunnel which runs the whole length of the organ of Corti. The hair cells, or specific sensory termini, are arranged in a series internal, and one external, to the rods of Corti, the inner series comprising a single row of hair cells, the outer series three or four rows. All of these cells are supported by other indifferent epithelium cells. Running outward from the axis is a so-called tectorial membrane, which lies upon the free ends of the hair cells, and is supposed to act as a damper to their hairs, which project freely into the endolymph. Some authorities, however, believe that the tectorial membrane is an artifact, being really the long hairs of the hair cells broken off and matted together. The nerve-fibres terminate about the bases of the hair cells in arborizations similar to those found in the sense organs of the vestibule. As to the functions of the parts just enumerated, the most diverse opinions prevail; and as a matter of fact, we have no definite knowledge on these points. (H.H.)

Functions. Helmholtz early adopted a resonance theory of audition, and was first attracted to the rods of Corti as the possible resonators by which tones are analysed in the ear. The fact that they are not present in birds, and, further, that they are practically all the same length, size, and shape, led him to abandon them. He next fixed upon the fibres of the basilar membrane. These increase gradually in length from base to apex of the cochlea, and thus satisfy one of the requirements of the theory. Ayers maintains that the fibres of the basilar membrane are inadequate on account of their number, their physical constitution, and their arrangement with reference to the sensory cells, and he advances the theory that the hairs of the sensory cells are the only structures present that can properly act as resonators. The objection that the hairs are too short and too nearly the same length no longer holds, if we accept Ayers' results; and in this way the number of resonators is greatly increased, from 24,000 fibres of the basilar membrane to, according to Ayers' estimate, 385,000 sensory hairs.

Another theory that is gaining in prominence is the appropriately named 'telephone theory' of Rutherford. According to this the organ of Corti vibrates as a whole, giving to the auditory nerve the same number of stimuli as there are movements of the tympanic membrane and stapes, and these stimuli are analysed by the auditory centres in the brain. See AUDITORY SENSATION below in this article (III).

Lee considers the organ of Corti, or in the animal series the papilla acoustica basilaris, co-extensive with the function of audition in vertebrates, and is inclined to think that all the other sensory structures of the labyrinth mediate only sensations of equilibrium. His statement is: 'Wherever among vertebrates undoubted audition exists, there is present an additional group of sensory organs, the papilla acoustica basilaris. This does not exist in fishes, but appears first in the amphibia as an offshoot of the lagena, and in higher vertebrates constitutes the nervous portion of the organ of Corti of the cochlea.'

Lee's table of functions of various parts of the labyrinth is as follows:—

'I. Dynamical functions, in recognition of—
    1. Rotary movements, mediated by cristae acousticae.
    2. Translatory movements, mediated by maculae acousticae.

II. Statical functions, in recognition of—
    3. Position in space, mediated by maculae acousticae.
III. Auditory functions, in recognition of—
    4. Vibratory motions, mediated by papilla acoustica basilaris.' (C.F.H.)

The auditory, or eighth, cranial nerve has two divisions corresponding roughly, though not exactly, to the different sensory functions served by the internal ear. The vestibular branch supplies the superior and external ampullae and the macula utriculi, while the so-called cochlear branch supplies, in addition to the cochlea, the posterior ampulla and the macula sacculi. The last two branchlets are more properly separated from the cochlear nerve under the name ramus medius. The cochlear nerve in the strict sense is the chief, if not the only, nerve of audition, the other branches being chiefly concerned with the static sense. Accordingly their central connections within the brain are very different from those of the cochlear nerve. The ganglion (of Scarpa) of the vestibular nerve lies in the internal auditory meatus, and the central processes of its cells form the vestibular, mesial, or anterior root of the auditory nerve, which enters the brain ventrally and cephalad of the cochlear root, and connects with many different brain centres, but chiefly with the cerebellum. The ganglion (spirale) of the cochlear root lies in the axis of the bony cochlea. The central connections of this root are even more intricate than those of the vestibular root. In general it may be stated that these fibres first enter either the dorsal or the ventral cochlear nucleus. The central auditory path extends from the ventral nucleus by way of the trapezoid body, and from the dorsal nucleus by way of the striae acusticae (both root-fibres and secondary fibres in each case), to the region of the superior olive, partly crossed and partly uncrossed. The path then goes up by way of the lateral fillet to the inferior member of the corpora quadrigemina (postgeminum), which appears to be the general centre for the elaboration of higher auditory reflexes, and which is absent in animals which do not possess the cochlea. Its reflex connections are very numerous, notably with lower centres and with the pregeminum (optic reflex path). Other fibres extend from the postgeminum to the corpus geniculatum mediale, where they terminate among the cells of this nucleus. The cortical acoustic path begins from these cells, and terminates in the auditory sense area in the temporal lobe of the cerebral cortex.

Literature : H. AYERS, A Contribution to the Morphology of the Vertebrate Ear, with a reconsideration of its Functions, J. of Morphol., vi (1892); L. F. BARKER, The Nerv. Syst. and its Constituent Neurones (1899); A. BARTH, Beiträge zur Anatomie des Ohres, Zeitsch. f. Ohrenh., xvii; Ueber die Darstellung des häutigen Labyrinthes, Arch. f. Anat. u. Physiol., Physiol. Abth. (1889); H. BEAUREGARD, Recherches sur l'appareil auditif chez les mammifères, J. de l'Anat. (1893); W. BECHTEREW, Ueber die innere Abtheilung des Strickkörpers und den achten Hirnnerven, Neurol. Centralbl., iv (1885); BOETTCHER, Rückblicke auf die neueren Untersuchungen ü. d. Bau der Schnecke, im Anschluss an eigene Beobachtungen, Arch. f. Ohrenh., xxiv (1886); H. HELD, Die centralen Bahnen des Nervus acusticus bei der Katze, Arch. f. Anat. u. Physiol., Anat. Abth. (1891); Die centrale Gehörleitung, ibid. (1893); P. C. LARSEN, Ein anatomisch-physiologischer Beitrag zur Lehre von den Ossicula auditus, Anat. Anz. (1890); F. S. LEE, The Functions of the Ear and the Lateral Line in Fishes, Amer. J. of Physiol., i (1898); M. v. LENHOSSEK, Die Nervenendigungen im Gehörorgan, Verh. d. Anat. Gesell., Anat. Anz., viii (1893); Die Nervenendigungen in den Maculae und Cristae acusticae, Anat. Hefte, ix (1893); J. NIEMACK, Maculae und Cristae acusticae mit Ehrlich's Methylenblaumethode, Anat. Hefte, viii (1892); B. ONUFROWICS, Experimenteller Beitrag zur Kenntniss des Ursprungs des Nervus acusticus des Kaninchens, Arch. f. Psychiat., xvi (1885); B. A. RANDALL and H. L. MORSE, Photographic Illustrations of the Anatomy of the Human Ear, together with Pathological Conditions of the Drum Membrane and Descriptive Text (Philadelphia, 1887); RAUBER, Ueber d. Bau des Gehörlabyrinthes, Sitzber. d. Naturf.-Gesell. zu Leipzig, xii (1886); G. RETZIUS, Das Gehörorgan d. Wirbelthiere (Stockholm, 1884); also Biol. Untersuch., iii and v (1892 and 1893); N. RUDINGER, Zur Anatomie und Entwickelung des inneren Ohres, Monatssch. f. Ohrenh., xxii (1888); L. SALA, Ueber den Ursprung des Nervus acusticus, Arch. f. Mikr. Anat., xlii; G. SCHWALBE, Lehrb. d. Anat. d. Sinnesorgane (Erlangen, 1887); Beiträge zur Anthropologie des Ohres, Festschrift f. Virchow, i; E. ZUCKERKANDL, Beitrag zur vergleichenden Anatomie d. Ohrtrompete, Arch. f. Ohrenh., xxiii (1886). (H.H.)

II. SOUND [Lat. *sonus*]: Ger. *Schall*; Fr. *son*; Ital. *suono*. Sound, the stimulation of certain nerve-endings of hearing in the ear, is due to the vibration of some portion of matter, such as a tuning-fork, a bell, and so on.

Sounds are divided into two classes—noises and musical notes. It may be shown by direct experiment that a noise is due to the irregular, interrupted vibration of a portion of matter, such as the tearing of a piece of paper or the rattling of a cart-wheel over cobble stones. On the other hand, a musical note can be proved to be due to a regular, uninterrupted vibration of a portion of matter, such as that obtained from a stretched string or tuning-fork. The presence between the ear of the observer and the vibrating instrument of some form of matter, such as air, water, or a solid body, is essential for the production of sound sensation. To analyse, therefore, different sounds, it is necessary to study different kinds of vibrations and the effect of these vibrations on surrounding matter. It may be shown that the most general possible vibration of matter is what is called a complex one. That is, it may be regarded as the superposition of an indefinite number of simple harmonic vibrations, such as those of simple pendulums. To completely understand, therefore, the nature of a complex vibration, it is necessary to know the component simple vibrations, then to determine the amplitude and the frequency of each of these components, and finally to observe the difference in phase of the component vibrations. As the result of the vibration of any portion of matter, such as a tuning-fork or a bell, there will be, in general, waves produced in the surrounding medium—air, or whatever gas is present. This is true provided the rate of vibration of the body is sufficiently rapid; otherwise the air or gas will not be compressed, but will flow round the matter as it vibrates. If, however, the vibration exceeds a certain number in frequency, there will be compressional waves produced in the surrounding matter, and these will spread away with a velocity which is characteristic of the medium itself, and which is independent of the frequency of the vibration.

A simple harmonic vibration will produce a simple harmonic wave, the amplitude of the wave varying directly as the amplitude of the vibration. A complex vibration will, on the other hand, produce a complex wave, which can be analysed into simple harmonic waves in the same manner as a complex vibration can be. The waves will have different forms, depending not alone on the component vibrations, but also on their phases. These waves are propagated through a medium from the vibrating body, and in case they reach the ear of a hearing individual, a sound sensation is in general produced. Individuals differ, however, in their range of hearing, so it may happen that the frequency of the vibration has given rise to waves which are either too short or too long to affect the sense of hearing of the individual.

Corresponding to the peculiarity of the waves which reach the ear, it is to be expected that there will be differences in the sounds heard. Musical notes are distinguished by being either complex or simple, and it may be shown by experiment that a simple note is in every case due to a simple vibration; that a complex note is due to a complex vibration, it being noted, however, that differences in phase of the component vibrations, and therefore of the component waves, do not affect the character of the sound heard. The complexity of a given note seems to depend simply on the nature of the component vibrations, and not on their relative phases. A complex note is therefore to be regarded as a complex sensation due to a simultaneous production of simple notes. Simple notes differ among themselves in intensity or loudness, and in pitch or shrillness. It is found by experiment that the greater the amplitude of the original vibration, the louder is the sound; while the greater the frequency of the vibration, the higher is the pitch. Two vibrations which have the same frequency will in general produce two sounds of the same pitch. If, however, one of the vibrating bodies is approaching the ear or receding from it, the pitch of the sound produced by it is altered. This is known as Doppler's principle. It is shown by theory and verified by experiment that if the vibrating body is approaching the ear, or if the hearing individual is approaching the vibrating body, the pitch of the note is raised, whereas the contrary is true if the motions of the vibrating body and the hearing individual are reversed—more vibrations reaching the ear in the one case and less in the other, than if the body is not approached.

In general, of course, the medium separating the vibrating body from the ear is air, and in this medium compressional waves travel at a rate which is found by experiment to be very nearly 332 metres per second at a temperature of 0° Centigrade. At higher temperatures the velocity increases. These waves in the air obey the laws common to all wave motions. They can be reflected by large obstacles, thus causing echoes and giving rise to the phenomena of whispering galleries, and so on. They can be refracted, diffracted, and can be made to interfere in the same manner as waves in the ether.

Literature : textbooks of physics ; POYNTING and THOMSON, Sound ; HELMHOLTZ, Sensations of Tone (Eng. trans., Ellis) ; RAYLEIGH, Theory of Sound ; PREYER, Ueber die Grenzen d. Tonwahrnehmung (1876) ; Ak. Untersuch. (1879) ; HÖFLER, Psychologie (1897), 95 ff. ; DROBISCH, Ueber d. musikalische Tonbestimmung und Temp., Abhandl. d. k. sächs. Gesell. d. Wiss., ii. (1855) 35 ff. ; VOLKMANN, Lehrb. d. Psychol., § 38 ; BEZOLD, Ueber die functionelle Prüfung d. menschl. Gehörorgans (1897) ; Das Hörvermögen d. Taubstummen (1896); MELDE, MAYER, STUMPF, Wiedemann's Annalen (1898) ; SCHÄFER, Zeitsch. f. Psychol. (1899) ; ABRAHAM and BRÜHL, Zeitsch. f. Psychol. (1898) ; EXNER, Pflüger's Arch., xiii ; AUERBACH, Wiedemann's Annalen, vi ; KOHLRAUSCH, ibid., x (1880) ; PFAUNDLER, Sitzber. d. Wien. Akad., ii (1877) ; BRÜCKE, ibid. (1884); MACH, Lotos (1873); APPUNN, Ueber Wahrnehmung tiefer Töne (1889) ; HERBART, Ueber d. Tonlehre, Werke, vii. 224 ff. ; LUFT, Philos. Stud., iv ; SCHISCHMANOW, ibid., v ; LORENZ, ibid., vi ; MARTIUS, ibid., vi ; SCHULZE, ibid., xiv ; MÜNSTERBERG, Beiträge, iv ; KÖNIG, Quelques expériences d'acoustique (1882) ; MAYER, Amer. J. of Sci. (1874), viii ; Philos. Mag., xlix ; SCHWARTZE, Handb. d. Ohrenh., i ; BARTH, Zeitsch. f. Ohrenh. (1887), xvii ; WIEN, Wiedemann's Annalen, xxxvi ; ZWAARDEMAKER, Zeitsch. f. Psychol., vii ; MEYER, ibid., xi.   (J.S.A.)

III. AUDITORY (or HEARING) SENSATION : Ger. *Gehörsempfindung* ; Fr. *sensation auditive* ; Ital. *sensazione uditiva*. Auditory sensations fall into two great groups : sensations of tone and sensations of noise. In actual experience, the two are combined in the most various ways, though not so constantly as are the visual sensations of colour-tone and brightness. The stimulus to the sensation of noise is a single aperiodic movement—a shock—of the air particles ; or, if this movement be physically impossible, a small number of wave movements, of which all but a very few are exceedingly weak. The stimulus for tone is a simple periodic vibratory movement of the air particles, continued for a certain length of time. The physical limit between noise and tone lies at about two complete vibrations ; that between noise and a tone recognized as of a determinate pitch at five to sixteen vibrations.

The discrimination of tone is best in the middle region of the musical scale, decreasing above and below. Külpe has estimated the total number of discriminable tones at 11,000 ; that of simple noises—though this latter estimate is very uncertain—at 600. The limits of tonal hearing are usually set at 16 and 50,000 vibrations per second ; but the position of the upper boundary must, in the light of recent work, be very considerably lowered. MUSIC (q. v.) employs less than 100 tones ; and the reasons for the selection of these constitute an important psychological problem.

Tones form a one-dimensional manifold, which can hardly be represented in a geometrical figure. A straight line does justice to the continuity of the scale, but not to the degrees of FUSION (q.v.) of its terms. A spiral figure used by Drobisch shows the relation of each fundamental to its octave, but suggests that the approximation is gradual and constant, which is not the case.

The following theories of auditory sensation have more or less currency :—

(1) The Helmholtz-Hensen Theory. The cross-strings of the basilar membrane function as a series of resonators—or the backboard of a piano. Each string is specifically tuned to a single wave-movement of the air particles, though it may vibrate weakly to neighbouring vibration-rates. Beats arise when the fibres intermediate between those of the two primary tones are thrown into interfering vibratory movements, and can occur only ' when the two exciting tones lie near enough to the prime tone of the sympathetic body for the latter to be set into sensible sympathetic vibration to both the tones used.' Combination tones are the result of the asymmetrical oscillations of the drum and ossicles of the ear. Noise sensations are set up through the basilar membrane, as tones are, by their own stimulus. The general theory has been confirmed by the proof of partial tone-deafness, i. e. deafness to a portion or portions of the musical scale. See TONE ISLANDS.

(2) The Rutherford-Waller Theory. This may be called the 'telephone,' as Helmholtz' is the 'piano' theory. The basilar membrane is set swinging by every stimulus, though more in some parts than in others, and thus gives 'acoustic pressure patterns' between the tectoria and the subjacent field of cell-hairs. The cells transmit the stimulation unanalysed

to the brain, as the telephone transmits the sound of the voice.

(3) Ebbinghaus' modification of Helmholtz' theory affords a simpler explanation of beats and combination tones. In the first place, a tone sensation corresponds to the vibration of a number of basilar strings; the SPECIFIC ENERGY (q. v.) of each string—the Helmholtz doctrine of one string for each tone—is, in so far, given up. Secondly, every air wave sets in motion not only its own string but also, by the formation of nodes, other strings that are tuned to its harmonics. These assumptions enable Ebbinghaus to relate beats to combination tones, and to explain the relative intensity of the latter.

Noteworthy are further: (i) Wundt's theory of a direct oscillatory stimulation of the acoustic nerve (*Physiol. Psychol.*, 4th ed., i. 478); (ii) Mach's theory of two specific energies (*Analyse d. Empfindungen*, 121); (iii) Hermann's and König's critiques of Helmholtz (Hermann, *Pflüger's Arch.*, xlix, lvi; König, *Quelques expériences d'acoustique*, chap. ix); (iv) Meyer's sketch of a new theory (*Zeitsch. f. Psychol.*, 1897; *Beitr. z. Ak. u. Musikwiss.*, 1898; *Pflüger's Arch.*, 1899); also citations under BEATS; (v) Stumpf's assumption of a specific noise energy, and doctrine of (simple) tone colour (*Tonpsychologie*, ii).

For special definitions see TIMBRE, NOISE, TONE, PITCH, INTERVAL, BEATS, and COMBINATION TONE.

Literature: EBBINGHAUS, Psychologie, 313; HELMHOLTZ, Sensations of Tone, 145; WALLER, Human Physiol., 461; BLASERNA, Theory of Sound (Ital. original, 1875); STUMPF, Tonpsychologie, i, ii; HENSEN, in Hermann's Handb. d. Physiol., iii. 2; especially NOEL, art. Audition in Richet's Dict. de Physiol. (with extensive bibliography); also BIBLIOG. G, 2, *u*, and the authorities cited above. (E.B.T.)

Hearing (defects of): Ger. *Hördefekte*; Fr. *défauts de l'ouïe* (or *auditifs*); Ital. *difetti dell' udito*. Defects of hearing, like those of vision, consist in a deficient capacity to obtain the characteristic forms of distinction and information normally yielded by the sense. Cf. DEAFNESS AND THE DEAF.

The factors of auditory perception are fewer and simpler, and contain a smaller element of interpretation than do those of vision. The characteristic forms of information yielded by the sense of hearing are the presence of sounds, their direction, their loudness, their pitch, their quality, their

duration, and the endless varieties and combinations of these, of which speech, music, and noises are composed. Any serious defect in the detection of sounds is called deafness, which may be partial or total. In partial deafness, sounds of low intensity are not heard, but those of a greater intensity may be distinctly perceived. If the sound is of constant loudness, its intensity will vary in an inverse ratio with the distance from the ear. To illustrate by a common test: if a watch which can be heard by the normal ear at 36 inches was heard by a defective ear only at 12 inches, the hearing power would be said to be 12:36 or 1:3. Cf. TESTS (psychophysical). Tests of the ability to distinguish between sounds of different intensity show a considerable variation in different individuals, some of whom undoubtedly possess a subnormal amount of such discriminative sensibility. In regard to defects of pitch, cases occur in which the ear, while deaf to sounds of certain pitches, is sensitive to lower or higher ones. This condition is termed TONE DEAFNESS (q. v.), or asonia. The range of pitch-hearing may be tested with regard to the highest audible tones by a Galton's whistle or by a set of steel bars, and for lowest tones by Appunn's forks. Tones which are audible to some ears are quite beyond the range for others; some persons fail to hear the chirp of a cricket, or the squeak of a mouse.

Similarly, there is a great variation among individuals in regard to the ability to appreciate musical effects and distinctions (largely a matter of pitch, interval, and quality). A considerable number are non-musical, or defective in musical hearing; but these distinctions, like most qualitative changes, are incapable of accurate determination. Cf. AMUSIA. Difficulties in the determination of the direction of sounds have been noticed, and have been traced to diseases which affect one ear alone, or the two ears unequally.

There are conditions of exalted or exaggerated hearing (hyperchusis or *hyperaesthesia acustica*) in which tones and noises produce more than their usual effect, owing to an irritable or sensitive condition of the nervous system; as in fevers, brain disease, &c. Of anomalous forms of hearing may be mentioned the subjective pulsating sounds, termed *tinnitus*; a double hearing in which each sound seems to be heard twice; paradoxical hearing in which hearing is better when a considerable noise (as in a railway train) is present; and several forms of subjective hearing. Hearing may take place not only through the normal conducting mechanism from the tympanum to the acoustic nerve, but indirectly through the skull; such conduction by the bones is of importance in the diagnosis of the nature of auditory defect.

Literature: GRUBER, Diseases of the Ear (Eng. trans.; 2nd ed., 1893); BUCK, Diseases of the Ear (3rd ed., 1898); LOVE and ADDISON, Deaf-Mutism (1896), chap. ii; citations made above, and under DEAFNESS. (J.J.)

Heart [AS. *heorte*]: Ger. *Herz*; Fr. *cœur*; Ital. *cuore*. A hollow muscular organ, in the path of blood or lymphatic vessels, whose rhythmic contractions, beats, furnish the initial motive force for movement of blood or lymph. Hearts may be simple, tubular or saccular, or chambered. (C.F.H.)

Heat and Cold Sensations: see TEMPERATURE SENSATION.

Heat Spot: Ger. *Wärmepunkt*; Fr. *point chaud*; Ital. *punto termico di calore*. See TEMPERATURE SPOT.

Heathen [Gr. ἔθνος, a body of men, tribe, nation]: Ger. *Heide*; Fr. *païen*; Ital. *pagano*. To the Jews: those who had no knowledge of the true God.

Just as among the Greeks a distinction gradually grew up between Greeks and barbarians, so amongst the Hebrews a similar contrast developed between the Jews and the 'nations' (*Goiim*). While the former contrast was based on the idea that the Greeks alone enjoyed the opportunities amid which a truly human life could be led, the latter depended upon a religious difference. The heathen were those who had no knowledge of the true God. This contrast naturally and inevitably passed over into Christianity; and although Christianity broke down the racial exclusiveness of the Jews, yet, as the Church grew up, a similar attitude towards the heathen was produced. As a matter of fact, on a true interpretation of Christianity, the contrast is, not of race, but of inner spirit, of ethical attitude. But the tendency to look down upon non-Christians, and even to persecute them—a tendency wholly at variance with the Christian spirit—has never been overcome altogether.

In modern scientific investigations of the history of religions, the word heathen, when it is employed, is commonly used to indicate a very low form of religion, something that can be called religion only by an extension of the term which it is difficult to warrant.

Literature: see RELIGION (evolution of). (R.M.W.)

Heaven [etymology uncertain: possibly Lat. *camera*, a chamber, or *capere*, to hold]: Ger. *Himmel*; Fr. *ciel* (*cieux*); Ital. *cielo*. Strictly, the abode of God; the place whence Christ came, and to which he returned; the place prepared for the saved.

For philosophy it has no prominent interest, for it connects God with a definite locality, and is therefore a concession to that anthropomorphism which falls to be considered rather by history and science of religions than by philosophy. It ought to be added that many of the theological conjectures on the subject are without warrant in Scripture; and naturally so, for the matter offers free play equally to mystic spiritualism and to gross realism. See ESCHATOLOGY.

Literature: SALMOND, in Hastings' Dict. of the Bible; DORNER, Hist. of Christ. Doctrine (Eng. trans.), iv. 415 f., both giving full literature. (R.M.W.)

Hedonic (1) and **Hedonics** (2) [Gr. ἡδονή, pleasure]: Ger. *Lust- und Unlust-bringend* (1), *Lust- Unlust-lehre* (2); Fr. *agréable ou pénible* (1), *théorie de la sensibilité* (2); Ital. *edonico* (1), *edonologia* (suggested—E.M.) (2). (1) Having pleasurable or painful colouring. (2) The science of pleasurable and painful conditions of consciousness.

Although by derivation hedonic refers to pleasure only, its use for both pleasurable and painful states is now well established. It is, therefore, not necessary to adopt algedonic and algedonics for this twofold reference, as Marshall (*Pain, Pleasure, and Aesthetics,* 9) suggests, seeing that pleasurable sufficiently well covers the narrower meaning of hedonic.

The science of hedonics treats of the nature of pleasurable and painful states of mind, their variations and development, their causes and effects, both mental and physical, &c.

Literature: see PAIN AND PLEASURE. (J.M.B., G.F.S.)

Hedonic Tone: Ger. *Lust und Unlust*; Fr. *plaisir et peine, élément hédonique* (suggested); Ital. *elemento edonistico*. The colouring of pleasure or pain attaching to a state of mind of any kind. See the recommendation made under AFFECTIVE TONE.

Following the broad connotation of hedonic as covering both pleasure and pain, hedonic tone serves as a substantive to that adjective. It is better than feeling tone, suggested by Stout, seeing that has the meaning given it by Wundt (translation of Gefühlston). See AFFECTIVE TONE. It is also better than algedonic tone, for the same reason that hedonic and hedonics are better than alge-donic and algedonics (Marshall). There is a tendency to abbreviate the phrase into 'tone' and 'toned,' as 'tone of sensation' (Baldwin), 'pleasurably toned' (Stout), but that may lead to confusion with affective tone, and should not be done. The objection to the compound term pleasure-pain (Marshall) is that it does not allow the distinction between hedonic tone and the sensations of pleasure and pain, which many psychologists insist upon. See also PAIN AND PLEASURE, and FEEL-ING. In French élément affectif is often used, but it fails, as 'affective element' fails in English, to mark the distinction between feeling tone and hedonic tone ; and we recom-mend that it be reserved for the former.

Literature: STOUT, Analytic Psychol., i. 121 f.; MARSHALL, Pain, Pleasure, and Aesthetics, chap. i ; BALDWIN, Handb. of Psychol., Senses and Intellect, 114 ; Feeling and Will, chap. v ; and the citations under the terms referred to. (J.M.B., G.F.S.)

Hedonism: Ger. *Hedonismus* ; Fr. *hédo-nisme* ; Ital. *edonismo*. The theory that plea-sure is the ultimate standard (or constituent) of moral value. See ETHICAL THEORIES, and EUDAEMONISM. (W.R.S.)

Hegel, Georg Wilhelm Friedrich. (1770–1831.) Born at Stuttgart, he entered the university at Tübingen as a student of theology, receiving a master's degree in philo-sophy, 1790. In this same year Schelling entered the university at the age of sixteen, and seems to have stimulated Hegel to greater activity. Hegel had already read Rousseau, and knew something of the Wolffian philosophy. In 1793 he left Tübingen, and became a private tutor in a family at Berne. He wrote a life of Christ, studied Kant and Benjamin Con-stant, and read for the first time Fichte's *Wissenschaftslehre*, which had just appeared. In 1797 he became a tutor at Frankfort, and there read Plato and Sextus Empiricus. In 1801 he removed to Jena, and began lecturing. Closing his lectures at Jena in 1806, on account of the war, he edited a newspaper in Bamberg until 1808, when he took charge of the gymnasium at Nuremberg. In 1816 he be-came professor of philosophy at Heidelberg. In 1818 he removed to Berlin to take the place left vacant by Fichte's death. Died at Berlin. See the following topics.

Hegelianism or **Hegelism.** After HEGEL (q. v.). See HEGEL'S TERMINOLOGY (especially II), IDEALISM, EPISTEMOLOGY, PHILOSOPHY, and METAPHYSICS.

Hegel's Terminology (in relation to the Hegelian Philosophy).

I. GENERAL NATURE AND ORIGIN OF HEGEL'S TERMINOLOGY.

Amongst the thinkers who, since Aristotle, have undertaken to work out a relatively independent terminology adequate to the complexity and to the organization of a com-plete philosophical system, Hegel occupies a very prominent place. His terms are chosen, on the whole, with a very careful regard to his own central theories. They are, in a number of instances, decidedly novel. Where they are familiar terms, their meaning is altered to such a characteristic doctrine of the system, according to which the process, or other object which Hegel names by any term, is the fulfilment, or 'truth,' i. e. the complete expression, of the meaning and purpose of the processes familiarly known under the same name. The method of nomenclature thus indicated is viewed by Hegel himself as justified by general practice ; and so far this seems indeed plain, since a familiar source of technical names is the deliberate employ-ment of an already familiar term in a meaning which is not only specialized, but specialized through an emphasis laid upon tendencies or purposes latent in the popular usage. In Hegel's case, however, this fashion of creating his own terminology, by employing familiar terms in new ways, is rendered decidedly more baffling than usual by the twofold fact: (1) that the terms whose sense is thus transformed are already old technical terms, of a past usage no longer vague, but, as Hegel himself holds, rather too abstractly sharp in definition ; and (2) that the change from the traditional usage is frequently very considerable, and concerns some of the most original features of the Hegelian system. The result is that brief summaries of the philosophy of Hegel, in his own terminology, are, as this first case illus-trates, extremely misleading ; and many of the most familiar criticisms of his system as 'panlogism,' as reducing life to 'mere thought,' as recognizing 'no reality but the thinking process,' or as 'identifying the philo-sophizing intelligence with the absolute,' whatever may be the ultimate justification of these criticisms, actually express, as they occur, mere impressions resulting from such a view of the whole system, obtained without grasp-ing the sense of its terms. In any case it is not at all easy to restate Hegelian definitions, without summarizing the whole of the *Logik*.

As for the sources and development of Hegel's terminology, a considerable proportion of his terms are of course Aristotelian and scholastic in origin, although then usually much influenced by the Kantian usage. A portion are specifically Kantian terms. Another portion are of distinctly independent and German origin. A considerable influence of popular usage appears (in such cases as *aufheben*). Hegel was fond, like Plato and Aristotle, of etymological comments on the supposed origin and meaning of his terms; and in view of the state of the science of language at the time, his etymologies are often decidedly arbitrary. Deliberate plays upon words are also frequent. At the point where we first meet with Hegel's technical vocabulary in any really free expression, viz. in the *Phänomenologie des Geistes* (1807), it appears very fully developed, although not as rich as later in the *Logik*. In the former work, some of the categories (e.g. *Wirklichkeit*, as opposed to *Dasein, Sein*, &c.) are not uniformly used in the pregnant sense later obtaining, and a certain number of vaguer or of more poetically formed terms or phrases do not later reappear; while, on the other hand, the relative poverty of the categories of the *Phänomenologie* has been a frequent topic of complaint, especially amongst the Hegelian critics of that work. The *Logik*, in its longer form, was first published 1812–16. In the *Encyklopädie der Philosophischen Wissenschaften* (1st ed. 1817, 2nd ed. 1827), the general statement of the whole system, together with its psychological, ethical, theological, and other terminology, appears.

II. Fundamental Features of the System as determining the Terminology.

a. If we now approach a little more closely our task of explaining the main features of Hegelian usage, a few preliminary observations as to the system, viewed as a whole, will help us. To know, with Hegel, as with many other thinkers, is a process involving two factors, namely, the factor usually called experience, and a factor including various constructive processes, of lower or of higher grades. The distinguishing features of Hegel's doctrine depend upon three central theses: (1) that the factor usually called experience, and the other factor (Kant's 'spontaneity' of the thinking process), can never be sundered, but

are universally present, in all grades of knowledge, however low or high. (2) that the lower stages of the knowing process itself are identical in their essential nature with the higher, so that the various grades of knowledge usually distinguished as *perception, understanding, reflection, reason*, &c., are not essentially different mental processes, but are merely successive phases in the evolution of a single process; (3) that the knowing process, in these its phases, in its evolution, and in its entire constitution, not only precisely corresponds to, but is identical with, the essential nature of the world, the object or true being, which is known, so that not only the theory of knowledge cannot be separated from metaphysic, but also the theory of the constitution of the universe is identical with the theory of the process by which we come to know the universe. All these theses are, in a measure, common to the idealism of Fichte, Schelling, and Hegel; but Hegel's working out of the theory is in many ways different from that of his idealistic contemporaries. Of these three theses, the first is the one most commonly misunderstood by opponents of the dialectic method (e.g. by Trendelenburg, in the latter's famous criticism in his *Logische Untersuchungen*). It has been supposed by such critics that Hegel deliberately intended to deduce the empirical element in knowledge wholly from the other, or spontaneous, factor of 'pure thought'; and Hegel has been blamed for failing in this essentially hopeless enterprise. But the criticism is founded upon a mistaken interpretation of Hegel's perfectly explicit statement of his position, as will easily appear from what follows.

b. Since knowledge and its object, what Hegel himself ultimately means by thought and by being, are not only thus correlative, but in essence identical, the exposition of the system in the *Logik* naturally proceeds in such a form as to bring this result as clearly as possible to light. Quite apart from the technicalities of the method, its spirit may in general be summarized by saying that, in our philosopher's opinion, all the necessary concepts which lie at the basis of human science, the categories of our thought, can be made rightly to appear as themselves particular stages in the one process whose general character has just been pointed out. The *Logik* itself will be the system of these concepts, with an account of the way in which higher concepts are rationally evolved out of lower ones. Of every one of these concepts it will be true, according to the general theses of the theory before us, that it is at once a concept of a type or grade of object, and a concept of a stage of knowledge. But not always will this double aspect be easy to seize as we consider any one concept in question. The objective and subjective meanings, as we here might call them, belonging to the various terms, will be always present ; but sometimes the stage in the evolution of knowledge represented by the concept in question will be in itself either too objective or too subjective, and sometimes the mere accidents of traditional usage will direct the reader's mind too much to one side or the other of the meaning. Examples of categories that, by virtue of the stage of evolution which they represent, undertake to be categories of fact rather than categories of knowledge, are furnished by such terms as *Sein, Dasein, Existenz, Ding, Eigenschaft*, &c. Examples of categories that are explicitly categories of the knowing process, are represented by the terms *Urtheil* and *Schluss*, i. e. *judgment* and *syllogism*. More neutral terms, which in common usage, or at certain stages of the actual history of philosophical discussion, have had both their objective and subjective meanings emphasized, are *das Allgemeine* and *die Idee*. For the Platonic ideas were originally purely objective truths ; and the reality of universals has often been discussed. The term *Reflection* is an interesting example of a term which first suggests to the reader's mind the process of subjective reflection, while Hegel frequently emphasizes its objective meaning as a name for a real process. As a fact, so far as the stage in the evolution of the subject-matter at any point permits, all the terms alike are intended to apply *both* to stages of what tradition calls the subjective knowing process, and to grades of what are usually regarded as external objects or processes. Thus Hegel speaks of judgment and syllogism (*Urtheil* and *Schluss*) as objective processes, present in nature or in history, frequently applying the former of these two terms to name processes of differentiation and division (especially those occurring on higher conscious levels), and the latter to name processes of reorganization and of the reconciliation of divided tendencies. This tendency in Hegel's terminology, while its justification, to the author's mind, forms one of the theses of the system, often gives his language, to one who first meets it, a fantastic, or at all events an allegorizing, appearance, which does not easily pass away, but which in any case must be regarded as a result of the author's deliberate intent, so far as it illustrates the general theses of the unity of *Sein* and *Denken*.

III. The Dialectical Method: General Features.

a. The method of procedure by which Hegel passes from the lower to the higher stages, in the development of his *Logik*, is of course the most characteristic feature of the entire system. This is the famous dialectical method. Stated still apart from its technical details, it takes two principal forms. The first form especially applies to categories that are defective by being too abstract, and that lay too much stress upon the objective aspect of the truth which they contain. They, in general, are more or less entirely the categories of *Immediacy* (*Unmittelbarkeit*), or, in other words, are categories of the world viewed as fact, or as *datum*. They are, by the general doctrine of the system, imperfect categories. Rightly criticized, they are therefore to lead to higher categories. The process of accomplishing this end is a process of showing that the fact-world is really a world of relations amongst facts, or that its truth is *relative*, so that what a given category attempts to define as *a* alone, or as *b* alone, turns out, upon analysis, to mean *a related to b*. This relation of *a* to *b* also appears to our author's mind as a fact that we grasp only in the transition (*Uebergang*) from *a* to *b*; so that in general we find that, if we first try to hold *a* alone, and then to determine what *a* means, we discover, often to our surprise, and generally with a clear sense of some contradiction thus brought to light, that *a* means *b*, either as one of its own aspects or (especially in the lower and therefore less stable categories) as something opposed to *a* itself, into which *a* nevertheless turns under our very hands, as we endeavour to state its meaning. Hereupon, we observe that the true *a* can be defined only by taking explicit account of *b*, only by transition from one category to the other, and only by the further explicit recognition of the *unity* (*Einheit*) of *a* and *b* in something whose nature appears as one involving the aforesaid *a related to b*. This new unity, made explicit, now gets some name, let us say *c*, and appears as a higher category of the series, which, in general, will have to be treated in the same fashion. The *Einheit* itself of *a* and *b* does not mean their simple identification; but just as any one space before us involves both right and left directions, or both up and down, and is thus the *unity* of up and down, right and left, without involving the mere confusion of these various directions, so in *c, a* and *b* are brought into unity, without our now losing sight of their differences, which the whole procedure has only made more explicit. The contradiction latent in trying to define *a* alone has thus been first brought to light, and then sublated or *aufgehoben*.

b. A simple example of this form of the dialectical method is found at the outset of the *Phänomenologie*, where common sense is challenged to point out some object which is certainly known for what, in our experience, it is. The first answer undertaken by common sense is: *This object,* viz. the object that I here and now see or touch; *This is known to me directly.* Hegel's reply is: But *what* is *this object?* What does *this* mean? He then points out, in various ways, that the name *this, ipso facto,* applies to any object whatever found in experience, so that, instead of reporting its knowledge of a single fact as such, common sense has to define its knowledge, so far, as the most general, vague, and indefinite knowledge possible, a mere knowledge of *thisness* in general, or of a *somewhat here and now*; so that *this,* merely as *this,* means as yet anything, or as good as nothing. The result, so far as it here concerns us, is, that the only knowable objects are much more than merely single facts given as such, viz. as *this.* The known objects of experience involve relations between *this* and *that, now* and *then, here* and *there,* and are accordingly interrelated masses of differentiated experience—e.g. an object seen against a background, or a thing which is *one* by virtue of and in contrast to its *many* qualities, &c.

The other form of the dialectical method often involves, at the precise point where it occurs, less apparent paradox, largely because we are better prepared for it when its stage is reached. It is, moreover, of a type more generally characteristic of modern idealistic systems, whether Hegelian or not. It is used when our categories have reached some more explicitly subjective stage, when the relativity of our world is already recognized, and when the purpose is to show that the subjective meaning in question is also an objective meaning, or that our more explicitly ideal processes are also expressive of the essence of

absolute facts. Here the method in general consists in showing that the development of the ideal process, and of all the complex interrelationships which this involves, is itself a fact, a law of truth, relatively independent, through its very universality, of the single subjective stages through which it has become explicit, so that, in discovering the inevitable character of a given process of thinking, we have discovered the only truth that, at this stage, there is to know. This truth now becomes once more, in a higher sense, *unmittelbar* or immediate. We now experience its actuality. This form of the dialectical method is used in Hegel's restatement of the ontological proof of God's existence; it appears very notably in the transition from *Subjektivität* to *Objektivität* in the third part of the *Logik.* In general it is used against sceptics, against Kant, against Fichte, and against subjectivism of all sorts. In substance it consists in saying, first, that some point of view, or ideal construction, has now given us a demand, or a fully developed need, for a certain system of conceptions, or of relationships, *a, b, c, d,* &c.; secondly, that the question hereupon arises, whether any objective truth corresponds to this ideal demand; and thirdly, that, carefully considered, the ideal demand, by its very universality and necessity, has shown itself to cover the whole ground which any object could here occupy, so that the fully grown *Begriff* is itself the object sought, the curtain is the picture, and the thought is the being. The basis for this use of the dialectical method is the same as that employed by any idealist who intends to show that the completed meaning of a system of ideas is identical with all that the mind seeks in looking for objective truth.

These two forms of the dialectical method, although developed with great thoroughness and originality by Hegel, are in origin not at all peculiar to himself. The two principles involved, viz. *That facts are knowable only as interrelated,* and *That the universal laws of ideal processes, taken together with the processes which embody these laws, are equivalent to all that is properly to be meant by reality,* are not unfamiliar to students of philosophy, quite apart from Hegel's system. The peculiar relation which Hegel brought to pass between these principles and the logical principles of identity, contradiction, and excluded middle, has led to considerable misunderstanding, and the form of statement has rendered the system difficult to survey in its wholeness.

Literature: TRENDELENBURG, Ueber die dialektische Methode, in vol. i of Logische Untersuchungen; J. ELLIS MACTAGGART, Studies in the Hegelian Dialectic; GEORGES NOËL, La Logique de Hegel; WALLACE, Prolegomena to Hegel's Logic (2nd ed.), are among the best discussions of the special topic here in question. Trendelenburg's view has been, for Hegel's critics, extremely influential, and is very skilfully stated, despite its defects.

IV. THE MOST GENERAL TERMS OF THE SYSTEM; EXPERIENCE OF THE DIALECTIC PROCESS.

In following the various stages of the dialectical process, one meets with a good many terms which are repeatedly used, not to define any of the individual categories, but to characterize the presuppositions and occurrences which are more or less universal throughout the process. These may here best be taken, first in order, as the *most general* terms of the entire system.

a. The word *unmittelbar*, or *immediate*, as employed by Hegel, is the first of the terms of most general use in the system. This term primarily refers both to the *presence* and to the apparent *lack of relationships* which first seem to characterize objects when taken as sense takes them, or when viewed as a falsely abstract thinking views them. Aristotle's propositions called ἄμεσα would be viewed by Hegel as also relatively immediate, but Hegel applies the word to numerous other objects. But *immediate*, in a secondary and higher sense, also refers to a character observable in all truth, even from the highest point of view.

Unmittelbar, in a relative sense of the term, is, for the first, any starting-point, or beginning, or presupposition; *vermittelt*, or *mediated*, on the contrary, is any result or consequence (cf. *Werke*, 2nd ed., iii, *Logik*, 39). In a still more obvious way, however, facts, taken as such, things, mere sensations, first appear to us as *unmittelbar*, and we only gradually discover that they are *vermittelt*, in so far as they stand in *relations*, without which they prove to be meaningless; and so are the *result* of conditions, both subjective and objective, which forbid us to treat them as alone. Numerous special shadings are given to the meaning of these two terms, *unmittelbar* and *vermittelt*, by the subject-matter and the con-

text; but these meanings are all derived from the general meanings:—*unrelated* and *related*; *given* and *explained*; *elementary* and *developed*; *initial* and *resultant*. In matters of practical import, *unmittelbar* can often be translated by *unwon* or *unearned*. Thus the object of a given vague plan appears as merely *unmittelbar*, when we have as yet no idea of the means by which to win it; the possession of unearned powers involves an immediacy to which we have as yet no explicit right, &c.

b. The universal law, principle, or process of *Vermittelung*, or of the whole evolution, both of thought and of things, is termed *Negativität*. This term, one of the most difficult in Hegel's usage, suggests in one word the entire system.

Negativität is a principle both of destruction and of production. That which *Negativität* produces, on the positive and objective side of its work, is first precisely the world that at the outset the philosopher empirically finds as the realm of immediacy, the whole universe of experience. Upon its destructive and subjective side, *Negativität*, as the principle determining the process of knowledge, next appears as denying or sublating the appearance of *mere* immediacy which characterizes this world, and so as both destroying abstractions and reducing the world of fact to a realm of universal relativity. *Negativität* finally, as the 'negation of the negation,' appears, in a new constructive task, as the process whereby the rational unity of thought, and of things of immediacy and mediation, of experience and reason, comes to light, in the positive system of the philosopher. In consequence, *Negativität* explicitly names a law or process both of things and of knowledge. This law, again, on its objective side, is the principle that everything merely immediate is false, transient, and illusory, but that the very constitution and evolution of the real world, as a whole, depends upon this very fact. In the process of displaying this transiency of every finite fact, in the conflicts due to the resulting contradictions, and in the bringing to light of the illusions, the very life and actuality of the whole outer or objective universe consists. Even the positive construction of the objective empirical world by the principle of *Negativität* is consequently full of relatively destructive processes. The visible universal is thus the incorporation of the principle called *Negativität*, which, as Hegel sometimes says, might be called *die Seele der Welt*.

The absolute possesses *Negativität* as its

own principle or law. If one takes the absolute abstractly, views it apart from the world in which it expresses itself (as the philosophical mystics love abstractly to view the absolute), or in a similar manner regards any principle as if it could be isolated from its manifestations, the absolute, or the principle in question, then possesses what Hegel calls *reine oder sich auf sich beziehende Negativität,* '*pure* or *self-related,* or *self-centred, Negativity.*' This implies that such absolute, taken thus *in abstracto,* would be a *self-denying* essence, a *sich auf sich beziehende Negativität,* or an idea which was self-related only in this negative way (cf. *Logik,* 2nd part, *Werke,* iv. 17, 31).

c. Any unity, i.e. any whole meaning or object, which exemplifies in a particular case the principle of negativity, by combining within itself differentiated, opposed, but related contents, is frequently called a *negative Einheit* (see *Logik,* 2nd part, *Werke,* iv. 42). So the unity of consciousness is a notable case of *negative Einheit.*

The exercise of *Negativität,* or an act which exemplifies it, especially in its first or more destructive aspect, but also, on occasion, in its constructive aspect, is an act for which Hegel uses the verb *aufheben.* Of this word he gives a full account in *Logik, Werke,* iii. 104. *Aufheben* and *vermitteln,* he here tells us, are very largely synonymous. In popular language *aufheben* is already ambiguous, since it means both to destroy and to lay aside for keeping. Hegel is attracted by this double sense, which seems to him an instance of unconscious speculative thought. He accordingly gives the verb its technical usage.

V. Further General Terminology. The Stages of the Development of 'Vermittelung.'

We now come to a series of generally applied expressions, for the various degrees in which any object, or category, may manifest either a relatively pure immediacy, or some form of explicit mediation. These expressions are the characteristic phrases and epithets: *Abstrakt, Concret, an sich, an sich oder für uns, an ihm* or *an ihm selbst, für sich, an und für sich, gesetzt, bestimmt;* together with various abstract nouns, such as *Ansichsein, Fürsichsein, Bestimmung, Bestimmtheit, Beschaffenheit,* which, while having a place amongst the categories, are principally useful as charac-

terizing the stages in the development of other categories.

a. Abstrakt and *Concret* have, in Hegel, an opposition not identical with the more familiar technical usage. With him an individual object may be so taken as to make appear *abstract,* while any universal principle becomes concrete just in proportion as it becomes true. Hegel's use of *abstrakt* includes, however, most of the ordinary applications, and is more extensive. Any object is *abstract,* in so far as it is viewed in a false isolation from its genuine relations, or if it is something in the world of objective things and processes, when it appears as a fact apart. In the objective sense, Robinson Crusoe alone on the island would be a relatively abstract individual, because he could not live a whole human life; when the man Friday came, Crusoe and his life were already more concrete, for man lives in relation to his kind. *Abstrakt* differs from *unmittelbar,* in so far as the former more easily applies to the cases which ordinary usage also calls *abstract,* viz. to cases where a relation is abstracted from its terms, a principle from its applications, &c. But it is true, of course, that *reine Unmittelbarkeit* is in Hegel's sense an abstraction. However, *unmittelbar* connotes *presence,* while *abstrakt* primarily refers only to isolation. *Concret,* on the other hand, is any whole, especially when its organization is explicit. 'The unity of various contents is the concrete' (*Gesch. d. Philos., Werke,* xiii. 37, Einl. — a passage in which the concept of the concrete is very fully developed and illustrated). Philosophy, therefore, instead of being confined to abstractions, really deals, according to our philosopher, with the most concrete object, namely, the organic unity called the world or the absolute.

The expressions next on our foregoing list, *an sich* and its correlatives, form a closely connected and very characteristic phraseology, which recurs in our philosopher's discussion of categories of every grade.

b. If deliberately dwelt upon in its *Unmittelbarkeit,* any object is viewed *an sich.* It is so viewed especially when one returns to such immediate view by a deliberate ignoring of other objects. But thus viewed it is not only falsely viewed, but is a basis for truer views, an abstraction out of which the more concrete form of these truer views develops. In this way *an sich* comes to mean *latent, undeveloped, not overt,* as one can speak of the infant Shakespeare as already, or *an sich,* a *born* poet. For even in dwelling upon the infant as infant, one necessarily interprets the infant in terms of what is to come. For the same reason, *an sich* may become wholly equivalent, in some contexts, to the scholastic *in potentia*. In case of mental processes, *an sich* may mean *unconscious*, as the man who hates his brother is *an sich* a murderer (or a murderer *in his heart*), although he perhaps does not recognize how murderous his hate is. This sense of *unconscious* is frequent in the *Phänomenologie*. All these meanings have both objective and subjective applications. The Kantian sense of *an sich*, according to which *an sich* means *independent of consciousness*, is often enough used in citations from Kant, and in criticisms of that philosopher, and is by Hegel connected with the notion of abstract (and secondary) immediacy, which according to Hegel belongs to objects, precisely in so far as they are conceived to be independent either of consciousness or of other things. *An sich* in all its meanings differs from *unmittelbar*, mainly by its greater intensity, viz. by virtue of the still more deliberate ignoring of relations which is in mind when an object is taken, not merely *as it comes*, but with express effort to sunder it from other objects, and to view it by itself; or again, when an object appears in the world in such wise as thus to lay stress upon the absence, or the complete latency, of its relations. *Das Unmittelbare*, in its first or lower forms, has as yet no relations; but what is *an sich* tries, as it were, to disown them (*Logik, Werke*, iii. 119: 'In so far as anything is in itself, it is withdrawn from relation to other, and from otherness').

c. The peculiarly Hegelian phrase *an ihm*, equivalent according to the author to AN *sich*, with an emphasis laid upon the AN (loc. cit., 120), is most naturally to be used either in the form, '*Etwas hat an ihm* any given character,' or also in the form, '*Es ist an ihm*, namely, *an etwas*, this same character.' Hegel justifies the usage so far by appeal to such popular phrases as, *Es ist nichts daran*. Hegel, however, in a sufficiently barbarous fashion, is capable of saying *dass das Etwas das, was es an sich ist, auch an ihm ist* (loc. cit., 123), so that *an ihm* becomes a predicative phrase, which is not easily intelligible apart from the technical explanation. This explanation is that *an ihm* refers to a character which is, in a more external and overt fashion, so *in* a subject, or rather, as one might say, attached *to* this subject, as to determine the subject's relations to others. If a man's latent traits of character, never yet expressed in his conduct, were supposed to be revealed by his features, a physiognomist would say that what the man *in himself* (*an sich*) is, is also *an ihm*, that is, belongs to him as feature, or is *in him* after all (Stirling, *Secret of Hegel*, new edition of 1898, 399, renders the force of *an ihm* as 'the manifestable peculiar nature' of its object). In brief, then, while the *an sich* of any being is a name for characters which are, if possible, to be dwelt upon by ignoring this being's relations to others, and while the *an sich* is therefore a name for abstract, fundamental, but latent and barely potential features, *an ihm* refers to characters that seem externally attributed to the being in question, so that they are more manifest, and are more such characters as indicate relations. A name for the characters which a being, as a consequence of its *an sich*, or original and latent nature, has *an ihm*, is the *Bestimmung*, or *vocation, destiny, power, capacity*, of a being, its *fitness* for external relationships (*Logik*, loc. cit., 123). This term is translated by Stirling (op. cit., 259) as *qualification*, and is interpreted by the same author (op. cit., 399) as 'that to which the something (*Etwas*) is adequate.' *Bestimmung* is opposed to *Bestimmtheit* by Hegel (loc. cit.) as capacity to the particular state, the definite condition or activity embodying this capacity. If the *Bestimmung* is fulfilled, one has a *Bestimmtheit* proper, the relation between the two being much that of *first act* and *second act* in scholastic terminology. Thus the *Bestimmung des Menschen*, the *vocation* or *capacity* of man, is to be reasonable, or is Reason (so Hegel himself, loc. cit.); but his thinking activity, his *Denken*, the fulfilment of this capacity, is his *Bestimmtheit*.

d. In general, any being is *bestimmt*, in so far as its determinate features bring it into contrast with external beings. *Bestimmen* is the verb which expresses the process of adding the specific differences, or *differentiae*, to the more general characters of anything. *Bestimmtheit* involves, when externally viewed, a *Beschaffenheit* (by Stirling ingeniously rendered *talification*), whereby a thing appears like this or that when involved in chance relations to other things. The *Beschaffenheit* is thus nearly allied to Aristotle's *accident*, as in the well-known Aristotelian example: 'You are not cultivated in so far as you are you (i. e. in yourself), but in so far as this has *occurred* to you.' So the *Beschaffenheit* reveals the *Bestimmung*, but in more accidental and external ways.

e. A being is *für sich* in a sense still more advanced. When characters no longer latent have been so developed, when relationships no longer ignored have become so explicitly included in the definition of a being, that it now appears capable of a genuine independence, as an internally related whole of meaning, it is taken *für sich* when this independence is insisted upon, or when, in the objective world, such independence appears to assert itself. An atom, a Leibnitzian monad, or a Kantian autonomous moral subject, undertakes to be *für sich. Fürsichsein* is therefore such *independent being* as, *for some definite reason,* appears to include a system of internal relations, and to cut off external relations (cf. *Encyk., Werke,* **vi.** 189; *Logik, Werke,* iii. 165).

A being is *an und für sich* in so far as its asserted independence is altogether the developed result of its nature, so that what it is *in itself* fully justifies its asserted independence of external relations. This stage is also called *Beisichsein,* and the compound *An-und-fürsichsein* is also employed (*Encyk., Werke,* vi. 161; *Logik, Werke,* iv. 5). *An-und-fürsichsein* belongs, in the highest sense only, to the absolute, but is often attributed to the later categories and to conscious beings of higher grades.

f. As to the terms *gesetzt* and *Gesetztsein,* it must be observed that any character is *gesetzt* in so far as it is *explicitly* shown to result from the nature of the object to which it is referred. *Gesetztsein* means the condition or state of being thus *gesetzt.* Thus the born poet, or poet *an sich,* who shows himself in youth to have the *Bestimmung* of a poet, or to have poetry *in him* (*an ihm*), or to bear the marks of a poet *about* him (still *an ihm*), is not yet *gesetzt* as a poet until by original production he has *lived up to* his early promise. *Gesetzt* is directly translated as *posited.* Stirling points out (op. cit., 368) how numerous are the consequences of this central conception of *Gesetztsein.* 'It is *gesetzt,*' says Stirling, 'means, it is developed into its proper explication, statement, expression, enunciation, exhibition, &c. Again, a *Gesetztes,* as not self-referent, is but lunar, satellitic, parasitic, secondary, derivative.' Still other derived senses appear in Stirling's view, in various passages; but these can usually be made clear from the context.

A final observation must here be made, in closing this series of terms, as to the interesting and frequent expression, *An sich oder für uns.* As Hegel is extremely anxious to distinguish, in the progress of the dialectical method, between what is so far explicit (*gesetzt*) and what is thus far only *latent* or *potential* in the development of any conception, he frequently has occasion to insist that a given feature, asserted to belong to any object, is not yet the explicit result of presuppositions, or is not yet *vermittelt,* but appears as a fact whose potentialities we, the philosophizing readers, predict in advance, or observe, while they are yet, in the object itself, only latent. What is latent thus becomes the same as what we externally observe to be in the object; and therefore what is *an sich* is so far just *for us,* or is observable from our point of view.

VI. OTHER TERMS.

a. Very characteristic of this system is the series of grades of being, or of gradations of the existential predicate. These are: *Sein, Dasein* (including *Realität*), *Existenz, Wirklichkeit, Substantialität,* and *Objektivität.* To say of a given object merely, *Es ist,* is not, for Hegel, as pregnant an assertion as to say, *Es existirt.* Still more do you say if you assert, *Es ist wirklich.* The most pregnant assertion on the list would be, *Es hat Objektivität.* An object may possess *Sein* without having *Existenz.* When Hegel asserts, in a well-known passage, *Alles Vernünftige ist wirklich, und alles Wirkliche ist vernünftig,* he does not mean that whatever *exists* is rational, for it is a part of Hegel's thesis that much of the merely phenomenal, but still existent, world contains chance, i.e. irrational contingency, while only the notion is *actual* or *wirklich.* Hegel's ontological phraseology must therefore be carefully considered in interpreting his meaning. This, to be sure, is less true of the *Phänomenologie* than of Hegel's later works, since in the *Phänomenologie* the ontological vocabulary is less clearly differentiated. In particular our terms mean as follows:—

Sein is the name for pure immediacy as such. Everything and anything *is*—the vaguest fancy or dream, in so far as it possesses immediacy. But pure immediacy taken absolutely in itself, as merely itself, without definitions and contrasts, would be the same as nothing. Hence the actual cases of immediacy all possess *Dasein,* or determinate being, i.e. being that has some sort of

Bestimmtheit, or contrast with other beings. *Dasein* would be possessed, so far, by any object with characters, e. g. a house, or any part of the universe, viewed merely as distinguishable part, but also by a rainbow, a flash of lightning, a taste or smell, or any *Etwas.* But such an *Etwas* is primarily *bestimmt,* its *Dasein* involves its determination. Only the *precisely* determinable, then, is present in the world of *Dasein.* If one says that he experiences *something,* we naturally ask, *What ?* If there is no answer naming the determinations of the *Etwas* in question, we have to say that it is *nothing in particular,* and this indefiniteness, if complete, would send us back to *reines Sein,* which is again equal to *Nichts.* But now, as Spinoza affirmed, *omnis determinatio est negatio,* and so determination, or *Bestimmtheit,* implies contrast with, and so negation of, some other determinate character, and every *Etwas* is opposed to *ein Anderes,* its negation or other (as light is contrasted with darkness, &c.). Such contrast, as a universal feature of *Dasein,* includes the twofold character that every *Etwas* is *positive,* in so far as it is what it is, and *negative,* in so far as it excludes the other. The *positive* character, whereby light, for instance, is light, as opposed to the *negative* character, whereby light is not darkness, Hegel calls the *Realität* of any *Etwas,* as opposed to its *Negation.* So that the term *Realität* is used, in the sense of the Kantian table of categories (see KANT'S TERMINOLOGY), to mean the positive aspect of the *Bestimmtheit* or *differentia* of any determinate being whatever (cf. *Encyk., Werke,* vi. 180; *Logik, Werke,* iii. 109 ff.). The difference between this usage and either the scholastic usage or the senses of *reality* more common in recent discussion must be noted.

b. Existenz, as opposed to *Sein, Dasein,* and *Realität,* is a much higher category, and, although it expresses a later form of immediacy, belongs to the world of *Wesen,* i. e. of explicitly mediated or relative being, to the world of principles and of phenomenal expressions of principles. The typical case of *Existenz* is any physical *thing,* with *qualities.* This has a grade of being, not merely involving, like *Dasein,* or like colours and rainbows, contrasts with other beings of the same grade, but pointing back to explanations, through principles, of the *basis* (*Grund*) upon which the thing's existence depends, or which it manifests, even in its immediacy. What has *Existenz* is also in interaction with its environment.

Wirklichkeit is a still higher category. What has *Existenz* is a relatively immediate fact, but appears as the result of conditions, and as related to an environment. But what has *Wirklichkeit* not only has a basis, or is explicitly the expression of a principle, but contains this basis within itself, so that it is relatively (in the complete case wholly) independent of any environment. It is, then, a higher instance both of *Fürsichsein* and of *An-und-fürsichsein.* If a physical thing with qualities has *Existenz,* an organism, a commonwealth, a solar system, or any such relative *totality* (*Totalität*), possesses *Wirklichkeit.* In the most genuine sense, only the absolute would be *wirklich,* but the term is often employed for finite but relatively organic beings (*Logik, Werke,* iv. 113, 115 ff., 120, 176 f., 178 ; *Encyk., Werke,* iv. 250, 253, 282 ff. ; and cf. the introd. to the *Encyk.,* iv. 10).

The type of *Wirklichkeit* historically represented by Spinoza's substance possesses, for Hegel, the grade of being which he names *Substantialität,* namely, *Wirklichkeit* conceived as a fully developed necessary nature of things.

c. Objektivität is the grade of being possessed by an object which explicitly fulfils or expresses a system of rational ideas, thoughts, or laws that is also subjectively conceived. This category differs from *Wirklichkeit* chiefly by virtue of the more explicit prior sundering of the ideal aspect of the world from its immediate aspect. To say that a thing is *wirklich* implies, indeed, that it expresses what can be defined as a law or rational character ; but one may first accept the *Wirklichkeit* as an immediate fact, and then observe its constitution, as a student of politics first regards the state as an actuality, and then analyses its structure. But when one affirms *Objektivität,* one does so *after* defining laws, subjective principles, systems of rational interrelationships, which already have their inner or *a priori* validity and necessity.

When one asserts of these systems that they also possess the immediacy exemplified, on lower stages, by *Dasein, Existenz,* &c., then, and not till then, is one dealing with the grade of being defined as *Objektivität.* The systems of things subject to law or expressive of purpose, which we find in nature and in history, possess therefore not only *Wirklichkeit,* but also *Objektivität* ; as, for instance, one may say : 'Purpose is an objective fact in the universe' (*Encyk., Werke*, vi. 365 ff.; *Logik, Werke*, v. 167 ff.).

Objektivität is possessed, in its own highest grade, by the completely fulfilled or expressed *Wahrheit*, or *truth*, which Hegel calls the *Idee*, or, in other words, by the *life* or *self* of the universe, the concrete embodiment of the principle of *Negativität*, also technically called the *Subject-Object*. The *Idee* is at once a name for the absolute, and for the world-process, taken in all its stages, but here viewed as a logical category (*Logik, Werke*, v. 229 ff.).

d. In contrast to the terms for the categories of immediacy stand the terms for the processes and results of mediation or of the process of thought. The term *Gedanken* is often used by Hegel to name what are by ordinary usage called *thoughts*, namely, *abstract thoughts*—the ordinary *concepts*. In this narrower sense, however, *Gedanken* are but fragments of the true *Denken*; and it is the purpose of the philosopher to lead such mere *Gedanken* to the unity of the *Begriff*. For the general definition of *Gedanke*, as subjective and individual occurrence, see *Encyk., Werke*, vii. 2, 355; the frequent narrower use is exemplified in the *Vorrede* to the *Phänomenologie, Werke*, ii. 7, 24 f.

The term *Begriff* itself has been variously translated; but Stirling's choice of *notion*, accepted also by Wallace, has now, on the whole, possession of the field. A good deal could be said in favour of the term *meaning*, as a translation of *Begriff*, were it possible to fix this essentially fluent popular term to any technical usage. The very fluency of the term *meaning* would tend to suggest Hegel's conception of what the *Begriff* is to accomplish, and its neutral reference *either* to objective *or* to subjective meaning, and *either* to volitional end *or* to intellectual significance, would be in conformity with the purpose of Hegel.

The term *Begriff* is, to the process of active mediation called *Denken*, precisely what the term *Sein* is to the contents and processes of the world of immediacy in the first division of the *Logik*. *Begriff*, namely, is: (1) a general name for any of the individual or relatively separable processes and products of *Denken*, and here especially for the earlier stages of *Denken*; (2) a name for the principle, law, or living meaning which expresses itself in the whole evolution of *Denken*; (3) a collective, or better, here, an organic name for the whole course of the evolution itself, conceived as an objective world of rational fact.

In sense (1) we can speak of various *Begriffe*, e. g. of the *Begriffe* of individuality, of the universal, of the syllogism; or, again, we can speak of all the previous categories of *Sein* and *Wesen* as, on their subjective side, *Begriffe*. So far *Begriff* is then a class name.

In sense (2), which is the most important of the three, and which one may call the first concrete sense, the term *Begriff* has *both* an objective and a subjective application. It names (*a*) the principle which, just because it is that of *Denken*, is the real principle which governs the whole universe, and which expresses itself therein; and this use of the term is very frequent in Hegel's terminology, not only here, but in other works than the *Logik*. Or (*b*) it names the philosophical process of subjectively appreciating the nature and meaning of this principle. This subjective use of the term *Begriff* is, on the whole, predominant in the *Phänomenologie*, and is never abandoned. It appears in the *Logik*, and Hegel himself uses the terminology *subjektiver und objektiver Begriff*.

Sense (3) appears in the title to this division, and is very easily derived from sense (2). It is the second concrete sense in which *Begriff* is used.

As for the further nature of this principle (the *Begriff*) itself, we now know it, in general, from the account already given of *Negativität*; only that term is explicitly an abstract noun. But *Begriff*, when employed with objective reference in sense (2), is generally – apart from special meanings, almost always—employed to name *concrete embodiments of the principle*, or the *principle as concretely embodied*. *Negativität* therefore stands to *Begriff* very much in the relation in which, in scholastic terminology, *Deitas* stands to *Deus*. *Negativität* is the *Qualität* of the *Begriff*. Sense (3) above enables us, also in concrete fashion, to speak of the whole world as the *Begriff*.

The *Begriff* (in senses 2, 3), as Hegel often declares (e.g. *Logik, Werke*, v. 12), is Spinoza's *Substanz* 'set free,' or turned into a *subject*. In this same sense, taken with objective reference, one can speak of the *Begriff* in the terms above used in speaking of the *Idee*; only that in the *Idee*, as the final form of the *Begriff* itself, the aspect of immediacy has fully returned to this principle of the universal mediation of thought and of things, by virtue of the discussion of the categories of *Objektivität*. In any case, what was first expressed as *Sein*, and then as *Wesen*, is now to be fulfilled as *Begriff*. That alone can be real which is of the nature of the life, principle, or meaning that determines the whole process of *Denken*. So much, then, for the terms *Denken*, *Gedanke*, and *Begriff*.

e. The way in which *Negativität* appears as the character of the *Begriff* is next notable. The *Begriff*, as the principle which determines both thought and things, is to be not only a self-related and self-differentiating process, but a process whose differentiations have exactly the type observable in *self-consciousness* of all grades. Self-consciousness, as Hegel is never weary of telling us, is a unity, at first *immediate* or *abstract*. This unity, however, preserves itself just by exercising itself in overcoming, and reducing to the service of its own desire, or will, or conception, or insight, countless facts that at first view are foreign to its own nature. It thus involves mediation, with constant rewinning of immediacy. That is how any man lives, whether materially or spiritually. The logical account of the *Begriff* will have therefore first to state the universal dynamics of this self-conscious process in the most universal form. Hegel here calls the *first*, or *immediate*, aspect of the *Begriff*, its *abstract* universality (*abstrakte Allgemeinheit*). Its mediation through variety of life, will, experience, meanings, finite individuals, &c., he calls in general its *Sich-Bestimmung* or its *Besonderheit*, its *particularity*. The developed *Begriff*, in differentiating itself into a variety of *Bestimmungen*, which, while held *within* the developing universal, may still in their immediacy seem at first foreign to its one meaning, 'comes to itself' precisely so far as, with concrete *Allgemeinheit* (or concrete universality), it recognizes these particulars as within itself, and as even in their immediacy still its own *meaning*. The finite facts of the life of the *Begriff*, the individuals of finite experience, the various *Existenzen*, &c., are thus within the *concrete universal* of the whole life of the true *Begriff*. The three terms, universal, particular, and singular (or individual), like the original terms *unmittelbar* and *vermittelt*, may frequently change places in their application; but throughout their discussion the main conception remains, as just stated, constant. The process present is the one originally called *Negativität*, but now it is present as a *conscious* process. It is a process of asserting unity through self-differentiation, and through bringing the results again into organic rela-

tions. The outcome of the process is a unity, essentially the unity of Self-Consciousness, wherein all finite individuality is present within a union (*Einheit*) of *Allgemeinheit* and *Besonderheit* ('The one undivided soul of many a soul' of Shelley's familiar phrase). Hegel, in general, defines this union as the category of *Einzelnheit*, or *individuality*, the category, one might say, of the unity of the many in the one.

These three, the categories of the *Begriff*, viz. *Allgemeinheit*, *Besonderheit*, and *Einzelnheit*, are to be understood, like the rest of the discussion, with reference to the special nature of Hegel's own *Begriff*. They are then not the merely tradition conceptions known under these names. In the later developments of this division of the Logic, the *concrete universal* becomes explicitly identical with an *infinite individual* (in Hegel's technical sense of infinite as developed above in (7), viz. a completely self-determined individual).

f. The particular mediations of the *Begriff*, in its primary or more subjective forms, occur through the development of the doctrines of *Urtheil* and *Schluss*. These, the principal sections of the traditional Logic, are incorporated by Hegel into his own theory in a greatly altered form, and with a deliberate effort to give them an interpretation which may also be stated as an objective process. An *Urtheil* is a process of making differentiation and the opposition of related terms explicit. No judgment, therefore, is subjectively expressive of a whole truth, and no corresponding objective process is a final one. Every judgment is one-sided, is a particular expression of *Negativität*, and passes away into some higher form of judgment, or into that truer expression of the *Begriff*, the *Schluss*. In particular, judgment depends upon opposing finite individuals, particulars and universals, in various degrees of abstraction, one to another, and then endeavouring to hold their unity also abstractly before the mind, despite the opposition. The higher forms of judgment express more nearly the organic union of finite individuals or particulars in inclusive universal wholes; but no judgment can reach the final unity, and the truth of the judgment is the *Schluss*. The *Schluss* is, as subjective process, an effort to express the uniting principle or *Mitte* (*middle term*), namely, the very selfhood of truth itself, which binds the many particulars of a differentiated experience in the unity of a single conscious whole. The objective correspondent of the subjective process called *Schluss* is any expression of an organically unifying principle in the realm of truth itself. The categories of *Schluss*, precisely as the necessity of such union becomes manifest, tend themselves to assume a more one-sidedly objective character, and the truth of the *Schluss* is the realm of *Objektivität* already considered (see above, (7))—a realm where objects are known as expressing rationality in its wholeness. When these objects are once more reflectively regarded as objects due to ideal demands, and so not merely as corresponding to *Denken*, but produced by it, the circle of this form of idealism is completed in the *Idee*. The *Idee* itself, in its freest manifestation as *absolute Idee*, is the highest possible logical definition of Hegel's Absolute itself. (J.R.)

GLOSSARY.

(The numbers and letters refer to the sections and paragraphs of this article.)

Absolute Idee, VI. *f.*
Abstrakt, V. *a.*
Abstrakte Allgemeinheit, VI. *e.*
Allgemein, II. *b.*
An etwas, V. *c.*
An ihm, V. *c.*
An sich, V. *b.*
An sich oder für uns, V. *f.*
An und für sich, V. *e.*
An-und-fürsichsein, V. *e.*
Aufheben, I, III. *a*, IV. *c.*

Begriff, III, VI. *d.*
Beisichsein, V. *e.*
Beschaffenheit, V. *d.*
Besonderheit, VI. *e.*
Bestimmt, V. *d.*
Bestimmtheit, V. *c, d,* VI. *a.*
Bestimmung, V. *c.*

Concret, V. *a.*
Concrete Allgemeinheit, VI. *e.*

Dasein, I, II. *b*, VI. *a.*
Denken, II. *b,* VI. *d.*
Ding, II. *b.*

Eigenschaft, II. *b.*
Einheit, III. *a*, IV. *c.*
Einzelnheit, VI. *e.*
Es existirt, VI. *a.*
Es hat Objektivität, VI. *a.*
Es ist, VI. *a.*
Es ist wirklich, VI. *a.*
Etwas, VI. *a.*
Existenz, II. *b,* VI. *b.*

Für sich, V. *e.*
Fürsichsein, V. *e.*

Gedanke, VI. *d.*
Gesetzt, V. *f.*

Gesetztsein, V. *f.*
Grund, VI. *b.*

Idee, II. *b,* VI. *c.*

Logik, II. *b.*

Mitte, VI. *f.*

Negation, VI. *a.*
Negativität, IV. *b,* VI. *c.*
Nichts, VI. *a.*

Objektivität, III. *b,* VI. *c.*

Realität, VI. *a.*
Reflection, II. *b.*
Reines Sein, VI. *a.*
Reine Unmittelbarkeit, V. *a.*

Sein, I, II. *b,* VI. *a.*
Schluss, II. *b,* VI. *f.*
Setzen, V. *f.*
Sich-Bestimmung, VI. *e.*
Subjekt-Objekt, VI. *c.*
Subjektiver und objektiver Begriff, VI. *d.*
Subjektivität, III. *b.*
Substantialität, VI. *b.*

Totalität, VI. *b.*

Uebergang, III. *a.*
Unmittelbar, III. *b,* IV. *a,* V.
Unmittelbarkeit, III. *a.*
Urtheil, II. *b,* VI. *f.*

Vermitteln, IV. *a, c,* V.
Vermittelung, IV. *b.*
Vernünftig, VI. *a.*

Wahrheit, VI. *c.*
Wesen, VI. *b.*
Wirklich, VI. *a.*
Wirklichkeit, I, VI. *b.*

Heliotropism : see TROPISM.

Hell [AS. *helan*, to hide]: Ger. *Hölle* ; Fr. *enfer* ; Ital. *inferno.* The place where lost sinners abide, suffering endless punishment, and keeping company with the devil and with devils.

Like many other words which have gathered an import that is the result of the associations of centuries, the term hell is commonly used without any very exact conception of its meaning ; it is taken symbolically. To gain further information, one turns naturally to the Scriptures. There, the word hell, with all its mediaeval materialistic associations, has been used to translate no less than three widely different terms. These are :—(1) The Hebrew *Sheol*, with its Greek equivalent HADES (q.v.) ; for this, hell in its modern significance is no fair translation. (2) The Greek Τάρταρος, for which, once more, hell is no proper equivalent, Τάρταρος being the place to which rebel immortals have been consigned, or where the corrupt are pent up for ever. (3) The Greek Gehenna (Γέεννα), the place where the impenitent suffer the penalties they have brought upon themselves. Gehenna is associated with the 'Valley of the children of Hinnom,' a place connected traditionally with defilement, foulness, and corruption. For this term hell furnishes a fair enough equivalent, because there can be little doubt that, in the centuries preceding Jesus, this valley came to be associated in popular Jewish usage with the place where irrevocable vengeance overtook the wicked.

The clause in the Apostles' Creed—' He descended into hell '—must be taken in connection with this subject. It is probably a late addition to this symbol ; and, having little Scripture warrant, it has been interpreted very variously. The Greek Church teaches that the human soul of Christ descended into hell to preach the gospel for the redemption of those who were there on account of original sin. The Roman Catholic Church teaches that the God-Man made the descent in order to release the 'saints of Israel.' The Lutherans hold that the God-Man descended on the morning of the Resurrection only (the interval since death having been passed in Paradise), and for the purpose of pronouncing sentence on sin. The Reformed theologians regarded the expression as wholly figurative, and as indicating the sufferings which Christ endured through the crucifixion. In other words, the phrase merely emphasized Christ's humiliation in the state of death. Others, like Schleiermacher and the Wesleyans, hold that the doctrine is without scriptural warrant. The details of the journey and sojourn are to be found in the extraordinary 'Gospel of Nicodemus.' Similar stories, it may be noted, are current in other religions.

It is well to remember that, on all the matters discussed under this head, the most striking feature of Scripture is its silence. Consequently, philosophical discussion of the subject must be based more on the ideas of the destiny of mankind formulated at various periods and by various races than upon documentary evidence. See ESCHATOLOGY, and cf. HEAVEN.

Literature: PFLEIDERER, Philos. of Religion (Eng. trans.), iv. 154 f.; ALGER, Crit. Hist. of the Doctrine of a Future Life; ATZBERGER, Eschatologie; KLIEFOTH, Eschatologie; DELITZSCH, Bib. Psychol. (Eng. trans.); KABISCH, Die Eschat. d. Paulus. On the descent into hell: PFLEIDERER, loc. cit., and iii. 101; PEARSON, Exposition of the Creed; KÖNIG, Lehre v. Christi Höllenfahrt; SCHWEIZER, Hinabgefahren z. Hölle als Mythus ohne bibl. Begründung; BOYER, (Amer.) Luth. Quart. (1894).   (R.M.W.)

Hellenistic (Civilization, &c.) or Hellenism [Gr. Ἑλληνιστής, an imitator of the Greeks]: Ger. *hellenistisch*; Fr. *hellénistique*; Ital. *ellenizzante, Ellenismo*. (1) The term characterizing the composite civilization which flourished in the lands round the Mediterranean, but particularly in Egypt and Syria, from the time of Alexander the Great.

It was composite because it consisted in the junction of Greek with oriental influences and characteristics. One aspect of it is of supreme importance for philosophy of religion—the influence of Greek civilization upon the Jews, and the results of this. A juster appreciation of the subject—its circumstances and consequences—has become possible only during the last generation, and is still in progress. Its prime importance may be gathered from the fact that, notwithstanding the lamentable destruction of many of the monuments of Graeco-Jewish literature, three of them remain practically unimpaired. Those are the Greek translation of the Hebrew Scriptures, known as the Septuagint; the writings of Philo of Alexandria; and the New Testament books. Hellenistic civilization is therefore hardly to be overestimated for the understanding of the rise and early history of

Christianity, as well as for the religious and spiritual condition of the world into which Jesus was born. Possibly, it may not be inapposite to add that few fields offer richer material to the student.

(2) The name Hellenistic is applied also to the Greek idiom or diction which sprang up when the Jews came into contact with Hellenic civilization. In contradistinction to the Romans, the Jews came by Greek rather through commerce than through literature; hence, to a large extent, the formal defects incident to their use of the Greek language. Something must also be set down to the changes which had taken place in the language itself under pressure of the universalism of Alexander. Hebrew, further, reacted on Greek; and from these influences, along with others of less moment, sprang the language and style of which the New Testament is the chief monument, and the Septuagint and Philo the great historical exemplars.

Literature: For (1): SCHÜRER, Hist. of the Jewish People in the Time of Christ (Eng. trans.), giving full literature. For (2): REUSS, Hist. of the New Testament (Eng. trans.), giving full literature.   (R.M.W.)

Helmholtz, Hermann von. (1821–94.) Born at Potsdam, Prussia, and educated for military surgery. He received his Ph.D. degree from Berlin University, 1842, and became surgeon in the army; assistant in the anatomical museum at Berlin; professor of physiology after 1849 at Königsberg, after 1855 at Bonn, and after 1858 at Heidelberg. After 1871 he was professor of physics at Berlin, and in 1888 took charge of the Physikalisch-Technische Reichsanstalt. His fame rests upon valuable contributions to the physiology of the nervous system, to the theory of mathematical physics, and to the psychology of sight and sound. One of the founders of experimental psychology, and one of the most famous scientific men of the 19th century.

Helvétius, Claude Adrien. (1715–71.) A French philosopher, an Encyclopedist, born and died in Paris. Educated at the College of Louis le Grand, and prepared by an uncle for a career as financier, in 1738, through the queen, he received the lucrative position of farmer-general, and later became chamberlain of the queen's household. Gaining a fortune, he retired to an estate at Voré in 1751, devoting the remainder of his life to the care of his property and to literature. While in Paris he had associated with Diderot,

Holbach, d'Alembert, and the other French ENCYCLOPEDISTS (q. v.).

Hemeralopia [Gr. ἡμέρα, day, + ὄψ, eye]: Ger. *Hemeralopie, Nachtblindheit*; Fr. *héméralopie*; Ital. *emeralopia*. This term and the term nyctalopia are used by different authors in exactly opposite senses, according as the term is regarded as etymologically equivalent to 'seeing at daytime,' or 'blind at daytime'; 'seeing at night-time,' or 'blind at night-time.' Nyctalopia is used by ancient and mediaeval writers as the equivalent of night-blindness. The conditions referred to are described under the terms DAY-BLINDNESS and NIGHT-BLINDNESS (q. v.). See also Hemeralopia and Nyctalopia in Quain's *Dictionary of Medicine*. (J.J.)

Hemi- [Gr. ἡμι-]: Ger. *halb-*; Fr. *hémi-*; Ital. *emi-*. A prefix used to indicate limitation to one half or side (of the body); thus hemianaesthesia denotes the loss of tactile sensibility in one half of the body; hemiplegia, a paralysis affecting one side of the body; hemispasm, a spasm of one side of the body only; hemianopia or hemianopsia, a special form of visual defect affecting the separate halves of the retina; and so on.

The existence of these several forms of defect, limited, and often most sharply limited, to one half of the organ concerned, is an evidence of the dual and symmetrical structure of most portions of the nervous system, and of the frequent special association of the centres in one hemisphere with the organs of one side of the body, either directly or by a decussation of the connecting fibres. (J.J.)

Hemianopsia [Gr. ἡμι-, half, + ἀ privative, + ὄψ, eye]: Ger. *Hemianopsie*; Fr. *hémianopsie*; Ital. *emianopsia*. A complete or partial loss of vision affecting one half of the field of vision, and accordingly one half of each retina. When this defect is described with reference to the field of vision, it is called hemianopsia or hemianopia; when with reference to the retina, hemiopia; thus temporal hemianopsia corresponds to nasal hemiopia.

Hemianopsia results from the manner of connection of the fibres of the two optic nerves with their subcortical and cortical centres. Owing to the great diversity of cases described, as well as of opinions relative to the manner of the central connections, the description must be limited to a few prominent and most generally accepted relations. Lateral homonymous hemianopsia (perhaps the most usual variety, and also termed equi-lateral or corresponding) involves loss of either the right or left half of the field of vision of each eye, while crossed or symmetrical hemianopsia involves loss of vision in either the two temporal or the two nasal halves of the field of vision. If the left optic tract (back of the crura), or these fibres in their further central connections, be injured, right lateral hemianopsia results; and left lateral hemianopsia if the injury is in the right optic tract. Double temporal hemianopsia might result from lesion over the centre of the commissure, or from a lesion of the central connections of each of the fibre systems which cross there, while double nasal hemianopsia (rare) would require a lesion affecting part of each optic tract or parts of their central connections. The differences in symptoms according as the lesion is in the tract, subcortical centres, or cortical centres, are most minute and in part uncertain. Cf. LOCALIZATION (cerebral). Some have supposed that the manner of decussation and central distribution of the fibres of the optic nerves is itself variable in man. The irregular forms consist of combinations of other disturbances in the retinal field with hemianopsia, of affections of the superior or inferior halves of the special quadrants of the field of vision—known as inferior and superior hemianopia—and the like. Tetranopsia signifies symmetrical quadrant defects in the two visual fields.

Hemianopsia of cortical origin in the occipital lobe is apt to occur in connection with MENTAL BLINDNESS (q. v.), this connection being significant of the functional nature of this visual centre. No simple formulation can be given of the relation of lesions in this area when limited to one hemisphere and when present in both, further than that the latter is more certain to produce mental blindness. It is clear that the centre, the incapacitation of which produces hemianaesthesia of the retina, is not the same as that, the injury of which appears as mental blindness. Cases of colour hemianaesthesia without true hemianopsia are not infrequent. Central hemianopsia is extraordinarily distinct when it occurs as a symptom of MIGRAINE (q.v., with figure, after Baldwin), and its progress as a symptom exhibits the development of the central disturbance.

Literature: art. by WILBRAND, in Norris and Oliver's Syst. of Diseases of the Eye, ii. 189–315 (with references); ROSS, Nerv. Diseases, i. 382 ff.; GOWERS, Nerv. Diseases, 145–62; Wood's Ref. Handb. of the Med.

Sci., sub verbo; BALDWIN, Hemianopsia in Migraine, Science (May 4, 1900). (J.J.)

Hemiparesis: see PARALYSIS.

Hemiplegia: see PARALYSIS.

Hemming, Nicolaus. (1518–1600.) A Danish philosophical writer, a pupil of Melanchthon.

Hemorrhage [Gr. αἷμα, blood, + ῥαγάς, a burst]: Ger. *Blutaustritt, Blutfluss*; Fr. *hémorragie*; Ital. *emorragia*. The flowing of blood from a ruptured blood-vessel. Occurring in the brain—cerebral hemorrhage—it causes apoplexy. The portion of the brain supplied by the ruptured vessel, or affected by pressure of the escaping blood, being suddenly thrown out of function, causes sudden loss of motion, sensation, and consciousness. Cerebral hemorrhage is frequently the cause of hemiplegia, i.e. paralysis of one side of the body. (C.F.H.)

Henotheism [Gr. ἕν, one, + θεός, God]: Ger. *Henotheismus*; Fr. *hénothéisme*; Ital. *enoteismo*. 'The worship of a single god.'

This term was first used by Max Müller in a paper on 'Semitic Monotheism,' which appeared in *The Times* (London) in 1860, to designate what he maintains to be an earlier stage in the history of religion than either Polytheism or Monotheism. 'The primitive intuition of God,' he says, 'was in itself neither monotheistic nor polytheistic, though it might become either. . . . Polytheism must everywhere have been preceded by a more or less unconscious theism. In no language does the plural exist before the singular. The primitive intuition of God, and the ineradicable feeling of dependence on God,' cannot however be correctly called monotheistic. 'A belief in God as exclusively One involves a distinct negation of more than one God, and that negation is possible only after the conception, whether real or imaginary, of many gods.' The belief, he says, might be formulated as 'There is a God,' but not yet as 'There is but one God' (see his selected *Essays*, ii). The term is put forward in similar phraseology in a lecture on the Vedas, delivered in 1865, and reprinted in the same volume. He there points out that, though the number of gods invoked in the hymns of the Rig-Veda is very considerable, the poet frequently 'seems to know, for the time being, of one single god only. In the momentary vision of the poet his divinity is not limited by the thought of any other god.' See also *Physical Religion*, 180–1. (A.S.P.P.)

A similar point of view is to be found in Schelling's *Philosophie der Mythologie*, 6te Vorles., under the term 'relative monotheism.' (K.G.)

Heraclitus. Born about 500 B.C. at Ephesus, Asia Minor. A Greek philosopher of noble birth. He took no part in public affairs, refusing, it is said, positions of honour and influence which were offered to him. Known to have written one work, *On Nature*, fragments of which have come down to us. He is called Heraclitus the Dark, because of the obscurity of his teachings. Cf. PRE-SOCRATIC PHILOSOPHY.

Herbart, Johann Friedrich. (1776–1841.) German philosopher, educated in the gymnasium of Oldenburg, his native town, and at Jena under Fichte. For some time he was private tutor in Switzerland. Began lecturing at Göttingen in 1802, and became professor extraordinary, 1805. In 1809 he was called to Königsberg to the chair once held by Kant. Recalled to Göttingen in 1833, he died there. He devoted much attention to pedagogy. See HERBARTIANISM.

Herbartianism (after HERBART, J. F., q.v.): Ger. *Herbart'sche Lehre*; Fr. *Herbartianisme*; Ital. *Herbartianismo*. Philosophical, psychological, and pedagogical views due to or much influenced by Herbart.

The Herbartian Metaphysics. Herbart's conception of metaphysics is a conscious return to the type of solution found in Aristotle; except that it goes further back and lays under contribution something of the method of Socrates (cf. SOCRATIC METHOD). The first task of metaphysics, on his view, is to 'rectify' and justify concepts. This can be done only by an adequate criticism, both of thought and of experience. Only on the basis of patient criticism and mutual adjustment of meanings can philosophy proceed at all. The true question is: What must we think about cause, self, change, reality, God, &c., that our thoughts may be consistent and our lives true? Knowledge cannot, in the last analysis, contradict experience; for experience, in the last analysis, is knowledge. So the real must ultimately be reached through such knowledge as is found to be the full teaching of experience, interpreted consistently with itself. On this basis and by this method Herbart reached his doctrine of atoms or 'reals,' which had the properties both of objective existence and of presentation—a view which is, in the work of other thinkers, also the historical outcome of such a conception of philosophy and its method, as e.g. the

468

'atomism' of Leibnitz and the 'real beings' of Lotze. Metaphysics therefore builds itself upon all science, and takes light from every experiential—as well as from every rational—source (revised quotation from the writer's article 'Metaphysics,' in *Johnson's Universal Cyc.*, new ed., 1894). (J.M.B.)

The Herbartian Psychology. As the title of his great work (*Psychol. als Wiss.*, &c., cited below) indicates, Herbart's psychology is founded on the threefold basis of metaphysics, mathematics, and experience. It is its foundation in experience which gives it abiding interest and value. Experience yields at once a point of departure and the means of verifying hypotheses. The point of departure is found in the problematic and sometimes contradictory character of certain results of introspection. The chief instance of a datum of introspection involving an inner contradiction is found in the fact of self-consciousness. This is contradictory, because it implies at once the sameness and the duality of subject, and also because the self of which we are conscious has no content apart from particular states, of thinking, willing, &c., and yet it cannot be identified with these particular states, being the common centre to which they are all referred. Psychology must give such an account of the nature and genesis of self-consciousness as will remove these contradictions. But experience not only yields such points of departure for the framing of psychological hypotheses, it also supplies the means of verifying them. Psychological theories must be tested by their power to explain the actual facts of mental life as they are found in concrete experience.

Herbart derives from his metaphysics the conception of the soul as being intrinsically a simple unchanging being without any plurality of states, activities, or powers. In its actual working as a psychological principle, this conception translates itself (1) into the denial of innate ideas or faculties, (2) into certain fundamental laws of the interaction of psychical states. All psychological explanation is based on the interaction of certain ultimate states of the soul, which arise in it through its various relations to other simple beings ('reals'), and are called by Herbart presentative activities.

Apart from the changes which they undergo through their action on each other, these presentative activities are contents of consciousness or presentations. Presentations may be entirely alike in quality—as, for instance, my sensation of green yesterday and my sensation of the same green to-day; or they may be entirely disparate in quality—e. g. sweetness and redness; in both these cases they merge in a single complex presentation or conscious presentative activity. If, on the other hand, they are neither identical nor disparate in quality—as, for example, the colours red and green—they are more or less contrary, and for that reason they tend to exclude each other from consciousness. When one presentative activity is completely excluded from consciousness or 'arrested' by others of contrary quality, it remains in existence as a tendency to become conscious. It will become a conscious presentation so soon as the arresting conditions are removed, just as a bent spring of perfect elasticity will recover its original position on removal of the pressure by which it is held down. But arrest need not be complete. The mutual antagonism of presentations may result only in their diminished intensity—the partial reduction of conscious to unconscious presentative activity. If we suppose a case in which only two simple presentations are in conflict, neither of them will be completely arrested. A certain 'sum of arrest' is distributed between them in the inverse ratio of their respective intensities. When the sum of arrest is distributed among a larger number of presentative activities only a few can escape complete arrest. Hence the narrowness of consciousness, which is thus for Herbart not a mere empirical fact, but a necessary consequence of his fundamental assumptions.

Those presentative activities which are in consciousness at any moment are said to be above the threshold, and those which are unconscious are said to be below the threshold. Throughout our mental life, presentative activities are continually rising and sinking. They are sinking in so far as they gradually lose conscious intensity owing to arrest, and so approach or pass below the threshold; they are rising when they gradually increase in conscious intensity or gradually approach the threshold of consciousness owing to the removal of arresting conditions.

We have so far spoken of arrest as if it concerned only single simple presentations. We must now consider it in connection with the union of presentations. For Herbart the union of presentations is an alliance against antagonistic forces. The united presentations resist as a whole the arrest of any one of them by sharing in the 'sum of arrest,' and for the same reason the rise of any of them above the threshold tends to raise the others.

The necessary and sufficient condition of union is co-presentation—the simultaneous existence of presentative activities above the threshold. Not only disparate and qualitatively identical, but also contrary presentations unite with each other.

The union of disparate presentations is called complication, that of contrary or qualitatively identical presentations is called fusion. Fusion takes place between the presentation residua which remain after the partial arrest of presentative activities. It also takes place while the process of arrest is still going on.

It is important for the Herbartian theory of reproduction that complications and fusions are formed between presentative activities only in so far as they are simultaneously above the threshold. If a has entered into union with b, and both a and b afterwards sink below the threshold, the subsequent emergence of a into consciousness will tend to raise b also into consciousness, but only in that degree of conscious intensity which b possessed at the moment of its original co-presentation with a. When b has reached this degree of intensity it ceases to receive further support from a. On the other hand, the conscious intensity of a when the union was formed determines the strength of the support which it gives to b. Herbart explains from this point of view the fact that 'in a series of associated presentations, A, B, C, D, E, such as the movements made in writing the words of a poem learned by heart, or the simple letters of the alphabet themselves, we find that each member recalls its successor, but not its predecessor' (Ward, *Encyc. Brit.*, art. 61). The Herbartian explanation is as follows: in the original experiences A first rises into full conscious intensity, and it is then gradually arrested by the occurrence of B. When B has risen to its full height above the threshold, A has sunk towards it; similarly, when C has attained its maximum of conscious intensity, B has become obscured, and A has become still more obscured; the same holds for D and E. Now, suppose the whole series to have passed from consciousness, and that on a subsequent occasion C recurs. The fusion of C with A and B took place when C itself was at its maximum intensity; and its tendency to revive A and B will be proportionate in strength to this intensity: on the other hand, A and B were both on the wane at the time of co-presentation, A being nearer the threshold than B. C will therefore reproduce A and B in a state of obscuration, and the revived A will be more obscured than the revived B. On the other hand, since C was co-presented in its maximum intensity both with A and B, it will reinstate these simultaneously and rapidly. Thus there will be no successive emergence of B and A into full distinctness, but only a simultaneous reproduction of them in different degrees of obscurity. D and E, on the contrary, will emerge successively into full conscious intensity. For D had reached its maximum when it fused with A, B, and C, and A, B, and C will therefore tend to reinstate it in full intensity. But since A, B, and C were waning at the time of co-presentation, they will reinstate D slowly and gradually, and for a similar reason they will tend to reinstate E still more slowly.

This is a good example of the way in which Herbart applies his abstract principles to the elucidation of psychological matter of fact. In this instance his own ingenuity is perhaps more conspicuous than any actual service-rendering to psychological theory. But at other points his explanations are more felicitous, and have, in fact, proved epoch-making. In particular we may refer to his account of the genesis of spatial and temporal presentation as distinctive forms of serial order due to different modes of fusion, to the doctrine of presentation masses and of APPERCEPTION (q.v.), and to his classical investigation of the nature and development of SELF - CONSCIOUSNESS (q. v.).

The doctrine of apperception variously modified and improved has become the common property of modern psychologists; and all modern accounts of the stages in the growth of the consciousness of self are under a deep debt, recognized or unrecognized, to Herbart. His theories of the origin of temporal and spatial presentations are in many respects highly suggestive; and though on the whole they must be regarded as failures, it ought to be remembered that they are the first systematic attempts to solve these problems.

The most noteworthy among those who can be called in the strict sense disciples of Herbart in psychology are T. Waitz, M. Drobisch, W. Volkmann (v. Volkmar). The *Zeitschrift für exacte Philosophie* was, until recently, the recognized organ of the school. It has now given place to the *Zeitschrift für Philosophie und Pädagogik*. Steinthal and Lazarus have applied the Herbartian doctrine of apperception to the psychology of language and of primitive thought. (G.F.S.)

With Herbart's name is also associated one

of the most fruitful movements in modern educational theory, and to this the term Herbartianism is also applied (cf. PEDAGOGICS). In this, his theory of apperception is the central doctrine. The principal writers of the school are Ziller, Rein, and Lange. Herbart's own pedagogical work is *The Application of Psychology to the Science of Education* (Eng. trans., 1898). (J.M.B.)

Literature: Herbart's complete works have been edited by G. HARTENSTEIN (latest ed. in 13 vols., 1883–93). His most important psychological writings are Psychologische Untersuchungen über die Stärke einer Vorstellung (1812; Werke, vii), Ueber die Möglichkeit und Nothwendigkeit Mathematik auf Psychologie anzuwenden (1822; Werke, vii), Psychologie als Wissenschaft neu gegründet auf Erfahrung, Metaphysik und Mathematik (1824–5; Werke, v, vi). The Lehrbuch zur Psychologie (1st ed. in 1813, 2nd ed. revised and enlarged in 1834; Werke, v; also in Eng. trans.) gives a brief account of his psychological doctrine adapted for beginners. For general accounts of Herbart see the histories of modern philosophy, especially HÖFFDING; on the psychology, F. A. LANGE, Grundlegung d. math. Psychol. (1865); G. DUMDEY, Herbart's Verhältniss z. engl. Associationspsychol. (1890); STOUT, Mind, 1898, 321, 473, and 1899, 1, 353; RIBOT, Ger. Psychol. of To-day (Eng. trans.), 24 ff.; ZIEHEN, Verhältniss d. Herbart'schen Psychol. z. physiol.-exper. Psychol. (1900); on the pedagogics, DE GARMO, Herbart and the Herbartians. (G.F.S.–J.M.B.)

Herbert, Edward, of Cherbury. (1581–1648.) Born in Montgomery castle in northern Wales, and educated at Oxford, he became knight of the Order of the Bath in 1603. In 1608 he journeyed to France, and in 1610 to Flanders, where he joined the army of Prince Moritz of Oranien as a volunteer. After several years spent in Germany, Switzerland, and Italy he became (1616) emissary to the French court, and peer of Ireland in 1625. In 1629 Charles I made him peer of England with the title Baron of Cherbury. He is an important figure in the history of English DEISM (q. v.).

Herder, Johann Gottfried von. (1744–1803.) An important figure in modern German literature. As a philosopher, he belongs with J. G. Hamann, Jacobi, and others, who vindicate feeling or faith against reason, which Kant had chiefly emphasized.

Heredity [Lat. *hereditas*]: Ger. *Vererbung*; Fr. *hérédité*; Ital. *eredità*. (1) Organic or physical: the transmission from parent to offspring of certain distinguishing characters of structure or function.

(2) Social: the process of social transmission; that by which individuals of successive generations accommodate to a continuous social environment, thus producing TRADITION (q. v.). Suggested by J. Mark Baldwin (*Amer. Naturalist*, June, July, 1896). Cf. also *Soc. and Eth. Interpret.* (1st ed., 1897).

(1) Organic. Many of the general facts of organic heredity have long been known. The theory of evolution has opened up fresh questions with regard to its nature, origin, and limitations. Of late the question has been raised whether ACQUIRED CHARACTERS (q.v.) are thus transmitted. As in the case of so many biological problems, the discussion has been transferred from the organism to the cell. According to the CELL THEORY (q.v., 7), there is a continuity of cell life; and, in REPRODUCTION (q.v.), this continuity is maintained in the germ-plasm; cf. the diagram given under CELL. Any transmission of acquired characters must be by some mode of influence of the body-cells on the germ-cells, the exact nature of which is at present unknown. Assuming that such influence of other than a general kind (e.g. in nutrition, poisoning, &c.) is unproven, and omitting the cases of transference of microbes as in some diseases (e. g. syphilis), there remains the question of the nature of hereditary transmission in the germ-cells. How do the characters of the adult lie enfolded in the fertilized ovum? And how do they become unfolded in the course of development? It is generally admitted that the IDIOPLASM (q.v.) contains the hereditary substance which in some way controls cell-development. According to one hypothesis there are present in the sexual cells minute germinal representatives of all the parts of the adult; of these the 'gemmules' of Darwin are derived from all parts of the organism (cf. PANGENESIS); the 'biophores' and 'determinants' of Weismann belong to the germ-plasm alone.

According to a second great hypothesis, the differentiation results from the mutual influence of the cells, the nature of each being determined by the environment made by the others. Other hypotheses combine, in different degrees, the conception of nuclear distribution and environing influence. But we are still far from anything like an ultimate solution of the problem. (C.LL.M.,E.B.P.,J.M.B.)

It is now evident, however, that characters are inherited, not so much from, as through, the parent organisms, and that the reason why the offspring resembles the parent is that they both develop from a substance of essentially the same structure and composition, held to be identically the same by those who advocate the doctrine of the 'continuity of germ-plasm.'　　　　　　　(E.S.G.)

The question of the origin of heredity has been recently discussed, and taken form in connection with the researches into VARIATION (q. v.). Heredity giving more or less close lack of variation — what is called 'breeding true' to stock—from parent to offspring, is the opposite of variability, which is departure from the 'true' or like. It has generally been assumed that heredity—at least in the simple form seen in cell-division, the so-called daughter-cells being parts of the original mother-cells—was an original property of living matter, and variation from the true was the thing to account for. Recently, however, the theory has been advanced by Bailey (*Plant Breeding*, 1895, and especially *Survival of the Unlike*, 1896) and Williams (*Geol. Biology*; *Science*, July 16, 1897; *Amer. Naturalist*, Nov., 1898), and advocated independently by Adam Sedgwick (*Nature*, Sept. 21, 1899), that variation is normal, and heredity acquired by the restriction and limiting of variation to the extent seen in the relative amount of 'breeding true' that is actually found in nature. It would seem *a priori* more reasonable to ask why such an unstable compound as protoplasm, acted upon by a complex environment, should not vary (i. e. should have heredity), than the reverse. And, moreover, the complicated apparatus necessary for sexual reproduction and transmission, itself showing the wide variations it does in different organisms in different life conditions, must have been acquired, even though it be the direct descendant of the earliest cellular multiplication.

A recent more exact statistical treatment of heredity has been made by Galton and Pearson, the results leading to the formulation of GALTON'S LAW of ancestral inheritance (q. v.). Pearson, who has worked out quantitative mathematical methods of treating vital phenomena, finds the solution of three great problems essential to an exact science of evolution — VARIATION (q. v.), SELECTION (q. v.), and heredity (see a series of papers, 'Mathematical Contributions to the Theory of Evolution,' *Proc. Roy. Soc.*, 1894 ff.,

summarized in *The Chances of Death* and in *Grammar of Science*, 2nd ed., 1900).

The evidence for and against the inheritance of acquired characters, in cases of sexual reproduction, is about as follows :—There are no clear and unambiguous cases of transmission of specific modifications. The arguments for such transmission are largely presumptive, based upon the requirements of the theory of EVOLUTION (q. v.). Of such arguments the following seem to be strongest. (1) Incomplete or imperfect instincts—together with complex instincts, which must at some time have been imperfect—cannot be due to NATURAL SELECTION (q. v.); for their early stages would involve partial correlations of movement of no use to the animal. Selectionists meet this by saying that (*a*) the organism as a whole must be considered, not the single organs or functions, in the matter of individual survival; (*b*) a certain degree of intelligence usually accompanies and supplements such instincts; (*c*) the intelligence, together with individual accommodations of all sorts, screen the variations which occur in the direction of the particular function, and so allow its evolution under natural selection (see ORGANIC SELECTION); (*d*) many of the instances cited under this head are not congenital characters at all, but are functions re-acquired by the young of each succeeding generation (see TRADITION).

(2) Paleontologists find bony structures whose initial and early stages are thought to have had no utility, and appeal is made generally of the so-called non-useful stages of useful organs. This is conceded to be the gravest objection now current to the universal applicability of natural selection. It is met— when urged as giving presumptive evidence of the transmission of acquired characters—by saying : (*a*) that it proves too much ; for the bony structures are least subject to modification by external influences, and, if such inheritance appear in them, it should appear more strongly in other structures where we do not find evidence of it ; (*b*) that even if such an objection hold against natural selection, still some unknown auxiliary factor may be operative; (*c*) that actual utility can be pointed out in most cases, and may be fairly assumed in others ; (*d*) organic or indirect selection again has application here, as supplementary to natural selection; (*e*) the principle of 'change of function' (Functionswechsel ; see A. Dohrn, *Der Ursprung der Wirbelthiere und das Princip des Functionswechsels*, 1875) is cited, according to which, in such 'non-useful' stages,

the organ in question served another and useful function.

Other objections of a general sort—such as that geological time is not sufficient for so slow a process as evolution by natural selection, that small variations could not produce such large differences, that variations are not sufficiently numerous nor sufficiently wide in distribution—are considered by selectionists to be mainly of an *a priori* character, even as objections to natural selection, and, hence, to offer no positive ground whatever for belief in the inheritance of acquired characters.

The advocates of the hypothesis of Lamarckian inheritance often fail to distinguish between the effects of the general influences of the environment upon the whole organism —e.g. malnutrition, toxic agents such as alcohol, &c.—and the specific modifications of particular parts and functions, arising from mutilation, use, the stimulation of particular organs, &c. The former are not denied by selectionists; but they claim that the sort of effect thus produced upon the offspring is rather a disproof than a proof of Lamarckism. For example, the effect of alcoholic excess is not an increased tendency to drink alcoholic beverages—the tendency itself shown in the children is accounted for as already congenital to the parent—but certain general deteriorating or degenerative changes in the nervous system or constitution of the offspring, as in hysteria, scurvy, idiocy, malformations, &c., which the parent did not have at all. Furthermore, the mechanism required to accomplish the two sorts of effect respectively are widely different. The general effects of the first sort upon the offspring are due simply to the influences which work upon the organism as a whole, through the ordinary metabolic physiological processes. But to accomplish the transmission of specific modifications of particular parts, a most complex special mechanism would be necessary, whereby the part affected in the parent would impart some sort of special modification to the germ-cells, which would again cause the same modification of the same part in the offspring (see the address of Sedgwick before the British Association, in *Nature*, 1899). It is suggested also by Stout that such a complex mechanism of transmission would be a highly specialized adaptation, and if it be necessary to Lamarckian heredity, it would itself have to be accounted for without such heredity, which is what the Lamarckians declare impossible. For a recommendation as to terms see TRANSMISSION.

Again, it has been argued (Weismann, Baldwin) that if the Lamarckian principle were in general operation we should expect to find many functions, such as speech in man, reduced to the stereotyped form of reflexes or animal instincts (see, however, on the other side, as regards this particular function, Romanes, *Darwin and after Darwin*, iii).

The philosophical defence of the Lamarckian principle is usually made from the point of view of teleology, that is, of getting determinate evolution, which is, in some form, the realization of a purpose or end. It is thought that through the accommodations secured by individual animals—provided they be inherited—a determinate direction of evolution toward such a realization is secured; while, on the other hand, the principle of natural selection, working upon so-called fortuitous variations, is 'blind' and mechanical (cf. Ward, *Naturalism and Agnosticism*; so also Wundt). There seem to be certain confusions lurking in this view. In the first place, it confuses teleology, in the process of evolution, with purpose in the individual. There are two errors here. (1) It is not seen that the evolution process might realize an end or ideal without aid from the individual's efforts or conscious processes. Indeed, even on the Lamarckian principle, most of the inherited modifications would not be directly due to the individual's purpose or conscious effort, and so the purpose of the whole could not be interpreted in terms of the teleology of the individual; for those who maintain a general teleological view in cosmology must hold that the cosmic evolution as a whole, and not merely biological evolution, is in some sense purposive. (2) It is not seen that the reverse is also true, i.e. that in spite of purpose in the individual, together with the inheritance of acquired modifications, the outcome might, on the whole, be the same as that due to simple probability with the natural selection of favourable variations from a great many cases. This has been shown, in fact, to be the case in recent investigations in MORAL STATISTICS (q.v.); e.g. suicide follows the laws of probability, and varies with climate, food supply, &c., in a way which can be plotted in a curve, despite the fact that each suicide chooses to kill himself. That is, the result is as regular and as liable to exact prediction, if we take a large population, as are deaths from disease or accident, or other 'natural' events in which purpose and choice have no part. In such cases, indeed, we have results which are as subject to law and as definite as those of mechanics, although the data are teleological. This case and the reverse, indicated above, show the fallacy of claiming that the exercise of individual purpose and the teleology of evolution must go together.

But there is another supposition open to objection in the view which requires Lamarckian heredity in order to secure teleology in evolution; the position that natural selection, working on so-called fortuitous or chance variations, is 'blind' and non-teleological. It has been found that biological phenomena—variations in particular—follow the definite law of PROBABILITY (q. v.); in short, that there is no such thing as the really fortuitous or unpredictable. Natural selection, therefore, working upon variations, themselves subject to law, gives a possible method of realizing a cosmic design, if such exists, just as adequate as any other natural process subject to law. Combining this with the result mentioned above, that even moral events are found to be subject to law when taken in large numbers—thus including events in which individual purpose plays a part—we are driven to the conclusion that the law of probabilities upon which natural selection rests is the vehicle of teleology in evolution—lawful replacing fortuitous variations.

A good illustration may be seen in the use made of vital statistics in life INSURANCE (q. v.). We pay a rate based on the calculation of the probability of life, and thus by observing this law realize the teleological purpose of providing for our children more effectively, though indirectly, than if we each carried our money in a bag around our necks, and gradually added to it of our savings. And furthermore, the insurance company is a great teleological agency, both for us and for itself; for it secures dividends for its stockholders also on the basis of charges adjusted to the 'chances' of life drawn from the mortality tables. Why is it not a reasonable view that the cosmic purpose—if we may call it so—works by similar, but more adequate, knowledge of the whole—*whether in conformity to or in contravention of our individual striving*—and so secures its results? Can such results be called blind or unteleological?

Indeed, we may go further, and say that this working out of cosmic purpose through some law of the whole rather than through the individual is necessary to teleology as such. In biology the law of REGRESSION (q.v.) provides just such a 'governor' or

regulator of the process. According to it, individuals which depart widely from the mean are not able to transmit their characters fully; but there is a regression towards a value which represents the mean attainment of the species up to date. Thus evolution is kept consistently to a determinate direction, and not violently wrenched by what might be called cosmic caprice. So it is necessary that the 'choice,' the capricious will, of the individual should be neutralized, and a consistent plan carried out despite the uncalculable variations of our private purposes. This principle of 'regression' or 'conservation of type' holds whether the inheritance of acquired modifications be true or not—whether the effects of personal effort and purpose be transmitted or not—and as it deals with all the cases, variations and modifications alike, the purposeful deeds of the individual can, in any case, be only a factor of minor importance to the result. Its real importance would depend upon its relation to the whole group of agencies entering into heredity. In so far as this fact should be in a direction divergent from that of the movement in general, it would, by the law of regression, be ineffectual; in so far as it should be in harmony with it, it would be unnecessary and unimportant; although in the latter case, no doubt, the Lamarckian factor, if real, would accelerate biological evolution. Cf. TELEOLOGY.

Special topics are GALTON'S LAW (q. v.) of ancestral inheritance, REGRESSION (q. v.), VARIATION (q. v.), and ATAVISM (q. v.).

Literature (organic): the best general work is DELAGE, Structure du Protoplasma, containing full literary lists to 1895, continued annually as the Année Biologique. See lists also in the annual Zoological Record, the Anatomischer Jahresbericht, and in WILSON, The Cell in Devel. and Inheritance. Recent general works are W. K. BROOKS, The Foundations of Zool. (1899); HEADLEY, The Problems of Evolution (1901). Other works are cited under BIOLOGICAL SCIENCES, ACQUIRED CHARACTERS, and the topics cited above. More psychological references occur in the literature of COMPARATIVE PSYCHOLOGY, INSTINCT, and PLAY. See also BIBLIOG. G, 1, *f.* (Social): see SOCIAL EVOLUTION.

(J.M.B., E.B.P., C.I.L.M., G.F.S.)

Heresy and **Heterodoxy** [Gr. αἵρεσις, selection]: Ger. *Häresie, Ketzerei*; Fr. *hérésie*; Ital. *eresia*. Dissent from the fundamental dogmas of the Church, springing up within its own membership. Heterodoxy, though often used as synonymous, has not the same ecclesiastical reference. It implies, rather, opposition to generally received opinions (e. g. in economics); when applied to religious matters, it often imports departure from the usual interpretation of doctrine or dogma— departure which yet does not amount to heresy.

As a rule, in the New Testament the word heresy indicates merely a party (see, e. g., Acts xv, xxiv, xxvi, xxviii), though occasionally it is used to designate doctrinal error (Titus iii. 10; 2 Pet. ii. 1). When Christianity had embodied itself in a formal organization, heresy came to mean dissent from or opposition to the doctrine deemed necessary to salvation. Till the time of Augustine, the name was applied chiefly to those who persisted in error, particularly if they were moved by enmity to the Church. The terrible severity of the Church towards heresy in later times is well known. When the civil power was called upon to assist the ecclesiastical in inflicting punishment, bigotry was at the height of its prosperity. The so-called 'liberal' theologian is the ordinary representative of heterodoxy. See ARIANISM, GNOSTICISM, MONTANISM, and PELAGIANISM.

Literature: the works (against various heretics) of the following Fathers: JUSTIN MARTYR, IRENAEUS, TERTULLIAN, CLEMENT of Alexandria, HIPPOLYTUS, EPIPHANIUS, PHILASTRIUS of Brescia, AUGUSTINE, THEODORET; HILGENFELD, Ketzergesch. d. Urchristenthums; HAHN, Ketzer im Mittelalter; BLUNT, Dict. of Sects, Heresies, and Eccles. Parties. (R.M.W.)

Heritage: see INHERITANCE, HEREDITY, and GALTON'S LAW (of ancestral inheritance).

Hermaphrodite [Gr. Ἑρμῆς, Apollo, + Ἀφροδίτη, Venus]: Ger. *Zwitter*; Fr. *hermaphrodite*; Ital. *ermafrodito*. Having the essential organs of both sexes united in the same individual (as in the earthworm); a condition common amongst the invertebrates, often found as a teratological feature, but amongst vertebrates found only very exceptionally in some fishes and Cyclostomes (Myxine and Bdellostoma).

It is often employed for abnormal monstrosities in man and higher animals with malformations of the sexual organs, representing double sex. (C.LL.M.—E.S.G.)

Hermeneutics [Gr. ἑρμηνεύειν, to interpret]: Ger. *Hermeneutik*; Fr. *herméneutique*; Ital. *ermeneutica*. That department of exegetical theology which treats of the science or theory of literary interpretation.

It lays down the principles which exegesis applies. In early Christian times the schools of Alexandria and of Antioch were ranged against one another in such hermeneutics as then existed. The former employed the allegorical, the latter the literal (or emphatic), method. It cannot be said that great progress was made beyond either of these schools before the Reformation. Flacius (1567) and Glassius (1629) are the first scientific hermeneutists. They were followed by Bengel (1740), Ernesti (1765), and especially by Winer (1822). Among later hermeneutists Hermann and his school may be mentioned. See EXEGESIS.

Literature: IMMER, Hermeneutics of the New Testament (Eng. trans.); S. DAVIDSON, Sacred Hermeneutics; HOFMANN, Bib. Hermeneutik; TERRY, Bib. Hermeneutics. (R.M.W.)

Hermes, Georg. (1775–1831.) A German teacher of philosophical theology. Educated at Rheine and at Münster, he became a teacher in both the gymnasium and the university at Münster. From 1820 until his death he was professor of theology at Bonn. J. E. Erdmann classes him as a semi-Kantian, because he insisted that in faith we have presentiments of the nature of being-in-itself, without being able definitely to conceive it.

Hermes Trismegistus. Hermes is Greek for Thoth, the name of an Egyptian god, who is said to be the author of the sacred books of the Egyptians. The name Trismegistus is probably from an epithet attached to the name Thoth in the Nubian hieroglyphic writings, meaning 'thrice-great.' These sacred books being lost, others were prepared in Greek, two or three centuries afterwards, purporting to be reproductions of the originals.

These grew at the hands of unknown authors to include a very considerable literature. It consists of a synthesis of Neo-Platonic, Judaic, and cabalistic ideas, which is intended as a substitute for Christianity. Some passages are almost Christian, but contain also mystic numerical symbolisms of Egyptian, and mystical elements of Philonic, origin. (R.M.W.)

Hero-worship: Ger. *Heldenverehrung*; Fr. *culte des héros*; Ital. *culto degli eroi*. Religious exercises directed towards prominent individual persons.

Inspection of primitive religions proves that many objects are worshipped—stones, fire, trees, and so forth. Among these objects are men—the departed, ancestors, saints, heroes. Hero-worship is difficult to differentiate from ANCESTOR WORSHIP (q. v.). The latter is essentially a private affair; the former, on the contrary, is usually public. If, then, a single ancestor come to be viewed as the progenitor of a large 'corporate' family, and if, in this way, his worship become quasi-public, the path is open for hero-worship. When the ancestor becomes publicly recognized as a 'heros eponymos,' hero-worship ensues. The central fact is that the hero is regarded as being the author or mediator of benefits. Apotheosis and canonization are its ecclesiastical forms.

Literature: see ANCESTOR WORSHIP, and APOTHEOSIS. (R.M.W.)

Heterodoxy: see HERESY.

Heterogamy [Gr. ἕτερος, other, + γάμος, marriage]: Ger. *Generationswechsel*; Fr. *hétérogamie*; Ital. *eterogamia*. See ALTERNATION OF GENERATIONS.

Heterogeneity: see HOMOGENEITY.

Heterolecithal [Gr. ἕτερος, other, + λέκιθος, yolk]: Ger. *heterolekithal*; Fr. *hétérolécithe* (rare—Y.D.); Ital. *eterolecito*. Of the ovum: having unequally distributed yolk. A term proposed by Mark (1892) to include both telolecithal and centrolecithal ova. Cf. HOMOLECITHAL, and CLEAVAGE. (C.LL.M.)

Heteromorphosis [Gr. ἕτερος, other, + μορφή, shape]: Ger. *Heteromorphose*; Fr. *hétéromorphose*; Ital. *eteromorfosi*. The production by some organisms, under the stimulus of external forces, of organs or parts where such do not occur normally.

REGENERATION (q. v.) is the reproduction of parts which have been lost; whereas heteromorphosis is the production of parts unlike those which have been lost, as the replacing of eye-stalks by antennary structures.

If, for example, *Tubularia mesembryanthemum*, a hydroid polyp with stalk, head, and base, have its base and head removed and be then placed in the sand inverted (i. e. with the head end buried), the other end produces a head in a position which is abnormal.

Literature: the term was proposed by LOEB, Untersuchungen zur physiologischen Morphologie der Thiere, Organbildung u. Wachsthum, Heft 122 (1892–3); C. HERBST, Ueber die Regeneration von antennenähnlichen Organen, Arch. f. Entwicklungsmech., ii (1896). (C.LL.M.)

Heteronomy: Ger. *Heteronomie*; *hétéronomie*; Ital. *eteronomia*. See AUTONOMY. (W.R.S.)

Hetero-psychological Ethics: Ger. *hetero-psychologische Ethik* (suggested — K.G.); Fr. *morale hétéro-psychologique* (suggested—

TH.F.); Ital. *morale eteropsicologica* (suggested — E.M.). See IDIO-PSYCHOLOGICAL ETHICS. (W.R.S.)

Heterotelic: see AUTOTELIC, where a recommendation is made (which has been seen and adopted by Hirn, *The Origins of Art*, 1900). (J.M.B.)

Heuristic Method (in education) [Gr. εὑρίσκειν, to find out]: Ger. *heuristische Methode*; Fr. *méthode heuristique*; Ital. *metodo euristico*. A method that stimulates to invention or discovery. See METHOD (in education). (C.DE G.)

Hibernation [Lat. *hibernare*, from *hiems*, winter]: Ger. *Winterschlaf*; Fr. *sommeil hibernal*; Ital. *ibernazione*. The state of torpor in which some animals which inhabit cold or temperate latitudes pass the winter.

Long looked upon as a specially created provision, this peculiar state is now regarded as an adaptation fostered by natural selection.

Literature: art. Hibernation, in Todd's Cyc. of Anat. and Physiol.; WESLEY MILLS, Hibernation and Allied States in Animals, Trans. Roy. Soc. of Canada (1892). (C.LL.M.)

Hickok, Laurens Perseus. (1798–1888.) An American theologian and philosopher, born in Bethel, Conn., educated at Union College. After twelve years of pastoral labour, he became professor of theology in Western Reserve College, 1836, and in Auburn Theological Seminary, 1844. In 1852 he became vice-president, and professor of mental and moral philosophy, in Union College. In 1866 he became president, and retained the position until 1874.

Hierarchy: see CATHOLICISM.

High Treason: Ger. *Hochverrath, Majestätsverbrechen*; Fr. *lèse-majesté*; Ital. *lesa maestà, alto tradimento*. Treason against the sovereign power of the state.

Petit treason, on the contrary, is a violation by a subject of his allegiance to his liege lord, or of the duty of subjection to one to whom services are legally due. In the United States there is no treason but high treason, and it is called simply treason; the nature of the offence being defined by the Constitution. See WAR. The term haute trahison is one of English origin (*Dict. de l'Acad. Franç.*, 'Trahison'). It is also found in early English law books in the Latinized form of *alta proditio* (Cowell's *Interpreter*, Treason).

High treason in English law extends to grave offences against the family or official representatives of the king, e.g. killing one of the justices of his courts.

Literature: LIEBER, On Civil Liberty,

chap. viii; BLACKSTONE, Commentaries on the Laws of England, iv. chap. vi.   (S.E.B.)

Highest Good: Ger. *höchstes Gut*; Fr. *souverain bien*; Ital. *bene supremo*. That which is possessed of highest intrinsic worth, or that which is most worthy of desire.

The term is frequently used to signify the ideal of human conduct. Cf. GOOD, and GOODNESS.   (W.R.S.)

Hilary of Poitiers, Saint. Born near the beginning of the 4th century, died 368 A.D. in Poitiers. Converted about 350, he was made bishop of Poitiers about 353. In 356, for not sanctioning the condemnation of Athanasius, he was banished into Phrygia, but permitted to return in 359. He reached Poitiers in 362. He opposed Arianism constantly and with great vigour.

Hindoo Philosophy: see ORIENTAL PHILOSOPHY (India).

Hinrichs, Hermann Friedrich Wilhelm. (1794–1861.) German philosopher, originally a jurist. Professor of philosophy at Breslau, 1822; at Halle, 1824. He was a disciple of Hegel.

Hipp Chronoscope: see LABORATORY AND APPARATUS, III, C, (1).

Hippias of Elis. A sophist contemporary with Prodicus and Protagoras. See PRE-SOCRATIC PHILOSOPHY (Sophists).

Hippolytus, Romanus. Born about the middle of the 2nd century A.D., in Italy. A pupil of Irenaeus. Banished by the Emperor Severus, he was martyred, probably by drowning. He wrote a work called *Philosophumena*, a refutation of all heresies, in eight books, part of which have been lost.

Histogenesis: see NERVOUS SYSTEM, II.

Histology: see NERVOUS SYSTEM, II.

Histonal Selection: see INTRASELECTION, and cf. SELECTION (in biology).

Historical School (in economics): see ECONOMIC METHOD.

Historism: not in use in Fr. and Ital. Used, mainly in the German Historismus, to denote a spiritual as opposed to a mechanical or naturalistic (sense 2 under NATURALISM) world-view; and more particularly applied to the Hegelian philosophy. Cf. HEGEL's TERMINOLOGY (especially II).   (J.M.B.)

History [Gr. ἱστορία, information, narrative]: Ger. *Geschichte*; Fr. *histoire*; Ital. *storia*. (1) The succession of events through which anything passes; (2) the knowledge of that succession of events; (3) the interpretation and explanation of events in their succession in accordance with general principles of science and philosophy. These are distinguished as (1) the actual history or the facts of history; (2) recorded history, the complete statement of events; and (3) the science or philosophy of history.

Under the second definition, what is historic or recorded in some form of narrative is contrasted with what is prehistoric (Sir D. Wilson) or antecedent to the use of records, though on the first definition the prehistoric still belongs to real history. The so-called traditional or orally transmitted statement of real facts occupies a sort of midway position, and is the subject of much discussion. The question of tradition, however, raises what is really the question of the canons of construction of records out of real history; seeing that an element of tradition or oral reporting is involved in all recording of that which is not the historian's personal experience. An exact science of history would include the application to all testimony of a calculus of probability worked out for 'first-hand' (eye-witness), 'second-hand,' and more remote stages of evidence. The relative absence of the requirement of a precise criterion of the reliability of evidence leaves room for what may be called the historian's equation of credulity; and when combined with the demand for literary treatment, it creates variations which forbid the use of the term science in any exact sense. Cf. the topic immediately following.   (J.M.B.)

History (philosophy of): Ger. *Philosophie der Geschichte, Geschichtsphilosophie (-wissenschaft)*; Fr. *philosophie (science) de l'histoire*; Ital. *filosofia della storia*. The term philosophy of history is used in several different senses: (1) To denote the principiant consideration of the meaning, the methods, and the canons of historical science in general. (2) To denote inquiry into certain highly complex phases and products of historical development—as the history of institutions or of civilization (cf. Guizot, *Hist. de la Civilisation en Europe*), the history of intellectual development (cf. Draper, *The Intellectual Devel. of Europe*), &c. (3) In its stricter meaning, to denote the explanation, from philosophical principles, of historical phenomena at large or the entire course of historical development. See HISTORY (3), and cf. STATE (philosophy of).

The principles of explanation adopted in this last endeavour may be empirical or speculative. Commonly, they include members of both these classes, the emphasis varying with the personal equation of the individual historian and the tenets of the school to which he belongs. The nature of the conclusions reached is also variable, in dependence upon similar causes : illustrations are F. Schlegel, *Philos. d. Gesch.*; Hegel, *Philos. d. Gesch.*; Comte, *Cours de philos. positive*, iv–vi. 51–7 ; Buckle, *Hist. of Civilization in England*; Lotze, *Mikrokosmos*, iii. 7. On account of this divergence of opinion, and in view of the inevitable incompleteness, in the present state of knowledge, of the best attempts to give a philosophical view of history, it is maintained by many writers that a tenable philosophy of history must remain for a long time to come, if not for ever, an unattainable ideal.

It is evident that these different meanings of 'philosophy of history' are intimately related ; in particular, (2) and (3) are distinguishable rather than fully separable. It is further to be remarked that 'philosophy' is used here in its broader significance ; a philosophy of history conceived entirely from the metaphysical point of view would be out of harmony with the tendencies of most modern thinkers. (A.C.A. Jr.)

Literature : in addition to the works cited above, DROYSEN, Grundriss d. Historik ; ROCHOLL, Philos. d. Gesch., i ; FLINT, Hist. of the Philos. of Hist., I. France (1897).

The two principal and metaphysically opposed points of view in the philosophical treatment of history, the Hegelian and the Positivistic, rest alike on certain presuppositions : the continuity of the material of history, and the theory of evolution, which affords ground for a genetic method. These two presuppositions go together, and it is their acceptance which distinguishes the modern from the earlier treatment of the subject. Possibly Herder alone of the earlier pre-evolution writers realized both these points (cf. Barth, as cited below, 203).

Hitherto history had been empirical in its method no less than in its data ; for instance, Lewes, *Biographical History of Philosophy*, belongs to the earlier class. But such works as Caird, *Evolution of Religion*, and Crozier, *History of Intellectual Development*, though opposed in point of view, still have these two presuppositions in common. This common ground may be said to be the real gain of the 19th century in history, as it is also in the sociological sciences in general. Extremes in the treatment of history arise from the pressing of particular theories of evolution : as in the attempts of the Hegelians to deduce historical movements, or to treat them as illustrating

phases of an idealistic dialectic ; and in those of the Positivistic evolutionists, who, with Comte and the 'descriptive' sociologists, construe history by preconceived formulas of progress, or account for historical and general social movements strictly in the naturalistic terms of biological analogy or of geographical, climatic, and other external environmental conditions (Spencer, Buckle). Other, less important, views are the so-called Great Man theory of history (M. Lehmann, James), which is hardly a philosophy (cf. GENIUS); the Social Environment theory, which eliminates the great man (Taine) ; and the theory of Special Providence, which is opposed, as in biology, to all forms of evolution.

What we may call the 'autonomic' or sociological view of history (cf. especially Barth, as cited below) maintains the essential irreducibility of the factors essential to human evolution, considers them psychological in their nature and subject to their own laws of development, and identifies the historical problem with that of the science of sociology. This programme may be carried out strictly as science ; or it may be taken in connection either with an idealistic monistic philosophy (Hegel's 'historism,' Lotze's 'spiritualistic monism'), which makes the essential factor thought, or with a voluntarism (Schopenhauer, Wundt, Barth, Paulsen) to which the essential factor is will broadly defined.

Barth gives the following classification of theories or 'interpretations' of history (Geschichtsauffassungen), all of which he calls 'one-sided,' as opposed to the sociological view called above autonomic.

Interpretations of History :

   I. Individualistic (Lehmann) : Great Man theory.

  II. Anthropo-geographical (Ritter, Ratzel, Mougeolle): Environment.

 III. Ethnological (Comte, Taine, Gumplowicz): Struggle of Races.

 IV. Culture History (Morgan, Tylor, Waitz): Conquest of nature, Invention, &c.

  V. Political (Lorenz, Schäfer, G. B. Vico): the State.

 VI. Ideological (Hegel, W. v. Humboldt, Buckle, Lazarus): Ideas (logical, religious, &c.).

VII. Economic (Durkheim, Marx, Engels, Loria): Division of labour, Production, Class-rivalry.

Literature: besides the titles cited above see HERDER, Ideen z. Philos. d. Gesch. d. Menschheit; BOURDEAU, L'Hist. et les Historiens; LAMPRECHT, Alte u. neue Richtungen in d. Geschichtswiss. (1896); RATZEL, Anthropogeographie; ROCHOLL, Die Philos. d. Gesch.; MOUGEOLLE, Les Problèmes de l'Hist. (1886); TAINE, Hist. of Eng. Lit.; GUMPLOWICZ, Der Rassenkampf (1883), and Sociol. u. Politik (1892); VIERKANDT, Naturvölker u. Kulturvölker (1896); TYLOR, Introd. to the Study of Anthropol. and Civilization; WAITZ, Anthropol. d. Naturvölker; LORENZ, Die Geschichtswiss. (1886); SCHÄFER, Das eigentl. Arbeitsgebiet d. Gesch. (1888); LAZARUS and STEINTHAL, Zeitsch. f. Völkerpsychol., i; LAZARUS, ibid. iii; STEINTHAL, ibid. xvii; DURKHEIM, La Division du Travail social (1893); MARX, Zur Krit. d. polit. Oekonomie (1859), and Das Kapital (3rd ed., 1883); LORIA, Die wirtschaftl. Grundlagen d. herrschenden Gesellschaftsordnung; LACOMBE, Hist. considérée comme Science; LECKY, Hist. of European Mor.; JAMES, The Will to Believe, 216–62; MÜNSTERBERG, Psychol. and Life, 179–228; BARTH, Die Geschichtsphilos. als Sociol., i. See also many of the titles given under SOCIOLOGY and under RIGHT (philosophy of). (J.M.B.)

History (political). That species of history which treats of the affairs of political communities.

It is difficult to give any definite meaning to the term history. Usually, however, when we employ the term without any qualifying epithet, we mean the history of states or political communities. Such a history will be more or less comprehensive according to the received conception of history. In most communities which have reached any appreciable degree of civilization, a record has been kept of matters of public interest, such as the succession of kings and magistrates or priests, and wars and treaties. These records have usually been very meagre. When private persons first began to write history, they had for the basis of their narrative little more than these records supplemented by tradition or rumour. They had no conscious purpose either of tracing the development of political institutions or of inculcating political lessons. They did not confine themselves to political events, but chronicled all occurrences which affected the life of the community, or were thought to possess a religious significance, or seemed likely to interest or instruct, such as remarkable instances of individual goodness or wickedness, strange reverses of fortune affecting eminent persons, romantic adventures, curious natural phenomena, plagues, famines, and earthquakes. But as knowledge increased, and other forms of prose literature were elaborated, the field of history was narrowed. It became more and more the record of political and military affairs. This change is well illustrated by a comparison of the histories of Herodotus and Thucydides. Hardly anything of human interest is excluded from the narrative of Herodotus. Thucydides adheres, with rigorous self-restraint, to the story of the Peloponnesian War. In this restriction of the field of history there was not yet any definite scientific purpose. The object of the historian was partly literary, partly didactic. He wished to give a noble and beautiful narrative of great events. He wished to record the experience of the past for the benefit of the future, to supply statesmen with a store of precedents, to enforce lessons of wisdom and virtue, by setting forth the deeds and sufferings of great personages. These were the aims of such writers as Thucydides and Tacitus, and indeed of most of the eminent historians who flourished between the revival of letters and the new critical movement which began in Germany. In the course of the last hundred years this movement has transformed the conception of history and historical methods. (1) It is now fully admitted that historical knowledge is desirable for its own sake—not merely for the morals which it may afford—and must be sought without reference to edification. (2) Whilst political history is more stringently defined than formerly, it is seen that the state is not co-extensive with society, and that war and politics do not exhaust the activity of mankind. Therefore, whilst literature, art, science, religion, economics, and social life are reserved for separate treatment by historians who have made one or other of these subjects their special study, the writer of political history is expected to study the general life of society, and show how religious, or economic, or literary, or other influences have affected its political development. (3) The closer attention now paid to the manifold life of society, and to the development of ideas and institutions, has enabled us to realize more vividly the conditions under which great men work, and the limits to individual action and influence. History has therefore become less biographical, less exclusively concerned with great men, and also less epical, less exclusively concerned with great deeds. More pains are bestowed on explaining the structure of society and the prevailing tendencies of thought at any given period. Dull ages and dull countries are thought deserving of study because they contribute, if not to our list of heroes, at least to our knowledge of political evolution. (F.C.M.)

History of Philosophy (main divisions and schools): Ger. *Geschichte der Philosophie*; Fr. *histoire de la philosophie*; Ital. *storia della filosofia*. The history of PHILOSOPHY (q. v.), as a whole, may be divided into two great portions, that which treats of ORIENTAL PHILOSOPHY (q. v.), and that which has to do with Occidental or European and American philosophy.

European philosophy is first of all the ancient, and especially the Greek philosophy (see GREEK TERMINOLOGY, PRE-SOCRATIC PHILOSOPHY, SCHOOLS OF GREECE, and the names of special movements below); secondly, the philosophy which attended the development of Christian theology, the period of the Church Fathers (see PATRISTIC PHILOSOPHY) down to and including the philosophy of the scholastic period (see LATIN AND SCHOLASTIC TERMINOLOGY, and ST. THOMAS, philosophy of); and, thirdly, the philosophy since, and including, the period of the RENAISSANCE (q. v.). The more general philosophical tendencies and movements of modern philosophy are treated in separate articles sub verbis. The purpose of the present sketch is simply to indicate the general historical position which the various schools of philosophy most prominent in the course of development have occupied.

Oriental (Hindoo) Philosophy. Confining attention here to the part of oriental philosophy represented by Hindoo thought, a word may be said as to its origin and most general tendencies. Hindoo philosophy was an outgrowth of Hindoo religion. At the close of the Vedic period of Indian literature, an elaborate ritualistic development, on the one side, came to be accompanied with an equally vigorous development of reflection, upon the fundamental meaning of the religious ideas of the Hindoo people of the age in question. This reflection was from the outset determined by practical motives, but was left singularly free from any violent dogmatic interference; and was soon able to develop great theoretical skill. In the works known as the *Upanishads* sages and thinkers interested in a reform

of life and, in part as well, of faith, set on record cosmological speculations, as well as discussions, of the ultimate nature of being, the plan of salvation, and the fundamental problems of self-consciousness. Theories appear which are well described by the customary word PANTHEISM (q. v.). It would be fairer to call these early thinkers extreme idealists, and in some respects it would be still better to call them mystics, using that term in a sense which the theology of the Christian middle ages came to understand. Out of the philosophy of the Upanishads developed a number of different schools, whose names appear in the special article on ORIENTAL PHILOSOPHY (India, q. v.). Of these schools, however, the principal, namely, the Sankhya Vedanta, were divided upon the question of realism and idealism. The Sankhya were rationalistic realists, who rejected the authority of the Hindoo sacred scriptures, broke away from the tradition of the Upanishads, maintained a sharp dualism between matter and mind, and sought for salvation by means of an utter abstraction of mind from all dependence upon bodily conditions. On the other hand, the Vedanta, following closely the tradition of the Upanishads, developed in the end a highly technical, but still mystical, theology, with an absolute idealism as their theory of the universe, an ascetic life as their practical plan of existence, and a mystic absorption in the absolute as their goal. Upon the basis of the controversies with these schools, and in opposition to them, developed the ethical philosophy of Buddhism (see ORIENTAL PHILOSOPHY). After the downfall of Buddhism a revival of the ancient philosophical schools led to developments which were not original in fundamental conceptions, and which found expression in elaborate scholastic commentaries upon older treatises. While dualistic and pluralistic forms of theology have never been unknown in India, the extreme rationalism of the Sankhya became gradually modified, or passed away altogether; and the Vedanta has remained in modern India, in spite of the very complex development of religious sects, the most important and representative tendency of philosophical thought.

Occidental (European and American) Philosophy, in its ancient phase, began in Greece about 600 B. C., and continued as the Graeco-Roman philosophy, until the edict of the Emperor Justinian in A. D. 529 closed the philosophical schools still existing at Athens.

The principal periods of Greek philosophy are as follows :—

(1) The early cosmological or Pre-Socratic period (see PRE-SOCRATIC PHILOSOPHY). To this belongs first of all the development of the Ionic speculation regarding nature. There then follow the Eleatic and Pythagorean schools, and the later members of the cosmological period, including the Atomists. A transition to the second great period of Greek philosophy is made by the age of the Sophists, who were already contemporaries of Socrates.

(2) The second period of Greek philosophy opens with Socrates, who was born in 469 B.C., and died in the year 399 B.C. It is the period of Socrates, Plato, and Aristotle. It contains by far the greatest developments of ancient thought. The death of Aristotle occurred in 322 B.C. See SOCRATIC PHILOSOPHY, and GREEK TERMINOLOGY.

(3) The ethical period, including the development of the Stoical, Epicurean, and Sceptical schools, and extending from the death of Aristotle to a period not far from the Christian era, is usually united in historical treatment with the more theological period into which it passed, and to which later Stoicism also belongs. See SCHOOLS OF GREECE (Academy, Cynic, Cyrenaic, Epicurean, and Stoic schools), and SCEPTICISM (Greek). In this sense, what is sometimes called the Hellenistic and Roman philosophy may be considered as extending until the close of the whole movement of ancient thought. To this third period of ancient thought may belong then, in addition to the before-mentioned schools, the Alexandrian philosophy and the Neo-Platonic schools. See ALEXANDRIAN SCHOOL, and NEO-PLATONISM. Cf. SOCRATICS (Plato).

Christian philosophy, which forms the second great division in the history of European thought, begins already in the 2nd century A.D. as the early PATRISTIC PHILOSOPHY (q. v.). The Patristic period extends to St. Augustine, who himself may be said to stand on the border-land between the Patristics and SCHOLASTICISM (q. v.). St. Augustine died in A.D. 430. The first division of the scholastic philosophy extends to the beginning of the 13th century, and is closed by the reappearance of the writings of Aristotle in Western Europe. It is followed by the great period of scholastic philosophy, that of the 13th century itself, in which the doctrine of Aristotle was laid at the basis of an elaborate and, as the event has proved, definitive statement of the theoretical theology of the Roman Catholic Church. See ST. THOMAS (philosophy of). From the beginning of the 14th century dates the gradual downfall of scholasticism.

The philosophy of the RENAISSANCE (q. v.) period belongs to the 15th and 16th centuries, and is characterized by the revival of Platonic influences, by the general breaking-up of the scholastic movement, and by the appearance of numerous tendencies due to the revived study of nature.

Modern philosophy begins with the 17th century, and extends to the present time. Its principal periods are: first, that of the 17th century, characterized by RATIONALISM (q. v.), by a marked dualism between matter and mind (see PRE-ESTABLISHED HARMONY, and OCCASIONALISM), and by the beginnings of English empiricism (see NATIVISM AND EMPIRICISM).

Secondly, the philosophy of the 18th century up to the appearance of Kant's *Critique of Pure Reason*, in 1781. This period is characterized by a continuation and development of the conflict between rationalism and empiricism, by the rapid development of ethics, by the French materialism of the middle of the 18th century, and by the philosophical scepticism which, in a measure, formed a prelude to the revolutionary period. The philosophy of Kant opens a new epoch in the history of thought, and more recent philosophy may be in general styled post-Kantian philosophy (see KANT's TERMINOLOGY, and NEO-KANTIANISM). Of the post-Kantian philosophy, the principal sub-periods are, the idealism of Fichte, Schelling, and Hegel (see HEGEL's TERMINOLOGY and philosophy); second, the period of the dissolution of the Hegelian school, the reappearance of MATERIALISM (q. v.), and the rise of POSITIVISM (q. v.) in France, and of a revived empiricism in Great Britain. The important movement called the Scottish philosophy (see NATURAL REALISM) is contemporaneous both with the development of the post-Kantian philosophy, and with the post-Kantian period, down to the time of the appearance of the new empiricism in Great Britain. The year 1860 may be said to begin the last sub-period in the history of European thought. This is the age of what may be called the philosophy of evolution, the revived idealism of recent times, and the new logical and cosmological, as well as historical, speculations, which mark the present era of discussion. It was not possible in the foregoing sketch to name all the schools, whether of scholastic or modern thought, which are important enough to deserve separate articles. One may add the names of the Thomistic school in scholastic thought (see ST. THOMAS, philosophy of); the Cartesian school (see OCCASIONALISM, and PRE-ESTABLISHED HARMONY) in modern thought, under which name the rationalistic movement from Descartes to Leibnitz is frequently comprised; the English empiricism from Locke to Berkeley, the school of Herbart (see HERBARTIANISM) in modern German philosophy, and the various tendencies of so-called real-idealism or ideal-realism (see REALISM) in post-Hegelian German thought.

Literature: see BIBLIOG. A.   (J.R., J.D.)

Hobbes, Thomas. (1588–1679.) An eminent English thinker, born at Malmesbury, Wiltshire. Sent to Oxford, he studied Aristotle and scholastic philosophy especially. As tutor to the earl of Devonshire, he travelled through France, Italy, and Savoy. Later, he became intimate with the leading thinkers of his day, Bacon, Ben Jonson, Herbert of Cherbury, Galileo, Descartes, Gassendi, Harvey, &c. He early became interested in questions of state, and continued to devote attention to them as long as he lived. He moved to Paris in 1640, and in 1647 became mathematical instructor to Charles, prince of Wales. To escape persecution he fled from Paris to England in 1653. After the Restoration he was pensioned by Charles II.

Hodge, Archibald Alexander. (1823–86.) An American clergyman and theologian, born, educated, and died at Princeton, N. J. He graduated from both Princeton College (1841) and Seminary (1847). In 1877 he was chosen associate professor of didactic and polemic theology at Princeton, to assist his father, Charles Hodge, whom he succeeded (1878).

Hodge, Charles. (1797–1878.) An American theologian of Scotch-Irish descent, educated and died at Princeton, N. J. Graduated from Princeton College (1815) and Seminary (1819). In 1820 he became assistant in oriental languages in the seminary; 1822, professor of oriental and Biblical literature. In 1840 he became professor of exegetical and didactic theology, and in 1852 polemical theology was added to his field.

Holbach, Paul Henri Thiry, Baron d'. (1723–89.) One of the ENCYCLOPEDISTS (q.v.). The heir of a large fortune, he moved to Paris in early life, and remained there until his death. He was a prolific writer, *Le Système de la Nature*, 'the Bible of atheism,' being perhaps best known.

Holiness (of God) [AS. *halig*, holy]: Ger. *Heiligkeit* (*Gottes*); Fr. *sainteté* (*de Dieu*); Ital. *santità* (*di Dio*). One of the attributes of Deity. God is absolutely intolerant of sin, being himself free from any taint of impurity.

In the Old Testament, the holiness of God indicates partly that Israel can rely on his fidelity, and partly that holiness is itself the essence of his being. With regard to the latter, the implication is that holiness is something more than moral purity. In the New Testament, God alone is holy, in the sense that his will is completely at one with his ethical purposes. Here, too, the idea of God as active in his holiness—revealing himself as holy—receives expression. As a result, conformity to holiness becomes the human ideal. See ATTRIBUTES (of God), and GOD.

Literature: articles in Herzog's Encyc., Schenkel's Lexicon, Hastings' Bible Dict.; ISSEL, Der Begriff d. Heiligkeit im N. T.; BAUDISSIUS, Stud. z. semit. Religionsgesch., ii.   (R.M.W.)

Holoblastic [Gr. ὅλος, whole, + βλαστός, a bud]: Ger. *holoblastisch*; Fr. *holoblastique*; Ital. *oloblasto*. Of ova: those which undergo complete as contrasted with partial cleavage. The term is due to Remak. See MEROBLASTIC, CLEAVAGE, and EMBRYO.   (C.LL.M.)

Holy Ghost: see HOLY SPIRIT.

Holy Spirit: Ger. *heiliger Geist*; Fr. *Saint-Esprit*; Ital. *Spirito santo*. The name given to the third Person in the Trinity of Christian dogma. In dealing with such a subject, it is exceedingly important to bear in mind the complete distinction between the rational standpoint of philosophy and the views which are primarily dogmatic or fiducial.

The conception of the Holy Spirit, in its definitely authoritative and so far completed form, dates so late as the Constantinople revision of the Nicene Creed (381). It was afterwards rendered even more definite dogmatically in the paradoxical propositions of the so-called Athanasian Creed, which grew up in the 8th century under the influence of AUGUSTINIANISM (q. v.). Prior to the middle of the 4th century, the dogmatic conception of the Holy Spirit is to a large extent inchoate; and although a triad was recognized as early as Novantian (250), it was still possible for Gregory Nazianzen to make the following statement, which shows the status of the question so far as dogma is concerned : 'As the Old Testament declared the Father clearly, but the Son more vaguely, so the New Testament has revealed the Son, but only suggested the divinity of the Spirit. Now, however, the Spirit reigns among us, and makes himself more clearly known to us ; for it was not advisable to proclaim the divinity of the Son, so long as that of the Father was not recognized, or to impose upon the former—if we may use so bold an expression—that of the Spirit, while it (viz. the divinity of the Son) was not accepted' (after 360).

As great misconception exists on this subject, especially in view of the fact that there is no ontological speculation in the Old or New Testaments, and that the formulated dogma of the Holy Spirit is almost exclusively ontological, it may be said that philosophy of religion is confronted with the following questions. Does the Old Testament contain any reference to such a Spirit as is defined in the creeds ? Here the problem might be suggested : Is not Heraclitus much more truly the forerunner of the doctrine of the Holy Spirit than any Old Testament writer ? Did Jesus (except in the passage John xiv. 16) go much beyond Old Testament conceptions ? What value is to be attached to this passage in St. John ? What is St. Paul's teaching as to the Holy Spirit ? Did it undergo any transformations of significance ? How far is it traceable to rabbinical angelology ? What is the historical value of the story of Pentecost ? Is the Holy Spirit, recognized early (150) by the Christian community, more than an expression (1) for the unity which Christians experienced among themselves ?—or (2) for the 'change of heart' that individuals felt they had undergone ? What is the history of the doctrine of the Holy Spirit in the Roman Church (i. e. the primitive Christian community at Rome from St. Paul to the Council of Nice) ? What in the other churches (e.g. Eastern, Alexandrian) ? How was it related to and affected by Platonic, Gnostic, Sabellian (modalist) teachings ? Why did the Synod of Constantinople extend the Nicene profession of the Holy Spirit ? What is the history and value of the so-called Athanasian Creed ? Only when, by a genetic treatment of the development of the religious consciousness, these questions are answered, and the problems they suggest solved, can a rational estimate be made of the precise import of the phrase

Holy Spirit. Philosophically viewed, it is, obviously, without authority.

Literature : this is extensive. It is enumerated in the various Encyclopedias—Herzog's, Lichtenberger's, Hastings'; PFLEIDERER, Philos. of Religion (Eng. trans.), iv. 60 f. ; HARNACK, Hist. of Dogma (Eng. trans.), i, ii, iii ; HAUSRATH, Hist. of N. T. Times, Times of the Apostles (Eng. trans.). iii. 82 f. ; MOZLEY, The Word ; BUCHANAN, Office and Work of the Holy Spirit ; KAHNIS, Lehre **v.** h. Geist, i ; HEBER, Bampton Lectures. A late work is CLARK, The Paraclete (1900).

(R.M.W.)

Home, Henry (Lord Kames). (1696–1782.) A Scottish judge, called to the Edinburgh bar (1724), and appointed a judge of the Court of Sessions (1752), when he became Lord Kames. He published, besides a number of works on ethical and religious themes, *The Elements of Criticism.*

Homogamy [Gr. ὁμός, like, + γάμος, marriage] : Ger. *Homogamie* (suggested) ; Fr. *homogamie* (not commonly used—Y.D.) ; Ital. *omogamia.* That 'discriminate' mode of isolation which gives rise to segregate breeding. The term was suggested by Romanes (*Darwin and after Darwin*, iii, 1897). Cf. APOGAMY, and ISOLATION.

(C.LL.M.)

Homogeneity and **Heterogeneity** [Gr. ὁμός and ἕτερος, same and other, + γένος, kind] : Ger. *Homo-(Hetero-)genität* ; Fr. *homo-(hétéro-)généité* ; Ital. *omo-(etero-)geneità.* Absence and presence respectively of differences.

Applied commonly to the structure and properties of bodies ; as 'homogeneous medium,' 'homogeneous mass.' The terms are used by Spencer (*First Principles*) to characterize the lack and subsequent presence of more or less differentiation in the cosmic material.

(J.M.B.)

Homogeneity (law of) : see PRINCIPLE.

Homogeny : see CONVERGENCE (in biology).

Homoiomeriae [Gr.]. Applied by Aristotle (*De Coel.*, iii. 3) to the atoms of Anaxagoras. Cf. PRE-SOCRATIC PHILOSOPHY (Atomists).

(J.M.B.)

Homoiousia [Gr. ὁμοιούσιον, of similar substance ; contrasted with ὁμοούσιον, of the same substance]. These two Greek words were the technical terms used by the parties to the Christological controversy associated with the name of Arius in the 3rd and 4th centuries. The former term expressed the doctrine of the semi-Arians ; the latter that of the Athanasians, which became the orthodox deliverance of the Church. Heteroousia was the term used by the full Arians; it means of different substance. The entire verbal framework of this controversy as to the real relation between God and Christ is derived from Platonic and Gnostic sources. See HOMOOUSIA, and cf. ARIANISM, GNOSTICISM, and CHRISTOLOGY.

Literature: HARNACK, Hist. of Dogma (Eng. trans.), iv. (R.M.W.)

Homolecithal [Gr. ὁμός, like, + λέκιθος, yolk]: Ger. *homolekithal*; Fr. *homolécithe* (not commonly used—Y.D.); Ital. *omolecito*. Of the ovum: having little food-yolk, and that equally distributed. Proposed by Mark (1892). Balfour used Alecithal in this sense. See CLEAVAGE. (C.LL.M.)

Homologous Organs: Ger. *homologe Organe*; Fr. *organes homologues*; Ital. *organi omologhi*. Those parts or organs of animals or plants which are of similar origin in development and phylogenetic history. Similar and homologous organs may, in the course of evolution, come to differ entirely in structure and function. Cf. ANALOGOUS ORGANS.

The term in its present biological use, as contrasted with analogous, was introduced by Richard Owen (1848). E. Ray Lankester has since suggested the terms homogenetic, for similarity of origin due to inheritance, and homoplastic, where the close agreement in form is due to similar moulding conditions of the environment without genetic connection. Homoplastic organs are therefore merely analogous.

Literature: R. OWEN, The Archetype and Homologies of the Vertebrate Skeleton; E. R. LANKESTER, On the Use of the term Homology in Modern Zoology, Ann. and Mag. of Nat. Hist. (1870). (C.LL.M.—E.S.G.)

Homologue and **Homology:** see HOMOLOGOUS ORGANS.

Homology (in biology): see HOMOLOGOUS ORGANS, and CONVERGENCE (in biology).

Homonymous [Gr. ὁμός, like, + ὄνομα, a name]: Ger. *homonym*; Fr. *homonyme*; Ital. *omonimo*. Homonymous terms are defined by Aristotle as those which are identical in name, but of which the definitions (the essential natures) relative to that common name are different. Thus castle would be homonymous when it is applied to a picture and to a building, while the natures of the objects named and the definitions of the names would be wholly different. The distinction is grammatical rather than logical. See Aristotle, *Categ.*, chap. i. (R.A.)

Homoousia [Gr. ὁμοούσιον, from ὁμός, same, + οὐσία, essence]: Ger. *Homoousia*; Fr. *homoousie*; Ital. *omousia*. The term used by early Church writers, and in the Nicene Creed, to express the oneness of Christ's nature with that of God, the term signifying not simply essential, but also numerical, identity with the divine substance. Cf. HOMOIOUSIA.

The term homoousia was employed to express the respect in which all the persons of the Trinity are one and the same being. The separate personal natures as distinguished from this unitary essence are expressed by the terms πρόσωπον, τριπρόσωπον, or ὑπόστασις. The latter term is the one generally used since the Nicene Council as a name for the separate personal subsistences which inhere in the unitary divine nature.

Literature: SUICER, Thesaurus Ecclesiasticus, tom. ii, Ὁμοούσιον Ὑπόστασις; STANLEY, Hist. of the Eastern Church, 'The Homoousion,' lect. ix. (A.T.O.)

Homoplasy: see HOMOLOGOUS ORGANS, and CONVERGENCE (in biology).

Homotaxis [Gr. ὁμός, like, + τάξις, order]: Ger. *Homotaxie*; Fr. *homotaxie* (not in use—Y.D.); Ital. *omotassi*. Similarity of succession in organic types in different regions.

A term introduced by Huxley (*Collected Essays*, viii. 276, 1862) to express the fact that strata containing a similar succession of organic forms are in the same relative position to the general sequence, though not necessarily contemporaneous. (C.LL.M.)

Honesty [Lat. *honestus*, honourable]: Ger. *Ehrlichkeit*; Fr. *honnêteté*; Ital. *onestà*. Due regard (1) for moral rights, (2) for the rights of property. (W.R.S.—J.M.B.)

The former or more general meaning of the term is the original meaning. Cicero distinguishes the *honestum*, or morally good, from that which is merely *rectum*, or in accordance with the rule, and examines cases of supposed conflict between the *honestum* and the *utile* (*De Officiis*). St. Augustine distinguishes the *honestum*, or that which is to be desired on its own account, from the *utile*, which is desired because it leads to something else (cf. Aquinas, *Summa*, II. ii. Q. 145).

This more general usage of the term honesty is now almost obsolete, though it is still sometimes used with other implications than that of regard for proprietary rights, as opposed to deception of any kind, especially interested deception. (W.R.S.)

Honour [Lat. *honor* or *honos*]: Ger. *Ehre*; Fr. *honneur*; Ital. *onore*. (1) RESPECT (q.v.) for excellence of any sort; applied also to any sign or mark of such respect. (2) Respect or reputation enjoyed by persons in certain—more or less elevated—social stations, conditionally on the observance of certain rules of conduct. (3) Recognition of personal obligations which are conditioned upon one's social relationships; honour is thus contrasted with ethical right.

The concept of honour in the third meaning seems to involve both a certain system of reciprocal rights and obligations belonging to a social station or relation, and also the individual's recognition of these. The 'honour among thieves,' the 'soldier's honour,' the 'husband's honour,' the 'honour of a gentleman,' the 'honour of a citizen,' &c., have in common a certain recognition of self as a member of this or that class, organization, or society; and the requirements of honour vary in different cases. Such requirements are usually supplementary to ethical rules.

The instances cited above show the existence of the second meaning, as well as of the third; e.g. a 'husband's honour' is impaired by a breach of conjugal duty on the part of his wife, even though he is in no way to blame; similarly, the honour of a family is impaired by the cowardice or fraud of one of its members. In both these cases it is not the recognition of personal obligations, but the reputation conditional on such recognition, which seems to be meant.

The relation of honour and right has not been fully cleared up. Simmel (*Année Sociol.*, i, trans. in *Amer. J. of Sociol.*, iii, 1897–8) makes honour a function of social organization, which plays a most important conservative rôle in securing 'the persistence of social groups.' To those who hold that ethical right is absolute and genetically independent of social progress, honour is an unethical reflex of custom or convention. On theories of right which allow a large social ingredient, or which make the ethical genetically a function of social organization, honour is ethical, and may be viewed either as right in the making, or as the sort of right which attaches to a lower or less developed social whole, in contrast with that which attaches to the relatively higher or more developed. In either case the conflicts arising between honour and right are equally well explained. For whether there is or is not an objective standard of right and wrong, there can be no doubt that men have commonly believed in the existence of such a standard; and the distinction in mediaeval and modern times

between the code of honour and the moral code—no such objectivity being attributed to the former so far as it diverges from or conflicts with the latter—may be regarded as a purely sociological distinction quite independent of ethical theory. This distinction, however, is not found in all stages of society. Indeed, it seems characteristic of Hellenic civilization that the distinction is not found there: in the idea of καλοκἀγαθία the code of honour and the moral code are not differentiated.

Some of the finest points of casuistry, however, arise here, as in the case of the freemason who betrays his country rather than another member of his chapter (honour *versus* honour), or that of the witness who perjures himself rather than give evidence against a comrade (honour *versus* right). The solution of these positions waits upon the theory of the morally right. (J.M.B.–H.S.)

Hope (1) and (2) **Despair** [AS. *hopian*, to hope; Lat. *de + sperare*, to hope]: Ger. *Hoffnung und Verzweiflung*; Fr. *espérance et désespoir*; Ital. *speranza e disperazione*. Modes of EXPECTATION (q. v.) which excite respectively

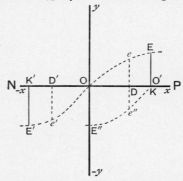

Ordinates in quadrant *y*P are values (D*e*) of hope from zero (O) to positive knowledge (K). Ordinates in quadrant −*y*N are values (D′*e*′) of fear from zero (O, despair) to negative knowledge (K′). The relation of hope and fear to each other in reference to the same state of expectation is given by transferring O for the negative values to O′, drawing the new curve O′E″, and extending the ordinates (D*e*) to this curve (D*e*″). When hope is at its maximum limit (knowledge, KE), fear is zero, O′; and when fear is at its maximum limit (despair, OE″), hope is zero, O.

pleasure and pain, and in which the chain of ideas necessary to the realization of a desired event is considered (1) in some degree, and (2) in no degree, likely of fulfilment. They represent respectively positive and negative modes of assurance as to future occurrences.

Hope is itself subject to many degrees, from

'faint' to 'lively.' Despair is applied for the most part only to very strong degrees of assurance, as to a coming disagreeable event. The term fear is used for the emotion accompanying moderate degrees of uncertainty. A curve may be roughly constructed, as in the figure, to show degrees of hope and fear (despair) with reference both to possible progressive differences of emotion based on differences of knowledge (ordinates of the curve EOE'), and also the relative presence of both hope and fear in the same state of mind for each stage of knowledge (the extended ordinates ee'', &c., as divided by the abscissa $-xx$). As with all such schemes for representing psychological states, however, this diagram should not be considered as aiming at artificial exactness. The phenomenon of affective CONTRAST (q. v.), both simultaneous and successive, enters in all cases. (J.M.B., G.F.S.)

Hopkins, Mark. (1802–87.) An eminent American divine, author, and educator. Educated at Williams College, he became professor of moral philosophy there (1830), and president (1836). In 1872 he resumed his former position as professor. He wrote in Christian apologetics and moral philosophy.

Horde [Pers. *ordu*, a camp]: Ger. *Horde*; Fr. *horde*; Ital. *orda*. A small social group composed of a few families, and comprising not more than from twenty-five to a hundred persons in all.

The horde is the lowest and most nearly primitive social organization of human beings. Examples : Veddahs of Ceylon ; Mincopis of the Andaman Islands ; Bushmen of South Africa ; the Fuegians of Tierra del Fuego ; and some of the Inunit of the northern coasts of North America. The horde has no governmental organization. It is never identical with a CLAN (q. v.). Hordes by combination may form a TRIBE (q. v.). (F.H.G.)

Horopter [Gr. ὅρος, a boundary, + ὀπτήρ, one who looks]: Ger. *Horopter*; Fr. *horoptère*; Ital. *oroptero*. The sum total of the luminous points that find representation upon corresponding points of the retinas, i. e. that are seen single by the two eyes. (E.B.T.)

It is capable of geometrical representation ; in the primary positions of convergence it consists of MÜLLER'S CIRCLE (q. v.) and a line through the fixation-point, and directed towards the feet of the observer. For a distant fixation-point, the horopter is the ground ; in walking, therefore, obstacles are seen single, and this furnishes the reason for the convergence of the vertical meridians of the eye. Helmholtz has given an exhaustive mathematical treatment of the horopter. This has been much simplified by Hering ; he applies to it the methods of projective geometry, which are peculiarly well fitted for dealing with it. (C.L.F.)

The term was coined by Aguilonius (*Opticorum libri*, vi, 1613). Vieth, J. Müller, and Prévost occupied themselves with the problem; but the modern theory begins with Meissner (*Beitr. z. Physiol. des Sehorgans*, 1854).

Literature : HELMHOLTZ, Physiol. Optik (2nd ed.), 860 ; SANFORD, Course in Exper. Psychol., expt. 210, App. II ; HERING, in Hermann's Handb. d. Physiol., III. i. 375 ff., 401 ; Beitr. z. Physiol., iii, iv (1863–4); WUNDT, Physiol. Psychol. (4th ed.), ii. 189 ff. ; LE CONTE, Sight (1881), 192 ff. ; HILLEBRAND, Zeitsch. f. Psychol., v. (1893), 1 ff. ; AUBERT, Physiol. Optik, 610 ff. ; HANKEL, Pogg. Ann. (1863), cxxii. 575. (E.B.T.)

Hotho, Heinrich Gustav. (1802–73.) A German Hegelian ; born, educated, and died in Berlin, where he became professor. Originally a jurist, his attention was turned to philosophy through the influence of Hegel.

Hours of Labour : Ger. *Arbeitstag(-stunden)* ; Fr. *durée* (or *heures*) *de travail* ; Ital. *ore di lavoro*. The length of time per day which is spent in work under the direction of an employer.

To the individual workman so far as he exercises his judgment, it seems desirable to prolong the hours of labour as long as the utility of the earnings outweighs the pain of production. But experience proves that the length of working day thus determined will not always prove advantageous to the public. Some labourers do not determine it for themselves (e. g. child-labour); some sacrifice the future to the present in the determination. Therefore efforts are everywhere made, wisely and unwisely, both by combination and by legislation, to restrict the hours of employment. (A.T.H.)

Hugo of St. Victor. (1096–1141.) Count of Blankenburg, born in his ancestral castle in the Hartz mountains, and educated in German schools, until in 1114 he entered the Augustinian cloister of St. Victor, where he remained until his death.

Humanism [Lat. *humanus*, human]: Ger. *Humanismus* ; Fr. *humanisme* ; Ital. *umanesimo, umanismo*. (1) Any system of thought, belief, or action which centres about human or mundane things to the exclusion of the divine (cf. the *New English Dict.*, sub verbo).

(2) The spirit, ideals, and doctrines of the Humanists—the scholars who, in the age of the RENAISSANCE (q.v.), devoted themselves to the study of the classical literatures and the culture of the ancient world.

The home of the earlier humanism was Italy, whose historical connection with classical antiquity was more direct than that of the other nations of Western Europe; where, in spite of the destruction of the Dark Ages, there remained remnants of ancient, especially Roman, literature and art; and which in the 15th century came into closer relations with the scholarship and the literary treasures of the Eastern empire. The growth of individualism, consequent upon political decentralization, and its aesthetic development had, furthermore, prepared the Italian mind for an active, as well as a receptive, interest in ancient literature and life. From Italy the humanistic movement passed northward and westward to Germany, the Netherlands, Spain, France, and England. The distinctive notes of the movement were, on the negative side, its opposition to the mediaeval type of thought and culture, and, positively, its accentuation of the worth and meaning of human nature and mundane life. To the men of the later middle age it revealed a classical world which had been forgotten or concealed, one, moreover, whose civilization had been superior to their own in political and intellectual freedom, in literary and speculative development, in artistic and social culture. With the Aristotelianism of ecclesiastical orthodoxy it contrasted new interpretations of Aristotle, gathered from a study of the sources, as well as the system of Aristotle's master, Plato. As philology, it aided in the birth of criticism; in history, it extended the horizon beyond the narrow limits of mediaeval Christendom; in religion, it initiated the comparative study of religious systems, often, however, with a disintegrating effect upon positive faith. Humanism came into connection, sometimes into alliance, with the Reformation through its opposition to scholasticism, its impatience of authority, and its linguistic and literary tendencies. In particular, the philological investigations of the humanists, which in the south had centred about the classical writings, were in the north often utilized to secure a new and better understanding of the Bible. For the most part, however, the humanists lacked the uncompromising spiritual determination of the leaders of the religious reform, and therefore in many cases parted company with the latter, as the reforming movement entered upon its more militant phases.

Literature: VOIGT, Die Wiederbelebung des classischen Alterthums; BURCKHARDT, Die Cultur der Renaissance in Italien, iii; GEIGER, Renaissance und Humanismus in Italien und Deutschland; SYMONDS, Renaissance in Italy, ii, The Revival of Learning; art. Renaissance, Encyc. Brit. (9th ed.), xx. 380–94. (A.C.A.Jr.)

Humanity: see CULTURE, ANTHROPOLOGY, and RELIGION OF HUMANITY.

Hume, David. (1711–76.) Born and educated at Edinburgh, he spent a brief period in commercial life; took charge of the Advocates' Library in Edinburgh for five years; accompanied General St. Clair on an embassy to Vienna and Turin, also the earl of Hertford on an embassy to Paris; was appointed under secretary of state by General Conway, and took charge of Scottish affairs, including the patronage of the churches. He died at Edinburgh. Cf. Huxley's *Hume*, and (for a detailed criticism) Green and Grose's ed. of the *Treatise on Human Nature*, Introd. See SCEPTICISM, SENSATIONALISM, EPISTEMOLOGY, and NATIVISM AND EMPIRICISM.

Humiliation of Christ [Lat. *humus*, the ground]: Ger. *Erniedrigung Christi*; Fr. *humiliation de Christ*; Ital. *umiliazione di Cristo*. The technical name given in dogmatic theology to one of the two states or conditions in which Christ is known to man. These are the state of humiliation (exinanition), and the state of exaltation.

The former embraces all that belongs to Christ in his earthly career: the miraculous conception, birth, circumcision, education and other vicissitudes of daily life, passion, death, burial. The latter has particular reference to the resurrection, ascension, and glorification at the right hand of God. See CHRISTOLOGY.

Literature: POWELL, The Principle of the Incarnation. (R.M.W.)

Humility [Lat. *humilis*, low, from *humus*, the ground]: Ger. *Demuth*; Fr. *humilité*; Ital. *umiltà*. Disposition to rank oneself low in character and achievements, especially in reference to the essential requirements of morality, religion, &c.

Humility is an emotional disposition, mood, or habit of mind. It seems to be more independent of reasons than is modesty, also to have less reference to other persons; and in both respects it is more deep-seated and rooted

487

in temperament. Possibly for this reason it is a religious virtue, which in the Christian conception of righteous character is not only consistent with manliness, but is an element of it. (J.M.B.)

Humour and **Humorous** [Lat. *humor*, moisture]: Ger. *Stimmung, Laune*(1), *Fröhlichkeit* (2), *Humor* (3); Fr. *humeur* (1) (3), *bonne humeur* (2); Ital. *umore* (1), *buon umore* (2), (3) *umorismo*. (1) Any disposition of mind, as in good or bad humour. (2) That special disposition which has the feeling of mirth. (3) A complex feeling (or corresponding quality) composed of an element of the comic and an element of sympathy. According to the varying degrees in which these elements are present, it shades from the COMIC (q. v.), on the one hand, to the PATHETIC (q. v.) on the other.

The humorous was treated as equivalent to the ludicrous (Shaftesbury, to whom it was equivalent to ridicule), or as a species of it (Richter, *Vorschule d. Aesthetik*, 1804). Its complex character was pointed out by Solger (1815), who regarded it as a union of comic and tragic. It was given special treatment by Trahndorf, Schopenhauer, Vischer, Lazarus, Zeising, Carriere, and Kirchmann. It seems desirable to use the term in the sense (3), although this is not perfectly established.

Literature: LAZARUS, Leben d. Seele (3rd ed., 1883); LIPPS, Komik u. Humor (1898); HARTMANN, Aesthetik, 451 ff.; SANTAYANA, Sense of Beauty, 253 ff. See also under COMIC. (J.H.T.)

Hutcheson, Francis. (1694–1746.) Of Scottish descent, he was born at Drumalig, Ulster, Ireland, and died at Dublin. Educated in theology at Glasgow; was a public teacher in Dublin for twelve years; appointed professor of moral philosophy at Glasgow, 1729. He holds a prominent place in the history of Scottish philosophy. See NATURAL REALISM.

Huxley, Thomas Henry. (1825–95.) Born at Ealing, Middlesex, and educated there and at the University of London. He was assistant surgeon of the royal navy (1846–53); a member of the party which sailed round the world in H. M. S. *Rattlesnake*; F.R.S. (1851); professor of natural history at the School of Mines, and Fullerian professor of physiology (1854); Hunterian professor at the Royal College of Surgeons (1863–9); president of the Geological and Ethnological Societies (1869–70); royal commissioner (1870); member of the London School Board

(1870–2); secretary of the Royal Society, and rector of the University of Aberdeen (1872); president of the Royal Society (1883); and Privy Councillor (1893). See *Life and Letters of Thomas Henry Huxley*, by Leonard Huxley (1900), and cf. AGNOSTICISM.

Hybrid [Lat. *hybrida*, spurious, possibly from Gr. ὕβρις]: Ger. *Bastard-* (*hybridisch*); Fr. *hybride* (offspring of two natural species —Y.D.), *métis* (offspring of two races of domestic animals; mongrel—Y.D.); Ital. *ibrido*. The result of a fertile cross between two species.

The existence of hybrids (e. g. mules) has long been known. Govelin is said to have first observed hybridism in plants, but Kölreuter during the latter half of the last century laid the foundations of our knowledge on the subject. Herbart, Gärtner, Wichert, Nägeli, and many others carried on the work, which Focke (1881) has summarized and extended. Darwin considered the question of hybridization in connection with the origin of species. Early observers held that hybrids were in all cases sterile. Later observations show that this is not always the case either among plants or animals. In connection with this subject the origin of cross-sterility between species has been discussed recently by Romanes in connection with his theory of PHYSIOLOGICAL SELECTION (q. v.).

Literature: C. DARWIN, Animals and Plants under Domestication; W. A. FOCKE, Die Pflanzen-Mischlinge; G. J. ROMANES, Darwin and after Darwin, iii. (C.LL.M.)

Hydrocephalus (or **-ly**) [Gr. ὕδωρ, water, + κεφαλή, head]: Ger. *Hydrocephalus, Wasserkopf*; Fr. *hydrocéphalie*; Ital. *idrocefalia*. An abnormal accumulation of fluid within the cranium; popularly termed 'water on the brain.'

The disease is most apt to be congenital, or to appear in the first months of life. Its most marked result is an enlargement of the head. The mental condition of developed cases of hydrocephalus is that of dullness, impaired mental action, and imbecility; muscular weakness is also apt to be present. Hydrocephalus is distinguished as internal (the usual form) when the serous fluid is in the ventricles; or external when it is in the meninges. It is termed chronic, infantile, or congenital when of slow growth and early appearance; acute when it appears as the result of meningitis.

Literature: HUGUEMIN, in Ziemssen's Encyc., xii, sub verbo; HEUBNER, in Eulenburg's Real Encyk., sub verbo. (J.J.)

Hydrotropism: see TROPISM.

Hyle [Gr.]: see PLATONISM, IDEALISM, passim, and MATTER AND FORM.

Hylotheism: see THEISM.

Hylozoism [Gr. ὔλη, matter, + ζωή, life]: Ger. *Hylozoismus*; Fr. *hylozoïsme*; Ital. *ilozoismo*. The doctrine which endows matter with an original and inherent life, and conceives life and the spiritual process in general as a property of matter.

In the philosophy of antiquity, hylozoistic tendencies were often associated with the crude attempts at a philosophy of nature (Thales, Anaximenes), or with speculations concerning the soul of the world (the Stoic view of the cosmos and the immanent divine reason). Similar tendencies appeared in the Renaissance philosophy of nature (Paracelsus, Cardanus, Bruno, Gassendi), and among the Cambridge Platonists (Cudworth, More). In later times hylozoistic views have been, in part, suggested by the results of physical, in particular of organic, science.

Literature: DIDEROT, Entretien entre d'Alembert et Diderot, and Le Rêve d'Alembert; ROBINET, De la Nature; HAECKEL, Der Monismus; cf. EISLER, Wörterb. d. philos. Begriffe, 331, and the histories of philosophy. (A.C.A.Jr.)

Hyper- [Lat. *hyper-*; Gr. ὑπέρ, over, above]: Ger. *über-*; Fr. *hyper-*; Ital. *iper-*. (1) In pathology: a prefix indicating an unusual, abnormal, or excessive degree of the condition named in the compound.

Thus, hyperaesthesia, an excessive or exalted state of sensibility to sensory impressions in general, or to tactile ones in particular; hyperbulia, an excessive tendency for desire to lead to action; hyperaemia, an excessive supply of blood, &c. The conditions thus indicated are frequently the result of an irritation or inflammation of a portion of the nervous system; and are opposed to conditions denoted by the prefix *hypo-*, or the prefix *a, an,* or *ab*, which indicate a defect or lack of the normal condition indicated (as anaesthesia, abulia, hypaesthesia, hypobulia). (J.J.)

(2) In philosophy: a prefix denoting a higher or limiting outcome or determination (so also Super-).

Thus hyperpersonal or superpersonal is that which is of the nature of personality, but to which the predicates of personality, some or all, do not apply; that which personality pressed to its limits would or might be. The hyperphenomenal is that which grounds or explains phenomena, while yet not itself phenomenal. Cf. LIMITING NOTION. (J.M.B.)

Hypermetropia (also **Hyperopia**) [Gr. ὑπέρ, over, + μέτρον, measure, + ὤψ, eye]: Ger. *Hypermetropie*; Fr. *hypermétropie*; Ital. *ipermetropia*. That defect of the eye in which, with the accommodation relaxed, parallel rays come to a focus behind the retina; the opposite of myopia; long-sightedness.

It forms one of the common defects of refraction, or ametropia. Its most frequent cause is a shortness of the eyeball in its anterior-posterior axis (axial hypermetropia); yet it may be due to deficient refracting power, or deficient convexity of the refractive mechanism (curvature hypermetropia). It is further distinguished according to its degree and mode of manifestation, particularly whether or not it can be overcome by accommodation. The axial form is nearly always congenital. The hypermetropic eye requires accommodation for very distant objects, for which the emmetropic eye need not accommodate at all. For nearer distances an unusual degree of accommodation is required, which is aided by the use of convex lenses. It is said that in old age the normal eye acquires a low degree of hypermetropia, while in the absence of the lens (APHAKIA, q.v.) a very high degree of it is usually present. See also STRABISMUS, and VISION (defects of). (J.J.)

Hyperopia: see HYPERMETROPIA.

Hyperpersonal: see HYPER- (2).

Hyperplasia: see HYPERTROPHY.

Hyperspace: see SPACE (in mathematics).

Hypertrophy [Gr. ὑπέρ, over, + τροφή, nutrition]: Ger. *Hypertrophie*; Fr. *hypertrophie, hyperplasie, hypergenèse*; Ital. *ipertrofia*. (1) Excessive growth of an organ by enlargement of its tissue elements.

(2) Abnormal multiplication of elements, for which Hyperplasia is preferred. (H.H.)

In the French, when a distinction is made between hypertrophie and hyperplasie, hyperplasie means more especially an increase of the organ by an increase of the number of its cells; hypertrophie, the same by an increase of the size of its cells. When this distinction is not made, the proper word is hypertrophie. (Y.D.)

Hypnagogic [Gr. ὕπνος, sleep, + ἀγωγός, leading]: Ger. *hypnagogisch, Halbschlaf-(Zustand)*; Fr. *hypnagogique*; Ital. *ipnagogico*. Inducing to sleep, and thus synonymous with hypnogenic; but specifically used of the condition introductory to sleep, the half-waking condition experienced in going to sleep or in coming out of sleep, or resulting from the action of a general anaesthetic (ether, chloroform, &c.). The appearances and fancies of this transitional condition are termed hypnagogic hallucinations or illusions, and often determine the content of the dream state.

Literature: the term was introduced by A. MAURY, Le Sommeil et les Rêves, and his description of hypnagogic images is classic. See also MANACEÏNE, Sleep (Eng. trans., 1897). (J.J.–E.M.)

Hypnogenic, -genetic, -genous [Gr. ὕπνος, sleep, + γένεσις, production]: Ger. *schlaf-bringend, hypnogen*; Fr. *hypnogène*; Ital. *ipnogeno*. Sleep-producing; more specifically applied to agencies which induce the hypnotic state.

The term is applied to the physical accessories that are used in the production of the hypnotic state, such as the strained fixation of a bright object, rotating mirrors, a sudden light or sound, stroking the face or hands, &c.; also to the mental methods of suggestion, direct or indirect. See HYPNOSIS. (J.J.)

Hypnology: see HYPNOSIS.

Hypnosis [Gr. ὕπνος, sleep]: Ger. *Hypnose*; Fr. *état hypnotique* (*hypnose*—-Th.F.); Ital. *ipnosi, stato ipnotico*. An artificially induced sleep-like or trance-like condition of mind and body.

On the physiological side, the condition resembles that of normal sleep, except in the phase called somnambulism, which is similar to normal somnambulism or sleep-walking. On the mental side—to which the term hypnosis especially applies—the state of somnambulism is characterized by 'suggestibility,' alterations of memory, and personal 'rapport' with the hypnotizer. Many authorities bring all the phenomena under these three heads; but different writers show the widest differences in their explanations of the details, and also in their theories of hypnosis as a whole. In general, the theory of 'suggestion,' advanced and developed by the 'Nancy school,' is now adopted, in opposition to the theory of the 'Paris school,' to which, however, much of the earliest and best investigations of the phenomena are due.

The suggestion theory brings hypnosis within the normal workings of consciousness in relation to personal and other stimulations, including the normal phenomena of sleep and dreaming. The Paris school held, on the other hand, that hypnosis is a pathological condition, having certain well-marked stages ('catalepsy,' 'lethargy,' 'somnambulism'), with which certain equally well-marked physiological conditions were connected. Janet notes that these three stages were recognized by Déspine in 1840. This position gave rise to an elaborate method of dealing with hypnosis in its different stages, which those who criticize the Paris school hold is based largely upon suggestion.

The terminology of the subject includes 'animal magnetism' (a synonym of hypnotism), 'suggestive therapeutics' (hypnotic treatment of diseases), 'post-hypnotic' or 'deferred' suggestion (suggestions given in hypnosis to be carried out after return to normal life), 'auto-suggestion' (suggestion to one's self; in this case self-hypnotization), 'exaltation' (increased acuteness of the senses and all the faculties), 'criminal suggestion' (hypnotic suggestion of crime). For early designations of the whole field, see HYPNOTISM. Hypnosis is often called 'Hypnotic Suggestion' and classed under SUGGESTION (q. v.), and illustrates the group of phenomena somewhat loosely termed FASCINATION (q. v.). Hypnology (Liégeois) has been used for the science of artificially induced sleep and trance-like states. A state in animals analogous to hypnosis is called CATAPLEXY (q. v.).

Literature: JAMES, Princ. of Psychol., ii. chap. xxvii; JANET, Automatisme psychol.; CHARCOT, Œuvres complètes, ix; LEHMANN, Die Hypnose; WUNDT, Hypnotismus u. Suggestion; DESSOIR, Bibliog. des modernen Hypnotismus (with supplements); FOREL, Hypnotismus; SCHMIDKUNZ, Psychol. d. Suggestion; MYERS, The Subliminal Consciousness, in Proc. Soc. Psych. Res. (since 1892); OCHOROWICZ, Mental Suggestion; MOLL, Hypnotism (3rd ed.); BERNHEIM, Suggestive Therapeutics, and Études nouvelles sur l'Hypnotisme; BINET, Alterations of Personality, and (with FÉRÉ) Animal Magnetism; E. MORSELLI, Magnetismo animale (1886). Early works are JAMES BRAID, Neurypnology; GRIMES, Electro-Biology; DURAND (de Gros), Électro-dynamisme. See also the psychological journals, especially the Zeitsch. f. Hypnotismus, the Rev. de l'Hypnotisme, and Ann. d. Sci. Psych., and many of the titles given under SUGGESTION. (J.M.B.)

Hypnotism (and **Mesmerism**): Ger. *Hypnotismus*; Fr. *hypnotisme* (*mesmérisme*); Ital. *ipnotismo*. The theory and practical manipulation of HYPNOSIS (q. v.), sometimes known as Braidism.

The term hypnotism was first used by the

English surgeon James Braid. The term mesmerism belongs—with such other terms as neurypnology (Braid), electro-biology, odology, &c. — to the older ante-scientific period of knowledge of the subject; it arose from the name of Mesmer (F. A.), a physician who practised hypnotism in Europe in the last third of the 18th century. His 'cures' were unfavourably reported upon by a royal French commission appointed in 1785. (J.M.B.)

Hypo- [Gr. ὑπό, under] : Ger. *unter-*; Fr. *hypo-*; Ital. *ipo-* or *sub-*. A prefix indicating a subnormal degree of the condition indicated in the compound, as hypobulia, a defective power of exercising the will; hypokinesia, deficiency of reaction to a stimulus; hypomania, a moderate degree of mania; hyposmia, deficiency of smell, &c.

Its use is not so general as might be expected, owing to the use of the prefix *a*, *ab*, or *an*, not in the strict sense of total lack of, but to include also any serious deficiency. Hypo- is also used in the anatomical sense of under (hypoglossus, hypogastrium), and in a chemical sense (hypochlorite, &c.). (J.J.)

Hypoblast [Gr. ὑπό, under, + βλαστός, bud] : Ger. *inneres Keimblatt* ; Fr. *hypoblaste* (= *endoderme*) ; Ital. *ipoblasto*. The inner of the two primitive layers of the embryo animal. Also termed ENDODERM (q. v.).

The term is due to Michael Foster; first published in Huxley's *Vertebrated Animals* (1871). The hypoblast arises in some cases by INVAGINATION (q. v.), in others by DELAMINATION (q. v.). Which of these two modes of origin is to be regarded as the more primitive is a matter of discussion. See GASTRAEA THEORY, PLANULA THEORY, ENDODERM, and EMBRYO. (C.LL.M.)

Hypochondria (or **-iasis**) [Gr. ὑπό, under, + χόνδρος, a cartilage] : Ger. *Hypochondrie* ; Fr. *hypocondrie* ; Ital. *ipocondria*. A condition of nervous origin characterized by consciousness and morbid anxiety about the physical health and functions.

As the derivation of the term implies, the disease was supposed to be connected with the hypochondriac region (the liver and parts of the digestive organs). As a symptom variable in degree, it is characteristic of certain temperaments and of weakened conditions of the nervous system; but in its extreme development it becomes a symptom of insanity, and frequently constitutes the main factor of diagnosis of the insanity, which is then termed hypochondriacal insanity or hypochondriacal melancholia.

It is closely allied to melancholia, with its depression of spirits and concentration of mind upon self, but it differs from it in that the melancholic is absorbed in his own thoughts, often to indifference regarding his health and food, while the hypochondriac is constantly busy with his bodily sensations. These may be vague and general, or formulated with regard to certain organs. The hypochondriac reads medical literature, consults various physicians, examines his own secretions, fears this or that trouble, analyses and exaggerates every minute symptom, is conscious of his digestion, respiration, or circulation, administers endless remedies, and changes them as rapidly for others. He may entertain definite delusions as to the specific cause of his ill health, but he may be free from delusions and simply absorbed in his bodily feelings and misery. Such disorder is allied to hysteria as well as to melancholia, into which it often develops. It may be further distinguished according to the particular organs (the head, the digestive tracts) which are supposed to be affected; but the mental type is similar throughout.

Literature: art. Hypochondriasis, in Tuke's Dict. of Psychol. Med.; the textbooks of mental diseases, in locis; TANZI, in Tratt. ital. di Med. (1898); BINSWANGER, in Nothnagel's Spec. Pathol. u. Ther., xii. (J.J.)

Hypophysis or **Pituitary Body**: see BRAIN, Glossary, sub verbo.

Hypostasis [Gr.]. Scholastic term for SUBSTANCE (q. v.). See LATIN AND SCHOLASTIC TERMINOLOGY (11).

The verb to hypostasize (sometimes written hypostatize) is used of the making actual or counting real of abstract conceptions. (J.M.B.)

Derived from Stoic thought, hypostasis was in common use amongst Christians during the Christological and Trinitarian controversies of the 3rd and 4th centuries. Literally, the word means 'a support'; in theosophical and theological discussions, it came to mean 'substance,' essential nature, modality; and finally, as accepted in Christian dogma, 'subject' or person. Subject at first had merely the *nuance* of a mode of existence; latterly it came to imply a distinct, self-conscious personality. Its precise meaning in this last sense was doubtless rendered clearer to those who used it by the developed implications of the word *persona* in Roman law. This definite meaning was not fully attained till 362 ; and it probably grew out of the necessity for preserving the definite (personal) being of the Son even as sharing the essence of the Father. The history of the matter is still far from being clearly understood.

Literature: HARNACK, Hist. of Dogma (Eng. trans.), iv. 33 f.; STENTRUP, in Innsbrucker Zeitsch. f. kath. Theol. (1877), 59 f. (R.M.W.)

Hypostatical Union: Ger. *persönliche Einheit*; Fr. *union hypostatique*; Ital. *unione ipostatica*. A Christological term used to denote the relation between the divine and human natures in Christ.

It is set forth in the Creed of Chalcedon (451) as against the errors of EUTYCHIANISM (q. v.) and NESTORIANISM (q. v.). It consists in the declaration that the two natures are supernaturally united inseparably, and this by means of the Incarnation. They remain distinct, notwithstanding they together form a single personality. They are not to be thought of as merely absorbed or confused or mystically united. For, as Leo says, 'the same who is true God is also true man, and in this unity there is no deceit; for in it the lowliness of man and the majesty of God perfectly pervade one another.' Hypostatical union is to be carefully distinguished from the *unio mystica* (or internal communion) of the individual Christian with Christ. See CHRISTOLOGY.

Literature: HARNACK, Hist. of Dogma (Eng. trans.), iv. (R.M.W.)

Hypothesis [Gr. ὑπόθεσις]: Ger. *Hypothese*; Fr. *hypothèse*; Ital. *ipotesi*. Hypothesis, expressed in its most general terms, is a name given to any assumption of a fact or connection of facts from which can be deduced explanation of a fact or connection of facts already known.

The formation of hypotheses, thus defined, is therefore to be regarded as but the exposition in concrete fashion of the 'explanatory tendency,' which is the vital spring of all thought. It is not necessary, though it is natural, that the term hypothesis should be restricted to the more organized departments of thought called sciences. In this quarter, however, questions arise of general logical interest regarding the kinds, conditions, and limits of hypothesis, and the exact place they hold in relation to other distinguishable parts of the whole process of tentative explanation. To such questions definite answers are probably impossible, on account of the continuous alteration in the contents of acquired knowledge and the varying boundary between established truth and conjecture. Without detailed specification, it is hard to maintain the distinction, on which Mill insists, between a hypothesis which defines conjecturally the law or laws of a collocation of facts already known to exist and to be concerned in the facts sought to be explained, and a hypothesis whose content is the assumed existence of a fact either not known to exist or not known to enter into the collocation determining the phenomenon to be explained. It is only on the grounds supplied by already established knowledge that we can formulate even the most general restrictive conditions for the formation of a hypothesis. The treatment of the testing of hypotheses too often proceeds with neglect of the two considerations: (1) that the establishment of a law and the formation of a hypothesis are two distinct things occupying different positions in the order of thought, and (2) that there are no special conditions of proof in the case of hypothesis; the conditions are those of proof in general. Cf. THEORY.

Literature: an excellent summary of the chief views regarding the nature and place of hypothesis is given in NAVILLE, La Logique de l'Hypothèse (1880); also JEVONS, Princ. of Sci., generally, and especially chaps. xxiii, xxiv, xxvi; BOSANQUET, Logic, Bk. II. chap. v. Some good remarks on the philosophical issues involved will be found in LIEBMANN, Die Klimax d. Theorien. (R.A.)

Hypothetical: Ger. *hypothetisch*; Fr. *hypothétique*; Ital. *ipotetico*. (1) Dependent or conditioned.

(2) In logic: the general character of the hypothetical judgment and syllogism is defined by the relation of dependence which is expressed by the one and which enters into the premises of the other.

Examples:

Hypothetical Judgment:
  If you go, you will be killed.

Hypothetical Syllogism:
  If you go, you will be killed,

(1) You will go, hence you will be killed   or (2) You will not be killed, hence you will not go.

As to the more precise definition of this relation, there has been, and is yet, great divergence of view among logicians. According to some the only relation truly hypothetical is that formally expressed in the principle of reason and CONSEQUENT (q.v.), the relation of logical dependence or consequence; and even in respect to this, there is permissible the more refined difference between the interpretations of the relation as either merely stating such dependence or as implying what Mill called 'inferribility.' According to others, the relation includes all types of general statement of a law connecting two facts in such fashion that the one indicates the other, or serves as a sign of it. The difference depends to some extent on the varying views taken as to the scope and import of categorical assertion. It is probable that a reconciliation of the divergent views is to be found by the method of genetically surveying the types of judgment; for in each of them a gradual ascent is discernible from concrete to more and more abstract relations. In all cases the hypothetical judgment rests upon the assertion of some general relation as holding good; and all are agreed as to the general principle of the judgment—that given the antecedent, the consequent must be accepted, and that from denial of the consequent there follows denial of the antecedent. According to the different interpretations taken of the judgment, there will be different doctrines, as (1) to the admissibility of distinctions of quantity and quality, (2) as to the possibility of applying the formal premise of conversion, and contraposition and opposition. From the more psychological side, the question has to be considered, how thought comes to express itself in hypothetical fashion; and here stress may be laid on the element of doubt, which is clearly of like nature with the thought involved, and may affect not the general relation represented, but the concrete cases in which it is embodied; or on the factor of supposition, i.e. ideal experiment, which again rests on a general relation implied. The hypothetical syllogism is generally defined as syllogism having a hypothetical major premise, and a minor which either categorically affirms the antecedent (*modus ponens*)—(1) above—or denies the consequent (*modus tollens*)—(2) above. Such a syllogism is perhaps more strictly to be designated hypothetico-categorical. There is obviously possible a form of reasoning, purely hypothetical, in which premises and conclusion are all hypothetical judgments.

Neither hypothetical judgment nor syllogism was formally recognized by Aristotle. What he called reasonings from a hypothesis or proposition assumed to be true, were treated by him in connection with indirect proof; and though they closely resemble the later hypothetical syllogisms, were not recognized by Aristotle as having any special features. The treatment of them was carried much further by the early Peripatetics; and in the Stoic logic there is clear recognition of the peculiar thought of ' consequence,' 'logical dependence' as the import of the hypothetical judgment, a judgment which they, however, grouped along with copulatives and disjunctives. Most points of the modern theory are discussed by Boethius, from whose elaborate treatment the later logic mainly drew. In modern logic the discussion has been largely influenced by the decisive view taken by Kant, who connected the hypothetical judgment with the principle of reason and consequent, and therefore assigned to it a quite special place distinct from and co-ordinate with the categorical judgment. Kant's predecessor Wolff had, on the other hand, tended towards the view, frequently taken, and to some extent encouraged by the current mode of defining the hypothetical judgment, that the hypothetical judgment is a subordinate form of the categorical, the real assertion being the consequent which is put forward not absolutely, as in the categorical, but subject to an expressed condition. (R.A.)

From this point of view (which indeed is the only tenable one), hypotheticals are characterized only by their composite character—they are statements concerning possible statements, instead of concerning terms; that is to say, 'if *a* is *b*, *c* is *d*' affirms the invariable sequence (whether empirical or inferential) of '*c* is *d*' upon '*a* is *b*.' It is an essential part of this doctrine that the hypothetical proposition does not deserve the extreme amount of attention that has been given it—it is of no greater consequence for logic than many other relations that are constantly affirmed to hold between statements (some universal in quality and some particular); as, unless *a* is *b*, *c* is *d*; not only if *a* is *b*, is *c d*; never when *a* is *b*, is *c d*; though *a* is *b*, *c* is sometimes *d*. Sigwart, returning to the doctrine of the Stoics, showed (1871) that the hypothetical judgment asserts the sure following of the validity of the consequent upon the validity of the antecedent, and that by this alone it deserves the name of judgment. (C.L.F.)

Herbart, from his modification of the formal doctrine, was led to raise the question as to the categorical judgment, and deciding that it was not existential, practically identified it with the hypothetical, a view from which conceptualist logic can hardly free itself. His follower, Drobisch, introduced a distinction between qualitative predications and predications of relation, the latter embracing the hypothetical. Boole, accepting the view that the hypothetical is an assertion about the truth of an assertion, called it a secondary proposition, defined the 'universe of discourse' in such secondary propositions as being the time at which they together hold good, and so brought them within the scope of his general symbolic method.

Venn's treatment from this point of view (*Symbolic Logic*, chap. viii), and his discussion of the more philosophical questions involved (*Empirical Logic*, chap. x), are of special interest. Much acute discussion will be found in Keynes (*Formal Logic*), who adopts and works out a distinction between the conditional and the hypothetical, resembling that above indicated between concrete and abstract relations. The best historical account of views is that of Sigwart (*Beitr. z. Lehre des hyp. Urth.*, 1871); see also his *Logik*, §§ 35–6, 49–50. A psychological discussion of judgments and syllogisms, in which a classification is reached on the basis of belief, and the hypothetic is made a fundamental form, is to be found in Baldwin, *Handb. of Psychol.*, i. chap. xiv. Cf. JUDGMENT, CATEGORICAL JUDGMENT, SYLLOGISM, and INFERENCE. (R.A.)

Hypothetical Dualism. COSMOTHETIC IDEALISM (q. v.). See IDEALISM, passim.

Hypothetical Imperative: see CATEGORICAL IMPERATIVE.

Hypothetical Morality: see ABSOLUTE ETHICS.

Hysteria [Gr. ὑστέρα, the womb]: Ger. *Hysterie*; Fr. *hystérie*; Ital. *isterismo*. The term hysteria is used in so many different senses that it should hardly be accepted as a serious term unless the context shows what definition is implied. The common but objectionable usage covers states of deficient emotional control and states of 'imaginary' diseases. The common medical usage is a little less crude, but fails to rise to a clear definition of what is implied by 'imaginary.' In neurological literature there is a growing tendency to limit the term to those psychogenic disorders which Charcot and his school have worked out: disorders of function depending usually on subconscious states of mind of the nature of those observed in hypnotism. Lloyd defines it as a psychoneurosis, of which the physical symptoms are the most conspicuous, tending to disguise the (really fundamental) mental phenomena and to simulate superficially the effects of various organic diseases. (A.M.)

The etymology of the term reflects the supposed connection of this disorder (a view dominant until within recent times) with uterine troubles. While the name is retained this view is abandoned, and even the special association of hysterical symptoms with the female sex must be modified.

If insanity may be considered as a disorder in the functionally highest layers of the cortex (which involve the most complex intellectual processes, and inhibition of which renders control impossible), hysteria may be considered to involve the next lower level of functional action, which is amenable to control. Its disturbance is consistent with intellectual ability, and is liable to bring with it sensori-motor disorders (Mercier). Hysteria is best considered a special type or tendency of neurotic or psychopathic instability which comes either as an abnormality of development (constitutional inferiority) or as a feature of acquired nervous disturbances. In accordance with the view that hysteria is a tendency or diathesis rather than a disease, and that mental characteristics form its distinctive features, these aspects may be first considered.

Subjects of Hysteria. Hysteria exhibits its connection with other forms of nervous disorders in its hereditary relations; neuropathic families present cases of distinct insanity, of epilepsy, and of hysteria in close connection. While it may come on earlier, it is most apt to appear soon after puberty, the ages between fifteen and twenty being most productive of it. The complex unfoldment and enlargement of emotions and ideas which ensue at this time make it a period of special stress and strain, a crisis in which any latent nervous instability is especially apt to become manifest. The more marked suddenness of onset of this period in woman, its more automatic relations with her physical economy, her deeper emotional development and the greater restraint of expression and action which social custom places upon her, contribute to a feminine preponderance of hysteria. But this is by no means so marked as was formerly considered; hysteria in males is quite common, and certain French statistics show that in the lower classes hysteria is more common in men than in women, while in the higher social strata the reverse is the case. It is certain that lack of rational interests and occupations, of wholesome outlets for natural instincts, as well as hereditary taint, contribute to the development of hysteria. Emotional shock, long-continued anxiety or strain, and a large number of special disorders which deplete or unbalance the nervous system may act as special excitants of hysteria.

Mental Symptoms. Exaggerated impressionability, the liability to tremulous emotion on slight provocation, undue concentration upon self, a craving for sympathy, a limited power of adaptation to circumstances, irresoluteness, imperfectly controlled action—these are some of the prominent characteristics of the hysterically disposed temperament. They do not constitute insanity, and indeed the mental disorder may be very slight. The outrageous and improper actions at times performed are recognized by the patient to be the result of a want of control. As in all temperamental abnormalities, there are endless degrees, from the lowest to the highest; and in hysteria especially the variety of the mental symptoms and the doubt which is cast on their genuineness by a probable admixture of imposture renders the state most difficult to describe. While the craftiness and subtlety of certain hysterical subjects must be fully admitted, it is a mistake to regard the disease itself as in any way a sham; although one must admit the proneness to deception, which in some cases becomes a dominant passion for falsehood and deceit, and in others is only the natural resource of a temperament longing for sympathy and interest. Apart from the sensory and motor disorders, the true nature of which is indicated by their amenability to suggestion and psychic influences, it is difficult in many cases to detect any tangible mental abnormalities.

Sensory Disorders. Hyperaesthesia, anaesthesia, pain, and perverted forms of sensibility (dysaesthesia, paraesthesia) are most common. Excessive tenderness in certain regions (abdomen, epigastrium, spine, ovary, joints) is a frequent symptom, the hysterical nature of which can be determined only by elimination of true objective causes. Certain spots or areas may exhibit anaesthesia or analgesia; these may be superficial or so deep that needles may be thrust into the skin without evoking pain or sensation. The conjunctiva may be quite insensitive to touch. There may be hemianaesthesia, limited to the entire half of the body and affecting the special senses as well, or affecting only certain unilateral tactile areas. Frequently the patient is unaware of the anaesthesia.

The psychical origin of such anaesthesias is indicated by their sensibility to suggestion and 'transfer' (see below). In the sphere of the special senses may occur intoler-ance of light, abnormal acuity of vision, subjective sensations of flashes, bad tastes or odours, partial deafness, &c. The craving for unnatural and distasteful articles of food is referred to disorders of taste. Specially noteworthy are the visual troubles; the most frequent being the narrowing of the visual field, usually affecting both eyes, but one more than the other. The absence of ocular and tactile reflexes is frequently noted, as well as the capricious and variable character of the sensory disorders in general. These are extremely common, and again indicate a participation of centres lower than those connected with the mental symptoms.

Motor Disorders. These occur mainly in the form of (1) spasms, (2) convulsions, and (3) various paralyses. (1) Characteristic forms of spasms are the globus hystericus, which is described as though a lump were rising from the epigastrium to the throat and there causing a choking and flow of tears. Spasmodic cough, respiratory difficulties, vomiting, stomachic or intestinal spasms, and both tonic and clonic spasms of muscles may be present, and in some cases may disappear suddenly after enduring for months or years. The mixture of laughter and weeping is perhaps the commonest example of hysterical spasm. Contractures have been noted, especially by French observers. They may persist during sleep, resist slight etherization, and yield only to electric stimulation. It is noteworthy that they may be aroused by slight tapping or excitation as well as by psychical causes. (2) Convulsive seizures are of common occurrence in pronounced hysteria. These may be preceded by a feeling of choking, a pain, headache, vertigo, or the like; they rarely come with extreme suddenness, and are frequently resisted by the patient for some time. If the patient falls, severe injury or dangerous positions are avoided (unlike the epileptic). The resulting spasms are irregular (seldom clonic); opisthotonos—a position in which the body is arched backwards and rests on the head and heels—is noted by French observers. The avoidance of injury in falling, the use of language, and other symptoms indicate that the unconsciousness in the hysterical fit is partial only. (3) Lessened muscular power and any degree and form of paralysis may occur affecting the visceral or voluntary system. Hysterical aphonia is a common variety. In this the voice alone is affected, and a characteristic whisper is used. In hysterical mutism the defect is more psychical, and all spoken language is lost, even the most common words, so often retained in true aphasia; intelligence is unimpaired, there is a desire to speak, and writing proceeds fluently. The legs are apt to be concerned in paresis, with rigidity in thighs and feet, and, to a less extent, the arms. Paraplegias and abnormalities in response to electrical stimuli are frequent. Hysterical paralysis can be distinguished from true organic paralysis only by carefully noting the absence of symptoms of true organic disorders. There is, too, in hysteria, a characteristic want of effort, indicating a defect in will power, resembling that in awaking from sleep. The tendency to sudden disappearance, to modification by suggestion, with the accompanying mental symptoms, is a significant mark of hysterical paralyses.

To sum up, it may be said that the characteristic change is the predominance of disorders of whole psychogenetic complexes of movements, e. g. disorders of the use of the legs for walking, while the patient can still climb; without involvement of those features which are not under psychic control, i. e. without influence on reflexes, electric reaction of nerves and muscles, &c.

Bodily Condition. Disorders of circulation and digestion are common. A tendency to syncope, palpitation, high temperatures of short duration, unusual sensations of cold and heat, have been noted; as have also vomiting, accumulation of gas in the digestive tract, abnormal secretions, difficulty in taking food, constipation, and the like.

Hysterogenic Zones. The existence of certain areas, stimulation of which by pressure may provoke or arrest the paroxysm of hysteria, was indicated by Charcot (1873); not only in the ovarian region, but particularly the definite regions of the head and trunk. They are frequently associated with dysaesthesias, and may be related to these. Their variability in some cases, and the fact that pressure may both provoke or arrest the attack, indicate the psychic factor in this process.

Hysteria and Hypnosis. Whether one maintains, with Charcot and his supporters, that hypnosis is a neurosis with definite stages and somatic symptoms, or, with the Nancy school, that mental suggestion is the one sufficient clue to the entire range of phenomena, the existence of a special relation between hysteria and hypnosis cannot be denied. It is certainly easier to produce the deeper stages and the more unusual phenomena of hypnotic suggestion in hysterical

subjects than in others. According to Charcot the relation is more intimate; the grande hypnotisme with its definite forms (lethargy, catalepsy, and somnambulism), its marked bodily stigmata and symptoms, its hypnogenic spots, its spasms, &c., occurs almost wholly in hysterical patients. Hypnotism has also been used as a means of study of the hysterical condition; it has been found, for instance, that while the anaesthetic or paralytic arm of an hysterical subject is apparently devoid of sensation and voluntary control, it does respond to the suggestions made in the hypnotic condition by touches and movements. Such observations, which have been ingeniously varied (see Janet, *L'Automatisme psychologique*), are of importance in the study of automatism and disorders of PERSONALITY (q.v.). Cf. HYPNOSIS, and HYSTERO-EPILEPSY.

Historical. Apart from the variations in the conceptions of this malady, and particularly its relations with ovarian troubles and its dependence upon nervous conditions (see Féré, as cited below, 551 ff.), hysteria has been of importance historically because it furnishes the clue to many of the phenomena of possession and ecstasy, of WITCHCRAFT (q.v.), demonomania, and mental epidemics (Féré, loc. cit., 451 ff.). The paroxysm of hysteria so suggestive of possession, the anaesthetic spots found in witches, the marvellous sudden cures at holy shrines, as well as the special susceptibility of hysterical persons to suggestion and contagion, indicate some of the directions in which modern study illuminates the phenomena of the past (cf. White, *The Warfare of Science with Theology*, 1896, chap. xvi; and Lehmann, *Aberglaube u. Zauberei*, 1899).

Literature: art. Hysteria in Tuke's Dict. of Psychol. Med. (1892); GILLES DE LA TOURETTE, Traité de l'Hystérie (3 vols., 1896–8); A. PITRES, Leçons sur l'Hystérie (2 vols., 1891); PRESTON, Hysteria and allied Conditions (1897); JANET, État mental des Hystériques (1894); CH. FÉRÉ, Hysteria, in Twentieth Cent. Pract. of Med., x (1897, with bibliography); BREUER and FREUD, Stud. ü. Hysterie (1895); general works on PATHOLOGY (q. v., notably CHARCOT). (J.J.–A.M.)

Hystero-epilepsy: Ger. *Hystero-epilepsie*; Fr. *hystéro-épilepsie*; Ital. *istero-epilessia*. A term which has its origin in the difficulty of distinguishing between many forms of convulsions of true epilepsy or true hysteria. It is also applied to those cases of hysteria in which convulsions occur (grande hystérie of Charcot).

The paroxysms in this form of disorder may be violent; the patient often, after distinct aura, falls with a cry, more completely loses consciousness than in ordinary hysteria, presents tonic convulsions usually more marked on the side where dysaesthesia or paralysis has been manifested, and may go through a series of flexions and extensions of the whole trunk, which are either general writhings or movements coarsely suggestive of the influence of various passions. This epileptic stage, which comes first, has many of the characteristic symptoms of true epilepsy: the suspension of respiration, the swelling of the neck, the foaming at the mouth, the position of the limbs. But the subsequent irregular movements, the admixture of speech mimicry and other mental elements, as well as the personal history of the patient and the absence of other epileptic symptoms, are sufficient to differentiate the one from the other. Fixed positions or contractions are apt to occur, and are often maintained during sleep and for a long time. In addition the dysaesthesias and paralyses, the pain and hysterogenic zones, the curious disorders of vision and voice, which have been described as characteristic of severe cases of hysteria, are equally characteristic of hystero-epilepsy. See HYSTERIA.

Literature: CHARCOT, Leçons sur les Maladies du Système nerveux (1886), i. chap. iii ; RICHER, L'Étude clinique sur l'Hystéro-épilepsie (1881); also citations under HYSTERIA. (J.J.)

Hysteron Proteron [Gr. ὕστερον πρότερον]. A form of the FALLACY (q. v.) of *Petitio Principii*, consisting in reversal of the true objective order of reason and consequent, or sign and signified.

In the concrete the fallacy—a very common one—occurs partly because the order of acquiring knowledge is generally different from the logical, objective order, partly because the interconnectedness of conditions in nature prevents our recognizing the true order of dependence. It is possible that the time-order of our perceptions, e. g., may reverse the real order of dependence. (R.A.)

I

I and Me. Synonymous with subject-self and object-self. See SELF (also for foreign equivalents). (J.M.B.)

I (in logic). Symbol for the particular affirmative judgment: 'Some men are fools.' Cf. A (in logic). (J.M.B.)

Iamblicus (or **Jamblicus**). Lived in the 3rd and 4th century A.D. A Neo-Platonic philosopher, who was a disciple of Porphyry. Many of his writings are extant. See ALEXANDRIAN SCHOOL.

Iconolatry: see IMAGE-WORSHIP.

Id : see IDANT, and BIOPHORE.

Idant [no specific formation according to Weismann—E.B.P.] (the same in other languages). The hypothetical unit resulting from the aggregation of biophores, determinants, and ids (all Weismann's terms). Suggested by Weismann, 1891 (*Germ-Plasm*, Eng. trans., 1893). (C.LL.M.)

Idea [Gr. ἰδέα]: Ger. *Idee, Vorstellung* (presentation); Fr. *idée*; Ital. *idea, rappresentazione.* The reproduction, with a more or less adequate IMAGE (q. v.), of an object not actually present to the senses. (G.F.S.—J.M.B.)

The partial reproduction by the image is distinguished from actual perception by various alleged characteristics—on which, however, authorities differ—such as difference in degree of intensity and, perhaps, in kind of intensity, comparative absence of detail, comparative independence of bodily movement on the part of the subject, and comparative dependence on mental activity.

The earlier English usage is well exemplified by the following passage from Locke : 'I must at the entrance beg pardon for the frequent use of the word idea which he [the reader] will find in the following treatise ; it being that term which I think best to stand for whatever is the object of the understanding when a man thinks. I have used it to express whatever is meant by phantasm, notion, species, or whatever it is which the mind can be employed about in thinking ; and I could not avoid frequently using it' (*Essay on Human Understanding*, I. vi. § 8). In this passage the term is applied to objects apprehended, and not to the subjective state or process of apprehending them. Further, objects as perceived by means of actual sensations are included under the term, as well as objects represented independently of actual sensations. In Hume the subjective process of apprehension is simply confused with the object as apprehended ; but he makes a sharp distinction between perceptual experiences, which he calls impressions, and ideas, which are, according to him, always fainter reproductions of previous impressional experiences.

The German Vorstellung is not uncommonly used so as to cover both perception and idea in the narrower sense (cf. PRESENTATION). There has been a tendency to give the term 'idea' the same wide application in English. It is, for instance, so used in Titchener's *Outline of Psychology*. But the English tradition since Hume is against this usage, and there seems to be no good reason for adopting it. The definition either of percept or idea, or both, as a group of sensations or sensory elements, so-called 'centrally initiated sensations' (see SENSATION), implies a particular psychological theory. The definition we have given might be provisionally adopted by all psychologists.

Literature: LOCKE, loc. cit.; HUME, Treatise

of Human Nature, Bk. I. Pt. I. § 1 ; TITCH-ENER, Outline of Psychol., Pt. II. chap. vii. § 43, with which contrast Primer of Psychol., chap. vi. §§ 38–9 ; WARD, art. Psychology, Encyc. Brit. (9th ed.), 57 ff.; WUNDT, Physiol. Psychol., ii. 1 ff. ; BALDWIN, Elements of Psychol., glossary. (G.F.S., J.M.B.)

Idea (in philosophy): see IDEALISM, and PLATONISM. Cf. also extensive citations in Eisler, *Wörterb. d. philos. Begriffe*, 'Idee.'

Idea-force. An idea considered as having a dynamic property or as being a force.

A rendering of the French Idée-force used by Fouillée (*Psychol. des Idées-forces*), who has developed the theory that mental development proceeds by the interplay of original idea-forces. (J.M.B.)

Ideal: Ger. (1) *vorstellend* (= ideating), (2) *ideal*; Fr. *idéal*; Ital. *ideale*. (1) The adjective of IDEA (q. v.). See also IDEATION, for distinction from ideational.

(2) That which we suppose would be completely satisfying, if we were able to attain it, is called the ideal of its kind : the moral ideal is the morally satisfying ; the ideal self, the self which would have no lack to itself ; the aesthetic ideal, that which satisfies the demand for beauty ; the ideal gun, one that satisfies the requirements of accurate shooting.

The mode of consciousness involved in 'setting-up,' 'entertaining,' or 'having' an ideal is complex and obscure. Many writers consider the ideal a conception, but one rarely, if ever, realized in knowledge, life, &c. But it seems to be a part of this state of consciousness that the demand goes out beyond the actual conception ; it never stops with the relatively satisfying, but aims always at what is still more satisfying.

Other writers accordingly find the ideal to be not an actual thought or conception, but a mixed conative-affective mode, which is a function of the actual thought : a mode which essentially anticipates further thought, and so demands something that can never be actually apprehended by thought. This meets the great difficulty that no one can state his ideal, in any department of knowledge. The case is not different in those instances in which the ideal seems to be fulfilled, as when we say that the circle fulfils the ideal of roundness ; for there the term ideal has the meaning merely of adequate definition, and the peculiar mode of consciousness in question is not present at all.

The conative element in the psychosis is so strong that the term is mainly significant in spheres demanding achievement and practical adjustment ; in philosophical construction, art, and conduct. The term is used in ethics (see IDEAL, moral, and END) for the theoretical determination of the highest end. But great confusion has arisen from the failure to distinguish what such an ideal would consist in, and the individual's state of mind of which his ideal is a function. It is quite possible that the nearest approximation to the ideal of the ethical life is realized when the individual's end is subserving an ideal of a very different character.

But the intellectual characteristics of the ideal are embodied in the constructions actually made, and progress toward the ideal is made only by a series of such embodiments. It is this which differentiates and marks off an ideal. In this sense the ideal is thought or conceived. It is a sort of imminent end which dominates the scheme of development ; although for this very reason consciousness cannot anticipate its own outcome, nor grasp the ideal itself in a single act of thought. Cf. INTENT.

Literature: general works on psychology and ethics. (J.M.B., G.F.S.)

Ideal (in aesthetics). (1) Consisting in ideas, having meaning or significance, as contrasted with the formal or sensuous element in a work of art; e.g. the ideal content of a picture, of music, &c. (2) A self-existing, changeless archetype, of which all finite forms or human images of beauty are imperfect copies, i.e. Plato's idea of beauty (see BEAUTY, I). 'The true and absolute ideal is God' (Cousin). (3) The embodiment in an individual (real or imaged) of what is valued aesthetically by an individual, a race, &c.; e.g. 'Apollo was the Greek ideal of manly beauty.' This may take three distinct forms : (*a*) what belongs especially to the TYPE (q. v.) may be emphasized to the neglect of the distinctively characteristic (so Winckelmann's conception of the Greek ideal); (*b*) what is distinctively characteristic of the individual may be intensified (rare); (*c*) the representation may be modified freely under the influence of more subjective considerations, viz. the artist's own personal selection of the point of view, or of the aspects of the subject or scene which appeal to his aesthetic feeling (the more usual popular conception of the term). (4) Actually embodying some concept or value, as 'He made an ideal Hamlet' (this is similar to (3), but is wider as involving the notion of corresponding to a concept as well as a value, and is thus akin to the mathematical and physical use of the term; e.g. an ideal solid is one that is perfectly rigid). (5) Existing merely in idea, opposed to real. This use seems to be derived from both (1) and (3 c). (6) Arising from an idea and having the unity characteristic of an idea, in the phrase 'ideal motion' used by Gurney to describe the process of perceiving musical form (*Power of Sound*, chap. viii).

For the discussion as to the nature of the ideal see IDEAL, BEAUTY, IV, and ART, III, and cf. CHARACTERISTIC, and EXPRESSION. For the process of forming ideals, see IMAGINATION, and IDEALIZATION.

Literature: see the general histories of aesthetics, given under ART, and BEAUTY; for the present usage, the works under AESTHETICS, and especially those under IDEALIZATION and REALISM. See also BIBLIOG. D, *a, d.* (J.H.T.)

Ideal (moral). (1) That which we suppose would satisfy our moral nature if we were able to attain it. Cf. IDEAL (2).

As contrasted with moral END (q.v.), the ideal is a state of attainment reached by the pursuit of the end. It is, therefore, rather an INTENT (q.v.) than an end. It is important that this distinction should be made, since the question of the ideal is often made the same as that of the end; that is, it is sought to determine the ideal in terms of the individual's end. (J.M.B.)

(2) The conception by reference to which man's conduct should be regulated, or to which his character should be assimilated.

Wherever independent ethical reflection has arisen, a rule or standard has been sought for the discrimination of right from wrong; and this rule or standard is either itself the ideal for man's conduct and character or results from that ideal. The term arose from the Platonic use of 'idea' for the true nature or essence of a thing. The moral ideal is thus the essence of goodness; and, in modern usage, the employment of the term 'ideal' instead of 'idea' indicates that this essential goodness is not actually realized, but in need of realization.

Different conceptions of the ideal of man fix the differences of ethical schools. Thus the various hedonist and utilitarian schools maintain that the realization of pleasure, in some form or other, is the ideal; while other schools hold it to be the perfection of the individual and social nature or the performance

of the moral rules laid down by each man's conscience. Cf. ETHICAL THEORIES. (W.R.S.)

Ideal Realism: see REAL IDEALISM.

Idealism [Gr. ἰδέα, idea]: Ger. *Idealismus*; Fr. *idéalisme*; Ital. *idealismo*. (1) In metaphysics: any theory which maintains the universe to be throughout the work or the embodiment of reason or mind.

(2) In epistemology: the view which holds, in opposition to REALISM (q.v.), that the reality of the external world is its perceptibility.

(1) In this reference, the so-called absolute idealism of Hegel, with its thesis of the convertibility of the real and the rational, is a consistent and ultimate formulation of the position. But any theory which seeks the explanation, or ultimate *raison d'être*, of the cosmic evolution in the realization of reason, self-consciousness, or spirit, may fairly claim to be included under this designation. For the end in such a system is not only the result, but, as the determining *prius* of the whole process, is also the true world-building power.

The diametrical opposite of idealism in this sense is materialism or, as it has sometimes been styled, NATURALISM (q.v., 2). According to this view, consistently formulated, the universe is simply a brute fact, or collocation of brute facts, under the sway of mechanical law. 'Verily, not by design,' as Lucretius puts it, 'did the first beginnings of things station themselves each in its right place guided by keen intelligence, but because, many in number and shifting about in many ways throughout the universe, they are driven and tormented by blows during infinite time past; after trying motions and unions of every kind, at length they fall into arrangements such as those out of which this our sum of things has been formed, and by which it is preserved through many great years when once it has been thrown into the appropriate motions' (*De Rerum Natura*, i. 1020). In other words, the apparently rational system of the present cosmos is represented as a happy accident, resulting from one of the infinite casts of nature's dice. This system might be fitly called the Democritic, as the idealistic might be styled the Platonico-Aristotelian. The principle of the one is ἀνάγκη, blind necessity or fate; the principle of the other is purposive reason.

The first historical system to which the name of idealism is applied by common consent is that of Plato. In Plato's system reality does not belong to the ever-changing world of sense; true being is found in the incorporeal essences or ideas, which communicate to phenomena whatever permanent existence and knowability they possess. These pure forms exist in a supersensuous world by themselves, and their relation to the world of phenomena is indicated by Plato only by the help of metaphors. The ideal world of Plato is thus not so much a world of spiritual or self-conscious existence as of abstract reason— a system of abstract rational conceptions, regarded as substances and powers. It must be allowed, however, that in his account of the Idea of the Good, the highest and, in some ways, the all-embracing concept, he formulates in his own way the same idea of an absolute self-realizing End which is the central thought of the Aristotelian system. But idealism, when it fails to demonstrate its thesis of the omnipotence and omnipresence of mind as the all-sufficient explanation of the facts of existence, relapses into dualism; and this relapse is represented in Plato by the necessity of invoking, besides the world of true being, a secondary or accessory cause τὸ μὴ ὄν, which he elsewhere designates ἀνάγκη, and which has to a certain extent the power of hindering the perfect realization of the ideas, and thus of thwarting the purposeful working of the Good. Aristotle, by his profound conception of development, goes far to overcome the dualism involved in the transcendent form of Plato's statement, but he also fails to eliminate the non-rational element involved in phenomenal existence. The Aristotelian πρώτη ὕλη, or wholly unformed matter, is defined as mere possibility which is not actual. Yet, says Windelband, it is not merely that which is not-being, but the accessory cause, which evinces itself as such through real effects (τὸ οὗ οὐκ ἄνευ—sine qua non). Its reality is shown in the fact that the forms do not completely realize themselves in individual things, and that from it side-workings (παραφυάς) proceed, which are without connection with the purposively active form, or are even in contradiction to it. From matter arises that which is conceptually indeterminate (συμβεβηκός) or the accidental (αὐτόματον)—the lawless and purposeless in nature. Hence the Aristotelian doctrine distinguishes, in its explanation of nature, as did Plato in the Philebus, between final causes (τὸ οὗ ἕνεκα) and mechanical causes (τὸ ἐξ ἀνάγκης): the former are the forms which realize themselves in matter; the latter reside in matter, out of which proceed side-workings and counter-workings. Thus the cosmic processes are regarded by Aristotle ultimately under the analogy of the plastic artist, who

finds in the hard material a limit to the realization of his formative thought. This material is, indeed, so far related to the idea that the idea can present itself in it, at least in general, and yet it is in so far a foreign, and thus an independent, element, that it in part opposes itself as a retarding principle to the realizing of the forms. Ancient philosophy did not overstep this dualism between the purposive activity of the form, on the one hand, and the resistance of matter on the other

In modern philosophy the term idealism, in this metaphysical significance, has been mostly used in connection with the speculative systems developed by Fichte, Schelling, and Hegel, out of the critical philosophy of Kant. Kant speaks of his own philosophy as 'transcendental idealism,' but, as so applied, the term is used in an epistemological reference which will presently be explained. The Kantian scheme might, indeed, be described as idealism in the metaphysical sense, inasmuch as it regards the kingdom of ends— the ethical commonwealth of self-legislating spirits—as the noumenal world or ultimate reality, of which the world of sense is the phenomenalization. 'Nature,' Kant says, 'assumes a unity which does not otherwise belong to it, and becomes a realm or system, only when viewed in relation to rational beings as its ends.' (Werke, iv. 286, ed. Hartenstein, 1868). But the term is not so used by Kant himself. Fichte, however, accepting from Kant the primacy of the practical reason, claims the name idealism as the distinctive appellation of his own system, and draws an elaborate series of distinctions between idealism and the opposite point of view, which he calls dogmatism. The ego, not as a fact or a thing but as a self-realizing activity (Thathandlung), constitutes the principle of his own theory; every doctrine, on the contrary, is dogmatic which starts with the existence of things and, taking the ego as a thing among things, explains it in the last instance as their product (see the 'First Introduction to the Wissenschaftslehre,' Werke, i. 419 f.; also i. 119 f.).

It used to be customary to describe Fichte's system as 'subjective' idealism in contrast to the 'objective' idealism of Schelling and the 'absolute' idealism of Hegel. The justification for such a usage was found in his method of starting with the ego, and regarding the non-ego simply as the antithesis or opposite of the ego—the obstacle (self-imposed, no doubt, and necessary, but still an obstacle) to the realization and complete self-expression of the intelligent and ethical self. But the usage is misleading, in so far as the ego with which Fichte starts is not the individual but the absolute ego. Moreover, the term subjective idealism has come to be used exclusively in an epistemological reference. Fichte himself describes his idealism as 'practical.' 'Our idealism is not dogmatic but practical, that is, it determines not what is but what ought to be' (*Werke*, i. 156). Nature, according to him, is simply the material for the realization of duty, and duty is an eternal sollen or thou shalt, inspired by 'the idea of our absolute existence.' 'The ego demands that it shall embrace all reality and fill infinity. At the bottom of this demand there lies necessarily the idea of the absolutely posited infinite ego' (i. 277). But this 'idea of the ego' exists only as an ideal. The completion of the task would mean that the ego had subdued all things to itself, and was able to view them as determinations of its own existence, but the extinction of opposition would signify the cessation of the strife on which morality and consciousness depend. Hence the ideal is in its very nature unrealizable. It was this 'practical' character of his idealism which made Fichte an ethical reformer, and inspired his famous *Addresses to the German Nation*. But from a metaphysical point of view the theory was attacked by Schelling and Hegel as an imperfect statement of the idealistic position, inasmuch as it presents the idea as a mere sollen—an ought-to-be, which never completely is. Schelling's 'objective' idealism regards 'nature as visible intelligence, and intelligence as invisible nature.' In other words, nature, apart from the moral activity of conscious beings, is already a system of ideal forms, and is therefore to be regarded not merely as non-ego, or an obstacle to be overcome, but as itself the expression of the same reason which comes to self-consciousness in man. Or, according to the somewhat later version of Schelling's theory, known as the IDENTITY PHILOSOPHY (q. v.), subject and object are parallel expressions of absolute reason, which, in itself, 'coincides precisely with the indifference-point of subjective and objective.' Hegel's 'absolute' idealism regards both nature and history as applied logic. Nature is merely 'the other' of reason—a petrified intelligence, as he says in the Schellingian manner—and in history we have the process of absolute

spirit, the necessary stages on its way to complete self-realization. The universe is claimed, therefore, as rational through and through and to the smallest detail; 'the real is rational and the rational is real.' Or, as he says again in the *Philosophy of Right*, 'the task of philosophy is to understand the "what is," for "what is" is reason.' In marked antithesis to Fichte, he disclaims for philosophy the rôle of the reformer; the idea is in fact eternally realized. Hegel even goes occasionally so far as to represent progress as, from this, the speculative point of view, an illusion. 'The consummation of the infinite end consists merely in removing the illusion which makes it seem still unaccomplished. This illusion it is under which we live, and it alone supplies the actualizing force on which our interest in the world depends. In the course of its process, the idea makes itself that illusion by setting up an antithesis to confront itself, and its action consists in getting rid of the illusion which it has created' (Wallace, *Logic of Hegel*, 304). Even Hegel, however, seems, in those passages in which he speaks of 'the range of the contingent' in nature and history, to surrender the claim to demonstrate the utter rationality of existence. 'Who but a Hegelian philosopher,' says Professor James trenchantly, 'ever pretended that reason in action was *per se* a sufficient explanation of the political changes in Europe?' (*Princ. of Psychol.*, i. 553). Whether, therefore, we look at Aristotle or at Hegel, it would seem as if it were impossible for the finite mind to carry through in detail a demonstration of the rationality of existence, and as if faith, accordingly, must unite with insight in the idealistic creed.

(2) Quite a different sense of the term 'idealism' emerges in connection with epistemology or theory of knowledge. In this reference, which belongs entirely to modern philosophy, idealism, more precisely defined as 'subjective idealism,' is opposed to realism. The realist is one who considers that in sense-perception we have assurance of the presence of a reality, distinct from the modifications of the perceiving mind, and existing independently of our perceptions. The idealist, on the other hand, asserts that the reality of the external world is its perceptibility; as Berkeley, the founder of modern idealism, expressed it, the *esse* of things is *percipi*. Mill's so-called 'psychological' theory of the belief in an external world, which resolves its reality into actual sensations and permanent possibilities of sensation, is pro-

bably the most typical recent form of the theory. Kant's definition of idealism in the *Prolegomena*, framed with Berkeley in view, applies equally to the more modern version: 'Idealism consists in the assertion that there are no other than thinking beings, that the other things which we believe ourselves to perceive are only ideas in thinking beings— ideas in fact to which there is no correspondent object outside of or beyond the thinking beings.' Idealism, in this sense, may be said to be the outcome of the belief that the mind is primarily limited in knowledge to a perception of its own subjective states, or, as Locke puts it, that 'the mind in all its thoughts and reasonings hath no other immediate object but its own ideas which it alone does or can contemplate' (*Essay*, IV. i. 1). 'It is evident,' he says elsewhere, 'the mind knows not things immediately, but only by the intervention of the ideas it has of them.' This may be said to be the common presupposition of modern philosophy from Descartes to Hume. It is common to Descartes and Locke, who believe in the independent existence of the external world, and to Berkeley and Hume who deny any such inference. It is inherent in Leibnitz's conception of 'windowless' monads, and in Spinoza's view of the attribute of thought as self-contained. Reid calls it 'the ideal theory' or 'the theory of ideas,' and traces to this root the scepticism of Hume, to which he opposes his own doctrine of natural realism or natural dualism. Kant's *Refutation of Idealism* is directed against the same presupposition—namely, that the only indubitable certainty is the certainty of our own internal states, and that this certainty constitutes (as Descartes makes it do) the starting-point of knowledge. From this point of view, the term idealism acquires in the hands of Kant and of Hamilton (elaborating the doctrine of Reid with Kantian additions) a wider application. Thus the doctrine of Descartes, who is, of course, not an idealist in the sense of denying the independent existence of the external world, is called by Kant 'problematical idealism,' because, by treating the *res extensa* as a matter of inference and belief, it places its reality on a lower level of certainty than that of our internal states. Hamilton applies the term 'cosmothetic idealism' (or 'hypothetical dualism'), in the same reference, and with precisely the same implication, to 'the great majority of modern philosophers' (*Lects. on Met.*, i. 295). As distinguished from such a position, idealism

in the stricter sense—the subjective idealism of Berkeley—is called by Kant 'dogmatic idealism.' He also uses the term 'material idealism' to include both varieties—the problematic and the dogmatic—in contradistinction to his own theory of 'formal,' 'critical,' or 'transcendental' idealism.

Consistent subjective idealism would seem to involve not only a denial of the reality of other persons (solipsism), but a sensationalistic scepticism like that of Hume, which resolves the thinker himself into a series of 'perceptions,' regarded as facts pure and simple, without any cognitive value whatever. Hence it is explicable how Spencer, in his polemic against idealism (*Princ. of Psychol.*, Pt. VII), persistently links idealism with scepticism—a conjunction which aptly illustrates the wide divergence between the epistemological sense of the term idealism, and the metaphysical usage which was discussed in the first part of this article.

The term 'transcendental idealism,' as applied by Kant to his own theory, refers only to the formal elements of experience— space and time and the categories. These constitute 'the pure schema of possible experience,' but do not apply to things in themselves; in Kant's language, they are 'transcendentally ideal,' that is to say, of merely subjective validity. In a general regard, Kant's theory of knowledge is to be classed as realistic or dualistic, inasmuch as, according to his own statement, it had never entered into his head to doubt the existence of things in themselves. Cf. PHILOSOPHY, EPISTEMOLOGY, METAPHYSICS, REALISM, KANT'S TERMINOLOGY, and HEGEL'S TERMINOLOGY.

Literature: PAULSEN, Introd. to Philos., ii. chap. i; KÜLPE, Introd. to Philos., §§ 5, 26; EUCKEN, Grundbegriffe d. Gegenwart, 244 f. (A.S.P.P.)

Idealism (in aesthetics): (1) An aesthetic standpoint or theory which emphasizes the ideal or content element in beauty, opposed to FORMALISM (q.v.), IMPRESSIONISM (q. v.), and SENSUALISM (q. v.). It may be either (*a*) abstract, ideas being transcendental copies or ideals (Plato, Schelling); or (*b*) concrete, the idea being an immanent principle (v. Hartmann, *Aesthetik*, i. 27). See under BEAUTY, IV. (J.H.T.–K.G.)

(2) As opposed to realism, a theory of art which lays emphasis on the artist's idealization or modification of his material and construction of his work, according to subjective values, as contrasted with an objective

reproduction. This in common usage often implies a less concrete and individualistic representation. Cf. IDEAL (in aesthetics), (3, *a* and *c*).

Literature: see under FORMALISM, IMPRESSIONISM, and REALISM. (J.H.T.)

Ideality: Ger. *Idealität*; Fr. *idéalité*; Ital. *idealità*. Ideal quality; used (in aesthetics) especially with reference to meanings (1), (3, *a* and *c*) of IDEAL (in aesthetics, q.v.). (J.H.T.)

Idealization (aesthetic): Ger. *Idealisierung*; Fr. *idéalisation*; Ital. (not in use). (1) The apprehension of truths or facts as fit for construction in an ideal.

The limits of idealization would seem to be, (*a*) the partial embodiment of the particular sort of ideal already in the truths or facts which are idealized. This partial embodiment prescribes the direction or character of the idealization. (*b*) The carrying over of the particular value—aesthetic, moral, &c.—attaching to the truths idealized, to the ideal, with exclusion of what is opposed or inharmonious. The ideal interpretation, it is felt, is thus and thus on the basis of these items of knowledge; that is, it is the sort of ideal which these particulars suggest. (J.M.B.)

(2) The process of giving meaning as under IDEAL (in aesthetics (1), q.v.), or of forming an ideal in either of the senses given under IDEAL (in aesthetics (3), q.v.).

Literature: VOLKELT, Aesth. Zeitfragen (1895), chaps. ii–iv; FECHNER, Vorschule d. Aesth. (1876); SANTAYANA, Sense of Beauty (1896), 112 ff.; SIEBECK, Das Wesen d. aesth. Anschauung (1875); SÉAILLES, Essai sur le Génie dans l'Art (1897); HODGSON, Met. of Experience (1898), iii. 384 ff.; SULLY, Human Mind, i. 377 ff.; BALDWIN, Feeling and Will, 198 ff.; DEWEY, Psychology, chap. vii; ALLEN, Physiol. Aesth. (1877), chap. ix. (J.H.T.)

Ideas of the Reason: see KANTIAN TERMINOLOGY, 10–21.

Ideation: Ger. *vorstellende Thätigkeit*; Fr. *idéation*; Ital. *attività rappresentatrice ideazione*. Mental process which takes the form of a succession of ideas. Suggested and explained by J. S. Mill, *Logic*, ii. 216.

The adjective form 'ideational,' as applied to such a process, is more exact than is ideal. (G.F.S.—J.M.B.)

Ideatum [Lat.]. The OBJECT (q. v.) of cognition. (J.M.B.)

Identical Points: Ger. *identische Punkte*; Fr. *points identiques des rétines*; Ital. *punti identici*. Retinal points which, when the eyes are in the primary position, occupy coincident positions in relation to the centre of the retina, and correspond to coincident image points of an infinitely distant object.

The identical points are for anatomy what the corresponding or CONGRUENT POINTS (q.v.) are for physiology. Their discussion in modern times dates from J. Müller (Helmholtz, *Physiol. Optik*, 2nd ed., 914; Wundt, *Physiol. Psychol.*, 4th ed., ii. 222). A theory of visual space perception, long current (more especially in physiology), and represented in modified form by Brücke and Volkmann, was based upon them.

Literature: HELMHOLTZ, Physiol. Optik (2nd ed.), 844, 913; WUNDT, Physiol. Psychol. (4th ed.), ii. 173; HERING, in Hermann's Handb. d. Physiol., III. i. 354, and Beitr. z. Physiol., i. (1861) 20 ff., ii. (1862) 81 ff.; AUBERT, Physiol. Optik, 605; BRÜCKE, Müller's Arch. (1841), 459; VOLKMANN, Arch. f. Ophthal., V. ii. (1859) 86; and art. Sehen in Wagner's Handwörterb. d. Physiol., III. i. 316 f., 340 f. (E.B.T.)

Identity (apprehension of individual) [Lat. *idem*, the same]: Ger. (*Erkenntnis der*) *individuellen Identität*; Fr. (*perception de l'*) *identité individuelle*; Ital. (*percezione dell'*) *identità individuale*. (1) Recognition of a thing as different from all other things, and including in its unity all its inner changes and other diversities. Such a thing is said to remain the same or to have sameness.

(2) Sometimes used for PERSONAL IDENTITY (q.v.).

The recognition seems in general to depend on unity, continuity, and exclusiveness of interest. Thus a thing may be regarded either as identical or not identical, according to the varying subjective point of view. See RECOGNITION, and cf. INDIVIDUAL. (G.F.S.—J.M.B.)

For instance, various qualities and modes of behaviour presented through the separate senses of touch, sight, hearing, &c., combine for our apprehension in the unity of a single thing, because the presentations of these different senses co-operate in processes having unity of practical interest. The nucleus or unifying centre is the experience of resistance connected with the actual manipulation of things at close quarters, by which we change or endeavour to change their position and shape by our effort. Practical efficiency in the attainment of the ends of animal life is predominantly constituted by movements which either take the form of effort put forth against resistance or prepare the way for such effort.

But the sensations of sight, touch, sound, smell, and taste, proceeding from the same material thing, co-operate in the most intimate way in leading up to and guiding movements of manipulation. It is primarily through this unity and continuity of practical interest that they become united for consciousness as constituting one and the same external object. Similarly, a series of changes in time is included in the unity of a single thing if the changes do not disturb, or if they actually subserve, the development of the distinctive interest which is aroused. The cat chasing a bird apprehends the bird as one and the same individual in all its changes of position and posture. Such changes merely serve to determine successive phases and stages in the development of its own activity. Similarly, the bird when killed is identified with the bird alive. The death of the bird is only a stage in the process which finds its end-state when the bird is eaten.

Mere unity and continuity of a distinctive interest are not in themselves sufficient to constitute the cognition of individual identity. As Royce has recently pointed out, the interest must be 'exclusive.' A child 'has a plaything, say a lead soldier. He loves it. He breaks it. Now offer him . . . another plaything—another lead soldier, as nearly as possible like the one just broken. Were the broken one not as such before the child's mind, the new one might prove in all respects satisfactory. But now, will the child . . . be very likely to accept the new soldier as a compensation for the broken one? No! . . . Now at this moment, I say, when the child rejects the other object—the other case that pretends to be an apt appeal to his exclusive love for the broken toy—at this very moment he *consciously individuates* the toy.' Royce seems to be clearly right in insisting on the necessity of exclusive interest. But the present writer cannot agree with him in demanding that the exclusiveness shall assume the highly developed form which attaches to it in the example of the broken toy. Before the toy was broken, the child must already have taken an exclusive interest in it. The accident and the proffered substitution only brings home to him the fact that his interest in it is exclusive. But to have an exclusive interest is one thing; to distinctly recognize that the interest is exclusive is another. The exclusive interest and the correlated apprehension of individual identity are the precondition of the passionate rejection of a

substitute. Royce's statement therefore puts the cart before the horse. His view breaks down in such simple cases as that of the cat chasing the bird. The bird is throughout the same individual for the cat which is pursuing it. But it would make no difference to the cat if another bird exactly like it were substituted. The exclusive interest arises from the fact that no other bird is substituted. No others may be present; and if they are, the cat can only chase one of them at a time, because it has itself only one body, and can therefore only execute one set of movements at once. Exclusiveness of this kind is the necessary presupposition of exclusiveness in Royce's sense. Unless the child is, to begin with, able to recognize his tin soldier as just this individual tin soldier numerically distinct from others, he cannot learn to love it in an exclusive manner. The exclusive love is due to growth of memories, associations, and connected sentiments, which attach to this individual object as such, and not to others. But this would be impossible unless the object were, to begin with, apprehended in its individual distinctness. The growth of these memories, associations, and sentiments constitutes a second and more advanced stage in the process of individuation. A third stage arises with the loss of the loved object, and the felt impossibility of compensating for this loss by substituting any other.

Literature: WARD, art. Psychology, Encyc. Brit. (9th ed.), 80 f.; ROYCE, The Conception of God, v (Suppl. Essay), Part III. Also citation under INDIVIDUAL. (G.F.S.)

Identity (apprehension of material): Ger. (*Erkenntnis der*) *inhaltlichen Identität*; Fr. (*appréhension de l'*)*identité matérielle*; Ital. (*percezione dell'*) *identità materiale*, or *identificazione*. RECOGNITION (q.v.) based on complete apparent likeness. Cf. Ward, art. Psychology, in *Encyc. Brit.* (9th ed.), 80 f. (G.F.S., J.M.B.)

Material identity is the limiting case of RESEMBLANCE (q.v.). When I say that the green of this leaf is identical with the green of that, I mean that the colours are exactly alike, and mean to assert material identity. When I say that I have the same body which belonged to me as a baby, I mean to assert individual identity (see the preceding topic).

Identity (in metaphysics). The principle of absolute equality with itself of what is real; the principle that the law of IDENTITY (in logic, q.v.) is also a principle of reality.

Identity is both an assumption of thinking

and a postulate concerning the nature of reality. The hypothesis of 'bare identity,' or 'distinctionless being,' is opposed by that of 'identity in difference,' according to which identity and difference are correlative and mutually dependent conceptions, identity being relative to difference and difference presupposing identity. This is undoubtedly sound as a criticism of these categories of thought as such; but it is mere tautology in relation to concrete matters of fact or of science, or, more broadly, to the process of knowledge as concretely determined. For here it is always one side or the other— identity or difference—which subserves the interest of the thought or action, and the determination of an identity in difference says nothing as to the extent or form of either. For example, to say that heredity is a law of identity in difference, leaves the extent of likeness and variation quite untouched; so also to say (see Bosanquet, *Mind*, April, 1899) that imitation and invention are both covered by the formula 'identity in difference.' Difference as a conception is fruitful as lending itself to one sort of method and to one sort of data, identity to another sort of each; just as in the genetic development of consciousness, the discernment of difference and distinction is a later and more complex act than that of the vague generalization which proceeds upon resemblances. So while they are logically correlative, and existence is always both, yet to the thought which makes use of these categories identity is an abstraction from differences and difference from identities.

Identity considered as principle of permanence and changelessness in being, contrasted with the flux of the phenomenal, dates back to the Eleatics. See PRE-SOCRATIC PHILOSOPHY. Cf. also CHANGE, and, for the place of identity in the Hegelian dialectic, HEGEL'S TERMINOLOGY, III, IV.

Literature: works of general metaphysics, as in BIBLIOG. B, 1, *c*; also see the indications under the other topics IDENTITY.

(J.M.B., G.F.S.)

Identity (logical). The principle that a logical term is always equal to itself ($A = A$) and to nothing else. Cf. CONTRADICTION, and see LAWS OF THOUGHT.

This principle states a logical demand or ideal of thinking rather than a psychological fact. The identity which formal logic supposes is an abstract or symbolic representation requiring a sameness in the content of the term which is never fully realized. The substitution of A for A is valid only without the psychological context in which A is a matter of experience. In dealing with universals and with definitions the principle of identity is both logically and psychologically valid, since, in the former case, the limit of material modification has been reached, or is formally assumed, and, in the latter case, material modification is expressly excluded. The hypostatizing of identity as a metaphysical principle assumes the metaphysical validity of this logical category. Cf. the other topics IDENTITY.

(J.M.B.)

Identity (personal): see PERSONAL IDENTITY.

Identity in Difference: see IDENTITY (in metaphysics).

Identity-philosophy: Ger. *Identitätsphilosophie*; Fr. *philosophie de l'identité*; Ital. *filosofia dell' identità*. (1) The theory which, metaphysically, reduces mind and matter, the ideal and the real, thought and being, to unity in the absolute (cf. IDEALISM, MONISM, and PANTHEISM); or, phenomenally, looks upon the physical and the psychical series as correlative 'sides' or 'aspects' of one and the same process. Cf. DOUBLE ASPECT THEORY, and PARALLELISM (psychophysical).

(2) In particular, the system propounded by Schelling in the second and most significant stage of his philosophical development (Falckenberg, *Hist. of Mod. Philos.*, 447, 456–61), in which, through a combination of Spinozistic and Fichtean principles, he reaches the conclusion that object and subject, real and ideal, nature and spirit, are one in the absolute, which is the identity or indifference of both (Ueberweg, *Hist. of Philos.*, ii. 213).

Fichte, in his subjective or transcendental idealism, had subordinated the objective or real element in the world to the subjective or ideal. Schelling adds the philosophy of nature to the science of knowledge with co-ordinate rank, and then interprets nature and spirit as alike proceeding from a neutral ground which is above them both. This identity divides by polar opposition into the negative or real pole (nature, object) and the positive or ideal pole (spirit, subject); but in itself it is the identical ground or indifference of the two. This system of identity was set forth in a series of writings which appeared in rapid succession in the first decade of the 19th century (*Darstellung meines Syst. d. Philos.*, 1801; *Bruno, oder ü. d. göttliche u. natürliche*

Prinzip d. Dinge, 1803 ; *Vorlesungen ü. die Methode des akademischen Studiums*, 1803).

Of contemporaries and followers of Schelling, Wagner, Friedrich Krause, Schleiermacher, and Hegel may be mentioned among those who felt the influence of the doctrine. In his absolute idealism, Hegel developed a monism of logical reason which combined the Fichtean emphasis of spirit with Schelling's insistence upon the philosophy of nature; but he energetically repudiated the conception of the absolute as an indeterminate neutrum, as well as the intellectual intuition by which Schelling claimed to attain a knowledge of the identical ground, together with his (lack of) derivation of nature and spirit therefrom (Hegel, *Phänomenologie des Geistes*, Vorrede ; Schwegler, *Hist. of Philos.*, xliv ; Falckenberg, op. cit., xii. 1). Cf. Simone Corleo, *La Filosofia dell' Identità* (1879-80). (A.C.A.Jr.)

Ideogenetic Theory (of judgment). Brentano's view of the original character of JUDGMENT (q. v., also BELIEF), known by his school (Hillebrand, Meinong, Höfler) as the ideogenetische Urtheilstheorie. (J.M.B.)

Ideogram (or **-graph**) [Gr. ἰδέα, idea, + γράφειν, to write]: Ger. *Ideogramm* ; Fr. *idéogramme* ; Ital. *ideogramma*. A written sign or symbol, not a name, which conveys its meaning by its own form, being often a pictorial representation (a pictograph) of the object symbolized.

The ideograph characterizes an important stage in the primitive evolution of writing. It is contrasted with a phonogram, which is a written representative of a thing or idea through the vocalized name for the thing or idea; occasionally, as in imitative sounds, onomatopoesis, it represents the sound itself. Our own language and those from which it is derived are of course phonographic. As examples of ideographic records may be cited the pictographs of North American Indians, and (in part) Mexican writings and Egyptian hieroglyphics. Ideographic survivals in current usage are the Roman numerals, I, II, III ; zodiacal, astronomical, and certain zoological signs, e. g. ♃, denoting Jupiter—an arm grasping a thunderbolt. Ideographic elements in the letters of the alphabet are abundant. Such characters, however, pass quickly into conventional stages and lose much of their original form.

Literature : works on the origin of writing ; HOFFMAN, The Beginnings of Writing (1895), 209 ; BRINTON, Essays of an Americanist (1890). (J.J.)

Ideogram (in psychology). The curve or tracing secured with a recording apparatus (Ideograph) arranged to exhibit variations of muscular movement occasioned by changes in thought. See Morselli, *Semej. mal. ment.* ii (1895), for its use in pathology. (J.M.B.)

Ideology [Gr. ἰδέα, idea, + λόγος, discourse]: Ger. *Ideologie* ; Fr. *idéologie* ; Ital. *ideologia*. The continuation and development, in the period of the Revolution and the immediately succeeding period, by Destutt de Tracy (the author of the term), Cabanis, and others, of the French sensationalism of the 18th century (Condillac). The ideologues made the analysis of ideas, and, in particular, the investigation of their origin, the fundamental philosophical discipline, which at the same time was expected to furnish the basis of the moral and political sciences.

Literature : DESTUTT DE TRACY, Éléments d'Idéologie, especially i (1808), Preface and Introd. ; UEBERWEG-HEINZE, Gesch. d. Philos., III. ii. (8th ed., 1897) 36 ; PICAVET, Les Idéologues. (A.C.A.Jr.)

Ideo-motor: Ger. *ideomotorisch* ; Fr. *idéomoteur* ; Ital. *ideomotore*. Applied to action considered as following upon thought. It is contrasted with SENSORI-MOTOR (q. v.) and REFLEX (q. v.).

The term is sometimes limited to actions which are non-voluntary or involuntary ; but the better usage includes voluntary action in the ideo-motor class. (J.M.B.-G.F.S.)

Ideoplastic (1) and **Ideoplasy** (2) [Gr. ἰδέα, idea, + πλαστός, formed]: Ger. *ideoplastisch* and *Ideoplasie* ; Fr. *idéoplastique* and *idéoplasie* ; Ital. *ideoplastico* and *ideoplasia*. (1) Applied to the physiological functions considered as liable to modification from suggested ideas (used originally by Durand de Gros —L.M.). (2) Suggestions operative in the production of physiological changes. Used by Ochorowicz (*Ment. Suggestion*, Eng. trans.), where the noun-form is mistakenly given 'ideoplasty.' (J.M.B., G.F.S.)

Idiocy [Gr. ἰδιωτεία, uncouthness, want of education ; ἰδιώτης, a person private or apart]: Ger. *Idiotie* ; Fr. *idiotie* ; Ital. *idiotismo*, *idiozia*. Deficiency in the ordinary mental powers, due to disease or failure of development of the central nervous system. More especially, idiocy often relates to the severer forms of such mental deficiency, while children of subnormal capacity or backward development are spoken of as feeble-minded, or mentally deficient children. There is some tendency to use the term feeble-minded to include all degrees of defect from the slightest to the most severe. (J.J.—J.M.B.)

Description. A general description may be profitably confined to an average case of idiocy. The typical idiot shows not merely mental, but physical defect: a blunted growth, a stooping attitude, a coarse skin, weak and flabby muscles, a sluggish circulation, a defective mastication and digestion of food, perverted or undeveloped sexual functions, a defective co-ordination of movements, a tendency to repeat a few simple automatic movements, a lowered sensibility (or sensory disorder), indistinct speech, and a general absence of alertness, with weak memory and mental initiative. Inability to take care of his person, a defective moral sensibility, and lack of appreciation of the feelings of others render the idiot socially unfit, apart from the more strictly intellectual deficiency. Variations from the type are considered below.

Frequency and Causes. The frequency of idiocy is most difficult to ascertain, owing to the unwillingness of the parents to report it, and varies markedly in different countries; certain varieties, as CRETINISM (q. v.) in Switzerland, being apparently related to local influences. General statistics indicate that one idiot to every 500 of the population is a conservative estimate, and that there are probably nearly as many idiots as insane, and more than the blind and deaf together (Ireland). Heredity or predisposing causes are most influential in the production of idiocy; physical defects being quite as pronounced as mental defects, according to the results of Shuttleworth and Beach. A phthisical family history was present in 28·31 per cent. of the cases, inherited disease in 21·38 per cent., and in an additional 20 per cent. a neurotic inheritance, in which epilepsy (8·69 per cent.) was frequent. The frequency of deafness in idiots has also been noted. Parental intemperance is a prominent predisposing cause, being found in from 13 per cent. to 20 per cent. of all cases, but in as many as 38 per cent. (Kerlin) if the grandparents also be counted. Idiocy may result from shock or ill health of the mother during gestation, and is more frequently the result of accidents, &c., incidental to birth. Many accidental causes after birth (epilepsy, injury to the head, fevers, sunstroke, fright) may be inducing causes of idiocy, but it is estimated that in at least two-thirds of all cases there are some marked congenital defects. These several factors frequently act in com-

bination, the inducing cause serving only to bring to the foreground an inherited taint. It should also be noted that while in some cases idiocy is sequential to epilepsy, the epileptic tendency is a marked concomitant of idiocy, being one of the frequent degenerative stigmata of the idiotic condition.

Pathological. The appearances of gross brain defect observable in cases of idiocy comprise most of the serious abnormalities to which this organ is liable; and certain forms of idiocy have been differentiated according to the pathological cause. Idiocy may result from mere deficiency of brain substance, which is termed microcephalic; from hypertrophy of the brain, one prominent form of which is HYDROCEPHALUS (q. v.). Softening or sclerosis of the brain, tumours and affections of the membranes and blood-vessels, asymmetries of development, atrophy of the cerebellum, defects of the corpus callosum, unusual forms of cortical cells in microscopical examination, &c., have been observed. Such defects may be distinguished according as they are formative or developmental, and as they result from inflammatory or degenerative diseases.

Varieties. The classification of cases of idiocy has proceeded in part upon the time of appearance of the defect, upon the degree of intelligence retained, upon the specific pathological basis for the condition, and upon the general appearance of the case. It is thus described as congenital, developmental, and accidental; each of which, especially the first, fall into many subdivisions suggestive of their pathology. Idiocy is also described as 'true' idiocy, imbecility, weak-mindedness, &c., or as microcephalic, hydrocephalic, eclampsic, epileptic, cretinism, &c., or as Mongolian, Negrolike, Malay, &c. Practically the pathological form of classification has been most influential, the other modes of description serving as supplementary. In a measure the various forms have been correlated with physical peculiarities and psychological defects, but not sufficiently to enable any brief formulation of these to be made. For descriptions of illustrative cases the reader may be referred to the standard works cited below.

Psychological Status. Idiocy is often spoken of as a state of arrested mental development, the unfoldment of mental power being cut off at the infantile or childish state. To a large extent this is true; and, as indicated by the process of education, there is spread out over a long period the slow steps of progress usually acquired quickly, spontaneously, and almost without effort. There is, however, an unequal development which is characteristic of idiocy. Adolescent and adult instincts appear, muscular strength and skill exceeding that of childhood lead into new fields of activity, while the mere aggregation of sensory and motor experiences, however poorly assimilated, produces some differentiation. In a few cases, sometimes known as idiot-savants or idiot-geniuses (see Peterson, *Pop. Sci. Mo.*, 1896, 237), one special group of faculties, such as music, linguistic faculty, memory, drawing, construction, is well developed, although the general mental operations are of a simple character. It is seldom that such facility is infused with great intelligence, but resembles more a freak of receptive or constructive facility. Morally, idiots are remarkably deficient; it is difficult to arouse in them the sense of shame and propriety; their love of approbation and capricious likings for certain individuals are often the most promising means of influencing their conduct. The analogy which has been drawn between the mental state of idiots and of animals, and the conception of idiocy as an atavistic condition, are on the whole misleading. In the one case the nature and direction of exercise of the intelligence is too diverse to be readily comparable, while the best authorities deny that in the character of the brain and other abnormalities of idiots atavistic tendencies are particularly marked.

Training of Idiots. The methods of educating the feeble-minded to the maximum degree of usefulness of which each is capable serve to illustrate the different degrees of defect, as well as its nature. The form of training now introduced is aptly termed physiological, and is one of the main contributions associated with the name of Seguin. It begins with the principle that a cultivation of muscular co-ordination is the necessary starting-point of the education of the feeble-minded. The apathetic torpid idiot is induced by such exercises as the throwing of a bean-bag, clapping the hands in time to music, marching, &c., to convert a simple imitative action into a purposive movement. If there is more serious defect in the movements of legs or arms, walking on flat rounds of ladders placed on the floor, to induce regularity of step, balancing exercises, grasping of blocks, placing marbles or pegs in designated holes in a board, the taking apart and putting together of boxes and simple contrivances, and other devices,

are used to induce and exercise co-ordinating movements. Their senses must be aroused by the handling of objects of different textures and shapes; their ears, with which they hear but do not listen, must be excited by systematic exercises in music, rhythm, and characteristic noises. Similarly for sight, the fixation of attention, the transition from seeing to looking must be aided by such devices as the kaleidoscope, coloured balls, diagrams, pictures, drawing. The training of speech offers a wide and difficult field. Some idiots do not speak at all, or at best only a few isolated words, and comprehend only a few simple directions. In many the natural speech tendency is slight, but may be considerably developed. Some pick up speech slowly and at a later period than is normal; but few, if any, of the feeble-minded have a normal control over articulation and readiness of expression. Articulation is induced and developed by progressive exercises in the movements of tongue, lips, and vocal chords. Imitation, chorus exercises, and patient correction of faults, together with general improvement in physical power, will bring motor control; yet the use of language will always be limited to the degree of mental capacity which is present. As the subjects of such training grow older, more elaborate occupations and handiworks are open to them; perhaps 20 per cent. of them will become self-supporting, and another 20 per cent. useful and in a measure able to take care of themselves. The psychological interest in this process is its illustration of the relations between motor and mental effort, and the substitution of the slow and deliberate acquisition for the quick spontaneous self-education of normal children. Apart from mental training, relief has been obtained by appropriate medical treatment, or even surgical operation, but this only in cases when the idiocy was evidently the result of a definite pathological condition which was thus reached. Cf. IMBECILITY, and CRETINISM.

Historical. The modern phase in the study and training of the mentally defective may be said to start with Seguin, who began to instruct an idiot child in 1837, and in 1846 issued his important book on the education of idiots. Under the view which was thus displaced the idiot was considered, and often treated, as little more than a human beast, and many cases of idiocy were described as wild men, wolf-boys, and the like.

Literature: W. W. IRELAND, The Mental

Affections of Children (1898); MORSELLI and TAMBURINI, in Riv. di Freniat. (1876–8); SHUTTLEWORTH, Mentally Deficient Children (1895); SOLLIER, L'Idiot et l'Imbécile (Paris, 1891), and art. Idiocy, in Twentieth Cent. Pract. of Med. (1897); LANGDON-DOWN, The Mental Affections of Childhood (1887); E. SEGUIN, Idiocy and its Treatment by the Physiol. Method (1866).   (J.J.)

Idiopathic [Gr. ἰδιοπαθεῖν, to feel for one-self alone]: Ger. *idiopathisch*; Fr. *idiopathique*; Ital. *idiopatico*. A term applied to a morbid condition or disease which is primary and distinctive; not a secondary effect of another disorder, nor a symptom of such disorder, nor the result of accident or injury. It thus often implies the typical and hereditary form of the disease, as idiopathic epilepsy, idiopathic insanity.   (J.J.)

Idioplasm [Gr. ἴδιος, the same, + πλάσμα, a thing formed]: Ger. *Idioplasma*; Fr. *idioplasme*; Ital. *idioplasma*. The nuclear chromatin substance that forms the physical basis of heredity.

Suggested by Nägeli (*Mechanisch-physiologische Theorie der Abstammungslehre*, 1884). Practically equivalent to the GERM-PLASM (q. v.) of Weismann.   (C.LL.M.)

Idio-psychological Ethics: Ger. *idio-psychologische Ethik*; Fr. *morale idio-psychologique* (suggested—TH.F.); Ital. *morale idio-psicologica*. A theory of ethics which depends upon 'the inner facts of conscience itself' (Martineau).

The term is used by Martineau (*Types of Ethical Theory*, 1885), who distinguishes idio-psychological ethics from hetero-psychological ethics (that is, the theories of ethics which derive moral phenomena from other mental categories). These two classes of theories, together with the unpsychological theories (which base ethics upon metaphysical or physical doctrines), make up his classification of ethical theories.   (W.R.S.)

Idio-retinal Light: Ger. *Eigenlicht der Netzhaut* (*Augengrau, Augenschwarz*); Fr. *lumière propre de la rétine*; Ital. *luce propria della retina*. The hazy or cloudlike patches of dull grey in the field of vision when the eyes are free from stimulation and after-images. Cf. Helmholtz, *Physiol. Optik* (2nd ed.), 242, 409, 1007.

It is important for the Helmholtz-Fechner theory of after-images (loc. cit., 502). G. E. Müller refers it to the cortex (*Zeitsch. f. Psychol.*, xiv. 40), in order to reduce Hering's retinal 'antagonism' to the single category of

'subtractive' (with elimination of 'relative') antagonism (Ebbinghaus, *Psychol.*, i. 259 262). For its measurement, cf. Fechner, *Elem. d. Psychophysik*, i. 168. See Visual Sensation under VISION.   (E.B.T.)

Idiosyncrasy [Gr. ἰδιοσυγκρασία, a peculiar temperament or habit of body]: Ger. *Idiosynkrasie*; Fr. *idiosyncrasie*; Ital. *idiosincrasia*. Idiosyncrasy denotes peculiar reactions of the individual to certain external influences, and further implies that such response or affection is not readily correlated with known physiological or psychological principles.

The term is thus distinguished from temperament or constitution or racial characteristics, all of which are expressions of the individual's special variation in regard to the normal and regular distribution of endowment. Peculiar likes and dislikes, the special effects of sensory stimuli, the actions on the secretions and vaso-motor system, the behaviour under the action of drugs and stimulants, peculiar habits of mental work, are types of idiosyncrasies. One person has the peculiar sensation of the blood running cold at the squeezing of a dry sponge, another at the creasing of paper or the scraping of the finger-nail; the odour or the mere presence of a certain animal, flower, or fruit is painfully disturbing to some individuals. In the use of drugs the normal effect at times fails to appear, and marked variations in the quantity needed to produce the same effect are readily noticeable. What is one man's meat is another man's poison; what conduces to productive mental energy in one defeats this object in another. The story of Schiller requiring the odour of decaying apples to stimulate him in his composition, or of Kant requiring the sight of a button on a student's coat to hold the course of his lectures, are cases of mental idiosyncrasies. During pregnancy and during adolescence the temporary appearance of special idiosyncrasies—unusual tastes and susceptibilities—is frequently observed. That many of these are somewhat imaginary in type, or partake of that peculiar admixture of feigning and reality characteristic of hysteria, cannot be doubted; but as all idiosyncrasies are expressions of the reactions of the nervous system, these are no less so. (J.J.)

Idol [Gr. εἴδωλον, an image]: Ger. *Idol*; Fr. *idole*; Ital. *idolo*. An object, usually an image or representation of a human or animal form, with which some mysterious and superhuman power is associated, and which is supposed to be propitiated by the worship paid to the object.

An immediate object of worship is not an idol, even though it may be an animal or something wholly unworthy of the religious sentiment. An idol is, in the first instance, an indirect object of worship, and is more or less symbolical. It would have its rise in the need the primitive mind would feel for some tangible symbol or representative of the mysterious object of its worship. Idol-worship could not exist, therefore, as a primitive form of religion.

Literature: see references under FETICHISM; also SPENCER, Princ. of Sociol., i. chaps. xxi, xxii; MAX MÜLLER, Is Fetichism an Original Form of Religion?, 38, 110, 196.　(A.T.O.)

Idol (Baconian). Prejudices natural to man, whether native or acquired, which hinder the discovery and advancement of truth; used first (Lat. *idola*) by Giordano Bruno (1582 ff.).

The list of 'idols' is given by Bacon in his *Nov. Org.*, i. 38 ff. They are cited in concise quotation in Eisler, *Wörterb. d. philos. Begriffe*, 'Idol.'　(J.M.B.—E.M.)

Idolatry: Ger. *Abgötterei*; Fr. *idolâtrie*; Ital. *idolatria*. (1) The worship of idols. Cf. IDOL.

(2) A name applied to any religious belief or worship that is conceived to be not only false but also degrading.

In the strict sense of the term idolatry is not a primary form of religious worship. It is devoted to an object which at first symbolized some unseen power, and has gradually become itself an object of superstitious regard. Image-worship is a species of idolatry in which this process is clearly manifested. The image or picture is at first merely representative, but tends gradually to become identified with the object itself.　(A.T.O.)

Ignorance (in law) [Lat. *ignorantia*]: Ger. *Unwissenheit*; Fr. *ignorance*; Ital. *ignoranza*. Want of knowledge as to a certain point; lack of information as to a certain matter.

Ignorance of law: ignorance as to what the law is; as when a man, not knowing bigamy to be unlawful, marries a woman already married to another. It is a legal maxim that *ignorantia legis neminem excusat*.

Ignorance of fact: ignorance as to what the facts are; as when a man marries a woman already married to another, not knowing of the former marriage. The maxim is *ignorantia facti excusat*. Ignorance is a cause of error, but a different thing from error, which is a want of conformity between our notions of things and their real state or nature.

The Roman law placed important limitations on the doctrine that ignorance of law is no excuse. It was an excuse to minors, women, and soldiers, under certain circumstances, and a broad distinction was drawn between its effect on public and on private wrongs. It is also, in some cases, a ground for relief or of defence in courts of equity. Cf. Pomeroy, *Equity Jurisprudence*, ii. § 842.

Literature: PHILLIMORE, Princ. and Maxims of Jurisprudence, xix; Dig. xxii. 6, De Iuris et Facti Ignorantia; HOLLAND, Jurisprudence, chap. xiii, viii. 94; HOLMES, On the Common Law, 47; MERLIN, Répertoire de Jurisprudence, 'Ignorance'; and SOHM's Inst. of Roman Law, § 29, on Error in Substantia.　(S.E.B.)

Ignoratio Elenchi: see FALLACY.

Illation and **Illative**: see INFERENCE.

Illegitimate (in law): see LEGITIMATE.

Illicit Process: see FALLACY (1), and DISTRIBUTION (in logic).

Illogical: see LOGICAL.

Illumination: see ENLIGHTENMENT.

Illusion [Lat. *in + ludere*, to play]: Ger. *Illusion, Täuschung*; Fr. *illusion*; Ital. *illusione*. (1) The construction, on the basis of data which are real in their sphere, of a mental object which is accepted as real but is not so.

(2) The mental object thus constructed.

(3) In general, mental acceptance of the unreal.

Meaning (1)—with (2)—is the recommended psychological definition. Illusion is thus any mistaken mental construction which has reliable data as its point of departure. The distinction from HALLUCINATION (q. v.) is twofold: (*a*) in hallucination, the trustworthy data are absent; that is, the determining elements in the construction are either of purely imaginative or of organic origin— both these cases being illustrated under that topic, and both being on the border, or over the border, of the pathological. (*b*) Hallucination is confined to the perceptual—to objects of sense in contrast with the DELUSION (q. v.) of higher mental processes. Illusion is thus broader, in that it covers those errors of the logical operations as well which are not of the persistence or of the indirect determination—in a system of beliefs—which characterize delusions.

The limits of the three terms *inter se* are, however, largely practical. The central processes of illusion and of hallucination, arising from organic causes, are the same; and in most cases of either, the influence of delusional elements, due to the earlier condition of mind —notably to emotional states—is marked. The cases of pure SENSE ILLUSION (q. v.), on the other hand, are cases really of perception, not of illusion; since they are normal, constant, and common to all individuals, and are exposed by resort to tests outside the sphere of the particular senses concerned. Cf. OPTICAL ILLUSIONS, and ILLUSIONS OF MOTION AND MOVEMENT.

Illusions occur in connection with all the senses, and with certain obscure modes of consciousness. Cf. ORIENTATION (illusions of), and PRESENTIMENT.

Literature: BIBLIOG. G, 2, *n*; titles cited under HALLUCINATION; list of references in BALDWIN, Senses and Intellect, 269. (J.M.B.)

Illusion (aesthetic) or **Self-illusion**: see SEMBLANCE. Also cf. ART, BEAUTY, and CLASSIFICATION (of the fine arts).

Illusion (pathological). A distinction between the usual and normal sense-deceptions and the unusual and somewhat abnormal false interpretation of sensory stimuli is much to be desired. Such normal illusions are considered under the preceding topic; and the general relations of hallucinations and illusions, both in the sane and insane, are considered under HALLUCINATIONS.

Illusions in the specific sense may be illustrated from the case of the whitewashed tree, which is momentarily mistaken by the belated wanderer in a lonely road for something more mysterious; to the raving of the maniac who sees in the wall-paper patterns the spiteful faces of his persecutors, and hears in passing footsteps or everyday noises their curses and insults. Some misinterpreting mental attitude or factor seems necessary to the formation of the typical illusion; it may be expectant attention, or fear, or the preponderance of a limited train of thought, or the poisoning of the brain by opium or hashish, or the disordered reasoning of insanity. When such misinterpretations are slight, the resulting illusion is assimilated to the normal sense-deception; when it becomes more marked, and particularly when the interpretation or inferential element becomes more prominent, it passes gradually into the abnormal type, and then its aetiology and nature is quite similar to that of the hallucination. This is well illustrated in the illusions of the insane; in many of these it is difficult to decide whether there exists an illusion or a pure hallucination, correlated with sensory and bodily disorders. A patient suffering from anaesthesia believes his legs to be made of wood or glass, or that he is dead; ringing in the ears is construed into warning voices; digestive troubles lead to the belief that the patient has no stomach; peculiar head-sensations, that he is possessed by another spirit; while total strangeness of disordered sensibility may lead to the belief in a changed personality. In dreams, likewise, illusions may occur; the fancies may have a sensory starting-point; while in hypnotism such are readily suggested. Cf. also DREAMS, and HYPNOSIS. (J.J.)

Illusions of Motion and Movement: Ger. *Bewegungstäuschungen*; Fr. *illusions du mouvement*; Ital. *illusioni di movimento*. False interpretation of sense data, resulting in the apparent perception of motion or MOVEMENT (q. v.) where it does not exist, or in the misjudgment of some circumstance attending actual motion, such as the rate, the direction, or the object that moves.

I. MOTION. Illusions of change of place may occur in any sense which is capable of giving impressions of position; they are found most commonly in vision, touch, the muscle sense, and the equilibrium sense. If we limit the term motion to displacements which are not the manifestation of subjective or organic activity, and designate the latter by the term MOVEMENT (q. v. for the distinction), as is customary, the illusions belonging to vision and touch will fall for the most part in the first category, and those of the muscle sense in the second. In many cases the illusion arises from the combination of data of several senses.

Visual Illusions. The interpretation of the rate of motion and of its source (i. e. the object that moves) is largely relative. If the eye follow a moving body, the motion will appear much less rapid than with the eye at rest, even though the entire motion be attributed to the moving object in both cases. In a moving train, the motion is attributed sometimes to the train, sometimes to the objects that pass by; but in the latter case the rate appears much greater. A similar effect is obtained from an endless belt of figured oil-cloth revolving over rollers; when the oil-cloth is near enough to fill the field of vision, the subject attributes the motion to the field or to himself, according as his eyes follow the patterns or remain fixed. Objects seen in indirect vision appear to move more rapidly than those viewed in direct vision, *ceteris paribus*, owing probably to the tendency of the eye to follow the object in the latter case. If the eye be fixed on a point at rest, the latter after a time will appear to move about slightly; the motion is especially marked when the object fixated is the only clearly defined point in the field of vision; it is really due to involuntary eye movements. Exner terms the experience 'autokinetic sensations.' If the eye-ball be pressed from side to side with the finger, the objects in the field of vision appear to move; but no such interpretation occurs when the eye moves normally.

A somewhat different instance of relativity is observed in the apparatus called *anortho-scope*. This consists of a paper with a narrow vertical slit, which is held before one eye, and a circle slightly less in diameter than the length of the slit; when this circle is moved rapidly from side to side behind the slit, it appears as an ellipse, the horizontal axis becoming shorter as the rate is increased; when the motion is slow, the illusion disappears, or is reversed, the horizontal axis becoming longer than the vertical.

Illusions of the direction of motion may be due to a false judgment of perspective, or to the undue prominence of certain factors and overlooking of others. An example of the former appears when we observe the motion of a windmill from an oblique angle at a distance; either side of the mill may be made to appear the nearer, so that the upper vanes seem to move now towards, now away from us. A similar illusion of perspective may be observed with vessels on the water. An illusion of direction due to the obscurity of certain factors is observed when a spiral figure is rotated rapidly about its centre on a colour-wheel; the rotary motion is indistinguishable, and there appears instead a motion of all points of the spiral towards the centre, or away from it, according to the direction of rotation. If a card with a number of broad concentric circles like a target be moved in a circle before the eyes without rotation of the card, the figure becomes partly blurred, and the blurred sectors appear to rotate in the direction of the actual movement. If a figure consisting of a circle with teeth projecting inwards or outwards (like cogs) be moved in a similar manner, the cogs will appear to rotate around the circumference of the circle. Figures of this sort are known as strobic circles.

The illusion of rest is illustrated in a rapidly rotating wheel, whose spokes present the appearance of a continuous, motionless, and semi-transparent surface. In the thaumatrope different pictures or letters are printed on the two sides of a card, which is rotated by twirling two strings attached to the right and left edges; the two pictures combine into one, or the letters into words, which appear to remain stationary before the eyes. An opposite illusion appears in the stroboscope. This consists of a circular card with a number of axial slits, and another circular card, placed behind it, with a series of dots or figures placed around the circumference, representing different phases of an object in motion. The two cards may be rotated in the same or in opposite directions; looking through the slits as they pass, we catch momentary glimpses of the successive images, and when the rotation is rapid they appear as a single object having a continuous motion. The figures may be placed on the back of the first card, and reflected by a mirror, which is substituted for the second card. There are various forms of stroboscope, called dedalium, phenakistoscope, zoetrope, &c. In the zoetrope the slits are cut in the side of a short cylinder, like the cover of a bandbox, while the figures are on a strip, which is placed upright around the inside of a cylinder; with a series of instantaneous photographs a very realistic appearance of continuous motion is obtained. In these forms of stroboscope the pictures must be the same distance apart as the slits. Recent applications of the stroboscopic illusion are found in the kinetoscope, mutoscope, vitascope, cinematograph, biograph, &c. Here the pictures follow one another in rapid succession, remaining in view for a period which is much longer than the time occupied by the transition; the latter is so short as to make the real motion imperceptible, while the pictures at rest are clearly perceived; this avoids the necessity of slits. The pictures represent very near phases of motion, and the result is an illusion of motion which is perfect in proportion to the degree of perfection of the apparatus; the rate of the illusory motion may be made the same as in life. The pictures may be enlarged and projected upon a screen by means of a lantern.

With certain coloured diagrams a continuous to-and-fro motion gives rise to the appearance of a sudden springing of the figures from side to side; this illusion is known as the 'fluttering heart,' or chromatokinopsia.

Similar is the so-called Münsterberg-Jastrow phenomenon. A circular disk with sectors of two alternating colours is rotated rapidly, while a pencil or thin stick is moved to and fro in front; alternate bands of the colours on the disk appear in place of the blurred image of the pencil; the width of the bands varies with the rate of motion.

After-images play a part in some of the above illusions, and give rise to others. In connection with the spiral illusion cited above, a distinct after-image may be observed; if the figure be suddenly brought to rest, motion in the opposite direction appears to set in and to continue for some time. An after-image illusion of motion in the same direction may also be observed; if a moving object be regarded for a time with unmoving eyes, and the eyes be suddenly closed, an after-image will appear, which seems to move onward for a brief period.

Tactile Illusions. These occur usually in connection with active touch, and combine with the illusions of muscular movement to be described later. In some cases, however, they arise independently. If a string be drawn through the subject's fingers by another person, it seems to be longer when drawn slowly than when drawn rapidly; that is, the amount of motion appears greater in the former case. An object passing over the finger-tips, forehead, &c., gives rise to an impression that the member in question is also moving, but in the opposite direction. Illusions of direction, more or less marked, are often observed in objects moving over the skin. Tingling is often interpreted as motion of something upon the skin.

II. Movement and Bodily Position. *Muscle Sense Illusions.* Our judgment of the rate and direction of muscular movement is very accurate. It is noted, however, that an object appears heavier as the rate of lifting is slower. When the member moved is seen, not directly, but in a mirror, the visual impression of direction may supplant the muscular, so that the member is felt to move in the same direction as the reflected image. In Stratton's experiment, in which the visual field was entirely reversed by lenses worn over the eyes, the location and direction of muscular movement came gradually to conform to the new visual field.

When one part of the body is moved over another (e. g. the finger over the forehead), the movement may be referred to the wrong source, or both members may appear to join in

the movement. In the similar tactile illusion mentioned above, there is often an illusory muscular sensation present also. The removal of resistance to one set of muscles may be interpreted as a force applied to the antagonistic set. If a string bearing a heavy weight be held in the subject's hand, with closed eyes, and the weight be suddenly pulled upward by another person, the subject's hand tends to fly up, and the movement is attributed to the application of an outside force. A similar illusion is observed in pouring water from a pitcher; the constant loss of weight from the escaping water is involuntarily interpreted as a force resisting our effort to lower the mouth of the pitcher.

An illusion regarding the amount of movement executed may arise when part of the movement is unconscious. If the head be turned to one side, with closed eyes, and an attempt be made to point at a given object in front of the former position, an error in direction is observed, owing to the unconscious 'lagging' of the eyes when the head is turned. Unconscious eye movements are responsible for several of the visual illusions described above. Where one of the eye muscles is partly paralyzed, movement of the eyes in that direction is exaggerated.

Another muscular illusion arises from the tendency of the two hands to assume symmetrical positions. If one hand be placed somewhat higher than the other, and we attempt to describe equal downward movements with both hands together (with eyes closed), the higher hand tends to make the greater movement, so as to approximate the level of the other. This tendency to symmetry has definite limits, however; if we endeavour to bring the hands together in front of the body, one is constantly found to be slightly higher or further out than the other.

An illusion of movement in an immovable member is noted if one hand be placed, palm down, with the last three fingers resting flat on a table, and the forefinger bent under and resting against the side of the table; after the forefinger has been bent in as far as possible, a sensation of apparent movement can still be felt if an effort be made to bend it further.

Equilibrium Sense Illusions. Although muscular and visual sensations are important data in affording knowledge of the passive movements and position of the whole body, the basis of these sensations is the special sense whose organs are the semicircular canals of the ear. The illusions connected with these sensations are due for the most part to the rapid fatigue of the equilibrium sense, and to faulty combination of its data with the visual and muscular.

The chief motor illusions of the equilibrium sense are observed with the 'rotation table.' This consists of a long, flat board, on which the subject lies, and which is made to rotate in the horizontal plane. If the subject's eyes remain closed, and a uniform rate of rotation be maintained, the movement gradually appears to become slower, and finally to stop; if the table now be actually stopped (or nearly so), the subject will experience an illusion of movement in the opposite direction. The same illusions appear in connection with progressive movement in any direction ; but in experiences of the latter sort, the effects are usually masked by the jolts or vibrations which accompany the motion, and which are interpreted in terms of movement forward or backward. In a railway train, for example, the sense of movement proper is lost soon after the train attains its speed; but by closing the eyes we still feel the train to be moving at the same rate, either forward or backward. The character and frequency of the jolts give the clue to the speed, so that in travelling over a smoother road-bed than usual we tend to underestimate the rate of progress, and vice versa. The illusion of reversal in progressive movement may be assisted by vision, if we look in a mirror placed perpendicular to the direction of motion; but when the train makes a curve the two senses part company; the equilibrium sense then asserts itself, and the landscape appears to fly around in the same direction as the train. If the train slows up while the illusion of reversal is being experienced, the muscular data become prominent, and the train appears to be going uphill, and vice versa. The equilibrial and visual data may be combined as follows. The subject is stretched at full length on the rotation table, with head slightly raised ; the room is darkened, so that some vertical white strips on the dark wall are barely visible. If, then, a mirror be placed before him, which rotates with the board, so that the strips seen in front (being really behind him) appear to move in the same direction as his feet, the rotation is interpreted as progress sideways, in the direction in which the head actually moves; that is, the data of the equilibrium sense serve for the head only, while the reversed visual data make the feet

appear to move in the opposite direction from the true one ; this is direct evidence of the location of the equilibrium sense in the head.

The feeling of dizziness that ensues upon rapid rotation is (apart from the nausea connected with it) a phenomenon of the equilibrium sense ; the illusion of motion that constitutes dizziness is the after-image belonging to this sense. A muscular-visual illusion is present also when the movement has taken place with open eyes ; the objects in the field of vision appear to continue moving after the subject ceases to rotate. This is known as Purkinje's dizziness ; it is due to unconscious eye movements. A kindred illusion, due to the unconscious control of the muscles through the equilibrium sense, is illustrated in a well-known parlour diversion. The subject stands with his body bent forward from the hips and his head resting on a cane which extends vertically from the floor; he walks around the cane three times, then raises his head and attempts to walk across the room, with the result that he staggers and usually falls. The equilibrium sense has been adjusted to the rotary horizontal movement, and this is suddenly transformed into a sense of vertical rotation when he rises ; in his involuntary muscular adjustments to this supposed motion he is thrown over in the opposite direction. The illusion of rocking which is experienced on land after an ocean voyage is due to the same cause. In the haunted swing illusion, the subject is seated on a swing in a perfectly closed room ; the swing remains stationary, while the entire room moves like a pendulum. The motion is attributed to the swing. The feeling of dizziness is very marked.

Illusions concerning the position of the body as a whole arise when the visual and muscular data are withdrawn or greatly altered. If the subject be strapped to the tilt-board and blindfolded, any rotary motion in the vertical plane is perceived almost wholly by the equilibrium sense, whose data are thus exaggerated, any deviation from the horizontal appearing much greater than it actually is ; this is more noticeable in the uncommon positions, with head lower than the feet, the head seeming to point directly downward when the actual angle is 45° or more short of that position. An illusion of position arises also when only the visual data are withdrawn. If the subject stand with closed eyes, and throw his head backward, forward, or on to one shoulder, his judgment of position, measured by a rod held in what he considers a horizontal line in the plane of his movement, will show a constant error; the inclination of the rod is usually contrary to the direction of his movement. (H.C.W.)

Literature: visual illusions: SANFORD, Course in Exper. Psychol., expts. 128, 134, 159, 222–31, and references there given; HELMHOLTZ, Physiol. Optik, 2. Aufl., 494, 498, 533, 711, 749, 763, 770 (full descriptions of apparatus and methods); STERN, Zeitsch. f. Psychol. (1894), vii. 321–86; MACH, Analysis of Sensations (Eng. trans.), 69 (oil-cloth illusion); EXNER, Zeitsch. f. Psychol. (1896), xii. 313–30 (autokinetic sensations); ZÖLLNER, Pogg. Ann. (1862), cxvii. 477–84 (anorthoscope); S. P. THOMPSON, Brain (1880), iii (strobic circles); SCRIPTURE, New Psychol., 108–20 (stroboscopes, kinetoscope, &c.). Tactile and muscle sense illusions: SANFORD, Course in Exper. Psychol., expts. 5, 12, 36–45, and references; STRATTON, Psychol. Rev. (1897), iv. 341, 463 (visual reversal). Equilibrium sense and dizziness: SANFORD, Course in Exper. Psychol., expts. 46–51, and references; MACH, Grundlinien d. Lehre v. d. Bewegungsempfindungen, 83, 128; DELAGE, Physiol. Stud. ü. d. Orientirung (deutsch v. Aubert); PURKINJE, Ueber d. Schwindel (repr. by Aubert with above); WARREN, Psychol. Rev. (1895), ii. 273; WOOD, Psychol. Rev. (1895), ii. 277. Apparatus for visual illusions, in Milton Bradley Co.'s 'Pseudoptics,' section D. (H.C.W.–E.C.S.)

Illusions of Orientation: see ORIENTATION (illusions of).

Image [Lat. *imago*, a likeness]: Ger. *Bild*; Fr. *image*; Ital. *immagine*. The mental scheme in which sensations or the sensory elements of a perception (or earlier image) are revived. The images of the mind taken collectively are known as imagery. Cf. IMAGINATION, and TYPE (mental). (J.M.B.–G.F.S.)

We speak of images of fancy, of memory, 'visual images,' 'auditory images,' 'tactual images,' &c. Cf. AFTER-IMAGE, and DOUBLE IMAGES. The image played a large part in the older associationist psychology, which taught that memory and recognition depend upon the comparison of the given presentation with its memory image. Recent experimental work and theories have established cases in which the image appears to play no essential part. (E.B.T.)

The theory of the mental DISPOSITION (q.v.) is proposed (by Stout, Meinong, Höfler, Ehrenfels) as a general way of accounting for many cases for which the associational-image theory is artificial; especially in the hands of those who make dispositions in the main motor tendencies and attitudes of interest, attention, &c. An interesting instance of the different points of view is seen in the experiments and discussions on the perception of time (see Schumann, in *Zeitsch. f. Psychol.*, xvii. 106, and Meinong, ibid., xxi. 182), and the critical *résumé* and discussion by Stout (Perception of Change and Duration, *Mind*, N.S., Jan., 1900). (J.M.B.)

Literature: in general, the psychologies, under Memory and Recognition. Also BERGSON, Matière et Mémoire; TAINE, L'Intelligence, i. 76–165, ii. 70; N. MICHAUT, De l'Imagination (1876); F. GALTON, Inquiries into Human Faculty, 83–113; PARISH, Illusions and Hallucinations (1898); STOUT, Manual of Psychol., 393 ff. (L.M.)

Also STERN, Psychol. d. individuellen Differenzen (1900), 47 ff.; J. M. BALDWIN, Philos. Rev., ii. (1893) 385; J. M. CHARCOT, Œuvres complètes, iii (trans. by S. Freud, 1886, as Neue Vorlesungen ü. d. Krankheiten d. Nervensystems, insb. ü. Hysterie); G. T. FECHNER, Elemente d. Psychophysik ii. (1889) 469 ff.; F. GALTON, Mind, O.S., v. (1880) 301; W. LAY, Psychol. Rev., Monog. Suppl. 7 (1898); C. UFER, Ueber Sinnestypen u. verwandte Erscheinungen (1895). (E.B.T.)

Imagery: see IMAGE.

Image-worship (or **Iconolatry**) [Lat. *imago*, a copy]: Ger. *Bilderdienst*; Fr. *culte des images*; Ital. *culto delle immagini, iconolatria*. The paying of divine honours to an object which is supposed to be, in some sense, a likeness or imitation of the divinity for which it stands. See IDOL, and IDOLATRY.

Image-worship (or iconolatry) may be regarded as a species of idol-worship. An idol need not be a likeness or imitation of the divinity, but may represent it by mere association. It is the characteristic of an idol that it gradually displaces the divinity it represents, and tends to become itself the object of worship. This is true of image-worship, although its supposed resemblance keeps the thought of the object before the mind of the worshipper, tending to check the process of identification. The evil of image-worship arises out of the temptation to materialize the spiritual. Historically, image-worship is of ancient date, being forbidden in the second commandment of the Decalogue. The controversy over the use of images in worship has played a great rôle in the history of the Christian Church, leading at one time to a conflict which practically disrupted Christendom. The Romish Church is more tolerant of the use of images and pictures than the Reformed, while in the latter the Calvinistic communions are most uncompromising in their opposition.

Literature: GOLDAST, Imperialia decreta de cultu Imaginum (1608); MAIMBOURG, Hist. de l'Hérésie des Iconoclastes (1679); K. SCHENCK, Kaiser Leon III: ein Beitr. z. Gesch. d. Bilderstreites (1880). (A.T.O.)

Imagination: Ger. (1) *Phantasie*, (2) *Einbildungskraft*; Fr. *imagination (constructive)*; Ital. *immaginazione*. (1) The general power or process of having mental images. See IMAGE, and IDEA. In this sense it seems better to use the terms imaging and imagery than imagination.

In its primary application imagination is simply equivalent to imaging, and is synonymous with the Greek φαντασία. Hobbes defines it as 'nothing but decaying sense'; but he goes on to distinguish two kinds of imagination, the one simple, 'as when one imagineth a man or horse which he hath seen before'; the other compounded, 'as when from the sight of a man at one time and of a horse at another, we conceive in our mind a Centaur' (Molesworth's ed., iii. 6). According to Berkeley 'imaginatio nihil aliud est quam facultas representatrix rerum sensibilium, vel actu existentium vel saltem possibilium' (*De Motu*, § 53). With him both senses of the word are united. 'I find I have a faculty of imagining or representing to myself the ideas of those particular things I have perceived, and of variously compounding and dividing them' (*Principles*, Introd. 10). The connection is that we can image combinations that we never have perceived, and never will perceive. Similarly, in modern usage, it is customary to use imagination in both senses, and, where more precise distinction is required, to call the one reproductive, and the other productive, imagination. It seems better to adopt the current usage of popular language, and to restrict the term to that forming of new combinations which is made possible by the absence of objective limitations confining the flow of ideas (meaning 2).

(2) The process of forming new ideal combinations, which depends on the relative absence of objective restrictions, and the consequent freedom of subjective selection.

The mind is relatively unrestricted when it passes from sense-perception to its selective dealings with mental imagery. We can image combinations which we have never perceived. This relative freedom forms the connecting link between imagination in the sense of imagery and in the sense of free selective combination. Again, the man of science when he is looking for a possible explanation may 'give the reins to his imagination' in framing hypotheses; when the facts become more fully known, his freedom becomes correspondingly restricted. The imagination of the poet and the novelist is free from objective restrictions, inasmuch as their mental activity is not immediately directed to the development of knowledge of the real world, or to the attainment of practical ends.

There are two kinds of imagination: fancy, which is relatively passive, and constructive imagination, which is relatively active. Constructive imagination is dominated by a systematic unity of plan controlling the process of selective combination. It has what Coleridge called an *esemplastic* character (from εἰς ἓν πλάττειν, i. e. to shape into one). Fancy, on the contrary, forms new combinations, which are relatively detached and sporadic instead of being integral parts of a whole. Coleridge quotes as an example of fancy the following verse from *Hudibras*:

> 'The sun had long since in the lap
> Of Thetis taken out his nap,
> And like a lobster boyl'd, the morn
> From black to red began to turn.'

As an example of constructive imagination he refers to Milton's description of the approach of the Messiah to battle. The words 'far off their coming shone' gather the whole into the unity of a single picture. It is manifest that constructive imagination requires more sustained and strenuous activity than the mere play of fancy; for it can only utilize those suggested ideas which subserve the development of the general plan and enhance the total effect. Fancy, on the contrary, is free to pass from one combination to another with only a comparatively slight thread of connection, e.g. harmony, with the predominant mood, as gay, comic, pathetic, pensive, &c. The dividing line between constructive imagination and fancy is not sharply marked. There are border cases which may with equal show of reason be referred to either head.

Inasmuch as imagination is conditioned by absence of the objective control which belief essentially involves, belief and imagination are mutually exclusive. What is called aesthetic illusion or SEMBLANCE (q. v.) partly excludes the belief-attitude, and even 'reality-feeling.' The spectators at a theatrical performance do not act as they would if the same scenes occurred in real life. But it should be noted that the freedom from objective control which characterizes imagination is only comparative, not absolute, and that it admits of very varying degrees. Combinations which involve explicit contradictions are always excluded, even in the most unrestricted play of fancy. There are also almost always other objective limitations. So far as objective control exists at all, the attitude of belief (or reality-feeling) is present. A man may mentally frame a narrative concerning normal men and women which has no reference to any actual man or woman. 'The flow of his ideas will be relatively free; it will not be bound down by conditions of date, place, &c.; none the less it will be tied, inasmuch as he is not at liberty to introduce into his mental construction features at variance with the normal constitution of human beings. . . . There is no belief in the narrative as historical fact; but belief about human nature is involved in it through and through' (Stout, *Manual of Psychol.*, 545 f.).

Literature: the treatises on psychology and BIBLIOG. G, 2, *j*; AMBROSO, L'Immaginazione (1898); RIBOT, L'Imagination créatrice (1900). (G.F.S.–J.M.B.)

Imaging (in logic): Ger. *Abbildung*; Fr. (in mathematics) *représentation*; Ital. *rappresentazione*. A term proposed to translate Abbildung in its logical use. In order to apprehend this meaning, it is indispensable to be acquainted with the history of the meanings of Abbildung. This word was used in 1845 by Gauss for what is called in English a map-projection, which is an incorrect term, since many such modes of representation are not geometrical rectilinear projections at all; and of those which Gauss had in view, but a single one is so. In mathematics Abbildung is translated *representation*; but this word is pre-empted in logic. Since Bild is always translated *image, imaging* will answer very well for Abbildung. If a map of the entire globe were made on a sufficiently large scale, and out of doors, the map itself would be shown upon the map; and upon that image would be seen the map of the map; and so on, indefinitely. If the map were to cover the entire globe, it would be an image of nothing but itself, where each point would be imaged by some other point, itself imaged by a third, &c. But a map of the heavens does not show the map itself at all. A Mercator's projection shows the entire globe (except the poles) over and over again in endlessly recurring strips. Many maps, if they were completed, would show two or more different places on the earth at each point of the map (or at any rate on a part of it), like one map drawn upon another. Such is obviously the case with any rectilinear projection of the entire sphere, excepting only the stereographic. These two peculiarities may coexist in the same map.

Any mathematical function of one variable may be regarded as an image of its variable according to some mode of imaging. For the real and imaginary quantities correspond, one to one and continuously, to the assignable points on a sphere. Although mathematics is by far the swiftest of the sciences in its generalizations, it was not until 1879 that Dedekind (in the 3rd edition of his recension of Lejeune-Dirichlet's *Zahlentheorie*, § 163, p. 470; but the writer has not examined the second edition) extended the conception to discrete systems in these words: 'It very often happens in other sciences, as well as in mathematics, that there is a replacement of every element ω of a system Ω of elements or things by a corresponding element ω' [of a system Ω']. Such an act should be called a substitution. . . . But a still more convenient expression is found by regarding Ω' as the image of Ω, and ω' of ω, according to a certain mode of imaging.' And he adds, in a footnote: 'This power of the mind of comparing a thing ω with a thing ω', or of relating ω to ω', or of considering ω' to correspond to ω, is one without which no thought would be possible.' [We do not translate the main clause.] This is an early and significant acknowledgment that the so-called 'logic of relatives'—then deemed beneath the notice of logicians—is an integral part of logic. This remark remained unnoticed until, in 1895, Schröder devoted the crowning chapter of his great work (*Exakte Logik*, iii. 553–649) to its development. Schröder says that, in the broadest sense, any relative whatever may be considered as an imaging—'nämlich als eine eventuell bald "undeutige," bald "eindeutige," bald "mehrdeutige" Zuordnung.' He presumably means that the logical universe is thus imaged in itself. However, in a narrower sense, he says, a mode of imaging is restricted to a relative which fulfils one or other of the two conditions of being never *undeutig*, or being never *mehrdeutig*. That is, the relation must belong to one or other of two classes, the one embracing such that every object has an image, and the other such that no object has more than one image. Schröder's definitions (however interesting his developments) break all analogy with the important property of the imaging of continua noticed above. If this is to be regarded as essential, an imaging must be defined as a generic relation between an object-class and an image-class, which generic relation consists of specific relations, in each of which one individual, and no more, of the image-class stands to each individual of the object-class, and in each of which every individual of the image-class stands to one individual, and to no more, of the object-class. This is substantially a return to Dedekind's definition, which makes an *imaging* a synonym for a substitution. (C.S.P., H.B.F.)

Imago [Lat.]: (the same in the other languages). The perfect or winged stage of those insects which pass through a complete METAMORPHOSIS (q. v.); it is in this stage only that the sexual organs are mature.

Literature: COMSTOCK, Introd. to the Study of Insects; PACKARD, Entomology; KORSCHELT and HEIDER, Entwickelungsgesch. d. Wirbellosen. (C.S.M.)

Imbecility [Lat. *imbecillitas*, weakness, feebleness]: Ger. *Imbecillität, Schwachsinn*; Fr. *imbécilité*; Ital. *imbecillità*. Generally, a weakness of mind; specifically, a degree of this defect inferior to idiocy.

It is applied more often to states of congenital mental enfeeblement. Imbecility may be said roughly to imply a sufficient defect of memory, reasoning, and mental initiation to incapacitate the subject for the ordinary duties of life and to make necessary a special form of education. Cf. IDIOCY. (J.J.)

Imitation [Lat. *imitatio*]: Ger. *Nachahmung*; Fr. *imitation*; Ital. *imitazione*. (1) The performance in movement, thought, or both movement and thought, of what comes through the senses, or by suggestion, as belonging to another individual.

This is the traditional and customary usage. It makes essential the fact that another person serves to set the copy imitated. This usage is that of Preyer and Lloyd Morgan. To distinguish imitation in this limited sense from the wider meanings designated below, it has been suggested that this be called 'conscious imitation' (when the repetition as such is conscious to the thought of the imitator), 'imitative suggestion' (when imitative to the onlooker only), and 'plastic imitation' (the subconscious conformity to types of thought and action, as in crowds).

(2) Any repetition in thought, action, or both, which reinstates a copy. This definition of imitation is wider than the foregoing. It includes what is called 'self-imitation,' or repetition of what is in one's own mind. This usage requires a certain identity as between the copy and the result made, but the conscious relating of copy to result, as in (1), is not essential. This usage is that of Tarde, James, Royce, Baldwin. As signifying simply 'mental reproduction' of nature, especially in art, it goes back to Plato and Aristotle. This usage is of value in discussions in social psychology, sociology, and the theory of art, as in the 'inner imitation' of K. Lange and Groos (for which see SEMBLANCE).

(3) An organic reaction of the stimulus-repeating or self-sustaining type. Organic imitation was used with this meaning as synonymous with CIRCULAR REACTION (q. v.) by the present writer. As this is a purely neurological and physiological conception, the use of the term imitation no doubt leads to confusion, and circular reaction expresses the meaning better. The question may then be discussed as to whether imitation always requires circular reaction.

As to the two first usages, it would seem to be wise to keep the broader meaning (2). Where ambiguity is likely to arise, it is well to use 'conscious imitation,' 'imitative suggestion,' 'self-imitation,' 'plastic imitation,' 'instinctive imitation,' all considered forms of the wider notion MIMETISM (q. v.), which covers also the pathological use of the term imitation. The wider meaning would seem necessary also as covering the imitative impulse before its character, as repeating a copy, becomes clearly conscious.

Distinctions have been made between 'spontaneous' and 'deliberate' imitation (Preyer), both being at first voluntary, but the former having become secondary—automatic; and between 'simple' and 'persistent' imitation (Baldwin), the former being involuntary repetition by imitative impulse and suggestion, and the latter being voluntary 'try-try-again' to reproduce a copy. The need of recognizing a class of relatively simple reproductions of the imitative type is seen in the growing belief that there is a native impulse to perform acts of the imitative sort.

A further distinction (Stout) is between 'impulsive' imitation, arising mainly from the direct impulse to imitate, and what may be called 'remote' imitation, springing from an ulterior motive.

Literature: psychological and biological: ARISTOTLE, Poetics, 4 ff.; J. S. MILL, Anal. of the Phenom. of the Human Mind (1829), ii. chap. xxiv; PREYER, The Mind of the Child (Eng. trans. and 4th Ger. ed.); BAIN, Senses and Intellect (3rd ed.), 413 ff., and Emotions and Will (3rd ed.), 344 f.; WALLACE, Natural Selection, v; LLOYD MORGAN, Habit and Instinct, chap. viii; GROOS, Play of Animals, in loc., and Play of Man, in loc.; ROYCE, Psychol. Rev., ii. (1895) 217, and The Imitative Functions, Century Mag., May, 1894; STOUT, Manual of Psychol., Bk. III. 269 ff.; BALDWIN, Mind, Jan., 1894, and the titles given below (general); LE DANTEC, Rev. Philos., Oct., 1899. Sociological: BAGEHOT, Physics and Politics; TARDE, Les Lois de l'Imitation; BOSANQUET, Mind, Apr., 1899, and Philos. Theory of the State, chap. ii. 3; DURKHEIM, Le Suicide, chap. iv; GIDDINGS, Princ. of Sociol.; TOSTI, Psychol. Rev., v. (1898) 247, and Polit. Sci. Quart., xii. 3; see also under CROWD. Neurological and pathological: PFLÜGER, Pflüger's Arch., xv (1877); citations made under MENTAL PATHOLOGY and MIMETISM. In art: PLATO, Republic, iii 400 B and D; ARISTOTLE, Poetics; works cited under ART THEORIES, especially titles by HEGEL, K. LANGE, v. HARTMANN, JOUFFROY, GROOS, GROSSE, BOSANQUET (Hist. of Aesth.); HIRN, The Origins of Art, chap. vi, General: TARDE, Lois de l'Imitation, and Social Laws (Eng. trans.); BALDWIN, Ment. Devel. in the Child and the Race, and Social and Eth. Interpret.; GROOS (titles cited above); WASHBURN, Philos. Rev. (Jan., 1899). (J.M.B., G.F.S.)

Imitation (in biology): see MIMICRY, and MIMETISM.

Imitative Arts: see CLASSIFICATION (of the fine arts).

Immaculate Conception (dogma of): Ger. *Lehrsatz der unbefleckten Empfängniss*; Fr. *dogme de conception immaculée*; Ital. *Immacolata concezione (dogma della)*. That the Virgin Mary, from her conception by her mother, Anne, became, by the grace of God, the subject of a peculiar application of the merits of Christ, whereby she escaped all taint of original sin.

A dogma of the Roman Catholic Church promulgated by Pope Pius IX in 1854. According to Roman Catholic doctrine, Mary, as Mother of God, has received certain privileges from the Deity. These are: perfect sinlessness, perpetual virginity, and the immaculate conception. As a matter of history, the Dominican doctors, especially Thomas Aquinas, opposed the doctrines of the privileges of Mary; in this they were supported by St. Bernard. But the Scotists revived the controversy and finally gained the victory. The doctrine of the immaculate conception is closely connected with the Roman Catholic view of Mary as a 'co-redeemer.' (R.M.W.)

Immanence: see TRANSCENDENCE AND IMMANENCE, and CAUSE.

Immanence (in theology) [Lat. *in* + *manere*, to remain]: Ger. *Immanenz*; Fr. *immanence*; Ital. *immanenza*. The indwelling and inworking of the Deity in nature and man.

Immanence as defined does not exclude TRANSCENDENCE (q. v.), and may coexist with it. But as often conceived, it is exclusive of that conception. Naturalistic and pantheistic conceptions of immanence are those which tend to identify the Deity completely with the inworking force of nature. This leaves no place for transcendence. It is possible, however, for God to work in nature, grounding its existence and phenomena, and yet to be something more in himself, to possess a being that is not identical with his operations. In this sense transcendence seems to be the presupposition of immanence. (A.T.O.)

Immanence - philosophy: Ger. *immanente Philosophie*; Fr. *philosophie de l'immanence*; Ital. *filosofia dell' immanenza*. The immanence-philosophy (philosophy of the immediately given or science of pure experience) is the doctrine of a group of recent German thinkers (Schuppe, Rehmke, Leclair, Schubert-Soldern, and others), who reduce all reality to conscious-contents or elements immanent in consciousness, and seek to explain the world therefrom (Eisler, *Wörterb. d. philos. Begriffe*, 371). In addition to the individual consciousness, some members of the school affirm the existence of Bewusstsein überhaupt, especially in order to escape the solipsistic consequences of their position. The doctrine has also been termed 'monism of consciousness' (Bewusstseinsmonismus). In certain respects it echoes Berkeley and Hume as well as Neo-Kantian and positivistic positions. (A.C.A Jr.)

Literature: the Zeitsch. f. immanente Philos., founded 1895, is the organ of the school (see especially a brief account in Heft 1, by M. R. KAUFFMANN); UEBERWEG-HEINZE, Gesch. d. Philos., III. ii. 21 (8th ed., 1897); SCHUPPE, Logik, is the leading work of the school. (A.C.A. JR.–K.G.)

Immanent and Transeunt Activity. Defining activity as any series of changes of a sufficiently regular and continuous character (see ACTIVITY, 2), the cases may be looked at as of two general sorts : 'transeunt' activity, on the one hand, in which one object is acted upon by another ; and 'immanent' or 'self'-activity, in which the changes observed take place within the active object with little or no influence from other things.

The activities of physical science are almost entirely of the transeunt sort : one body, molecule, atom, or system acts upon some other so that the results of the changes in the other are taken as a measure of the activity of the first. In the biological and mental sciences we have activity of the 'immanent' type: the series of changes seems to evolve within the organism or the mind, with a kind of determination called self-determination or immanence. They cannot be entirely or even largely construed as having been produced by the influence of things outside the organism or the mind. Theories, however, of life and mind turn just upon this question, as to whether both life and mind can be reduced ultimately to changes illustrating activity of the transeunt type ; or, on the other hand, whether the activity of nature, which seems to involve the action of two or more separate things upon each other, may not be viewed as the immanent activity of a larger system of which the things are parts (Lotze), or interpreted after analogy with social community (Ormond). The controversy between freedom and determinism turns upon the interpretation of mental activity in answer to this question.

Literature : LOTZE, Metaphysics ; STOUT, Analytic Psychol., i. Bk. II. chap. i ; BRADLEY, Appearance and Reality, 95 ff. ; ORMOND, Foundations of Knowledge, Pt. II. chap. vii ; and the references given under ACTIVITY.

(J.M.B.)

Immaterialism [Lat. *in* + *materialis*, material]: Ger. *Immaterialismus* ; Fr. *immatérialisme* ; Ital. *idealismo spiritualistico*, *immaterialismo*. Immaterialism is a term which has been applied chiefly to the theory of Berkeley, which asserts that 'nothing properly but persons does exist. All other things are not so much existences themselves as manners of the existence of conscious persons' (Commonplace Book, in Fraser's *Life and Letters of Bishop Berkeley*, 469).

It is considered more applicable than subjective idealism to such a theory, inasmuch as Berkeley accepts the trans-subjective reality of other finite spirits and of the Divine Spirit. It is only the material world whose substantial or independent existence he denies ; its *esse* is *percipi*, or it exists simply as an ordered system of signs by which conscious beings communicate with one another. This system of signs, although it may be supposed to be conceptually present to the mind of God, by whom it has been instituted, has otherwise no reality for Berkeley except in the recurrent experiences of conscious beings. (A.S.P.P.)

Immediacy : see IMMEDIATE AND MEDIATE.

Immediacy and **Mediacy** (Hegel's use): see HEGEL'S TERMINOLOGY, Glossary, 'unmittelbar,' 'Unmittelbarkeit,' 'vermitteln,' 'Vermittelung.'

Immediate and **Mediate** [Lat. *in* + *medius*, middle]: Ger. *unmittelbar* and *vermittelt* ; Fr. *immédiate* and *médiate* ; Ital. *immediato* and *mediato*. (1) Psychological : so far as new conscious process is a development of previous conscious process, it is said to be psychologically mediate ; so far as it is determined by conditions independent of previous conscious process, it is said to be psychologically immediate. The corresponding substantives are immediacy and mediacy.

Speaking psychologically, careful analysis seems to show that no knowledge is purely immediate or purely mediate. All cognition is both immediately and mediately determined. Immediacy is a characteristic belonging most conspicuously to the perception of external objects or the apprehension of subjective processes. But the immediacy is never pure immediacy ; it is inextricably blended with the self-development of mental process. The play of external impressions on the organs of sense contributes an element of immediacy to all sense-perception. But this is only one factor in the process. Previous experience also contributes to the result and determines its nature. I raise my eyes from my book and look out of the window. There on the grass I see a robin hopping about. No previous experience of mine could have enabled me to predict that a robin would present itself at this time and place. There is an immediacy in the cognition which cannot be explained away. But critical reflection shows that there is also a mediacy which is equally indispensable. It is owing to previous experience that I am able to distinguish and identify the object I call a robin, or even the red colour of its breast. Even the shape and distance of things seen exist for my consciousness only as an outcome of my previous mental development. But can we not push our analysis further so as to extract from the total experience the immediate element, the pure datum, and exhibit it in isolation? The attempt is worth making; but its value will be found in its failure, not in its success. The first step we must take is to pass from external to internal apprehension. In asserting the actual presence of the external thing as such, there is always an element of mediacy and a theoretical possibility of error. We may be subject to an illusion or hallucination. In the pursuit of pure immediacy we must retire into the citadel of our own self-consciousness. I affirm not that there is a robin, but that I see or think I see one. But even this is not purely immediate knowledge. The mere appearance of a robin as contrasted with the reality presupposes the identification of this object in distinction from others. Moreover, when I affirm that I see, or think I see, I must have learnt to discriminate those modes of consciousness which I call thinking and seeing from other modes of consciousness. Besides this, it is important to note that 'thinking' and 'seeing' mean more to some persons than to others. They mean more to those who have studied and analysed these processes than to those who have not, just as the sight of a robin means more to a naturalist than to those who are not naturalists. But the fuller of meaning perception is, the larger is the part played in it by interpretation based on previous experience. This is a point of the utmost importance. The more purely immediate a cognition is, whether it be of material things or of subjective process, the more meagre and empty it is, and the less value it has for the system of knowledge as a whole. The attempt to discover an absolutely pure datum of consciousness, without psychological preconditions—a matter of fact which is pure and immediate—ends in the discovery of nothing at all, or of something quite insignificant. The immediacy of internal cognition, like the immediacy of external perception, is valuable, not in itself, but because of its relation to the work of the mind. It is valuable only in so far as it confirms, modifies, corrects, or overthrows that body of inferences which constitute the system of knowledge as a whole.

But if no knowledge is, in a psychological sense, purely immediate, we have still to inquire if any is purely mediate. It will be granted that all knowledge psychologically presupposes data as its point of departure which are not mere products of subjective process. But it may be said that, given certain data, we can evolve further knowledge from them without the aid of fresh data. Given the general constitution of the number-series, we can deduce a multitude of consequences without any further datum. This is true in the sense that no further datum is required which is not contained in the constitution of the number-system itself. But the nature of this system reveals itself gradually in the process, and each new revelation may be regarded as a fresh datum which we do not make, but find. We exercise subjective activity on the object, but the result depends on it, and not on us. In this sense all experience partakes of the nature of experiment, whether it be trying the taste of a fruit, or following the dialectical transitions in Hegel's logic. (G.F.S., J.M.B.)

(2) Psychical or mental: the immediacy or mediacy of an experience, either in a psychological or in a logical sense, (1) or (3), as it exists for the subject of that experience at the time at which it occurs.

We may distinguish two forms, which may or may not coexist. The first has reference only to cognition as such. Psychical immediacy from this point of view consists in the absence of conscious inference, and mediacy consists in the presence of conscious inference. A cognition which is psychically immediate enters the consciousness of the subject without any recognition of its dependence on other cognitions. The second kind of psychical immediacy consists in the absence of reference, not to reasons for a belief, but to the psychological conditions of the experience. For example, we usually accept ideas as they occur without inquiry into the mode in which they suggest each other by association: we are not continually asking—'What made me think of that?' If we do ask this question, the occurrence of our ideas becomes psychically mediate in the second sense. (G.F.S.–J.M.B.)

The force of the distinction between (1) and (2) is seen in the cases of perception, &c., given under (1), in which the psychologically mediate is taken to be (i.e. is, psychically) immediate. The difference between (1) hallucinatory and (2) strict sense illusions is that between the presence of (1) psychical and (2) psychological elements of immediacy. As is said above, the psychically immediate is not always psychologically so; and it is also true, though not so frequent, that the psychologically immediate is not always psychically so. For instance, pathological emotions, due to organic causes, which the patient 'justifies' by the belief in persecution, possession, &c., have elements of psychological, but not of psychic, immediacy. Cases within the sphere of cognition are furnished by hypnotic, and more clearly by post-hypnotic, or deferred, suggestion. Cognitions of various sorts are 'immediate' suggestions in the psychological sense; but are 'accounted for,' 'justified,' 'explained' by the subject; that is, they are psychically mediate.

The distinction between (1) and (2) is the general one between PSYCHIC AND PSYCHOLOGICAL (q. v.). Cf. the two headings in the case of ANALYSIS. It is important in this case, notably for ethics, the discussion of the immediacy of ethical value being confused by the failure to make the distinction, a confusion which the use of the undefined terms 'derived' and 'immediate' only accentuates. Its epistemological value also becomes evident when one recalls the use of the notion of immediacy as one of the TESTS OF TRUTH (q. v.), under such phrases as 'self-evidence,' 'direct intuition,' &c. It is difficult to see how mere psychical immediacy to the individual—at its purest in sensation and intense feeling, that is, in anoetic consciousness—can be taken as a test of validity in what is over-individual and absolute; for it does not even guarantee psychological immediacy. And even if it did, the question would remain as to whether immediacy in any form is not the purest sort of relativity.

Kant, while showing this fallacy in the case of the ideas of the reason, nevertheless makes similar use of the psychical immediacy of the practical reason. Spencer's criticism of immediacy of both sorts—as being a function of race adaptation and not necessarily avoiding, but to him requiring, an agnostic position—goes to show that the resort to immediacy in epistemology is everywhere futile. The latest reasoned appeal to it is that of Bradley, who, like Kant, though for different reasons, fails to find comfort in the mediate. The FAITH PHILOSOPHY (q. v.), down to its recent advocacy of the 'will to believe,' always puts its trust in some data of psychical immediacy. Ultra-rationalism or intellectualism which deduces its absolute makes much appeal to mediacy, but is in turn criticized by positivists for not going the whole way. Cf. Ormond, *Foundations of Knowledge*, Pt. I. chap. iii. (J.M.B., G.F.S.)

(3) Logical or epistemological. From a logical or epistemological point of view a cognition is immediate when it requires no proof; and it is mediate when it requires proof.

I see an ink-pot before me on the table: I perceive it as having an existence distinct from and independent of my own existence, both bodily and mental. This cognition is psychologically mediate inasmuch as it is a product of previous mental process. Psychically it is immediate, inasmuch as I am not aware, in the moment of perception, of its dependence on grounds or reasons. But let some one question or deny that the ink-pot exists as I perceive it. I may then think it necessary to justify my perceptual judgment by assigning reasons for it. I may begin by saying that the ink-pot exists in the manner I affirm, because I perceive it as existing in this manner. This is to assign a psychical fact as the logical ground of a physical fact. The doubter may then proceed to unmask the whole battery of subjective idealism, and bombard my position. In the end I may find it necessary to develop a series of complicated arguments to establish what, in the first instance, came before consciousness as an immediate datum. In taking this course I admit that what was the psychically immediate datum really required justification by grounds and reasons. In other words, I admit that it is logically mediate. On the other hand, I might have adopted a different course. I might have resolutely refused to argue, affirming that the existence of the inkstand is for me a self-evident fact which requires no proof, and that all arguments to the contrary must, from the nature of the case, be irrelevant or nonsensical. I should then be maintaining that my perceptual judgment is logically immediate. Cf. KNOWLEDGE (in logic).

Literature: see EPISTEMOLOGY, and BIBLIOG. B, 1, d. (G.F.S., J.M.B.)

Immediate Creation: see CREATION.

Immediate Inference: see INFERENCE.

Immensity: see ATTRIBUTES (of God).

Immortality [Lat. *in* + *mortalis*, mortal]: Ger. *Unsterblichkeit*; Fr. *immortalité*; Ital. *immortalità*. The doctrine that the human soul survives the death of the body, and is the bearer of an endless life.

Belief in immortality, in some vague form

at least, has been a feature of most religions, although it is perhaps only in Christianity that it has become an assured conviction. In the Greek mysteries, notably the Eleusinian, it is taught rather by implication than dogmatically. In philosophy it has played a prominent part. Plato held the doctrine and developed a number of proofs of immortality, connecting it in his eschatology with the process of metempsychosis. Aristotle's doctrine of the perishability of the passive intellect leaves the attitude of his philosophy towards personal immortality in doubt. The Stoics taught a doctrine of limited immortality. Mediaeval thought divided on Aristotelian grounds, the Arabians tending to deny, while the leading schoolmen affirmed, personal immortality. In modern thought the question became involved with that of the substantiality of the soul. On the soul's knowledge of itself as a substance Mendelssohn's famous proof of immortality is founded. Kant refutes this proof by calling in question the presupposition on which it rests—namely, the soul's ability to know itself as a substance. Kant founds his own proof of immortality on the demands of the moral reason. Since Kant the tendency has been gaining strength to rest the doctrine of immortality mainly on moral and aesthetic grounds, or on what Lotze calls considerations of value. The most recent tendency is to ground the persistence of the individual soul in its relation to God on the Absolute.

Literature: W. R. ALGER, A Crit. Hist. of the Doctrine of a Future Life (1871); W. E. CHANNING on Immortality, in Essays (1839); PLATO, Phaedo, and the Apology; G. TEICHMÜLLER, Über die Unsterblichkeit d. Seele (1874); E. ABBOT, Literature of the Doctrine of a Future Life; LOTZE, Microcosmus; Ingersoll Lects., by JAMES and ROYCE. (A.T.O.)

Immutability [Lat. *in* + *mutabilis*, changeable]: Ger. *Unveränderlichkeit*; Fr. *immutabilité*; Ital. *immutabilità*. Changelessness. A theological term used to designate the attribute of changelessness in the divine nature. See ATTRIBUTE (of God), and ABSOLUTE. (J.M.B.)

Impenetrability [Lat. *in* + *penetrabilis*, penetrable]: Ger. *Undurchdringlichkeit*; Fr. *impénétrabilité*; Ital. *impenetrabilità*. That property of matter by virtue of which every portion or particle of it prevents any other portion or particle from occupying the same space with itself at the same time.

It is known by universal experience that, whenever the attempt is made to bring two masses of matter into the same position, an irresistible force comes into play which prevents coincidence. The masses with which we are most familiar, solid and liquid bodies, seem to us to have definite boundaries, forming geometric surfaces; and the force in question comes into play instantly when two such surfaces are brought into contact. To this familiar fact the conception of the parts of matter in general, how minute soever they may be, as having extension in space and absolute impenetrability may be supposed due. But careful analysis does not justify the conclusion that the properties of extension and impenetrability grow out of the fact that the parts of matter have absolutely definite boundaries. The really observed phenomenon is that of a repulsive force coming into play when two particles are brought into apparent contact. We may therefore, with Boscovisch, abandon the idea of a definite boundary to the parts of matter, and consider the latter as simple centres of attractive and repulsive forces acting at distances so minute as to elude our senses.

Impenetrability thus becomes a secondary quality arising from an unlimited increase of the repulsive force as two centres are brought nearer together. (S.N.)

Imperative: see CATEGORICAL IMPERATIVE.

Imperative Idea or **Conception**, also **Insistent Idea**: Ger. *Zwangsvorstellung*; Fr. *obsessions, impulsions intellectuelles*; Ital. *idee coatte* (or *coartanti*), *ossessione*. An idea or train of thought which dominates or harasses the individual in spite of his struggle to escape from it and his recognition of its unreasonableness.

The imperative idea is not a DELUSION (q.v.) nor a FIXED IDEA (q.v.), which actually moulds the individual's intellectual processes; but it is rather an idiosyncrasy, the nature of which the victim fully recognizes but seems powerless to dispel. It is not a form of insanity, but seems associated with unstable or susceptible nervous conditions. The experience is a common one of being annoyed by the frequent occurrence of a word, a line of verse, a train of thought, a suggestion to say or do some trifling absurdity or impropriety; and the imperative idea is only the more marked and established form of such an idea or habit. It is related psychologically to conditions of impairment or weakness of will (see WILL, diseases of); and the imperative idea may at times prevent or check normal action, or incite to actions which it is the purpose and policy of the individual to inhibit. Examples of imperative ideas which affect both thought and action are : agoraphobia, the nervous dread of open places ; claustrophobia, the dread of shut-in places ; arithmomania, the impulse to count all sorts of objects and speculate uselessly and endlessly on numerical relations. Such tendencies as coprolalia, the impulse to use blasphemous or obscene expressions ; and such habits of thought as constant speculation about intellectual trifles, fear of contamination in the slightest and most exaggerated forms, may come to dominate so much of the intellectual processes as to approximate to a condition of insanity. It is to be noted that these unwelcome but insistent ideas (well characterized by the German Zwangsvorstellung) often cause intense fear, worry, and anxiety, even when they do not influence action ; the patient fears that he may yield to certain impulses, and maintains a struggle against a habit which he recognizes to be absurd. Rather few of the imperative ideas are purely intellectual, most of them being related to morbid motor impulses. Those that are sensory may be regarded as similar to SYNAESTHESIAS (q. v.) or Zwangsempfindungen, or the inevitable association of one sensation with another ; while those which are entirely motor become nothing more than eccentric habits ; e.g. the trick of feeling some obligation to touch with a cane every post or tree, or some particular object on an accustomed walk. What is common to all cases is a bondage or impulse which the victim feels ' to pursue a certain trivial or disagreeable line of thought, often associated with vocal utterance, or motor acts (and with emotional disturbance, such as fear, anxiety), along with sanity in other respects' (Tuke).

Literature : art. Imperative Ideas in Tuke's Dict. of Psychol. Med., and literature there cited ; MICKLE, Obsessions and Besetments, J. of Ment. Sci. (1896), xlii. 691 ; THOMSEN, Lehre von den Zwangsvorstellungen, Arch. f. Psychiat., xxvii (1895) ; KRAFFT-EBING, Arch. f. Psychiat. (1890), 68, 529 ff. ; JANET, Névroses et Idées Fixes (1898) ; TUKE, in Brain (1894), xxii. 179–97 ; JACKSON (and others), in Brain (1895), 318–51. See also works of MAGNAN, KOCH, LEGRAND-DE-SAULLE, and MORSELLI, as cited under DOUBTING MANIA, and DEGENERATION. (J.J.)

Imperceptible [Lat. *in* + *percipere*, to perceive]: Ger. *unmerklich*; Fr. *imperceptible*; Ital. *impercettibile*. Applied to stimulations or differences of stimulation which are too weak to be distinguished by consciousness.

Such stimulations are said to be below the conscious THRESHOLD (q. v.), as those which are 'least or just noticeable' are just above it. The discussion as to whether there are sensations which are imperceptible is not raised here. Cf. UNCONSCIOUS. (J.M.B., G.F.S.)

Impersonal Judgment: see PROPOSITION.

Implicate and **Implication:** see IMPLICIT AND EXPLICIT.

Implicit and **Explicit:** Ger. *miteinbegriffen, implicit* (*Implikation*), and *ausdrücklich, explicit*; Fr. *implicite* (*implication*; means also contradiction—TH.F.) and *explicite*; Ital. *implicito* and *explicito*. That which is outwardly, definitely, or expressly included in any whole is explicit to the whole ; that which belongs to a whole but is not explicit is implicit to it.

Inferable, nascent or incipient, immanent, all present shades of meaning expressed in various contexts by implicit. That which is, especially logically, implicit is called an implicate or an implication. Both implicit and explicit are applicable in particular to wholes of meaning or intent. Cf. the next topic. (J.M.B.)

Implicit (in logic). Said of an element or character of a representation, whether verbal or mental, which is not contained in the representation itself, but which appears in the strictly logical (not merely in the psychological) analysis of that representation.

Thus, when we ordinarily think of something, say the Antarctic continent, as real, we do not stop to reflect that every intelligible question about it admits of a true answer ; but when we logically analyse the meaning of reality, this result appears in the analysis. Consequently, only concepts, not percepts, can contain any implicit elements, since they alone are capable of logical analysis. An implicit contradiction, or contradiction *in adiecto*, is one which appears as soon as the terms are defined, irrespective of the properties of their objects. Thus there is, strictly speaking, no implicit contradiction in the notion of a quadrilateral triangle, although it is impossible. But, owing to exaggeration, this would currently be said to involve not merely an implicit, but an explicit contradiction, or contradiction in terms.

Any proposition which neither requires the exclusion from nor the inclusion in the universe of any state of facts or kind of object except such as a given second proposition so excludes or requires to be included, is implied in that second proposition in the logical sense of implication, no matter how different it may be in its point of view, or otherwise. It is a part of the meaning of the copula ' is ' employed in logical forms of proposition, that it expresses a transitive relation, so that whatever inference from the proposition would be justified by the *dictum de omni* is implied in the meaning of the proposition. Nor could any rule be admitted as universally valid in formal logic, unless it were a part of the definition of one of the symbols used in formal logic. Accordingly, whatever can be logically deduced from any proposition is implied in it; and conversely. Whether what is implied will, or will not, be suggested by the contemplation of the proposition is a question of psychology. All that concerns logic is, whether all the facts excluded and required by the one proposition are among those so excluded or required by the other.   (C.S.P.)

Import [Lat. *in + portare*, to carry]: Ger. *Bedeutung*; Fr. *portée, signification*; Ital. *importanza, significato*. Import is almost synonymous with signification or meaning. It is therefore used in logic as equivalent to COMPREHENSION (q. v.), e. g. in the case of notions. In reference to judgment, import must be taken to mean the precise thought-relation which is asserted, positively or negatively, in the judgment. Cf. JUDGMENT.   (R.A.)

Impregnation: see FERTILIZATION.

Impression [Lat. *impressus*]: Ger. *Eindruck*; Fr. *impression*; Ital. *impressione*. (1) Used by Hume to designate experiences of the perceptual order as contrasted with ' ideas ' (fainter revived impressions).

(2) The physiological process of stimulation apart from the corresponding sensation which it arouses.

(3) In sociology: sometimes used for CONSTRAINT (q.v.).   (J.M.B., G.F.S.)

Impression (aesthetic). The effect produced by the intrinsic qualities of an aesthetic object, as distinguished from its expression or suggestion of a meaning pointing beyond itself.

For example, the impression of a straight line as compared with that of a curve, and the impression of either of these as compared with the expression of a face, whose features chanced to contain both (cf. Santayana, *The Sense of Beauty*, 1896). See IMPRESSIONISM.   (J.R.A.)

Impressionism [Lat. *impressio*, from *in + premere*, to press in or upon]: Ger. *Impres-*

sionismus; Fr. *impressionisme*; Ital. *impressionismo*. A school or tendency of art, in which the aim is to record or render the immediate and personal impressions received or felt by the artist.

The impression may be derived from an outer scene, or from inner experience. The media concerned are chiefly those of painting, music, and literature. In painting, the term has meant more definitely the effort to portray the momentary effect produced by some aspect of nature, seen at once and as a whole, without details, but with no alteration of colour. An especially prominent phase of impressionist painting has been the rendering of the effects of light, notably of sunlight or *plein air*.

In contrast with IDEALISM (q.v.) in art, which emphasizes meaning or EXPRESSION (q.v.), impressionism requires that the artist should abstract himself from memory, seeing only that which he looks upon, and that as for the first time.

It is distinguished from certain other phases of REALISM (q.v.) and NATURALISM (q.v.) in art, in that its aim is to present not a literal transcript of nature, but the impression or emotion which nature gives to the artist. It is opposed also to formalism (see FORM, in aesthetics). This shows itself in painting and drawing by emphasizing ' values,' or light and shade effects in mass, rather than accurate delineation, and in music by the presentation of a series of tone-colour effects instead of the development of a theme. In literature, impressionism aims to tell its story by a series of vivid pictures, and in criticism to record the critic's impression as immediately felt, with no attempt at analysis or objective evaluation.

The term came into use in connection with the paintings of E. Manet and others, which were exhibited in Paris in the seventies. Although disowned by the school itself, which preferred to be known as that of the ' Independents,' it has passed into general use and has been extended to other arts. It is useful to indicate an aspect of the work of many artists who are not impressionists in a narrow sense. Such, among painters, were Corot and Millet; among writers, Sterne and Keats; among musicians, Wagner and Grieg.

Literature: MUTHER, Hist. of Mod. Painting, ii. chap. xxxiii; LECOMTE, L'Art Impressionniste (1892); DURANTY, La nouvelle peinture (1876); DURET, Les peintres impressionnistes (1879); HUYSMANS, L'Art moderne (1892); WEDMORE, in Fortn. Rev., Jan., 1883;

T. Child, Art and Criticism (1892), 70 ff., 162 ff.; The Desire of Beauty (1892), chap. ix; Art J., xlv. 28, 103; Quart. Rev., clxxxv. 173; Blackwood's Mag., clxiii. 630; Francis Bate, The Naturalistic School of Painting (2nd ed., 1887). (J.H.T.)

Impulse [Lat. *impulsus*, from *impellere*, to impel]: Ger. *Trieb*; Fr. *impulsion*; Ital. *impulso*. A conation in so far as it operates through its intrinsic strength, independently of the general system of mental life. Action on impulse is contrasted with action due to deliberation. As a typical instance of impulse we may refer to the motor tendencies connected with a Fixed Idea (q. v.) See also the next topic.

In the experience which has been called the 'fascination of a precipice,' the idea of throwing oneself over the edge into the depths below acquires an insistent vivacity, which may lead to its realization, though the whole organized system of our mental life is up in arms to resist it. Animal cravings, such as that for drink or opium, may operate in a similar way. In general the activity of the lower animals is impulsive; for in them conative tendencies do not seem to be co-ordinated and subordinated in an organized system of motives. The mental processes of the lower animals are mainly of the perceptual type. But when conscious life is mainly perceptual, the several trains of activity which compose it are relatively disconnected with each other. Each arises out of the circumstances of the present moment, instead of being part of a general plan of life. On the other hand, in the deliberate action peculiarly characteristic of human beings, the impulse arising from the circumstances of the present is brought into relation with a general system of ends, and is repressed, strengthened, or modified accordingly.

It will be seen that impulsiveness is a relative conception. Any conation may be regarded as having a certain strength of its own, and also in other circumstances as forming part of a mental system.

A special case of impulse is the so-called Instinct-feeling (q.v.), the conation of rising strength, before its expenditure in an instinctive action. The term is useful as marking off this class of impulses, and so preventing the use of the term Instinct (q v.) for impulse.

The use of the word as a technical term is modern. There is a confusing variety of definitions. 'A conation initiated and fused with a feeling of craving, in view of some object of sense-perception or imagination, with a tendency to discharge in a complicated form of purposeful movements' (Ladd, *Psychol. Descrip. and Explan.*, 592). 'An emotional state which tends to express itself in external movements of the body of such a character that their result is the increase of a pre-existing pleasure or the removal of a pre-existing pain. Consciousness of the result previous to its occurrence is not implied' (Wundt, *Grundzüge d. physiol. Psychol.*, ii. 410). Our definition attempts to give the common element in the varying usages. It is also in accordance with popular usage.

Literature: see the textbooks of psychology; also Bibliog. G, 2, s. (G.F.S.—J.M.B.)

Impulse (abnormal). An abnormal impulse appears in mental disorders as an impairment of the will, owing to which the transition from thought to action is too sudden and too little controlled. An uncontrollable impulse is thus a state of defective inhibition, which is often a characteristic factor in mania, in excited melancholia, and in the first stage of general Paralysis (q. v.).

Clouston and others speak of certain cases in which this is the dominant symptom, as impulsive insanity. Homicidal and suicidal impulse, destructive impulses, the unconscious acts of an epileptic are types of pathological impulses. It is customary also to include under impulse the feeling of a marked tendency towards an action even when control takes place. The morbid impulse which many normal persons feel to throw themselves from a height or to commit some glaring impropriety are of this type. In many such cases the intellectual aspect is more prominent, and they become akin to cases of Phobia (q.v.) and Mania (q.v.). Such an impulse also resembles the Imperative Idea (q.v.). (J.J.)

Imputation (in law) [Lat. *imputare*, to impute]: Ger. *Zurechnung*; Fr. *imputation*; Ital. *imputazione*. The attribution to a particular person of legal responsibility for an act; it is properly used only of free actions and their natural consequences (see Wolff's *Inst.*, chap. i. § 3).

Imputation is also used by civilians to signify an appropriation of payments where there are several debts and enough is not paid to satisfy all. (S.E.B.)

Imputation (in theology). The doctrine (1) of the attribution of the guilt of Adam's sin to his posterity; (2) of the attribution of the merit of Christ's righteousness to believers.

It is generally agreed that imputation is a forensic term, and that the transfer of guilt and merit is to be understood legally and not morally. The attempt to rationalize the putative act has developed great divergences of view, ranging from extreme Augustinianism on the one hand to Pelagianism on the other. On the question of the imputation of Christ's righteousness, if we leave out of view the moral theory of the Atonement as practically denying imputation, there is substantial agreement that the transfer rests on a substitutionary act of free grace on the part of Christ.

Literature: SCHAFF, Creeds of Christendom; FISHER, Imputation; DORNER, Gesch. d. Protestantischen Theol., ii ; EDWARDS, The Great Doctrine of Original Sin; STEVENS, The Pauline Theol.; C. HODGE, Bib. Repertory, July, 1830, 1831; October, 1839.   (A.T.O.)

In and for itself: see HEGEL'S TERMINOLOGY, Glossary, 'An und für Sich,' and 'An Sich,' and KANT'S TERMINOLOGY, Glossary, 'Ding an Sich.'

In esse, in intellectu, in re [Lat.]. Expressions denoting different forms of REALITY AND EXISTENCE (q.v.). See also LATIN AND SCHOLASTIC TERMINOLOGY, 'Esse,' and 'Realitas.'   (J.M.B.)

In posse [Lat.]: see POTENTIAL AND POTENTIALITY.

Inability (in theology) [Lat. *in* + *habilis*, manageable]: Ger. *Unzulänglichkeit*; Fr. *incapacité* (?); Ital. *inabilità*. The want of power to do the will or to obey the law of God this want of power being either natural, arising from the lack of capacity, or moral, arising from the absence of disposition.

Man's inability is ordinarily regarded as an effect of the Fall. In early Christian thought the opposite poles are found in Pelagianism, which denies inability, and Augustinianism, which asserts it in a radical sense. In mediaeval theology the doctrine of Aquinas is representative, who affirms man's moral power to will and desire the good, but denies his ability to realize it without divine help. In modern theology a less radical difference separates Calvinism from Arminianism. Among Calvinists the old school adheres to the doctrine of Augustine, while the new school denies natural inability and asserts that man could do good if he would. Arminianism differs from old-school Calvinism in asserting gracious ability; that is, man's power to co-operate with divine grace in his own salvation.

Literature: C. HODGE, System. Theol., ii. 257-77; HODGSON, New Divinity examined, Brit. Quart. Rev., July, 1867; New Englander (1868), 486-90, 496-9, 511, 553.   (A.T.O.)

Inattention [Lat. *inattentio*]: Ger. *Unaufmerksamkeit*; Fr. *inattention*; Ital. *disattenzione*. A relative term denoting more or less absence of attention to a particular object when attention is normally possible. It includes the more restricted terms ABSTRACTION, DISTRACTION, and AB-SENT-MINDEDNESS.   (J.M.B., G.F.S.)

Incantation: see MAGIC.

Incapacity [Lat. *in* + *capacitas*, ability to contain]: Ger. *Dispositionsunfähigkeit*; Fr. *incapacité*; Ital. *incapacità*. Inability arising from mental disease.

It raises an important practical question, especially in relation to legal or testamentary rights. Technically, the question is one which the laws and courts decide; and while a considerable change of opinion has taken place in recent years, and some attempt has been made to reconcile legal practice with medical views, the question of incapacity must always be somewhat arbitrarily decided. The question is not so broad as that of general responsibility for one's action; but in both cases a knowledge of the distinction between right and wrong, an appreciation of the probable consequences of one's action, and an ability to resist undue influence on the part of others are usually regarded as the most essential requisites. The absence of these powers would be regarded as an indication of incapacity.

Literature: MAUDSLEY, Responsibility in Mental Disease (1874); CLEVENGER, Med. Jurisprudence, ii. (1898); DELBRÜCK, Gerichtl. Psycho-Pathol. (1897).   (J.J.)

Incarnation [Lat. *in* + *caro*, flesh]: Ger. *Fleisch-* (or *Mensch-*) *werdung*; Fr. *incarnation*; Ital. *incarnazione*. The assumption by Deity of mortal (generally human) form. In Christian theology, the doctrine of the union of divine and human nature in the person of Jesus Christ. Cf. SPIRITISM.

The belief that the gods assume mortal form is imbedded in the religious traditions of most nations. Whether or not some form of this belief is essential to religion, it is certainly true that in precisely those religions that are most spiritual does it hold the most prominent and central place. The Christian conception of the Incarnation has tended to vary according as the greater emphasis has been placed on the humanity or the Divinity of Christ, but all Christian creeds agree in affirming that in him the Divine Word has somehow become flesh.

Literature: DORNER, Hist. of the Doctrine of Christ, &c. (Ger. and Eng.); B. F. WEST-COTT, The Incarnation and Our Common Life, 7 (1894); textbooks of systematic theology. (A.T.O.)

Incipient: see NASCENT.

Inclination [Lat. *inclinatio*]: Ger. *Neigung*; Fr. *inclination, penchant*; Ital. *inclinazione, tendenza*. (1) Used loosely in the general sense of APPETENCE (q. v.). (2) A disposition to act on considerations of personal ease or pleasure. In this sense, inclination is often contrasted with duty. (J.M.B.–G.F.S.)

Inclusion (in logic): see SUBORDINATION.

Incoherence [Lat. *in + cohaerens*, sticking together]: Ger. *Incohärenz, Verwirrtheit*; Fr. *incohérence*; Ital. *incoerenza*. Want of orderly connection in thought and speech; it thus implies an abeyance of the voluntary selecting and co-ordinating processes of the intelligence, and a consequent exposure of the train of ideas to the caprices of the imagination or to accidental association.

Incoherence thus becomes characteristic, and somewhat permanently so, of certain types of mania and of dementia; it appears as a transitory state in the delirium of disease, in the effect of psychic poisons (see PSYCHIC EFFECTS OF DRUGS), in dreaming, &c. It is important psychologically as showing that consistent, rational thought is a selective process controlled by the highest cortical centres, while the several factors and materials of such thought may be present in a less developed process controlled by a lower range or level of centres. (J.J.)

Income: see EARNINGS.

Incompatible. Not COMPATIBLE (q. v.).

Incomprehensible: see COMPREHENSION; and for relation to inconceivable and UN-KNOWABLE see the latter topic.

Inconceivable and **Inconceivability**: see UNKNOWABLE, and TESTS OF TRUTH.

Inconceivableness (of the contrary): see UNIVERSAL POSTULATE.

Inconsistency [Lat. *in + con + sistere*, to stand]: Ger. *Unvereinbarkeit*; Fr. *inconsistance*; Ital. *incompatibilità*. The relation between two assertions which cannot be true at once, though it may not be a direct contradiction; as between a statement of items and a statement of their total. Cf. CONSISTENCY.

A logical discrepancy, on the other hand,

is a difference between two statements either difficult or impossible to reconcile with the credibility of both. It is said to be negative if one assertion omits an inseparable part of the fact stated in another; as when one witness testifies that *A* pointed a pistol at *B*, and another that *A* shot at *B*. It is positive if one asserts what the other denies. But even then it may often be conciliable (verträglich); that is, may not prove that either statement is in other respects untrustworthy. See Bachmann, *Logik*, §§ 214 ff.

'Inconsistent' is applied to an assertion, or hypothesis, which either in itself, or in copulation with another proposition with which it is said to be inconsistent, might be known to be false by a man devoid of all information except the meanings of the words used and their syntax.

Inconsistent differs from contradictory (see CONTRADICTION) in being restricted usually to propositions, expressed or implied, and also in not implying that the falsity arises from a relation of negation. 'That is John' and 'It is Paul' are inconsistent, but hardly contradictory. Moreover, contradictory is also used in a peculiar sense in formal logic. Cf. OPPOSITION. (C.S.P.)

Inco-ordination [Lat. *in + co-*, together, + *ordinare*, to arrange]: Ger. *Unkoordiniertheit* (*Ataxie*); Fr. *incoordination* (*ataxie*); Ital. *incoordinazione*. Lack of ability or defective ability to control movements and to combine them into orderly, useful, and purposive actions. See ATAXIA. (J.J.)

Increasing Return: Ger. *steigende Produktivität*; Fr. *loi des débouchés*; Ital. *prodotto crescente*. The converse of DIMINISHING RETURN (q. v.).

The increasing profit when we enlarge the output of a factory is often contrasted with the diminishing profit when we attempt to do the same thing on a farm; and some writers say that the factory is subject to a law of increasing return which contrasts with the law of diminishing return that prevails in agriculture. We quote two different but not conflicting views of the subject from Marshall's *Principles of Economics* and from Hadley's *Economics*.

'An increase of capital and labour leads generally to an improved organization; and therefore in those industries which are not engaged in raising raw produce it generally gives a return increased more than in proportion; and further, this improved organization tends to diminish or even override any increased resistance which nature may offer to raising increased amounts of raw produce. If the actions of the laws of increasing and diminishing returns are balanced, we have the *law of constant return*, and an increased produce is obtained by labour and sacrifice just in proportion' (Marshall).

'With a given amount of fixed capital, whether invested in agriculture or in manufactures, any increase of output diminishes the charges on such capital per unit of product. The *current* expenses per unit of product do not thus tend to diminish, but rather to increase. Whether with an increase of output the gain from fuller use of fixed capital outweighs the loss from increased current expenses, depends chiefly on the degree to which the fixed capital was previously utilized. If it was not fully utilized, we shall see the phenomena of increasing return; if it was already fully utilized, we shall see those of diminishing return. The apparent contrast between agriculture and manufactures in this respect is chiefly due to the fact that population habitually approaches a limit set by the arts of food production, so that its agricultural improvements are always employed nearly to the limit of profitable output; while in manufactures there is no such necessary increase of demand, and fixed capital is often quite inadequately employed' (Hadley).   (A.T.H.)

Increment [Lat. *incrementum*, increase]: Ger. (1) *Zunahme*; Fr. (1) *incrément*; Ital. *incremento, aumento*. (1) In psychophysics: relative increase in amount of stimulation. It is expressed as a fractional part of the stimulation existing before the increase is made.

(2) In mathematics: equivalent to an INFINITESIMAL (q. v.) increase.   (J.M.B.)

Indefinite: see INFINITE (notion of, ad fin.), QUANTITY (in logic), and DETERMINATE (in biology).

Indemnity (in law) [Lat. *indemnis*, from *in* + *damnum*, hurt]: Ger. *Entschädigung, Indemnität*; Fr. *indemnité*; Ital. *indennità*. (1) What is given by or due from one in behalf of whom another acts, to make the latter good for any consequent loss. An obligation to indemnify is implied in favour of agents and sureties. Indemnity against mere liability to loss can be claimed only under an express contract.

(2) Compensation for losses or expenses for which the party making it is or agrees to be held responsible, as e. g. a war indemnity.

Act of Indemnity: a statute or sovereign decree absolving from its penalties certain persons or classes of persons who have transgressed the law.   (S.E.B.)

Independence [Lat. *in* + *de* + *pendere*, to hang]: Ger. *Unabhängigkeit*; Fr. *indépendance*; Ital. *indipendenza*. (1) Two subjects are independent in so far as the possession of any character by the one does not require nor prevent the possession of any character by the other, unless these characters are directly or indirectly relative to the other individual.

(2) Two events are independent if either is equally probable whether the other takes place or not.   (C.S.P.)

(3) See FREEDOM (political).

Indeterminism [Lat. *indeterminatio*]: Ger. *Indeterminismus*; Fr. *indéterminisme*; Ital. *indeterminismo*. (1) The theory according to which mental change or development cannot in all cases be fully accounted for by pre-existing psychological or external conditions. Cf. DETERMINATION (mental).   (G.F.S.—J.M.B.)

(2) The extreme form of the free-will theory. It represents volition as, to some extent or in certain circumstances, independent of the strength of motives, or as itself determining which motive shall be the strongest. See FREEDOM, and WILL.

The term indeterminism (2) is given to mark the opposition to the theory of the complete causal connectedness of motive and volition, commonly called DETERMINISM (q.v.). It describes best what is also called 'liberty of indifference,' and is defined by Windelband (*Hist. of Philos.*, II. i. 16, 194, Eng. trans.) as 'a choice between different possibilities that is determined by no causes.' But upholders of free will usually deny that their theory can be correctly described as indeterminism. Thus Kant (*Relig.*, Erstes Stück, sub fin.; *Werke*, ed. Hartenstein, vi. 144 n., Abbott's trans., 359 n.) says: 'Freedom does not consist in the contingency of the action (that it is not determined by reasons at all), that is, not in indeterminism (that it must be equally possible for God to do good or evil, if his action is to be called free), but in absolute spontaneity.' Calderwood (*Handb. of Mor. Philos.*, 182, 10th ed.) says: 'In the history of philosophy there are no thinkers to be classified under the latter designation [indeterminists].' The term is, however, used by W. James to describe his own view (accepted on extra-psychological grounds) that the causal connection of psychical phenomena is not complete, and leaves room for an undetermined choice of will (*Princ. of Psychol.*, ii. 573); and he further allows that this theory of 'indeterminism is rightly described as meaning chance' (*Will to Believe*, 159). (W.R.S.)

Index (in craniometry) [Lat. *index*, from *indicare*, to point out]: Ger. *Index*; Fr. *indice*; Ital. *indice*. The relation of two dimensions of the skull to one another.

The most important index is the cephalic, which (if one neglects detailed differences in the mode of measurement) may be described by the formula:

$$\frac{\text{Maximum transverse diameter} \times 100}{\text{Maximum antero-posterior diameter}}.$$

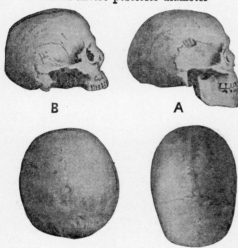

B   A

B, the figures on the left side, represents a brachycephalic skull with length 177 mm., breadth 156 mm., or cephalic index of 88·1. In this skull the orbital index was 87·5 and the nasal index was 49·1. A, the figures on the right, represents a dolichocephalic skull of length 204 mm., breadth 143 mm., or cephalic index of 70·1. In this skull the orbital index was 87·2, the nasal index 42. Upper and side views of skulls of long and round barrow races: after Haddon.

Long-headed skulls in which this index is 75 and under are called dolichocephalic; those with an index of 77·78 to 80·00 are mesaticephalic; index 80·01 to 83·33, sub-brachycephalic; index 83·34 and above, brachycephalic (Broca). Roughly speaking, the index 80 : 100 is that of a medium skull (mesocephalic), while the index 75 : 100 is quite a long skull (dolicho-), and the index 85 : 100 quite a short skull (brachy-) (for variations in these terms, &c., see references cited under CRANIOMETRY). Of other indices the following may be mentioned as most frequently employed. The vertical index, or relation of maximum height to length of head (*B, Bg* to *Gl, O* in the figure under CRANIOMETRY), varies from 69 to 78; the facial index, which is the ratio of the width of the face (horizontal distance between the two zygomatic arches) to the height of the face, and varies from 61 to 73 (see also FACIAL ANGLE); the nasal index, or proportion of length to width of nose, from below 48 : 100 to above 53 : 100; orbital index, or ratio of height to width, from below 84 : 100 to above 89 : 100. If the breadth of the head is expressed in terms of the height, we should have a transverse vertical index (86 : 104), and so on.

Literature: art. Indices, in Dict. d'Anthropol.; MANOUVRIER, Année Psychol., v. (1899) 558 (a review of recent work); the references under CRANIOMETRY. Cf. also BRAIN, IV. (J.J.)

Index (in exact logic). A sign, or representation, which refers to its object not so much because of any similarity or analogy with it, nor because it is associated with general characters which that object happens to possess, as because it is in dynamical (including spatial) connection both with the individual object, on the one hand, and with the senses or memory of the person for whom it serves as a sign, on the other hand.

No matter of fact can be stated without the use of some sign serving as an index. If *A* says to *B*, 'There is a fire,' *B* will ask, 'Where?' Thereupon *A* is forced to resort to an index, even if he only means somewhere in the real universe, past and future. Otherwise, he has only said that there is such an idea as fire, which would give no information, since unless it were known already, the word 'fire' would be unintelligible. If *A* points his finger to the fire, his finger is dynamically connected with the fire, as much as if a self-acting fire-alarm had directly turned it in that direction; while it also forces the eyes of *B* to turn that way, his attention to be riveted upon it, and his understanding to recognize that his question is answered. If *A*'s reply is, 'Within a thousand yards of here,' the word 'here' is an index; for it has precisely the same force as if he had pointed energetically to the ground between him and *B*. Moreover, the word 'yard,' though it stands for an object of a general class, is indirectly indexical, since the yard-sticks themselves are signs of the Parliamentary Standard, and that, not because they have similar qualities, for all the pertinent properties of a small bar are, as far as we can perceive, the same as those of a large one, but because each of them has been, actually or virtually, carried to the prototype and subjected to certain dynamical operations, while the associational compulsion calls up in our minds, when we see one of them, various experiences, and brings us to regard them as related to something fixed in length, though we may not have reflected that that standard is a material bar. The above considerations might lead the reader to suppose that indices have exclusive reference to objects of experience, and that there would be no use for them in pure mathematics, dealing, as it does, with ideal creations, without regard to whether they are anywhere realized or not. But the imaginary constructions of the mathematician, and even dreams, so far approximate to reality as to have a certain degree of fixity, in consequence of which they can be recognized and identified as individuals. In short, there is a degenerate form of observation which is directed to the creations of our own minds—using the word observation in its full sense as implying some degree of fixity and quasi-reality in the object to which it endeavours to conform. Accordingly, we find that indices are absolutely indispensable in mathematics; and until this truth was comprehended, all efforts to reduce to rule the logic of triadic and higher relations failed; while as soon as it was once grasped the problem was solved. The ordinary letters of algebra that present no peculiarities are indices. So also are the letters *A*, *B*, *C*, &c., attached to a geometrical figure. Lawyers and others who have to state a complicated affair with precision have recourse to letters to distinguish individuals. Letters so used are merely improved relative pronouns. Thus, while demonstrative and personal pronouns are, as ordinarily used, 'genuine indices,' relative pronouns are 'degenerate indices'; for though they may, accidentally and indirectly, refer to existing things, they directly refer, and need only refer, to the images in the mind which previous words have created.

Indices may be distinguished from other signs, or representations, by three characteristic marks: first, that they have no significant resemblance to their objects; second, that they refer to individuals, single units, single collections of units, or single continua; third, that they direct the attention to their objects by blind compulsion. But it would be difficult, if not impossible, to instance an absolutely pure index, or to find any sign absolutely devoid of the indexical quality. Psychologically, the action of indices depends upon association by contiguity, and not upon association by resemblance or upon intellectual operations. See Peirce, in *Proc. Amer. Acad. Arts and Sci.*, vii. 294 (May 14, 1867). (C.S.P.)

Index Number: Ger. *Indexzahl*; Fr. (Eng. term in use); Ital. *numero-indice*. A figure calculated to show the relative level of prices in a certain year as compared with that in preceding years, so that we may know whether prices in general have risen or fallen.

The index numbers of *The Economist*, which were the first calculated, consisted of simple additions of prices of a number of articles for successive years. An improvement was made when these numbers were reduced to a percentage basis, some one year which is taken as the basis of comparison being given the index number 100. A still further improvement was made by taking, instead of an arithmetical average of prices, a 'weighted' average of prices, which considers the relative amounts of the different articles used in trade or consumption.

Literature: principally in the economic journals. The chief authorities on the subject are SAUERBECK and LOETBRER. (A.T.H.)

India (philosophy and religion in): see ORIENTAL PHILOSOPHY (India).

Indictment [Med. Lat. *indictare*, to declare]: Ger. *Anklage*; Fr. *accusation, jugement* (to indict, *mettre quelqu'un en jugement*); Ital. *accusa*. (1) A formal charge of crime.

(2) In English and American law: a written charge of crime or misdemeanour, presented to a court for prosecution, by a grand jury. It is drawn up by the prosecuting officer, and at that stage is termed a bill of indictment. If the grand jury are satisfied that there is probable cause for supporting it, their foreman indorses it as 'a true bill,' and returns it to court, whereupon it becomes an indictment. The party accused is then entitled to trial before a petit jury.

The grand jury is an English institution for the protection of the individual against unjust prosecution. In cases of grave crimes most American constitutions require the return of an indictment before the accused can be brought to trial. (S.E.B.)

Indifference [Lat. *in* + *differens*, different]: Ger. *Gleichgültigkeit*; Fr. *sentiment d'indifférence*; Ital. *indifferenza*. (1) The state of mind in which a mental object, although noticed or thought of, fails to excite further interest for its own sake.

The state of indifference is ascribed to the subject, and the adjective indifferent is applied both to the agent and to the object or thought. The indifference thus defined may refer to mere intellectual interest, to interest leading to voluntary determination, or to the determination of a moral attitude (see the next topic).

(2) Emotional neutrality or lack of excitement or of affection of any sort. For this the term neutral is to be preferred. Cf. IN-DIFFERENCE POINT. (J.M.B.–G.F.S.)

Indifference (moral). That which is outside the application of moral law, and without tendency to promote or retard moral ends, is said to be morally indifferent and to have the quality of moral indifference.

Actions neither required nor forbidden by the moral law, or which do not affect morality, are called morally indifferent. The doctrine of 'things indifferent' (ἀδιάφορα) arose in the Stoic school. Owing to the abrupt opposition of 'good' and 'bad,' a large class of objects were at first regarded as indifferent. But within this class, three sub-classes came to be distinguished: things to be preferred because they helped the life according to nature; things to be avoided because they hindered it; and things indifferent in the narrower sense. The conception of things indifferent is, according to Kant, extra-moral.

Literature: CICERO, Acad., ii., De Fin. iii. 15, 16; ZELLER, Philos. d. Griechen, III. i. 259 ff. (3rd ed.); KANT, Relig., Erstes Stück (Werke, ed. Hartenstein, vi. 116); ABBOTT, Kant's Theory of Ethics, 329 (3rd ed.). (W.R.S.)

Indifference (in philosophy). (1) The principle of ἀδιάφορα, common to the Stoics, Cynics, and Sceptics of Greece, that all is indifferent save virtue and vice, which alone have absolute value. See SCHOOLS OF GREECE (Cynics), STOICISM, and SCEPTICISM; cf. also RELATIVITY OF KNOWLEDGE.

(2) The view of certain scholastics (e. g. Adelard of Bath) that a thing is indifferently an individual or a universal according to the point of view. (J.M.B.)

Indifference Point: Ger. *Indifferenz-punkt, Nullpunkt*; Fr. *point d'indifférence*; Ital. *punto d' indifferenza*. The theoretical zero or point of transition on a scale of positive and negative values; applied in psychology to the theoretical point at which neither of two contrasted sense or other qualities, which are supposed to depend on the same sort of stimulation, is experienced: as the indifference point on the scale of temperature, of hedonic tone, &c.

The indifference point as thus defined is, with the threshold, much discussed; many holding that both are merely conceptions convenient for the purposes of graphic representation, and in no sense psychological values. On this view, the indifference point of temperature is simply no temperature sensation, not a point on a scale of real sensation values; and the attempt to establish thresholds for positive heat-values and positive cold-values itself shows this: for the part of the curve between the two thresholds would be a distance, not a point, and we should have two sensation curves, one for each quality, not at all connected with each other. This is emphasized by the relative character of the THRESHOLD (q. v.). (J.M.B., G.F.S.)

Indirect (in logic): see PROOF, REASONING (inference), and SYLLOGISM.

Indirect Selection: see ORGANIC (or INDIRECT) SELECTION.

Indirect Vision: Ger. *indirektes Sehen*; Fr. *vision indirecte*; Ital. *visione indiretta*. Visual perception of objects when the regard is directed to something else. (J.M.B.)

Indirect vision takes place with the peripheral portions of the retina. It differs from central vision in three ways: (1) the power of space discrimination of the retina falls off rapidly outside of the fovea—more rapidly above and below than in a horizontal direction; (2) after the eye has suffered adaptation (regeneration of the visual purple), all lights, except those near either end of the spectrum, appear surprisingly brighter when indirectly viewed than when their images fall upon or near the fovea; (3) the colour sensitiveness of the retina alters from the centre outwards. The innermost or paracentral zone is entirely sensitive to colour; then follows a zone of red-green blindness; the outermost zone is wholly colour-blind. Cf. Sanford, *Course in Exper. Psychol.*, expts. 117 b, 136, 137, 161.

Early experiments on peripheral colour vision were made by Clerk Maxwell and Woinow in 1870. Hess' results (*Arch. f. Ophthal.*, XXXV. iv. 1 ff., 1899) show that the red and green which do not change colour before becoming invisible, in the middle zone, are Hering's fundamental red and green. V. Kries has recently found that the distribution of brightness in the spectrum of the outermost zone, with bright adaptation, is that of the normal spectrum (*Zeitsch. f. Psychol.*, xv, 1897, 247). The fact, as it stands, is thought to tell against Hering's theory. Cf. PURKINJE PHENOMENON, and VISION.   (E.B.T.–C.L.F.)

Literature : on the general topic, EXNER. Arch. f. Ophthal., xxxii. 1, 233 ff. (1886); A. E. FICK, Pflüger's Arch., xliii. 441 ff. (1888); KIRSCHMANN, Philos. Stud., v. 447 ff. (1889), viii. 592 ff. (189); HERING, Arch. f. Ophthal., xxxv. 4, 63 ff. (1889), xxxvi. 1, 264 (1890); Pflüger's Arch., xlvii. 417 ff. (1890) ; A. PICK, Pflüger's Arch., xlvii. 274 ff. (1890) ; Hermann's Handb. d. Physiol., iii. 1, 206 ff. ; AUBERT, Physiol. Optik, 495, 539 ff., 585 ff. ; Physiol. d. Netzhaut, 89 ff., 116 ff. ; HELMHOLTZ, Physiol. Optik (2nd ed.), 255 ff., 268, 372 ff. ; HOLDEN, Arch. f. Ophthal., xxiii. 40 ff. ; v. KRIES, Zeitsch. f. Psychol., ix. 81 ff. ; Arch. f. Ophthal., xlii. 3, 95 ff. ; Zeitsch. f. Psychol., xv. 247 ff. ; LUCKEY, Amer. J. of Psychol., vi. 489 ff. ; GUILLERY, Zeitsch. f. Psychol., xii. 243 ff. ; WILLIAMS, J. of Amer. Med. Assoc. (1898), xxxi. 767 ; HELLPACH, Philos. Stud., xv. 524 ff. For illusions of form in indirect vision see SANFORD, Course in Exper. Psychol., expt. 172 ; for the indirect perception of movement, ibid., expt. 224.   (E.B.T.–C.L.F.)

Indiscernibles (principle of sameness of) [Lat. *indiscernibilis*, indistinguishable] : Ger. *Ununterschiedbaren*; Fr. *indiscernables* ; Ital. *indiscernibili*. Leibnitz maintained this principle, i. e. that no two monads — in general, no two things in the universe — are exactly alike, else they would be not two, but one (*Monadologie*, 9 ; *Nouveaux Essais*, ii. 27, 1–3).

This *principium identitatis indiscernibilium* was a characteristic element in the Leibnitzian view of the world (Falckenberg, *Hist. of Mod. Philos.*, 278–80). Similar views have been held by other thinkers, ancient and modern (the Stoics, Ueberweg, *Hist. of Philos.*, i. 196 ; Giordano Bruno). See LIKENESS, and DIFFERENCE ; and cf. INDIVIDUAL.   (A.C.A.Jr.)

Individual [Lat. *individuus*, undivided] : Ger. (1, 3) *einzeln* (*Wesen*, &c.), (2, 4) *individuell* (adj.), *Individuum* (n.) ; Fr. *individuel* (adj.), *individu* (n.) ; Ital. *individuale* (adj.), *individuo* (n.). (1) A single being, as distinct either from a collection of beings or from the logical object of the general concept ; a unique being ; a being at least numerically distinct from all other beings. (2) A being that cannot be divided into parts to which the name of this being will apply. Thus a

general name applies to a class of objects which can be divided into classes, to any one of which the class-name can still be applied, as Frenchmen, Germans, or Russians are all equally Europeans. But the name of an individual being, as for instance Socrates, cannot be applied to any of the parts, such as the hand or foot, into which Socrates can be divided. (3) An independent, separable being, capable of existing alone. (4) In ethics : a person, an individual as opposed to a corporation or a collection of men, or to a social group or organization of any kind.

The concept of the individual is at once one of the most familiar and the most difficult both in the world of common sense and in the world of philosophy. That the beings which are to be found in the world, whether inanimate objects or living beings, whether material or mental, are individuals, i. e. are distinct, singular, and unique, is a matter of common belief and report. But what constitutes individuality, or what is the principle of individuation, has been a matter of controversy both within the realm of special science and from the point of view of logical and metaphysical definition.

In logic the individual is opposed to the various kinds of universal concepts and classes, as, for example, to genus or species, or property, or accident. In psychology it has been frequently asserted that individual objects are the immediate objects of our perceptive experience ; so that it has been frequently maintained, as sufficiently defining the nature of an individual being, that an individual is any object perceived by the mind as an external or as a real object. From this point of view the idea of individuality as a character of beings is derived directly from experience, and is irreducible to simpler ideas. As against this view, it has been maintained that the direct object of our perceptual experience is always a series or complex of definable or indefinable qualities, characters, relations, and behaviours of objects. Thus we observe that an orange is coloured, is round, is of a given weight, is in given relations to other observed objects, as for instance lying on a plate. But to observe these characters, however great their number and complexity, is still to observe characters that might be shared by other oranges, and frequently by other objects, so that it seems as if the individuality of the object were precisely what we least directly perceive. In case of individual persons, it is plain that we mean by personal identity a character which could never be made the object of any simple perceptive act ; and in general the concept of individual being, in the various special sciences, as well as in metaphysical inquiry, shows many characters that cannot be derived from mere perception in any case. It is somewhat easier to regard the idea of individuality as an ultimate and indefinable idea, without giving any ground whatever, in experience or in articulate thought, for our overwhelming assurance that the objects with which we deal are individuals. Nevertheless, this way of treating the problem would be merely an abandonment of the question as insoluble ; and accordingly we find in the history of thought a considerable number of efforts to define what has been called the principle of individuation. Such efforts have also played a part in the definitions of the individual that have been framed to meet the exigencies at various special times.

The problem of the nature of individuality is first reached in European philosophy as the result of those efforts at the definition of the logical method which assume definite form in the Socratic, Platonic, and Aristotelian doctrines. The Platonic ideas were beings supposed expressly to correspond to our general conceptions. A discussion of the nature of these ideas, and of their relations to one another and to the world of facts, of sense, and of ordinary experience, made prominent the question : What is meant by an individual ? The problem in question is very explicit in the mind of Aristotle, though it cannot be said that he gave any very explicit solution of the questions that he himself raised. According to Aristotle, all beings in the universe are individuals, and universals have being only as realized in individual entities. On the other hand, science, according to Aristotle, is necessarily concerned with the universal, that is, with the laws and the ideal general characters possessed by facts. And yet, according to Aristotle, science undertakes to know being. Thus arises the familiar paradox of the Aristotelian system, that just that character of facts which science best knows is not that character which constitutes the true being of anything, since this true being is individual, and what science knows is universal. As to the principle of individuation, Aristotle is not explicit, except in the case where he is speaking of obviously corporeal entities, when he upon occasion says that their material aspect is that which constitutes the individuality of any one being ; while what he calls the form or general nature is common to many individuals.

The problem of the definition of the individual became prominent in the philosophy of the Christian Church in the Middle Ages, especially owing to the importance which ethical individuality had acquired in Christian doctrine, and in consequence of the relation of individuality to the doctrine of the Trinity. In the early ages of scholastic philosophy, the discussion regarding the nature of universals was especially prominent, while from the age of Thomas Aquinas onwards, scholastic philosophy made especially important the principle of individuation and the nature of individuality. Here it was a classic Thomistic doctrine that, in the realm of nature, matter is the individuating principle, so that the purely incorporeal entities, such as the angels, could be individuated only by their form, and so that consequently, as the well-known Thomistic theory maintained, two angels of the same species do not exist. The ethical individuals in the human world, according to Thomas, are genuine individuals, but they are individuated primarily by the different bodies to which the souls belong, so that when absent from the body, the soul, between death and the judgment, would be individuated by reason of what Thomas calls its *inclinatio* to a particular corporeal embodiment, an *inclinatio* which at the resurrection would be met by the presence of the glorified body of the saved or of the equally permanent material organization of the lost. To the Thomistic theory, Duns Scotus opposed the doctrine that a special form, called by him the *haecceitas*, is responsible for the individuation of every being, corporeal or incorporeal. This *haecceitas*, different in each individual, is something that is said to be 'fused with the common nature,' in such wise that the doctrine of Duns Scotus especially lays stress upon the fact that the difference between individual beings is a real and ultimate, non-corporeal, but not necessarily indescribable, character of each being — a character which a higher type of intelligence than our own may be able to appreciate, although it is admitted by Duns Scotus that this character is indefinable for our own human intellect.

In the philosophy of Leibnitz an effort is made to solve the problem of the individual by the famous principle of the identity of indiscernibles. According to this principle it is impossible that two individuals in the universe could be precisely alike. And the unlikeness between individuals is always of an essentially describable or intelligible character. Were two individuals in all respects precisely alike, so that whatever was predicated of one was true of the other, these two individuals would be *ipso facto* identical, and difference of individuality means difference of quality or character.

Post-Kantian thought, during the idealistic period, laid most stress upon the definition of the ego, or of the ethical and epistemological person, and dealt with the problem of individuality mainly in this case. New in this period of thought, therefore, especially after Kant's theory of the unity of self-consciousness, are the Fichtean and Schellingean attempts to define the relations between a finite individual and the absolute ego. New is also the Hegelian definition of the individual as 'the unity of the universal and the particular.' In other words, Hegel held that when a universal law or principle, of the type that he defined as the Begriff, gets a complete development and expression, in respect of all the particular or specific aspects which the nature of this Begriff involves, such total expression of a universal law is as such an individual being, so that the problem with regard to the individual becomes identical with the problem as to the way in which universal principles can find complete or wholly satisfying expression in nature or in mind, or in general in experience.

Since the close of the idealistic period the problem of the individual has received discussion especially from three points of view. In the first place, in modern psychology and epistemology, efforts have been made to deal afresh with the problems of the nature of individuality in its most general form. The most familiar of these efforts is one not wholly unknown to earlier thought, very plainly stated by Schopenhauer, and frequently developed in recent works—an effort to make time and space the essential principles of individuation, to define the primary individual object as that which is in a given place, and at a given time, and to make the other forms of individuality derivable from this primary form of the idea by means of various associations between time and space, localization, and the various other characters possessed by moral or other types of individuals. The second point of view from which the problem has been discussed has been that of the biological sciences, and of the related branches of inquiry. Into these discussions this is not the place to go. The third point of view with regard to the individual has been that suggested by the ethical problem of the rights of the individual as a person, and of his relations to the social order. The revolt against certain eighteenth-century doctrines concerning the rights and position of the individual man has led to a number of forms of socialism and of ethical universalism, which have made light of the historical importance and of the moral value of the individual man. A frequent reaction against these very tendencies has led to a reassertion of individualism, which has been associated with various more or less novel efforts to restate the definition of the ethical individual.

If we survey the problem of the individual apart from its history, it is easy to see that the question has several distinct forms, which may indeed be ultimately connected, but which are usually presented to our attention in quite different regions of inquiry. Amongst the sciences mathematics is prominent in dealing with individual objects and systems of individual objects, which as artificial creatures of definition, or as very simple abstractions from our experience of space, ought apparently to be topics of easy and final agreement. Yet regarding the nature of all these forms of mathematical individuality considerable difference of opinion has existed amongst mathematical experts. Examples of mathematical entities that appear more or less obviously as individuals are the unit in arithmetic, the point in geometry, the line, when regarded as an elementary concept in some forms of geometrical investigation, and several other cases of objects which are regarded as the elements of given mathematical systems. The question of the individuality, or at any rate of the singularity of such objects as space and time, viewed in their wholeness, has interested the mathematicians as well as the philosophers. In theoretical natural science, such concepts as the modern concept of energy, when compared with the usual concepts of matter, may well introduce the question whether recent theory is not really as much concerned with the problem whether universals exist, or whether individuals alone are real, as was ever scholastic doctrine. For energy as usually described appears to be an entity whose individuation is altogether problematic, and whose known character seems to be entirely of universal type. In the biological sciences the problem as to the living individual introduces entirely different questions and interests; and the problems of ethical individuality belong to still another realm of a decidedly special character. Finally, the problem of the ultimate place of the category of individuality in the world at large remains as an issue for general metaphysics. It is, nevertheless, a fair question for philosophical inquiry whether all these so various problems are not really much more closely connected than they seem, and whether a final definition which will hold for all forms of individuality may not yet be discovered. Cf. IDENTITY (individual).

Literature: the classic scholastic view of the problem is to be found in ST. THOMAS AQUINAS, Summa Theologica, P. 1, passim—in particular, Q. xxx. art. iv; Q. xxix. arts. i, iii, and iv; Q. l. art. iv; Q. lxxvi. art. ii. DUNS SCOTUS, in his commentary upon the Sentential, in the first half of the sixth volume of his collected works (London ed. of 1639), discusses the problem of individuality in connection with his Angelology. See, in particular, 374 ff., 403 ff., 487 ff. SUAREZ, in his Disputationes metaphysicae, sums up the scholastic opinions on the whole range of the problem in Disp. v: De unitate individuali, eiusque principio. Father HARPER, in his Metaphysic of the School, i. 208–90, reviews the same issues at length. See also the youthful dissertation of LEIBNITZ, De principio Individuationis, and his later discussions of the problem, in particular in the Nouv. Ess., Lib. II. chap. xxvii. HEGEL treats our problem, in connection with the theory of universals, at the outset of the third part of his Logik. SCHOPENHAUER frequently, but always summarily, discusses the principle of individuation. For a collection of the passages in Schopenhauer see FRAUENSTADT, Schopenhauer Lexikon, i. 351. Amongst recent discussions that of SIGWART, Logik, Th. III. Abschn. II. § 78, may be mentioned. ROYCE has treated the topic at length in The Conception of God, 217–322, and in The World and the Individual; see also ORMOND, Foundations of Knowledge, Pt. II. chap. xii. (J.R.)

Individual (in biology): a single ORGANISM (q.v., in biology). (J.M.B.)

Individual (in logic) [as a technical term of logic, *individuum* first appears in Boethius, in a translation from Victorinus, no doubt of ἄτομον, a word used by Plato

(*Sophistes*, 229 D) for an indivisible species, and by Aristotle, often in the same sense, but occasionally for an individual. Of course the physical and mathematical senses of the word were earlier. Aristotle's usual term for individuals is τὰ καθ' ἕκαστα, Lat. *singularia*, Eng. *singulars*.] Used in logic in two closely connected senses. (1) According to the more formal of these an individual is an object (or term) not only actually determinate in respect to having or wanting each general character and not both having and wanting any, but is necessitated by its mode of being to be so determinate. See PARTICULAR (in logic).

This definition does not prevent two distinct individuals from being precisely similar, since they may be distinguished by their hecceities (or determinations not of a generalizable nature); so that Leibnitz' principle of indiscernibles is not involved in this definition. Although the principles of contradiction and excluded middle may be regarded as together constituting the definition of the relation expressed by 'not,' yet they also imply that whatever exists consists of individuals. This, however, does not seem to be an identical proposition or necessity of thought; for Kant's Law of Specification (*Krit. d. reinen Vernunft*, 1st ed., 656; 2nd ed., 684; but it is requisite to read the whole section to understand his meaning), which has been widely accepted, treats logical quantity as a continuum in Kant's sense, i. e. that every part of which is composed of parts. Though this law is only regulative, it is supposed to be demanded by reason, and its wide acceptance as so demanded is a strong argument in favour of the conceivability of a world without individuals in the sense of the definition now considered. Besides, since it is not in the nature of concepts adequately to define individuals, it would seem that a world from which they were eliminated would only be the more intelligible. A new discussion of the matter, on a level with modern mathematical thought and with exact logic, is a desideratum. A highly important contribution is contained in Schröder's *Logik*, iii, Vorles. 10. What Scotus says (*Quaest. in Met.*, VII. 9, xiii and xv) is worth consideration.

(2) Another definition which avoids the above difficulties is that an individual is something which reacts. That is to say, it does react against some things, and is of such a nature that it might react, or have reacted, against my will.

This is the stoical definition of a reality; but since the Stoics were individualistic nominalists, this rather favours the satisfactoriness of the definition than otherwise. It may be objected that it is unintelligible; but in the sense in which this is true, it is a merit, since an individual is unintelligible in that sense. It is a brute fact that the moon exists, and all explanations suppose the existence of that same matter. That existence is unintelligible in the sense in which the definition is so. That is to say, a reaction may be experienced, but it cannot be conceived in its character of a reaction; for that element evaporates from every general idea. According to this definition, that which alone immediately presents itself as an individual is a reaction against the will. But everything whose identity consists in a continuity of reactions will be a single logical individual. Thus any portion of space, so far as it can be regarded as reacting, is for logic a single individual; its spatial extension is no objection. With this definition there is no difficulty about the truth that whatever exists is individual, since existence (not reality) and individuality are essentially the same thing; and whatever fulfils the present definition equally fulfils the former definition by virtue of the principles of contradiction and excluded middle, regarded as mere definitions of the relation expressed by 'not.' As for the principle of indiscernibles, if two individual things are exactly alike in all other respects, they must, according to this definition, differ in their spatial relations, since space is nothing but the intuitional presentation of the conditions of reaction, or of some of them. But there will be no logical hindrance to two things being exactly alike in all other respects; and if they are never so, that is a physical law, not a necessity of logic. This second definition, therefore, seems to be the preferable one. Cf. PARTICULAR (in logic). (C.S.P.)

Individual (social). (1) A single human being. (2) Hence, by development of the ideas of separateness and completeness, a human being in a marked degree differentiated from others: a centre of social influences.

The history of the concept individual is important both in psychology and in sociology. The individual has been conceived as independent of and antecedent to society, as correlative with society, and as dependent on and created by society. All of these conceptions are presented in Aristotle's *Politics*, where the distinctions are made that in genesis individual and society are inseparable, that in will and

conduct the individual is independent or free, while in moral perfection he is created by the state. The political philosophy of Hobbes' *De Corpore Politico* assumes the antecedent completeness and sufficiency of the individual. Modern psychology and sociology demonstrate the interdependence of individual and society (cf. Baldwin, *Social and Eth. Interpret.*). See also INDIVIDUALISM. (F.H.G.)

Individual Psychology: Ger. *Individualpsychologie*; Fr. *psychologie individuelle*; Ital. *psicologia individuale*. That department of psychology which investigates the psychological individual considered as different from others, i. e. having for its subject-matter psychological variations among individuals.

Particular questions on which work has been done are: (1) the psychology of TEMPERAMENT (q. v.); (2) of mental TYPE (q. v.); (3) of mental differences of the sexes (see SEXUAL CHARACTERS); (4) of GENIUS (q. v.); (5) of mental DEFECT (q. v., also special types of defect); (6) of the CRIMINAL (q. v., also CRIMINOLOGY); (7) of classes, professions, &c., considered as based upon individual differences. Cf. VARIATIONAL PSYCHOLOGY.

Literature: BIBLIOG. G, 1, *e*; lists, sub verbo, in the Psychological Index, 1 ff.; BINET and HENRI, Année Psychol., ii. (1896) 411 (a *résumé* and exposition); DILTHEY, Sitzber. Akad. Wiss. Berlin (1896), 295. (J.M.B., G.F.S.)

Individual Selection: Ger. *Personalselektion* (Weismann); Fr. *sélection entre individus* (Y.D.), *sélection individuelle* (better than *personnelle*—J. A. Thomson); Ital. *selezione individuale*. The survival of the individual organism or animal under the operation of NATURAL SELECTION (q. v.), as distinguished from the survival of parts, cells, germinal elements, &c. (cf. INTRASELECTION), which are supposed to be selected by an analogous method.

This rendering of Weismann's Personalselektion for the original Darwinian view of the survival of the individual—for which, moreover, it was earlier used—is better than the literal translation 'personal selection.' Personal selection suggests 'conscious selection' by a person, and it is better to reserve it for that. See SELECTION. (J.M.B., C.LL.M.)

Individualism: Ger. *Individualismus*; Fr. *individualisme*; Ital. *individualismo*. (1) Exclusive or excessive regard for self-interest.

(2) The doctrine that the pursuit of self-interest and the exercise of individual initiative should be little or not at all restrained

by the state, and that the functions of government should be reduced to the lowest possible terms.

Definition (2) is a product of the thought of the middle of the 19th century. The views of Bentham, Ricardo, and the elder Mill were derived largely from Adam Smith and the French Encyclopedists, and they found complete formulation in J. S. Mill's *Liberty* and Spencer's *Social Statics*. These works remain the standard defence of individualism, which differs from anarchism in recognizing the rightfulness of government to maintain order and to enforce equality of liberty. In his later work Spencer defends individualism on the ground that individual initiative is a normal and state action, in most instances an artificial factor in social evolution. The views opposed to individualism are classed together under the term SOCIALISM (q. v.). (F.H.G.)

Individualistic: Ger. *individualistisch*; Fr. *individualiste*; Ital. *individualistico*. (1) In sociology: applied to theories which advocate or imply INDIVIDUALISM (q. v.). (J.M.B.)

(2) In ethics: applied to those theories which derive the moral ideal or standard from the nature—desires or conscience—of the individual man.

All forms of EPICUREANISM, as well as the MORAL SENSE theory of ethics, and most forms of INTUITIONISM are thus individualistic (see those terms and ETHICAL THEORIES). The chief difficulty of such theories lies in bringing out the grounds and place of social duty. Cf. Sorley, *Eth. of Nat.*, chaps. ii–iv. (W.R.S.)

Individuality: Ger. (1) *Einzelheit*, (2, 3) *Individualität*; Fr. *individualité*; Ital. *individualità*. (1) The quality or character belonging to an individual, as single. (2) The ethical qualities or dignity properly pertaining to an individual. (3) In case of character, the qualities which especially distinguish one individual person from another. See INDIVIDUAL, and IDENTITY (the different topics). (J.R.)

Individuation: see INDIVIDUAL, and IDENTITY (individual).

Indivisibility: see DIVISIBILITY.

Induction [Lat. *inductio*, from *in + ducere*, to lead; a word applied by Cicero—and probably first by him, as Quinctilian seems to think—to transfer Aristotle's ἐπαγωγή]: Ger. *Induction*; Fr. *induction*; Ital. *induzione*. (1) Inference from particular cases to a general conclusion. See INFERENCE, and REASONING.

(2) The method of procedure known as inductive reasoning, which makes large or exclusive use of inductive inference. See BACONIAN METHOD, and SCIENTIFIC METHOD.

The two forms of inductive inference generally distinguished are 'perfect' and 'imperfect.' In the former the conclusion rests upon confirmatory knowledge of all the cases which this general conclusion covers; in the latter, the conclusion covers cases which have not been actually experienced. 'Simple' or 'raw' induction by simple enumeration (*inductio per enumerationem simplicem*) is also distinguished from critical or methodical induction, which is inductive method criticized and organized for the purposes of research. This latter takes cognizance of the proportion of positive to negative cases, of variations of all sorts, of partial and compound results, and makes use of hypothesis and experimentation.

In the history of induction the names of Aristotle, Bacon, and Mill are eminent. Aristotle made the ideal of induction (ἐπαγωγή) perfect enumeration of cases. With Bacon induction was reinstated as scientific method (see BACONIAN METHOD for particulars). Mill grounded inductive inference as such upon the 'uniformity of nature,' which he makes the foundation of all knowledge, finding in it the 'natural tendency of the mind to generalize its experiences' (*Logic*, Bk. III. chap. ii. § 1). Mill, following Whately, made induction not a distinct type of argumentation, but a SYLLOGISM (q. v.; see also REASONING), of which the major premise, stating the universal principle of uniformity, is suppressed. Mill's discussion is a classical contribution to the theory of scientific method; the criticisms of it are aimed not so much at the theory of inductive procedure, as at the metaphysics which underlies his theory of UNIFORMITY OF NATURE (q. v.).

The principal theoretical question arising in connection with induction is that of the universality or universal validity of the conclusion. Here a critique is necessary in which discriminations are made concerning the nature of the assertion arrived at in the particular case. If, for example, we are dealing with judgments based on experience—*a posteriori* synthetic judgments, such as 'the stone is hard'—the conclusion, apart from other grounds of inference, is limited to what has been called a 'reasonable expectation' as to the hardness of other stones; an expectation which, however, rapidly gains in force as uniform experience continues. In the case, however, of a judgment of cause—such as 'the sun warms the stone'—the inference to other cases would include the condition—which in this instance we call cause—of the presence of the sun; and the warmness of future stones will be said to be necessary when that condition is fulfilled. In this latter case we are no longer dealing with the 'natural tendency to generalize,' but with an application of a universal judgment, from which we deduce the particular cases. It is only in these latter cases that the principle of uniformity, which is the logical justification for our expectation, is really invoked. We count on uniformity in the logical sense only where we postulate necessity or universal connection; and it is genetically the growth of experience which leads us to abandon reasonable expectation and develop inductive method as opposed to mere inductive inference. The child would say, 'All stones are warm'; the scientist, 'Stones exposed to heat become warm.' The progress of science is by (1) the formulation of a 'reasonable expectation,' embodied in a hypothesis; (2) the devising of crucial experiments or observations wherewith to test the hypothesis by bringing the phenomenon under a category of necessary dependence; that is, to show that the connection observed is not merely a repetition of like cases, but includes some one or more antecedent conditions without which the consequent phenomenon would not occur. So we have Mill's method of DIFFERENCE (q. v.) and the other rules called 'canons of induction.' See CONCOMITANCE (logical), and AGREEMENT (method of); cf. also ANALOGY (in logic).

(3) The actual prediction of cases in kind, or the deduction of new phenomena from the conclusion thus arrived at.

Literature: BACON, Nov. Org.; MILL, Logic; the textbooks on logic (notably those of SIGWART, LOTZE, WUNDT) and on inductive logic; the literature cited under REASONING and SCIENTIFIC METHOD (notably the works of WHEWELL, JEVONS, VENN). See also BIBLIOG. C, 2, *p*, and extensive citations in EISLER, Wörterb. d. philos. Begriffe, 'Induction.' (J.M.B.)

Induction (in education). The process of reasoning from particulars to generals as a stage in educational method.

In Herbartian terminology, induction is the second of the three chief stages of a rational method; the first being the apperception of observed facts, and the last the deductive application of the generalizations derived by means of the middle, or inductive, process. See METHOD (in education).

Literature: McMURRY, Method of the Recitation, 170–87, and General Method, 122–44; HARRIS, Psychologic Foundations of Educ., 78–89. (C.DE G.)

Industrial [Lat. *industrialis*, pertaining to industry]: Ger. *gewerbthätig, industriell*; Fr. *industriel*; Ital. *industriale*. (1) Pertaining to industry, without restriction.

(2) Pertaining to manufacturing industry in particular.

Industry in the general sense (of human labour of any kind) is as old as the Latin *industria*. Industry, as manufacture, is distinguished from agriculture and trade by Quesnay (*Tableau Économique*, 1758) and by Adam Smith (*Wealth of Nations*, iii, i, end, &c., 1776). The adjective has shared the fate of the noun, and the restricted sense is now the more common. In either its wide or its narrow sense it is to be distinguished (as colourless) from 'industrious,' a term of praise. It seems to owe currency to St. Simon. Cf. INDUSTRIALISM. (J.B.)

Industrialism: Ger. *Industriesystem, Industrialismus*; Fr. *industrialisme*; Ital. *industrialismo*. The organization of labour in manufacture.

Lotz (*Grundbegriffe d. Nat.-ök.*, 1811) used Industriesystem for Adam Smith's economic system, as opposed to physiocracy and mercantilism. The word Industriesystem would now mean the system of large production in manufacture (see Lexis, sub verbo, in *Handwörterb. d. Staatswiss.*). St. Simon used système industriel for his own organization of labour, and industrialisme as its synonym. Comte used this last, as Spencer 'industrialism,' to express the condition of a people or an age devoted mainly to manufacture as opposed to war ('militarism' indicating the dominance of the last). Cf. INDUSTRIAL. See Palgrave's *Dict. of Polit. Econ.*, 'Industrial Régime.' (J.B.)

Industry [Lat. *industria*, diligence]: Ger. *Gewerbe, Industrie*; Fr. *industrie*; Ital. *industria*. (1) Organized economic activity.

(2) Specifically, the application of labour to goods in such a manner as to presumably increase their value.

Industry, in this second sense, is distinguished from trade, where the profit is made by buying and selling; also, less sharply, from agriculture, where the labour is applied to land rather than to goods. (A.T.H.)

Inebriety [Lat. *in* + *ebrietas*, drunkenness]: Ger. *Trunkenheit*; Fr. *inébriété*; Ital. *ebbrezza, ubbriachezza*. The effects of an over-indulgence in alcoholic liquors, either occasionally or habitually.

General drug intoxication is considered under PSYCHIC EFFECTS OF DRUGS (q. v.), and the special effects of indulgence in alcohol under ALCOHOLISM (q. v.). Inebriety is often used in reference to the medico-legal relations incidental to actions committed by persons in a more or less irresponsible condition through alcoholic indulgence. (J.J.)

Inertia (nervous) [Lat. *inertia*, lack of skill or activity]: Ger. *Trägheit*; Fr. *inertie*; Ital. *inerzia*. A name applied, by physical analogy, to that peculiarity of nervous substance, or of a particular sense-organ, which conditions the 'rise' and 'fall' of sensation; i.e. the fact that the sensation requires an appreciable time to reach its maximal clearness, and an appreciable time to disappear, after the presentation and the removal respectively of the stimulus.

Some of the facts of inertia are as follows: (1) The interval separating the 'primary' and 'secondary' pressures from the skin may be due to the inertia of the central grey matter of the cord (Goldscheider, 'Verh. d. physiol. Gesell. zu Berlin,' 1890, in *Arch. f. Physiol.*, 1891, 168 f.; Sanford, *Course in Exper. Psychol.*, expt. 11, and cf. expt. 32; but see von Frey, *Abhandl. d. kgl. sächs. Gesell. d. Wiss.*, 1896, 243; Külpe, *Outlines of Psychol.*, 85, 92). (2) Initial and terminal inertia can be demonstrated in the case of the auditory apparatus (Sanford, op. cit., expt. 64; Stumpf, *Tonpsychologie*, i. 16, 211 f., 277, 391; ii. 516 f.; Urbantschitsch, *Pflüger's Arch.*, xxv. 323 ff.); (3) and in that of the visual (Fick, in Hermann's *Handb. d. Physiol.*, iii. 1, 211; Sanford, op. cit., expt. 144; Ebbinghaus, *Psychol.*, 230, 241; Helmholtz, *Physiol. Optik*, 2nd ed., 530 ff.; Fechner, *Pogg. Ann.*, xlv. 227 ff.; Brücke, ibid., lxxxiv. 418 ff.; Exner, *Pflüger's Arch.*, iii. 214 ff.; Aubert, *Physiol. Optik*, 560; Rood, *Colour*, 92 ff.; *Amer. J. of Sci.*, 1860, Ser. 2, xxx. 182 ff.; Nichols, ibid., 1884, Ser. 3, xxviii. 243 ff.; Charpentier, *C. R. de l'Acad. d. Sci.*, cxiii. 147 ff., 217 ff.; cxiv. 1423 ff.). (4) The length of reaction-time to smell, taste, and temperature may be due in part to initial inertia of their organs (Wundt, *Physiol. Psychol.*, 4th ed., ii. 317). (5) Cutaneous pain shows an initial inertia as compared with cutaneous pressure (Sanford, op. cit., expt. 32; von Frey, *Ber. d. kgl. sächs. Gesell. d. Wiss.*, 1894, 294). (E.B.T.)

Inertia (in physics): Ger. *Trägheit, Beharrungsvermögen*; Fr. *inertie*; Ital. *inerzia*. That property of matter by virtue of which it does not, even when free to move, change its velocity *per saltum* under the influence of a force, but continually resists the change which the force tends to produce, so that the force must persist in order to effect a change.

Inertia affords the absolute measure of the mass of a body, and seems to be absolutely invariable. The use of the term in physics has therefore been deemed unnecessary, since it may be avoided by the use of the word 'mass.' Maxwell compared the resistance expressed by it to a supposed resistance of coffee to the sweetening power of sugar, since the necessity of adding more and more sugar to make the coffee sweeter and sweeter is analogous to the necessity of employing more and more force to make a body move faster and faster. This is, however, misleading, since the resistance is not in the coffee; but the fact illustrates WEBER'S LAW (q.v.) of the relation of stimulus to sensation. Yet the use of the term may be justified, as introductory to the conceptions of the fundamental laws of force and motion, and as being, at worst, quite harmless. (S.N.–J.M.B.)

Infallibility [Med. Lat. *infallibilis*, not liable to mistake or error]: Ger. *Unfehlbarkeit*; Fr. *infaillibilité*; Ital. *infallibilità*. (1) Of the Church: the doctrine that the Church, as a whole, by reason of the indwelling Divine Spirit, is rendered inerrant in matters of faith and teaching.

(2) Of the Pope: the doctrine that the Pope, when he speaks *ex cathedra*, is, through the divine assistance promised him in blessed Peter, endowed with inerrancy in defining doctrine about faith and morals.

The infallibility of the Church, in the sense defined, has been held from the beginning by the Roman Catholic Church, its warrant being such passages as Matt. xxviii. 20; John xiv. 16; 1 Tim. iii. 15. The Protestant churches as a rule reject the doctrine or hold it in a very much modified form. The infallibility of the Pope, though not foreign to the belief of the Church, was authoritatively enunciated for the first time by the Vatican Council of 1870. Infallibility should be distinguished from impeccability, which it does not involve, and it is to be construed as an official rather than as a personal prerogative.

Literature: MANNING, The True Story of the Vatican Council (London, 1877); WENNIGER, Apostolical and Infallible Authority of the Pope (1874); GLADSTONE, The Vatican

Decrees, &c. (1874), also Vaticanism (London, 1875); Döllinger, Über die Unfehlbarkeits-adresse (1870); Reinkens, Über päpstliche Unfehlbarkeit (1870); Gueranger, De la Monarchie Pontificale (1870). (A.T.O.)

Infancy [Lat. *infans*, infant]: Ger. (1) *Kindheit*; Fr. (1) *enfance*; Ital. (1) *infanzia*. The period of immaturity during which the individual is dependent on parental care; it extends (1) from birth to the period of self-support (in a biological sense); and (2) to maturity or self-support (in a social, legal, and economic sense).

(1) The origin and meaning of infancy is an important biological problem. From the point of view of evolution, especial significance attaches to this period. It is thought to have arisen correlatively with the parental instincts in the animal world, and to have direct relation to the Gestation (q. v.) period; indeed the term infancy is sometimes used to cover both periods, a division being made between the intra-uterine (gestation or prenatal) period and the extra-uterine (post-natal) period. The relation of these periods is somewhat thus: a relatively short prenatal period is correlated with swift embryonic development in creatures which are born equipped for immediate or very early independent self-support. The extreme case is found in those insects which are born practically adult or fully developed. On the other hand, a relatively long post-natal infancy goes with relatively long and slow embryonic development, relative immaturity at birth, and relatively complex nutritive and protective adaptations for the young after birth. The significance of this is that by this arrangement higher endowments, involving plasticity, intelligence, complex social relationships, &c., are made possible; for the young, not having to begin immediately at birth to take care of themselves, need not have the fixed instinctive and reflex nervous and other special adaptations, but may have the general capacity for learning by slow accommodation to a varied set of conditions, while nourished and protected by their parents. The infancy period, therefore, adds directly to the resources of the species for the production of individuals of a higher order. With this goes the evolution of the brain in quality and complexity in the grey matter, with its convolutions and differentiations of function. Stated in terms of heredity, the meaning of it seems to be that by having an infancy period the individual may inherit less and

acquire more—have less fixity and more Educability (q. v.).

(2) See Infant (in law).

Literature: Fiske, Cosmic Philos.; Milnes-Marshall, Biol. Lectures, xiii; Baldwin, Ment. Devel. in the Child and the Race (from the psychological point of view). (J.M.B.—C.LL.M.)

Infant (in law): Ger. *Unmundiger*; Fr. *mineur*; Ital. *minore, minorenne*. One not of full age.

Full age in the United States and England is twenty-one years. Infants cannot bind themselves by contract, except for necessaries of life. For acts of violence or wrong they are civilly responsible. An infant under seven years of age is incapable of committing a felony.

By the older Roman law, infancy, so far as the right of control over property was concerned, ended at puberty; later the *tutor*, who till then had charge of an infant *sui iuris*, was replaced by a *curator*, the time of full majority being twenty-five. (S.E.B.)

Infant Psychology: see Child Psychology.

Inference [Lat. *in + ferre*, to bear]: Ger. *Schliessen, Schluss*; Fr. *inférence*; Ital. *illazione (conclusione)*. (1) In logic: (*a*) the act of consciously determining the content of a cognition by a previous cognition or cognitions, in a way which seems generally calculated to advance knowledge.

In this sense the word differs from Reasoning (q. v.) only in referring strictly to a single step of the process, or to what seems a single step. Unless the act is consciously performed, no logical control can be exercised; and this is sufficient reason for separating such acts from any operations otherwise analogous which may take place in the formation of percepts. To be conscious of determining a cognition by another, and not merely of making the one follow after the other, involves some more or less obscure judgment that the pair of representations, the determining and determined, belong to a class of analogous pairs, so that a general maxim is virtually obeyed in the act. There is, besides, a purpose of learning more of the truth. The representations concerned in inference are, it appears, always judgments (or propositions). Probably, if a pair of percepts were, in the very act of determining the one to accord with the other, looked upon as special cases of a class of pairs of percepts so related to one another that if one were true the other ought to be accepted, they would, *ipso facto*, become judgments.

(*b*) A pair (or larger set) of judgments, of

which one (or all of them together but one) determines the remaining one, as in (a) above, the whole set being regarded as constituting together a cognition more complete than a judgment.

In this sense, inference is synonymous with argument. The latter word, it is true, only implies that the set of propositions might be thought, being perhaps written down and no longer even accepted by the author, while the former word implies that the movement of thought takes place. Moreover, an inference creates belief in the mind that makes it, while an argument may be a system of propositions put together with a view of creating belief in another mind, or perhaps merely to exhibit the logical relation between different beliefs. But these distinctions often vanish or lose all importance. When the determining judgment is a copulative proposition, its members may either be called the premises, or their compound may be called the PREMISE (q.v.). But when different beliefs are brought together in thought for the first time to form a copulative judgment, the premises must be taken as plural.

Several other logical meanings are in general use as more or less permissible inaccuracies of language. Thus, the determined judgment, or conclusion, may sometimes be conveniently called an 'inference.' The popular use of the word for a dubious illation, as in such a sentence as 'This is proof positive, while that is only an inference,' is quite inadmissible.　　　　　　　　　　(C.S.P.)

(2) In psychology: the determination in the form of judgment, and as belonging to a mental whole, of any of the relations involved in that whole.

The matters of psychological interest are (a) the passage of consciousness from the antecedent to the subsequent or inferred content, covering the two cases of mediate and immediate inference, according as there are or are not elements common to both contents which serve explicitly to carry the mind over from one to the other and so determine them both in one whole. Immediate inference—e.g. John is human, therefore John is mortal—is the isolating in judgment of a phase of analysis of the whole 'human.' The humanity of John is analytically judged to involve his mortality. In mediate inference — the forms of reasoning involving a middle term—there are several cases, concerning all of which the question arises as to whether, from the psychological point of view, a reduction to the immediate form is possible. In the universal affirmative syllogism —e.g. John is human, all human beings are mortal, therefore John is mortal—we have no new psychological act or function; the process is, however, one of different emphasis, for the two contents, John and mortality, before not consciously judged in one whole, are explicitly joined, by an act of judgment, through the assertion of the minor premise. This distinction is more evident in cases of particular and hypothetical reasoning. See what is said of the 'conceptual interpretation' of judgment under ANALYTIC AND SYNTHETIC JUDGMENTS.

The various forms of inference, SYLLOGISM (q.v.), dialogism (a disjunctive conclusion following from a single premise), &c., fall in general under one or other of these headings, mediate or immediate.

(b) The other psychological point of discussion is that of so-called 'unconscious inference': the application of the term inference to the cases of mental construction or determination of objects as psychically immediate which are psychologically or logically mediate. Cf. PSYCHIC AND PSYCHOLOGICAL, and IMMEDIATE AND MEDIATE. The theory of unconscious inference was propounded by Helmholtz (*Die Thatsachen in d. Wahrnehmung*, and *Physiol. Optik*, 1st ed.) to explain colour contrast, was used in the theory of 'unconscious judgment' and in the explanation of optical illusions by Wundt (*Physiol. Psychol.*, 1st ed.) and others, and made much of by Binet (*Psychol. de Raisonnement*, Eng. trans., 1899). It is now largely obsolete. The ordinary processes of perception which cover these phenomena do not yield explicit judgments of relation; and the theory of inference is now constructed rather on the basis of mediate inference as type. It would be well to follow this tendency of usage. The psychological questions are brought to full consciousness in the theory of the thought function as the progressive determination of concepts as wholes. For the distinction between INDUCTION and DEDUCTION as forms of inference, see those terms. A little-used synonym for inference is Illation. Cf. also PROBABLE INFERENCE, and PROBABILITY.

Literature: see REASONING, and BIBLIOG. C, 2, *p*, *q*; especially the general works on logic (e.g. WUNDT, SIGWART) and on psychology (e.g. STOUT, Analytic Psychol., Bk. II. chap. vi; BALDWIN, Senses and Intellect, chap. xiv).　　　　　　　　(J.M.B., G.F.S.)

Infidelity [Lat. *in* + *fides*, faith] : Ger. *Un-glaube* ; Fr. *infidélité* ; Ital. *infedeltà*. (1) Denial or rejection of the distinctive tenets of any religion.

(2) More specifically, the denial or rejection of the distinctive tenets of Christianity, and particularly its claims as a divine revelation.

In view of the etymology of the word, infidelity is to be carefully distinguished from moral obliquity, which may accompany it, but is not necessarily implied in it. Again, it must be distinguished from such terms as atheism, deism, agnosticism, naturalism, and rationalism, with which it may or may not coincide, but with which it is neither generally nor specifically identical. It must also be distinguished from scepticism, of which, however, it is a species. The term infidelity is so closely associated in the popular belief with moral depravity, that its employment in cases of simple doctrinal unbelief is rarely justifiable.

Literature: PEARSON, Infidelity, its Aspects, &c. (1860) ; CHRISTLIEB, Christianity and modern Unbelief (Ger. and Eng.) ; FARRAR, Crit. Hist. of Free Thought (1863) ; McClintock and Strong's Cyc. of Bib. and Eccles. Lit., 'Infidelity' ; Schaff-Herzog's Encyc., 'Infidelity.' (A.T.O.)

Infinite (the) and the **Finite** [Lat. *in* + *finis*, end] : Ger. *unendlich* ; Fr. *infini* ; Ital. *infinito*. The object of the notion of infinity (see INFINITE, notion of), considered as having independent reality, is the infinite ; all other mental objects are, in opposition to it, in their mode of reality, finite.

The infinite has played an important part in the history of thought in certain connections : (1) the discussion as to the sort of reality the notion of the infinite carries with it. Here we have the views that (*a*) the infinite is an intuition having direct cognitive validity, or realized by mystic contemplation ; (*b*) it is thought as the perfect, and so must have existence (its being *in intellectu* is also being *in se*, Anselm : see ONTOLOGICAL ARGUMENT, and THEISM) ; (*c*) it is an 'idea of the reason' (Kant), and so a noumenon or rational presupposition of the phenomenal world. (2) The discussions of RELATIVITY OF KNOWLEDGE (q. v.) ; see also RELATIVE AND ABSOLUTE. (3) The discussions of the antithesis of finite and infinite, notably with reference to the implication of an infinite being or experience in finite experience ; particularly in later metaphysical discussions of an idealistic sort. See IDEALISM, and THEISM. (4) The discussion of the ABSOLUTE (q. v.) conceived as all-comprehensive and so transcending all limitation (Spinoza). (5) The theories of Agnosticism (see UNKNOWABLE), which either (*a*) deny the conceivability of the infinite (pure empiricism, Lewes) ; or (*b*) treat the infinite as an unknowable absolute (Hamilton, Spencer). (6) In the discussions of REALISM and NOMINALISM (q. v.). (7) In discussions of TIME, SPACE, and the WORLD (see those terms).

Little has been done in the way of utilizing the mathematical conceptions of LIMIT (q. v.) and INFINITESIMAL (q. v.)—see also INFINITE (in mathematics)—in philosophical discussion. The logical pitfalls of the subject are illustrated in the arguments of Zeno, the Eleatic, concerning infinite divisibility, and in the 'first antinomy' of Kant (cf. KANTIAN TERMINOLOGY, 21).

Literature: recent books on METAPHYSICS and EPISTEMOLOGY (see those topics ; also BIBLIOG. B, 1, *c*, *d*), especially COHN, Gesch. d. Unendlichkeitsproblems ; BRADLEY, Appearance and Reality ; ROYCE, The World and the Individual ; ORMOND, Foundations of Knowledge ; LADD, Philos. of Reality ; RÉCÉJAC, The Bases of the Mystic Knowledge ; FULLERTON, The Infinite. (J.M.B.)

Infinite (in mathematics). A quantity considered as always greater than any quantity to which we assign a definite value, and therefore itself having no definite value or boundary.

Such a quantity is used in investigation as an auxiliary one, to discover relations between other quantities in certain special cases. See INFINITESIMAL. (S.N.)

Infinite (notion of) and **Infinity**. The conception of any sort of mental object as having quantity which cannot be exhausted by any succession of experiences, however prolonged. Such an object is said to have infinity.

This definition is intended to assign the least that can be involved in any conception of infinity. A not uncommon way in which the child first forms this conception is by imagining himself as falling over the 'edge of the world' into empty space. He sees at once that if no physical obstacle exists, there is no reason why he should ever cease falling. When reflective analysis comes into play, the mere thought that there is 'no end' is completed by the insight into the reason why there can be 'no end.' Space, for instance, is seen to be endless, because any spatial boundary is a boundary between parts of space, and therefore implies space beyond it.

So the number-series is seen to be constituted by a process which at every step supplies the conditions essential for its own repetition.

The usual phrase 'idea of the infinite' is not strictly exact. Notion or concept of the infinite is better. Cf. INFINITE (in mathematics), and INFINITESIMAL.   (G.F.S.–J.M.B.)

Psychologically, the infinite is a LIMITING NOTION (q.v.) on the side of quantity, its correlative limiting notion being the infinitely small; a conception used in mathematics under the term INFINITESIMAL (q. v.). It is always thought in connection with a qualitative determination to which the attribution of infinity is confined. It is different from the metaphysical notion of the absolute in this restriction to a sphere of application which makes the infinite always a general. Spinoza's doctrine of the 'infinitely infinite' is a second generalization of infinites, in which again the limiting notion of infinity is of a quantitative (numerical) series, each term of which is a qualitative determination itself quantitatively infinite. This possible generalization of quantitative infinites is well represented by Spinoza's figure of an infinite number of infinite lines, making up one of an infinite number of infinite planes, which in turn constitute an infinite sphere; such a sphere being the limiting notion of three-dimensional space. Hamilton (*Logic*, iv), following Descartes, distinguishes the infinite from the 'indefinite' (that whose limits are not determined).   (J.M.B., G.F.S.)

Infinitesimal (in mathematics): Ger. *infinitesimal*; Fr. *infinitésimal*; Ital. *infinitesimale*. Denoting a quantity considered as always less than any quantity to which we assign a definite value, and therefore indefinite in value. Such a quantity is used in mathematics as an auxiliary one to discover relations between other quantities in certain special cases. See FINITE (in mathematics).

Quantities are not conceived in mathematics as having absolutely infinite or infinitesimal values. Quantities are compared by comparing their boundaries, and in all operations upon them, *qua* quantities, they are conceived as bounded. But infinite quantities have no boundaries, and therefore can neither be compared together nor operated on with definite results; and the attempt to do so often leads to contradictory or fallacious conclusions. For example, if a particle falls towards an immaterial centre attracting it as the inverse square of the distance, it would,

on reaching the centre, be acted on by an infinite force. In such a case we can equally prove that it would pass through the centre, or that it would return from it on the straight line by which it fell. An absolutely infinitesimal quantity would be one smaller than any quantity whatever, and therefore simply zero, as an infinitesimal line would be, at most, a point, and therefore not a line at all. In attempting to use such quantities we are met by the antinomy of Kant and Hamilton, that we can neither conceive of space and time as absolutely unbounded, nor yet as having boundaries. The difficulties thus arising are completely evaded by a mathematical method of using infinites and infinitesimals in the way we have defined them.

Their use grows out of the inapplicability of the ordinary methods of reasoning about finite quantities to the case of continuously varying quantities. We can compare two straight lines by bringing them into coincidence. If we have two polygons of any number of sides, however great, we can divide them into triangles, and measure the area of these triangles. But we cannot divide a circle or any other curve into measurable parts, nor divide two different curves into congruent parts. Arithmetical numbers express only fixed quantities, not continuously varying ones. In all such cases we have, when attempting to apply ordinary methods of reasoning, to deal with an infinite number of quantities, each infinitesimal. These are treated by the method of LIMITS (q. v.). (S.N.)

Infinity (in mathematics): Ger. *Unendlichkeit*; Fr. *infinité*; Ital. *infinità*. That region of space or quantity which we treat as being or lying beyond all limits whatever. A line is said to extend to infinity when it extends without end, a point to be at infinity when its distance is infinite, and a quantity to increase to infinity when it increases beyond all assignable limits. Cf. INFINITE (in mathematics), and INFINITESIMAL.   (S.N.)

Infinity (in philosophy): see INFINITE AND FINITE (the), and INFINITE (notion of).

Inflammation [Lat. *inflammatio*, a burning]: Ger. *Entzündung*; Fr. *inflammation*; Ital. *infiammazione*. Diseased condition of an organ or part characterized by swelling, pain, and discolouration—generally redness—and disturbed function.

The above results are in the main due to certain abnormal conditions of the bloodvessels, which permit passage through their walls of great quantities of lymph (swelling) and also of blood corpuscles (discolouration). (C.F.H.)

Inflation [Lat. *inflatio*, a blowing up]: Ger. *Uebermass, Inflation*; Fr. *extension de (papier-)monnaie*; Ital. *espansione dell' emissione*. An increase of debased currency beyond the amount of the better currency which it displaces (see GRESHAM'S LAW), resulting in depreciation.

'A permanent excess of the circulating money of a country, over that country's distributive share of the money of the commercial world, is called inflation' (Walker). (A.T.H.)

Inflection [Lat. *inflexus*, bent]: Ger. *Inflexion*; Fr. *inflexion*; Ital. *inflessione*. The general term including all the various modifications in the form of a word by which its relations to other parts of a proposition are expressed.

In the 'isolating' languages (Chinese, &c.), relations, if not indicated by distinct formwords, are left to be inferred from context or word-order; in the 'agglutinative' languages (Turkish, &c.), relations are indicated by elements which combine with the substance words and form composites in which the constituents maintain a consciously distinct existence; in the 'inflectional' languages the relations are expressed by changes in the word, generally of the ending. (B.I.W.)

Influence [Lat. *in + fluere*, to flow]: Ger. *Einfluss*; Fr. *influence*; Ital. *influenza*. That which enters in any way into the determination of a thing (1) is an influence, (2) has an influence, (3) exerts an influence; that is, the influence is (3) an element in the determination, (2) the capacity to contribute this element to the determination, (1) the thing which has such a capacity.

This term is useful from its very generality and vagueness; it applies to physical forces, mental elements, moral and social factors of change. (J.M.B.)

Influxus Physicus [Lat.]: see INTERACTION, and MIND AND BODY. Cf. also OCCASIONALISM, passim.

Infralapsarianism [Lat. *infra*, within, + *lapsus*, a fall]: Ger. *Infralapsarianismus*; Fr. *infralapsarisme*; Ital. *infralapsarianismo*. The doctrine that God's decree in relation to the fall of man was permissive and in view of the divine foreknowledge of that catastrophe.

Infralapsarianism is to be distinguished from supralapsarianism, which represents the decree as logically prior to the foreknowledge; also from sublapsarianism, which practically denies the decree and regards God's relation to the Fall as simply one of foreknowledge. Infralapsarianism is the doctrine of moderate Calvinists, while a few high Calvinists have held to the supralapsarian doctrine. Sublapsarianism belongs to a point of view that is essentially hostile to Calvinism. The doctrine of the Fall usually stands second in a series of divine determinations: (1) to create the world, (2) to permit the fall of man, (3) to elect a portion of the fallen to salvation, (4) to send Jesus Christ for their redemption, (5) to leave the residue to perish in their sins.

Literature: Schaff-Herzog Encyc. (sub verbo); JACKSON, Concise Dict. of Religious Knowledge; McClintock and Strong's Bib. Encyc., 'Sublapsarianism'; HEGENBACH, Dogmengeschichte (3rd ed.), t589; SCHNEITZER, Ref. Dogmatik, ii. 129 f.; HODGE, System. Theol., ii. 319–20; SHEDD, Dogmatic Theol., i. 441–3. (A.T.O.)

Inherence [Lat. *inhaerere*, to stick to]: Ger. *Inhärenz*; Fr. *inhérence*; Ital. *inerenza*. The relation which properties or accidents are thought to sustain to the substances to which they belong. See SUBSTANCE. (J.M.B.)

Inheritance (or **Heritage**) [Lat. *in + haeres*, heir]: Ger. (1) *Erbschaft*, (2) *Erbtheil*; Fr. *héritage*; Ital. *eredità, retaggio*. That which is inherited (1) physically; (2) socially or legally, that is, figuratively.

Sometimes used loosely as equivalent to HEREDITY (q. v.). See also GALTON'S LAW (of ancestral inheritance). (J.M.B.)

Inhibition (mental) [Lat. *inhibere*, to restrain]: Ger. *psychische Hemmung*; Fr. *inhibition mentale*; Ital. *inibizione mentale*. Inhibition exists in so far as the occurrence of a mental process prevents the simultaneous occurrence of other mental processes which might otherwise take place.

There are two distinct conditions which may give rise to mental inhibition—conflict and competition. In conflict there is intrinsic incompatibility between two processes. Thus I cannot judge the same thing to be at once black and white. This is sometimes called, in the case of images, contradictory representation. If one person tells me it is white and another that it is black, conflict arises. There is a tendency to judge it black and a tendency to judge it white, and the two tendencies arrest each other. There is consequently a block in the flow of mental activity, so far as it depends on the formation of a judgment on the point raised. Strictly speaking, conflict arises only between alternative continuations of the same mental process. The judgments 'this crow is black' and 'this crow is white' have a common starting-point and divergent continuation. It is divergent continuation from the same point which constitutes the conflict. Conflict arises only between connected processes—between processes which claim to occupy in some degree the same position in a system of relations. The ultimate explanation of conflict rests, therefore, in the ultimate theory of mental system as such. Theories which locate conflict in the direct incompatibility of mental images would, however, deny this. Yet, except in cases of directly antagonistic processes, such as black-no-black, round-not-round, there would seem to be no intrinsic reason that such conflicts should take place. Theories which find the ground of conflict in the rival claims of different elements in the same system are as varied as the theories of mental SYSTEM (q.v.). Motor theories, however, have the evident advantage in the fact that channels of co-ordinated action are fewer than those of incidental stimulation; the conflict of the stimulations may thus be due to their rival claim upon the motor channels (cf. Baldwin, *Ment. Devel. in the Child and the Race*, 286, 308 f., 322 f.; and Münsterberg, *Grundzüge der Psychol.*, i. 534).

Competition, on the contrary, occurs between disconnected processes. It is due merely to the narrowness of consciousness, to the fact that mental activity in a given direction more or less completely excludes activity in other directions. 'The typical instance is what we call *distraction of mind*, in which attention is solicited simultaneously by a plurality of objects so disconnected in their nature that they cannot be attended to together' (Stout, *Analytic Psychol.*, i. 285).

Both conflict and competition are illustrated in hypnotic somnambulism. The attention is held upon one object to the exclusion of all possible competing objects; and the objects of actual perception in the environment are inhibited by conflict with the suggestions of the hypnotizer. In many instances of the latter case only partial inhibition takes place, and there is a partial adjustment of elements of objective reality with those of the suggested image.

Literature: BINET, L'Inhibition dans les Phénomènes de Conscience, Rev. Philos., Aug., 1890; A. BINET and V. HENRI, Les Actions d'Arrêt dans les Phénomènes de la Parole, Rev. Philos., Jan., 1894; EXNER, Entwurf

z. ein. physiol. Erklärung d. psychischen Erscheinungen (1894); BALDWIN, loc. cit.; STOUT, loc. cit.; ODDI, L'Inibizione (1898); COLOZZA, Del potere di inibizione (1898); citations under ATTENTION, and in BIBLIOG. G, 2, *d*. See also the following topic.

(G.F.S.—J.M.B.)

Inhibition (nervous): Ger. *Hemmung, Inhibition*; Fr. *arrêt, inhibition*; Ital. *inibizione, arresto*. Interference with the normal result of a nervous excitement by an opposing force.

It differs from paralysis, in case of which the nervous action is prevented, while in case of inhibition it is overcome, diverted, or neutralized. The normal effect of a higher upon a lower centre of a series is the partial inhibition of the lower. Reflexes may be inhibited voluntarily or by the strong stimulation of sensory nerves up to a certain point.

The conception of inhibition is due to Brown-Séquard. Setschenow attempted to demonstrate a special centre for inhibition (*Ueber den Hemmungsmechanismus f. d. Reflexthätigkeit im Gehirn des Frosches*, 1863), but it is now conceded that inhibition is a general peculiarity of the interference of nervous activities, which tend to modify each other either by augmenting or repressing (inhibiting) each other. Physiologically, inhibition is a necessary condition in preserving the balance and tone of bodily function. The ganglion cells of the heart, for example, are constantly inhibited by the vagus nerve, and similar control is exercised over all other vital processes. As James says, 'we should all be cataleptics and never stop a muscular contraction once begun, were it not that other processes simultaneously going on inhibit the contraction. Inhibition is therefore not an occasional accident; it is an essential and unremitting element in our cerebral life.' The exact nature of the process remains obscure. Cf. SUMMATION.

Literature: BOMBARDA, Les neurones, l'hypnose et l'inhibition, Rev. Neurol., No. 11 (1897); BROWN-SÉQUARD, Faits nouveaux relatifs à la mise en jeu ou à l'arrêt (inhibition) des propriétés motrices ou sensitives de diverses parties du centre cérébro-rachidien, Arch. de Physiol., 2e sér. vi (1879); Recherches expérimentales et cliniques sur l'inhibition et la dynamogénie, application des connaissances fournies par ces recherches aux phénomènes principaux de l'hypnotisme, de l'extase et du transfert, Gaz. hebd. de Méd., 2e sér. xix (1882); Inhibition de certaines puissances réflexes du bulbe rachidien et de la moelle épinière, sous l'influence d'irritations de diverses parties de l'encéphale, C. R. Soc. de Biol. (1884); EULENBURG and LANDOIS, Die Hemmungsneurose, ein Beitrag zur Nervenpathologie, Wien. med. Wochensch. (1866); JAMES, The Reflex Inhibitory Centre Theory, Brain (1881–2); LANGENDORF, Ueber Reflexhemmung, Arch. f. Anat. u. Physiol. (1877); LISTER, Preliminary Account of an Inquiry into the Functions of the Visceral Nerves, with special reference to the so-called Inhibitory System, Trans. Roy. Soc. (London, 1858); LOEB, Einleitung in die vergleichende Gehirnphysiol. u. vergleichende Physiol. (Leipzig, 1899); McKENDRICK, On the Inhibitory or Restraining Action which the Encephalon exerts on the Reflex Centres of the Spinal Cord, Edinburgh Med. J., xix (1873–4); MUNK, Ueber Erregung und Hemmung, Arch. f. Physiol. (1881); NOTHNAGEL, Beobachtungen über Reflexhemmung, Arch. f. Psychiat., vi (1875–6); ODDI, L'inibizione dal punto di vista fisio-patologico, psicologico e sociale (Turin, 1898); PAL, Ueber Hemmungscentren im Rückenmark, Wien. klin. Wochensch. (1895); SETSCHENOW, Physiol. Stud. ü. Hemmungsmechanismen f. die Reflexthätigkeit des Rückenmarks (Berlin, 1863); SETSCHENOW and PASCHUTIN, Neue Versuche am Hirn u. Rückenmark des Frosches (Berlin, 1865); STEINACH, Ueber die viscero-motorischen Functionen der Hinterwurzeln und über die tonische Hemmungswirkung der Medulla oblongata auf den Darm des Frosches, Pflüger's Arch., lxxi (1898); VERWORN, Erregung und Lähmung, Verh. d. Ges. deutsch. Naturf. u. Aerzte zu Frankfurt, I.Theil(1896); also Deutsch.med.Wochensch., xxii (1896); WUNDT, Grundzüge d. physiol. Psychol. (Leipzig, 1893, 4th ed.); see also the other textbooks of physiological psychology and psychology; BREESE, On Inhibition, Psychol. Rev., Monog. Suppl., No. 11 (1899); DANILEWSKY, Ueber die tonischen Reflexe und ihre Hemmung, Arch. f. d. ges. Physiol., lxxviii (1899); HEYMANS, Untersuchungen über psychische Hemmung, Zeitsch. f. Psychol., xxi (1899); MELTZER, Inhibition, N. Y. Med. J., lxix (1899); PEAVY, Inhibitory Action of the Cerebrum, J. of Amer. Med. Assoc., xxxiii (1899); B. ONUF, A Tentative Explanation of some of the Phenomena of Inhibition on a Histo-physiological Basis, including a Hypothesis concerning the Function of the Pyramidal Tracts, N. Y. State Hosp. Bull. (1897), ii; L. HOFBAUER, Ueber Interferenz zwischen verschiedenen Impulsen im Centralnervensystem, Arch. f. d. ges. Physiol., lxviii (1897); M. HEIDENHAIN, Neue Erläuterungen zum Spannungsgesetz der centrirten Systeme, Morphol. Arb. (Schwalbe), (1897), vii; LOURIE, Riv. di Filos. Scient. (1887–8). (H.H.)

Initiation [Lat. *initio*, from *in + ire*, to go]: Ger. *Anfang, Initiative*; Fr. *initiation*; Ital. *iniziazione*. A general term for the starting of a relatively new series of changes.

The term is mostly used in discussions : (1) as to whether the mind, simply by its own act, can initiate changes in its motives or functions generally (the theory of indeterminism : see FREEDOM, and WILL); (2) as to whether consciousness can initiate changes in the brain (see MIND AND BODY); and (3) as to the causes from which spring relatively new movements in history.　　(J.M.B.–G.F.S.)

Injustice : see JUSTICE.

Innate (in biology) [Lat. *in + natus*, born]: Ger. *eingeboren*; Fr. *inné*; Ital. *innato, ingenito*. Equivalent to congenital. See ACQUIRED AND CONGENITAL CHARACTERS.　　(J.M.B.)

Innate Ideas, &c. (in philosophy): Ger. *angeborene* (*Ideen*); Fr. (*idées*) *innées*; Ital. (*idee*) *innate*. Belonging in some sense to the individual himself.

The distinction between ideas which are 'innate' and those which are 'acquired' is an old one in the history of thought. It came to full expression in Descartes, who laid down certain characteristics of innate ideas by which their certainty and value were attested. Locke gave the matter further statement by arguing that there were no innate ideas as such—meaning notions or actual thoughts inborn with the individual. Kant gave a further turn to the discussion, showing that there were—as he thought—certain forms or categories of thought in which all the material of experience was cast and organized in a system of knowledge. To him these forms were universal principles of mental action which could not themselves arise from experience, and which consequently were to be considered innate. In connection with each of these phases of theory the 'acquired' ideas were those items or elements of knowledge which did come through the experience of the individual. The verbal antithesis between the actual words 'innate' and 'acquired' came into use with the Scottish philosophers, who inquired, in a more psychological way, and in detail, into the actual conditions of the rise in the mind of such ideas as cause, space, time, &c.

In current discussion the controversy over innate ideas has taken on a more psychological phase in two directions. First, the question has been removed largely from the sphere of the individual's knowledge to that of the origin of the categories of thought in the race as a whole, called universal. Spencer opened the question, maintaining that although experience might be inadequate to generate these ideas in the individual—that is, although certain principles of knowledge may seem to be innate to the individual—still they have been acquired by mankind in human evolution through a larger and continuous race experience. Second, the question—like so many others in the remoulding of the traditional psychology—has taken on what has been called the 'functional' phase. It is not now claimed by any one that the child is born with a stock of actual ideas, complete and adequate—the view which Locke combated; on the contrary, it is now asked whether the child comes to his experience with a readiness for certain mental functions, certain characteristic ways of mental action; if so, then these tendencies, of a functional sort, are innate or native, and his experience requires his actual use of such native tendencies. In other words, the mind is not a *tabula rasa*—a blank tablet—as Locke supposed, upon which his experience is gradually inscribed; but experience serves to stimulate the functions and processes which, as a being with a mind, he is constituted to exercise. The insufficiency of the term innate for this new conception has led to its disuse; the terms native and nativism, with modifying words, being now widely current. For further historical matter and literary references see INTUITIONALISM, and NATIVISM AND EMPIRICISM. Innateness is used broadly to cover all the forms of what is innate or native.   (J.M.B.)

Innateness: see INNATE (in philosophy), ad fin.

Inner and **Outer:** see INTERNAL EXPERIENCE, and EXTERNAL OBJECTS; cf. OUTNESS.

Inner Imitation: see SEMBLANCE.

Innervation (sensation of) [Lat. *in* + *nervus*, nerve]: Ger. *Innervationsempfindung*; Fr. *sensation d'innervation*; Ital. *senso di innervazione*. A mode of consciousness having the characteristics of actual sensation, supposed to accompany discharge from the central nervous system into the motor apparatus, and to vary in intensity with the intensity of the out-going current. See EFFORT (bodily), and KINAESTHETIC (sensations and equivalents).   (G.F.S.—J.M.B.)

The existence of such a sensation in experiences of effort was maintained by certain psychologists (e.g. Biran, Carpenter, Helmholtz) previously to the analysis of the articular, tendinous, and muscular sensation complexes which are called kinaesthetic. An innervation sensation of this kind is still accepted by Bain, Waller, Ladd, Mach, &c.; and Wundt maintained it in his earlier books (e. g. *Physiol. Psychol.*, 1. Aufl.).   (E.B.T.—J.M.B.)

Literature: SANFORD, Course in Exper. Psychol., expts. 36–8; BERTRAND, La Psychol. de l'Effort, 96 ff.; CARPENTER, Ment. Physiol. (6th ed.), 388; HELMHOLTZ, Physiol. Optik (2nd ed.), 742 ff.; MACH, Analyse d. Empfind., 57 ff.; WUNDT, Physiol. Psychol. (1st ed.), 316, 488; cf. 3rd ed., i. 404; 4th ed., i. 431, and later books; BAIN, Senses and Intellect (3rd ed.), 77 ff.; LADD, Psychol., Descrip. and Explan., 221; WALLER, Brain (1891), 189 ff.; JAMES, Princ. of Psychol., ii. 493 ff.; DELABARRE, Bewegungsempfindungen (1891); STUMPF, Tonpsychologie, i. 166, 426, ii. 306, 550; also citations under EFFORT (bodily).   (E.B.T.—J.M.B.)

Innocence (in law): see IGNORANCE, and INTENTION.

Inorganic: see ORGANIC (1).

Inquisition [Lat. *inquisitio*]: Ger. *Inquisition, Glaubensgericht*; Fr. *Inquisition*; Ital. *Inquisizione*. An ecclesiastical court of the Roman Catholic Church, called officially the Holy Office, and instituted for the suppression of heresy and certain other offences against morality and canon law.

The Inquisition was formally organized toward the close of the 12th and the beginning of the 13th centuries under Popes Innocent III and Gregory VII, and the principal theatre of its operations included France, Spain, Italy, Portugal, and Germany. It was reorganized in Spain in the 15th century on an ecclesiastico-political basis, and became noted for the severity of its proceedings, especially in connection with the Netherlands. The Inquisition reached its height in the 16th century. It was suppressed in France in 1772, in Portugal under John VI, and in Spain in 1834.

Literature: LEA, Hist. of the Inquisition of the Middle Ages (1887–8); GANS, Kirchengesch. Spaniens (1862–79), iii. 1–93; C. DONAIS, Les Sources de l'Histoire de l'Inquisition, &c., in Rev. des Quest. Hist., xxx (1881); RANKE, The Popes; HEFELE, Cardinal Ximenes (Eng. trans., 1860). (A.T.O.)

Insanity (and **Sanity**) [Lat. *insanitas*, from *in + sanus*, sound]: Ger. *Wahnsinn*; Fr. *démence, folie* (mania); Ital. *pazzia, follia* (pop.), *infermità mentale* (in law). A serious departure from the normal in the sphere of thought, emotion, or rational action, by way of defect or irregularity. (J.J.–J.M.B.)

The conventional use of the term implies that the disorder is not merely temporary or incidental to a temporary physical condition (a person in a fit of anger, or under the influence of an intoxicant, or in the delirium of fever is not considered insane); while a more special usage eliminates as well the conditions of primary defect (idiocy) and of simple loss or decay of faculty (dementia), and thus confines the term to perversions or aberrant forms of mental functioning (Verrücktheit) which constitute in many cases the salient characteristics of the insane state. There is, too, the legal or practical conception of insanity, which proposes such tests as the ability to distinguish between right and wrong, the being 'of sound mind, memory, and understanding,' the capacity to conduct one's affairs. However necessary and admittedly useful the popular, the legal, and the clinical conceptions of insanity may be, they do not contribute to a clearer understanding of the nature of the defects to which they refer. In distinction from them are the psychological and the pathological or somatic modes of viewing insanity, both founded upon scientific principles, but both also lamentably incomplete; the former considers, mainly, abnormal forms of mental function; the latter diseased conditions of the brain looked upon as the substratum of such function. Both consider insanity not in the restricted or conventional sense, but comprehensively, as the totality of abnormal mental and cerebral conditions. The terms mental pathology and psycho-pathology are better suited to describe what is thus considered than insanity.

Psychology. The factors of greatest importance in the determination of psycho-neuroses (or less accurately the insanities) are precisely those that most profoundly influence normal mental life. Such are heredity and the conditions of existence; inherited natural capacities, and environmental nurtural experiences. Again, mental functions as thus determined are psychologically different, particularly as they involve what are commonly characterized as intellectual, moral, or volitional elements. The various insanities are thus distinguished from one another by their inherited or acquired character, by their special relations to periods of growth or decay, by the symptoms which characterize them, by their relation to known conditions of the nervous system. All of these factors may, and several of them frequently do, combine to the production of a given form of insanity; so that its distinctive name or characteristic may vary according as one or another factor becomes especially prominent. The factors thus enumerated may be spoken of as (1) aetiological, the general causes and conditions of insanity; (2) symptomatic, the mental and bodily abnormal phenomena; and (3) somatic or pathological in the narrow sense, the specific dependence upon diseased conditions of the nervous system. Of these the symptoms are for the psychologist, and probably also for the psychiatrist, the most instructive.

The insanities are also profitably viewed as exaggerations of normal tendencies; and this both generally as abnormalities in the aggregate mental endowment, but still more, specifically, in the distribution and balance of faculties. Insanity is lack of poise and balance more frequently than it is defect or degeneration. Fluctuations in emotional susceptibility, in intellectual power, in practical energy, are normal and psychological, but when these fluctuations exceed normal limits there is insanity; and between there is a wide and vaguely determined borderland. In other words, while despondency and excitement are in themselves normal occurrences, the temperament that gives way upon slight or ordinary occasions to violent fits of dejection, or is prone to periods of exaggerated and wild excitement, is closely akin to that of the victim of melancholia or of mania; while the borderland of eccentricity, of high endowment in a limited sphere combined with marked deficiency in other directions, readily yields illustrations of many typical forms of mental irregularities.

While it may be maintained (Mercier, Morselli) that insanity, like mental processes in general, is to be judged by conduct, this should not be construed to disparage the source of information to be derived from the patient's own description of his feelings and thoughts. It is false to judge insanity, as it is to judge normal action, wholly from without. Perverse motives may lead to wise conduct; a sound decision may be provoked by absurd deliberations and doubts; abnormal tendencies may be resisted and concealed. The very inconsistency between inner feelings and outer conditions often constitutes the psycho-neurosis. It is equally true that an action must be judged in the light of its environment. The ecstatic expression of joy by a child might be a symptom of insanity if manifested by an adult; an action normal for one temperament or in one grade of social life might be so foreign to another as to suggest a mental disorder; the belief in witches and zeal in the persecution of them which was held laudable a few centuries ago might well be regarded to-day as the product of insanity.

Finally, it is well to emphasize again that insanity must not be too exclusively viewed as an intellectual disorder. Perverted thinking, the entertainment of delusions, eccentricities of conduct naturally attract attention; but an abnormality in the emotional sphere, an insensibility to the ordinary motives of action, a personal uncleanliness and indecency which is born of deep alteration of personal and social feelings, a waywardness of action, are far more common than the more picturesque intellectual irregularities, and often determine the latter. In this field, too, lies the basis of the social unfitness of the insane.

Aetiology. The causes of insanity are profitably considered as predisposing and exciting; the former refer to the general concomitant conditions affecting insanity, the latter to the particular occasions and accidents likely to bring it on. Of the former a most prominent factor is the social environment. Insanity has been termed a disease of civilization; its rareness among savages has been noted; its increase in cities and populations most markedly characteristic of modern life has been claimed. It is certainly true that social relations and obligations constitute a preponderant factor in the mental life of sane and insane alike; it is true that the maladaptation and imperfect adaptation of certain portions of all civilized communities is a factor in the production of insanity. But it can hardly be inferred that civilized life, properly developed, in itself predisposes to insanity, however readily it may be admitted that a more complex mental structure with more delicate parts and nicer construction is more liable to faults of mechanism and varieties of derangement than the simpler and more vacant minds of primitive peoples. As between the different strata of society,

there seems to be evidence that most of all the very poor—those upon whom lack of proper nutrition, proneness to alcoholic indulgence, unsuitable hygiene and moral surroundings have worked most severely—contribute most to the aggregate of insanity; and that again those in easy circumstances, with too little or irrational occupation, prone to much self-indulgence, and over-attention to personal longings and sensations, yield a considerable percentage of the insane. Regarding excessive strain or overwork, the preponderance of opinion seems to indicate that as a factor of insanity this has been highly overrated. It is not work and occupation, but the worry and anxiety accompanying many of the forms of earning a livelihood, the ambition and the strain that incites to unhealthy forms and habits of activity, that should be enumerated as more important aetiological factors of insanity.

Next to the social, the hereditary factors demand notice. One-fourth, or one-third, or even a greater proportion of all regularly enumerated cases of insanity appear in individuals whose families present other cases of insanity or nervous taint. Insanity is graved in the nervous structure. This should not be taken to mean that the insanity, least of all the particular form of it, is handed down from generation to generation; on the contrary, the frequency with which certain members of a family escape the taint which passes on to others in direct or collateral descent, the variety of forms which the taint assumes—mania here, epilepsy there, neurasthenia or hysteria in a third case, marked but eccentric ability in a fourth—are most characteristic. What is inherited is properly spoken of as a diathesis (and as such enumerated as a separate aetiological factor), an instability of organization which at certain critical periods of life, or as a result of stress, exhibits the characteristic degeneration. Age is an important factor, especially in relation to the special forms of insanity. Apart from idiocy and imbecility, insanity in the first fifteen years of life is rare; between fifteen and twenty attacks increase, while the two most predisposing decades are those between twenty and thirty, and between thirty and forty, the former perhaps predominating. The period of maturity and fullest expansion of brain power is the danger period of derangement. For different periods different insanities are characteristic: idiocy, spasms, convulsions, epilepsy in the earliest periods;

paroxysmal mania, hysteria, great motor and emotional rather than intellectual disturbance in early manhood and womanhood; active mania and delusions in the prime of life, and later melancholia, with dementia in old age. Statistics regarding sex must be interpreted with regard to the proportion of men and women in the general population and the relative low mortality of women; when that is done it is probable that an excess of insanity among males will appear, although this becomes significant only when the special liability of men to certain mental diseases and of women to others is taken into account. (See MANIA, MELANCHOLIA, HYSTERIA, and PARALYSIS.) The effect of consanguineous marriages in the production of insanity is frequently asserted, but it is difficult to determine how far such a factor exists apart from the concentration thus possible of a neurotic diathesis.

Of more specific factors (most of which may be termed exciting) may be mentioned disease of the mother during pregnancy, injury in parturition, accidental injury in later years, intemperance, sexual excess, the stress occasioned by the crises of life, and an endless series of mental, and particularly emotional, shocks or strains. Such exciting causes usually co-operate with the predisposing causes in the production of a specific abnormal state. This is best illustrated in connection with the periods of adolescence, child-birth, the climacteric, &c., at which times latent tendencies to mental break-down become manifest. Such influences have been well discussed by Mercier, under the headings of direct and indirect stress, and again as stress of internal and external origin. The special aetiology of the several forms of insanity has been carefully studied, especially in regard to the exciting causes; these are mainly of interest to the clinical alienist. For a brief tabulation of them see Shaw, as cited below, 137–45.

Varieties of Insanity. An almost endless number of varieties of insanity has been described, particularly by clinical alienists. In the article on Insanity in Tuke's *Dictionary of Psychological Medicine* some one hundred and thirty varieties are enumerated without exhausting the terms current in medical literature. The classification of these insanities is a vexed question which requires only slight notice in the present connection. A classification is valuable only with reference to the purpose for which it is to be used. The purposes of clinical diagnosis are quite different from those of psychological analysis. The purely practical classifications have attempted to select the salient characteristics of actual cases of insanity, and to group about them as main types subordinate varieties which deviate more or less from them. The result is logically indefensible, but practically useful. Thus Clouston's clinical classification includes, among others, general paralysis, traumatic insanity, alcoholic insanity, phthisical insanity, senile insanity (for details see his work); while his symptomatological classification groups the various forms of defect about states of (1) mental depression, (2) mental exaltation, (3) mental alternation, (4) fixed and limited delusion, (5) mental enfeeblement, (6) mental stupor, (7) defective inhibition, (8) insane diathesis—all of them variations of psychological functions. But in actual description such terms are supplemented by characteristic groups of symptoms, such as epilepsy, hysteria, general paralysis, &c. In addition to the clinical, the symptomatological, and the psychological classifications, there are those that consider mainly the pathological cause; those that consider mainly the time of appearance, or specific exciting cause; those that consider the association with specific bodily diseases. The psychologist will find most interest in the symptoms of insanity, but cannot afford to neglect the natural groups of which these symptoms are characteristic; while the specific study of the derangements of mental processes in insanity falls under ABNORMAL PSYCHOLOGY (q.v.). For examples of classification consult Shaw, as cited below.

Insanity and the Brain. That normal and abnormal functions alike depend upon cerebral conditions follows necessarily from the modern conception of their nature. But the imperfect state of knowledge regarding the nervous concomitants of mental processes renders it desirable (in this connection) to indicate only a few general and typical correlations. In general abnormal appearances are strikingly frequent in insanity; some of them are local and specific, others general and in part secondary in character. They may be considered as macroscopic and microscopic; as related to insanity in general or to the specific form of it which is present; as related to gross defect or derangement, or to the abnormal symptoms manifested. Thus an abnormally large or small or misshapen cranium, an adherent dura mater, opacity of the arachnoid, arachnoid cysts, hyperaemia or congestion or anaemia or inflammation of the pia mater, atrophy of the cerebral substance, smallness of brain, hydrocephalus, softening of the brain, &c., are some of the pathological appearances frequently met with. More specifically, severe mental defect is generally associated with marked and coarse brain lesions. Thus in idiocy and dementia and epilepsy, abnormality of size and weight of brain, tumours, softening, atrophy, &c., are common, while in mania and melancholia there is frequently nothing to be observed except hyperaemia and slightly uncertain microscopic irregularities. (For the discussion of the special pathology of such conditions see references cited under MANIA, MELANCHOLIA, IDIOCY, and EPILEPSY.) In regard to symptoms the results of localization of function have received corroboration in the field of insanity. Disorders of sight and hearing, of tactile and motor sensibility, paralyses and spasms, motor and sensory speech defects, have been more or less completely correlated with lesions or irritations in definite portions of the brain cortex. EPILEPSY (q. v.) and aphasia (see SPEECH, defects of) best illustrate the extent to which such LOCALIZATION (q.v., cerebral) has been carried. Furthermore, in a great majority of instances we have reason to suspect cerebral changes, which, however, elude any attempt to locate them accurately (cf. Shaw, cited below, chap. vii). See PSYCHOSIS.

Literature: most psychological in treatment are: MERCIER, Sanity and Insan. (1890); HYSLOP, Ment. Physiol. (1895); EMMINGHAUS, Allg. Psycho-Pathol. (1878); MAUDSLEY, Pathol. of Mind (1895); E. MORSELLI, Semej. malat. ment. (3rd ed., 1899); SOMMER, Lehrb. d. psycho-pathologischen Untersuchungsmethoden (1899). For general data of Insanity see KRAEPELIN, Psychiatrie (6th ed., 1899); SPITZKA, Manual of Insan. (1893); KAHLBAUM, Gruppirung d. Psychosen (1863); ZIEHEN, Psychiatrie (1894); FORBES WINSLOW, Aids to Psychol. Med. (1882); KRAFFT-EBING, Lehrb. d. Psychiat. (1879); ADAMKIEWICZ, Functionsstörungen d. Grosshirnrindes (1898); CLOUSTON, Ment. Diseases (1887; 5th ed., 1898); BUCKNILL and TUKE, Manual of Psychol. Med.; SAVAGE, Insanity (1884 and 1896); CHURCH and PETERSON, Nerv. and Ment. Diseases (1898); BEVAN-LEWIS, Ment. Diseases (2nd ed.); MEYNERT, Klin. Vorlesungen ü. Psychiatrie (1890); SÉGLAS, Leçons cliniques sur les Malades mentales (1887–94); G. BALLET, Les Psychoses (Ital. trans. by MOR-

SELLI with additions, 1895). Many of the systems of diseases contain excellent contributions on mental diseases, particularly Ziemssen's Cyc. of the Pract. of Med., The Twentieth Cent. Pract. of Med., &c. J. SHAW, Epitome of Mental Diseases (1892), is a convenient reference book. (J.J.)

Insanity (in law). Such lack of mental soundness as makes one who does a particular act incapable of appreciating its real character.

Law deals in all instances with particular acts, and (except with reference to putting an alleged lunatic under guardianship) the question of sanity or insanity is to be determined in each instance with reference to the act in question. Monomania does not destroy testamentary capacity, unless it touches something involved in the particular will. So, though one has been put under guardianship as a lunatic, this action does not necessarily deprive him of the ability to make a will or to commit an actionable wrong or crime.

Literature: see chapter on Insanity in its Medico-legal Bearings, in HAMILTON, Syst. of Legal Med., ii. 19. (S.E.B.)

Insects [Lat. *in* + *secare*, to cut]: Ger. *Insekten*; Fr. *insectes*; Ital. *insetti*. The insects, or Hexapoda, form a class of the phylum Arthropoda, in which the body is divided into three regions: head, thorax, and abdomen.

There are typically a pair of sensory antennae, eyes, a pair of mandibles, and two pairs of maxillae on the head; three pairs of legs and two pairs of wings on the thorax. The ventral genital pore is situated near the extremity of the abdomen. The Hexapoda are typically air-breathing and tracheate animals, of terrestrial or aërial habit in the adult state; they are remarkable for the perfection of their sense-organs, and the high development of their instincts and ability to perform acts which seem intelligent. This is especially true of those which form social communities.

Literature: J. LUBBOCK, Origin and Metamorphoses of Insects (1874); Ants, Bees, and Wasps, Int. Sci. Ser. (1882); and On the Senses of Animals, Int. Sci. Ser. (1888); D. SHARP, Insects, in the Cambridge Nat. Hist., Pt. I (1895), Pt. II (1899); A. S. PACKARD, Textbook of Entomol. (1898); W. KIRBY and W. SPENCE, Introd. to Entomol. (1816–28); G. W. and E. G. PECKHAM, The Instincts and Habits of the Solitary Wasps, Wisc. Geol. Survey Bull., No. 2, 1898 (valuable). Cf. COMPARATIVE PSYCHOLOGY, and INSTINCT; and see BIBLIOG. G, 1, *f*. (E.S.G.)

Insensibility: see ANÆSTHESIA.

Insight [in + sight]: Ger. *Einsicht, Anschauung*; Fr. *connaissance profonde* (no exact equivalent); Ital. *intuizione*. (1) Apprehension of the more subtle and profound aspects of truth in a relatively immediate and direct way.

(2) The organ of higher intuition or reason, held to afford direct contemplation of truth.

The use of the term varies from the more refined and penetrating processes of thought to the supposed faculty of CONTEMPLATION (q. v.) of the mystics.   (J.M.B.)

Insistent Idea: see IMPERATIVE IDEA.

Insolubilia [Lat. *in + solvere*, to loose; trans. of Aristotle's ἀπορία; used mainly in plural]. A class of sophisms in which a question is put of such a nature that, whether it be answered affirmatively or negatively, an argument unimpeachable in form will prove the answer to be false.

The type is this. Given the following proposition:

This assertion is not true:

is that assertion, which proclaims its own falsity, and nothing else, true or false? Suppose it true. Then,

Whatever is asserted in it is true,

But that it is not true is asserted in it;

∴ By Barbara, That it is not true is true;

∴ It is not true.

Besides, if it is true, that it is true is true. Hence,

That it is not true is not true,

But that it is not true is asserted in the proposition;

∴ By Darapti, Something asserted in the proposition is not true;

∴ The proposition is not true.

On the other hand, suppose it is not true. In that case,

That it is not true is true,

But all that the proposition asserts is that it is not true;

∴ By Barbara, All that the proposition asserts is true;

∴ The proposition is true.

Besides, in this case,

Something the proposition asserts is not true,

But all that the proposition asserts is that it is not true;

∴ By Bokardo, That it is not true is not altogether true;

∴ That it is true is true;

∴ It is true.

Thus, whether it be true or not, it is both true and not. Now, it must be either true or not, hence it is both true and not, which is absurd.

Only two essentially distinct methods of solution have been proposed. One, which is supported by Ockham (*Summa totius logices*, 3rd div. of 3rd part, cap. 38 and 45), admits the validity of the argumentation and its consequence, which is that there can be no such proposition, and attempts to show by other arguments that no proposition can assert anything of itself. Many logical writers follow Ockham in the first part of his solution, but fail to see the need of the second part. The other method of solution, supported by Paulus Venetus (*Sophismata Aurea*, sophisma 50), diametrically denies the principle of the former solution, and undertakes to show that every proposition virtually asserts its own truth. This method, therefore, denies the premise of the antithesis that 'all that the proposition asserts is that it is not true,' since, like every other proposition, it also asserts its own truth, and is therefore contradictory and false, not in what it expressly asserts, but in what it implicitly asserts. Some writers (as Fries) hold that because every proposition asserts its own truth, therefore nothing is a proposition which asserts its own falsity. See Aristotle, *Sophisticae Elenchi*, cap. 25. Other proposed solutions of little importance are given by Paulus Venetus, loc. cit.   (C.S.P.)

Insomnia [Lat. *in + somnus*, sleep]: Ger. *Schlaflosigkeit*; Fr. *insomnie*; Ital. *insonnio*. Sleeplessness, inability to sleep.

The amount of normal sleep varies with the period of life and the individual; any marked deficiency in habitual sleep might be termed insomnia, although the term is usually restricted to a more or less chronic defect due to some disturbance of the nervous system. Defective sleep may consist of a deficiency in quality as well as in quantity, although insomnia refers usually to the latter alone. The two frequently exist together. The causes of the insomnias are various; some are due to bodily disorders, but most are of nervous origin. It is common among the insane, and is often the most distressing accompaniment of melancholia. In weakened conditions of the nervous system in those temperamentally disposed to nervous disorders, insomnia is apt to be caused by slighter degrees of the same influences—such as worry, grief, excitement—that produce it in others.

For artificially produced loss of sleep see SLEEP.

Partial sleeplessness may lead to SOMNAMBULISM (q. v.) and AUTOMATIC ACTION (q. v.). The medical literature is concerned with the treatment of insomnia; and for this purpose PSYCHO-THERAPEUTICS (q. v.) have been tried with considerable success.

Literature: H. M. LYMAN, Insomnia (1885); MACFARLAND, Insomnia (1890); C. EDGELOW, Modern Sleeplessness (1891); E. YUNG, Le Sommeil normal et le Sommeil pathologique (1893); BROWN, Disorders of Sleep, in Twentieth Cent. Pract. of Med., x. 813. (J.J.)

Inspiration [Lat. *inspiratio*, from *inspirare*, to breathe into]: Ger. *Eingebung*; Fr. *inspiration*; Ital. *ispirazione*. (1) An illumination or stimulation of the human mind which is conceived to be of supernatural origin.

(2) The doctrine that the writers of the Christian Scriptures were so informed and guided by the Holy Spirit as to make them truly express the mind and produce the word of God.

In the first sense Socrates was inspired by the suggestion of his daimon. So also the divine illumination of Philo and the intuition of the mystics are inspiration in the first sense. In the narrower and more technical sense of the term it is distinguished by exact writers from Revelation, which means original communication of truth, and is confined to the process of its transmission. Theories of inspiration have been various, as for example (1) verbal, the dictation of the words of the message by the Holy Spirit; (2) plenary, that the Scripture is fully inspired in all its parts; (3) limited or partial, that only parts of the Scripture are fully inspired or that only certain elements are inspired.

Literature: DELITZSCH, De Inspiratione Scripturae Sacrae (Leipzig, 1872); ROHNERT, Die Inspiration d. heiligen Schrift (Leipzig, 1889); RABAUD, Hist. de la Doctrine de l'Inspiration (Paris, 1883); JOHN DE WITT, What is Inspiration? (N. Y., 1893); WESTCOTT, Introd. to the Study of the Gospels; LADD, Doctrine of Sacred Scriptures (N. Y., 1883). (A.T.O.)

Instability [Lat. *in* + *stabilis*, stable, from *stare*, to stand]: Ger. *Unbeständigkeit*; Fr. *instabilité*; Ital. *instabilità*. Relative liability to DISSOCIATION AND DISAGGREGATION (q. v.), either mental or nervous.

Instability is a general word for all sorts of retrograde or disintegrative tendencies. In psychology it is applied particularly to lack of persistence or effectiveness in the functions which involve synthesis and organization. Cf. Duprat, *Instabilité mentale*, and the textbooks of mental diseases (in which the term is often used without clear definition). (J.M.B.)

Instinct [Lat. *instinctus*]: Ger. *Instinkt*; Fr. *instinct*; Ital. *istinto*. (1) An inherited reaction of the sensori-motor type, relatively complex and markedly adaptive in character, and common to a group of individuals.

(2) Native endowment of any kind; the adjective instinctive is frequently used in this sense. This meaning is not recommended; the terms congenital, innate, and impulsive serve this purpose adequately.

(1) This definition makes instinct a definitely biological, not a psychological conception. No adequate psychological definition of instinct is possible, since the psychological state involved is exhausted by the terms sensation (and also perception), Instinct-feeling, and IMPULSE (q. v.). This definition, it will be seen, rules out the application of the term instinct to tendencies and impulses which do not have definite native motor channels of discharge. The line of difficulty with this definition lies in the distinction of instinct from reflex action; but the facts that instinct is definitely associated with stimulation through the higher centres (sensori-motor), and that it is highly adaptive and relatively complex, while reflexes are relatively simple and not always evidently adaptive, serve to differentiate them. On the other hand, the distinction of instinct from action of the secondary-automatic type is in their origin respectively, the former being congenital, the latter acquired. Further, they differ psychologically in that instincts may involve a high degree of consciousness, with attention; and also inasmuch as secondary-automatic acts exhibit the progressive conative determination, described under HABIT (q. v.), as the instincts do not.

The much discussed question of the origin of instincts has given rise to various theories. There are two main views, called respectively the 'lapsed intelligence' and the 'reflex' theory. According to the former, instincts have arisen through intelligent accommodations which have become secondary-automatic actions, and have been transmitted by physical heredity. This theory is held by Wundt, Eimer, Cope, &c. The principal difficulty with it is the lack of evidence of the actual transmission of acquired characters, together with the difficulty of supposing sufficient intelligence so far back in the history of life. The psychological differences between instinct and secondary-automatic actions also create a difficulty (Stout). The other great class of theories—the reflex theories—hold that the instincts have arisen by the gradual accumulation of reflex adjustments to the environment; a compounding of such adjustments, which may be both congenital adaptations, or variations, and individually acquired organic accommodations (as think those who hold to the inheritance of acquired characters, e.g. Spencer), or only congenital adaptations (those who do not so hold). The main objections to this theory are that it does not account for the survival of the early beginnings of an instinct before it is of utility, and also that it does not account for the facts of co-ordination of muscular groups. The two views are held by some (Romanes) to be both partly true. A third point of view consists in the application of the principle of ORGANIC SELECTION (q. v.) to some instincts; according to which accommodations of all kinds, whether intelligent or organic, may serve to supplement incomplete endowment and so keep a species alive until variations are secured sufficient to make the instinct relatively independent (Ll. Morgan, Baldwin, Groos, Stout). Cf. COINCIDENT VARIATION.

Literature: general works on psychology, and works on COMPARATIVE PSYCHOLOGY (q. v.); also many of the titles given under EVOLUTION, and BIBLIOG. G, 1, *f*, 2, *l*. Further: LL. MORGAN, Some Definitions of Instinct (Nat. Sci., May, 1895), Habit and Instinct, and Animal Behaviour (1900); GROOS, The Play of Animals, and the Play of Man (Eng. trans.); ROMANES, Ment. Evolution in Animals (especially the Appendix, a posthumous paper by CHARLES DARWIN), and Darwin and after Darwin, Pt. I; BALDWIN, Science, March 20 and April 10, 1896, and Story of the Mind, chap. iii; LICATA, Fisiologia dell' istinto (1879); MASCI, Teorie sulla formazione naturale dell' istinto, R. Accad. Sci. (Napoli, 1893); WHITMAN, in Woods Holl Biol. Lects. (1899).

(J.M.B., G.F.S., C.LL.M.)

Instinct-feeling : see IMPULSE.

Instinctive Morality : Ger. *instinktive Moralität*; Fr. *moralité instinctive*; Ital. *moralità istintiva*. (1) Conduct exhibiting the external marks of moral conduct, but due to instinctive action of the individual nature

in given circumstances, and not to deliberate choice.

Instinctive morality is thus without knowledge of the nature of morality (of the distinction between good and evil) and accordingly without choice of the good as good.

At the same time it may be the basis upon which conscious morality is built up in the individual character. The facts of instinctive morality are exhibited in the conduct of races and of children before the stage of moral reflection has been reached. Thus the social instinct is held (as by Hutcheson, *Inquiry*, iii. 15) to be a 'principle of virtue.'

(W.R.S.)

(2) The term is also used to indicate a supposed moral instinct by which conduct is regulated without further intellectual or other preparation or cultivation. It is in so far a form of the native or intuitive theory. (J.M.B.)

Institution [Lat. *institutio*]: Ger. *Institution*; Fr. *institution*; Ital. *instituzione*. Any established and successful arrangement for carrying out a purpose, such as business, education, &c.

Certain of the most important, apart from private establishments, are (1) social institutions—those belonging to or administered by SOCIETY (q. v.); and (2) political institutions—those belonging to or administered by the STATE (q. v.). (J.M.B.)

Instruction [Lat. *instructio*, from *in* + *struere*, to build]: Ger. *Unterricht*; Fr. *instruction*; Ital. *istruzione*. The teaching act whereby the pupil is informed and also trained and stimulated to acquire knowledge and mental power. (C.De G.—J.M.B.)

It concerns itself chiefly with three things: the materials, the course, and the methods of instruction. The materials of instruction are the literature and science that constitute human knowledge. Its first stage is to enable the pupil to master the symbols that pertain to the acquisition and expression of knowledge; that is, the pupil must first be taught to read, to write, and to compute. He must next be taught the most patent facts that influence his intellectual, moral, and social life. The curriculum of study has varied with the complexity of life and the national ideals of the place and function of the individual. Democratic society demands the open door into every department of human activity, hence the ideal elementary curriculum in a system of universal education furnishes the essential elements of all human culture. It lays the foundations for the mastery of the quantitative sciences by mathematical training, and for the humanities by its instruction in history, literature, grammar, civics, and geography. In the secondary period the curriculum is usually limited to fewer branches, but still to those typical of all culture. It differs chiefly from the elementary course of study by its more intensive character and its more scientific methods.

The course of instruction depends upon the age, ability, and natural interests of the pupils. In the earlier years of school life its course of procedure is governed more by the psychological needs of the pupil than by the logical unfolding of the subject. During the high school period, however, the course of instruction follows much more closely the order of scientific procedure, causal relations being more emphasized than accidental ones. Herbart recommends the blending of three orders of progress, namely, (1) the merely presentative, which gives facts; (2) the analytic, which separates wholes into their elements; and (3) the synthetic, which presents in proper order and relation the manifold material of human culture.

The method of instruction varies with the knowledge and capacity of the pupil. In the early years the steps must be short, the relations of subject-matter simple, the strain upon the attention brief; while the presentation should be varied, vivacious, and interesting. In the high school the methods of instruction follow more closely the analogies of scientific investigation, being for the most part inductive in character and involving the lesser systems of relationship; thus, for example, botany will involve the function of organs as well as the naming and classification of plants; it will involve also a study of the relations of the plant to its environment of earth, air, temperature, and light. See METHOD (educational), ANALYSIS, and SYNTHESIS.

Literature: HERBART, Sci. of Educ. (trans. by Felkin), 135–93; ADAMS, Herbartian Psychol. applied to Educ., 81–187; H. SPENCER, Education; ROSENKRANZ, Philos. of Educ., 106–43; HARRIS, Psychol. Foundations of Educ., 321–400; BAIN, Educ. as a Science, 146–396; BALDWIN, Story of the Mind, chap. iii; DE DOMINICIS, Linee di Pedagogia, 3 vols. (1897); R. ARDIGÒ, La Scienza dell' Educazione (1893).   (C.DE G.)

Insurance [OF. *enseurer*, to insure]: Ger. *Versicherung*; Fr. *assurance*; Ital. *assi-*

curazione. A contract whereby the person insured pays a relatively small sum, in order to receive a larger sum in case of a contingency which would otherwise cause him a loss. The term assurance is also used, especially for other forms than life insurance.

It is the last clause which distinguishes insurance from GAMBLING (q. v.). Insurance contracts and gambling contracts are both wagers, and may be exactly alike in form; but if such a contract is made for contingent gain, it results in loss of utility and in commercial demoralization; while if it is made to prevent contingent loss, it results in increase of utility and in commercial security. See Jevons, *Theory of Political Economy*.   (A.T.H.)

A special theoretical interest attaches to insurance from the fact that it is based upon a statistical treatment of PROBABILITY (q. v.). The unit payment of premium, p, represents— apart from cost and profits to the insurance company — a sum which, multiplied by the coefficient a, gives the quantity b, that is

$$ap = b.$$

The quantity a is a function of the serial distribution of the annual payments with the subordinate coefficients a', a'', a''', &c.— the calculated numbers of years' payments of the insured based on (e. g.) vital statistics; that is

$$ap = (a' + a'' + a''' + \dots)\, p.$$

The quantity b is the sum of the face values of all the policies issued—apart from the settling of disputed claims, forfeitures, &c. We accordingly have, disregarding corrections for the fluctuations of b,

$$p = \frac{b}{a' + a'' + a''' + \dots},$$

giving a value of p which insures the company against loss. The point of interest is that p is a function of the a values, which are calculated probabilities of life in years of persons of different ages. The application of the method, in practice, to all sorts of social and moral facts only awaits the gathering of statistics to furnish data for the preparation of tables like those for mortality.   (J.M.B.)

Integral [Lat. *integer*, whole]: Ger. (1) *ganz*, (2) *ergänzend*; Fr. *intégral*; Ital. *integrale*. (1) Made up of parts in some way—primarily spacially—distinct: as in the phrase 'an integral whole.'

(2) Belonging, as one of distinct parts,

to a whole: as in the phrase 'an integral part.' Cf. INTEGRATION (different topics).

The phrase 'in some way distinct' leaves open the question of the separateness of the parts when taken out of relation to the whole. Distinct means here more than distinguishable, and in most cases—though possibly not always—it means separable also, an integral whole meaning a whole of integrated parts. (J.M.B.)

Integral (in mathematics): see CALCULUS.

Integration (and **Disintegration**) [Lat. *integer*, complete]: Ger. *Verknüpfung*; Fr. *intégration* (suggested); Ital. *integrazione*. Integration is the act or process of bringing together as parts of a whole, disintegration the act or process of separation into component parts.

According to Herbert Spencer and his school, the integration ('aggregation,' 'concentration,' 'consolidation') of matter is one of the two most general momenta of the evolution process, and disintegration of the process of dissolution: 'Evolution, under its simplest and most general aspect, is the integration of matter and concomitant dissipation of motion; while dissolution is the absorption of motion and concomitant disintegration of matter' (*First Princ.*, § 97).

These transformations are undergone not only by every aggregate, but also by its more or less separate parts, and are exemplified also by the combinations of the parts. The local integration of like units is segregation. Directly or indirectly, integration and disintegration characterize the development not only of physical and biological phenomena, but also of psychical and social phenomena (*First Princ.*, §§ 107–15; *Princ. of Psychol.*, §§ 58–76, 380–3; *Princ. of Sociol.*, §§ 224–7, 448–53, 763–7). They hold, moreover, of the totality of things; for 'the entire process of things, as displayed in the aggregate of the visible universe, is analogous to the entire process of things as displayed in the smallest aggregates' (*First Princ.*, § 183). Cf. INTEGRATION (in psychology). (A.C.A.Jr.)

Integration (in mathematics). The method of the integral CALCULUS (q. v.). (J.M.B.)

Integration (in psychology). (1) A mental combination in which the composing elements remain qualitatively distinguishable.

Used loosely for combination, association (see REDINTEGRATION), &c., until given this technical sense by Baldwin (*Elements of Psychol.*, 1893, Glossary). The suggestion of the term 'colligation,' as a translation of Verknüpfung (see Külpe, *Grundriss d. Psychol.*, 21, 285; Eng. trans., 1895, 21, 277), is directly in the face of this earlier use of integration, besides having been used (Ger. Colligation) in a different sense by earlier writers. See COLLIGATION; cf. COMBINATION, COMPLICATION, and FUSION. It also has analogy with the more general use of the term and with its mathematical use. (G.F.S.–J.M.B.)

(2) The combination of qualitatively different contents of presentation in the apprehension of a single object (cf. Stout, *Manual of Psychol.*). This is a special case of meaning (1); and as another term, COLLIGATION (q. v.), has been used in this sense (as opposed to the union of disparate elements of all sorts), the first meaning is preferred.

(3) Spencer's use carried over into psychology. See the preceding topic. (J.M.B., G.F.S.)

Intellect (or **Intelligence**) [Lat. *intelligere*, to understand]: Ger. *Verstand*; Fr. *intellect* (*intelligence*); Ital. *intelletto* (*intelligenza*). The faculty or capacity of knowing; intellection or, better, COGNITION (q.v.) denotes the process. The corresponding adjective is intellectual (together with intellective, adjective of intellection). (G.F.S.–J.M.B.)

The earlier English psychologists used the word understanding rather than intellect. Locke's great work was entitled *Essay on the Human Understanding*. The corresponding title in Reid is *Essay on the Intellectual Powers*; but even he makes little use of the word intellect. In general, intellect is used in some kind of antithesis to sensation. But the contrast takes different forms in different writers. In Locke it is the contrast between sensations as material on the one hand, and the mind's elaboration of this material on the other. In Cudworth and similar writers the antithesis is between higher and lower faculties of knowing, and assumes a Platonic form. 'There is a superior power of intellection and knowledge of a different nature from sense which is not terminated in mere seeming and appearance only, but in the truth and reality of things, whose objects are the eternal and immutable essences and natures of things and their unchangeable relations to one another' (Selby Bigge, *Brit. Moralists*, § 831).

There is a tendency to apply the term intellect more especially to the capacity for conceptual thinking. This does not hold in the same degree of the connected word intelligence. We speak freely of 'animal intelligence'; but the phrase 'animal intellect' is unusual. However, the restriction of the term to 'conceptual process' is by no means so fixed and definite as to justify us in including it in the definition.

As 'intellect' stands for the capacity, intellection stands for the process of knowing. Here again there is a tendency to restrict the term to conceptual thinking. Ward does so definitely and consistently. Croom-Robertson, on the other hand, gives the word the widest possible application, making it cover all forms of cognitive process. On the whole, if the term is to be employed at all, Robertson's usage appears preferable, as corresponding better to the generality of the words intellect and intelligence. See also CLASSIFICATION (of the mental functions). (G.F.S., J.M.B.)

Literature: see the textbooks of psychology; BIBLIOG. G, 1, *c*, 2, *p*; EISLER, Wörterb. d. philos. Begriffe, 'Intellect' (especially for scholastic distinctions under *Intellectus*).

Intellection: see INTELLECT.

Intellectualism: Ger. *Intellectualismus*; Fr. *intellectualisme*; Ital. *intellectualismo*. (1) In psychology: the theory which finds the intellectual or cognitive function more fundamental than the affective and conative, and accounts for the other functions in terms of it.

Applied especially to Herbart's doctrine of the 'mechanics of presentations,' of which feeling and will are functions.

(2) In philosophy: the theory which (*a*) makes the ultimate principle of the universe some form of thought or reason, or (*b*) holds that reality is completely intelligible to thought. Cf. IDEALISM (1).

It is opposed to VOLUNTARISM (q. v.) and to what might be called affectionism, which make will and feeling respectively the ultimate explaining principles. In this meaning it is especially applied to the philosophy of T. H. Green (*Prolegomena to Ethics*), who finds all reality to consist in 'intellectual relations.' (J.M.B.)

Intellectualism (aesthetic). Emphasis upon the intellectual content or ideal element in the aesthetic object, and the derivation of aesthetic value from this element. It is contrasted with SENSUALISM (q. v.) and FORMALISM (q. v.), and especially with emphasis upon the emotional aspects of aesthetic value. The theory of Hegel represents an intellectualistic tendency (see BEAUTY, IV). Cf. also RATIONALISM.

Literature: BERGMANN, Über das Schöne

(1887). See also under the topics referred to above. (J.H.T.)

Intelligence: see INTELLECT.

Intelligible: see LATIN AND SCHOLASTIC TERMINOLOGY, Glossary, 'intelligibilis'; and mundus intelligibilis under MUNDUS; also cf. Eisler, *Wörterb. d. philos. Begriffe*, 'Intelligibel.' (J.M.B.)

Intemperance: see TEMPERANCE.

Intension (in logic): for foreign equivalents see COMPREHENSION (in logic), with which it is generally in modern logic taken as synonymous.

The name is derived from the scholastic use of the term *intentio*. On the history of the word see Baynes, *New Analytic*, ii. 92. (R.A.)

Intensity (measurement of mental): see WEBER'S LAW, and FECHNER'S LAW, and cf. the following topic.

Intensity (mental) and **Intensive Magnitude** [Lat. *in* + *tendere*, to stretch]: Ger. *Intensität, Stärke* (strength, applied rather to stimulus), *intensive Grösse*; Fr. *intensité, grandeur intensive*; Ital. *intensità, quantità intensiva*. Intensive magnitude is a kind of quantity, inasmuch as it admits of the distinction of more and less. Besides saying absolutely that what possesses intensive magnitude exists or does not exist, we can say that it exists in various degrees. On the other hand, it is held to be distinguished from extensive quantity or magnitude, because the difference between one intensity and another cannot be exhibited as a separate intensive magnitude; whereas the difference between one extensive magnitude and another is itself an extensive magnitude.

In the gradual transition from blue to green, through intervening blue-greens and green-blues, each colour in the series is bluer than that which follows it and greener than that which precedes it. Such differences of more and less are intensive. If a green-blue be regarded as a compound of green and blue, such intensive variations may be described as variations in the relative degrees of green and blue. If the sensation called a green-blue is regarded as simple, the intensive variation must be supposed to affect merely the relative degrees of resemblance of the green-blue to pure green on the one hand and pure blue on the other. On either hypothesis the term degree is preferable to intensity. Degree may be used to denote all kinds of intensive magnitudes. But it seems convenient to give the term intensity a more restricted application. It means more especially that intensive quantity of sensation which is a function of the quantity of physical energy expended in its production. Thus a sound, without varying in pitch, may vary in intensity (loudness) according to the amplitude of the vibrations which affect the organ of hearing. On the other hand, variation in pitch, with approximately unaltered loudness, is a variation in intensive magnitude or degree, but not in intensity.

It is a question how far, if at all, the intensity of sensation is revivable in the corresponding mental image. Most psychologists assume that the difference is only one of degree. Others, like Lotze, say that mental images do not possess intensity at all.

It has been maintained, by Münsterberg and others, that intensity does not belong intrinsically to the sensation which is said to be more or less intense, and that it is not really an intensive magnitude. On this view, what we take for an intensive quantity is in truth the extensive quantity of some concomitant experience (kinaesthetic according to Münsterberg).

Others regard intensive distinctions as really not quantitative mentally, but in all cases qualitative. See QUANTITY, QUALITY, and PSYCHOPHYSICS. (G.F.S., J.M.B.)

Literature: the textbooks of psychology and treatises on psychophysics; KANT, Krit. d. reinen Vernunft (Eng. trans., Müller), 136. (J.M.B.)

Intent (psychical): Ger. *Meinen* (nearest; cf. Eisler, sub verbo), *Sagen-Wollen, im Sinne haben*; Fr. *intention*; Ital. *intento* (cf. foreign equivalents given for CONTENT and INTENTION). What intelligent consciousness 'means or intends' (James).

The word is not in general use in this sense. But some term is needed, and 'intent' seems peculiarly appropriate. The intent of consciousness at any moment is virtually identical with the object of consciousness at that moment. But the word 'intent,' in the application we propose, marks a certain point of view from which the object may be regarded.

In any process having unity of interest there must also be corresponding unity of object. If our interest be merely in attaining more full, definite, or vivid knowledge, the object as it becomes more perfectly known must be identified as the same with the object as less perfectly known. Hence it can be regarded in two aspects. As the process advances, the object progressively receives or tends to receive further specification. At any moment

its detail is only partially presented. Yet these partial presentations come before consciousness as appearances of one and the same total object which it is endeavouring to know in its completeness. Now this total object, considered as the goal of conscious endeavour, may be called with great appropriateness the intent of consciousness. For it is what the mind consciously means or intends, but has not yet attained. The same remarks apply to the case in which the interest involved is practical—in which there is an endeavour after the production of some result other than mere knowledge. The end pursued becomes progressively defined in the process of its achievement. So far as it is as yet indefinite, and therefore only partially developed in consciousness, it is an 'intent.'

The word CONTENT (q. v., 2) has sometimes been used in a sense more or less analogous to that which we propose for intent (i. e. by Bradley). But this usage is unfortunate. In the first place, the intent is precisely what consciousness does not contain. In the second place, the phrase 'content of consciousness' has a different application in current usage. It is applied to all special modifications of conscious experience, whatever may be their nature, and not merely to objects of consciousness. Indeed, it is sometimes questioned whether we ought to apply it to objects at all. In perceiving the distance of things in space, the experiences connected with movements of the eyes play an important part. These experiences are contents of consciousness; but they are not objects. We do not perceive them. What we do perceive is the external object and its spatial relation. Again, when we are pleased or displeased with anything, the pleasure or pain is a content of consciousness. But it is by no means always an object or an intent of consciousness. It only becomes so if, and so far as, we reflect on our subjective state. The same holds true of the self. There are always present in consciousness contents which belong to the self as distinguished from the not-self. But we are not always thinking of ourselves. Self-consciousness may be present in every moment of our waking lives. But the consciousness of self as a self is not invariably present. Finally, it would be correct to speak of the content of a 'merely feeling-consciousness' in the sense in which that phrase is used, among others, by T. H. Green. But it would not be correct to speak of such a consciousness as having an intent.

In relation to allied conceptions we may

remark that the intent is the consciousness of the general nature of the END-STATE (q. v.) of an intellectual process before it is reached; and in mental progress toward an IDEAL (q.v.) we have successive stages of 'intent.'

(G.F.S.—J.M.B.)

Intention [Lat. *in + tendere*, to stretch]: Ger. *Absicht*; Fr. *dessein*; Ital. *intenzione*. The purpose in view in any action, along with all the consequences of the action, so far as foreseen to be certain or probable.

The distinction in any act of *intentio, actio*, and *finis* is found in Gregory I (540–609 A. D.): cf. Ziegler, *Gesch. d. christ. Eth.*, 247. The definition above given agrees with that of Sidgwick (*Meth. of Eth.*). The intention is thus the action from the internal or agent's point of view; and the internal character of morality is brought out by laying emphasis on the intention rather than on the external results or consequences. Intentions have been distinguished as immediate or remote, outer or inner, direct or indirect, conscious or unconscious, formal or material. See J. S. Mackenzie, *Manual of Ethics* (3rd ed.), 60, 61.

(W.R.S.)

The best German usage of Absicht seems to be in agreement with this, the distinction between means and ends (Zwecke) being marked. Absicht is the end for which there may be alternative means (Meinong, *Psych.-eth. Untersuch. zur Werttheorie*, 94, 95; Höfler, *Psychologie*, 473, 518). Where, according to Meinong (loc. cit.), the end is directly pursued, without means, Absicht becomes Ziel—a usage not general, however. Cf. DESIGN, and see TERMINOLOGY (German). Intention, in the broader ethical sense of entire moral INTENT (q. v.), a determination of disposition or character, is rendered by the German Gesinnung (Höfler, loc. cit.). (J.M.B.)

Intention (first and second, in philosophy) [Schol. Lat. *intentio, prima et secunda*]. Used in a series of scholastic distinctions (both *intentio* and *intentionalis*), for which see LATIN AND SCHOLASTIC TERMINOLOGY, 13, 14; revived in modern philosophy to indicate the distinction of knowledge as direct (first) and reflective (second) intention. See INTENTION (in logic), and cf. REFLECTION.

Literature: HODGSON, Philos. of Reflection, Index; citations in EISLER, Wörterb. d. philos. Begriffe, 'Intentio'; GOCLENIUS, Lex. Philos., 253. (J.M.B.)

Intention (in law). The purpose of an act; it is often imputed, without regard to its actual existence.

A man acts at his peril. If loss to another naturally ensues from his voluntary act, he is liable, although it is neither intended by him nor due to his negligence (Holmes, *The Common Law*, 82; Holland, *Jurisprudence*, chap. viii. 93; Pollock, *Jurisprudence*, chap. vi. 138). Crime rests on intention; but he who does a criminal act is held to have intended the actual and natural result, although in fact he may have intended only a much less grave offence. Contracts rest on agreement, presupposing an intent to assume an obligation, but the law often implies the intent. 'Such an intent may be implied, although it be certain that it never actually existed, but not unless the parties are in such relations that each ought to have had it' (Beers *v.* Boston and Albany Railroad Co., 67 Conn. Law Reports, 425). Cf. RESPONSIBILITY (legal).

Literature: authorities cited above; also BENTHAM, Mor. and Legisl., i. chaps. vii, xii. § 2. (S.E.B.)

Intention (in logic) [Lat. *intentio*, with the same meaning in Aquinas (*Summa Theol.*, I. 9. 53, is the principal passage); in classical writers an act of attention (and so Aquinas, ibid., I. ii. 9. 38, art. 2, and elsewhere); from *in + tendere*, to stretch. Aquinas seems sometimes to use the term for a mode of being (ibid., I. ii. 9. 22) and sometimes for a relation (ibid., I. 9. 29, art. 1; 9. 76, art. 3, and esp. art. 4)]. A concept, as the result of attention.

First intentions are those concepts which are derived by comparing percepts, such as ordinary concepts of classes, relations, &c. *Second intentions* are those which are formed by observing and comparing first intentions. Thus the concept 'class' is formed by observing and comparing class-concepts and other objects. The special class-concept, *ens*, or what is, in the sense of including figments as well as realities, can only have originated in that way. Of relative second intentions, four are prominent—identity, otherness, co-existence, and incompossibility. Aquinas defined logic as the science of second intentions applied to first. (C.S.P.)

Interaction [Lat. *inter + actio*, action]: Ger. *Wechselwirkung*; Fr. *interaction*; Ital. *interazione*. (1) The relation between two or more relatively independent things or systems of change which advance, hinder, limit, or otherwise affect one another.

(2) The relation of mere uniform occurrence of such systems together.

An important case of supposed interaction is that of MIND AND BODY (q. v.), in the discussions of which interaction is usually used in the first sense (under the phrase *influxus physicus*). The theory of PRE-ESTABLISHED HARMONY (q. v.), which holds that mind and body are absolutely independent—their changes merely occurring together—sometimes construes interaction in the second sense, while retaining the term (in English). The more general application is to the relation of objects which 'act and react' in the external world. Cf. MUTUALITY, and RECIPROCITY (for which interaction is sometimes used as translation of the term Wechselwirkung in Kant's table of categories).

Literature: books on metaphysics. The classical citation is LOTZE, Metaphysics, Bk. I. chaps. v, vi. A late discussion is in ORMOND, Foundations of Knowledge, Pt. II. chap. vii. (J.M.B.)

Intercession [Lat. *intercessio*, from *intercedere*, to pass between]: Ger. *Fürbitte*; Fr. *intercession*; Ital. *intercessione*. (1) The office undertaken by Christ on his ascension into heaven, of perpetual mediation before the Father in behalf of those whom he had redeemed by his death. (2) Prayer offered by saints in heaven to God or Christ in behalf of persons still on earth or in purgatory.

The intercession of Christ is a common doctrine of all Christians, while that of the saints is an accepted article in the creeds of the Roman and Greek Catholic churches only. Some traces of belief in the efficacy of the intercession of the saints may be found among Protestants, but with the rejection of prayer to the saints as idolatry, belief in their intercessory function largely disappeared. (A.T.O.)

Interdependence: see DEPENDENCE, and RECIPROCITY.

Interest [Lat. *interest*, it concerns]: Ger. *Interesse*; Fr. *intérêt*; Ital. *interesse*. (1) The consciousness which accompanies mental tendencies of any sort, so far as they terminate upon mental objects or stimulate to the construction of them.

Considered in abstraction from the content or object upon which the tendency or disposition goes out, interest is usually considered a phase of feeling, and classed with the 'intellectual feelings.' Interest is always manifested by voluntary attention, to which it may be considered a stimulus, or of which it may be considered a result. 'Exploring' interest, or 'interest of curiosity,' is often distinguished from interest of 'custom,' habit, or preference; the former seeming to be more of the nature of a stimulation to intellectual function, and the latter a result of frequent function. This latter aspect it is which underlies the popular use of the term in the plural, 'interests' meaning prevailing and more permanent dispositions. We suggest that the distinction be marked by the terms 'actual' and 'dispositional' interest.

(2) Loosely used for personal advantage or good; as in the phrase 'it is in his interest to do so.' This meaning is not sufficiently exact to be technically useful. For the pedagogical doctrine of interest see below.

Literature: the general works on psychology and pedagogy. Special discussions of the psychology of interest are in the larger psychologies of JAMES, SULLY, and BALDWIN. (J.M.B.—G.F.S.)

Interest (doctrine of, in education). The doctrine that the interest naturally attaching to the ends for which pupils study should be awakened in the means (i. e. the studies) used for reaching them; and, conversely, that permanent interest in the ends should be fostered through the means.

When interest attaches to the end, but not to the means for reaching it, we have drudgery, as in the case of a workman who thinks only of the dollar, taking no pride or interest in the labour that earns it; on the other hand, when there is interest in the means but none in the end, we have play, not work. Interest is then only amusement. When, however, there is interest in the end to be attained by activity, and also in the means for reaching the end, we have the type of work desirable in education. A direct interest, therefore, should be aroused in the studies as the means of reaching the ends of education; this interest when thoroughly aroused has a reflex influence in developing true ideals of life and conduct. The mental attitude of the sculptor is the ideal one for the pupil, since the interest he feels in the statue as an end attaches to every stage of its creation. When this direct interest is moral as well as intellectual and aesthetic, then instruction becomes truly educative. See EDUCATIVE INSTRUCTION, and DISPOSITION.

Literature: HERBART, Sci. of Educ. (trans. by Felkin), 122–99; ZILLER, Allg. Päd., 330–89; McMURRY, Gen. Meth., 49–68; DE GARMO, Herbart and the Herbartians, chap. v; DEWEY, Interest as related to Will (2nd suppl. of the First Year-book of the

Herbart Society); HARRIS, Professor Dewey on Interest and the Will, Educ. Rev., May, 1896; Herbart's Doctrine of Interest, Educ. Rev., x. 71; BARNES, A Study of Children's Interests, Stud. in Educ.; SHAW, A Comparative Study on Children's Interests, Child-Study Mo. (July–August No., 1896); LUCKEY, Children's Interests, North-Western Mo., vii. 67, 96, 133, 156, 221, 245, 306, 335; BALDWIN, Story of the Mind, chap. viii; ARDIGO, Sci. dell' Educ. (1897). (C.DE G.)

Interest (in economics): Ger. *Zins*; Fr. *intérêt*; Ital. *interesse*. A payment for the use of capital; habitually expressed in terms per cent. per unit of time.

Payments in this form were regarded with grave disfavour by the canon law, and were veiled under the forms of compensation for loss suffered by the owner of the capital while it lay in others' hands; or also of a fictitious rent-charge (Ger. *Zins, Census*). But the historical starting-point of the modern interest system seems to be found in the contract of assurance whereby some of the partners in an enterprise would virtually insure the others against industrial risks (compare Ashley, *Eng. Econ. Hist.*).

The practical justification of interest is to be found in the large amount of capital which can be utilized by this motive, and the relatively small price which the community has to pay for the results achieved. The theoretical justification is more difficult. Some have sought to base it on the abstinence of the capitalist; others on the productivity of the capital. These productivity theories of interest were in past generations for the most part rather crude; under the influence of the Austrian theory of value they have been made extremely complex (compare Wieser, *Natural Value*). Still others (Jevons) have laid stress on the economic value of time as a basis of interest. Boehm-Bawerk's theory, which is perhaps the most influential one at the present day, is to be regarded as a development of the latter view.

It may be questioned whether the thing which these authors explain has any very close connection with the commercial phenomenon of interest, which is really an average or commutation of profits rather than a marginal increment of productivity.

Literature: BOEHM-BAWERK, Kapital und Kapitalzins (trans. into Eng. by Smart), a work of monumental excellence. (A.T.H.)

Interference [Lat. *inter + ferire*, to strike]: Ger. *Interferenz*; Fr. *interférence*; Ital. *interferenza*. (1) If two sound-waves of the same length are travelling in the same direction, we have a strengthening of the sound when the phases are coincident, and a neutralization of sound when they differ by half a wave-length. These phenomena are termed phenomena of auditory interference (Helmholtz, *Sensations of Tone*, 160). See BEATS.

(2) Similar phenomena arise from the interference of light-waves (visual interference). Many natural colour effects, among them iridescence, are due to the interference of rays reflected from thin films (see Tyndall, *Light*, 1885, 61).

(3) The word interference is used analogically of the mutual inhibition or cancellation of physiological or mental processes, as judged by the results (see Bergström, *Amer. J. of Psychol.*, v. 356, vi. 433). Similar conceptions are the *Vorstellungsconcurrenz* of the Herbartians, and the 'interference of imitation waves' discussed by Tarde, *Les lois de l'imitation*, 26 ff. See INHIBITION. (E.B.T.)

Intermediate State: Ger. *Zwischenzustand*; Fr. *état intermédiaire*; Ital. *stato intermedio*. The condition of souls during the interval between the death of the body and the final consummation or last judgment.

The belief in an intermediate state is a feature of Platonism, which connects it with the transmigration cycle. The Stoics also believed in a state of soul-existence after the death of the body, which was to continue till the end of the cycle of cosmic existence to which it belonged when it ceased to exist. The consummation, then, was to be dissolution. There is, properly speaking, no intermediate condition in Hindu eschatology. The soul perishes at death, and only Karma survives to lead to a reincarnation. The soul does not properly exist in the interval. Of the Christian confessions, the Roman Church teaches distinctly the existence of an intermediate state of purification (purgatory) for those who die penitent. Reformed Christianity does not dogmatize on the subject, though the condition of the soul between death and the judgment is conceived to be different from its condition after that event. Cf. HADES, and PURGATORY. (A.T.O.)

Intermittence Tone [Lat. *inter + mittere*, to send]: Ger. *Intermittenzton, Unterbrechungston*; Fr. *son (ton) d'intermittence*; Ital. *suono* (or *tono*) *d'intermittenza*. If a tone is interrupted at short intervals (by passing a card, e.g., to and fro between a tuning-fork and the ear), we have artificial BEATS

(q. v.); if, then, the intervals are made short enough, we have not beats, but a new tone, called the intermittence or interruption tone. The tone is theoretically important, as suggesting the origin of combination tones in rapid beats.

Literature: HELMHOLTZ, Sensations of Tone, 533; KÖNIG, Quelques Expériences d'acoustique, 139; MAYER, Amer. J. of Sci., 3 ser., viii. 241, and Philos. Mag., xlix. 352, 428; WUNDT, Physiol. Psychol. (4th ed.), i. 473, 476; EBBINGHAUS, Psychologie, i. 312. (E.B.T.)

Internal [Lat. *internus*]: Ger. *inner*; Fr. *interne*; Ital. *interno*. As applied to an individual experience the term has certain implications: (1) That conscious experience is in some way inside the body, and is so contrasted with things external to the body, and in more refined thought with the body itself (when the 'something inside the body' comes to be identified with the brain). (2) That individual experience, as such, is unshared by other individuals, and is so contrasted with external objects which can be present to different persons. (3) That the consciousness of experience is direct or immediate as opposed to the 'indirect' apprehension of external things through the medium of the senses. See discussion under EXPERIENCE; and cf. INTROJECTION, and KANT'S TERMINOLOGY (6, 7). (G.F.S.—J.M.B.)

Internal Speech (and **Song**): Ger. *inneres Sprechen* (*und Singen*); Fr. *parole* (*et chant*) *intérieure*; Ital. *parola* or *linguaggio* (*e canto*) *interni*, *endofasia* (Morselli). The content when speech is mentally revived with or without actual utterance. (J.M.B.—G.F.S.)

It indicates the class of mental states denoted popularly by the phrases having something to say 'in mind,' 'musing,' 'having tunes in one's head or ear' (internal song), together with the part played by such internal revivals in actual speech or song. Cf. KINAESTHETIC EQUIVALENTS. For the defects of speech which arise from the disturbance of this function see SPEECH (defects of), and AMNESIA. The adoption of Morselli's term Endophasia in English, French, and German (*Endophasie*) is recommended, and with it the term Endomusia is suggested for internal song (melody).

Literature: STRICKER, Ueber die Bewegungsvorstellungen; BALLET, La Parole intérieure; SÉGLAS, Les Troubles du Langage chez les Aliénés; JANET, Automatisme psychologique, and Rev. Philos., Nov., 1892; BASTIAN, Brain as Organ of Mind; STUMPF,

Tonpsychologie, i. Also (together with internal song): EGGER, La Parole intérieure; STRICKER, Langage et Musique; WALLASCHEK, Vtljsch. f. Musikwiss. (1891), Heft 1, and Zeitsch. f. Psychol., vi. Heft 1; LOTZE, Medicinische Psychol., 480; G. E. MÜLLER, Grundlegung d. Psychophysik, 288; BRAZIER, Rev. Philos., Oct., 1892; BALDWIN, Ment. Devel. in the Child and the Race, chap. xiv, and Philos. Rev., ii. (1893) 389 (in the last three many titles are given); MORSELLI, Semej. malat. ment. (1895). The literature of APHASIA may also be consulted. (J.M.B., G.F.S.)

International Law: Ger. *Völkerrecht*; Fr. *droit international*; Ital. *diritto internazionale*. The body of rules generally observed by civilized, sovereign states in their dealings with each other, and with one another's citizens or subjects. Less correctly termed the *law of nations*. D'Aguesseau was the first to remark that it was a law between nations, rather than a law of nations (*Œuvres*, ii. 337). Private international law: see CONFLICT OF LAWS.

The *ius fetiale* in ancient Rome was the law expounded by a priestly college, which determined the circumstances under which hostilities might be commenced against a foreign power, the forms of declaring war, &c. It was only a law for Rome. International law first grew into form under the hand of Grotius, mainly through his *Mare Liberum* (1608) and *De Iure Belli et Pacis* (1624), and received this name from Bentham (*Morals and Legislation*, chap. xvii. § 25).

Literature: VATTEL, Le Droit des Gens, &c.; WHEATON, Elements of Int. Law; PHILLIMORE, Int. Law; HAUTEFEUILLE, Des Droits des Nations neutres, &c.; FIELD, Draft Outlines of an Int. Code; BLUNTSCHLI, Das moderne Völkerrecht, &c.; CALVO, El Derecho Int.; WOOLSEY, Introd. to the Study of Int. Law. (S.E.B.)

Interpretation (in law) [Lat. *interpretatio*]: Ger. *Interpretation, Erklärung*; Fr. *interprétation*; Ital. *interpretazione*. The process of fixing the application of legal rules in particular cases (Pollock, *Jurisprudence*, 219, 224-5). It is legal or authoritative when it is the work of the proper representatives of the state; doctrinal when it is a mere matter of grammatical or logical construction proceeding from a private individual. In England and the United States the judicial interpretation of the law on any point, by the highest court, is itself law, but only as an official statement of what the law is and was before the decision upon that point (Markby's *Elements of Law*, § 72).

In Roman law interpretation was ordinarily sought in the first instance from jurisconsults holding no official station, and their opinions, certified for use in court, were received as authority. In the early empire a legal sanction was given to such opinions, when proceeding from certain persons who were invested with the *ius respondendi*, or found in certain treatises. In countries following the principles of the civil law, judicial precedents, in the line of interpretation, have little weight except that due to their intrinsic reasonableness.

Literature: PUFFENDORF, De Officio Hominis et Civis, i. chap. xvii, de Interpretatione; WOLFF, Inst. of the Law of Nature and of Nations, ii. chap. xix, de Interpretatione; LIEBER, Hermeneutics; DWARRIS, Statutes and Judicial Interpret.; BON, Instituzioni del Diritto pubblico internazionale. (S.E.B.)

Intersubjective [Lat. *inter* + *subiectus*, thrown under]: Ger. *intersubjectiv*; Fr. *intersubjectif*; Ital. *intersuggettivo*. (1) Applied to 'intercourse' between different consciousnesses at any stage of their development (Ward, *Naturalism and Agnosticism*).

(2) Applied to what is immediately present in each individual consciousness (was jeder in seinem Bewusstsein unmittelbar vorfindet; Volkelt, *Erfahrung und Denken*, 42; quoted by Eisler, *Wörterb. d. philos. Begriffe*, sub verbo). (J.M.B.)

Interval [Lat. *intervallum*, a space between]: Ger. *Zwischenzeit, Intervall*; Fr. *intervalle*; Ital. *intervallo*. (1) The time between two concrete events abstracted from the intervening events: a duration concretely determined.

Psychologically, an interval is always determined as a relative function of the events from which it is abstracted; objectively, an interval is determined by a controlled series of events (chronometric devices). (J.M.B., G.F.S.)

(2) In experiments upon the temporal consciousness: the 'filled' or 'empty' duration lying between two limiting stimuli. See TIME SENSE.

Literature (to 2): on the 'just noticeable interval' see MACH, Sitzber. d. Wien. Akad., 2, li. 142; EXNER, Pflüger's Arch., xi. 403; HAMLIN, Amer. J. of Psychol., vi. 564; WUNDT, Physiol. Psychol. (4th ed.), ii. 390 ff.; WEYER, Philos. Stud., xiv. 616, xv. 67. (E.B.T.)

Interval (in music). A musical term for difference of pitch between two tones.

'When two notes have different pitch numbers there is said to be an interval between them' (Helmholtz, *Sensations of Tone*, 13).

The intervals of the musical scale are sharply defined, and have, besides their distinctive names ('octave,' 'fifth,' &c.), various technical characterizations, as harmonic and melodic, simple and compound, augmented and diminished, consonant and dissonant, &c. Psychophysics has borrowed the word 'interval' from music, but employs it more freely, with sole reference to vibration ratios (Stumpf, *Tonpsychologie*, ii. 135). (E.B.T.)

Intoxication [Lat. *intoxicatus*, poisoned]: Ger. *Berauschung*; Fr. *enivrement*; Ital. *intossicazione*. (1) The effects of certain drugs or poisons.

(2) Frequently limited to alcoholic intoxication.

The state of intoxication usually makes itself felt soon after the absorption of the toxic substance. The mental symptoms which characterize it differ considerably according to the poison used; but a very typical characteristic is a state of excitement, release of inhibition, unrestrained conduct, inactivity, exaltation, incoherence. But these are only the characteristics outwardly most conspicuous; effects often differing from those just mentioned, and extending into less obvious alteration in mental processes, characterize the various forms of drug intoxication. These are described in general, and with regard to the more important intoxicants, under PSYCHIC EFFECT OF DRUGS. For the effects produced by alcohol, see ALCOHOLISM. For further details consult the works cited under those topics. (J.J.)

Intraselection [Lat. *intra*, within, + *selectio*]: Ger. *Intraselection, Kampf der Teile* (Roux); Fr. *sélection interne*; Ital. *selezione interna*. A process, held to be analogous to that of natural selection, by which the fittest cells, tissues, or parts within an organism prevail over others and ultimately supplant them.

Incidentally employed by Herbert Spencer in 1860 as an illustration in discussing social phenomena; the conception is generally attributed to Wilhelm Roux, 1881, and has been adopted by Weismann, to whom the term is due. Weismann thus summarizes: 'Just as there is a struggle for survival among the individuals of a species, and the fittest are victorious, so also do even the smallest living particles within the organism—not only cells and tissues, but also the smallest living particles or "biophores"—contend with one another, and those that succeed best in securing food and place grow and multiply rapidly, and so displace those that are less suitably equipped.' Weismann subsequently suggested the phrase 'histonal selection' for this process, and finally reached the hypothesis of struggle between the germinal elements. He speaks of the three principal stages of selection as (1) INDIVIDUAL (Ger. Personal-) SELECTION (Darwin and Wallace); (2) Histonal Selection (Roux); and (3) GERMINAL SELECTION (Weismann). See those topics; also SELECTION, and EXISTENCE (struggle for). The particular case of the selection of alternative functions, such as movements, has been called Functional Selection (see EXCESS).

Literature: HERBERT SPENCER, The Social Organism, Westminster Rev. (1860); W. ROUX, Der Kampf der Theile im Organismus (1881); A. WEISMANN, Effect of External Influences upon Development, Romanes Lecture (1894), and Germinal Selection, Monist (1895); DELAGE, La Structure du Protoplasma, &c.; BALDWIN, Ment. Devel. in the Child and the Race (2nd ed.), chap. vii. (C.LL.M.)

Intrinsic (1) and (2) **Extrinsic** [Lat. *in-* and *extrinsecus*]: Ger. *innerlich* (or *wesentlich*) and *äusserlich*; Fr. *in-* and *extrinsèque*; Ital. *in-* and *estrinseco*. (1) Necessarily, and (2) not necessarily, belonging to a thing or object of thought. (J.M.B.)

Intrinsic Value: Ger. *innerer Werth*; Fr. *valeur intrinsèque*; Ital. *valore intrinseco*. WORTH (q.v.) which belongs to an object or action in itself and is not due to its tendency to lead to some other object, or to promote a result. (W.R.S.)

Introjection [Lat. *intro*, within, + *iacere*, to throw]: Ger. *Introjection*; Fr. *introjection*; Ital. *introjezione*. The name given by Richard Avenarius to a certain theory, which he considers fallacious, of the relation between the cognitive consciousness of the individual and the external world cognized by it. This theory rests upon two assumptions: (1) that the individual consciousness is locally enclosed within the individual organism; (2) that its presentations of external things are merely internal images or copies of these things, taken to be so by reason of the process described below.

'Introjection' is closely akin to that 'ideal philosophy' which Reid ascribes to his predecessors, and in particular to Descartes, Locke, Berkeley, and Hume. There is no doubt that Reid was largely right in his account of the position of these philosophers. In the case of Descartes, we may refer to his theory of 'ideas' in the corporeal phantasy to which the mind directly applies itself, and which intervene between it and external things. Indeed, the whole of the Cartesian philosophy is dominated by the antithesis between 'ideas' as objects that lie exclusively within subjective consciousness, constituting its private property, and the world outside which these ideas are supposed to resemble or to which they correspond. Further, it is clear that Descartes is apt to confuse existence within the individual consciousness with existence within the individual organism. The soul is for him situated within the pineal gland, and it cannot directly cognize material objects unless they are in local proximity to it. As for Locke, we may refer to a passage quoted by Reid: 'Methinks the understanding is not much unlike a closet wholly shut from light, with only some little opening left to let in external visible resemblances or ideas of things without. Would the picture coming into such a dark room but stay there, and lie so orderly as to be found upon occasion, it would very much resemble the understanding of a man in reference to all objects of sight and the ideas of them.' The same kind of assumption is illustrated by Hamilton's theory that the primary qualities are perceived as 'in our organism,' and by his doctrine of sense-perception throughout (his ed. of Reid, ii. 881).

Avenarius describes and analyses this point of view with great precision, and he shows that it must emerge naturally and necessarily at a certain stage of mental growth. This feature of his theory has been considered especially original, and it is this to which many of the expositions of introjection as a process have been confined. He also shows the essential fallacy involved in it, and traces the disastrous consequences of this fallacy in philosophy and psychology. But Avenarius was anticipated, on the psychological side at least, by Herbart. Herbart, in his account of the growth of self-consciousness, traces the emergence of a point of view essentially the same as that which Avenarius calls introjection. 'The child at a certain stage comes to distinguish between those living things which contain within them representations of things external to them and those which do not.' This point of view is crude, but it constitutes an essential step in the development of the consciousness of self. The mode in which it originates will be most clearly exhibited by an example. 'A child sees a dog run away from a stick which is raised to strike it. He figures the stick as present to the dog, i. e. as in some sense inside the dog. Otherwise the dog would not run away (for in running away it is moved from within, not from without).' But it is obviously not the real stick which he thinks of in this way; for he sees the real stick outside of the dog. It is, therefore, an unreal stick, i. e. the representation or image or idea of the stick. For an image is that which is like a thing and is nevertheless not the thing itself. Thus the child regards the dog as having a representation in the way of an image or copy of what is without it. This point of view, acquired in the first instance by observation of other living things, he easily and inevitably transfers to his own case, inasmuch as he comports himself towards external things in an essentially similar way. He is now, therefore, able to regard the various objects of his consciousness as representative images of something other than themselves. These images he can carry about inside him, whether the reality they represent is present to his senses or not. He thus has an idea of what an idea or perception is. It is the counterpart inside him of a thing outside him. The conception is crude and inaccurate, and will not stand the test of reflective criticism. But it is none the less an indispensable step in the development of self-consciousness (Herbart, *Psychol. als Wiss.*, § 133). Avenarius gives the name introjection to the view which results from the carrying over to or into one's own body of this dualism between images and things.

As Reid waged war on the 'ideal theory,' so Avenarius wages war on the philosophical and psychological developments of 'introjection' as a point of view. He opposes to it the doctrine of 'essential co-ordination.' The self and the environment of which it takes cognizance are in direct and essential relation. The one cannot exist apart from the other. When a man says that he sees a tree before him, he means the actual tree, not an image of it. He means that he sees something outside him, not inside him. He ought to interpret the same words as used by another man in strictly the same sense. He ought to infer from them that the other man sees a tree outside him, and not a picture of the tree inside him. To adopt the second alternative is the fallacy of introjection. It is a fallacy because the interpretation of another man's

words depends on the analogy of our own experience. But in our own experience the object as part of our own external environment is the object seen; and if we suppose it absent, the seeing of it is logically abolished also. Hence, in the case of the other man, we must infer that what he sees is part of his external environment, not a complex of sensations inside him (e. g. somehow localized in his brain) and 'projected' outside him. The fallacy of introjection does not end here. Avenarius, like Herbart, lays stress on the fact that the point of view gained first by a crude inference from the actions of our fellow men or of animals is transferred by a back-stroke to ourselves. Hence the introjection theory may be expressed in the general formula, 'all perceived parts of our environment—as perceived—are nothing but presentations in us' (R. Avenarius, 'Bemerkungen zum Begriff des Gegenstandes der Psychologie,' in *Vtljsch. f. wiss. Philos.*, xviii. 143 ff.).

Literature: AVENARIUS, as cited, also Menschlicher Weltbegriff, and Krit. d. reinen Erfahrung. For a brief statement in English see WARD, Naturalism and Agnosticism, ii. 172; also BALDWIN (for a development somewhat similar), Ment. Devel. in the Child and the Race, chap. xi. § 3.   (G.F.S.)

The point of view of introjection is defended (as against Avenarius) by Jerusalem (*Urtheilsfunction*; see also in *Vtljsch. f. wiss. Philos.*, xviii. 170), who calls his own theory of judgment 'Introjectionstheorie.' See also the notice, with citations, in Eisler, *Wörterb. d. philos. Begriffe*, sub verbo.   (J.M.B.)

Introspection [Lat. *intro*, within, + *spectus*, seen]: Ger. *innere Wahrnehmung, Selbstbeobachtung*; Fr. *introspection, observation interne*; Ital. *introspezione, coscienza riflessa in sè*. Attention on the part of an individual to his own mental states and processes, as they occur, with a view of knowing more about them.

Locke uses the term reflection for 'the notice which the mind takes of its own operations' (*Essay*, ii. chap. i. § 4). Other writers speak of an 'inner sense' or 'inner perception.' The suggested analogy to 'outer sense' and 'outer perception' is misleading.

Literature: see INTROSPECTIVE METHOD.
                    (G.F.S.—J.M.B.)

Introspective Method: Ger. *Methode der inneren Wahrnehmung* (or *Selbstbeobachtung*); Fr. *méthode introspective*; Ital. *metodo introspettivo*. The systematic use of introspection for scientific purposes.

The introspective method is essential to psychology, and it has been followed by psychological writers in all ages, from Plato and Aristotle downward. A main advantage of the method of experiment in psychology is that it gives opportunity for introspection under test conditions. Some psychologists may be called introspective in a special sense, because they make more exclusive use of the method than others. Among these are St. Augustine, Hobbes, Locke, Berkeley, Hume, and the earlier English psychologists in general. But no psychologist ever confined his procedure to mere introspection. It was always more or less supplemented by inference from resulting products to producing processes, and by observation of the manifestations of mental process in other minds. Cf. PSYCHOLOGY.

Literature: BENEKE, Die neue Psychol., Aufsätze 1 und 2; HERBART, Psychol. als Wiss., Zweiter Theil, Erster Abschnitt, chap. v; BRENTANO, Psychol., chap. ii; JAMES, Princ. of Psychol., i. 115 f.; LADD, Psychol., Descrip. and Explan., chap. ii; VIGNOLI, La legge fondamentale dell' intelligenza (1876); VILLA, Psicol. contemporanea; and textbooks of psychology in general. (G.F.S.)

Intuition [Lat. *intueri*, to look at]: Ger. *Anschauung*, *Intuition* (see TERMINOLOGY, German, sub verbo); Fr. *intuition*; Ital. *intuito*, *intuizione*. (1) Sense intuition: the final stage in the mental determination of an external object, consisting in a synthesis of elements in space and time.

This meaning is in so far common with the philosophical meaning of intuition that it leaves open to analysis the discovery of the sensational and other elements which go into the determination, and in default of such analysis makes the intuition of objects an act of direct apprehension. See INTUITION (in philosophy).

(2) Motor intuition: ready command of a complex action or series of actions independently of conscious preparation; and the act itself considered as a motor synthesis.

Applied to the act itself which is thus performed; a phrase which corresponds to percept, the object of sense-intuition. Some writers use synergy for the process of motor synthesis itself, and synerg might be employed for the resulting action, co-ordinate with percept. This would be convenient in various discussions, such as the loss or impairment of the 'synerg' in apraxia, the relation of motor and sensory elements—that is, of percept and synerg—in all concrete determinations of objects. The adjective form, 'synergic,' would also lend itself to use.

Literature: sense intuition: see the general works on psychology and the titles given under EXTERNAL WORLD, PERCEPTION, and EPISTEMOLOGY. Motor intuition: besides the foregoing, see the titles under HABIT, SYNERGY, and APRAXIA; also WARD, Mind, July, 1893, and Oct., 1894; MÜNSTERBERG, Die Willenshandlung; MOSCI, Le forme dell' intuizione (1881). (J.M.B., G.F.S.)

Intuition (in educational method). Primarily, the grasp of knowledge through the use of the senses; concrete ways of apprehending knowledge.

The middle ages had departed far from sense methods of teaching; they emphasized the word or the symbol above the thing symbolized. Comenius and Pestalozzi brought the world of words and that of things into intimate relation again, by laying much stress on sense-perception in education. Herbart made a further advance by urging the importance of apperception. The perception itself is important only when fully apprehended. Cf. METHOD.

Literature: COMENIUS, The Great Didactic; PESTALOZZI, How Gertrude teaches her Children; BOWEN, Froebel, 4, 156, 159; ROSENKRANZ, Philos. of Educ., 76–81. (C.DE G.)

Intuition (moral): Ger. *sittliche Intuition*; Fr. *intuition morale*; Ital. *intuizione morale*. The immediate apprehension, apart from experience, of moral principles or of the moral quality of action.

Whether there are any moral intuitions, in the strict sense of the term, is a question of controversy between intuitive and empirical writers; whether, if there are such intuitions, they are perceptions of the moral quality of particular actions, or of general principles of morality, is a question which divides the intuitionist writers themselves. See INTUITIONAL ETHICS. (W.R.S.)

Intuition (in philosophy): Ger. *Intuition*, *Anschauung* (see TERMINOLOGY, German); Fr. *intuition*; Ital. *intuizione*, *intuito*. Immediate or direct apprehension, perception, judgment, cognition, and the results of such processes.

The root-idea of this term is that of directness or IMMEDIACY (q. v., different forms) in contrast to abstractive or representative knowledge, or, more frequently, to forms of knowledge which are mediated by a discursive process. This fundamental idea appears in all, or nearly all, of the various senses in which the term is used.

(1) Of sense-perception: to denote its presumed immediacy; to denote perception proper as objective in contrast to sensation as subjective; to denote the perception of present objects in contrast to reproductive and productive imagination; to denote the perception of individual objects in contrast to conception and thought. Sensuous cognition in general is sometimes termed sense-intuition or intuitive knowledge. See INTUITION (second topic above). (2) Of self-consciousness as the perception of inner states (internal sense). Also, by many writers, of self-consciousness as the perception of the ego: see below, (5). (3) In aesthetics: to designate the act of aesthetic appreciation or contemplation, or the insight of the artist into aesthetic values. (4) Of cognition or knowledge: to denote sense-perception or self-consciousness, see above, (1) and (2); to distinguish intuitive knowledge, in which all the component elements can be directly presented, from symbolic knowledge (Leibnitz, *Meditationes de Cognitione, Veritate et Ideis*, 1684); to denote the immediate perception of the connection between subject and predicate, this connection being conceived as the essence of knowledge (Locke, *Essay concerning Human Understanding*, IV. ii. 1); to denote the knowledge of first truths, see below, (5). (5) To denote original, self-evident, and necessary first principles, both theoretical and practical, and the (primary) consciousness of them (Sir William Hamilton, *Reid's Works*, note A, v. 3; see also INTUITIONALISM). (6) By Kant, who distinguished between empirical intuitions of objects through sensation (empirische Anschauungen, intuitions *a posteriori*) and pure intuition (intuition *a priori*: space and time as the form of sensibility; *Krit. d. reinen Vernunft, Werke*, Hartenstein, 2nd ed., iii. 55–6, 60, 65). It is to be noted, however, that high authorities have of late questioned the equivalence of intuition and the Kantian Anschauung (E. Caird, *The Crit. Philos. of Kant*, 1889, i. p. xi; see also KANT'S TERMINOLOGY). (7) In the phrase intellectual intuition: to denote an immediate function of thought or understanding akin to the direct perception of sense. Such would be required, according to Kant, to secure a positive knowledge of things-in-themselves, while the absence of it is the condition which necessitates for human understanding the distinction between mechanism and teleology as well as between possibility

and actuality, necessity and contingency (*Werke*, Hartenstein, 2nd ed., iii. 216–24, v. 408–23). Fichte ascribes to intellectual intuition the self-knowledge of the ego; Schelling makes it the medium of man's knowledge of the absolute (*Philos. Briefe ü. Dogmatismus u. Kriticismus*, viii). See also below, (8). (8) To denote the spiritual illumination of the mystics and the supernal vision of God. Intellectual intuition is used in this sense among the German mystics. The term without the adjective is employed also, by many writers who are not to be classed as mystics, to describe the moral and the religious consciousness considered as immediate organs of spiritual truth.

Literature: general works on philosophy and psychology; references under INTUITIONISM, and the other topics INTUITION; EISLER, Wörterb. d. philos. Begriffe, 'Anschauung.' (A.C.A.Jr.)

Intuitional Ethics: Ger. *Intuitions-Ethik*; Fr. *morale* (or *éthique*) *intuitive* (or *intuitionniste*); Ital. *etica intuitiva*. Any theory which recognizes moral intuitions. See ETHICAL THEORIES.

Intuitional ethics depends upon the assumption that man has a special faculty or capacity for recognizing moral distinctions. According to the different views held as to the nature and objects of this faculty, three main forms of intuitional ethics have been distinguished: (1) aesthetic or perceptional intuitionism, according to which the moral value of particular actions and affections is apprehended intuitively either singly (as held by Shaftesbury and Hutcheson) or relatively to one another (as in the view of Martineau, *Types of Ethical Theory*, 1885, that motives or stimuli to action form a sort of moral hierarchy, in which the preference of a lower to a higher is always condemned, and the preference of a higher to a lower always approved by conscience); (2) dogmatic intuitionism (the common scholastic theory, and the view of Butler in his *Dissertation on Virtue*, of Richard Price and Thomas Reid, and more recently of McCosh and Calderwood), according to which the rightness or wrongness of classes or kinds of actions—or, as some writers hold, of classes or kinds of motives—is intuitively known; (3) philosophical intuitionism, in which a complete synthesis of practical rules is sought, and the practical reason or conscience is held to lay down one universal rule capable of distinguishing good from evil (e. g. the categorical imperative of Kant). Cf. Sidgwick, *Meth. of Eth.*, I. vi, viii; III. (w.r.s.)

Intuitionism or **Intuitionalism**: Ger. *Intuitionismus*; Fr. *intuitionnisme*; Ital. *intuizionismo*. (1) These terms are sometimes employed to describe that form of ethical and religious philosophy which looks on the moral and the religious nature as immediate organs of spiritual truth. See INTUITION (in philosophy), 8.

(2) They are also used in designation of systems of philosophy which are based upon an (assumed) intellectual intuition of absolute reality. See INTUITION (7).

(3) They are employed most specifically, and most frequently in the history of later modern thought, to denote the philosophy which makes knowledge and life dependent on a body of immediately given self-evident and necessary first truths. See INTUITION (5).

These last constitute the fundamental principles alike of theory and of practice. They are held to be independent of experience, in that they are not derived from it nor established by it, but supply it with a basis and with norms, and so make it possible. Associationism, on the contrary, looks on these principles and their apparent evidence as products of experience; while evolution, enlarging the doctrine of associationism by the addition of heredity, views them as native to the individual but developed in the race (Spencer, *Princ. of Psychol.*, § 208; *Princ. of Eth.*, §§ 40–7). The intuitive first truths are variously enumerated by different writers. All intuitionalists may be said to include under the first principles of knowledge the formal (concepts and) judgments which make up the organic framework of thought, although the list is variously drawn (the causal principle is, perhaps, the one which is postulated with the nearest approach to universality after the first principles of logic and mathematics). Others, and especially the members of the Scottish school, add to these principles judgments (or perceptions) of content, maintaining, for example, that there is an immediate, self-evident, and necessary knowledge of external reality, or, at least, that sense-perception includes such a factor among others, that self-consciousness supplies a direct and indubitable cognition of the ego, &c. The existence of intuitive first principles of religion is also asserted, but less frequently: the majority of intuitionalistic thinkers, for instance, now recognize that there is no immediate intuition of God.

Cf. INTUITIONAL ETHICS, A PRIORI, ASSOCIATIONISM, COMMON SENSE, INNATE IDEAS, INTUITION, REALISM, SCOTTISH PHILOSOPHY, and TESTS OF TRUTH.

Literature: TH. REID, Intellectual and Active Powers; Sir WM. HAMILTON, Reid's Works, note A; J. S. MILL, Exam. of Hamilton's Philos.; J. McCOSH, The Scottish Philos., The Intuitions of the Mind, and Realistic Philos.; H. CALDERWOOD, Handb. of Mor. Philos.; H. SIDGWICK, Meth. of Eth., iii; J. MARTINEAU, Types of Ethical Theory, ii; R. FLINT, Theism, 79–86, and Appendix X. (A.C.A.JR.)

Besides the Scottish philosophers proper—and their successors—by whom the intuitional philosophy has been developed under that name, a point of view essentially intuitional has been held by certain French realistic thinkers (Laromiguière, Maine de Biran, Cousin, Janet) who were influenced directly by Reid. A similar influence has coloured philosophy in America (McCosh, Porter, Hopkins). Intuition has further lent itself in turn to the uses of theological philosophy, both Catholic and Protestant, most conspicuously again in Scotland and the United States, in both of which countries, however, the intuitionalistic and realistic point of view is rapidly yielding to certain forms of idealistic thought. (J.M.B.)

Intuitive Morality: see INTUITION (moral).

Invagination [Lat. *in* + *vagina*, a sheath]: Ger. *Einstülpung*; Fr. *invagination*; Ital. *invaginazione*. The inpushing or folding process whereby a simple cell-layer may more or less completely enclose a cavity.

In development many organs arise by invagination, and the hollow vesicle or BLASTOSPHERE (q. v.) is thus generally converted into a two-layered cup or GASTRULA (q. v.).

The generalization that the formation of a two-layered BLASTODERM (q.v.) is typically produced by the invagination of a hollow spherical one-layered vesicle is due to Haeckel. See GASTRAEA THEORY.

Literature: HAECKEL, Generelle Morphol. (1866); F. M. BALFOUR, Compar. Embryol. (1880); and the citations given under EMBRYO. (C.LL.M.–E.S.G.)

Invariability: see VARIABLE, and UNIFORMITY.

Invention [Lat. *in* + *venire*, to find]: Ger. (1),(3) *Erfindung (Erdichtung)*,(2) *Erneuerung* (Barth); Fr. *invention*; Ital. *invenzione*. (1) In psychology: a relatively new determination in the sphere of imagination and thought, judged by the thinker to be true or valuable.

Inventions are, in a general way, distinguished from mere fancies, on the one hand, by their acceptance as true or valuable; and they are more than the reinstatement of old thoughts, being 'relatively new.' Narrower restriction of the term would bring it within the range of controversy. Some of the questions which arise about invention are: the distinction of inventions from other sorts of mental constructions within the so-called imaginative function; the process of selection of inventions as true or valuable; the mechanism in general whereby relative novelty is reached; the plane of attainment from which the particular invention is projected; the relative independence of the individual thinker in appraising his inventions, as over against the influence of social suggestion. The terms SELECTION (mental), SELECTIVE THINKING, DETERMINATION (mental), RELATIVE SUGGESTION, &c. (see those terms), are used for the progressive advance of the inventive process through successive stages. The process of reaching inventions is also called invention.

Considerable literature has been devoted to the development of the child with more particular reference to his active life. The principles of his activity had heretofore seemed to fall under one or other of the two principles of invention and imitation; and in so far as they were considered separate and independent types of action, the child's conduct was interpreted in one category or the other. There was no common meeting-place for these two types. This is the older view; a view set in the usages of language itself, which contrasts strongly the imitative, copying, uninventive action (and child) with the inventive, self-active, spontaneous action (and child). This contrast as usually made is, however, too sharp. The recent psychological analyses of the child's activities show that imitativeness and inventiveness are really two phases of all action; that the terms are expressions of emphasis rather than of real and vital difference.

The first consideration which tends to diminish the degree of separation between an imitative and an inventive action concerns the definition of IMITATION (q. v.) itself. A more adequate analysis of imitation has shown that we cannot limit that term to the intentional conscious procedure of the child by which he closely observes some other person and then himself carries out the action which that person performs before him. In the first place, many imitations are performed without the child's consciously observing the model or knowing that he is acting with reference to a particular deed of another. Again, it is not necessary that the child should imitate another person, or another thing, than his own self. When he looks at his own hands accidentally placed in this position or that, or at any attitude of his into which the circumstances of the time may have forced him, these he may imitate, aiming to do intentionally or spontaneously what was done before by his members accidentally or by external constraint. So also he may imitate his own mind as well as his own body. When he has before him something to imitate—that is, before his mind—it does not matter whether there be or be not outside of him another person actually doing the thing he is imitating. It may be that the model he aims to reproduce is the result of his own thought, imagination, fancy. Suppose a child opening his mind in the early morning, as he lies in bed in the dark, and thinking over the doings of the preceding day. Something of a striking character comes into his mind from the preceding day's sport, and he proceeds to jump from his bed and perform the act again and again. In this case he is imitating his own action of the preceding day, or—if we interpret his present state—he is imitating the image or memory which has arisen in his mind spontaneously. All this is so plainly the same sort of action as that in which the model is set up by some one else, that it is now called 'self-imitation.' Whenever the child thinks of anything he can do, and then proceeds to do it in a way which reproduces a result like that of which he thinks, then he is imitating, and his act is self-imitation.

When we come to inquire into invention, we get a result which at once brings that form of action into connection with self-imitation. The old idea that the mind can create things, ideas, plans, &c., 'out of whole cloth,' so to speak, has been given up. We now know that the mind, even that of the great genius, is held down to the actual store of materials which he has acquired in his lifetime. He must call up from the stores of his memory images, earlier thoughts, reminiscences of action, &c., which are 'fit' to go into the scheme of his invention. 'Imagination never creates' has now become a proverb, and recent advances have tended in the direction of making it more than ever true.

So what the inventor does is really to meditate on what he already knows, to consider the possibilities of new combinations of the data with which he is already so familiar. That is the reason we never hear of a farmer inventing an electric light, nor of a statesman getting rich by taking out patents for new machines. Each invents only in the field in which he has worked so thoroughly and so long that his mind is stored with knowledge, both of facts and of principles. This means that the inventor must, as a preliminary, fall into the state described above as one of self-imitation. He must bring up before his mind materials already familiar, to be used as a more or less adequate copy for the new construction which he is to make. He must cause to pass before him this and that possible combination, this and the other possible situation, in order that his sense of fitness may go forth critically for the selection of the more available.

Putting together the two points now made, we see that the relation of invention to imitation is very close indeed. The child, or the man, must be a facile imitator before he can be an inventor. He must become an adept in the methods of using his materials of memory and imagination. He must by constant self-imitation practise the combinations he already knows, and by so doing come to see the possible forms of novelty into which the materials may be cast.

Furthermore, the study of children has shown that the connection between these functions is even closer than this. We find that the child goes on to invent largely in proportion as he actually carries his imitations out into action. He sets out to reproduce something which another person or his own fancy suggests, and just by carrying out this purely imitative purpose he falls into new ways of action or thought which seem to him more valuable. This is especially true when the function in question allows of large variations; when the hand is used or the tongue—members which, by their great flexibility, give various possibilities of modified result. The child soon learns these possibilities, begins to use his imitative functions with view to securing variations on the models, and loves to produce relatively new and inventive results. So, too, as he becomes strenuous, using his members vigorously and with less exact control, the performance flows over the limits of the model, so to speak, and gives to the result new and possibly valuable phases.

The general conclusion, therefore, is that the child is not 'either an imitator or an inventor'; on the contrary, he is always in some degree both at once. Teachers tend sometimes to disparage the imitative scholar in contrast with the more inventive one. But this is generally a mistaken attitude. Imitation is the natural schoolmaster to invention. Imitation may, of course, be made parrot-like, a matter of mere repetition, especially when the teacher approaches it with such a disparaging attitude. But the average scholar is dependent upon imitation for the normal growth of his faculties—more, much more, upon that than upon any other one factor—and the recognition of the essential union of imitation and invention which psychology now teaches is, in the teacher's hand, the best means of furthering this progress.

(2) In sociology : any relatively new idea which gains currency in society. For the part assigned to invention by current sociological theories see Social Organization (also for literary references).

(3) A mechanical device for utilizing power, doing work, &c. The popular distinction between invention and discovery—the former giving something not found in nature, and the latter something realized in nature—is only partially justified from a psychological point of view.

The German term Erdichtung is applied to the more poetic and fanciful, and so to the less strictly true, and even to the false, productions of the imagination. It is more nearly equivalent to the English fancy or imagination in the phrases 'drawing on the imagination,' 'fanciful fabrication,' &c., a meaning expressed in the terms 'practising,' 'romancing,' &c., which do not imply intentional deception. The German Erneuerung is suggested by Barth (*Philos. d. Gesch. als Sociol.*, i. 212) to include both invention (3) (Erfindung) and discovery (Entdeckung).

Literature (psychological): Paulhan, Rev. Philos.; Royce, Studies in Good and Evil, chap. ix, and Psychol. Rev., v. (1898) 113; James, The Will to Believe, 216 f., 255 f.; Stout, Analytic Psychol., Bk. II. chap. vi; Simmel, Arch. f. syst. Philos., i. 34 ff.; Baldwin, Soc. and Eth. Interpret., Pt. II, and Psychol. Rev., January, 1898. (J.M.B., G.F.S.)

Invention (in anthropology): see Invention (in psychology), particularly meaning

(3), as depending upon or arising from meaning (1). (J.M.B.)

The anthropologist's interest in invention lies in its relation to mental evolution, as indicated by an increased utilization of natural resources for comfort and material prosperity, for the arts and sciences, for the pleasures and civilization of life. In the early history of human invention is thus contained the beginning of that struggle for human supremacy which constitutes the true culture history of mankind. The directions which such studies of the evolution of invention have taken are various : on the material and industrial side may be mentioned the arts and implements concerned with the cultivation of the earth, with the elaboration of fibrous textures for clothing, with war and the chase, with the preparation of food ; the habitations of man in cave and shelter, in tent and hut and house ; the transportation of man and goods by land and sea. On the mental side may be mentioned the development of the social life through the invention of money and a system of barter ; the development of writing and drawing ; the inventions of art and decoration, of music and the dance, the composition of poetry, myth, and tradition ; the discoveries of nature's laws ; the means of counting and weighing and measuring, and other rudiments of scientific lore.

The history of invention likewise suggests the problem of individual variation. The capacity for independence and originality is always opposed by the conservative tendencies in society and the power of the *status quo*. The psychology of invention considers the determining factors in such original variations, and the processes which constitute or promote it.

Literature: general treatises on ANTHROPOLOGY (q. v.) and the history of CULTURE (q. v.). Also especially O. T. MASON, The Origin of Invention (1895); discussion in Psychol. Rev., v. 1, 113, 307; GROOS, The Play of Man (Eng. trans.), on play-experimentation as a factor in invention (orig. p. 55); SOURIAU, Théorie de l'Invention ; RIBOT, L'Imagination créatrice (1900); PAULHAN, Psychol. de l'Invention (1901). (J.J.)

Inversion (sexual): see PERVERSION (sexual).

Invertebrate [Lat. *invertebratus*, without vertebrae]: Ger. *wirbellos* ; Fr. *invertébré* ; Ital. *invertebrato*. Applied to any animal not belonging to the sub-kingdom of vertebrates.

Originally it was supposed that the presence or absence of a vertebral column was a sufficient diagnostic mark. It is known now that the lowest undoubted members of the true vertebrata have no vertebrae, the vertebral axis being replaced by the notochord and its fibrous sheaths (marsipobranchs, i. e. lampreys, &c.); but their entire structure proves that these animals are closely related to the vertebrates only, and not to any invertebrate, hence the term invertebrate is still used with the original limitations, although in the strict etymological sense it is not correctly applied. (C.S.M.)

Investment [Lat. *investire*, to invest]: Ger. *Kapitalanlage* ; Fr. *placement* ; Ital. *investimento*. The use of capital with a view to profit ; also, the form which the capital takes when thus used.

Looking at the transaction from the private standpoint, a property owner transfers a certain amount of money either to labourers or to other property owners, in the hope of receiving a larger amount of money in the future by the sale of products acquired or made. Looking at it from the public standpoint, the property owners as a class put the labourers in a position to consume the wealth over which the property rights have extended, in the expectation that the products of the labour to which they thereby acquire rights will more than replace the wealth thus consumed. In practice, the term investment is chiefly applied to permanent investments like real estate or securities. (A.T.H.)

Invisible World: see WORLD.

Involuntary (**Action,** &c.): Ger. (1) *widerstrebend* ; Fr. (1) *contre-volontaire* (suggested); Ital. (1) *controvolontario* (or *antagonistico*), (2), (3) *involontario*. (1) Action contrary to an actual volition, or to a volition which would have existed had there been time and opportunity to form it : contraconative action. (2) NON-VOLUNTARY (q. v.) or aconative action. (3) NON-VOLITIONAL (q. v.) action, i. e. action which is not due to an express 'fiat' of the will.

Meaning (1) is recommended in accordance with the scheme given under ACTION.
(G.F.S.–J.M.B.)

Involuntary Action (pathological): Ger. *unwillkürliche Thätigkeit* ; Fr. *action involontaire* ; Ital. *azione involontaria*. In a pathological sense an involuntary action is one which takes place in spite of the effort of the will to prevent it, thus implying some defective state of control or inhibition. Such states are considered under WILL (defects of). (J.J.)

Involution [Lat. *in* + *volvere*, to roll]: Ger. *Involution*; Fr. *involution*; Ital. *involuzione*. A term of SYMBOLIC LOGIC (q.v.) borrowed from algebra, where it means the raising of a base to a power. In logic it has two different senses. (1) Relative involution: let *lwm* denote any lover of a well-wisher of a man. That is, any individual *A* is denoted by *lwm*, provided there are in existence individuals *B* and *C* (who may be identical with each other or with *A*), such that *A* loves *B*, while *B* wishes well to *C*, and *C* is a man. Further, let $l\,^{w}m$ denote any individual *A*, if, and only if, there is in existence an individual *C*, who is a man, and who is such that taking any individual *B* whatever, if *B* is a well-wisher of *C*, then *A* is a lover of *B*. The operation of combining *l* and *w* in this statement is termed 'progressive involution.' Again, let $l^{w}m$ denote any individual *A*, if, and only if, there is in existence an individual *B*, who is loved by *A*, and who is such that taking any individual *C* whatever, if *C* is wished well by *B*, then *C* is a man. The operation of combining *w* and *m* in this statement is termed 'regressive involution.' These designations were adopted because of the analogy of the general formulae to those of involution in the algebra of quantity.

These kinds of involution are not, at present, in use in symbolical logic; but they are, nevertheless, useful, especially in developing the conception of continuity. These two kinds of involution together constitute relative involution.

(2) Non-relative involution: consisting in the repeated introduction of the same premise into a reasoning; as, for example, the half-dozen simple premises upon which the Theory of Numbers is based are introduced over and over again in the reasoning by which its myriad theorems are deduced. In exact logic the regular process of deduction begins by non-relatively multiplying together all the premises to make one conjunctive premise, from which whatever can be deduced by using those premises as often as they are introduced as factors, can be deduced by processes of 'immediate inference' from that single conjunctive premise. But the general character of the conclusion is found to depend greatly upon the number of times the same factor is multiplied in. From this circumstance the importance and the name of non-relative involution arise. (C.S.P.)

Ionics: see PRE-SOCRATIC PHILOSOPHY (Ionics).

Ire: see WRATH.

Irenaeus. Born probably in the first quarter of the 2nd century A.D. One of the most important of the early church fathers. Educated under Polycarp among others, he became a presbyter at Lyons. In 177, upon the martyrdom of Photinus, he became bishop of Lyons. He championed orthodoxy against Gnosticism. The place and manner of his death are uncertain; possibly he suffered martyrdom in 202 or 203 A.D.

Iron Age: see SOCIALIZATION.

Irony [Gr. εἴρων, a dissembler]: Ger. *Ironie*; Fr. *ironie*; Ital. *ironia*. Assumed ignorance with an implied conscious superiority. (1) Socratic irony: see SOCRATIC METHOD.

(2) Romantic irony: used by a set of writers (Schlegel, Tieck, Solger) to characterize an aesthetic standpoint which emphasizes the artist's or critic's self-consciousness as the only reality and standard, and from this position of superiority regards the world of so-called reality, with its laws, morality, &c., as futile, unreal, and illusory. This conception grew out of Fichte's emphasis upon the ego as the central principle of philosophy. The 'genius' as critic showed this irony by his exposition of the futility of the works criticized; as artist he should set forth characters or situations which bring out the futility of life and its supposed principles.

Literature: LOTZE, Gesch. d. Aesthetik in Deutschland (1868), 370 ff.; SCHASLER, Gesch. d. Aesthetik (1872), 779 ff.; HEGEL, Philos. of Fine Art (trans. by Bosanquet), 121 ff.; J. H. SCHLEGEL, Die neuere Romantik (1863). (J.H.T.)

Irradiation [Lat. *irradiare*, to radiate]: Ger. *Irradiation, Ausstrahlung*; Fr. *irradiation*; Ital. *irradiazione*. The lateral diffusion of nervous stimuli out of the path of normal discharge, as a result of which the excitation of one peripheral end-organ may excite other central organs than those directly correlated with it or anatomically related to it by direct nervous connection.

Where it takes place is not certainly known. Dogiel shows that in skin areas subject to great irradiation (genital organs) the end-organs of one order are connected by communicating rami, suggesting peripheral irradiation. There are also indications of irradiation of excessive stimuli in the spinal cord. The stimulus may not be excessive, but in that case the entire part of the system implicated is in a state of expectant innervation. It has been suggested that irradiation (or an analogous process) is at the foundation of all or most pleasurable sensations (Herrick).

Literature: A. S. DOGIEL, Die Nervenendigungen in der Schleimhaut der äusseren Genitalorgane des Menschen, Arch. f. mikr. Anat., xli (1893); C. L. HERRICK, Modern Algedonic Ideas, J. of Compar. Neurol., v (March, 1895); also Wood's Ref. Handb. Med. Sci., ix (1893). (H.H.)

Irrational: see RATIONAL.

Irrational Action: Ger. *unvernünftige Handlung* (i. e. *Handlung wider besseres Wissen*); Fr. *action irrationnelle*; Ital. *azione irrazionale*. The choice of an action which (1) is opposed to what is objectively right or reasonable in the circumstances, or (2) is opposed to what the agent sees to be right or reasonable in the circumstances.

In both senses the phenomenon of irrational choice, or unreasonable action, has given rise to difficulties. The former difficulty, which is discussed by Aristotle (*Eth. Nic.*, III. iv) under the question whether it is the true or the apparent good that is the object of a man's wish, is not so much a difficulty concerning choice or activity, as the difficulty of understanding unreason at all—how things can 'appear' other than they are, how error or false opinion is possible. The difficulty commonly referred to is the second, namely, to understand how knowledge and choice can be at variance in the same mind at any given time. The Socratic paradox that vice is ignorance is a denial of the existence of the phenomenon called incontinence or ἀκρασία. This is analysed in detail by Aristotle, *Eth. Nic.*, VII.

Literature: SIDGWICK, Pract. Eth., ix; BALDWIN, Social and Eth. Interpret., chaps. ix, x. (W.R.S.)

The confusion of the meanings (1) and (2) is very common (e. g. Kidd, *Social Evolution*); that which is irrational from the observer's or philosopher's point of view being treated as irrational also from the actor's point of view, when it may be simply non-rational, or even rational. See further discussion under RATIONAL, and SANCTION. (J.M.B.)

Irrelevant [Lat. *in + relevare*]: Ger. *unanwendbar*; Fr. *sans rapport à, inapplicable*; Ital. *irrilevante*. Not pertinent to the question. Irrelevant may be applied either (1) to the conclusion of an argument, which is erroneously taken to be decisive of the ques-

tion, or (2) to any premise suggested which is declared to have no logical connection with the conclusion to which it leads. The former is identical with the *ignoratio elenchi* of the Aristotelian logic; the latter, a special form of confusion, includes the fallacy called by Aristotle *non causa pro causa*. See FALLACY. (R.A.)

Irreligion [Lat. *in + religio*, religion]: Ger. *Religionsverachtung, Unglaube*; Fr. *irréligion*; Ital. *irreligione*. A state of indifference or opposition to the theoretical or practical claims of religion.

It is to be observed of the term irreligion that it applies to an attitude rather than to any specific content, and is, therefore, more subjective than the term religion. It is privative rather than negative, and, like many privatives, has a positive force in English implying not merely the absence of the religious attitude from a being who normally possesses it, but also the presence of a different attitude, one of indifference or opposition. Irreligion is to be distinguished from unbelief or impiety, with which it may be associated, but which it does not necessarily include. Cf. Guyau, *L'Irreligion de l'avenir* (Eng. trans.), for a sociological defence of irreligion. (A.T.O.)

Irritability [Lat. *irritabilis*, irritable]: Ger. *Reizbarkeit*; Fr. *irritabilité*; Ital. *irritabilità*. Power of an active tissue, nerve, muscle, gland, to respond to appropriate stimulation. See EXCITABILITY, NERVE STIMULATION AND CONDUCTION, and LIVING MATTER. (C.F.H.)

Irritant [Lat. *irritare*, to excite]: Ger. (1) *Reizmittel*, (2) *Reiz*; Fr. (1) *irritant*, (2) *stimulant*; Ital. (1) *irritante*, (2) *stimolo*. (1) In physiology: an agent, chemical, mechanical, or acting through the nervous system, which causes inflammation. See STIMULANT. (C.F.H.)

(2) In neurology: that which excites irritability; a STIMULUS (q. v.). (J.M.B.)

Isidorus Hispalensis. (560–636 A. D.) A prominent and learned ecclesiastic of the Western Church. A Spaniard, he succeeded his brother as bishop of Seville. He was ranked as the fifth *Doctor Ecclesiae* for his great learning. In his *Sententiarum libri tres* he gathers together a large number of propositions by himself and others, depicting the entire doctrine of salvation—a compendium of ecclesiastical doctrine of the time.

Islam: see MOHAMMEDANISM.

Isolation [Ital. *isolare*, from Med. Lat.

insulare, to separate]: Ger. *Isolirung*; Fr. *ségrégation*; Ital. *segregazione, isolamento*. The separation of a group of organisms into two permanent groups by any means which prevents interbreeding. The term segregation is also much used.

Moritz Wagner, in 1868, drew attention to the importance of geographical isolation. Gulick and Romanes developed and extended the conception. Romanes divides the effects of isolation into two classes, APOGAMY (q. v.) and HOMOGAMY (q. v.). His theory of PHYSIOLOGICAL SELECTION (q. v.) involves isolation by the barrier of sterility. By regarding the survivors who mate together, and the organisms eliminated before they produce offspring, as two isolated groups, he brings natural selection itself under the category of isolation, a view not generally adopted. Gulick and Romanes contend that in the absence of isolation (other than natural selection) evolution is monotypic (without divergent lines from common ancestors), and that all polytypic (or divergent) evolution involves isolation.

The distinction between (1) discriminate and (2) indiscriminate isolation (homogamy and apogamy) is that between the dividing off of a group (1) having some common mark or character already which differentiates them from others, or (2) not having such a differentiating character. Gulick and Romanes hold to so-called accumulative segregation, leading to polytypic evolution, even in the second case, on the ground that in the group separated off the average or mean of the characters would not be exactly that of the larger group from which they were divided off, and this difference would be cumulative under the operation of natural selection. This sort of isolation Weismann calls AMIXIA (q. v.). (C.LL.M.–J.M.B.)

One of the most important applications of isolation in the form called by Romanes Physiological Selection is that which finds in it the origin of the STERILITY (q. v.) of species *inter se*. (J.M.B.)

Literature: MORITZ WAGNER, Die Darwinsche Theorie u. das Migrationsgesetz (1868); Ueber d. Einfluss d. geographischen Isolirung (1870); J. J. GULICK, Divergent Evolution through Accumulative Segregation, Linn. Soc. J. Zool., xx (1887); G. J. ROMANES, Darwin and after Darwin, Pt. III (1897), criticized by BALDWIN, Psychol. Rev., v. (1898) 215 f. Expositions may be found in CONN, The Method of Evolution (1900), and HEADLEY, The Problems of Evolution (1901). (C.LL.M.–J.M.B.)

Issue [Lat. *exire*, to go forth, through Fr.]: Ger. *Streitpunkt*; Fr. *issue*; Ital. *questione*. A topic of discussion or controversy.

Recently given a quasi-technical meaning by James (*The Will to Believe*), who distinguishes issues of various sorts with reference to belief and conduct. (J.M.B.)

Itch (or **Itching**) **Sensation**: Ger. *Kitzelempfindung*; Fr. *sensation de gale*; Ital. *sensazione della rogna*. See TOUCH SENSATION, and ORGANIC SENSATION.

J

JACKSONIAN EPILEPSY — JANSENISM

Jacksonian Epilepsy : Ger. *Jackson'sche Epilepsie* ; Fr. *épilepsie Jacksonienne* ; Ital. *epilessia Jacksoniana* (or *corticale*). A form of attack of an epileptic character with definite march or progress of spasms, relatively unaffected consciousness, and other characteristics by which it is differentiated from true or ordinary EPILEPSY (q. v.). The state was described and its significance pointed out by Hughlings Jackson. (J.J.)

Jacksonian Re-evolution : Ger. *Jackson'sche Wiederentwicklung* ; Fr. *réévolution Jacksonienne* ; Ital. *reintegrazione di Jackson.* The principle, ascribed to Hughlings Jackson, that the order of the recovery of the mental functions after severe injury or disease is the reverse of that of their loss, and the same as that of their original normal development or acquisition.

Literature : H. JACKSON, J. Ment. Sci., Oct., 1888, 352 ; PICK, Arch. f. Psychiat., xxii, 1891, 756 ; BALDWIN, Ment. Devel. in the Child and the Race, chap. xiii. § 4, 4 (from the German translation of which, p. 370, the equivalent is taken). (J.M.B.)

Jacobi, Friedrich Heinrich. (1743–1819.) Educated for commercial life at Frankfort and Geneva ; engaged in business for seven years, 1763–70 ; councillor of finance for Jülich and Berg ; called to Munich, 1804, as a member of the Academy of Science ; president of this Academy, 1807–13. See FAITH PHILOSOPHY.

James-Lange Theory. The 'peripheral' or 'effect' theory of the relation of emotion to its so-called expression. Named from Wm. James and K. Lange. Cf. EMOTIONAL EXPRESSION (also for literary citations).

The theory has become the starting-point of discussions of emotion. Anticipations of it have been attributed to Bastian (*Brain as an Organ of Mind*, 1880), to Maudsley (*Physiol. and Pathol. of Mind*, 1867), to Lotze, and to Descartes. Cf. Stumpf, *Zeitsch. f. Psychol.*, xxi, 1899, 47. (J.M.B.)

Janet, Paul. (1823–99.) Born at Paris and educated at the École Normale, Paris. He was professor of philosophy, first at Bourges (1845), then at Strassburg (1848), later at Paris, in the Lycée Louis-le-Grand (1857), and the Sorbonne (1864). In 1864 he was elected member of the Academy of Moral and Political Sciences. He was, in the main, eclectic, a disciple of Cousin.

Jansenism : Ger. *Jansenismus* ; Fr. *Jansenisme* ; Ital. *Giansenismo.* The system of Cornelius Jansen, the distinctive feature of which is its reassertion, in an extreme form, of the Augustinian doctrine of human inability ; to wit, that Adam's fall has totally destroyed man's power to do good, and that his salvation must be the work of sovereign and irresistible grace.

Jansenism was condemned by the Roman Catholic Church, which holds the more moderate doctrine of St. Thomas. By Protestants, to whom Thomism savours of semi-Pelagianism, it has been generally looked on as a reaction toward a sounder faith. Its appearance was the occasion of a long and bitter controversy, the Port Royalists, Arnauld and Pascal, making the cause of Jansenism their own, while the Jesuits championed the orthodox view of the Romish Church. Jansenism as an organized movement was finally suppressed and the doctrine condemned as a heresy.

Literature : DUMAS, Hist. des cinq Propositions ; ST. BEUVE, Port Royal (Paris) ;

BOURIER, La Vérité sur les Arnaulds (1877); RAPIN, Hist. du Jansénisme. (A.T.O.)

Jave, Yahweh, Jehovah [Heb.]: Ger. *Jehovah*; Fr. *Jéhovah, Jaweh*; Ital. *Jeova*. The title applied to Deity in the Hebrew Scriptures when the intent is to represent the one self-existent and immutable God as entering into progressive moral relation with men, and especially with the Jewish people.

Of the two appellations of the Deity used in Hebrew Scripture, Elohim and Jehovah, the former is generally used of God in his unethical relation to nature, while the latter expresses a personal and moral relationship with men. The root conception of Jehovah includes a synthesis of being and manifestation, and, as employed in the Old Testament, represents the Being who not only creates man, but makes a revelation of himself to him. Jehovah is not purely transcendent and unsearchable, but comes into loving, intelligible relations with humanity. The germ of the LOGOS (q. v.) is already in the conception of Jehovah.

Literature: HENGSTENBERG, Authen. of the Pentateuch; ALDIS WRIGHT, Smith's Bible Dict., sub verbo; THOLUCK, Literarischer Anz. (1832); BALLANTINE, Import of the Name Jehovah, Bib. Repository, iii. (A.T.O.)

Jealousy (1) and (2) **Envy** [OF. *jalous*, and Lat. *invidere*, to grudge, through Fr.]: Ger. (1) *Eifersucht*, (2) *Neid*; Fr. (1) *jalousie*, (2) *envie*; Ital. (1) *gelosia*, (2) *invidia*. (1) Jealousy is envy (as below) with the added factors that the individual one envies is thought of as sustaining and profiting by a relation to a third individual which properly belongs to oneself; there is an added consciousness of personal injury.

This is what is known as the higher or reflective form of jealousy, in which the grounds for the emotional state are conscious to the individual. A simpler form, sometimes called 'organic' jealousy, is that seen in action which duplicates the expression of reflective jealousy without consciousness of its conditions, i. e. a reaction fitted to convey to an onlooker the impression that the individual is jealous.

(2) Envy is the emotion aroused by the presentation of enjoyment on the part of another under conditions considered desirable for oneself.

Analyses of these states have usually set out from an earlier analysis of sympathy, involving the placing of self in some way in the mind or 'in the shoes' of the person sympathized with. They are thought to involve the double reflection: (*a*) that the self is represented in the other, and (*b*) that the experience thus attributed to the self is not one's own. Another view makes the 'other' an identical content with the self, fitted to excite the same attitudes as in sympathy, but prevented from doing so by the actual difference between the fancied and the real experience; jealousy and envy are emotions of this conflict. See further under SYMPATHY. The lower, organic, or instinctive jealousy, like the same form of sympathy, is exhibited by the animals, and is accounted for, like the other organic emotions, by the laws of utility and survival; this type of reaction being of use in prompting the animal to secure the gain which another is getting. It is very difficult to assign to the animal consciousness the elements involved, and yet the reaction may be the characteristic one of jealousy, as well as that of mere envy.

Jealousy is further characterized by the direction it takes to reach the object; it may wreak itself on either of the individuals in the relation which excites the jealousy. The injured husband punishes the intruder and also upbraids the wife. His emotion leads him, however, to exaggerated suspicion and ill-treatment of the latter. In envy the object is simply the one individual envied considered as being in a fortunate and enviable case. Covetousness is another name for envy.

Literature: see references under EMOTION, COMPARATIVE PSYCHOLOGY, and (especially) SYMPATHY. Special treatment may be found in ADAM SMITH, Theory of the Moral Sentiments; SPINOZA, Ethics, Pt. V. prop. 50 ff.; BAIN, Emotions and Will; BALDWIN, Social and Eth. Interpret., sect. 146. (J.M.B.–K.G.)

Jehovah: see JAVE.

Jerome, Sophronius Eusebius Hieronymus, Saint. (cir. 340–cir. 420 A.D.) His careful education was completed in Rome. He travelled in Gaul, journeyed into the East (373), and retired (374) into the desert of Chalcis, where he spent four years in ascetic practices and in study. Ordained a presbyter by Bishop Paulinus of Antioch, he went to Constantinople (380) to hear Gregory Nazianzen. In 382 he returned to Rome, whence in 386 a wealthy noble woman, Paula, followed him into Palestine and built in Bethlehem four convents, three for nuns and one for monks. Over the latter she placed Jerome, and he remained there until his death. His translation of the Bible into Latin was his greatest work.

Jesuitism : Ger. *Jesuitismus* ; Fr. *jésuitisme* ; Ital. *Gesuitismo*. The system of the Jesuits, a society of the Roman Catholic Church, called also the Society of Jesus, instituted for the propagation and defence of the Romish faith, and noted for the perfection of its organization and discipline and the devotion of its members to the ends of the society.

The Society of Jesus was founded in 1540 by Ignatius Loyola for the express purpose of defending Catholicism against the inroads of the Reformation. In this it was eminently successful, and for over a century was the most powerful agent of Roman Catholic propaganda. Whether justly or not, it fell under the suspicion of unscrupulous ambition and laxity in practical morals. The term Jesuitism has become a synonym in the popular mind for supple diplomacy and an accommodating conscience which substitutes the standard of permissibility for that of right and obligation.

Literature: F. SUAREZ, De Religione Societatis Jesu ; F. J. BUSS, Die Gesch. d. Gesell. Jesu (1883) ; RAVIGNAN, De l'Existence et l'Instinct des Jésuites (7th ed., Paris, 1855–83 ; Eng. trans., London, 1844). (A.T.O.)

Jesus [Lat. *Iesus* ; Gr. Ἰησοῦς ; Heb. *Yeshua*, or *Yoshua, Yeheshua*, the salvation of Jehovah] : Ger. *Jesus* ; Fr. *Jésus* ; Ital. *Gesù*. The Saviour of the Christian Church, called the Christ. The four Gospels are accounts of his life. (J.M.B.)

The teaching of Jesus, as distinguished from the history of his life and from the doctrine of his work and of his person, has its source in his dominating consciousness of his Divine Sonship. Speaking out of this consciousness, he seeks to lead men to realize the same essential relationship. From this point of view the highest virtue is filial obedience to the will of a Heavenly Father. The supreme principle of living is love, which binds men first and supremely to God and secondly to one another as brethren. Out of this springs brotherly love, peace, gentleness, and a forgiving spirit. The great practical law of life is that of self-devoted service, in which the private individual life is lost in the larger life of the community. The last judgment, the resurrection, and the life beyond the grave were also important elements of his personal teaching. Cf. the special topics of Christian theology. (A.T.O.)

Jevons, William Stanley. (1835–82.)

English logician and political economist. Educated at University College, London. Held an appointment in the royal Mint at Sydney, Australia, 1854–9 ; became fellow of University College, 1864 ; and in 1866 professor of logic, mental and moral philosophy, and Cobden lecturer on political economy in Owens College, Manchester. Moved to London, 1876, and was drowned in 1882.

Jewish Philosophy and Religion : see JUDAISM.

John of Salisbury. (cir. 1115–80.) Born in southern England, he left his native land in 1136, and went to Paris and to Chartres to study. He returned in 1148 with Archbishop Theobald of Canterbury, and lived as the latter's secretary, continuing in the office under Theobald's successor, Thomas à Becket, until 1163. From 1163 to 1170 he spent in the abbey of St.-Rémy, near Rheims, occupied with literary pursuits. After a few years in England he became bishop of Chartres, where he died. See SCHOLASTICISM, I.

Joint Cost : Ger. *gemeinsame Kosten* ; Fr. *frais non répartis* ; Ital. *spese non ripartite*. Expense attaching to the production of a number of articles collectively, and not naturally assignable to one rather than to the other.

Thus it is impossible to tell the respective costs of freight and passenger service on a railroad, because many of the items of expense apply to the road as a whole, and not to any special part of the railroad service.

Mill called attention to the difficulty of applying the adjustment of value to cost of production in certain cases of this kind, especially in the matter of by-products, where a concern established for the supply of one article, like gas, finds itself in a position to sell another, like coke. But the difficulty is far more widespread than Mill assumes. It applies not merely to the apportionment of expenses among different articles simultaneously produced, but among varying quantities of the same article.

The supply of different commodities produced under these conditions is known as a joint supply ; such products are sometimes known as joint products. A somewhat difficult transfer of the same conception from the phenomena of production to those of consumption leads to a conception of joint demand.

Literature: MARSHALL, Princ. of Econ., Bk. V. (A.T.H.)

Joint-sensation : Ger. *Gelenkempfind-*

ung; Fr. *sensation articulaire*; Ital. *sensibilità articolare* (or *delle giunture*). Sensation from the joints. See ARTICULAR SENSATION. (E.B.T.)

Josephus, Flavius. (37–cir. 103 A.D.) Born and educated in a noble family at Jerusalem, he passed through the schools of three Jewish sects, spent three years in a desert with the hermit Banus, and adopted the views of the Pharisees. He was sent on a diplomatic errand to Rome in 63 A.D., and commanded in Galilee during the Jewish revolution. Becoming a captive in the Roman army, he ingratiated himself in the royal families, and returned to Rome with Titus after the destruction of Jerusalem to spend the remainder of his life.

Jouffroy, Théodore Simon. (1796–1842.) Born at Pontets, and educated partly by his uncle at the college of Pontarlier, and partly at the college of Dijon. He was taken into the École Normale, Paris, in 1814, where Victor Cousin instructed him in philosophy. In 1817 he became doctor of philosophy and instructor in philosophy at the École Normale. The government closed the latter in 1822, but he continued to lecture in his own dwelling. In 1832 he opened a course of lectures on 'natural right,' and in 1833 became a member of the Académie for the class of moral and political sciences. On account of illness he spent the winter of 1835–6 at Pisa, and in 1838, on returning to Paris, exchanged his position for that of university librarian, made vacant by the death of Laromiguière.

Joy [Lat. *gaudere*, through Fr.]: Ger. *Freude*; Fr. *joie*; Ital. *gioja*. A pleasurable emotional state accompanying consciousness of gain or advantage of any sort to oneself or another.

Joy is the contrary emotion to GRIEF (q.v.). The nature of such pairs of contrary emotions is explained under HOPE AND DESPAIR. The expressions of joy are also antithetic to those of grief: expansive, as opposed to depressive, vaso-motor and muscular effects show themselves in attitudes and movements exhibiting, like those of grief, little practical adjustment, such as clapping of hands, jumping up and down, social demonstrativeness, and laughter.

Literature: see EMOTION, and BIBLIOG. G, 2, *k*. (J.M.B., G.F.S.)

Judaism [Lat. *Iudaismus*]: Ger. *Judenthum*; Fr. *Judaïsme*; Ital. *Giudaismo*. The religious system of the Jews, founded on the law of Moses and enjoining the exclusive worship of Jehovah as the one and only true God, together with their religious and ethical philosophy. Cf. CABALA.

Judaism is the oldest of the three great monotheistic religions of the world. The creed of ancient Judaism is to be found in the Old Testament, and includes Messianic hope as one of its essential features. The creed of modern orthodox Judaism was drawn up by the celebrated Moses Maimonides in the 11th century, and includes the doctrines of the Messianic hope and belief in the resurrection of the body. Modern Judaism is divided into two branches, the conservative or orthodox and the reformed. The latter have expunged from their creed the Messianic hope and the dogma of the resurrection, while maintaining the immortality of the soul and the perfectibility of human nature. An ultra-liberal wing has practically eliminated the religious feature from Judaism, and aims to turn it into a purely ethical cult.

Literature: CASSEL, Lehrb. d. jüdischen Gesch. u. Literatur; JOST, Gesch. d. Judenthums. (A.T.O.)

Judge (in law): see JUDICIAL.

Judgment [Lat. *iudex*, judge]: Ger. *Urtheilskraft, Urtheil*; Fr. *jugement*; Ital. *giudizio*. The mental function and act of assertion or predication; applied also to the resulting assertion or predication. Cf. BELIEF, and PROPOSITION.

The definition is necessarily broad, since controversies about judgment are now in the air. Logic had the field until recent times and defined judgment in terms of verbal or some other sort of predication expressed in propositions. This did not do justice to judgment as a mental act whereby the assertion is reached. The act or attitude of judgment is not exhausted psychologically in the formulated content of predication. This is in brief the motive of the newer way of looking at judgment, in which Brentano was a pioneer, and in which both logicians and psychologists have recently done much work. Brentano finds the judging function an original form of mental determination over and above presentation or apprehension of content. This assimilates judgment as a mental act to belief, defined by J. S. Mill as an irreducible form of acceptance of a content. (Windelband has suggested that the German term Beurtheilung be used for judging in Brentano's sense. Cf. Eisler, *Wörterb. d. philos. Begriffe*, 'Beurtheilung.')

Consequently, the problem now before psychologists is not that of the recognition of judgment as an operation over and above that of presentation, but the analysis of the general state of psychological acceptance in its various forms, with view of its elements and primary roots. Is judgment identical with belief? If not, in what way is assertion with predication, or possibly without explicit predication, something added to acceptance? Does the determination of belief carry with it also the assertion of what is believed? Or is assertion not at all necessary to the predication of judgment? What are the different kinds of judgment (hypothetical? categorical? existential? disjunctive?), and how are they accounted for on the basis of the psychological theory reached by analysis? Cf. PROPOSITION. These questions indicate that, in the newer way of looking at judgment, psychologists are finding it difficult to define belief and judgment without overlapping; and if a real distinction is to be made between these two terms, the only line of demarcation seems to be in the act of assertion and the manner of it, with or without predication, as distinct from the acceptance of belief.

Another older and logical way of looking at judgment made the explicit relation of one term to another—that is, as involving 'acts of comparison' (Hamilton) or explicit predication—necessary to it, as in the verbal categorical judgment. The analysis, however, of psychologists shows that no such trait can be universally maintained. The existential, ejaculatory, impersonal forms of assertion do not lend themselves to this treatment except by verbal abstraction and supplementation, in which the psychological state loses its purity. Moreover, the more primitive forms of judgment do not deal with two presentations or ideas, but with one. In fact some hold (e. g. the writer) that all sorts of judgment can be constructed as re-determinations of the content of conception through a progressive series of changes. Cf. ANALYTIC AND SYNTHETIC JUDGMENTS.

The need of analysis is seen in the conflicting views of judgment, logical and psychological, now current. The current divergence of view is shown by the comparison of Erdmann's *Logik* and Hillebrand's *Die neuern Theorien der kategorischen Schlüsse*. Hillebrand accepts Brentano's view of judgment and develops it in its logical bearings. This view seems to be psychological in two of its factors. (1) It emphasizes an aspect of existential judgments which is not covered by the ordinary predicative theory; namely, if existence is a predicate in the ordinary attributal sense, it must have a notional content of its own—it must be itself a content, an earlier presentative experience—an error which Kant refuted once for all in his criticisms of the ontological proof for the existence of God. But the formal logicians (i. e. Erdmann) reply: if existence is not a predicate, the distinction between presentation and judgment is subverted. This last is unanswerable, but it leaves unrelieved the acute strain between the psychological and logical views of the existential, pointed out by Brentano. (2) The Brentano-Hillebrand view does justice for the first time to the 'unitary' or 'conceptual' meaning of judgment and syllogism; a point of view from which the formal strictly predicative or 'two-membered' doctrine of judgment is seen at a great disadvantage. When I say 'The dog is fierce,' my content is a single object, *fierce dog*—this much certainly, whether or no we go over to the existential view which says 'The fierce dog is' is equivalent to the original statement (cf. Baldwin, *Handb. of Psychol.*, i. 285, 301). Indeed, Brentano seems to go over to the existential view, thus saving himself from the criticisms to which his doctrine is open, at the same time that he has cut himself off from a predicative theory by his unitary view of the judgment content.

Yet it is curious to note how the logical progressus of doctrine may be reversed. Erdmann holds the predicative theory, yet maintains the unitary view properly belonging to the existential theory. This he does by upholding what may be called the 'declarative' as opposed to the synthetic function of judgment (*Logik*, i. 205, 261). For this there is much to be said. As the present writer has said (loc. cit., i. 283, 285): 'The essential feature of judgment is this, that it sets forth, in a conscious contemplative way, the actual stage of the thought movement.' Erdmann holds (loc. cit., i. 262) that it is always expressed in a proposition. But how easy it would be to reverse this chain of argument, and to say that because there is this declaration of relationship between parts of the objective whole which is the content of judgment, there must have been originally more than one content, and that, therefore, judgment, as a synthetic thing, precedes presentation and renders it possible.

The view of judgment which is desiderated, therefore, should have the following features:

first, it should find some way of holding that existence is a true predicate and yet not an attribual content; second, that the content of judgment is a single concept; third, that reference to existence accompanies all judgment; and fourth, that judgment is declarative of results already reached in conception. The first and third of these four points are essential, if the existential and predicative theories of judgment are to find common ground.

On the first point—the nature of the existence predicate—introspection seems to throw light. Reality is at first simply presence, sensation, presentation; we have here the fundamental phase of affective consciousness, reality-feeling. There is no judgment at all, because there is no occasion for assertion. There is no acceptance of reality as such, because there is no category into which to put it. But now let experience come in like a flood, let pleasures of gratification be succeeded by pains of want, let impulse seek its end, finding it here and losing it there; and amid the contradictions and reiterations, the storm and stress of the accommodation of life to the world, a few great relief-points begin to stand out in consciousness. They recur, they satisfy, they stand together, they can be found when wanted. They are not new as objects of apprehension; they are the same objectives as before. But somehow, after we have gratified our appetites by them, and have sought and found them, again and again, standing firm together, while other objectives have shifted, faded, and disappeared—then the mental part of us which envelops them becomes different. Our affective consciousness now assumes the colouring which we call belief; that sense of acceptance, assurance, and confirmation which succeeds doubt and perplexity. This is feeling; a feeling of the methodical way in which certain objectives manœuvre in consciousness, in contrast with the unmethodical way in which other objectives manœuvre; the feeling of a reality-coefficient.

This, then, is the primary meaning of belief in reality or existence. It is the sense of the confirmed presence of an objective, as satisfying the demands of conscious life. But so far, belief is not judgment, and existence is not an idea. But as soon as such an objective is labelled as real, is pictured with this coefficient, then the declarative, assertive phase of consciousness arises, and the '*S* is' is born—a true predicative judgment. What

was before the feeling-envelope, so to speak, of the presentation, is now itself presented as part of the content. Hillebrand seems to be right in saying that the idea of existence does not arise before, but in and through, the existential judgment.

In the predicate of the existential, therefore, what we assert is not content over and above the subject *S*, but the feeling-category in which the *S*-content is enveloped in consciousness: the way consciousness feels in consequence of the presence of this particular content in it. This is, in the writer's view, the true explanation of the existential. It is a judgment, because in its declarative function it renders in intelligible form the endorsement which distinguishes belief from simple presentation. But the predicate is only a sign of this endorsement, not an added objective element.

The other desideratum of the theory is now clearly in sight, i. e. the presence always of an existence-value in judgment. As experience broadens, our reality-coefficients are so well established as categories of feeling-consciousness, that each presented content has its familiar envelope of belief, its endorsement in kind—so familiar and natural that it is not formally asserted at all. And the new marks which accrue to a content in conception come to be declared in the ordinary 'two-membered' form of judgment, all inside of a tacit (felt) reality-coefficient. The *is* of 'The man is white' is, therefore, very different from the *is* of 'There is a white man.' The former is merely the sign of conceptual synthesis: the judgment might be true on any 'world of reality,' e. g. of Adam Bede. The existence-value of the judgment is simply the environment of feeling which an accepted proposition carries, with no indication of any particular kind of existence. But in the true existential — 'There is a white man'—the feeling factor is taken up as a quasi-logical predicate, and the coefficient of external reality is declared. The *is* now expresses the conscious ratification and declaration of belief.

The employment of the belief criterion as a norm of classification of judgments (see Venn, *Empirical Logic*, 243; Baldwin, loc. cit., 1st ed., i. 293) is fruitful in further confirmation of this general result. If we look at the belief-attitude of the mind in cases of assertion, we find two clear truths not brought out by the ordinary division of the logics. First, the disjunctive judgment is seen to be a categorical form of expression. The disjunctive form of the predicate P or P' means that the same belief-feeling accompanies either of two or more declarations concerning the subject S. It expresses the belief-value of the concept S so far as constructive experience of it (i. e. the evidence) is of value for belief. With more evidence the parity of P and P', as claimants upon belief, disappears, and the judgment takes the regular categorical form. Second, the hypothetical judgment lies, with reference to belief, midway between the ordinary categorical and the existential. We may approach it from either extreme. For example, the judgment 'If a is b, c is d,' means that the same degree of reality, or belief-feeling, accompanies the conceptual synthesis ab on the one hand, and the synthesis cd on the other hand. But it does not determine the particular coefficient of reality belonging to either ab or cd. Or we may approach the hypothetical from the side of the existential, getting the hypothetical judgment of existence, 'If ab exists, so does cd.' In this case, not only does the belief-feeling envelop both ab and cd, as before, but, further, the particular coefficient of reality attaching in common to them both is now expressed. This last form of judgment is, therefore, from our present point of view, the richest and most notable. In it we catch both belief as felt coefficient, and existence as asserted predicate (i. e. the reality-coefficient itself made the P of predication).

The above account, it will be seen, suggests an explanation also of the negative existential judgment—a point of great difficulty to Herbart, Brentano, and Hillebrand—by saving the predicative force of the existence sign. Yet by the negation in this judgment, as now explained, no element of content is cut off from S; what is denied is belief in a positive coefficient of reality, or, as Erdmann (loc. cit., i. 349 ff.) and Sigwart say, it is the rejection of an attempted positive judgment of existence.

The element of belief which accompanies all judgment, described above as felt recognition of a reality-coefficient, gives us the line of connection between formal and material logic. The judgments A, E, I, O cannot be purely formal, nor can the syllogisms constructed from them; for every S and P in each one of them has its belief-value—its reality-coefficient—and every actual case of inference means the development of concepts subject to the limitations of thought in that particular sphere of reality. The truth of

every conclusion rests upon the presupposition—from the supplying of which the hypothetical syllogism arises, just as the hypothetical judgment arises from the supplying of the ground of belief in the categorical judgment—that the two premises have the same kind of reality. The syllogism

$$A \text{ is } B$$
$$B \text{ is } C$$
$$\overline{A \text{ is } C,}$$

to be valid, really requires belief that the proposition 'If A is B and B is C, then A is C,' applies to the particular elements of content in question. Without this presupposition, securing the same coefficient to both premises, the conclusion would be false; as for example:—

All men who have died will rise again.
The man Romeo died.
The man Romeo will rise again.

The 'man Romeo' and the 'all men' have different coefficients of reality — different material reference — and the conclusion is invalid.

Additional questions are: the relation of judgment to language and to other forms of mental symbolism (see Erdmann, *Logik*, i. 23, 224, 234; and cf. LANGUAGE FUNCTION); the social or 'communication' element in judgment; the interpretation of the 'material' reference of judgment (another way of asking as to the presence of belief); the interpretation of negative judgment (does it implicate belief to the same extent as the affirmative judgment?).

Literature: logical: see under PROPOSITION, and BELIEF, and in BIBLIOG. C, 2, r (especially the works of MILL, VENN, SIGWART, ERDMANN, WUNDT, BOSANQUET). Psychological: HAMILTON, Metaphysics, lect. xxxvii; the larger Psychologies of BRENTANO, STOUT, JAMES, LADD, JODL, VOLKMANN, BALDWIN (also in Mind, 1892, 403, from which quotations are made above); HILLEBRAND, Die neu. Theor. der kat. Schlüsse; JERUSALEM, Die Urtheilsfunktion; MACLENNAN, The Impersonal Judgment; ORMOND, The Negative in Logic, Psychol. Rev., iv. (1897) 231.   (J.M.B.)

Judgment (in law) [from Lat. *iudicare*, through Fr.]: Ger. *Gericht*; Fr. *jugement*; Ital. *giudicato* (*passato in . . .*). The judicial determination of a matter in litigation. It may extend only to the determination of a matter coming up for decision in the course of a lawsuit, before its conclusion, and is then an interlocutory judgment, as distinguished from a final judgment. On a jury trial the verdict of the jury precedes the judgment, and is the ground of it. (S.E.B.)

Judgment (in logic) : see PROPOSITION.

Judgment (last): Ger. *jüngstes Gericht*; Fr. *jugement dernier*; Ital. *giudizio finale* (or *universale*), *l' ultimo giudizio*. In Christian theology, the great day of final award, following the general resurrection, in which the destiny of the righteous and the wicked shall be finally determined. See ESCHATOLOGY (also for literature). (A.T.O.)

Judgment of Taste. Aesthetic appreciation; an expression sometimes used as the English equivalent of Kant's Urtheilskraft and of the earlier *cognitio sensitiva* of Baumgarten's *Aesthetica*. Cf. HIRN, *Origins of Art* (1900), I. See AESTHETICS, and TASTE; and cf. WORTH. (J.M.B.)

Judicial (in law) [Lat. *iudicialis*]: Ger. *juristisch, gerichtlich*; Fr. *judiciaire*; Ital. *giudiziario*. That which pertains to a court of justice in the exercise of its proper functions.

An opinion of a court volunteered upon a matter not properly before it for decision would be *extra-judicial*. *Quasi-judicial* powers are exercised by administrative tribunals, such as boards of railroad commissioners or of city aldermen when disposing of a proceeding for the removal of an officer for cause. *Judicial notice*: the notice taken by judges, without proof, in the disposition of a cause, of the existence of facts of universal knowledge (e. g. the day of the week or month, the name of the chief magistrate, the intoxicating qualities of brandy, or the explosive character of gunpowder).

'Judicial notice takes the place of proof, and is of equal force. As a means of establishing facts, it is therefore superior to evidence. In its appropriate field it displaces evidence, since, as it stands for proof, it fulfils the object which evidence is designed to fulfil, and makes evidence unnecessary. The true conception of what is judicially known is that of something which is not, or rather need not, unless the tribunal wishes it, be the subject of either evidence or argument—something which is already in the court's possession, or at any rate is so accessible that there is no occasion to use any means to make the court aware of it. If, in regard to any subject of judicial notice, the court should permit documents to be referred to or testimony introduced, it would not be, in any proper sense, the admission of evidence, but simply a resort to a convenient means of refreshing the memory, or making the trier aware of that of which everybody ought to be aware' (State *v.* Main, 69 Connecticut Reports, 123, 136; Thayer's *Cases on Evidence*, 20; Brown *v.* Piper, 91 United States Reports, 43). (S.E.B.)

Judicial Notice: see JUDICIAL.

Jural [Lat. *ius*, right]: Ger. *rechtlich*; Fr. *juridique*; Ital. *giuridico*. Pertaining to right, as distinguished from that which pertains to law or to morals.

'The jural sphere includes only external actions. . . . The moral comprehends the jural' (Woolsey, *Polit. Sci.*, i. 17, 14). It relates 'to such right actions (or abstinences) as are required to satisfy the rightful claims of others' (cf. Sidgwick, *Hist. of Eth.*, chap. i. 9). The word jural was coined by Lieber in his *Political Ethics*. (S.E.B.)

Jurisdiction (in law) [Lat. *iurisdictio*]: Ger. *Jurisdiction, Rechtssprechung*; Fr. *juridiction*; Ital. *giurisdizione*. (1) In respect to a state: the territory over which its laws are in force, namely, that under its flag. Treaties may concede an extra-territorial jurisdiction, as do those of China with the Western powers.

(2) In respect to a court: (*a*) the extent of its power to adjudicate; (*b*) the territory over which its process can run.

Original jurisdiction is that over a cause from the time it is first instituted, as distinguished from appellate jurisdiction, which attaches only upon proceedings in the nature of an appeal from a court in which the action has been previously pending. (S.E.B.)

Jurisprudence [Lat. *iurisprudentia*, from *ius*, law, + *prudentia*, knowledge]: Ger. *Jurisprudenz*; Fr. *jurisprudence*; Ital. *giurisprudenza*. (1) Law viewed as a science.

(2) The system of laws in force in a particular state.

Holland defines it as 'the formal science of positive law' (*Jurisprudence*, chap. i. 12). 'Iurisprudentia est divinarum atque humanarum rerum notitia; iusti atque iniusti scientia' (*Inst. of Just.*, i. 1, *De iustitia et iure*, 1). Modern jurisprudence is viewed mainly from its human side. See COMPARATIVE JURISPRUDENCE.

Literature: BENTHAM, Mor. and Legisl., ii. chap. xvii. § 2; SIDGWICK, Outlines of the Hist. of Eth., 8, 95; POLLOCK, First Book of Jurisprudence; AMOS, Sci. of Law, and System. View of the Sci. of Jurisprudence; AUSTIN, Lects. on Jurisprudence; POST, Bausteine f. eine allg. Rechtswissenschaft; RATTO, Sociol. e Filosofia del Diritto, chap. v (1894). (S.E.B.)

Jurist [L.L. *iurista*, a lawyer, through Fr.]: Ger. *Jurist, Rechtsgelehrter*; Fr. *juriste*; Ital. *giurista*. One who has shown himself to have a scientific knowledge and comprehension of the principles of law. (s.e.b.)

Juristic: see ACT (in law).

Just (or **Least**) **Noticeable** (or **Perceptible**) **Difference**: see DIFFERENCE (least noticeable).

Justice [Lat. *iustitia*]: Ger. *Gerechtigkeit*; Fr. *justice*; Ital. *giustizia*. (1) Psychological and social: (*a*) the recognition and observance of the requirements incidental to social status and of those prescribed by custom; together with (*b*) the enforcement of such recognition and observance upon others personally, or by means of an institution common to all. (j.m.b.)

(2) Ethical: the habit of voluntary activity, or virtue, which consists in due regard for the ethical rights of others. Cf. RIGHT (ethical).

Injustice is used for the positive failure of either factor in (1), or for the lack of (2).

A history of the views of moralists concerning justice would be almost a history of ethics. In Plato's ideal state justice is made to consist in the perfect harmony of the whole, which is brought about by each part doing its own work and abstaining from interference with its neighbours: so that the nature of justice in detail depends upon the due assignment of function to each factor in the social organism. Aristotle's analysis proceeds upon an examination of the actual social order. To him are due the important distinctions: (*a*) between 'universal justice,' which consists in regard for the laws or social requirements generally, and is therefore equivalent to complete virtue; and 'particular justice,' a special virtue, the fundamental characteristic of which is a certain regard for equality. The use of the term for Aristotle's 'universal justice' is now obsolete in English. (*b*) Within the special virtue, between 'distributive' and 'corrective' justice—the latter coming into operation only when a defect in the original distribution requires to be righted. The weight of this view therefore falls upon the doctrine of distributive justice, where the guiding idea of equality is necessarily transformed into a proportion according to merit. Subsequent attempts to define justice have been largely influenced by Aristotle's analysis. Either the actual social order and the 'normal expectations' it produces are accepted as the final arbiter of 'rights,' or these are held to be determined by regard to some ideal—commonly either to the ideal of 'equality' (as

in modern socialist writers) or to that of 'liberty' (Kant, Spencer, &c.).

The impulsive basis of justice seems to lie in the feeling of revenge (described by Bacon as a 'wild justice'), which becomes moralized when the intention of the agent and his individual responsibility are recognized. When private revenge is superseded by the organized force of the community, the infliction of punishment has to be preceded by proof of injury, that is to say, of infringement of the rights of another. In the determination and maintenance of these rights consists social justice, while the just man is one in whom respect for such rights has become a habit of will.

Of recent discussions of justice, one of the most notable is that of Sidgwick, in which stress is laid on the distinction between 'conservative justice' (or respect for 'normal expectations') and 'ideal justice,' which may be described as respect for the rights involved in the ideal of social manhood, however that ideal may be determined. (w.r.s.)

The conception of justice is correlative with those of LAW and RIGHT (q.v.), and the evolution of the three concepts seems to have proceeded *pari passu*. Social justice and right, like the unformulated requirements described by the words 'status' and 'custom,' on which they depend, are relative terms, lying at one extreme, as purely legal justice and right lie at the other. The social sense of justice seems to come first both in race development and in the child. Apart from the conditions of its rise and from its ultimate relation to ethical and legal justice, it is the fundamental category of objective social organization and development. Two essential psychological elements seem to be present at every stage of its growth: (1) the recognition of a personal situation through which individuals are involved in a set of relationships *inter se* acknowledged by them; (2) the limitation of this situation not only by the recognition *inter se* of the members of the group which it involves, but also by the equally positive recognition of the foreignness to the group-situation of other individuals, who constitute other groups or exist in more or less independence. Justice to the king is very different in its requirements from justice to the slave, although both are outside my group, and hence outside the requirements of justice to my coequals. Justice, then, is psychologically a function of social organization everywhere, whose essential character is that its development and relationships are recognized more or less adequately by the individuals whom it concerns. It is this psychological relativity which has often made political and social use of the idea of justice mistaken and disastrous. Absolute and abstract standards of justice have been aimed at—ethical right reacting upon the rights of status. The social justice of communities of low development cannot embody the ideas of social or ethical right of higher communities, nor devise the legal procedure to interpret and enforce them.

The second (*b*) element of social justice—the enforcement of the recognition and observance of social requirements—is altogether subordinate to the other, psychologically: it is a sort of demand for the correction of outraged justice rather than an intrinsic element in justice. Yet it is a utilitarian factor of the first importance. For it is in this that the embodiment of justice in law appears to have its root; for legal justice, apart from its merely interpretative function, means essentially enforcement, whether by prevention or by punishment, and enforcement is necessary for the persistence of social order. 'Criminal justice and law (Strafrecht), born of a very primitive impulse, revenge, is the oldest of all forms of justice. We shall see, as Durkheim has rightly indicated, that primitive people have perhaps only criminal justice, and that civil justice is a later growth' (Barth, *Die Philos. d. Gesch. als Sociol.*, i. 86).

On the other hand, in the fact of enforcement, both social and legal justice differ from ethical, which is essentially a matter of internal personal sanction. Ethical justice is not enforced by law—except so far as ethical precepts are embodied socially and legally. This enforcement aspect it is which appears to be reinforced, or anticipated, by the emotional states and impulses of revenge and desire to punish, with their correlative notions of guilt and retribution. When private revenge came to be recognized as a social right, it was positively restricted and limited, the demands of social and ethical justice being united with it, as in the regulations respecting the cities of refuge among the Hebrews. This recognition, as socially valid, of a spontaneous personal sanction, attaching to what were relatively acts of injustice, may have radically advanced or even initiated the development of justice in its legal form. And the reflective forms of the analogous emotions

and impulses, springing up when persons were recognized as in a system of relationships—as described above—would create an essentially similar demand for the legal embodiment of justice; a state of things illustrated in other emotions, of which a lower organic phase develops, without changing its methods of expression or its social form of embodiment, into a higher reflective phase.

The relation of ethical to social justice is one of subordination. Social justice may or may not be ethical according as the organization in which it is found is or is not of individuals having the ideals of self and conduct which developed ethical standards embody.

The actual tracing of the idea of justice and its embodiment in institutions is nothing less than the history of law, in all its aspects, in sociology, and the history of social, ethical, and religious sanctions in social psychology. Cf. the various topics RIGHT (especially philosophy of), PUNISHMENT, and SANCTION. (J.M.B.–H.S.)

Literature: titles given under the topics named (especially ROUSSEAU, ADAM SMITH, HEGEL, GREEN). Recent works are IHERING, Zweck im Recht (3rd ed., 1899); BOSANQUET, Philos. Theory of the State. For the psychology, see titles under SOCIAL ORGANIZATION; also PLATO, Rep., iv; ARISTOTLE, Eth., v; KANT, Rechtslehre (trans. by W. Hastie, Kant's Philos. of Law, 1887); SIDGWICK, Meth. of Eth., iii; SPENCER, Princ. of Eth., Pt. V ('Justice'); ARDIGÒ, Sociologia, in Opere filos., iv (1886). (W.R.S.–J.M.B.)

(3) In law: the right application of the rules of law to the decision of a matter in controversy. 'Legal justice aims at realizing moral justice within its range, and its strength largely consists in the general feeling that this is so' (Pollock, *Jurisprudence*, chap. ii. 31).

'Iustitia est constans et perpetua voluntas ius suum cuique tribuens' (*Inst. of Just.*, i. 1, *De iustitia et iure*, 1). Cf. RIGHT (in law). (S.E.B.)

(4) In theology: an attribute of God in the sphere of his relation to his sentient and rational creatures, by virtue of which he as legislator wills equal laws, and as judge makes awards that are equal and proportionate to merit or demerit. See (also for literature) ATTRIBUTES (of God).

This attribute is to be distinguished from the righteousness of God, which it presupposes as the source of the distinction between equity and inequity; also from the divine holiness, which it presupposes as the source of the distinction between merit and demerit. It is objective in its reference, and is distinguishable into the two species legislative and judicial. Justice is contrasted with love, which wills good rather than equity, and with mercy, which awards favour without regard to merit or demerit. The relations of justice and mercy to sin and redemption supply a central problem in the Christian doctrine of the atonement. (A.T.O.)

Justification: see SANCTION.

Justification (in law) [Lat. *iustificatio*]: Ger. *Rechtfertigung*; Fr. *justification*; Ital. *giustificazione*. (1) Establishing a defence to an action, which, while admitting that the act charged was done, shows that it was done in the exercise of a lawful right. (2) Proof that one offered as a surety is able to satisfy the obligation which he proposes to assume. (S.E.B.)

Justification (in theology). The method by which, in the Christian doctrine of redemption, the sinner passes out of the state of guilt and condemnation into that of righteousness and peace with God.

Justification is to be distinguished from conversion, which it presupposes; from remission, which is its negative aspect; from imputation, which is a means to it; and from sanctification, which is rather its end and completion. Historically, the most important distinction has arisen between the evangelical Protestant and the Roman Catholic doctrines of justification; the former conceiving it as forensic and putative, conditioned by faith in the believer, and by virtue of which he is counted, not actually made, righteous; the latter as a process, conditioned by good works on the part of the believer, by virtue of which the merit of Christ is not simply imputed, but communicated, and in which the believer is actually made righteous. Some of the more philosophical of recent theologians tend to conceive justification as the generation of a new personality grounded in Christ.

Literature: see THEOLOGY. (A.T.O.)

Justin Martyr, or **Flavius Justinus.** (cir. 105–cir. 165 A.D.) An early Christian apologist. Studied philosophy in Asia Minor, Greece, and Egypt. About 132 he abandoned philosophic systems and embraced Christianity. Nothing is known of his life. He suffered martyrdom in Rome. His writings are among the most important of the Christian literature of the 2nd century. See PATRISTIC PHILOSOPHY (4).

K

Kames, Lord : see HOME, HENRY.

Kant, Immanuel. (1724–1804.) Born, lived, and died at Königsberg. Studied theology, philosophy, and mathematics in the University at Königsberg. Engaged as private tutor, 1746–55. Became doctor of philosophy and Docent in the University in 1755, and professor of logic and metaphysics in 1770. In 1797 his age compelled him to retire. See the following topics: also IDEALISM, EPISTEMOLOGY, and PHILOSOPHY.

Kantian Philosophy : see KANT'S TERMINOLOGY.

Kantian Terminology : see KANT'S TERMINOLOGY.

Kantianism(or **Kantism**): Ger. *Kantianismus*; Fr. *Kantianisme*; Ital. *Kantismo*, *Kantianismo*. The philosophy which holds to the distinctive doctrines of Immanuel Kant. See KANT'S TERMINOLOGY, and the principal philosophical topics generally.

The features of Kant's philosophy, which have given name to later thought as Kantian, are mainly (1) the critical method, which consists in a 'criticism' of reason (Vernunftsvermögen) with a view to discovering the *a priori* elements in knowledge; (2) the doctrine of *a priori* mental forms, which, as a theory of knowledge, is characterized as formalism; (3) the resulting antithesis between the 'phenomenal,' or that world of things or appearances to which these forms are applied, and the 'noumenal,' or that world of things in themselves, the transcendental thought-postulates, to which the forms do not apply, and which (4) are consequently unknowable; this is the agnostic element in Kantianism, especially as developed with reference to the ideas of reason—'God, Freedom, and Immor-

tality of the Soul'—and in the theory of the antinomies or contradictions which reason falls into in applying the category of infinity; (5) the recognition of the validity of the ideas of reason as postulates of the moral life (practical reason). These features at least should be included in Kantianism, though any one of them would justify the use of the adjective Kantian.

Literature: see CRITICISM, and BIBLIOG. A, 'Kant'; in English, especially the works by STIRLING, CAIRD, and WATSON; for German citations see EISLER, Wörterb. d. philos. Begriffe, in locis; a study of Kant's Psychology has been made by BUCHNER, Monog. Suppl. (No. 4) to the Psychol. Rev.; a Kant Bibliography is by ADICKES, Monog. Suppl., i, to the Philos. Rev. (J.M.B.)

Kantism : see KANTIANISM.

Kant's Terminology (in relation to the **Kantian Philosophy**).

(1) At the outset of the history of philosophical terminology, amongst the Greeks, the problem of the thinker was to adapt his native language to the novel business of expressing philosophical ideas. The word and the conception then often came into existence together. The power of mere tradition was at its minimum. Creation was relatively free. At the outset, however, of the efforts of modern philosophers to discuss their problems in the vernacular tongues, the situation was wholly different. An elaborate, and in fact often extremely difficult terminology, the result of several successive great movements of human thought—the terminology of Scholasticism—stood in the way of novelty in expression. The modern thinker sometimes, like Locke, endeavoured to escape altogether from this tradition, and was then

driven, by this very effort, into a certain disorganization of technical language, which, upon occasion, gave to his terms a capricious seeming, without freeing them altogether from the influence of the past. Locke's struggles with the term *Substance* furnish an instance of the resulting inconveniences. Or again, like Meister Eckhart, or in another way and time, like Wolff, one might make a systematic effort to find translations for a great number of terms of scholastic origin. The result varied according to the genius of the thinker. But in any such case this latter procedure was at least guided by a definite principle. New terms arose, to be sure, side by side with the old. But the process attempted to win a certain unity and continuity.

(2) In the case of Kant, however, the situation is still far more complex and problematic than that present at the outset of modern philosophy. Comparable though he is, in originality of conception, with the great thinkers of antiquity, Kant cannot, like a Plato or an Aristotle, freely invent terms, in his own vernacular, to meet his new needs. He must appeal to tradition; and in so far he is like his modern predecessors. On the other hand, he is not content to translate scholastic, nor yet simply to accept Wolffian, terminology. Nor yet is he, like Locke, in a conscious revolt against the traditions of language which all the while bind him. He wishes to reform without unnecessary transformation. He intends to select and to adapt for his own purpose. But since he cannot select and adapt with the freedom of an ancient Greek, and since the originality of his ideas equally forbids him to remain content with what he finds, in the way of means of expression, he is led to efforts at reform which follow no one principle, and which seldom seem wholly to satisfy even himself. His training and his method often appear to us to savour of pedantry. Yet as a fact, he loves his meanings so much better than his words, that he is impatient with merely terminological researches; and he has an imperfect acquaintance with the history either of thought or of usage. Moreover, while the terms used by his contemporaries and immediate predecessors are known to him in great masses, his thoughts are still far richer than his vocabulary, and at the critical stages of his mental evolution they develop much faster than his most elaborate displays of terminological skill can follow them. In consequence, there are extended passages in Kant's works, e. g. in the 'Deduction of the Categories' in the *Kritik der reinen Vernunft*, where the terminology alters in the course of the same discussion. Such changes are doubtless often due to Kant's habit of making up his longer works out of fragments, which were written down at various times, and afterwards collected and ordered. But the result, as we find it in Kant's printed text, is often baffling enough. His usage in such cases seems to be in a sort of Heraclitean flux, so that we do not twice step into the same river of expression while we wander in search of the thought.

(3) A thorough history of Kant's terminology is still to be written. Much of importance is already to be found in the authoritative, but too diffuse, *Commentar zu Kant's Kritik der reinen Vernunft*, by Professor Hans Vaihinger, of which two volumes have so far appeared (i, Stuttgart, 1881; ii, 1892). But the most important portions of the *Kritik* and of its terminology still await their treatment in Vaihinger's work. Paulsen, in his admirable volume, *Immanuel Kant, sein Leben und seine Lehre* (Frommann's *Klassiker der Philosophie*, Stuttgart, 1898), has discussed (especially 144–55) a number of Kant's most characteristic and important concepts and expressions. Adickes, in his edition of the *Kritik der reinen Vernunft* (Berlin, 1889), has introduced into his crisply written notes a large number of explanations of Kantian expressions. The general historical relations of the Kantian terminology are treated by Eucken, *Geschichte der philosophischen Terminologie* (139–50). The psychological vocabulary of Kant, with especial reference to its relations to the Ethics, is extensively and carefully expounded by Alfred Hegler, *Die Psychologie in Kant's Ethik* (Freiburg, 1891). The fullest of all collections of Kant's terms and expressions is Mellin's *Encyclopädisches Wörterbuch der kritischen Philosophie, oder Versuch einer fasslichen und vollständigen Erklärung der in Kant's kritischen und dogmatischen Schriften enthaltenen Begriffe und Sätze* (Züllichau and Leipzig, 1797). Mellin, who also published other contributions to the terminological comprehension of Kant, here undertakes what is to be at once an encyclopedia of Kant's doctrine, and an exposition of the sense of his expressions and ideas. The result, however, is rather a thesaurus of Kantian statements than any thorough explanation of their forms and meanings. Mellin is a

harmonizer, who smooths over difficulties as skilfully as Vaihinger, in his commentary, emphasizes or even magnifies them. Mellin's book is published in six volumes (having eleven parts). Krug's *Philosophisches Lexikon* contains also the Kantian vocabulary, but without the modern effort at a philological treatment of the Kantian usage. The recent *Wörterbuch der philosophischen Begriffe und Ausdrücke*, by Eisler (Berlin, 1899), so far as it has yet appeared, contains much valuable material for comparing Kant's usage with that of his predecessors. The monographic literature upon Kant furnishes an immense number of discussions of Kant's terms,—discussions which are, however, generally found only in subordination to some more general expository or critical interest. No attempt can here be made at any bibliographical analysis of this literature with reference to its bearings upon Kantian terminology. The original materials upon which Kant's own selection of his terms is based are to be found in the Latin and German works of Wolff; in the textbooks of Baumgarten, whose *Metaphysica* (which reached its seventh edition in 1779) was long Kant's favourite textbook in that subject; and finally in the general literature, philosophical and psychological, of Kant's day. In following the evolution of Kant's thought, upon the basis of these contemporary influences, one has constantly to deal, of course, with terminological questions, which accordingly find their place in the important monographic treatises of Benno Erdmann (*Kant's Kriticismus in der ersten und in der zweiten Auflage der Kritik der reinen Vernunft,* Leipzig, 1878), and of Adickes (*Kant-Studien,* Kiel and Leipzig, 1895)—treatises which we may select from this whole literature for especial mention in this connection. The student of Kant's language should pay due attention to Jäsche's edition of Kant's *Logik* (published in the eighth volume of the chronological edition of Kant's works, by Hartenstein, 1868, 1–141); and, in regard to Kant's psychological terminology, should also consult his *Anthropologie in pragmatischer Hinsicht,* published in 1798. Kant's own formal definitions of his terms are seldom to be accepted as final; nor are his reports of the historical or of the current usage of a term, such for instance as *a priori,* to be regarded as authoritative. Kant was once for all no historian of thought or of usage; and his resolutions as to the use of his own

terms are merely expressions of a present and serious effort, which may or may not prove permanently efficacious, to use a particular device for clarifying and organizing his ideas. In general, he is a great lover of analysis; so that while, like Aristotle and the Scholastics, he makes systematic use of the method of distinctions for the sake of explaining or removing the contradictions of thought and opinion, he is much more radical than any of his predecessors in the distinctions that he draws, and his world largely consists of definable barriers and chasms. Kant loves, meanwhile, synthesis, but is never as successful in this direction as in the other (see the excellent observations of Eucken, op. cit., 143–5). One synthetic aspect of his systematic undertakings he especially emphasizes, namely, the ideal of an exhaustive enumeration of all the provinces of reality, and of all the problems of thought, which come within his scope. Many of the devices of his terminology have to do with the pursuit of this ideal. Thus the table of categories is the outcome of an effort, whose development occupied several years, to obtain a complete table of the fundamental conceptions of the understanding. Associated with this table is a list, equally intended to be complete, which enumerates the *a priori* principles of the understanding; and so on. In order to obtain such formal completeness, Kant sometimes is led to arbitrary inventions, whereby a scheme is filled out, in a way whose importance is clear only to himself. The methods of Kant's work while he was engaged in the construction of his doctrine and of its various expressions can best be studied in the *Reflexionen,* edited by Professor Benno Erdmann, and in the *Lose Blätter aus Kant's Nachlass,* edited by Rudolf Reicke. The *Reflexionen* are notes made by Kant in connection with his lectures upon Baumgarten's *Metaphysik.* The *Lose Blätter* contains a great variety of fragmentary notes, made upon various occasions. The terminology used in these notes is by no means always in agreement with that known through Kant's published works.

(4) Kant never lived to write the sort of encyclopedic statement of a system of philosophy which he himself desired to produce. His most important works, the *Kritik der reinen Vernunft,* the *Kritik der praktischen Vernunft,* and the *Kritik der Urtheilskraft,* constitute, in his own opinion, merely introductory discussions, indispensable, but needing

in their turn to be followed by a reconstruction of doctrine made in the light of these critical researches. In general, Kant conceives philosophy as the sum total of what he terms *reine Vernunfterkenntniss aus Begriffen*—an expression most easily translated as 'conceptual knowledge gained through pure reason alone.' The two antitheses which define philosophy are (1) the contrast with mathematics, and (2) the contrast with empirical science. Mathematics makes use of ideas of pure reason, but does so only by the intermediation of the process of construction, whereby Kant means any process such as gets expressed in a diagram or figure, when the diagram or figure is intended as the visible embodiment of a rational conception. Philosophy is not thus dependent upon a voluntary construction of its objects in sensuous form. It conceives them in their purity, and reflects upon their meanings and their connections. In contrast to empirical science, philosophy uses no empirical data, as such, amongst its presuppositions. This latter contrast in Kant's definition of philosophy was, in its origin, Wolffian, and the whole tendency of Kant's own thought is to deprive it of much of its positive meaning; since, as Kant in the end discovers, there is no theoretical knowledge *aus reiner Vernunft* except the knowledge of the necessary structure which must belong to the whole realm of experience. In consequence, a better name for Kant's theoretical philosophy would be the Theory of Experience; and this name, whose accuracy is implied by many of Kant's expressions, has been actually adopted by some modern Kantians (e. g. Cohen). Philosophy in general is divided into the two great divisions, *Theoretical* and *Practical*. Another, and coordinate, division of philosophy is that into its critical or preparatory portion, called *Transcendentalphilosophie*, and its systematic portion, called *Metaphysik*. The *Transcendentalphilosophie* has to deal with the sources and scope of our rational knowledge. *Metaphysik* has to set forth the sum total of our purely rational, i. e. non-empirical knowledge, concerning both the objects of theory (God, Nature, the Soul) and the objects of rational choice as such, or of freedom (Duty, the Moral Law, the Absolute Good). It is the *Transcendentalphilosophie* which Kant has most fully developed. On Kant's division of philosophy, one may consult his own essay *Ueber Philosophie überhaupt* (1794) in Hartenstein's edition (1868), vi. 373; also, the *Kritik*

der reinen Vernunft, Methodenlehre, 3tes *Hauptstück*. On the contrast between mathematics and philosophy, see the *Methodenlehre*, 1tes *Hauptstück*, 2nd ed. of the *Kritik der reinen Vernunft*, 751. [As is now customary in citations from Kant, the *Kritik der reinen Vernunft* is here to be cited after the pages of the second edition; while in case of difference between the editions, the paging of the first edition is to be cited for passages that occur only in that edition. Other Kantian works are to be cited after the Hartenstein edition of 1868.] One may compare, upon the same topic, Mellin's articles *Encyclopädie*, *Metaphysik*, *Transcendentalphilosophie*; and Paulsen, op. cit., 108 ff. Kant is by no means quite uniform in his account of these main divisions of philosophy.

(5) All further classifications of Kant's doctrines and conceptions are greatly influenced by his psychological conceptions. 'We can,' he says (*Werke*, vi. 379), 'reduce all the powers of the human mind to three:—*Intellect* (*Erkenntnissvermögen*); *Feeling* (*das Gefühl der Lust und Unlust*, a power always to be defined in terms of this contrast of *pleasure and pain*); and *Will* (*das Begehrungsvermögen*, or the power whereby mental states come to be viewed as the *causes of the existence of objects*).' The *Erkenntnissvermögen* itself is first divided into a *passive* aspect, the *Sensibility* (*Sinnlichkeit*), the *lower* portion of the *Erkenntnissvermögen*; and an *active* aspect, the *intellectuelles Erkenntnissvermögen*, whose general activity is called *Denken* (*Anthropologie*, *Werke*, vii. 451). For this latter, the *higher* portion of the *Erkenntnissvermögen*, or the intellect proper, the words *Verstand* and *Vernunft* are upon occasion used almost interchangeably, both of them in a broader or more inclusive sense (e. g. *Verstand* in the *Anthropologie*, loc. cit.; *Vernunft* in the title of the *Kritik der reinen Vernunft*, where it also even includes the *a priori* aspect of the *Sinnlichkeit*). In more exact usage, however, the *Verstand* is only one of three special divisions of the *oberes Erkenntnissvermögen*. The three are *Verstand*, *Urtheilskraft*, and *Vernunft*. The *Verstand*, in this more special sense, is the power that forms *concepts* (*Begriffe*), or that knows, or furnishes, or applies the *rules* of the formal constitution of conceptual objects. The *Verstand* also is the power to apprehend the unity which gets expressed in our judgments. And in this sense the *Verstand* can even be called (*Krit. d. reinen Vernunft*, 2nd ed., 94) the *Vermögen*

zu urtheilen. But as distinct from the *Verstand*, the *Urtheilskraft* proper is the power to find what cases fall under given concepts, or the power to 'subsume under rules.' And the *Vernunft*, in contrast with both of these powers, is the power to systematize into unity, and by means of inclusive *principles*, the less inclusive *rules* of the *Verstand* (*Krit. d. reinen Vernunft*, 2nd ed., 359). Thus the *Vernunft* is the power which conceives God, the Universe, and the Moral Law. Yet while Kant makes these distinctions, or related ones, repeatedly, he remains in his usage consistent with no one of them (cf. Vaihinger, *Commentar*, i. 123, 166, 454 note, and in many other passages). Permanent only is the *tendency* to define the *Verstand* as the power of thought in so far as it is expressed in *single* acts of judgment or of conception, and the *Vernunft* as the systematizing tendency of thought in its search for all embracing unities; while the *Urtheilskraft*, standing between the two former powers, does excellent service to Kant in completing the schematism of his accounts of intellectual processes, by taking charge of whatever the two other powers may seem to have neglected. That the three powers of the higher *Erkenntnissvermögen* have a peculiarly apt one-to-one relation, in their turn, to the three general powers of the mind (in that our objective knowledge of reality is properly to be limited to the field of the empirically applied *Verstand*, while the principles for the free self-determination of the Will belong to the *Vernunft*, and the *Urtheilskraft* is of especial service in expressing the definable aspect of the *values* present to the *Gefühl*),—all this is a characteristic thesis which Kant expounds in the essay on *Philosophie überhaupt*, and which enables him to explain the title of his *Kritik der Urtheilskraft*—the treatise wherein Kant's doctrine of the Beautiful, and his Teleology, are both contained (see the cited essay, *Werke*, vi. 402 f.).

(6) In general, this psychological terminology of Kant, while of the most constant use as a means of determining the divisions of his work, and the trend of his various researches, is of a bewildering complexity and changeableness. The bewildering effect is, however, due not so much to the mere changes themselves, as to the fact that Kant repeatedly makes much of the importance and exactness of distinctions amongst the various mental powers and processes, while he himself is the first soon to alter or to ignore these very

distinctions. Of considerable and very baffling importance, in Kant's psychological vocabulary, is the term *Gemüth*, used on the whole very much as recent English writers employ the term *Mind*. In general, this word is evidently felt by Kant to be relatively presuppositionless, and he so expresses himself, vi. 458. Thus the term seems not to imply any decision as to the problems of rational psychology, or as to the various aspects of the ego; so that, as Hegler well points out (*Psychol. in Kant's Ethik*, 52), this term takes the place of the more metaphysically coloured term *Seele*, where Kant has to speak of the empirical processes wherein the various mental powers co-operate, and so get their concrete expression. Yet, as the *Gemüth* can 'affect itself' and thereby produce the phenomena of the *innerer Sinn*, and has a life that evidently goes beyond what is directly revealed by consciousness (Eisler, s. v., seems incorrectly to identify *Bewusstsein* and *Gemüth* in Kant's usage), the precise implications of the term become puzzling whenever we have to deal with the problem as to the sense in which the *a priori* principles are *original*, or are innate (in so far as they are in any sense innate) in the *Gemüth*. The manifold uses of the term *Gemüth* have been well collected by Hegler (loc. cit.).

(7) There remain two psychological terms of Kant which cannot be passed over without some mention even in the most general sketch. These terms are *innerer Sinn* and *Einbildungskraft*. The *innerer Sinn* is a term in very general use in the psychology of the 18th century. In origin it dates back to the Aristotelian-Scholastic doctrine of the *sensus communis*; but its 18th-century form was largely due to Locke's well-known passage upon 'the notice that the mind takes of its own operations.' As the term had to compete, in its pre-Kantian history, with the Leibnitzian term *Apperception* (also used by Kant), and with still other terms for the general nature of consciousness, its place remained indefinite. In Kant's usage it is rendered perplexing because of its relations, as a *passive* power, to the intimately associated *active* processes of consciousness with which it is bound up. In a very few passages (of which two are given by Hegler, op. cit., 54), the *inner sense* even appears as itself active – even as thinking and judging. In this sense it would assume the functions of the *Verstand*. In general, however, it is a capacity, within the mind or the ego, to receive, passively, the influence

of the active understanding or *Einbildungs-kraft*, and so to get presented the more or less organized facts of the inner life. Like the outer sense, it presents to us phenomenal and not ultimate reality, and does not show us the ego in itself, but only the self as empirical. Its form is time, just as space is the form of the outer sense. But the parallel between inner and outer sense proves to be hopelessly incomplete, and the term is an unhappy and superfluous one despite its frequent use. The *Einbildungskraft* plays a more important part. It occupies, in Kant's doctrine, the place of an essentially mediating principle. In all the history of philosophy (and also of theology) the principles that may be called in general the mediators have played an important part. The *Logos* in Stoic and Alexandrine philosophy; the *Pneuma* in later ancient psychology and theology; the *Nous* and the *Soul* in the doctrine of Plotinus; the *attributes* of the substance in Spinoza, and the *infinite modes* in the same system; the so-called *Platonic ideas* as interpreted by Schopenhauer for the purposes of his own system:—all these are examples of such mediating concepts. In terminology the names of these mediators are always confessedly more or less ambiguous. The ambiguity goes along with the synthetic tendency which gives rise to these conceptions, and this ambiguity constitutes at once the convenience and the defect of such terms. In depth of implication they are superior to the more sharply defined and abstract terms that name the opposed and extreme principles which the mediators are to bring into unity. But this depth is purchased by vagueness. The mediators suggest the actual life of things better than do the comparatively dead extremes; but they have the disadvantages of their very concreteness. The *Einbildungs-kraft* is such a mediator. It has many functions, *reproductive* and *productive*. The former are the more familiar; the latter are the more important, since it is through them that the data of sense are brought into synthesis, and the *Verstandesbegriffe* or forms of the understanding—the categories—get applied to experience. The *Einbildungskraft*, as productive, is at once sensuous and intelligent. It is the minister of the *Verstand*, and is in fact the *Verstand* in action, so that in places it seems to make the very concept of the *Verstand* itself superfluous. Its functions are more or less antecedent to, and apart from, our actual consciousness. We are aware, from moment to moment, rather of the results than

of the original synthetic processes of the *Einbildungskraft*. In our practical life the same power has also its important place. The stress laid upon the *Einbildungskraft* in its distinction from the rest of the higher *Erkenntnissvermögen* thus threatens to destroy the finality of the usual threefold division of the latter; but Kant is preserved from admitting this consequence because of the intimate relations which the *Einbildungskraft* all the while establishes with its neighbours. See upon this term *Anthropologie*, vii. 495–7; *Krit. d. reinen Vernunft* (1st ed.), 103 ff., especially 119, where the *Einbildungskraft* is brought into relation to *Verstand* and *Apperception* (2nd ed.), 151 ff. One may also consult Hegler (op. cit., 143 ff.); Adickes in the notes to the deductions of the two editions of the *Kritik*; and E. F. Buchner, *A Study of Kant's Psychology* (Monog. Suppl., No. 4, to the *Psychol. Rev.*), 114–17. See also Paulsen, op. cit., 175.

(8) Between Kant's psychological and his epistemological terminology stand the important terms *Apperception* and *Einheit der Apperception*, the general names for the *active unity of consciousness*, a principle whose tendency is expressed by the fact that, in view of the presence of this apperception, or in view of the unity of apperception, every conscious state is *capable of being viewed as mine*, or as, in its form, the product of *my activity*. In its most explicit form, *Apperception* is identical with *self-consciousness*, since when I know my states definitely, I know them as *my own*. But one can speak of apperception when the *Ich denke* is viewed merely as the *possible* accompaniment of every conscious state. The idea of the self, the consciousness that *it is I who think this*, may be either clear or obscure at any moment; but, says Kant (1st ed., 117 note): 'The possibility of the logical form of all knowledge necessarily depends upon its relation to this apperception as a capacity' (*Vermögen*). So too, in the 2nd ed., 131–2, he uses the often quoted expression: 'Das *Ich denke* muss alle meine Vorstellungen begleiten können.' This *Ich denke*, however, must be an act of spontaneity, opposed in nature to the passivity of sense. Through the work of the *Einbildungs-kraft*, which applies the forms of the *Verstand* to the data of sense, I come to be thus able to say, *Ich denke*. The one original act of referring all to the self is at the basis of the entire process, and the result expresses the meaning of this act, which is at first a

latent or subconscious act, in conscious form. The term *Apperception* comes to Kant from Leibnitz. Descartes had earlier employed the corresponding verb.

(9) The special terminology of the theory of knowledge in the *Krit. d. reinen Vernunft* is so complex, and the interdependence of the various terms is so intimate, that no complete account of this terminology could be given without a lengthy exposition of the whole system. One must confine the following statement to a very few important points; and in general, the remainder of this article must be devoted merely to specimens of Kant's terminology.

(10) Kant's theory of knowledge, as is well known, maintains that the internal process of applying the forms of the understanding to the facts of sense introduces into our whole conceptual world that conformity to law which the earlier rationalistic theories of knowledge had supposed to be the revelation of an absolute external truth, but which Kant views as no revelation of anything absolute. While our experience has to conform to law, and is known in advance to be thus subject to necessary principles, the lawful connectedness of our experience is due to the unity of apperception, to the synthetic work of the *Einbildungskraft*, to the activity of the *Verstand*, to the spontaneity of our thought (*Denken*) in general, and not to our knowledge of any absolute or external truth. All these expressions dwell, as we have now seen, upon various aspects of what is, for Kant, the same great fact. It is the *intellect* that weaves the unity of its own world. Meanwhile, the intellect, or the *Einbildungskraft* in particular, is indeed *produktiv* but not creative (*schöpferisch*). It needs, namely, material for its weaving, and without such *given material* it can do nothing. This material is furnished to it by the *Sinnlichkeit*. The latter, although passive, has its Forms. These are usually called the forms of the *Anschauung*, i. e. of perception. They are space and time; and these forms (especially the latter form, time) predetermine what *schemes*, or general types of objects (*Schemata*), the *Einbildungskraft* can weave, when it applies the forms of the *Verstand* to the facts of sense. Thus there are two types of *forms*, or of characteristic *conditions of knowledge*, which are determined for us by the original nature of our sort of intelligence: viz. the forms of the *Verstand*, and the forms of the *Sinnlichkeit* or of the *Anschauung*. The forms of the *Anschauung* Kant considers in

the first division of the critical analysis of our knowledge in the *Kritik*. This division is called the *Aesthetik*, as being the doctrine of *sense*. The forms of the *Verstand* are studied in the *Analytik*, whose name Kant derives from the known terminology of the Aristotelian Logic.

(11) The most general terms which express the central thoughts of the resulting theory of knowledge can be brought together by means of a series of theses. As Kant teaches:— (*a*) We can know only *phenomena* (*Erscheinungen*), not *things in themselves* (*Dinge an sich*), or *Noumena*. (*b*) But we can know, *a priori* or *aus reiner Vernunft*, that the *Erscheinungen* are subject to universal and necessary *laws* (*Regeln*), so that *a priori Grundsätze*, upon which all empirical science depends, are possible, and can be exhaustively stated, on the basis of a complete enumeration of all the categories or the understanding or of the fundamental concepts or *Begriffe*. (*c*) In view of this limitation and accompanying necessity to be found in the world of our knowledge, the field of human insight can be defined as *Erfahrung*. *Erfahrung* constitutes, in a sense, *one whole*; for although empirical facts are countless, and although the brute data of sense are not controlled by the understanding, the order of the realm of experience is due to the categories, and the *Einheit der möglichen Erfahrung*, or *unity of possible experience*, is assured in advance, by virtue of the relation of all special facts of experience to the *Ich denke* or to the original unity of *Apperception*. (*d*) The knowledge of this whole theory is, for Kant, a *transcendental* knowledge. Applied to the interpretation of the problems of philosophy, it frees us from the *Antinomien* with which human thought has thus far been beset. It rids us from bondage to the necessary *illusions*, the *Dialectic* of the *Vernunft*; and so at once sets the due limits to our knowledge, and assures us of the sovereignty of rationality within the sphere that is open to our science. Hereby the possibility (*Möglichkeit*) of experience, of science, and of synthetic judgments *a priori*, is established.

(12) All the terms thus named are of central importance for Kant; and many of them are difficult. We may begin here with one of the most famous and puzzling of the list—the adjective *transcendental*. The word had in scholastic terminology its established usage, which is very different from the Kantian usage. It was an adjective applied to those predicates which the scholastic doctrine re-

garded as *transcending in generality* even the Aristotelian categories themselves. These *transcendentals* were *unity, truth,* and *goodness,* together with *thing* and *something.* But the term *transcendentals* referred solely to the high degree of generality of these predicates, and had no relation to the possibility of our knowing them, or to the conditions of our knowledge of them. In Baumgarten's *Metaphysica* (§§ 72–123), while these same predicates, *unum, verum, bonum,* are treated upon the basis of the scholastic tradition, stress is laid upon the fact that, in every being, these predicates are in some sense present of *necessity*; and *unum transcendentaliter* is translated, in Baumgarten's note (§ 73), by the German phrase *wesentlich eins,* while *veritas transcendentalis* (§ 89) is translated in the note by *nothwendige metaphysische Wahrheit.* The *twofold* character of the epithet *transcendental,* as thus known to Kant in former usage, appeared to him to warrant an analogous, but novel usage. For *transcendental* had thus been (*a*) no direct predicate of any *object,* but a predicate technically applied to certain *predicates,* viz., as we have seen, to the predicates *unum, verum, bonum.* (*b*) It had also (in Baumgarten's usage) come to imply a certain necessity and universality about these predicates themselves. Having once proposed to himself the problem of a theory of necessary knowledge, or of knowledge valid in advance of all experience, Kant needed a predicate to characterize the type of knowledge which should constitute this new theory. He chose *transcendental,* and declared (*Krit. d. reinen Vernunft,* 2nd ed., 25) that by *transcendentale Erkenntniss* he intended (*a*) to mean not any kind of knowledge of objects, but a knowledge concerned with a particular *type of knowledge* (*Erkenntnissart*), viz. of that type of knowledge which (*β*) his new theory of the *necessary principles* of the understanding was to embody. This new usage thus imitated, for the purposes of Kant's theory, *both* of the aspects of Baumgarten's former usage.

(13) But the meaning of *transcendental* as *theoretical knowledge about the necessary principles of all knowledge about objects* never remains steadfast in Kant's usage, just because he had so long lectured upon Baumgarten's text, and because the old usage entered into all sorts of curious psychological complications, in his own mind, with the ideas associated with his new enterprise. The term is otherwise explained in the *Krit. d. reinen Vernunft,* 352–3. It is otherwise used in a fashion which

Adickes calls *weitherzig* (see his note to p. 25 of the 2nd ed. of the *Krit. d. reinen Vernunft*), and which Vaihinger declares to constitute the 'most difficult terminological problem' in Kant, and even in 'all modern philosophy' (*Commentar,* i. 467). The term is often confused with *transcendent,* and then means going beyond, or transcending, the limits of human knowledge. Of the other meanings, no complete account has yet been published by any student. They must be made out from the context, each time afresh.

(14) Our necessary knowledge about the world of experience is founded upon *a priori* principles. The term here used has its origin in the well-known Aristotelian distinction between what is *prior in nature* and what is *prior for us.* In modern thought, ever since the scholastic period, the Aristotelian distinction had been familiar; and the special expressions *a priori* and *a posteriori,* used as adjective phrases qualifying especially the noun *demonstration,* had been employed since the later scholasticism. To know or demonstrate *a priori* is, in this sense, to know through *causes* or *principles,* as opposed to a knowledge gained wholly through the particular facts of experience. Kant gives the term a new and more special meaning. Knowledge *a priori* is for him knowledge *in advance of all experience,* and hence is a knowledge of the content of any of the necessary concepts or principles of thought. These necessary principles are themselves *a priori,* because they are independent of experience.

(15) But by virtue of this knowledge, which we get through the *a priori* principles, we become acquainted with phenomena, and not with *Noumena,* with *Erscheinungen,* and not with *Dinge an sich.* The terms here used have become extremely familiar in recent literature. Their Kantian usage still suggests, however, many topics of controversy. The phrase *an sich* goes back to the well-known Greek usage, in both Plato and Aristotle, according to which anything that truly exists, or that truly is known, exists or is known καθ' αὐτό, i. e. *per se* or *in se* (cf. Aristotle, *Met.,* VII. 4. 1029 b). Kant's relative novelty in usage lies in the fact that in speaking of the *Ding an sich* he emphasizes the thing in itself, not in an abstract contrast to *other things* in general, or to its relations to such other things, but in a contrast with *knowledge only.* This contrast of the thing in itself with the thing's seeming or appearance was indeed not new; but Kant expressly emphasizes it as against

all other aspects of the *an sich*. The *Ding an sich* then is the thing as it exists independently of and apart from all knowledge. The principal problems as to the *Ding an sich* are: (*a*) whether Kant really assumes its existence as a positive fact; (*b*) how he conceives that existence; and (*c*) how he reconciles such affirmation of the thing's existence *an sich* with the theory of the subjectivity of all our knowledge. While a discussion of these problems belongs elsewhere, there can be no doubt that Kant does assume the independent reality of *Dinge an sich* as a positive fact, and does not make any serious attempt to demonstrate that reality. The correlate of the *Ding an sich* is the *Erscheinung*, to which, however, Kant attributes not mere existence in our private and isolated experience from moment to moment, but a certain secondary type of reality, or of *objectivity*, due to the fact that the *Erscheinung* follows universal laws, which are equally valid for all men. An *Erscheinung* is no mere *Schein*; it is a fact for all of us men,—a verifiable content of *possible experience*.

(16) In addition to the term *Ding an sich*, Kant uses for the objects of the metempirical realm two other terms: *Noumenon* and *transcendentaler Gegenstand*. The former of these terms comes to Kant from his own dogmatic period (cf. his Inaugural Dissertation, *Werke*, ii. 403). It is the relic of the stage when he still opposed to the phenomenal world the world of true Being, knowable, in abstraction from all sensuous facts, through the pure intellect. A *Noumenon* is a reality such as one *would* know who could seize ultimate truth through his understanding alone, *without the aid of sense*. As a positive concept, this is wholly rejected by Kant in his critical period. Viewed negatively, the concept of the *Noumenon* as the object which we (who are bound to sense whenever we seek to win any positive knowledge) do *not* know and cannot know,—this *Noumenon* becomes, in *denotation*, identical with the *Ding an sich*; but the two concepts have a different origin. The *Ding an sich* is a concept expressing a *selbstverständliche Voraussetzung* (see Benno Erdmann's work before cited, *Kant's Kriticismus*), viz. the presumption that phenomena somewhat independently real must correspond. The *Noumenon* is a concept reached by first conceiving an object of the pure intellect, and by then observing that such an object must for ever lie beyond our ken, since what we know is a phenomenal world, where sense-facts are subject to the *a priori* laws of the *Verstand*.

(17) The *transcendentaler Gegenstand* is a concept of still a different origin. The *Verstand* refers all content of sense to an object. This is the very nature of the *Verstand*. Hereby it accomplishes its task of conceiving the facts of sense as in unity. But any object once conceived, through an intellectual synthesis of sense-data, e.g. *this house*, *this stone*, remains, as an object present to our experience, still but a *Vorstellung*, i.e. a particular *idea*, or content of our consciousness. So soon as we view this *Vorstellung* as such, we are again led to seek for its object; and so on. The limit of this process of referring the contents of experience to still further objects as their basis is given by the concept of an *Etwas = x*, whereof we can only say that it is an *Etwas*, a *something* in general. This is the *transcendentaler Gegenstand*, the *object that I am trying to know through every particular act of my empirical knowledge*. This object, the permanently sought *beyond* of my empirical search for truth, can never be presented in experience. I therefore can only define it as *beyond every experience*. It is the law of my consciousness thus to seek for, but never to find, the ultimate correlate of my own conscious activity, namely, *the final object that I am trying to know*. While the *Noumenon*, then, as such, is first positively conceived as the object of the pure intellect, and is thereafter found to be nothing knowable to us, the *transcendentaler Gegenstand*, as such, is first conceived as that which would finally determine, and if present would satisfy, my *empirical* search for the truth of my own objects. The latter, then, is *der gänzlich unbestimmte Gedanke von Etwas überhaupt*, or *der Gegenstand einer sinnlichen Anschauung überhaupt*. Since it can never be found within experience, but is driven, through the essential endlessness of the search, *beyond all experience*, the *transcendentaler Gegenstand* comes at last to *denote*, once more, the absolute *beyond*, for which the *Ding an sich* was the first name.

(18) The three terms then, with different origin and connotation, come, in most passages where they are used, to denote the same object, the inaccessible reality. See *Krit. d. reinen Vernunft*, 1st ed., 109, and the section 'Von dem Grunde der Unterscheidung aller Gegenstände überhaupt in Phenomena und Noumena,' in both editions. Compare the *Doctor-Dissertation* of Rudolf Lehmann, *Kant's Lehre vom Ding an sich* (Berlin, 1878); Cohen's discussion in *Kant's Theorie der Erfahrung*

(2nd ed., Berlin, 1885), 501 ff.; and the accounts of Benno Erdmann (op. cit.) and Paulsen (pp. 153–5 of his op. cit.).

(19) The realm of our actual knowledge is *Erfahrung*. Here again we have a word of ambiguous meaning. In general it is used in two senses: (1) as the sum total of facts so far as they are determined not by necessary principles, but by the immediate data of sense; (2) as the sum total of facts in so far as they are determined to unity by the application of the principles of the *Understanding*, and are so brought under the *unity of apperception*. In the first sense, *Erfahrung* is the source of knowledge in so far as it is not *a priori*. In the second sense, *Erfahrung* is a realm of *possible perceptions*, all of which are woven into unity by their universal and synthetic relations to the self.

(20) The judgments which we can make, in advance, concerning all objects of possible experience, are *synthetic judgments a priori*. Such judgments are opposed, as *synthetic*, to *analytic* judgments. The latter judgments express in their predicates nothing but what was already contained in the explicit or known meaning of their subjects; e.g. *Every triangle has three angles*. But a synthetic judgment passes *beyond* the direct meaning of its subject to bring this meaning into unity with that of a *new* predicate; e.g. *Every change has a cause*. That such synthetic judgments *a priori* can be made regarding the whole constitution of our experience is Kant's principal thesis in his *Deduction of the Categories*. The categories themselves (by no means identical either in name or in character with the original Categories of Aristotle, despite some points of agreement) are the fundamental concepts *a priori* of the *Verstand*, the forms in conformity with which the *Einbildungskraft* weaves into unity the data of sense. The list of the categories can be given exhaustively, as Kant thinks, and upon this basis an equally exhaustive list of the *Grundsätze* of the understanding, the principles or basal synthetic judgments *a priori*, can be drawn up.

(21) The *Analytik* of Kant's *Kritik* is devoted to the development of this theory of *Erfahrung*. The *Dialektik* is devoted to an examination of the inevitable claims and efforts of the *Vernunft*, our organ of *principles*, to transcend *all* experience by attempting to weave the provisional unities of the *Verstand* into *absolute unities*. These efforts of the *Vernunft* are as necessary as they are doomed to failure. We cannot primarily avoid the illusions of reason, but we can detect them. In doing so we deal, first, with the *Antinomien* or necessary conflicts between contradictory propositions, to which the *Vernunft* is led. We solve these contradictions by showing that they are due to our tendency to view as absolutely true of things in themselves, principles which apply only to phenomena. The later discussions of the *Dialektik* lead to the problems of Rational Psychology and of Rational Theology. But henceforth, in the *Krit. d. reinen Vernunft*, while the terminology remains intricate enough, it is oftener in touch with that of the older metaphysic; and one who has proceeded so far has grappled with the most serious of the terminological difficulties of the *Kritik*.

(22) The foregoing must serve merely as specimens of some of the most famous of Kant's terms, and as instances of the general principles regarding the nature and growth of his usage which have been discussed in the early portion of this article. No space can here be given to the terminology of the later works of Kant, except in so far as the foregoing discussions already give guidance.

GLOSSARY.

[The numbers refer to the paragraphs of this article.]

A priori, 14.
Aesthetik, 10.
Analytic Judgments, 20.
Analytik, 10, 21.
Anschauung, 10; see also TERMINOLOGY (German).
Antinomien, 21.
Apperception, 8, 11.
Begriff, 5, 7, 11.
Categorien, 7, 11.
Denken, 5, 10.
Dialektik, 11, 21.
Ding an sich, 11, 15; in relation to Noumenon and to transcendentaler Gegenstand, 16–18.
Einbildungskraft, 7; produktive, 10.
Einheit der Apperception, 8; Einheit der möglichen Erfahrung, 11.
Erfahrung, 11, 19.
Erkenntnissvermögen, 5.
Erscheinung, 11, 15.
Forms of Sense and Understanding, 10.
Gefühl, 5.
Gemüth, 6.
Grundsätze *a priori*, 11.
Ich denke, 8, 11.
Innerer Sinn, 6, 7.
Intellect, 10.
Kritik der reinen Vernunft, general character of terminology, 9; terminology of its principal theories, 10–21.

Metaphysik, 4.
Möglichkeit der Erfahrung, 11.
Noumenon, 11, 16–18.
Oberes Erkenntnissvermögen, 5.
Phenomena, 11.
Philosophie in general, 4.
Praktische Philosophie, 4.
Produktive Einbildungskraft, 10.
Regeln, 5, 11.
Schein, 15.
Schemata, 10.
Seele, 6.
Sinnlichkeit in general, 5. See also 10.
Synthetische Urtheile, 11, 20.
Theoretische Philosophie, 4.
Transcendent, 13.
Transcendental, 11–13.
Transcendentaler Gegenstand, 17, 18.
Transcendentalphilosophie, 17, 18.
Urtheilskraft, 5.
Vernunft, 5, 21.
Vernunfterkenntniss, 4.
Verstand, 5, 17.   (J.R.)

Karma [Sansk. *Karman*, from *Kar*, to do or create]. In Hindu philosophy, the principle of individual existence by virtue of which the sum of moral desert in the life of one sentient being becomes the germ which develops another in whose destiny it is a predetermining factor.

Whether the Brahmistic metaphysic of the Vedanta or the more negative conceptions which underlie Buddhism be regarded as the truer expression of Hindu thought, it is still true that in the phenomenal world of causation and change the only persistent feature is the process of metempsychosis, which is an endless re-creation of the world in obedience to moral necessity. The source of this necessity is Karma, which is the seed out of which a new life emerges. A man dies but leaves his Karma, the sum of his moral desert, which necessitates another life as the bearer of its retribution. The process is unending, but the motive of it is Karma exerting the pressure of a moral destiny that is imperishable and inexorable. The only escape from this fatality is through the suppression of Karma itself, which can be attained only by travelling the Hindu road of salvation. The suppression of Karma means freedom from the necessity of existence and absorption into Nirvana, which is either Brahm, the universal life, or nothingness. See ORIENTAL PHILOSOPHY (India).

Literature: DEUSSEN, Die Sûtras des Vedanta (Leipzig, 1887); Appendix to his Metaphysics; and art. Buddhism, in Encyc. Brit. (9th ed.); Buddhism, in Oriental Religions Series (ed. by Max Müller).   (A.T.O.)

Karyokinesis [Gr. κάρυον, a nut, + κίνησις, movement]: Ger. (the same); Fr. *cariocinèse*; Ital. *cariocinesi*. Indirect nuclear division, involving the formation of a spireme or nuclear thread, its segmentation into CHROMOSOMES (q. v.), and the splitting of the chromosomes.

A term suggested by Schleicher in 1878; equivalent to the mitosis of Flemming (1882). See MITOSIS.

Literature: SCHLEICHER, Die Knorpelzelltheilung; FLEMMING, Zellsubstanz. (C.LL.M.)

Karyoplasm [Gr. κάρυον, a nut, + πλάσμα, a thing formed]: Ger. *Zellkernsubstanz*; Fr. *carioplasme*; Ital. *carioplasma*. The nuclear, as opposed to the cytoplasmic, substance of the cell.

A term due to Flemming (1882). In the same year Strasburger introduced the term nucleoplasm for the same substance.

Literature: FLEMMING, Zellsubstanz; STRASBURGER, Ueber den Theilungsvorgang der Zellkerne. (C.LL.M.)

Katabolism [Gr. κατά, down, + βάλλειν, to cast]: Ger. *Katabolismus*; Fr. *catabolisme*; Ital. *catabolismo*. The distinctive METABOLISM (q. v.) whereby complex organic substances break down into less complex forms with concomitant liberation of energy.

A term introduced by Gaskell in 1886. Cf. ANABOLISM. (C.LL.M.)

Katatonia [Gr. κατά, down, + τείνειν, to stretch tightly]: Ger. *Katatonie, Spannungsirrsinn*; Fr. *catatonie*; Ital. *catatonia*. A mental disorder with marked neuro-muscular symptoms, described by Kahlbaum in 1874.

Although not admitted by all writers as a distinct disorder, but only as the presence of a group of symptoms in cases of mental stupor or of circular insanity, &c., yet clinically, as well as theoretically, the term has been recognized in recent literature (cf. Kraepelin, *Psychiatrie*, 441 ff.).

In typical cases the disease shows at first a condition of depression, melancholia, and distress; which condition is at times preceded by a period of nervousness, unsettlement, headache, languor, desire for solitude, and the like. With the depression are apt to occur hallucinations and illusions, mostly connected with the self-accusations and distress of the patient. The depression gives place to, or is at times replaced by, a condition of excitement and agitation, of wild, senseless actions and exciting hallucinations; and it is in this stage that the more distinctive symptoms of katatonia are observed. There is an abeyance or absence of movements, even movements of respiration and of the eyelids being much less frequent. A fixed attitude, and often an uncomfortable one, is rigidly maintained. As soon as passive movements of the patient's limbs are attempted the antagonistic muscles contract energetically; this symptom is termed negativism. If this is slight or is overcome, then the patient's limbs may be set in any posture, however unusual or uncomfortable (*flexibilitas cerea*). The rigid immobility is often interrupted by repetitions of simple stereotyped movements (*Bewegungsstereotypie*). Quite characteristic in many cases is the presence at times of suggestibility, particularly of movement and attitudes and the automatic repetition of peculiar actions or words, along with an obstinate resistance to movement at other times. There is often mutism or complete absence of speech or refusal of food, although not always from purely psychical cause. The disease may terminate in stupor and dementia.

Literature: KAHLBAUM, Die Katatonie; art. Katatonia, in Tuke's Dict. of Psychol. Med.; PH. CHASLIN, La Confusion mentale primitive (1895); SÉGLAS, Troubles du Langage. (J.J.–P.J.–L.M.)

The term is also used (Ger. *katonischer Zustand*; Fr. *catatonie*; Ital. *catatonismo*) by Arndt, Schüle, Morselli, and other alienists to indicate this neuro-muscular condition as a symptom of various mental diseases, e. g. stupidity, amentia, hysteria, &c.

Literature: ARNDT, Lehrb. d. Psychiat.; SCHÜLE, Klin. Psychiat.; MORSELLI, Semej. malat. ment. (E.M.)

Keller, Helen: see BRIDGMAN, LAURA.

Kenosis and **Kenotism** [Gr. κενός, empty]: Ger. *Kenosis, Kenotismus*; Fr. *kénose*; Ital. *chenosi, chenotismo*. That theory of the dual nature of Jesus Christ which represents his divinity as adapting itself by an act of self-emptying or self-limiting to the conditions of a developing human experience.

The doctrine of the kenosis is a modern revival of the ancient controversies over the nature of Jesus Christ. It arose in the 17th century out of a controversy between the theologians of Giessen and Tübingen, the former maintaining that during his earthly career Jesus actually divested himself of his divine attributes, while the Tübingen group held that these attributes were present but concealed from view. The controversy dealt with a profound mystery in a way that developed no new insight.

Literature: Herzog's Real-Encyc., vii. 511 f.,

xiv. 786; DORNER, Doctrine of the Person of Christ, and Amer. Presb. Rev. (July, 1861), 651; McClintock and Strong's Cyclopedia, art. Kenosis. (A.T.O.)

Kierkegaard, Sören. (1813–55.) Born and educated at Copenhagen; his special branches were philosophy and theology. In 1841–2 he visited Germany; after his return he lived in retirement at Copenhagen, engaged in philosophical writing. As a thinker he is related to Hamann, Jean Paul, Feuerbach, and Trendelenburg.

Kinaesthetic (1) **Memory** and (2) **Equivalent**: Ger. (1) *Bewegungsvorstellung, kinaesthetisches Bild*, (2) *kinaesthetisches Aequivalent*; Fr. (1) *image kinesthésique, image motrice* (in use, but inexact—L.M.), (2) *équivalent kinesthésique*; Ital. (1) *immagine cinesica* (or *di movimento*), (2) *equivalente cinestesico*. (1) All images which represent movements of the body, whether the original sensations were immediate or remote in the sense given under KINAESTHETIC SENSATION (1).

(2) Any mental content of the kinaesthetic order which is adequate to secure the voluntary performance of a movement. Suggested by Baldwin, as cited below.

Kinaesthetic sensations and images go to make up kinaesthetic equivalents. The term 'equivalents' is recommended to sum up the formulation that unless a kinaesthetic content, 'equivalent' to a movement, be reinstated in consciousness, the voluntary performance of that movement is impossible. In other words, a movement must be thought of before there can be a volition to perform it, and, according to this formulation, thought of in kinaesthetic terms, i. e. of earlier experiences of movement. In particular, the term is useful (*a*) in connection with the theory of the child's or others' acquisition of voluntary movements, i. e. by getting 'kinaesthetic equivalents'; (*b*) in connection with the pathology of will and attention when the equivalents are disturbed or destroyed; (*c*) with the analysis of particular motor functions, in determining just what elements the equivalents involve. As illustrating these three classes of cases, we may cite (*a*) the child's acquisition of the equivalents of vocal utterance; (*b*) the cases in which certain of the kinaesthetic images are gone, and the patient can only perform a movement when he sees the limb (depending on visual sensational equivalents); and (*c*) such analysis of equivalents as those cited under HANDWRITING

(q. v.). The use of the term, moreover, does not prejudice the discussion of the facts.

Literature: see the indications given under KINAESTHETIC SENSATION. Of special importance are JAMES, Princ. of Psychol., ii. chap. xxvi ; PICK, Die sogenannte 'Conscience Musculaire,' Zeitsch. f. Psychol., iv (1892), 161 ff. ; JANET, Automatisme psychol. ; BALDWIN, Story of the Mind, 16 ff. See also the textbooks of psychology on Voluntary Movement. (J.M.B., G.F.S.)

Kinaesthetic Sensation [Gr. κινεῖν, to move, + αἴσθησις, perception] : Ger. *kinaesthetische Empfindung, (b) Bewegungsempfindung* ; Fr. *sensation kinesthésique* (or *motrice), (b) de mouvement* ; Ital. *sensazione cinestetica* (or *cinesica*—E.M.), *(b) di movimento*. Any sensation which informs us of the movement of the body or of a part of it.

Here belong sensations (*a*) other than those from the moving member, such as those of sight, hearing, &c., of the movement, as well as (*b*)—and to these the adjective 'kinaesthetic' is sometimes restricted—the sensations from the member actually in movement: a group of muscular and other sensation qualities.

The words 'kinaesthesis' and 'kinaesthetic' were first used by Bastian (*Brain as Organ of Mind*, 543). He speaks of the sense of movement, or kinaesthesis, as 'a separate endowment of a complex kind, whereby we are made acquainted with the position and movement of our limbs, whereby we judge of "weight" and "resistance," and by means of which the brain also derives much unconscious guidance in the performance of movements generally, but especially in those of the automatic type.' (E.B.T., J.M.B.)

James has distinguished (*a*) and (*b*) as 'resident' (*b*) and 'remote' (*a*) effects of movement (*Princ. of Psychol.*, 488, 491, 493). This is useful, since it allows free analysis of the entire set of sensations involved. It is accordingly better to follow James's preference (now expressed here) for 'keeping the word a generic one.' Its advantage appears in the discussion of the KINAESTHETIC MEMORY AND EQUIVALENT (q. v.).

Literature: generally the same as for INNERVATION SENSATION, and EFFORT (q.v.); see also BIBLIOG. G, 2, δ, ε. (J.M.B.)

Kind [AS. *cynd*, nature, from *cynde*, natural ; same root as Gr. γένος, Lat. *genus*] : Ger. *Art* (the word 'kind' is also used to translate Ger. *Gattung*, for which see HEGEL'S TERMINOLOGY) ; Fr. *genre* ; Ital. *genere, specie*. Before 'class' acquired its logical

signification in Queen Anne's reign, kind was sometimes used for any collection of objects having a common and peculiar general character, simple or complex.

Thus, in Blundevile's *Arte of Logicke*, we read : '*Genus* is a generall kind which may be spoken of many things differing in speciall kind.' At other times, and more accurately, it was restricted to the species, or narrowest recognized class, or that which was supposed to be derived from one stock. Thus Wilson's *Rule of Reason* (1551) has : '*Genus* is a generall woorde, vnder the whiche diuerse kindes or sortes of thinges are comprehended.'

But before persons who picked their words had become ready to use 'class' as a mere logical extension, they had begun to avoid 'kind,' except when the emphasis of attention was placed upon the logical depth rather than the breadth. Watts's *Logick* (1724) illustrates this. This last is the ordinary popular sense of the word to-day ; so that 'of this kind,' 'of this nature,' 'of this character' are interchangeable phrases. J. S. Mill, however, in his *System of Logic*, Bk. I. chap. vii. § 4, erected the word into a technical term of logic, at the same time introducing the term 'real kind.' His meaning, so far as it was determinate, was that classes are of two orders, the first comprising those which, over and above the characters which are involved in their definitions and which serve to delimit their extension, have, at most, but a limited number of others, and those following as 'consequences, under laws of nature,' of the defining characters ; and the second, the real kinds, comprising those each of which has innumerable common properties independent of one another. As instances of real kinds, he mentions the class of animals and the class of sulphur ; as an instance of a kind not real, the class of white things. It is important for the understanding of Mill's thought here, as throughout his work, to note that when he talks of 'properties,' he has in mind, mainly, characters interesting to us. Otherwise, it would not be true that all white things have few properties in common. By a 'law of nature' he means any absolute uniformity ; so that it is hardly enough to assert that if all white things had any property *P*, this would be a 'consequence, under a law of nature,' of their whiteness ; for it would be itself an absolute and ultimate uniformity. Mill says that if the common properties of a class thus follow from a small number of primary characters 'which, as the phrase is, *account for* all the rest,' it is not a real kind. He does not remark that the man of science is bent upon ultimately thus accounting for each and every property that he studies. The following definition might be proposed: Any class which, in addition to its defining character, has another that is of permanent interest and is common and peculiar to its members, is destined to be conserved in that ultimate conception of the universe at which we aim, and is accordingly to be called 'real.' (C.S.P.)

Kind (in biology) [AS. *cynd*, from *cyn*, family]. Another term for SPECIES (q. v.), as in the phrase 'each after his kind' (Gen. i. 21 ff.). See also CLASSIFICATION (in biology).

The term has been extended to apply to various groupings analogous to biological species, and has been used in sociology in the phrase CONSCIOUSNESS OF KIND (q.v.). (J.M.B.)

Kind and **Degree:** for the foreign equivalents see the separate topics. A distinction applied to differences or transformations according as they are (degree) or are not (kind) stated entirely in terms of QUANTITY (q. v.).

The distinction, as popularly used, covers many ambiguities and confusions. (J.M.B.)

Kindergarten [Ger. *Kinder*, children, + *Garten*, garden]: Fr. *jardin de petits enfants*; Ital. *giardino d' infanzia*. A school for very young children, in which play is utilized as an instrument of instruction in the facts of nature and the customs and ideals of society.

According to Froebel, its founder, the object is as follows:—'It shall receive children before the school age, give them employment suited to their nature, strengthen their bodies, exercise their senses, employ the waking mind, make them acquainted judiciously with nature and society, cultivate especially the heart and temper, and lead them to the foundation of all living—to unity with themselves.'

Literature: FROEBEL, Educ. of Man; BOWEN, Froebel and Educ. by Self-activity. (C. DE G.)

Kinesis (1) and (2) **Metakinesis** [Gr. κινεῖν, to move, μετά, beyond]: not in use in Fr. and Ger.; Ital. *cinesi* and *metacinesi* (suggested—E.M.). (1) Physical movement as characterizing the material world; and (2) its supposed correlative or accompanying aspect which is psychical or quasi-psychical. Cf. MIND DUST THEORY.

Terms of the DOUBLE ASPECT THEORY (q.v.), introduced by Lloyd Morgan, for the two aspects in the case of physical changes in which the psychic aspect is not apparent. A metakinesis is assumed, according to the requirements of the theory, to accompany the kinesis. See Lloyd Morgan, *Animal Life and Intelligence* (1891), and cf. K. Pearson, *Grammar of Science* (2nd ed., 1900), 339 ff. (J.M.B., C.LL.M.)

Kinesodic [Gr. κίνησις, movement, + ὁδός, road]: Ger. *impulsleitend, kinesodisch* (see note on Ger. equiv. for AESTHESODIC); Fr. *kinésodique*; Ital. *cinesiodico*. Originative rather than receptive; said of tracts and centres which convey or give origin to centrifugal impulses. Cf. AESTHESODIC. More inclusive than 'motor' in the same connections, and not implying that the impulse necessarily issues in muscular contraction. Stimuli which produce or regulate secretion, digestion, and the like, or even inhibitory impulses, may be kinesodic. (H.H.)

Kinetic [Gr. κινεῖν, to move]: Ger. *kinetisch*; Fr. *cinétique*; Ital. *cinetico*. Relating to or growing out of motion, especially motion as an element of energy.

Kinetic theory of gases: the theory that air and other gases are formed of disconnected molecules in rapid motion and constantly colliding; that their heat is only the energy of these molecules due to their motion, and that their elasticity is only apparent, and is really due to the collisions of the molecules against the sides of the containing vessel.

Kinetic energy: see ENERGY. (S.N.)

Kinetics: Ger. *Kinetik*; Fr. *cinématique*; Ital. (*teoria*) *cinetica, cinematica*. The science of the motion of bodies as produced by the forces acting upon them, especially the particular forms which this science assumes when based upon the relations of kinetic energy to energy of position.

Introduced by Maxwell as a substitute for the term dynamics in the former limited sense of that word, the actual sense being now extended so as to include the general laws of force action. (S.N.)

Kingdom and **Sub-kingdom** (in biology): see CLASSIFICATION (in biology).

Kinship [AS. *cyn*, kin]: Ger. *Verwandtschaft*; Fr. *parenté, consanguinité*; Ital. *consanguineità*. Blood-relationship.

The word kin belongs to a group of derivatives from roots that originally meant womb. In a series of essays collected in *The Chances of Death and other Studies in Evolution*, Karl Pearson has traced the history of these words in detail. The weight of evidence from all sources now shows that kinship was by every part of the human race originally traced through the mother. Cf. MATRIARCHATE.

Literature: McLENNAN, Kinship in Ancient Greece and other essays collected in Stud. in Ancient Hist. (1st and 2nd series); ROBERTSON SMITH, Kinship and Marriage in Early Arabia; LEWIS H. MORGAN, Systems of Consanguinity and Affinity. (F.H.G.)

Knee-jerk or **Patellar Reflex**: Ger. *Kniephänomen, Patellarreflex*; Fr. *réflexe patellaire*, or *rotulien*; Ital. *reflesso patellare* (or *rotuleo*). A tendon reflex: a sudden straightening of the knee-joint caused by contraction of the quadriceps femoris muscle. It is usually evoked by tapping the patellar tendon (front knee region) while the lower leg hangs freely suspended from the knee.

It is abolished by destruction of the motor roots supplying this muscle, by destruction of the sensory root of the corresponding area (the fifth lumbar root in man), and by the destruction of the descending paths from the cerebellum and mid-brain, or by any cause, such as shock, which reduces the nervous tone of the reflex centre in the spinal cord. It is exaggerated by destruction of the pyramidal or cortico-spinal tract, showing that the cerebrum normally exerts an inhibitory influence upon the reflex centres. It is extensively employed clinically as a sign of various physiological and pathological conditions of the nervous system, this being one of the most convenient tests of the nervous tonicity of the reflex mechanism. It has also been found of psychological interest as reflecting alterations of attention, stages of fatigue, &c., being locally convenient for experimentation.

The patellar reflex is sometimes followed by a 'crossed adductor jerk.' The ordinary patellar reflex follows about $\frac{1}{8}$ sec. after the stimulus, and this is followed after a similar interval by a twitching of the other leg produced by the adductor muscles.

Abolition of the patellar reflex has frequently been described as a result of cerebellar lesions, though this view has been recently actively combated on the ground that such injuries never produce this effect unless accompanied by destruction of the 'reflex bundle of the patellar reflex' in the oblongata.

Literature: H. P. BOWDITCH, The Reinforcement and Inhibition of the Knee-jerk, Boston Med. and Surg. J., cxviii. 542 (1888); H. P. BOWDITCH and J. W. WARREN, The Knee-jerk and its Physiological Modifications, J. of Physiol., xi. 25–64; C. EISEN, Studien über das Verhalten der Reflexe bei gesundem und krankem Nervensystem, Inaug.-Diss., Erlangen (1897); C. FÉRÉ, Note sur les Réflexes tendineux du Genou, et en particulier sur la Contraction réflexe successive, C. R. Soc. de Biol., Paris, 9e sér., i. 530 (1899); A. VAN GEHUCHTEN, Le Mécanisme des Mouvements réflexes, J. de Neurol. et d'Hypnol. (1897); W. R. GOWERS, A Study of the so-called Tendon-reflex Phenomena, Med.-Chir. J., London, lxii. 269–305 (1879); An Address introductory to a Discussion on the Diagnostic Value of the so-called 'Tendon-reflexes,' Lancet, London, ii. 839–42 (1885); A. JARISCH and E. SCHIFF, Untersuchungen über das Kniephänomen, Med. Jahrb., Wien, 261–308 (1882); W. P. LOMBARD, The Variations of the Normal Knee-jerk, and their Relation to the Activity of the Central Nervous System, Amer. J. of Psychol., i. 5–71 (1887) also trans. in Arch. f. Physiol., Leipzig, Suppl.-Bd. (1889); On the Nature of the Knee-jerk, J. of Physiol., x. 122–48 (1889); MARIE, Le Bulletin Médical, Paris, Apr. 15, 1894 ('Crossed Knee-jerk'); H. NETTER, Zur Geschichte der Lehre vom Kniephänomen bei Geisteskranken, Inaug.-Diss., Freiburg i. B. (1897); NONNE, Patellarreflex bei Kleinhirnerkrankung, Neurol. Centralbl. (1897), 285; C. S. SHERRINGTON, Brit. Med. J., March 12, 1892; Lancet, London, May 6, 1893; P. STEWART, Experimental Observations on the Crossed Adductor Jerk, J. of Physiol., xxii. Nos. 1 and 2 (1897); T. ZIEHEN, Corresp.-Bl. d. allg. ärztl. Ver. v. Thüringen, Weimar, xviii. 1–8 (1889); SEPPILLI, Riv. di Fren., 1887. (H.H.)

Knowledge [Lat. *gnoscere*]: Ger. *Erkenntniss*; Fr. *connaissance*; Ital. *conoscenza*. (1) The cognitive aspect of consciousness in general.

From this point of view it has been proposed to distinguish two kinds of knowledge, named respectively 'knowledge of acquaintance' and 'knowledge about,' corresponding to γνῶναι and εἰδέναι, *noscere* and *scire*, *Kennen* and *Wissen*, *connaître* and *savoir*. 'To know may mean either to perceive or apprehend, or to understand or comprehend.' Knowledge in the first sense is only recognition; knowledge in the latter sense is the result of intellectual comparison, and is embodied in a judgment. Thus a blind man, who cannot know light in the first sense, can know about light in the second (Ward, art. Psychology in *Encyc. Brit.*, 9th ed., 49). The terms 'knowledge of acquaintance' and 'knowledge about' are due to John Grote (*Exploratio Philosophica*, 60). The distinction is elaborated by James (*Princ. of Psychol.*, i. 221).

(2) Knowledge is also used in contrast to the form of mere opinion sometimes called belief. In this application it signifies certitude based on adequate objective grounds. There may be belief or subjective certitude without adequate objective foundation. Yet, strictly speaking, this distinction is not psychological.

(3) Knowledge is further used for 'what is known' as such. Thus we may speak of chemistry as a 'body of knowledge.'

For literature see the psychologies; on the questions as to the origin, meaning, and validity of knowledge, see EPISTEMOLOGY. (G.F.S.—J.M.B.)

Knowledge (in logic). This word is used in logic in two senses: (1) as a synonym for COGNITION (q.v.), and (2), and more usefully, to signify a perfect cognition, that is, a cognition fulfilling three conditions: first, that it holds for true a proposition that really is true; second, that it is perfectly self-satisfied and free from the uneasiness of doubt; third, that some character of this satisfaction is such that it would be logically impossible that this character should ever belong to satisfaction in a proposition not true.

Knowledge is divided, firstly, according to whatever classification of the sciences is adopted. Thus, Kantians distinguish formal and material knowledge. See SCIENCE. Secondly, knowledge is divided according to the different ways in which it is attained, as into immediate and mediate knowledge. See IMMEDIACY AND MEDIACY (logical). Immediate knowledge is a cognition, or objective modification of consciousness, which is borne in upon a man with such resistless force as to constitute a guarantee that it (or a representation of it) will remain permanent in the development of human cognition. Such knowledge is, if its existence be granted, either borne in through an avenue of sense, external or internal, as a percept of an individual, or springs up within the mind as a first principle of reason or as a mystical revelation. Mediate knowledge is that for which there is some guarantee behind itself, although, no matter how far criticism be carried, simple evidency, or direct insistency, of something has to be relied upon. The external guarantee rests ultimately either upon authority, i.e. testimony, or upon observation. In either case mediate knowledge is attained by REASONING, which see for further divisions. It is only necessary to mention here that the Aristotelians distinguished knowledge ὅτι, or of the facts themselves, and knowledge διότι, or of the rational connection of facts, the knowledge of the how and why (cf. the preceding topic). They did not distinguish between the how and the why, because they held that knowledge διότι is solely produced by SYLLOGISM (q.v.) in its greatest perfection, as demonstration. The term empirical knowledge is applied to knowledge, mediate or immediate, which rests upon percepts; while the terms philosophical and rational knowledge are applied to knowledge, mediate or immediate, which rests chiefly or wholly upon conclusions or revelations of reason. Thirdly, knowledge is divided, according to the character of the immediate object, into apprehensive and judicative knowledge, the former being of a percept, image, or Vorstellung, the latter of the existence or non-existence of a fact. Fourthly, knowledge is divided, according to the manner in which it is in the mind, into actual, virtual, and habitual knowledge. See Scotus, *Opus Oxoniense*, lib. I. dist. iii. quest. 2, paragraph beginning 'Loquendo igitur.' Fifthly, knowledge is divided, according to its end, into speculative and practical. (C.S.P., C.L.F.)

Knowledge (theory of): see EPISTEMOLOGY, and GNOSIOLOGY.

Knutzen, Martin. (1713–51.) A mathematician in Königsberg; a teacher of Immanuel Kant.

Koran [Arab. *Quran, Qoran*, book]: Ger. *Koran*; Fr. *Coran*; Ital. *Corano*. The sacred book of Islam, claimed to have been communicated to the Prophet directly by Allah, and containing the religious and moral system of the Mohammedan religion.

The Koran was composed by Mohammed at intervals during his prophetic career. Its materials are largely derived from Hebrew, Christian, and Arabian traditions, but these are fused into a homogeneous product by the powerful genius of the Prophet. It is comprised of 114 suras or chapters, which were collected and given their present form by Zaid, an amanuensis of the Prophet, under the direction of the Kaliph Abubekr. The Koran is creed, code, and cult combined. The central religious doctrines of the Koran are its monotheistic conception of God and its doctrine of unconditional predestination. It contains a very high and pure system of morality. Cf. ORIENTAL PHILOSOPHY (India).

Literature : NÖLDEKE, Gesch. des Qorans (1860); MUIHR and R. B. SMITH, Lives of Mohammed ; KUENEN, Hibbert Lectures ; WEIL, Einleitung in den Koran (2nd ed., 1878); GARCIA DE TASSY, L'Islamisme d'après le Coran (1874); SEYD AMED, Essays (1871); TOY, Johnson's Univl. Cyc., art. Koran. (A.T.O.)

Kratylus. A pupil of the sophist Protagoras, who adhered to the teachings of the Ephesian philosopher Heraclitus in Athens. Plato was his pupil, and, later, honoured him with the dialogue *Kratylus*.

Krause, Karl Christian Friedrich. (1781–1832.) German philosopher, educated at Jena. Privat-docent in Jena 1802, and in Berlin 1814. He died when about to habilitate in Munich. He developed a system called panentheism, 'All in God.'

Kritias. A pupil of Socrates, who later became one of the thirty tyrants, an adherent to the school of the Sophists, and the opponent of Socrates.

Krug, Wilhelm Traugott. (1770–1842.) German philosopher, educated in theology and philosophy at Wittenberg. Professor of philosophy in Frankfort-on-the-Oder, in Königsberg (1805), and in Leipzig (1809).

Kymograph : see LABORATORY AND APPARATUS, II (general).

L

Labials: see PHONETICS.

Laboratory (of psychology) **and Apparatus:** Ger. *psychologisches Institut, Institut für experimentelle Psychologie, Apparate, Instrumente;* Fr. *laboratoire de psychologie, appareils, instruments;* Ital. *laboratorio, apparecchi, strumenti.* A room or series of rooms fitted up for psychological experiments. By apparatus is meant all the instruments or material means of investigation, training, or demonstration.

I. *Laboratory.* Psychological experiments had been made in physical and physiological laboratories and in private quarters, but the first laboratory of psychology was established by Professor Wundt in Leipzig in 1879. The second laboratory, now discontinued, was that of the Johns Hopkins University (Professor Hall, 1883), and the third—the first in which undergraduate work in the laboratory was undertaken—was that of the University of Pennsylvania (Professor Cattell, 1888). Laboratories have now been established in the leading Universities of Germany; at the Sorbonne, Paris, and elsewhere in France; in some thirty American colleges and universities. In England beginnings have been made, but the only laboratory planned and adequately equipped for experimental psychology in the British Empire is still that of the University of Toronto (Professor Baldwin, 1890). Laboratories for the investigation of pathological mental conditions have been established in various institutions, e. g. at the Salpêtrière, Paris (Professor Janet), at Heidelberg, Germany (Professor Kräpelin), at Reggio Emilia, Italy (Professor Tamburini), and at the Physiological Institute, Turin (Professor Mosso). Cf. PSYCHOLOGY (various topics).

A laboratory of psychology should have the same general position and arrangement as laboratories for the other sciences. A series of small rooms is, however, preferable to one or more large rooms; a dark room is needed for work on vision, and a quiet room for work on hearing, attention, &c. A workshop for wood and metals is very desirable. There should be light from the north and south, and it is important to have throughout good light and quietness. Electric light and power (including a current of low potential) are needed, as also water and gas. It is also desirable that such a laboratory should comprise facilities for physiological as well as simply experimental work, and this is often accomplished by arranging for local proximity to special laboratories in physiology, neurology, and histology, and for some degree of co-operation with them. (J.McK.C.–J.M.B.)

II. *Apparatus. General.* The quantitative measurements of psychology rest on the same general principles as the investigations of physics and physiology, and the apparatus employed are to a large extent the same. Since any direct measurement of sensations, thoughts, feelings, or emotions appears to be out of the question, the investigator aims to obtain an expression of their value in terms of their most immediate causes or effects. The individual experiencing the sensations, &c., can indicate their inequality, alteration, and the like, but the numerical value of such differences or alterations must be supplied from material phenomena open to external measure. Thus the measurements of mental phenomena depend on measurements of either the stimuli (i. e. physical processes) of the mental state or the (physiological) motor effects which follow the stimuli or the mental state.

605

The stimulus may be measured with respect to its duration, intensity, or spatial extent, and with reference to the least sensation or the least difference in sensation under each aspect.

The least sensation is measured by the least stimulus that will produce a sensation: called threshold of sensation; the least difference of sensation by the least change in stimulus that will produce a different sensation: called threshold of difference. Where measurements of the quality of sensation are possible, as in sight and hearing, they are of the same character. See THRESHOLD. The motor effect is generally measured with reference to variation in the amount, force, and direction of movement. By comparison or other treatment of these data, inferences are drawn regarding the central processes and the accompanying mental changes.

Records are obtained in two ways. In the first or visual method, an index moves along a scale and stops at a number representing the measurement obtained. This principle is involved in the apparatus whose names end in *-meter* or *-scope*. The index is usually constructed so as to stop at the point desired, while the mechanism either continues to work, as in the chronoscope, or returns to its starting-point, as in the dynamometer. A number of records may thus be obtained in rapid succession. An electric current is often used to start the mechanism or stop the index.

In the second or graphic method, a quill point moves to and fro across a cylinder covered with blackened paper, at the same time that the cylinder rotates; a record or curve is thus obtained in two dimensions, one of which represents time. This principle is involved in the apparatus whose names end in *-graph*. The quill may be attached directly to the special apparatus, as in the ergograph, or the record may be transmitted by air-pressure or an electric current. For air-pressure transmission the *Marey tambour* is used. This consists of two drums of wood or metal (called tambours), connected by an inelastic rubber tube, each drum having an elastic rubber head. The movement to be recorded takes the form of an inward pressure on the elastic head of the first or exploring tambour; this compresses the air in the tube and in the second or receiving tambour, and the elastic head of the latter is raised. A quill, extending over the receiving tambour, rises and falls with the movement of the head. This principle is used in the sphygmograph and similar apparatus. The electric mode of transmission is illustrated in the *Deprez signal*. Here the quill is fastened to the armature of an electro-magnet. When the circuit is made, the quill is drawn to the magnet; when the circuit is broken, it is released and drawn away by a spring. A record of the points of time at which the circuit is made and broken is thus obtained on the paper. This principle is used in the chronograph.

The devices for holding and running the recording cylinders are numerous. The *kymograph* consists of a clockwork to turn the cylinder, and several adjustments for altering the rate of rotation, the angle of its axis, and its position along the axis. The *polygraph* is used for obtaining several records simultaneously. Near the cylinder is an upright rod, to which several receiving tambours may be clamped; their quills recording at different heights on the cylinder, but at corresponding points of its circumference; these records generally include a time indication, so as to fix the duration of the phenomena, should the cylinder fail to rotate uniformly. The records are obtained on glazed paper that has received a uniform coating of lamp or candle black; they are made permanent by bathing the paper in some fixing solution.

Necessary accessories are electric batteries and circuits, keys, sounders, current testers, resistance boxes, standards and clamps, and a compact switch-board, by which the entire electric supply to the different rooms is regulated and utilized in various combinations.

III. *Apparatus for special investigations.* In the more complex tests, special apparatus are necessary, which must be devised by the investigator for the particular problem. The following descriptions embrace apparatus in general use. They are suitable for demonstration purposes; and with certain adaptations, according to the problem in hand, they may be used for special investigations as well.

A. *Motor Recording Apparatus. General.* Apparatus for measuring the extent of movement are described elsewhere (space relations, muscular sense); its duration and rate are measured by a simple application of the kymograph; its force may be determined by the pressure exerted against a spring (Cattell). There are various apparatus for measuring one or more of these data. Delabarre's apparatus for finding the components of movement along vertical and horizontal axes consists of a vertical and a horizontal string, each attached to the finger and passing over a pulley; at the other end they are attached to recording quills, which are pulled one way by the finger, the other by an elastic band. The *dynamometer* is used to determine the maximum force of a muscle, or to compare movements of the same estimated force. It is an oval of flexible steel, which can be compressed at the sides or pulled apart at the ends; the amount of force exerted in either case is indicated on scales by a pointer, which remains at the highest point reached. The hand dynamometer is grasped in the hand and squeezed; a larger form is used for the arm and other muscles. In the *dynamograph* the force exerted is recorded on a revolving cylinder by means of tambours. This shows the rate and variation, as well as the amount of force exerted. Mosso's *ergograph* measures the work done by a single set of muscles, and its rate of fatigue and exhaustion. The forearm is placed on a cushioned board and held immovable by two sets of clamps; the second and fourth fingers are held fast in tubes, and the middle finger is attached to a string bearing a heavy weight; in raising and lowering the weight this finger moves alone without bringing any other muscles into play. The recording part of the ergograph consists of a carriage, to which the string from the finger is attached; it moves on two rods; from this carriage another rod extends, with a quill which marks on a revolving cylinder. There is also the 'spring' ergograph (Cattell, Binet). The *myograph* measures the form and rate of simple muscular contraction. It consists of a bridge placed over the muscle in question and bound fast. A rod extends down and rests on the muscle. As the muscle contracts, the rod is pressed up, and this acts on a tambour, which records the movement.

The form of movement of various organs in speech is measured and recorded by apparatus which are applied to the proper organs in the same way as the myograph, and which work on the same principle. The *labiograph*, *laryngograph*, and *palatometer* measure the movements of the lips, larynx, and palate respectively. By means of the polygraph (described above) these records may be obtained simultaneously. (H.C.W.)

Physiological Processes. The rate and form of certain physiological processes furnish a measure of the condition and changes of consciousness. A record of such processes under normal conditions may be compared with other records, taken during hard thinking or strong emotion, or after intellectual effort, fatigue, &c. The rate and intensity of the heart-beat is measured by the *cardiograph*; the *sphygmograph* measures the rate and form of the pulse; the *pneumograph* measures the movements of the thorax in breathing. These are similar in principle to the myograph. In one form of pneumograph a flexible rubber bottle is bound to the chest; it is compressed by the expansion of the chest in breathing, and the pressure recorded by a tambour. The *plethysmograph* is used to measure changes in the volume of the arm, &c., due to changes in the blood-supply. It consists of a vessel into which the arm is inserted; the opening about the arm is tightly closed, after the vessel has been filled with, e. g., water. Any increase in volume of the arm forces the water out into a second jar and causes a weight to fall, and vice versa; these changes are registered on a scale.

B. *Sensation and Perception.* We have the following groups: (1) Demonstration apparatus; physical and physiological instruments and models. Here belong models of eye, ear, brain, &c.; models of the horopter, the field of vision, &c.; large wooden copies of metal instruments, made to show the working of the latter; models illustrating the stream of consciousness, the course of feeling, &c.; apparatus for purely physiological tests, for astigmatism, for the change of the lens in accommodation (phacoscope), for demonstration of the form of vowel waves by means of manometric flames, for recording muscular strength, work, and contraction (dynamometer, ergograph, and myograph), for the registration of pulse, respiration, volume (sphygmograph, pneumograph, plethysmograph), for exploring the eye (ophthalmoscope). Many of these pieces should be included also under group (4); they may be turned to direct psychological account. (2) Apparatus for class experiments. These are instruments of the type of group (4), enlarged and simplified, to permit of the obtaining of results from a small class of students (on the average, from ten or twelve persons), or from very large numbers (two or three hundred). (3) Apparatus for drill experiments. These are cheap and simple forms of the pieces of group (4), intended for use with junior classes in the laboratory. Sanford (ref. below) figures and describes a large number of such instruments. (4) Research apparatus. Under the limits of the present heading, the psychological instruments proper fall into three larger and two smaller groups—optical, acoustical, and haptical pieces (the word Haptics, q. v., being taken in its widest sense), and apparatus for the investigation of taste and smell. (e.b.t.)

(*a*) *Optical.* The instruments employed in the study of psychological optics fall into the following groups :—

(1) Apparatus for indirect vision. Near the periphery of the retina the power of space discrimination falls off considerably, and the colour-sense is entirely lost. These phenomena are investigated by means of the *perimeter*; this consists, essentially, of a fixation point for the eye, and a circular arm with scale rotating about the line of direct vision. To determine the peripheral limits of any colour, a small piece of coloured paper is placed at the end of the scale and gradually approached to the centre of vision until the colour is correctly distinguished; this is repeated for as many points of the periphery as desired. To determine the peripheral variations of the space threshold the coloured piece is replaced by a white surface having two black dots a small distance apart; the piece is moved in till the spots are distinguished as two. The *campimeter* is similar to the perimeter; instead of a circular scale, a large flat sheet of white paper is used; the colour limits, &c., are marked directly on this. Both perimeter and campimeter are used for mapping the Blind Spot (q. v.). A small dot on a white background is moved about near the centre of vision; the points where it disappears and reappears indicate the edges of the blind spot. In this case the eye moves and the stimulus is constant.

A useful instrument for general purposes is Hess' indirect vision colour-mixer (*Arch. f. Ophthal.*, xxxv). (h.c.w.)

(2) Apparatus for the testing of Colour-blindness (q. v.). See also that subject under Vision.

(3) Quality and wave-length; sense discrimination of spectral qualities; instruments for analysing rays of light—the *spectroscope*, *spectrometric* apparatus, and—for combining them—the *chromatoscope*. Cf. Uhthoff, *Arch. f. Ophthal.*, xxxiv; Brodhun, *Zeitsch. f. Psychol.*, iii; Mentz, *Philos. Stud.*, xiii. See Spectrum, and Light under Vision.

(4) Purkinje phenomenon; liminal values. As (3). Also dark room or dark box, with arrangement for graduation of light intensity (e. g. an *episkotister*, or partial disk composed of a retaining rim and variable black sectors); colour-mixers (rotating disks), Aubert's diaphragm, and gelatine sheets.

Bruecke, *Sitzber. d. Wien. Akad.* (1878), 3. Abth.; Hillebrand, ibid., 3. Abth. (1889); Hering, *Pflüger's Arch.*, xlix and lx; König, *Helmholtz-Festschrift* (1891); König and Brodhun, *Sitzber. d. Berl. Akad.* (1888 and 1889); Langley, *Philos. Mag.* (1889).

(5) Apparatus for Colour Mixture (q. v.).

(6) Apparatus for contrast. Demonstration pieces may be prepared from coloured cards. The phenomena can be well shown on rotating disks, or by means of shadows. An elaborate arrangement for quantitative work is described by Hess and Pretori, *Arch. f. Ophthal.*, xl. See Lehmann, *Philos. Stud.*, iii; Ebbinghaus, *Sitzber. d. Berl. Akad.*, xlix; Kirschmann, *Philos. Stud.*, vi; Pretori and Sachs, *Pflüger's Arch.*, lx. Cf. Meyer's Experiment, Side-window Experiment. (e.b.t.)

[(2) to (6)]. The threshold of difference of light intensity is found by comparing different shades of grey on the *colour-wheel*. This apparatus has an axle, on which black, white, and coloured disks or sectors may be clamped and rotated rapidly by means of a series of geared wheels or a motor. The disks used are slit along one radius, so that they can be fitted into one another, giving sectors of different colours or shades. The adjustable colour-wheel has an axle in three parts, one within another; the disks are fitted to each, interlocking as in the simple colour-wheel; but by moving a lever the proportion of each disk visible may be altered while they are rotating. To find the threshold of difference, one black and one white disk are fitted together in a certain ratio, which is slowly altered till a difference is noted. The shade of grey is measured in terms of the proportion of black and white in the circumference. Another method used in this problem is to compare the shadows from two lights, one of which is varied in intensity or distance.

The thresholds of colour-sensation and colour-difference, and various phenomena of saturation, colour mixing, contrast, &c., are investigated by means of colour-mixers. There are several forms, including the colour-wheel just described. The *reflection colour-mixer*, in its simplest form, consists of a clear pane of glass, standing perpendicular to a black velvet surface. Strips of differently coloured paper are placed on the velvet at each side; the subject looks through the glass at an angle and sees the reflection of one strip over the image of the other. The intensity of the reflected colour, and hence the character of the mixture, alters with the angle of regard. Another form is Hering's *binocular colour-mixer*. Glasses of different colours are placed before the two eyes, which are directed upon three white spots; the left spot is seen with the left eye alone, and in the colour of the glass before that eye; the right spot similarly with the right eye; the central spot is seen with both eyes, and gives a binocular mixture of the two colours, which may be compared with each separately. (H.C.W.)

(7) After-image apparatus. Hering and Wundt have devised demonstration pieces. An arrangement for the study of fatigue by spectral colours is described by Hess, *Arch. f. Ophthal.*, xxxvi; an arrangement for work on positive after-images, by the same author, *Pflüger's Arch.*, xlix. Cf. Bidwell, *Proc. Roy. Soc.*, lvi (1894).

(8) Apparatus for the study of geometrical-optical illusions. These consist of frames, cards, &c., so arranged that lengths, directions, &c., of the lines entering into the represented figures may be independently varied. See Sanford, op. cit., expts. 187–203. (E.B.T.)

The well-known OPTICAL ILLUSIONS (q.v.) of the size of angles, relation of horizontal to vertical lines, relation between filled and empty space, &c., may be measured by taking such variable figures and altering their form till the illusion is allowed for and apparently corrected. Baldwin's two-area illusion apparatus is an example of this. It consists of a smaller and a larger square with a slit connecting the mid points of their sides or two circles similarly joined; behind this slit moves a pointer, which the subject stops (by pressing a key) when the middle of the line appears to be reached; this judgment is affected by the relative size of the area; the amount of error—the centre being located too far towards the larger area—is indicated on a concealed scale, and constitutes a measure of the illusion, which varies with the ratio of the two areas to each other. See Baldwin, *Psychol. Rev.*, ii. (1895) 244 ff. (with figure), and *Story of the Mind*, 135. (H.C.W.)

(9) Apparatus for the study of the visual perception of motion. Artificial waterfall, and spirally lined disk, for investigating after-images of movement. Rotating drum, with lines, dots, &c., for the perception of movement in direct and in indirect vision. Synthesis of movement: by *stroboscope*, *anorthoscope* (in the former, phases of a movement are combined by positive after-images;

in the latter, distorted phases are righted by positive after-images, or a figure is distorted owing to a false estimate of the rate of movement. See ILLUSIONS OF MOTION AND MOVEMENT. Cf. Sanford, op. cit., expts. 222–31.

(10) Apparatus for the study of visual space-perceptions (distance, size, direction, &c.). VISUAL AREA (q. v.) measurement apparatus: a black screen, with movable white lines, points, &c. *Stereoscope; pseudoscope*: the latter an instrument which interchanges the normal perceptions of the two eyes. Tele-stereoscope: increases the difference between the images thrown by an object upon the two retinae. Haploscope: a stereoscope presenting to each eye a field invisible by the other. Apparatus for study of perception of depth by means of movements of accommodation and convergence: in principle, a box, in which threads or sharp edges can be moved in, towards, or out from the observer, without appreciable alteration of the retinal images. See Sanford, op. cit., expts. 170–86, 204–21; also the catalogues of Jung (Heidelberg) and Rothe (Leipzig). (E.B.T.)

[(9), (10)] Visual perception of motion. A series of instantaneous pictures appearing in rapid succession will give the effect of continuous motion. The *stroboscope* is based on this principle; it consists of a round box with slits at intervals in the side; opposite each slit is a picture; when the box is rotated horizontally, the pictures appear in rapid succession, giving the appearance of continuous motion. The rate of change necessary to accomplish this is measured by the apparatus described under 'least duration' (below, C. 2), or by a stroboscope whose speed is variable and measurable. Other forms of apparatus having the same principle as the stroboscope are the zoetrope or zoötrope, vitascope, mutoscope, and kinetoscope.

The space threshold is measured by means of a series of alternate black and white strips of the same width. The distance of the strips from the eye, or their width, is varied, till they are barely distinguishable. The threshold of difference is determined by numerous methods. Münsterberg's apparatus for the measurement of visual area consists of a long black surface, across which extend three movable white strips. Two of the strips are placed a certain distance apart, and the subject endeavours to place the third so as to make an equal distance. A concealed scale indicates the actual distances. Other forms of apparatus are similar in principle. In some the strip or point moves automatically, and is merely stopped by the subject at the point desired. To measure discrimination of depth a different instrument is necessary. Cattell's apparatus consists of a box with eye-holes at one end and threads within, stretched vertically across. These threads can be placed at various distances from the eye, the distance being measured on a scale. The subject judges their absolute or relative distance with one eye or with both together. See Münsterberg, 'Augenmass,' in *Beitr. z. exper. Psychol*, H. 2. (H.C.W.)

(b) *Acoustical.* The following are some of the more important instruments required for work upon psychological acoustics. (1) Limits of stimulation: Politzer's *acoumeter*, for distance threshold (see ACOUMETRY); Galton's whistle or small forks, for upper tone limit; large fork, or wire forks, or lamella, for lower tone limit; Mayer's pierced disk and fork with resonator, for limits of tone and noise; pendulum carrying small fork, with Y-piece and tubing, for inertia. (2) Production of pure tones (for fusion experiments, &c.) and noises: forks on resonance boxes, some electrically driven, others sounded by bows or rubber hammers; steel cylinders, or vibrating steel rods; bottles with gutta-percha blow-pieces; Quincke's tubes; 'singing' tubes; air-hydrogen bubble apparatus; series of small corked phials, for 'pops.' (3) Production and analysis of tones: *piano*; *harmonium*; *harmonical* (pure scale, with 24 overtones of the tone of 66, and 16 of the tone of 132 vibrations per sec.: see Helmholtz, *Sensations of Tone*); *sonometer* (strings stretched over a long, thin-topped resonance box); organ pipes, closed and open (preferably with manometric flame attachments); *resonators*; bellows tables and compressed air supply. (4) Sense discrimination: reed-boxes, giving intervals smaller than the musical semitone; Stern's continuous-change apparatus (bottle to blow over, while slowly filled with or emptied of water or mercury, at a rate determined by a 'variator'); Gilbert's tone-tester (adjustable pitch-pipe, with scale); set of mistuned forks; sound-pendulum, *phonometer*, for giving sounds of varying degrees of intensity. Here may be placed the toothed wheel (Savart's) and the siren. (E.B.T.)

[(1) to (4)] The threshold of difference in sound intensity is determined by dropping an ivory ball from varying heights upon a wooden stand; the ball is held by a clamp and released automatically; the length of fall is determined by a scale on the rod to which the clamp is fixed. Instead of ivory, a steel ball is sometimes used; it is held by the armature of an electro-magnet, and drops when the circuit is broken. In the *audiometer* a sound of constant intensity is used; the intensity is varied by altering the size of certain apertures through which it passes. The *sound-pendulum* consists of a swinging metal rod, tipped with a hard rubber ball, which strikes against an ebony block at the lowest point of its arc. A clamp holds the ball at any desired point of the arc and releases it. The intensity of the sound is calculated from the length of arc, which is measured by a scale on the arm bearing the clamp.

Quality or pitch differences. The lowest audible pitch (see HEARING) is determined by means of large tuning-forks; a fork is fitted with an adjustable weight, by which its rate may be varied from 16 to 24 vibrations per second; the rates for various positions of the weight are indicated on the fork. *Appunn's reed*, or *lamella*, is a blade surmounted by a flat bulb, and held below by a clamp; the length of the blade, and consequently its rate of vibration, is varied by adjusting the clamp. The highest audible pitch is determined by the *Galton whistle*. This is a very short pipe, whose length may be diminished to zero by a screw piston. The sound is made by squeezing a bulb attached to the pipe, the pitch being determined by the length of pipe, as indicated by a fine scale. Another means of determining the highest audible pitch is a set of steel cylinders, which, when struck with a steel hammer, give very high notes, the highest in the series being inaudible. To determine the threshold of pitch difference, tuning-forks of nearly the same pitch are compared, or a standard fork is compared with an adjustable one. The *Savart wheel* consists of a disk with a large number of teeth at uniform distances on the circumference; when placed on an axis and rotated against a tongue, it produces a tone which varies in pitch with the rate of speed. Beats and difference-tones are investigated by means of the *siren*. Or a *piston whistle* is sounded at the same time as a constant one; starting with the two at the same pitch, the pitch of the former is gradually altered, giving beats and finally difference-tones. Pitch intervals and overtones are investigated with the *sonometer*.

This is a long sounding-board, over which two wires are stretched; on the board are marked off various fractions of the length, and the interval noted by which the pitch is altered when the wire is held or dampened at these points. (H.C.W.)

(5) Apparatus for the study of auditory localization: wire circles, revolving chair, snapper-sounders, telegraph receivers, &c. (E.B.T.)

[(5)] Our auditory space-perception consists chiefly of estimates of direction. It may be investigated by means of a graduated horizontal circle in the plane of the ears, with other arcs in various planes. A sound is made with a telegraphic snapper at different points on these circles, and the subject's estimate compared with its actual direction. (H.C.W.)

(6) Auditory time-sense apparatus: kymograph-drum, with revolving hand for instantaneous make and break of contacts, electrical sound-hammer, &c. See *Time-sense Apparatus* (below, C. 4).

(7) Apparatus for study of rhythm and auditory span of consciousness: *metronome*; interrupter-clock, with chronograph, keys, hammer, &c.

Special arrangements, involving the use of interference tubes, silent boxes, dampers, Marey tambours, &c., are apt to be required in an acoustical investigation. Besides the pieces mentioned above, there are a large number of instruments on the market which have been devised or employed for some particular end. See catalogues of Appunn (Hanau) and König (Paris).

(c) *Haptical*. The principal pieces used in haptical investigation ('haptics' being taken in the widest sense, as noted above) are the following:—

(1) Cutaneous sensation. *Kinesimeter* (regulated moving point, for exploration of the cutaneous surface). Pressure-point apparatus (cork or pith or hair points, for discovering the pressure spots). Temperature-spot apparatus (metal tubes, pointed, for hot and cold water). Pain-spot apparatus (pointed hairs are most useful for pain exploration). Thermometers, Roux regulators, plaster casts, &c., are employed in this exploratory work.

For intensity. Series of minimally different weights; or pressure balance (an arrangement whereby weights can be laid upon the resting skin, either discretely or continuously). Temperature apparatus, as before. *Algometer* (or algesimeter), as described below.

(2) Deeper-lying sense organs. Induction coil, for faradization of muscle; ether spray, &c., for producing cutaneous and subcutaneous anaesthesia.

[(1), (2)] Sense of pressure. The threshold of difference is measured with a set of *test-weights*. Jastrow's test-weights are cylinders of the same size and appearance, whose weight may be regulated by pouring in or taking out shot. One cylinder, called the standard, is placed on the subject's hand; it is then replaced by another, and he compares the two. The standard is next compared with another in the same way, and so on, till we find the one least different from the standard which the subject observes to be different. Verdin's (also Griesbach's) aesthesiometer, described just below, under *Space Apparatus* (3), has a scale showing the amount of pressure exerted when it is applied to the skin.

Kennedy's pressure balance consists of a lever, one end of which presses on the finger-tip. On the other end rests another lever. When the latter is lifted, the pressure on the finger is increased; when it is applied, the pressure is diminished—in either case without fluctuations in pressure due to jar or momentum. The weights on both levers may be regulated to give any desired pair of pressures.

Heat and cold sensations. The threshold of difference in these two senses is determined by the *thermaesthesiometer*. One form of this apparatus consists of two tubes filled with water, whose temperature is measured by a thermometer and regulated by spigots. One tube is maintained at constant temperature, while the other is heated or cooled till a difference between the two is observed. Münsterberg's aesthesiometer (described below, 3) is also adapted for this investigation.

Pain sense. The thresholds of pain and difference for pain, and greatest endurable pain, are measured by the *algometer* or *algesimeter* (Beaunis, Cattell). It consists of a piston-rod, which works against a heavy spring. At the end of the rod is a button-like tip which may be covered with flannel. This is pressed against the skin with increasing force, till it becomes painful; the amount of pressure is indicated on a scale.

Muscular sensations. The threshold of difference is measured with the test-weights as in the sense of pressure; in investigating the muscle sense, however, the weights are grasped and lifted by the subject, instead of resting on the palm of his hand. (H.C.W.)

(3) Perception of space. Aesthesiometric compasses; elbow-board (for minimal elbow-

joint movement perceptions); movement apparatus (rectilineal, Münsterberg; circular, Stoerring); electrodes, to suit different parts of the skin (for fusion of pressures, and resultant localization); tilt and rotation table, with apparatus for showing a glowing platinum wire at different places in the dark field; interrupted-extent apparatus (for giving continuous and uninterrupted touch-stimulations to the resting and moving skin).

[(3)] In addition to the thresholds of space and space-difference, the space relation gives rise to a threshold of direction, which is obtained by comparing two lines or pairs of points differing slightly in direction.

Space relations of touch and pressure. The several threshold values are determined by means of points brought in contact with the skin; for these investigations the aesthesiometer is used. *Verdin's aesthesiometer* consists of a long horizontal beam, on each half of which slides a vertical rod tipped with a rounded ivory point; the distance apart of the two points is indicated by a scale on the beam. The lower part of each rod holds a piston, which works against a spring; when the points are pressed on the skin the spring is forced up, the amount of pressure being indicated on another scale. *Jastrow's aesthesiometer* is a simplified form without the spring; the instrument is held by a handle which slides on a vertical rod; when the points touch the skin the handle is free to move downward, thus avoiding any additional pressure by the operator. *Münsterberg's aesthesiometer* is a flexible rod, terminating at one end in a handle, at the other in a sheath, into which various contact-pieces may be inserted. Among the contact-pieces used are points arranged in various figures, continuous squares and circles, and surfaces of various sizes, for investigating the thresholds of sensation and difference; a set of small pans is used for investigating the temperature senses. For reaction-time experiments a circuit is made, when the skin is touched, by the bending of the flexible rod.

Space relations of heat and cold. Besides the application of Münsterberg's aesthesiometer just noted, the space relations of the temperature senses are investigated by moving a warm or cold point along the skin. A brass cylinder tapering at one end to a fine point is used. Two cylinders are necessary, one being kept in hot or cold water while the other is in use, with frequent changes on account of the rapid loss or gain of temperature from the skin. This apparatus is used for mapping out the position of the heat and cold spots. The thermaesthesiometer is also used for this investigation. Crawford's transparent transfer frames are serviceable for comparing different records for the same area (cf. *Psychol. Rev.*, v. 1898, 63).

Space relations of muscular sense. The usual apparatus for measuring the appreciation of small differences of movement consists of a carriage which travels freely on a track. One finger is inserted into a loop attached to the carriage, and the latter is moved a certain distance; the carriage is then brought back, and the subject endeavours to make another movement of the same length. The distance travelled each time is indicated by a pointer on a scale.

The sense of passive rotary movement is investigated with the *rotation table*. This is a long board on which the subject lies, and which rotates freely in the horizontal plane. A fixed scale, over which a pointer moves, indicates the amount of rotation, and the beats of a metronome, or electric contacts at various points on the scale, record its rate. The apparatus measures the least perceptible movement, and demonstrates the fading away of these sensations under continuous motion. (H.C.W.)

The sense of bodily position and movement. For investigating the subjective estimate of bodily position the *tilt board* is used. This is a long, flat board (like the rotation table) placed across a saw-horse, so as to swing in a vertical plane. The subject is strapped to the board with bandaged eyes; it is then swung into any position, and he makes a judgment as to the angle. The actual angle is shown by a scale and a plumb-line or pointer.

(4) Sense illusions. Weights, of same weight and different size; weights, of same size and different weight. (E.B.T.)

[(4)] The illusion of weight as affected by size is measured by comparing a series of objects, of different weight and size but uniform material, with a standard weight of different material. The subject determines which one of the series is apparently equal to the standard. (H.C.W.)

(5) Involuntary movement. Sommer's *analyser* (records the excursions of tremor movements in three dimensions); *automatograph* ('planchette').

[(5)] Jastrow's *automatograph* consists of a horizontal pane of glass resting on three perfectly spherical balls, which rest on another pane—this last firmly set and carefully levelled before the experiment. The hand rests lightly on the upper pane, which moves without friction with the movements of the hand. A rod extending out from this pane bears a hard rubber pencil, which moves over a flat sheet of blackened paper. When the eyes are closed the hand makes slight involuntary movements, differing according to the nature of the mental processes, and these movements are recorded on the blackened paper. This is a scientific application of the popular planchette. (H.C.W.)]

(6) Many other pieces for haptical work are on the market, used for special purposes at the various laboratories. The forms of aesthesiometric appliances, e.g., are very numerous; and there are several devices for investigating the perception of weight (keyboard pressure, weight bags, weight funnels, &c.).

Besides the apparatus mentioned, the following materials are needed: corks, blackboard and chalk, string with attached weight, rods of varying size and weight, metal disks, sticking-plaster, tuning-fork (for tickling, &c.), millimetre scales, &c.

(d) *Taste*. The apparatus needed for the study of taste perception and sensation consists of a concave (enlarging) mirror, a series of fine camel's-hair brushes, and a supply of solutions; see Sanford, op. cit., 370. Various anaesthetizing agents will also be found useful.

(e) *Smell*. The chief instrument is the olfactometer, the theory of which is that intensity of smell varies directly as extent of odoriferous surface exposed. Zwaardemaker has a cheap clinical olfactometer, which does well for psychological drill-work; and a large, double olfactometer, which (though its use requires extreme caution) answers every purpose for research work (Sanford, op. cit., 371; Zwaardemaker, *Physiol. d. Geruchs*, 1895).

The olfactometer will probably fulfil all laboratory requirements (for minimal odours, discrimination of smell, complementarism of smell, &c.). It is, however, useful to have a series of solutions (standard synthetic products) and a stock of solvents (glycerine, odourless paraffin, &c.) on hand for occasional use. Such a supply is, indeed, required for the double olfactometer. (E.B.T.)

[(d) and (e)] The means used are solutions of sugar, quinine, tartaric acid, salt, &c. The substance is diluted in water until it can no longer be distinguished, or solutions

of different strength are compared. Zwaardemaker's olfactometer consists of a pair of horizontal tubes, turned upward at one end for insertion in the nostrils. Over the other end are fitted in turn various tubes with odoriferous substances. A board conceals the other end from the subject's view, and prevents the odours from reaching the nostrils except through the tube. The strength of the odour varies with the distance that the odour-tubes project out beyond the inhaling tubes, and this furnishes a measure for the thresholds of sensation and difference. (H.C.W.)

Other olfactometric devices are those of Passy, *Année Psychol.*, ii; Mesnard, *C. R. Acad. d. Sci.*, June 19, 1893, and *Rev. de Botanique* (1894), 97; Ch. Henry, *Rev. Philos.*, xxxi. 447, and *C. R. Acad. d. Sci.*, Feb. 9, 1891; Buccola (for reaction-time experiments), *Riv. di Filos. Scient.*, 1882. (L.M.—E.M.)

C. *Apparatus for investigating the Time-relations of Mental Processes*: (1) REACTION TIME (q. v.). Reaction time is measured by means of the chronoscope or chronograph.

The *Hipp chronoscope*, the form in general use by psychologists, is a clock whose hands are connected with the mechanism by making an electric circuit, and disconnected by breaking it or *vice versa*. There are two dials, each divided into one hundred parts: the hand on the upper dial makes a circuit in one-tenth of a second, the lower in ten seconds; by reading the two together, the time is indicated in thousandths of a second (called σ, sigma; 1,000 σ = 1 sec.). In practice the clockwork is first started; then the stimulus is given, which also makes the circuit, thereby starting the hands at the same instant; when the proposed mental act is completed, the subject presses a reaction key, which stops the hands; the reaction time is the entire time during which the hands of the clock have moved.

A simpler form of chronoscope is the *d'Arsonval chronometer*. This has but one dial, marking hundredths of a second; it is portable and almost noiseless, and is intended for pathological use; once wound the clockwork continues to go till run down. The arrangement for starting and stopping the hand is essentially the same as in the Hipp. The *pendulum chronoscope* is a pendulum which swings along a scale, graduated to mark the time occupied in swinging. The pendulum is held at the upper end of the arc by an electro-magnet, and released when the stimulus is given; when the subject reacts, another electro-magnet draws a pointer to the scale and holds it, while the pendulum continues its course. The position of the pointer indicates the reaction time. The chronoscope is usually 'controlled' or verified from time to time by a control hammer or electric tuning-fork.

The *chronograph* used in psychological experiment is some form of revolving cylinder, such as the kymograph or polygraph, described above (II, general). The time is measured by a tuning-fork, metronome, or seconds pendulum, and recorded by means of tambours or an electric circuit. The electric tuning-fork gives the most accurate results. An electro-magnet near one prong of the fork draws that prong; this breaks the circuit, and the prong, released, flies back, makes the circuit again, and so on. The fork is thus kept in vibration, and as the circuit is made and broken with each vibration, it is recorded on the cylinder by the Deprez signal. When the circuit is finally broken by the reaction movement, the record ceases, though the fork continues for a time to vibrate. A continuous time record may be obtained by a quill attached to a prong of the fork and touching the cylinder. In other forms, the record is made by another tuning-fork vibrating in 'sympathy.'

The reaction-time apparatus includes also the *stimulus releaser* and the *reaction key.* For visual stimuli, such as light, colours, letters, and words, a screen with an aperture is attached to a pendulum; as the latter swings, the stimulus, behind it, is exposed for a time to view; the instant this exposure begins, the chronoscope or chronograph circuit is made. The two apparatus are combined in the pendulum chronoscope. Instead of a pendulum, a heavy falling screen with an aperture may be used to expose the stimulus. For sensations of sound a bell or hammer is struck, and this contact completes the circuit, which starts the time apparatus. For sensations of touch a blunt point is pressed against the skin, and this movement completes the circuit.

The most common form of *reaction key* is for the hand; it is similar to a telegraphic key; the circuit is broken (or made) by pressing a knob at the end of a lever. For reacting with the vocal organs a lever is fastened to the jaw or pressed against the teeth; when the mouth is opened to speak a circuit is broken. In another (Libbey-Baldwin) form the mouth is placed at the large end of a funnel; a puff of air is sent through the funnel, moving

a swinging metal tongue at the other end and breaking the circuit. For reaction with choice a complex key is used, with a lever for each finger; if one stimulus appears, the thumb lever is pressed; if another stimulus, the forefinger lever, and so on, as agreed on beforehand. Or two simple keys may be used and the reaction made with right or left hand respectively.

(2) *Least Duration.* The least duration of stimulus consistent with a given kind of perception is measured as follows: a disk with alternate sectors of black and white is rotated on a colour-wheel (described above, B. *a*, (4)); when the speed is increased beyond a certain rate the flickering ceases, and we see a uniform grey; from the rate of speed and width of the sectors the duration of the separate stimuli is calculated. Or, using a screen with aperture, attached to a pendulum, and taking a printed word as stimulus, the speed of the pendulum is increased or the width of the aperture diminished till the word is no longer distinguishable; the least time of exposure at which the word can be read is thus determined. Arrangements with auditory limiting stimuli have also been used.

(3) *Time Relations of Different Senses.* The relation between simultaneous perceptions of visual and auditory stimuli is measured by the *complication pendulum.* This consists of a disk with a scale, over which swings a pointer attached to a pendulum. Concealed behind the disk is a bell, which can be adjusted so as to sound as the pointer passes any given point on the scale. The subject notes the point at which the bell seems to sound; the direction and amount of error depends upon certain conditions of attention, &c.

(4) *Appreciation of Time.* To measure the least noticeable difference between two periods of 'empty' time, the *time-sense apparatus* is used. It consists of a disk with circular scale. Three levers, which project from the disk, may be placed at any points on the scale. Another disk, with a single pointer, rotates over this, and the pointer strikes the three levers in turn, making an electric circuit, and causing a bell or hammer to sound each time. The position of the first two levers being fixed, the third is varied till the time between the second and third taps is just noticeably different from the time between the first and second. The time-sense apparatus of Schumann is described in *Zeitsch. f. Psychol.,* iv. 1 ff.

D. *Apparatus for investigating the Intellec-*

tual Functions: (1) *Attention*. If the attention be maintained at a maximum, this maximum will rise and fall at intervals. The rate of fluctuation is measured for vision by means of the *Masson disk*. This is a white surface, along one radius of which is a black line of uniform thickness but broken into segments; when the disk is rotated, the inner segments of the line, being broader in proportion to the whole circumference than the outer segments, will give a darker grey. The breadth of the line is such that four or five rings are always distinguishable with close attention; the ring next beyond alternately appears and disappears; the alternating intervals are measured by the chronograph. For hearing, the ticking of a watch at the furthest audible distance is used, or the faint sound of sand dropping continuously on a metallic surface; the 'buzzer' of an induction coil, electric forks, singing tubes, &c., have also been used. For experiments on distraction no special apparatus is required; but the sort of distraction must be carefully chosen and certain conditions fulfilled.

(2) *Memory*. Ebbinghaus has measured the falling off in accuracy of memory trains and their latent force by means of nonsense syllables. Having memorized a series of these of given length after a certain number of repetitions, he observed the number of errors made in repeating the series after the lapse of one day, two days, &c. The number of repetitions required to relearn the series furnished a measure of the latent force of memory. Memory of intensity and intensity-difference has been measured in several of the senses for short intervals. The apparatus is the same as that used for the threshold of intensity-difference. Memory of visual size has been measured by means of a series of squares, circles, or lines of nearly the same dimensions. One of these, the standard, is shown and removed; after an interval, another, or others. The falling off in accuracy is shown by the increase of the threshold value as the time is lengthened.

(3) *Imaging*. Scripture's apparatus for measuring the intensity of images consists of a telescope tube, through which the subject observes a screen of white paper. The latter is illuminated, faintly in front and by a variable flame behind. The subject is asked to imagine threads like the cross hairs of a telescope on the white surface, and to describe their changes as the illumination is increased. On the back of the paper, unknown to him, is a real line, which he finally sees and compares with his imagined lines. When they are equal in intensity the intensity of the real line furnishes a measure of the intensity of his visual imagination.

E. *Apparatus for Anthropometrical Measurements*. Measurements of height, weight, diameter of chest, &c., are made by direct means. The capacity of the lungs is measured by means of a *spirometer*. One form of spirometer consists of an inverted jar resting in water and counterbalanced by weights. When air is blown through a tube into this jar the latter is lifted, the amount of air sent in being indicated on a scale. The subject takes a full breath and breathes out through the tube. The dimensions of the head are measured by means of the *craniometer*. One form of this apparatus is the hatter's *conformateur*, which is set on the head and indicates the outline of the largest horizontal area of the head. The *pupillometer* is used to measure the diameter of the pupil of the eye. The *ophthalmometer* determines the curvature of the cornea. The dynamometer, colour-blindness tester, perimeter, Galton's whistle, reaction-time, and other apparatus described above are also employed in anthropometrical tests. (H.C.W.)

Literature. Laboratories, historical: BALDWIN, Psychology Past and Present, Psychol. Rev. (1894), i. 4, and Princeton Contrib. to Psychol., i. 1; DELABARRE, Année Psychol. (1894), i; BINET, Psychol. Expér. (1894, inexact); VILLA, Psicol. Contemp. (1899). Descriptions of single laboratories are: BALDWIN, Lab. Univ. of Toronto, Science, O.S. (1892); FLOURNOY, Notice sur le Lab. Psychol. de Genève (1896); TITCHENER, as below (Cornell laboratory). In general: TITCHENER, Mind, N.S., vii. 311 (with bibliography), and Amer. J. of Psychol., xi. 251; BUCCOLA, Legge del tempo; MANTOVANI, Psicol. Fisiol.; KROHN, Amer. J. of Psychol. (1892), iv (German labs.), and Rep. of U. S. Comm'r. of Educ. (1892) (labs. in U. S.); BECHTEREW, Cong. de Zool. de 1892 (1893), iii (lab. at Kasan); HENRI, Rev. Philos. (1893), xxxv. 12 (German labs.); SANFORD, Amer. J. of Psychol. (1893), v (suggestions of equipment); Psychology in American Colleges and Universities (by various authors), Amer. J. of Psychol. (1890), iii (2); DE VARIGNY, Rev. Scient. (1894), 4th S., i. (lab. at Univ. of Wisc.); STRATTON, Science (1896), N.S., iv. (Leipzig lab.); TOKARSKY, Zapiski Psichol. Lab. (1896) i (Moscow lab.); BÉRILLON, Notice sur l'Institut Psychophysiologique de

Paris (1897); CASSLANT, Le Lab. de Physiol. des Sensations de la Sorbonne (1897); VASCHIDE, Rev. d. Rev. (1898), xxiv (Paris lab.); JASTROW, Official Catalogue of the World's Columbian Exposition (1893), Pt. XII (psychological exhibit). (J.MᶜK.C.–H.C.W.)

Apparatus: see especially the reports (with discussions) of the Committee on Tests of the Amer. Psychol. Assoc., Psychol. Rev., 1895 ff., and the topic TESTS (psychophysical); SANFORD, Course in Exper. Psychol.; WUNDT, Physiol. Psychol. (4th ed.); MÜNSTERBERG, Psychol. Lab. of Harvard Univ. (1893); H. C. WARREN, art. 'Recording Apparatus' (psychological), in Johnson's Univl. Cyc. (new ed.), Appendix (which has been quoted, by permission, in this article); SCRIPTURE, The New Psychol.; TITCHENER, Outline of Psychol.; Exper. Psychol., i. 1. 2 (1901); Mind (as cited above), and Amer. J. of Psychol., Jan., 1900; Année Pyschol., esp. i. 460, 530, 531, ii. 776, iii. 652 ff., iv. 245, 253, 303; many papers in the Philos. Stud., Psychol. Rev., Zeitsch. f. Psychol., Amer. J. of Psychol., Arch. f. Ophthal., Pflüger's Arch., Riv. Sperim. di Freniat., describe special instruments. Pathological appliances and their use are described by MORSELLI, Semej. malat. ment. (1895–8). See also the catalogues of the various instrument dealers: Verdin, König, Appuun, Rothe, Zimmermann, Petzold, Cambridge Scientific Instrument Company, Queen, Biddle, Meyrowitz, Chicago Lab. Supply Co., Columbia, Yale, and Clark Universities' Psychological Instrument Makers. (E.B.T.–H.C.W.–J.M.B.)

Labour [Lat. *labor*]: Ger. *Arbeit*; Fr. *travail*; Ital. *lavoro*. Effort directed towards a more or less remote economic end.

The conscious separation of the end from the means is essential to the idea of labour.

The first labour of importance under the limits of this definition arose from the system of slavery. For this labour the motive was fear. With the progress of emancipation reward takes the place of compulsion as a stimulus.

It is a mooted question whether all labour involves *pain*. The presumption generally is that it does; for if there is a future happiness to be attained, men will generally continue to work for it until stopped by a present discomfort, which counterbalances the anticipation of future good as a present motive. But there would appear to be exceptions to this rule, i. e. counterbalancing motives not properly classed as pains. (A.T.H.)

La Bruyère, Jean de. (1639–96.) Born at Dourdan, he was educated in Paris for the law and admitted to the bar in 1665. In 1684, through the influence of Bossuet, he became tutor to the duc de Bourbon in the house of Condé, to which he remained attached until his death. Admitted to the Academy in 1693.

Lactantius, Firmianus. Also called Lucius Caecilius, or Caelius. One of the Church fathers, born near the middle of the 3rd century A. D., either in Italy or in Africa. Studied rhetoric under Arnobius, and became distinguished for his eloquence and learning. About 301 he was made professor of Latin eloquence in Nicomedia, became a Christian, and wrote in defence of the new religion. Called to Treves by the Emperor Constantine as tutor of his son Crispus, he is supposed to have died there about 330. See PATRISTIC PHILOSOPHY (4).

Laissez-faire [Fr.]: also used in German; Ital. *lasciar fare, lasciar passare*. 'Let things take their own course.'

A maxim of practical economics, based on the observation that the dangers from too much government interference are greater than those from too little government interference. Sometimes, but erroneously, made the basis of a theory of commercial ethics.

This phrase was apparently first used by the Marquis d'Argenson in an anonymous letter to the *Journal Économique* in 1751. It is less correctly attributed to de Gournay.

Literature: ONCKEN, Die Maxime laissez-faire (1886). (A.T.H.)

Lalling [Lat. *lallare*, Gr. λαλεῖν, to speak]: Ger. *Lallen, Stammeln* (stammering); Fr. *balbutiement*; Ital. *balbuzie, balbettamento*. A defect in precision of articulation such as characterizes the speech of childhood.

It becomes a disorder if it fails to disappear in due time with education, as is frequently the case with backward and defective children. Specific lalling may appear as a difficulty in pronouncing accurately single sounds or groups of sounds, and may thus characterize individuals, classes, or races. Cf. DYSLALIA. See also ANARTHRIA, and SPEECH AND ITS DEFECTS. (J.J.)

Lalo- [Gr. λαλεῖν, to speak]: Ger. *Lalo-*; Fr. *lalo-*; Ital. *lalo-*. The term lalo- (used in combination) indicates the articulatory factor of speech, as distinguished from the intellectual factor on the one hand, and the association factor on the other.

In general, disturbances in speech utterance would thus be lalopathies; in the formation of thoughts preliminary to speech, logopathies; and in the associative bonds between thought and speech, aphasias or dysphasias (see LOGO-, and SPEECH AND ITS DEFECTS). Stuttering and stammering are common forms of lalopathy. Likewise laloplegia has been used to indicate a paralysis affecting speech utterance. (J.J.)

Lamarck, Jean-Baptiste Pierre Antoine de Monet, Chevalier de. (1744–1829.) A well-known French naturalist. He was the eleventh child, and intended for the Jesuits. Deserting them for the army, he was very soon named to a lieutenancy. An accident disqualified him for service, and he went to Paris to study medicine. In 1781–2 Buffon obtained for him an appointment as botanist to the king, and he travelled extensively in Europe. In 1788 he received a botanical appointment in the Jardin des Plantes, Paris, and in 1793 was offered a chair in zoology. Stricken soon afterwards with blindness, he did not cease to labour, and between 1815 and 1822 published his greatest zoological work. The devotion of his family, and particularly of his eldest daughter, redeemed these later years for science. See LAMARCKISM, and HEREDITY.

Lamarckism or **Lamarckianism**: Ger. *Lamarck'ische Lehre*; Fr. *Lamarckisme*; Ital. *Lamarckismo.* (1) The doctrine that use and disuse, broadly considered, are the main determinants of adaptations of structure in animal species. (2) The view that specific modifications or 'acquired characters' of individuals are inherited by their offspring is also called Lamarckism, Lamarckian Inheritance, or Neo-Lamarckism. Cf. ORTHOGENESIS.

(1) This doctrine was summarized by Lamarck in his 'Third' and 'Fourth Laws,' which are: (*a*) The development of organs and their power of action are constantly determined by the use of these organs; (*b*) All that has been acquired, begun, or changed in the structure of individuals during the course of their life is preserved in reproduction and transmitted to the new individuals which spring from those which have experienced the changes.' More generally he elsewhere says, 'The gains or losses of organic development, due to use or disuse, are transmitted to offspring.'

(2) It is now generally admitted that use and disuse, together with the direct effects of environing forces, may determine modifications of structure in the course of individual life; but many zoologists contend that such

modifications are not inherited, and are therefore inoperative in the evolution of species. The latter therefore reject the essentially Lamarckian doctrine of the transmission of the effects of use and disuse. On the other hand, Lamarckian inheritance is often emphasized in opposition to natural selection. Hyatt and Cope in America, Eimer in Germany, Cunningham and Henslow in England, Canestrini and Cattaneo in Italy, support the views of Lamarck. The trend of opinion in the last decade has been distinctly against the Lamarckian view. Cf. HEREDITY. (C.LL.M.–J.M.B.)

The Lamarckian or Orthogenesis theory of evolution may be illustrated by the diagram given below; it is sufficiently described by its lettering. It may be compared with the analogous diagrams given under NATURAL SELECTION and ORTHOPLASY.

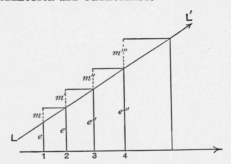

LL', line of evolution. **1, 2,** &c., successive generations by physical heredity. *e, e'*, &c., congenital endowment. *m, m'*, &c., acquired modifications. The modification of one generation is added to the endowment of the next (USE-INHERITANCE (q. v.)).

Literature: LAMARCK, Philos. Zool. (1809), and Hist. Nat. (1816–22). See also under EVOLUTION, ACQUIRED CHARACTERS, HEREDITY, and NATURAL SELECTION. (J.M.B., C.LL.M.)

Lambert, Johann Heinrich. (1728–77.) Born in Elsass. He travelled as tutor to two young Swiss noblemen. In 1764 he went to Berlin and was made member of the Academy of Sciences by Frederick II. He wrote in mathematics, natural science, and metaphysics.

La Mettrie, Julien Offray de. (1709–51.) Born at St. Malo, Brittany. Physician in the army of the duke of Gramont, he was discharged because one of his publications was materialistic and atheistic. He was also compelled to leave France in 1746, and repaired to Holland, but was expelled again. Frederick II invited him to Berlin, and he accepted, living in close intimacy with the emperor until his death.

Lancaster and **Lancastrian System**: see BELL AND LANCASTER (Monitorial System).

Land, Land Value [AS. *land, lond*]: Ger. *Land, Land-* (or *Boden-*) *Werth*; Fr. *terre, valeur de la terre*; Ital. *terra, valore della terra*. The original and indestructible powers of the soil; the price which is paid for the right to use those powers.

The separation of land from capital has been found impossible in practice and difficult in theory. The value of a piece of real estate is attributed to land rather than to capital (1) so far as it is due to location rather than to improvements (original powers), (2) so far as it can be used recurrently rather than used up (indestructible powers).

We can determine the original value of capital directly, and then estimate the return at the market rate of interest. Deducting this interest from the total net income of the property, the remainder is economic rent; from which we deduce the land value by applying a rate of capitalization, which is the inverse of the rate of interest.

Literature: GEORGE, Progress and Poverty; WALKER, Land and its Rent; LORIA, Analisi della proprietà capitalista (1889). (A.T.H.)

Land Tenure: see TENURE.

Lange, Friedrich Albert. (1828–75.) Educated at Zürich and Bonn. Teacher in the gymnasium at Köln, Privat-docent at Bonn and then at Zürich, professor of philosophy at Marburg, where he died. His *History of Materialism* is his greatest work.

Language [Lat. *lingua*, tongue]: Ger. *Sprache*; Fr. *langage*; Ital. *linguaggio*. Language is the communication of thought through speech-sounds. The expression of thought through signs, as in the system of communication employed among deaf-mutes, is based in general upon the written form of vocal speech; and the systems of communication by gesture, common among roving, uncivilized tribes, and serving to supplement or replace language, are not included under the head of language proper, inasmuch as they involve few of the problems of speech-psychology and speech-history. Cf. SPEECH FUNCTION, and SPEECH AND ITS DEFECTS.

Language cannot be defined as merely the expression of thought, for its character and history are determined quite as much by the consideration of intelligibility as by that of expression. The impulse to expression is individual, but the function of speech is social. The form which individual expression shall take is determined in the main by what the hearer can understand. As the hearer on different occasions listens to different speakers, and in turn addresses different hearers, the necessities of general intelligibility and common currency make speech a community possession, and hence a social, and not an individual, product. As tradition fixes its validity practically beyond the conscious power of the individual to make or change, it is historically determined, and ranks as a socio-historical institution.

The normal individual is born with the faculty of speech, but not with its endowment. If he is deaf, he will be in consequence dumb. Born of a certain race or tribe or nation, he inherits nothing of the speech-characteristics or the speech-materials of either. An English child born and brought up in the exclusive environment of the Chinese language will speak that language without a trace of his English parentage in tone or idiom. What we call the Scotch accent and the Irish brogue are not due to any peculiarity in the form or texture of the speech-organs in the individual speaker, but to the influences which governed his early imitative reception of language. He speaks as he heard. Language is therefore, in its distinctive character, purely socio-historical, and not racial or physical. The individual receives his language as he does in general the manners and customs of the society about him, not as he does the colour of his hair or the tint of his skin.

The process by which the child comes into possession of language is a process of accommodation to its environment. The first vague articulations of the infant treat the organs of speech as a new-found toy. They are handy instruments for the production of interesting noises. Gradually, through continued use and practice, the little individual gains control of the various parts of the mechanism. Soon it begins to imitate crudely the speech-sounds it hears in its environment; then it begins to note the connection these sounds have in usage with objects and qualities. Therewith it starts on its career as a language-user. The beginning of this career is marked by the acceptance of speech as a social instrument, and by a self-adjustment therein involved in a traditional social order. During the second year of the child's life the acquisition of new words as speech-signs advances rapidly, but always subject to the limitations arising from incomplete control of the mechanism of articulation, incomplete registration of the content of hearing, or incomplete co-ordination of hearing and reproduction in speaking. See SPEECH AND ITS DEFECTS. At any period in the development of the child's control of the linguistic apparatus it will be noticed that the same sound or combination of sounds is alike treated in different words. A child who says *pĭk* for 'speak' will say *poŏn* for 'spoon,' &c., or who says *punny* for 'funny' will say *poŏt* for 'foot.' The following words taken from the usage of a child of twenty-five months illustrate this regularity in the treatment of sounds and groups of sounds; the words are given in simple phonetic writing: *pī*, 'fish'; *poŏt*, 'foot'; *pig*, 'figs'; *pai*, 'fire'; *pŏl*[1], 'fall'; *pī*, 'please'; *hau*, 'house'; *ki*, 'kiss'; *tŏn*, 'tongs'; *bŏ*, 'box'; *pĭ*, 'fish'; *bed*, 'bread'; *ōtmĭ*, 'oatmeal'; *kŏ*, 'cross,' also 'cloth'; *pa*, 'fast'; *de*, 'dress'; *bœk*, 'black'; *dum*, 'drum'; *pin*, 'pink'; *šēn*, 'change'; *tĭtŏ*, 'sea-shore'; *tūgĭ*, 'sugar'; *tœ*ə, 'chair'; *kŏpĭ*, 'coffee.' All this shows that the acquisition of speech does not proceed as the haphazard acquirement of individual words. The incompleteness of control is not a matter of incomplete articulation alone; it is incompleteness in the control of the linguistic faculty as a whole. It is a significant fact that the uniformities observed are valid only for a single individual. Different children differ greatly in their progress towards complete mastery of speech, but each has its own laws of uniformity within the compass of its own vocabulary.

In any inquiry concerning the attitude of the individual towards his language, it is necessary to make rigid discrimination between what we may call the naïve attitude and that which is affected by reflection, i. e. by the more or less thorough review and comparison of the materials contained in the language, or by instruction based upon such review, such as is given by grammars, dictionaries, and teachers. The reflective attitude succeeds in partially isolating language from its thought-stimulus, and observing it as an objective phenomenon. The naïve attitude receives it as it comes in full and undisturbed association with its content.

The naïve attitude is characterized by a consciousness that language and content, name and thing, belong to each other absolutely;

or rather by an absence of any consciousness to the contrary. The thing is unthinkable without a name. If the name be unknown, it is an unfortunate accident, for surely there is a name, and to know it gives power and control. It is indicative of Jehovah's power that he 'telleth the number of the stars, and calleth them all by name' (Ps. cxlvii. 4). The name is not a mere convenient tag, but is a form of the thing itself. A change of name involves a change of character, and *vice versa*; thus, in the case of proper names, Saul to Paul, Jacob to Israel. A thing has one native, inherent name, and that name betrays its nature. 'The swine is rightly so named,' says the old proverb; and the true attitude of the son of nature towards language is revealed in the naïve remark of the peasant: 'That the astronomers can tell how far off the stars are, and how they move, that I can understand; but how in the world can they ever get at their names?' Cf. Polle, *Wie denkt das Volk über die Sprache?* (1889).

So profound is the naïve sense for the natural connection of words with the things they denote, that one's own language in comparison with stranger tongues is regarded as the standard from which the others have departed. The sound of conversation in a foreign language excites compassionate mirth, for, forsooth, it is a pitiful perversion of the one standard speech. If a foreigner cannot understand you, instinct suggests louder enunciation. Deafness is the natural explanation of his failure to understand. Prejudice against dialect and brogue is one of the hardest snakes for reason to strangle. Stranger words are felt to be approximations to our own. Meaning is read into them, or they are corrected to our standard. The naïve interpretation of French *frontispice* (Lat. *-spicere*) is betrayed in the telltale orthography—*piece*. Gk. γλυκύρριζα, 'sweetroot,' becomes *liquiritia* by virtue of *liqueo*!

The linguistic sense 'abhors the vacuum of a meaningless word.' It refuses to treat names as tags. It insists that names contain a clue to the character of the thing. Hence arise the legions of folk-etymologies involving perversion of native words—*coatplaster* for *courtplaster*, *ashfelt* for *asphalt*, and the like. But subtler and far more insidious are the cases where meanings creep into the empty shells without changing the outward shape of the shells, and betray their presence only incidentally. Thus *shoplifter* is very commonly associated in thought with *lift*, though its

---

[1] *ŏ* is here, and in following, a symbol for open *o* in *not*; *ō* for close *o* in *note*; *œ* for open *e*, as in *back*; *ē* for close *e*, as in *pain*; ə for the 'obscure' vowel.

latter component is connected with Greek κλέπτειν, 'to steal'; bric-a-brac conveys to many minds the notion of fragments; preface, despite Lat. praefatium, is likely to shape its use according to a false suggestion of face; duel (O. Lat. duellum = bellum) has indeed changed its value in deference to the intruding idea of duo, just as par- in parboil has shifted from the value 'very' (Lat. per-) under the misleading influence of part; hostler (cf. hostel, hôtel) has certainly suffered from association with horse; miniature, a derivative of minium, 'red lead,' has come to involve the suggestion of smallness through influence of minimus. These few illustrations represent a widespread influence of tremendous power which is continually at work honey-combing, undermining, reshaping the whole fabric and structure of language.

Closely akin to this first characteristic of the naïve attitude towards language is a second, which is indeed scarcely more than its corollary. Words are regarded not only as the native and inherently proper names of things, but in their relations to other words maintain a form which sets forth their relation in value. Form and content are believed to consort naturally together. This naïve belief manifests itself in the incessant pressure towards endowing like content with like expression. It may be the content which yields, as in the cases we have already cited, e. g. parboil and duel, or it may be the form. It matters little from which side the impulse comes; the goal of the tendency is one—to give like content like expression.

The phenomena of change commonly classed under the head of the action of analogy belong to the adjustment of form to content. The child who changes know, knew to know, knowed, after the analogy of love, loved, or think, thought to think, thunk, after the analogy of sing, sung, is frankly following a tendency which the maturer man resists, only because the traditional irregularity is more firmly impressed upon him by usage; but the way of the child is the way the current sweeps.

Among the phenomena of analogy are to be noted cases where (1) words diverse in form are brought into association by likeness of signification. Such words appearing together on the level of consciousness in response to an idea may become confused, and a case of 'telescoping' result; thus exactly and precisely may yield prezackly; similar are withstrain, begincement. In the field of syntax

appear phenomena like Greek τίς πόθεν εἶ; 'That's the book of which I was telling you about,' &c. (2) Words diverse in form are associated by affinity of signification, i. e. by sharing some like category of idea, and through this association a change of form results intended to mark the like category of idea with a like body of form. Thus Latin *olle (cf. olim) becomes ille after the analogy of iste, ipse. February becomes Febyuary after the analogy of January. Female displaces *femel after the analogy of male.

Most notable under this head is the drift towards the adoption of like function signs, as for the expression of like moods, tenses, cases, &c. Thus on the analogy of Lat. tribui, tributus, &c., habui, habitus become habui, *habutus, as shown in the Italian avuto, Fr. eu; and debui, debitus become debui, *debutus (Fr. dû), &c. Lat. esse yields to the more familiar type of regĕre and becomes *essĕre, as shown in Fr. être.

The same general tendency which causes like cases of different nouns to take the same endings forces different cases of the same nouns to use the same stem. It is a tendency to express like by like. Thus Lat. honos, honoris, &c., become honor, honoris. Eng. cloths as plural of cloth displaces the phonetically consistent clothes, which however survives in the isolation of a special significance. Vulg. Eng. threble for treble through influence of three belongs under this head.

The creation of the new form in the interest of completer system does not of necessity involve the entire abandonment of the old. Such older forms surviving through attachment to some peculiar signification or peculiar use, or through relegation to another grammatical category, are known as 'isolated' forms, and are of the highest scientific importance as furnishing a clue to the status anterior to the levelling. Thus Fr. dû represents a Latin *debūtus, but the older debitus, debita survives in dette, being rescued by its employment as a noun. Lat. pondus, -eris, is a neuter, but its earlier condition as a noun of the masc. o-declension is betrayed by the adverb pondo. Despite pennies the older plural pence survives through its peculiar use; so brethren versus brothers; cf. elder versus older.

The process of levelling and systematizing in language is continually producing a superfluity of forms. The new and the old are in perpetual struggle. Sometimes the old prevails through force of tradition; and this occurs most commonly in the case of the most used words, which show, in consequence, the greatest 'irregularity' of inflection. The 'regular' is in general modern, the irregular antique. Sometimes the new prevails, displacing the old; sometimes the new asserts its place in the system, leaving the old in the isolation of a special use. Language frequently avails itself of the superfluity of form to acquire the means of differentiating signification and use. It does not create the superfluity for the sake of the differentiation.

To return now to our inquiry concerning the naïve attitude of the individual toward his language, we may note as a third main characterization that the value and power of words and expressions is not determined by any consideration of their history or etymology, nor by any thorough or conscious review of their various uses such as dictionaries summarize in 'definitions,' but by a direct and unconsciously formulated feeling for their character derived from experience of their use in the various associations of speech. One who could not possibly define the difference between *big* and *great* might use them correctly. Words carry with them an atmosphere derived from association in use which gives them a character. Forms like *doth, hath, wist, thou*, have now a stately effect, not from anything inherent in this form, but because of their association with Holy Writ, the liturgy, and prayer. When first used in the translation of the Bible they were common words and carried no such effect. The judgments of taste in language and style are generally based upon this feeling concerning the character of words rather than upon any rational criteria which etymology or scientific grammar can supply.

The standards of 'correctness' in language must also be ultimately based upon this feeling, so far as they are really trustworthy. The canons of the purists have often however been found, when put to the test, to rely upon superficially conceived criteria; for instance, the pronoun *'em* in *go and get 'em* would probably be condemned as involving careless and lax pronunciation of *them*. This however is not the fact; *em* is not historically an abbreviation of *them*, but an independent pronoun, and the apostrophe is misleading. If it be true that good taste condemns the use of *em*, then the canon can be based on that observed fact, and not on the false historical statement. The feeling against *em*, at least in dignified speech, is probably due to a feel-ing that it is an abbreviation. In a similar way the word *victuals* has been demeaned in the eyes of linguistic taste by the notion that its pronunciation *vittles* is a perversion; yet *vittles* is the correct historical representative of Middle English *vittailles*, just as *battles* is of *battailles*. It is the rococo orthography *victuals* which has been the word's undoing. The historically correct pronunciation of *arctic* is *artic*, which was indeed the Old French and Middle English form, but the elegant spelling, remodelled after the Greek, has in recent years started up a bastard pronunciation *arktik*, which with its appearance of genuineness is dispossessing the true heir; so *leftenant*, the correct pronunciation of *lieutenant*, is in America shrinking before *lūténant*. The purism which attempts to separate the word *don't-you* (*dóntšu*) into *don't* and *you* is utterly false to historical phonology; *you* is an enclitic, and *-ty-* yields *ch* (*tš*), as in *orchard* from *ortyard*. The sentiment, so far as it exists, against the pronunciation *dóntšu, nétšur* (nature), &c., appears to have been awakened by the false humour of *dontchoo* and *natchoor*. It is doubtful, however, if so falsely conceived a sentiment will make itself in this case a permanent position in taste. Etymologies, furthermore, as they can only show by what processes a word reaches a present or any given stadium of use, can never be properly employed to fetter or direct the application and use of a word of established position in a language.

Finally, it may be said of the naïve attitude towards language that it is not the attitude of the critic, but that of good faith. It presumes that the speaker's language will fit and express his thought. It does not expect errors, or seek for them, and the reason of this is that language is not commonly differentiated from its content or rendered an object of attention in itself. The pun is man's first tottering venture out upon the way of differentiation.

The folk-mind accepts the speaker's language as he means it, so far as it can divine what that meaning is. Hence it is that language is full of expressions which the logical sense of the critic discerns to be illogical, but which the natural man accepts in unhesitating good faith. It is the logician who discerns that 'two negatives equal an affirmative'; the folk-mind knows better, and usually recognizes in the double negative only a twofold negation. The grammar which undertakes to be applied logic is false to language and an abuse of nature. Standards of 'correctness' which are based upon logical determinations are artificial and perversive. It is unavoidable, in fact it is desirable, that systematic effort should be made in the interest of establishing a common and well authenticated medium of intercourse between the dialectally diverse communities of a nation ; but such an effort must consult the linguistic consciousness, the current usage, and the historical conditions, rather than the categories of logic.

Language is primarily and originally a matter of sounds and not of writing. The idea of committing language to record is an afterthought. The first primitive writing was a record of things rather than of language. Writing based on pictures of the things denoted by words is called ideographic. The transition to language-writing begins when the value of an ideogram is extended to include homonyms; thus, as if the ideogram of *mail* (armour) were used to denote also *mail* (post) and *male*. The next step in the development of phonetic writing is taken when the symbol associates itself with a body of sounds which may be used merely as a syllable; thus, to continue our fictitious illustration, as if our symbol were used for the first three sounds of *male*volent, or even for *ma*. The final step is taken when by the use of vowel signs (cf. the Hebrew vowel points) the various syllables of like consonant are differentiated ; e. g. *ma, me, mi, mo, mu* ; so as to provide at least an approximate denotation of separate sounds.

Though in general it may be said that writing assumes to be no more than a record of spoken language, and that reading should properly be, as indeed in the earlier phases of literary civilization it always was, a *viva voce* reproduction of the language suggested by the written symbols, yet with the wide extension of the habit of reading and the consequent development of the paradoxical usage of 'reading to one's self,' the written form comes to have a validity of its own, and may in its turn exercise an influence upon the spoken language, if not dictate to it; thus words, especially unusual words and foreign names, are pronounced 'as they are spelled' ; cf. the American pronunciation of *almonds* which re-establishes the *l*, of *traits* (Eng. *trēz*), of *Berwick* (Eng. *Berrik*).

Orthography as a conventionalized form of writing has the advantage of rising above the irregularities of dialect and the historical changes of sounds, and binding together the forces and expressions of a civilization in defiance of time on the one hand and of space as expressed in provincial boundaries and dialect, on the other. A language which is to be the unifying force of a nation must be garbed in an orthography. Phonetic spelling, great as its advantages in restoring the spoken form to its primacy, and lessening the difficulty of learning to read, would, for instance in the case of English, make the language of Shakespeare and the English Bible an antique, almost a foreign, speech, and scatter the present unitary English of literature into a score of diverse idioms. English orthography, as to a greater or less extent all orthographies, involves a mass of quaint errors, pedantries, and vain embellishments, which it may well be the task of prudent reform to eliminate ; e. g. *foreign* and *sovereign* seem to have their *g* from *reign*, cf. Middle English *foreine, soverain* ; *island* has its *s* from *insula* ; *delight* (M. E. *delit*) its *gh* from analogy with *right, light*, &c. ; *science* its *c* from Lat. *scientia*, and *scent* (Lat. *sentio*) has followed it ; *scissors* (M. E. *sisoures*) has been misguided by Lat. *scindere* ; *could* (older *coude*) by *would* and *should*, &c. Still the fundamental idea of an orthography is correct. The literary language as the bond of a civilization and the voice of a nation must be regarded first as a *written* language, though it must not, if it is to remain vital, relax its connection with speech.

In passing from generation to generation a language undergoes gradual change in the stock of its words, in the meanings which they bear, in the sounds which compose them. The investigation of the processes by which this change takes place is the task of the historical grammar. While descriptive grammar arranges the facts of language according to the form and relation which they present in actual use, historical grammar deals with them as standing in a line of historical development. Among the phenomena of language it is the sounds which have submitted to the most systematic treatment and discovered in their changes the clearest acceptance of laws. The department of historical grammar dealing with the history of sound-changes is called historical phonology.

The most interesting problem of phonology concerns the nature of the so-called phonetic laws. It has been noted that a sound-change occurring in a given word at a given period in a given speech-community is prone to manifest itself in all the other words of the language which contain the same sound under like environment; thus, for illustration, the primitive Indo-European *oi*, which appears in Gothic as *ai*, changes in High German to *ei*, in Old English to *ā*, which becomes in Mod. Eng. *ō*, thus :—

Goth.	Ger.	O. Eng.	Mod. Eng.
haims	*heim*	*hām*	*home*
aiths	*eid*	*āth*	*oath*
hlaifs	*laib*	*hlāf*	*loaf*
ains	*ein*	*ān*	*one*
dails	*theil*	*dāl*	*dole*
wait	*weiss*	*wāt*	*wot*
twai	*zwei*	*twā*	*two*
hails	*heil*	*hāl*	*whole*

This uniformity manifesting itself in distinct words apparently separated from mutual influences is naturally a subject of wonder. The main problem is this: what bond unites the like sounds in these different words, that should compel them to like change? It cannot be said that any satisfactory solution has thus far been found. A view which has been widely held and ably defended during the past two decades is that which is most clearly stated in Paul's *Principien der Sprachgeschichte*. This treats the change as a gradual shifting of the sound-image, made up of impressions both upon the ear and upon the apparatus of sound-reproduction. This image is common for all the occurrences of the sound in whatever words, and common to the mass of speakers in a speech-community by reason of like experiences and like demand for intelligibility. It is the resultant of numberless experiences, and gradually shifts under the impact of individual divergences. This theory seems, however, to be in plain conflict with the following facts: (*a*) the changes appear to effect themselves by way of a temporary confusion between the old and the entirely differentiated new, and not by a gradual shifting from old to new in all words alike; (*b*) the changes appear to move from word to word, and not *pari passu* through the entire vocabulary. The fact, however, remains that after a period of confusion uniformity is the practically unvarying and certain result; i.e. the change reaches to the uttermost recesses of the vocabulary. The problem therefore remains: if *hām* changed to *hōm*, why should *stān* change to *stōn*, and *gāt* to *gōt* (*goat*)? What possible tie could bind the new *hōm* to *stān* and *gāt*, so that it should influence them to change—for their vowels are now entirely diverse? The observed

facts of language lead us to the belief that for a certain period, both in the usage of a community and of the individual speaker, *hām* and *hōm* existed as variants of one word; *ō* was felt to be one way of reproducing the sound-image *ā*, and hence an occasional *stōn* might appear beside *stān*, &c. Those of us who as children pronounced *Tuesday* as *Tūzdē*, and *new* as *nū*, are aware of a like impulse, when under the influence of standard English we substitute *Tyūzdē* and *nyū*, and then through a false feeling for *yū* as a proper variant for *ū* extend the new pronunciation to make *dyū* and *tyū* out of *do* and *two*. Between *hōm* and *stān* there is indeed no bridge, but between the confusion of *hām* : *hōm* there is a bridge to *stān* : *stōn* and *gāt* : *gōt*. The compelling power which then carries the new into every recess of the vocabulary is the feeling that when *ō* rises to claim the place of *ā* it is the newer and better. Only in case that feeling becomes fully established does the 'law' assert itself; most innovations die, throttled of their own unintelligibility. The tie then which binds together the like sounds in different words remains the sound-image, but the means by which the new in one word reaches to the old in another is the persisting old of the former.

For a full appreciation of the extent to which the sound-laws produce uniformity we must eliminate certain elements of confusion and aberration; thus :—

(1) We must not be misled by spelling; we say, e. g., *musnt*, but in deference to *must* write *mustn't*; we say *cubbud*, but write *cupboard*; we write the older *knife* (French *canif*) and *knee* (Ger. *knie*) and *knew* (Ger. *kennen*), but drop the *k*; we write one and the same sound *s* with *sh* in *shall*, *s* in *sugar*, *ce* in *ocean*, *ch* in *chaise*, *sci* in *conscious*, *ti* in *motion*. In periods of unsettled orthography different spellings often mean the same thing, as Eng. *ax, axe*; *sunne, sun*; *cuppe, cup*; *beauty, beute, bewtie, beautie, beawtye*, &c.; sometimes different spellings of the same word are utilized to mark its distinct uses, as *base* (low) and *bass* (in music); Ger. *stadt, statt*.

(2) Words borrowed from another language evade the action of laws which had operated before their introduction: thus Fr. *mobile* is a late-comer from Latin, while *meuble* has borne the burden and heat of the day; so *débit* beside *dette*, *régale* beside *royal*; the English *ar, er* in *sergeant, Derby, 'varsity, clerk*, &c., involve mixture of dialect. Names like *Bill* (William), *Dolly* (Dorothy), *Bess*

Elizabeth) are borrowed from the 'dialect' of the nursery.

(3) In like manner it may happen that after a sound-law has completed its action, a sound which would have been subject to its action comes into existence through some other law; thus in Attic-Ionic *ā* becomes *ē*, as τιμή for τιμά, but πᾶσᾰ keeps its *ā*, being for *pántša*.

(4) One law may be crossed by another: thus Indo-European *t* becomes Teutonic *th*, as Lat. *tres*, Eng. *three*; but *kt* becomes *ht*, as Lat. *octo*, Eng. *eight*.

(5) Different positions of words in the sentence, especially with reference to the sentence-accent, may expose them to different laws of change; thus, Eng. *an* and *one* are both resultants of Old Eng. *ān*, but the former as proclitic submitted to shortening.

(6) The action of analogy, which has been already discussed, is a potent means of obscuring the results of the phonetic laws. Thus, *s* is dropped in *cherry* for *cherrys* (Fr. *cerise*), but not through the action of a phonetic law; it is the result of the analogy, as *trees*, *tree*; *cherrys* (conceived as plural), *cherry*; *effigies*, *effigy*; *pease* (Fr. *pois*), *pea*; *chinese*, *chinee*; *chaise*, *shay*, &c.

In the last analysis, sound-changes must be found to originate in individual inaccuracies of pronunciation. Only when these become frequent enough, or for any reason potent enough, to influence the community does a phonetic tendency develop capable of formulating a 'law.' One individual has of course more influence in establishing a tendency than another, so one class than another. What should determine the inception of a tendency, or what should make a certain individual accuracy or aberration in reproduction so acceptable as to give it currency, must in most cases evade observation. Attempts to connect these tendencies with influence of climate, &c., have usually proved failures so soon as any considerable range of facts is taken into account. The point of view most hopeful of result is that which finds in race-mixture and bilingualism the initial impulse towards change. A language forced outside its frontiers by conquest or intercourse always suffers thereby, for the people which adopts a stranger tongue, whether as a substitute or as a colleague of its own, will surely speak the language with phonetic as well as syntactical colourings of its own. Syntactical solecisms, like Swiss *es macht warm* (*il fait chaud*) or Alsatian French *il a frappé* (*geschlagen*)

dix heures, are common in the bilingual communities near the great speech frontiers. It is furthermore notably the case that in such communities the common man speaks both the current languages in one and the same general phonetic mould, so that the distinct acoustical character of each is seriously impaired. It has furthermore been noted that dialectal differentiations in languages may often be explained as marking the persistent influence of displaced languages; thus the dialects of Italian may be connected with the influence of the pre-Latin languages of Italy (cf. Ascoli, 'Ueber die ethnologischen Gründe der Umgestaltung der Sprachen,' *Verh. d. Berl. Orient. Congr.*, II). The second mutation of consonants which gave to the High German group its distinctive character had its origin on the extreme southern frontier of German speech, and sweeping northward, gradually lost its vigour as it departed from its source. The law by which *ū* became *au* in like manner began its action at the extreme east in Austria, and swept westward by the Main valley to die out at the Rhine. In these, as in many other cases, phonetic change may be identified as a corruption spreading from some part of the language domain where the ordinary conditions of transmission are rudely disturbed. Similar disturbances have been noted in cities whose population has rapidly grown and developed a violent mixture of dialects.

From the foregoing discussion it is apparent that the term law as used of phonetic uniformity represents a different conception from that attaching to the term in natural sciences. Phonetic law deals with observed uniformities, and presents no basis upon which to predict or expect; i. e. it is law in the sense of the socio-historical laws.

The study of historical changes in the meaning of words constitutes a branch of historical grammar called sematology. These changes are found to be due to an interplay between the general and the special meanings of words. The general meaning of a word covers the range of ideas it is capable of evoking in the mind of hearers. The special meaning is that which is in the mind of the speaker when speaking. Special significations of the word 'tongue' are involved in each of the following: 'Hold your tongue;' 'Every man in his own tongue;' 'Boiled tongue;' 'Hitch the horses to the tongue.'

Change of signification implies change in the general signification; this takes place by way of the special significations. A special may itself become the general by displacing all the other specials. Thus *smith* becomes a proper noun *Smith* by limitation to one special application. Furthermore, new special significations may gain general currency and add to the scope of the term; or old special significations may become obsolete, and the scope of the term be narrowed.

The study of the sounds of language as produced by the speech-organs is called PHONETICS (q. v.), or the physiology of speech. It is a natural science, and an auxiliary rather than a branch of the science of language, which is an historical science.

The earliest records of language carry us back perhaps about 10,000 years, but this gives us no clue to the antiquity of language. Neither have we any further clue to the origin of language than such as we gain from a consideration of the processes which language is continually employing under our eyes for the creation of new material. Neologisms like *clubbable* show that a condition of intelligibility for new words is the establishment of an appreciable connection between thing and name. This may be effected through the intermediation of an already accepted name, or through sound, which onomatopoetically suggests the act or object which might produce it. The mass of imitative words in any language is always great. Such elements evade etymology and establish direct connection with act or object; cf. *fizz, hiss, whizz, clang, clink, pop, jingle, whack, thump, smack, ding-dong, coo, purr, mew, moo, buzz, quack,* &c. Interjections are undeveloped sentences expressing feelings which seem to stand in causal connection with the sound; thus, *phew! whew! ssh!* (cf. *hush!*) *aau! aautch!* In all these existing phenomena of existing speech we discern the way to a connection between name and thing which might have served in the beginnings of speech to advance expression into intelligibility. Cf. Wedgewood, *Origin of Language*; Paul, *Principien d. Sprachgeschichte*, chap. ix; Whitney, *Life and Growth of Language*, chap. xiv; Lefèvre, *Race and Language*, Pt. I. chap. ii; Taylor, *Anthropology* (1881).

The existing languages of the world submit to definite grouping only on the basis of historical connection, and even here the number of groups is so great and their relative extent and importance so various that no general statement is possible concerning them. Between such well-distinguished groups as the Aryan (Indo-European) and Semitic, the Aryan and Ugrian (Finnish-Hungarian), earlier connection has been surmised, but on such uncertain basis that no sure advance has been made toward demonstration of any common ancestry for the various tongues of men. Investigations and discussions make it apparent that the distribution of languages forms no guide to the history and distribution of races. The Indo-European languages which emerge upon history, stretching across the map from India by way of Iran, Armenia, Russia, and Central Europe to the Atlantic coasts, were formerly believed to represent the speech of a fair-haired, blue-eyed, long-skulled, stout-willed race called the Aryans, whose original home we are now inclined to place by the Baltic, either in Scandinavia or Lithuania; but, in the light of present knowledge, we are uncertain whether the Aryans may not have been the recipients rather than the apostles of the Indo-European (cf. Taylor, *Origin of the Aryans*, 1890; Penka, *Herkunft d. Arier*, 1886; Sweet, *The Hist. of Language*, chap. vi, 1900).

The classification of languages according to structure or style is rough and approximate at the best, and has little or no reference to the historical connections. Isolating languages express thought by successions of independent words, whose grammatical relations are betrayed by the context and the relative position, aided occasionally by particles. Chinese affords the best illustration of such a language. Agglutinative languages are characterized by words whose grammatical relations are betrayed by prefixes, suffixes, or infixes, these elements being so loosely combined with the word that their separate value is clearly felt. Turkish is a good illustration of this type. Inflectional languages indicate grammatical relations, preferably through elements which are so intimately combined with the word-body as to have no distinct meaning identified with them in the consciousness of the speaker. The Indo-European and Semitic languages are inflectional. The incorporating languages tend to treat the sentence as a single word by forcing the verb to cover and include the whole proposition. The American languages are commonly of this type, the Old Mexican Nahuatl furnishing a good illustration. The devices which prevail in each of these types may be, and often are, utilized by other languages. The classification is based upon the preference of a language for a given device, not upon the exclusive use thereof. Thus in English an expression like *You find John a six-foot stick* is thoroughly 'isolating' in character—as much so as any Chinese sentence. Formations like *un-fail-ing-ly* and *talk-a-tive-ness* are agglutinative. Latin *venumdedit* is incorporating. The isolating type represents the highest economy of material, and is the creation of an order of society whose stable conditions rest upon fully recognized conventions. The agglutinative type is the most 'regular,' leaving least to convention, and plainly expressing each modification of idea by a distinct body of sound definitely committed to such office. It is the type of language best suited to the use of tribes scattered over wide areas who are obliged, however, to maintain communication with each other (cf. the Swahili of Central Africa and the Mongol languages of Central Asia). The inflectional type seems to represent a progress of the agglutinative type towards the conventionalism of the isolating; it is agglutination smitten with crystallization.

Literature: H. PAUL, Principien d. Sprachgesch. (3rd ed., 1898); G. VON DER GABELENTZ, Die Sprachwiss. (1891); A. H. SAYCE, Princ. of Compar. Philol. (4th ed., 1893); F. MÜLLER, Einl. in die Sprachwiss. (1876–88); H. STEINTHAL and F. MISTELI, Characteristik d. haupts. Typen des Sprachbaues (1893); H. SWEET, The Hist. of Language (1900); W. D. WHITNEY, Life and Growth of Language (1875); STRONG-LOGEMAN-WHEELER, Introd. to the Study of the Hist. of Language (1891); I. TAYLOR, The Origin of the Aryans (1889); B. DELBRÜCK, Introd. to the Study of Language (2nd ed., 1885). See also LANGUAGE FUNCTION, and cf. SPEECH AND ITS DEFECTS. (B.I.W.)

Language Function: Ger. *psychische Funktion der Sprache*; Fr. *fonction du langage*; Ital. *funzione del linguaggio*. The essential function of language is control over the flow of ideas by means of the control we possess over the signs which express ideas.

This control is exercised by the individual over the flow of his own ideas and also over the flow of ideas in another mind. From a genetic point of view the two kinds of control are inseparably connected, and cannot be understood apart from each other.

The control which we possess over the signs both of the language of imitative gesture and of that of conventional speech and its equivalents is primarily motor. Hence the control over the ideas with which these signs are associated is also primarily motor.

Indeed, we might almost venture to define language, in the widest sense, as 'motor control of the course of ideas in our own minds and in the minds of others.'

This is peculiarly clear in the case of the imitative gesture. The imitative gesture is a consequence, on the one hand, of the inherent tendency of ideas to act themselves out, and on the other of that mutual interdependence of men in society, which makes thinking and willing co-operative processes. The motor tendencies involved in ideas, in so far as they cannot take form in practical adjustment to a present environment, are reduced to mere movements of expression. The idea of eating will not enable a man to eat, unless food be within his reach. But he can at least open his mouth and raise his hand to it, or he can place his hand on his stomach. Similarly, the idea of his own warlike prowess will not enable him to fight, unless an enemy be at hand. But there is nothing to prevent him from brandishing his weapon and going through the pantomime of fighting. Such action, of the kind called SELF-IMITATION (q. v.) or CIRCULAR (q. v.) reaction, expresses his ideas, but, at the same time, it is a means of sustaining and developing them in consciousness. It gives him a motor control over his own ideational processes, which may be regarded as a rudimentary beginning of language. But it would at the most remain only a rudimentary beginning apart from social intercourse. If a hungry man A is in presence of another man B, who may be expected to supply his want, the idea of the food will be the idea of food as coming from B, and the imitative gesture will be made with reference to B. In other words, it will be used by A as a means of determining the flow of ideas in the mind of B, and so of obtaining food for himself.

The next point to be noted is that any isolated bit of pantomimic expression is usually vague and ambiguous, owing to its generality. Thus, carrying the hand to the mouth might mean 'I am hungry,' but it might also mean 'Are you hungry?' It might signify thirst as well as hunger. Again, it might express the idea not of needing food, but of having already eaten. There is nothing to connect it specially with any one of these experiences to the exclusion of others. This deficiency may be supplied by the particular circumstances under which the sign is used. But in very many cases, more will be needed for social understanding. It will be necessary to combine different expressive signs in a context, so that each defines and determines the meaning of the others. In this way language is an instrument of conceptual analysis and synthesis. The isolated sign represents only some partial aspect of concrete perceptual experience, and fixes attention on this. By the combination of signs the ideal wholes are constructed out of these indeterminate and fragmentary ideas. In this way it is possible to communicate to another ideal combinations corresponding to complex experiences which have never been theirs. We can, for instance, convey to a person by description the idea of a scene such as he never himself saw. Our description analyses the total experience into its conceptual constituents, each of which has its counterpart in the mind of the person we are talking to. At the same time, the order and connection of the signs determines a progressive combination of these conceptual constituents answering to their combination in the original experience. This of course presupposes co-operation on his part; he must endeavour to shape the course of his thought in accordance with the prompting cues supplied by our discourse.

All this may be accomplished in a certain measure by imitative gestures and other natural signs. But conventional signs are far more convenient and manageable, and they are vastly more powerful as instruments of conceptual analysis and synthesis. The primary and essential procedure of the language of natural signs is to represent things and processes by imitating the broad features of their sensible appearance or of the sensible appearance of something naturally connected with them. But the concepts which are capable of being represented in this manner are of a comparatively low grade of generality or abstractness. 'To make,' says Tylor, 'is too abstract an idea for the deaf-mute; to show that the tailor makes the coat, or that the carpenter makes the table, he would represent the tailor sewing the coat and the carpenter sawing and planing the table.' It is difficult or impossible to represent by natural signs what is common to all kinds of making in abstraction from what is specific in this or that kind of making. But if we use a conventional sign, such as the word 'to make,' the difficulty disappears.

It should be remarked, however, that the child has the advantage that society is in possession of spoken and written language, and that his imitative learning is therefore not the process of slow personal experience and slower adoption of means of expression. This advantage profoundly modifies, in many ways, the child's method both of acquiring and of utilizing the language function. Connected topics (q.v.) are LANGUAGE, and SPEECH AND ITS DEFECTS.

Literature : the controversy between NOMINALISM and REALISM (see these terms) first brought into prominence the essential part played by language in human trains of thought. Among the classical English psychologists HOBBES, LOCKE, and J. S. MILL have made the most important contributions to the subject. See HOBBES, Human Nature, chap. iv (Molesworth's ed. of Works, iv); LOCKE, Essay, Bk. III; MILL, Logic, Bk. IV. chaps. iv, v. Among modern works may be mentioned STEINTHAL, Psychol. u. Sprachwiss.; VICTOR EGGER, La Parole Intérieure; TAINE, On Intelligence, Pt. I. Bk. I. chap. iii; MARTY, Ueber Sprachreflex, Nativismus und absichtliche Sprachbildung, in Vtljsch. f. wiss. Philos. (1889–92); G. H. LEWES, Problems of Life and Mind (3rd series), prob. iv; WARD, art. Psychology, Encyc. Brit. (9th ed.), 75–7. The more psychological aspects are treated by STOUT, Manual of Psychol., Bk. IV. chap. v; BALDWIN, Ment. Devel. in the Child and the Race, chaps. xiv, § 1, and xv, § 3, and Social and Eth. Interpret., chap. iv, § 1; MONCALM, Origine de la Parole et de la Pensée (1899). (G.F.S.–J.M.B.)

Languor [Lat. *languere*, to be faint, languish]: Ger. *Schlaffheit*; Fr. *langueur*; Ital. *languore*. A listless unwillingness to exert oneself; a form of depression or lack of tone (atonia), with sensations of fatigue, feebleness, or faintness.

It is a frequent symptom in depleted conditions of body and mind, in convalescence, &c. It also represents a temperamental characteristic; and as a temporary symptom is perfectly normal and usual. Atmospheric and temperature conditions frequently induce the state of languor, as in what is called 'spring fever.' (J.J.)

Lao Tsze : see ORIENTAL PHILOSOPHY (China).

La Rochefoucauld, François VI, duc de, Prince of Marsillac. (1612–80.) Banished from court by Cardinal Richelieu, he returned after the latter's death. Lived a troubled political and private life, which is reflected in his work *Réflexions*.

Laromiguière, Pierre. (1756–1837.) Teacher of philosophy in the Collège d'Esquille in Toulouse, he came to Paris during the Revolution, won the friendship of Siéyès, and became professor in the Normal School, 1810–13. At the same time he became a member of the Academy of Moral and Political Sciences. Afterwards he lived a life of learned seclusion until his death.

Larva [Lat. *larva*, ghost, mask]: Ger. *Larve*; Fr. *larve*; Ital. *larva*. An immature young stage of an animal, characterized by independent self-feeding and the absence of functional sexual organs. An embryo differs from a larva primarily in not having to secure its own food, consequently its locomotive and digestive systems remain undifferentiated, whereas in a larva they are both necessarily differentiated and functional. (C.S.M.)

The term was applied by Linnaeus because the young stage masks or hides the future mature or perfect form of the species.

Literature: SEDGWICK, Zoology (1898); COMSTOCK, Introd. to the Study of Insects; MINOT, Biol. Centralbl., xv. 577; F. M. BALFOUR, Compar. Embryol. (1881); SIR J. LUBBOCK, Origin and Metamorphoses of Insects (1874); C. CLAUS, Zoologie; D. SHARP, art. Insecta, in Camb. Nat. Hist. (C.S.M.–E.S.G.)

Larynx: see SPEECH AND ITS DEFECTS.

Lasalle, Ferdinand. (1824–64.) Born at Breslau, he was educated for mercantile pursuits, but afterwards studied philology and philosophy at Breslau and Berlin. In 1856 he returned to Berlin and lived as a private scholar.

Lassitude [Lat. *lassitudo*, from *lassus*, faint]: Ger. *Müdigkeit, Mattigkeit*; Fr. *lassitude*; Ital. *stanchezza*. A state of diminished vigour of functions of body and mind.

The energies may be actually weakened by fatigue, although the term frequently refers to a condition in which the sensations of exhaustion and weakness are prominent, with little actual fatigue. It thus approaches the condition of languor. (J.J.)

Latency [Lat. *latere*, to lie hidden]: Ger. *Latenz*; Fr. *latence*; Ital. *latenza*. (1) An older term used to characterize the general group of phenomena now covered by the term 'subconsciousness,' as in the expressions 'latent knowledge,' 'latent memories,' &c. (cf. Hamilton, *Lects on Met.*, xviii, and his references). See SUBCONSCIOUS.

(2) In philosophy and in physics: equivalent to POTENTIAL (q. v.); especially the adjective latent. (J.M.B.)

Latent Heat: Ger. *latente Wärme*; Fr. *chaleur latente*; Ital. *calore latente*. Heat which has been absorbed, or the energy of which has been expended, in changing the interior constitution of a body without altering its temperature.

Its most familiar form is that of the heat absorbed while ice is melting over a fire. The temperature of the mass (ice + water) remains unchanged during the melting, the heat absorbed being expended in the work of liquefaction. (S.N.)

Latent Period: Ger. *Latenzdauer*; Fr. *période d'excitation latente, temps perdu du muscle*; Ital. *periodo* (or *tempo*) *latente*. Time elapsing between stimulus and beginning of reaction, especially of a muscle.

The latent period was first measured for contractions of frog's muscle by Helmholtz, who found it to be about 0·01 of a second. Tigerstedt (1885), by more delicate apparatus, reduced the time for frog's muscle to 0·004 of a second; and Burdon-Sanderson (1890) was able to demonstrate that the electrical condition of a muscle changed 0·0025 of a second after the stimulus had been applied, and concluded that the actual change in the muscle took place even sooner than this, at practically the instant of stimulation. Mendelssohn (1880) estimated the latent period for human muscles at 0·008 of a second. This is probably too large. Bernstein (1871) has analysed the phenomenon of latency by stimulating a muscle directly and indirectly through its nerve. The longer latent period, in case of indirect stimulation, led him to attribute the chief loss of time (0·002–0·003 of a second) to passage of stimulus through the end-plate of the nerve. (C.F.H.)

Latin and Scholastic Terminology: with reference principally to the PATRISTIC and SCHOLASTIC philosophy, and to THOMISM (see those terms). Cf. the glossary below, and also the LATIN INDEX (in vol. ii), where the Latin terms throughout the entire work, including those mentioned in this article, are alphabetically arranged.

(1) Amongst the numerous influences to which the complex terminology of the scholastic philosophy is due, that of Aristotle is notoriously the most important. Yet this influence reached the scholastic thinkers, for a long time, only indirectly, and in part through decidedly circuitous paths. Only in the 13th century and later did it become relatively direct. The other most prominent external influences were those of the Neo-Platonic philosophy, of the patristic theology (especially

as represented by St. Augustine), and of the Arabic commentators of Aristotle. But the inner development of the scholastic doctrine itself had much to do with the formation especially of the later scholastic vocabulary.

(2) A detailed account of these various influences would be equivalent to a history of the whole philosophy of the school. For the purpose of the outline sketch, which is here alone in question, a brief mention of a few of the aids to the study of our subject must first be mentioned; and then the remainder of the account must be limited to illustrative selections from the enormous mass of the facts. The great influence of the scholastic upon the whole of our modern philosophical terminology, and the significance of the recent revival of the Thomistic philosophy under the influence of Pope Leo XIII, combine to make the subject well worthy of a fuller study than is here possible.

(3) The terminology of Roman and mediaeval philosophy occupies, in Eucken's brief *Geschichte der philosophischen Terminologie*, pp. 48–78. Prantl, in his *Geschichte der Logik*, summarizes the early Latin adaptations of Greek terminology (i. 511–27); discusses the *Isagoge* of Porphyry (626–31), with mention of many of the terms there used; and gives a similar attention to Boethius (681–721). In Prantl, Bd. ii, where the early period of scholastic logic is discussed, one may mention especially the treatment of the influence of the Arabic philosophy (in Abschnitt xvi. 297 ff.). The discussion of Albertus Magnus and of St. Thomas (in Bd. iii) is rendered inadequate by reason of Prantl's somewhat lively prejudices; but Duns Scotus (202–33) is more fairly treated. Prantl's work ends (in Bd. iv) with an account of the later scholastic logic. Each volume has its separate index, in which terms are duly entered. Amongst the general histories of philosophy, that of Ueberweg, especially in the latest editions, contains many useful remarks and literary references bearing upon the study of mediaeval usage. Windelband's general history, while very summary in its treatment, is valuable in this region by reason of the prominence that it gives to the history of concepts. Weber's compend is decidedly less trustworthy in regard to scholastic doctrine than it is elsewhere. Siebeck's *Geschichte der Psychologie* is summary, but important. The monographic literature of the history of scholasticism, prepared in the full light and in the true spirit of modern historical inquiry, is still far too small. One may mention at once, as an example of what is needed, a recent careful study of the work and influence of a single scholastic doctor of the 12th century—'Die Philosophie des Alanus de Insulis im Zusammenhange mit den Anschauungen des 12. Jahrhunderts, von M. Baumgartner' (*Beiträge zur Geschichte der Philosophie des Mittelalters*, Münster, 1896). This monograph contains an account of many of the most fundamental terms of the earlier period of scholasticism, with summary statements of the relations between the thought and speech of this period and the thought and speech of the greater scholasticism which followed. No index of terms appears; but the detailed classification of the material, and the extended references to the literature, make this little volume useful for the history of a considerable number of fundamental terms. The numerous compends and expositions of scholastic doctrine by modern Catholic writers usually contain a great many definitions of terms; and it is therefore never hard, with such books at hand, to find the scholastic usage of single words and expressions, where these are such as are at all common. For the doctrine of the school is fond of formal definition, and follows the tradition of St. Thomas and of Socrates in employing simple and often homely illustrations to show the application of the more doubtful definitions. But on the other hand, such textbooks, in recent times, are written almost wholly in the interest of the Thomistic doctrine, and undertake few discussions of the varieties either of usage or of opinion within the history of scholasticism itself, and say little of the origin of the prevailing and adopted terminology. A general appeal to the authority of Aristotle, and an occasional mention of this or of that point in which the recognized usages vary—such is all that these textbooks commonly find space to offer in the way of a history of their terms, beyond the mere report of the Thomistic, or, on occasion, of the later-established definitions of such terms or usages as came into vogue after St. Thomas. Amongst the summaries of scholastic philosophy, the great but unfinished treatise of Father Harper, *The Metaphysics of the School* (London, 1879–84, 3 vols.), holds, in English, the most important place, and contains extensive accounts of the meaning of terms and expressions. A number of these accounts are condensed into alphabetically arranged vocabularies at the close of the various volumes. But Father

Harper, in some respects, deliberately adapts his usage to the habits of modern English readers; and his avowed intent to harmonize some of the most difficult of the apparent conflicts of his authorities (namely, of Suarez and of the Dominican Thomists) renders certain of his statements inadequate to the actual differences of opinion that have found expression in scholastic teaching. Different in precisely this respect is Suarez himself, whose great work, *Disputationes Metaphysicae* (2 vols. fol., Geneva, 1614), was written for readers who still required no apology for the complexities and doubtful disputations of the doctrine of the school. Whoever, therefore, wishes to find a thesaurus of scholastic distinctions, in the shape which they assumed at the close of the whole movement, must look directly to Suarez, in whose work the citation of manifold scholastic opinions, and consequently of the terminology needed to express those opinions, is carried out with the most scholarly thoroughness, yet, as Eucken remarks (op. cit., 73), with a real desire, upon the part of Suarez, to avoid whatever seemed to him useless complications of the technical vocabulary. The treatise of Suarez is supplied with elaborate indices; and the *Index Rerum*, in particular, could be laid at the basis of a very extended vocabulary of scholastic expressions. Yet it must of course be borne in mind that this treatise of Suarez is a textbook of metaphysics, and not of theology proper, and is so far limited as to its embodiment of the usage of the school. St. Thomas's works have been elaborately indexed in the older editions; and when the Papal edition now in course of publication is completed, the final index of that edition may be expected to bring much new light as to the Thomistic vocabulary. St. Thomas is himself accustomed, especially in the great *Summa*, to assume not too much previous knowledge of the language of the school upon the part of the reader, but to explain his most important expressions as he proceeds, so that few great philosophers have done so much as he has there done to furnish a running commentary upon their own work; and in the Papal edition, marginal references often aid in the collation of the various points of this commentary, while the formal commentary of Cajetan upon the *Summa*, published in the same edition, adds still further aid. But at best the complexity, both of the subject and of the speech, makes St. Thomas, while always a lucid writer, still a thinker,

whose usage is hard to survey in its entirety. In consequence, lexicons of scholastic, and in particular of Thomistic usage, have been undertaken. Of these, two here especially concern us: first, that of J. Z. Mellinius, *Lexicon Peripateticum* (Naples, 1872); and secondly, that of Ludwig Schütz, *Thomas-Lexikon* (Paderborn, 1881). The latter (in German) is especially full and clear, and contains many illustrative citations. The expositions of Thomistic doctrine by Kleutgen and Werner, and the general histories of scholastic philosophy by Haureau and Stöckl (see the *General Bibliography of Philosophy*), are of standard importance, but may be merely mentioned here; while, of the shorter textbooks in English, the *Manuals of Catholic Philosophy* (Stonyhurst Series) and the *Elementary Course of Christian Philosophy*, by Louis of Poissy (translated and adapted by the brothers of the Christian Schools, New York, 1893), contain, the one more extended discussions of difficult conceptions, the other extremely concise and, in view of the small size of the book, numerous definitions of scholastic terms. The relations of scholastic to modern terminology have received increasing attention in recent literature, although no adequate account exists. Baumann, in his *Lehre von Raum, Zeit und Mathematik in der neuern Philosophie* (2 vols., Berlin, 1868–9), devotes the opening section of his first volume (1–67) to the exposition of such terms and concepts in the *Disputationes* of Suarez as bear upon the topics treated in the subsequent work. Baumann urges as his reason for this procedure, the importance of the work of Suarez as a generally used textbook during the period in which the early modern philosophers grew to maturity. In the early portion of his exposition (5–14), Baumann discusses such general scholastic terms as *essentia, a priori, materia*; while the later pages of the section in question pass to the concept of quantity, and to the more mathematical terminology of Suarez. Baumann's collection of historical materials, in the entire book mentioned, has been somewhat unjustly neglected. A number of the scholastic terms used by Descartes find their place in the notes to Veitch's translation of the *Discourse on Method and Meditations of Des Cartes* (9th ed., Edinburgh, 1887; see 274–92). The scholastic elements in the thought and speech of Spinoza have been emphasized in an important essay by Freudenthal, 'Spinoza und die Scholastik' (in the

Philosophische Aufsätze, E. Zeller gewidmet, Leipzig, 1887, 85 f.). See also, in the *Archiv für die Geschichte der Philosophie,* the article of Siebeck, 'Ueber die Entstehung der Termini Natura Naturans und Natura Naturata' (iii. 370–8). Other papers in the same *Archiv* bearing upon scholastic doctrine and usage are: Siebeck, 'Zur Psychologie der Scholastik' (*Archiv f. Gesch. d. Philos.,* i. 375–90, 518–33; ii. 22–8, 180–92, 414–25, 517–25, iii. 177–91); Rabus, 'Zur Synteresis der Scholastik' (ii. 29–30). On the single, but important, term last mentioned, one may consult Appel, *Die Lehre der Scholastiker von der Synteresis* (Rostock, 1891, *Gekrönte Preisschrift*). On the development of the psychological concepts of scholasticism one may also compare Werner, 'Der Entwickelungsgang der mittelalterlichen Psychologie von Alcuin bis Albertus Magnus' (*Wiener Akademie,* 1876,—also separately printed). Plusanski in his thesis, *La Philosophie de Duns Scot* (Paris, 1887), undertakes a study of an author recently too much neglected.

(4) The translation of Greek terms into Latin, together with the difficulties that the different character of the two languages made inevitable in such an undertaking, began already with Roman Epicureanism, Stoicism, and Eclecticism. The authors principally in question in this connection are Lucretius, Varro, Cicero, Seneca, and Quintilian. To this earlier period belong such words as *substantia* and *essentia* (as rival translations of οὐσία), *proportio* (as translation of ἀναλογία), *elementa* (for elements), *forma, materia, definitio, absolutus, notio, qualitas, individuus, positio, intelligibilis, sensibilis, quantitas, possibilis, universalis.* The Fathers of the Church added many new terms; and amongst these writers St. Augustine is of the greatest importance. His special psychological terminology was long of very great influence, and was not wholly displaced by the later predominance of the Aristotelian terminology (cf. Eucken, op. cit., 56). The logical terminology of later times was greatly under the influence of the *Isagoge* of Porphyry (in the translation of Boethius), and of the translations and commentaries made by Boethius as expounder of the Aristotelian logic. In this sense, the Aristotelian influence determines an important portion of the terminology of the whole scholastic period. To Porphyry's treatise, the *Isagoge* (an introduction to the Aristotelian treatise called the *Categories*), is due

the transmission to the middle ages of the terminological distinctions between *genus, species, difference, property,* and *accident,* in the form in which these *quinque voces,* or *five words,* became the centre of the early discussions between Nominalism and Realism, and later entered into the standard textbooks of Logic (see Ueberweg, *Gesch. d. Philos.,* 8th ed., Th. II, 161–8). Boethius both translated and commented upon a portion of the Aristotelian logical treatises; and both the preservation of an older logical terminology, and the addition of some new terms, are due to him. Of his new terms, Prantl names especially *contradictio, disparatum,* the fixing of the later terminology of the logical 'square of oppositions,' and the introduction of *affirmatio infinita* and of *negatio infinita* to name the forms of affirmation and negation in which a negation goes with the predicate (e. g. 'The man is, or is not, unjust'). The early period of scholasticism, up to the 12th century inclusive, was further influenced by the writings attributed to Dionysius the Areopagite, and by other Neo-Platonic documents, which had their effect upon terminology. A Latin translation of a portion of the *Timaeus* of Plato (made by Chalcidius in the 4th century) was the only portion of Plato's writings directly known in this period; and of Aristotle, apart from the portion of the logical treatises translated by Boethius, nothing was accessible, even in translations, until the 12th century itself. To the Latin translations of the Arabic commentators of Aristotle, who became known to European scholars during the 12th century, there are due a number of new terms and expressions :— e. g. *quidditas* (Prantl, ii. 325), *intentio* (in the technically scholastic meaning), *principium individuationis* (Eucken, 68), and the later so much used distinction between the *universalia* as *ante rem, in re,* and *post rem* (Prantl, ii. 350; Ueberweg, 8th ed., Th. II, 231). The acquaintance with the philosophy of Aristotle, first in very imperfect Latin translations made from the Arabic, but later in translations made directly from the original, rapidly reformed the scholastic terminology of the 13th century, which in St. Thomas assumed a form that later tended, as the Thomistic influence increased, to become the definitive and official standard of scholastic usage. But at the time, and for a good while after the generation of St. Thomas, rival influences (e. g. the skill and authority of Duns Scotus, the later revival of Nominalism, &c.) tended to complicate the situation;

and the later scholasticism is a period of great complication, both in usage and in method. The official revival of the study of St. Thomas has of late set the seal of the authority of the Church upon a return to the more classic terminology of St. Thomas.

(5) In offering a few examples of scholastic usage, we are naturally led to begin with the terms for the fundamental metaphysical concepts. These, even before the Aristotelian period proper, were already to a considerable extent of Aristotelian origin (see the summary in the before-mentioned monograph of Baumgartner on *Alanus de Insulis*, 39–69); and the Thomistic usage only presents in a more finished form what had already been, in large measure, prepared by the discussions up to the 12th century inclusive. For the Neo-Platonic and other late classical terminology already indirectly represented Aristotelian influences; and the translations and commentaries of Boethius were especially interesting to the earlier scholastics for their metaphysical suggestions. We therefore must not think of the Peripatetic elements in the terminology here in question as due to any one line of tradition. The terms *essentia* and *substantia*, together with the related terms, *ens*, *esse*, *realitas*, *existentia*, *actus*, and the rest of the distinctively ontological vocabulary, have their origin in part in Platonic as well as in Aristotelian usage, and form an undoubtedly difficult, not to say over-wealthy, collection of terms for expressing the various aspects and types of Being. *Being*, as Aristotle already pointed out, is a word of many meanings. The scholastic efforts to reduce these and their interrelationships to a system led to a number of relatively new distinctions, especially in the later period of scholasticism. *Ens*, in the classic scholastic usage, is employed, like Aristotle's τὸ ὄν, as the term for *Being* in general, — a term whose various usages are first distinguished, as nearly as possible, in Aristotle's way. *Ens* is first divided into (i) *entitas rei*, or being such as belongs to any *object*, and (ii) *entitas quae significat veritatem propositionis* (Aristotle's ὄν ὡς ἀληθές). In the first sense, *ens* is classified, after Aristotle, according to the ten categories, as the being of *substance*, of *quality*, &c.; and is in this sense also to be called *ontological* being proper. In the other sense, *ens* is *logical being*. *Ens* as ontological, and when also definitely regarded as external to the mind that knows it (*extra animam*), is *ens in rerum natura*, or *ens reale*. *Ens reale*, how-

ever, may still be classified as *ens in actu* and *ens in potentia*, according to a very well-known Aristotelian doctrine. If *ens* is conceived as belonging to a fictitious object, real, *not without*, but *only in* the mind, we have *ens rationis*, concerning whose precise relations to *logical being* the usage of various writers somewhat differs (compare Harper, op. cit., i. 47, with Schütz, *Thomas-Lexikon*, s. v. *ens*). *Ens rationis*, according to Suarez (*Disp.*, ii. 504), is most strictly to be defined as that 'which is conceived by the intellect as a being, while yet in itself it has no entity.' *Blindness*, *darkness*, the *chimera*, &c., are favourite examples of entities of this type. And *logical being*, as just defined, would of course also come under this general definition. But since logical being, taken as the *veritas propositionis*, whose form turns upon the use of the copula, has its own peculiar character, distinct from that of privations, negations, and chimeras, some writers (such as Schütz in his *Lexikon*) prefer to speak of *ens rationis* as a class of *ontological* being, and so as different from logical being proper. In this case the latter is defined as the truth of a statement, without regard to the externally real or internally fictitious character of any object. In any case *real* ontological being belongs to objects in so far as they are not *mere entia rationis*, but either exist or may exist outside of the mind. *Being*, taken ontologically, can be further distinguished as to its usage, in so far as *ens* (i) may be taken *participially*, as expressing the *existence* of the object whose *ens* is in question; or (ii) may be viewed as an abstract noun, which names the *nature* or *essence* of the object in question, whether or no it at any time actually exists. Thus, to say that a given object *comes into being*, is to use *being* or *ens* in the participial sense. What comes into being then and there *exists*. But to say of an object, without regard to whether it exists or no—perhaps even without regard to whether it is a fiction, an *ens rationis* or no—that its very *being* implies such and such characters (e. g. that the very being of a *man* requires him to be an *animal*), this is to use the term *ens* as a noun. To take *ens* thus as a noun is to speak of the *essentia*, *quidditas*, or *natura* of an object without regard to the existence of this object. Any object taken thus, without regard to its existence, does not, however, thereby become an *ens rationis*; for a being that is to be and is *not yet*, or that *was* and is no longer, has *quidditas* or essence, and has not existence, but still is no fiction, and no mere product of the human intellect. In fact, the men not yet born have no existence; but they have perfectly *real essence*.

(6) Like the participle or noun *ens*, the infinitive form *esse*, or in fact the verb *esse* in all its forms, has the same tendency to a variety of meanings. *Esse* has its logical use as the copula, and also its ontological use, as expressing the fact, or at least the appearance, of being. But even when taken in an ontological reference, *esse* may still be viewed as *esse in intellectu* (in the usage which St. Anselm's discussion of the ontological proof made famous), i. e. as what Thomas calls the *esse intentionale*; not as if this latter were always identical with the *esse* of the *mere* fiction, but in so far as *esse in* the mind, while it may well represent a real being independent of the mind, is still different from *esse in re*, or real external being as such. The distinction between *essence* and *existence* also often finds its expression in various phrases that include *esse*. The word *esse*, taken simply, is often used (when in contrast with any of the special terms for *essence*) as in itself sufficient to express *existence*. More formally expressed is the contrast between *esse essentiae* and *esse existentiae*, employed to name respectively the essence and the existence of things. This contrast is often used in later scholasticism. But these later expressions are pleonastic, as Suarez (*Disp.*, ii. 115) points out. The first of them, as he there says, adds nothing to the term *essentia* beyond the mere fashion of conception or of expression. And *esse*, when taken in contrast with *essentia*, already sufficiently distinguishes, in the opinion of Suarez and in the frequent usage of St. Thomas, the existence of things from their nature or essence. Very frequent in scholastic writers is the expression *esse in actu* for existence, and the explanatory phrase *extra causas suas* is also constantly used by such writers to express the sense in which a created thing exists. But of course the *esse in actu*, or the *actualitas*, which is thus attributed to any existent thing, implies laying stress upon a somewhat different aspect of reality from the one directly emphasized in the term *esse*, when the latter is taken as simply equivalent to *existence*. For *existence*, as such, is in contrast with *essence*; but *actus* is contrasted with *potentia*. In brief, then, to sum up the truly important features of this overwealthy collection of technical terms for existence, an object is said to be *real*, in scholastic usage, in so far

as it is viewed as *outside of the knowing mind*, and so as in contrast to a mere idea. It is said to possess *esse*, or *esse existentiae*, or to be an *existent* object, so far as it is taken in contrast to its own mere *essence* or *quiddity*, or, again, in so far as it is conceived as *outside of its causes*. It is said to be *in actu*, or to possess *actuality*, in so far as it is contrasted with the *potential* being to which the Aristotelian metaphysic opposes whatever is a realized being. These four contrasts—(1) of the *external* object, with the object viewed as *in* the mind; (2) of the existent object and its mere *essence*; (3) of the existent thing and *other* existent things (especially its causes, *outside* of which it exists); and (4) of the *actual* thing and the merely *potential* thing—are all of them founded in the Aristotelian doctrine, and play a great part not only in scholastic, but in all later metaphysical discussions. They are, however, seldom very sharply or permanently sundered in metaphysical discussions, but they are emphasized, upon occasion, in various ways; and the only objection to this part of the scholastic vocabulary is that it is not sufficiently settled as to its use of the means for distinguishing the four, and that it has for all of them, and especially for the first and second, a confusing wealth and variety of expressions. That just this way of classifying the ontological expressions is not to be found so formally emphasized by Aristotle as are other classifications is indeed true. But it is not, in spirit, at all opposed to his treatment of the subject.

(7) Passing from the terminology of *existence* to that more directly concerned with the *essence* or *nature* of things, we find, as in fact we have already found, that here, too, there is a perplexing variety of expressions. The word *οὐσία*, in Aristotle, is one of his most puzzling terms, even when one abstracts from all direct reference to the precise meaning of *existence*, and when one dwells alone upon the *nature* of that which is said, according to Aristotle's doctrine, to exist. The scholastic doctors did much to clarify, but little to simplify, the situation here in question. The starting-point of the older scholastic discussion of the term *substantia* was, of course, the Aristotelian treatise upon the categories. *Substantia* and *essentia* are frequently employed as synonymous terms. But when they are distinguished, *substantia* (in its more proper sense) is that which, whenever it exists at all, exists *in itself*, as opposed to that which (namely as an *accident*) exists *in another as*

its subject. *Substantia* is also often spoken of as that which *supports or sustains its accidents*—an ancient metaphor, for emphasizing which the scholastic doctrine later had to pay dear, when a modern empiricism became suspicious of whatever seemed to be *merely* beneath or behind the verifiable facts. But, as a fact, the scholastic doctrine of substance is in general far more directly empirical in its nature than are the technical concepts of substance prevalent, since the rise of modern science, in the more speculative doctrines of recent realism. For the school, in what it has to say about substance, lays stress upon two decidedly *empirical* aspects of the known world. The first is that the world comes to us differentiated into various beings (the substances), each one of which seems to be relatively independent of the others, so that it exists, or may exist, by or in itself. The second aspect is that, on the other hand, there are facts (namely qualities, relations, and the like) which exist, yet which cannot exist alone, but which exist as belonging to the substances, and needing the substances to *sustain* them. The latter facts (the accidents) are, in language, *predicated* of the substances. In existence, the accidents seem to be only *in* the substances. The consequence of this situation is that, when one tries to conceive how the accidents and the substances can be related to each other, the empirical dependence of the accidents, for their very being, upon the fact that they are the accidents of substances (e. g. the fact that colour is always the colour of something), and the permanence of the substances through many changes of state and relation, seem together to warrant the view that the substances have some central or centralizing nature about them, whereby they *support*, or *carry*, the accidents, while the latter merely belong to and *rest upon* the substances. This view of substance (whereby it seems a *substratum*) was indeed much emphasized for the scholastics by the speculative problems to which the dogma of transubstantiation gave rise. Apart from the difficulty due to such supernatural aspects of the matter, however, the scholastic *substantia* was far from assuming anywhere nearly the metempirical form of Kant's *Ding an Sich.* The concept is primarily intended not as a theory of an unknown *substratum* behind the scenes, but as an expression of the known fact that while *things* are found existing in relatively separable and independent ways, *accidents* are, in the natural order, incapable of existing separately. Substances were distinguished, after the fashion of the treatise on the categories, into *first substances* (*individual* things), and *second substances* (*genera* or *species*). But this distinction involves no new difficulties.

(8) Returning, however, once again to the terms for the *nature* of things, the term *essentia*, in so far as it is *not* merely equivalent to *substantia*, refers to the definable nature of *any* object, to whatever one of the Aristotelian categories it may belong. Even an *ens rationis* might be conceived as if possessing, in a sense, its essence; but usually and properly *essentia*, in metaphysical discussions, is used of beings conceived as either actual or possible. God also has his essence, although, in case of the divine, one must not view the essence as distinct from the existence, God being the one reality wherein essence and existence are indistinguished. But in created beings essence and existence are different. In such beings, the scholastic doctrine often defines the essence as *that which possesses the existence.* Taking an essence in itself, and apart from existence, we can still speak of an essence as *real* in the sense above pointed out; for the essence of an object that has been, or that is to be, but that does not now exist, is still something *outside the mind.* In particular, the essence of any object is *that which the definition of the object rightly sets forth*, or that which primarily *characterizes* this object, or that which we name when we answer the question as to *what* this object really is. The essence, as defined or definable, is *real*, first, negatively speaking, in so far as it is not self-contradictory, and is *not a mere fiction* of the mind; and secondly, positively speaking, it is *real* in so far as it *can be produced* by an act of divine creation, or in so far as, considered in itself, it possesses *aptitude for existence* (Suarez, *Disput.*, i. 42; Schütz, *Thomas-Lexikon*, s. v.). For *essentia* the words *quidditas* and *natura* are often used; as well as, upon occasion, the word *substantia* ('uno modo,' says St. Thomas, *Summa Theolog.*, i, Quaest. 29, art. 2, 'dicitur substantia quidditas rei, quam significat definitio, . . . quam quidem substantiam Graeci οὐσίαν vocant, quod nos essentiam dicere possumus'). The word *quidditas*, due, as we have seen, to the translations of the Arabian commentators, is used quite synonymously with *essentia.* *Natura*, a word of manifold meaning, like the Greek original from which it is derived, has as its

principal technical sense (Harper, op. cit., i. 46) 'the principle of operation, or of the tendency of each thing towards its constitutive end' (cf. *Thomas-Lexikon*, s. v.). And since natural things are (for the Peripatetic view) the products of operations directed towards ends, and since the end of these operations is the realization of some essence, *natura* and *essentia* can be thus identified, despite their difference of primary meaning. For the concept of essence, St. Thomas also uses the expressions *quod est* and *quod quid est*; and the essence can also be identified with the *form, except* in the case of substances which are compounded of form and matter. In these substances the matter also belongs to the essence.

(9) In beings supposed to be real, the scholastic doctrine distinguishes, after Aristotle, (*a*) the *formal* and the *material* aspects, and (*b*) the *potentia* and the *actus*. Notable, however, in the scholastic terminology, is the tendency to use these familiar Peripatetic terms as the basis for derivatives and usages which go beyond the original Aristotelian usage. *Materia* itself, as that *out* of which anything may come to be formed, is called, in its principal Aristotelian sense, the *materia ex qua*. In this sense *materia* is *in potentia* with reference to that which may be formed out of it, while form is the *actus*, the attainment, which realizes the matter. *Materia* is divided in various ways, e. g. into *materia communis* and *materia signata*. The former is that out of which any member of a given species may come to be, in such wise that this *materia* is common to all members of the *species*. The *materia signata* is the quantified or spatially determinate *materia* which is peculiar to a single corporeal individual; in St. Thomas's doctrine, the *materia signata* is the *principium individuationis*, or that whereby an individual is distinguished from others of its species, in case of all the *corporeal* individuals (but not in case of wholly incorporeal beings). *Materia* is further divided into *materia intelligibilis* and *materia sensibilis*, &c. But the same term *materia*, in a transferred sense, comes to be used for any *object towards which* a given activity or power is directed; and in consequence of the various ways in which the distinction between matter and form can be applied to various grades or types of beings, one has a complex series of meanings of the two terms which Harper summarizes (op. cit., ii. 750–1). Thus quantity is the matter of figure, free-will the matter of the moral act; bodies are the matter towards which sense-activities are directed; facts are the matter of history, &c. The well-known and manifold modern popular uses of the ancient Aristotelian contrast between Form and Matter have thus been developed out of a scholastic usage, which tended constantly more and more to diversify Aristotle's already extremely complex way of employing the terms. The term *forma*, used not merely in its direct antithesis to *materia*, but by itself, tends also to a great variety of applications. Thus *forma exemplaris* is the type-model of an object as thought or reason may possess it; *forma individualis* is a form that, when it is united with matter, constitutes an individual; the angels are called *formae subsistentes*—forms or essences existing *by themselves*, apart from matter, &c. Schütz, in the *Thomas-Lexikon*, enumerates twenty-seven of these various special uses of *forma* with an adjective or other modifying expression attached. In general, the scholastic use of the distinction between form and matter tended, despite the close connection of the two, to make the two terms not mere correlatives, but relatively separable terms, and to give to each of the two manifold new, and often greatly transferred, applications. Hereby what was originally a distinction of aspects tended to become more decidedly than in Aristotle a division of the world into the spheres of different real principles. On the other hand, the numerous applications of the same distinction often also tended, by reason of the unity of the terminology, to restore a sense of the connectedness of various facts; and the extreme dualism, which later became so prominent in the European thinking of the 17th century, is indeed foreign to the genuine spirit of scholasticism.

(10) The adjectives *formalis* and *materialis*, the adverbs *formaliter* and *materialiter*, are typical examples, in scholastic usage, of the consequences of such a process as the terms *form* and *matter* in general illustrate. A highly technical and often convenient, but dangerously flexible, employment of these modifying words results. In Harper's summary (loc. cit., 752–4), a number of the most frequent of these usages are brought together. Thus, the *formal object* of an activity or a power (e. g. of sight) is the object that is *adapted to* or is *fitted to become* such an object (e. g. colour is the formal object of sight). But the *material object* is the object viewed

in itself, and not taken as possessed of such aptitude. Thus the *material object* of an act of vision may be something that is *heavy*; while, as heavy object, it would be the formal object of the various sense-processes by which we directly test its weight. An act contrary to moral law is a *material* sin when ignorantly, and therefore innocently, committed; it is a *formal* sin if knowingly committed. In consequence 'an act materially bad may be formally good.' In a concept, one can distinguish between what is *formally* and what is *materially* part of the concept; and in this sense Harper points out that 'possible essence is formally negative and conceptual; materially it does not differ from existing essence.' But the further developments of this distinction may easily tend to become, as one may venture to say, 'formally' exact, but 'materially' very arbitrary and unenlightening. And this has been the result in the familiar modern popular usage of all such expressions.

(11) Amongst the names for the actually existent beings, the scholastic terminology possessed an interesting group of terms: *Subsistentia, subsistere, persona, hypostasis, individuum*, the adjective *individuus*, the abstract noun *individuatio, substantia separata*, the later (Scotistic) term *haecceitas*, and still others—all of which have in common that they were developed for the sake of defining some aspect of the nature of the individual beings of some grade, high or low. In so far as any *substance* exists alone and in itself, it *subsists*; and *subsistentia* is a term for expressing the sort of existence especially due to substances. A subsistent being of rational grade is a *persona*, or an *hypostasis* (St. Thomas, *Summa Theolog.*, P. I. Q. 29); any subsistent being is an *individual*. As such it is within itself *undivided*; it is *distinct* from any other individual; and it has a form of being *incommunicable* to any other. The last of these characteristics of the individual being led to an especially difficult series of discussions, in later scholasticism, as to the *principium individuationis*, i. e. as to the metaphysical means whereby there is secured to every being a nature that *no other* being can conceivably possess. It was to this incommunicable nature that Duns Scotus applied the term *haecceitas*, and this term was later generally used. The theological use of the terms *persona* and *hypostasis* is very well known; and in the discussion of the dogma of the Trinity, the relations of *persona, substantia*, and *essentia*, as applied to God

become of the most critical importance. A *substantia separata* is one that, by its nature, is a truly spiritual substance, having no commerce with matter. Man's soul is no such substance, but by nature has a tendency or *inclinatio* to an individual body.

(12) After these examples of the metaphysical terminology, a few instances must be mentioned of the vocabulary relating to thought, knowledge, and ideas, in their relations to objects. That the traditional vocabulary of formal logic is in the main of scholastic authorship is well known, although we have also seen how far back lies the historical origin of this vocabulary. The scholastic epistemology is that of Aristotle, rendered simpler and sharper in outline, and intermingled, upon occasion, with Neo-Platonic elements. The discussion as to the nature of Universals is one of the oftenest mentioned features of the scholastic movement; and comparatively familiar is the terminology in which was expressed the classic solution of the difficulty during the great period of scholastic philosophy. As before pointed out, this terminology has its origin with the Arabian philosophers. Universals, according to this distinction, have their being, *ante rem*, in the mind or intent of the divine source of the universe, *in re*, in so far as the general nature is in the existent individual, and *post rem*, in so far as the intellect, by an abstraction from the individuality of a thing known, rediscovers the divine type through a contemplation of its expression in individual form. This solution, as Prantl points out, became almost common property in the 13th century, and is not to be attributed either to Albertus Magnus, or to his disciple, St. Thomas. The *five words* (*quinque voces*), *genus, species*, &c., above referred to, and the rest of the regular vocabulary of the logic textbooks, need not here be in particular discussed.

(13) The contrast between what belongs to the *mind*—to the process of knowledge, to ideas, to the reason—and what belongs to the *external* facts, or to the *world*, divine or created, *beyond* the human mind, receives rich expression in scholastic doctrine. Here a full account would involve the exposition both of the scholastic psychology, and of the whole theory of knowledge in question. Only a few terms can be mentioned. The modern terminological opposition between the *objective* and *subjective* had, in this particular form, its origin in the 18th century, and came into

general use only since Kant. The terms are old; their precise present application is very recent. The school expressed the contrast in question otherwise, and employed the terms *subject* and *object* with a different and older connotation, which, however, we still also in part retain. *Subiectum*, in St. Thomas, is either used for the *subject* of a proposition, or as equivalent to *substantia*, or in the sense of the *topic* of a discussion, or of a science. This usage is, of course, modelled after the Aristotelian, and is not wholly strange to us to-day. *Obiectum*, especially with reference to the already mentioned contrast between *formal* and *material object*, is *that with which any process or activity is concerned*, or in which it *terminates*. Such an object may be, of course, that with which our *knowledge* is concerned, since knowing is also a process or an activity. And so far, of course, the *object* of knowledge may be either a mental fact, or, on the other hand, the known external fact itself (just as in the modern usage). So here, too, the Thomistic-Aristotelian usage has much in common with ours. But in later scholastic usage (namely from Duns Scotus onwards) we meet with an opposition between the terms *subjective* and *objective* (and the various cognate expressions), which has its foundation in the former usage, but which has a new technical importance. This usage is explained by Prantl (iii. 308, *note*) thus :—' *Subiectivum* means that which relates to the *subjects* of judgments, that is, to the concrete facts about which one thinks (*Gegenstände des Denkens*); while, on the contrary, *obiectum* means what is involved merely in *obiicere*, that is, in the act of *bringing before the mind*; and *obiectivum* falls to the account of the mind before which the fact is brought.' This usage is, in the main, directly opposite to our own at the present day. In one of the *Opuscula* attributed to Thomas, but of questionable authenticity, the same usage occurs (Prantl, iii. 293). Suarez (*Disp.* i. 31), in discussing the nature of our conception of being, states very clearly the definition of a *conceptus obiectivus*, which he here opposes to *conceptus formalis*, the distinction being, as he points out, a well-known one (*vulgaris distinctio*). The *conceptus formalis* is the mental act or process itself whereby we get before us the idea, say, of a man. It is called *formalis*, Suarez continues, perhaps because it is an *ultima forma mentis*, i.e. a type of mental product, a *Vorstellung*, a state of mind, a fact belonging to the formal life of the intellect.

In this sense the *conceptus formalis* is the idea taken as an actual psychical occurrence, or product, or possession—as a way of conceiving of the object—or as the offspring of the mind, *veluti proles mentis*—or as the more permanent *acquisition* of the mind that has it. But the *conceptus obiectivus* is that which *we ourselves mean to conceive*, or *intend to get before our minds*, when we think of a man. It is the *obiectum et materia circa quam versatur formalis conceptio*; it is that which forms the *topic* of this whole business of conceiving man as man. Since Averroes, Suarez continues, many have called this *conceptus obiectivus* the *intentio intellecta*—the *meaning* or *intent* of the mind. (As a fact the term *intentio* is the one generally used by St. Thomas in this connection.) Suarez goes on to say that the *conceptus formalis* is always a *vera* and *positiva res*—an actual mental occurrence or possession; but the *conceptus obiectivus* may have as its content a mere *ens rationis* (e.g. blindness, darkness, or a chimera). If one attempts to think of *nothing*, the *conceptus formalis* is still an actual and positive state of mind, but the *conceptus obiectivus* is wholly negative, and contains no entity. In the same way, when one conceives of any *universal*, the *conceptus formalis* is itself an individual fact, and the universal, as such, belongs merely to the *intentio*. The usage of *obiectivus* here in question does not perfectly correspond to the *ordinary* sense either of *objective* or of *subjective* of post-Kantian usage; for the *conceptus formalis* here defined might be viewed, in the post-Kantian sense, as either *subjective* (in so far as it is a *mental* fact) or *objective*, in so far as it stands for the *actual psychical occurrence* or possession which retains its own type of actuality, despite the possible vacuity or absence of its intended meaning, or, as we should now often say, despite the failure of the *subjective intent* of the one whose idea this is. While then it is misleading to say that the terms *subjective* and *objective* have *merely* changed places in the transition to the modern usage, it is true that the foregoing account, as given by Prantl, sufficiently indicates why, especially in later scholastic usage, and in the 17th century, the adjective *obiectivus* came to be so frequently used precisely as we now should employ the opposed word *subjective*, namely to characterize anything in so far as it is *within* or *before* the mind, or especially in so far as it is the object, topic, creation, or figment, of a mental *intention.* The use of *subjective* to characterize the *external* fact, especially the *substantial* fact, has likewise its perfectly obvious basis in the original Aristotelian meaning of the corresponding word. And the link between the scholastic and our usage of this term is obviously determined by the fact that the mind, or the self, is itself conceived as a *substance,* and so (in the older sense) as a *subject,* while, on the other hand, its states, *subjective* (in the post-Kantian sense) because they thus belong to a *subject,* can also be taken as having the value which the scholastics, as we have now seen, often called *intentional,* or also *objective.* Very common, in later scholasticism, is the employment of *formalis* in the sense of our modern *objective,* and as the opponent of the scholastic *obiectivus.* Here the obvious sense is that since, as St. Thomas says, and as the whole Peripatetic doctrine teaches, *forma per se ipsam facit rem esse in actu* (or, as it is often expressed, *a form is an act*), *formal existence,* or *formal being,* can be identified with *real* or with *existent* being, for the purposes of most discussions, and despite the above-mentioned distinctions between *actuality, existence,* and *reality* (see § 6). That these later scholastic usages are the constant ones in Descartes and Spinoza is a generally known fact (see also on the whole series of distinctions, Veitch on Descartes, in his op. cit., 283–6). Meanwhile, as we have just seen, there is indeed a sense in which *formal,* even when opposed to *obiectivus,* may still admit of the translation by the *modern use* of *subjective.* So Harper (op. cit., i. 579) translates the *conceptus formalis* of Suarez by *subjective concept,* and interprets the latter expression, in the now usual sense of *subjective,* as 'the idea which is formed in the subject (the man who is thinking).' In brief, from the very nature of the distinction here in question, no absolutely sharp line can be drawn between the scholastic and the modern usage, marked as is, in some cases, the contrast.

(14) The term *intentio,* now several times exemplified, means, in its primary sense, *intent, purpose,* or *intention,* as we ordinarily use the word. In a somewhat transferred sense, it is employed for *attention* (see examples in Schütz, *Thomas-Lexikon,* s. v.). In a still more technical sense it is a representative mental *image, idea,* or *meaning,* particularly the last (as in the passage just cited from Suarez). St. Thomas sometimes uses *intentio* in its intellectual significance, as

quite synonymous with *ratio* in the sense of *concept.* With the *intentio* of the intellect as the *deliberate* or definitive meaning, resulting from the operation of the intellect, is contrasted the *species intelligibilis,* the natural and primary abstraction that the intellect first makes when it knows any general nature of things (see the quotation made by Schütz to illustrate this difference); but both the *intentio* of the intellect and the *species intelligibilis* are names for intellectual states having a *representative meaning*— representations in the mind of intelligible objects external to the mind. And just as there is the *species intelligibilis,* and the *intentio* upon the intellectual level, so, since sense also, in its own way and degree, represents the *forms* of objects, the scholastic theory speaks of the *species sensibilis,* and, especially in later scholasticism, of the *species sensibilis intentionalis,* or *representative sensuous idea of the object.* *Species,* in general, is used, in the *epistemological* discussions of scholasticism, for the form of an object in so far as this form is cognitively represented, whether by sense or by intellect; and thus *species* and *intentio* come to possess intimately related meanings, while *intentionalis* is especially the adjective to express *mentally representative,* or sometimes representative taken more in general. The distinction between *first* and *second* intentions is a familiar one. The *first intention (intentio prima)* is the concept as primarily formed by the mind. Its object is the reality external to the mind. The *intentio secunda* or *second intention* is the *logically reflex* concept, i. e. the concept which has the logical law or form of thought, or of any thought, for its object. Its object is therefore *in* the mind, and has no reality beyond. This distinction is due to Avicenna, and, from the time of Albertus Magnus on, played a great part in all the logical discussions of later scholasticism (see Prantl, ii. 321, iii. 91, and further passages in the index to that and later volumes).

(15) These illustrations of the metaphysical and psychological vocabulary of scholasticism tend to throw the sort of light upon the origin, and the general character of this terminology, which it is the purpose of a general article upon terminology to give. The central character of the whole scholastic vocabulary remains its elaborate use of *distinctions.* The method of distinctions had already been carried far by Aristotle. He

used it (see GREEK TERMINOLOGY) to solve apparent contradictions, and so to prepare the way for synthetic views of his world. Scholasticism made the method of distinctions more and more an ideal. Hereby the complex problems of theology, and the always serious tasks of defining, avoiding, and disarming heresies, were brought within the range of what seemed to those concerned a highly exact method. The result, whatever its speculative value, was of the utmost importance for the history of philosophical language. For literature see section (3) above.

GLOSSARY.

[The figures refer to the sections of this article. See also the fuller LATIN INDEX referred to at the beginning of this topic.]

Absolutus, 4 : ABSOLUTE (q. v.).
Accidens, 4 : ESSENCE, and SUBSTANCE.
Actualitas, 6.
Actus, 5, 9 : ACTIVITY (q. v.).
Affirmatio (infinita), 4.

Conceptus (and in phrases), 13.
Contradictio, 4 : CONTRADICTION (q. v.).

Definitio, 4 : DEFINITION (q. v.).
Differentia, 4 : see DEFINITION.
Disparatum, 4 : DISPARATE (q. v.).

Elementa, 4.
Ens (and in phrases), 5 : cf. ENTITY, and BEING.
Entitas (and in phrases), 5.
Esse (and in phrases), 5, 6 : BEING (q. v.); cf. EXISTENCE.
Essentia, 5 (οὐσία), 4, 7, 8.
Existentia, 5 : EXISTENCE (q. v.).

Forma (and in phrases), 4, 9, 10 : form; cf. MATTER AND FORM.
Formalis, 10.
Formaliter, 10.

Genus, 4 : GENUS (q. v.).

Haecceitas, 11.
Hypostasis, 11.

Inclinatio, 11.
Individuatio, 11 : Individuation ; see INDIVIDUAL.
Individuum (and -us), 4, 11 : INDIVIDUAL (q. v.).
Intelligibilis, 4 : Intelligible.
Intentio (and in phrases), 4, 13, 14 : INTENTION (in philosophy, q. v.) ; cf. INTENT, and MEANING.

Materia (and in phrases), 4, 9, 10 : MATTER (q. v.) ; cf. MATTER AND FORM.
Materialis, 10 : cf. MATTER.
Materialiter, 10 : cf. MATTER.

Natura, 8 : NATURE (q. v.).
Negatio (infinita), 4 : cf. NEGATIVE.
Notio, 4 : NOTION (q. v.), CONCEPT (q. v.).

Obiectum (and -tivum), 13 : OBJECT (q. v.).

Persona, 11 : PERSON (q. v.).
Positio, 4 : POSITION (q. v.).
Possibilis, 4 : POSSIBLE (q. v.).
Potentia, 9 : cf. POTENTIAL.
Principium Individuationis, 4, 9, 11 : see INDIVIDUATIO.

Property, 4.
Proportio (ἀναλογία), 4 : ANALOGY (q. v.).

Qualitas, 4 : QUALITY (q. v.).
Quantitas, 4 : QUANTITY (q. v.).
Quidditas, 4, 5 : QUIDDITY (q. v.).
Quinque voces, 4.
Quod est and quod quid est, 8.

Ratio, 14 : cf. RATIO, and CONCEPT.
Realitas, 5 : REALITY (q. v.).

Sensibilis, 4 : SENSUOUS (q. v.).
Species (and in phrases), 4, 14 : cf. DEFINITION.
Subiectum (and -tivum), 3 : SUBJECT (q. v.).
Subsistentia, 11.
Subsistere, 11.
Substantia, 5 (οὐσία), 4, 7, 8, 11 : SUBSTANCE (q. v.).

Universalia (ante rem, in re, post rem), 4, 12 : cf. UNIVERSAL.
Universalis, 4 : UNIVERSAL (q. v.).

Veritas propositionis, 5.   (J.R.)

Latitudinarianism [Lat. *latitudo*, breadth]: Ger. *Latitudinarianismus*; Fr. *latitudinarisme*; Ital. *tollerantismo* (suggested—E.M.) The doctrine of a body of English churchmen of the 17th century who sought a *modus vivendi* between Dissenters and the Church of England by emphasizing only common grounds of belief, and, while adhering to the Episcopal form of government and ritual, yet denying its divine origin and authority. In general, a latitudinarian is one who exercises a breadth of view and of toleration which verges on indifference.

Literature (on ecclesiastical latitudinarianism): TULLOCH, Rational Theol. and Christ. Philos. in the 17th Cent. (1872); CHURTON, Latitudinarianism from 1671 to 1787 (1861).   (A.T.O.)

Laughing Philosopher (the): see DEMOCRITUS, and PRE-SOCRATIC PHILOSOPHY.

Law [ME. *lawe*, Lat. *lex*]: Ger. *Gesetz*; Fr. *loi*; Ital. *legge*. Any formulation of sequences which from demonstration, experimental proof, successful application, or for any other reason, is accepted as having the highest degree of probability.

Since conviction based on the highest degree of probability expresses practical certainty, this definition of law escapes the discussion of the absolute validity of laws of nature and of other empirical determinations. The laws which are based on observation rest upon the principle of UNIFORMITY OF NATURE (q. v.); and that principle expresses the highest degree of probability—an assumption indeed upon which the law of probability itself rests. On the other hand, whatever the law of causation—or other law having grounds of universality apart from those of empirical observation—may rest upon besides, as guarantee of its holding good, it is yet true that it also has the highest degree of probability. The law of universal causation, therefore, which rests upon what is called necessity, no less than the principles of mechanical and physical science, which rest upon experimental proof and assume uniformity of nature, comes under the formula of the definition.

This aspect of law, which may be described as law in its theoretical or logical aspect, is contrasted with the modal and legal aspects of the same term—what may be called law of action or practice, or law in its practical aspect. In the latter the determination of conduct with reference to a prescription, requirement, or ideal, makes appeal essentially to persons as such, for recognition and obedience; in the sphere of the theoretical, however, this appeal is not present except in the general sense which is true of all knowledge, i. e. that being true, such laws must be allowed for and observed. In the one case, the penalty is what has been called natural, and is of the nature of an effect; in the other, it is modal or legal, and is called SANCTION (q. v.). Cf. the other topics LAW (jural and moral).

The ordinary warning against making law something apart from the sequences which it formulates may be repeated here. Natural events cannot be said strictly to obey law; rather they establish and illustrate law by their behaviour. The law is an abstract statement of certain observed ways of behaviour, and the law cannot have any meaning except as formulating aspects of phenomenal existence.

As to applying the term law to formulations of less than the highest degree of probability, scientific usage does not sanction it. Law is commonly compared with HYPOTHESIS and THEORY (see those terms) just in this, that these latter terms carry less than the highest probability, and are still in waiting for the demonstration, crucial testing, or final observation which, by conferring what amounts to certainty, raises them to the dignity of law.

On the logical aspects of the topic, see LAWS OF THOUGHT, and PRINCIPLE. (J.M.B.)

Law (economic): see ECONOMIC LAW.

Law (jural): Ger. *Gesetz*; Fr. *loi, droit*; Ital. *legge, diritto*. A rule of action, declared or created by competent authority. Cf. definition of *vera lex*, by Cicero, *De Republica*, iii. 22; *De Legibus*, ii. 4; *Inst. of Just.*, i. 2, 11. See the other topics LAW.

Law may be regarded, in its essence, analytically, as a command from a superior to an inferior; or historically, as a rule judicially declared to be entitled to general observance, and therefore obligatory. 'Law, for the practical purposes of lawyers and citizens, means the sum of those rules of conduct which courts of justice enforce, the conditions on which they become applicable, and the manner and consequences of their application' (Pollock, *First Book of Jurisprudence*, 217). Any particular law, properly so called, is 'a general rule of human action, taking cognizance only of external acts enforced by a determinate authority, which authority is human, and among human authorities is that which is paramount in a political society' (Holland, *Jurisprudence*, 36, 5th ed.). A proper law necessarily carries with it a sanction, that is, it involves the conception of the consequent employment of power, in case of necessity, to enforce obedience or punish disobedience, or annul the effect of disobedience. See ADJECTIVE LAW, POSITIVE LAW, STATUTE, and SANCTION.

Municipal law is a rule of external human action declared or created by or under power granted by a political, sovereign authority, for those subject to such authority; or an aggregate body of such rules. The former may be termed 'a law,' the latter 'the law' (Austin, *Jurisprudence*, i. 91).

Public law is law ordained for public purposes, to regulate conduct or rights in which the state as a whole is interested. *Private law* is law ordained for private purposes, to regulate conduct or rights interesting only, or primarily, the relations of private individuals between themselves (*Digest*, I. i. 1, 2). See PUBLIC LAW, and PRIVATE LAW.

Public law ordinarily is, and always should be, a general law affecting equally all those subject to the jurisdiction of the state, who may come within its provisions. A bill of attainder is a penal law aimed at a particular individual, and is generally prohibited by American constitutions. Private law may lay down a special rule for a particular individual, and often does. Such a rule may even, so far forth, change the course, as to that particular case, of the general public law, affecting all others in a similar situation: e. g. by granting a divorce to a particular individual for a cause not recognized by the general laws, and thus changing his personal status in the community (Maynard *v.* Hill, 125 United States Reports, 209).

The English language fails to discriminate in precise terms between law in the abstract, and a particular law, ordained by the political sovereign, which are represented in most other languages by distinct terms: e. g. *ius* and *lex.* 'Right' and 'law' present these notions inadequately, because although formerly the former was used by the Anglo-Saxons like the German *Recht*, as in folc-riht, with us it now includes the whole domain of morals.

Literature: MAINE, Ancient Law (law is developed from the unwritten to the written; from the formal to the equitable; from the personal to the territorial); BRUNNER, Deutsche Rechtsgesch., i. 3, §§ 33, 38; SMITH, Right and Law, chap. ii. 2; BENTHAM, Mor. and Legisl., chaps. xvii, xxiii; RATTO, Sociologia e Filosofia del Diritto (Rome, 1894; *subjective* and *objective* law well contrasted in chap. vi); FILOMUSI GUELFI, Del Concetto del Diritto Naturale e del Diritto Positivo (Naples, 1874). Cf. ADJECTIVE LAW, ADMINISTRATIVE LAW, CANON LAW, CASE LAW, CIVIL LAW, COMMON LAW, CONFLICT OF LAWS, CONSTITUTIONAL LAW, LEGAL, PRIVATE LAW, ROMAN LAW. (S.E.B.)

Law (moral): Ger. *Sittengesetz*; Fr. *loi morale*; Ital. *legge morale.* A rule of conduct resulting from the application of the moral ideal to life, or laid down by the moral authority, however this may be conceived.

The influence upon ethics, both of theology and of positive law, has led to the statement of morality as in essence a system of moral rules. See DUTY. (W.R.S.)

Law of Parcimony: see PARCIMONY.

Laws of Thought: Ger. *Denkgesetze*; Fr. *lois de la pensée*; Ital. *leggi del pensiero.* The three formulas of identity, contradiction, and excluded middle have been widely so known, though the doctrine that they are three co-ordinate and sufficient laws of all thought or of all reasoning has been held by a comparatively small party which hardly survives; and it is not too much to say that the doctrine is untenable. But the designation is so familiar and convenient that those formulas may very well be referred to as 'the so-called three laws of thought.' The formulas have usually been stated by those who upheld the doctrine as follows:—

I. *The Principle of Identity*: *A* is *A.*

II. *The Principle of Contradiction*: *A* is not not-*A.*

III. *The Principle of Excluded Middle* or *Excluded Third*: everything is either *A* or not-*A.*

It is noticeable that two of these propositions are categorical and the third disjunctive, a circumstance demanding explanation for those who hold the distinction of categorical, conditional, and disjunctive propositions to be fundamental.

The meaning of the formula of identity presents only one small difficulty. If the copula 'is' be taken in the sense of 'is, if it exists,' then the meaning of the formula is that no universal affirmative proposition having the same term as subject and predicate is false. If, however, the copula be understood to imply existence, the meaning is that no universal affirmative proposition is false in which the same term is subject and predicate, provided that term denotes any existing object. Or, the meaning may be that the same thing is true when the subject and predicate are the same proper name of an individual. In any case, it may properly be required that the precise meaning attached to the copula should be explained; and this explanation must in substance involve one or other of the above three statements; so that in any case the principle of identity is merely a part of the definition of the copula.

In like manner, if the word 'not' is to be used in logical forms, its force should be explained with the utmost precision. Such an explanation will consist in showing that the relation it expresses belongs at once to certain classes of relations, probably not more than two, in view of the simplicity of the idea. Each of these two statements may be embodied in a formula similar, in a general way, to the formulas of contradiction and excluded middle. It has, therefore, seemed to Mill and to the 'exact' logicians that these two formulas ought together to constitute a definition of the force of 'not.'

Other writers have regarded all three laws as 'practical maxims.' But practically nobody needs a maxim to remind him that a contradiction, for example, is an absurdity. It might be a useful injunction to tell him to beware of latent contradictions; but as soon as he clearly sees that a proposition is self-contradictory, he will have abandoned it before any maxim can be adduced. Seeing, then, that such formulas are required to define the relation expressed by not, but are not required as maxims, it is in the former aspect that their true meanings are to be sought.

If it is admitted that they constitute a definition, they must conform to the rules of definition. Considered as part of a definition, one of the commonest statements of the principle of contradiction, '*A* non est non-*A*,' offends against the rule that the *definitum* must not be introduced into the definition. This is easily avoided by using the form '*A* est non non-*A*,' '*A* is not not-*A*,' or every term may be subsumed under the double negation of itself. If this form is adopted for the principle of contradiction, the principle of excluded middle ought to be 'What is not not-*A* is *A*.' If, however, we prefer to state the principle of excluded middle as 'Everything is either *A* or not-*A*,' then we should state the principle of contradiction as 'What is, at once, *A* and not-*A* is nothing.' There is no vicious circle here, since the term 'nothing,' or 'non ens,' may be formally defined without employing the particle 'not' or any equivalent. Thus, we may express the principle of contradiction as follows:

Whatever there may be which is both *A* and not-*A* is *X*, no matter what term *X* may be.

In either formula, *A* may be understood to be restricted to being an individual, or it may be allowed to be any term, individual or general. In the former case, in order to avoid conflict with the fundamental law that no true definition asserts existence, a special clause should be added, such as 'if not-*A* there be.' In the latter case, it should be stated that by 'not-*A*' is not meant 'not some *A*,' but 'not any *A*,' or 'other than whatever *A* there may be.'

Bearing these points in mind, the formula '*A* is not-not-*A*,' or '*A* is other than whatever is other than whatever is *A*,' is seen to be a way of saying that the relation expressed by 'not' is one of those which is its own converse, and is analogous to the following:

Every rose is similar to whatever is similar to whatever is a rose;

which again is similar to the following:

Every man is loved by whatever loves whatever is a man.

But if we turn to the corresponding formula of excluded middle, 'Not-not-*A* is *A*,' or 'Whatever is not anything that is not any *A* is *A*,' we find that its meaning cannot be so simply expressed. Supposing that the relation *r* is such that it is true that

Whatever is *r* to whatever is *r* to whatever is *A* is *A*,

it can readily be proved that, whether the multitude of individuals in the universe be finite or infinite, each individual is either non-*r*

to itself and to nothing else, or is one of a pair of individuals that are *non-r* to each other and to nothing else; and conversely, if the universe is so constituted, the above formula necessarily holds. But it is evident that if the universe is so constituted, the relation *r* is converse to itself; so that the formula corresponding to that of contradiction also holds. But this constitution of the universe does not determine *r* to be the relation expressed by 'not.' Hence, the pair of formulas,

A is not not-*A*,

Not not-*A* is *A*,

are inadequate to defining 'not,' and the former of them is mere surplusage. In fact, in a universe of monogamously married people, taking any class, the *A*'s,

Every *A* is a non-spouse to whatever is non-spouse to every *A*,

and

Whatever is non-spouse to whatever is a non-spouse to every *A* is an *A*.

No such objection exists to the other pair of formulas:

Whatever is both *A* and not-*A* is nothing,

Everything is either *A* or not-*A*.

Their meaning is perfectly clear. Dividing all ordered pairs of individuals into those of the form *A* : *B* and those of the form *A* : *A*,

The principle of contradiction excludes from the relation 'not' all of the form *A* : *A*,

The principle of excluded middle makes the relation of 'not' to include all pairs of the form *A* : *B*.

From this point of view, we see at once that there are three other similar pairs of formulas defining the relations of identity, coexistence, and incompossibility, as follows:

Whatever is *A* is identical with *A*; i. e. Identity includes all pairs *A* : *A*.

Whatever is identical with *A* is *A*; i. e. Identity excludes all pairs *A* : *B*.

Whatever is *A* is coexistent with *A*; i. e. Coexistence includes all pairs *A* : *A*.

Everything is either *A* or coexistent with *A*; i. e. Coexistence includes all pairs *A* : *B*.

Whatever is both *A* and incompossible with *A* is nothing; i. e. Incompossibility excludes all pairs *A* : *A*.

Whatever there may be incompossible with *A* is *A*; i. e. Incompossibility excludes all pairs *A* : *B*.

Much has been written concerning the

relations of the three principles to forms of syllogism. They have even been called Die Principien des Schliessens, and have often been so regarded. Some points in reference to the meanings they have borne in such discussions require mention. Many writers have failed to distinguish sufficiently between reasoning and the logical forms of inference. The distinction may be brought out by comparing the moods Camestres and Cesare (see Mood, in logic). Formally, these are essentially different. The form of Camestres is as follows:

Every P is an M,

Every S is other than every M;

∴ Every S is other than every P.

This form does not depend upon either clause of the definition of 'not' or 'other than.' For if any other relative term, such as 'lover of,' be substituted for 'other than,' the inference will be equally valid. The form of Cesare is as follows:

Every P is other than every M,

Every S is an M;

∴ Every S is other than every P.

This depends upon the equiparance of 'other than.' For if we substitute an ordinary relative, such as *loves*, for 'other than' in the premise, the conclusion will be

Every S is loved by every P.

(See De Morgan's fourth memoir on the syllogism, *Cambridge Philos. Trans.*, x. (1860) 354.) The two forms are thus widely distinct in logic; and yet when a man actually performs an inference, it would be impossible to determine that he 'reasons in' one of these moods rather than in the other. Either statement is incorrect. He does not, in strict accuracy, reason in any form of syllogism. For his reasoning moves in first intentions, while the forms of logic are constructions of second intentions. They are diagrammatic representations of the intellectual relation between the facts from which he reasons and the fact which he infers, this diagram necessarily making use of a particular system of symbols—a perfectly regular and very limited kind of language. It may be a part of a logician's duty to show how ordinary ways of speaking and of thinking are to be translated into that symbolism of formal logic; but it is no part of syllogistic itself. Logical principles of inference are merely rules for the illative transformation of the symbols of the particular system employed. If the system is essentially changed, they will be quite different. As the Boolians represent Cesare and Camestres, they appear, after literally translating the algebraic signs of those logicians into words, as follows:

A that is B is nothing,

C that is not B is nothing;

∴ A that is C is nothing.

The two moods are here absolutely indistinguishable.

From the time of Scotus down to Kant more and more was made of a principle agreeing in enunciation, often exactly, in other places approximately, with our principle of contradiction, and in the later of those ages usually called by that name, although earlier more often *principium primum, primum cognitum, principium identitatis, dignitas dignitatum*, &c. It would best be called the *Principle of Consistency*. Attention was called to it in the fourth book of Aristotle's *Metaphysics*. The meaning of this, which was altogether different, at least in post-scholastic times, from our principle of contradiction, is stated in the so-called *Monadologie* of Leibnitz (§ 31) to be that principle by virtue of which we judge that to be false which involves a contradiction, and the denial of the contradiction to be true. The latter clause involves an appeal to the principle of excluded middle as much as the former clause does to the formal principle of contradiction. And so the 'principle of contradiction' was formerly frequently stated. But, in fact, neither is appealed to; for Leibnitz does not say that the contradiction is to be made explicit, but only that it is to be recognized as an inconsistency. Interpreted too strictly, the passage would seem to mean that all demonstrative reasoning is by the *reductio ad absurdum*; but this cannot be intended. All that is meant is that we draw that conclusion the denial of which would involve an absurdity—in short, that which consistency requires. This is a description, however imperfect, of the procedure of demonstrative Reasoning (q. v.), and deos not relate to logical forms. It deals with first, not second, intentions. (C.S.P.)

It is unfortunate that 'contradictory' and 'principle of contradiction' are terms used with incongruent significations. If a and β are statements, they are mutually contradictory, provided that one or the other of them must be true and that both cannot be true; these are the two marks (essential and sufficient) of contradiction, or precise denial, as it might better be called. If a and b are terms, b is the precise negative of a (or the contradictory term to a), provided it takes in *all* of that which is *other than a*—that is, if everything must be one or the other (*a* or *b*) and if nothing can be both. These two properties constitute the definition of a pair of contradictories (whether terms or propositions), namely, they are mutually exclusive, and they are together exhaustive; expressed in the language of 'exact logic,' these properties are (writing $\bar{x}$ for the negative of x and $+$ for *or*) :

(1) $x\bar{x} < 0$, what is at once x and $\bar{x}$ does not exist, or, in the language of propositions, the conjoint occurrence of x and $\bar{x}$ does not take place.

(2) $\infty < x + \bar{x}$, everything is either x or $\bar{x}$, or, in the language of propositions, what can occur is either x or $\bar{x}$, or, reality entails x or $\bar{x}$—there is no *tertium quid*.

Together these properties constitute the requirements of contradiction or of exact negation; it is a very inelegant piece of nomenclature (besides that it leads to actual confusion) to refer to (1) alone as the 'principle of contradiction.' Better names for them are (1) exclusion and (2) exhaustion (in place of excluded middle). In the common phraseology we are obliged to commit the absurdity of saying that two terms or propositions may satisfy the 'principle of contradiction' and still not be contradictory (since they may lack the quality of being exhaustive). The mere fact that (1) has been called the principle of contradiction has given it a pretended superiority over the other which it by no means deserves; they are of equal importance in the conducting of reasoning processes. In fact, for every formal argument which rests upon (1) there is a corresponding argument which rests upon (2): thus in the case of the fundamental law of TRANSPOSITION (q. v.), which affirms the identity of these two propositions, (*m*) the student who is not a citizen is not a voter; (*n*) every student is either a citizen or not a voter; that (*m*) follows from (*n*) depends upon one of these principles, and that (*n*) follows from (*m*) depends upon the other. These two names, exhaustion and exclusion, have the great advantage that they permit the formation of adjectives; thus we may say that the test for the contradictoriness of two terms or propositions which are not on their face the negatives one of another is that they should be (1) mutually exclusive and (2) together exhaustive.

It may be noticed that if two terms are exhaustive but not exclusive, their negatives are exclusive but not exhaustive. Thus within the field of number, 'prime' and 'even' are exclusive (no number can be both) but not exhaustive (except in the limiting case of two, some numbers can be neither), while 'not even' and 'not prime' are exhaustive and not exclusive.

In the case of propositions, 'contrary' and 'subcontrary' are badly chosen names for the OPPOSITION (q. v.) of *A* and *E*, *O* and *I*, respectively, of the traditional logical scheme; they do not carry their meaning on their face, and hence are unnecessarily difficult for the learner to bear in mind. *A* and *E* should be said to be mutually exclusive (but not exhaustive), *O* and *I* to be conjointly exhaustive (but not exclusive). This relation of qualities is then seen to be a particular case merely of the above-stated general rule.

Again, 'no *a* is *b*' and 'all *a* is *b*' are exclusive but not exhaustive, while 'some *a* is *b*' and 'some *a* is not *b*' are exhaustive but not exclusive (provided in both cases that *a* exists).

Laws of thought is not a good name for these two characteristics; they should rather be called the laws (if laws at all) of negation. Properly speaking, the laws of thought are all the rules of logic; of these laws there is one which is of far more fundamental importance than those usually referred to under the name, namely, the law that if *a* is *b* and *b* is *c*, it can be concluded that *a* is *c*. This is the great law of thought, and everything else is of minor importance in comparison with it. It is singular that it is not usually enumerated under the name. Another law of thought of equal consequence with those usually so called is, according to Sigwart, the law that the double negative is equivalent to an affirmative, $\bar{\bar{x}} = x$, or

(3) $x < \bar{\bar{x}}$,   (4) $\bar{\bar{x}} < x$.

But these are not fundamental, for from the principles of

Exclusion,	Exhaustion,
(1) $x\bar{x} < 0$,	(2) $\infty < x + \bar{x}$,
it follows	
by (2) that	by (1) that
$x < \bar{\bar{x}}$,	$\bar{\bar{x}} < x$.

(C.L.F.)

Literature: for the history of these principles see UEBERWEG, Syst. d. Logik, §§ 75–80; PRANTL, Gesch. d. Logik (see 'principium' in the indices to the four volumes). There are additional notes in an appendix to HAMILTON, Lects. on Logic.

(C.S.P.)